CHILDREN –
THE MODERN LAW

Third edition

CHILDREN –
THE MODERN LAW

Third edition

ANDREW BAINHAM
Fellow of Christ's College, Cambridge
Reader in Family Law and Policy,
University of Cambridge

Family Law
2005

Published by Family Law
an imprint of Jordan Publishing Limited
21 St Thomas Street
Bristol
BS1 6JS

British Library Cataloguing-in-Publication Data
A catalogue record for this book is available from the British Library.

ISBN 0 85308 939 6

Typeset by MFK-Mendip, Frome, Somerset
Printed by MPG Books Ltd, Bodmin, Cornwall

TO MY CHILDREN, SAM AND RHYS

PREFACE

My central aim in writing this third edition has not changed. It is principally to provide students of children law and family law with an overview of the many different areas of law which affect children and to highlight the central issues of principle and policy with which the law has to engage. It has not, of course, been possible to discuss all of the issues which are of relevance to children, but I hope that I have been able to focus on most of the ones which will be important to students undertaking modules in children law or family law courses in which there is a major children component.

Six years have elapsed since the previous edition; six years in which the changes to the law affecting children have been profound and extensive. Foremost among these was the integration in 2000 of the European Convention for the Protection of Human Rights and Fundamental Freedoms (ECHR) into English law through the implementation of the Human Rights Act 1998. It is true that the ECHR had long before this had a significant impact on family law, particularly in relation to the abolition of corporal punishment in schools and procedural protections for parents in care and related proceedings. Yet, the effect of the Human Rights Act has been nothing less than revolutionary on the development of children law, accepting that some are more enthusiastic about this revolution than others. It has been necessary in preparing this edition to take full account of the jurisprudence of the European Court of Human Rights throughout the book. But such is the importance of the Convention that I have also devoted a separate section to it, and this has involved some reorganisation of the book. In the second edition, I included a few pages on the likely impact of the ECHR in the final chapter which was concerned more generally with children in the international community. Such an approach could no longer be defended, and I have accordingly expanded the discussion. I have also brought it forward to its rightful place in Chapter 2, alongside the two other key sources and influences on children law, the Children Act 1989 and the United Nations Convention on the Rights of the Child (UNCRC).

Chapter 17 remains concerned with children in the international community, but I have now used this chapter to concentrate on what are perhaps the two great international problems affecting children, international child abduction and intercountry adoption. So far as the latter is concerned I have taken the opportunity to include a discussion of the issues in the context of Romania, drawing on my own direct experiences of involvement in that country throughout the period of writing this edition. I have also been able to include a section on the new Council of Europe Convention on Contact concerning Children. Apart from these structural changes, the shape of the book has not greatly changed.

If the implementation of the Human Rights Act 1998 has been the single most important development since 1998, there is no doubt about what takes second place. It is the Adoption and Children Act 2002 which radically, and in my view controversially, reforms the law of adoption. Chapter 7 has been largely rewritten to take account of the legislation, and I have also attempted to highlight in this chapter why I believe that there is a tension between the Act and the new-found commitment to human rights in the family. Indeed the Act in its final form and the Government's declared objective of driving up the figures for public law adoptions raise questions about the Government's commitment to, indeed understanding of, the requirements of the ECHR. This is especially so in relation to attempts at reunification of the child with the natural family where the child is in substitute care.

I wonder also how sound is the Government's understanding of rights in the context of contact between parents and children in the private law. In its recent Green Paper it acknowledges that there is a problem in the way the legal system is responding to cases of disputed contact. But there is a reluctance on the part of the Government to concede that adults, as well as children, have rights in relation to preservation of their relationship, perhaps giving the impression that it is more enthusiastic about some of the rights it has 'brought home' than others. Neither, in my view, have the judges of the European Court of Human Rights shown the commitment which might have been expected in relation to the fundamental relationship of parent and child. The Court has persisted in its view that whereas 'family life' arises between mother and child at birth, it may or may not arise between father and child at that time. This is difficult to square with Article 7 of the UNCRC, which clearly envisages that the child's right to know and be cared for by both parents is indeed a right which arises *from birth*. This is a contradiction of which the Court appears to be quite oblivious. It also perhaps invites more general consideration of the extent to which the content of children's own Convention rights under the ECHR should be informed by the content of the UNCRC.

Other major legislative changes have occurred since the last edition. In the criminal law, perhaps the major event has been the enactment of the Sexual Offences Act 2003, a well-motivated but strikingly illiberal piece of legislation which proceeds on the assumption that all sexual activity involving children is by definition wrong. This has the potential for damaging the harmless, and some would say entirely positive, sexual experimentation which is a common feature of growing up. Major changes have also been made to the law governing children's evidence by the Youth Justice and Criminal Evidence Act 1999. Two other pieces of legislation, the Children Act 2004 and the Domestic Violence, Crime and Victims Act 2004, had not made it to the statute book in time for inclusion in this edition. It has nonetheless been possible to make some reference to some of the more significant provisions in the respective Bills as they stood at the time of writing. More generally, I have endeavoured to state the law as at 1 October 2004, but it has been possible to note some developments since then, especially some recently reported cases.

There has been no shortage of major decisions in the courts affecting children and it would be possible to provide a rather large catalogue of these, not least of the burgeoning jurisprudence of the family courts as they grapple with the implications of the Human Rights Act 1998. But some decisions stand out. In the private law these include the Court of Appeal's attempt to deal with the problem of a conflict of interests between two children in the harrowing case of *Re A (Conjoined Twins: Medical Treatment)* and its attempt to balance the human rights of mothers, fathers and children in 'relocation' cases in *Payne v Payne*. These and other decisions expose to some degree the apparent tension between the traditional welfare or paramountcy principle and human rights considerations – a fertile area of academic debate in recent years. In the public law there have been major decisions of the House of Lords concerning the statutory threshold for public intervention where the child has been injured by an unknown perpetrator, and the extent to which the courts may review the care plan of the local authority.

As on previous occasions I would like to express my gratitude to those friends and colleagues who have been kind enough to assist in various ways with the preparation of this edition, but who bear no responsibility for what is said in these pages. Chapter 1, which provides an historical sketch of the law as it applies to children, is still very largely the chapter written by Stephen Cretney for the first edition and updated by me, especially to take account of recent demographic changes. The same is true to a lesser extent of Chapter 9. This has entailed some substantial rewriting to take account of recent important reforms to the child support scheme and the introduction of tax credits. I continue to owe Stephen Cretney a considerable debt, both for his initial work on these chapters and for being kind enough to read and comment on the latest versions. I am grateful also to Loraine Gelsthorpe, Neville Harris, Steve Hedley and Rosemary Pattenden for their input into certain chapters. Members of the Cambridge Socio-Legal Group, which it has been my privilege to chair, have contributed much to my understanding in certain areas of the law, particularly on the subjects of contact with children and sexuality with which the Group has been concerned in its recent seminars. I owe a special debt of gratitude to Belinda Brooks-Gordon, both for the many stimulating discussions I have had with her on the subject of sexual offending and for introducing me to materials which would otherwise have escaped my attention.

I would like to express my appreciation of the staff at Jordans and especially of Tony Hawitt for his patience as deadline after deadline slipped and Jo Morton who has handled the proof stage with her characteristic dedication and commitment. Completing this edition has been a struggle of momentous proportions, undertaken against the backdrop of constant interruption which seems to be such a feature of the academic condition these days. I know that I am not the only one who feels a warm sense of gratitude to the late Joseph James Zimmerman, inventor of the answerphone. But finally, in the last few months of writing, I was fortunate to find the love and support of Hsin-Ping Lu in her haven in Essex where the telephone never rang – at least for me.

ANDREW BAINHAM
Christ's College Cambridge
November 2004

CONTENTS

TABLE OF CASES

References are to page numbers.

TABLE OF STATUTES

References are to page numbers.

TABLE OF STATUTORY INSTRUMENTS, STATUTORY GUIDANCE, ETC

References are to page numbers.

TABLE OF EC AND INTERNATIONAL LEGISLATION

References are to page numbers.

TABLE OF FOREIGN ENACTMENTS

References are to page numbers.

TABLE OF ABBREVIATIONS

CA 1989	Children Act 1989
CAFCASS	Children and Family Court Advisory and Support Service
CAO	child assessment order
the Children Act	Children Act 1989
COTS	Childlessness Overcome Through Surrogacy
CPS	Crown Prosecution Service
CSA 1991	Child Support Act 1991
CSPSSA 2000	Child Support, Pensions and Social Security Act 2000
DDA 1995	Disability Discrimination Act 1995
DFE	Department for Education
DfEE	Department for Education and Employment
DfES	Department for Education and Skills
DPP	Director of Public Prosecutions
DTO	detention and training order
ECHR	European Convention on Human Rights and Fundamental Freedoms
ECtHR	European Court of Human Rights
EPO	emergency protection order
ESO	education supervision order
FAO	family assistance order
FLA 1996	Family Law Act 1996
GAL	guardian ad litem
HFEA 1990	Human Fertilisation and Embryology Act 1990
HRA 1998	Human Rights Act 1998
ILO	International Labour Organization
LEA	local education authority
LMS	local management of schools
MCA 1973	Matrimonial Causes Act 1973
MHA 1983	Matrimonial Homes Act 1983
NSPCC	National Society for the Prevention of Cruelty to Children
Ofsted	Office for Standards in Education
PACE 1984	Police and Criminal Evidence Act 1984
PCC(S)A 2000	Powers of Criminal Courts (Sentencing) Act 2000
PRO	parental responsibility order
QCA	Qualification and Curriculum Authority
RE	religious education
SACRE	standing advisory council on religious education
SAO	school attendance order
SATs	standard assessment tasks
SEN	special educational needs
SENDA 2001	Special Educational Needs and Disability Act 2001
SENDIST	Special Educational Needs and Disability Tribunal
UNCRC	United Nations Convention on the Rights of the Child
VAA	voluntary adoption agencies

PART I
BACKGROUND AND SOURCES OF CHILDREN LAW

Part I of the book aims to introduce the student to the historical evolution, sources and fundamental principles of the law affecting children. Chapter 1 sketches the profound historical and demographic changes which have influenced the attitude of society towards children and which provide the context in which legal change has occurred.

Chapter 2 is concerned with the three most important sources of children law domestically and internationally. Part I of the chapter focuses on the immediate background to the Children Act 1989, its basic principles and underlying philosophies. There is now no question that the Act constitutes the single most important source of children law. Even where it does not have direct application, its influence is, nonetheless, likely to be pervasive. Part II of the chapter examines some of the more important Articles and principles set out in the United Nations Convention on the Rights of the Child (UNCRC). This is, equally clearly, the most important international source. Part III is concerned with the application of the European Convention for the Protection of Human Rights and Fundamental Freedoms (ECHR) to children. The ECHR and the jurisprudence of the European Court of Human Rights (ECtHR) have since 2 October 2000 been an integral part of English domestic law following implementation of the Human Rights Act 1998. While account has to be taken throughout the book of the Convention and the case-law it has generated, Part III of Chapter 2 attempts to introduce the main provisions of the Human Rights Act 1998 and the principal Articles of the ECHR which are liable to be invoked in children cases. Chapter 3 attempts to identify some central issues which recur throughout the book. These relate to basic questions about the nature of childhood, parenthood and the interaction of children's rights with parents' rights and responsibilities.

Some understanding of these fundamentals is essential before embarking upon an examination of the substantive areas of law which are covered in the remainder of the book.

Chapter 1

CHILDREN AND THE LAW:
A DEMOGRAPHIC AND
HISTORICAL SKETCH

INTRODUCTION

The law reflects changing social and cultural attitudes and assumptions, and this is particularly true of family law. The history of those changes is a fascinating subject of study which, in recent years, has attracted much scholarly writing[1]. Considerations of space make it impossible to give even a brief summary of this research in

---

1   The history of family law in England is the subject of a seminal work by Stephen Cretney. See S Cretney *Family Law in the Twentieth Century: A History* (Oxford University Press, 2003). Specifically on the aspects of family law relating to children, see Part IV – 'Children, the Family and the State'. Another useful introduction is to be found in WR Cornish and G de N Clark *Law and Society in England 1750–1950* (Sweet & Maxwell, 1989) (particularly chs 5 and 6); and both AH Manchester *A Modern Legal History of England and Wales 1750–1950* (Butterworths, 1980) and RH Graveson and FR Crane (eds) *A Century of Family Law 1857–1957* (Sweet & Maxwell, 1957) are valuable. RA Houlbrooke *The English Family 1450–1700* (Longman, 1984) is a study from a modern perspective, as is L Stone *The Family, Sex and Marriage in England, 1500–1800* (Weidenfeld & Nicolson, 1977). Reference may also usefully be made to the standard, if now dated, general legal history texts: F Pollock and FW Maitland *The History of English Law before the Time of Edward I* (Cambridge University Press, 1898); and Sir William Holdsworth *A History of English Law* (Methuen, 1966). For a scholarly collection of essays examining the problems of family law reform from an historical perspective, see S Cretney *Law, Law Reform Reform and the Family* (Clarendon, 1998). For an evaluation of the achievements and failings of the twentieth century from the perspective of children's rights see M Freeman 'The End of the Century of the Child?' (2000) 53 *Current Legal Problems* 505. An authoritative volume of essays on the development of family law and policy in the United States and England is S Katz, J Eekelaar and M Maclean (eds) *Cross Currents* (Oxford University Press, 2000). For an assessment of the state of family law at the beginning of the twenty-first century, see S Cretney (ed) *Family Law – Essays for the New Millenium* (Family Law, 2000).

  The most accessible general social history is probably I Pinchbeck and M Hewitt *Children in English Society* Vol I (Routledge, 1969) and Vol II (1973) – although this work is not universally admired: see PEH Hair 'Children in Society 1850–1980' in T Barker and M Drake (eds) *Population and Society in Britain 1850–1980* (Batsford, 1982) at p 57. The evolution of public policy is traced in J Packman *The Child's Generation: Child Care Policy in Britain* (2nd edn) (Blackwell, 1981). For an authoritative study of the history of social policies for children, see H Hendrick *Child Welfare: England 1872–1989* (Routledge, 1994). A more discursive and international approach is taken in P Ariès *Centuries of Childhood* (Jonathan Cape, 1962). Demographic factors are addressed in P Laslett and R Wall (eds) *Household and Family in Past Time: Comparative Studies in the Size and Structure of the Domestic Group over the Last Three Centuries in England, France, Serbia, Japan and Colonial North America, with further materials from Western Europe* (Cambridge University Press, 1972); EA Wrigley and RS Schofield *The Population History of England 1541–1871, A Reconstruction* (Cambridge University Press, 1989); and in J Eekelaar and D Pearl (eds) *An Aging World – Dilemmas and Challenges for Law and Social Policy* (Clarendon Press, 1989). For more specialist works, see L deMause (ed) *The History of Childhood* (Harper & Row, 1975); and L Pollock *A Lasting Relationship: Parents and Children over Three Centuries* (Fourth Estate, 1987). Useful comparative demographic material is to be found in the *Proceedings* of the *Seminar on present demographic trends and lifestyles in Europe* (Council of Europe, 1991).

this book, but it may be helpful for the reader to have a sketch of a number of key areas, such as the rules governing legal decision-taking within the family, the role of the State from the Elizabethan Poor Law through the child protection measures of the late nineteenth century down to the development of child-centred services as part of the post-Second World War Welfare State, and the development of legal procedures designed to shield children from the worst consequences of the breakdown of their parents' relationships. These historical developments must be seen in the context of rapidly changing demographic factors, and a brief account of the most relevant data therefore follows.

Demographic factors: children and families[1]

The first issue relates to the proportion of children in the population and to the size of family units in which they are reared. There are two conflicting trends to note: on the one hand the number of live births[2] has fallen sharply since the early twentieth century[3], but on the other hand there has been a dramatic improvement (paradoxically most marked in the Second World War[4]) in infant mortality rates. The proportion of the population represented by children aged under 16 years in the UK fell from 23.5 per cent (25 per cent boys and 22 per cent girls) in 1961 to 20 per cent in 2000 (21 per cent boys and 19 per cent girls). It is estimated that this trend will continue and that by 2011 the figure will be 17.5 per cent (18 per cent boys and 17 per cent girls)[5].

An ageing population, and its impact
The life expectancy of a boy born in 1901 was 45 years and of a girl born that year 49 years; the life expectancy of a boy born in 2001 was over 75 years and that of a girl over 80 years[6]. This significant improvement means that young people form a

---

Stimulating general works include J Weeks *Sex, Politics and Society: The Regulation of Sexuality Since 1800* (Longman, 1981); J Donzelot *The Policing of Families* (Hutchinson, 1980); JE Goldthorpe *Family Life in Western Societies: a Historical Sociology of Family Relationships in Britain and North America* (1987).

1   See generally C Gibson 'Changing Family Patterns in England and Wales' in S Katz, J Eekelaar and M Maclean (eds) *Cross Currents* (Oxford University Press, 2000).

2   The number of children in Britain probably increased decade by decade from the mid-eighteenth century to the early twentieth century: see PEH Hair 'Children in Society 1950–1980' in T Barker and M Drake (eds) *Population and Society in Britain 1850–1980* (Batsford, 1982); and, generally, EA Wrigley and RS Schofield *The Population History of England, 1541–1871, A Reconstruction* (Cambridge University Press, 1989).

3   In the first decade of the twentieth century the average number of live births was approximately 1.1 million each year, but – after the 'baby boomer' years of the 1960s when, once again, more than a million live births were recorded – the number in the 1980s and 1990s stabilised at around a figure of 750,000 annually. There were 669,000 births in the UK in 2001 and it is expected that the number of births will remain reasonably constant over the next 40 years: *Social Trends* 33 (2003) Tables 1.7 and 1.8.

4   In 1901 the rate of infant mortality approached 160 for every 1,000 live births, but by 1961 it had fallen to 22.1 for every 1,000 live births. In 1991 the rate had fallen to 7.4: *Population Trends* 70 (1992) Table 8. By 1996 it had fallen yet further to 6.1: *Population Trends* 90 (1997) Table 8. The downward trend is continuing and by 2001 the figure had dropped to 5.5: *Population Trends* 108 (2002) Table 2.1.

5   *Social Trends* 32 (2002) Table 1.3. Latest projections are that the percentage of the population who are children will fall to 18% by 2011: *Social Trends* 33 (2003) Table 1.2.

6   *Social Trends* 33 (2003) Chart 7.1.

much smaller proportion of the population. Indeed, by 2014 it is predicted that those aged over 65 will exceed the number of those aged under 16 and that by 2025 there will be more than 1.6 million more people over the age of 65 than people under 16[1]. The proportion of the population which is of pensionable age has risen sharply and can be expected to continue to rise: in 1961, 4 per cent of the people in the UK were aged 75 or over: by 2000 the figure was 7 per cent (5 per cent men and 9 per cent women) and those aged over 65 represented 15.6 per cent of the population. It is estimated that by 2025 those over 75 will form 10 per cent of the population (9 per cent men and 11 per cent women) and those over 65 will make up 20 per cent[2].

These changes have had (and will continue to have) a dramatic effect on the composition and size of kinship groups. Whereas the modern child expects to know both his parents throughout his childhood and some at least of his grandparents, eighteenth-century children often knew none of their grand-parents, frequently knew only one of their parents, and not uncommonly knew neither of their parents[3]. So the modern child is much more likely to have at least the possibility of knowing his or her parents, grandparents and siblings. But, in fact, the family unit has become much smaller. Whereas the typical mid-Victorian family contained four or more children (and it was not uncommon to find families with up to 10 children), by 1991 only 5 per cent of households had three or more dependent children and by 2000 this had fallen further to just 4 per cent[4]. This trend towards a much smaller functioning family unit is reinforced by the increase in the number of single-parent families. The percentage of all dependent children living in lone-parent families has trebled since 1972 to reach 22 per cent by 2001[5] with the great majority of the parents being lone mothers rather than lone fathers[6].

Remarriage and step-children

There are about 150,000 divorces each year in England and Wales and there has been a very large increase in the number of children who experience the divorce of their parents: 20 years ago it was estimated[7] that one in five children would experience a parental divorce by the time the child was 16 years of age. Many divorcing parents remarry[8] and in 1990 there were more than 40,000 births within marriage to women who had remarried. This figure had, however, sharply declined to 32,600 by 1996[9]. In recent years there has been a further significant

---

1   *Social Trends* 33 (2003), Table 1.3.
2   *Social Trends* 32 (2002), Table 1.3.
3   Hair 'Children in Society 1850–1980' in Barker and Drake (above) at p 44.
4   The figures for the proportion of households with one or two dependent children is of course much higher at 20% in 1991 and 19% in 2001: *Social Trends* 32 (2002) Table 2.2.
5   *Social Trends* 32 (2002) Table 2.16.
6   Ibid. But the majority – 78% in the Spring of 2002 – of dependent children still live in a household headed by a couple: *Social Trends* 33 (2003) Table 2.4.
7   J Haskey 'Children of Divorcing Couples' in *Population Trends* 31 (1983).
8   Remarriages increased by about one-third between 1971 and 1972 following the liberalisation of divorce brought about by the Divorce Reform Act 1969. Since then the number of remarriages has remained fairly constant. In 2000 there were 126,000 remarriages for one or both partners – about 40% of all marriages that year: *Social Trends* 33 (2003) Figure 2.10.
9   *Population Trends* 70 (1992) Table 11 and *Population Trends* 90 (1997) Table 11.

decline to 23,900 by 2001[1]. Such children will have kinship links with more than one family. The law's response to this phenomenon has not always been consistent[2]. Concern has also been expressed about the difficulties which children and parents encounter in keeping in contact after the breakdown of the parents' relationship[3] although there have been some important studies in recent years which challenge the orthodox view that divorce is necessarily harmful for children and which focus instead on the quality of parental relationships both before and after divorce in the new social situation of increasingly fragmented households[4].

Births outside marriage

Perhaps the most striking of all the demographic changes which have occurred since the end of the Second World War is the dramatic increase in the proportion of births which take place outside marriage. In 1961 there were 48,500 live births in England and Wales outside marriage (ie some 6 per cent of all births)[5]; but by 1996 there were 232,700, representing well over one-third (35.8 per cent) of all births and by 2000 the figure of 238,600 constituted almost 40 per cent of the total[6]. These figures are all the more remarkable in the light of the fact that a large number of pregnancies are now legally terminated by abortion. In 1991 over 167,000 legal abortions were carried out on residents in England and Wales (the great majority on unmarried women) and in 1996 the figure was just under 167,000[7]. Around one-third of pregnancies outside marriage are terminated by an abortion[8]. In fact the percentage of all pregnancies terminated by abortion has remained relatively constant over the last decade at between 19 and 22 per cent[9]. Although a high proportion of lone-parent families are headed by a single woman[10], it should not be assumed that the child born outside marriage is likely to be brought up in a one-parent household: in 2001 more than three-quarters of all births outside marriage were registered jointly by both parents, and three-quarters of these parents were parents living at the same address[11]. Teenage mothers

---

1   *Population Trends* 108 (2002) Table 3.3.
2   The Children Act 1975 introduced provisions intended to discourage the use of legal adoption by couples wishing to integrate children of a previous relationship into their family, while the Children Act 1989 is more neutral on the issue: see Chapter 7 below and generally J Masson et al *Mine, Yours or Ours?* (1983).
3   See, generally, MPM Richards and M Dyson *Separation, Divorce and the Development of Children: a Review* (1983).
4   See generally Chapter 4. See also C Smart and B Neale *Family Fragments?* (Polity Press, 1999). The question of why some children survive these family transitions better than others is explored in J Pryor and B Rodgers *Children in Changing Families: Life After Parental Separation* (Blackwell, 2001). For a study which examines children's own perspectives of family life after divorce see C Smart, B Neale and A Wade *The Changing Experience of Childhood: Families and Divorce* (Polity, 2001).
5   *Population Trends* 70 (1992) Table 10.
6   *Population Trends* 90 (1997) Table 10 and *Population Trends* 108 (2002) Table 3.2.
7   *Population Trends* 70 (1992) Table 16 and *Population Trends* 90 (1997) Table 17.
8   *Social Trends* 32 (2002) Chart 2.11.
9   *Population Trends* 108 (2002) Table 4.1.
10 Almost ten times as many as are headed by a man although there has been a noteworthy increase in the number of single-parent households headed by men in recent years. In 1999 18% of all such households with dependent children were headed by women and just 1% by men. Later figures indicate 20% by women and 2% by men: *Social Trends* 32 (2002) Table 2.17.
11 *Social Trends* 33 (2003) Figure 2.18.

account for a significant proportion of births outside marriage and of births registered without details of the father. In 2000 almost 9 in 10 live births to women aged under 20 in England and Wales occurred outside marriage. Just over one-quarter (27 per cent) of births to teenage mothers were registered solely by the mothers[1].

It seems that to some extent social reality and legal institutions in this area have not been so closely related as is often assumed. Research has revealed, for example, that many cohabiting, but unmarried, fathers were quite unaware of the legal position that they lacked parental responsibility in the legal, as opposed to social, sense in relation to their children[2]. The legal and social positions have now been brought much closer together by the long-awaited reform introduced by the Adoption and Children Act 2002 which confers automatic parental responsibility on the man registered as the father of the child of an unmarried mother[3].

THE CHILD AS A LEGAL PERSON

All legal systems give parents or other adults powers in respect of the upbringing of children, but the extent of those powers differs from time to time and from place to place. In England, Blackstone (writing in the eighteenth century) accepted that the power of parents over their children was derived from the need to enable a parent more effectually to perform his duty to the child (although he also saw parental rights as being, to some extent, a recompense for the care and trouble taken by the parent in the faithful discharge of his duties)[4]. Blackstone also pointed out that the assessment of the scope of parental power varied from time to time and from nation to nation:

'the ancient Roman laws gave the father a power of life and death over his children; upon this principle, that he who gave has also the power of taking away. Moreover a son could not acquire any property of his own during the life of his father, but all his acquisitions belonged to the father, or at least the profits of them for his life.'

Parental power in English law was still 'sufficient to keep the child in order and obedience'[5]; and Blackstone's description of the eighteenth-century parent's right bears extended citation. The parent (he said):

'... may lawfully correct his child, being under age, in a reasonable manner: for this is for the benefit of his education. The consent or concurrence of the parent to the marriage of his child under age, was also directed by our ancient law to be obtained ... and this is also another means, which the law has put into the parent's hands, in order the better to discharge his duty; first, of protecting his children from the snares of artful and designing persons; and, next, of settling properly in life, by preventing the ill consequences of too early and precipitate marriages. A father has no other power over his son's estate, than as his trustee or guardian; for, though he may receive the profits during the child's minority, yet he must account for them when he comes of age. He may indeed have the benefit of his children's labour while they live with him, and are maintained by him: but this is no more than he is entitled to from his apprentices or servants. The legal power of a father (for a mother, as such, is entitled to no power, but only to reverence and

---

1 *Social Trends* 32 (2002) p 47 and Chart 2.14.
2 See R Pickford *Fathers, Marriage and the Law* (Family Policy Studies Centre for the Joseph Rowntree Foundation, 1999).
3 See Chapter 5.
4 Blackstone *Commentaries on the Laws of England* (4th edn) (1770) Book 1, ch 15, section 2.
5 Ibid.

respect) over the persons of his children ceases at the age of 21: for they are then enfranchised by arriving at years of discretion, or that point which the law has established (as some must necessarily be established) when the empire of the father, or other guardian, gives place to the empire of reason. Yet, until that age arrives, this empire of the father continues even after his death; for he may by his will appoint a guardian to his children. He may also delegate part of his parental authority during his life, to the tutor or schoolmaster of his child; who is then *in loco parentis,* and has such a portion of the power the parent committed to his charge, viz. that of restraint and correction, as may be necessary to answer the purposes for which he is employed.'

Legal power and social reality

Although it is difficult to make any confident assessment of the way in which parental authority was exercised in times past[1], there is ample evidence that the right to a child's services was widely regarded as being an economically valuable asset. As recently as 1921[2], it was said to be 'no uncommon thing, when a child has reached an age at which it can work and earn wages, for parents who have habitually neglected it and left it to be brought up by a relative or even a stranger, to claim it back simply in order to take its earnings'; and there is some evidence that child stealing – not a crime until 1814 – was sometimes practised by those who wanted a cheap supply of labourers for trades such as chimney sweeping and prostitution[3].

At the upper end of the socio-economic scale, it appears that parents and guardians did not hesitate to exercise parental rights in respect of matters such as education. In one of the (comparatively few) reported cases[4], a young man of 16 was told by the court that the guardian was the best judge of his education, and that, since the boy had no reasonable complaint against the master at Eton, he would be compelled to return there if he did not go voluntarily. And even in the latter part of the nineteenth century the courts were reluctant to give any real weight to a child's views. In *Re Agar-Ellis*[5], the parents of a 16-year-old girl were separated. The father exercised his legal right[6] to take his daughter away from her mother, to send her to boarding school and to have her looked after by clergymen and others during the holidays, moving from one lodging to another. The court refused an application for the daughter to spend the holiday with her mother and, indeed, for the mother to have any access to her. It was said that in the absence of any fault on the father's part the court had no jurisdiction to interfere with the father's legal right to control the custody and education of his daughter.

The father's exclusive entitlement to parental authority

As already seen, in Blackstone's time, parental authority was vested exclusively in a child's father: the mother was not entitled to any power with respect to the child, but 'only to reverence and respect'[7]. One of the most remarkable features of the development of English law is that this remained the underlying principle of the

---

1   See, generally, I Pinchbeck and M Hewitt *Children in English Society* (Routledge, 1973) Vol 2 at chs 12 and 13.
2   See *Report of the Committee on Child Adoption* (1921) (Cmnd 1254) at para 13.
3   I Pinchbeck and M Hewitt (above) at p 360.
4   *Hall v Hall* (1749) 3 Att 721.
5   (1883) 23 ChD 317.
6   On parental 'rights' in the modern law, see Chapter 3 below.
7   Blackstone *Commentaries on the Laws of England* (4th edn) (1770) at p 453.

law until 1973. Only in that year did Parliament enact that, in relation to the legal custody or upbringing of a minor and in relation to his property or the application of income therefrom, a mother was to have the same rights and authority as the law had previously allowed to a father[1]. The fact that, for so long, a mother had no legal rights in respect of a legitimate[2] child may prompt the reader to ask how far the law is, in reality, relevant in practical terms. How many mothers, fathers, or children born before 1973, were aware of the legal position which denied the mother any parental authority? How far did this rule of law affect their behaviour?[3] Perhaps the reality is that the denial of parental authority to a mother was rarely noticed in the functioning family, but this is not to say that the 1973 reform was irrelevant. Although such things may be difficult to measure, the law presumably has some impact on attitudes and, in any event, it is, no doubt, important that the law should reflect a position which is defensible, both socially and morally. It may be argued, for example, that it is important for the law to assert the principle of contact between parents and children even if enforcement of contact is difficult or even impossible. This issue is discussed in Chapter 4.

Erosion of the father's legal rights
The evolution of the law is of more pressing practical significance in cases in which the parental relationship is no longer harmonious, and very slowly – but then at an increasing pace – nineteenth-century parliaments began to allow the courts to intervene between father and mother in such cases. It was no longer regarded as acceptable that mothers who had separated from adulterous or cruel husbands should be deprived of the care of their children, and even denied any form of contact with them; or for the children to be handed over to complete strangers or perhaps even to the father's mistress[4].

Talfourd's Act
The first legislative interference with the father's virtually absolute right to have the possession of his children and to deny the mother any contact with them was the Custody of Infants Act 1839 which empowered the court to make orders giving custody of any child up to the age of seven to the mother and to make orders giving her access to her children during their infancy[5].

1　Guardianship Act 1973, s 1(1).
2　The position in respect of an illegitimate child was different: see Chapter 5 below.
3　As noted above, similar questions have been raised more recently in relation to unmarried fathers who have lacked parental responsibility. See Pickford (above).
4　See *R v de Manneville* (1804) 5 East 221 and *de Manneville v de Manneville* (1804) 10 Ves 52 in which a father forcibly took an eight-month-old unweaned baby from the house in which it was living with the mother; and see *R v Greenhill* (1836) 4 Ad&E 624 where the Court of King's Bench ordered Mrs Greenhill to hand over her three small daughters (all under six years of age) to their father, notwithstanding the fact that he had been guilty of considerable cruelty to the wife and children and intended to hand the children over to the care of his mistress. When Mrs Greenhill refused to comply with the order she was committed to prison for contempt of court.
5　The Act, known as Talfourd's Act, was promoted by Serjeant Talfourd, a lawyer with experience of some remarkable cases, and the parliamentary proceedings were protracted and bitter: see I Pinchbeck and M Hewitt *Children in English Society* Vol 2 at pp 371–375 and, generally, as to the scope and objects of the Act, see *Warde v Warde* (1849) 2 Ph 786. The Act was restrictively interpreted: see *Re Halliday* (1853) 17 Jur 56; *Shillito v Collett* (1860) 8 WR 683; *Re Winscom* (1865) 2 H&M 540.

The Matrimonial Causes Act 1857

The introduction of judicial divorce by the Matrimonial Causes Act 1857 required the legislature to consider the consequences of granting a decree of divorce both in respect of financial matters and in respect of the upbringing of the parties' children; and the Act gave the court a wide discretion in judicial separation, nullity or divorce proceedings to make such orders with respect to the custody, maintenance and education of the children of the marriage 'as it may deem just and proper'[1]. The Act also empowered the divorce court to direct that proper proceedings be taken for placing such children under the protection of the Court of Chancery[2]. The Act thus accepted – for the first time – the important principle that, whenever there were matrimonial proceedings, a father's rights might be overridden by the court, and it also gave effect to the view that the child of divorced (or legally separated) parents might need the ongoing supervision, available in wardship, of all important steps in his or her life[3].

Later Victorian legislation[4]

The extensive discretion conferred on the court by the divorce legislation was not easy to reconcile with the restrictive approach underlying the Custody of Infants Act 1839: on divorce or judicial separation, the court had a complete discretion, but in other cases its discretion was greatly circumscribed. Not without difficulty and hesitation it came to be accepted that a wide discretion vested in the courts was necessary in cases relating to the upbringing of children; and the Custody of Infants Act 1873 empowered the court[5] to give custody of a child up to the age of 16 (rather than seven) to the mother. That Act also removed the bar established by the Custody of Infants Act 1839 against access or custody petitions by an adulterous mother; and it provided that no agreement contained in a separation deed should be held to be invalid by reason only of its providing that the father of an infant should give up the custody or control of the infant to the mother. But the parties were not to be allowed to oust the court's powers, since the Custody of Infants Act 1873 provided that the court should not enforce any agreement if it was of the opinion that it would not be for the benefit of the infant to give effect thereto[6].

---

1   Matrimonial Causes Act 1857, s 33.
2   Ibid.
3   For the wardship jurisdiction, see pp 13 et seq below.
4   The text deals only with legislation conferring powers on the superior courts, but the last quarter of the nineteenth century also saw the creation of the magistrates' jurisdiction – for long particularly significant in the case of the working classes. The Matrimonial Causes Act 1878, s 4, provided that when a husband was convicted of assault the court might order that the legal custody of any children of the marriage under the age of 10 years be given to the wife (although no order was to be made in favour of a wife proved to have committed adultery). The Summary Jurisdiction (Married Women) Act 1895 greatly extended the magistrates' powers.
5   The Court of Chancery.
6   See, for example, the notorious case of *Re Besant* (1878) 11 ChD 508, in which the court overrode a provision in a deed of separation made between a Church of England clergyman

Father rules from beyond the grave: guardianship

At common law, a father's parental authority survived his death: a father could appoint a testamentary guardian[1] for his child, and the guardian then, effectively, stepped into the position of the father on the father's death. The mother had no right to interfere with the exercise of the testamentary guardian's authority[2]. But the principles underlying the statutes passed in 1839, 1857 and 1873 made it 'difficult to accept that in a free country a widowed mother might be robbed of her young children, even if they were babes in arms, by a stranger appointed guardian by her late husband against her wishes or by her late husband's distant relative whom she had never seen'[3]. A vigorous public campaign eventually lead to the enactment of the Guardianship of Infants Act 1886 which provided[4] that, on the death of the father of an infant, the mother, if surviving, should be the infant's guardian, either alone (when no guardian had been appointed by the father) or jointly with any guardian appointed by the father. The 1886 Act also empowered the court to appoint a guardian or guardians to act jointly with the mother where no guardian had been appointed by the father, or where the guardians or guardian appointed by him had died or refused to act.

Freestanding custody applications

The problem of guardianship and abuse of paternal power were the matters which precipitated the enactment of the Guardianship of Infants Act 1886, but in conceptual terms that Act can today be seen as having a far greater significance. The reality is that the Act destroyed the concept of the family as a domestic kingdom ruled by the father. This was done by conferring on the court – which for this purpose included the county court as well as the High Court[5] – an unrestricted power on the mother's application to make such order as it thought fit regarding the custody of an infant and the right of access, thereto, of either parent, 'having regard to the welfare of the infant, and to the conduct of the parents, and to the wishes as well of the mother as of the father'[6]. It was no longer necessary to bring any other issue (such as the termination of the partners' marriage) before the court if either parent wanted the court to assume jurisdiction to deal with the upbringing of children; it was sufficient that either parent wanted the court to deal with the questions of custody and access.

---

and his wife. The mother (the founder of the ethical code known as theosophy) had written works which the Court of Appeal considered 'disgusting to decent English men and women, a violation of morality, decency and womanly propriety', and had proselytised on behalf of her atheistical beliefs, and the court directed that custody of the daughter be given to the father. For the background, see R Dinnage *Annie Besant* (1986).

1   Under the Tenures Abolition Act 1660, as amended by the Wills Act 1837.
2   *Talbot v Earl of Shrewsbury* (1840) 4 My&Cr 672 at 683.
3   See I Pinchbeck and M Hewitt *Children in English Society* Vol 2 at p 381.
4   Section 2.
5   Section 9.
6   The Act also provided that the court could alter, vary or discharge such orders on the application of either parent or, after the death of either parent, on the application of a guardian appointed under the Act.

The unfit parent

The Guardianship of Infants Act 1886 also[1] gave the divorce court power to include, in decrees of divorce and judicial separation, a declaration that one spouse was unfit to have the custody of the children. The person declared unfit lost the right to custody or guardianship of the child which he or she would otherwise have had on the death of the other parent; but, in theory at least, a declaration of unfitness did not mean that the parent was to be deprived of all contact with the child, nor did it debar the unfit parent from seeking and being given custody or access[2].

The family and outsiders

The 1886 legislation – the substance of which remained on the statute book until the enactment of the Children Act 1989 – gave effect to the principle that the child's welfare should be the determining factor in disputes between parents over their child's upbringing, but the position was very different when the dispute was between the parents and an outsider – typically a foster-parent who had provided a home for a destitute child. In particular, parents often sought to reclaim a boy or girl of an age to earn wages from one of the children's homes established by the philanthropist Dr Barnardo[3] in an attempt to provide vagrant and destitute children with care, training and a sound upbringing, according to the tenets of evangelical protestantism; and these parents were not deterred by the fact that Barnardo required the parents of those whom he 'rescued' to renounce all claim to the child[4]. On a number of occasions, Barnardo was ordered to return children to the legal parents[5]; but, in due course, Parliament responded to what was seen to be a scandalous situation. In the words of Lord Herschell:

> 'When a parent has abandoned or deserted his child, has cared nothing for it, and has left it to be cared for by others, it is outrageous that he should be allowed to go before a Court and say, although I have neglected every duty which I owed my child, and although to deliver up to me now would be most disastrous for the child, still I have a legal right to the custody of the child, that custody I will have, and you must give it to me ... All that this legislation proposes to do so is that where the court is satisfied that a parent has so behaved as to disentitle him to the custody of the child it shall have power to refuse its writ to procure the delivery of that child back to the parent.'

The Custody of Children Act 1891 (which remained on the statute book until repealed by the Children Act 1989) empowered the court in its discretion to decline to issue a writ of habeas corpus or make an order for the production of a child if the court considered that the parent had abandoned or deserted the child or that he had otherwise so conducted himself that the court should refuse to enforce his right to the custody of the child. More generally, the Act provided[6]

---

1   Section 7.
2   *Re A & B* [1897] 1 Ch 786 at 795. A modern manifestation of the unfitness question is the debate about whether the behaviour of some parents is so bad that there should be power to deprive them of parental responsibility. As the law stands only the unmarried father, but not married parents or the unmarried mother, may have parental responsibility removed by the court. See Children Act 1989, s 4(3) and Chapters 4 and 5 below.
3   For a comprehensive account, see G Wagner *Barnardo* (Weidenfeld & Nicolson, 1979) at ch 13. See also J Rose *For the Sake of the Children: Inside Dr Barnardo's* (1988).
4   Such an agreement was without legal effect: see Chapter 4.
5   See *R v Barnardo* (1889) 23 QBD 305, (1890) 24 QBD 283, [1891] 1 QB 194; *Barnardo v McHugh* [1891] AC 388; *Barnardo v Ford* [1892] AC 326.
6   Section 3.

that the court should not make an order for the delivery of a child to a parent who had abandoned or deserted the child or who had allowed the child to be brought up by another person at that person's expense (or by the poor law guardians) for such a length of time and under such circumstances as to satisfy the court that the parent was 'unmindful of his parental duties', unless the parent had satisfied the court that 'having regard to the welfare of the child' the parent was a fit person to have the custody of the child.

Religion: the first recognition of children's rights

Perhaps the most remarkable provision of the Custody of Children Act 1891, however, was that dealing with religious education. Some, at least, of the *Barnardo* cases were prompted by parents being brought to believe that the child's spiritual health was at risk by reason of the religious teaching given in the Barnardo homes; and, in an attempt to allay fears on this score, the Act provided[1] that a court denying a parent custody of his child might, nevertheless, take such steps as it thought fit to secure that the child be brought up 'in the religion in which the parent had a legal right to require that the child should be brought up'. To this extent, the parental right to control the child's spiritual upbringing was firmly reasserted, even though the parental right to have the physical care of the child was removed; but – remarkably for legislation of the period – it was also provided that nothing in the legislation should interfere with or affect the power of the court to consult the *wishes of the child* in considering what order ought to be made, or diminish the right which the child possessed to the exercise of the child's own free choice. It can plausibly be argued that this – little noted – provision marks the first statutory recognition of the child's legal right to autonomy.

The role of the Court of Chancery: wardship

The Court of Chancery exercised the prerogative jurisdiction of the Crown over infants; and it would, in so doing, apply the principle that the primary consideration was the child's welfare. However, the court was reluctant to override the wishes of the father[2]; and, in practice[3], it would at this time only act in cases in which it had the means of applying property for the use and maintenance of the

---

1   Section 4.
2   'It is not the benefit of the infant as conceived by the court, but it must be the benefit to the infant having regard to the natural law which points out that the father knows far better as a rule what is good for his children than a Court of Justice can': see *Re Agar-Ellis* (1883) 24 ChD 317 at 337–338, per Bowen LJ. A similar approach was taken nearly a century later by Lord Templeman in *Re KD (A Minor) (Access: Principles)* [1988] 2 FLR 139 at 141, HL: 'The best person to bring up a child is the natural parent. It matters not whether the parent is wise or foolish, rich or poor, educated or illiterate, provided the child's moral and physical health are not endangered'. An even more recent example is provided by Waite LJ in *Re T (Wardship: Medical Treatment)* [1997] 1 FLR 502 at 514: '... in the last analysis the best interests of every child include an expectation that difficult decisions affecting the length and quality of its life will be taken for it by the parent to whom its care has been entrusted by nature'. In practice today, however, the courts are prepared to override even the strongly held, religiously inspired and reasonably held convictions of parents if the welfare of the child, as perceived by the court, demands intervention. The leading authority is now *Re A (Children) (Conjoined Twins: Surgical Separation)* [2000] 4 All ER 961. See further Chapter 8.
3   Although not in theory: see generally NV Lowe and RAH White *Wards of Court* (2nd edn) (Barry Rose/Kluwer, 1986) at p 3.

children concerned[1]. Indeed, the promoters of the Custody of Children Act 1891 sought to explain the necessity for legislation by arguing that legislation would give to the poorer child the same protection as that traditionally given by the Court of Chancery to wealthier children who had had property bestowed upon them[2].

Principles on which the court would exercise its discretion: the paramountcy of the child's welfare

Much of the late nineteenth-century legislation was influenced by the movement for achieving legal equality for women[3], particularly in relation to property and, although the child custody legislation gave the court a wide discretion, it did not give any specific guidance in respect of the *principles* upon which this discretion should be exercised. In practice, the courts seem often to have regarded the welfare of the child as identical to the father's wishes.

The Guardianship of Infants Act 1925[4] made its objectives clear in the preamble:

'... whereas Parliament by the Sex Disqualification (Removal) Act 1919, and various other enactments, has sought to establish equality in law between the sexes, and it is expedient that this principle should obtain with respect to the guardianship of infants and the rights and responsibilities conferred thereby.'

The Act provided that where, in any proceedings before any court[5], the custody or upbringing of an infant, or the administration of any property belonging to or held on trust for an infant, or the application of the income thereof, was in question, the court, in deciding that question, should regard the welfare of the infant as the first and paramount consideration, and should not take into consideration, whether from any other point of view the claim of the father, in respect of such custody, upbringing, administration or application was superior to that of the mother, or the claim of the mother was superior to that of the father.

There would seem to be little room for doubt that this legislation was designed to secure equality of rights *as between father and mother* in relation to their children, and to make the welfare of those children paramount in relation to the two, henceforth equal, interests of their parents[6]. The Act did not, in terms, apply to cases in which the dispute was between a parent and an outsider; and for many years it seems to have been thought that a parent – certainly an 'unimpeachable' parent – still had 'rights' in respect of a child's upbringing, which would prevail as against a stranger. For example, in *Re Thain*[7]:

'... a father who on his wife's death had no means of looking after his eight month old daughter, accepted an offer by the child's uncle and aunt to look after her. Six years later he had re-married

---

1 See *Wellesley v Duke of Beaufort* (1827) 2 Russ 1 at 21, per Lord Eldon.
2 See Lord Thring *Hansard* 3rd series (1891) Vol 349, cols 1508–10.
3 Culminating in the Married Women's Property Act 1882.
4 For a detailed examination of the legislative history of the Act, see SM Cretney '"What Will the Women Want Next?": The Struggle for Power Within the Family 1925–1975' (1996) 112 LQR 110.
5 The Act thus extended the principles applied by the Chancery Division of the High Court to the magistrates' court.
6 *A v Liverpool City Council* [1982] AC 363 at 377, per Lord Roskill; see also *Richards v Richards* [1984] 1 AC 174 at 203, per Lord Hailsham of St Marylebone.
7 [1926] Ch 676.

and was in a position to provide the child with a permanent and suitable home. He applied for and obtained an order that she be handed back to him. The trial judge said[1] that he could quite understand that the little girl would be "greatly distressed and upset" at the parting from her foster parents, but "at her tender age, one knows from experience how mercifully transient are the effects of partings and other sorrows, and how soon the novelty of fresh surroundings and new associations effaces the recollection of former days and kind friends" . . .'

It was only in the landmark case of *J v C*[2], more than 40 years later, that the House of Lords unequivocally ruled that the principles of the 1925 legislation were applicable whether the dispute was between parents, or between parents and outsiders. In *J v C*:

'. . . the question was whether a 10 year old boy should be returned to his natural parents (Spanish nationals resident in Spain) or whether he should continue to be in the care of English foster parents who had looked after him for all save some 18 months of his life. The House of Lords upheld the decision of the trial judge and Court of Appeal that the boy should stay in the care of the foster parents in England. The consequences of returning a boy who scarcely knew his natural parents and had been brought up as an English boy with English ways to a foreign country might have been disastrous, the more so since the parents would have been unable to cope with the problems of adjustment and consequent maladjustment and suffering. The fact that the parents were "unimpeachable" could not prevail. The legislation required the child's welfare to be treated as the paramount consideration.'

Child still not entitled to access to courts

This clear acceptance of the paramountcy of the child's welfare establishes a principle which is comprehensible, however difficult it may be to apply it in practice[3]. But for many years it was an inflexible rule that a child could not, directly, bring or participate in legal proceedings in the superior civil courts, and that a guardian ad litem or next friend must act on the child's behalf[4]. The child's father was, in principle, entitled to act in that capacity, and would only be removed if it could be shown that he was acting improperly. The difficulties to which this rule gave rise – as well as the difficulty of deciding what precisely is in a child's best interests, even in the context of legal and financial matters – was vividly demonstrated in *Re Taylor's Application*[5]:

'The defendants in actions brought on behalf of children claiming to have been damaged by the drug Thalidomide made an offer of settlement on terms that all the 365 plaintiffs accepted. The parents of five children refused to do so; and the defendants sought to remove the father from his position as next friend with a view to a person being appointed who would accept the proposed settlement. The court rejected the application: the only impropriety alleged against the father was that he was in a small minority in believing that the settlement was not in his child's best interests; but (as Lord Denning MR remarked) being in a minority is not itself evidence of unreasonableness.'

---

1 Eve J at 684.
2 [1970] AC 668.
3 See Chapters 2 and 4 below.
4 In certain circumstances, a child may now participate in family proceedings without it being necessary for a guardian or litigation friend to act: see Chapter 13 below.
5 [1972] 2 QB 369, CA. For the situation today, see Chapter 13 below.

The age of majority

A child is not entitled to full legal capacity[1] until he or she attains the age of majority. For many years, this was fixed at 21 years of age, but the Family Law Reform Act 1969 reduced the age of majority to 18 years[2].

THE ROLE OF THE STATE

The Poor Law

Lord Scarman has said that the historic base from which Parliament advanced to meet the needs of the orphans, the deserted, and the abandoned child was the Poor Law[3]; and it is certainly true that, for centuries, the problems associated with poverty, and particularly the problems of fatherless children begging and vagrancy, have been a major concern of Government. The statute which established the Elizabethan Poor Law in 1601 put legal sanctions, for the first time, behind the observance of what had formerly been regarded as the ordinary obligations of kinship[4]. Parents, grandparents and children were statutorily obliged to support their relatives, and this general principle survives in the obligation imposed on 'liable relatives' for income support purposes and in the provisions of the Child Support Act 1991 imposing maintenance obligations on absent parents. It should, however, be noted that the scope of the obligation has now greatly narrowed since the days of the Poor Law (which was abolished by the National Assistance Act 1948). The obligation is now restricted to husbands and wives and to parents and children; and the National Assistance Act 1948 also limited the extent of the liability to the recovery of sums paid out by way of supplementary benefit or income support[5].

The impact of the Poor Law was not confined to financial obligations; and two, often related, developments of practice in relation to the care of children can, in retrospect, be seen to have played a major part in the development of child care law and practice.

---

1 Until the *Gillick* decision (*Gillick v West Norfolk and Wisbech Area Health Authority* [1986] 1 AC 112), it was widely assumed that a child was legally incapable for all purposes (except where capacity was specifically conferred on the child by statute) until he or she attained full age, but that case held that this view was erroneous: see, particularly, Chapters 3 and 8 below.
2 Following the *Report of the Committee on the Age of Majority* ('the Latey Report') (1967) (Cmnd 3342). The position is the same in Scotland but it should be noted that under the Age of Legal Capacity (Scotland) Act 1991 children over the age of 16 enjoy a large measure of active legal capacity to enter into civil transactions. See JM Thomson *Family Law in Scotland* (3rd edn) (Butterworths, 1996) ch 9, and see Chapter 15 below. Most developed countries have 18 as the age of majority. Austria has recently lowered its age of majority from 19 to 18 to bring it in line with the other States in the Council of Europe. See B Verschraegen 'The New Austrian Child Law 2001' in A Bainham (ed) *The International Survey of Family Law (2002 Edition)* (Family Law, 2002) p 57 at p 58.
3 *Leeds City Council v West Yorkshire Metropolitan Police* [1983] 1 AC 29 at 41.
4 *Report of the Finer Committee on One-Parent Families* (1974) (Cmnd 5629) Vol 2, Appendix 5, para 51.
5 The Child Support Act 1991 imposes a much more extensive obligation, although one which was moderated by sweeping changes to the child support scheme introduced by the Child Support, Pensions and Social Security Act 2000: see Chapter 9 below.

Boarding-out: assumption of parental rights

In the latter part of the nineteenth century, it increasingly became the practice for pauper children to be 'boarded out' under the authority of the Poor Law Board with foster-parents[1]; and the Poor Law Act 1889 empowered the Poor Law guardians to assume all the powers and rights in respect of a child deserted by his parents and maintained by the Poor Law guardians[2]. The Poor Law Act 1899 extended the grounds on which such action could be taken – it sufficed if the parent (for example) was thought to be unfit to have control of the child 'by reason of mental deficiency, or of vicious habits or mode of life'[3]. These procedures were seen to provide a means of caring for poor children without institutionalising them in a workhouse or other Poor Law institution, and a further stimulus to the practice of boarding-out was provided by the Poor Law Institutions Order of 1913, which made it illegal to retain a healthy child over the age of three years in a workhouse for more than six weeks.

Local authorities' responsibilities for child care

In some ways, the most significant step in the evolution of modern child care practice[4] came in 1929, when the responsibilities of the Poor Law guardians were taken over by local authorities[5]. The Second World War impeded any comprehensive reforms, but also provided a stimulus for further reform. A growing sense of dissatisfaction[6] led to the appointment of a committee 'to enquire into existing methods of providing for children who, from loss of parent or from any cause whatever, are deprived of a normal home life with their own parents or relatives; and to consider what further measures should be taken to ensure that these children are brought up under conditions best calculated to compensate them for parental care'.

---

1 See I Pinchbeck and M Hewitt *Children in English Society* (Routledge, 1973) Vol 2 at p 522. For further discussion of the powers of the Poor Law authorities in the context of the social and legal background to the introduction of legal, as opposed to informal, adoption in 1926, see S Cretney 'From Status to Contract?' in FD Rose (ed) *Consensus Ad Idem: Essays in the Law of Contract in honour of Guenther Treitel* (Sweet & Maxwell, 1996) pp 251 et seq, especially at pp 252–255.

2 Poor Law Act 1889, s 1(1).

3 Ibid, s 1. The Poor Law Act 1889 is commonly described as the Poor Law Adoption Act; and informal adoption was statutorily recognised by the Poor Law Act 1899, s 3, which dealt with the case where a child had been adopted notwithstanding the fact that at the time there was no legal machinery for adoption.

4 See the Literature Surveys by RA Parker in 'Residential Care, The Research Reviewed', commissioned by the *Independent Review of Residential Care Chaired by Gillian Wagner OBE PhD* (I Sinclair, ed) (HMSO, 1988).

5 Local authorities could also be appointed as 'fit persons' to whom the care of children removed from their parents under the child protection legislation could be committed.

6 For an account of practice, see *Report of the Care of Children Committee* ('the Curtis Report') (1946) (Cmnd 6922).

The Curtis Report

In 1946, the Committee (under the chairmanship of Miss Myra Curtis) published its report[1] which led directly[2] to the enactment of the Children Act 1948. That Act sought to give effect to a policy that, so far as possible, all children deprived of a normal home life should have the advantages of which they had been deprived, and to that end the Act required local authorities to provide care for extended categories of children. The Act remained the cornerstone of the structure of children's social services for more than 40 years; and marked a significant step away from the traditional reliance on voluntary organisations, family doctors, the clergy and neighbours for dealing with welfare problems, and towards reliance on paid, trained, professional social workers employed by local authorities.

Caring involves paying

Although the Children Act 1948 imposed a duty on local authorities to provide care for children deprived of a normal home life, it soon came to be recognised that prevention was better than cure, and children's departments tried to forestall the need for children to come into care by working, in co-operation with the other community services, to keep the family in being whenever this was in the best interests of the children. But the legal basis on which such help could be given was often obscure; and in 1960 the Ingleby Committee[3] pointed out that authorities had no power to give help in cash or kind to the families of children in care or of children who might have to be received into care because of their home circumstances. The Children and Young Persons Act 1963 sought to deal with this problem by imposing on local authorities a duty 'to make available such advice, guidance and assistance as may promote the welfare of children by diminishing the need to receive children into or keep them in care' or to bring children before a juvenile court under the provisions then in force.

The range of services which could be provided under the Act was wide: authorities would provide general social work support, and also specific facilities such as the relief of overburdened mothers by admitting young children to day care and older children to after-school play schemes, and assistance with housekeeping and budgeting; while there was power for a local authority to provide housing for a family if the children would otherwise stand in peril of being received into care[4]. The Act[5] also empowered local authorities to make provision 'in kind or, in exceptional circumstances, in cash', and this power enabled local

---

1   *Report of the Care of Children Committee* (above). See, generally, J Packman *The Child's Generation* (2nd edn) (Blackwell, 1981). For a brief account of the background, see the speech of the Lord Chancellor moving the second reading *Hansard* (HL) Vol 153, cols 913–925.

2   The death of two children while in the care of foster-parents and the subsequent inquiry by Sir Walter Monckton, *Report on the circumstances which led to the boarding out of Dennis and Terence O'Neill* . . . ('the Monckton Report') (1945) (Cmnd 6636), highlighted some of the issues and may have contributed to the creation of a climate of opinion favouring change; but it seems that the Monckton Report did not directly influence the legislation: R Parker in Bean and MacPherson *Approaches to Welfare* (Routledge, 1983). For a more detailed examination of the legislative history and influences which contributed to the enactment of the Children Act 1948, see S Cretney 'The Children Act 1948 – lessons for today?' [1997] CFLQ 359 and 'The State as a Parent: The Children Act 1948 in Retrospect' (1998) 114 LQR 419.

3   *Committee on Children and Young Persons* (1960) (Cmnd 1191).

4   See *Attorney-General, ex rel Tilley v Wandsworth London Borough Council* [1981] 1 WLR 854, CA.

5   Child Care Act 1980 (a consolidating measure), s 1(1).

authorities to pay off rent arrears in order to keep a roof over the family's head, and to give help with fuel debts.

Child care: a subject for specialists?

The Children Act 1948 accepted the need for specialisation in the provision of the child care service. Each local authority had to have a children's committee, and each local authority was obliged to appoint a specialist children's officer and adequate staff. However, the Local Authority Social Services Act 1970 gave effect to the view that family needs were best integrated with all other relevant social services; and Directors of Social Services were thenceforth to manage integrated social services departments. The Children Act 1989 (as will be seen[1]) gives further impetus to the concept that services for families and children in need should be developed on the basis of a collaborative and inter-disciplinary approach and this is given yet further emphasis in the Children Bill 2004.

The voluntary principle and its erosion

The emphasis of the Children Act 1948 was on the need to return children to their parents; and the main purpose of so-called voluntary care was to cater for short-term difficulties without overriding the rights and duties of a parent and without recourse to the courts[2]. The legislation imposed a duty on local authorities to receive children into their care in certain circumstances; it did not give the local authorities any right to compel a parent to place a child in care. Parents needed to be confident that, in using the child care service, they would not run any greater risk of losing their child than if they had made private fostering arrangements; and the 1948 Act provided that a local authority was not to keep a child in its care if any parent or guardian desired to take over the care of the child. It also imposed a duty on local authorities, in all cases where it appeared to them consistent with the welfare of the child so to do, to endeavour to secure that the care of the child would be taken over by a parent or guardian or by a relative or friend. It is true that local authorities could, in certain conditions – mostly involving parental culpability[3] – pass a resolution vesting the parental rights and duties in the local authority, but this could only be done[4] if the child was already in care. Moreover, the decision could be tested in the courts. The principle was thus clearly established that a child was not to be 'removed from his home or family against the will of his parent save by the order of the court, where the parent will have the opportunity to be heard before the order is made'[5].

---

1 See particularly Chapter 10 below.
2 See, per Lord Scarman, *Lewisham London Borough Council v Lewisham Juvenile Court Justices* [1980] AC 273 at 306, HL: 'No court proceedings are required for action under these subsections. The Act provides for social casework to relieve a child's distress and anger: it is not concerned to vindicate rights or to set a scene for litigation. The rescue of a lost or abandoned child, advice and help to a parent in difficulty are the objectives of the legislation. An emergency must be met, and the child protected. This is the world of social administration, not a legal battlefield. The purpose of the Act is to help in an emergency which will at best be only temporary but may be prolonged.'
3 See *O'D v South Glamorgan County Council* (1980) LGR 522 at 526, per Sir J Arnold P.
4 A court could, in certain circumstances, make a care order in favour of a local authority: see Children and Young Persons Act 1969, s 1; see also Chapter 11 below.
5 See *Lewisham London Borough Council v Lewisham Juvenile Court Justices* [1980] AC 273 at 307, per Lord Scarman.

However, it came to be thought that the voluntary principle sometimes led to the long-term future of children who were in voluntary care being neglected, since it was difficult to make plans for them. The Children Act 1975 was much influenced by the perceived dangers of allowing children to 'drift' in care; and that Act, accordingly, contained provisions which may be thought significantly to have undermined the parents' rights over a child who had been received into voluntary care. First, once a child had been in care for a period of six months, a parent or guardian would be guilty of a criminal offence if he removed the child from the accommodation provided for him by the authority unless the parent or guardian had given the authority not less than 28 days' notice in writing of his intention or had the authority's consent; and, if a parent did give such a notice, the local authority would no doubt consider whether to take other action – for example, making the child a ward of court[1] – to enable it to protect the child's interests. Secondly, it was provided that the foster-parents of a child who had been boarded out with them for three years were to be entitled to seek a custodianship order[2] giving them legal custody of the child. Finally, the fact that a child had been in the care of a local authority for three years was made a ground on which the authority could pass a parental rights resolution assuming the parental rights and duties over a child in their care. Taking these three provisions of the Children Act 1975 together, it was clear that the rights of parents whose children had been in care for any length of time had been significantly eroded: consideration of the parents' rights should no longer be allowed to inhibit proper long-term planning for the welfare of children. As will be seen, the Children Act 1989 marks a decisive swing away from the philosophy of the 1975 Act, whilst still seeking to protect children from the dangers of drift. As we shall see, the voluntary principle is now underscored by the European Convention for the Protection of Human Rights and Fundamental Freedoms (ECHR). The opportunities for parents to challenge in the courts the various actions which local authorities take in relation to their children may be expected to increase significantly now that the Human Rights Act 1998 has been implemented[3].

Adoption

Background
It has already been mentioned that the Poor Law Act 1889 empowered poor law guardians to assume parental rights in respect of children who had been deserted, and legislation[4] sometimes referred to this procedure as 'adoption'. In fact – in marked contrast to other systems of law, which had long accepted the possibility of transferring a child from one family unit to another – English law made no provision for legal adoption until 1926, but it appears that the practice of informal

---

1   See Chapter 11 below.
2   See Chapter 6 below.
3   For a good introduction to the issues see R Tolson QC *Care Plans and the Human Rights Act* (Family Law, 2002), a special bulletin on the House of Lords decision in *Re S (Minors) (Care Order: Implementation of Care Plan); Re W (Minors) (Care Order: Adequacy of Care Plan)* [2002] 1 FLR 815.
4   For example, the Poor Law Act 1899.

adoption grew considerably in the first part of the twentieth century[1]. There were a number of reasons for this[2]. First, the First World War led to an increase in the numbers of orphans who were available for adoption. In addition, it may have led to an increase in the number of those who were unable or unwilling to look after their own children. Secondly, growing knowledge of child psychology led to a preference in informed circles for bringing up children as a member of a family in a normal home surrounding rather than in an institution. Thirdly, there was an increasing tendency on the part of those who had no children of their own, or desired another child, to value a child's life and to desire association with and companionship with children. Finally, societies formed to encourage adoption gave publicity to the practice.

Not surprisingly, there was considerable dissatisfaction about the lack of any legal framework to regulate the practice of adoption. This dissatisfaction came from two main sources. First, there were those who were primarily concerned to provide security for the adopters: the law forbade a parent to bargain away his parental rights, and a parent might at any time seek to reclaim his child from the 'adopters'; conversely, a parent who had placed her child with adopters might then, at any time, be forced to take the child back. Secondly, there were those who were primarily concerned with the evils of child trafficking. Under the law as it stood before 1926, children could be handed from one person to another, with or without payment, or sent out of the country without any record being kept; intermediaries could accept children for adoption, and dispose of them as and when they chose; and 'homes' and institutions for the reception of children existed which were not subject to any system of inspection or control. A particularly obtrusive feature was the use of newspaper advertisements, often inserted by professional agents who would charge, both the natural parent and the adopters, large fees. For example, one individual was found to have inserted advertisements in these terms:

'Good refined home required for an army officer's twin boy and girl, fortnight old.'

'Adoption – beautiful blue-eyed boy wishes to be adopted where he would give love in return for parents and home.'

Pressure led to the appointment of the Hopkinson Committee on Adoption, in 1921. This Committee was favourably disposed to the introduction of legislation legalising adoption; and it considered that adoption was the next best thing to a stable home with natural parents. It thought that it was a proper object of the law to satisfy the natural desire of the childless to have the care and upbringing of the child, and it considered that this was often, in itself, the best guarantee of an adopted child's welfare. The Committee recognised that legal adoption would never be more than one link in the chain and proposed measures to prevent abuse of long-term child care arrangements.

There was still a reluctance, however, to legislate. Ultimately, the Government appointed a second Committee under the chairmanship of Mr Justice Tomlin.

---

1 On the history of legal adoption in England, see S Cretney 'From Status to Contract?' in FD Rose (ed) *Consensus Ad Idem: Essays in the Law of Contract in honour of Guenther Treitel* (Sweet & Maxwell, 1996) at pp 251–268, and N Lowe 'English Adoption Law: Past, Present, and Future' in S Katz, J Eekelaar and M Maclean (eds) *Cross Currents* (Oxford University Press, 2000).

2 See *Report of the Committee on Child Adoption* (1921) (Cmnd 1254) and *Report of the Child Adoption Committee* (1925) (Cmnd 2401).

That Committee was unenthusiastic about the validity of the arguments for legal adoption, but concluded that a case had been made for giving some legal recognition to the link between the adopter and the adopted child, and for creating a procedure for the transfer of parental rights and duties. The Adoption of Children Act 1926, which laid the foundation for the modern law, followed.

The changing nature of adoption

The picture so far presented of adoption corresponds with its popular image; it is a legal procedure enabling those who are unable to have children to adopt a baby whom the adopters will thenceforth treat in all respects as if the child had been born to them. But, in fact, adoption increasingly came to be seen as an appropriate legal technique to be employed by local authorities concerned to provide a secure home for children in their care – often older children (who might have been in care for some years) and disabled children. In recent years, the nature and purposes of adoption and adoption law have been the subject of an extensive review culminating in the Adoption and Children Act 2002. One of the prime objectives of this legislation is to make increased use of adoption as a permanent solution for children in long-term care. But, as will become apparent, there are tensions between this policy direction and the demands of human rights legislation which require that action to protect children be limited to that which is necessary and proportionate. This requires that every effort be made by the State to reunify children with their birth families. These developments are considered in Chapter 7.

Child protection legislation

What part does the criminal law have to play in promoting the welfare of children? One technique which has been increasingly used is to prohibit activities, such as caring for children for reward, unless certain formalities, for example registration, are met. In recent years there has been heightened concern about the fitness of those working with children, reflected particularly in the Protection of Children Act 1999 and the Care Standards Act 2000. The first example of such legislation is the Infant Life Protection Act 1872[1], which was concerned to eradicate the worst evils of baby farming – then, often described as adoption. It seems that a pregnant unmarried woman would arrange for her child to be delivered in a private lying-in house, and pay the owner a lump sum (perhaps as little as £5) in exchange for the owner agreeing to arrange the baby's adoption. The baby was soon removed to the 'worst class of baby farming house', where children were 'so culpably neglected, so ill-treated, and so badly nurtured' (for example on a diet consisting of a mixture of laudanum, lime, corn flour, water, milk and washing powder) 'that with rare exceptions they all of them die within a very short time'. In response to a number of notorious cases, the Infant Life Protection Act 1872 required registration of persons who, for payment, took charge of two or more infants under one year of age for more than 24 hours. As will be seen[2], legislation now requires registration and supervision of a wide range of activities, including the provision of private fostering, day care, residential care, and so on.

---

1   Following the *Report of the Select Committee on Protection of Infant Life* (1871).
2   See Chapter 10 below.

Punishment for ill-treatment of children

The Prevention of Cruelty to, and Protection of, Children Act 1889 was the first of many statutes seeking by the imposition of criminal penalties to deter mistreatment of children. Thus, it is an offence for a person over the age of 16 to assault, ill-treat, neglect or abandon any child for whom he has responsibility[1]. Over the years, criminal offences have often been created in the wake of particular well-publicised scandals – for example, it was made an offence to allow a child to be in a room containing an unguarded heating appliance if this resulted in serious injury to the child, and it was made an offence to cause the death of a child under the age of three by overlaying it in bed if the defendant was under the influence of drink when the defendant went to bed[2]. Legislation also criminalises conduct which is thought to expose children to danger – it is, for example, an offence under the Crossbows Act 1987 to sell or hire a crossbow to a person under the age of 17; the Children and Young Persons (Protection from Tobacco) Act 1991 creates offences intended to prevent children having access to that drug; while the Tattooing of Minors Act 1969 made it an offence to tattoo a person under the age of 18 except for medical reasons. It is not always clear that such legislation serves any long-term need.

Preventing the economic exploitation of children

The Act to regulate the labour of children and young persons in the mills and factories of the UK enacted in 1883 was the first of many legislative attempts to prevent the economic exploitation of children, and the statute book contains general rules (for example, that no child be employed so long as he is under 14, or before 7 am and after 7 pm[3]) as well as specific prohibitions or regulations in respect of certain kinds of activity – such as acrobatics[4].

Compulsory child care measures

As discussed earlier, the Poor Law allowed the Poor Law guardians to assume parental rights in respect of pauper children in some circumstances and, latterly, juvenile courts were allowed to commit children who were found to be in danger to the care of a local authority. The juvenile courts were primarily concerned with children who were accused of criminal offences, but in the 1960s it was asked increasingly whether the social control of harmful behaviour by the young on the one hand, and social measures designed to protect and help the young on the other, should remain distinct and separate processes. The view that the aim of protecting society from juvenile delinquency and the aim of helping children in trouble to grow up into mature and law-abiding persons were essentially complementary[5] became increasingly accepted, and with it came a reluctance to classify children in need into two distinct groups – the deprived and the depraved.

The Children and Young Persons Act 1969 was influenced by these views. The court was given power to make orders – including a care order committing a child to the care of a specified local authority – if any one of a number of primary conditions was proved, but the court was only to make an order if the so-called

---

1   The legislation is now embodied in the Children and Young Persons Act 1933, s 1, as amended.
2   Children and Young Persons Act 1933, s 1(2)(b).
3   Ibid, s 18(1), as amended.
4   Ibid, ss 23, 30; and see Chapter 15 below.
5   *Children in Trouble* (1968) (Cmnd 3601) para 7.

'care and control' test was satisfied – that is to say, if the court considered that the child was in need of care and control which he was unlikely to receive unless the court made an order[1]. The primary conditions included[2] the condition that the child was guilty of an offence[3], and it is fundamental to an understanding of the 1969 legislation that a primary focus of its concern was the delinquent child and that it was intended that care proceedings under the Act should routinely be used instead of prosecution in cases of delinquency.

This policy was always controversial; and it was abandoned by a Conservative government. Although the 'offence' condition remained in force, it was rarely used: the great majority of delinquent children against whom legal proceedings were taken continued to be prosecuted. Care proceedings were, in practice, taken by local authorities who considered that a child was being ill-treated or that his health or development was being avoidably impaired or neglected[4]. But the legislation was drafted to deal with both the delinquent and the needy, and this duality of function led to considerable ambivalence about the nature of the proceedings. For example, it seemed reasonable that the child accused of delinquency should be protected by strict rules of evidence, and that a high standard of proof be required if a finding of guilt was to be made. However, it increasingly came to be seen that these considerations sometimes prevented appropriate action being taken to protect a child who was suffering neglect. This ambivalence was only resolved by the provisions of the Children Act 1989 which impose a strict division between the prosecution of child offenders – now to be dealt with in special youth courts[5] – and taking measures for the care and protection of children at risk of significant harm[6], a matter usually handled in the first instance by the family proceedings court, also a magistrates' court but quite distinct from the youth court.

SPECIAL PROTECTION FOR CHILDREN ON PARENTAL DIVORCE

Background

Since judicial divorce become available in the UK in 1858, there has been a substantial upward trend in the divorce rate. In 1858 there were only 244 divorce petitions. In 1914, for the first time, the number exceeded 1,000, and in 1942 the number of petitions rose above 100,000[7]. These figures may seem small by comparison with the 150,000 or so divorces which were the annual average in the last decade of the twentieth century, but there was grave concern about the impact

---

1   Children and Young Persons Act 1969, s 1(2). On the evolution of policy, see generally
    JM Eekelaar, R Dingwall and T Murray 'Victims or Threats? Children in Care Proceedings'
    (1982) JSWL 67.
2   Children and Young Persons Act 1969, s 1(2)(f).
3   Excluding homicide: ibid, s 1(2)(f). Homicides continued to be dealt with under the provisions
    of the Children and Young Persons Act 1933, s 53 and are now governed by s 90 of the Powers
    of Criminal Courts (Sentencing) Act 2000. See Chapter 14.
4   Children and Young Persons Act 1969, s 1(2)(a).
5   See the Criminal Justice Act 1991; and see Chapter 14 below.
6   See Chapter 11 below.
7   See the *Royal Commission on Marriage and Divorce* (1956) (Cmnd 9678) Appendix 2, Table 1.

of divorce on children, and there was also widespread agreement that the divorce process should do everything possible to mitigate any adverse effects. In the 1950s, divorce was not necessarily available to all who sought it: a matrimonial offence had to be proved, amongst other conditions[1], and there were those who thought that the interests of the children might be regarded as being of secondary importance. In particular, if the divorce was not opposed and there was no dispute about the custody of the children, the court would have no way of knowing whether the parties had done what was really best for the children, or whether (perhaps) one party had only agreed to the divorce in return for an assurance that he or she would be allowed custody. The traditional adversarial procedures of the courts – albeit, theoretically, not governing the practice of the divorce courts – did not enable the court to look behind the evidence which the parties chose to put before it, or to make orders which neither party had sought. There was, thus, a significant risk that the interests of the children would not be adequately safeguarded on divorce and, indeed, in 1947 the Denning Committee[2] expressed the view that, in divorce proceedings, the welfare of children was wrongly subordinated to the interest of the divorcing parents.

This concern weighed heavily with the Royal Commission on Marriage and Divorce in 1956 and the Commission concluded[3] that a procedure was needed to ensure that parents themselves had given full consideration to the question of their children's future welfare, and that the court had an effective control over the children's welfare.

Legislation

The scheme which was adopted was to enact that a decree nisi of divorce should not normally be made absolute unless, and until, the court had satisfied itself that the arrangements proposed for the care and upbringing of children were the best that could be devised in the circumstances. Legislation to give effect to this proposal was first enacted in 1958[4], and was re-enacted with modifications in 1970[5].

When this legislation was enacted, it was assumed that the divorce court would always hold a hearing but, in 1977, the 'special procedure' – under which undefended divorces are granted without the parties' attendance – was extended to cases involving children[6]. It was evidently thought important to ensure that the extension of the special procedure did not jeopardise the protection of children, and the Lord Chancellor said that he 'attached considerable importance' to the duty of the judges to protect children involved in divorce, and to the judges' ability to discuss the proposed arrangements with petitioners[7]. It was, accordingly, provided that if children were involved in divorce, a judge would hold a special

---

1 See the brief summary in SM Cretney, JM Masson and R Bailey-Harris *Principles of Family Law* (7th edn) (Sweet & Maxwell, 2002) at ch 12.
2 *Final Report of the Committee on Procedure and Matrimonial Causes* (Cmnd 7024) at para 31.
3 Ibid, para 372.
4 Matrimonial Proceedings (Children) Act 1958, s 2.
5 The legislation was consolidated in the Matrimonial Causes Act 1973, s 41.
6 In 1973 (when it was first introduced) the special procedure had been confined to undefended cases, based on living apart for two years, in which there were no children of the family: Matrimonial Causes Rules 1977, SI 1977/334, rr 33(3), 48.
7 *Hansard* Vol 371, col 1218.

children's appointment and would look into the arrangements to be made for the children's upbringing.

It was hoped that this procedure would be more effective than that available under the old system for the trial of undefended divorces in open court (which usually involved no more than the making of a formal enquiry to the petitioner as to whether there was anything to be added to the details already given in the papers). It was said that the greater informality of the children's appointment procedure would make for easier communication between parents and judge; and this would, in turn, help to uncover problems, as well as enabling judges to offer parents advice and encouragement. However, a major research project[1] demonstrated many imperfections in the system and, influenced by these considerations, Parliament amended the relevant statutory provisions. As explained below[2], the parties now have to give extended details about the arrangements which are proposed for their children, but these will be considered privately by a district judge sitting in his chambers. There is no necessity for a hearing or for any further investigation unless the district judge believes that there is ground for concern or further enquiry, and the circumstances in which a decree of divorce can be held up have been greatly restricted[3].

The Family Law Act 1996 was intended to reform radically the law of divorce[4]. However, in early 2001 the Government announced that it intended to repeal Part II of the Act, which dealt with divorce and which had never been implemented[5]. The divorce aspects of the legislation as they affect children are considered further in Chapter 4. From an historical perspective there are perhaps two features of the now defunct Part II which ought to be highlighted. The first is that, by generally requiring a statutory period for 'reflection and consideration' to be extended by six months in cases where there were minor children[6], the Act would have been a departure from the philosophy hitherto accepted by law reform bodies that divorce ought not to be made more difficult where there are children than where there are none[7]. Secondly, and most unusually for English legislation[8], the Act sets out a list of 'general principles' in Part I, which has been brought into force and which are to be given effect by the court and 'any person, in exercising functions under or in consequence' of those parts of the legislation which deal with divorce and mediation. These principles refer, inter alia, to the

---

1   E Elston, J Fuller and M Murch 'Judicial Hearings of Undefended Divorce Petitions' (1975) 38 MLR 609.

2   See Chapter 4.

3   Ibid.

4   On the Act generally, see M Freeman *The Family Law Act 1996* (Sweet & Maxwell, 1996), and on the divorce aspects specifically, see R Bird and S Cretney *Divorce: The New Law* (Family Law, 1996). A more academic analysis is to be found in SM Cretney, JM Masson and R Bailey-Harris *Principles of Family Law* (7th edn) (Sweet & Maxwell, 2002) at pp 297 et seq. See also Dame Brenda Hale 'The Family Law Act 1996 – the death of marriage?' in C Bridge (ed) *Family Law Towards the Millennium: Essays for PM Bromley* (Butterworths, 1997).

5   The reasons for this volte-face are a matter of considerable speculation. For the author's views on why it may have happened, see A Bainham 'Exciting Times in England – Human Rights, Children and Divorce' [2001] IFL 71 at pp 74–76 and, generally, Chapter 4 below.

6   Section 7(11) and (13).

7   A principle accepted by the Law Commission in its report of 1990. See Law Com No 192 *Family Law: The Ground for Divorce* (1990) at para 5.28.

8   But not for Continental civil codes, as to which see MA Glendon *The Transformation of Family Law* (University of Chicago Press, 1987) at ch 3.

need when bringing a marriage to an end to do so in a way which minimises distress or the risk of violence to children and which promotes 'as good a continuing relationship between the parties and any children affected as is possible in the circumstances'[1]. These statutory principles may be viewed by some as a bold attempt to adjust the existing balance by giving greater emphasis to the interests of children, as opposed to those of adults, on divorce. Whether the substance of divorce practice matches this rhetoric and how indeed the law *should* seek to balance the interests of children and parents on divorce are issues considered further in later chapters[2].

---

1 Section 1(c) and (d). See also s 11(3)(c).
2 Chapters 3 and 4.

Chapter 2

FUNDAMENTAL PRINCIPLES:
THE CHILDREN ACT 1989, THE UNITED NATIONS
CONVENTION ON THE RIGHTS
OF THE CHILD, AND HUMAN RIGHTS

Coincidentally, the United Nations Convention on the Rights of the Child (UNCRC) was adopted by the General Assembly in November 1989 – the same month that the Children Act reached the statute book in England. Together, these two basic sources of children law represented a fresh beginning for children in domestic and international law. Then on 2 October 2000 the Human Rights Act 1998 was implemented. This had the effect of transplanting directly into English law the rights and freedoms guaranteed by the European Convention for the Protection of Human Rights and Fundamental Freedoms (ECHR) and conferring on children so-called 'Convention rights'.

Together, these three sources now represent the most important sources of children law and for that reason they are examined in juxtaposition in this chapter. There needs to be an awareness of the inter-relationship between them. It is necessary, for example, to keep under review the extent to which the provisions of the Children Act are compatible with the ECHR. It is also necessary to bear in mind the UNCRC, which may not take exactly the same position as domestic legislation on the various issues affecting children, and these three sources may even be thought, in some instances, to be inconsistent with one another. In this chapter we consider the fundamental principles of children law as derived from these sources.

I THE CHILDREN ACT 1989

THE SCOPE OF THE LEGISLATION

General

The Children Act 1989 ('the Children Act') is now, undoubtedly, the most important single source of children law[1]. It was described by the then Lord Chancellor as 'the most comprehensive and far-reaching reform of child law which has come before Parliament in living memory'[2]. It constituted a completely new statutory code governing the 'public' and 'private' law affecting children and drew those two branches much closer together[3]. It removed, in one fell swoop, much of the complex and technical statutory law which had grown up in characteristically English, piecemeal fashion over several decades. It was, in every sense, a fresh start. As if to emphasise this break with the past, the legislation was brought into force in its entirety on 14 October 1991, thereby avoiding the delay and disjointed implementation which had previously bedevilled this area of law[4].

The Children Act established parenthood as the primary legal status in relation to children and reformed the law of guardianship to reflect this. It introduced 'parental responsibility' as the central organising concept in children law and reasserted the significance of children's welfare as the paramount consideration in disputes concerning their upbringing. It gave to the courts wide-ranging and

---

1   The Children Act has been the subject of extensive commentary and generated an unprecedented number of books within a short time of Royal Assent. These include: A Bainham *Children: The New Law* (Jordans, 1990); R White, P Carr and N Lowe *A Guide to the Children Act 1989* (3rd edn) (Butterworths, 2002); J Eekelaar and R Dingwall *The Reform of Child Care Law* (Routledge, 1990); J Masson *The Children Act 1989, Current Law Statutes Annotated* (Sweet & Maxwell, 1990); N Allen *Making Sense of the Children Act 1989* (Longman, 1990); J Bridge, S Bridge and S Luke *Blackstone's Guide to the Children Act 1989* (Blackstone Press, 1990); L Feldman and B Mitchels *The Children Act 1989: A Practical Guide* (Longman, 1990); and S Bell MP *Shaw's Annotated Acts: Children Act 1989* (Shaw & Sons, 1990). The Department of Health also issued its official guidance on the 1989 Act under the title *An Introduction to the Children Act 1989* (HMSO). Other commentaries on the legislation, which take account of the regulations and rules of court made under it, are: MDA Freeman *Children, Their Families and the Law* (Macmillan, 1992); and J Masson and M Morris *Children Act Manual* (Sweet & Maxwell, 1992). For more recent commentaries which take account of the extensive case-law under the Act, see SM Cretney, JM Masson and R Bailey-Harris *Principles of Family Law* (7th edn) (Sweet & Maxwell, 2002) Part V; M Hayes and C Williams *Family Law: Principles, Policy and Practice* (2nd edn) (Butterworths, 1999) chs 1–4; K Standley *Family Law* (4th edn) (Palgrave Macmillan, 2004) Part V; and J Herring *Family Law* (2nd edn) (Pearson, 2004) chs 7–11. For a very succinct, yet scholarly, commentary, see R Probert *Cretney's Family Law* (5th edn) (Sweet & Maxwell, 2003) Part III. See also G Douglas *An Introduction to Family Law* (2nd edn) (Clarendon, 2004) especially ch 5, and M Freeman 'The Next Children Act?' [1998] Fam Law 341.

2   *Hansard* (HL) Vol 502, col 488.

3   The expressions 'public' and 'private' law are used extensively throughout this book to indicate, respectively: the law governing care and related proceedings; and family proceedings involving disputes between private individuals such as divorce, guardianship, wardship or adoption.

4   The staggered implementation of the Children Act 1975 was a notorious example of this. While that Act, inter alia, introduced the concept of custodianship, it was a decade before this was eventually brought into force. See Part II of the 1975 Act; and the Children Act 1975 and the Domestic Proceedings and Magistrates' Courts Act 1978 (Commencement) Order 1985, SI 1985/779.

flexible powers to regulate the exercise of parental responsibility and introduced sweeping procedural and jurisdictional changes. In the public law, the legislation made fundamental adjustments to the powers and duties of local authorities regarding the family and to the relationship between local authorities and the courts in fulfilling their complementary child care functions. It established a wholly new basis for compulsory care or supervision and, while leaving intact the ancient wardship jurisdiction, imposed severe limitations on its use. New procedures for protecting children in emergencies were introduced and major changes made to the legal regulation of substitute care arrangements.

Much of the detail of the reformed law is contained in the Act's many Schedules as amended, including the code now governing the courts' powers to make financial provision for children[1], the specific duties of local authorities to children looked after by them and, more controversially, the radically reformulated supervisory role of the divorce court. The law and procedure applying to children on divorce are considered in Chapter 4. A vast amount of practical detail is consigned to the many regulations, rules of court and guidances issued under the Children Act's enabling provisions[2]. The regime established by the Children Act has been subjected to considerable scrutiny since the implementation of the Human Rights Act 1998 and it may well be that some amendments to the Act will be required to create more opportunities for parents and others to challenge the actions of local authorities in relation to children looked after by them[3].

The legislation substantially replaced all the existing private law governing the custody and upbringing of children, and the public law applying to social services for families, voluntary and compulsory care and supervision. This was no small feat. It entailed the repeal of eight post-war statutes, namely, the Nurseries and Child Minders Regulation Act 1948, the Guardianship of Minors Act 1971, the Guardianship Act 1973, the Children Act 1975, the Child Care Act 1980, the Foster Children Act 1980, the Children's Homes Act 1982 and the Children and Young Persons (Amendment) Act 1986. The Children and Young Persons Act 1969 and the Domestic Proceedings and Magistrates' Courts Act 1978 were significantly amended.

Children issues in adult litigation: beyond the Children Act 1989

Despite this extensive coverage, the Children Act still represents only one source of children law. The interests of children are affected, directly or indirectly, by a mass of statutory provisions and common law rules, many of which were left quite untouched by the Act. While, for example, the Children Act brought about some minor changes to adoption law, adoption continues to be governed by an essentially separate code[4].

---

1 The legislation largely consolidated the existing law on this, although major changes, which have severely restricted the jurisdiction of the courts, were subsequently introduced by the Child Support Act 1991, as to which see Chapter 9 below.
2 The principal enabling provisions are contained in ss 92 and 93 and Sch 11.
3 See the House of Lords decision in *Re S (Minors) (Care Order: Implementation of Care Plan)* [2002] 1 FLR 815, and Chapter 11 below.
4 Formerly the Adoption Act 1976 and now the Adoption and Children Act 2002. See Chapter 7 below.

It is clear that the student will need to look well beyond the Children Act for a proper understanding of the many and varied legal issues which concern children and young people. Thus, there are many matters which are conceptualised as 'adult issues' because it is thought that they relate *predominantly* to the competing interests of two or more adults. The interests of any children are not considered the central concern. This is evidently so in the case of divorce. The general principles set out in s 1 of the Family Law Act 1996, as noted above, do attempt to give greater prominence to children's interests on divorce[1] but do not go so far as to allow the interests or wishes of children to influence the essential basis or 'grounds' for divorce[2]. The welfare principle, which makes the best interests of children paramount, has no application to this question. Adult interests are also deemed to be relevant in varying degrees on other questions which clearly affect children. The interests of minor children are the 'first' but not paramount consideration where a court is considering what financial and housing provision to make for a parent and dependent children on divorce[3]. Since the decision of the House of Lords in *White v White*[4] and the Court of Appeal decision in *Cowan v Cowan*[5] it seems that considerations of equality and fairness as between the adult parties should be the court's principal focus, although how precisely this will relate to the duty of the court to give first consideration to the interests of minor children is not entirely clear. The issue does not directly relate to the upbringing of the child, so this is a question which falls outside the provisions of the Children Act and continues to be governed by the Matrimonial Causes Act 1973.

Likewise, where the issue is whether an order should be made excluding a husband or partner from the family home, the interests of children (while relevant) are neither the 'first' nor the 'paramount' consideration. The Matrimonial Homes Act 1983, s 1(3) specified as a factor the needs of the children alongside the conduct of the adult parties and their needs and resources. It is fair to say that the Family Law Act 1996 does attempt to give greater weight to the interests of children on applications for occupation orders since, in the case of 'entitled applicants' and former spouses, there is in effect a *presumption* that an order be made where 'the applicant or any relevant child is likely to suffer significant harm attributable to conduct of the respondent' unless at least as much, or more, harm is likely to be suffered if the order is made. The position is complex, however, in that no such presumption applies in the case of 'non-entitled' cohabitants or former cohabitants, although the court must still have regard to the 'balance of harm' criterion[6].

In all these instances, the welfare of children is bound to be affected by the various outcomes and, to the uninitiated, the way in which the law ascribes more or less relevance to this may appear somewhat arbitrary. Yet this may simply be a reflection of the relative importance which society is prepared to attach to the often competing claims of children and adults. It is not really surprising that this

---

1   See Chapters 1 and 4.
2   For a full discussion of the ground for divorce, see Law Com Report No 192 *The Ground for Divorce* (1990) and Chapter 4 below.
3   Matrimonial Causes Act 1973, s 25(1). For a case in which the interests of a child had a significant influence on the outcome, see *C v C (Financial Relief: Short Marriage)* [1997] 2 FLR 26.
4   [2000] 2 FLR 981.
5   [2001] 1 FLR 192.
6   See Family Law Act 1996, ss 33(6) and (7), 35(6)–(8) and 38(4) and (5).

should vary depending on the question which is being asked or that a different answer to the same question may be given at different times. It must, moreover, be acknowledged that, notwithstanding the current trend to deny the existence of independent 'rights' for parents, the reality is that the law does not always give precedence to children's interests. Increasingly also there will be difficult questions about how to balance the 'Convention rights' of parents and children under the ECHR. This difficult question of balancing the claims of children with those of parents and other adults is considered below[1].

Impact of the Children Act 1989 on other legislation

Broadly, the Children Act incorporates those jurisdictions and those issues which can conveniently be termed 'children jurisdictions' and 'children issues'. 'Adult jurisdictions' and 'adult issues' are governed by separate pieces of legislation. At the same time, proceedings under certain other enactments are 'family proceedings' for the purposes of the Children Act[2]. Where this is so, and a 'children issue' arises in family proceedings, that issue will fall to be determined by applying the welfare principle and the other principles in the Children Act which apply to all family proceedings. To that extent the Children Act has a direct impact on other legislation.

Take the example of an application for an occupation order, a matter involving the criteria in Part IV of the Family Law Act 1996. The ouster issue itself must be determined by the criteria in that legislation. But the proceedings are 'family proceedings' and the question of the residential arrangements for any children is, clearly, highly relevant. This latter issue relates to the upbringing of children, falling directly within s 1 of the Children Act, and is governed by the welfare principle. The child's welfare is only one of several factors relevant to the occupation issue but is the sole consideration on the residence issue. The beauty of the Children Act was that it enabled the court, for the first time, to hear these obviously related issues together in the same proceedings. This can, of course, give rise to further difficulties concerning the proper balance to be struck between the interests of children and adults in this context.

The Law Commission considered whether it might be possible to collect, in a single statute, all the courts' powers over upbringing and financial provision for children. But it concluded that it was 'convenient for the statutes dealing principally with the affairs of adults to contain those of the provisions relating to children which cannot readily be separated from those relating to adults'. Where these powers related exclusively to children, the Law Commission felt that they could be conveniently collected in one place and the Children Act gave effect to this[3].

Other children issues

The Children Act does not provide the answer to certain other fundamental questions regarding the legal position of children. The very nature of the legal

---

1   See Chapter 3 below.
2   Section 8(3) and (4). Section 8(4) was amended to include proceedings under the Family Law Act 1996 and the Crime and Disorder Act 1998. See further Chapter 4.
3   Law Com Report No 172 *Review of Child Law: Guardianship and Custody* (1988) at para 1.8.

relationship between parents and children still largely falls to be determined at common law. The Children Act did little more than repeat the open-ended and imprecise definition of 'parental rights and duties' in its definition of 'parental responsibility'[1]. Certain aspects of upbringing, notably education, are substantially regulated by separate statutory regimes[2]. The principles of child support are now substantially contained in the Child Support Acts 1991 and 1995, as amended by the Child Support, Pensions and Social Security Act 2000, and cannot be properly understood without some knowledge of social security legislation[3]. In fact, a host of issues concerning the position of children in society, and their involvement with individuals and institutions outside the family, are governed by a mixture of common law and statutory rules[4]. This is true of employment, contractual capacity, tortious liability and criminal responsibility. There is also a plethora of ad hoc statutory provisions reflecting society's concern to protect children from harmful activities and influences which arise from time to time[5]. Increasingly, also, it is necessary to take account of the international dimension. There is, in particular, a burgeoning growth in domestic and international law dealing with the problem of child abduction[6]; and there is now strong international recognition of the 'rights' of children as an aspect of human rights, most obviously reflected in the UNCRC and the ECHR, and, increasingly, under other Conventions[7].

The student of children in the modern law must therefore be prepared to search well beyond the confines of the Children Act, but it would be idle to deny the key significance of the Act. A good part of this book is thus concerned with the application of the Children Act in particular contexts. This can only be properly understood in the light of the central principles which are expressly enunciated by the Children Act and some of the underlying philosophies which those principles may be thought to encapsulate.

THE HISTORY OF THE LEGISLATION

The Children Act was not the product of one single influence. It rather emerged in its final form as a result of the happy coincidence of two independent reviews, and a general climate of opinion in which there was impatience to rectify what were seen as intolerable deficiencies in existing law and practice.

The public law review

In 1982, the House of Commons Social Services Select Committee began an inquiry into aspects of the practice relating to children in care. Its report ('the *Short Report*') produced in 1984, concluded that a thorough-going review of the

---

1   Children Act 1975, s 85(1) and Children Act 1989, s 3(1).
2   The various Education Acts from 1944 to 2002 are discussed in Chapter 16 below.
3   See Chapter 9 below.
4   Part IV of this book is largely concerned with the law affecting the position of children in wider society.
5   Examples are the Tattooing of Minors Act 1969 and the Protection of Children Act 1978.
6   See Chapter 17 below.
7   See, generally, G Van Bueren *The International Law on the Rights of the Child* (Martinus Nijhoff, 1995) and Chapter 17 below.

whole body of child care law was overdue. The Department of Health and Social Security (as it then was) set up an interdepartmental working party comprising civil servants from relevant government departments and representatives from the Law Commission. This Committee produced a lengthy consultation paper in October 1985, entitled the *Review of Child Care Law* ('the *Review*'). Most, but not all, of the recommendations were accepted by the Government in its White Paper entitled *The Law on Child Care and Family Services*[1] ('the White Paper') published in January 1987. It is important to appreciate that the bulk of the reforms to the public law now embodied in the Children Act derive from these two sources. The former document is the more significant since it sets out, in some considerable detail, the reasoning behind the reforms. The White Paper needs to be taken together with the *Review*, not least because it rejected certain of the *Review*'s recommendations, including the original proposal to retain the concept of 'voluntary care' and to sub-divide it into 'respite' care and 'shared' care[2]. In the event, the very idea of voluntary care was abandoned in favour of a new concept of 'looking after' or 'accommodating' children on a voluntary basis[3].

It had been a popular misconception that the legislation in general, and the reforms to care procedures in particular, were a reaction to the crisis concerning the investigation of child sexual abuse which occurred in Cleveland in June 1987 and was the subject of a subsequent report by Lady Justice Butler-Sloss[4]. It is quite evident that this was not the case since, chronologically, the *Review* and the White Paper pre-date even the first murmurings of the crisis. Yet it is probably fair to say that, more than any other single influence, what happened in Cleveland contributed to the gathering impetus for early reform. Just as Cleveland had alerted public opinion to the dangers of 'over-reaction' to the problems of child abuse, so a succession of public inquiries into the domestic homicide of individual children exposed the opposite danger of 'under-reaction'. Among these, the more influential were probably those relating to Jasmine Beckford, Tyra Henry and Kimberley Carlile[5]. Other major influences on the legislation were several decisions of the European Court of Human Rights[6] (which found aspects of English child care procedures incompatible with the ECHR) and the House of Lords decision in the *Gillick* case[7] (which highlighted children's claims to have

---

1 Cmnd 62.
2 The *Review*, at chs 6 and 7. Cf the White Paper, at para 26.
3 See Chapter 10 below.
4 *Report of the Inquiry into Child Abuse in Cleveland 1987* (1988) (Cmnd 412). See also Chapters 11 and 12 below.
5 *A Child in Trust: The Report of the Panel of Inquiry into the Circumstances surrounding the death of Jasmine Beckford* (London Borough of Brent, 1985); *Whose Child? The Report of the Public Inquiry into the death of Tyra Henry* (London Borough of Lambeth, 1987); *A Child in Mind: Protection of Children in a Responsible Society: Report of the Commission of Inquiry into the Circumstances surrounding the death of Kimberley Carlile* (London Borough of Greenwich, 1987); and more recently see Lord Laming *The Victoria Climbié Report* (London: The Stationery Office, 2003). For academic assessments of the role of public inquiries in children cases, see R Dingwall 'The Jasmine Beckford Affair' (1986) 49 MLR 489 and N Parton and N Martin 'Public Inquiries, legalism and child care in England and Wales' (1989) 3 IJLF 21. More recently, see B Corby, A Doig and V Roberts 'Inquiries into Child Abuse' (1998) 20 JSWFL 377 and B Corby 'Towards a new means of inquiry into child abuse cases' (2003) 25 JSWFL 229.
6 *R v UK, O v UK, W v UK* [1988] 2 FLR 445, ECtHR.
7 *Gillick v West Norfolk and Wisbech Area Health Authority* [1986] 1 AC 112. See Chapter 8 below.

their views heard as an aspect of children's rights)[1]. Other provisions in the Children Act are the result of the many amendments to the Children Bill during its passage through Parliament, of which the most significant was probably the introduction of the 'child assessment order'[2]. This was not mentioned in the *Review* or the White Paper, was rejected by the Butler-Sloss report and only emerged at the eleventh hour following lengthy debate in Parliament.

The private law review

Contemporaneously with the review of child care law, the Law Commission had been conducting its own review of child law which was concerned with the 'private' law of custody, guardianship and wardship. Between 1985 and 1987 it produced four working papers on, respectively, *Guardianship*[3], *Custody*[4], *Care, Supervision and Interim Orders in Custody Proceedings*[5] and *Wards of Court*[6]. After consultation, the Commission unveiled its final report on *Guardianship and Custody*[7] in July 1988. It is this report which is the foundation for the private law reforms and the central principles which appear in Parts I and II of the Children Act. The content of the first three working papers was largely subsumed in the 1988 report but the fourth, on wardship, remains an important source of reference in its own right. This is because the Commission, after consultation, decided not to make final recommendations on the future of the wardship jurisdiction. Despite this, the Children Act (to the surprise of many) imposed drastic restrictions on the hitherto liberal use of wardship and the inherent jurisdiction by local authorities. In future, the procedure would be largely confined to the private sphere, and there was some speculation on whether it could, or should, survive at all the radical remodelling of legal procedures effected by the Children Act[8].

The position in 1988, when the Law Commission reported, was that the Government had already announced its proposals for the reform of child care law. This convenient conclusion of the two reviews presented, as the former Lord Chancellor, Lord Mackay, put it, 'an historic opportunity to reform the English Law into a single rationalised system as it applies to the care and upbringing of children'[9]. The draft Bill, which the Commission annexed to its report, reflected and incorporated the results of both reviews. This not only enabled all the public and private law to be gathered together in one place, it also presented the

---

1 For discussion of the provisions in the Children Act which reflect this aspect of children's rights see A Bainham 'The Children Act 1989: Adolescence and Children's Rights' [1990] Fam Law 311.

2 Section 43. See Chapter 12 below.

3 Law Com Working Paper No 91 *Review of Child Law: Guardianship* (1985).

4 Law Com Working Paper No 96 *Review of Child Law: Custody* (1986). See also Law Com Supplement to Working Paper No 96 *Custody Law in Practice in the Divorce and Domestic Courts* (1986).

5 Law Com Working Paper No 100 *Review of Child Law: Care, Supervision and Interim Orders in Custody Proceedings* (1987).

6 Law Com Working Paper No 101 *Review of Child Law: Wards of Court* (1987).

7 Law Com Report No 172 *Review of Child Law: Guardianship and Custody* (1988).

8 See, for example, N Lowe 'Caring for Children' (1989) 139 NLJ 87 and A Bainham 'The Children Act 1989: The Future of Wardship' [1990] Fam Law 270. Cf J Eekelaar and R Dingwall 'The Role of the Courts under the Children Bill' (1989) 139 NLJ 217.

9 Child and Co Lecture, April 1988.

Commission with a unique chance to formulate common principles and establish common remedies which would apply, as far as possible, in both the public and private spheres[1]. Therefore, while the private law and public law remain distinct in certain important respects, the Children Act brought about a partial fusion of what were previously seen as two substantially distinctive codes.

CENTRAL PRINCIPLES

Part I of the Children Act contains a number of fundamental principles which apply throughout the legislation and are common to the public and private law. It also introduces and defines the key concept of 'parental responsibility' which, again, has application in the public and private spheres. In the following pages, the principles themselves as they appear in the Children Act are considered, after which the philosophies and ideologies which may be reflected in those principles are explored.

The welfare principle

Paramount or sole consideration
Section 1(1) of the Children Act re-enacted, in slightly modified form, what is the cardinal principle in children law. It provides:

'When a court determines any question with respect to:
(a)   the upbringing of a child, or
(b)   the administration of a child's property or the application of any income arising from it,
the child's welfare shall be the court's paramount consideration.'

The former provision in the Guardianship of Minors Act 1971 made the welfare of the child the 'first and paramount' consideration, but, in 1970, the House of Lords in *J v C*[2] interpreted similar wording in the Guardianship of Infants Act 1925 to mean that the child's welfare should be the court's *sole* concern. All other considerations were to be excluded, except insofar as they had a bearing on the determination of the child's best interests. The principle, as Lord MacDermott put it, means:

'. . . more than that the child's welfare is to be treated as the top item in a list of items relevant to the matter in question. [The words] connote a process whereby, when all the relevant facts, relationships, claims and wishes of parents, risks, choices and other circumstances are taken into account and weighed, the course to be followed will be that which is most in the interests of the child's welfare as that term is now to be understood. That is the first consideration because it is of first importance and the paramount consideration because it rules upon or determines the course to be followed.'[3]

Since, according to this interpretation, welfare is the *only* consideration, the Law Commission took the view that to describe it also as the 'first' consideration

---

1   For a succinct explanation of the general aims of the legislation, see B Hoggett 'The Children Bill: The Aim' [1989] Fam Law 217.
2   [1970] AC 668.
3   Ibid at 710–711.

would be otiose[1]. Hence, this is the preferred formulation, but it should be noted that no change of substance was intended, and Lord MacDermott's settled interpretation applies as much today as it did in 1970.

Can paramountcy survive the Human Rights Act 1998?

In recent years the welfare principle has been subjected to a good deal of academic analysis[2] and there has been much speculation about whether it can survive the incorporation of the ECHR into English law by the HRA 1998.[3]

Is Lord MacDermott's classic interpretation of the principle compatible with the balancing exercise which the courts are required to perform under the ECHR where children's interests may clash with the rights of adults? The problem, in a nutshell, is this: if the welfare of the individual child is the *sole* consideration for the court, does this not mean, as Lord MacDermott seemed clearly to say, that any adult rights in issue would simply be subsumed in the process of investigation of the child's best interests? On that basis adult rights as such would be regarded as *irrelevant* except in so far as they shed light on the central question of the child's best interests. This has been the understanding in English law for the last 30 years or so, although it must be said that in reality there has always been an awareness that children disputes are clearly about adult interests too.[4] But can this approach continue to be taken, particularly under Article 8 of the ECHR which seems to require something quite different.[5] Adult rights to respect for private and family life *must* be respected and must not be interfered with unless the specific justifications envisaged by Article 8(2)[6] exist and only then when they are *necessary* and *proportionate* to a legitimate State aim. This is prima facie very much more prescriptive than merely leaving it to a court to decide at large what course of action is in the best interests of a child.

---

1 Law Com Report No 172 *Review of Child Law: Guardianship and Custody* (1988) at paras 3.12–3.16. In fact the Commission proposed that the welfare of the child should be the court's 'only concern' and this form of wording appeared in its draft Bill. In the event, the word 'first' was dropped while the 'paramount consideration' formula was retained.

2 See especially J Eekelaar 'Beyond the Welfare Principle' [2002] CFLQ 237; H Reece 'The Paramountcy Principle – Consensus or Construct?' (1996) 49 *Current Legal Problems* 267; and N Lowe 'The House of Lords and the Welfare Principle' in C Bridge (ed) *Family Law Towards the Millennium: Essays for PM Bromley* (Butterworths, 1997).

3 See J Herring 'The Human Rights Act and the Welfare Principle in Family Law – Conflicting or Complementary?' [1999] CFLQ 223; J Herring 'The Welfare Principle and the Rights of Parents' in A Bainham, S Day Sclater and M Richards *What is a Parent? A Socio-Legal Analysis* (Hart Publishing, 1999); J Fortin 'The HRA's impact on litigation involving children and their families' [1999] CFLQ 237 and A Bainham 'Can we Protect Children and Protect their Rights?' [2002] Fam Law 279.

4 See, for example, A Bainham 'Children Law at the Millennium' in S Cretney (ed) *Family Law: Essays for the New Millennium* (Family Law, 2000) and M Freeman 'Disputing Children' in S Katz, J Eekelaar and M Maclean *Cross Currents* (Oxford University Press, 2000).

5 See further Chapter 3 below.

6 Article 8(2) provides:
  'There shall be no interference by a public authority with the exercise of this right except such as is in accordance with the law and is necessary in a democratic society, in the interests of public safety, for the protection of public order, health or morals, or for the protection of the rights and freedoms of others.'

So what is the answer? There has been no shortage of suggestions. Fortin's view[1] is that the welfare of the child acts as a qualification or limitation on the adult rights in Article 8. These rights must be respected and upheld except where to do this would be contrary to the best interests of the child. An objection to this approach put forward by Eekelaar is that it 'may place the interests of children too low. The sequence is: have regard first to the rights of adults and apply these, *unless* it can be shown that it is necessary in a democratic society to depart from them on account of the welfare of the child'[2]. Eekelaar has himself tentatively suggested a new approach which might involve abandonment of the welfare principle as we know it. Under this approach the concept of welfare would be replaced by the concept of 'well-being' since welfare is an expression which 'can be too easily used to cover anything someone else thinks is good for you'. The concept of 'well-being' would offer a more 'nuanced approach' and would be 'indicated by the degree of success achieved in realising the person's significant goals in life'[3]. He goes on to suggest a formulaic approach under which the well-being of all concerned, children and adults, is measured and favours the course of action which 'avoids inflicting the most damage on the well-being of any interested individual'. He prefers this to a 'crude utilitarian attempt at maximising the well-being of the greatest number ... since this would pay insufficient regard to the extreme adverse effects of certain outcomes, on the well-being of particular individuals'. It is impossible to do justice to Eekelaar's complex thesis here but it repays closer attention because it does represent one attempt to accommodate the interests of *both* children and adults in an era of human rights which surely requires this[4].

If there is a criticism which can be made of most of the commentaries on this issue it is that they all appear to take the position that the question under the ECHR is how to reconcile adult rights with the welfare of children where the two may appear to conflict, and there is a good deal in the jurisprudence of the courts to suggest that this is how they also view the dilemma. But this leaves out of account a further dimension. This is that, quite apart from a commitment to the child's welfare, the child also has 'Convention rights' as do adults. The child has as much right to respect for family life under Article 8, for example, as does a parent. Therefore, one answer to Eekelaar's objection that to put rights before welfare would be to attach too great an importance to adult interests and too low a priority to children's, is that this need not be the position even under what he calls the 'Convention approach'. This is because the court would be having regard from the outset not merely to the child's welfare as perceived by the court but to that child's *Convention rights*[5].

Take, for example, the facts of *Payne v Payne*[6] which is considered in greater depth in Chapter 4. A mother wishes to relocate with her child on the other side of

---

1   J Fortin 'The HRA's impact on litigation involving children and their families' [1999] CFLQ 237.
2   Ibid at p 240.
3   Ibid at p 243.
4   See further A Bainham 'Non-Intervention and Judicial Paternalism' in P Birks (ed) *The Frontiers of Liability* (Oxford University Press, 1994).
5   See further A Bainham 'Can We Protect Children and Protect their Rights?' [2002] Fam Law 279. For a recent case in which the content of a child's Convention rights was explored judicially, see *Re Roddy (A Child) (Identification: Restriction on Publication)* [2004] 2 FLR 949.
6   [2001] 1 FLR 1052.

the world, leaving behind in England the father and the paternal family who have regular contact and a good relationship with the child. This could be presented as a straightforward clash between the rights of the father and his family to respect for family life with the child and the best interests of the child which might be thought to be associated with the mother's happiness as primary carer. This indeed has been largely how the case has been perceived. But it might be presented rather differently by focusing more closely on the child's own *Convention rights*. The starting point then would be that the child would have a right to respect for family life with *both* mother and father, and any interference with this should be justified as proportionate and necessary to a legitimate aim. It is more than likely that the result would be the same, except perhaps that greater attention might have been paid by the court to the need to safeguard in the longer term the contact between the child and the paternal family[1]. But such an approach would take into account the interests of all concerned and would perhaps also meet Eekelaar's objection that the rights of adults are being given precedence over the interests of the child. The answer, it is submitted, is to make sure that children's *own* Convention rights are ranked and considered alongside the Convention rights of adults. The difficulty of course is that this involves further complex questions about how the child's Convention rights are to be defined. This is something which is explored further in Chapter 3.

The conclusion for the moment is that it will be increasingly difficult to apply the *paramountcy principle* alongside respect for children's rights and that *some* more sophisticated approach which explicitly takes account of the *rights* of all concerned is going to be necessary. None of this should detract, however, from the undeniable fact that the ECtHR has shown a willingness on many occasions to uphold the decisions of domestic courts which have in the final analysis been substantially grounded in the best interests of the child[2]. Attaching *priority* to the best interests of the child seems not to be a problem as long as adult interests are not ignored in the process. The welfare of the child plays a *preponderant* role but cannot be regarded as *paramount* in the sense of being the *sole* matter under consideration.

Welfare 'checklist' introduced

Lord MacDermott referred, in his now famous dictum, to welfare 'as that term is now to be understood'. This begs the question of how precisely the term *is* understood at any given time. The truth is that the 'welfare' or 'best interests' of children are notoriously indeterminate concepts, so much so that it has been argued that the really crucial issue is not the concept of welfare itself but the choice of decision-maker[3]. What is or is not in children's interests depends largely on who is asked the question. Thus, there are those who have asserted that the psychological well-being of children following divorce is best protected by 'exclusive' custodial arrangements which provide them with the security of one

---

1   Specifically for the author's view on the Court of Appeal decision see A Bainham 'Taking Children Abroad: Human Rights, Welfare and the Courts' [2001] 60 CLJ 489.

2   For one such example of many, see the ECtHR's decision in *Söderback v Sweden* [1999] 1 FLR 250.

3   RH Mnookin 'Child Custody Adjudication: Judicial Functions in the Face of Indeterminacy' (1975) 39 *Law and Contemporary Problems* 226 and 'Thinking about Children's Rights – Beyond Kiddie Libbers and Child Savers' (1981) 16 *Stanford Lawyer* 24.

'psychological parent'[1]. But, equally, there are others who have taken the very different position that children fare best where contact with *both* divorcing parents is maximised and maintained[2]. It is, perhaps, inevitable that individual value judgments must intrude to some extent into the determination of a child's best interests. However, in an effort to structure judicial discretion, the Children Act broke new ground and incorporated a statutory 'checklist' of factors for courts applying the welfare principle.

The court must have regard in particular to:

'(a) the ascertainable wishes and feelings of the child concerned (considered in the light of his age and understanding);
 (b) his physical, emotional and educational needs;
 (c) the likely effect on him of any change in his circumstances;
 (d) his age, sex, background and any characteristics of his which the court considers relevant;
 (e) any harm which he has suffered or is at risk of suffering;
 (f) how capable each of his parents, and any other person in relation to whom the court considers the question to be relevant, is of meeting his needs;
 (g) the range of powers available to the court under this Act in the proceedings in question.'

The application of these factors in individual cases is discussed below[3]. At this stage, it is sufficient to note that the checklist applies only in *contested* private proceedings, whereas it applies to all public proceedings under Part IV of the Act whether or not they are opposed[4]. The absence of a duty to apply the checklist in unopposed private proceedings is consistent with what some may see as an essentially 'non-interventionist' role for the courts. The implication appears to be that where all parties are in agreement about what should happen to children, the court's role may be limited to sanctioning officially that agreement. It has been suggested that the presence in the checklist of the final factor might also 'be taken as a tacit warning that too much should not be expected of court intervention'[5].

No premium is attached to any of the factors in the list. They are all apparently to be accorded equal weight, along with any others which the court may think relevant[6]. A considerable amount of discretion must, accordingly, remain vested in individual judges. There would appear to be nothing to prevent one judge from attaching greater importance to a child's wishes (factor (a)) than to considerations of the relative capabilities of the two parents (factor (f)). Another judge might, equally legitimately, place greater emphasis on the latter. While such differences might be put down to the distinctive features of individual cases, they might also be explained by divergent judicial attitudes on the value of children's views.

---

1   J Goldstein, A Freud and AJ Solnit *Beyond the Best Interests of the Child* (The Free Press, New York, 1973).
2   J Wallerstein and JB Kelly *Surviving the Breakup* (Grant McIntyre, 1980). This certainly seems to be the thinking which informs some of the so-called 'general principles' in s 1 of the the Family Law Act 1996. See Chapter 4 below.
3   See Chapter 4 below.
4   Section 1(4).
5   SM Cretney 'Defining the Limits of State Intervention' in D Freestone (ed) *Children and the Law* (Hull University Press, 1990) at p 65.
6   Unlike other statutory checklists, this one does not contain a 'sweeping-up clause' but the clear implication, since the court must have regard to the specified factors 'in particular', is that the court may consider all other relevant circumstances not enumerated in the list.

The problem of checklists

The problem (if it is a problem) of largely unfettered discretion in family law is not a new one. This particular checklist was not a revolutionary experiment, since similar devices had operated for some years to structure judicial discretion in relation to property and financial adjustments on divorce and ouster orders, now replaced by 'occupation' orders under Part IV of the Family Law Act 1996[1]. The Adoption and Children Act 2002 also introduces a checklist into adoption law for the first time. The list of factors is similar to that in the Children Act 1989 with additional factors relevant only to the particular context of adoption[2].

The experience under the Matrimonial Homes Act 1983 is instructive. For a considerable number of years it was not appreciated that the statutory criteria (previously enshrined in the Matrimonial Homes Act 1967) applied at all in ouster applications brought under the Domestic Violence and Matrimonial Proceedings Act 1976. During this period, individual judges and differently constituted divisions of the Court of Appeal had taken widely differing positions on the relative importance of children's welfare (especially housing needs) and the conduct of the adults[3].

In 1984 the House of Lords in *Richards v Richards*[4] held that all ouster applications were governed by the criteria in the Matrimonial Homes Act 1983. Ostensibly, this meant that the needs of children should, in principle, be given equal weight to the conduct of the adults, their own needs and financial resources, and all other circumstances of the case. Yet this ruling did nothing to preclude individual judges from taking the view that one or other of these factors should predominate in an individual case and there is plenty of evidence that they did just that[5]. Under Part IV of the Family Law Act 1996 the introduction of the so-called 'balance of harm' test was an attempt to give greater weight to the needs of the applicant and children. Whether or not this has succeeded, in the light of reported cases, is discussed later[6]. Thus, while checklists or statutory criteria may serve the limited function of trying to ensure that all relevant factors are taken into account[7] they cannot affect the fundamentally indeterminate nature of concepts like 'welfare', 'best interests', 'significant harm'[8], 'children in need'[9], and so on.

---

1 Matrimonial Causes Act 1973, s 25(1); Matrimonial Homes Act 1983, s 1(3); and Family Law Act 1996, ss 33(6) and (7), 35(6)–(8) and 38(4) and (5).
2 See Chapter 7.
3 *Samson v Samson* [1982] 1 All ER 780. Cf *Myers v Myers* [1982] 1 All ER 776.
4 [1984] AC 174.
5 Contrast, for example, *Lee v Lee* [1984] FLR 243 and *Summers v Summers* [1986] 1 FLR 343.
6 See Chapter 12.
7 Failure to take one of the statutory criteria into account, such as a failure to explore the child's own views, ought to be a ground of appeal. See, for example, the pre-Children Act decision in *M v M (Minor: Custody Appeal)* [1987] 1 WLR 404. But in *H v H (Residence Order: Leave to Remove)* [1995] 1 FLR 529 at 532, Staughton LJ said that the checklist was not 'like the list of checks which an airline pilot has to make with his co-pilot, aloud one to the other before he takes off'. It is sufficient if the judge takes all the statutory factors into account.
8 This is the key concept in care and emergency proceedings. See particularly ss 31, 43 and 44, and Chapters 11 and 12 below.
9 This is now the principal concept in preventive work and family support. See Part III of the Children Act, and Chapter 10 below.

Application of the welfare principle: public and private law

Notwithstanding these practical limitations of the welfare principle, there is widespread agreement that the welfare of children should be an important priority in any civilised society. It may also be argued that the extent to which a legal system can offer effective protection of the rights of its most vulnerable members is a reasonable litmus test of the efficacy of that system. Perhaps it is these aspirations which have led to the bold assertion that the welfare principle has general application in English law and that parents and others who deal with children are legally bound by it[1]. Is there any substance in this contention?

It can certainly be said that the welfare principle in s 1(1) of the Children Act, as interpreted in Lord MacDermott's technical sense, applies only in certain well-defined and restricted circumstances. It has already been noted that it does not apply in relation to issues deemed to be 'adult issues', even where children's interests are liable to be affected. The principle also applies in quite different ways in public and private proceedings. Only in the latter does it function in Lord MacDermott's sense. In public law proceedings there is no question of care or supervision orders being made on the sole basis of a broad welfare criterion and, indeed, this was specifically rejected as a ground for State intervention in both the *Review* and the White Paper[2]. The welfare principle only comes into play if the minimum 'threshold' condition relating to 'significant harm' has been established to the court's satisfaction so that there is, in effect, a 'threshold stage' and a 'welfare stage'[3]. It would, therefore, be fundamentally misleading to imply that the welfare principle has *equal* application in public and private law. This is not to deny that its application in care proceedings is a significant feature in the court's final determination at the 'welfare stage' when the court has to decide what, if any, orders to make. The significance of the child's welfare in the context of adoption proceedings has long been a matter of controversy. Traditionally, the welfare principle has not applied in adoption proceedings but the Adoption and Children Act 2002 controversially extends it to adoption law. It will henceforth govern not only the decision on whether adoption is the best option for the child but also whether a court should dispense with the consent of a parent opposed to adoption. Whether this new approach is compatible with parents' rights under the ECHR is discussed later[4].

What is the situation where no court is involved at all? Are local authorities bound by the welfare principle in performing their statutory functions? The answer to this must be an unequivocal 'no'. It is true that social services departments have a general legal duty 'to safeguard and promote the welfare of children within their area who are in need'[5]. But they are not obliged to regard the welfare of those children as their paramount or sole consideration. Indeed,

---

1 See, for example, S Sedley 'Child's welfare limits parents' rights to punish or restrain' (1986) 26 *Childright* 18.

2 The *Review*, at para 15.10, and the White Paper, at paras 59 and 60. The welfare principle will apply, however, where a local authority succeeds in obtaining leave to invoke the inherent jurisdiction of the High Court but the principle does not itself govern the question of whether leave should be granted. See ss 8(4) and 100(3). There have been a number of controversial uses of this jurisdiction which are discussed in Chapter 11 below.

3 Section 31(2).

4 See Chapter 7.

5 Sections 17(1)(a) and 22(3)(a).

their former statutory duty to give 'first consideration' to their welfare was removed by the Children Act[1]. Clearly, local authorities must have regard to factors other than the welfare of individual children when discharging their statutory obligations of which one (expressly mentioned in the legislation) is the need to protect members of the public from serious injury[2]. The Court of Appeal has also held that the issue of the use of secure accommodation in relation to children in care is governed by the criteria in s 25 of the Act and *not* by the welfare principle. The court went on to say that the welfare principle, significantly, did not apply to *any* of the decisions taken by local authorities under Part III of the Act[3].

What if there is more than one child?

The courts have also had to grapple with the problem of conflicting interests between two or more children. The answer they originally gave was that it was the child who was the subject of the application whose interests were paramount. Thus, where care proceedings relate to the child of a mother who is herself a minor, it is the baby's and not the minor mother's interests which are paramount. This applies both to the question of contact with the child who has been taken into care[4] and on the initial application for the care order[5]. The same logic has been applied where the interests of siblings are thought to conflict[6]. Whether the interests of one child *should* as a matter of policy be preferred over the interests of another merely because the first child was technically the subject of the application and the other was not was doubted by some commentators[7]. A better approach, as the Law Commission had suggested[8], might have been for the court to have regard in an even-handed way 'to the welfare of any child likely to be affected'.

Then in 2000 the Court of Appeal was faced with a situation in which it could not resolve a conflict of interest between two children on the convenient basis that only one of them was the subject of the application. In *Re A (Conjoined Twins: Surgical Separation)*[9] the majority of the court felt that they were faced with an irreconcilable conflict of interest between conjoined twins since the inevitable result of surgical separation with a view to saving the life of the stronger twin would be the almost immediate death of the weaker twin. The case is discussed in depth in Chapter 8. We are only concerned for the moment with the court's approach to the application of the welfare principle in the event of a conflict of interest between two children *both* of whom were the subject of the application. The court ultimately resolved this issue by applying a test of the 'least detrimental

---

1 Formerly contained in the Child Care Act 1980, s 18(1), which was repealed by the Children Act.
2 Section 22(6).
3 *Re M (Secure Accommodation Order)* [1995] 1 FLR 418. See also *R on the application of W v Lambeth Borough Council* [2002] 2 FLR 327.
4 *Birmingham City Council v H (No 3)* [1994] 1 FLR 224.
5 *F v Leeds City Council* [1994] 2 FLR 60.
6 *Re F (Contact: Child in Care)* [1995] 1 FLR 510 and *Re T and E (Proceedings: Conflicting Interests)* [1995] 1 FLR 581.
7 For a critique of these decisions, see A Bainham 'The Nuances of Welfare' [1995] CLJ 512.
8 Law Com Report No 172 *Review of Child Law: Guardianship and Custody* (1988) at para 3.13 and cl 1(2) of the draft Bill appended to that Report; and Working Paper No 96 *Custody* (1986) at para 6.16.
9 [2001] 1 FLR 1.

alternative'. This in its view was to authorise surgery, since it would offer the chance of life to one child in circumstances where the death of the other was inevitable[1]. This approach, which involves balancing the welfare of one child against the other, with the scales starting even, is not very far removed from the view of the Law Commission noted above. Another way of expressing it might be, taking both children's interests into account, to follow the course which maximises the total welfare of all concerned and, indeed, this is an approach which might be adopted where the interests of children conflict with those of adults[2].

Are parents and others bound by the welfare principle?

It can hardly be argued that parents, in taking family decisions affecting a child, are bound to ignore completely their own interests, the interests of other members of the family and, possibly, outsiders. This would be a wholly undesirable, as well as unrealistic, objective. Again, it is sometimes said that third parties dealing with children and young people are legally obliged to act consistently with their best interests. There is more than a suggestion of this in Lord Fraser's speech in *Gillick* where he stated that a doctor should not provide contraceptive advice or treatment to a girl under 16 unless, inter alia, he regarded it as in her best interests to do so. But he did not say that this was to be the doctor's *sole* concern. In fact, he made it clear that he was obliged also to have regard to the interests of the girl's parents (by seeking to persuade the girl to involve them), and to her own *views* (as opposed to interests), judged in the light of her maturity and understanding. Lord Fraser clearly had in mind the application of a different kind of welfare test than that applied by the courts under Lord MacDermott's formulation. It is submitted that it would be a distortion to say that outsiders dealing with children are legally bound by the welfare principle.

Those who imply that the welfare principle has this much wider application are really expressing the hope that society in general, and individual adults, will, in their decisions, feel it appropriate to act in the best interests of children, as they see them. This hope appears to be behind many of the provisions in the Children Act as they affect parents. The Act reposes a great deal of trust in parents that they will know what is best for their children and act accordingly. Whether this level of trust is justified by the historical record is something which at least one commentator was quick to question[3].

The no order principle

The welfare principle must be read in conjunction with another fundamental principle which has come to be widely known as the 'no order' or 'non-intervention' principle. This states:

---

1 For commentaries on the case see the sources cited in Chapter 8. For the author's own view, see A Bainham 'Resolving the Unresolvable: The Case of the Conjoined Twins' [2001] CLJ 49.

2 Such an approach would involve a complex calculus. See J Eekelaar 'Beyond the welfare principle' [2002] CFLQ 237.

3 J Eekelaar 'Parental Responsibility: State of Nature or Nature of the State?' (1991) JSWFL 37.

'Where a court is considering whether or not to make one or more orders under this Act with respect to a child, it shall not make the order or any of the orders unless it considers that doing so would be better for the child than making no order at all.'[1]

The express purpose of this provision is to emphasise that there should be a demonstrable benefit to the child in any order which the court is contemplating. The Law Commission was concerned, specifically in the context of divorce, that orders for custody and access (as they were then known) were routinely made, notwithstanding that a very high percentage were uncontested. They had, in reality, become 'part of the package' of divorce. The Commission's position was that the law should not intrude unnecessarily into the divorce process. Where divorcing parents were able to reach amicable and workable arrangements concerning children it was not desirable for these to be embodied in court orders. It was concerned also to avert the danger of polarising parents who were already co-operating with each other[2]. This view of the role of court orders also accorded with the notion of parenthood as a continuing responsibility. Thus, the responsibility of *both* parents should survive the process of divorce, and court orders should be reserved for those cases in which there was a clear need to regulate the exercise of that responsibility. Most, if not all, of those instances, it was thought, would be situations in which the parties themselves failed to reach agreement.

The principle again applies equally to public orders. Before making a care or supervision order the court should be satisfied not only that this would be in the child's best interests but also that the order can achieve something which is unlikely to be achieved without it. This requires consideration of the other ways, falling short of compulsory action, in which social services might assist a family in difficulty[3]. Such an approach is congruent with the jurisprudence of the ECtHR, which has emphasised that taking children into care is, for example, to be regarded as a temporary measure and that the ultimate aim should be that of reuniting parent and child[4].

The no order principle may, on one view, be seen as complementary to the welfare principle, since it cannot be in the best interests of children to be the subject of unnecessary court orders. If it is not better for a child that an order should be made, than that it should not, then the welfare of the child is ex hypothesi not furthered by the order. Looked at in this way, the principle might almost be regarded as superfluous, since it appears to add little to the welfare principle itself. Yet the intention is clear enough. It is to emphasise the need for courts to apply their minds specifically to the various options open to them, and not to assume that any order is better than none. The onus is on the applicant, whether a private individual or institution, to convince the court of the alleged benefits of the order sought. While it can be argued that this was always the case under the former law there was an undoubted shift of emphasis which has led to suggestions that there is now a *presumption* against court orders. This interpretation is open to doubt. It should be noted that the statute does not contain express

---

1 Children Act 1989, s 1(5).
2 Law Com Report No 172 *Review of Child Law: Guardianship and Custody* (1988) at paras 3.2 et seq.
3 These services are discussed in Chapter 10 below. The principle does not, however, govern applications for financial provision (see *K v H (Child Maintenance)* [1993] 2 FLR 61).
4 See especially *Johansen v Norway* (1996) 23 EHRR 33 and Chapter 11 below.

language which presumes orders to be unnecessary. It merely says that they ought not to be made *if they are unnecessary*. It is also clear that the Law Commission's Report which is the source of the principle did not presume court orders to be unnecessary either[1]. And whether the principle may accurately be described as 'the non-intervention principle' or properly thought to embody a wider 'non-interventionist philosophy' about the relationship between the State and the family, as many commentators have been inclined to assert, is highly questionable[2].

Delay is prejudicial

Section 1(2) of the Children Act enshrines another central and innovative principle applying equally in public and private proceedings. It states:

> 'In any proceedings in which any question with respect to the upbringing of a child arises, the court shall have regard to the general principle that any delay in determining the question is likely to prejudice the welfare of the child.'

It has been known for a long time that delays in residence and related proceedings can have an adverse effect on children as well as prejudice the legitimate interests of the adult parties. In the context of care proceedings, it has been bluntly stated that there are 'cases where children have clearly suffered significant harm as a result of the court process itself'[3]. Such delays have regrettably often occurred and have long been the subject of judicial censure[4]. The major concerns have been the uncertainty which delay engenders in the lives of children, and the prejudice which it can cause to the party who is not living with the children. Delay reinforces the status quo and makes it more difficult to argue effectively for a change of residential arrangements. This so-called 'status quo principle' is indirectly acknowledged in the statutory checklist which refers to 'the likely effect on [the child] of any change in his circumstances'[5].

It is, of course, one thing to bemoan delay in resolving disputes over children and quite another to do anything about it, but the Children Act attempted to underscore the principled objection to delay by giving the courts new powers and duties to ensure the expeditious disposal of cases. Thus, in both public[6] and private[7] cases the court is required to draw up a timetable with a view to determining the questions before it without delay and to give appropriate directions to ensure, as far as possible, that the timetable is followed. Rules of court spell out in greater detail the procedural requirements which may be

---

1 Law Com Report No 172, para 3.2.
2 See A Bainham 'Changing Families and Changing Concepts: Reforming the Language of Family Law' [1998] CFLQ 1 at pp 2–4.
3 A McFarlane QC 'Delay: A Cause of Significant Harm' [2003] Fam Law 453.
4 See, for example, Ewbank J in *Stockport Metropolitan Borough Council v B; Stockport Metropolitan Borough Council v L* [1986] 2 FLR 80. See also *Re S (Contact: Grandparents)* [1996] 1 FLR 158, in which there had been 17 hearings between 1992 and the end of 1994, and in which the Court of Appeal said that there had been an inappropriate use of the 'no order principle' in s 1(5); and the report by Dame Margaret Booth *Avoiding Delay in Children Act Cases* (Lord Chancellor's Department, 1996).
5 Section 1(3)(c).
6 Section 32.
7 Section 11.

imposed[1]. The wording in the Children Act concedes that there may be some instances (perhaps many) in which *some* delay is readily justifiable. There is only a *presumption* that delay is prejudicial and the Law Commission thought that this could be rebutted where, for example, the benefit to be derived from a full welfare report could outweigh the delay of having to wait for it[2]. Clearly this is a relative matter, and much will turn on the extent of the delay. The enactment of this principle injected into what might have been thought a hitherto largely adversarial system an inquisitorial feature, since it envisages that the court, and not the parties, should dictate the pace of children proceedings.

Despite these reforms and no shortage of good intentions, the problems of delay in children cases have increased rather than decreased in recent years. A scoping study for the then Lord Chancellor's Department[3] attempted to identify the principal causes of delay and to report on whether the Children Act was in need of fundamental reform or whether the problems of delay could be tackled by improvements in the practical operation of the Act. Like the Booth Report[4] before it, the study concluded that it was the *operation* of the system and not the Act which was in need of reform. It identified the principal causes of delay as a lack of available experts, not having the right judges in place at the right time and defective judicial case management[5]. The Lord Chancellor's Department then consulted on the idea of an over-arching 'Family Justice Council' to cover the whole family justice system for England and Wales[6]. The Family Justice Council, which reports to the newly established Department of Constitutional Affairs, is chaired by the President of the Family Division and was established on 1 July 2004. The Council's remit is to facilitate the delivery of better and quicker outcomes for families and children who use the family justice system.

Specifically in the context of public law Children Act cases, a Protocol for Judicial Case Management has set guidelines designed to reduce delay[7]. In particular it has set timetables, established a 'road map' and prescribed a guideline of a maximum of 40 weeks for the conclusion of care cases, while acknowledging that some cases will need to take longer whereas many more should take less. The Protocol applies to all courts and was implemented from 1 November 2003.

---

1   See, particularly, the Family Proceedings Rules 1991, SI 1991/1247.
2   Law Com Report No 172 *Review of Child Law: Guardianship and Custody* (1988) at para 4.57. For some early empirical findings on the operation of these provisions, see I Butler et al 'The Children Act and the Issue of Delay' [1993] Fam Law 412. *The Children Act Advisory Committee Final Report June 1997* (Lord Chancellor's Department, 1997) Appendix 2, Table 5 contained statistics on the time taken for the disposal of care and supervision cases. These revealed a considerable regional variation, but showed that on average it took almost a year (48.3 weeks) from the date of application to the final hearing in the High Court; and 43.7 weeks in the county court. The time-lag, as might be expected, was significantly shorter in the magistrates' (family proceedings) courts, being in the region of 30 weeks.
3   *Scoping Study on Delay in Children Act Cases: Findings and Action Taken* (Lord Chancellor's Department, March 2002).
4   Fn 4 at p 47 (above).
5   Ibid at para 52.
6   See Consultation Paper, *Promoting inter-agency working in the family justice system* (Lord Chancellor's Department, 2002).
7   *Protocol for Judicial Case Management in Public Law Children Act Cases* (June 2003) reproduced at [2003] 2 FLR 719. See also *Practice Direction: Care Cases: Judicial Continuity and Case Management* [2003] Fam Law 606.

PHILOSOPHIES AND IDEOLOGIES

It would be surprising if a statute which was the product of such disparate influences embodied a single philosophy throughout. What exactly the values are which inform the legislation must, of necessity, be a matter of opinion. Different commentators have read different things into the Act[1] and it should be borne in mind that what follows is only one view of the Act. One commonly held view is that the Children Act attempted to bring about a substantial shift in the relationship between the State and the family. By emphasising that the *primary* responsibility for raising children rests with parents, the law might be thought to be 'in retreat from the private realm of family life'[2]. This change of direction was thought by some to be consistent with, if not positively inspired by, the neo-conservative political ideology of the 1980s, which in Britain has often been referred to as 'Thatcherism'[3]. An analogy has been drawn with the privatisation programme of the Thatcher administration, such that the Children Act might be seen as a move (perhaps a substantial move) towards 'privatising' the family. Others have noted the same phenomenon but prefer the term 'de-regulation'[4]. The issue is a complex one, not least because there is no unitary concept of the 'the State'. It is not clear how precisely the interaction between the State and the family is to be measured. Should we, for example, concentrate on the policies of central government as they affect families and, if so, should an attempt be made to evaluate their specific impact on children and young people?

The need to consider the impact of national policies on children led to calls for the creation of a Children Rights Commissioner such as had existed in certain other countries, notably in Scandinavia[5]. Following devolution, Britain's first Children's Commissioner was established in Wales by the National Assembly for

---

1 These include LM Fox Harding 'The Children Act 1989 in Context: Four Perspectives in Child Care Law and Policy' (1991) JSWFL 179 and 285; SM Cretney 'Defining the Limits of State Intervention' in D Freestone (ed) *Children and the Law* (Hull University Press, 1990) at p 58; SM Cretney 'Privatising the Family: The Reform of Child Law' (1988) *Denning Law Journal* 15; A Bainham 'The Privatisation of the Public Interest in Children' (1990) 53 MLR 206; G Douglas 'Family Law under the Thatcher Government' (1990) 17 *Journal of Law and Society* 411; J Eekelaar 'Parental Responsibility: State of Nature or Nature of the State?' (1991) JSWFL 37; M Ryan 'The Children Bill 1988 – The Philosophy and the Reality' (1989) 1 JCL 102; and M Freeman 'In the Child's Best Interests? Reading the Children Act Critically' in *The Moral Status of Children* (Martinus Nijhoff, 1997). For a re-evaluation of the Act's ideologies in the light of the experience since it came into force, see M Freeman 'The Next Children's Act?' [1998] Fam Law 341.

2 An expression originating in the decision of the US Supreme Court in *Prince v Massachussetts* 321 US 158 (1944) and borrowed by SM Cretney in 'Defining the Limits of State Intervention' (above).

3 SM Cretney 'Defining the Limits of State Intervention' (above) at pp 67–68. For a discussion of the influence of neo-conservative philosophies on family law developments in North America, see B Dickens 'The Modern Function and Limits of Parental Rights' (1981) 97 LQR 462.

4 See, for example, G Douglas (above), and K O'Donovan *Sexual Divisions in Law* (Weidenfeld & Nicolson, 1985) at ch 1.

5 See M Rosenbaum and P Newell *Taking Children Seriously – A Proposal for a Children's Rights Commissioner* (Gulbenkian Foundation, 1991) and critique by A Bainham (1992) JSWFL 552.

Wales under the Care Standards Act 2000[1]. The UN Committee on the Rights of the Child recommended that a Commissioner for England be established. This will be achieved by the Children Bill 2004[2].

The general function of the Commissioner will be to 'promote awareness of the views and interests of children in the United Kingdom'. Five aspects of their well-being are identified in the Bill as important to children, namely physical and mental health; protection from harm and neglect; education and training; the contribution made by them to society; and social and economic well-being. The Commissioner will be required to take reasonable steps to involve children themselves in the discharge of his functions and, in performing them, must have regard to the principles of the UNCRC. The Commissioner will not generally be permitted to conduct investigations into the cases of individual children, but will be allowed to do so where the case has a wider policy relevance for other children not directly invovled. The Commissioner will be required to produce an Annual Report covering the way in which he has discharged his function, what he has found during the exercise of that function and the matters he intends to consider or research during the next financial year.

It should also be noted that the first Minister of State for Children (Margaret Hodge) has been appointed. The Minister, in the Department for Education and Skills, is responsible for children's services, child care and provision for under-fives, together with family policy (including parenting support and family law). The transfer of, inter alia, responsibility for children's social services from the Department of Health, the Family Policy Unit from the Home Office and family law policy from the former Lord Chancellor's Department, all to the Department for Education and Skills is intended to integrate children's policy into one department[3].

Should we, perhaps, look more closely at adjustments to the powers and duties of local authorities in view of their primary functions regarding family support and child protection? And how significant are changes to the role of the courts, as an organ of the State, in upholding the interests of parents, children and others, vis-à-vis each other and defending them against unwarranted action by other public agencies? All of these questions need to be explored if any meaningful attempt can be made to evaluate the effect of the legislation on the balance between the State and the family.

There can be no doubt that the legislation also affected the balance of other relationships. It redrew the division of responsibility for child welfare between the courts and local authorities, it altered the relative legal positions of men and women (in their respective roles as fathers and mothers), and it redefined the

---

1   See also the Children's Commissioner for Wales Regulations 2001, SI 2001/2787. For discussions of the Commissioner's work, see O Rees 'Beyond the Hype – A Year in the life of the Children's Commissioner for Wales' [2002] Fam Law 748, J Williams 'The Children's Commissioner for Wales' (2001) 1 *Wales Law Journal* 203, and K Hollingsworth and G Douglas 'Creating a Children's Champion for Wales? The Care Standards Act 2000 (Part V) and the Children's Commissioner for Wales Act 2001' (2002) 65 MLR 58.
2   The Bill follows the Green Paper *Every Child Matters* (2003) (Cm 5860) and the White Paper *Every Child Matters: Next Steps* (2004). See further Chapter 10 below.
3   For a short critique of these changes see 'A Policy for Families?' [2003] Fam Law 918, summarising the views of S Cretney presented to the Centre for Public Law, University of Cambridge in October 2003.

relationship in law between children and adults. Below, some views are offered on how the legislation may have impacted on these various relations.

One arguably consistent theme throughout the legislation is that of 'partnership'[1]. The concept of a 'voluntary partnership' between parents and the State was crucial to the thinking behind the public law reforms. This implies public support for parents in discharging their primary responsibilities, social work assistance where families experience difficulty, and continuing co-operation with parents in the more extreme circumstances where it has proved necessary to remove a child from the family.

This was the classic use of the partnership notion in the debates leading up to the reforms but it is by no means the only sense in which the legislation underscores the essential nature of partnerships. The persistence of parental responsibility means that, increasingly, it will be shared between two (or conceivably more) individuals. It has been seen that divorced parents will, in law, each retain parental responsibility. If this is to be taken at all seriously it must imply that the law expects a degree of co-operation between them. Similarly, where a foster-parent obtains parental responsibility through a residence order, this will be shared with the current holder or holders of parental responsibility (usually parents). This must surely give rise to a similar implication of co-operation between all those who now hold parental responsibility. It is equally clear that courts and local authorities are expected to work together to secure the welfare of children. Thus, for example, the court in family proceedings may direct an authority to investigate the circumstances of a child[2]. The same may also be said of the various statutory and voluntary agencies having particular responsibilities which may affect children. The urgent need to improve inter-agency co-operation was a significant feature of various public inquiry reports[3], and the legislation sought to give effect to this in a number of ways. Local education, housing and health authorities were thus placed under new statutory duties to assist social services departments where a request for help is made[4]. And the increased importance which the legislation attaches to children's views means that parents, social workers, judges and others now have to bring them into deliberations about their future more than has traditionally been the case[5].

The general thrust of all these developments may be seen as consistent with the partnership ideal. People and institutions having the care of children or dealings with them are apparently expected to work together to promote their welfare. In so doing they are expected to take account of what children want for themselves. This must surely mean that there is bound to be much more of what used to be

---

1   The White Paper, at para 5. It should be said that this idea of partnership between parents and the State is not a new one. Sir William Beveridge, in producing his report which laid the foundations for the post-war Welfare State, clearly proceeded on the assumption that the financial responsibility for the cost of raising children should be shared between parents and the wider community through a system of family allowances. See *Report of the Committee on Social Insurance and Allied Services* (1942) (Cmnd 6404).

2   Section 37(1).

3   See, particularly, *A Child in Trust: The Report of the Panel of Inquiry into the Circumstances surrounding the death of Jasmine Beckford* (London Borough of Brent, 1985).

4   Section 27.

5   See Chapter 3 below.

described as the 'fragmentation' of parental rights[1]. This conveys the idea that the legal powers and responsibilities for children are not centralised in one carer but shared or allocated between two or more individuals or institutions.

The impact of the Children Act on these various 'partnerships' will now be addressed briefly.

The State and the family

Strengthening of the parental position

Most commentators agreed that the Children Act strengthened considerably the legal standing of parents (and others with parental responsibility) vis-à-vis social services[2]. Foremost among those changes was the abolition of the 'parental rights resolution', an administrative mechanism for retaining compulsory control of a child originally placed voluntarily in the care of social services[3]. Although susceptible to a subsequent judicial challenge, the resolution procedure failed to extend to parents the minimum participatory rights mandated by the ECHR[4]. In the same vein, the Children Act placed important restrictions on the length of time for which a child might be kept away from home without an opportunity for challenge under emergency procedures[5].

Other provisions which marked a distinct shift of power away from local authorities have been criticised as emanating from an ideological stance which takes insufficient account of the practicalities involved. These include the abolition of the requirement of notice where parents wish to resume the care of a child voluntarily 'accommodated' by social services[6]. Here, there was an obvious unwillingness to allow any period of notice, however short, to detract (even in theory) from the apparently strict demarcation of voluntary services and compulsory care which the Children Act establishes[7]. Other provisions which involve a distinct loss of control by local authorities are those which were designed to ensure that parents are allowed to participate fully in decision-making[8]. These

---

1　An expression originally coined by J Eekelaar in 'What are Parental Rights?' (1973) 89 LQR 210 at p 229 and taken up by S Maidment in 'The Fragmentation of Parental Rights' [1981] CLJ 135.

2　See SM Cretney 'Defining the Limits of State Intervention' in D Freestone (ed) *Children and the Law* (Hull University Press, 1990) at p 68; J Eekelaar 'Parental Responsibility: State of Nature or Nature of the State?' (1991) JSWFL 37; and A Bainham 'The Children Act 1989: The State and the Family' [1990] Fam Law 231.

3　For a critique of the resolution procedure, see M Adcock, R White and O Rowlands *The Administrative Parent* (BAAF, 1983) and LM Harding 'The Hundred Year Resolution' (1989) 2 JCL 12.

4　See *R v UK, O v UK, W v UK* [1988] 2 FLR 445, ECtHR.

5　Section 45, and see Chapter 12 below.

6　Formerly parents were required to give 28 days' notice. Failure to do so constituted a criminal offence under s 13 of the Child Care Act 1980.

7　There was great concern that voluntary arrangements should not be allowed to slip into compulsion, as had frequently happened under the existing law, since this was thought to discourage some families in difficulty from seeking voluntary assistance. See the discussion of the 'voluntary principle' in BM Hoggett *Parents and Children: The Law of Parental Responsibility* (3rd edn) (Sweet & Maxwell, 1987) at pp 130 et seq.

8　These participatory rights are, to some extent, implicit in the very notion of continuing parental responsibility, but the Children Act also confers on parents specific rights to be consulted. See particularly s 22, and Chapter 10 below.

new 'participatory' rights can be viewed merely as the logical accompaniments of the statutory commitment to reuniting children with their families[1]. But, equally, some may see in them the potential for inhibiting local authorities in the discharge of their statutory functions, for no better reason than an ideological commitment to the primacy of natural parenthood[2].

Despite these apparent shifts of power away from local authorities, it should be said that in several important respects the Children Act strengthened their powers to take protective action. These include the re-casting of the grounds for care and supervision orders to embrace prospective harm[3], and the introduction of child assessment orders alongside emergency protection orders, thereby increasing the short-term options for protective action[4].

Restriction of court intervention in divorce

In the private sphere, there is an equally strong affirmation of the parental role and the need to restrict public intervention through the courts. Nowhere is this thinking more strikingly obvious than in the reforms to the court's supervisory role on divorce. These changes are considered in Chapter 4.

Agents of the State: the courts and local authorities

Former use of wardship by and against local authorities

Courts and local authorities may be seen as partners in upholding the public interest in child welfare[5]. While local authorities are given primary responsibility for the protection of children, they may take compulsory action only with the sanction of the courts. More importantly, perhaps, the courts have long performed an independent role in safeguarding the welfare of children in a variety of family proceedings. The archetypal protective jurisdiction has been wardship, where the courts have traditionally exercised wide and flexible powers to deal with any serious issues affecting individual children[6]. The existence of this potentially unlimited jurisdiction alongside the statutory powers and duties of local authorities gave rise to much litigation in the decade or so preceding the 1989 legislation[7]. The result which had appeared to emerge was that, whereas local authorities were at liberty to seek the 'supplementary assistance' of the courts in discharging their child care functions, it was not open to parents and others to

---

1 See s 23(6) and Sch 2, para 15, discussed by M Ryan 'The Children Bill 1988 – The Philosophy and the Reality' (1989) 1 JCL 102 at p 104.
2 See the views of J Eekelaar 'Parental Responsibility: State of Nature or Nature of the State?' (1991) JSWFL 37 at pp 48 et seq.
3 Section 31(2) overcoming the technical difficulties exposed in *D (A Minor) v Berkshire County Council* [1987] 1 All ER 33, discussed in Chapter 11 below.
4 Sections 43 and 44. See Chapter 12 below.
5 See A Bainham *Children, Parents and the State* (Sweet & Maxwell, 1988) at p 103.
6 On the nature of the wardship jurisdiction, see particularly NV Lowe and RAH White *Wards of Court* (2nd edn) (Barry Rose/Kluwer, 1986) at ch 1; and Cross 'Wards of Court' (1967) 83 LQR 200.
7 The leading cases were *A v Liverpool City Council* [1982] AC 363 and *Re W (A Minor) (Wardship: Jurisdiction)* [1985] AC 791.

invoke wardship to question the merits of decisions taken by social services[1]. A clear disparity had therefore grown up in the treatment of local authorities and other applicants.

The Children Act addressed this disparity in dramatic fashion by curtailing drastically the circumstances in which local authorities might have access to the inherent jurisdiction of the High Court[2]. The broad effect is that neither social services nor anyone else may act outside the statutory regime. The authority must prove the statutory ground for care and supervision orders if it wishes to take compulsory action, and it cannot resort to wardship or the inherent jurisdiction as an extra-statutory alternative. Similarly, any judicial challenges to the actions of the authority must be based on an alleged failure to satisfy the criteria in the legislation. By way of exception, where impropriety or ultra vires action is alleged against the authority this may be challenged through the judicial review procedure but no longer in wardship proceedings. There is now also the possibility of challenges under the HRA 1998[3].

Parliament and the courts

The restriction on the use of wardship, outlined above, proved controversial from the start and the arguments will be discussed later[4]. The main concern here is to explore the essential thinking in the legislation about the proper relationship between the different organs of the State. The first point concerns Parliament and the courts, and here the reasoning is patently clear. Where Parliament has through legislation defined with particularity the basis for State intervention in the family, it is not for the courts to gainsay this by allowing a 'back-door' entry into care. Authorities must operate within the statutory framework either by proving the grounds for compulsory action or by securing the voluntary co-operation of the family concerned. By the same token, it is improper for the courts to countenance extra-statutory challenges to the legitimate exercise of statutory discretion. To allow them to do so on the strength of some broad or open-ended welfare criterion would make a complete nonsense of that which Parliament has ordained[5]. As a matter of pure logic this is impeccable, despite the practical ramifications of removing from local authorities what some regarded at the time as the crucially important safety net of wardship[6]. If it is illegitimate for the courts to ignore Parliament's scheme at the behest of parents and relatives then, logically, it must be improper for them to do so at the behest of local authorities.

---

1   An example of the former type of case was *Re CB* [1981] 1 All ER 16, where the local authority had insufficient grounds for passing a parental rights resolution. Examples of the latter type of case are the two cases cited above at p 53 in fn 7.
2   Section 100. On the distinction between wardship and the other uses of the inherent jurisdiction of the High Court, see R White, P Carr and N Lowe *A Guide to the Children Act 1989* (3rd edn) (Butterworths, 2002) at paras 12.1–12.3.
3   See Chapter 10 below.
4   Ibid.
5   It is also the case that to allow a wider, welfare-based criterion for compulsory intervention could be an unjustifiable violation of both parents' and children's rights to respect for family life under Article 8 of the ECHR.
6   N Lowe 'Caring for Children' (1989) 139 NLJ 87.

Relationship between local authorities and the courts

It is more difficult to discern a consistent philosophical position regarding the appropriate relationship between local authorities and the courts[1]. The limitations imposed on wardship are characteristic of a number of provisions which assert the primary responsibility of local authorities (rather than the courts) for children falling within their statutory functions. It is for the authority to determine what level of social work involvement is appropriate to safeguard the well-being of children in families experiencing difficulties. It is not for the courts to act unilaterally of their own volition. Thus, it is no longer possible for a court, in family proceedings, to direct that a child be taken into care or put under supervision, unless the authority itself seeks such an order in those proceedings. All the court may do, where it is concerned about the welfare of a child before it, is to direct the authority to investigate his circumstances with a view to determining what level of intervention (if any) is necessary[2].

This represented a significant re-casting of the respective roles of the courts and social services. Before the reforms, the court might, of its own motion in wardship and certain other family proceedings, commit a child to care[3]. It could, thereafter, give directions to the authority about aspects of upbringing and, in wardship, it preserved for itself an ongoing supervisory role[4]. The reasoning under the Children Act was that the courts were not equipped to perform this kind of 'managerial' role and that the local authority should be firmly in control of case management provided only that it does not exceed its statutory powers[5]. This reasoning is apparent in the decision to improve the review procedures within authorities and the requirement that every authority establish an internal procedure to deal with representations or complaints[6]. Here, again, it was thought inappropriate that the detailed matters concerning the treatment of children 'looked after' by social services should be subject to external review by the ordinary courts. Instead, the concentration should be on trying to ensure good practice through a better system of internal reviews[7].

The courts' role: adjudicative or managerial?

These developments suggest strongly that the courts' role in children cases is conceptualised as an adjudicative rather than managerial one. Yet it has been observed that the legislation may not be entirely consistent on this since, in certain respects, the courts are now required to involve themselves much more with the

---

1   See SM Cretney 'Defining the Limits of State Intervention' in D Freestone (ed) *Children and the Law* (Hull University Press, 1990) at pp 71–74; J Dewar 'The Courts and Local Authority Autonomy' (1995) 7 JCL 15; and M Hayes 'The proper role of the courts in child care cases' [1996] CFLQ 201. And see now R Tolson QC *Care Plans and the Human Rights Act* (Family Law, 2002) for a discussion of the human rights issues involved in this question.

2   Section 37.

3   Under, for example, Guardianship Act 1973, s 2(2)(b) or Matrimonial Causes Act 1973, s 43(1).

4   For a good example of the implications of this ongoing role, see *Re E (SA) (A Minor) (Wardship)* [1984] 1 All ER 289.

5   Where it does exceed its statutory powers the appropriate procedure is now judicial review rather than wardship. See *Re DM (A Minor) (Wardship: Jurisdiction)* [1986] 2 FLR 122.

6   Section 26.

7   See the White Paper at para 31.

substance of case management[1]. Nowhere is this more obvious than in relation to the vexed issue of contact (formerly access) with children in care[2]. Local authorities are now required to justify to the courts, to a greater extent than ever before, decisions to terminate or restrict contact between the child and prescribed individuals[3]. The impact of this greater level of scrutiny should not be under-estimated given the crucial significance of the issue for the prospects of the child returning to the family and longer-term management of the child's case. It is also, without doubt, the single issue which generated the greatest number of wardship applications by parents and others[4]. Alongside this, the more inquisitorial role expected of the courts has been noted, with regard to the progress of proceedings. The House of Lords has held in effect that the courts remain in control of the interim stage of care proceedings, namely after making an interim care order but before the final hearing[5].

It may, therefore, be that there is some ambiguity in the way that the role of the courts is perceived. But it is fair to say that, in general, while the courts exercise significant control over entry into, and discharge from, care, most issues concerned with the treatment of children once in care (with the exception of the sensitive questions concerning contact, the use of secure accommodation and issues arising at the interim stage) were, following the Act, seen as internal matters for the local authority. Whether this is the appropriate distribution of functions is, naturally, debatable[6].

The whole issue has now been reopened by the implementation of the HRA 1998 and by the necessity for compatibility with the ECHR. Article 6 of the ECHR in particular requires that parents have effective access to the courts to determine disputes in relation to major issues affecting the life of the child following the making of a care order. In *Re S (Minors); Re W (Minors)*[7] the House of Lords did not go so far as to find the public law regime of the Children Act incompatible with the Convention but found that there was a 'lacuna' in it which could lead to actions under the HRA 1998 unless the gap were to be filled by amending legislation. Accordingly, it seems likely that the balance of power between local authorities and the courts will shift again in the foreseeable future back in the direction of greater control by the courts[8]. These matters are discussed further in Chapter 10.

---

1   See SM Cretney 'Defining the Limits of State Intervention' in D Freestone (ed) *Children and the Law* (Hull University Press, 1990) at p 68.
2   This is governed by a modified statutory code contained in s 34 and the regulations made under that section.
3   Under the former law, the courts had jurisdiction over decisions to 'refuse' or 'terminate' access but not over decisions regulating the amount or frequency of access; see the Child Care Act 1980, ss 12A–12G. It has been emphasised that the courts now have the final say on the whole question of contact. See, particularly, the remarks of Hale J in *Berkshire County Council v B* [1997] 1 FLR 171.
4   The leading wardship case of *A v Liverpool City Council* [1982] AC 363 was such a case in which a mother's access had been curtailed by the local authority to one hour per month under supervision at a day nursery.
5   See *Re C (Interim Care Order: Assessment)* [1997] 1 FLR 1 discussed in Chapter 11 below.
6   Discussed in Chapter 11 below.
7   [2002] 1 FLR 815.
8   See also R Tolson QC *Care Plans and the Human Rights Act* (Family Law, 2002).

Children and adult society

The Children Act, more than any legislation before it, gave recognition to the views of children and young people. As such, it can be argued that it marked a distinct movement away from the perception of children as recipients of welfare and towards the view that they are juristic persons with distinctive rights. While it would be absurd to equate simplistically a multi-faceted concept like 'children's rights' with autonomy claims, there is a close association between the two ideas exemplified by the *Gillick* saga[1].

In several different instances, the legislation requires the wishes of children to be taken into account, to an extent appropriate to the individual child's age and understanding. This is a requirement which binds courts[2], local authorities, voluntary organisations and private children's homes[3] and, arguably (following *Gillick*), school authorities, medical personnel and other outsiders[4]. Curiously, there is no corresponding legal duty placed on parents and others with parental responsibility, but the Scottish Law Commission proposed that such an obligation should be introduced into Scots law[5]. This has now been achieved by s 6(1) of the Children (Scotland) Act 1995, under which the parent, when reaching any major decision in fulfilling parental responsibilities or exercising parental rights, must have regard so far as practicable to the views of the child if he or she wishes to express them. The Children Act also gives greater autonomy to young people aged over 16 by providing that court orders should not generally be made or extended beyond that age[6], that they should be able to seek a 'self-referral' into 'care'[7] and that those leaving substitute care should be given more assistance in making the transition to independent living in the community.[8]

The Children Act does not go so far as to confer complete independence on adolescents. It should be appreciated that parental responsibility continues right up to the age of majority, but the degree of control exercised by parents gradually diminishes as the child grows older[9]. There is, however, a more radical view that parental powers (responsibility if this is preferred) should terminate completely

---

1 See Chapter 3 below.
2 Section 1(3)(a).
3 Sections 22(4) and (5), 61(2) and (3) and 64(2) and (3).
4 Since *Gillick* decides that it is lawful for outsiders to have direct dealings with mature adolescents this might arguably imply an obligation to consult with them on major matters rather than to deal exclusively with their parents or other carers. Later Court of Appeal decisions have, however, cast doubt on this analysis. See Chapters 3 and 8 below.
5 Scottish Law Com Discussion Paper No 88 *Parental Responsibilities and Rights: Guardianship and the Administration of Children's Property* (1990) at paras 2.41–2.42, and Law Com Report No 135 *Report on Family Law* (1992) at paras 2.64–2.65.
6 Sections 9(6) and (7) and 91(10).
7 'Care' is used here in the non-technical sense since, by definition, a child who asks voluntarily to be accommodated is not in 'care' in the technical sense in which that term is now used in the legislation. See s 20, and Chapter 10 below.
8 Sections 23A and 24. The duties of local authorities towards such children have been significantly increased by the Children (Leaving Care) Act 2000, as to which see Chapter 10.
9 This was the classic view of the relationship between parents and adolescents expressed by Lord Denning MR in *Hewer v Bryant* [1970] 1 QB 357 at 369 and apparently accepted by the House of Lords in *Gillick*. For a perspective on Lord Denning's contribution in *Hewer v Bryant* itself see A Bainham 'Lord Denning as a Champion of Children's Rights: The Legacy of Hewer v Bryant' (1999) *Denning Law Journal* 81.

when a child has sufficient level of competence to be able to make his own decisions[1]. There is little in the Children Act to support this theory except, perhaps, the mature child's right to refuse a medical or psychiatric examination or other assessment[2]. Instead, the Children Act generally supports the notion of participatory decision-making which gives to young people a degree of self-determination. This general principle to have regard to children's views[3] marked an important adjustment in the balance of power between children and adult society.

Fathers and mothers

It is not difficult to discover in the Children Act provisions which adjust the relative positions of men and women in their role as parents. The Act does not openly differentiate between men and women but perpetuates significant distinctions between parents inside and outside marriage, although these have been reduced by the Adoption and Children Act 2002. The courts, too, have abandoned in theory their former practice of applying presumptions to the effect that young children should be with their mothers or that older boys should be with their fathers. Nonetheless, the House of Lords has (in a case from Scotland) reasserted the value of mothers to young children in a way which some may think goes close to applying a presumption. In *Brixey v Lynas* Lord Jauncey of Tullichettle (who gave the only speech) said:

> '... the advantage to a very young child of being with its mother is a consideration which must be taken into account in deciding where lie its best interests in custody proceedings in which the mother is involved. It is neither a presumption nor a principle but rather recognition of a widely held belief based on practical experience and the workings of nature. ...'

He went on:

> 'Where a very young child has been with its mother since birth and there is no criticism of her ability to care for the child only the strongest competing advantages are likely to prevail.'[4]

More recently Thorpe LJ referred, in a residence dispute in which the father had acted as 'house husband' but the mother proposed to give up a lucrative career and move from London to Scotland with the two children, to 'the very different role and functions of men and women'[5].

The abolition of parental guardianship, primarily to distinguish parenthood from guardianship, removed the anachronistic rule that the married father was

---

1 J Eekelaar 'The Eclipse of Parental Rights' (1986) 102 LQR 4.
2 Sections 38(6), 43(8), 44(7) and Sch 3, para 4(4). See Chapter 8 below. The courts, however, have controversially taken the view that a child's objections, even under these provisions, may be overridden where his or her best interests require it by invoking the jurisdiction of the High Court. See, particularly, *South Glamorgan County Council v W and B* [1993] 1 FLR 574, and Chapter 11 below.
3 See, particularly, ss 1(3)(a) and 22(4) and (5).
4 [1996] 2 FLR 499 at 505.
5 *Re S (Children)* (unreported, 17 April 2002), CA. The husband unsuccessfully applied for leave to appeal the judge's decision to make a residence order in the mother's favour. The Court of Appeal rejected the argument that this was gender discrimination on the part of the judge in that, if the roles had been reversed, it was inconceivable that a father who proposed to give up a successful career to look after two young children would have been given a residence order. See further Chapter 4.

the sole guardian of his child. When the Guardianship Act 1973 gave to the married mother equal parental rights and authority, it left untouched the sole guardianship of the father[1]. The Children Act thus completed the process of conferring on married parents equal parenthood (by giving to each of them parental responsibility)[2]. More significantly, the Children Act adjusted the legal position of unmarried parents and strengthened, in a number of respects, the legal position of the father. While the unmarried mother remained exclusively entitled to automatic parental responsibility[3], the Children Act widened the mechanisms whereby the father might acquire it by agreement with the mother or by court order[4]. The Children Act did not confer on the unmarried man automatic parental responsibility, although it did bring him within the definition of 'parent' for most other purposes[5]. Thus, although the Act attached greater significance to unmarried fatherhood, especially in the context of stable cohabitation, it still preserved the essential inequality of motherhood and fatherhood outside marriage while supporting equality within marriage[6]. These differences have been greatly reduced, though far from eliminated, by the amendment introduced by the Adoption and Children Act 2002, the effect of which is to confer automatic parental responsibility on the great majority of unmarried fathers who are registered as such at the time of the child's birth[7].

Where parental responsibility is shared between father and mother, either in marriage or where an unmarried father has acquired it by legal process, the law takes a gender-neutral view of parenthood, at least in theory. The father or mother may exercise parental responsibility independently and each has an equal say in upbringing[8]. There has, nonetheless, been some speculation concerning the possible effect of the legislation on the respective child-rearing roles of men and women. One viewpoint is that the statutory framework was grounded in the notion of 'time-sharing' and a legal presumption of co-parenting which disguises and perpetuates substantial inequalities of power and responsibilities between men and women[9]. Some feminists have long argued that the concept of joint custody enabled 'absent' men to exercise control over their ex-wives without shouldering the responsibility of child care[10]. The idea of continuing parental responsibility could be viewed as a variant on this theme. Another manifestation of this

---

1 See Law Com Working Paper No 91 *Review of Child Law: Guardianship* (1985) at paras 2.7–2.8.
2 Section 2(1), and see Chapter 4 below.
3 Section 2(2).
4 Section 4, and see Chapter 5 below.
5 This arises by virtue of the incorporation of s 1 of the Family Law Reform Act 1987 by s 2(3) of the Children Act.
6 These issues are discussed further in Chapter 5 below.
7 See Chapter 5 below.
8 Section 2(7).
9 See, particularly, J Brophy 'Custody Law, Child Care, and Inequality in Britain' in C Smart and S Sevenhuijsen (eds) *Child Custody and the Politics of Gender* (Routledge, 1989) at p 217.
10 See, for example, A Bottomley 'Resolving Family Disputes: a critical view' in MDA Freeman (ed) *The State, the Law and the Family* (Tavistock, 1984) at p 293. For a collection of essays offering feminist perspectives on the law affecting children see J Bridgeman and D Monk *Feminist Perspectives on Child Law* (Cavendish, 2000).

argument is perhaps the backlash against what is said to be too rigorous an enforcement of contact post-divorce[1].

Against this, it has been argued that the legislation, if anything, further strengthened the relative position of women by placing so much weight on parental agreements[2]. There is overwhelming evidence that a very high percentage of these agreements result in women obtaining the primary, if not exclusive, child care role[3]. The legislation did not attempt to redress this, as it might have done, by creating a legal presumption in favour of joint residence or time-sharing[4].

It is unclear whether the Children Act has had any significant impact on the way in which society perceives the parenting responsibilities of men and women. But in asserting parenthood as a primary and gender-neutral status and in making it so difficult for either parent to divest himself or herself of parental responsibility, the Children Act has given tacit encouragement to the notion of equal co-parenting, and the principles enunciated in s 1 of the Family Law Act 1996 would appear to take this notion further, as discussed in Chapter 4 below[5].

THE STATUTORY SCHEME

This section describes the essential framework established by the Children Act. Before considering the application of the Children Act in distinctive contexts it is necessary to have an initial grasp of the function of parental responsibility, the way in which court orders relate to it, and the jurisdictional arrangements under which these orders are made.

One important effect of the legislation was to render less important the distinctions previously drawn between parents and non-parents and different categories of non-parent. Under the old law, the kind of proceedings and the kind of orders available to interested individuals varied considerably and were largely governed by technical rules on standing[6]. Thus, for example, it could make a difference whether a step-parent had married a divorced parent, a previously

---

1 See, particularly, C Smart and B Neale 'Arguments Against Virtue – Must Contact be Enforced?' [1997] Fam Law 332. See also J Wallbank 'Castigating Mothers: The Judicial Response to Wilful Women in Cases concerning Contact' (1998) 20 JSWFL 557, and C Smart and B Neale *Family Fragments?* (Polity Press, 1999) especially at pp 188 et seq; and Chapter 4 below.

2 A Bainham 'The Privatisation of the Public Interest in Children' (1990) 53 MLR 206 at pp 216–219.

3 The empirical evidence of the Law Commission testified to this. See Priest and Whybrow, Law Com Supplement to Working Paper No 96 *Custody Law in Practice in the Divorce and Domestic Courts* (1986). There are approximately 10 times as many lone parent households headed by women as there are by men. See Chapter 1.

4 As in certain other jurisdictions. See Chapter 4 below.

5 This objective is certainly implicit in much of the Law Commission's work leading up to the reforms. Thus, when discussing the need for court orders the Commission offered the view that 'anything which can be done to help parents to keep separate the issues of being a spouse and being a parent will ultimately give the children the best chance of retaining them both': Law Com Report No 172 *Review of Child Law: Guardianship and Custody* (1988) at para 3.3.

6 The general position can best be appreciated by referring to the relevant chapters of leading family law texts published before the Children Act, such as SM Cretney *Principles of Family Law* (4th edn) (Sweet & Maxwell, 1984) Part IV, particularly chs 13–18, or PM Bromley and NV Lowe *Bromley's Family Law* (7th edn) (Butterworths, 1987), particularly ch 9.

unmarried parent or a widowed parent[1]. The fact that access to the courts should depend on such technicalities reflected no credit on the legal system, and most have been swept away to be replaced by a new 'open-door' policy. In general, *anyone* with a genuine interest in a child's well-being may apply to the court (albeit that in some cases they may need leave) in family proceedings although some important distinctions, especially between parents and non-parents, remain[2].

Another salient feature of the statutory scheme is its flexibility and the attempt to achieve a degree of uniformity in the orders available in different kinds of proceedings. 'Family proceedings' are defined expansively, with the result that, subject to certain qualifications, the same orders are available to the court whatever the nature of the particular proceedings. This has the added advantage of making available common remedies in public and private proceedings in accordance with the common principles discussed earlier.

The function of parental responsibility

Parental responsibility is now the central legal concept which establishes the link between a child and the person or persons who have authority to care for him, or take decisions concerning his upbringing. It replaces the former concept of 'parental rights and duties' which performed a similar function. The change in terminology is intended to reflect changes in the way that the relationship between parents and children is perceived. The objective was to move away from the proprietorial connotations of 'rights' towards a more enlightened view which emphasises that children are persons rather than possessions[3]. According to this, parental powers and authority exist only to enable parents to discharge their responsibilities. In fact, the Children Act defines parental responsibility to include, inter alia, 'rights', and the new definition was remarkably similar to the old definition of parental rights and duties[4]. Thus, the unitary concept of parental responsibility includes within it 'all the rights, duties, powers, responsibilities and authority which by law a parent of a child has in relation to the child and his property'[5].

It should be appreciated that, as a legal concept, parental responsibility performs two distinct but inter-related functions[6]. First, it encapsulates all the legal duties and powers concerning upbringing which exist to enable a parent to care for a child and to act on his behalf. These duties and powers relate to all the

---

1 The step-parent who married a divorced parent had the advantage of recourse to the matrimonial and divorce jurisdictions under the Domestic Proceedings and Magistrates' Courts Act 1978 and the Matrimonial Causes Act 1973. These jurisdictions were not open to other step-parents.
2 See Chapter 6 below.
3 On the view of children as property, see MDA Freeman *The Rights and Wrongs of Children* (Frances Pinter, 1983) at pp 13–18, and J Montgomery 'Children as Property?' (1988) 51 MLR 323.
4 Children Act 1975, s 85(1), which provided that the expression 'the parental rights and duties' meant 'all the rights and duties which by law the mother and father have in relation to a legitimate child and his property'.
5 Section 3(1).
6 These two senses in which the term 'parental responsibility' is used are brought out very helpfully by J Eekelaar in 'Parental Responsibility: State of Nature or Nature of the State?' (1991) JSWFL 37 at pp 38–39.

obvious concerns such as the child's material needs and health care, the manner of his education and religious upbringing, legal representation, and administration of his property. There are many difficult questions about the extent of these powers and duties and how they relate to the capacities and responsibilities of children themselves[1].

Secondly, the concept of parental responsibility exists not only to determine the way in which the law expects a parent to behave towards his child, but also to determine that *someone* (usually, but not necessarily, a parent) is entitled to bring up a child without interference from others who do not have parental responsibility. It has been said that the focus here is *not* on the nature of the duties owed to a child 'but rather upon the distance between the parent and others in making provision for the child; indeed, on the degree of *freedom* given to parents in bringing up their children'[2]. The acquisition of parental responsibility thus becomes crucial in determining which individuals or institutions have decision-making authority concerning a child. It is this legal status which is all-important, however close or distant the de facto relationship with the child may be. A grandparent physically caring for a child may have less power and authority in law than an absent parent who scarcely ever sees the child. And it is for this reason that court orders are available, to regulate the acquisition and exercise of parental responsibility[3]. The blanket statement that parental responsibility confers a legal status which others do not have to act in relation to a child requires qualification. First, it should always be remembered that parental responsibility may be vested in more than one person[4]. But, even where it is, the 'sharers' each have a status in relation to the child which distinguishes them from everyone else who does not have parental responsibility for that child. Secondly, it can be important to distinguish between the rights which parental responsibility confers, and the *enforcement* of the rights. For, while parental responsibility clearly implies freedom from external interference, it is by no means clear what legal action (if any) may be taken to prevent this interference[5].

The effect of court orders on parental responsibility

The general thinking in the legislation has already been noted: that the primary responsibility of parents for raising children should not be unnecessarily disrupted by court orders. Accordingly, the intention is that court orders should be confined to those instances in which it is necessary to resolve specific disputes about upbringing or to pre-empt such disputes by regulating in advance possible areas of disagreement. The courts were therefore given flexible new powers modelled on those which were traditionally available in wardship. These included a new range of orders and a general power to attach conditions and give

---

1 See Chapter 3 below.
2 J Eekelaar (above) at p 39.
3 Thus, in this example, the grandparent could seek a residence order or one of the other 's 8 orders' in order to prevent the parent from trying to exercise parental responsibility against the child's best interests as she (the grandparent) sees them. The parent, although retaining parental responsibility, would then be precluded from exercising it in a way which was incompatible with the court order: s 2(8).
4 Section 2(5) and (7).
5 See A Bainham 'Interfering with parental responsibility: a new challenge for the law of torts?' (1990) 3 JCL 3, commenting on *F v Wirral MBC* [1991] 2 WLR 1132.

directions[1]. The principal 'private' orders (s 8 orders) comprise the residence order, the contact order, the prohibited steps order, and the specific issue order[2]. The main 'public' orders are the care order and the supervision order[3]. Although private orders will usually be made in private proceedings and public orders in care proceedings, it should be remembered that both are, in principle, available in either type of 'family proceedings'. Thus, s 8 orders may be made in care proceedings as an alternative option to a care or supervision order. Likewise, a local authority may intervene in private proceedings and seek a care or supervision order. There is much more interchangeability and flexibility than existed under the old law where there was a more rigid demarcation between public and private proceedings.

It is vital to appreciate that no order (with the exception of an adoption order or an order under s 30 of the Human Fertilisation and Embryology Act 1990)[4] actually *removes* parental responsibility from parents. A residence order *does* vest parental responsibility in the person in whose favour it is made (assuming he or she does not already have it), but it does not transfer it *from* anyone else[5]. The effect of the order is simply to regulate the child's residence[6]. In practical terms, this means that the 'non-residential' parent is simply precluded from exercising that aspect of parental responsibility which relates to the question of where the child is to live. This is because parental responsibility must not be exercised in a way which is incompatible with a court order[7]. But parental responsibility itself remains intact, unaffected by the order, and may be exercised to the full extent that is compatible with the order.

Exactly the same reasoning applies to the other s 8 orders. Again, these orders simply regulate contact or other specific matters, such as religious upbringing or medical treatment, but do not otherwise affect parental responsibility or its exercise. Remarkably, these principles also apply to care orders. Hence, even where a child has been compulsorily removed from home on account of some parental failing, the parental responsibility of the parent concerned is preserved

---

1 These powers are largely contained in ss 10 and 11.

2 These orders are not exhaustive of the 'private' orders which can be made. The Children Act also introduced a new 'family assistance order' (s 16) and the unmarried father may obtain a 'parental responsibility order' (s 4(1)). It should also be noted that the court has power to attach conditions or make directions regarding any of the s 8 orders (s 11(7)) and this has had the effect of giving the court very wide-ranging powers of regulation going well beyond the straightforward effect of the order itself.

3 Section 31(1). Again, these are not exhaustive of 'public' orders. Others include the 'education supervision order' (s 36 and Part III, Sch 3), the 'child assessment order' (s 43), the 'emergency protection order' (s 44) and the various orders relating to the regulation of substitute care arrangements for children (see Chapter 11 below). Part IV of the Family Law Act 1996 also amended the Children Act to enable the courts in specified circumstances to include 'exclusion requirements' in interim care orders and emergency protection orders (Children Act 1989, ss 38A, 44A; and see Chapter 12 below).

4 See Chapter 7 below.

5 Section 12(2).

6 Section 8(1) provides quite simply that a residence order 'means an order settling the arrangements to be made as to the person with whom a child is to live'.

7 Section 2(8).

and is shared with the local authority which acquires it by virtue of the care order[1]. This was a considerable departure from the effect of a care order under the old law which was to *transfer* the bulk of parental rights exclusively to the local authority[2]. Similarly, despite some contrary dicta in the Court of Appeal[3], it was widely thought that the effect of a custody order was to transfer to the custodial parent exclusively most of the major decision-making powers over the child. Now the theory in all of these instances is that court orders are strictly limited in their effect to the specific issues they purport to govern on their face. A note of caution should perhaps be sounded. While, in theory, there will be many situations in which someone living physically apart from a child will retain parental responsibility, the extent to which this can be effectively exercised must be a matter of some doubt[4]. It is not clear how far theory and practice coincide on this issue.

Jurisdictional arrangements[5]

There have been many calls for the establishment of a 'family court' in England[6]. The Children Act did not create a family court, in the sense in which that expression is normally used, but it was the Government's view that the new jurisdictional arrangements brought about by the reforms constituted a substantial move in that direction[7]. The Government felt that the substantive law affecting children should be rationalised before fundamental reforms to the court system were introduced. At the same time, it hoped that the jurisdictional and procedural reforms could incorporate some of the more desirable features associated with the concept of a family court[8].

The Children Act created a concurrent jurisdiction in 'family proceedings' to be exercised by magistrates' 'family proceedings courts', county courts and the High Court[9]. The definition of 'family proceedings' is drawn sufficiently wide to

---

1   Sections 2(5) and (6) and 33(3). For an extreme example, see *Re M (Care Order: Threshold Conditions)* [1994] 2 AC 424, where the father retained parental responsibility despite serving a life sentence for killing the mother in the presence of the children. (The case is discussed in Chapter 11 below.)

2   Section 10(2) of the Child Care Act 1980. For an analysis of the legal effect of the various routes into care under the old law, see S Maidment 'The Fragmentation of Parental Rights and Children in Care' [1981] JSWL 21.

3   *Dipper v Dipper* [1981] Fam 31; and, on the confusion surrounding the term 'custody', see M Parry 'The Custody Conundrum' [1981] Fam Law 213.

4   In the public context it is specifically provided that the local authority has the power 'to determine the extent to which a parent or guardian of the child may meet his parental responsibility for him': s 33(3)(b), discussed in Chapter 11 below. In the private context, it is not wholly clear how far the 'non-residential' parent has a right to be consulted by the 'residential' parent. See Chapter 4.

5   See also Chapter 13 below where the position of the child in court is discussed.

6   See, particularly, B Hoggett 'Family Courts or Family Law Reform – which should come first?' (1986) 6 *Legal Studies* 1. Family courts have been operating in Australia since the mid-1970s. For a full evaluation of the Australian model, see A Dickey *Family Law* (2nd edn) (The Law Book Co, 1990) at ch 4, and S Parker, P Parkinson and J Behrens *Australian Family Law in Context* (The Law Book Co, 1994) at ch 7.

7   This at least was the view expressed by the Solicitor General: *Hansard* (HC) Vol 158, col 547.

8   It should not be thought, however, that the concept of family court, or informal justice in family matters, commands universal support. The Australian experience revealed remarkable public hostility, initially, to such matters as the derobing of the judiciary. See A Dickey (above).

9   Section 92(7).

cover virtually all proceedings, public and private, in which issues affecting a child's upbringing might be raised. Thus, the definition[1] includes:

(i) proceedings under the inherent jurisdiction of the High Court (these include, but are not synonymous with, wardship); and

(ii) proceedings under:
    (a) Parts I, II and IV of the Children Act;
    (b) the Matrimonial Causes Act 1973;
    (c) ...
    (d) the Adoption and Children Act 2002;
    (e) the Domestic Proceedings and Magistrates' Courts Act 1978;
    (f) ...
    (g) Part III of the Matrimonial and Family Proceedings Act 1984;
    (h) the Family Law Act 1996; and
    (i) ss 11 and 12 of the Crime and Disorder Act 1998.

Although expansive, the definition is not quite all-embracing. In particular, it does not include proceedings under Part V of the Children Act which are concerned with the short-term protection of children, often emergency protection. There is, in effect, a special code governing these cases and it would have been inappropriate to make available the whole range of orders under the Children Act in that context. Also, it hardly needs saying that many proceedings which can affect the interests of children in some way are not in the nature of family proceedings and consequently fall outside the definition. The obvious examples are criminal proceedings and ordinary civil actions such as contractual or tortious claims[2].

The broad objective of creating a concurrent jurisdiction is to achieve, as far as possible, uniformity of orders, flexibility and consistency in the procedure and remedies applying in different levels of court. This end is also promoted by rules of court which regulate the allocation of cases between the different courts and facilitate the transfer of cases either vertically between the various levels or horizontally within tiers. Thus, cases may be transferred sideways from one magistrates' court to another; upwards from the magistrates' court to the county court or from the county court to the High Court; or downwards from the High Court to the county court or from the county court to the magistrates' court[3]. *The Children Act Advisory Committee Final Report June 1997*[4] contained statistics on upward transfers of public law cases from the magistrates' court which revealed that gravity of the case was the most important reason for such transfers (accounting for approximately 70 per cent). While, in principle, concurrent jurisdiction means that a case could be heard at any of the three levels, in practice, cases are directed to the most appropriate court, depending on such factors as the complexity or gravity of the issues, the need to consolidate proceedings and the degree of urgency.

It has already been observed that the Children Act attempts to incorporate the more valuable features of the wardship jurisdiction. An aspect of this is the

---

1 In s 8(3) and (4), as amended.
2 See Chapter 15 below.
3 Schedule 11, and the Children (Allocation of Proceedings) Order 1991, SI 1991/1677.
4 (Lord Chancellor's Department, 1997) Appendix 2, Table IB.

procedural changes designed to emphasise the non-adversarial nature of family proceedings. It has long been regarded as a distinguishing feature of wardship that the proceedings are essentially inquisitorial rather than adversarial[1]. The legislation seeks to emulate this (and thereby reduce the need to resort to wardship) by promoting a non-adversarial style of proceedings. The increased role for the court was noted in controlling the progress of cases. In addition, the rules require all family proceedings to be commenced by application (rather than complaint or summons), to have preliminary hearings, and to require advance disclosure of the nature of the case, the orders sought and proposed plans for the child's future. Full rights of appeal are conferred on all parties to care proceedings, and appeals now lie to the High Court rather than the Crown Court to emphasise the civil nature of the proceedings[2]. The appointment of children's guardians (formerly guardians ad litem) to represent the independent interests of children in public proceedings has become the normal course, and further adds to the inquisitorial flavour of public family proceedings[3].

Whether or not the courts were fully equipped to respond to the new challenges posed by this radical change of approach has been questioned. While informal or participatory justice has an undoubted appeal, it has been said that 'the danger of adjudicators who have the responsibility of deploying the coercive power of the State appearing to "descend into the arena" is a real one'[4]. That said, these fundamental procedural reforms are consistent with the general aim of encouraging a thorough investigation of a child's welfare, untrammelled by technicalities, which may be thought not only desirable but essential if the paramountcy of children's welfare is to be more than rhetoric.

II THE UNITED NATIONS CONVENTION ON THE RIGHTS OF THE CHILD

The United Nations Convention on the Rights of the Child (the UNCRC) now constitutes the most authoritative and comprehensive statement of the fundamental rights of children covering civil and political, social, economic, cultural,

---

1   See NV Lowe and RAH White *Wards of Court* (2nd edn) (Barry Rose/Kluwer, 1986). Whether other children cases could really be described as 'adversarial' is debatable since the judges were often reluctant to insist on such matters as adherence to the strict rules of evidence. This is discussed further in Chapter 13 below.

2   Section 94(1). Under the old law, only the child had a right of appeal and this was to the Crown Court, an unlikely situation which arose from the 'criminal' model of care proceedings established by the Children and Young Persons Act 1969.

3   Section 41. It should be noted that the Family Law Act 1996, s 64 empowers the Lord Chancellor to make regulations providing for the separate representation of children in certain classes of 'private' proceedings under that Act and other legislation. See further Chapter 13 below.

4   SM Cretney 'Defining the Limits of State Intervention' in D Freestone (ed) *Children and the Law* at p 74.

recreational and humanitarian rights[1]. The expression 'rights' must be treated with some caution, since many of the aspirations for children set out in the UNCRC could arguably never be enforced as *legal* rights by *individual* children in the courts[2]. They are of a progressive and programmatic nature and, thus, dependent on political will and the availability and commitment of resources in individual countries. Others are more specific, and many of these were arguably already implemented in English law before the advent of the UNCRC.

The legal effect of the UN Convention

The UK ratified the UNCRC on 16 December 1991, but this does not mean that its substantive provisions form part of English domestic law[3]. In this respect its effect is quite different from that of the ECHR since implementation of the HRA 1998. An important question addressed below is the relationship between these two Conventions in the process of defining children's rights. In broad terms, the UK Government is legally bound to follow policies which are in conformity with the general and specific obligations set forth in the UNCRC. It is not, however, open to individual children to bring proceedings before the national courts, based solely on alleged violations of the UNCRC which affect them[4]. In order to achieve this result it would be necessary to *incorporate* the UNCRC into English law. Some

---

1   See, generally: D McGoldrick 'The United Nations Convention on the Rights of the Child' (1991) 5 IJLF 132; B Walsh 'The United Nations Convention on the Rights of the Child: A British View' (1991) 5 IJLF 170; and see also (1992) 6 IJLF at Part I which issue is devoted entirely to a re-evaluation of the concept of children's rights in the light of the UNCRC. It is also published as a separate volume: see P Alston, S Parker and J Seymour *Children, Rights and the Law* (Oxford University Press, 1992). For more detailed treatment, see LJ LeBlanc *The Convention on the Rights of the Child* (University of Nebraska Press, 1995), and G Van Bueren *The International Law on the Rights of the Child* (Martinus Nijhoff, 1995). For a critical evaluation of how far English law complies with the Convention, see M Freeman *The Moral Status of Children* (Martinus Nijhoff, 1997) at ch 6. For further assessments of the contribution of the Convention to the cause of children's rights see M Freeman 'The End of the Century of the Child?' (2000) 53 *Current Legal Problems* 505, CM Lyon 'Children and the Law – towards 2000 and beyond' in C Bridge (ed) *Family Law Towards the Millennium: Essays for PM Bromley* (Butterworths, 1997). And for a volume of essays evaluating the first decade of the Convention's operation see D Fottrell (ed) *Revisiting Children's Rights: 10 Years of the UN Convention on the Rights of the Child* (Kluwer, 2000).

2   Nonetheless, it can be persuasively argued that it is important to ascribe 'rights' to children even if some are unenforceable. See J Eekelaar 'The Importance of Thinking that Children have Rights' (1992) 6 IJLF 221, and M Freeman (above), especially ch 2.

3   For a general discussion of the enforceability of the UNCRC, see G Van Bueren 'The United Nations Convention on the Rights of the Child: The Necessity of Incorporation into United Kingdom Law' [1992] Fam Law 373.

4   It is not, however, improbable that the spirit if not the letter of the UNCRC will increasingly be used in legal arguments in future. For a good example, see Ward LJ's judgment in *Re H (Paternity: Blood Test)* [1996] 2 FLR 65 which was clearly influenced by Article 7 of the Convention. See also *Re H and A (Paternity: Blood Tests)* [2002] 1 FLR 1145; and see further Chapter 5 below. The principles of the UN Declaration of the Rights of the Child 1959 are, however, now likely to be of less assistance, especially where they may be thought to conflict with, or at least be superseded by, the 1989 UNCRC. Thus, in *Re A (Children: 1959 UN*

countries, for example the Netherlands and Spain, have a tradition of incorporating human rights treaties such as this directly into national law, but this is not the case in the UK[1].

It should not be concluded from this that the UNCRC is of no use to British children, but it does mean that the accountability of the Government is likely to be achieved more through political than legal means. Quite apart from legal redress, Van Bueren has noted that human rights treaties may be utilised as educational instruments and as evidence of the need for reform of national laws. So far as education is concerned, there is a specific obligation on States, under Article 42, to make the UNCRC's provisions and principles, by appropriate and active means, widely known to adults and children. It may also be the case, as argued below, that the substantive Articles of the UNCRC may assist in defining the *content* of children's Convention rights under the ECHR.

Political accountability leading to reform of national laws and practices is perhaps the key to enforcement of the UNCRC at the national level. In this respect, the Committee on the Rights of the Child, established under Article 43, has a vital role.[2] This Committee consists of 'ten experts of high moral standing and recognized competence in the field covered by [the] Convention'[3], elected by the States parties. The main function of the Committee is to produce periodic reports on the operation of the UNCRC under Articles 44 and 45. States have undertaken to report on the 'measures they have adopted which give effect to the rights recognized . . . and on the progress made on the enjoyment of those rights'[4]. These 'Reports' must indicate factors and difficulties affecting the degree of fulfilment of the obligations in individual countries[5]. The Reports are to be made public, and the Committee must report biennially to the General Assembly through the Economic and Social Council[6]. More significantly, the Committee may make suggestions and general recommendations on the strength of the information which it receives under Articles 44 and 45. These are then transmitted to the General Assembly and the State concerned, together with any comments made by that State[7].

A poor track record of implementation by individual States may, through these procedures, become a matter of public record and accountability within the international community. It is conceivable that this may have a potentially greater

---

Declaration) [1998] 1 FLR 354, the Court of Appeal held that the judge had erred in granting residence to the mother in relation to a toddler and rejecting the welfare officer's recommendations for a residence order to be made in favour of the father. The mother had relied in part on Principle 6 of the 1959 Declaration to the effect that a child of tender years should not, save in exceptional circumstances, be separated from its mother. The court said that the relevance and value of the 1959 Declaration, now being 40 years old, was most doubtful. Moreover, the UNCRC of 1989 was gender-neutral. See also *Brixey v Lynas* [1996] 2 FLR 499.

1   See Van Bueren (above) for further discussion. In English law domestic legislation is required for this purpose, as in the case of the HRA 1998.
2   But for criticism of the effectiveness of the Committee and the reporting system under the UNCRC, see L Woll 'Reporting to the UN Committee on the Rights of the Child: A catalyst for domestic debate and policy change?' (2000) *International Journal of Children's Rights* 71.
3   UNCRC, Article 43(2).
4   Ibid, Article 44(1).
5   Ibid, Article 44(2).
6   Ibid, Article 44(5).
7   Ibid, Article 45.

impact than recourse to an international tribunal might have done. The Committee's first report on the UK was less than glowing about the Government's record under the Convention. Among the matters it criticised were the extent of child poverty, the law permitting corporal punishment of children, the low age of criminal responsibility and the lack of children's rights in the educational sphere.[1] In 2000 Michael Freeman gave this scathing assessment of the lack of an effective enforcement mechanism under the UNCRC[2], after drawing attention to the lack of provision for national or individual petition. In his view, the committee was 'under-resourced, severely overwhelmed by the volume of work with which it is expected to cope and, not surprisingly, is years behind. Perhaps taking a cue from this, many States parties are overdue with their initial reports (these are due two years after ratification) and many more are overdue in submitting their periodic reports. In short, the system is breaking down'[3]. It had been suggested, in the English context, that an office of 'Commissioner for children's rights' was required, inter alia, to monitor the effective implementation of the UNCRC in England[4]. In particular, the point was made that responsibility for different pieces of legislation and areas of policy affecting children was fragmented between a number of different government departments. No single department had responsibility for children. One of the Commissioner's functions would be to require all these separate departments to consider specifically the impact of legislation and policies on the rights and interests of children. Children's 'ombudsmen' existed in certain other countries, notably in Scandinavia and New Zealand, and it was argued that the ratification of the UNCRC highlighted the need for a similar office to be established in the UK.

A Children's Commissioner for Wales, as noted above, was established by the National Assembly for Wales. A major influence was the publication of the Waterhouse Report[5] on the abuse of children in institutional care in Wales and the subsequent enactment of the Care Standards Act 2000. Provision for a Children's Commissioner for England is now made in the Children Bill 2004[6].

---

1 See United Nations *Concluding Observations of the Committee on the Rights of the Child: United Kingdom of Great Britain and Northern Ireland* CRC/C/15Add34 (1995), and see U Kilkelly, 'The UN Committee on the Rights of the Child – an evaluation in the light of recent UK experience' [1996] CFLQ 105. These criticisms were substantially repeated in the Committee's Second Report on the UK. See United Nations Committee on the Rights of the Child, Thirty-First Session *Concluding Observations: United Kingdom of Great Britain and Northern Ireland* (2002).

2 M Freeman 'The End of the Century of the Child?' (2000) 53 *Current Legal Problems* 505 at 509–510.

3 Ibid.

4 M Rosenbaum and P Newell *Taking Children Seriously* (Gulbenkian Foundation, 1991; revised edn March 2000).

5 *Lost in Care* – Report of the Tribunal of Inquiry into the Abuse of Children in the Former County Council Areas of Gwynedd and Clwyd since 1974 (HMSO, 2000).

6 See below.

General aims and general obligations

The general aims of the UNCRC have been referred to as the '4 Ps' – *Prevention, Protection, Provision,* and *Participation*[1]. As to *prevention,* there are Articles relating to preventive health care[2], preventing child abduction[3] and prohibiting discrimination against children[4]. As to *protection,* the UNCRC seeks to protect children from all forms of torture, cruel, inhuman and degrading treatment and punishment, abuse and exploitation[5]. As to *provision,* there are Articles creating rights of recipience in education[6] and social security[7], the right to rest and leisure[8], as well as the more general right to an adequate standard of living[9]. Rights of *participation* are recognised in Articles which provide for access to information[10], freedom of expression[11] and the right of the child to express his views[12].

The UNCRC applies to 'every human being below the age of eighteen years unless, under the law applicable to the child, majority is attained earlier'[13]. Parties to the Convention are required to 'respect and ensure' that the rights in the UNCRC are extended to all children within their jurisdiction 'without discrimination of any kind, irrespective of the child's or his or her parents' or legal guardian's race, colour, sex, language, religion, political or other opinion, national, ethnic or social origin, property, disability, birth or other status'[14].

Article 3 arguably contains the most important principle in the UNCRC, since it is the general standard which must be applied throughout the Convention to the more specific rights guaranteed by it. The Declaration of Geneva 1924 and the Declaration of the Rights of the Child 1959 had both embodied the general principle that 'mankind owes the child the best it has to give'. The UNCRC provides:

> 'In all actions concerning children, whether undertaken by public or private social welfare institutions, courts of law, administrative authorities or legislative bodies, the best interests of the child shall be a primary consideration.'[15]

Family lawyers will immediately detect echoes of the 'welfare principle' in English law but will also be struck by the difference in wording between the two provisions. First, the best interests of the child are expressed to be *primary,* but not paramount, and secondly, they are only *a* primary consideration and not *the* primary consideration. As argued above, it may be that a reformulation of the

---

1 See the discussion in G Van Bueren 'The UN Convention on the Rights of the Child' (1991) 3 JCL 63.
2 UNCRC Article 24.
3 Ibid, Article 11.
4 Ibid, Article 2.
5 Ibid, Article 37.
6 Ibid, Article 28.
7 Ibid, Article 29.
8 Ibid, Article 31.
9 Ibid, Article 27.
10 Ibid, Article 17.
11 Ibid, Article 13.
12 Ibid, Article 12.
13 Ibid, Article 1.
14 Ibid, Article 2(1).
15 Ibid, Article 3(1).

welfare principle in the Children Act, making children's welfare the primary but not paramount consideration, might be more realistic in the light of human rights obligations towards adult parties. On the other hand, the domestic welfare principle applies only to courts and only in those instances in which the upbringing of the child is the central issue. The UN principle, in contrast, applies to a much wider range of public and private institutions, courts, authorities and bodies[1]. Quite apart from all the difficulties of interpretation of 'welfare'[2], it is plain that States may, under the UNCRC, have regard to other factors in discharging their obligations and may, conceivably, find that these outweigh the interests of the children in issue. Article 3[3] goes on to provide:

> 'States parties undertake to ensure the child such protection and care as is necessary for his or her well-being, taking into account the rights and duties of his or her parents, legal guardians, or other individuals legally responsible for him or her, and, to this end, shall take all appropriate legislative and administrative measures.'

Reading this with the preamble, which talks of taking due account of 'the importance of the traditions and cultural values of each people for the protection and harmonious development of the child', Eekelaar has commented that, prima facie, 'the way seems open for almost unrestricted welfarism by the injection of adult values into a conception of what constitutes the "best interests" of the child', but he notes that this must be read 'in the context of the series of explicit rights which the Convention protects'[4]. Thus, the apparently open-ended discretion which States have in promoting the best interests of children is circumscribed by a whole range of specific duties. This is not unlike the position of parents themselves, exercising parental responsibility[5]. Difficult questions can undoubtedly arise concerning the application of the best interests doctrine in very different cultural contexts[6].

The obligations of States to children are also in a sense qualified by specific duties owed to parents and other carers. The UNCRC assumes that many of the child's welfare needs will be met by his primary carers[7] but also requires States to respect the rights and duties of these adults. Article 5 provides:

> 'State parties shall respect the responsibilities, rights and duties of parents or, where applicable, the members of the extended family or community as provided for by the local custom, legal guardians or other persons legally responsible for the child, to provide, in a manner consistent with the evolving capacities of the child, appropriate direction and guidance in the exercise by the child of the rights recognised in the present Convention.'[8]

One way of looking at this provision is to regard it as merely reflecting the realities of life. Children do not exist in a vacuum and 'the Convention is not simply an exercise in abstraction'[9]. The rights of children must inevitably be

---

1   See Part I of this chapter for a discussion of the nuances of the welfare principle.
2   Ibid.
3   UNCRC Article 3(2).
4   J Eekelaar 'The Importance of Thinking that Children have Rights' (1992) 6 IJLF 221 at p 231.
5   See Chapter 3 below.
6   This question is explored in depth in P Alston (ed) *The Best Interests of the Child* (Clarendon, 1994).
7   UNCRC Article 3(2).
8   See also Article 14(2) which similarly recognises the parental role in the context of the child's right to 'freedom of thought, conscience and religion'.
9   J Eekelaar (above) at p 233.

secured in large measure by the actions of adults, usually those with their primary care, but in exercising these adult rights and duties in relation to children, the UNCRC requires those concerned to provide direction and guidance which is *consistent* with the rights set out in the Convention and not inconsistently with them[1]. Another way of viewing the Article is that it imports into the international arena all the uncertainties and difficulties which surround the interaction of children's rights and parental rights and responsibilities in domestic law[2]. The fact is that there may be a conflict between adults' and children's rights, and the UNCRC acknowledges this[3]. As McGoldrick has astutely observed, 'those charged with providing "appropriate direction and guidance" to the child on the exercise of its rights may well have an interest, personal or institutional, in ensuring that the child does not exercise its rights'[4]. The practical application of the concept of evolving capacities of the child may, therefore, be no less fraught than it is in English domestic law.

Specific rights

It is not possible here to provide a comprehensive analysis of each and every Article of the UNCRC or of what the various rights may mean for children in English law[5]. Instead, an attempt will be made to identify some of the more significant Articles commenting, where appropriate, on the current state of English law. It should also be noted that Optional Protocols to the Convention governing, respectively (i) the sale of children, child prostitution and child pornography, and (ii) the involvement of children in armed conflicts, came into force early in 2002[6].

The right to life and development
Article 6 requires States to recognise that every child has the inherent right to life and to ensure, to the maximum extent possible, the survival and development of the child. This provision clearly has implications for medical decision-making but, as discussed later, the right to life and survival may have to be qualified in those instances in which a minimal quality of life is not sustainable[7].

The right to an identity
Two Articles are concerned with this. Article 7(1) requires that the child 'shall be registered immediately after birth and shall have the right from birth to a name, the right to acquire a nationality, and, as far as possible, the right to know and be

---

1 J Eekelaar (above) at p 233.
2 As to which, see particularly Chapter 8 below.
3 For further discussion see A Bainham 'Children Law at the Millennium' in S Cretney (ed) *Family Law: Essays for the New Millennium* (Family Law, 2000) especially at pp 113–114.
4 D McGoldrick 'The United Nations Convention on the Rights of the Child' (1991) 5 IJLF 132 at pp 138–139.
5 See, generally, the sources cited at fn 1 at p 67 above.
6 See U Kilkelly 'Annual Review of International Family Law' in A Bainham (ed) *The International Survey of Family Law (2004 Edition)* (Family Law, 2004) p 1 at pp 17–18.
7 The right to life is also enshrined in Article 2 of the ECHR. Neither of these Articles, it must be said, greatly influenced the Court of Appeal in *Re A (Conjoined Twins: Medical Treatment)* [2001] 1 FLR 1, a case in which the right to life was surely at issue. See further Chapter 8 below.

cared for by his or her parents'[1]. This is fast becoming one of the most significant and frequently cited provisions in the Convention since it is closely associated with recent claims that children have a right to knowledge of their biological origins[2]. It will be noted here that the UNCRC does not distinguish between married and unmarried parents and also that Article 2, the anti-discrimination provision, prohibits discrimination on the basis of status. The implications for English law, and for the laws of many other countries, may be that procedures for establishing paternity and giving recognition to the parental responsibility of unmarried fathers need to be improved[3].

Under Article 8, States undertake to 'respect the right of the child to *preserve* his or her identity, including nationality, name and family relations as recognised by law without unlawful interference'. This Article was an Argentinian initiative inspired by the 'disappearance' of an estimated 150–170 children in Argentina between 1975 and 1983[4].

The English reforms providing for the continuity of parental responsibility, especially post-divorce, may be viewed as an aspect of preserving the child's identity, as may the shift towards more open adoption[5]; and preserving family relations clearly has implications for rights of ongoing contact between parent and child[6].

Separation from parents

Article 9 requires States to 'ensure that a child shall not be separated from his or her parents against their will, except when competent authorities subject to judicial review determine, in accordance with applicable law and procedures, that such separation is necessary for the best interests of the child'[7]. Where the child *is* separated, the State must respect the right of the child 'to maintain personal relations and direct contact with both parents on a regular basis, except if it is contrary to the child's best interests'[8].

This is reinforced by the ECHR which imposes *positive* obligations on the State to seek reunification of parent and child[9].

The right of the child to express views

Article 12(1) is another of the Convention's most important Articles. It requires States to 'assure to the child who is capable of forming his or her own views the right to express those views freely in all matters affecting the child, the views of the

---

1   See K O'Donovan 'Interpretations of Children's Identity Rights' in D Fottrell (ed) *Revisiting Children's Rights* (Kluwer, 2000).
2   This is an issue in many different contexts such as where there is a dispute over paternity (see Chapter 5), where the child has been conceived with the use of donated gametes (see Chapters 3 and 6) and following the adoption of a child (see Chapter 7).
3   See Chapter 5 below.
4   See Van Bueren (above) at pp 118–120.
5   See Chapters 4 and 7 below.
6   See Chapter 4.
7   UNCRC, Article 9(1).
8   Ibid, Article 9(3).
9   See especially *Johansen v Norway* (1996) 23 EHRR 33, and Chapters 10 and 11 below.

child being given due weight in accordance with the age and maturity of the child'[1].

This is close to the formulation which appears in several places in the Children Act[2] but its ambit extends well beyond those specific instances. Rather more troubling from an English perspective is Article 12(2), which states that 'the child shall in particular be provided the opportunity to be heard in any judicial and administrative proceedings affecting the child, either directly, or through a representative or an appropriate body, in a manner consistent with the procedural rules of national law'. Although it has been doubted that this necessarily entails separate representation of the child[3] it is the case[4] that representation in England is patchy, and there must also be doubt about whether the lack of independent representation of children's views in the educational sphere conforms with the spirit, if not the letter, of this Article[5]. Article 12(2) should now be considered alongside the European Convention on the Exercise of Children's Rights 1996, which has as its essential aim to grant *procedural* rights to children in family proceedings and to improve their rights of participation in such proceedings[6].

Civil rights

Articles 13 to 17 deal with some of the classic civil liberties recognised by liberal democracies and expressly apply these to children. Thus, subject to certain qualifications, Article 13 recognises the child's right to 'freedom of expression'. Article 14 requires States to respect the right of the child to 'freedom of thought, conscience and religion' but this is qualified by the rights and duties of parents to give direction to the child[7]. Article 15 upholds the right of the child to 'freedom of association and to freedom of peaceful assembly'. Article 16 protects the child against interference with 'his or her privacy, family, home or correspondence', while Article 17 requires States to ensure that the child has 'access to information' on a range of material, especially that aimed at the promotion of his or her social, spiritual and moral well-being and physical and mental health.

Parental responsibilities

Under Article 18(1), States must 'use their best efforts to ensure recognition of the principle that both parents have common responsibilities for the upbringing and development of the child'. They must also recognise that parents or guardians 'have the primary responsibility for the upbringing and development of the child'.

This would, again, appear to have implications for the law applying to unmarried fathers. The Scottish Law Commission was clearly of the view that it required *automatic* rights for parents whether they were married or not and proposed changes to Scots law to give effect to this. These proposals were not

---

1   Many useful articles, case reports and other materials relating to the general issue of the representation of children in legal proceedings are to be found in the journal *Representing Children* published by the National Youth Advocacy Service.
2   Especially that in s 1(3)(a).
3   D McGoldrick 'The United Nations Convention on the Rights of the Child' (1991) 5 IJLF 132 at p 141.
4   See Chapter 13 below.
5   See Chapter 16 below.
6   This Convention is examined in Chapter 17 below.
7   See text and fn 8 at p 71.

accepted by the Westminster Parliament and did not find their way into the Children (Scotland) Act 1995[1]. The reference to the *primary* responsibility of parents implies a *secondary* responsibility in the State. This is borne out by Article 18(2) which requires States to 'render appropriate assistance to parents and legal guardians in the performance of their child-rearing responsibilities and [to] ensure the development of institutions, facilities and services for the care of children'. Article 18(3) also requires them to 'take all appropriate measures to ensure that children of working parents have the right to benefit from child-care services and facilities for which they are eligible'. It is arguable that English law, in failing to provide comprehensive nursery provision, is in breach of the spirit, if not the letter, of this provision[2].

Child protection

Articles 19 to 24 can all be said to relate to aspects of the protection of children, either generally, or specifically, to such groups of children as refugees[3] or disabled children[4]. Article 19 requires States to 'take all appropriate legislative, administrative, social and educational measures to protect the child from all forms of physical or mental violence, injury or abuse, neglect or negligent treatment, maltreatment or exploitation, including sexual abuse, while in the care of parent(s), legal guardian(s) or any other person who has the care of the child'. Article 20 provides that a child 'temporarily or permanently deprived of his or her family environment ... shall be entitled to special protection and assistance provided by the State'. It also states that, when considering solutions, 'due regard shall be paid to the desirability of continuity in a child's upbringing and to the child's ethnic, religious, cultural and linguistic background'. As discussed later[5], these considerations are now incorporated in the Children Act, and the adequacy of Part IV, regulating care and supervision, should be evaluated in the light of the above Articles.

Article 21 regulates various aspects of adoption. Of particular interest is the requirement that States which 'recognize and/or permit the system of adoption shall ensure that the best interests of the child shall be the paramount consideration'. This is now the position under the Adoption and Children 2002, whereas under the Adoption Act 1976 the child's welfare was the 'first' but not 'paramount' consideration. This controversial change is discussed in Chapter 7. Article 24 deals with protection of the child's health, and requires States to 'recognize the right of the child to the enjoyment of the highest attainable standard of health and to facilities for the treatment of illness and rehabilitation of health'[6]. This and several other Articles have major resource implications and the State's obligations must be viewed as programmatic or progressive.

---

1   See Chapter 5 below. For an assessment of the situation in Scotland see E Sutherland 'How are Children Faring in the "New Scotland"?' in A Bainham (ed) *The International Survey of Family Law (2001 Edition)* (Family Law, 2001) p 363, especially at pp 368 et seq.
2   See Chapter 10 below.
3   UNCRC, Article 22.
4   Ibid, Article 23. English law has responded to some extent to the concerns of this Article in the Carers and Disabled Children Act 2000 and the Health and Social Care Act 2001.
5   See Chapters 10 and 11 below.
6   UNCRC, Article 24(2) also importantly requires States to take appropriate measures in relation to various forms of preventive medicine.

Recipience of social welfare

Articles 26 to 31 are a cluster of Articles dealing with the right of the child to receive various forms of social welfare. Article 26 protects the child's right to social security while taking into account in particular 'the resources and the circumstances of the child and persons having responsibility for the maintenance of the child'.

Article 27(1) requires States to recognise 'the right of every child to a standard of living adequate for the child's physical, mental, spiritual, moral and social development'. However, this is then qualified by references to the 'abilities and financial capacities' of the child's carers[1] and the national conditions and means of States[2]. Subject to this, States are required to assist carers to implement the child's right by providing material assistance and support programmes directed, in particular, towards nutrition, clothing and housing. Article 27(4) is an interesting provision from the English perspective since it would seem to provide some justification for the controversial principles of the child support legislation[3]. It requires States to 'take all appropriate measures to secure the recovery of maintenance for the child from the parents or other persons having financial responsibility for the child ...'. While the motivation behind this provision is undoubtedly to benefit the child rather than the Exchequer (as contrasted with that of the English Child Support Acts), this must be seen in the light of the principle that the *primary* responsibility for the child's financial support under the UNCRC is the *parent's*, and the State's responsibility, through social security, is *secondary*. This is, to say the least, contentious in the English context, since there are some who would argue that the *primary* responsibility for the casualties of family breakdown is the State's, and that parental responsibility is secondary. This is especially so where the parent concerned now has other responsibilities towards the children in his reconstituted household.

Articles 28 and 29 relate to education and are considered later[4]. Article 30 deals with rights of minority groups and provides that, in those States 'in which ethnic, religious and linguistic minorities or persons of indigenous origin exist, a child belonging to such a minority or who is indigenous shall not be denied the right, in community with other members of his or her group, to enjoy his or her own culture, to profess and practise his or her own religion, or to use his or her own language'[5]. Article 31(1) upholds the child's recreational rights. It requires States to recognise 'the right of the child to rest and leisure, to engage in play and recreational activities appropriate to the age of the child and to participate freely in cultural life and the arts'.

---

1   UNCRC, Article 27(2).
2   Ibid, Article 27(3).
3   See Chapter 9 below.
4   See Chapter 16 below.
5   For an excellent discussion of children's rights and cultural issues, which addresses the rival philosophical positions of monism, cultural relativism and cultural pluralism, see M Freeman *The Moral Status of Children* (Martinus Nijhoff, 1997) ch 7. See also M Freeman 'Children and Cultural Diversity' in D Fottrell (ed) *Revisiting Children's Rights* (Kluwer, 2000). Also useful, especially in the context of medical procedures, is C Bridge 'Religion, Culture and the Body of the Child' in A Bainham, S Day Sclater and M Richards (eds) *Body Lore and Laws* (Hart Publishing, 2002).

Protection against exploitation

Articles 32 to 35 recognise the child's right to protection from various forms of exploitation, including economic exploitation[1], protection against narcotics[2], sexual exploitation and sexual abuse[3], and trafficking in children[4]. Other Articles: protect the child against torture or other cruel, inhuman or degrading treatment or punishment[5]; require States to abide by the rules of international humanitarian law regarding children and armed conflicts[6]; place States under rehabilitative duties towards child victims of the kinds of harm contemplated by the UNCRC[7]; and regulate the treatment of children under the criminal law[8].

Evaluation of the UNCRC

Critics of international law often question its value and whether it is truly law at all, in view of the difficulties of enforcement. It is fair to say that there is much in the UNCRC which can only be achieved with political will and a massive commitment of resources. Yet the UNCRC, like domestic law, should not be evaluated solely on the basis of its legal enforceability. Arguably more important is the educative and symbolic effect of internationally agreed norms against which domestic standards may be measured. In particular the process of defining children's Convention rights under the ECHR may be expected to be influenced to an appreciable extent by the content of the UNCRC. McGoldrick has pointed out that the UNCRC is evidence that the international community has adopted a broad consensus on what rights children have and on what the obligations of the family, society and the international community should be[9]. The UNCRC also has a distinctive place in applying or extending to children, many of the human rights incontestably possessed by adults. The hope is that this will enable a more child-orientated or child-centred jurisprudence of human rights to develop. A possible criticism is that it fails to go far enough in the direction of empowerment rights and is over-concerned with protection. It is certainly true that the majority of its Articles are protectionist in nature. One commentator's view is that it is a decidedly conservative instrument, built on compromise and concession, which is largely confined to reiterating existing human rights norms in their application to children[10].

It has been seen that the UNCRC gives explicit expression to the primary duties of parents but, importantly, it reaffirms the secondary role of the State. At the same time, it goes beyond merely listing a range of duties owed by adults to children and underlines the importance of recognising children as persons capable of possessing rights. It is, moreover, the possession of these rights which

---

1 UNCRC, Article 32.
2 Ibid, Article 33.
3 Ibid, Article 34.
4 Ibid, Article 35.
5 Ibid, Article 37.
6 Ibid, Article 38.
7 Ibid, Article 39.
8 Ibid, Article 40.
9 D McGoldrick 'The United Nations Convention on the Rights of the Child' (1991) IJLF 132 at p 158.
10 LJ LeBlanc (above). See also M Freeman (above), especially ch 4.

has the potential for transforming, not simply childhood, but adulthood as well. The point has been eloquently made by Eekelaar:

> 'The strength of the rights formulation is its recognition of humans as individuals worthy of development and fulfilment. This is not an appeal to narrow self-interest. On the contrary it recognizes the insight that people can contribute positively to others only when they are respected and fulfilled. And to recognize people as having rights from the moment of their birth continuously into adulthood could turn out, politically, to be the most radical step of all. If all *young people* are secured all the physical, social and economic rights proclaimed in the Convention, the lives of millions of adults of the next generation would be transformed. It would be a grievous mistake to see the Convention applying to childhood alone. Childhood is not an end in itself, but part of the process of forming the adults of the next generation. The Convention is for all *people*. It could influence their entire lives. If its aims can be realised, the Convention can truly be said to be laying the foundations for a better world.'[1]

III   CHILDREN AND HUMAN RIGHTS: THE EUROPEAN CONVENTION FOR THE PROTECTION OF HUMAN RIGHTS AND FUNDAMENTAL FREEDOMS, AND THE HUMAN RIGHTS ACT 1998

The combined effect of the ECHR and the HRA 1998[2] is that the rights under the ECHR and the jurisprudence of the ECtHR interpreting those rights form an integral part of English law. It is therefore necessary to take account of the Convention principles as they affect every aspect of the law concerning children, and reference will be made to the implications of the ECHR throughout this book. At this stage it is necessary merely to set out the fundamental principles of the HRA 1998, to look briefly at the main Articles which are likely to affect children and families and to offer a preliminary view on the impact of this comparatively new regime in children cases.

---

1   J Eekelaar 'The Importance of Thinking that Children have Rights' (1992) 6 IJLF 221 at p 234.
2   On the Convention generally, see M Janis, R Kay and A Bradley *European Human Rights Law* (2nd edn) (Oxford University Press, 2000) and C Ovey and R White *The European Convention on Human Rights* (3rd edn) (Clarendon, 2000). For a digest of cases decided by the ECtHR, see S Nash and M Furse *Essential Human Rights Cases* (2nd edn) (Jordans, 2002). Specifically on the HRA 1998, see J Wadham and H Mountfield *Blackstone's Guide to the Human Rights Act 1998* (2nd edn) (Blackstone Press Ltd) and E Shorts and C de Than *Human Rights Law in the UK* (Sweet & Maxwell, 2001). The most comprehensive treatment of the ECHR and HRA 1998 from the perspective of family law is H Swindells, A Neaves, M Kushner and R Skilbeck *Family Law and the Human Rights Act 1998* (Family Law, 1999). For a major collection of papers on human rights and the family see P Lødrup and E Modvar (eds) *Family Life and Human Rights* (Gyldendal Akademisk, 2004). U Kilkelly *The Child and the European Convention on Human Rights* (Ashgate, 1999) is essential reading for a perspective on the ECHR as it applies to children. Relevant articles are J Fortin 'Rights brought home for children' (1999) 62 MLR 350; A Bainham 'Family

The Human Rights Act 1998

The HRA 1998 was implemented on 2 October 2000 and from that date the ECHR became part of English law[1]. Before that time the ECHR was occasionally invoked in English family cases and there was ultimately a right of individual petition to the European Commission and, if declared admissible, from there to the ECtHR. This was a lengthy process which could take many years but there were nonetheless some significant successes, especially in relation to the eradication of corporal punishment in schools[2] and the improvement of procedural rights for parents in care proceedings[3].

The broad effect of the HRA 1998 is that 'Convention rights' are now directly enforceable in the English courts[4]. It is now possible for a person who claims that a 'public authority' (which includes a court or tribunal)[5] has acted in a way which is incompatible with his Convention rights to bring proceedings against that authority directly in the English courts[6]. It is also the case that domestic courts and tribunals, in arriving at their decisions, are required to take into account the judgments, decisions and opinions of the European Court and Commission 'so far as, in the opinion of the court or tribunal, it is relevant to the proceedings in which the question has arisen'[7]. English courts are therefore required to apply the existing and evolving jurisprudence of the ECtHR. Moreover, the effect of applying the Convention directly is that already a substantial domestic jurisprudence has been generated which takes much greater account of human rights arguments than was ever so before. It is now the case that a significant proportion of children cases which reach the higher courts will involve arguments under the ECHR[8]. While it may well be that the outcome would not have been greatly different if they had been decided before 2000[9] the process of reasoning, which involves a careful balancing of rights, has had to change. And already, in some areas, it seems reasonably clear that the longstanding position taken by the law has

---

Rights in the Next Millennium' (2000) 53 *Current Legal Problems* 471; H Swindells ' "Crossing the Rubicon" – Family Law post the Human Rights Act 1998' in S Cretney (ed) *Family Law: Essays for the New Millennium* (Family Law, 2000), and U Kilkelly 'The impact of the Convention on the case-law of the European Court of Human Rights' in D Fottrell (ed) *Revisiting Children's Rights* (Kluwer, 2000).

1 For a useful article looking at the effect of implementation from a family law perspective, see G Kingscote 'Incorporation of the European Convention on Human Rights' [1998] Fam Law 195. See also J Fortin *Children's Rights and the Developing Law* (2nd edn) (Butterworths, 2003) at pp 50–63. The Act followed the Government's White Paper *Rights Brought Home: The Human Rights Bill* (Home Office) (Cm 3782).

2 See especially *Tyrer v UK* (1978) 2 EHRR 1; *Campbell and Cosans v UK* (1982) 4 EHRR 293 and *Costello-Roberts v UK* (1995) 19 EHRR 112.

3 *W, O, H and B v UK* (1988) 10 EHRR 29.

4 'Convention rights' under s 1 of the HRA 1998 are essentially the 'rights and fundamental freedoms' set out in the Convention and the Protocols to it.

5 HRA 1998, s 6.

6 Ibid, s 7.

7 Ibid, s 2.

8 This has been true, for example, of a succession of recent cases considering the procedural rights of unmarried fathers in adoption proceedings. For an assessment of these cases and the general attitude of the English courts to children's Convention rights, see A Bainham 'Children's Rights and Human Rights' (2002) *Human Rights* 142.

9 The strong adherence of the judges to the application of the welfare principle is a major factor here.

been eroded. One example, discussed in Chapter 7, is the traditional right of the unmarried mother to place her child confidentially for adoption[1].

So far as it is possible, primary and subordinate legislation must be read and given effect in a way which is compatible with Convention rights[2]. The higher courts are empowered to make declarations of incompatibility where this is not the case[3]. Legislation affecting children may therefore be scrutinised to examine its compatibility with the ECHR[4], and the domestic judicial precedents are also liable to be attacked on the basis that they no longer conform with the requirements of the Convention[5].

The ECHR: key Articles for children and families

While any part of the ECHR could potentially be invoked in cases involving children and families, it is plain that some Articles are of key importance. What follows is no more than an attempt to introduce the more important Articles which will resurface throughout the book.

Article 8

The most important Article in the ECHR for families is undoubtedly Article 8[6]. This provides:

'1. Everyone has the right to respect for his private and family life, his home and his correspondence.

2. There shall be no interference by a public authority with the exercise of this right except such as is in accordance with the law and is necessary in a democratic society in the interests of national security, public safety or the economic well-being of the country, for the prevention of disorder or crime, for the protection of health or morals, or for the protection of the rights and freedoms of others.'

The Article guarantees to children and parents and, to a lesser extent, wider members of the family the right to respect for their family life with one another. As we shall see, this implies, in the private law[7], mutual rights of contact between parent and child and, in the public law, that the emphasis should be on reuniting parent and child where it has been necessary for the child to spend time in substitute care[8]. 'Family life' for these purposes is not confined to marriage but difficult questions have arisen concerning when family life comes into being between a genetic, unmarried father and a child[9]. The Article has implications for when the adoption of a child should, or should not, be allowed[10].

---

1 Bainham 'Children's Rights and Human Rights' (above).
2 HRA 1998, s 3.
3 Ibid, s 4.
4 A good example being the House of Lords decision in *Re S; Re W (Minors)* [2002] 1 FLR 815.
5 A good example here is the practice of the courts relating to the granting of leave to take children out of the jurisdiction which came under attack (unsuccessfully) from a human rights perspective in *Payne v Payne* [2001] 1 FLR 1052.
6 For the most important case-law generated under Article 8, see M Janis et al (above) at ch 6 and Swindells et al (above) at pp 119 et seq.
7 See Chapter 4 below.
8 See Chapter 11 below.
9 See Chapter 5 below.
10 See Chapter 7 below.

Article 6

Article 6 has very significant implications for the procedural rights of family members, including children, in the many kinds of legal proceedings in which their interests may arise[1]. It provides:

'In the determination of his civil rights and obligations or of any criminal charge against him, everyone is entitled to a fair and public hearing within a reasonable time by an independent and impartial tribunal established by law.'

Article 6 has been interpreted to require effective access to the courts[2]. As we shall see it is already having an impact in relation to the public law regime of the Children Act where issues have arisen about whether there are adequate opportunities for parents to challenge the decisions of local authorities in relation to important matters affecting children in care[3].

Article 14

Article 14 constitutes a general prohibition on discrimination in the delivery of Convention rights. It is not a freestanding provision and may only be taken in conjunction with other Articles. It provides:

'The enjoyment of the rights and freedoms set forth in this Convention shall be secured without discrimination on any ground such as sex, race, colour, language, religion, political or other opinion, national or social origin, association with a national minority, property, birth or other status.'

Specifically in relation to children, this Article invites consideration of whether the differential treatment of children and adults by the State can be justified and, if so, to what extent. It will be recalled that Article 14, inter alia, prohibits discrimination on the basis of 'birth or *other status*'. Could 'childhood' or 'minority' be regarded as falling within the term 'other status'? If so, the onus would be on the State to justify the different application of its laws to children and adults. The legal disabilities which attach to minority[4] would, for example, need to be kept under review and it is not difficult to imagine challenges under the ECHR to the kinds of paternalistic interventions in relation to adolescents which we have seen in recent years[5]. It may well be that greater State paternalism or protectionism is justified towards children than towards adults but the starting point in future may have to be that children are persons with fundamental rights and the burden will be squarely on those who seek to interfere with these rights. If the jurisprudence of the ECHR does develop along these lines it will only, in a sense, reflect what the United States Supreme Court has been doing under the United States Constitution for decades[6].

---

1 For discussion of the jurisprudence under Article 6 see Janis et al (above) ch 8 and Swindells et al (above) at pp 23–38 and ch 8.

2 See particularly *Airey v Ireland* [2002] 2 FLR 631 in which it was held by the ECtHR that, in certain circumstances, this could imply an obligation to provide legal aid. On the question of publicly funded legal representation see also *P, C and S v United Kingdom* [2002] 2 FLR 631.

3 See Chapter 11 below.

4 See Chapter 3.

5 See Chapters 3 and 8.

6 See particularly *Re Gault* 387 US 1 in which the Supreme Court acknowledged that 'neither the Fourteenth Amendment nor the Bill of Rights is for adults alone'. See also *Tinker v Des Moines Independent Community School District* 393 US 503 (1969), which was concerned with children's rights to freedom of speech, and *Goss v Lopez* 419 US 565 (1975), which was concerned with the

Other Articles

These are perhaps the three most important Articles affecting children. Other Articles can come into play on certain children issues. Article 12 enshrines the right to marry and found a family, but is clearly of greater relevance to adult family members than to children. More important for children, perhaps, are Article 2, which protects the right to life and which has an obvious relevance to serious medical decisions affecting them[1], and Article 3, which prohibits torture or inhuman and degrading treatment and which has had an important impact on the evolution of English law governing corporal punishment in schools[2] and latterly on the parental right to discipline the child[3].

The potential of the ECHR for children

The whole idea of children's Convention rights is a new one for the English courts which have been much more accustomed to thinking in terms of *interests* and applying the welfare principle, largely unfettered by other considerations. Since the HRA 1998 came into force there is plenty of evidence that, while the family judges have embraced and applied the idea of adult Convention rights, they have followed an approach which ultimately involves deciding disputes as hitherto, in accordance with the welfare principle[4].

Accordingly, the notion of children's Convention rights itself, to say nothing of how it might relate to adult Convention rights, remains at the time of writing largely under-developed. Indeed, as yet, there appears to be no clear appreciation either from the judiciary or from many commentators that giving effect to children's Convention rights might not be synonymous with applying the welfare principle[5]. It was argued earlier that part of the problem lies in the definition of children's Convention rights[6]. Here there is an immediate and obvious issue. The ECHR was drawn up with adults and not with children in mind. Indeed children are scarcely mentioned in the Convention and its Protocols[7]. Children are the holders of rights under the ECHR, not because they are children but because they are *persons* and all persons enjoy the rights and freedoms guaranteed by the Convention except to the extent that the Convention itself permits interferences with them.

How then are we to determine the substance of children's Convention rights? One answer to this is given by Ursula Kilkelly[8]. She argues that the content of

right to a hearing in school discipline cases. Perhaps the case which best illustrates the issue of the differential treatment of children and adults is *Ginsberg v New York* 390 US 629 (1968), where it was held that prohibitions on the sale of obscene materials to minors could be constitutional but that they might be unconstitutional if imposed on adults.

1 Although this Article did not greatly influence the Court of Appeal decision in *Re A (Conjoined Twins: Medical Treatment)* [2001] 1 FLR 1 where it certainly might have done. See Chapter 8.

2 See cases cited at Chapters 15 and 16.

3 See particularly *A v UK (Human Rights: Punishment of Child)* [1998] 2 FLR 959 and *R v H (Assault of Child: Reasonable Chastisement)* [2001] 2 FLR 1024. See also the Government's consultation document *Protecting Children, Supporting Parents* (2000).

4 See Bainham 'Children's Rights and Human Rights' (above).

5 Ibid.

6 At p 39 above.

7 For the exceptional instances in which the Convention and its Protocols make express reference to 'children', 'minors' or 'juveniles', see Kilkelly in Fottrell (ed) (above) at pp 89–90.

8 See the two works cited above.

children's Convention rights should be influenced by the comprehensive rights set out for children in the UNCRC. She takes the position that the much better enforcement mechanisms under the ECHR (and in the context of the UK under the HRA 1998) could combine with the much clearer articulation of the substance of rights in the UNCRC to become a potent force for the advancement of children's rights. She goes on to give examples of ECHR case-law, which has often been informed by the provisions of the UNCRC and indeed those of other international Conventions. We consider further the potential for this development in relation to individual issues as we come to them.

Another under-explored issue is how clashes between the Convention rights of adults and children might be resolved. This is clearly related to the earlier discussion of the relationship between adult rights and the application of the welfare principle but, as argued above, it ought not necessarily to be regarded as the same process – especially since the child may be an applicant under the Convention and be asserting *rights*, not merely a claim to have his or her best interests determined. There was perhaps a flavour of this dilemma in *X, Y and Z v United Kingdom*[1]. The case is discussed in depth in the second edition of this work[2]. It remains an unresolved issue for the future.

---

1   (1997) 24 EHRR 143, and for commentary, see A Bainham 'Sex, Gender and Fatherhood: Does Biology Really Matter?' [1997] CLJ 512 and C Lind 'Perceptions of sex in the legal determination of fatherhood' [1997] CFLQ 401.

2   See pp 601–602.

Chapter 3

THE CENTRAL ISSUES

What is a 'child' and what is a 'parent'? Do children have 'rights' and do parents have 'rights' or only 'responsibilities'? What duties or responsibilities (if any) may legitimately be expected of children? And if both children and parents have rights, how is the law to resolve a conflict between them? All of these questions attract simplistic answers, but on closer examination it is quickly apparent that each is an issue of considerable sophistication.

CHILDHOOD AND PARENTHOOD

The concepts of 'childhood' and 'parenthood' are both social and legal constructs. They are not immutable classifications, and who may be regarded as a 'child' or a 'parent' by a society, or under the law of that society, is liable to revision and re-evaluation[1]. This most obviously occurred in England in 1969 when the status of childhood, or more accurately 'minority'[2], was redefined with the reduction in the age of majority from 21 to 18[3]. The effect of this was to regard as adults many young people previously denied this status. Yet the position is more complex than this. It has already been noted that children of various ages below majority nonetheless have legal capacity to take certain actions and decisions so that, to that limited extent, they might be viewed as equivalent to 'adults' for some purposes and 'children' for other purposes[4]. It should also be remembered that although the expression 'child' is apposite to include all those aged from one day to 17 years and 364 days, there is a great deal of practical difference, in terms of the kinds of problems the law has to resolve, between the position of a newborn baby and that of a 17-year-old approaching majority.

---

1   On the changing historical conceptions of childhood, see P Ariès *Centuries of Childhood* (Jonathan Cape, 1979) and I Pinchbeck and M Hewitt *Children in English Society* Vol I (Routledge and Kegan Paul, 1969) and Vol II (1973). See also MDA Freeman *The Rights and Wrongs of Children* (Frances Pinter, 1983) at ch 1, and *The Moral Status of Children* (Martinus Nijhoff, 1997) at ch 2. For a recent volume of essays explaining ideas of childhood in different legal contexts see J Fionda (ed) *Legal Concepts of Childhood* (Hart Publishing, 2001). For an explanation of the relationship between the sociology of childhood and children's rights see M Freeman 'The Sociology of Childhood and Children's Rights' (1998) *International Journal of Children's Rights* 433.
2   The term 'minor' includes both 'children' and 'young persons', who have been distinguished for certain purposes, especially in connection with juvenile justice, in English law. Scots law, until fairly recently, drew a distinction between 'minors' and 'pupils'.
3   Family Law Reform Act 1969, s 1, following the recommendations of the Latey Committee. See the *Report of the Committee on the Age of Majority* (1967) (Cmnd 3342).
4   The age of 16 years is particularly important in this respect, since children who have attained this age have a significant number of legal capacities in common with adults.

WHAT IS A CHILD?

A 'child' is normally defined as a 'person' below the age of majority, and this is the position taken in the Children Act 1989 and in the UNCRC[1]. This inevitably gives rise to definitional difficulties at either end of the spectrum since there may be legitimate disagreement about when precisely personhood (and hence childhood) begins and when childhood ends.

The beginning of childhood

The beginning of childhood raises directly the status of the foetus or unborn child. English law generally takes the position that personhood is established at birth and not before. This is the assumption underlying much of the criminal law governing offences against the person, which depends on the child having achieved a separate existence from the mother[2]. The criminal law and the law of tort do offer certain protection to the foetus or unborn child but not on the basis that it is a 'child'. A good example is the case of *Attorney-General's Reference (No 3 of 1994)*[3] in which the Court of Appeal held that the doctrine of transferred malice could in principle apply where a defendant stabbed a pregnant woman causing the premature birth and subsequent death of her child. The defendant could be liable for the murder or manslaughter of the child on the basis of his intention to cause injury to the mother since, before birth, the foetus might be taken to be *part* of the mother. The House of Lords rejected the Court of Appeal's analysis on the basis that a foetus is 'neither a distinct person separate from its mother nor merely an adjunct of the mother' but 'a unique organism'. While holding that the doctrine of transferred malice could not be invoked so as to found a conviction for murder the House contrived to find a basis for liability in manslaughter. It held that it was a sufficient mens rea for constructive manslaughter that the defendant had intended to commit an act which was unlawful and which all sober and reasonable people would have recognised as creating a risk of harm to some other person. It was unnecessary to show that the person who died was the intended victim. Although a foetus was not a living person, the possibility of a dangerous act directed at a pregnant woman causing harm to the child to whom she subsequently gave birth made it permissible on public policy grounds to regard that child as within the scope of the defendant's mens rea when committing the unlawful act.[4] Much the same view is taken in the USA, where the unborn child is not regarded as a person under the Constitution[5]. It does not follow that no legal protections should be extended to the foetus but merely that, if they are, they are

---

1   A child is defined, subject to limited qualifications relating to financial support, as 'a person under the age of eighteen' (s 105(1) of the Children Act). In the UNCRC, 'a child means every human being below the age of eighteen years unless, under the law applicable to the child, majority is attained earlier' (Article 1).

2   See, generally, JC Smith *Smith and Hogan: Criminal Law* (10th edn) (Butterworths, 2002), especially at pp 354–356, and Chapter 14 below.

3   [1996] 2 WLR 412 (CA) and [1997] 3 WLR 421 (HL).

4   For commentary, see J Keown 'Homicide by Prenatal Assault Revisited' [1998] CLJ 240.

5   *Roe v Wade* 410 US 113 (1973). For a discussion of some of the Canadian cases, see Alison Diduck 'Child Protection and Foetal Rights in Canada' (1993) 5 JCL 133. See also the decision of the Scottish Court of Session in *Kelly v Kelly* [1997] 2 FLR 828.

not based on the status of childhood or personhood[1]. The issue has caused particular difficulty where social services wish to take early action to protect a newly born baby from potentially inadequate or irresponsible parents. Here, it has been held that an authority may not take a pre-emptive strike by making the foetus a ward of court since a foetus is not a 'child', however well-developed or close to birth[2]. On the other hand, it was held that the authority might intervene immediately following birth, and might found its intervention largely, if not exclusively, on the mother's behaviour towards her unborn child while pregnant[3].

Under the Children Act 1989, it is now more likely that intervention would be based on the new prospective element in the threshold test of 'significant harm' which applies in care proceedings. An alternative would be, with leave, to use the inherent jurisdiction of the High Court. In one case this was used to authorise a Caesarean section to be performed on a 17-year-old crack cocaine addict, and thereafter to detain her for medical treatment, using reasonable force if necessary, in a maternity ward[4].

Another effect of drawing the line for childhood at birth is to prevent the status of parenthood, and the legal responsibilities which go with it, from coming into being until that point. Thus, the prospective father of an unborn child has no legal standing to prevent the mother from undergoing an abortion[5].

The end of childhood

The end of childhood can also be problematic. The existence of an age of majority and the attainment of adulthood suggests, prima facie, a termination of the legal significance of the parent–child relationship and the disabilities of minority. Yet it is undeniably true that many young adults remain in the parental home, and some degree of factual dependency will often continue to exist[6]. This can cause acute difficulties in the case of mentally disabled young adults who, in reality, are as dependent on their parents as are young children. Thus, the cessation of parental responsibility and the wardship jurisdiction at majority has left the courts struggling to find a legal basis for protective action where, for example, a

---

1 A useful and well-balanced discussion of the role of the law in regulating pregnancy is to be found in E Sutherland 'Regulating Pregnancy; Should We and Can We?' in E Sutherland and A McCall Smith (eds) *Family Rights: Family Law and Medical Advance* (Edinburgh University Press, 1990) at p 100. For a detailed examination of parental responsibility towards a child before birth, see M Brazier 'Parental responsibilities, foetal welfare and children's health' in C Bridge (ed) *Family Law Towards the Millennium: Essays for PM Bromley* (Butterworths, 1997) at ch 8.

2 *Re F (In Utero)* [1988] Fam 122.

3 *D (A Minor) v Berkshire County Council* [1987] 1 All ER 20. Whether such early intervention is justified as a matter of policy is a contentious issue. See Chapter 11 below.

4 *A Metropolitan Borough Council v DB* [1997] 1 FLR 767. See further Chapters 8 and 11.

5 *Paton v British Pregnancy Advisory Service Trustees* [1979] QB 276, upheld by the ECtHR in *Paton v United Kingdom* (1980) 3 EHRR 408 and *C v S* [1987] 1 All ER 1230.

6 Legal liability can sometimes remain with parents to provide financial support for adult children who have left home and are in advanced education, and in some jurisdictions there is, conversely, liability on adult children to support their parents. See *B v B (Adult Student: Liability to Support)* [1998] 1 FLR 373, and Chapter 9 below.

sterilisation operation is thought necessary[1]. In certain limited respects, the relationship of parent and child endures for life, particularly for the purposes of succession. It is also the case that a few legal disabilities endure beyond majority, such as that relating to the holding of public offices, which is dependent on attaining the age of 21[2]. This was, until 1994, also true of private acts of buggery between consenting males, but the requisite age was reduced to 18 in that year[3] and then to 16 by the Sexual Offences (Amendment) Act 2000 to bring it in line with the age of consent for heterosexual intercourse[4]. It is also generally the case that applicants for adoption should have attained the age of 21, subject to certain qualifications which apply to married couples adopting together[5].

WHAT IS A PARENT?

The concept of 'parenthood' is just as elusive[6]. Many people would instinctively identify the natural mother and father of a child as his parents and, of course, this presents no problems in perhaps the majority of cases. The difficulty is that the notion of parenthood has been traditionally located in the conventional family centred on marriage. In recent decades there has been a gradual erosion in the relative significance of this form of family arrangement, and modern ideas of parenthood have to accommodate the many different forms which the 'new family' may take[7]. The growth in the divorce rate, remarriage and cohabitation outside marriage have meant that large numbers of children spend much of their childhood either in single-parent households or with at least one 'social' or 'psychological' parent who is not biologically connected to them[8]. Those that perform the social role of parents may also have a claim to be regarded as such by the law. Moreover, even the issue of who is a biological parent may now be unclear with the advent of the new reproductive technologies[9].

An initial point relates to terminology or language[10]. Many people may be known socially as 'parents', usually because they are performing what is thought to be the social role of parents by looking after and raising a child. These could include step-parents, foster-parents, grandparents or other relatives, cohabitants

---

1   See *T v T* [1988] Fam 52 and *Re F (Mental Patient: Sterilisation)* [1990] AC 1, discussed in Chapter 8 below. See also on the contact issue *Re C (Mental Patient: Contact)* [1993] 1 FLR 940. Cases involving judicially authorised Caesarean sections raise at the same time issues about the protection of the foetus and paternalistic interventions in relation to adults. See *Norfolk and Norwich Healthcare (NHS) Trust v W* [1997] 2 FLR 613 and *Re MB (Medical Treatment)* [1997] 2 FLR 426. But see now *St George's Healthcare National Health Service Trust v S* [1998] 3 All ER 673 and Chapter 8 below.
2   Representation of the People Act 1949.
3   Criminal Justice and Public Order Act 1994, s 143, amending Sexual Offences Act 1967, s 12(1).
4   See further Chapter 14 below.
5   Adoption and Children Act 2002. See further Chapter 7.
6   For a collection of essays exploring the subject see A Bainham, S Day Sclater and M Richards (eds) *What is a Parent? A Socio-Legal Analysis* (Hart Publishing, 1999).
7   See, for example, the discussion in B Dickens 'Reproductive Technology and the "New Family"' in E Sutherland and A McCall Smith (above).
8   'Social' or non-biological parenthood may take many forms. The issues surrounding social parenthood are discussed in Chapter 6, while adoption is discussed in Chapter 7.
9   See pp 91 et seq below.
10 See further p 100 below.

of parents, and so on. There is nothing, for example, to prevent a step-father or the mother's cohabitant from being known locally as the child's 'father' despite the absence of a genetic connection. But this will not make him the *legal* father. This raises two key questions. The first is whether it matters to social carers, like the man in this example, to be *called* a 'parent' or a 'father' or whether 'step-father' will do. The second is whether, if it does matter, it is appropriate for the law to confer on the social parent the *legal* status of being a parent. Here, matters are complicated further by the distinction which English law draws between the status of being a parent and the status of possessing *parental responsibility*[1]. To return to the example, it may be that to give to the man in question the status of *parent* would be inappropriate, but to give him *parental responsibility*, and with it most of the powers and duties which parents possess in raising children, would be appropriate and desirable. This raises yet another question which is whether there is something special about the full legal status of *being a parent* or *parenthood* which suggests that it should be largely (if not exclusively) withheld from those who lack a genetic connection with the child.

John Eekelaar has said that the concept of parenthood can in reality be broken down into three distinguishable elements[2]. The first is *biological parenthood*[3]. This is the question of whose sperm as a matter of biological truth led to the conception of the child, and which woman gave birth to the child. The question of the child's biological mother has, however, become more complex since it is now possible, in some cases of surrogacy, for there to be a genetic mother and a gestational mother. In these instances the biological process of becoming a 'mother' is divided between two women and it is not so easy to give a straightforward answer to the question of who is the 'biological mother'. The law does, however, give a very clear answer to the question of who is the 'legal mother' in these cases[4]. This initial biological inquiry, it is submitted, is what is ordinarily understood by the concept of *parentage*, although many writers use the terms *parentage* and *parenthood* interchangeably and do not distinguish between the two. If we say, in ordinary language, 'there is a dispute over A's parentage' what we mean is that there is uncertainty about who is the *biological* parent (usually the father). So *parentage*, arguably, is the term used to describe the establishment of the initial connection between a child and a parent. Indeed, the *Concise Oxford Dictionary* defines *parentage* as 'descent from parents, lineage'. *Parenthood* on the other hand perhaps implies, in ordinary parlance, an ongoing status and role in relation to a child. John Eekelaar's second element is *legal parenthood*, which gives rise to certain legal incidents. But it is distinct from biological parenthood in that there are clear instances, mainly in the context of assisted reproduction and adoption, in which

---

1 See A Bainham 'Parentage, Parenthood and Parental Responsibility: Subtle, Elusive, Yet Important Distinctions' in A Bainham, S Day Sclater and M Richards (above).

2 J Eekelaar 'Parenthood, Social Engineering and Rights' in D Morgan and G Douglas (eds) *Constituting Families: A Study in Governance* (Franz Steiner Verlag, Stuttgart, 1994), especially at pp 85–89.

3 For further examination of the meaning of biological parenthood see M Johnson 'A Biomedical Perspective on Parenthood' in A Bainham, S Day Sclater and M Richards (above). And for a legal perspective on biological parenthood see J Hill 'What Does It Mean To Be a "Parent"? The claims of biology as the basis for parental rights' (1991) 66 *New York University Law Review* 353.

4 See p 91 below.

the biological parent is not initially, or is no longer, the legal parent[1]. Eekelaar's third element of parenthood is *parental responsibility*. This is distinct from both biological and legal parenthood in that, while it confers extensive powers and duties normally exercised by parents, it does not create the status of legal parenthood and it can be vested in many categories of carers who are not biologically connected with children. What makes this scheme so complex is that all three elements – biological parenthood, legal parenthood and parental responsibility – may be vested in the same person (as is the case with the parents of a child born to their marriage) but they may also be split up between individuals or between individuals and institutions (in the case of care and adoption)[2].

In *Law and Parenthood*[3], Barton and Douglas present a stimulating and challenging thesis about parenthood which they call 'a doctrine of intention'[4]. They describe a continuum of State regulation of parenthood, from minimal regulation, as for example in the case of birth by an unmarried mother, to lengthy State investigation in the case of adoption. A second dimension to the analysis is a second continuum with biological parenthood at one end and social parenthood at the other. Their central argument is that 'the extent to which legal recognition is given to a person's intention or desire to be regarded as a parent, and to fulfil the functions of a parent, has increased over time, so that it is now the *primary* test of legal parentage'[5]. One response which can be offered to this thesis is that it fails to distinguish sufficiently between the different elements of parenthood outlined above. It may well be that the law has given increased recognition to the parental role of social parents but, more often than not, this has been by conferring on them *parental responsibility*. Whether it should go further and confer the full legal status of *parent* is a very different matter, and this question has been given added significance by the growing acceptance of the child's right to knowledge of his biological origins. It is moreover clear that the law confers the status of parent on many of those who through intentional sexual relations *unintentionally* conceive a child[6]. It may be that in future the law will need a clear concept through which to recognise and preserve the biological link. It is certainly arguable that this should be the concept of *parenthood*, leaving *parental responsibility* as the status-conferring concept for non-biological carers[7].

---

1   For the 'status provisions' which apply in cases of assisted reproduction, see pp 91 et seq below. For adoption, see Chapter 7.
2   Eekelaar (above) at p 87 gives an example of how convoluted the situation can become:
    'Suppose a child is born from sperm donated by A to an unmarried couple (a woman, W, and a man, B) who jointly underwent treatment from a licensed facility. If the couple subsequently separate and the mother marries another man (C), in whose favour a Residence Order is made, then, while W is the biological and legal mother, and has parental responsibility, A is the biological father, B the legal father (without parental responsibility) and C shares parental responsibility with W.'
3   (Butterworths, 1995).
4   At pp 50 et seq.
5   Barton and Douglas (above) at p 51.
6   See A Bainham 'Unintentional Parenthood: the Case of the Reluctant Mother' [2002] CLJ 288 commenting on *Re B (Adoption: Natural Parent)* [2002] 1 FLR 196, as to which see further Chapter 7.
7   It is conceded, of course, that this is not the direction in which the law has consistently moved thus far.

Who is the mother?

In general, the question of who is a child's mother will be straightforward and a self-evident fact of childbirth, although in some jurisdictions, notably France, the mother has been permitted to give birth anonymously in the sense that her name need not be registered with the details of the birth[1]. In *Odièvre v France*[2] the ECtHR held by majority that there had been no violation of Articles 8 and 14 of the ECHR by the French legislation on *accouchement sous X* which allows mothers to give birth anonymously. The majority rejected the argument that it was an infringement of the applicant's right to respect for her private life and family life to withhold from her information which would give her access to her birth mother's identity. The Court was swayed by the consideration of the right to confidentiality which had been requested at the time of the birth and it can be argued that the decision is deficient in failing to engage sufficiently with the argument surrounding the applicant's right to 'family life'. It can be argued that the decision is inconsistent in this respect with the Court's own earlier decision in *Marckx v Belgium*[3] and with Article 7 of the UNCRC which confers on the child the right to know both parents *from birth*. The biological mother will also be the legal mother, whether the child is born in or out of wedlock, and the mother will also automatically acquire parental responsibility[4]. It has, of course, long been the case that the parental status of the mother may be terminated and transferred through the process of adoption[5]. But in recent years the question of who is the biological and legal mother has caused greater difficulty in the context of surrogacy arrangements which rely on techniques of assisted reproduction.

Where the surrogate mother has merely been inseminated with the sperm of the commissioning father (or that of a donor) she will be both the genetic and gestational mother and there is no question that she is appropriately described as the 'biological' mother. Where, on the other hand, she is implanted with an embryo created by in vitro fertilisation and involving the ova of the commissioning mother or donated ova, she will be the gestational or carrying mother but *not* the genetic mother. In these cases of 'full surrogacy', the concept of biological parenthood is difficult to apply. Is the biological link primarily about genetics or is it more to do with the process of gestation and childbirth? Whatever the biological position, the legal position is clear. For policy reasons[6], the law deems the woman who gives birth to the child, whether or not she is genetically related to the child,

---

1 See J Rubellín-Devichi 'France: How Matters Stand Now in Relation to Family Law Reform' in A Bainham (ed) *The International Survey of Family Law (2000 Edition)* (Family Law, 2000) p 143 at pp 146–148.
2 [2003] 1 FCR 621. For a detailed commentary on the case, see E Steiner 'Desperately seeking mother – anonymous births in the European Court of Human Rights' [2003] CFLQ 425.
3 (1979) 2 EHRR 330.
4 See Chapters 4 and 5 below for the allocation of parental responsibility between parents within and outside marriage respectively.
5 See Chapter 7 below.
6 Explored in Chapter 6 below.

to be the child's *legal* mother with all that this implies for parental status and the acquisition of parental responsibility[1].

Who is the father?

The question of who is the 'father' of a child has always been a matter of proof since paternity, unlike maternity, is not biologically obvious in the process of parturition. Certain legal presumptions as to paternity apply where the mother is married. These usually result in her husband being presumed to be the biological father and, from that, the legal father, whatever may be the biological truth of the situation[2]. Where the mother is unmarried no such automatic presumptions apply. Cohabitation with a man may give rise to such a presumption in some jurisdictions but not under English law. The determination of paternity depends primarily on birth registration and, failing that, on scientific tests which may or may not be directed in the event of a dispute. Important questions are raised by the development of the DNA testing technique which, unlike conventional blood-testing, now enables paternity to be determined with virtual certainty. We explore some of these issues when we look at the position of children born to two parents who are not, or may not be, married to one another[3].

At this stage, we address only the question of who is the father in cases of assisted reproduction under the so-called 'status provisions' of the Human Fertilisation and Embryology Act 1990 (HFEA 1990)[4]. These techniques which enable the artificial transfer of gametes have been considered by Dickens to have comparable implications for family life to:

'. . . modern developments in social lifestyle that accommodate unmarried and serial married reproduction, in that they contribute to the creation of families in which children may be genetically unrelated to their social or psychological parents, and in which children in the same households may not genetically have both or either such parents in common.'[5]

In coming to the complex rules which determine who is the *legal* father in these cases it should be noted at the outset that they result in a situation in which English law is now prepared to treat quite openly, as the legal father, a man who is manifestly *not* the genetic father. While it is true that many married men have long been treated as the legal fathers of children to whom they may not in fact be

---

1   HFEA 1990, s 27(1) provides:

'The woman who is carrying or has carried a child as a result of the placing in her of an embryo or of sperm and eggs, and no other woman, is to be treated as the mother of the child.'

However, this result is not inevitable. In the Californian case of *Johnson v Calvert* 5 Cal 4th 84 (1993) the genetic commissioning mother in a surrogacy arrangement was held to be the legal mother largely on the basis of her intention to act as such.

2   See Chapter 4.

3   See Chapter 5.

4   For academic discussions of the determination of paternity in cases of assisted reproduction, see RG Lee and D Morgan *Human Fertilisation and Embryology: Regulating the Reproductive Revolution* (Blackstone Press, 2001) at pp 236–241 and S Bridge 'Assisted Reproduction and the Legal Definition of Parentage' in A Bainham, S Day Sclater and M Richards (above). The Government has announced (21 January 2004: see www.dh.gov.uk) a wide-ranging review of the 1990 Act, including a full public consultation during 2005.

5   B Dickens 'Reproductive Technology and the "New" Family' in E Sutherland and A McCall Smith (eds) *Family Rights: Family Law and Medical Advance* (Edinburgh University Press, 1990) at p 28.

genetically connected, it should be remembered that this is on the basis of a *presumed genetic link* arising from the fact of marriage to the mother. That said, the starting point, and indeed the conclusion if the status provisions do not result in another man being treated in law as the father, is that the man whose sperm leads to the conception of the child will be the legal father. In other words, all other things being equal, the genetic father of a child will also be the legal father[1]. He will not, however, necessarily have parental responsibility for the child, which will depend essentially on whether he is married to the child's mother or, following recent amendments to the Children Act 1989 by the Adoption and Children Act 2002, he is registered as the father of the child. This is of course an excellent illustration of the severance of genetic and legal parenthood from the independent concept of parental responsibility[2].

What then are the exceptions to the general rule? The first is that where a married woman is artificially inseminated or has infertility treatment involving the placing in her of an embryo, sperm or eggs but this does *not* involve the use of her husband's sperm, the husband will nonetheless be deemed to be the *legal* father of the child 'unless it is shown that he did not consent' to the treatment which took place[3]. A second exception clearly has in mind the situation of an unmarried couple in a stable relationship but has been drafted in such a way that difficult questions have arisen about its possible application outside that context. The rule is that, where no man is treated as the father under the first provision above, if a woman is artificially inseminated or receives infertility treatment 'in the course of treatment services provided for her and a man together' that man is treated as the father of the child[4]. Where a man is deemed to be the father under either of these provisions, the legislation goes on to provide that 'no other person is to be treated as the father of the child'[5]. Neither of the rules operates to rebut the normal presumption of legitimacy which arises in the context of a birth to a married woman[6]. Finally, it is expressly provided that sperm donors are *not* to be treated as the legal fathers of any resulting children[7], nor is a deceased man whose sperm

---

1   For a particularly good illustration of this principle, see the judgment of Bracewell J in *Re B (Parentage)* [1996] 2 FLR 15. See also *Re M (Child Support Act: Parentage)* [1997] 2 FLR 90. In this case, although the mother's husband had consented to her artificial insemination by donor, the resulting child had been born prior to 4 April 1988 and hence before the provisions of the HFEA 1990 and its predecessor, s 27 of the Family Law Act 1987, came into effect. The legislation was held not to have retrospective effect. Hence, the husband was not to be regarded as the legal father and was not liable for child support.

2   See Chapter 5.

3   HFEA 1990, s 28(2).

4   Ibid, s 28(3).

5   Ibid, s 28(4).

6   Ibid, s 28(5).

7   However, the Government announced in 2004 that gamete donors are to lose their anonymity. Under the Human Fertilisation and Embryology Authority (Disclosure of Donor Information) Regulations 2004, SI 2004/1511, children born as a result of the donation of sperm, eggs or embryos donated on or after 1 April 2005 will have the right on attaining the age of 18 to identifying information provided by donors to the relevant clinics. It should also be noted that this exclusion from legal parentage applies only to licensed sperm donation. Someone donating sperm on a 'do-it-yourself' basis will be the legal father of the resulting child. See *Re M (Sperm Donor Father)* [2003] Fam Law 94 where the man concerned replied to an advertisement by a lesbian couple.

was used after his death[1]. This second rule has now been substantially qualified by the enactment of the Human Fertilisation and Embryology (Deceased Fathers) Act 2003. The Act enables certain mothers who have conceived children using assisted conception techniques after the death of their husbands or partners to register the deceased as the father of the child on the child's birth certificate. The Act followed a ruling of the High Court in March 2003 that the restrictions in s 28(6) were incompatible with the rights of the children concerned under Article 8 and/or Article 8 taken in conjunction with Article 14 of the ECHR.

In essence the Act allows a man to be registered as the father where a child was conceived after his death using his sperm or using an embryo created with his sperm before his death[2]. The Act also allows a man to be registered after his death where the child was conceived using donor sperm before his death[3]. In neither case will the registration (which is intended as a symbolic acknowledgement of the father) confer on the child concerned any legal status or rights as a consequence of that registration. In each case the mother must elect in writing within 42 days of the child's birth that the deceased be treated as the father. In each case also the deceased must have consented in writing to the use of his sperm or the placing in the mother of the embryo after his death and not withdrawn that consent.

These provisions are exceptionally convoluted and have given rise to serious difficulties of interpretation, perhaps because they have been invoked in situations to which they were not really designed to apply. In essence, the policy of the law is clear enough – where a married or unmarried couple together undergo licensed fertility treatment involving donated gametes, *they* should be regarded together as the child's legal parents, thus excluding the gamete donor. But difficulties have arisen where the couple in question become estranged following the treatment and also in the context of surrogacy arrangements.

In *Re CH (Contact: Parentage)*[4], a child was born to a married couple with the assistance of donated sperm. The husband had consented to the procedure. Following the birth of the child, the parties separated and the mother sought to deny the husband contact with the child on the basis that he was not the child's *genetic* father. He was of course the *legal* father under the above provisions, and Judge Callman held that he should not be denied contact unless there was a compelling reason against it. The presence or absence of the genetic link was not the crucial factor in a contact determination.

Three decisions have considered the proper interpretation of the notoriously vague s 28(3). *Re Q (Parental Order)*[5] involved a surrogacy arrangement and an application for a parental order under s 30 of the Human Fertilisation and Embryology Act 1990. We consider the decision more closely when we examine the law applying to surrogacy arrangements[6]. The central question was whether

---

1   HFEA 1990, s 28(6). The problems associated with the posthumous use of sperm sprang to the attention of the public with the 'Diane Blood' saga, although the legal difficulties here concerned the absence of the late Mr Blood's consent to the use of his sperm to inseminate his wife after his death. See *R v Human Fertilisation and Embryology Authority ex parte Blood* [1997] 2 All ER 687.

2   Section 1, inserting new s 28(5A) (husbands) and (5B) (partners) into the HFEA 1990.

3   Section 1, inserting new s 28(5C) (husbands) and (5D) (partners) into the HFEA 1990.

4   [1996] 1 FLR 569.

5   [1996] 1 FLR 369.

6   See Chapter 6.

the commissioning father and surrogate mother should be regarded as a man and woman who were 'together' provided with licensed treatment services. Crucially, the commissioning father's own sperm had not been used. Johnson J, in a restrictive interpretation, held that Parliament must have intended that *the man himself* should be provided with treatment services in order to trigger the provision. That was thought not to be the case here. The commissioning father was therefore *not* the legal father and his consent to a s 30 order was not required. In *Re B (Parentage)*[1] (a case which did not directly involve s 28(3)) Bracewell J took a less restrictive view suggesting that providing sperm and attending a hospital together with the mother might be sufficient although she agreed with Johnson J in *Re Q* that the provision would not apply merely because a man was living with the woman who received treatment. Finally, in *U v W (Attorney-General Intervening)*[2], an unmarried couple together received infertility treatment in Rome. IVF treatment took place using both the male partner's sperm and donor sperm. The resulting embryos were known to be created by the donor sperm and in due course twins were born. When the parties returned to England and their relationship broke down, the question arose as to whether the man was the legal father and thus liable for child support. Wilson J held that he was not the father since the provision had no application to unlicensed treatment. The treatment in Italy fell outside the licensing system, and the safeguards established under it which would have applied if the treatment had been provided in England. But he did take the view that the parties had received treatment services together as envisaged by s 28(3) since the doctor had been 'responding to a request for that form of treatment by the woman and the man as a couple, notwithstanding the absence in the man of any physical role in such treatment'.

This case reveals the legal pitfalls of fertility treatment which takes place outside the licensing system established by the 1990 legislation. Difficulties may also arise where the extra-territorial complications of *U v W* are not present. The rule that a sperm donor is not to be treated as the father will only apply to licensed sperm donation so that those who operate outside the statutory scheme will be caught by the primary rule that the genetic parent is also the legal parent. Thus, failure to follow licensed procedures could have major disadvantages for both the mother and sperm donor. The former will run the risk that the donor might seek parental responsibility in relation to the child as he would be entitled to do as a 'parent'. The latter will risk being pursued for child support.

The above decisions illustrate that, in cases of assisted reproduction, legal parentage can be conferred to reflect the intention that a man should be a parent in the course of a joint enterprise between that man and a woman, whether they are married (s 28(2)) or unmarried (s 28(3)). But what is the position where the common intention of the man and woman is frustrated by subsequent events unforeseen at the time when treatment commenced? This was the situation in two remarkable cases which have come before the courts. In each case the pregnancy was achieved in circumstances which went beyond those contemplated by the couple concerned.

---

1   [1996] 2 FLR 15.
2   [1997] 2 FLR 282.

In *Leeds Teaching Hospitals NHS Trust v A*[1] a white couple, Mr and Mrs A, and a black couple, Mr and Mrs B, sought infertility treatment involving the injection of the respective husbands' sperm into the eggs of their respective wives to be followed by implantation. Mrs A became pregnant and gave birth to twins who were of mixed race. Clearly Mr A could not be the genetic father, and tests revealed that, following a mix up, Mr B's sperm had been used. It was not disputed that the twins should remain with Mr and Mrs A who were given a residence order to reinforce their right to look after them. But the question of their legal paternity arose. Dame Elizabeth Butler-Sloss P held that the common law presumption of legitimacy was displaced and, further, that Mr A was *not* to be treated as the legal father by virtue of s 28(2) since he had only consented to the use of *his* sperm in the treatment and not to the use of any other man's sperm. The mistake which the hospital had made was not trivial but fundamental and vitiated consent. Neither could Mr and Mrs A be regarded as a man and woman who had been provided with treatment services together for the purposes of s 28(3) since that provision was intended to apply only to those who were *unmarried* to each other. In any event the fundamental mistake which had been made would have vitiated the whole concept of treatment together[2]. Thus, Mr B (the genetic father) and not Mr A was the legal father.

In *Re R (IVF: Paternity of Child)*[3] an unmarried couple underwent infertility treatment involving the use of donor sperm. The man acknowledged that he would be the legal father of any resulting child. No pregnancy was achieved from the initial embryo placement but the second cycle of treatment succeeded and a child was born. However, just prior to the second placement the relationship between the couple had terminated and the woman had acquired a new partner. She did not reveal this change of circumstances to the clinic. The original partner then brought legal proceedings claiming that he was the legal father under s 28(3) on the basis that the embryos had been placed 'in the course of treatment services provided for' the mother and him 'together'. The Court of Appeal, allowing the mother's appeal, held that this was not the correct construction of the legislation. The relevant time at which to ask the question whether treatment services were being provided for a man and a woman together was the time of the successful implantation. It was not sufficient to demonstrate that the man in question had participated *at some stage* in the course of treatment which ultimately resulted in the pregnancy and subsequent birth. Hale LJ (as she then was) emphasised the seriousness of the judgment to be made under s 28(3) which was

---

1 [2003] 1 FLR 1091. For commentary see L Terry and A Campbell 'Delicate Bonds and Blunt Instruments' [2003] Fam Law 599, and M Ford and D Morgan 'Addressing a Misconception' [2003] CFLQ 199. For commentary on this and on *Re R (IVF): Paternity of Child)* [2003] 1 FLR 1183 see A Bainham 'Whose Sperm is it Anyway?' [2003] CLJ 566.

2 In *Evans v Amicus Health Care Limited (Secretary of State for Health Intervening)* [2004] 2 FLR 766 the Court of Appeal held that the concept of the provision of services for a man and woman together was a condition which was satisfied as long as the couple were united in their pursuit of treatment, whatever might otherwise be the nature of the relationship between them. In this case the withdrawal of consent by the man, following the end of the relationship, prevented both the use and the continued storage of embryos fertilised with his sperm despite the fervent wish of his former partner to the contrary.

3 [2003] 1 FLR 1183. For commentary on the case, see C Lind 'Unmarried Paternity under the Human Fertilisation and Embryology Act 1990' [2003] CFLQ 327, and A Bainham (above).

'an unusual provision, conferring the relationship of parent and child on people who are related neither by blood nor by marriage'.

Fatherless children

The effect of the above provisions, illustrated by some of the cases, is to create in certain circumstances a category of 'fatherless' children. This can also arise where a single woman, without a partner and without any intention of having an involvement with any man, gives birth following licensed sperm donation. Inevitably, this raises questions about whether children can be conceptualised as possessing a 'right' to two parents or whether women have a superior right to produce a child without the physical and emotional involvement of a man[1]. Whatever view is taken of this potential clash of interests, it is fair to say that there are already very many instances in which children are effectively 'fatherless', either because paternity has never been established or because they are being brought up in single-parent households headed by mothers. There must also have been many instances of what has been termed 'genetic passing off' where a person regarded in law as the father is not in fact the genetic father[2]. Seen in this light, the 1990 provisions, which openly recognise as legal fathers social or non-genetic fathers, were not perhaps such a remarkable or contentious development.

THE CONCEPT OF CHILDREN'S RIGHTS

The whole issue of children's rights, always a difficult one, has in recent years become yet more complicated by the Human Rights Act 1998. As we have seen, the broad effect of this is to admit directly into the English courts arguments about children's 'Convention rights'. It is now therefore necessary to consider, in addition to the various theories about the nature of children's rights, the specific question of the definition of their Convention rights and how these may relate to the Convention rights of others, most obviously parents. How does this as yet largely unexplored concept of children's Convention rights relate to our previous understanding? It would be tempting to argue that the concept of Convention rights is concerned with the child's rights against the State whereas the more general theories of children's rights are more to do with the child's relationship with parents or other individuals. Yet, as will become apparent, this would be far too simplistic an analysis both because the child's Convention rights clearly extend to the relationship between children and adults in the *private* as well as the public context and because general theories of children's rights have also embraced the child's relationship with the State. We look first at the development of the concept of children's rights. Then we consider some of the more influential English theories. Finally, we speculate on where the concept of children's Convention rights may fit into the broader picture.

---

1   For the arguments from a children's rights perspective, see L Neilsen 'The Right to a Child versus the Right of a Child' in J Eekelaar and P Sarcevic (eds) *Parenthood in Modern Society: Legal and Social Issues for the Twenty-First Century* (Martinus Nijhoff, 1993). Related issues can arise in connection with the controversial question of the adoption of children by homosexuals, as to which see Chapter 7.

2   D Morgan and RG Lee (above). This can arise most obviously where no one takes steps to rebut the presumption that the husband of a married woman is the father of any child born to her.

There is an initial difficulty in seeking to pin down the concept of children's rights. This is that whatever rights or interests children may have, they do not exist in a vacuum. It is quite impossible to evaluate the claims of children without considering their interaction with the claims of others, whether parents or others in the community. The very notion of children possessing rights implies the existence of legal or moral duties in *someone*, or indeed everyone, and this raises immediately the issue of the interests of the adult world which can often clash with children's interests. This should be borne in mind throughout this discussion. It has become an even more important question in English law with the advent of children's Convention rights under the ECHR and the HRA 1998[1].

'Welfare' versus 'rights'

An obvious question is whether there is any difference of substance between protecting the 'welfare' of children and protecting their 'rights'. English law has a strong theoretical commitment to the welfare or best interests of children, but is this the same as upholding their rights?

Some liberationist writers are inclined to draw a sharp distinction between the two ideas, expressed most graphically by Farson, who differentiated between protecting *children* and protecting their *rights*[2]. For Farson, the critical birthright which children possess is self-determination and this overrides all other rights. The extreme liberationist school represented by Farson and others would treat children as adults and extend to them all the liberties normally associated with adulthood. A child of *any* age would, in principle, have contractual freedom, sexual freedom, the right to work, the right to vote and so on. These 'kiddie libbers', as Mnookin has called them, stand in stark contrast to the 'child savers'[3]. The latter stress the vulnerability of children and the need to protect them from others and indeed from themselves[4]. According to this position, restrictions on contractual capacity, the prohibition of certain forms of sexual activity with minors, restrictions on child labour, and the disenfranchisement of children may all be justified. The very status of minority, with its attendant disabilities, has, as its *raison d'être*, children's assumed inability to act in their own best interests. Child protectionism is thus a highly paternalistic notion[5] for it supports the right of adults to take decisions for children and not the right of children to act for themselves[6].

There can be no doubt that the English law affecting children, although historically dominated by such influences as the devolution of property and

---

1 See generally A Bainham 'Can We Protect Children and Protect Their Rights?' [2002] Fam Law 279.

2 R Farson *Birthrights* (Harmondsworth, 1978). See also J Holt *Escape from Childhood* (Penguin, 1975).

3 RH Mnookin 'Thinking About Children's Rights – Beyond Kiddie Libbers and Child Savers' (1981) *Stanford Lawyer* 24.

4 These protectionist concerns can clearly justify interferences with the civil liberties of children which would be unacceptable if imposed on adults. In the United States, certain forms of intervention, such as the prohibition of the sale of obscene materials to minors, may be constitutional as they apply to children, but would be unconstitutional if imposed on adults. See *Ginsberg v New York* 390 US 629 (1968).

5 On the philosophical justifications of paternalism in the writings of Hobbes, Locke and Mill, see MDA Freeman *The Rights and Wrongs of Children* (Frances Pinter, 1983) at pp 52–54.

6 This is why it is argued that the choice of decision-maker is crucial. See RH Mnookin (above).

preservation of the social order rather than the protection of children for their own sake[1], has had a strongly protectionist orientation[2]. It is certainly arguable that it has been the concentration on safeguarding the welfare of children which has obscured the issue of their rights and which explains, at least until the last quarter of a century or so, the absence of a generally accepted theory of children's rights.

Children's rights in the USA

Meanwhile, in the USA, the issue of rights had to be directly confronted because of the written constitution and bill of rights enshrined within it[3]. In the 1960s, the Supreme Court firmly grasped the nettle by holding that children were persons under the constitution and thus capable of possessing fundamental rights[4]. This did not mean that *all* those rights enjoyed by adults would automatically be extended to children[5], but it did mean that apparent infringements of those rights in the case of children would have to be justified by some other legitimate interest protected by the constitution[6]. Children's rights accordingly have a strong theoretical foundation in the USA since there is, in effect, a presumption that they are entitled to all the normal civil liberties possessed by adults. The onus is firmly on those who would withhold them to find a legal justification for doing so. Parents are also self-evidently persons under the Constitution, and have rights both as individuals and in their capacity as parents[7]. This can give rise to a clash of constitutional rights between parents and children which the courts have occasionally had to resolve[8]. These conflicts of interest have been confronted less openly and more subtly in England[9].

Development of children's rights in England

Despite the absence of a written constitution or bill of rights in England, the rights of children have been firmly on the agenda since the early 1980s, and the cause received major boosts from the *Gillick* decision in 1985 and the Children Act

---

1   See, particularly, JM Eekelaar and T Murray 'Childhood as a Social Problem: A Survey of the History of Legal Regulation' (1984) *Journal of Law and Society* 207 and J Eekelaar, R Dingwall and T Murray 'Victims or Threats? Children in Care Proceedings' (1982) JSWL 68.

2   Perhaps epitomised by the all-embracing wardship jurisdiction in which a 'ring of protection' is thrown around a ward of court.

3   The earlier developments of the constitutional guidelines affecting children's rights are discussed and extracted in W Wadlington, CH Whitebread and SM Davis *Children in the Legal System* (Foundation Press, 1983) at ch II. There were also calls there for a Bill of Rights for children. See Foster and Freed 'A Bill of Rights for Children' (1972) 6 Fam LQ 343. For a more recent commentary on the development of children's rights in the USA, see BB Woodhouse 'The Status of Children: A story of emerging rights' in SN Katz, J Eekelaar and M Maclean *Cross Currents* (Oxford University Press, 2000).

4   *Re Gault* 387 US 1 (1967).

5   See RH Mnookin (above).

6   In the case of children, the standard is a 'significant state interest' – a somewhat lower standard than the 'compelling state interest' required in the case of adults.

7   See, for example, *Prince v Massachusetts* 321 US 158 (1944).

8   See H Wingo and SN Freytag 'Decisions Within the Family: A Clash of Constitutional Rights' 67 (1982) *Iowa Law Rev* 401.

9   Chapter 2 above discussed the different weightings given to children's welfare which may be seen as one manifestation of this.

1989[1]. The debate has tended to focus on the autonomy claims of adolescents and there has been a strong inclination to associate, if not equate, the concept of children's rights with the claim to self-determination[2]. Yet, in reality, the notion of children's rights is a multi-faceted idea, far too complex to be looked at in a one-dimensional way. At the very least, any serious theory must acknowledge and admit elements of both protection and self-determination, and most do.

The concept of children's rights, although distinct from welfare, therefore includes within it welfarist or protectionist concerns. We should, moreover, question the assumption, sometimes made, that welfare as an idea is antithetical to self-determination. It can be cogently argued that the welfare of children dictates that they be allowed a *degree* of self-determination or qualified autonomy. Ronald Dworkin brings this out rather well in his philosophical analysis of distributional equality[3]. Dworkin discusses the various theories of welfare, one species of which is the 'success theories' which suppose that 'a person's welfare is a matter of his success in fulfilling his preferences, goals and ambitions'[4]. Although Dworkin is talking specifically about the distribution of resources, the welfare of children can be similarly viewed as a matter of individual self-fulfilment which must, by its nature, imply an element of independence from adult control. It was also noted that, under the statutory checklist governing the application of the welfare principle, the wishes of children must, in principle, be taken into account[5]. It is submitted that the converse is also true. As we shall see, the jurisprudence of the ECtHR makes it very plain that it will uphold, as consistent with the notion of children's Convention rights, determinations of domestic courts which in the final analsyis are based on the court's assessment of the child's best interests[6].

In one respect, the concept of rights performs a valuable function for which the concept of welfare is ill-adapted. It draws attention to the *universality* of children's claims. The concept of welfare, as interpreted in English case-law, is a highly individualistic notion which is inadequate to embrace the multifarious legal and moral claims which children may be thought to have as a matter of social justice. The concentration is wholly on doing what is best for an individual child in an individual set of circumstances and it is often said that each case must turn on its own facts. Rights, on the other hand, although clearly capable of assertion in individual cases, are designed to safeguard the interests of *all* children as a class. Indeed, it has been said that 'a necessary feature of children's rights is that they be genuinely universal, appropriate for children everywhere'[7]. It is this aspect which was, at least until recent decades, rather neglected in England.

---

1   Other significant developments were the International Year of the Child in 1979 and the establishment of the Children's Legal Centre in London. Children's rights have now received a further boost since the ECHR has been incorporated into English law.

2   This might well have been a reaction to what might have been seen as the over-paternalistic attitude of English law before the *Gillick* ruling.

3   R Dworkin 'What is Equality Part I: Equality of Welfare' (1981) 10 *Philosophy and Public Affairs* 185.

4   Ibid at p 191.

5   Children Act 1989, s 1(3)(a).

6   See below.

7   V Worsfold 'A Philosophical Justification for Children's Rights' (1974) 44 *Harvard Educational Review* 142 at p 149.

The significance of language and terminology

Does it really matter whether the law's protection of children's interests is analysed in terms of 'rights' or 'welfare', or that parents are described as having 'rights' or 'responsibility', or whether someone is described as a 'parent' or in some other way? There is some truth in the assertion that playing with conceptual labels will not necessarily have any effect on the substance of family relations[1]. Perhaps there ought to be some healthy scepticism about the limits of what the law can achieve for children[2]. There are dangers in indulging in 'rights-talk' too loosely since it has been said that this can be a reductionist device for lawyers, reducing the complexity of human relationships (with which the law is ill-equipped to deal) to manageable concepts[3]. Against this, it can be argued that the use of certain expressions can have an influence on society. If this is correct, the modernisation of terminology *is* an important issue because it may have a symbolic or educative effect on social attitudes. There is no question that one of the most striking features of the reform of family law has been the reformulating of concepts and that behind this reformulation lie shifting values[4]. Seen in this light, it becomes important to assert and defend rights for children, but it should be acknowledged that the *substance* of the relationships between children and the adult world are, in the final analysis, of greater significance than any theoretical description applied to them.

SOME THEORIES OF CHILDREN'S RIGHTS

Before attempting to explore the substantive rights which children have, the initial question of what is a 'right' arises and this is a matter of considerable controversy[5]. Yet it is of crucial significance since someone who denies, for example, that children have a right to 'love and affection' may be saying one of two things. Either he may be saying that children have no claim or interest of any kind, whether legal or moral, in receiving love and affection or, alternatively, he may be saying that any such claim or interest is not properly classified as a 'right'. The second is the more likely interpretation, since almost everyone would recognise the moral claims of children in this respect while there may be substantial doubt about whether they could ever be elevated to the status of legal rights, far less enforceable ones.

---

1 See A Bainham *Children, Parents and the State* (Sweet & Maxwell, 1988) at pp 57–61.
2 See M King 'Playing the Symbols – Custody and the Law Commission' [1987] Fam Law 186. See also M King *A Better World for Children?* (Routledge, 1997) for a wide-ranging critique of decision-making, policy formulation and moral campaigns designed to improve the lot of children from the perspective of autopoietic theory – a social theory of self-regulation systems in 'society' of which law is said to be one.
3 M King and C Piper *How the Law Thinks About Children* (Gower, 1990) particularly at pp 68–70.
4 See A Bainham 'Changing Families and Changing Concepts: Reforming the Language of Family Law' [1998] CFLQ 1.
5 For a discussion of the problem of children's rights in the context of the general dispute about rights, see WNR Lucy 'Controversy About Children's Rights' in D Freestone (ed) *Children and the Law* (Hull University Press, 1990) at p 213. For a succinct review of the literature on the concept of rights and the principal theories of rights more generally see NE Simmonds *Central Issues in Jurisprudence: Justice, Law and Rights* (2nd edn) (Sweet & Maxwell, 2002) Part III.

This general difficulty should always be kept in mind since there are many statements, particularly in international instruments[1], about the alleged rights of children which go well beyond what is normally understood by lawyers to constitute rights. It may be that much of this can be accounted for by distinguishing between legal rights and moral claims. The issue of children's rights is further complicated by the uncertainties surrounding the *content* of individual substantive claims. While it may be possible to conclude that children have rights to adequate food, medical care and education, the content of these rights may be uncertain. Thus, it may be fairly obvious what is adequate care and nourishment for a newborn baby, but far less clear what is an adequate education for an older child. How far the child's basic right to an education extends may well be something on which there is no consensus. This problem is compounded by the case of children's Convention rights under the ECHR where the content and extent of the rights can only be established by judicial interpretation.

With these initial difficulties in mind, a brief examination will now be made of three of the more influential British theories of children's rights, put forward by MacCormick, Eekelaar and Freeman respectively. This is followed by a short section summarising the views of Onora O'Neill, whose distinctive contribution to the debate is to argue that a concentration on children's rights is misplaced and that the emphasis should rather be on the duties or responsibilities of adults towards children. This leads neatly on to the following section which asks the question whether children themselves have, or ought to have, any duties.

MacCormick's test case

In an article first published in 1976[2], Neil MacCormick used the claim that children have rights as a test case for theories of rights in general. MacCormick pointed out that before substantive theories of particular rights of children could be constructed it was necessary to address the fundamental issue of whether they have rights at all.

The 'will theory' and the 'interest theory'

There are broadly two competing theories of the nature of rights – the 'will theory' and the 'interest theory'. MacCormick sought to demonstrate that the former could not accommodate the rights of children and was accordingly suspect as a general theory. However, in his view, it was possible to make sense of the claim that children have rights by formulating a variant of the interest theory. The will theory is based on the notion that to have a legal or moral right is to be able to exercise individual choice over the enforcement or waiver of duties imposed on someone else. The essence of the theory is the pre-eminence of the right-holder's will over the will of others with respect to the subject-matter of the right. The interest theory concentrates on the protection of an individual's interests by the imposition of duties on others – what MacCormick refers to as 'the imposition of (legal or moral) normative constraints on the acts and activities of other people with respect to the object of one's interests'. Therefore, an important element in both

---

1   See, particularly, the United Nations Declaration of the Rights of the Child 1959 and the United Nations Convention on the Rights of the Child 1989.

2   N MacCormick 'Children's Rights: A Test-Case for Theories of Right' (1976) 62 *Archiv für Rechts und Sozialphilosophie* 305; also published as ch 8 in *Legal Right and Social Democracy* (1982).

theories is the existence of duties in others, correlative to the rights asserted[1]. The critical difference is that the will theory regards as crucial the capacity for individual autonomy, ie the ability to waive or enforce the duty in question, whereas under the interest theory it is sufficient for the existence of a right that there is an identifiable interest and a corresponding duty.

The will theory

MacCormick drew attention to the difficulty (in his view impossibility) of accommodating the concept of children's rights within the will theory. He took as an example the right of a baby to care, nurture and love[2]. The will theory is inept as a foundation for this, essentially for two reasons. First, a baby clearly lacks the physical and mental capacity to exercise any will or choice about whether to relieve his parents from their duty to provide him with these things. Secondly, and more importantly, it was MacCormick's contention that neither the baby, nor anyone acting on the baby's behalf, should be allowed to waive the parents' duty or acquiesce in its non-performance. For MacCormick it is the fundamental interest and moral claim of the infant to care and nurture which justifies the imposition of the duty on the parent. The duty is not constitutive of the right but rather a means of securing that right. When outside agencies, such as social services, intervene where parents have failed to provide adequate care, this does not remove the duty placed on parents. Rather, such action constitutes substituted performance of the duty as opposed to a waiver or release for parents. MacCormick concludes that to see such powers as constitutive of the child's right is to confuse the substantive right with ancillary remedial provisions.

The interest theory

MacCormick, instead, saw the rights of children as being located somewhere in the interest theory and grounded in the basic jural precept of respect for persons. Thus, to argue[3]:

> '. . . that each and every child is a being whose needs and capacities command our respect, so that denial to any child of the wherewithal to meet his or her needs and to develop his or her capacities would be wrong in itself (at least in so far as it is physically possible to provide the wherewithal) and would be wrong regardless of the ulterior disadvantages or advantages to anyone else – so to argue, would be to put a case which is intelligible as a justification of the opinion that children have such rights.'

Although MacCormick conceded that rights require the imposition of duties, for him the existence of a right preceded the imposition of a duty. It is *because* children have a right to care and nurture that parents have a duty to care for them[4].

If this is correct, it means that it may be possible to recognise that children have rights even where there is uncertainty about who is to bear the corresponding duty. MacCormick gives the example of education. While there may be a wide measure of agreement that children have a right to be educated to the limits of their abilities, it is far less clear who has the duty or power to provide it as between

---

1 Correlativity was crucial to Hohfeld – see *Fundamental Legal Conceptions* (Yale University Press, 1919).

2 N MacCormick 'Children's Rights: A Test-Case for Theories of Right' (above).

3 Ibid at pp 310 et seq.

4 Ibid at p 313.

parents, local authorities, central government, a church or the children them-selves[1]. MacCormick attempted to fit this reasoning into a general interest theory. His thesis was that to ascribe to all members of a class C (for present purposes, children) a right to treatment T (in the above examples, care and nurture or education) is to presuppose that T is, in all normal circumstances, a good for every member of C and that T is a good which it would be wrong to withhold from any member of C.

It should be noted that MacCormick's theory, as applied to children (especially young children) incorporates a measure of paternalism. Whereas in a liberal democracy it is generally accepted that a right-holder should be allowed the liberty to determine when to enforce his rights, this is not so, according to MacCormick, in the case of children – an exception acknowledged by the exponents of classical liberalism including JS Mill[2]. This is based on a contentious argument which will be discussed later: 'Children are not always or even usually the best judges of what is good for them'.

The emergence of children's rights according to Eekelaar

In a seminal article, published in 1986[3], John Eekelaar assessed the current status of the concept of children's rights in English law in the context of an historical overview and two (then) recent decisions of the House of Lords[4]. Like MacCormick, Eekelaar relied on the interest theory of rights, especially that version propounded by Joseph Raz that 'a law creates a right if it is based on and expresses the view that someone has an interest which is sufficient ground for holding another to be subject to a duty'[5].

Historical background

Eekelaar was at pains to demonstrate that, historically, the earliest legal duties towards children emerged not to protect the interests of children themselves but to further other interests, usually the interests of fathers or the wider community. Thus, the legal enforcement of parental support obligations in the sixteenth century arose primarily from the threat to social stability posed by the growth of mass unemployment and labour mobility. Insofar as this advanced the interests of children it did so only incidentally and was not its aim or purpose[6]. The same, he argues, may be said of the limited incursions into the father's right to custody of his legitimate children during the nineteenth century. Although, apparently, conceived as protective of the child's independent interests, the reality was that the father's interests were seen as paramount unless his behaviour posed a severe threat to the child's well-being. But the courts would only hold this to be so where it consisted of such matters as 'immorality, profligacy, impiety and radical social views, all of which might undermine the child's commitment to the dominant social values'[7]. For Eekelaar these judicial interventions had the effect of equating

---

1   N MacCormick 'Children's Rights: A Test-Case for Theories of Right' (above).
2   JS Mill *Essay on Liberty* (1859).
3   J Eekelaar 'The Emergence of Children's Rights' (1986) 6 *Oxford Journal of Legal Studies* 161.
4   *Richards v Richards* [1984] AC 174 and the *Gillick* case.
5   J Raz 'Legal Rights' (1984) 4 *Oxford Journal of Legal Studies* 1 at p 13.
6   J Eekelaar 'The Emergence of Children's Rights' (above) at pp 166–169.
7   See, for example, *Shelley v Westbrooke* (1817) Jac 266 and *Symington v Symington* (1875) LR 2 SC and Div 415.

the welfare of children with the transmission of conventional social norms. In other words, their thrust was to uphold the prevailing community interest rather than the independent interests of children.

Isolation of interests

The key precondition for rights in Eekelaar's theory is the social perception that an individual or class of individuals has certain interests. Crucial to this is that the interests in question must be capable of isolation from the interests of others. Thus, to assert the existence of a particular right for children is to identify an independent interest which they have in the subject-matter or, as Eekelaar puts it, 'those benefits which the subject himself or herself might plausibly claim in themselves'. He gives the example of a parent's power to take decisions concerning his daughter's medical welfare. Although the parent might claim that this power is in the child's interests, the parental interest is not identical with the child's interest. Her interest or right is that only the *best* medical decisions are taken for her. Accordingly, it cannot per se be enough to see the child's interests as synonymous with those of the parent, despite the force of parental autonomy claims. Eekelaar's thesis is that no child would plausibly claim parental independence as an end in itself. If it is claimed at all it must be because it is perceived to advance other ends such as material or emotional stability[1]. He acknowledged, however, that children might lack the information or ability to evaluate their own best interests and, accordingly, the construction of a theory of children's rights involves 'some kind of imaginative leap and guess what a child might retrospectively have wanted once it reaches a position of maturity'.

Eekelaar identified three separate kinds of interest which might form the foundation of these retrospective claims. These he described as 'the basic interests', 'the developmental interests' and 'the autonomy interests'.

Basic interests

The 'basic interests' relate to what might be described as the essentials of healthy living, including physical, emotional and intellectual care[2]. The duty to secure these interests is placed initially on the child's parents but, where this is abused or neglected, the State may intervene in care proceedings[3]. These interests are 'basic' because they require compliance with minimally acceptable standards of upbringing. The parents' duty is 'to refrain from the actual prevention or neglect of proper development or natural health rather than the maximum promotion of these qualities'.

Developmental interests

The 'developmental interests' are wider and may be asserted not just against parents but against the wider community. They are more nebulous than the basic interests and, hence, more difficult to categorise as legal rights. The developmental interest, according to Eekelaar, is that, subject to the socio-economic constraints in a particular society, 'all children should have an equal opportunity to maximise the resources available to them during their childhood (including

---

1 J Eekelaar 'The Emergence of Children's Rights' (above) at p 170.
2 Ibid at pp 171–172.
3 Under s 31(2) of the Children Act 1989, discussed in Chapter 11 below.

their own inherent abilities) so as to minimise the degree to which they enter adult life affected by avoidable prejudices incurred during childhood'. Eekelaar doubted that these interests, while the subject of moral claims, could legitimately be classified as legal rights since, beyond education, the law imposes no duty on parents to fulfil children's developmental interests, which depend rather on 'the natural workings of the economies of families which are themselves dependent on the wider social and economic mechanisms of the community'[1].

Autonomy interest

The 'autonomy interest', which a child might retrospectively claim, is 'the freedom to choose his own lifestyle and to enter social relations according to his own inclinations uncontrolled by the authority of the adult world, whether parents or institutions'. This is, of course, the classic claim of the child liberationists which was alluded to above. Eekelaar argued that this could be interpreted as a version of the developmental interest, no doubt on the basis that healthy development implies a measure of self-determination or autonomy. The justification for adopting a separate categorisation is that the autonomy interest has the potential for conflicting with the developmental interest or the basic interest. It is, for example, likely that the removal of age restrictions on drinking or driving would further the autonomy interest but would also result in more deaths or injury among children from road accidents, thereby infringing their developmental and basic interests. Eekelaar, agreeing with Freeman[2], would rank the autonomy interest as subordinate to the other two interests, since it is likely that the majority of adults would not give their retrospective approval to exercises of autonomy while children which damaged their life chances in adulthood when compared with other children.

The value of Eekelaar's thesis is that it alerts us to potential conflicts both between the distinctive interests or rights which children may claim and between those interests and rights and the competing claims of the adult world, especially those of parents. Eekelaar has subsequently attempted to build on his earlier theory by suggesting a way in which furthering the best interests of children may be reconciled with treating them as possessors of rights. His theory, which is based on the concept of 'dynamic self-determinism', relies on the argument that the welfare principle, or best interests principle, should be properly understood to accommodate an opportunity for the child to determine what those best interests are[3]. He proposes, subject to two limitations, that a competent child's decision should determine the outcome of the issue in question. These are 'compatibility with the general law and the interests of others' and, more controversially, situations in which a child might take a decision which is 'contrary to his or her *self-interest*, . . . narrowly defined in terms of physical or mental well-being and integrity'[4]. This, of course, raises again the central question of precisely what are the acceptable limits of paternalism.

---

1 J Eekelaar (above) at p 173.
2 MDA Freeman *The Rights and Wrongs of Children* (Frances Pinter, 1983).
3 J Eekelaar 'The Interests of the Child and the Child's Wishes: The Role of Dynamic Self-Determinism' in P Alston (ed) *The Best Interests of the Child* (Clarendon, 1994) at p 42. Also published at (1994) 8 IJLF 42. See further J Eekelaar 'Beyond the Welfare Principle' [2002] CFLQ 237.
4 J Eekelaar (above).

Freeman's liberal paternalism

The most extensive study of children's rights in England is probably *The Rights and Wrongs of Children* by Michael Freeman[1]. This has now, to a degree, been superseded by his collection of essays, *The Moral Status of Children*[2], which in some respects is intended by Freeman to serve as a second edition to his earlier work. The principal change is a shift of emphasis. He is now inclined to believe that he underestimated the importance of giving children participatory rights in *The Rights and Wrongs of Children*. Freeman stressed the importance of rights for children as against benevolence towards children, or other morally significant values such as love, friendship or compassion. Rights enable, at least in theory, the right-holder to stand with dignity and demand or insist on certain treatment without embarrassment or shame. They represent entitlements and avoid the need to grovel, beg or show gratitude for favours. At the same time, Freeman was quick to warn that the enactment of legal rights could become merely an abstract affirmation of principle if the will was lacking to put it into practice. He pointed to examples from juvenile justice in which well-intentioned measures, designed to enhance the rights of children, back-fired and had the opposite effect of eroding them[3].

Freeman's distinctive contribution to the children's rights debate was to demonstrate the extremely diverse nature of the substantive rights which children might claim and to fit a categorisation of these rights into an over-arching theory of liberal paternalism. His theory adapts Rawls' influential 'Theory of Justice'[4] to apply to children. Freeman produced a fourfold classification of children's rights, comprising rights to welfare, rights of protection, rights to be treated like adults and rights against parents[5].

Rights to welfare

Freeman's first category, welfare rights, was located in the more general notion of human rights and he drew freely on the statements on children's rights in the United Nations Declaration of the Rights of the Child[6]. Freeman regarded this as politically important because, by expressing children's rights as human rights,

---

1   (Frances Pinter, 1983).

2   (Martinus Nijhoff, 1997). See also M Freeman 'The End of the Century of the Child?' (2003) 53 *Current Legal Problems* 505 for a more succinct distillation of the author's views on the successes and failures of the twentieth century from a children's rights perspective.

3   *The Rights and Wrongs of Children* (above) at pp 32–34. Freeman's attacks were levelled particularly at the system of juvenile justice and the juvenile court where well-intentioned measures designed to decriminalise juvenile misbehaviour, particularly those embodied in the Children and Young Persons Act 1969, had the unintended effect of establishing, inter alia, a 'criminal model' in care proceedings. See Chapter 11 below.

4   J Rawls *A Theory of Justice* (Harvard University Press, 1972). A similar adaptation of the theory to children was put forward by V Worsfold in 'A Philosophical Justification for Children's Rights' (1974) 44 *Harvard Educational Review* 142.

5   MDA Freeman *The Rights and Wrongs of Children* (above) at pp 40–54.

6   Adopted by the General Assembly on 20 November 1959. See also the United Nations Convention on the Rights of the Child, adopted on the thirtieth anniversary of the Declaration, both discussed in Chapter 2 above.

'the United Nations was not saying that children ought to have these rights but, since children are undoubtedly human beings . . . they already have them'[1].

The rights in question are wide-ranging and include: entitlement to a name and nationality; freedom from discrimination based on, for example, race, colour or religion; social security extending to adequate nutrition, housing, recreation and medical care; entitlement to free education and equal opportunities; protection from all forms of cruelty, neglect and exploitation; and special treatment for the disabled. These rights are not, as Freeman acknowledged, easily formulated against anyone in particular. They are, in essence, 'manifestos' of the rights which children *ought* to have against everyone. Typically, these types of 'rights against the world' are vague, perhaps deliberately so, to reflect cultural and economic differences between societies. Some, such as the provision of adequate nutrition and medical care, are clearly fundamental since they relate to survival and fall within what Eekelaar termed the 'basic interests'. The rights listed are essentially protectionist rather than liberationist and, to that extent, there is an overlap with Freeman's second category, rights of protection. But 'welfare rights' is a wide enough idea to include within it rights of *recipience*, ie rights to receive *positive* welfare benefits such as education, social security or (perhaps more controversially in rights analysis) love, understanding and affection.

Rights of protection

Freeman's second category, protective rights, was more overtly concerned with protection from *negative* behaviour and activities[2] such as inadequate care, abuse or neglect by parents, exploitation by employers or environmental dangers. Whereas welfare rights are pitched at a high level and are grounded in the assumption that society owes children the best it has to offer, protective rights are concerned that minimally acceptable standards of treatment are observed and, as such, are largely, although not exclusively, the province of the criminal law[3].

The first two categories of rights have a common paternalistic approach. They are rights which the adult world would deem to be appropriate for children whether or not they would be claimed by children for themselves. They contrast sharply with Freeman's third and fourth categories, both of which belong more to the liberationist school.

The right to be treated like adults

Freeman's third category was the right of children to be treated like adults. This right is grounded in social justice and egalitarianism. It is essentially that the rights and liberties extended to adults should also be extended to children as fellow human beings, unless there is a good reason for differentiating between them. Comment has already been made on this in the context of the USA. The point should now also be made that children, prima facie, enjoy the same fundamental civil liberties as adults, while making due allowance for protectionist concerns and

---

1   A point which can be made with even greater force now that children have 'Convention rights' under the ECHR.

2   MDA Freeman *The Rights and Wrongs of Children* (above) at pp 43–45.

3   As to which see Chapter 14 below. Civil care proceedings are also, of course, concerned directly with protection.

the role of parents, under both the UNCRC and the ECHR[1]. Although the UK has not had a bill of rights, there is, nonetheless, a strong tradition of respect for civil liberties and this must pose the question of how far the civil liberties enjoyed by adults are, or should be, extended to children and young people. Freeman regarded the claim that children should be treated as adults with some scepticism. While distinctions between children and adults are social and legal constructs which may appear arbitrary, Freeman's view was that respect for children as persons requires that society provides 'a childhood for every child'[2] and not an adulthood for every child. Yet Freeman also questioned the double standard involved in the differential treatment of children and adults[3]. He pointed out that the basis for this was the supposed incapacity or lack of maturity which would prevent children from taking sound decisions on their own behalf. He nonetheless rejected the removal of all age-related disabilities since to do so would ignore the evidence about the cognitive abilities of children provided by developmental psychology. But he argued that children's rights at least required that age-related restrictions be kept under review in the light of this evidence. His own preference was for legal capacity to be determined on a case-by-case basis, by assessing the *actual* capacity for particular activities of individual children. This, he argued, could be achieved by employing an objective test of rationality determined in accordance with a neutral theory of what is 'good' for children.

Rights against parents

Freeman's fourth category was rights against parents[4]. This is also concerned primarily with self-determination or autonomy but, whereas the third category is concerned with the justification of civil liberties and the child's position under the general law, this fourth category is concerned with the claim for independence from parental control[5]. Claims in this category range from the trivial (eg length of hair, choice of clothes, bedtimes, etc) to serious matters (eg consent to abortion or provision of contraceptives). Freeman noted two variants of this claim. The first is the claim that the child should be able to act entirely independently. The second is the claim that the child should be able to act independently but with the sanction of an outside agency, usually a court[6]. Freeman's general position on parent–child conflicts was to view the parental role as a representative one. Where parents' and children's views accord with one another there is no problem. Where they do not, Freeman would uphold parental decisions insofar as they are consistent with an objective evaluation of what Rawls called 'primary social goods'. These include liberty, health and opportunity and are, in short, the things which any rational person would want to pursue. Where parents purport to take

---

1   These include the rights to freedom of expression, conscience and religion, freedom of association and the right to privacy (see Articles 13–16 of the UNCRC and Articles 8–11 of the ECHR).

2   MDA Freeman *The Rights and Wrongs of Children* (above) at p 3. Freeman borrowed the quotation from M Gerzon *A Childhood for Every Child – Politics of Parenthood* (Outerbridge and Lazard, New York, 1973).

3   The legal capacities of children and young people are considered in Chapter 15 below.

4   MDA Freeman (above) at pp 48–52.

5   There is a discussion in the next section of the inter-relationship between children's capacities and parental control.

6   This solution has often been adopted in the USA. See Chapter 8 below.

decisions not in accordance with this objective, Freeman would hold that parental representation ceases at that point and that the intervention of an outside agency is justified, his own preference being a court.

Rawls' fundamentals of justice

It is clear from this analysis that Freeman favoured a degree of paternalism as a feature of children's rights[1]. The critical requirement of respect for persons was, he thought, that the potential capacity of children for taking responsibility as free and rational agents should be recognised. But, since in the case of children we are often talking about *potential* rather than actual capacity, a limited amount of intervention could be justified to protect them against irrational actions. The obvious question is, what kind of actions are to be considered irrational for these purposes? What test of rationality can be employed? Here, Freeman found that it was Rawls' idea of equality at the stage of a hypothetical social contract which best captured the idea of treating people as equals with regard to their capacity for autonomy.

Rawls was concerned with the principles which individuals would hypothetically choose in a just society in order to secure fair treatment for everyone[2]. Everyone in society would participate in choosing these principles in a hypothetical state ('the original position') and in ignorance of their own specific interest and circumstances (behind 'the veil of ignorance'). Since they would be hypothetically unaware of what would be to their own advantage or disadvantage, all individuals would choose principles of justice impartially and with a view to equality. According to Rawls, individuals in this state of ignorance, but acting in self-interest, would choose two fundamental principles of justice. These were, first, that each person should have as much personal liberty as was compatible with similar liberty for everyone else and, secondly, that social and economic inequalities should be tolerated only to the extent that they were to the greatest benefit of the least advantaged and attached to offices and positions open to everyone under conditions of fair equality of opportunity.

Rawls included children in the initial social contract when they reached the 'age of reason'. Freeman interpreted this as meaning participation to the extent that they were capable. Justice required, therefore, that children be brought to a capacity whereby they were able to take responsibility as free and rational agents. In order to achieve this, Freeman argued that they required two types of right. The first was equal opportunity extending to such matters as good parenting and good teaching. The second was liberal paternalism. This would allow intervention to protect the child's potential for development. The test propounded by Freeman is 'what sorts of action or conduct would we wish, as children, to be shielded against on the assumption that we would want to mature to a rationally autonomous adulthood and be capable of deciding our own system of ends as free and rational beings'[3]? Within this framework, protection from death or injury and compulsory education could be readily justified. While there was no guarantee that every individual would consent to these principles, Freeman's thesis was that they were

---

1   His theory of liberal paternalism is set out at pp 54–60 of his book.
2   See the explanation of Rawls' theory by V Worsfold in 'A Philosophical Justification for Children's Rights' (1974) 44 *Harvard Educational Review* 142 at pp 151 et seq.
3   MDA Freeman *The Rights and Wrongs of Children* (above) at p 57.

the ones which were most consistent with a neutral theory of the good and which would appeal to those in the 'original position'.

Common ground between the theories

This analysis has touched briefly on just three of the many theories of children's rights which have been advanced, and doubtless many more will emerge in the years to come[1]. There is much common ground between the three theories discussed above which, at the risk of over-simplification, might be summarised in the following propositions:

(1)   Children have rights which arise from the fundamental moral requirement of respect for persons which underlies all human rights.

(2)   The particular rights which children have are grounded in the interests which society recognises they possess and which justify the imposition of duties on others.

(3)   'Children's rights' is not a unitary concept but a catch-all expression for a range of legal and moral claims.

(4)   The imposition of a duty on *someone* (perhaps unspecified) is a necessary concomitant of any right asserted for children. Where this is imposed on an identifiable entity, especially a parent, it may be possible to recognise the existence of a legal right stricto sensu – a 'claim right' in the Hohfeldian sense[2]. Where, conversely, the right is asserted against the world, it is less clear that it can be regarded as a legal right but may have the status of a moral right. The existence of such a moral claim may itself justify the creation of a legal right and, but for potential difficulties of enforcement, many such claims probably would be.

(5)   Children's rights must embrace elements of both qualified self-determination and limited paternalism.

(6)   Rights, although asserted by individual children, must have a general or universal character such that they can be applied to all children as a class.

Perhaps the most controversial issue arising from these theories is the basis upon which paternalistic interventions are justified. Broadly, there would appear to be two schools of thought on this. The first, accepted by Eekelaar and Freeman, entails a hypothetical enquiry by adult decision-makers into what children would ideally want for themselves. The judgment of adult society is, as it were, substituted for that of the child who is (as yet) unable to exercise it for himself. This can only be made on the basis of a projection of what rational persons would have wished for themselves as children. The second, adopted by Ruth Adler in her study of

---

1   Many of these theories, particularly those put forward in North America, are cited by Freeman. For a Scottish perspective on children's rights, see R Adler *Taking Juvenile Justice Seriously* (Scottish Academic Press, 1985); and the review by J Eekelaar at (1986) 6 *Oxford Journal of Legal Studies* 439. For other significant collections of essays on the general subject of children's rights, see M Freeman and P Veerman (eds) *The Ideologies of Children's Rights* (Martinus Nijhoff, 1992) and P Alston, S Parker and J Seymour (eds) *Children, Rights and the Law* (Clarendon, 1992). See also C Smith 'Children's Rights: Judicial Ambivalence and Social Resistance' (1997) 11 IJLPF 103.

2   Hohfeld regarded these 'claim rights' as the only true legal rights: see Hohfeld *Fundamental Legal Conceptions* (Yale University Press, 1919).

juvenile justice in Scotland[1], is that adult decision-making reflects the value
judgments of the decision-maker about what is good for children and not the
decision-maker's projection of what children would want for themselves. Adler
would, accordingly, allow a form of modified protectionism based on external
assessments of what is good or necessary for children. Whatever may be the
theoretical merits of the former school of thought, it is likely that the latter is a
more realistic reflection of what actually happens in practice. We will return to this
issue in the context of medical decision-making, where the 'substituted judgment
test' has a certain following, especially in North America[2].

Onora O'Neill: Children's rights or adults' duties?

Onora O'Neill has made a distinctive contribution to the children's rights debate
by questioning whether 'children's positive rights are best grounded by appeals to
fundamental (moral, natural, human) rights'. Instead, she argues they are 'best
grounded by embedding them in a wider account of fundamental obligations'[3]. In
essence, her thesis is that regarding 'rights as fundamental in ethical deliberation
about children has neither theoretical nor political advantages'. Instead, she
thinks that the best way to achieve rights for children is to shift the concentration
on to the fundamental *obligations* of adult society.

O'Neill does not deny the force of the rhetoric of rights in the claims of those
who lack power but she is concerned that such rhetoric can lead to claims of
'spurious rights even when no corresponding obligations can be justified'. She
warns that:

> 'many of the rights promulgated in international documents are not perhaps spurious, but they
> are patently no more than "manifesto" rights . . . that cannot be claimed unless or until practices
> and institutions are established that determine against whom claims on behalf of a particular
> child may be lodged. Mere insistence that certain ideals or goals are rights cannot make them
> into rights . . .'[4]

Thus, the rhetoric of rights cannot, according to O'Neill, establish positive
rights for children. She goes on to consider whether the use of the language of
children's rights might have a *political* usefulness contributing to the 'realisation of
fundamental imperfect obligations'. Here, she rejects the analogy between
children and other (formerly) oppressed groups such as colonial peoples, the
working classes, religious or racial minorities and women, all of which 'have
sought recognition and respect for capacities for rational and independent life
and action that are demonstrably there and thwarted by the denial of rights'[5]. For
O'Neill, the 'crucial difference between (early) childhood dependence and the
dependence of oppressed social groups is that childhood is a stage of life, from
which children normally emerge and are helped and urged to emerge from by
those who have most power over them'. She concludes:

---

1   R Adler *Taking Juvenile Justice Seriously* (above).
2   See Chapter 8 below.
3   O O'Neill 'Children's Rights and Children's Lives' (1988) 98 *Ethics* 445, also reproduced in
    Alston, Parker and Seymour *Children, Rights and the Law* (Clarendon, 1992) at p 24.
4   Ibid at p 37.
5   Ibid.

'Those who urge respect for children's rights must address not children but those whose action may affect children; they have reason to prefer the rhetoric of obligations to that of rights, both because its scope is wider and because it addresses the relevant audience more directly.'[1]

O'Neill's thesis has provoked considerable disagreement as it was bound to do[2]. Its value is to remind us that where any 'right' is being asserted for children we ought to pause to consider on whom there is, or might be, a correlative obligation and whether such obligation is enforceable.

Do children have duties?

The whole children's rights debate raises one other important question. This is whether children *themselves* have any duties or responsibilities. Those rights which aim to protect children or secure positive welfare benefits for them largely entail, as perhaps O'Neill's thesis reminds us, the exercise of responsibility by others. But those rights which are autonomy based and would extend to children greater liberties, by treating them like adults or by giving them freedom from parental control, do invite consideration of how much responsibility children have for their own actions. It is striking how rarely the advocates of children's rights even mention, let alone deal with, this issue.

The short answer is that, whereas many jurisdictions do explicitly recognise the existence of certain obligations upon children and set them out in civil codes or legislation, English law is largely silent on the question[3]. Historically, the common law did enable a parent to sue for the loss of his child's services but this was only actionable where the child *in fact* performed some service for the parent – even if it was only making the tea![4] The action fell into disuse and was eventually abolished in 1982[5]. A more modern approach to the general obligation which children might be thought to have is a duty of respect for parents and this is acknowledged expressly in a number of jurisdictions[6]. In South East Asia, certain States provide expressly for the financial obligations of children (for these purposes including 'adult children') towards parents who are unable to support themselves[7].

---

1 O O'Neill (above) at p 39.
2 For a particularly readable critique, see M Freeman *The Moral Status of Children* (Martinus Nijhoff, 1997) at pp 25–29.
3 For a general discussion, see A Bainham '"Honour Thy Father and Thy Mother": Children's Rights and Children's Duties' in G Douglas and L Sebba (eds) *Children's Rights and Traditional Values* (Dartmouth, 1998).
4 So where a two-year-old was run down by the defendant's carriage no action would lie. See *Hall v Hollander* (1825) 4 B&C 660, and for a more detailed discussion, PM Bromley *Bromley's Family Law* (6th edn) (Butterworths, 1981) at pp 329–332.
5 Administration of Justice Act 1982, s 2(b).
6 Perhaps not surprisingly in Israel, given its traditions, but less obviously in Indonesia and the new family code of Croatia. See further Bainham (above) and the sources cited at fn 28 to that article.
7 This is so in Indonesia. See Wila Chandrawila Supriadi 'Indonesia: Indonesian Marriage Law' in A Bainham (ed) *The International Survey of Family Law 1995* (Martinus Nijhoff, 1997). More strikingly, Singapore passed the Maintenance of Parents Act 1995 which gives to parents, in specified circumstances, the right to obtain maintenance from their children. See P de Cruz 'Singapore: Maintenance, Marital Property and Legislative Innovation' in A Bainham (ed) *The International Survey of Family Law 1996* (Martinus Nijhoff, 1998).

In English law such legal obligations as children have really arise, if at all, by implication. These include criminal responsibility from the age of 10 and limited tortious liability[1]. There is no direct statutory obligation on the child to attend school, although this arguably arises by implication from the parental duty to ensure the child receives a proper education and from the very existence of the compulsory education system[2]. It can be argued that the express imposition of certain duties on children would be desirable, or is even a necessary concomitant, of the acquisition of limited autonomy. The younger the child the less actual and legal capacity that child will possess and the less justification there is for imposing duties or responsibilities on that child. As the child gets older and gradually acquires greater actual and legal independence so the case gets stronger for requiring increased actual and legal responsibility on the part of the child or, perhaps more accurately, young person. This might appear to justify, inter alia, a specific duty on the child to attend school and, it will be suggested later, a duty to remain in contact with parents – albeit one which would be qualified by the operation of the welfare principle[3]. Finally, it is noteworthy that the UNCRC gives all manner of *rights* to children but nowhere addresses this question of responsibility.

PARENTS: RIGHTS, RESPONSIBILITIES AND DISCRETIONS

The change in terminology from 'parental rights' to 'parental responsibility' has already been noted, and the function performed by these two concepts described. But did this reformulation of the parent's position represent any real change in the substance of the legal relationship between parents and children? During the late 1980s and the 1990s there was a marked reluctance to accept that parents have 'rights', and one commentator more or less coupled the 'eclipse of parental rights' with the 'emergence of children's rights'[4]. It was stressed frequently that any rights which parents had existed only to enable them to discharge their duties to their children[5]. The law was apparently seeking to express parenthood in a different way which played up the responsibility of parents and played down any legal rights which might arise from the relationship[6].

The best restatement of the parental position was perhaps that of the Law Commission in its first report on illegitimacy in 1982, taken up in its working paper on custody in 1986 in which it put it thus:

---

1   See Chapters 14 and 15 respectively.
2   See Chapter 16.
3   See Chapter 4. In its recent decision in *Hansen v Turkey* [2004] 1 FLR 142, the ECtHR held, inter alia, that although measures against children obliging them to reunite with one or other parent were not desirable in the sensitive area of contact, such action could not be ruled out in the event of non-compliance or unlawful behaviour by the parent with whom the children lived. Is this not implicit recognition that children may have an obligation to see a parent?
4   J Eekelaar 'The Eclipse of Parental Rights' (1986) 102 LQR 4 and 'The Emergence of Children's Rights' (1986) 6 *Oxford Journal of Legal Studies* 161.
5   For a post-*Gillick* restatement of this position, see the views of the Scottish Law Commission, in its Discussion Paper No 88 *Parental Responsibilities and Rights* at paras 2.1 et seq.
6   On the similar trend in North America, see KT Bartlett 'Re-Expressing Parenthood' (1988) 98 *Yale Law Journal* 293.

'Parenthood would entail a primary claim and a primary responsibility to bring up the child. It would not, however, entail parental "rights" as such. The House of Lords in *Gillick v West Norfolk and Wisbech Area Health Authority* has held that the powers which parents have to control or make decisions for their children are simply the necessary concomitant of their parental duties. This confirms our view that "to talk of parental 'rights'" is not only inaccurate as a matter of juristic analysis but also a misleading use of ordinary language.'[1]

This view of parenthood as embracing powers in order to discharge responsibilities accords with what has been termed the 'exchange view'. Parents have rights *because* they have responsibilities and they have responsibilities *because* they have rights[2]. On this view, the correct way of looking at parenthood is one which implies reciprocity.

The new emphasis on responsibility raises a fundamental issue. Whether or not it is jurisprudentially accurate to say that parents have 'rights', can it at least be said that they have *independent interests* which can be asserted in law? After a period in which it was fashionable to deny that they do, judicial decisions[3] and academic commentaries[4] began to acknowledge that they did.

The following section examines the substance of the parent's position in law. This revolves around the issue of the *control* which parents are required or allowed to exert over the lives of their children. Although there are many angles to this, the discussion can usefully be reduced to three distinct but inter-related questions.

(1) What are the legal incidents of parenthood and, in particular, over which areas of upbringing does the law charge parents with responsibility or allow them to exert control?
(2) What are the limits of parents' responsibilities and powers?
(3) How do these responsibilities and powers relate to the legal capacities and responsibilities of children themselves?

The legal incidents of parenthood

It has never been possible to state with complete confidence the legal incidents of parenthood. This is because they have never been set out in statutory form. The statutory definitions of 'parental rights and duties' and now 'parental responsibility' simply refer back to the general law. Therefore, in order to appreciate the full legal implications of the parent–child relationship, it has been necessary to piece this together by taking into account the legal effects recognised at common law and under various statutory provisions. A number of commentators attempted to do this[5] before the Children Act 1989, although the Law Commission eschewed

---

1   Law Com Working Paper No 96 *Custody* (1986) at para 7.16 and Law Com Report No 118 *Illegitimacy* (1982) at para 4.18.
2   See KT Bartlett (above) at pp 297 et seq.
3   See, for example, *Re K (A Minor) (Custody)* [1990] 2 FLR 64; and *Re K (A Minor) (Wardship; Adoption)* [1991] 1 FLR 57, discussed in J Eekelaar 'The Wardship Jurisdiction, Children's Welfare and Parents' Rights' (1991) 107 LQR 386. See also the decision of the ECtHR in *Hokkanen v Finland* (1995) 19 EHRR 139 which can surely only be explained on the basis that a parent has a right to and an independent interest in contact with his child. See further Chapter 4 below.
4   J Eekelaar (above), and A Bainham 'Growing Up in Britain: Adolescence in the post-*Gillick* Era' (1992) *Juridical Review* 155.
5   See, for example, J Eekelaar 'What are Parental Rights?' (1973) 89 LQR 210 and S Maidment 'The Fragmentation of Parental Rights' (1981) CLJ 135.

the opportunity to do so in its report on guardianship and custody. The Commission argued that, although it would be superficially attractive to provide a list, this would be a practical impossibility given the need for change periodically to meet different needs and circumstances[1]. It is nonetheless possible to collate with some accuracy the major incidents of parenthood. The following list is taken from one leading text on family law[2]:

(a) providing a home for the child;
(b) having contact with the child;
(c) determining and providing for the child's education;
(d) determining the child's religion;
(e) disciplining the child;
(f) consenting to the child's medical treatment;
(g) consenting to the child's marriage;
(h) agreeing to the child's adoption;
(i) vetoing the issue of a child's passport;
(j) taking the child outside the UK and consenting to the child's emigration;
(k) administering the child's property;
(l) protecting and maintaining the child;
(m) naming the child;
(n) representing the child in legal proceedings;
(o) disposing of the child's corpse;
(p) appointing a guardian for the child.

One could possibly add to this list, sharing responsibility for criminal offences committed by the child given the liability of parents to pay the child's fines or have parenting orders made against them[3]. Each of the listed matters requires qualification and there is considerable debate about their content and extent, but they do at least convey, in general terms, the areas of control which fall within parenthood. There is little cause for surprise since they relate to all the most important matters which can affect a child's upbringing and it would be expected that parents would exercise *primary* control over them.

The approach in Scotland

The Scottish Law Commission took a slightly different view of the nature of the parental position in law from that of the English Commission[4]. It agreed that it was correct to emphasise the *responsibility* of parents but recommended that parental *rights* should also be expressly recognised in legislation accepting that such rights would be subordinate to the child's best interests. The Commission also felt that it was helpful to set out the principal responsibilities and rights of parents in

---

1   Law Com Report No 172 *Review of Child Law: Guardianship and Custody* (1988) at para 2.6.
2   PM Bromley and NV Lowe *Bromley's Family Law* (9th edn) (Butterworths, 1998) at p 350.
3   See further Chapter 14.
4   See Scot Law Com No 135 *Report on Family Law* (Edinburgh HMSO, 1992) especially at paras 2.1–2.35.

legislation, and the Scottish legislation does just that[1]. Section 1 of the Children (Scotland) Act 1995 sets out the following *responsibilities* of parents:

(a) to safeguard and promote the child's health, development and welfare;
(b) to provide direction and guidance to the child in a manner appropriate to the stage of the child's development;
(c) if the child is not living with the parent, to maintain personal relations and direct contact with the child on a regular basis; and
(d) to act as the child's legal representative.

These responsibilities together with the rights set out below (which replace common-law, but not specific statutory, duties) must be exercised to the extent that it is practicable and in the interests of the child to do so.

Section 2 of the Act sets out a corresponding list of parental *rights* which a parent has in order to fulfil these responsibilities. They are:

(a) to have the child living with him or her or otherwise to regulate the child's residence;
(b) to control, direct or guide the child's upbringing in a manner consistent with the child's stage of development;
(c) if the child is not living with the parent, to maintain personal relations and direct contact with the child on a regular basis; and
(d) to act as the child's legal representative.

It will be noted that there is a close correspondence, almost direct correlation, between the above responsibilities and rights, emphasising the reciprocal nature of rights and responsibilities which essentially conforms with the 'exchange view' of parenthood discussed earlier.

Legal parentage and parental responsibility

It is important to appreciate that there is a distinction between the effects of 'being a parent' and the effects of having 'parental responsibility'. In most instances, of course, it will be the parents who have parental responsibility, so that their relationship with the child will be partly the result of being parents and partly the result of having parental responsibility. But where parental responsibility is vested in a non-parent, or where a parent does not have parental responsibility[2], the distinction is more significant. The essential point is that certain legal effects derive exclusively from being a parent[3] since they are dependent on being *related* to someone else in a particular way. As such, these incidents are not incorporated in the concept of parental responsibility in the sense that they are not acquired by a non-parent who obtains this by court order[4].

---

1 See generally JM Thomson *Family Law in Scotland* (3rd edn) (Butterworths, 1996) at pp 193 et seq, and E Sutherland 'Scotland: Child Law Reform – At Last!' in A Bainham (ed) *The International Survey of Family Law 1995* (Martinus Nijhoff, 1997). For a more recent evaluation see E Sutherland 'How Children are Faring in the New Scotland' in A Bainham (ed) *The International Survey of Family Law (2001 Edition)* (Family Law, 2001) at p 363.
2 This can only be the case regarding the unmarried father who is not registered as the father and who has not acquired parental responsibility by agreement with the mother or by court order.
3 Although some also apply to guardianship in view of the assimilation of the legal effects of guardianship and parenthood. See Chapter 6 below.
4 A residence order in the case of an individual, and a care order in the case of a local authority.

The clearest example is rights of succession. Neither the child nor the non-parent with parental responsibility will have any claim on the other's estate in the event of intestacy[1]. The acquisition of 'parental responsibility' does not make the child in the fullest legal sense a member of the family of the person acquiring it in the way that an adoption order does. The latter creates a new legal relationship of parent and child and does not merely confer parental responsibility. Thus, holding parental responsibility will not create a legally recognised relationship between the child and the wider kin of the holder. These wider kin (children, parents, siblings, uncles and aunts, etc) will not, for example, fall within the definition of 'relative' vis-à-vis the child under the Children Act 1989[2]. The Children Act 1989 also provides that certain powers which are considered fundamental to the status of being a parent or guardian are not to pass to a non-parent who obtains parental responsibility through a residence order[3], or to a local authority which obtains it under a care order[4]. These are the right to consent or refuse to consent to adoption and the right to appoint a guardian[5]. The right to change the child's name and the right to remove the child from the jurisdiction may also be restricted where a residence order is in force[6]. Thus, while parental responsibility includes within it the bulk of powers over upbringing which parents and guardians enjoy, it is a somewhat more limited notion than either parenthood or guardianship.

This explanation does not adequately convey the peculiar status of the unmarried father who has not acquired parental responsibility which is essentially the converse of the non-parent with parental responsibility. Although undoubtedly having the status of being a parent[7] (and with it, for example, succession rights), these unmarried fathers do not possess any of the powers included in parental responsibility which arguably constitute, in reality, the most important features of being a parent[8]. Despite this, such a father *is* liable to support the child financially. This gives rise to the rather incongruous result that a lawyer or other adviser may have to explain to such a man how it is that he does not possess parental responsibility but is still obliged to support his child[9]. Is, then, the notion of parental responsibility jurisprudentially accurate in conveying the legal position of parents and others having control over children?

---

1   This can, of course, be overcome by making a will.
2   See s 105(1) which defines 'relative' as 'a grandparent, brother, sister, uncle or aunt (whether of the full blood or half blood or by affinity) or step-parent'.
3   Children Act 1989, s 12(3).
4   Ibid, s 33(6)(b).
5   Additionally, a local authority may not 'cause the child to be brought up in any religious persuasion other than that in which he would have been brought up if the order had not been made' – ibid, s 33(6)(a).
6   Ibid, s 13.
7   This was not always the position under the old law since the unmarried father fell outside the definition of 'parent' or 'guardian' for several purposes including care proceedings and adoption.
8   They can only acquire this by registration as the father, by agreement with the mother or by court order. See Chapter 5 below.
9   Social Security Administration Act 1992, ss 78(6)–(9) and 105, and Children Act 1989, s 3(4)(a). See the comments of SM Cretney 'Defining the Limits of State Intervention: The Child and the Courts' in D Freestone (ed) *Children and the Law* (Hull University Press, 1990) at pp 66–67.

The nature and extent of parental responsibility

Bernard Dickens, in a seminal article published in 1981 on the modern function and limits of parental rights[1], attempted to apply to parents Hohfeld's analysis of legal rights[2]. Hohfeld's thesis was centred on correlative relations so that, for a right to exist, it was necessary to establish the existence of a correlative duty. Applying Hohfeld's analysis, Dickens described the parental 'right' as 'a parental discretion to act regarding a child in a way others have a co-relative duty to permit, or a duty to forbear from preventing'[3]. Yet Dickens recognised that certain powers which parents possess are more a question of duties than of rights. Parents have clear legal duties to provide their children with essential health care, food, shelter and clothing[4] and education[5]. These are absolute duties in the sense that failure to secure these minimal provisions for children may result in legal action against the parents.[6] It is therefore possible to say that children have correlative rights to be provided with these essentials of life. Insofar as parents have rights or powers over these matters, such rights or powers appear to exist only to enable parents to discharge their duties and 'the function of parenthood may appear to be the protection of children against physical, psychological, social and moral harm'[7].

Dickens moved on to consider the area of discretion which parents have once they have complied with these minimal duties. He noted that 'parental duties and related rights appear to be defined by reference not to the positive standard of achieving good for children, but by reference to the negative standard of protecting children from harm'. He concluded that this leaves open 'a parental discretion to employ control over children for purposes not violating children's interests, but equally not advancing their welfare or best interests'[8].

Many examples could be given of this area of parental discretion which is left open once basic obligations to children are met. Thus, while parents cannot elect not to educate their children at all, the *manner* of that education is left largely to parents themselves and parental choice has become an increasingly significant feature of education law[9]. Parents have a completely free hand over religious education. They may bring up their children in any religion or none at all[10]. In the medical sphere, while parents clearly do not have the sole say in matters of life and death[11], they have considerable influence over what non life-saving treatment or

---

1   BM Dickens 'The Modern Function and Limits of Parental Rights' (1981) 97 LQR 462.
2   Hohfeld *Fundamental Legal Conceptions* (Yale University Press, 1919).
3   BM Dickens (above).
4   Children and Young Persons Act 1933, s 1.
5   Education Act 1996, s 7, formerly Education Act 1944, s 36.
6   This could be in the form of criminal or care proceedings or, in the case of education, proceedings for an education supervision order, discussed in Chapter 16 below.
7   BM Dickens (above) at p 464.
8   Ibid.
9   This was very much the hallmark of the policy of the former Conservative administration, embodied particularly in the Education Act 1980 and the Education Reform Act 1988.
10   Discussed in Chapter 16 below.
11   See *Custody of a Minor* 379 NE 2d 1053 (1978) in which the Supreme Court of Massachusetts stated that parental rights 'do not clothe parents with life and death authority over their children'. But they do, it appears, have a significant say. See *Re T (Wardship: Medical Treatment)* [1997] 1 FLR 502; cf *Re A (Conjoined Twins: Medical Treatment)* [2001] 1 FLR 1; and see Chapter 8 below.

elective surgery a child should receive[1]. Whether a baby should be given the MMR vaccine is, for example, an issue which is left entirely to parents.

The concept of 'discretion' conveys the realities of parenthood very well, perhaps better than the notions of 'rights' or 'responsibility'. Ronald Dworkin has used the image of a ring doughnut in analysing the nature of legal discretion. For Dworkin, discretion is a relative concept which can exist meaningfully only 'when someone is in general charged with making decisions subject to standards set by a particular authority'. Accordingly, discretion 'like the hole in a doughnut does not exist except as an area left open by a surrounding belt of restriction'[2]. Dworkin was concerned primarily with the discretions exercised by judges, officials or others charged with public duties, but the imagery of the Dworkinian doughnut may usefully be borrowed. It is not a distortion to describe parents as discharging a public function in the sense that there is an undoubted public interest in the well-being of children[3]. Even if the private law model of the trust is used, as some commentators have done[4], it will be evident that trustees have certain basic duties to the beneficiaries of the trust, but, beyond that, they enjoy significant discretion in the administration of trust funds. Likewise, parents have a large area of discretion to determine all manner of issues related to the upbringing of their children, but they are surrounded by a belt of restriction which requires them to ensure that children are given certain basic protections to meet the necessities of life.

Returning to Dickens' view of parental discretion as a 'right', was he correct to assert that others have a correlative duty to permit, or forbear from preventing, parents from exercising that duty as they see fit? It may be that the answer to this question depends to some extent on who the 'others' are. Dickens had in mind those public and quasi-public officials who are charged with child protection, which in England would largely refer to social services and other welfare agencies[5]. It is fair to say that such agencies cannot intervene, certainly not compulsorily, in family life unless and until parents have failed to achieve the minimum standard of upbringing required by law[6]. It is debatable whether this is also true of the courts since it is, in principle, open to anyone to challenge the exercise of a parental discretion on the basis that it is not in the best interests of the child[7]. But, in practice, a court would be reluctant to entertain such an application unless it thought that what was proposed by a parent would be likely to have a seriously detrimental effect on the child[8]. Dickens himself conceded that it could not be said, even in 1981, that children themselves would necessarily be bound by a duty of tolerance or compliance with parents' wishes, and this is most definitely the case today.

---

1 See Chapter 8 below.
2 RM Dworkin 'Is Law a System of Rules?' in RM Dworkin (ed) *The Philosophy of Law* (Oxford University Press, 1977) at pp 52 et seq.
3 As to which, see J Eekelaar 'What is Critical Family Law?' (1989) 105 LQR 244 at pp 254–258.
4 C Beck, G Glavis, S Glover, M Jenkins and R Nardi 'The Rights of Children: A Trust Model' (1978) 46 *Fordham Law Review* 669; and R Dingwall, J Eekelaar and T Murray *The Protection of Children: State Intervention and Family Life* (Basil Blackwell, 1983) at p 224.
5 Particularly the National Society for the Prevention of Cruelty to Children.
6 Now defined in s 31(2) of the Children Act 1989.
7 Traditionally such 'single issues' have been heard in wardship proceedings but may now be the subject of an application in family proceedings for prohibited steps or specific issue orders.
8 Such as an irreversible procedure like sterilisation. See Chapter 8 below.

The most problematic category of 'others' are those who might be termed 'outsiders', which could include members of the extended family, other interested private individuals, and institutional authorities such as schools or hospitals. How far are such outsiders bound by a legal duty not to interfere with the exercise of parental discretions? There is considerable uncertainty about this. Few would disagree with the straightforward statement that parents have a primary claim to raise their children as they wish[1] and it is superficially attractive to conclude from this that external interference is, prima facie, unlawful. Yet the Court of Appeal has held that parents have no independent 'rights' capable of founding an action in tort for interference with parental rights[2]. Parents may be able to bring an action against outsiders for interferences which are tortious invasions of the child's own rights,[3] but they have no independent avenue of redress. Their former right to sue for loss of a child's services was thought to be based on outmoded proprietorial conceptions of parenthood and was finally abolished in 1982[4]. While it is true that parents can invoke the wardship jurisdiction, or seek a s 8 order, to prevent unwelcome activities or undesirable associations between a child and a third party, they may only obtain relief on the discretionary (and therefore uncertain) basis that these involvements are not in the best interests of the child[5]. This is not at all the same as saying that the third party concerned is in breach of a duty of non-interference with parental rights or discretion. Quite apart from anything else, the court might, in its discretion, uphold the view of the outsider and not that of the parent[6].

We might wish to conclude from this that parental discretions do not give rise to 'rights', at least in the sense of claim rights[7] giving rise to correlative duties – except perhaps against the State. Parental discretion is really a 'privilege' or 'liberty' in the Hohfeldian sense. In Hohfeld's scheme of jural relations, a privilege is the opposite of a duty and the correlative of the inelegantly phrased 'no-right'. In simple language, what this means in the case of parents is that when they are exercising their discretions, they are not subject to legal duties, but, equally, outsiders have no right to require parents not to exercise them as they choose. While parents may have difficulty founding a legal action to prevent dealings between their children and third parties, it can at least be said with

---

1 This was clearly the view of the Law Commission: see fn 1 at p 115 above.

2 *F v Wirral Metropolitan Borough Council* discussed in A Bainham 'Interfering with Parental Responsibility: A New Challenge for the Law of Torts?' (1990) 3 JCL 3. In limited circumstances, the crime of child abduction under the Child Abduction Act 1984, s 2 might be committed by an outsider removing a child from the lawful control of parents.

3 These will usually be physical interferences which constitute trespass to the child's person in the form of assault, battery or false imprisonment. Parents may also commit torts, or crimes, against their own children where they indulge in physical interferences with them which exceed the bounds of reasonable parental control. See *R v D* [1984] AC 778 and *R v Rahman* [1985] 81 Cr App R 349. The wardship jurisdiction might be used to intervene in such cases as it was in *Re KR (Abduction: Forcible Removal by Parents)* [1999] 2 FLR 542 where a 16-year-old Sikh girl had been forcibly taken to India by her parents with a view to an arranged marriage. Her elder sister successfully secured her return to England in wardship proceedings.

4 Law Reform (Miscellaneous Provisions) Act 1970, s 5 and Administration of Justice Act 1982, s 2.

5 See NV Lowe and RAH White *Wards of Court* (2nd edn) (Barry Rose/Kluwer, 1986) at ch 12.

6 As happened in *Re D (A Minor) (Wardship: Sterilisation)* [1976] Fam 185 where the view of an educational psychologist was upheld.

7 See fn 2 at p 111 above.

confidence that outsiders have no legal claim to prevent parents from determining issues of upbringing[1].

These principles must now be qualified by the added complication that the child himself may well have a view on what is proposed.

Parent–child conflicts

It is now clear, both at common law and under a variety of statutory provisions, that children have the capacity to perform certain acts and take certain decisions[2]. Sometimes this is dependent upon them having attained a certain age and sometimes it falls to be determined by the test of maturity propounded by the House of Lords in the *Gillick* case. That case will be discussed in depth later when medical issues are considered[3]. The present concern is to explore the interaction between children's capacity for decision-making and parental discretion[4].

The critical question is whether the child's acquisition of capacity, whether through age or maturity, *terminates* any parental claim to involvement, or whether the child's capacity and parental discretion co-exist in some form until the child reaches maturity. The traditional view was that parental rights 'dwindle' as the child approaches majority but at least survive until then. The older the child, the less likely it has been that a court would enforce parental control against his wishes[5]. But, although it was not always enforceable, it was thought that parental control continued to exist even where it amounted, in the case of older teenagers, to no more than a right to give guidance or advice[6].

A radical interpretation of *Gillick* would suggest that any right of parental control is completely eclipsed by the child's ability to act for himself[7]. Such a view relies heavily on the speech of Lord Scarman in which he said that 'the parental right yields to the child's right to make his own decisions when he reaches a sufficient understanding and intelligence to be capable of making up his own mind on the matter requiring decision'[8]. But Lord Scarman himself appeared to acknowledge that parental rights would *survive* until majority and he was in general agreement with Lord Fraser. Lord Fraser adopted a noticeably more cautious approach to the inter-relationship of adolescent capabilities and parental control. He evidently took the view that maturity alone should not be enough to justify the provision of contraceptives to 'under-age' girls without parental knowledge or consent[9]. Lord Fraser was especially concerned that, in every case, the medical personnel should attempt to persuade the girl to allow parental involvement in the decision, although it has been suggested that failure

---

1   Anyone wishing to do so would have the onus of bringing a legal action and seeking to persuade the court to overrule the parental view applying the welfare principle.

2   See Chapter 15 below for a further discussion.

3   In Chapter 8 below.

4   For these purposes it is assumed that the ratio of *Gillick* is sufficiently wide to govern a range of issues other than contraception or medical issues.

5   See *Krishnan v Sutton London Borough Council* [1970] Ch 181 and the views of Lord Denning MR in *Hewer v Bryant* [1970] 1 QB 357 at 369.

6   It could be argued that the adolescent child has a right of recipience to this parental guidance and advice. See A Bainham 'Growing Up in Britain: Adolescence in the post-*Gillick* Era' (1992) *Juridical Review* 155.

7   See J Eekelaar 'The Eclipse of Parental Rights' (1986) 102 LQR 4.

8   [1986] 1 AC 112 at 186.

9   In all, he laid down five preconditions. See Chapter 8 below.

to do so might be merely a breach of professional ethics rather than unlawful[1]. Taken as a whole, the majority opinion in *Gillick* did appear to recognise the potential value of parents' participation in adolescent decision-making but accorded *priority* to the views of a competent adolescent. On this interpretation, the decision could be viewed as supportive of a form of participatory or inclusive decision-making which involves parents, children and third parties (in the *Gillick* case, the medical profession). Further, it might be concluded that the final decision rests with neither parents nor children but with the third party with whom they are dealing and that they each have only consultative rights[2]. This might provide a way of reconciling the continuing responsibilities and discretions of parents, particularly to provide advice and guidance, with the gradual legal emancipation of children although later Court of Appeal decisions represent something of a retreat from *Gillick* in that they appear to support the right of outsiders to act on parental authority in the face of objection by the competent child[3].

PARENTS AND CHILDREN: BALANCING RIGHTS AND INTERESTS

It now seems clear that both children and parents possess rights and that the task for any legal system is to achieve a proper balance between them. Put in terms of interests, it can at least be acknowledged that children and parents have separate or independent interests which ought to be recognised in law. At the heart of the jurisprudential debate is the question of when the rights and interests of children and parents can truly be regarded as distinct and when they ought to be conflated. This is a problem deeply embedded in the welfare principle itself. For if the welfare of children is paramount and the sole consideration, the separate interests of parents (if they exist at all) are not only subordinate, they are actually irrelevant. This apparent denial of an independent parental interest cannot withstand scrutiny, as we have seen, in the context of human rights.

Alexander McCall Smith has produced an ingenious analysis which attempts to establish two independent categories of parental rights, namely 'child-centred parental rights' and 'parent-centred parental rights'[4]. McCall Smith's thesis is that certain powers which parents have are 'child-centred' in that their sole or principal purpose is to advance the welfare of their child. Other powers which parents have are 'parent-centred' since they are exercised predominantly for the benefit of the parent, although they may incidentally benefit the child. Into the first category McCall Smith would put parental restrictions on the hours when a child is allowed out of the home since these are intended to safeguard the child

---

1 J Eekelaar (above).
2 A Bainham (above) at pp 172 et seq.
3 See *Re R (A Minor) (Wardship: Consent to Treatment)* [1992] Fam 11, *Re W (A Minor) (Medical Treatment: Court's Jurisdiction)* [1993] Fam 64, and Chapter 8 below.
4 A McCall Smith 'Is Anything Left of Parental Rights?' in E Sutherland and A McCall Smith (eds) *Family Rights: Family Law and Medical Advance* (Edinburgh University Press, 1990) at p 4.

from harm[1]. Into the second category he would put the rights to determine the manner of the child's religious upbringing and secular education since these relate to the basic moral issue of the sort of child the parents wish to have. Thus, for McCall Smith, the parent-centred right is an area of control in which 'the parent has a wide range of discretion to pursue goals which society as a whole might find undesirable, but which it will tolerate'. He also includes within this, the right to the 'society' of the child, by which he is presumably referring to the former right of access (now contact). While he accepts that there is also a right of children to parental society, he sees this as a distinct and independent right. The key to identifying independent rights is, according to this argument, to focus on the beneficiary of the alleged right.

There is considerable force in what McCall Smith has to say. The right of access (now contact), although often regarded as a right of the child[2], is equally a crucial benefit to the parent concerned – evidenced by the mass of litigation which the issue has generated. Parents and children might both therefore be regarded as having rights to their mutual society. And it is in precisely this area that the courts started to edge cautiously away from the exclusivity of the welfare principle towards the recognition of independent parental rights or interests[3]. They have, as will be appreciated, been obliged to do so since an open denial of their existence, especially vis-à-vis the State, would not conform with the UK's obligations under the ECHR[4].

Increasingly, it is likely that the trend will be to admit the co-existence of independent rights and interests for children and parents whilst emphasising the *primacy* of the rights and interests of children[5]. This has led to the suggestion that the welfare principle should itself be reformulated as a principle 'giving *priority* to children's rights over those of parents (or others) in cases where they cannot be reconciled'[6]. In the final analysis this would probably represent a more realistic and theoretically accurate approach than that which attempts to subsume everything within the notion of parental responsibility and the welfare role of the courts. It would moreover chime better with the formulation of the welfare commitment in the UNCRC and with the notion of balancing rights under the ECHR.

This does rather make the assumption that children's interests *should* always be given precedence over adult interests and this is certainly open to question. An alternative approach might be to devise criteria for determining in specific instances whether the interests of children or parents (or other adults) should be

---

1   In fact it could be argued that this is not a good example since the restrictions imposed by parents may reflect their own value judgements about such matters as the kind of company they wish their children to keep.

2   The change in emphasis from access as a parental right to access as a child's right is usually traced back to the view of Wrangham J in *M v M (Child: Access)* [1973] 2 All ER 81.

3   See fn 3 at p 115 above.

4   As to which see *Re KD (A Minor) (Ward: Termination of Access)* [1988] AC 806, discussed by J Eekelaar in 'The Wardship Jurisdiction, Children's Welfare and Parents Rights' (1991) 107 LQR 368 at pp 387–388, and *Hokkanen v Finland* (1995) 19 EHRR 139.

5   But see *Re R (A Minor)* [1992] Fam 11 and *Re W* [1992] 3 WLR 758 discussed in Chapter 8 below which are rather against this trend.

6   J Eekelaar (above) at p 389.

preferred[1]. The conclusion would not be automatic that children's interests come first and others' second, or vice versa. Instead, there would be an exploration of which interest should be regarded as the more significant or serious. That interest might then be designated as the primary interest and given priority[2]. Matters can become yet further complicated when the wider family interest is thrown into the balance since children and parents are not merely individuals with independent interests but members of a family unit. It may be that the family as a whole has a collective interest which in some cases should outweigh the interests of its individual constituent members[3]. It is this position of the child in various family contexts which is the subject of Part II of the book.

---

1 See generally A Bainham 'Non-Intervention and Judicial Paternalism' in P Birks (ed) *The Frontiers of Liability*, Vol 1 (Oxford University Press, 1994), pp 161, 173–174. And see John Eekelaar's recent analysis of what might happen if we were to abandon the welfare principle as we know it, in J Eekelaar 'Beyond the Welfare Principle' [2002] CFLQ 237.

2 Ibid.

3 Discussed further in A Bainham in '"Honour Thy Father and Thy Mother": Children's Rights and Children's Duties' in G Douglas and L Sebba (eds) *Children's Rights and Traditional Values* (Dartmouth, 1998).

PART II
CHILDREN AND FAMILIES

The chapters in Part II are all concerned primarily with legal questions which relate to children's relationships with their families or carers. While a large number of children continue to experience childhood within the conventional family based on marriage, increasing numbers of children spend all or part of their childhood in households in which they are unrelated genetically to one or more of their carers. Many children also spend a substantial part of their childhood in one-parent households. Part II considers the legal issues surrounding the various kinds of family arrangements in which children may be raised.

Chapter 4 begins by looking at what might have been considered the 'typical' family centred on marriage and addresses the issues for children which arise on marriage breakdown and divorce. Chapter 5 examines the law's attitude to the very large number of children born to parents who are not married to each other. Chapter 6 looks at the different family arrangements in which children may live where one or both natural parents are, for whatever reason, not raising their children. The expression 'social family' is used as an umbrella term to embrace guardians, step-parents, foster-parents and families in which children are raised by relatives and others. Adoption is not considered in this chapter since the subject is of sufficient importance to merit a separate chapter (Chapter 7). The remaining two chapters in Part II deal with two of the most significant spheres of parental responsibility which have, particularly in recent years, been fertile areas of dispute. Chapter 8 considers medical decision-making which has often been the site of the most difficult questions concerning the interrelationship of children's rights and parents' rights and responsibilities. Chapter 9 discusses the principles which govern the ownership and management of children's property and responsibility for their financial support. The child support legislation radically adjusted the balance between the State and the family and has been the subject of further recent reform which, to an extent, has readjusted the balance.

Chapter 4

THE MARRIED FAMILY AND DIVORCE

INTRODUCTION

Married parents

The birth of a child within marriage gives rise to an automatic legal status for both father and mother. Historically, the married father was the sole guardian of his children to the exclusion of the mother, and it was not until the Guardianship Act 1973 that the mother became automatically entitled to equal rights and authority over the children. The Children Act 1989 now provides that, where a child's father and mother were married to each other at the time of the child's birth, each has parental responsibility for the child[1]. Being married to each other at the time of the birth is given an extended meaning for these purposes in accordance with the Family Law Reform Act 1987[2]. The broad effect of that legislation is that certain children will be *regarded* as being born to married parents. These include some children of void marriages, legitimated and adopted children, and children who are treated as legitimate. The legal significance of being born to parents who are not married to each other is explored later.

Proof of parentage

Proof of parentage within marriage is usually established by the fact of birth and by the application of legal presumptions. Maternity is almost always established by the fact of parturition[3], although it has already been noted that the definition of biological motherhood may have to be re-evaluated in certain cases of assisted reproduction[4]. The determination of paternity within marriage is usually just a matter of applying the legal presumption that any child born to the wife is the child of her husband[5]. But this may be rebutted under s 26 of the Family Law Reform Act 1969 by evidence which establishes, on the balance of probabilities, that the husband is not the father[6]. The test is less exacting than the former common law requirement that the matter be established beyond reasonable doubt. The courts have wavered in their attitudes to the amount of evidence required to rebut the presumption[7], but the availability of the DNA technique now means that paternity may be established virtually conclusively, thus overcoming the limitations of conventional blood tests. It is now provided that 'scientific

---

1 Section 2(1).
2 Section 2(3), incorporating, by reference, s 1 of the Family Law Reform Act 1987.
3 *The Ampthill Peerage* [1977] AC 547.
4 See Chapter 3 above.
5 Encapsulated in the maxim *Pater est quem nuptiae demonstrant.*
6 In *Kroon v The Netherlands* (1994) 19 EHRR 263 a Dutch law which prevented anyone other than the husband himself from seeking to rebut the presumption was found to violate the Convention. See further Chapter 5.
7 *S v S; W v Official Solicitor* [1972] AC 24. Cf *Serio v Serio* (1983) FLR 756, *W v K (Proof of Paternity)* [1988] 1 FLR 86 and *F v Child Support Agency* [1999] 2 FLR 244.

tests' are to be made available to determine parentage[1]. As from 1 April 2001, the courts have had power to direct that samples of bodily fluid or bodily tissue other than blood be used for scientific analysis. The reality is that, where the husband does not deny paternity, and no other man asserts that *he* is the father, the husband will be treated in law as the father whatever may be the true biological position. Whether this is consistent with the increasingly recognised right of the child to knowledge of his or her biological origins is a matter to which we return in Chapter 5.

What happens where a married woman, while pregnant, divorces? At common law, it appears that the courts will continue to apply the *pater est* presumption, provided that the child is born within the normal period of gestation. Some jurisdictions specify precisely the number of days within which the child must be born following divorce for the presumption to continue to apply. In Chile, for example, the period is 300 days[2]. In Estonia it is 10 months[3]. The English courts have also applied the presumption where the mother has remarried before the birth of the child[4]. In this situation, there may be a *clash* of presumptions. The child would be presumed the child of the first husband (H1), but birth after the second marriage would also trigger a presumption of paternity of the second husband (H2). It seems likely that if the mother and H2 jointly register the birth with H2 named as the father, and if H1 does not dispute this, then the presumption arising from registration of the birth will prevail. If H1 should dispute the paternity of H2, the matter would nowadays be likely to be settled by a direction for DNA testing[5].

Parental responsibility

The general philosophy has been observed that the primary responsibility for raising children rests with parents. And, despite the apparent neutrality of the welfare principle as between the competing claims of parents and non-parents, the courts have, from time to time, appeared to attach a premium to the natural blood tie[6]. In *Re D (Care: Natural Parent Presumption)*[7] the Court of Appeal was quite explicit about this in allowing the appeal of a natural father against the judge's order that a boy in care should be placed with his maternal grandmother rather than his father. The Court of Appeal decided the issue on the basis that it

---

1   Family Law Reform Act 1987, s 23(1), amending the Family Law Reform Act 1969, s 20(1) and (2).

2   See I Pardo de Carvallo 'Identifying Parentage and the Methods of Proof in the New Chilean Law' in A Bainham (ed) *The International Survey of Family Law (2000 Edition)* (Family Law, 2000) at p 83.

3   K Kullerkupp 'Family Law in Estonia' in A Bainham (ed) (above) at p 95.

4   *Re Overbury (deceased)* [1954] Ch 122. It should be noted, however, that this remarkable case arose from a birth which took place in 1869 and which occurred some eight months after the death of H1 and just two months after the mother's second marriage to H2. The case for allowing the first presumption to apply in such circumstances was a strong one, especially in the social conditions which prevailed in the mid-nineteenth century. Whether the preference for the first presumption would be appropriate in the very changed social circumstances of the early twenty-first century and in the context of divorce is questionable.

5   See Chapter 5.

6   For a modern example see, particularly, the views of Fox LJ and Waite J in *Re K (A Minor) (Ward: Care and Control)* [1990] 1 WLR 431.

7   [1999] 1 FLR 134.

should consider whether there were any compelling factors which overrode the prima facie right of a child to an upbringing by its surviving parent[1]. The assumption is often made that the responsibility of parenthood is a natural phenomenon and that the very fact of biological parentage, or at least *presumed* biological parentage within marriage, gives rise to moral obligations which are then translated into legal obligations. Whilst it is evident that most legal systems do place automatic legal obligations on parents to care for their children, the pre-existing moral basis for such obligations is elusive.

Eekelaar has convincingly demonstrated that contractarian theories of moral obligation (which rely heavily on the principle that the participants in a social contact are motivated at least in part by self-interest) cannot adequately account for parental obligations to children[2]. Eekelaar found the true basis for these moral obligations to children in the non-contractarian theory of human flourishing propounded by John Finnis[3]. According to this, there are moral obligations on *everyone* to respect the well-being of others, including children. This background moral duty may, according to Eekelaar, give rise to *special* obligations by reason of the social roles in which certain individuals are cast. Thus, the duty to care for children arises from the 'conjunction' of the general duty to promote human flourishing and the independent moral duty to comply with the social practice of particular societies – in this case the social practice that a *particular* responsibility for children should be placed on biological parents[4].

Responsibility is automatic

This automatic imposition of responsibility, which carries considerable powers of control over children, is not accompanied by any attempt to discover in the first instance whether individual parents are able and/or willing to perform the task. Whilst it is generally accepted that raising a child is no easy matter, there is self-evidently no regulatory system for biological parents such as applies to adoption and, to a lesser extent, certain other substitute care arrangements[5]. The State assumes that the natural family will properly discharge the obligation of child-rearing unless and until there is clear evidence to the contrary. It is therefore tempting to agree with the sentiments expressed by a Washington court that 'fortunately for the preservation of the human species ... a lot of people who would rate poorly on any scale of parental prospects have done rather well at it when confronted by the reality of a baby, in a crib, in the home ...'[6]. It has, nonetheless, been suggested that a system of licensing for parents would at least be feasible, using a variety of predictive screening techniques, the purpose of which would be to pre-empt the worst cases of child abuse or neglect by identifying in

---

1   For a critique of the decision see J Fortin '*Re D (Care: Natural Parent Presumption)*. Is blood really thicker than water?' [1999] CFLQ 435. The decision was followed by Johnson J in *Re D (Residence: Natural Parent)* [1999] 2 FLR 1023 where he preferred the claims of the natural mother over those of a paternal aunt with whom the child had temporarily stayed.

2   J Eekelaar 'Are Parents Morally Obliged to Care for Their Children?' (1991) 11 *Oxford Journal of Legal Studies* 340. The most well-known of modern contractarian theories is J Rawls *A Theory of Justice* (Harvard University Press, 1972).

3   J Finnis *Natural Law and Natural Rights* (1980), discussed by Eekelaar (above) at pp 348–349.

4   Eekelaar (above) at p 351.

5   See Chapters 6, 7 and 10 below.

6   In *Re Welfare of May* 14 Wash App 765 (1976) at pp 768–769, 545 P.2d 25 (1976).

advance 'very bad' parents[1]. It has even been argued that it might be possible to formulate a concept of 'responsible parenthood' which might generate an obligation not to have children or not to continue a pregnancy in certain circumstances[2]. Whilst no such approach exists in England, or would be likely to command much support, it has been the case for some time that legal powers have been utilised to remove certain babies from their parents at birth[3]. But such cases are exceptional and do not generally detract from the central principle that the status of parent gives rise to an automatic legal right and duty to care for the child.

Parenthood is for life

It is important to appreciate that being a parent is a legal status. As such, *all* the incidents of parental responsibility devolve automatically on the married parent. It has been said that parenthood is a package deal[4]. It is not open to a parent to pick and choose between the various responsibilities attaching to parental status. Parenthood is, in this respect, like marriage itself, the condition of belonging to a class of persons in relation to whom the law assigns particular rights and obligations[5]. This status is not lost except through the ultimate step of adoption (or, much more rarely, a 'parental order' under s 30 of the HFEA 1990) – a position neatly encapsulated in the catchphrase 'parenthood is for life'.

Parental responsibility cannot be transferred

An aspect of the lifelong nature of parenthood is that the legal status of parent and the parental responsibility which goes with it is 'non-transferable'[6]. While parents may delegate the exercise of parental responsibility, they may not surrender or transfer it[7]. Thus, they may arrange for someone to take temporary care of their children, or meet some aspect of parental responsibility, but this does not result in the temporary carer acquiring parental responsibility or in the parent losing it. Such an arrangement may be made with someone who already has parental responsibility as well as with someone who does not[8]. The former situation could cover married parents who might agree that one of them should take all the

---

1   H La Follette 'Licensing Parents' (1980) 9 *Philosophy and Public Affairs* 182, and C Pap Mangel 'Licensing Parents: How Feasible?' (1988) 22 Fam LQ 17. Cf Sandmire and Wald 'Licensing Parents – A Response to Claudia Mangel's proposal' (1990) 24 Fam LQ 53.
2   M Freeman 'Do Children Have the Right not to be Born?' in *The Moral Status of Children* (Martinus Nijhoff, 1997), ch 9.
3   As to which, see MDA Freeman 'Removing Babies at Birth: A Questionable Practice' [1980] Fam Law 131 and, generally, Chapter 12 below.
4   A McCall Smith 'Is Anything Left of Parental Rights?' in Sutherland and McCall Smith (eds) *Family Rights* (Edinburgh University Press, 1990) p 4 at p 7.
5   See Sir C Allen 'Status and Capacity' (1930) 46 LQR 277, especially at p 288.
6   This is subject only to the right of a parent to consent to the ultimate step of adoption of the child or to an order under s 30 of the Human Fertilisation and Embryology Act 1990, as to which see Chapters 7 and 6 respectively.
7   Children Act 1989, s 2(9). This was also the case at common law. See *Vansittart v Vansittart* (1858) 2 De G&J 249. The unmarried mother may, however, agree to share parental responsibility with the father (who does not otherwise have it through the process of birth registration), and a parent may agree to share it with a step-parent under an amendment to s 4 of the Children Act 1989 introduced by the Adoption and Children Act 2002. See further Chapter 6 below.
8   Ibid, s 2(9) and (10).

decisions on some aspect of upbringing, for example, education. It might be particularly appropriate to come to some definite arrangement where, for example, one parent is frequently absent from the home, perhaps for employment reasons. Where the delegate is a person without parental responsibility, that person will have the legal power (and arguably the duty) to 'do what is reasonable in all the circumstances of the case for the purpose of safeguarding or promoting the child's welfare'[1]. Yet even in these temporary arrangements the parent retains parental responsibility and may be held liable for 'any failure to meet any part of his parental responsibility for the child concerned'[2]. The natural parent could thus be civilly or criminally liable for any harm caused to the child arising from his failure to ensure satisfactory care[3].

SHARING PARENTAL RESPONSIBILITY IN MARRIAGE

Potential for sharing

Since both married parents have parental responsibility, they must share it. The Children Act 1989 confirms that parental responsibility may be held contemporaneously by more than one person[4]. Whilst this is self-evident in the case of married parents, it should be remembered that responsibility may also be shared between parents and non-parents, such as foster-parents or guardians. Indeed, it may be shared in a triangular relationship, as where a mother and step-father obtain a shared residence order but the divorced father retains his own parental responsibility. Since parental responsibility is not lost because someone else acquires it[5], the potential for a multiplicity of sharing arrangements is considerable. The precise legal effect of sharing parental responsibility is, therefore, a matter of some theoretical and practical importance. In particular, the regime which applies during marriage will be carried over into the post-divorce situation unless it is specifically altered by a court order.

What is involved in sharing?

In simple terms, the statutory scheme provides for *joint* and *several* parental responsibility. While both parents have equal powers and responsibilities, they may act independently as well as jointly in exercising them, and they are not obliged to consult each other before doing so. No doubt in a functioning marriage, all serious issues affecting the children will be discussed and real attempts will be made to reach agreement. This is not a legal requirement, but whether there is a legal right of consultation where parents separate or divorce is not wholly clear. This issue is discussed below.

The Children Act provides that where parental responsibility is shared between two or more people 'each of them may act alone and without the other (or others)

---

1 Section 3(5).
2 Section 2(11).
3 This issue is explored from a comparative perspective in C McIvor 'Expelling the Myth of the Parental Duty to Rescue' [2000] CFLQ 229, and see further Chapter 15 below.
4 Section 2(5).
5 Section 2(6).

in meeting that responsibility'[1]. There are just two limitations on this right of independent action. The first is where statute requires the consent of more than one person[2]. The second is that parental responsibility may never be exercised in a way which is incompatible with a court order[3]. The best example of the first limitation is adoption, which requires the consent of all parents or guardians[4]. The consent of others with parental responsibility[5] and local authorities who have a care order[6] is not required. Statute also imposes certain automatic restraints on changing a child's surname unilaterally or taking him out of the country. In both of these instances, the consent of all those with parental responsibility is normally required, unless the court orders otherwise[7].

Both of these restraints on independent action continue to cause difficulty in the modern law. So far as changing the child's surname is concerned there has long been an *automatic* restraint on unilateral action deriving originally from the concept of the residual rights of the natural guardian. While the courts have vacillated to some extent in their views of the importance of children's names, they have been consistent in upholding the prohibition[8]. They even did so on one occasion in a case in which three older children were all in favour of the change[9]. There was apparently some doubt following the Children Act about whether the automatic prohibition continued to apply otherwise than in the context specifically envisaged by the legislation, namely where a residence order has been made[10]. The suggestion was bizarre since, if correct, it would have meant that the mother without a residence order in her favour would have been in a stronger legal position in this respect than the mother who had one! The argument was rightly scotched by Holman J in *Re PC (Change of Surname)*[11], who held that where two or more persons have parental responsibility for a child, one of them may lawfully effect a change of surname only if everyone with parental responsibility consents. Where the parents are unmarried it is, in what has been until recently the majority of cases and will now be a minority, only the mother who holds parental responsibility (unless the father has taken steps to acquire it) and she alone is entitled to choose the name of the child[12]. It would seem, however, that, if she then wishes to change it, this would require agreement with the father or the

---

1 Section 2(7).
2 Ibid.
3 Section 2(8).
4 Adoption and Children Act 2002, s 47(2). This is subject to the court's power to dispense with consent on specified grounds. See Chapter 7 below.
5 Section 12(3).
6 Section 33(6).
7 Section 13; Child Abduction Act 1984, s 1, discussed in Chapter 17 below.
8 The leading authority before the Children Act was *W v A (Child: Surname)* [1981] Fam 114.
9 *Re B (Change of Surname)* [1996] 1 FLR 791. Cf *Re C (Change of Surname)* [1998] 1 FLR 549 where the children were younger (aged 7 and 8) and where the 'non-residential' mother failed to prevent an order that the 'residential' father be allowed to give his surname to the children along with the other members of his household.
10 Section 13(1)(a).
11 [1997] 2 FLR 730. But for a very different perspective, see J Eekelaar 'Do Parents Have a Duty to Consult?' (1998) 114 LQR 337. See also A Bond 'Reconstructing families – changing children's surnames' [1998] CFLQ 17, and M Ogle 'What's in a Name?' [1998] Fam Law 80.
12 *Dawson v Wearmouth* [1997] 2 FLR 629.

authority of the court[1]. *Re PC* (above) also illustrates that where there has been an unlawful change of name it does not necessarily follow that a reversion to the previous name will be in the children's best interests. The result in this case, applying the welfare principle, was to preserve the status quo. Orders were made allowing the children to continue to be known by their new name but prohibiting the mother from taking steps to 'cause, encourage or permit any person or body to use the new surname without the prior consent of the father or the court'.

Reported cases concerning disputes over children's names have continued unabated in recent years[2] perhaps indicating, as Gillian Douglas has pointed out, that 'disputes over surnames are really concerned with determining the child's "affiliation" with a particular parent'. And she continues, 'it is no surprise ... that parents may hold very strong, conflicting views on the child's surname where their own relationship has ended and they are no longer seen to constitute an "intact" family group'[3]. Not surprising, then, that Mr Mark Dawson strongly objected to the child he had fathered being registered with the surname of the mother's former husband Tony Wearmouth[4]. While upholding the Court of Appeal decision that the judge had erred in ordering a change of the surname to Dawson, two of the Law Lords clearly felt the significance of the name as a means of linking a child to the biological father. As Lord Jauncey put it, 'the surname is ... a biological label which tells the world at large that the blood of the name flows in its veins' and, in this case, the child had 'not a drop of Wearmouth blood in his veins'[5]. Neither has the significance of the name been lost on the international community. As we have seen, the question of the name is closely bound up with the child's right to an identity and to preservation of identity and family relations under the UNCRC[6].

At the same time, the courts have occasionally found it necessary to warn that too much importance should not be attached to the single issue of the child's name. In *Re R (Surname: Using Both Parents')*[7] Hale LJ offered the view that it was a matter of great sadness that it was so often assumed that fathers needed the outward and visible link of a shared surname in order to retain their relationship with and commitment to their child. For her, the crucial point was rather that it was important for there to be transparency about a child's parentage and for it to be acknowledged that a child always had two parents.

Two more recent decisions deal with novel issues in relation to children's names. *Re S (Change of Names: Cultural Factors)*[8] concerned a child born to a

---

1 At least there were dicta to this effect in the House of Lords in *Dawson v Wearmouth* [1997] 2 FLR 629. See also *Re W, Re A, Re B (Change of Name)* [1999] 2 FLR 930 where similar obiter remarks were made.

2 See, for example, *Re T (Change of Surname)* [1998] 2 FLR 620, *Re C (Change of Surname)* [1998] 2 FLR 656, *A v Y (Child's Surname)* [1999] 2 FLR 5, and *Re A (Change of Name)* [2003] 2 FLR 1. In this last case, the Court of Appeal allowed the mother's appeal against a change of name since her choice of her former husband's name was found to be in accordance with Muslim law. The child had been conceived within four months of the divorce.

3 G Douglas *An Introduction to Family Law* (2nd edn) (Oxford University Press, 2004) at p 88.

4 *Dawson v Wearmouth* [1997] 2 FLR 629.

5 For further commentary on this decision, see A Bainham 'In the Name of the Father?' [1999] CLJ 492.

6 Articles 7 and 8; and see Chapter 2 above.

7 [2001] 2 FLR 1358.

8 [2001] 2 FLR 1005.

Muslim mother and a Sikh father. The child had been given Sikh names but, following divorce, the mother wished to change his name to a Muslim name, arguing that socially and culturally the Muslim community would never accept a child with Sikh names. Wilson J held that in order to be accepted into the Muslim community it was necessary that the child be known on a day-to-day basis by Muslim names. Accordingly, he should be registered with Muslim names at schools and a health practice. However, nothing more than this should be formally done by deed poll since it was important to preserve the reality of his parentage and Sikh heritage.

This distinction between the formal and informal use of names surfaced again in *Re H (Child's Name: First Name)*[1], the first reported case to consider a dispute over the child's first names, as opposed to surname. Here the married parents separated when the mother was six weeks pregnant. The father then reappeared at the birth and, following a discussion with the mother in hospital about names, registered the child without her approval with the names of his choice. The mother then tried to register her own choice of name but the Registrar took the position that the first registration only was effective and that the mother's should be cancelled. The issue was whether the mother could use her own choice of names with educational and other authorities. Allowing her appeal, the Court of Appeal held that there was nothing to prevent the mother from using her choice of names in this way provided that it was recognised that the child had an immutable series of names by statutory registration. The court went on to say that, unlike surnames, which denoted the family to which the child belonged, a number of given names might legitimately be used over the course of a child's life.

The question of leave to take the children out of the jurisdiction has been the subject of a great deal of litigation both before and after the Children Act. We return to this issue in the context of the law governing child abduction because of its obvious relationship with that matter[2].

The right of independent action represents something of a change from the position before the Children Act. Under the old law it was provided that parents might exercise parental rights alone but this was thought to be qualified by a separate provision which restricted unilateral action where another joint holder of parental rights had signified prior disapproval of the proposed action[3]. There was some doubt whether this encompassed the situation of married parents or was confined to non-parental holders of parental rights. What is clear is that there was never any statutory duty of consultation between parents. The Law Commission was concerned with the practicalities of daily living and thought it would be unworkable to require parents to consult with each other[4]. There is evidently force in this argument with respect to the myriad of trivial actions parents perform on a daily basis, but its wisdom may be doubted where major or irreversible decisions are concerned. It is also questionable whether the scheme can work where parental responsibility is shared by two or more persons who do not live in the same household[5].

---

1   [2002] 1 FLR 973.
2   See Chapter 17.
3   Guardianship Act 1973, s 1(1); and the Children Act 1975, s 85(3).
4   Law Com Report No 172 *Guardianship and Custody* (1988) at para 2.10.
5   Such as, for example, a surviving parent and an appointed guardian, a natural parent and a
    foster-parent, or two divorced parents.

Disputes over children during marriage

It is unlikely that serious disagreements over children between married partners will as such lead to litigation. The former provision in the Guardianship Act 1973, which enabled a parent to bring such disagreements before the courts, was seldom, if ever, utilised[1]. The reason is obvious. Where disputes over children reach the point of litigation, it is a virtual certainty that the parents will be seeking divorce or some other more limited matrimonial relief, or a more comprehensive order relating to the care of the children[2]. This remains the case under the Children Act. Most s 8 orders are likely to be made in the context of divorce, but it should be noted that the court has jurisdiction to regulate any aspect of a child's upbringing during the marriage. It could do so, for example, on a freestanding application for such an order, where one of the spouses is seeking financial relief under the Domestic Proceedings and Magistrates' Courts Act 1978 or in wardship proceedings, all of which are 'family proceedings'[3].

The position of third parties

The effect of independent exercises of parental responsibility on third parties is an important practical matter. Since a single holder of parental responsibility may act alone, it follows that outsiders such as schools, hospitals or churches may safely deal with him or her alone without risking any legal liability. It would seem that this applies even where the third party is aware of a disagreement between those with parental responsibility, although the prudence of going ahead with a course of action in these circumstances is questionable[4]. But, in principle, the third party is free to choose between two equally valid yet discordant views and is, indeed, *obliged* to choose between them even if this involves inactivity. An added complication in the case of an older child is that the child may be '*Gillick*-competent' so that a third party could lawfully choose to comply with the wishes of a competent child rather than those of one or both parents[5].

Preventive court orders

In theory, at least, no *legal* (as opposed to practical) advantage is derived from having the physical care of the child. The non-resident[6] parent has just as much authority and responsibility as the parent with day-to-day care, but will inevitably have less opportunity of exercising it. This may well be an area in which theory and

---

1   Section 1(3).
2   Under the old law, this might have been under the Matrimonial Causes Act 1973, the Domestic Proceedings and Magistrates' Courts Act 1978 or the Guardianship of Minors Act 1971.
3   'Family proceedings' are defined in s 8(3) and (4) of the Children Act, discussed in Chapter 2 above.
4   Technically, for example, a doctor would be acting lawfully in performing an abortion on a minor which was supported by one parent but opposed by the other; but the more sensible course in this situation would be to seek the authority of the court. For further discussion, see J Herring 'Children's Abortion Rights' (1997) 5 *Medical Law Review* 257.
5   Although this proposition is more doubtful following the Court of Appeal decisions in *Re R (A Minor) (Wardship: Consent to Treatment)* [1992] Fam 11 and *Re W (A Minor) (Medical Treatment: Court's Jurisdiction)* [1993] Fam 64, discussed in Chapter 8 below.
6   The term 'non-resident' is used here in a non-technical sense to describe all parents who are not primary carers. It is not intended to describe only those situations in which a residence order has been made in favour of the primary carer.

practice diverge[1]. Where one parent wishes to assert superior control over any particular area of a child's upbringing, it will be necessary for that parent to seek a court order. The other parent will then be precluded from exercising responsibility inconsistently with the order, although this may lead to some awkward questions of interpretation[2].

DIVORCE AND CHILDREN

A problem?

The United Kingdom is the divorce capital of Europe with, as noted in Chapter 1, around 150,000 divorces per annum. These figures are bound to give rise to concern about the interests of the very large numbers of children involved and the possible adverse effects on them. It is frequently said, particularly in the media, that divorce has a harmful effect on children. Is this true and, if so, what (if anything) can the legal system do about it?

There is now clear evidence from a large number of research projects that there are negative associations between parental separation or divorce and the development of children and young adults[3]. No summary can do justice to this extensive body of research, but Martin Richards has described these associations as follows:

> 'Compared with those of similar social backgrounds whose parents remain married, children whose parents divorce show consistent, but small differences in their behaviour throughout childhood and adolescence and somewhat different life courses as they move into adulthood. More specifically, the research indicates on average lower levels of academic achievement and self-esteem and a higher incidence of conduct and other problems of psychological adjustment during childhood. Also during childhood a somewhat earlier social maturity has been recorded. A number of transitions to adulthood are typically reached at earlier ages; these include leaving home, beginning heterosexual relationships and entering cohabitation, marriage and child bearing. In young adulthood there is a tendency toward more changes of job, lower socio-economic status, a greater propensity to divorce and there are some indications of a higher

---

1 Especially, perhaps, in the context of divorce.
2 Thus, it will be important for the court to spell out these matters with particularity by attaching conditions to its orders or giving directions as to how they are to be carried into effect. The statutory scheme is quite flexible enough for this to be done. See s 11(7).
3 The published research is extensive and includes PR Amato and B Keith 'Parental divorce and adult well being: a meta-analysis' (1991) 53 *Journal of Marriage and the Family* 26; PR Amato and B Keith 'Parental divorce and the well being of children: a meta-analysis' (1991) 110 *Psychological Bulletin* 16; PR Amato 'Children's adjustment to divorce: theories, hypotheses and empirical support' (1993) 55 *Journal of Marriage and the Family* 23; KE Kiernan 'The impact of family disruption in childhood on transition in young adulthood' 46 *Population Studies* 213; and BJ Elliott and MPM Richards 'Children and Divorce: educational performance and behaviour, before and after parental separation' (1991) 5 IJLF 258. For an accessible and brief review of some of the research in the context of the then proposed changes to English divorce law, see C Piper ' "Looking to the Future" for Children' (1994) 6 JCL 98. For a more recent evaluation of the evidence from a comparative perspective relating to the experience of children in the context of divorce and reconstituted families see J Pryor and B Rodgers *Children in Changing Families: Life After Parental Separation* (Blackwell, 2001). This book aims especially to offer insights into why some children survive change in families better than others. See also B Rodgers and J Pryor *Divorce and Separation: the Outcomes for Children* (Joseph Rowntree Foundation, 1998).

frequency of depression and lower measures of psychological well-being. The relationships (in adulthood) with parents and other kin relationships may be more distant.'[1]

This all sounds rather drastic and might be thought to justify the mantra 'divorce is bad for children'. It is clear, however, that these findings must be treated with very great caution and are subject to significant qualifications.

The first and most important point is that there has frequently been a tendency on the part of the public, the media and, it must be said, governments of all complexion, to make the rather naïve assumption that *association* is to be equated with *cause*. It does not follow in the least that because an *association* can be established between the fact of divorce or parental separation and certain developmental disadvantages for children and young people, that the divorce or separation was actually the *cause* of those disadvantages. As Richards puts it:

> '... while it is relatively easy to establish associations, it is a great deal more difficult to unravel the processes that may produce them ... Simple cause and effect models of divorce are not very helpful.'[2]

Other factors which may have a bearing on outcomes for children are economic factors, 'welfare provision, housing policies, availability of child care, minimum wage legislation, as well as attitudes to divorce and marriage'[3].

The second qualification is that there is a great deal of variation in outcomes for individual children and between children of different social class or gender. The research findings are based on *averages* between groups of children whose parents stay together and those whose parents divorce. But this disguises the fact that 'some children whose parents divorce will do very well at school with excellent psychological well-being while others whose parents remain together will have unhappy or traumatic childhoods and do poorly at school'[4]. Allied to this is the third qualification that, in a sense, to compare the position of children whose parents divorce with those whose parents stay together is almost bound to be a flawed operation from a policy perspective since it is making the wrong comparison. What policy-makers might wish to know is whether there is evidence to show that the children of *unhappy* marriages do better if the parents stay together rather than separate, but the research does not, and probably cannot, isolate happy from unhappy marriages in the samples of parents who stay together. In other words, there is a qualitative element which is missing and which would be difficult, if not impossible, to pin down. What *is* beginning to be realised is that 'some (but not all) of the attributes in children which have been associated with divorce can be seen *before* a couple separate', but 'pre-divorce effects cannot account for all the differences which have been described after divorce'[5]. This again suggests that there should be greater emphasis placed on the *quality* of relationships between parents and children both pre- and post-separation.

---

1   M Richards 'The Interests of Children at Divorce' in M-T Meulders-Klein (ed) *Familles et Justice* (Bruylant, Bruxelles, 1997) at p 543.
2   Ibid at p 545.
3   Ibid at p 544.
4   Ibid.
5   Ibid at p 545, and Elliott and Richards 'Children and Divorce: educational performance and behaviour, before and after parental separation' (above).

In recent years the very conceptualisation of children as 'victims' of the divorce process has been challenged by a number of writers[1]. Smart, Wade and Neale criticise 'the prevailing discursive framework in which the couplet "children and divorce" is set as one in which children are unmistakably objects of concern'[2]. According to this 'it is clear that in popular imagery and narrative, children are inevitably hailed as the victims of divorce and harm to children is virtually unavoidable'. And they go on:

> 'It is almost impossible to find a counter-balance to this vivid imagery – even if the research on which it is based is far more equivocal than the popular image would suggest. On the one hand the image is employed by the anti-divorce lobby as a means to try to reform the divorce laws, on the other it is employed by those who wish to remoralise the family and to curb delinquency and school failure. So, although there is genuine concern about children intermingled with the rhetoric, there is very little room left in the public debate in which to refashion the child of divorced parents as a person rather than merely an object of concern.'[3]

These writers argue for the development of mechanisms which would allow children themselves to participate more meaningfully in the divorce process[4].

A key aim of policy ought, it is argued, to be to encourage and preserve a better *quality* of relationships between parents and children rather than to preserve marriages at all cost. We consider below what the largely unimplemented Family Law Act 1996 had to say about this. At this stage, it is sufficient to note that, in the light of available research, two policy conclusions do seem to have been drawn. The first is that exposure to parental *conflict* is bad for children, and the legal system should do what it can to minimise this. The second is that children are likely to do better if they can preserve a good ongoing relationship with *both* parents following divorce[5]. The first of these is relatively uncontroversial but the second represents a considerable shift in thinking over the last few decades and continues to provoke some disagreement. For some years, the dominant philosophy favoured sole custodial arrangements and a central role for the so-called 'psychological parent'[6]. This was, in part, reflected in England and Wales by the overwhelming number of sole custody orders in favour of mothers and an apparent preference for maternal care and control even where 'joint custody' orders were made[7].

1　See C Smart, A Wade and B Neale 'Objects of Concern? – Children and Divorce' [1999] CFLQ 365. See also S Day Sclater and C Piper (eds) *Undercurrents of Divorce* (Ashgate, 1999), and S Day Sclater and C Piper 'Social Exclusion and the Welfare of the Child' (2001) 28 *Journal of Law and Society* 409.

2　C Smart, A Wade and B Neale (above) at p 366.

3　Ibid.

4　There has been a recent increase in empirical work with children focusing on their own experiences of the divorce process. See, especially, C Smart, B Neale and A Wade *The Changing Experience of Childhood: Families and Divorce* (Polity Press, 2001).

5　The most influential research was probably JS Wallerstein and JB Kelly *Surviving the Breakup* (Grant McIntyre, 1980) and JS Wallerstein and S Blakeslee *Second Chances* (Bantam, 1989).

6　J Goldstein, A Freud and AJ Solnit *Beyond the Best Interests of the Child* (The Free Press, New York, 1980) was the classic exposition of this view.

7　Research conducted for the Law Commission, based on the statistical returns of 174 divorce registries, found, for example, that in 1985 sole custody orders were made in 86% of cases, 77.4% being in favour of the mother and 9.2% in favour of the father. See JF Priest and JC Whybrow *Custody Law in Practice in the Divorce and Domestic Courts*, Supplement to Law Com Working Paper No 96 (1986) at para 4.21.

This view was, in the 1980s and 1990s, largely supplanted by empirical evidence suggesting that the childen who suffer least from the breakdown of parental relationships tend to be those who are able to maintain good ongoing relationships with *both* parents. Conversely, those who suffer most are those whose parents carry on the conflict which was apparent during the marriage and at divorce[1]. This thinking originally manifested itself in the growth of 'joint custody' especially in the USA, but also in England[2]. It undoubtedly also influenced the principles established by the Children Act, although the concept of 'custody' itself was abandoned in favour of the new idea of minimal interference with the joint parental responsibility which exists during marriage. Increasingly these ideas have become intertwined with notions of human rights. Both parent and child are viewed as possessing fundamental rights to a continued relationship with one another. The rights-based discourse has, however, been challenged by some feminist writers who argue that there is a gendered aspect to it, favouring the claims of men over those of women, and that there has been too great an emphasis placed on the 'ethic of justice' and not enough on the 'ethic of care'. These arguments have surfaced strongly in connection with contact disputes and we examine them later in that context.

The legal background

Chapter 1 considered the origins of the post-war principle that divorce is an occasion for some form of public scrutiny of the interests of children. We saw that the former 'children's appointments' system was ultimately discredited as a perfunctory process. We must now turn to the changes brought about by the Children Act 1989.

The effect of the Children Act 1989

The no order principle
The essential regime of the Children Act, as has been seen, is that the responsibility of parents should not be unnecessarily disturbed and that orders should not be made unless they can positively achieve something for the child. This applies both during the marriage and on divorce. The technical distinctions between orders under the old law were swept away by the Children Act. The new law applies in all 'family proceedings', including divorce[3]. Thus, in a large number of cases, no order relating to children will be made on divorce, and the effect of this will be to preserve joint and several parental responsibility. It is *joint* in the sense that both parents retain it equally, and *several* in that it may be exercised independently and arguably without consultation. That at least is the theory. It has, however, become clear that, after an initial period following the implementation of the Children Act in October 1991 in which there was a major decline in orders relating to children on divorce, in recent years there has been an increase

---

1 See fn 5 at p 140 above.
2 JA Priest and JC Whybrow (above), at paras 5.2–5.6, found that joint custody orders were made in 12.9% of cases in 1985 but there were marked regional variations.
3 Defined in s 8(3) and (4). For an academic analysis of the no order principle, see R Ingleby *The Presumption of No Order* (Faculty of Law, University of Manchester, 1993).

in the number of such orders[1]. There is evidence too that the number of orders would have been substantially higher were it not for a reluctance on the part of the judges to make them even when they are sought. A number of commentators have drawn attention to the 'settlement culture' which pervades the family justice system[2]. In their view this can lead to an assumption that any solution produced by parental agreement is necessarily better than anything the court could impose. The danger with such an approach is that these agreements may be more apparent than real and may rather be the result of coercion or resignation[3]. In other words, agreements over children arrived at during the process of divorce may not always reflect what the parties really want, but may instead be the result of the pressure to agree which has been applied by their legal advisers and the court. In these cases the system may not meet the expectations of the parties which they had when they applied for a court order.

It is possible also to argue that there has been a misuse of the no order principle. Bailey-Harris, Barron and Pearce, drawing on an empirical study of appointments for Children Act matters in a number of courts in the West of England, put it this way:

> 'It is possible to argue from the evidence of our study that in practice the courts are using the "no order principle" in cases to which it was never intended to apply. In many cases where there is originally real conflict between parents who have invoked the court's jurisdiction specifically to resolve their dispute, the principle is invoked by judges to reinforce the promotion of parental autonomy and agreement as the preferred method of resolution: the court asserts that no order is needed where parents can eventually agree, even though their preferred intention was to obtain an order.'[4]

The requirement to act if necessary

Under the Children Act, the court is no longer required to declare itself satisfied with the arrangements proposed for the children. It has been given the more limited duty of considering whether it should exercise any of its powers in relation to any child of the family[5]. This is analogous to the duty placed on the magistrates' court under the old law[6]. Parents are, however, required to file a more detailed statement of arrangements in the hope that this may alert the court to problem

---

1 See the figures relating to residence, contact, prohibited steps and specific issue orders below. All of these orders increased significantly between 2000 and 2001.

2 See, for example, R Bailey-Harris, J Barron and J Pearce 'Settlement Culture and the use of the "No Order" principle under the Children Act 1989' [1999] CFLQ 53. See also G Davis 'Love in a Cold Climate – Disputes about Children in the Aftermath of Parental Separation' in S Cretney (ed) *Family Law: Essays for the New Millennium* (Family Law, 2000).

3 Bailey-Harris et al (above) at pp 54–55.

4 Ibid at pp 59–60.

5 Schedule 12, para 31, amending s 41 of the Matrimonial Causes Act 1973. By s 105, 'child of the family' means in relation to the parties to a marriage:
   '(a) a child of both of those parties;
   (b) any other child, not being a child who is placed with those parties as foster parents by a local authority or voluntary organisation, who has been treated by both of those parties as a child of their family.'
   The most important category of children (who are not the children of both parties) to be included in the expression are step-children. Other children, however, may also be regarded as children of the family, for example the grandchild in *Re A (Child of the Family)* [1998] 1 FLR 347. See further Chapter 6.

6 Domestic Proceedings and Magistrates' Courts Act 1978, s 8(1), now amended by the Children Act 1989, Sch 13, para 36.

cases and facilitate reference to mediation services[1]. The court has retained the power to direct that the decree of divorce or nullity should not be made absolute, or a decree of judicial separation not granted, in restricted circumstances, but such cases are rare[2]. The former rule that a decree absolute which was made without the necessary declaration was void was abolished along with the declaration requirement itself. Where the court is concerned about the proposed arrangements it may order a welfare report and, in disputed cases, will need to consider making one or more s 8 orders. But there is thought to be no reason why the decree itself should be delayed where the court made appropriate directions regarding the resolution of the children issues[3]. There is, thus, no requirement of judicial approval or, indeed, scrutiny in any real sense of the existing and proposed arrangements.

The Family Law Act 1996: the disappearing reform

The Family Law Act 1996 would have revolutionised divorce law and procedure. In the event the Government finally decided to abandon Part II of the Act which dealt with divorce. Accordingly, divorce continues to be governed by the Matrimonial Causes Act 1973, and a detailed description of the law and procedures which would have been introduced by the 1996 Act is no longer justified[4]. Nevertheless it would be wrong to ignore the Act completely for several reasons. First, Parts I and III of the Act, which relate respectively to general principles and mediation, were brought into force[5]. Secondly, the Act provides a fascinating insight into 'official thinking' about what is good for children and parents on divorce. Thirdly, the whole question of divorce reform, though temporarily jettisoned, is almost certain to resurface at some future point, and the Law Commission reports, government papers and debates in Parliament, to say nothing of the many academic commentaries which were generated by the attempt at reform, will continue to provide a rich source of information and argument when the question of divorce reform is eventually resurrected[6].

---

1 Law Com No 172 *Guardianship and Custody* (1988) at para 3.10, and *The Children Act 1989 Guidance and Regulations Vol 1 Court Orders* (HMSO, 1991) at paras 2.54 et seq.

2 Schedule 12, para 31(2), amending s 41(2) of the Matrimonial Causes Act 1973, provides:
   'Where ... it appears to the court that –
   (a) the circumstances of the case require it, or are likely to require it, to exercise any of its powers under the Act ... with respect to any such child;
   (b) it is not in a position to exercise that power (or as the case may be those powers) without giving further consideration to the case; and
   (c) there are exceptional circumstances which make it desirable in the interests of the child that the court should give a direction under this section,
   it may direct that the decree of divorce or nullity is not to be made absolute, or that the decree of judicial separation is not to be granted, until the court orders otherwise.'

3 The court has a duty to set a timetable in this respect under s 11.

4 For rather more detail, see the second edition of this work at pp 119–121. For a thorough examination of the divorce aspects of the 1996 Act, see R Bird and S Cretney *Divorce: The New Law* (Family Law, 1996) and M Freeman, *The Family Law Act 1996* (Sweet and Maxwell, 1996).

5 Part IV relating to domestic violence and occupation of the family home was brought into force in 1997 and, insofar as it affects children, is considered in Chapter 12.

6 Valuable commentaries include SM Cretney 'Divorce Reform in England: Humbug and Hypocrisy or a Smooth Transition?' in M Freeman (ed) *Divorce: Where Next?* (Dartmouth, 1996); M Freeman 'England: Family Justice and Family Values in 1995' in A Bainham (ed) *The International Survey of Family Law 1995* (Martinus Nijhoff, 1997); G Douglas 'England and Wales:

In this section, therefore, an attempt will be made to describe the essential features of the scheme which would have been established by the 1996 Act, highlighting those which would have had a particular relevance to children. We then consider briefly why the reforms may have failed. Finally, in the conclusion to this chapter we discuss some of the issues relating to children and divorce which remain unresolved.

The 1996 Act would have abolished fault as a basis for divorce and indeed would have swept away all the 'facts' required for proof of irretrievable breakdown[1]. Parties intending to initiate divorce would have been required to attend an information meeting not less than three months before doing so. Divorce proceedings would then have had to be commenced by a neutral 'statement of marital breakdown' being no more than a statement of belief by one or both parties that the marriage had broken down. There would then have been a 'period for reflection and consideration', the length of which would have varied depending on a number of factors. It would not have been less than nine months beginning with the fourteenth day after the statement of marital breakdown had been received by the court. And, significantly, this period would have been extended for a further period of six months where there was at least one minor child of the family. The period could be further extended where, for example, one party wished to 'stop the clock' for reconciliation attempts to be made. The six-month extension in the case of minor children would not have been imposed in cases where there was domestic violence. It was visualised that parties would use this period to make arrangements for the future concerning children and their financial affairs, and it would have been a feature of the process that the requirements in the Act relating to the settling of those arrangements should be satisfied before a divorce or separation order could be made. Finally, the divorce order would be made on application by either party if all the above requirements were satisfied and a declaration was made by that party that he or she believed that the marriage could not be saved. There would have been a limited power to refuse an order where the court was satisfied that to dissolve the marriage would result in substantial financial or other hardship to the other party or to a child of the family.

Another feature of the intended reforms would have been a stronger emphasis on mediation, which is discussed below. The Act also sought to give greater weight to the interests of children and it is that feature which perhaps concerns us most in the context of this discussion. There is no doubt that the former Conservative Government took the position that divorce, an evil to be avoided if possible, was even more of an evil where the children were concerned. Thus, in the Foreword to the Government's consultation paper on Mediation and the Ground for Divorce[2], the former Lord Chancellor, Lord Mackay, said:

"family values" to the fore?' in A Bainham (ed) *The International Survey of Family Law 1996* (Martinus Nijhoff, 1998); Dame Brenda Hale 'The Family Law Act 1996 – the Death of Marriage?' in C Bridge (ed) *Family Law Towards the Millennium: Essays for PM Bromley* (Butterworths, 1997) and Lady Justice Hale 'The Family Law Act 1996 – Dead Duck or Golden Goose?' in S Cretney (ed) *Family Law: Essays for the New Millennium* (Family Law, 2000). For a more extensive recent critique, see H Reece *Divorcing Responsibly* (Hart Publishing, 2003).

1 See the discussion of the ground for divorce under the Matrimonial Causes Act 1973 and the special procedure below.
2 Lord Chancellor's Department *Looking to the Future: Mediation and the Ground for Divorce* (1993) (Cm 2424).

'... Almost inevitably the breakdown of a marriage is hard for one or both of the parties and especially for the children. I believe that a good divorce law will support the institution of marriage ... it should seek to eliminate unnecessary distress for the parties and particularly for the children in those cases where a marriage has broken down irretrievably ...'

It is important to appreciate that the legislation, like all legislation, was the product of different influences both before and during the Parliamentary process. Yet the Family Law Act 1996 was more overtly ideological than most statutes, setting out in s 1 a list of *general principles* behind which, as Freeman pointed out, lay values[1]. It is not possible to gain a proper appreciation of the specific provisions which related to children without a realisation that some of these, controversially, were grounded in the notion that divorce is per se bad. Freeman rightly described the legislation as 'anti-divorce' and there is no question that one way in which it was seeking, rightly or wrongly, to protect the interests of children was by attempting to *prevent* the divorce itself from happening. And even where it was clear under the new procedures that one or both parties would have intended to go ahead with divorce, the Act still attempted to make this more difficult to achieve where there were minor children by extending by six months the period of time which had to elapse before a divorce order could be made. How well this would have squared with the other central feature of the new divorce law – the abandonment of fault[2] and the matrimonial offences of adultery, desertion and 'unreasonable behaviour' – is open to doubt. There was indeed a curious ambivalence about a law which in substance made divorce available as of right and without proof of grounds but, at the same time, procedurally would have made divorce more difficult to obtain[3].

The 'general principles' in s 1 referred to above do, however, to a limited extent and for the first time in English legislation, articulate an official view of what is good or bad for children in the context of divorce, and they would have been reinforced by s 11 of the Act had it been implemented. The final feature to note about the legislation was its emphasis on *mediation* (previously usually referred to as 'conciliation' in children cases) and this raises questions about the implications for children and their part (if any) in the mediation process. Why did these ambitious reforms fail?[4] The official reason came in a Press Release by the then Lord Chancellor's Department on 17 June 1999 to this effect:

'The Lord Chancellor, Lord Irvine, confirmed today in a written Parliamentary answer, that the Government did not intend implementing Part II of the Family Law Act in 2000.

Part II includes a requirement that married people considering divorce attend information meetings designed to save saveable marriages and where this is not possible, promote mediation in divorce as an alternative to adversarial litigation. Reiterating the Government's commitment

---

1   See the annotations to s 1 in M Freeman *The Family Law Act 1996* (Sweet & Maxwell, 1996), in which he identifies these values as 'pro-marriage, pro-children and anti-violence'.
2   On the place of fault in divorce and in family law generally, see A Bainham 'Men and Women Behaving Badly: Is Fault Dead in English Family Law?' (2001) 21 *Oxford Journal of Legal Studies* 219.
3   For critiques, see M Freeman 'England: family justice and family values in 1995' in A Bainham (ed) *The International Survey of Family Law 1995* (Martinus Nijhoff, 1997), and G Douglas 'England and Wales: "family values" to the fore?' in *The International Survey of Family Law 1996* (Martinus Nijhoff, 1998).
4   See especially Lord Justice Thorpe and E Clarke *No Fault or Flaw: The Future of the Family Law Act 1996* (Family Law, 2000). For a discussion of the political context of the reforms, see J Eekelaar 'Family Law: keeping us "on message"' [1999] CFLQ 387.

to reducing conflict in divorce and supporting families, the Lord Chancellor said that before implementing Part II the Government must be satisfied that these objectives are fulfilled. However, the interim results of extensive pilots testing information meetings had been disappointing: only 7% of those attending the pilots, for example, had been diverted into mediation and 39% of those attending had reported that they were more likely than before to go to a solicitor.

The final assessment of the pilot projects will be available early next year when the Government will consider whether any further research is necessary.'[1]

In due course on 16 January 2001 came a further Press Release indicating that the postponement of the implementation of Part II was to be permanent and that that part of the legislation would be repealed. There has been a good deal of speculation by commentators and those working in the many public services relating to divorce about what exactly went wrong and what should be done. One feature of the reactions to the loss of Part II is worth highlighting. This is that there appears to be something approaching unanimity among practitioners in the field, that no-fault divorce has become an unfortunate casualty of the failure of the reforms and that at some time it should be introduced. Others are inclined to attribute the failure of the reforms to a fundamental clash between conservative influences which had infiltrated the legislation and would have led to divorce becoming a lengthier (and in that sense a more difficult) process, and modern ideas held by perhaps the majority of the population that divorce is now to be regarded as an individual right. Hence, to make divorce a more difficult process would have been unacceptable to the majority of the electorate and politically dangerous[2]. We now consider briefly the general principles, the court's role where there are children (now governed, as before the 1996 Act, by the Matrimonial Causes Act 1973, as amended by the Children Act 1989) and, finally, the question of children and mediation.

The general principles

These are set out in s 1 of the Act and must be applied by 'the Court and any person, in exercising functions under or in consequence of Parts II and III'[3] which are the parts of the Act dealing with divorce and mediation. We set out below the principles as they stand but with emphasis added to highlight those which directly refer to children. We then return to these principles in the final section of the chapter, which considers some of the policy issues for the future.

The principles are:

'(a)   that the institution of marriage is to be supported;
(b)   that the parties to a marriage which may have broken down are to be encouraged to take all practicable steps, whether by marriage counselling or otherwise, to save the marriage;
(c)   that a marriage which has irretrievably broken down and is being brought to an end should be brought to an end –
    (i)   *with minimum distress to the parties and to the children affected;*
    (ii)   *with questions dealt with in a manner designed to promote as good a continuing relationship between the parties and any children affected as is possible in the circumstances;* and

---

1   LCD, Press Release, 17 June 1999.
2   This is the view of the author set out in greater detail in A Bainham 'Family Rights in the Next Millennium' (2000) 53 *Current Legal Problems* 471 at pp 498–503, and in A Bainham 'Exciting Times in England: Human Rights, Children and Divorce' [2001] *International Family Law* 71 at pp 74–76.
3   Although, in the light of the demise of Part II, now applicable only to Part III.

(iii) without costs being unreasonably incurred in connection with the procedures to be followed in bringing the marriage to an end; and

(d) *that any risk to one of the parties to a marriage, and to any children, of violence from the other party should, so far as reasonably practicable, be removed or diminished.'*

The basis for divorce

This book is about children and the details of the divorce process itself are beyond the scope of the present discussion. The intricate and convoluted procedure for obtaining a divorce which would have been introduced by Part II of the Family Law Act 1996 will not be discussed since, for the foreseeable future, the long-established special procedure under the Matrimonial Causes Act 1973 seems set to govern divorce. The changes to the procedure which had been enacted in the 1996 Act were covered in the previous edition of this work, and the reader is referred to the relevant section and the sources cited there[1].

Under the special procedure the sole ground for divorce is irretrievable breakdown of marriage but this may be established only on proof of one of five 'facts'[2]. The special procedure applies to all undefended divorces, which today are virtually all divorces. The procedure, though judicial in form, is largely administrative in nature. The petitioner presents a standard form petition together with a statement of arrangements relating to any children of the family which covers the current arrangements regarding such matters as where they live and attend school and their financial support and which also deals with the intended arrangements for them following divorce. These documents are then served on (posted to) the respondent. If the respondent indicates that it is not his wish to defend the petition, as is the case in the overwhelming majority of petitions, the petitioner will sign an affidavit (another standard form) and apply for 'directions for trial'. The district judge will then enter the case in the special procedure list and consider the evidence filed by the petitioner. If satisfied that the contents of the petition are proved, he will file a certificate to that effect. In due course a decree nisi will be pronounced by the judge in open court but the attendance of the parties is not required. The petitioner is automatically entitled to have the decree made absolute six weeks from the grant of decree nisi. It is not difficult to see why this process is sometimes referred to as 'postal divorce'.

The court's role in relation to children

The court's duty is the limited one of considering whether there are any relevant 'children of the family' and, if so, 'whether (in the light of the arrangements which

---

1 At pp 119–121.

2 The facts as set out in s 1(2) of the MCA 1973, are:

(a) that the respondent has committed adultery and the petitioner finds it intolerable to live with the respondent;

(b) that the respondent has behaved in such a way that the petitioner cannot reasonably be expected to live with the respondent;

(c) that the respondent has deserted the petitioner for a continuous period of at least two years immediately preceding the presentation of the petition;

(d) that the parties to the marriage have lived apart for a continuous period of at least two years preceding the presentation of the petition ... and the respondent consents to a decree being granted;

(e) that the parties to the marriage have lived apart for a continuous period of at least five years immediately preceding the presentation of the petition.

have been, or are proposed to be, made for their upbringing and welfare) it should exercise any of its powers under the Children Act 1989 with respect to any of them'[1].

This duty is exercised by the district judge on the strength of written statements about the arrangements for children filed with the court. The court has power in 'exceptional circumstances which make it desirable in the interests of the child that the court should give a direction' to direct that the decree of divorce or nullity is not to be made absolute or the decree of judicial separation not granted until the court orders otherwise[2]. This provision is not much used but there are a significant number of cases in which the district judge exercises his power to call for further evidence or for the attendance of the parties at a hearing in chambers, or to direct welfare reports in cases where it may be necessary to exercise the court's powers – usually but not invariably because the parties are not in agreement. Where a hearing is held, it is usual for a children and family reporter to be present and to attempt 'in-court conciliation' between the parties.

The court is required to regard the welfare of the child as the paramount consideration. The 1996 Act would have introduced the important modification that the court have particular regard to a checklist of factors in deciding whether it needed to exercise its powers[3]. These were:

'(a) the wishes and feelings of the child considered in the light of his age and understanding and the circumstances in which those wishes were expressed;
(b) the conduct of the parties in relation to the upbringing of the child;
(c) the general principle that, in the absence of evidence to the contrary, the welfare of the child will be best served by –
    (i)   his having regular contact with those who have parental responsibility for him and with other members of his family; and
    (ii) the maintenance of as good a continuing relationship with his parents as is possible; and
(d) any risk to the child attributable to –
    (i)   where the person with whom the child will reside is living or proposes to live;
    (ii) any person with whom that person is living or with whom he proposes to live; or
    (iii) any other arrangements for his care and upbringing.'

This checklist fell along with the rest of Part II of the Act.

The reality is that what parents agree about the children will initially be followed, and the cases in which the court seeks to intervene in any way are likely to be only a small minority of the total. Cretney, commenting on the unimplemented provisions of s 11, saw something of a philosophical inconsistency between the principles of the Children Act and those of the Family Law Act:

'The truth is that the provisions of the Children Act in general are based on a philosophy of non-intervention which does not sit easily with the more interventionist philosophy of the 1996 Act.'[4]

---

1 MCA 1973, s 41(1). See, generally, G Douglas, M Murch, L Scanlon and A Perry 'Safeguarding Children's Welfare in Non-contentious Divorce: Towards a New Conception of the Legal Process?' (2000) 63 MLR 177.
2 Ibid, s 41(2)(c).
3 Family Law Act 1996, s 11(3), (4).
4 SM Cretney *Family Law* (3rd edn) (Sweet & Maxwell, 1997) at p 53.

Children and mediation

One of the central features of the divorce process under the Family Law Act 1996 would have been the much increased role for mediation as opposed to the more traditional processes of negotiation by lawyers and adjudication[1]. Mediation is a process whereby the parties are assisted by an impartial third person, the mediator, to reach their own agreements on separation or divorce. Mediation, often referred to in the past as 'conciliation', has tended to be confined to children issues but, in recent years, there has been a growth in the idea of 'comprehensive' or 'all-issues' mediation[2]. After many years in which the former Conservative Government had shown an unwillingness to fund properly the existing mediation services, it then underwent what appeared to many to be a dramatic conversion[3]. The result was that the Family Law Act contained a whole range of provisions designed to bring to the attention of the divorcing parties the supposed benefits of mediation to enable them to take advantage of mediation services and, in those cases in which they were eligible for legal aid (now known as the Community Legal Service Fund), to have the costs of mediation borne by public funds. Part III of the Act was brought into force, including s 29 which made it a pre-condition for those qualifying financially for legal aid who sought legal representation to attend first a meeting with a mediator to determine whether mediation appeared suitable to the dispute and the parties' circumstances and, if so, to help the person applying for legal representation to decide whether instead to apply for mediation[4]. The clear implication is that legal representation will be refused where mediation is thought suitable, although the legislation specifically requires that any fear of domestic violence be taken into account in arriving at the determination.

Despite this strong push in the direction of mediation, the evidence is that the vast majority of family disputes have not, and still do not, involve recourse to mediation[5]. One view is that mediation is never likely to be more than a 'minority choice' but that it may have real value for those who wish to opt for it. But the

---

1 On the nature of family mediation, see J Haynes *Alternative Dispute Resolution: The Fundamentals of Family Mediation* (Old Bailey Press, 1993), and L Parkinson *Family Mediation* (Sweet & Maxwell, 1997); and on the characteristics of mediation more generally, see M Palmer and S Roberts *Dispute Processes* (Butterworths, 1998) ch 4.

2 For a discussion of mediation in the context of the interests of children at divorce, see M Richards 'The Interests of Children at Divorce' in M-T Meulders-Klein (ed) *Familles et Justice* (Bruylant, Bruxelles, 1997) especially at pp 554–557.

3 This change of heart was signalled in the Green Paper *Looking to the Future: Mediation and the Ground for Divorce* (1993) (Cm 2424) and was followed by a White Paper, *Looking to the Future* (1995) (Cm 2799).

4 See Access to Justice Act 1999, s 8(3) and the Community Legal Service Funding Code.

5 Cretney notes, for example, that National Family Mediation had, before the enactment of the 1996 legislation, been providing out-of-court mediation to some 6,500 families per annum while the equivalent figure for the Family Mediators Association was about 1,500 families. Set against the annual divorce rate of around 150,000 divorces per year, it is readily apparent that mediation was very much a minority activity before 1996. See SM Cretney 'Divorce Reform in England: Humbug and Hypocrisy or a Smooth Transition?' in M Freeman (ed) *Divorce: Where Next?* (Dartmouth, 1996) at p 49 and the sources cited there. For two very different perspectives on the place of mediation following the abandonment of the divorce reforms, see S Roberts 'Family Mediation after the Act' [2001] CFLQ 265 and G Davis 'Researching Publicly Funded Mediation' in Lord Justice Thorpe and E Clarke (eds) *No Fault or Flaw* (Family Law, 2000).

wisdom of official coercion or persuasion may be doubted[1]. The precise relationship between mediation and legal advice or adjudication has never been totally clear. What is clear is that to some extent this is a false dichotomy since many lawyers have trained as mediators and it is, in any event, necessary for mediation to operate in conjunction with legal advice, particularly in relation to the drawing up in legal form of agreements arrived at in mediation.

Where do children fit into all of this? While this is also not entirely clear, several points can be made with some confidence at the time of writing. The first is that hitherto only a tiny minority of divorcing couples have used mediation services at all. It is equally clear that a signficant proportion of divorcing couples will not be in dispute about children and that, in many cases, the arrangements for the children, as now, will be worked out by agreement under the procedures outlined above. Secondly, while the official assumption has been made that mediation is somehow 'better' in terms of outcomes for children there is scant evidence to support this beyond the intuitive feeling that it may enhance communication and assist in avoiding prolonged conflict where conflict is known to be bad for children[2]. And, as we have seen, there is a good daily of scepticism about whether solutions produced by agreement are necessarily more satisfactory than court-imposed solutions. Thirdly, it is not at all clear what part, if any, children themselves are expected to play in the mediation process but, in most cases at present, children play no direct role. Any benefits of mediation for them are therefore likely to be of an indirect nature. Recently, there have been some examples of children's views being obtained in separate sessions as an adjunct to the mediation itself. The question of how a conflict of interest between the parents and the children arising in mediation ought to be resolved is also uncertain[3].

The issue of the participation of children in mediation and the most appropriate way of ascertaining and accommodating their views is part of a much wider issue about the representation of children in legal processes, and we return to this in Chapter 13.

Private orders and the exercise of the court's discretion

Where it appears to the divorce court that it *should* exercise its powers, it may make one or more s 8 orders, the effect of which is to regulate the *exercise* of particular aspects of parental responsibility whilst leaving parental responsibility itself intact. Since divorce is by far the most numerically significant occasion when s 8 orders are made, consideration is given here to the circumstances under which these orders may be appropriate, their legal effect and the criteria which the courts must apply in deciding whether to make them. We look briefly at the court's flexible powers to attach conditions and give directions when making the orders. We also consider the powers which the courts have to make a 'family assistance order' or to direct a local authority to investigate the circumstances of a child which could lead to the making of a supervision or care order. It should be remembered that these powers are available generally in 'family proceedings', subject to certain restrictions, and that much of what is said here can be applied to litigation

---

1   Davis (above).
2   See M Richards 'The Interests of Children at Divorce' (above) at pp 554–557.
3   Ibid.

involving social parents[1]. Parents, unlike certain categories of social parents, may always apply in family proceedings for any s 8 order as of right and do not require the leave of the court[2]. *Any* child whose welfare arises in family proceedings may be the subject of an order and not simply a 'child of the family'[3]. Orders will not normally be made after the child has attained 16 years of age but may be made, in exceptional circumstances, such as those of a mentally disabled young person[4]. By virtue of the Adoption and Children Act 2002, s 114, inserting a new s 12(5) into the Children Act 1989, the court is given power to direct that a residence order in favour of a person who is not the parent or guardian of the child should continue until the child reaches the age of 18[5].

The range of orders

The residence order
Arguably, the most significant of the orders is the 'residence order'. This is defined as 'an order settling the arrangements to be made as to the person with whom the child is to live'[6]. In contested cases, it is important that the court should give adequate reasons for making or refusing a residence order[7].

Statistically, there are fewer residence orders made than contact orders. In 1996, an estimated 27,600 residence orders were made, an increase of 8 per cent on the 1995 figures. This compared with 40,330 contact orders in 1996, a 14 per cent increase from 1995[8]. By 2000 the figures were 25,809 residence orders and 46,070 contact orders. In 2001 there were 29,546 residence orders and 55,030 contact orders[9]. In many divorces, therefore, no residence order will be made,

---

1   See Chapter 6 below.
2   Section 10(1) and (4).
3   Sections 10(1) and 105(1) defining a 'child', subject to certain qualifications regarding financial support, as 'a person under the age of eighteen'.
4   Section 9(7). For the reasoning behind the change in the law (the age limit under the old law generally being 18), see Law Com Report No 172 (above) at para 3.25.
5   This power is one of a number of provisions introduced by the Adoption and Children Act 2002 which are designed to enhance the status and security of long-term substitute carers. See further Chapter 6 below.
6   Section 8(1). It was held in *Re B (A Minor) (Residence Order: Ex Parte)* [1992] 2 FLR 1 that the court has jurisdiction to make an ex parte interim residence order. The Court of Appeal in *Re P (A Minor) (Ex Parte Interim Residence Order)* [1993] 1 FLR 915 has, however, stated that such orders will rarely be appropriate except, for example, to thwart abduction. Another decision to similar effect is *Re G (Minors) (Ex Parte Interim Residence Order)* [1993] 1 FLR 910. Another case emphasising caution in the use and interpretation of ex parte residence orders is *Re J (Children: Ex Parte Orders)* [1997] 1 FLR 606.
7   *B v B (Residence Order: Reasons for Decision)* [1997] 2 FLR 602. In *Re W (Residence)* [1999] 1 FLR 869 the Court of Appeal remitted the residence issue for rehearing where the judge had failed to follow the recommendations of the welfare officer that the children should live with their mother and her new partner. The judge, it was found, had over-reacted to the practice of the mother and partner in allowing the two children aged nine and six to see them about the home in the nude and engaging in communal bathing. The Court of Appeal took the position that what had occurred was unwise in the context of someone else's child but that neither nudity nor communal bathing were abuse. The reaction of the judge had been extreme and his perception of a serious risk to the children had no substance and was not supported by the evidence.
8   *The Children Act Advisory Committee Final Report June 1997* (Lord Chancellor's Department, 1997), Appendix 2.
9   *Children Act Report 2001* (Department of Health, 2002).

and the expressions 'resident' and 'non-resident' parent might be thought somewhat ambiguous. They may be used where a residence order has been made, but they may just reflect the fact that there is a primary carer looking after the child with or without an order. One reason why a residence order might be made is to offer added security where there is a threat that the child might be removed from the country or contact with one parent deliberately impeded. In *Re K (Residence Order: Securing Contact)*[1] the Court of Appeal upheld a residence order in relation to a two-year-old child which had been made in favour of the father. The circumstances were unusual in that the court found the mother to be fundamentally untrustworthy and feared that, if she were given a residence order, she might abuse it by taking the child to India or otherwise impeding the father's contact with the child.

The effect of the order

In the case of married parents, who already possess parental responsibility, the order simply regulates where the child is to live and no more. This contrasts with the position of non-parents who *acquire* parental responsibility by virtue of the order and retain it as long as the order remains in force[2]. Divorcing parents will therefore retain, to the full, all aspects of parental responsibility which they exercised during the marriage, save only that the 'non-resident' parent will lose his right physically to look after the child except insofar as this is compatible with the residence order and any other order, condition or direction which the court may make[3]. In practical terms, the non-resident parent will be able to take all decisions on upbringing while the child is with him but it may be difficult to participate in the child's upbringing in the more common situation of the child being in the care of the resident parent. The Law Commission recognised this when it suggested that the reality of parental responsibility is that it 'runs with the child'[4]. But, technically at least, the non-resident parent is entitled to exercise parental responsibility even where the child is not physically with him. Whether this is more than a merely symbolic retention of parental responsibility may depend, to a large extent, on how far the non-resident parent wishes to assert his potential contribution to the upbringing of his child.

No express rights of consultation, even on major matters, were written into the legislation but judicial remarks have cast doubt on this analysis. In *Re G (Parental Responsibility: Education)*[5], Glidewell LJ said obiter that the non-resident mother should have been consulted by the resident father on the matter of changing the child's school from a day school to a boarding school. On the other hand, in *Re P (A Minor) (Parental Responsibility Order)*[6], Wilson J made remarks suggesting that the

---

1   [1999] 1 FLR 583.
2   Section 12(2).
3   Just what is incompatible with a residence order may prove contentious in practice. It seems that the concept of residence is a more restricted idea than the notion of physical possession or control associated with the old idea of custody. The order simply settles where the child is to live. Does this mean that the resident parent has the right to control the physical movements of the child and the non-resident parent would be acting unlawfully, for example, in taking the child away for an afternoon without the resident parent's consent? Clearly, it would be desirable for this kind of situation to be regulated by a contact order.
4   Law Com Working Paper No 96 (1986) at paras 4.51 et seq.
5   [1994] 2 FLR 694.
6   [1994] 1 FLR 578.

acquisition of parental responsibility by an unmarried father would not give him the right to question everyday decisions taken by the mother if she had a residence order in her favour. This rather suggests that the non-resident parent does not have an automatic right of consultation. But, again, in *Re J (Specific Issue Orders: Muslim Upbringing and Circumcision)*[1] the Court of Appeal held that circumcision of a male child was a 'serious' matter which should be carried out only with parental agreement or under court order. The decision suggests that there may be a need to distinguish between serious matters that require consultation and more trivial or minor day-to-day issues that do not require it. It is not clear which decisions would fall into each category. What is clear is that it was not the intention of the legislature, as expressed in the Act, to create this distinction, although such a distinction has been, and still is, a feature of the wardship jurisdiction. Only 'major', as opposed to 'minor', matters have to be brought back before the court in that jurisdiction[2]. The matter is in need of clarification by the higher courts. The factual superiority of the resident parent's position, if such it is, may be preserved on his or her death where the resident parent has appointed a guardian[3].

In most cases, therefore, despite theoretical equality and the ethos of continuing parental responsibility, it is the resident parent who, for practical purposes, will exercise parental powers. The legislation may, notwithstanding, have some influence on the way in which the role of parents is perceived following divorce. It might even be viewed as an attempt at social engineering. It is statutory recognition that ex-spouses remain parents and are expected to be able to distinguish between termination of their own legal and factual relationship and their continuing moral and legal obligations to their children. There is a clear expectation in the legislation that these obligations should not simply be off-loaded onto the other parent or the State[4].

Shared residence orders

There is no restriction in the Children Act which prevents a residence order being made in favour of more than one person. Since the Act was implemented, two separate and distinct uses of the shared residence order have emerged. The first is to give effect to what might be termed 'time-sharing' arrangements. The second is a status-conferring device to give parental responsibility to a social parent.

Time-sharing

The Children Act enables an order to be made 'in favour of two or more persons who do not themselves all live together' and it 'may specify the periods during which the child is to live in the different households concerned'[5]. The Law Commission considered that a joint residence order would be more realistic than a sole residence order coupled with a contact order where it is proposed that the child should spend substantial periods in the care of each parent. The effect was to introduce the possibility of 'time-sharing', a feature of some joint custodial

---

1   [2000] 1 FLR 571.
2   See further Chapter 11 below.
3   Section 5(7)(b), discussed in Chapter 6 below.
4   These expectations are reflected most obviously in the child support legislation and are reinforced by the general principles in the Family Law Act 1996.
5   Section 11(4).

arrangements elsewhere[1]. It marked a shift away from the attitude expressed judicially which was antagonistic to the idea of joint custody orders which included joint physical care and control on the basis that a child needed a settled home and such arrangements could be disruptive[2].

It is unlikely that orders like this will be made except where there is already a very high level of co-operation[3]. One instance will be where a child spends school holidays with one parent and term-time with the other. In *Re F (Shared Residence Order)*[4] the Court of Appeal held that the use of a shared residence order was not confined to the situation where children alternated between two homes evenly. Where the two parents lived a considerable distance apart there was the possibility that the children's year could be divided up between their homes in such a way as to validate the making of a shared residence order. If the home offered by each parent was of equal status and importance to the child a shared residence order could be valuable. A joint order may also be appropriate where the parties continue to reside geographically close to one another, thereby increasing the practicability of the arrangement and minimising the risk that the child will be 'shunted about'. It should be noted that the Children Act creates no presumption of joint physical care. Several reported cases have made it plain that joint residence orders contemplating shared physical care may be appropriate in some situations such as, for example, to accommodate the working patterns of a shift worker[5].

The leading case is *A v A (Minors) (Shared Residence Orders)*[6]. The Court of Appeal held that the pre-Children Act decision in *Riley v Riley* could not stand in the light of the new statutory framework. In many cases, it would be confusing for children to have two homes but joint residence orders were not to be confined to 'exceptional circumstances'. Sole residence orders would be more usual and it would need to be shown that there was some positive benefit to the child in making the unconventional order. Butler-Sloss LJ warned that such an order would be inappropriate where there were still concrete issues which required resolution, such as a dispute concerning the amount of contact. This view that the joint residence order ought not to be confined to exceptional circumstances was reiterated by the Court of Appeal in *D v D (Shared Residence Order)*[7] where the court emphasised that there was no onus on the person seeking the order to demonstrate that it would be of positive benefit to the child. It was sufficient that it was in the best interests of the child as required by the welfare principle. In this case the father had wanted the order to underline his standing in relation to third parties when seeking information about the child. He claimed that, without the order, he had been treated as a second-class parent. In *Re R (Residence Order:*

---

1   The American concept of joint custody, for example, envisages joint physical and legal custody.
2   *Riley v Riley* [1986] 2 FLR 429.
3   The extent to which the legal system should positively promote shared residence, perhaps by the creation of a rebuttable presumption for 50:50 time sharing, has been the subject of disagreement. See, for example, L McCallum 'Shared Residence – Just a Label?' [2004] Fam Law 528. Cf B Neale, J Flowerdew and C Smart 'Drifting Towards Shared Residence?' [2003] Fam Law 904. For a short discussion of the debate in Australia see S Leigh 'A Legal Presumption in Matters of Child Contact' [2004] Fam Law 533.
4   [2003] 2 FLR 397. See also *A v A (Shared Residence)* [2004] 1 FLR 1195.
5   *G v G (Joint Residence Order)* [1993] Fam Law 570.
6   [1994] 1 FLR 669.
7   [2001] 1 FLR 495.

Finance)[1], the Court of Appeal upheld a joint residence order where both parents worked full-time. The three-year-old son lived during the week with his father (although the care was actually provided by the paternal grandmother) and with his mother at most weekends and during holiday periods. The mother then declared her intention to give up work and sought a sole residence order. The court held that the judge had been entitled to have regard to the consequences of the mother giving up work and having to rely on State benefits. He could not be criticised for taking the view that the existing arrangement was the best of the alternatives on offer[2].

It should be remembered that in the great majority of divorces no order at all will be needed, or made, in relation to the children. In these cases, the parties will themselves work out informally the most practicable arrangements for them. It seems entirely likely that in some of these cases there will be a kind of *de facto* shared residence[3]. With or without residence orders, there will be in practice a very wide range of caring arrangements, from equal time-sharing at one end, to sole and exclusive residential arrangements at the other. Between these two extremes, there will be many variations, but the real change brought about by the Children Act was the demise of the stereotypical sole custody order which was so much a feature of the old law. The great variation in arrangements for the care of children merely reflects the rich kaleidoscope of family arrangements which are characteristic of Britain in the early twenty-first century.

Shared residence and parental responsibility

It has been noted that one effect of a residence order is to confer parental responsibility on the holder if he or she does not already have it, although this will only be for as long as the residence order itself lasts[4]. Two reported cases have shown an ingenious use of the joint residence order as a device for conferring this legal status on a social parent.

In *Re H (Shared Residence: Parental Responsibility)*[5], the mother's husband was the father of her younger child but not of her elder son. He was therefore step-father to the older boy and had accepted him as his own. After separation there had been a joint residence order by consent and both children continued to see a lot of the father with the mother's full co-operation. The mother sought to vary the order to a sole residence order but the court upheld the original order on the basis that it had value in giving the father parental responsibility in relation to the elder boy. In this way, the law could give its stamp of approval to the factual position that the boy was accepted by the man as his own.

An even more imaginative use of the joint residence order occurred in *Re AB (Adoption: Joint Residence)*[6]. An unmarried couple were foster-parents to a five-year-old child. They wanted to adopt the child but were precluded from doing

---

1   [1995] 2 FLR 612.
2   Cf the views of Thorpe LJ in *Re S (Children)*, at p 58 above.
3   For critiques of the use of the joint residence order, see C Bridge 'Shared residence in England and New Zealand – a comparative analysis' [1996] CFLQ 12, and Baker and Townsend 'Post-divorce parenting – rethinking shared residence' [1996] CFLQ 217. For an analysis of the essential scheme for joint parenting under the Children Act, see B Hoggett 'Joint parenting systems: the English experiment' (1994) 6 JCL 8.
4   Children Act 1989, s 12(2).
5   [1995] 2 FLR 883.
6   [1996] 1 FLR 27.

so since the then adoption legislation required that all *joint* adoptions be made by a *married* couple[1]. Cazalet J granted the foster-father an adoption order[2] (one effect of which was that the child could bear his surname) and made a shared residence order in favour of both of them. This had the effect of giving the foster-mother parental responsibility during the child's minority and was the next best thing to adoption. Unmarried couples are now permitted to adopt jointly[3].

The contact order

The contact order is 'an order requiring the person with whom a child lives, or is to live, to allow the child to visit or stay with the person named in the order, or for that person and the child otherwise to have contact with each other'[4]. The whole question of contact has become one of major importance. There are far more contact orders made than any other type of children order[5]. There are significantly more reported cases on this issue than on any other issue in family law with, possibly, the sad exception of child abduction[6]. Contact has also become one of the focal points for disputes under the ECHR and the Human Rights Act 1998 (HRA 1998). It has recently been the subject of a Report to the Lord Chancellor[7] and it has spawned an apparently endless amount of academic commentary[8].

There has been some difference of opinion about whether contact is the right of the parent or the right of the child[9]. We saw in Chapter 3 that the Scottish approach is to accept that parents have both responsibilities and rights and that contact falls into both categories. The view in Scotland must therefore be that contact is a right of *both* parent and child. The English contact order (replacing the former access order) is certainly 'child-centred' in form, providing for *the child* to visit or stay with a named individual. This is a deliberate change of emphasis from the old law, under which access orders were 'adult-centred' and allowed a named adult to visit the child. While it is now generally accepted in England that contact with parents is a fundamental right of children, it remains a matter of

---

1 Adoption Act 1976, s 14. See further Chapter 7.
2 Adoptions by single unmarried persons were allowed in some circumstances. See Adoption Act 1976, s 15, and Chapter 7 below.
3 See Chapter 7 below.
4 Section 8(1).
5 In 2001, 55,030 contact orders were made as compared with 29,546 residence orders. See *Judicial Statistics 2001*.
6 As to which see Chapter 17 below.
7 See *Making Contact Work: A Report to the Lord Chancellor on the Facilitation of Arrangements for Contact Between Children and their Non-Residential Parents and the Enforcement of Court Orders for Contact* (Lord Chancellor's Department, 2002).
8 These writings include C Smart and B Neale 'Arguments against Virtue – Must Contact be Enforced?' [1997] Fam Law 332; A Bainham 'Contact as a Fundamental Right' [1995] CLJ 255; J Masson 'Thinking about Contact – a Social or Legal Problem?' [2000] CFLQ 15; R Bailey-Harris 'Contact – Challenging Conventional Wisdom' [2000] CFLQ 361; and R Bailey-Harris, J Barron and J Pearce 'From Utility to Rights: The Presumption of Contact in Practice' (1999) IJLPF 111. See also J Eekelaar 'Contact – Over the Limit' [2002] Fam Law 271 for a sceptical view of the extent to which contact between the child and the non-resident parent should be pursued. Cf C Willbourne and G Stanley 'Contact under the Microscope' [2002] Fam Law 687.
9 It was first described judicially as a right of the child by Wrangham J in *M v M (Child: Access)* [1973] 2 All ER 81. For the view that it is *both* the child's and the parent's right, see A Bainham 'Changing Families and Changing Concepts: Reforming the Language of Family Law' [1998] CFLQ 1 at 5–8.

controversy whether it may also legitimately be regarded as a right of parents. It was suggested earlier that it is perhaps best regarded as a mutual interest and right of both parent and child[1].

This question must now be set in the context of the ECHR and the HRA 1998. What is abundantly clear from the jurisprudence of the ECtHR is that, whatever the domestic arguments about the concept of rights, contact is a *human right* or, put another way, a *Convention right* of both parent and child. This arises as an aspect of respect for their mutual family life under Article 8. Of course, this right is no more absolute than any other right under the ECHR, but it is the starting point. The right of either parent or child is liable to be displaced by the justifications for interfering with the right to respect for family life under Article 8(2). But it is important to emphasise, with the utmost vigour, that it is *only* those justifications expressly contemplated by the Convention which will provide a lawful basis for disrupting the mutual relationship between parent and child. As we shall see, this has important implications for the obligations of the State in this supposedly private area of law. A failure on the part of the State to take reasonable steps to enforce contact rights may lead to breach of the ECHR with all the consequences that entails. In this way, there is a very real *public* aspect to what is normally conceived as an issue of private law and what might be seen as a blurring of the public and private.

The ECtHR, as we have seen, has held on several occasions that States must take reasonable steps to enforce orders for contact. In its recent ruling in *Hansen v Turkey*[2] the Court found that Turkey had violated Article 8 in failing to make adequate and effective efforts, including realistic coercive measures against the Turkish father who was obstructing contact between the children and their Icelandic mother. A noteworthy feature of the judgment is the court's acknowledgement that, although not desirable, measures against reluctant children obliging them to see a parent could not be ruled out in the event of non-compliance or unlawful behaviour by the primary carer. The ruling is an indication of just how seriously the ECtHR views the importance of the State's obligation to foster and maintain contact between parent and child. This is apparent also from another recent judgment of the Court in *Kosmopoulou v Greece*[3]. Here the Court emphasised that the rights under Article 8 include a right for parents to have *positive* measures taken with a view to their being reunited with their children. The Court expressly states that the principle is not confined to cases where children are taken into public care, but also to private law cases involving contact and residence disputes. The obligation on States to facilitate reunion is qualified, however, and not absolute and requires that the national authorities strike a fair balance between the rights and interests of all concerned. Yet more recently, in *Re D (Intractable Contact Dispute: Publicity)*[4] Munby J held, inter alia, that it could not be assumed that the conventional domestic approach to the enforcement of contact meets the standards required by Articles 6 and 8 of

---

1   A particularly helpful discussion on the nature of the right to the 'society' of parents and child is to be found in A McCall Smith 'Is Anything Left of Parental Rights?' in McCall Smith and Sutherland (eds) *Family Rights* (Edinburgh University Press, 1990) at p 10.

2   [2004] 1 FLR 142.

3   [2004] 1 FLR 800.

4   [2004] 1 FLR 1226.

the ECHR. In this case there had been a staggering 43 court hearings before 16 different judges and numerous adjournments. The mother, who had sabotaged contact with the father by various means over a five-year period, had flouted court orders, which had resulted in penal notices, suspended prison sentences and eventually imprisonment itself. He said that in this case at least the father was fully entitled to blame the system[1].

The leading case of *Payne v Payne*[2] illustrates the way in which Article 8 operates in relation to contact. Following divorce the mother, a New Zealander, wished to return to New Zealand with the parties' four-year-old daughter. The effect would inevitably be to interfere drastically with the relationship between the child and the father and the paternal family, which was accepted to be extremely good. Mr Payne alleged that to give the mother leave to take the child out of the jurisdiction would be to infringe his right to contact which existed as an aspect of his right to respect for family life and would also be contrary to the principles of the Children Act 1989. He argued that there was in existing case-law a *presumption* in favour of giving leave which was incompatible with his Convention rights. The Court of Appeal disagreed. It found that there was nothing in the jurisprudence of the ECtHR which prevented the court from reaching the conclusion which it determined was in the best interests of the child. Here the child's welfare was bound up with the mother's happiness as primary carer and the effect of refusing leave might be that her 'unhappiness, sense of isolation and depression would be exacerbated to a degree that could well be damaging to the child'.

It is important to note, then, that this was not a denial that the father had a Convention right to contact with the child, but rather a determination that interference with this right was a necessary and proportionate response to the legitimate aim of protecting the best interests of the child, taking account also of the rights and interests of the mother[3]. In fact, the reasoning and conclusion in this case were not greatly different to the position taken by the House of Lords in the pre-Children Act decision in *Re KD (A Minor)*[4], perhaps indicating that the fundamentals have not really changed since then.

What is clear, beyond doubt, is that if it is a right, it is a qualified one. While parents may be thought to have a prima facie right to contact as an aspect of respect for their family life, protected by the ECHR, this is subject to the welfare principle and the courts' power of intervention.

Yet the power to deprive a parent and child of contact is not one which will be exercised lightly, and the courts will require a sound justification for doing so[5]. The mere fact that contact arrangements are difficult to operate, or that a parent

1   Cf *Re O (Contact: Withdrawal of Application)* [2004] 1 FLR 1258, in which Wall J held that it was not enough for a father to blame the system where he himself bore a substantial share of the blame for contact breaking down.
2   [2001] 1 FLR 1052. For the author's views on the case, see A Bainham 'Taking Children Abroad: Human Rights, Welfare and the Courts' [2001] CLJ 489. Other aspects of the case are discussed in Chapter 17 below.
3   One of the rights of the mother to which Thorpe LJ alluded was the right of mobility protected by Article 2, Protocol 4 to the ECHR, although not ratified by the UK.
4   [1988] AC 806.
5   See, for example, *Re C (Minors) (Access)* [1985] FLR 804, *Williams v Williams* [1985] FLR 509 and *Wright v Wright* (1981) FLR 276. See also *Re B (Minors: Access)* [1992] 1 FLR 140 in which the Court of Appeal held that 'eccentric, bizarre behaviour' ought not to deprive a father of defined access (now contact) provided that there was no suggestion of violence or verbal

or child would prefer not to have contact with the other parent, is not of itself a sufficient justification for refusing it. The leading case on the principles applicable to contact under the Children Act is the Court of Appeal decision in *Re M (Contact: Welfare Test)*[1]. It was a comparatively unusual case in that it involved denial of contact to a *mother*. The children were living with their father and had exhibited 'extreme distress' on previous attempts at contact. The mother argued that contact was a fundamental right of the child only to be displaced in 'wholly exceptional circumstances'. The Court of Appeal thought that this was going too far. There was a strong presumption in favour of contact but each case had to be examined on its merits. Wilson J said that the applicable principles now had to be cast in terms of the statutory checklist of factors in s 1(3) of the Children Act. Thus, the test would now be:

> '... whether the fundamental emotional need of every child to have an enduring relationship with both his parents [s 1(3)(b)] is outweighed by the depth of harm which in the light, inter alia, of his wishes and feelings [s 1(3)(a)] this child would be at risk of suffering [s 1(3)(e)] by virtue of a contact order.'

The public law governing contact is constituted by a separate code in Part IV of the Children Act[2]. This creates, inter alia, a *presumption* of reasonable contact in favour of parents and certain other individuals, and local authorities are placed under a statutory duty to promote contact between the child, his relatives and friends[3]. There are no corresponding provisions in the private law, although a presumption of contact with parents is implicit in what was said above and it was probably felt unnecessary to put it into statutory form. Although the hallmark of the scheme is flexibility, orders for 'reasonable contact', which leave the parties to work out the precise arrangements, are likely where a residence order is made. Indeed, without a contact order, the non-resident parent's right to see the child would be in doubt, notwithstanding his retention of parental responsibility, since to take physical control of the child for however short a period would arguably contravene the terms of the residence order[4]. Where, on the other hand, there is no residence order, parents will each have rights of contact as an aspect of parental responsibility and, provided they can work out an arrangement which is acceptable to both of them, a contact order will not be necessary[5]. A parent, while exercising contact, will also exercise parental responsibility to the full, but this arises quite independently of any order.

---

aggression in his personality or any suggested risk that he might use access to undermine the children's feelings of love and loyalty towards their mother. In this case the father had, inter alia, allegedly attempted to set fire to some of the grass on which the children were sitting. On another occasion it was alleged that he had walked down the street with a plastic bag over his head. See also *Re H (Minors) (Access)* [1992] 1 FLR 148 in similar vein.

1 [1995] 1 FLR 274, discussed alongside the ECtHR decision in *Hokkanen v Finland*, in A Bainham 'Contact as a Fundamental Right' (1995) CLJ 255.

2 Section 34 and Sch 2, para 15, which require local authorities to promote contact between children looked after by them and their families and friends. See also the Contact with Children Regulations 1991, SI 1991/891.

3 Ibid.

4 Although, as discussed earlier, this is a contentious issue.

5 This follows automatically from the no order principle in s 1(5).

The experience over many years has been that contact (formerly access) was at best difficult, and at worst impossible, to enforce[1] and the extent to which the courts should do so is a highly contentious issue. Children, especially older children, cannot be forced to see parents, 'absent' parents cannot be forced to be actively involved in parenting[2], and resident parents cannot be forced to be welcoming and co-operative towards an ex-spouse. Various enforcement mechanisms have been resorted to, including defining and varying the terms of contact, changing the residence of the child[3], making supervision or care orders[4] and imposing penal sanctions on the recalcitrant parent[5]. There has been some debate about how far the courts should go in their endeavours to enforce contact, much of which centres on the concept of 'implacable hostility'[6]. The notion that contact is a fundamental right which the courts should attempt to enforce in the absence of a very good reason to the contrary has been challenged. It has been said that 'the public and judicial treatment of contact has taken on an increasingly rigid and dogmatic form, which is becoming a harmful trend in family law'[7]. Against this it has been argued that the *attempt* to enforce needs to be made not least for ideological reasons. Unless the courts are seen to be taking the contact issue seriously, the message of the law that contact is an important right of the child may be lost. And caution needs to be exercised in equating too readily the interests of women (usually the so-called 'primary carers') and children in this matter[8]. Moreover, as we have seen, the ECHR *requires* the State to take action to enforce orders for contact.

The reported decisions illustrate the contrasting approach of the courts to the question of enforcement and reveal that they will examine carefully the reasons for refusal of contact.

In *A v N (Committal: Refusal of Contact)*[9] an order was eventually made committing a mother to prison for contempt where she refused to comply with the court's orders for contact for over a year and continued to dispute the father's paternity despite clear DNA evidence to the contrary. In *Re B (Contact: Stepfather's Opposition)*[10] the Court of Appeal made it plain that the mere fact of a step-father's

---

1 See, for example, *Churchard v Churchard* [1984] FLR 635 and *I v D (Access Order: Enforcement)* [1988] 2 FLR 286.

2 Although there is increasing support for the view that parents should be placed under a legal duty, as in Scotland, to maintain contact with their children.

3 But see *Re B (Residence Order: Status Quo)* [1998] 1 FLR 368 for an inappropriate change in the child's residential arrangements precipitated by contact difficulties.

4 A drastic example under the old law being *R v G (Surrey County Council Intervening)* [1984] Fam 100, where the child was eventually committed to care.

5 But see *Re F (Contact: Enforcement: Representation of Child)* [1998] 1 FLR 691 where the child in question was disabled, having been born with cerebral palsy, and where the Court of Appeal held that the judge had rightly not attached a penal notice to the contact order made in favour of the father.

6 See particularly J Parker and D Eaton 'Opposing Contact' [1994] Fam Law 636; S Jolly 'Implacable Hostility, Contact and the Limits of Law' [1995] CFLQ 228; and H Conway 'Implacable Hostility – Seeking a Breakthrough' [1997] Fam Law 109.

7 Smart and Neale 'Arguments against virtue – must contact be enforced?' [1997] Fam Law 332.

8 A Bainham 'Changing Families and Changing Concepts: Reforming the Language of Family Law' [1998] CFLQ 1 at 7.

9 [1997] 1 FLR 533. For another case of committal to prison, against which the mother successfully appealed, see *Re K (Contact: Committal Order)* [2003] 1 FLR 277.

10 [1997] 2 FLR 579.

opposition to contact between the child and the natural father would not prevent the court making a contact order if the best interests of the child required it. On the facts, however, the step-father's position was found to be justifiable since the child had had virtually no contact with the natural father since birth. *A v N* was an example of so-called 'implacable hostility'[1]. More recently it has been argued that there is a psychological form of child abuse, recognised by courts in the USA, known as 'parental alienation syndrome' which occurs, it is said, where one parent seeks to alienate their children from the other parent, consciously or sub-consciously[2]. It is then alleged that: 'severe PAS becomes self-perpetuating: the child refuses contact with the alienated parent, having internalised a host of powerful negative messages from the alienating parent'[3]. There is disagreement among psychologists about whether there is such a condition, and the English courts have been unimpressed by arguments based on so-called PAS in those cases in which it has been raised[4].

In contrast to cases of so-called implacable hostility are those in which it is transparently plain that a parent has a sound justification for refusing contact, of which fear of violence heads the list. Thus, in *Re D (Contact: Reasons for Refusal)*[5] the mother had a genuine fear of violence from the father and it was held that it would be wrong to categorise this as a case of implacable hostility[6]. In some cases a compromise has been reached which has resulted in an order for only indirect contact.[7] The leading case on the principles applicable to direct contact in the context of a violent parent is the Court of Appeal decision in *Re L (Contact: Domestic Violence)*[8], a consolidated appeal by four fathers who had been denied contact, all of whom lost their appeals. The following principles emerge. At the interim stage, before any allegations of violence have been properly investigated, the priority must be to secure the safety of the child and the resident parent. There is not, however, a presumption of no contact on proof of violence but violence is obviously a factor in the exercise of the judge's discretion. Where the allegations are proved, the court must engage in a balancing exercise, weighing the risk against the positive benefits of contact. The willingness of a party to change his

---

1   For a more recent example of the same phenomenon see *Re S (Unco-operative Mother)* [2004] 2 FLR 710. See also *V v V (Contact: Implacable Hostility)* [2004] 2 FLR 851, in which Bracewell J responded to a case of implacable hostility by the mother by transferring the children's residence to the father.

2   See T Hobbs 'Parental Alienation Syndrome and UK Family Courts' [2002] Fam Law 182. Cf C Bruch 'Parental Alienation Syndrome and Alienated Children – getting it wrong in child custody cases' [2001] CFLQ 381.

3   T Hobbs (above) at p 183.

4   See, for example, *Re C (Prohibition on Further Applications)* [2002] 1 FLR 1136 and *Re S (Contact: Children's Views)* [2002] 1 FLR 1156.

5   [1997] 2 FLR 48.

6   Sadly, there is no shortage of reported cases where contact has been refused in the context of domestic violence. See also *Re H (Contact: Domestic Violence)* [1998] 2 FLR 42; *Re M (Contact: Violent Parent)* [1999] 2 FLR 321; *Re S (Violent Parent: Indirect Contact)* [2000] 1 FLR 481; and *Re L (Contact: Genuine Fear)* [2002] 1 FLR 621.

7   As in *Re S* and *Re L* (above).

8   *Re L (Contact: Domestic Violence); Re V (Contact: Domestic Violence); Re M (Contact: Domestic Violence); Re H (Contact: Domestic Violence)* [2000] 2 FLR 334. On the general question of contact in the context of domestic violence, see C Humphreys and C Harrison 'Squaring the Circle – Contact and Domestic Violence' [2003] Fam Law 419. See also F Kaganas 'Contact and domestic violence' [2000] CFLQ 311.

conduct would be an important factor in this assessment. Finally, under the ECHR, where there is a conflict between the rights and interests of a child and those of a parent, the interests of the child must prevail under Article 8(2).

In *Re H (Contact Order) (No 2)*[1] Wall J had to consider how to perform this balancing exercise where violence and threats emanated from illness. In this case, the father suffered from Huntington's disease which could bring adverse effects on mood and personality. It had led the father to violence and indeed to threaten to kill the children, but it was not in doubt that he loved the children or that they loved him. He reached the conclusion that direct contact could not be risked in these circumstances but expressed the confidence that the mother would promote indirect contact through letters and telephone calls.

Just as the principles of contact applied by the courts must comply with the ECHR, so too must the principles governing enforcement. In this respect, the jurisprudence of the ECtHR makes it plain that there is a *positive* obligation on the State, acting through the courts and social welfare agencies, to make all reasonable efforts to facilitate contact between parent and child and to reunite them where they have become separated. Thus, in *Hokkanen v Finland*[2] the Court found that the State of Finland had breached Mr Hokkanen's right to respect for family life by the failure of the Finnish authorities over many years to enforce his right of access to his daughter who was in the care of her maternal grandparents following the death of her mother[3]. In contrast, in *Glaser v United Kingdom*[4] the father unsuccessfully argued that the UK authorities in England and Scotland had breached his Convention rights in their failure to enforce adequately English contact orders in relation to his three children. The mother had managed to disappear to Scotland with the child and dodged compliance with the court orders. Although the orders of the English court were registered in Scotland, they proved very difficult to enforce because of the mother's determination to be obstructive. The ECtHR concluded that the UK authorities had done all that could reasonably be expected of them. The most significant point to grasp about these decisions is the principle that the State is accountable for its actions in what might appear to be an essentially private law context.

Despite attempts at enforcement, it remains the case that many 'non-resident' parents (usually, but not invariably, fathers) lose all substantial contact with their children within a few years of divorce[5]. A major challenge is to discover why it is

---

1   [2002] 1 FLR 22.

2   [1996] 1 FLR 289.

3   See also *Ciliz v The Netherlands* [2000] 2 FLR 469 in which the deportation of the father and refusal to extend his residence permit by the Dutch authorities was held to breach his right to respect for private and family life. The father had separated from the mother and had only had intermittent contact with the child. Nevertheless, the ECtHR found that it was enough to amount to family life between them. The interference with this right, though in pursuance of the legitimate aim of preserving the economic well-being of the country, was not *necessary* in a democratic society since it prejudged the decision on the father's pending application for access (contact) and it interfered with his ability to develop family ties with the child. See also *Elsholtz v Germany* [2000] 2 FLR 486.

4   [2001] 1 FLR 153.

5   See J Bradshaw and J Millar *Lone Parent Families in the UK* (HMSO, 1991). For recent evidence from research in Australia, see P Parkinson and B Smyth 'Satisfaction and dissatisfaction with father–child contact arrangements in Australia' [2004] CFLQ 289.

that so many contact arrangements break down with the passage of time. Certainly there is a philosophical commitment in both the Children Act and the Family Law Act 1996 to continued dual parenting following divorce, but the question of whether the legal system can do much, or indeed anything, to achieve this remains unresolved.

The whole question of contact and how best to facilitate it was the subject of a report to the Lord Chancellor by the Children Act Sub-Committee of the Advisory Board on Family Law[1]. Among its recommendations were: the provision of better information about the principles of contact to be provided to separating and divorcing parents and to children themselves; that judges and magistrates should have the power to refer parties to mediation; that there should be better funding for contact centres[2]; and that there should be funding for additional facilities for resolving contact disputes by negotiation, conciliation and mediation. This recommendation was based on 'a widespread feeling that an application to the court should be the last resort'. As we have seen, this premise is one which might be challenged by some commentators who have warned of the dangers involved in over-reliance on the settlement approach. A further recommendation that the courts should be given much wider powers to ensure that their orders are obeyed and otherwise to facilitate their implementation was also controversial.

In December 2003, the Department of Constitutional Affairs published a report[3] containing a number of further recommendations designed to promote and facilitate safe and beneficial contact between children and non-resident parents. It has also published a report[4] containing the results of a survey on the level of contact which currently exists between children and non-resident parents. This reveals some differences in perception as between resident and non-resident parents about this. For example, while 14 per cent of non-resident parents reported that they never saw their children, twice as many resident parents, 28 per cent, said that the non-resident parent never saw the child. While 77 per cent of non-resident parents said that they saw their children either every day, at least once a week or at least once a month, the figure was only 60 per cent among resident parents who reported this. Even greater discrepancies in these perceptions were observed in relation to indirect contact. The survey also revealed that, while the law might not make the link between contact and child support payments, many parents did[5]. It also revealed that children who had direct contact at least once a week with the non-resident parent were more likely to receive support payments than children who had direct contact less frequently, while those who had no contact with the non-resident parent were the least likely to receive support.

---

1   *Making Contact Work* (Lord Chancellor's Department, 2002).
2   In February 2003 the Government announced that £2.5 million would be allocated with a view to promoting safe contact between children and separated parents, the bulk of which would go into developing supervised child contact centres.
3   *The Final Report of the Child Contact Facilitation and Enforcement Group* (Department of Constitutional Affairs, 2003).
4   A Blackwell and F Dawe *Non-Resident Parental Contact with Children* (Department of Constitutional Affairs, 2003).
5   For discussion of the issue, see G Brasse 'Contact and Money' [2002] Fam Law 691.

Finally, in July 2004 the Government published a Green Paper[1] launching a consultation on a number of significant changes it proposes with a view to facilitating contact between children and parents from whom they are separated. The Government rejects the view that there is a need for a change in the law or to the core principles in the Children Act but accepts that changes are needed to the way in which the legal system operates in order to resolve parental disputes more effectively. It notes that only 10 per cent of separating couples resort to the courts while the overwhelming majority already reach agreement without this. It rejects the perception of some fathers' groups that the courts are biased against them[2]. It favours an approach which does more to facilitate contact by agreement in this minority of cases which would otherwise be likely to result in protracted litigation. But it also proposes more diverse measures for enforcing agreements and court orders[3] relating to contact, should these prove necessary. This dual approach reflects the Government's view that facilitation and enforcement are not properly seen as alternatives but rather as points on a spectrum.

Alongside the consultation period, the Government is piloting a more intensive supportive intervention model called the 'Family Resolutions Project', the intention being to roll it out nationally if the results are good in the piloted areas[4]. The experiment is influenced by procedures for resolving family conflict in other jurisdictions, notably some US States. Participation in the scheme is on a voluntary basis. Components include screening for domestic violence, parents' attendance at information and support sessions which focus on co-parenting and the needs of children, and family resolution sessions designed to help parents produce a 'parenting plan' setting out how they intend to co-operate over the future parenting of their children.

In terms of essential philosophy, the Green Paper is strongly committed to the paramountcy principle. It rejects the notion that there should be a statutory 'presumption of contact' and an automatic 50:50 division of the child's time between the two parents, both for practical reasons and because 'children are not a commodity to be apportioned equally after separation'[5]. On the other hand, it is firmly accepted that 'in the event of parental separation, a child's welfare is best promoted by a continuing relationship with both parents as long as it is safe to do so'[6]. It is acknowledged, albeit rather cursorily, that 'rights' have a part to play in that the ECHR requires respect for private and family life and that 'this includes respect for the rights of both parents who enjoy family life with their children to have contact with those children, provided this is consistent with the welfare of the children, and also the rights of children to have beneficial relationships with their parents'[7].

---

1   *Parental Separation: Children's Needs and Parents' Responsibilities* (2004) (Cm 6273).
2   For a vehemently expressed opinion that they are so biased, see Bob Geldof 'The Real Love that Dare Not Speak its Name' in A Bainham, B Lindley, M Richards and L Trinder (eds) *Children and their Families: Contact, Rights and Welfare* (Hart Publishing, 2003) at p 171.
3   New powers would include referral of a defaulting parent to a variety of resources including counselling and parenting programmes, community-based orders and the award of financial compensation from one parent to another, for example where a holiday has been lost.
4   Inner London, Brighton and Sunderland.
5   Paragraph 42. For a further critique of the 50:50 time-sharing presumption, see F Kaganas and C Piper 'Shared Parenting – a 70% solution?' [2001] CFLQ 365.
6   Paragraph 4.
7   Paragraph 45.

These proposals represent a genuine attempt to address the issue of disputed contact. However, it is a pity that the notion of a legal presumption of contact appears to be rejected out of hand. It would, for example, be perfectly possible to enshrine a legal presumption in favour of *maximising* contact with both parents following divorce insofar as to do so would be consistent with the welfare of the child[1]. It does not follow that because a crude mathematical presumption for a 50:50 division of time is rejected that *no* presumption is appropriate. It will also be necessary for all those involved in the family justice system to have a sharp appreciation of rights, as required by the ECHR and UNCRC, and it is to be hoped that the Government will in due course give this issue greater prominence than is perhaps suggested by the solitary paragraph[2] it apparently merited in the Green Paper.

Prohibited steps and specific issue orders

These orders are designed to resolve what might be described as 'single issues' affecting children and are modelled on the powers of the court in wardship. It was an express aim of the Children Act to emulate and incorporate the better features of the wardship jurisdiction[3]. Both orders may be made in conjunction with other s 8 orders or on freestanding applications. They are intended to be subsidiary to residence and contact orders (which are the principal orders governing the exercise of parental responsibility) and they must not therefore be made with a view to achieving a result which could be achieved by the main orders[4] or in a way which is denied to the High Court in the exercise of its inherent jurisdiction[5]. The court in wardship exercises a degree of continuing control over a child's situation and retains parental responsibility (formerly 'custody') in the wider sense of the decision-making powers. The statutory powers are narrower (at least conceptually) than this all-embracing 'custodial' control. In wardship, every major issue affecting the ward must be referred back to the court for its determination[6]. The statutory orders do not vest parental responsibility in the court but do enable it to exercise control over particular areas of difficulty.

These orders should be considered alongside the court's wide powers to attach conditions and give directions in relation to residence and contact orders. These respective powers are two alternative ways of addressing problem areas. The orders may be pre-emptive or reactive in nature. Where it appears to the court, on making a residence or contact order, that there is likely to be a potential area of dispute, for example over education, it may wish to address the difficulty in

---

1 The author has argued for this elsewhere. See A Bainham 'Contact as a Right and Obligation' in A Bainham, B Lindley, M Richards and L Trinder (eds) *Children and their Families* (above) at p 61.

2 Paragraph 45.

3 Law Com Report No 172 *Guardianship and Custody* (1988), Part IV.

4 Section 9(5)(a). See *Nottinghamshire County Council v P* [1994] Fam 18; cf *Re H (Prohibited Steps Order)* [1995] 1 FLR 638, and Chapter 12 below.

5 Section 9(5)(b), and Law Com Report No 172 (above) at paras 4.18–4.20.

6 There were several good examples under the old law of a failure to refer issues back to the court. See, particularly, *Re GU (A Minor) (Wardship)* [1984] FLR 811 where a local authority was criticised by the High Court for arranging an abortion for an adolescent girl in its care, who was also a ward of court, without first referring the issue to the High Court. The ongoing control exercised by the court in wardship is best illustrated by the House of Lords decision in *Re E (SA) (A Minor) (Wardship)* [1984] 1 All ER 289.

advance. On the other hand, such difficulties may only manifest themselves sometime later, at which point it will be open to a parent to return to court for those difficulties to be resolved. Where the court is seised of a dispute over a matter of upbringing it must be prepared to adjudicate. In *Re P (Parental Dispute: Judicial Determination)*[1] the divorced parents disagreed over the private school the children should attend. The judge, favouring the mother's choice of school, made an order that 'in respect of both M and O, future questions which may arise about either child's schooling ... shall be finally determined by the child's mother following consultation with their father'. The Court of Appeal held that this amounted to the plainest failure to adjudicate, that the parent had a right to judicial determination and that the court should not abdicate from its primary obligation to decide.

A prohibited steps order is an order 'that no step which could be taken by a parent in meeting his parental responsibility for a child, and which is of a kind specified in the order, shall be taken by any person without the consent of the court'[2]. Around 8,730 applications and 5,780 orders were made for prohibited steps in 1996, approximately the same numbers as in 1995[3]; 5,345 orders were made in 2000 and there was a sharp increase to 7,343 orders in 2001[4]. The order is entirely prohibitive or negative in substance as its name suggests. The kinds of involvements with children which might be prohibited are infinitely various but, most obviously, contact between the child and an 'undesirable adult' could be restrained[5]. This example highlights one of the limitations of the order. In view of the reference to the exercise of parental responsibility, the order cannot be used to prohibit a mature child herself from having such contact. It may be that this is one instance in which the wardship jurisdiction will continue to have a special usefulness, especially in view of the Court of Appeal's ruling that the court in wardship or under the inherent jurisdiction has power to override the wishes of a mature minor[6].

An interesting use of the prohibited steps order occurred in *Re Z (A Minor) (Freedom of Publication)*[7] which concerned a child of famous parents who was receiving treatment at a special unit for her special educational needs. The courts had previously granted an injunction under the inherent jurisdiction restraining the media from publishing information which could lead to revelation of the child's identity. The mother then wished her daughter to take part in a television programme about the unit. It was held by the Court of Appeal that the child had a right of confidentiality concerning her attendance at the unit. The mother could, prima facie, waive this right of confidentiality on the child's behalf but to do so would amount to an exercise of parental responsibility. A prohibited steps order

---

1   [2003] 1 FLR 286.
2   Section 8(1).
3   *The Children Act Advisory Committee Final Report June 1997* (Lord Chancellor's Department, 1997).
4   *Children Act Report 2001* (Department of Health, 2002).
5   The so-called 'teenage wardship' cases would fall within this category – as to which, see NV Lowe and RAH White *Wards of Court* (2nd edn) (Barry Rose/Kluwer, 1986) at ch 12. Another use of the order, the subject of much recent litigation, is to restrain the removal of a child from the country, as to which see Chapter 17 below.
6   *Re R (A Minor) (Wardship: Medical Treatment)* [1992] 1 FLR 190, discussed in Chapter 8 below.
7   [1996] 1 FLR 191. For an analysis of the decision in the wider context of protecting children's privacy, see J Moriarty 'Children, Privacy and the Press' [1997] CFLQ 217, especially at pp 226 et seq.

could therefore be made to control the exercise of this aspect of parental responsibility. Here, the child's welfare prevailed over the freedom of publication and the order should be made.

A specific issue order is an order 'giving direction for the purpose of determining a specific question which has arisen, or which may arise, in connection with any aspect of parental responsibility for a child'[1]. In 2000 there were 2,457 such orders, a figure which increased significantly to 2,960 in 2001[2]. The order may be positive or negative, and its function is to *regulate* a sphere of upbringing. The order may be especially useful where a sole residence order is *not* made. Where the court makes a joint residence order, or no order at all, both parents will exercise full responsibility. However, it is possible that there may be an area of disagreement which could jeopardise the whole arrangement if it is not resolved. Here, the court might use the specific issue order in a variety of ways which, it has been suggested, could include imposing its own view, referring the issue to an appropriate third party such as a welfare officer or doctor, or reserving this one area of upbringing to one parent[3].

The reported cases illustrate the diverse uses of the specific issue order. In *Re HG (Specific Issue Order: Sterilisation)*[4], a specific issue order was used to authorise the sterilisation of a severely epileptic young woman with a chromosomal deficiency. Since she was under a legal disability, her father was allowed to apply for the order on her behalf as next friend. In *Re F (Specific Issue: Child Interview)*[5], the father of two boys was due to stand trial for assaulting the mother. The father's defence lawyers succeeded in obtaining a specific issue order to authorise them to interview the boys in order to prepare the father's defence. It was held that interviewing children involved an aspect of parental responsibility which could be controlled through s 8 orders.

In contrast, in *Re J (Specific Issue Order: Leave to Apply)*[6], it was held by Wall J that the determination of 'children in need' for the purposes of Part III of the Children Act was not intended by Parliament to be susceptible to adjudication by the courts through s 8 orders. Accordingly, a 17-year-old boy failed in his attempt to obtain leave to apply for a specific issue order requiring the local authority to deem him to be a child in need.

In *Re A (Specific Issue Order: Parental Disagreement)*[7] a French father succeeded in obtaining a specific issue order, as against the mother who had primary care, that the two children attend a French-speaking school, the Lycée Français in London. The court was influenced by the need to preserve the children's bi-cultural identity and by bilingual considerations. Rather in contrast to this outcome, in *Re J (Specific Issue Orders: Muslim Upbringing and Circumcision)*[8] the nominally Christian

---

1   Section 8(1).
2   *Children Act Report 2001* (Department of Health, 2002).
3   SM Cretney, JM Masson and R Bailey-Harris *Principles of Family Law* (7th edn) (Sweet & Maxwell, 2002) at p 596. It is of course fair to point out that too liberal a use of the order would jeopardise the principle of continuing parental responsibility, but the no order principle in s 1(5) ought to operate as a check on this.
4   [1993] 1 FLR 587. On sterilisation generally, see further Chapter 8 below. On the capacity of children to seek court orders, see Chapter 13 below.
5   [1995] 1 FLR 819.
6   [1995] 1 FLR 669.
7   [2001] 1 FLR 121.
8   [2000] 1 FLR 571.

mother, who was also the primary carer, was able to resist the application of the father, a non-practising Turkish Muslim, that their five-year-old child be circumcised and brought up in the Muslim faith[1]. Finally, in *Re K (Specific Issue Order)*[2] a natural father failed (controversially) to obtain an order requiring the mother to inform the child, aged 12 at the time of the proceedings, of his paternity and his existence. The merits of the decision are discussed later[3].

The power to attach conditions and give directions

The court has a general power when making a s 8 order to give directions or attach conditions to the order. These conditions may be imposed on the person in whose favour the order is made, a parent or a non-parent with parental responsibility, and anyone with whom the child is living. The court may also make 'such incidental, supplemental or consequential provision as the court thinks fit'[4]. The former distinction between interim and final orders has been abolished and all s 8 orders may be limited to a specific period and individual provisions in the orders may be subject to time-limits. There is also a general power to vary all orders which cease when the child reaches 16 years of age, other than in exceptional circumstances[5], although under amendments introduced by the Adoption and Children Act 2002 residence orders may be extended to 18 years of age[6].

The width and flexibility of these powers should enable the court to tailor its orders to the individual circumstances of the case. Where appropriate, the court may go into considerable detail about the future upbringing of the child, although to attempt to regulate this too closely might actually generate opportunities for dispute. Moreover, an extensive use of detailed orders would run counter to the ethos of continuing parental responsibility. The court has the power to dilute considerably the input of a non-resident parent by preventing the exercise of parental responsibility or by making it subject to extensive restrictions. It is, however, bound by the welfare and no order principles in deciding whether or not to make directions or conditions and this should operate as a restraint on the use of these powers.

Re E (Residence Order: Imposition of Conditions)[7] provides an illustration of an inappropriate use of conditions. Here, the judge made a residence order in favour of the mother but sought to impose a requirement that she should continue to reside at a named address. The Court of Appeal held that this was an unwarranted

---

1   For a detailed commentary on *Re J* and for an assessment of the place of religion and culture in decisions affecting children, see C Bridge 'Religion, Culture and the Body of the Child' in A Bainham, S Day Sclater and M Richards (eds) *Body Lore and Laws* (Hart Publishing, 2002). See also *Re P (Section 91(14) Guidelines) (Residence and Religious Heritage)* [1999] 2 FLR 573 which concerned orthodox Jewish parents who were seeking the return of their Down's syndrome child who had been fostered with nominally Roman Catholic foster-parents.
2   [1999] 2 FLR 280.
3   See Chapter 5 below.
4   Section 11(7).
5   Section 9(7).
6   Adoption and Childen Act 2002. See further Chapter 6 below.
7   [1997] 2 FLR 638. Cf *B v B (Residence: Condition Limiting Geographic Area)* [2004] 2 FLR 979 for an exceptional case in which a condition regulating the area in which the resident mother should live was made. For other illustrations, see *Re D (Residence: Imposition of Conditions)* [1996] 2 FLR 281 and *D v N (Contact Order: Conditions)* [1997] 2 FLR 797, both of which established the principle that the court ought not to make orders, which are injunctive in nature, dressed up as conditions under s 11(7).

imposition on the right of a parent to choose where she would live within the UK and with whom.

Orders restricting applications

Under s 91(14) of the Children Act it is possible for the court to prevent any further applications in relation to a particular child when it disposes of an application for any order under the Act. There have been several reported examples of the use of these restrictions which are designed to prevent the unsettling effect of successive and potentially endless applications to the court[1]. Where such a restriction has been enforced the party affected will be required to apply to the court for leave to lift it and allow a further application. It has been held by the Court of Appeal that the criteria in s 10(9) of the Act (which generally govern applications for leave to seek s 8 orders) are inappropriate in these circumstances[2]. The test is rather the simple one of whether the application for leave demonstrates that there is a need for renewed judicial investigations. It appears that the matter is not governed by the welfare principle[3].

Following the HRA 1998, there was some speculation that the order might be found to be incompatible with Article 6 of the ECHR. The relevant part of Article 6 provides: 'In the determination of his civil rights and obligations ... everyone is entitled to a fair and public hearing within a reasonable time by an independent tribunal established by law'. In *Re P (Section 91(14) Guidelines) (Residence and Religious Heritage)*[4] the Court of Appeal considered arguments under both this and the UNCRC. It was held that a s 91(14) restriction did not breach Article 6 because it did not deny access to the court, only access to an immediate inter partes hearing. It was of the nature of a partial and justified restriction which required the applicant to persuade the judge that there was an arguable case with some chance of success.

It is clear, however, that the restriction on applications should not be imposed lightly in the absence of evidence that repeat applications are likely to cause detriment to the child and are being pursued in an unreasonable manner[5].

Orders in problem cases

In a small minority of cases, the court may be positively unhappy, or at least concerned, about what is proposed for children on divorce. Whether problem cases will come to light at all, given the court's more limited duty, must be a matter

---

1   See, particularly, *B v B (Residence Order: Restricting Applications)* [1997] 1 FLR 139, *Re G (Child Case: Parental Involvement)* [1996] 1 FLR 857 and *Re N (Section 91(14) Order)* [1996] 1 FLR 356. For an inappropriate use of the restricting order, see *Re M (Contact: Restrictive Order: Supervision)* [1998] 1 FLR 721. See also *Re M (Section 91(14) Order)* [1999] 2 FLR 553, in which the Court of Appeal indicated that a time restriction on the order might be appropriate.

2   *Re A (Application for Leave)* [1998] 1 FLR 1.

3   *Re R (Residence: Contact: Restricting Applications)* [1998] 1 FLR 749.

4   [1999] 2 FLR 573.

5   See the detailed guidance on when the orders should be used by Hale J (as she then was) in *C v W (Contact: Leave to Apply)* [1999] 1 FLR 916. For a case in which it was held that there had been an improper use of the order affecting a litigant acting in person, see *Re C (Prohibition on Further Applications)* [2002] 1 FLR 1136. And for a case in which the restriction (imposed by the judge for the extent of the child's minority) was found to be excessive, see *Re B (Section 91(14)*

of doubt[1]. Under the old law, the court might, of its own volition, make a supervision or care order on the basis that there were 'exceptional circumstances making it desirable that the child should be under the supervision of an independent person'[2]. These orders were, by definition, not extensively used and, where they were, they were used in two quite different kinds of circumstances[3]. The Law Commission was concerned that a clear distinction should be drawn between those cases in which the court simply wished to assist with difficulties which might occur following relationship breakdown and those in which it was concerned to protect the child from possible harm[4]. The choice for the court under the Children Act is now between making a 'family assistance order' (intended to cover the first situation) and a 's 37 direction' to the local authority (intended to cover the second situation). It might also, in appropriate cases, seek to meet its concerns by making one or more s 8 orders with or without attaching conditions, or by giving directions. In practice, it is likely that the distinction between family assistance orders and s 37 directions may be less than clear cut and that the court's choice of order will be determined by the level of concern it feels for the child's situation.

The family assistance order
The family assistance order (FAO) was an innovation of the Children Act[5]. It is, in essence, a form of short-term voluntary assistance to the parties, usually in the immediate transitional period following breakdown of their relationship. It contrasts with the traditional form of supervision order which is now confined to cases in which the protection of the child is in issue. One use of the FAO may be to provide assistance with difficulties over contact[6]. The FAO may be made, in principle, wherever family proceedings take place, and the court has power to make it whether or not it makes any other order. Its effect is to require either a CAFCASS officer or an officer of the local authority to be made available 'to advise, assist and (where appropriate) befriend anyone named in the order'[7].

Order: Duration) [2004] 1 FLR 871. In this case the Court of Appeal held that the judge had not correctly struck the balance between preventing unwarranted litigation and the primary objective of restoring the child's relationship with her father and reduced the length of the moratorium to two years.

1　It may be that the combined effect of the no order principle and the court's reformulated duty on divorce will be to make the court's role in practice a more reactive rather than proactive one. Unless a party before the court raises a problem, it is possible that it may go unnoticed.

2　Such orders could be made in a range of family proceedings including guardianship, divorce and adoption.

3　Discussed in Law Com Report No 172 *Guardianship and Custody* (1988) at paras 5.10 et seq.

4　Ibid.

5　Section 16 and Law Com Report No 172 (above) at paras 5.19–5.20. For a discussion of the use of the order, see J Seden 'Family Assistance Orders and the Children Act 1989: Ambivalence about Intervention or a Means of Safeguarding and Promoting Children's Welfare?' (2001) IJLPF 226.

6　As in *Re M (Contact: Family Assistance: McKenzie Friend)* [1999] 1 FLR 75. In *Re E (Family Assistance Order)* [1999] 2 FLR 512 the order was used against a local authority which was reluctant to provide facilities for supervised contact between a mother and her child.

7　Section 16(1).

This could be a parent or guardian, any person with whom the child is living or in whose favour a contact order has been made, or the child himself[1].

The order may only be made in 'exceptional circumstances' and requires the consent of every person named in it other than the child[2]. The consent requirement underlines the voluntary nature of the order but it is noticeable that there is no obligation to obtain the child's consent or, it would appear, to ascertain or take into account his wishes[3]. Those persons named in the order must keep the specified officer informed of their addresses and must permit visits by that officer. The order will last for a maximum of six months or such shorter period as the court specifies[4]. The officer's powers are limited to referring to the court the question of whether an existing s 8 order should be varied or discharged[5]. He has no power to seek a supervision or care order but, where he expresses concern for the child's situation, this may prompt the court to direct an investigation by the local authority.

Re C (Family Assistance Order)[6] shows the potential limitations of the order in practice. In this case, a boy of 10, who had left home to live with his uncle and aunt, succeeded, with leave, in obtaining a residence order in their favour. The court also made a family assistance order directed to the local authority with a view to repairing the damaged relationship between the boy and his mother. The local authority complained that it lacked the resources to carry out the order and Johnson J, noting the limited options for enforcement of the order, felt that it was not in the child's best interests to attempt to force the authority to carry it out.

In 2000 there were 979 family assistance orders and 1,096 were made in 2001[7].

Section 37 directions

Prior to the Children Act, the courts had powers in a variety of family proceedings to take the initiative and make a supervision order or, in cases of more serious concern, to commit a child to care[8]. While the local authority might itself have been intervening in the proceedings and seeking an order, there was nothing to preclude the court from, in effect, over-ruling the authority and imposing an order on it. A major objective of the reforms in the public sphere was to spell out and standardise the basis upon which a child might be placed compulsorily under supervision or committed to care. There was concern that the courts in private proceedings, particularly but not exclusively wardship, could reserve to themselves a wider power of compulsory intervention based not on the criteria laid down by Parliament but on some more open-ended criterion such as 'best

---

1   Section 16(2). In *Leeds City Council v C* [1993] 1 FLR 269, Booth J held that the FAO was the correct order to achieve local authority supervision of contact between a mother and her three children. The court should not try to achieve this result by making directions under s 11(7).

2   Section 16(3).

3   The statutory checklist, which applies to s 8 orders and care and supervision orders, does not apply to family assistance orders. Nonetheless, it is suggested that, as a matter of good practice, the wishes of the child concerned should be explored.

4   Section 16(4) and (5).

5   Section 16(6).

6   [1996] 1 FLR 424. See also *S v P (Contact Application: Family Assistance Order)* [1997] 2 FLR 277, in which the court refused to make the order, the effect of which would have been to provide an 'escort service' for the children to visit their father in prison.

7   *Children Act Report 2001* (Department of Health, 2002).

8   Law Com Report No 172 (above) at paras 5.2–5.9.

interests' or 'exceptional circumstances'[1]. The Children Act removed this power to act independently, except the power to make interim care orders[2]. The new principle is that the local authority, which has primary statutory responsibility for child protection, must seek care or supervision orders which must only be made where the statutory threshold is crossed[3].

The court is, however, given a more limited power of independent action. It may, in any family proceedings, direct an authority to investigate a child's circumstances[4]. In this way, the court can still take the lead in the sense of triggering action by the authority. The power to make the direction exists wherever 'a question arises with respect to the welfare of any child' and 'it appears to the court that it may be appropriate for a care or supervision order to be made with respect to him'. This power is additional to the authority's right to intervene in family proceedings to seek such orders[5]. Where a direction is made, the authority must investigate and consider whether any action is required and, if so, what this should be[6]. It must then report back to the court within eight weeks but, significantly, where it decides to take no action, the court may not overrule it by imposing a care or supervision order. This is one area in which the Children Act effected a clear shift in the balance of power for child protection away from the courts and towards local authorities although, as we shall see, the requirements of the ECHR and the HRA 1998 may well shift the balance back in the direction of the courts[7].

The remarkable case of *Re H (A Minor) (Section 37 Direction)* illustrates the use of the s 37 direction[8]. Here, a child was born to a couple who already had one child and did not want a second. They agreed to hand the baby over to a lesbian couple (A and B) who lived nearby and wanted to bring up the child as their own. In fact, the birth had taken place at their home. A and B wished to adopt or foster the child but were not permitted to do so. Scott Baker J made an interim residence order in A and B's favour, coupled with an interim supervision order and a s 37 direction to the local authority. While he made no criticism of the care offered by A and B, he thought that there were long-term concerns which justified investigation by the local authority.

In *Re L (Section 37 Direction)*[9] the Court of Appeal held that there had been an inappropriate use of the direction. In this case the child, a girl aged six, had been looked after with devotion by her maternal grandmother but the parents, though not wishing to challenge her as primary carer, were unhappy with the extent and detail of contact which they had with the child. The judge had, inter alia, made a s 37 direction on the basis that some evidence related to the mother might *eventually* justify a care or supervision order. The Court of Appeal thought this too speculative. The case came nowhere near the public law threshold and, in purely

---

1   See the DHSS *Review of Child Care Law* (1985) at paras 8.20–8.23 and 15.35–15.38, and the White Paper *The Law on Child Care and Family Services* (1987) (Cmnd 62) at para 36.
2   Section 38(3).
3   Section 31(2), and see Chapter 11 below.
4   Section 37(1).
5   Thus, under s 31(4) an application for a care or supervision order may be made 'on its own or in any other family proceedings'.
6   Section 37(2).
7   See Chapter 11 below.
8   [1993] 2 FLR 541. For another illustration, see *Re CE (Section 37 Direction)* [1995] 1 FLR 26.
9   [1999] 1 FLR 984.

private law proceedings, matters requiring investigation, it was held, should be conducted by other means. Perhaps this was a case in which an FAO would have been more appropriate. In contrast, in *Re M (Intractable Contact Dispute: Interim Care Order)*[1] the s 37 procedure was invoked by Wall J to address an intractable contact dispute where the children were found to be suffering significant harm by being denied all contact with the non-resident parent in breach of the court's orders. Although the consequences of making the direction should be seriously thought through, it could be used as a means of removing children who were being obstructed from having contact with a parent because of the primary carer's false and distorted beliefs about the non-resident parent.

Applying the welfare principle: the court's discretion

It was noted that the court, in applying the welfare principle, is obliged in contested private proceedings, to have regard to a checklist of factors[2]. While it is not required to do so in uncontested private cases, it remains bound in those cases by the welfare principle and the no order principle and, in applying these, it is likely to take into account factors similar to those in the checklist. These factors represent, for the most part, those which were habitually taken into account by the courts under the old law[3]. Reference is made here to decisions both before and after implementation of the Children Act in 1991[4].

Factors taken into consideration by the courts

Under the old law, the court had a largely unfettered discretion. Athough certain principles did emerge from appellate decisions it was probably incorrect to see them as creating hard precedents in view of the infinite number of variables which had to be taken into account and the court's overriding duty to do what it considered best for the *individual* child. It was also held by the House of Lords[5] that the Court of Appeal should not interfere with the order of the judge unless satisfied that his decision was plainly wrong. It was, nonetheless, possible to discern the kind of factors which the courts took into account and the sort of reasoning which formed the basis of their decisions[6]. Thus, for example, it was generally thought desirable that siblings be kept together where possible[7], that matrimonial 'misconduct' should be ignored except where it was directly relevant

---

1 [2003] 2 FLR 636.
2 See Chapter 2 above.
3 The reasoning behind the introduction of a statutory checklist is to be found in Law Com Report No 172 *Guardianship and Custody* (1988) at paras 3.17–3.21.
4 For a useful historical perspective on the resolution of children disputes over the period of the second half of the twentieth century, see M Freeman 'Disputing Children' in SN Katz, J Eekelaar and M Maclean *Cross Currents* (Oxford University Press, 2000).
5 *G v G (Minors) (Custody Appeal)* [1985] 1 WLR 647. A principle reasserted emphatically, but controversially on the facts, by the House of Lords in the context of adoption in *Re B (Adoption: Natural Parent)* [2002] 1 FLR 196. See further Chapter 7 below.
6 See, particularly, SM Cretney, JM Masson and R Bailey-Harris *Principles of Family Law* (7th edn) (Sweet & Maxwell, 2002) at pp 651–664. On assumptions made within the family justice system about children's best interests, see C Piper 'Assumptions about Children's Best Interests' (2000) 22 JSWFL 261.
7 See, for example, *C v C (Minors: Custody)* [1988] 2 FLR 291. The principle, however, has never been an inflexible one. For a case in which the Court of Appeal upheld the judge's decision to keep siblings apart, see *B v B (Residence Order: Restricting Applications)* [1997] 1 FLR 139.

to parenting capacity[1], that disparities in material circumstances should not generally be decisive except in extreme cases[2], that existing arrangements for the child's care should not be unnecessarily disturbed[3], and that the courts should remain neutral as between different religious persuasions except where they were thought to have a clearly deleterious effect on their adherents[4]. Although the Children Act ushered in a completely new set of principles and orders, well-established principles like those above are, to an extent, still applied under the Children Act.

We will now consider briefly some of the principles which emerged from previous decisions of the higher courts and which are likely to carry weight when applying the statutory criteria[5]. In view of the infinite number of variables which are inevitably present in individual cases, these should be treated with caution – the more so, since the scheme introduced by the Children Act has no precise equivalence with what existed before[6].

---

1   Thus, a matrimonial 'offence', such as adultery, would certainly not per se affect the custody issue – see, particularly, *Re K (Minor) (Children: Care and Control)* [1977] Fam 179. Neither would other sexual proclivities of a parent such as lesbianism – see *C v C (A Minor) (Custody Appeal)* [1991] 1 FLR 223 and *B v B (Minors) (Custody, Care and Control)* [1991] 1 FLR 402. On the other hand, sexual abuse of the child could be decisive but, even here, contact might be allowed in appropriate cases – see, for example, *H v H (Child Abuse: Access)* [1989] 1 FLR 212 and *L v L (Child Abuse: Access)* [1989] 2 FLR 16. And see *Re H (Minor: Custody Appeal)* [1991] Fam Law 422, in which the Court of Appeal held that 'reprehensible' behaviour towards a spouse or former spouse did not of itself disentitle either or both spouses from being good or adequate caretakers of the children. Thus, the judge had not erred in failing to make findings concerning the father's allegations that the mother had, inter alia, committed perjury, theft, blackmail, assault and battery, as well as adultery.
2   Thus, in *Richards v Richards* [1984] AC 174 at 205, Lord Hailsham said that 'the court ought not to confine itself to a consideration of purely material requirements or immediate comforts'. But the courts would, nonetheless, wish to satisfy themselves that a parent had the practical resources to ensure that the child's material needs were adequately looked after, as to which see *D v M (Minor) (Custody Appeal)* [1983] Fam 33.
3   Whether or not it ought to be disturbed would, of course, depend, to some extent, on how satisfactory was the existing arrangement. As Ormrod LJ said in *S v W* (1981) Fam Law 81 at 82, 'the status quo argument depends for its strength wholly and entirely on whether the status quo is satisfactory or not. The more satisfactory the status quo, the stronger the argument for not interfering. The less satisfactory the status quo, the less one requires before deciding to change'.
4   The most striking example of judicial disapproval of a religious sect and the effect of this on custody arrangements is probably the Court of Appeal's diatribe against Scientology in *Re B and G (Minors) (Custody)* [1985] FLR 493. Discrimination based purely on a parent's religion (as opposed to its effects on the child) might indeed amount to a breach of that parent's rights under the ECHR. See *Hoffmann v Austria* (1993) Series A, No 255C, and Chapter 16 below. The courts have, with few aberrations, consistently refused to allow a parent's religious views to prevent the child from receiving necessary medical care, especially in life-threatening cases. See Chapter 8 below.
5   These are discussed in greater depth in SM Cretney, JM Masson and R Bailey-Harris *Principles of Family Law* (7th edn) (Sweet & Maxwell, 2002) at pp 651–664. For a concise trawl through the checklist, see R Probert *Cretney's Family Law* (5th edn) (Sweet & Maxwell, 2003) at pp 300–311.
6   While there may, for example, be similarities between custody and residence orders or between access and contact orders, there are also important differences.

The ascertainable wishes and feelings of the child concerned (considered in the light of his age and understanding)

The increased importance attached to the views of children in the legislation has already been noted[1]. We have also noted that the importance of listening to children is underlined by Article 12 of the UNCRC[2]. In this context, despite the argument (following *Gillick*) that the courts might be obliged to follow the wishes of mature children[3], the Children Act merely requires the court to ascertain those wishes and to take them into account. Its overriding duty is to do what is *best* for the child and that may not always coincide with what the child wants[4].

Precisely how old or how mature an individual child has to be before the court's duty bites must, inevitably, be rather uncertain. But it would appear that the onus is on the court to justify its failure to seek out and consider the wishes of an older child. Even before the Children Act, the Court of Appeal had held that failure to accord proper weight to the strongly held views of a 12-year-old girl was a good ground of appeal[5]. Now, it is quite clear that a demonstrable failure to have regard to *any* factor in the checklist would sustain an appeal. How much weight individual courts may give to the views of particular children must be speculative. Traditionally, there has been some inconsistency among the judiciary on this. The message of the modern law is that the capacity of children of all ages to express a valid opinion on matters affecting them must not be underestimated but must be taken seriously. This is also a noteworthy feature of developments in the public law and the law governing children's evidence[6]. The Children Act makes no express provision for the court to take into account the wishes of parents or other interested adults in private proceedings, although this is required of local authorities looking after children[7]. In practice, the court will, of necessity, be presented with these views and it is implicit in the legislation that it should take them into account.

How, then, should the court discover children's views? The answer to this will depend to some extent on the kind of proceedings in question and the ages of the

---

1   See Chapter 2 above. On the practical problems involved in ascertaining and conveying the views of children in family proceedings, see C Piper 'Ascertaining the Wishes and Feelings of the Child' [1997] Fam Law 796. For a thorough examination of the question of children's participation in the different kinds of proceedings in which their interests may arise, see N Lowe and M Murch 'Children's Participation in the Family System – Translating Principles into Practice' [2001] CFLQ 137.

2   See Chapter 2 above.

3   J Eekelaar 'Gillick in the Divorce Court' (1986) 136 NLJ 184. In *Re P (Minors) (Wardship: Care and Control)* [1992] 2 FLR 681. Butler-Sloss LJ emphasised that the court was not *bound* by the wishes of the children, in this case brothers aged 13 and 11 years respectively, and should depart from them when their future welfare required it.

4   For a striking example of the court's refusal to follow children's wishes, see *Re B (Change of Surname)* [1996] 1 FLR 791. For a case in which the child's views proved decisive, see *Re P (A Minor) (Education)* [1992] 1 FLR 316, discussed in Chapter 16 below. In *Re S (Contact: Children's Views)* [2002] 1 FLR 1156 the court was highly critical of the father's failure to accord sufficient respect to the views of his young adolescent children in relation to contact. Judge Tyrer said that children of that age were entitled to have their views respected and that they should have been allowed to make decisions without the pressure of being asked to select between one parent or another.

5   *M v M (Transfer of Custody: Appeal)* [1987] 2 FLR 146.

6   See Chapter 13 below.

7   Section 22(4) and (5).

children. In public proceedings, the child will usually be represented by a children's guardian (formerly known as a guardian ad litem) whose duties include conveying the child's views to the court[1]. In private proceedings, children will usually be unrepresented. The judge may decide to interview older children in private[2] or may rely on the report of a children and family reporter (formerly known as a court welfare officer). In wardship, the Official Solicitor has traditionally acted as the child's representative. Representation of children is one area in which a major distinction still exists between the public and private law. In public cases, representation of the child is the norm, whereas in private proceedings it is exceptional. It must, at least, be questioned whether this dichotomy is wholly justifiable[3]. On the other hand, there would be massive resource implications in any proposal for the routine representation of children in, for example, divorce proceedings and it can certainly be argued that this degree of intervention would be contrary to the philosophy of the legislation[4].

The physical, emotional and educational needs of the child
The court's task is to take a broad and wide-ranging view of the various needs of the child. Needs other than those specifically mentioned may be taken into account. It is well-established that the court will not allow itself to be unduly swayed by considerations of the child's material needs[5]. The fact that one parent can offer a higher standard of living than the other should not weigh heavily unless the standard of living which one of the parents is able to provide is wholly inadequate. The court is much more likely to be influenced by the quality of the relationship which the child has with each parent[6].

Educational needs ought not to be decisive in determining who has the care of a child, since they can usually be met by attaching conditions to the court's principal orders or by accepting undertakings from the primary carer, for example to preserve the existing religious education of the child[7]. Whilst the assessment of needs is supposed to be wholly objective, the value judgments and prejudices of

---

1   Section 41; Family Proceedings Rules 1991, SI 1991/1247, rr 4.11(4) and 4.11A and Family
    Proceedings Courts (Children Act 1989) Rules 1991, SI 1991/1395, rr 11(4) and 11A.
2   See, for example, *H v H (Child: Judicial Interview)* [1974] 1 WLR 595.
3   See, for example, M Richards 'But what about the children? Some reflections on the Divorce
    White Paper' [1995] CFLQ 223.
4   As has been noted, the Family Law Act 1996 did provide for the possibility of increased
    representation of children in certain private proceedings. See Chapter 13 below.
5   As Griffiths LJ put it in *Re P (Adoption: Parental Agreement)* [1985] FLR 635 at 637: 'Anyone with
    experience of life knows that affluence and happiness are not necessarily synonymous'.
6   The spirit of the court's approach to ascertaining welfare is captured particularly well in the
    following passage from the judgment of Hardie Boys J, in the New Zealand case of *Walker v
    Walker and Harrison* noted in [1981] *NZ Recent Law* 257:
      ' "Welfare" is an all-encompassing word. It includes material welfare, both in the sense of an
      adequacy of resources to provide a pleasant home and a comfortable standard of living and
      in the sense of an adequacy of care to ensure that good health and due personal pride are
      maintained. However, while material considerations have their place, they are secondary
      matters. More important are the stability and the security, the loving and understanding care
      and guidance, the warm and compassionate relationships, that are essential for the full
      development of the child's own character, personality and talents.'
7   For a case which did apparently turn on the relative capacities of the parents to provide
    educational stimulus and discipline, especially in the periods immediately before and after the
    school day, see *May v May* [1986] 1 FLR 325.

the judiciary have occasionally appeared to intrude[1]. This is perhaps an inevitable hazard with indeterminate welfare tests[2].

The likely effect on the child of any change in his circumstances

We have already alluded to the status quo principle. There is a wealth of empirical evidence that courts, applying the old law, made orders which preserved the existing child care arrangements predominantly involving sole care by mothers[3]. It has been said that this was much more a reflection of what parents agreed themselves than any conscious maternal preference on the part of the judges[4]. The application of this factor should be seen alongside the new principle that delay is prejudicial and the court's proactive role is to eliminate it. There is, in any event, some evidence that, in certain contexts, especially 'snatching' cases, the weight being attached to this factor had already diminished[5]. More fundamentally, the courts are increasingly likely to explore a variety of ways in which parental responsibility may effectively be shared. Hence, the stereotypical notion of 'winners and losers' reflected in exclusive child care arrangements is fast becoming a thing of the past. The legislation appears to provide at least tacit encouragement for the exploration of a range of possible caring arrangements and it does not support any kind of presumption that existing arrangements should be preserved. Having said that, it remains true that the courts will wish to avoid unnecessary disruption to children where it cannot be demonstrated that a modification of present arrangements would positively advance their interests.

The child's age, sex, background and any characteristics of his which the court considers relevant

While the age or sex of a child has never determined conclusively which parent should have care of the child, the courts have traditionally applied certain rules of thumb which would normally be followed unless there was a good reason for not doing so. These embodied the view that young children, and girls of any age, were generally better off with their mothers, while older boys were more appropriately

---

1   An example is, perhaps, *B v B (Custody of Children)* [1985] FLR 166 where the judge's decision to deny custody to the father had been influenced by his alleged moral duty to find work and not to take advantage of welfare benefits.

2   Indeed, the view has been put forward that 'the heavily subjective nature of the power granted to the judge means that, so long as he does not claim to be applying it as a conclusive rule of law, a judge can consider almost any factor which could possibly have a bearing on the child's welfare and assign to it whatever weight he or she chooses'. See J Eekelaar *Regulating Divorce* (Clarendon Press, 1991) at p 125. It should also be recalled that no one factor in the checklist is accorded more weight than any other. See Chapter 2 above.

3   See the discussion in SM Cretney, JM Masson and R Bailey-Harris *Principles of Family Law* (7th edn) (Sweet & Maxwell, 2002) at p 646 and the studies cited there. For a more recent case which reaffirms the status quo principle, see *Re B (Residence Order: Status Quo)* [1998] 1 FLR 368. Here, the father had cared for the child since he was aged two. There were major difficulties concerning contact which culminated in the judge making a residence order in favour of the mother. By that time the boy was aged eight and the Court of Appeal took the view that the decision to transfer residence was plainly wrong and could not possibly be justified on the evidence. For an illustration of the status quo principle in the context of human rights see *Hokkanen v Finland* [1996] 1 FLR 289.

4   J Eekelaar *Family Law and Social Policy* (2nd edn) (Weidenfeld & Nicolson, 1984) at pp 79–80.

5   See Chapter 17.

looked after by their fathers[1]. The House of Lords, as we have seen, has now held that there is no such legal *presumption* but that, in practice, there would still be advantages to a very young child in being with his mother[2]. There was also a well-established principle that siblings should be kept together where possible[3].

The Children Act now requires local authorities in their decision-making to give due consideration to children's 'religious persuasion, racial origin and cultural and linguistic background'[4]. These factors are likely to be especially relevant to the child's placement[5]. Whether or not cultural factors ought to be taken into account by a court which is considering whether the ground for care or supervision is made out, is the subject of some dispute[6]. In the present context it ought to be the case that religious, racial and linguistic factors are relevant to the choice of home for the child, although some concerns might be met by conditions or directions[7]. The courts maintain that they take a neutral stance on religious beliefs except where the practices associated with a particular sect are thought to be potentially harmful to the welfare of children[8].

Any harm which the child has suffered or is at risk of suffering
Exposure of the child to a risk of physical or sexual abuse will be a strong reason for denying a residence order but not necessarily for refusing contact where this can be adequately supervised. Where the court considers the child to have suffered or be at risk of suffering harm, it may wish to direct the local authority to investigate that child's circumstances. Whether or not the court makes such a direction may be a question of degree, since only 'significant' harm is sufficient to found a care or supervision order. In other cases, the court might wish to give consideration to short-term protective remedies under the legislation governing domestic violence and occupation of the family home[9]. Where the court's concern is of a lesser degree, a family assistance order may be appropriate.

How capable each of the child's parents (and any other person in relation to whom the court considers the question to be relevant) is of meeting the child's needs
The most obvious 'other person' contemplated in the legislation will be any step-parent or partner of a former spouse. Where a parent has remarried, the

---

1   See, for example, *Bowley v Bowley* [1984] FLR 791; *Allington v Allington* [1985] FLR 586; and *W v W and C* [1968] 3 All ER 408. In *Re W (A Minor) (Residence Order)* [1992] 2 FLR 332, the Court of Appeal held that there was a rebuttable presumption that a baby's best interests were served by being with its mother. But cf *Re S (A Minor) (Custody)* [1991] 2 FLR 388, in which the Court of Appeal held that there was no presumption that one parent should be preferred to another parent for the purpose of looking after a child at a particular age. In this case the judge had erred by substituting his own discretion for that of the justices who had decided that a girl aged two years should live with her father rather than her mother. See also *Re A (A Minor) (Custody)* [1991] 2 FLR 394, another Court of Appeal decision in similar vein.
2   *Brixey v Lynas* [1996] 2 FLR 499.
3   See, for example, *C v C (Minors: Custody)* [1988] 2 FLR 291.
4   Section 22(5)(c).
5   See Chapter 10 below.
6   See Chapter 11 below.
7   See particularly the Court of Appeal decision in *Re M (Child's Upbringing)* [1996] 2 FLR 441, in which the court ordered that a Zulu boy should return to his natural parent in South Africa despite his being cared for in England for some years by a white Afrikaner woman. Cf *Re B (Residence Order: Leave to Appeal)* [1998] 1 FLR 520.
8   See Chapter 16 below.
9   Part IV of the Family Law Act 1996.

court may see advantages, especially material advantages, to the child living in a two-parent household rather than a one-parent household[1]. But where a new partner is thought 'undesirable' or likely to have a seriously negative impact on the child, the court may be reluctant to reinforce the position with a residence order[2]. The high incidence of step-parenthood and unmarried cohabitation following divorce has generated a significant number of applications for either adoption or joint residence orders in favour of a parent and the new married or unmarried partner. Under the old law there was, in effect, a legal presumption against step-parent adoption and in favour of what was then joint custody. The Children Act abandoned any form of statutory directive against adoption and the court now has an unfettered choice between adoption and alternative orders. Much is likely to turn, in individual cases, on the perceived value of the existing relationship between the child and the parent who does not have primary care[3]. Where a spouse is in full-time employment, his or her capacity to undertake the day-to-day care of the child will be limited and the court will want to be satisfied that adequate arrangements for day care have been proposed. This may be a problem for fathers more than for mothers, given prevailing employment patterns[4].

The range of powers available to the court under the Children Act in the proceedings in question[5]
It should be remembered that the court is not confined to making those orders specifically sought by the parties. It has power to make orders of its own volition[6]. A rather obvious example is that it might, in making a residence order in favour of a mother, wish to couple this with a contact order in favour of the father – even if this were not specifically sought. The critical question will be which order, if any, from the range of orders at the court's disposal, would best advance the welfare of the child.

The above factors are not exhaustive since the court is merely required to have regard 'in particular' to them. At the same time the Court of Appeal has held[7] that the checklist represents an extremely useful and important discipline in ensuring that all relevant factors are considered and balanced. Where the factors are finely balanced it is, moreover, important for the judge to give reasons for his decision.

In contested cases the court will pay particular regard to any recommendations in welfare reports[8] and, indeed, must give reasons where it decides not to follow

---

1   As in *Re DW (A Minor) (Custody)* [1984] Fam Law 17.
2   Cohabitation in a lesbian household, for example, has controversially proved a cause of concern, as in *Re P (A Minor) (Custody)* (1983) FLR 401.
3   The abolition of the former statutory directives is discussed in A Bainham 'The Privatisation of the Public Interest in Children' (1990) 53 MLR 206 at pp 214–216.
4   The fact that a father may have to give up employment or remain unemployed will not necessarily prevent an order in his favour. See *B v B (Custody of Children)* [1985] FLR 166.
5   This provision was discussed in Chapter 2 above.
6   Section 10(1)(b).
7   *B v B (Residence Order: Reasons for Decision)* [1997] 2 FLR 602.
8   For the argument that the legal system could usefully allow a greater role for primary prevention before children become embroiled in contested cases, see A Buchanan and V Bream 'Do some separated parents who cannot agree arrangements for their children need a more therapeutic rather than forensic service?' [2001] CFLQ 353.

them[1]. The court's power to order a welfare report in family proceedings is a general one whenever it is considering a question with respect to a child under the Children Act[2]. The report may be requested from a child and family reporter (formerly court welfare officer). Although the court may direct that the report should deal with specific matters relevant to the welfare of the child, it may be more wide-ranging[3]. Welfare reports are ordered much more frequently in contested than in uncontested cases[4]. The Law Commission resisted the suggestion that the court should be obliged to order a report in every case, partly because it was mindful of the need to target limited resources, and partly because of the delays which might otherwise be engendered[5].

The welfare report may be oral or in writing[6]. Where it is in writing, rules of court require its disclosure to the parties in advance of the hearing[7]. The court is entitled to have regard to any statement in the report, or any evidence in it insofar as the court thinks it is relevant to what it is considering[8]. There can, thus, in children cases, be a relaxation in the normal rules of evidence and, in particular, hearsay evidence may be permitted. Evidential issues involving children are discussed in greater depth later[9].

CHILDREN AFTER DIVORCE: UNRESOLVED ISSUES

Following the collapse of the divorce reforms, there is something of an absence of direction in the appropriate response of the legal system to the phenomenon of large numbers of children experiencing parental divorce and life in reconstituted families[10]. In some respects the focus is shifting away from the divorce process itself towards a concentration on the quality of the relationships which children have with parental figures in a wide diversity of family relationships. Smart and Neale have neatly encapsulated this shift in thinking as a focus on *parenting* and not on *partnerships*[11]. Perhaps one of the mistakes of the past has been to single out divorce as an occasion for official scrutiny of the interests of children to the

---

1 *Stephenson v Stephenson* [1985] FLR 1140. Failure to do so may be a ground of appeal: see *W v W (A Minor: Custody Appeal)* [1988] 2 FLR 505 and *Re CB (Access: Attendance of Court Welfare Officer)* [1995] 1 FLR 622. See also, more recently, *Re W (Residence)* [1999] 2 FLR 390.
2 Section 7(1). The court is not confined to ordering one report if it thinks a second report would be useful. See *Re W (Welfare Reports)* [1995] 2 FLR 142.
3 Section 7(2).
4 See the discussion in SM Cretney, JM Masson and R Bailey-Harris *Principles of Family Law* (7th edn) (Sweet & Maxwell, 2002) at pp 582–584.
5 Law Com Report No 172 *Guardianship and Custody* (1988) at para 6.15.
6 Section 7(3).
7 Family Proceedings Rules 1991, SI 1991/1247, r 4.17(1) and Family Proceedings Courts (Children Act 1989) Rules 1991, SI 1991/1395, r 17(1). In *Re C (A Minor: Irregularity of Practice)* [1991] 2 FLR 438, the Court of Appeal held that while it was permissible for a judge to see a court welfare officer privately in his chambers during the course of a trial he should only do so in exceptional circumstances, which did not exist in this case.
8 Section 7(4).
9 See Chapter 13 below.
10 For consideration of some of the recent initiatives of the Law Society in particular, see G Douglas and M Murch 'Taking Account of Children's Needs in Divorce – a study of family solicitors' responses to new policy and practice initiatives' [2002] CFLQ 57.
11 C Smart and B Neale *Family Fragments?* (Polity Press, 1999).

exclusion of concerns about the quality of relationships between children and adults before and after that event. Thus, Pryor and Rodgers have concluded that since change is not going to go away 'our energies are better used in supporting children and their parents in diverse family structures than yearning for a somewhat mythical bygone golden age of nuclear families'[1].

A key area of debate in the coming years is likely to be that of gender. Ought the legal system to treat women, in their role as mothers, and men, in their role as fathers, in a neutral way or are there distinctive roles for mothers and fathers which the law should recognise? Should 'equality', however that is defined, be achieved through formal neutrality or by the acknowledgement of difference? Family legislation today (in sharp contrast to the historical position) is almost entirely gender-neutral in form and speaks most of the time of the gender-neutral *parent* rather than the gender-specific *mother* or *father*[2]. One of the difficulties with an approach which openly differentiates between mothers and fathers is that the traditional roles have been gradually breaking down. Many more women are in employment and an admittedly much smaller, but still significant, number of men are now the primary caretakers of children.

Smart and Neale[3], on the basis of their empirical research, draw attention to what appear to be the very different perceptions of mothers and fathers following divorce. They found that the women in their sample rarely talked about *rights* but saw themselves rather as having *needs*. Men, on the other hand, were much more preoccupied with questions of rights and were largely conceptualised as the possessors of rights. Smart and Neale are critical of current legislation which they view as supporting a 'free-floating concept of rights which has no commensurate presumption about responsibilities or quality of fathering' and which is capable of enhancing 'gendered power without accountability'[4]. One challenge for the legal system may therefore be to impose stronger obligations on the non-resident parent to behave responsibly and make every effort to continue to participate in the life of the child. This would, however, surely imply a correlative obligation on the part of the resident parent to facilitate this involvement.

We ought not to leave this question of gender and the possession of rights without commenting that the perception which is clearly held by some, perhaps many, mothers that they have needs but not rights is not an accurate perception, certainly when considering the ECHR under which mothers, fathers and children all possess Convention rights. In the more unusual situation in which mothers have become separated from their children and denied contact with them by fathers, rights can be a powerful weapon.

A good illustration is the case of *Ignaccolo-Zenide v Romania*[5]. This case concerned a French mother and a father who had French and Romanian nationality. Following divorce, the French court had ruled that the mother should

---

1   J Pryor and B Rodgers *Children in Changing Families: Life After Parental Separation* (Blackwell, 2001) at p 276.

2   A rare exception is s 2 of the Children Act 1989 which distinguished between fathers and mothers where the child is born to parents who are not married to each other although, as we have seen, even this distinction has been significantly eroded by the Adoption and Children Act 2002.

3   (Above) at ch 8.

4   Ibid at p 167.

5   (2001) 31 EHRR 7.

have custody of the two children. The children visited the father in the USA during the summer holidays but he then refused to return them to the mother, taking them instead to Romania. A court in Bucharest ordered their return to the mother on the basis that the father had abducted the children contrary to the Hague Convention. The Romanian authorities then failed to enforce the order. Only one meeting was organised by them, and the mother saw her children only once between 1990 and 1997. She then complained to the ECtHR that their failure to enforce the order was a breach of her right to respect for family life under Article 8 and the Court agreed with her. In essence the Romanian authorities had failed to take adequate and sufficient steps to comply with the mother's right to return of her children. Romania was ordered to pay her FRF 100,000 and FRF 86,000 in costs.

This and many other cases reveal only too clearly that the concept of rights is no more redundant or inappropriate in the case of women than it is in the case of men. And we have only just begun to appreciate how valuable the concept of rights may be for children themselves.

Chapter 5

THE UNMARRIED FAMILY

INTRODUCTION

The assumption that natural parents have moral obligations, reinforced by legal obligations, to care for their children has not as readily been made in the case of parentage outside marriage. Historically, the child born out of wedlock was a social outcast, 'filius nullius'. When the law first began to impose obligations on unmarried parents through the Poor Law, this was motivated primarily by the desire to avoid unwanted children becoming a public burden[1]. In due course, it was recognised that the rights and obligations of unmarried mothers extended beyond purely financial concerns to the responsibility for safeguarding the welfare of their children, but the historical attitude to unmarried fathers persists to some extent today.

Nowadays, the remaining legal distinctions between children born in or out of wedlock, and the underlying policy issues behind these distinctions, revolve around the connection between children and fathers. For this reason, most of this chapter is concerned with how paternity is established and to what extent, and in what circumstances, a man who is found to be the genetic father of a child acquires the benefits and burdens of parenthood. It is again crucial in this context to bear in mind the distinction which the law makes between *being a parent* and possessing *parental responsibility*[2]. A further point which should be made at the outset is that this is not primarily a chapter about 'father's rights' although, inevitably, this dimension appears. The position taken here is rather that there is a *reciprocity* about the relationship between the child and the father so that legal distinctions or discrimination between fathers necessarily amount to distinctions or discrimination between children[3]. It is, moreover, obvious that the position the law takes on the presence or absence of a legal parental relationship between fathers and children has important legal and practical implications for the mothers of those children.

The law generally does not recognise the parental responsibility of unmarried fathers, except for limited purposes such as financial support and succession[4]. The law until very recently did not confer parental responsibility on most unmarried fathers, but the effect of recent reforms in the Adoption and Children Act 2002 is that those men registered as fathers in the register of births and on the

---

1   Useful materials tracing the development of illegitimacy laws in their historical context can be found in B Hale, D Pearl, E Cooke and P Bates *The Family, Law and Society* (5th edn) (Butterworths, 2002) at pp 488 et seq. See also M Maclean and J Eekelaar *The Parental Obligation* (Hart Publishing, 1997) at ch 3, especially pp 33 et seq.

2   See Chapter 3.

3   This is not something which has, thus far, been accepted by the English Law Commission or by the Lord Chancellor's Department (now the Department of Constitutional Affairs) or Parliament. See below.

4   This has, however, assumed a greater significance with the enactment of the child support legislation, as to which see Chapter 9 below.

respective children's birth certificates will acquire parental responsibility auto-matically by operation of law[1]. This will still leave a significant number of genetic fathers who are not so registered and who will not acquire parental responsibility merely by virtue of having paternity established. And, of course, there will be other cases where the identity of the father is not established at all, or at least not officially established. Determining paternity per se has much more limited effects relating to such matters as financial liability to support the child and succession. The expression 'unmarried father' is chosen throughout this chapter to describe the father of a child who is not married to the child's mother. Strictly speaking, it can be something of a misnomer since, as Stephen Cretney has pointed out, many such men are in fact *married* – but to someone other than the mother:

'... Charles II, King of England, enjoys a certain notoriety as the father of a number of illegitimate children; yet it would be absurd to describe him, in defiance of the facts, as "unmarried".'[2]

The use of the expression 'unmarried father' is for reasons of convenience and because it is extremely difficult to think of a satisfactory alternative. Some people have viewed the unmarried father as an unnecessary figure in the life of the child, except for his part in the reproductive process and his continuing financial obligation. In recent years, debate concerning the use of so-called 'virgin birth' techniques, where a single woman elects to have a child on her own, has even called into question the first of these functions[3]. It is, of course, possible for a child to be conceived without sexual involvement or any semblance of a relationship between the mother and the genetic father. Ruth Deech has described this rather extreme view of unmarried fatherhood thus:

'Men are nothing more than mobile sperm banks ... their rôle over as soon as conception has been achieved. They fulfil only decorative purposes. It could even be said that in England and in a number of other scientifically advanced countries, the unmarried father has come to be seen as sexually and socially unnecessary, merely a man who pays, or should pay: nicknamed in German a "Zahlvater", expressing the idea that the duties of paternity are a form of perpetual payment for sinful and stolen pleasures, the act of insemination as the occasion for a lifetime of financial obligation. Of the positive and familial aspects of fatherhood we hear little in law.'[4]

In recent years, rather more has been heard of the positive aspects of fatherhood outside marriage. The reasons for this are undoubtedly complex but may be thought to include a heightened awareness of children's rights, the growing numbers of children born into stable cohabitations and the more assertive claims of unmarried fathers themselves.

---

1   Adoption and Children Act 2002, s 111, amending Children Act 1989, s 4.
2   SM Cretney *Family Law* (4th edn) (Sweet & Maxwell, 2000) at p 218.
3   The matter came to public attention in 1991. See, for example, 'The Inviolate Conception' [1991] Fam Law 204 and 'Virgin Birth or Filius Nullius?' (1991) NLJ 433. The Human Fertilisation and Embryology Act 1990, s 13(5) does attempt to address this issue as follows:
    'A woman shall not be provided with treatment services unless account has been taken of the welfare of any child who may be born as a result of the treatment (including the need of that child for a father), and of any other child who may be affected by the birth.'
    For commentary on this provision, see G Douglas 'Assisted Reproduction and the Welfare of the Child' [1993] *Current Legal Problems* 53 and the scathing attack on it by Emily Jackson who sees it as incorporating 'the political and moral belief that the heterosexual, two-parent family is the optimum, or even the only legitimate, place to bring up children'. See E Jackson *Regulating Reproduction: Law, Technology and Autonomy* (Hart Publishing, 2001) at p 193.
4   R Deech 'The Unmarried Father and Human Rights' (1992) 4 JCL 3.

Human rights issues are also beginning to have a significant influence following the implementation of the HRA 1998 although, as we shall see, a great deal depends on whether 'family life' can be said to have arisen between the child and the genetic father.

Some of these concerns were expressed by Sir George Baker P, as long ago as 1982, when he said that 'children, whether born in wedlock or not, need fathers. If there is a father then he should have the opportunity of developing the relationship'[1]. Perhaps most importantly, it can be argued that there are international obligations which require the State to create the conditions in which these extra-marital familial relationships can develop[2]. The difficulty with such a policy is that it might be thought to detract from the support which a society wishes to give to the institution of marriage. Hence, the existence of a discriminatory status of illegitimacy historically can be explained on the basis that the family within marriage was considered to be the only acceptable social grouping in which to raise children.

The complementary concepts of legitimacy and illegitimacy also played a crucial role in achieving the orderly devolution of property. The modern law is much less concerned with this latter consideration and much more with the assertion of *parenthood* as the primary legal status in relation to children – perhaps now outstripping marriage as the central organising concept in family law.

Illegitimacy: before 1987

The history of the gradual reform of the illegitimacy laws in England is the story of an attempt to equalise the positions of children born in and out of wedlock by removing the legal disadvantages suffered by the latter but to do so in a way which did not unnecessarily weaken the institution of marriage. This was a piecemeal and incremental process over many years, culminating in the Family Law Reform Act 1987 which at least came close to removing the concept of illegitimacy[3].

The 'illegitimate' child suffered significant legal disadvantages and a considerable social stigma. The disadvantages at common law were principally the absence of succession rights, rights of financial support and the lack of a legal nexus with the father. These legal distinctions were slowly whittled away by widening the categories of those children who were regarded as legitimate[4] and by removing some of the specific disadvantages attaching to illegitimacy more directly by legislation[5]. When, at the end of the 1970s, the Law Commission came to examine the whole question of illegitimacy, a fundamental issue had to be addressed. This

---

1   S v O (*Illegitimate Child: Access*) (1982) 3 FLR 15 at 18.
2   See, for example, A Bainham 'When is a Parent not a Parent? Reflections on the Unmarried Father and his Child in English Law' (1989) 3 IJLF 208, NV Lowe 'The Meaning and Allocation of Parental Responsibility – A Common Lawyer's Perspective' (1997) 11 IJLPF 192, especially at pp 201–205, and R Collier, 'A Hard Time to be a Father?: Reassessing the Relationship between Law, Policy and Family (Practices)' (2001) 28 *Journal of Law and Society* 520.
3   The Family Law Reform Act 1987 removed most of the remaining legal disadvantages suffered by children born out of wedlock and it became a matter of some doubt whether the distinctions which remained were enough to add up to a discriminatory status.
4   Particularly through the process of legitimation under the Legitimacy Acts of 1926, 1959 and 1976.
5   Thus, under the Family Law Reform Act 1969, ss 14 and 16, an illegitimate child could claim under his father's intestacy or under his will.

was whether the removal of the residual legal discrimination could be achieved simply by sweeping away the few legal distinctions which were left, or whether the status of illegitimacy itself would have to be removed. The Law Commission provisionally preferred the more radical alternative[1] but later resiled from this position[2]. It concluded that the advantages of removing the status of illegitimacy were outweighed by the disadvantages which would flow from conferring automatic parental rights on unmarried fathers[3].

Meanwhile, the Scottish Law Commission was also considering this issue. It, too, concluded that it would be undesirable to give automatic parental rights to unmarried fathers but that all remaining legal distinctions between *children* could, nonetheless, be removed. Insofar as it was necessary to distinguish between fathers, this could be done by reference to the marital status of the parents and not by attaching labels to the children[4]. The English Commission subsequently produced a second report which substantially adopted the Scottish solution[5]. Consequently, s 1 of the Family Law Reform Act 1987 embodies a general rule of construction which applies to all legislation and instruments made after 4 April 1988. This is that:

'references (however expressed) to any relationship between two persons shall, unless the contrary intention appears, be construed without regard to whether or not the father and mother of either of them, or the father and mother of any person through whom the relationship is deduced, have or had been married to each other at any time.'

The position after 1987

The position, following the 1987 legislation, was that all but a few legal distinctions between children born in and out of wedlock had been removed, along with an attempt to remove the stigmatising language and terminology of illegitimacy. The only remaining differences (apart from the relationship with the father) relate to titles of honour[6] and citizenship[7]. In the light of this, it is an unresolved question whether it is still accurate to talk of a status of legitimacy and illegitimacy[8]. In 1992 the Scottish Law Commission recommended the complete abolition of the concepts of legitimacy, illegitimacy and legitimation in Scotland. The Commission's view was that a separate status could only be justified where the person possessing it was in a significantly different legal position from other people. Since this would no longer be so if the Commission's proposals were accepted, these concepts would be unnecessary, anachronistic and regarded by some as offensive.

---

1 Law Com Working Paper No 74 *Illegitimacy* (1979).
2 Law Com Report No 118 *Illegitimacy* (1982).
3 Ibid, particularly at paras 4.29–4.36.
4 Scot Law Com No 82 *Illegitimacy* (1984).
5 Law Com Report No 157 *Illegitimacy* (Second Report) (1986).
6 See *Re Moynihan* [2000] 1 FLR 113.
7 See *R on the Application of Montana v Secretary of State for the Home Department* [2001] 1 FLR 449 in which the Court of Appeal rejected the argument that the refusal to register the citizenship of a child born abroad to unmarried parents, where only the father was British (the mother being Norwegian), amounted to a violation of either the father's or the child's right to respect for family life under Article 8 of the ECHR.
8 The Scottish Law Commission concluded in 1992 that, at least in Scotland, the equivalent legislation (the Law Reform (Parent and Child) (Scotland) Act 1986) had not removed the status of legitimacy or illegitimacy: Scot Law Com No 135 *Report on Family Law* (1992) at para 17.3.

Thus, the Commission recommended that they all ought to be removed from Scots law, subject to certain savings relating to hereditary titles and existing deeds and enactments. As the Commission put it, 'In the new Scottish Family Law children should just be children, and people should just be people, whether their parents were married to each other or not'[1]. These proposals were not, however, accepted by the Westminster Parliament, and Scots law thus continues to distinguish between married and unmarried fathers[2].

What, then, is the current position in English law? There is no doubt that legal distinctions of substance do remain between children born in and out of wedlock and that the concepts of legitimacy and illegitimacy remain on the statute book, albeit in pre-1987 legislation not repealed by the 1987 Act. On the other hand, it is equally clear that it was an express purpose of the Family Law Reform Act to remove the discriminatory labelling of children and in this way to lessen any social stigma there might be attaching to birth outside marriage. As long ago as 1979 the English Law Commission recognised the force of the language used by the law. It said:

> 'We believe that the law can help to lessen social prejudices by setting an example clearly based upon the principle that the parents' marital relationship is irrelevant to the child's legal position. Changes in the law cannot give the illegitimate child the benefits of a secure, caring, family background. They cannot even ensure that he does not suffer financially ... But they can at least remove the *additional* hardship of attaching an opprobrious description to him.'[3]

Hence the policy of the 1987 legislation was to distinguish only between *parents* and not between children where it was still thought necessary to perpetuate legal distinctions. A reasonable question, therefore, if 'illegitimacy' is considered to have survived the 1987 reforms, is whether we should be talking about *illegitimate parents* rather than *illegitimate children*[4]. Rightly or wrongly, the evidence is that the media, judges, academics and society in general continue to use the language of illegitimacy in some cases apparently oblivious of the policy of the law over the last decade. Many illustrations could be given from post-1987 case-law[5], but one is the Court of Appeal decision in *Dawson v Wearmouth*[6] where the judgment (given by Hirst and Thorpe LJJ) is riddled with references to 'an illegitimate child'.

More recent is the single judgment in the Court of Appeal in *R on the Application of Montana v Secretary of State for the Home Department*[7]. In contrast, Hale J in *Re R (Surname: Using Both Parents')*[8] was outspoken in her view that the law reporters

---

1 Scot Law Com No 135 (above) at para 17.4.

2 For a critique, see E Sutherland 'Scotland: Child Law Reform – At Last!' in A Bainham (ed) *The International Survey of Family Law 1995* (Martinus Nijhoff, 1997) p 435 at pp 438–439 and, more recently, E Sutherland 'How Children are Faring in the "New Scotland"' in A Bainham (ed) *The International Survey of Family Law (2001 Edition)* (Family Law, 2001) p 363, especially at pp 368–369.

3 Law Com Working Paper No 74 *Illegitimacy* (HMSO, 1979) at para 3.15.

4 See B Hale, D Pearl, E Cooke and P Bates *The Family, Law and Society* (5th edn) (Butterworths, 2002) where there is a section headed 'Illegitimate children or illegitimate parents?'.

5 For illustrations of the use of the language of illegitimacy post-1987 in the press, by judges and by academics, see A Bainham 'Changing families and changing concepts: reforming the language of family law' [1998] CFLQ 1 at pp 8–11.

6 [1997] 2 FLR 629.

7 [2001] 1 FLR 449.

8 [2001] 2 FLR 1358 at 1362.

should avoid using the language of illegitimacy. What she said bears extended citation:

> 'It is a matter of huge regret that the Incorporated Council of Law Reporting chose to entitle that case *In Re W (A Child) (Illegitimate Child: Change of Surname)*[1]. It is now more than 14 years since the Family Law Reform Act 1987 sought to remove such language from our law, and in particular that no opprobrious adjectives should be attached to the child. If there is to be any opprobrium stemming from the birth of a child to parents who are not married to one another (and for my part I would not necessarily say that there was to be any such opprobrium), it should be attached to the parents, whose choice it was, and not to the child, whose choice it definitely was not. I very much hope that the Incorporated Council will pay attention to these observations, should the problem arise in the future.'

Perhaps Her Majesty's judges should also pay attention to them.

Is this use of language perhaps justifiable? If there are still distinctions of substance, and if the concepts of legitimacy and illegitimacy remain on the statute book, perhaps differentiating language is still required. Perhaps to refrain from using the language of legitimacy/illegitimacy in relation to children is to prefer 'political correctness' to accuracy[2]. An opposing view is that the spirit, if not the letter, of the 1987 legislation together with international obligations require that the language of illegitimacy be expunged from the law[3] even if certain substantive legal distinctions survive. The essence of this argument is that in the real world the question of status is going to be bound up to a large extent with the use of language. If those most involved with applying and interpreting the law continue to use the language of illegitimacy, it is not really surprising that it remains in common usage in society[4].

The rest of this chapter is devoted to these issues. The initial question of how paternity is established outside marriage is considered first. The nature of the legal relationship between the father and the child is then examined. The legal effects of establishing paternity are looked at and consideration is given to the initial allocation of parental responsibility and legal procedures which may be invoked by the unmarried father who wishes to acquire full parental responsibility. The chapter concludes by reviewing some of the very different perspectives on the future direction of the law.

ESTABLISHING PATERNITY AND FAMILY LIFE

The automatic position

Where a child is born to an unmarried woman, there is no presumption of paternity equivalent to that which applies where a child is born to a married woman[5], and this is so whether or not she is in a stable relationship or cohabiting.

---

1   [2000] 2 WLR 258.

2   This is certainly Cretney's view. See SM Cretney *Family Law* (4th edn) (Sweet & Maxwell, 2000) at p 218.

3   Mary Ann Glendon, writing in 1989, clearly thought that the Family Law Reform Act 1987 had succeeded in expunging the terminology of illegitimacy from English law. See MA Glendon *The Transformation of Family Law* (University of Chicago Press, 1989) at p 269.

4   A Bainham 'Changing families and changing concepts: reforming the language of family law' [1998] CFLQ 1 at p 11.

5   See Chapter 4 above and, generally, G Douglas and NV Lowe 'Becoming a Parent in English Law' (1992) 108 LQR 414.

The above statement requires some qualification where a child is born following assisted reproduction[1]. We considered the issue of the determination of paternity in cases of assisted reproduction in Chapter 3 and are concerned here only with children conceived in the ordinary way by sexual intercourse.

Proving paternity

Births outside marriage take place in a wide variety of circumstances, ranging from stable cohabitations equivalent to marriage in all but name, to the casual encounter, or even rape. In some instances the mother will have had intercourse with more than one man around the time of conception so that there may be doubt, even in her own mind, about who is the father. This was so in the case of *Re T (Paternity: Ordering Blood Tests)*[2] (discussed below) where the mother had sexual relations with four men other than her husband with a view to becoming pregnant. Hence, the law has to provide mechanisms for determining paternity, although in many cases the biological truth will in fact remain a matter of doubt. These mechanisms are declarations of parentage, the system of birth registration and the use of blood tests or other scientific tests, often, but not necessarily, in the context of legal proceedings. In 1998 the Labour Government issued a Consultation Paper which sought views, inter alia, on whether it would be possible to establish a single procedure for obtaining a declaration of paternity which would be valid for all purposes[3].

Declarations of parentage
Until recently there were two separate procedures for obtaining a declaration of parentage[4].

Under the Family Law Act 1986[5], s 56 it was possible for any person to obtain a declaration:

(a)   that a named person is or was his parent, or
(b)   that he was legitimate, or
(c)   that he had or had not become a legitimated person.

This was a procedure in essence only open to someone wishing to establish that he or she was a *child* of a particular person. In most cases the applicant would of course be an adult and would be seeking a declaration for purposes such as the right to amend a birth certificate, to establish a right to inherit property, or to acquire nationality or citizenship. Such a declaration, if obtained, was binding for *all* purposes but it should be noted that the procedure was limited in two significant ways. First, it was available only to someone seeking to establish that he or she was a *child* and to no one else. It was not, for example, open to someone to

---

1   As to which see Douglas and Lowe (above) at pp 418–422; G Douglas *Law, Fertility and Reproduction* (Sweet & Maxwell, 1992) at pp 127–132; RG Lee and D Morgan *Human Fertilisation and Embryology: Regulating the Reproductive Revolution* (Blackstone Press Ltd, 2001) at pp 221–228; and E Jackson *Regulating Reproduction: Law, Technology and Autonomy* (Hart Publishing, 2001) at pp 237–241.
2   [2001] 2 FLR 1190.
3   See Consultation Paper *1. Court Procedures for the Determination of Paternity*; and *2. The Law on Parental Responsibility for Unmarried Fathers* (Lord Chancellor's Department, March 1998).
4   Discussed ibid at paras 1–19.
5   The 1986 Act followed Law Com Report No 132 *Declarations in Family Matters* (1984).

seek a declaration that he or she was a *parent* of a person. Secondly, it was not possible to obtain a declaration that a named person was *not* the applicant's parent or a declaration of illegitimacy.

Alongside this procedure was a quite separate procedure for obtaining a declaration of parentage under the Child Support Act 1991, s 27[1]. This procedure was open to either the Secretary of State or the person with care of the child where a maintenance assessment was under consideration and there was a denial of paternity. But such declarations were limited to the single purpose of establishing whether or not there was liability for child support and could not be relied upon for other purposes. In particular, they could not be relied upon for the purposes of birth registration or for applying for contact with the child. One especially adverse consequence of this was that the process of s 27 declarations actually impeded the registration of some fathers since the obtaining of a court order for maintenance (one of the forms of evidence which allowed a man to register himself as father of a child) had been largely superseded by child support maintenance assessments which did not have this effect[2].

Accordingly, there was a need for a simplified and unified procedure for obtaining declarations of parentage. This is now achieved by a new s 55A inserted into the Family Law Act 1986[3]. Alongside this there are amendments to s 27 of the Child Support Act 1991[4]. The further effect of these amendments is to widen the availability of the procedure. Now *any person* may apply for a declaration of status, and the application need not relate to the applicant's own position. The procedure now extends to a declaration as to whether *or not* a named person is or was the *parent* of another person named in the application. Any person seeking a declaration that *he or she* is the *parent* of a named person may bring the application as of right[5]. Beyond this the court has a discretion whether or not to hear the application and may refuse to do so 'unless it considers that the applicant has a sufficient personal interest in the determination of the application'[6].

These reforms reflect in part the greater emphasis which is now being given throughout the law to establishing the biological truth of paternity, although they also recognise that there may be circumstances in which this might not be desirable especially where to do so might be considered to be against a child's best interests[7].

Birth registration

The effect of registration of the name of a man as father of a child is to create a rebuttable presumption that he is the father[8]. Accordingly, where registration takes place, the onus will shift to anyone wishing to dispute paternity. The circumstances under which registration may be effected are, therefore, all-important.

---

1 Law Com Report No 132 (above) at paras 20–25.
2 Ibid, para 29.
3 By s 83 of the Child Support, Pensions and Social Security Act 2000. For a helpful analysis of the reform see N Wikeley 'Child Support, Paternity and Parentage' [2001] Fam Law 125, especially at pp 127–128.
4 By virtue of the Child Suport, Pensions and Social Security Act 2000, Sch 8, para 13.
5 Family Law Act 1986, s 55A(4).
6 Ibid, s 55A(3).
7 Ibid, s 55A(5).
8 Births and Deaths Registration Act 1953, s 34(2).

Where parents are married, there is for both parents a statutory obligation to register particulars of the birth within 42 days of its occurrence[1]. Where the child is born to an unmarried mother, only the mother is under this obligation[2]. The father is neither under a duty, nor does he have an independent right, to register his paternity. The circumstances under which his name may be registered were significantly extended by the Family Law Reform Act 1987 and the Children Act 1989[3]. In essence, registration of the father's name will normally require the co-operation and joint attendance by both the mother and father. Independent registration of the father by either the mother or the father will be allowed only on production of a relevant court order or declaration of parentage which entails the determination of parentage together with a declaration that the order has not been terminated by a court. Such orders include parental responsibility orders under s 4 of the Children Act 1989 and an order that the father make financial provision for the child under the residual jurisdiction of the courts[4].

Where none of the above circumstances apply, the father's name will be left blank on the child's birth certificate but may subsequently be added to the register by re-registration, subject to the same conditions set out above[5], or where the parents have married following the birth[6]. We noted in Chapter 1 that a high percentage of births outside marriage are registered jointly by the personal attendance of the mother and father together[7] and, as we shall see, this has now become a much more legally significant event, since its effect, following the reform introduced by the Adoption and Children Act 2002, will be to confer automatic parental responsibility on the great majority of unmarried fathers. It is clearly the case that some men registered as fathers under these procedures will not in fact be the genetic fathers. As with the *pater est* presumption at common law, registration of paternity provides a means of *attributing* legal parentage which may or may not coincide with the biological reality. It is usually only in the event of a dispute that there will be an occasion to look behind the attribution of parentage arising from the fact of registration. Yet, although a man seeking registration as father will not have to establish an actual genetic link with the child he may, it seems, have to establish that he is himself a biological *male*. Such was the result of the decision of the ECtHR in the remarkable case of *X, Y and Z v The United Kingdom*[8].

Here, a female-to-male transsexual (X) sought to be registered as the father of a child (Z) with the co-operation of his female partner (Y) who was the mother of the child. The child had been conceived through artificial insemination by donor after X and Y had successfully obtained licensed fertility treatment together. The Registrar-General refused to register X as the father, taking the position that only a biological male could be so registered. For these purposes English law took the

---

1 Births and Deaths Registration Act 1953, s 2.
2 Ibid, s 10(1), and the Registration of Births and Deaths (Amendment) Regulations 1994, SI 1994/1948, which provide that the unmarried father is not required to give information concerning the birth.
3 Births and Deaths Registration Act 1953, s 10(1), as amended.
4 See further Chapter 9 below.
5 Births and Deaths Registration Act 1953, s 10A(1).
6 Ibid, s 14.
7 See p 6 above.
8 (1997) 24 EHRR 143. For a commentary on the case, see A Bainham 'Sex, Gender and Fatherhood: Does Biology Really Matter?' (1997) CLJ 512.

line that a person's sex is determined at birth, applying biological criteria, and did not recognise the 'psychological' sex of a post-operative transsexual[1]. The European Commission had found by 13 votes to 5 that the refusal of registration violated X's rights under the Convention, but the Court (with six dissenting opinions) found that there had been no violation of Article 8 taking into account the wide margin of appreciation enjoyed by States. In particular, it regarded as crucial the fact that there was, as yet, no common European standard about granting rights to transsexuals or about the manner in which the social relationship between a child conceived by donor sperm and the person performing the social role of the father should be reflected in law. It was not thought to be clearly demonstrated that to register X would benefit the child Z and it was pointed out that X and Y could together apply for a joint residence order, the effect of which would be to give X parental responsibility over Z.

This decision must now be reviewed in the light of the rulings by the ECtHR in *Goodwin v United Kingdom*[2] and *I v United Kingdom*[3]. In these decisions the Court found that the refusal of English law to recognise a change of status for post-operative transsexuals no longer fell within the State's margin of appreciation in view of an emerging consensus within the contracting States of the Council of Europe to grant such legal recognition. Although these cases did not on their facts raise directly the issue of a relationship between a transsexual social parent and a child, the reasoning ought to cover that situation. The recognition of a change of gender should cover not only change of the birth certificate and the right to marry and found a family but also the capacity to be a legal parent[4]. As the Court itself put it in *Goodwin*[5]:

> 'Where a State has authorised the treatment and surgery alleviating the condition of a transsexual, financed or assisted in financing the operations and indeed permits the artificial insemination of a woman living with a female-to-male (as demonstrated in the case of *X, Y and Z v the United Kingdom*) it appears illogical to refuse to recognise the legal implications of the result to which the treatment leads.'

Findings of paternity in legal proceedings

Questions of paternity may fall to be determined in many kinds of legal proceedings. They may arise as a secondary, yet necessary, issue in proceedings the primary purpose of which is something else. A child's upbringing or welfare may be in issue, for example where a man claiming to be the father is seeking a parental responsibility order or a s 8 order. To establish standing to seek these orders, he will need to prove that he is indeed the father of the child[6]. The principal issue may relate to property or financial claims. Thus, rights of inheritance may depend

---

1   *Corbett v Corbett (otherwise Ashley)* [1971] P 83. The European Court held that this approach did not itself violate the rights of transsexuals under the ECHR in *Rees v The United Kingdom* (1986) 9 EHRR 56, *Cossey v The United Kingdom* (1990) 13 EHRR 622 and *Sheffield and Horsham v United Kingdom* [1998] 2 FLR 928.

2   [2002] 2 FLR 487.

3   [2002] 2 FLR 518.

4   See now the Gender Recognition Act 2004, which recognises the acquired gender of transsexuals for many purposes. However, an existing parent will retain the status of father or mother, as the case may be, despite a change of gender. Gender Recognition Act 2004, s 12 provides that 'the fact that a person's gender has become the acquired gender under this Act does not affect the status of the person as the father or mother of the child'.

5   [2002] 2 FLR 487 at 506–507.

6   Otherwise he would require leave to seek a s 8 order. See s 10 of the Children Act 1989.

on being able to establish a biological connection[1]. Most obviously, the issue will often arise where a man is denying financial responsibility for a child under the child support legislation[2]. It has also been held that in principle the tort of deceit may apply as between a cohabiting couple. In principle, at least, a finding that a man was fraudulently deceived by the mother of a child into believing that he was the father of a child could in future lead to an action in damages, to recover in particular child support paid on the basis that he was the legal father[3]. Clearly a finding in legal proceedings that such a man was *not* in fact the father would be necessary. Alternatively, as we have seen, paternity may be the only question where, for example, a person is seeking a declaration of parentage or legitimacy.

Blood tests and other scientific tests

The most effective way of proving paternity in legal proceedings is through the use of tests, although other evidence may also be valuable[4]. Whilst tests will usually be court directed, there is no reason why they should not be undertaken voluntarily.

Traditionally, the best available evidence was the conventional blood test. This entailed a comparison of the blood of the mother, the child and the alleged father. Since blood has certain inherited characteristics it is possible to identify those which have been derived from the father. Such a test, however, could not identify conclusively who was the father, since the blood of more than one man may exhibit the relevant characteristics. Yet where these characteristics were absent, it was possible to *exclude* conclusively the man in question. Where the alleged father was not excluded by the test, his blood group characteristics were examined as a percentage of the general population. If the incidence of men in the group was small, this was strong evidence that he was the father, especially if supported by other evidence concerning, for example, the mother's sexual relationships at the relevant time.

The Family Law Reform Act 1987[5] extended the court's powers to order 'scientific tests' based on samples of genetic material other than blood. This power was finally implemented on 1 April 2001[6]. The DNA profiling technique now enables paternity to be established virtually conclusively, thus overcoming the limitations of the conventional blood test. The technique entails the analysis of genetic samples such as blood specimens, semen, saliva or hair roots. It examines the deoxyribonucleic acid in chromosomes which contains an individual's unique genetic pattern of characteristics transmitted by that individual's parents[7].

---

1 As we saw in Chapter 4, this was the case in *Re Overbury (deceased)* [1954] Ch 122.
2 See, for example, *T v Child Support Agency and Another* [1997] 2 FLR 875, *F v Child Support Agency* [1999] 2 FLR 244 and Chapter 9 below.
3 *P v B (Paternity: Damages for Deceit)* [2001] 1 FLR 1041. Here it was determined by consent that the man was not the father. On a preliminary issue, Stanley Burnton J held that the tort of deceit applied as between a cohabiting couple and that the claim for damages could proceed to trial. He continued, however, that it did not follow that any of the special damages were recoverable, even if liability were established.
4 Such as evidence of the mother's sexual relationships during the relevant period or the physical absence of her husband.
5 Family Law Reform Act 1987, s 23(1).
6 Family Law Reform Act 1987 (Commencement No 3) Order 2001, SI 2001/777.
7 See, particularly, R White and J Greenwood 'DNA Fingerprinting and the Law' (1988) 51 MLR 145, and K Kelly, J Rankin and R Wink 'Method and Applications of DNA Fingerprinting: A Guide for the Non-Scientist' [1987] Crim LR 105.

The court has a general power to direct such tests[1], but may not order a party to undergo them without that party's consent[2]. The consent of a person with care and control of a child under 16 years of age was until recently also required[3].

The question arose in two reported decisions as to whether the court had the power to *order* a parent to produce a child for testing where that parent objected. In *Re R (Blood Test: Constraint)*[4] Hale J held that there was such a power deriving from the parent's own right to compel a child to submit to a test. The court, she said, had power under its inherent jurisdiction to authorise the use of physical constraints against a child if satisfied that this was the right course of action. In this case the child, aged 22 months, was ordered to be delivered into the care and control of the Official Solicitor for the purposes of compliance with the court's direction. But in *Re O and J (Paternity: Ordering Blood Tests)*[5] Wall J reluctantly reached the conclusion that he lacked jurisdiction to oblige a mother to produce her child for testing. Amendments to the legislation introduced in 2000 now make it plain that a 'bodily sample' may be taken from a person under the age of 16 years, either if the person who has care or control of him consents or 'if the court considers that it would be in his best interests for the sample to be taken'[6].

The whole question of genetic testing without consent is controversial and the significance of the widespread use of 'DIY' testing, especially via the internet, should not be underestimated. In May 2002 the Human Genetics Commission produced a Report[7] which called for a code of practice on genetic testing to be introduced bearing in mind the sensitivity of these procedures. The Report makes a number of recommendations designed to protect individuals from the misuse of tests. It proposes, inter alia, that it should be a criminal offence to obtain or analyse personal genetic information for non-medical purposes without the individual's knowledge or consent and that the proposed code of practice should provide that parentage testing must not take place without the written consent of all participating adults and should be in the best interests of the child.

In contrast to the testing of a child, where an adult refuses to comply with a direction, the court may not compel him or her to submit to the test but may draw adverse inferences from a refusal[8]. This will often result in a finding of paternity against an alleged father and the very fact of refusal may amount to corroboration of the mother's evidence[9]. Refusal by a certain man to undergo a test may result in an adverse inference that he is the father[10]. Conversely, where a man believes he is the father and does not want to put his paternity to the test, he may have an adverse

---

1   Family Law Reform Act 1969, s 20(1), as amended.
2   Ibid, s 21(1).
3   Ibid, s 21(3).
4   [1998] 1 FLR 745.
5   [2000] 1 FLR 418.
6   Section 21(3) of the Family Law Reform Act 1969, as amended by s 82 of the Child Support, Pensions and Social Security Act 2000.
7   Human Genetics Commission *Inside Information: Balancing Interests in the Use of Personal Genetic Data* (May 2002). For a concise discussion of the Report's contents see A Northover and G Dennison 'Genetic Testing and the Impact on the Family' [2002] Fam Law 752.
8   Family Law Reform Act 1969, s 23(1).
9   *McVeigh v Beattie* [1988] Fam 69.
10 See *Re A (A Minor) (Paternity: Refusal of Blood Test)* [1994] 2 FLR 463, in which it was held that since a DNA test could have conclusively established who the father was, a man could put the issue beyond doubt by submitting to the test. See also *F v Child Support Agency* [1999] 2 FLR 244.

inference drawn against him that he is *not* the father[1]. The court has a discretion to direct tests and is not bound by the welfare principle in exercising this, since the child's welfare is not directly in issue[2]. It is clear that the court should have regard to the interests of the child in arriving at its decision, although it may not always be easy to determine where these lie. Undoubtedly, there is a case for saying that the child himself (in addition to the other parties) has an interest in discovering the truth about his identity[3], but this may have to be weighed against a possible risk to the disruption of existing relationships. Several decisions illustrate the dilemmas with which the courts have had to wrestle in these cases. They also reveal how the courts have wavered in the weight which they have attached to ascertaining the biological truth as opposed to considerations of family stability.

Re F (A Minor: Paternity Test)[4] shows the traditional preference of the courts for leaving the status quo undisturbed and refusing to direct tests where the child is being raised in an ongoing marriage. Here, the mother had had sexual relations with her husband and another man claiming to be the father at around the time of conception. This man's relationship with the mother had ceased but he nonetheless applied for a parental responsibility order and contact order in relation to the child. The Court of Appeal upheld the judge's refusal to direct blood tests. It was held that the child's welfare depended primarily for the foreseeable future on her relationship with her mother and the stability of the family unit and that this need was not outweighed by any advantage to the child which could accrue from knowledge of the biological truth.

A very different view was taken in *Re H (Paternity: Blood Test)*[5], but here there was a crucial distinguishing feature in that the mother's husband had had a vasectomy well before the birth of the child. Again, the child was being raised as a child of the marriage – the mother having become reconciled to her husband following an affair. Her former lover sought contact with the child and a parental responsibility order. Here, the Court of Appeal upheld the judge's decision to direct tests notwithstanding the mother's opposition to tests on her child. Ward LJ said that it was in the child's best interests to be told 'the truth' unless the child's welfare justified a 'cover up'. The mother ought not to be 'living a lie' but ought to be following the maxim which she should be teaching her children 'at her knee' that 'honesty is the best policy'. Moreover, the sooner the child was told the truth, the better. Importantly, the court did not see any necessary inconsistency between

---

1   *Re G (Parentage: Blood Sample)* [1997] 1 FLR 360.
2   *S v McC* [1972] AC 24. Such a test should not be directed where the court is satisfied that it would be *against* the best interests of the child concerned, but a direction can be made despite the opposition of a parent if it is consistent with the child's welfare. See *Re H (Paternity: Blood Test)* [1996] 2 FLR 65.
3   Discussed in K O'Donovan 'A Right to Know One's Parentage?' (1988) 2 IJLF 27, E Haimes ' "Secrecy": What Can Artificial Reproduction Learn from Adoption?' (1988) 2 IJLF 46, S Maclean and M Maclean 'Keeping secrets in assisted reproduction – the tension between donor anonymity and the need of the child for information' [1996] CFLQ 243, and K O'Donovan 'Interpretations of Children's Identity Rights' in D Foltrell (ed) *Revisiting Children's Rights: 10 years of the UN Convention on the Rights of the Child* (Kluwer, 2000) p 73.
4   [1993] 1 FLR 598.
5   [1996] 2 FLR 65. For comments, see A Bainham, 'Vasectomies, Lovers and Disputed Offspring: Honesty is the Best Policy (Sometimes)' (1996) CLJ 444, and B Gilbert 'Paternity, truth and the interests of the child' [1996] CFLQ 361.

upholding the *social* fatherhood of the husband while possibly establishing the *biological* parentage of the former lover.

A starkly different view of the importance of the truth of paternity to children was exhibited by Judge Hyam in the remarkable case of *Re K (Specific Issue Order)*[1]. Here paternity was not in dispute at all. The case concerned a child aged 12. His father was a well-known disc jockey from King's Lynn. The mother had told the child when he was aged 5 that his father was dead and had persisted with this story thereafter because of the father's adverse behaviour towards her. The child had originally been jointly registered and given the father's name but the mother later changed this to her own and resisted all forms of contact between the father and the child. The father applied for a specific issue order requiring the mother to inform the child of his paternity arguing that it was fundamental that he be told the truth and that, since it was inevitable that sooner or later the child would find out the true position when he looked at his birth certificate, it was better that he be told as soon as possible. Judge Hyam disagreed. Although generally a child had a right to be told the truth about his father's identity, his welfare was paramount. Here there was, he thought, a cogent reason for denying the right to know. The mother's hatred of the father was such that informing the child about him would cause emotional disruption to the child's life which would be seriously detrimental to his welfare.

Re K is probably best regarded as an eccentric aberration from the tide of case-law which is now flowing in the direction of establishing truth. Two more recently reported cases illustrate the strength of the current. In *Re H and A (Paternity: Blood Tests)*[2] the mother gave birth to twins following an extra-marital affair. She told the man concerned that he was the father and allowed him some contact with the children. When they fell out he brought a paternity suit which the mother successfully concealed from her husband for almost a year. She refused to consent to blood tests, and the husband's evidence was that he was likely to leave the family home if the tests established that he was not the father. The judge refused to order tests on the basis that this would risk the stability of the children's family life. The Court of Appeal, remitting the case for rehearing, disagreed taking the view that the judge had given insufficient weight to the benefits of certainty in a situation in which there had been much speculation and gossip. The judge had also concluded too readily that the children's family would be destroyed since he had based this on the assumption, not necessarily borne out by the evidence, that the marriage was sound. The court said that the paternity of a child was now to be established by science and not by legal presumption or inference. Most significantly, perhaps, the court gave a clear indication that there would be few cases where the best interests of children would be served by the suppression of truth.

Re T (Paternity: Ordering Blood Tests)[3] was not one of them. A married couple had been unable to conceive a child together. They agreed that the mother would have sex with someone else for this purpose and she tried unsuccessfully to produce a child with the applicant, who was a friend of the family. Ten years later she tried again, this time with four men including the applicant. She gave birth in

1   [1999] 2 FLR 280.
2   [2002] 1 FLR 1145.
3   [2001] 2 FLR 1190.

due course to a child who was raised by her and her husband as a child of the marriage. Initially the applicant saw the child regularly but the mother eventually found the visits too demanding and ended them. This led in due course to speculation in the wider family and local community about the child's paternity. The applicant applied for a parental responsibility order and a contact order. Having failed with his application he made another some six years later relying on his rights under the ECHR.

Bodey J ordered blood tests under the newly amended s 21(3) of the Family Law Act 1969[1] and considered the balance to be struck between the various interests under domestic law and under the ECHR. In most cases, he said, it was likely to be in the child's best interests to know the truth. In this case this was so because of the doubts which were already in the public domain and bearing in mind that the marriage was stable notwithstanding these doubts. Further, the result of the tests, depending on what it was, might well determine the applications for contact and parental responsibility. So far as the ECHR was concerned, it was a matter of balancing Convention rights. The child had a right to know his true identity and to have the possibility of contact with each of his parents, but this had to be set against the child's competing right to have the current stability of his family life protected. Likewise the mother, her husband and the applicant had conflicting rights under Article 8. These rights pulled in different directions but the child's rights and best interests fell particularly to be considered. The child's right to know here emerged as the weightiest. In his view the interference with other rights was *proportionate* to the legitimate aim of providing the child with the possibility of certainty of his real paternity.

It may be that increasingly in the future it will not be assumed that a choice necessarily has to be made between stability and truth or between potential fathers. With the very high incidence of social parenting and a growing emphasis on the child's right to knowledge of biological origins, the way forward may be to acknowledge the child's interests in *both* potential fathers albeit performing different roles. Certainly, the courts do not regard the genetic link as crucial to the contact question and have openly recognised in this context the importance to the child of the social father[2]. Part of the problem may be thought to arise from the legal position that there can only be *two* parents which in turn can create a mindset that the child can have only two significant adults in his life. This is a view which is likely to be increasingly questioned.

Human rights: when does family life begin?

Human rights issues arise in relation to the start of the relationship between parents and children just as they do throughout family law. Under the ECHR a key question is when 'family life' is established between parent and child. The significance of course is that the right to respect for family life under Article 8 will only come into being at all if it can be said that family life indeed exists between the child and an adult, whether a parent or someone else. So when does family life arise? The answer which the ECtHR has given to this question distinguishes between *mothers* and *fathers*.

---

1 See pp 193–194 above.
2 See, for example, *O v L (Blood Tests)* [1995] 2 FLR 930.

Mothers

Over a quarter of a century ago the ECtHR held in *Marckx v Belgium*[1] that family life
between a mother and her child arose *from the moment of birth*. This case concerned
the status of unmarried mothers in Belgian law. Here, the Court held that Belgian
law violated the rights of mother and child under Article 8, both independently
and in conjunction with Article 14, in failing to acknowledge the mother's
maternity from the moment of birth. As Belgian law stood at the time, the
unmarried mother was required to undertake a formal legal process of voluntary
recognition. No legal bond was recognised by the mere fact of birth. Alternatively,
maternity could be established in legal proceedings. These formal requirements
were not imposed in relation to legitimate children. The court held that it was
discriminatory to distinguish between legitimate and illegitimate children, since
all such children had an equal interest in establishing the maternal bond. It found
that there was no objective and reasonable justification for making this distinction. The most significant feature of the decision, however, was the interpretation
of Article 8 as imposing *positive* obligations on the State and not merely the
negative obligation not to interfere with family life. Thus, the State was obliged to
act in a manner calculated to allow ties between near relatives to develop normally.
In other words, the ECHR required States to promote the development of family
life whether within or outside the institution of marriage[2].

Another important feature of this case, confirmed by the Court's later decision
in *Johnston v Republic of Ireland*[3], was the recognition by the Court that the interests
of mother and child were inextricably linked, so that discrimination against one
was discrimination against the other. Thus, in the *Johnston* case it was said that 'the
close and intimate relationship between the third applicant (the child) and her
parents (a cohabiting unmarried couple) was such that there was of necessity also
a resultant failure to respect the family life of each of the latter'.

Fathers

Here, as in relation to establishing paternity, the position is far from straightforward. What is certain is that the *mere fact* of genetic parentage will not per se
establish family life between a man and a child. This is clear from the
jurisprudence of the ECtHR. The uncertainty surrounds how much more is
required. This is something which has exercised not just the ECtHR but also the
English courts in a string of cases concerning the right of a genetic father to
participate in adoption proceedings[4].

If family life were to be established by the genetic connection alone, it would
arise between, inter alia, a sperm donor and the resulting child. In *G v The
Netherlands*[5] the European Commission was unwilling to hold that it did. What is
required then beyond this? The answer which the Court gave in *Söderback v Sweden*[6]

---

1   (1979) 2 EHRR 330.
2   See JS Davidson 'The European Convention on Human Rights and the "Illegitimate" Child' in
    D Freestone (ed) *Children and the Law* (Hull University Press, 1990) p 75, especially at pp 88–89.
    See also NV Lowe 'The Meaning and Allocation of Parental Responsibility – A Common
    Lawyer's Perspective' (1997) 11 IJLPF 192, especially at pp 201–205.
3   (1986) 8 EHRR 203.
4   See further A Bainham 'Can we Protect Children and Protect their Rights?' [2002] Fam Law
    279 at pp 280–284.
5   (1990) 16 EHRR CD 38.
6   [1999] 1 FLR 250.

was that 'certain ties' must exist between father and child. However, we also know from this case that cohabitation between the mother and father is not an essential prerequisite to the establishment of family life – although doubtless where it has existed this will be a factor tending towards a finding that family life exists. In *Söderback* the natural father was attempting to prevent adoption of a child by the step-father. The Court found that certain ties did exist between the biological father and the child but that the interference with the father's family life with the child could be justified on the basis of the child's best interests. The ties here appear to have been the father's commitment to contact with the child, although little had in fact taken place. In *Kroon v The Netherlands*[1] family life was established on the basis that there was a relationship of sufficient constancy to create de facto family ties. The mother and father had had a relationship of considerable duration and had produced no less than four children together, but they had never cohabited.

Two further cases from the Netherlands have also been concerned with this question of when family life begins between a father and a child. In *Haas v The Netherlands*[2] the applicant was born out of wedlock and was seeking to establish that he was the son of the deceased and therefore entitled to the deceased's estate as against a nephew of the deceased. The deceased had never 'recognised' him as his son, but he had made payments for his care and upbringing, visited him and occasionally gone on day trips with the boy and his mother. The applicant argued that he had family life with the deceased and that Dutch laws which discriminated against the illegitimate and 'unrecognised' child violated Article 14 of the ECHR. Having failed in the Dutch courts, the applicant took his case to Strasbourg. The ECtHR held unanimously that there was no violation of the ECHR. In the Court's view, it was not truly faced with an issue of 'family life' or 'private life' within the meaning of Article 8 but with a question of evidence going to the issue of whether family ties between the applicant and the deceased should be recognised. It was held that the evidence was insufficient to establish this link and that the applicant could not derive from Article 8 a right to be recognised as heir of the deceased for inheritance purposes.

On the other hand, in *Yousef v The Netherlands*[3] 'family life' was found to have existed even though the mother (as she was entitled to do under Dutch law) had refused to permit the father to 'recognise' his child. Here there was no dispute as to biological paternity, and the mother and father had cohabited for a certain period. Further, after the mother's death, the father had some contact with the child. In these circumstances family life did exist between the father and the child[4]. The Court went on to hold, however, that there was no violation of the father's rights under Article 8 when engaging in the balancing exercise required

---

1   (1994) 19 EHRR 263.
2   [2004] 1 FLR 673.
3   [2003] 1 FLR 210.
4   See also *Lebbink v The Netherlands* [2004] 2 FLR 463, where family life was also found to exist between the father and child even though the mother and father had never cohabited. The ECtHR reiterated the principle that mere biological kinship, without further legal or factual elements indicating the existence of close personal ties, could not be enough to establish family life. Here, such ties were found to exist based on the fact that the father had been the child's 'auxiliary guardian' under Dutch law, had been present at the birth, had visited the mother, had changed the baby's nappy a few times and baby-sat once or twice, and had had contact with the mother concerning the child's impaired hearing.

by Article 8(2). The denial under Dutch law of the father's right to recognise his child was in accordance with the law and pursued a legitimate aim which was necessary in a democratic society in that it was considered to be in the child's best interests. The Court also held that, where it was necessary to balance the *rights* of parents and the *rights* of children, the child's rights must be the paramount consideration and, in any balancing of *interests*, the interests of the child must prevail.

The English courts have also had to grapple with this issue. The two cases of *Re H; Re G (Adoption: Consultation of Unmarried Fathers)*[1] provide an illustration of decisions coming down on different sides of the line. Both concerned mothers who placed their babies for adoption with the local authority on the basis that confidentiality would be observed. Both involved fathers who were known to the local authority, and guidance was sought as to whether the respective fathers should be consulted in the adoption process. In the first case, the mother and father had cohabited for a while and had another child together with whom the father had contact. Dame Elizabeth Butler-Sloss had no difficulty in finding that family life was established between the father and child and ordered the authority to identify and consult the father. However, in the second case, although the parties had been engaged at one point, they had never cohabited and had lost touch. The father was from overseas and was training for a profession in this country. Here she held that the relationship had insufficient constancy to come within the concept of family life. Accordingly, it was not necessary for the authority to give the father notice or to join him as a respondent in the proceedings.

A similar conclusion was reached in *Re J (Adoption: Contacting Father)*[2]. Here the relationship between the teenage parents ended just after the mother became pregnant. The father was unaware of the pregnancy or birth, and the child was diagnosed with severe cystic fibrosis. Bennett J granted a declaration that it was lawful for the local authority not to inform the father or his family of the existence of the child and for the authority to place the child for adoption without consulting him. There was found to be no family life between father and child. The mother and father did not have a strong commitment to each other, they had never cohabited and it was a short relationship in their teenage years. As such it did not have sufficient constancy to create de facto family ties. Moreover it was unlikely that the father would have wanted to look after the child given the child's medical condition. Thus, there was little to be gained by informing the father, and the mother had only revealed his identity believing that she would be protected by confidentiality.

A final question is whether a formal kinship relationship between someone and a child is per se enough to establish family life. The better view is that a legally recognised family relationship, such as that between a grandparent, uncle or aunt[3], would automatically give rise to family life between those relatives and the child. The same would probably apply to a *married* father who left the scene completely before the birth of the child. We consider in the conclusion to this chapter how satisfactory is the current position on when family life comes into being.

---

1   [2001] 1 FLR 646.
2   [2003] 1 FLR 933.
3   See *Z County Council v R* [2001] 1 FLR 365.

PARENTAL RESPONSIBILITY IN THE UNMARRIED FAMILY

The background

English law has long taken the position that whereas parental responsibility (formerly parental rights and duties) is automatically held by *both* parents where those parents are married to each other, where the parents are not married to each other parental responsibility is held only by the mother[1]. It has been and still is the case that biological paternity per se does not result in the automatic acquisition of parental responsibility by operation of law. At the same time the law has provided mechanisms for the acquisition of parental responsibility by the father. We consider these procedures and the case-law which they have generated below.

However, while it remains true that paternity alone will not result in the father obtaining parental responsibility, the position in practice will be radically transformed by recent amendments to the Children Act 1989 brought about by the Adoption and Children Act 2002[2]. Those fathers who are now *registered* as such (which as we have seen usually requires the personal attendance and co-operation of both father and mother[3]) will acquire parental responsibility by virtue of that registration[4]. Previous to this, parental responsibility could be acquired only by entering into a parental responsibility agreement with the mother or by obtaining a parental responsibility order (PRO) from the courts[5]. As we shall see[6], only a tiny *minority* of fathers acquired parental responsibility in these ways. But the effect of conferring parental responsibility on birth registration will be dramatic since it will lead to a very substantial *majority* of unmarried fathers acquiring it. This is on the reasonable assumption that the change in the law will not result in significant numbers of unmarried mothers refusing to co-operate in the registration of the father where they otherwise would have done. Therefore, on the basis of what is known about the patterns of birth registration, it can be predicted that about four-fifths[7] of all fathers unmarried to the mother will henceforth acquire parental responsibility more or less immediately after the birth of the child when the process of birth registration is completed.

This will still leave about one-fifth of unmarried fathers who will be 'parents without parental responsibility', along with a large number of men in this position because their children were born before December 2003 when the new provisions on registration took effect. This may arise because they themselves are unwilling to acknowledge their paternity through the process of registration perhaps because of indifference or perhaps because they deny it. But this may also be because the mother, for whatever reason, wants no further contact with the man concerned or, at any rate, does not wish him to have formal legal standing in relation to the child.

---

1 Children Act 1989, s 2(2).
2 Adoption and Children Act 2002, s 111, amending Children Act 1989, s 4. For a summary of the changes, see P Booth 'Parental Responsibility – What Changes' [2004] Fam Law 353.
3 See p 191 above.
4 The Adoption and Children Act 2002 amends s 4 of the Children Act 1989 so that it is now provided that the father shall acquire parental responsibility for the child if he becomes registered as the child's father under the Births and Deaths Registration Act 1953.
5 Children Act 1989, s 4.
6 See p 207 below.
7 See Chapter 1 above.

It is in this latter situation that the most difficult human rights issues are likely to arise if the father himself wishes to have contact with the child.

The question of the circumstances under which the unmarried father *should* acquire parental responsibility has been the subject of debate and of reports by the English[1] and Scottish Law Commissions[2] for a quarter of a century. Much attention has been focused on the different circumstances in which children may be conceived and on ways of distinguishing between so-called 'meritorious' and 'unmeritorious' men. Indeed, as we shall see,[3] much of the case-law governing the granting of PROs is in essence an attempt to do just that. Alongside this view there has been another to the effect that parental responsibility should flow automatically from the determination of legal paternity – a position adopted in almost all the States of Eastern Europe in the period after World War II and by Australia in 1975. The English Law Commission, after provisionally favouring this solution, came out against it in 1982[4] largely because of the perceived threats to the security of unmarried mothers raising children on their own. The Scottish Law Commission by contrast had come around to the view a decade later that this was the preferred solution and that it would have the additional advantage of being able to abolish illegitimacy conclusively[5]. This is not the result of the recent reform which makes *registration*, and not the determination of paternity, the key event. It will therefore continue to be necessary to distinguish between fathers with parental responsibility and those without it.

Where do human rights fit into all this? More than once it has been argued that for the law to differentiate between fathers in this way and between the children of those fathers is contrary to the ECHR[6]. The ECtHR has thus far rejected these arguments. In *B v United Kingdom*[7] an unmarried father applied for a PRO and contact but, shortly afterwards, the mother took the child to Italy. The English courts dismissed his claim that this amounted to child abduction since, following *Re B (Abduction) (Rights of Custody)*[8], he lacked 'formal rights of custody' which in this context largely hinged on his lack of parental responsibility[9]. He complained unsuccessfully of a breach of his rights under Article 8 of the ECHR taken in conjunction with Article 14. The essence of the argument was that unmarried fathers were discriminated against in the protection given to their relationships with their children when compared with that given to married fathers. The ECtHR, however, found the complaint inadmissible in that there was an objective

---

1   Law Com Working Paper No 74 *Illegitimacy* (1979); Law Com Report No 118 *Illegitimacy* (1982); and Law Com Report No 157 *Illegitimacy (Second Report)* (1986).
2   Scot Law Com Report No 82 *Illegitimacy* (1984) and Scot Law Com No 135 *Report on Family Law* (1992).
3   See pp 208 et seq below.
4   Law Com Report No 118 *Illegitimacy* (1982).
5   Scot Law Com No 135 *Report on Family Law* (1992). For a detailed account of the reasoning of the Scottish Law Commission see the second edition of this work at pp 172–173.
6   See especially *McMichael v United Kingdom* (1995) 20 EHRR 205.
7   [2000] 1 FLR 1.
8   [1997] 2 FLR 594.
9   The concept of 'rights of custody' under the Hague Convention on the Civil Aspects of International Child Abduction 1980 does not precisely translate into the possession of parental responsibility under English law since there are circumstances, where, for example, a father has the primary care of the child, in which he may be held to have rights of custody for the purposes of the Convention despite lacking formal parental responsibility. See Chapter 17 below.

and reasonable justification for the difference in treatment between married and unmarried fathers regarding the range of possible relationships between fathers and children. Specifically, fathers who had children in their care to any degree had different responsibilities to those who simply had contact. This, the Court held, justified the difference in treatment between those fathers with parental responsibility and those without it. It is important to appreciate that this decision is confined to the question of automatic parental responsibility. As we shall see, in a later decision,[1] the Court held that discrimination under German law between married and unmarried fathers in relation to the question of the right of access (contact) *did* breach the Convention.

Since then, it continues to be necessary under English law to differentiate between the legal position of married and unmarried fathers. We explore first the legal effect of this distinction and what it means to be a parent without parental responsibility. We then look at the acquisition of parental responsibility by agreement with the mother or by court order and the possibility of its termination. Consideration is then given to the decisions of the courts where unmarried fathers have been asking, perhaps in addition to PROs, for contact or residence orders where they have wanted a significant role in the upbringing of the child. The chapter concludes with some observations on the policy considerations and possible future direction for the law in the light of evolving human rights obligations.

A parent without parental responsibility

Where a child's parents were unmarried at the time of his birth[2], the mother has sole parental responsibility[3]. The father is, however, within the definition of 'parent' in the Children Act 1989 and is thus a 'parent without parental responsibility'. In order to become a legal parent in the fullest sense, the unmarried father must take steps to acquire parental responsibility through legal process. We have noted above that registration will now be the most numerically significant of these procedures by far. This discussion is only concerned with the minority of fathers who are not registered and who wish to acquire parental responsibility. The principles governing applications for contact or residence orders, however, apply to all fathers whether or not they acquired parental responsibility by registration. These procedures include an agreement with the mother, a parental responsibility order, a residence order or (in the event of the mother's death) guardianship. All of these mechanisms must be considered but, before doing so, it is important to have an appreciation of what it means, in law and in practice, to be a parent without parental responsibility.

As we have seen, certain legal consequences flow automatically from the legal status of *being a parent* and are not dependent on the possession of parental responsibility. The unmarried father is thus in the same position as all other parents for the purposes of succession. He may succeed to his child's estate, or the child may succeed to his, in the event of either of them dying intestate[4]; he has an

---

1   *Sahin and Others v Germany* [2002] 1 FLR 119.

2   This has an extended meaning in accordance with the Children Act 1989, s 2(3). In essence, the expression includes those regarded as legitimate under various enactments, and adopted children.

3   Children Act 1989, s 2(2).

4   Family Law Reform Act 1987, s 18.

obligation to maintain the child financially[1]; there is a presumption of reasonable contact in his favour where the child is in care and he has a right to be consulted by a local authority about decisions taken in relation to the child, where the authority is accommodating the child[2]; and, finally, he has standing to commence or participate in certain kinds of legal proceedings. Thus, as a parent, the unmarried father may apply without leave for any s 8 order[3]; he ought to be entitled to participate in care proceedings[4]; and, although his *consent* is not required for adoption of the child, he has certain procedural rights in adoption proceedings and, increasingly, human rights considerations require that he be notified, consulted and allowed to participate in adoption proceedings[5].

On the other hand, those legal effects which arise from holding parental responsibility do not accrue to the unmarried father despite his being a parent. He has no right to look after the child physically and no right to take or participate in decisions regarding upbringing[6]. Third parties have no duty to deal with him or to take his views into account. For these purposes, it must be appreciated that no distinction is made between the unmarried man in a stable cohabitation and the unmarried man who is living separately from the mother, except that the former is very likely now to acquire parental responsibility through birth registration. There will, of course, be practical distinctions since the cohabitant, unlike the non-cohabitant, is likely to be performing the role of social father. Indeed, it is the case that at least some unmarried cohabitants have been unaware of the male partner's lack of legal responsibility for the child[7]. While they are living together amicably it is unlikely that much will turn on the strict legal position between the parents and, of course, the father will, in any event, have the powers and responsibilities which are held by any de facto carer[8].

Other effects of withholding automatic parental responsibility

The father's lack of parental responsibility not only affects his relationship vis-à-vis the mother, but also, significantly, his standing in relation to the State[9]. He has no

---

1   Child Support Act 1991, ss 1(1) and 54. This obligation applies notwithstanding that the father has not acquired parental responsibility. See the Children Act 1989, s 3(4).

2   Children Act 1989, ss 34(1) and 22(4) respectively.

3   Ibid, s 10(4) and *M v C and Calderdale Metropolitan Borough Council* [1993] 1 FLR 505.

4   He is not automatically a party unless he has acquired parental responsibility but may apply to be joined. In any event, he is entitled to receive notice of the proceedings. See Family Proceedings Rules 1991, SI 1991/1247, r 4.7 and Appendix 3. For an exploration of the extent to which he is entitled to participate in care proceedings, see *Re B (Care Proceedings: Notification of Father Without Parental Responsibility)* [1999] 2 FLR 408.

5   See further Chapter 7 below.

6   A good example is *Dawson v Wearmouth* [1997] 2 FLR 629, where an unmarried father tried unsuccessfully to persuade the courts that the child should be known by his surname rather than the surname of the mother's ex husband which she had chosen. The initial choice of name is the mother's alone (as the person with sole parental responsibility) and the father's claims are limited to a possible change of name based on the child's best interests.

7   This was certainly what Pickford found in her study involving unmarried fathers. See R Pickford *Fathers, Marriage and the Law* (Family Policy Studies Centre/Joseph Rowntree Foundation, 1999). See also R Pickford 'Unmarried Fathers and the Law' in A Bainham, S Day Sclater and M Richards (eds) *What is A Parent? – A Socio-Legal Analysis* (Hart Publishing, 1999).

8   Section 3(5) of the Children Act 1989. In some ways his position is analogous to that of a step-father.

9   For a particularly good example of this under the old law, see the House of Lords decision in *Re M and H (Minors) (Local Authority: Parental Rights)* [1988] 3 All ER 5.

right to object to a voluntary arrangement between the mother and social services for the local authority to look after the child. This was a problem which surfaced in several reported cases under the old law[1]. Although the father does have standing to apply for a residence or contact order in these circumstances, the reality is that this may prove a difficult hurdle where the child has, in the meantime, been placed in substitute care. It is certainly not as effective, from the father's point of view, as an initial right of objection would be.

It has been noted that the unmarried father has no right to veto adoption although, as we have seen, human rights considerations will now result in the involvement of the majority of fathers in adoption proceedings, to the extent that they wish to be involved[2]. Neither does he have the right to appoint a guardian[3]. All of these limitations on the father's parental status will, however, be overcome if he succeeds, through one route or another, in obtaining parental responsibility.

Acquiring parental responsibility

The unregistered unmarried father may obtain parental responsibility by agreement with the mother, by obtaining a residence order or PRO or, possibly, where the mother has died, by being appointed guardian. Where he is only concerned to establish or preserve contact with the child, or question some aspect of the child's upbringing, the appropriate course will be to apply for a s 8 order.

Parental responsibility agreements

The Family Law Reform Act 1987 stopped short of allowing unmarried parents to share parental responsibility by agreement without the necessity of going to court. The Law Commission originally rejected the idea on the basis that it had the potential for eroding the institution of marriage by 'blurring the legal distinction between marriage and other relationships'[4]. This view was criticised by some commentators who felt that to recognise private agreements could be a means of allowing 'meritorious' fathers in stable relationships to acquire full parental status while excluding 'unmeritorious' men from parental participation[5]. The Law Commission was, in due course, persuaded of this view[6], and the Children Act 1989 gave effect to its recommendations. The Children Act provides that 'the father and mother may by agreement ... provide for the father to have parental responsibility for the child'[7]. The agreement must be made in prescribed form and recorded in the Principal Registry of the Family Division[8]. The purpose of these formalities is to warn parents that the agreement will seriously affect their legal position, to advise them to seek legal advice and to inform them about the

---

1　The right of objection extends only to those with parental responsibility, as does the subsequent right of removal of the child. See s 20(7) and (8) of the Children Act 1989.

2　But see the decision of the ECtHR in *Keegan v Ireland* (1994) 18 EHRR 342 which effectively held (in the context of Irish law) that a secret adoption deliberately concealed from the father is a breach of his rights under the ECHR.

3　The right extends only to parents with parental responsibility and guardians. See s 5(3) and (4) of the Children Act 1989.

4　Law Com Report No 118 (above) at para 4.8.

5　See, in particular, J Eekelaar 'Second Thoughts on Illegitimacy Reform' [1985] Fam Law 261.

6　Law Com Report No 172 *Guardianship and Custody* (1988) at para 2.18.

7　Section 4(1)(b).

8　Section 4(2), and the Parental Responsibility Agreement Regulations 1991, SI 1991/1478.

ways in which the agreement can be brought to an end. The court's function is a purely administrative one and it has no power to question the desirability of the agreement for the welfare of the child. The agreement is, however, revocable by the court on the application of anyone with parental responsibility, or on the application of the child himself where the court has given the child leave on being satisfied that he has sufficient understanding to make the application[1]. It has been held that it is open to parents to enter into a parental responsibility agreement notwithstanding the fact that the father (who had previously failed to obtain a PRO) was in prison and the children were in care[2].

The parental responsibility agreement was primarily designed for unmarried couples in stable relationships who wished to bring the legal situation into line with the factual position in which they were effectively raising a child together. It was also the case that at least some agreements were made to head off applications to the courts for PROs. Given the apparently liberal attitude of the courts to the making of such orders, in many instances the mother should be advised to share parental responsibility voluntarily rather than go to court. In fact, in most instances, cohabiting couples will now share parental responsibility automatically through joint registration of the birth and it may be that these agreements will become largely redundant. Under the old law, this sharing of parental status was not possible, even by court order[3]. Yet it was questionable from the outset how far these agreements would be used in practice. Parents living together amicably might see no advantage in formalising their arrangements, especially since some people choose to cohabit precisely because of their dislike of the formalities which attach to marriage. They might also be unaware of the disparity in their respective legal positions or of the provision for agreements[4]. There is yet a further possibility that the mother may not be sufficiently confident about the relationship, or the father's parenting role, that she would wish to dilute her own legal control by sharing parental responsibility. Indeed, one of the fears which was expressed concerning the automatic acquisition of parental responsibility by registration of the father is that this may result in a minority of mothers being unwilling to name the father on registering the child's birth because of the consequential sharing of parental responsibility. Some mothers may see this as undermining their central parental role.

The statistics for the registration of parental responsibility agreements reveal rather strikingly that these misgivings about the extent of the use of these

---

1   Section 4(3) and (4).
2   *Re X (Parental Responsibility Agreement: Children in Care)* [2000] 1 FLR 517.
3   It was possible for a legal custody order to be obtained by the father but this was unenforceable where he was cohabiting with the mother and lapsed after three months' cohabitation. See the Guardianship of Minors Act 1971, s 9(3). In effect, an order for joint legal custody was not possible.
4   This is certainly borne out by Pickford's research: see R Pickford *Fathers, Marriage and the Law* (above). There is little evidence of greater use of parental responsibility agreements in Scotland than in England. In 1998, there were just 230 agreements set against a figure of 22,319 children born to unmarried parents in Scotland that year. In 1999 there were 335 such agreements. See E Sutherland 'How Children are Faring in the "New Scotland" in A Bainham (ed) *The International Survey of Family Law (2001 Edition)* (Family Law, 2001) p 363 at pp 368–369. The Scottish Law Commission thought that these agreements were only a 'second best solution' and that an automatic status was preferable. See Scot Law Com Report No 135 *Report on Family Law* (1992) at para 2.51.

agreements were warranted. After an initial surge of interest which led to the registration of over 5,000 agreements in 1994, by 1996 there were only around 3,000 such agreements. In that year there were 5,587 PROs[1]. Yet, even taken together, agreements and orders made in 1996 totalled less than 9,000 and clearly accounted for only a tiny minority of births outside marriage[2] which amounted to 232, 663 in England and Wales in that year. Despite the fact that there appears to have been a slight increase in the number of PROs in later years[3], it remained the case that the overwhelming majority of unmarried fathers did not acquire parental responsibility by invoking either of these two mechanisms.

A final matter is guardianship. The mother might be prepared to appoint the father as guardian, in which case he would only acquire parental responsibility if she should die. In this event, if she had not appointed the father as a guardian, he might himself apply to the court to be appointed guardian[4].

Court orders

If the mother is unwilling to register the father or to share responsibility voluntarily, the father may apply to the court for a PRO or, if he wishes to take over the physical care of the child, a residence order. Clearly, this will most commonly arise where the father and mother are living apart and do not have an ongoing relationship.

The PRO is a reincarnation of the former 'parental rights order' introduced by the Family Law Reform Act 1987[5], and reflects the conceptual changes wrought by the Children Act 1989. The order, if granted, has the same effect as the parental responsibility agreement and may be similarly terminated by the court[6]. Its effect is to give the father an equal say in all matters of upbringing but it will not give him any superior claim vis-à-vis the mother to look after the child. If the father wishes to have the child in his care, he will need to apply for a residence order.

The parental responsibility order: a status-conferring device?

It was quickly established, even before the Children Act came into force, that the primary purpose of the former 'parental rights order' was to confer on the father the full status of legal parent and that the order was appropriately used even where it was not contemplated that the man in question would be actively involved in the child's upbringing. Thus, the order could be of value even where the child was in the care of the local authority since it could give him the standing to challenge the authority's plans for the child[7] or to resist a proposed adoption of the child[8]. It was not therefore fatal to an application that the father would not in practice be in a position to exercise parental rights or responsibilities[9].

---

1 Lord Chancellor's Department Consultation Paper (March 1998).
2 See Chapter 1 above.
3 In 1999, the number of orders made totalled 7,514. See *Judicial Statistics 1999* (Lord Chancellor's Department, 2000), Table 5.3.
4 On the appointment of guardians generally, see Chapter 6 below.
5 Section 4.
6 Section 4(3).
7 *D v Hereford and Worcester County Council* [1991] 1 FLR 205.
8 *Re H (Illegitimate Child: Father: Parental Rights) (No 2)* [1991] 1 FLR 214.
9 *Re C (Minors) (Parental Rights)* [1992] 1 FLR 1.

These principles have now been carried forward and reinforced by the jurisprudence of the courts dealing with applications for PROs[1]. The leading authority is *Re S (Parental Responsibility)*[2]. Here, the unmarried parents had intended to marry. The birth of their daughter was jointly registered[3] and the child took her father's surname. The relationship between the parents broke down when the father was convicted of possessing obscene literature. The mother suspected that he might be involved in paedophiliac activities and became reluctant to allow him contact with the girl. The father applied for contact (which ceased to be an issue) but also for a PRO which was refused by the judge. Allowing the father's appeal, the Court of Appeal set out the principles applicable to the use of these orders. The court emphasised that the purpose of the order was to give the father the full status 'for which nature had already ordained that he must bear responsibility'[4]. The order would not, however, entitle the father to interfere in matters concerned with the management of the child's life[5]. Any abuse of the order or any interference with upbringing which was inconsistent with the child's welfare could be controlled by the court through s 8 orders. The court went on to say that expert psychological evidence regarded it as important that a child should grow up with good self-esteem and have a 'favourable positive image' of the 'absent' parent. Ward LJ emphasised that, wherever possible, the law should confer the stamp of its approval on a committed father lest the child should grow up with a belief that the father was in some way disqualified from fulfilling his parental role. Butler-Sloss LJ emphasised the significance of the conceptual and linguistic change from the notion of parental 'rights' to that of 'responsibility':

> 'It is important for parents to remember the emphasis placed by Parliament on the order which is applied for. It is that of duties and responsibilities as well as rights and powers. Indeed the order itself is entitled "parental responsibility". A father who has shown real commitment to the child concerned and to whom there is a positive attachment ... ought ... to assume the weight of those duties and cement that commitment and attachment by sharing the responsibilities for the child with the mother.'

The result of this decision was to establish the three criteria of commitment, attachment and motivation in determining whether or not a PRO should be granted.

The reported cases and judicial statistics do indicate a readiness on the part of the courts to make PROs[6]. It should not, however, be assumed that such orders will be routinely granted simply because fathers ask for them. The court will want

---

1   See, for example, *Re H (A Minor: Parental Responsibility)* [1993] 1 FLR 484; *Re CB (A Minor) (Parental Responsibility Order)* [1993] 1 FLR 920; *Re G (A Minor) (Parental Responsibility Order)* [1994] 1 FLR 504; and *Re E (Parental Responsibility: Blood Tests)* [1995] 1 FLR 392.
2   [1995] 2 FLR 648. See also *Re C and V (Contact and Parental Responsibility)* [1998] 1 FLR 392.
3   Hence, under the new law, the father would have had parental responsibility automatically by virtue of being registered as the father.
4   On the 'natural' rights of parents, see Chapter 3 above.
5   As indicated in Chapter 4, this interpretation of the Children Act 1989 is open to question since, unless a s 8 order has been made, all holders of parental responsibility at least in theory have an equal and independent say in the child's upbringing.
6   Not even a failure to pay maintenance for the benefit of the child should by itself be enough to deprive a father of the order if he is otherwise devoted to the children. It was held in *Re H (Parental Responsibility: Maintenance)* [1996] 1 FLR 867 that withholding the order should not be used as a weapon to extract money from the applicant father even where the court was critical of his failure to contribute financially.

to make an evaluation of the individual father's potential contribution to the child's life. Adverse conduct may also lead to an order being refused. In *Re P (Parental Responsibility)*[1] an order was refused where the father was serving a long prison sentence for several offences of robbery. The Court of Appeal upheld the judge's decision which had properly taken into account the nature of the offence committed by the father and the effect of his incarceration as a restriction on his ability to exercise parental responsibility. In *Re H (Parental Responsibility)*[2], where the judge had found that the father had previously injured the child and the child of a former partner and had displayed cruel behaviour with an element of sadism, the Court of Appeal upheld the decision not to make a PRO (although the judge had allowed supervised contact) emphasising that the court was obliged to decide whether the order was in the best interests of the child. In this case the judge was entitled to conclude that the father posed a future risk to his son and that his previous behaviour rendered him unfit to have parental responsibility. The case also perhaps reveals that a PRO is not exclusively (even if primarily) a status-conferring device. In *Re P (Parental Responsibility)*[3] the Court of Appeal again upheld the judge's decision not to make a PRO on the basis that there was clear evidence that the father would use it inappropriately to interfere with and undermine the mother's care for the child. In *Re M (Contact: Parental Responsibility)*[4] the potential misuse of the order by the father was again a decisive factor in withholding parental responsibility from him[5].

If a father should wish to go beyond merely acquiring the full status of parenthood and actually seek primary care of the child, this would necessitate an application for a residence order[6]. If successful, the court is obliged to make a PRO at the same time[7] and this must not be terminated while the residence order remains in force[8]. Clearly, if the child is to live with the father, the father must be given the necessary legal authority to take decisions on upbringing.

The termination of parental responsibility

Parental responsibility orders and agreements terminate automatically when the child attains the age of 18[9], or by earlier order of the court[10]. Although a PRO cannot be terminated while a residence order is in force, the converse is not true. Thus, when a residence order is terminated, the father will continue to have parental responsibility unless the court specifically decides to terminate it, which

---

1 [1997] 2 FLR 722.
2 [1998] 1 FLR 855.
3 [1998] 2 FLR 96.
4 [2001] 2 FLR 342.
5 For two other cases in which fathers failed to obtain PROs, see *Re J (Parental Responsibility)* [1999] 1 FLR 784 and *M v M (Parental Responsibility)* [1999] 2 FLR 737 in which Wilson J had to take into account the difficult matter of adverse behaviour induced by the father's illness. He concluded that the father was unable because of his illness to exercise his parental responsibility properly.
6 See Chapter 4 above for the legal effect of residence orders.
7 Children Act 1989, s 12(1).
8 Ibid, s 12(4).
9 Ibid, s 91(7) and (8).
10 Ibid, s 4(3).

it may do where it considers that the welfare of the child requires it[1]. Applications to remove a father's parental responsibility are most likely to arise where, following an agreement, the relationship between the father and mother breaks down. In *Re P (Terminating Parental Responsibility)*[2], the child had suffered very severe non-accidental injuries when nine weeks old which were later attributed to the father. The father was convicted and sent to prison but sought contact with the girl, who by this time was in the care of foster-parents. The mother, unaware of the father's guilt, had previously entered into a parental responsibility agreement with him. She succeeded in having this revoked and in obtaining an order under s 91(14) preventing further applications by the father without the leave of the court. The court emphasised that, once obtained, parental responsibility ought not to be terminated except on solid grounds and there was a strong presumption in favour of its continuance. It was relevant to consider whether in the circumstances now obtaining the court would have made a PRO which required evidence of attachment and commitment to the child. These requirements were clearly not met in the circumstances of this case.

It should be noted that whether or not the father acquired parental responsibility while the parents' relationship lasted, there is no automatic judicial scrutiny of the arrangements for the child following relationship breakdown approximating to those which apply on divorce[3]. Since the issue of the parties' relationship (as opposed to marriage) is not itself before the court, the question of any child's welfare will not get there either unless someone takes steps to bring it there.

Section 8 orders: the court's discretion

What is the position where an unmarried father is seeking a residence or contact order in relation to the child? Is there any evidence that unmarried fathers are likely to find it more difficult than their married counterparts to obtain residence or contact orders? Can distinctions readily be drawn between the man who has, at some point, cohabited with the mother and the man who has not?

The reported cases do not give a clear message but it is evident that the unmarried man without parental responsibility starts from a weaker position than the married man who has parental responsibility from the outset. There is a perceptible feeling that the unmarried father wishing to secure a residence, or perhaps even a contact, order is likely to experience an uphill struggle in convincing the court of his case. This is an area in which there has been some judicial disagreement.

---

1   This is in contrast to the position in marriage where the parental responsibility of a married or divorced parent cannot be terminated through any legal mechanism short of adoption. For a particularly striking example, see *Re M (A Minor) (Care Order: Threshold Conditions)* [1994] 2 AC 424, where the father retained parental responsibility despite murdering the mother in the presence of the children. Ironically, he was one of several fathers of the mother's children but the only one who happened to be married to her. It might be argued that there *should* be power to terminate parental responsibility in such cases. See further Chapter 11.

2   [1995] 1 FLR 1048.

3   The question of whether there should be is a fascinating one, touched upon briefly in J Eekelaar *Regulating Divorce* (Clarendon Press, 1991), and in M Richards 'Private Worlds and Public Intentions – The Role of the State at Divorce' in A Bainham, DS Pearl and R Pickford (eds) *Frontiers of Family Law* (2nd edn) (John Wiley & Sons, 1995).

On the one hand, there have been cases in which the judges have gone out of their way to emphasise the importance of the blood tie and have not distinguished in this respect between married and unmarried parents. A striking example is *Re K (A Minor) (Custody)*[1]. Here, a boy aged four years went to live with his uncle and aunt following the suicide of his mother. The natural father had had regular contact at weekends and on Wednesday evenings. He applied for care and control of the child and was supported by the welfare officer and a psychiatric social worker. The judge found that the standard of care which would be provided by the uncle and aunt was far superior to that which the father would be able to offer since he was in full-time employment and would have to rely, to a large extent, on the back-up services of his own mother. Her long-term commitment was in some doubt and the judge concluded that the child's best interests would be served by giving care and control to the uncle and aunt. The Court of Appeal disagreed, taking the view that the best person to bring up a child was the natural parent. It mattered not whether the parent was wise or foolish, rich or poor, educated or illiterate, provided that the child's moral and physical health were not in danger. The court referred to the 'prima facie right' of the natural parent to raise his child which would require 'compelling factors' to be overridden. What the father could offer was considered adequate and his commitment to the child was not in doubt so that to make comparisons with someone who could provide a better home was an erroneous approach.

A similar view of the value of natural parenthood was expressed in *Re O (A Minor) (Custody: Adoption)*[2]. Here, the child was aged 15 months, the product of a brief relationship between a married woman and a divorced man whose relationship had ceased before the child's birth. The mother returned to her husband and placed the child, at birth, with an adoption society, who in turn placed him with short-term foster-parents where his welfare blossomed. The father had had a number of short-lived relationships with women but no settled home with any of them for any length of time. The Court of Appeal upheld the judge's decision granting custody to the father, coupled with a one-year supervision order in favour of the local authority. The court held that, where the natural mother could not look after the child for whatever reason, and the father desired to do so, he should be given first consideration as the long-term carer. It was not just a balancing exercise between the father and an unknown adoptive family. The issue was whether the father, despite the criticisms made of him, was fit to care for the child. Only if he was considered unfit should other options be looked at outside the family circle. The court went on to say, specifically, that no distinction should be drawn between those fathers who had not applied for parental responsibility, those who had parental responsibility and those who were married to the mother[3].

These were both cases in which an unmarried father was seeking to assert his claims against individuals other than the mother and this may have been the crucial factor in the decisions. Even so, they are difficult to reconcile with the

---

1   [1990] 2 FLR 64.

2   [1992] 1 FLR 77.

3   See also *Re D (Care: Natural Parent Presumption)* [1999] 1 FLR 134 in similar vein. There, the relevant child was the subject of an application for a care order by the local authority, and the contest was between his father and the maternal grandmother as to who should look after him. The case is discussed in Chapter 2 above.

traditional approach of integrating any parental or other adult claims into the general examination of the child's welfare and giving it no further weight than as an element in determining the child's best interests[1] although, as we have seen in Chapter 2, this process itself may need some fine tuning to comply with human rights requirements relating to adults. The position will almost certainly be very different where the contest is between the father and mother. *Re SM (A Minor) (Natural Father: Access)*[2] provides a striking contrast to the above decisions. It reveals that the father may face a considerable hurdle in securing even contact where the mother is opposed to this. Here again, the relationship between the parents broke down before the child's birth. The father subsequently had regular monthly access for 22 months. At that point the mother remarried her former husband and denied further access to the father. The magistrates awarded the father monthly access but their decision was overturned by Sir Stephen Brown P. What weighed with him was that the decision was largely founded on the 'theoretical general principle of access being maintained between a child and his or her natural parent'. The justices had taken insufficient account of the particular facts and the very strong reasons for denying access here. Insufficient account had been taken of the absence of a bond between the father and the child, and the risk of destabilising the mother's new family unit in which there was a bond between the child, herself and the step-father.

It might seem from this case that any prima facie claim which an unmarried man, as a natural parent, might have against 'outsiders' is not effective vis-à-vis the mother – not even to the extent of a presumption of contact[3]. The unmarried father, certainly in this context, has been required to show that he is responsible and has some practical benefit to offer to the child through contact. He has also to show much more than this if he is to succeed in securing the physical care of the child. There is no question that the courts have been heavily influenced by the history of the father's interest or lack of interest in the child from birth onwards. They have viewed unfavourably an application by a father who never lived with the mother, had no previous involvement with the child's upbringing, and limited or no contact with the child. On the other hand, the father who has cohabited with the mother for some time following the child's birth has been in a much stronger position, especially regarding contact with the child.

---

1   See, particularly, *Re KD (A Minor)* [1988] AC 806, where the House of Lords made it clear that any claims parents may have against third parties are liable to be displaced where the welfare of the child requires it.

2   [1991] 2 FLR 333 at 339. See also *Re F (A Minor) (Access)* [1992] Fam Law 484 which is in similar vein. See also *Re D (A Minor) (Contact: Mother's Hostility)* [1993] 2 FLR 1 in which the Court of Appeal stated that the principles regarding contact between unmarried fathers and children had not changed since the Children Act.

3   This is a principle which certainly seemed to have been affirmed by the House of Lords in an appeal from Scotland. In *S v M (Access Order)* [1997] 1 FLR 980, it was held that there was no *presumption* that the courts should seek to preserve the link between the child and the natural parent unless there were strong reasons to the contrary. The onus was on the parent to show on the balance of probabilities that an order (in this case for contact) was in the child's best interests. On the facts, the order denying contact to the father who had on occasions been violent and aggressive was justified. It has been pointed out that the onus on the unmarried father will be that much more difficult to discharge where he lacks automatic parental rights and responsibilities. See E Sutherland 'Scotland: From Birth to Death' in A Bainham (ed) *The International Survey of Family Law 1996* (Martinus Nijhoff, 1998) at p 383, especially pp 391–393. Whether *S v M* can stand with more recent rulings of the ECtHR is doubtful. See below.

Several reported cases have been concerned with the question of contact between children and unmarried fathers. In *Re C and V (Contact and Parental Responsibility)*[1] the Court of Appeal upheld the judge's decision to refuse contact where the child concerned had severe medical problems which required constant attention by the mother. The mother's ability to provide the necessary care might have been impeded if contact, which she strongly opposed, had been allowed. In contrast, in *Re M (Contact: Supervision)*[2] the Court of Appeal allowed the father's appeal against the judge's refusal to order supervised contact. The father had a background of drug and alcohol abuse and an unstable lifestyle but was gaining some control over his problems. The Court of Appeal reiterated the importance of contact between the child and his natural parent and took the view that the judge had been over-concerned with short-term considerations. The medium and long term pointed inexorably to the benefits of the child having meaningful, effective contact with her father. The importance of establishing contact as soon as possible was also the basis of the decision of Holman J in *A v L (Contact)*[3]. Here, the father had had a short-lived and violent relationship with the mother and now found himself in prison with an earliest release date in 2000. He had, however, applied for contact before his incarceration and was now pursuing indirect contact with the child. The magistrates refused this on the basis that the mother and her family would not co-operate in any arrangements. Allowing the father's appeal, Holman J emphasised the importance of introducing the child to the fact that he had two fathers (the mother's partner acting as social father). It was appropriate, given the young age of the child, to introduce him gently so that he could assimilate the biological facts about his parentage. An order for indirect contact at this early stage would enable the nettle to be grasped. He therefore ordered indirect contact through letters and modest presents, with the mother's solicitors acting as a conduit[4].

The approach of the English courts must now be re-evaluated in the light of human rights requirements and two decisions of the ECtHR bearing on the issue of contact between children and unmarried fathers.

In *Sahin and Others v Germany*[5] the ECtHR found by majority that German law, as it then stood, violated Articles 6, 8 and 14 of the ECHR in differentiating between married and unmarried fathers in relation to contact with their children. German law then[6] provided that the father of a child born within a marriage who did not have custody and care of the child had a right to personal access to the child. In contrast, where the child was born to unmarried parents, the father could only have contact with the child if the person with custody (usually the mother) permitted it or if the court ordered it. This amounted to discrimination contrary to Article 14 taken in conjunction with Article 8, since the aim of German law, the

---

1 [1998] 1 FLR 392.

2 [1998] 1 FLR 727.

3 [1998] 1 FLR 361.

4 See also *Re M (Contact: Family Assistance: McKenzie Friend)* [1999] 1 FLR 75 where the mother had a genuine fear of the father. Indirect contact was again ordered together with a family assistance order subject, in the case of the latter, to the mother's consent.

5 *Sahin v Germany; Sommerfeld v Germany; Hoffmann v Germany* [2002] 1 FLR 119.

6 German law had in fact been reformed before the ECtHR ruling by the Law on the Family Matters Act 1997. For commentary on the German reforms, see R Frank 'Germany : Parentage Law Reformed' in A Bainham (ed) *The International Survey of Family Law 1995* (Martinus Nijhoff, 1997) p 167.

protection of the interests of children and parents, could have been achieved without making this distinction. The Court also found a violation of Article 6 in that German law excluded the general right of further appeal against a first appeal decision in the case of natural fathers. This was a limitation on the right of access to a court which was not compatible with a father's right to a fair and public hearing under Article 6[1]. Subsequently the German government requested that the cases be referred to the Grand Chamber of the Court. The Grand Chamber[2] found violations of Article 8 in conjunction with Article 14 but did not find it necessary to consider separately the father's complaint under Article 6, either alone or in conjunction with Article 14. The Grand Chamber took the view that it would be going too far to say that domestic courts should always hear evidence from a child in court on the issue of access or that they were required to involve a psychological expert in every case. But the Grand Chamber reiterated that very weighty reasons had to be advanced for treating fathers of children born outside marriage differently from fathers of children born within marriage and that no such reasons had been discerned in these cases.

In *Elsholtz v Germany*[3] the unmarried father had cohabited with the mother. He acknowledged paternity, undertook to pay and did pay maintenance. He had frequent contact with the child for a few years following his separation from the mother. Then contact was terminated and a German court refused to order contact on the basis that *both* the mother and the child were opposed to it. The court failed to obtain an expert psychological opinion despite the recommendation of the Youth Office that it should do so. The father's appeal was then dismissed without a hearing. The ECtHR found violations of Article 8 and Article 6. The denial of continuing contact was held to be an unjustifiable interference with the father's right to respect for family life and there had been an insufficient involvement of the father in the decision-making process. Article 6 was violated in that the questions of fact and law could not be adequately resolved on written material alone and therefore the requirements of a fair and public hearing had not been met.

These two decisions taken together certainly support the view that, at least in the matter of contact (as opposed to the acquisition of parental rights or responsibility), there is a prima facie right of contact as an aspect of family life, and the courts need to take care not to discriminate between married and unmarried parents in their approach to disputes concerning contact.

---

1   It appears, however, that the general practice of hearing children cases *in private* is compatible with Article 6 requirements. See *B v United Kingdom* [2001] 2 FLR 261 in which two English fathers failed to establish a violation of Article 6 where they had been denied a public hearing of their cases.
2   [2003] 2 FLR 671.
3   [2000] 2 FLR 486.

PUBLIC POLICY, UNMARRIED PARENTHOOD AND HUMAN RIGHTS: SOME ISSUES FOR THE FUTURE

Despite the reform of the illegitimacy laws and the removal of most forms of discrimination against children born out of wedlock, the question of the relationship of such children with their fathers remains a controversial one for policy-makers. At its most basic, the central issue has been identified as how far mothers should be able to control the extent to which fathers may become legally involved in the lives of their children. In a seminal article considering the position of fathers (married and unmarried) in the legislation of Western European States, Marie-Thérèse Meulders-Klein observes that recent scientific and cultural developments have had the effect of reversing the historical dominance of men in relation to children[1]. It is now *women* who substantially control the conception, birth and upbringing of children. In England, as we have seen, it is still impossible for the unmarried man to make a voluntary acknowledgement of paternity without either the mother's co-operation or a relevant court order[2]. Acquisition of full parental responsibility where the father is not registered is, likewise, dependent on the father persuading either the mother or the court that he is deserving of this level of involvement. Automatic legal effects of paternity per se are limited to such matters as financial obligations and succession rights. Yet there is an ongoing debate about whether the father's moral and legal obligations ought to be only financial or whether they should be the more wide-ranging obligations which the law imposes on all married fathers. The conceptual shift from parental 'rights' to parental 'responsibility' has led some to question why it is that every biological father is not encouraged or required to accept more responsibility[3].

Of course it might be objected that English law is now compatible with the ECHR and that the reform brought about by the Adoption and Children Act 2002 will result in the substantial equalisation with married fathers of the position of the most significant and largest category of unmarried fathers, those who have acknowledged their responsibility for the child from the outset by joining in registration of the child's birth, the majority of whom are living in a continuing

---

1 M-T Meulders-Klein 'The Position of the Father in European Legislation' (1990) 4 IJLF 131.

2 This is not the case, for example, in France where the French Civil Code imposes no checks on voluntary acknowledgement of paternity. See Meulders-Klein (above) at pp 140–141. For a particularly stimulating review of the procedures for establishing paternity in France, Belgium, Luxembourg and The Netherlands, see P Senaeve 'Reform of Affiliation Law in France and the Benelux Countries' in J Eekelaar and P Sarcevic (eds) *Parenthood in Modern Society* (Martinus Nijhoff, 1993) at ch 6. Acknowledgement or recognition of children as their own by men is a feature of many civil law jurisdictions, for example in Latin America. For an account of establishing paternity in Chile, see I P de Carvallo 'Identifying Parentage and the Methods of Proof in the New Chilean Law' in A Bainham (ed) *The International Survey of Family Law (2001 Edition)* (Family Law, 2001) p 83.

3 For the nature and effects of parental responsibility see Chapter 2 above.

relationship with the mother.[1] It is submitted that there are two major difficulties with this view.

The first difficulty is that, as the Scottish Law Commission pointed out in 1992,[2] it is impossible to remove entirely the discriminatory status of illegitimacy and its concomitant legitimacy unless all distinctions between married and unmarried fathers vis-à-vis their children are removed. The question which needs to be asked is whether the continuation *at all* of the legal status of illegitimacy can be reconciled with a commitment to children's rights. The second difficulty is also concerned with the theme of rights. It is that the granting of automatic parental responsibility to registered fathers, most of whom are living with the mother, will not address most of the serious human rights issues which have been surfacing in the reported cases. The reason for this is that it is not likely to be the father who has a sound, co-operative relationship with the mother who is before the court. It is much more likely to be the man who is *not* living with the mother and who may *not* have been registered as the father, or even told of the pregnancy or birth in some cases. This sort of case will not be affected by what is, it is argued, only a partial rectification of deficiencies in the law.

There is a further, yet more significant, dilemma. This is that the jurisprudence of the ECtHR and the position taken by the English legislation both appear to be at odds with the requirements of the UNCRC. The key points are that the UNCRC, as we saw in Chapter 2[3], upholds the right of the child, admittedly only as far as possible, to knowledge of *both* parents, viz the mother and the father, *from birth* and the right thereafter to be cared for by them[4]. Further, it is explicit about States using their best endeavours 'to ensure recognition of the principle that both parents have common responsibilities for the upbringing and development of the child'.[5] Even allowing for the fact that these are not absolute, unqualified obligations there is an incongruity between what the UNCRC requires and what the ECtHR has held is required by the ECHR. There is an incongruity too between the UNCRC's requirements and English legislation, even after the recent reform.

The UNCRC has as its starting point the position that, once a child's parents are identified, the child has a right to knowledge of them and a relationship with them if this is possible to achieve. Specifically in the case of the father these requirements would appear to be satisfied automatically once paternity is established. Of course the child's rights cannot come into being in a concrete sense until paternity is established, but even that is not the end of the matter since it is more than plausible to argue that the UNCRC requires States to take positive action to try to establish both maternity and paternity whenever a child is born.

In contrast the ECtHR, as we have seen, has been unwilling thus far to accept that the determination of paternity per se gives rise to 'family life' between the child and the father. It is difficult to see how this can be reconciled with Article 7 of

---

1   There are those who have objected even to this reform. Wallbank, for example, believes that it will do nothing to promote and enhance the relationship between children and fathers but will represent a considerable incursion into the control that women, as primary carers, have in relation to their children. See J Wallbank 'Clause 106 of the Adoption and Children Bill: Legislation for the "good" father?' (2002) 22 *Legal Studies* 276.

2   Scot Law Com Report No 135 *Report on Family Law* (1992) (above).

3   At pp 72–73 above.

4   Article 7(1).

5   Article 18(1).

the UNCRC and this then raises a further question about how to resolve a possible conflict between the two Conventions[1]. In similar vein, English legislation has never conferred parental responsibility, and hence the full legal status of parent, on proof of paternity alone. This remains the case despite the amendments brought about by the Adoption and Children Act 2002.

The fundamental issue is the extent to which the father's involvement, if any, with the child should continue in effect to be controlled by the mother. The question of the mother's attitude is now especially significant in the light of the new provision on registration. The traditional view of English law has been that, except where she is in receipt of social security benefits and the State thus has a financial interest, it is largely a matter for her whether or not she wishes to identify the father and, thereafter, her attitude to his continuing involvement with the child is likely to have a significant bearing on the outcome of any application he might make for contact or parental responsibility. The central question which this poses is whether it is compatible with the notion of Convention rights for fathers and children, vis-à-vis each other, for access to those rights to be contingent on the view of another person, that is the mother.

There is recent evidence, in the context of adoption, that the English courts are now moving in the direction of holding that this general philosophy is no longer compatible with human rights requirements. In a series of reported cases a number of unmarried mothers were seeking to place their children confidentially (that is without the fathers' knowledge) for adoption, as they have been able to do since adoption was first introduced in England in the 1920s[2]. This traditional right has now been severely called into question by these decisions, which hold that the normal presumption should be that the father must be identified and consulted in the adoption process[3].

A question for the future is how far this new thinking might, or should, be taken. The child's right to knowledge of biological origins is recognised both in the UNCRC and in domestic adoption legislation which allows an adopted person, on attaining majority, access to his or her original birth certificate[4]. Yet the law does not assert this right to knowledge of origins as strongly as it might *while the child is still a child.* Under the ECHR the State's obligations in relation to family relationships are not merely *negative* obligations, not to interfere unjustifiably in their development, but *positive* obligations to foster them. We can therefore expect to see in the coming years further evolution in the extent of these positive obligations given that the ECHR is a 'living instrument'. We have suggested above[5] that the notion of children's Convention rights should be developed in accordance with the standards articulated in the UNCRC. This might suggest that the obligations of the State should extend to a responsibility, as in some of the Nordic countries, to attempt to ascertain paternity in *all cases* of childbirth. Such an approach would clearly carry the implication that the mother of the child would be under a legal duty to co-operate in disclosing the identity of the man believed by her to be the father and not just, as is presently the case, to enable the

---

1 See further Chapter 17 below.
2 Adoption of Children Act 1926.
3 See further Chapter 7 below.
4 Ibid.
5 In Chapter 2.

State to recoup the cost of child support. Social policy, it is submitted, should be concerned not simply with the financial liability of biological fathers but also with the wider aspects of parental responsibility[1].

---

1   For a very different view of the position of fathers in relation to human rights, which denies that
    they should have rights to family life except where they are cohabiting with the mother, see
    R Deech 'The Unmarried Father and Human Rights' (1992) 4 JCHL 3. Cf A Bainham 'When is
    Parent not a Parent? Reflections on the Unmarried Father and his Child in English Law' (1989)
    3 IJLF 208. See further the second edition of this work at pp 170–172.

Chapter 6

THE SOCIAL FAMILY

INTRODUCTION

This chapter considers the legal position of those persons who are not biological parents but who take care of children or are otherwise interested in their upbringing[1]. It is not easy to find a convenient generic term to describe the disparate categories involved but they have been variously described as 'social parents'[2], 'non-parents'[3], 'de facto carers' and 'substitute parents'. None of these labels does justice to the variety of circumstances which can arise. Here, the expression 'social family' is used to embrace any family unit in which a child is looked after wholly or partly by someone who is not his biological or legal parent. It includes, therefore, guardians, step-parents, foster-parents, relatives, and others such as the cohabitants of parents.

This chapter does not discuss adoption, for two reasons. The first is that the effect of the legal process of adoption in England is to create the full legal relationship of parent and child. This is not true of the other arrangements under consideration here, with the limited exception of 'parental orders' in surrogacy cases. The second reason is that adoption is a vast subject in its own right and has been the subject of a fundamental recent reform in the Adoption and Children Act 2002. Thus, the next chapter is devoted entirely to the subject of adoption.

The question of the legal controls on day care, foster-care and the different kinds of residential care are also discussed separately in another chapter, since it is convenient to deal with these when looking at the powers and duties of local authorities' social services departments[4].

References in this chapter are to the Children Act 1989 unless otherwise stated.

Parental responsibility

There are two fundamental features of the law affecting social parents. The first is that they do not have parental responsibility simply by virtue of looking after a child. The second is that they may acquire parental responsibility by court order. Guardians, however, are an exception. When guardianship comes into being this automatically carries with it parental responsibility[5]. The lack of any automatic legal status places the social parent in a precarious position, especially when faced with claims by a natural parent or someone else who *does* have parental responsibility. This vulnerability is well illustrated by *Re N (Minors) (Parental*

---

1   For a useful general guide to the pre-Children Act law, see J Priest *In Place of a Parent* (Jordans, 1986).
2   See, for example, J Dewar *Law and the Family* (2nd edn) (Butterworths, 1992) at ch 11.
3   See, for example, A Bainham 'The Children Act 1989: The Standing of Non-Parents' [1990] Fam Law 362, and C Barton and G Douglas *Law and Parenthood* (Butterworths, 1995) at pp 99 et seq.
4   See Chapter 10 below.
5   Discussed at pp 225 et seq below.

Rights)[1] decided 30 years ago. Here, the widowed step-father and maternal grandmother of orphaned children were in dispute over their upbringing. Without a court order neither of them had any parental right (now parental responsibility) and neither of them was in a stronger legal position than the other. In this case the matter had to be resolved in wardship proceedings.

In the absence of a court order, under the Children Act 1989, the social parent has the limited powers and duties of all de facto carers, namely to 'do what is reasonable in all the circumstances of the case for the purpose of safeguarding or promoting the child's welfare'[2]. While there is some doubt about the scope of this provision, it seems that it does not empower the carer to take 'major', as opposed to 'minor' or day-to-day, decisions and, more importantly, it does not give any legal right to retain the care of a child. These greater responsibilities and rights, as before the Children Act, can only be acquired by court order. The old law was full of technicalities about which proceedings and which types of order were available to persons other than parents. It is the policy under the Children Act to allow much more open access to the courts and greater consistency in the available orders[3]. The broad scheme of the legislation is to draw the various groups of social parents closer together by the elimination of the technical distinctions which the old law made between them and by substantially assimilating their legal position to that of parents where they acquire parental responsibility. One of the aims of the Adoption and Children Act 2002 is to give greater legal security, in a variety of ways, to social parents and it creates a new legal status of special guardianship as one device for this purpose.

It is, nonetheless, still necessary to differentiate between natural parents and social parents on the one hand and between different kinds of social parents on the other. Accordingly, after discussing the general scheme, we explore some particular considerations which apply to different types of social parents.

THE GENERAL SCHEME

The nature and effect of court orders in family proceedings were discussed earlier. Our concern now is with the circumstances in which these orders may be sought by social parents.

The private law

Subject to limited qualifications, *anyone* may, in principle, apply for a s 8 order in *any* kind of family proceedings[4]. A clear and relatively uniform set of rules now governs the standing of social parents to make applications, whatever the specific nature of the proceedings. The Children Act divides applicants into two categories – those who are entitled to apply for orders as of right, and those who require the leave of the court[5].

---

1 [1974] Fam 40.
2 Children Act 1989, s 3(5), and see Chapter 2 above.
3 See Chapter 2 above. But for a critique of the way this policy may operate in practice, see SM Cretney 'Litigation May Seriously Endanger Your Welfare: Locus standi and the family' (1993) 109 LQR 177.
4 The expansive definition of 'family proceedings' was discussed in Chapter 2 above.
5 Section 10.

Applications without leave

Parents, guardians and persons in whose favour a residence order has been made may apply for *any* s 8 order as of right[1]. These are people whose interest in the child is self-evident since they already possess parental responsibility. The legislation then prescribes a further category of persons whose presumed closeness to the child entitles them to apply for residence or contact orders, but not for other orders, without leave[2]. The reasoning for this distinction is not obvious, but it probably reflects the view that prohibited steps and specific issue orders are sufficiently unusual and intrusive that a preliminary filter is appropriate to weed out unmeritorious applications. The reason why these orders might be thought intrusive is that their effect is to interfere with and curtail the normal exercise of parental responsibility by a person who has it.

Those persons who are entitled to apply for residence or contact orders without leave include parties to a marriage in relation to whom the child is a 'child of the family'[3], persons with whom the child has lived for at least three years[4], and persons who have the consent of those with parental responsibility[5]. The first group covers, primarily but not exclusively, step-parents, whose position is discussed below. The other two groups essentially embrace those who would have qualified to apply for an order under the former custodianship procedure[6]. Rules of court may extend the categories of those entitled to apply without leave, of which grandparents were thought, by some, to be prime contenders, given that under the old law some grandparents did have an automatic right to intervene in certain proceedings. This was a rare example of the Children Act tightening, rather than relaxing, the rules on standing[7]. The thinking behind these provisions is that, in all the above cases, the genuineness of the concern for the child would be so palpable that in most cases a requirement of leave would be an empty ritual.

---

1   Section 10(4). For these purposes, 'parent' does not include a former natural parent after the child has been adopted. In *Re C (A Minor) (Adopted Child: Contact)* [1995] 2 FLR 431, it was held that the natural mother of an adopted child had rightly applied for leave (in this case to seek contact and specific issue orders) since the effect of the child's adoption had been to terminate her parental relationship with the child.

2   Section 10(5).

3   Defined in s 105(1) as:
    'in relation to the parties to a marriage ...
    (a) a child of both of those parties;
    (b) any other child, not being a child who is placed with those parties as foster parents by a local authority or voluntary organisation, who has been treated by both of those parties as a child of their family.'
    See further Chapter 4 above.

4   It is provided by s 10(10) that the period of three years need not be continuous but must not have begun more than five years before, or ended more than three months before, the making of the application.

5   This includes the consent of those who have parental responsibility while a residence order is in force, the consent of the local authority where the child is in care and, in other cases, the consent of each person with parental responsibility.

6   Under the Children Act 1975, s 33, but not implemented until 1985. The most comprehensive treatment of the subject is to be found in MDA Freeman *The Law and Practice of Custodianship* (1986).

7   Section 10(7). No such rules have been made at the time of writing.

Applications with leave

Where interested persons are unable to bring themselves within any of the above categories they may, nonetheless, make applications with the leave of the court[1]. The purpose of leave is to provide a 'filter to protect the child and his family against unwarranted interference in their comfort and security'[2]. The statutory scheme is designed to be flexible enough to obviate the need to resort to the wardship jurisdiction. The leave requirement should thus be relatively easily satisfied, except where the motives of the applicant are improper or where there is a sound reason for regarding the application as inappropriate[3]. The Children Act prescribes a checklist of factors for the court considering leave applications[4], including the nature of the proposed application, the applicant's connection with the child, the risk of disruption to the child's life and, where the child is being looked after by a local authority, the authority's plans and the feelings of the child's parents.

The Court of Appeal has held that the initial application for leave is not governed by the welfare principle[5]. In *Re A and W (Minors) (Residence Order: Leave to Apply)*[6], the mother had had a colourful personal life in which she had accumulated three husbands (two she divorced and one committed suicide), a cohabitant and six children. The application for leave to apply for a residence order was by the foster-mother of the four younger children. The judge granted her leave on the basis that the children's welfare was paramount. The local authority (supported by the mother) appealed. Allowing the appeal, the Court of

---

1   Section 10(2)(b). The procedure governing applications for leave is set out in r 4.3 of the
     Family Proceedings Rules 1991, SI 1991/1247, and r 3 of the Family Proceedings Courts
     (Children Act 1989) Rules 1991, SI 1991/1395. See, generally, E Hamilton *Applications for Leave
     and Joinder in Children Act Cases* [1993] Fam Law 263. In an urgent case, an application for leave
     may be made ex parte. In *Re O (Minors) (Leave to Seek Residence Order)* [1994] 1 FLR 172, an ex
     parte application for leave to apply for a residence order was granted to a paternal cousin who
     had been looking after two boys while the mother was in hospital. The mother was demanding
     their immediate return and was proposing to return to her alcoholic husband. Leave was
     granted together with an interim residence order, although the length of the latter was reduced
     on appeal.
2   Law Com Report No 172 *Guardianship and Custody* (1988) at para 4.41.
3   But it should be noted that this is, in some ways, more restrictive than the more traditional
     wardship proceedings in which there was never a leave requirement as such. The wardship
     could, of course, have been discontinued at the court's discretion. See also SM Cretney
     'Litigation May Seriously Endanger Your Welfare: Locus standi and the family' (1993) 109 LQR
     177.
4   Section 10(9). In *G v Kirklees Metropolitan Borough Council* [1993] 1 FLR 805, Booth J held that
     these guidelines are equally applicable where the applicant is seeking to be joined as a party to
     existing proceedings with a view to seeking a s 8 order. There is some common ground between
     this checklist and the checklist in s 1(3) but a notable distinction is that there is no mention of
     the wishes and feelings of the child among the leave criteria. However, in *Re A (A Minor)
     (Residence Order: Leave to Apply)* [1993] 1 FLR 425, Hollings J held that the factors in the
     checklist were not exhaustive and did not exclude consideration of the ascertainable wishes and
     feelings of the child concerned. In *Re M (Care: Contact: Grandmother's Application for Leave)*
     [1995] 2 FLR 86, the Court of Appeal held that, although the criteria in s 10(9) did not govern
     applications for contact to children in care, the court, in exercising its discretion in that
     context, should have in mind the factors in the checklist.
5   There has been some judicial inconsistency on this question where the application for leave is
     by a *child*. We consider this matter in Chapter 13.
6   [1992] Fam 182. For commentaries, see J Masson 'Leave, Local Authorities and Welfare' [1992]
     Fam Law 443, and R White 'Liverpool Revisited? *Re A and W (Minors)*' (1992) 4 JCL 190.

Appeal held that the leave application was governed by the particular statutory checklist in s 10(9), which included such matters as the local authority's plans for the children, the mother's wishes and feelings, any risk of disruption to the children's life, etc. The upbringing of the child was *not*, however, directly in issue. That would arise for determination on the substantive application if leave were granted. On the facts, the children were of an age where they could express a view, it was unlikely in the circumstances that a residence order would be made and leave should therefore be refused.

After considering the criteria in s 10(9), the crux of the matter will be whether the applicant has been able to establish an arguable case or whether the prospects of success on the substantive application are so remote that leave should be refused. But it has been said that the court should not approach the question of leave in a restrictive or inflexible manner[1]. In *G v F (Contact and Shared Residence)*[2] a lesbian couple embarked on an enterprise to have a child together by artificial insemination of one of them. The child was born and was jointly parented by both women. When in due course they separated amicably the intention was that the applicant should continue to play a substantial role in upbringing. For a period the applicant had regular staying contact with the child, and she applied for leave to make applications for contact and shared residence. Bracewell J reiterated the principles that the issue of leave was not governed by the welfare principle and that the proper approach was to ask whether there was an arguable case. Further, there was no presumption that, if leave were granted, the substantive application would succeed. It was necessary to consider the length of time and nature of the relationship between the child and the applicant. In this case it was a serious application stemming from a deep affection and concern which the applicant had about the child, and leave should be granted. It was also the case that there was no basis for discrimination because the parties lived in a lesbian relationship.

Since this case was decided the ECtHR has made it plain in *Salguiero de Silva Monta v Portugal*[3] that differential treatment based on sexual orientation in relation to the parenting of children will require very weighty reasons in order to be justified and not fall foul of the ECHR.

The public law

The extent to which social parents are entitled to participate in public family proceedings (ie those relating to care and supervision) is discussed later[4]. It is sufficient to note here that the policy of the legislation is to increase the opportunities for their participation in these proceedings[5]. Moreover, local authorities have wider duties under the Children Act to seek out and take into account the views of 'outsiders' when taking decisions regarding children 'looked after' by them[6]. The Children Act, on the other hand, prohibits applications for

---

1 See *Re M (Care: Contact: Grandmother's Application for Leave)* [1995] 2 FLR 86.
2 [1999] 2 FLR 799.
3 (2001) 31 EHRR 1055.
4 See Chapter 11 below.
5 See A Bainham 'The Children Act 1989: The Standing of Non-Parents' [1990] Fam Law 362, at pp 364–365.
6 Section 22(4) and (5).

s 8 orders, other than residence orders where a child is 'in care'[1] reflecting the general policy that outsiders ought not to be able to interfere with the proper discharge of local authority responsibilities to children in care. Local authority foster-parents are considered to be a special kind of social parent for much the same reason, and their position is examined below.

The nature and effect of orders obtained by social parents: parental responsibility not parenthood

It might be thought that the legal effect of the various s 8 orders is the same for a social parent as it is for a parent, but this would be misleading. The natural parent's legal position is constructed not simply by possessing parental responsibility but also by the status of being the legal parent. Thus, where a parent obtains a residence order, it has no effect beyond regulating where the child is to live. The parent already has parental responsibility and this is neither gained through the residence order nor lost if the order is revoked. The social parent, however, depends on the residence order for parental responsibility[2] and retains this only while the order subsists[3]. Further, the order does not pass on the wider rights attaching to the status of parenthood[4]. While a residence order remains in force, the holder will exercise parental responsibility (alongside the parent or other person already possessing it) and there may also be some important consequential implications of this enhanced status. Thus, a person with parental responsibility is automatically in a stronger position vis-à-vis the local authority[5] and has better standing in family proceedings[6].

Other s 8 orders will not give parental responsibility to the social parent but will merely regulate the exercise of parental responsibility by those having it. Most obviously, many social parents will be seeking contact orders. Prohibited steps and specific issue orders may prove especially useful where the social parent has a residence order but is in disagreement over the child's upbringing with someone else sharing parental responsibility. Alternatively, potential problems may be pre-empted by the court attaching conditions or giving directions when it makes a residence order in favour of a social parent[7]. The statutory regime is flexible enough to enable the court to regulate, in some detail, the complex relationships between parents, children and social parents[8].

---

1 Section 9(1). This restriction does not apply where the child is merely 'looked after' by the authority.
2 Section 12(2).
3 In this respect it should be noted that the court has a general power to vary or discharge s 8 orders since the definition of a s 8 order in s 8(2) of the Children Act includes 'any order varying or discharging such an order'.
4 Section 12(3) provides that the order does not confer the right to consent to or refuse adoption, or to appoint a guardian. Neither does the order, for example, affect succession rights or, more generally, the child's kinship relations in the wider family.
5 He has, for example, the right to object to the child being accommodated by the authority (s 20(7)) and the subsequent right to remove the child (s 20(8)). He must be consulted by the authority (s 22(4)) and may invoke the complaints procedure (s 26(3)). He has a right in due course to apply for discharge of a care order (s 39(1)(a)).
6 He may, for example, apply for s 8 orders without leave.
7 Section 11(7), and see Chapter 2 above.
8 The key point here is that no one may exercise parental responsibility in a way which is incompatible with an order of the court (s 2(8)).

A general underlying issue is how far it is desirable to support 'inclusive' networks of relationships or 'exclusive' substitute arrangements which are designed to centralise the child's existence in the social family and to shut out the natural family. While it is a truism that every case must turn on its own peculiar facts, there is little doubt that *inclusive* arrangements are more in keeping with the philosophy of the legislation, with adoption law[1] and with human rights requirements. Martin Richards has, perhaps, captured the mood of current thinking by criticising the 'very persistent prejudice that children should never have more than two parents and when a new one arrives, an old one has to go'[2]. We should, however, remember to take care to distinguish between an inclusive policy which contemplates relationships between children with more than two significant adults, perhaps by giving *parental responsibility* to more than two persons, and one which visualises more than two *parents* for a child. Being a legal parent is different from the possession of parental responsibility, and the case has not been convincingly made out, it is submitted, for conferring the status of parent on more than two adults.

In deciding whether to make an order (on the substantive application, as opposed to the initial application for leave), the court is bound by the welfare principle and the statutory checklist. It has been observed by Douglas and Lowe[3] that, whilst the court may order the preparation of a welfare report, there is no mandatory involvement of the local authority (as was the case under the former custodianship procedure)[4]. Douglas and Lowe characterise the procedure for obtaining parental responsibility by court order as embracing a degree of State regulation which is lower than that required for adoption but greater than that applying to guardianship which is largely a matter of private ordering. We now turn to the individual considerations which apply to different groups of social parents.

GUARDIANS

The nature of guardianship

The traditional concept of guardianship

Guardianship has a long history[5]. At common law, the father was the 'natural guardian' of his legitimate children. Thus, he exercised all parental rights, to the exclusion of the mother. When the mother was eventually given equal rights and authority by the Guardianship Act 1973, the father still remained, in theory, the sole guardian. Indeed, for quite some time, the father was, on losing custody, said to retain the 'residual rights of the natural guardian'. The concept was invoked by

---

1 See Chapter 7 below.
2 MPM Richards 'Private Worlds and Public Intentions: The Role of the State at Divorce' in A Bainham, DS Pearl and R Pickford (eds) *Frontiers of Family Law* (2nd edn) (John Wiley & Sons, 1995) 13 at p 21.
3 G Douglas and NV Lowe 'Becoming a Parent in English Law' (1992) 108 LQR 414 at 429.
4 In every case, the custodianship applicant was required to notify the local authority which was, in turn, obliged to prepare a full report.
5 The best account of this is probably to be found in Law Com Working Paper No 91 *Guardianship* (1985), especially Part II.

the courts as the basis for the father's right to object to a unilateral change of the child's surname by the mother, following divorce[1]. Alongside this natural or parental guardianship there was another kind of guardianship which arose where someone other than a parent took over legal responsibility for a child on the death of a parent[2]. Neither of these concepts of guardianship is to be confused with the office of *children's guardian* (formerly *guardian ad litem*) which is concerned with the representation of the child in certain kinds of legal proceedings. We consider this role in Chapter 13. Neither should it be confused with the wholly new concept of *special guardianship* introduced by the Adoption and Children Act 2002. Special guardianship is a new legal status introduced with a view to providing greater legal security for long-term carers of children but not amounting to adoption. We discuss this new regime for special guardianship below[3]. This section, therefore, is concerned only with those who act as guardians on the *death* of parents.

Abolition of parental guardianship

The policy of the Children Act, following the work of the Law Commission, was to abolish the notion of parental guardianship and replace it with the primary status of parenthood[4]. Henceforth, parents would just be parents, and guardianship would be confined to non-parents who stepped into the shoes of deceased parents. Yet it was recognised that guardians who do take over in this way, in practice, take on all the responsibilities of parents and are accordingly in an analogous position. Hence, the second aspect of the reforms was to assimilate the legal position of parents and guardians. By conferring parental responsibility on guardians as a matter of status, it was possible to do this and also to remove the anachronistic distinctions which the old law made between guardianship of the person and guardianship of the estate[5].

The legal effects of guardianship

Guardianship differs significantly from all other forms of social parenthood. It is by far the least regulated, the appointment of guardians being largely a private matter not subject to public scrutiny, judicial or otherwise. It is also the most far-reaching in its legal effects since it carries some of the incidents which are normally associated with legal parenthood but which do not arise merely by possessing parental responsibility[6]. Yet the status of guardianship, although closely resembling parenthood, is not identical. For example, guardians are not liable for child support as parents are[7]. More importantly, they may voluntarily disclaim their appointment, whereas the obligations of parenthood are imposed by operation of law and may not be voluntarily relinquished or transferred. The status of guardianship may also be revoked by court order, whereas parenthood survives all court orders except adoption.

---

1   The leading authority was *W v A* [1981] Fam 14, and see Chapter 4 above.
2   Guardianship was largely governed by the Guardianship of Minors Act 1971, and formerly by the Guardianship of Infants Act 1925.
3   See pp 250 et seq.
4   This had the incidental advantage of finally equalising the legal position of the married mother and father.
5   For an explanation of these distinct offices, see Law Com Working Paper No 91 (above) at paras 2.21–2.25.
6   See below.
7   See Chapter 9 below.

The view has been expressed that:

'Given the gamut of safeguards, or controls, ... existing to ensure that a transfer of parental responsibility to a non-parent is consistent with the child's welfare, their absence in the case of guardianship is striking.'[1]

This emphasis on private ordering may be accounted for partly by the principle of testamentary freedom. Just as testators enjoy a wide measure of independence from legal controls in disposing of their material wealth[2] on death, so also should they be able to plan appropriate arrangements for the care of their minor children should death be untimely. It is also, to some extent, consistent with the lack of legal controls on the acquisition of parenthood[3]. The Law Commission did consult on the question whether there ought to be restrictions on private appointments or the disqualification of certain individuals analogous to those applying to become private foster-parents but rejected the idea[4]. Indeed, the Law Commission thought guardianship was such a desirable institution that it wanted to encourage more private appointments by relaxing the formalities governing appointment; and the Children Act gives effect to this policy.

The appointment of guardians

The Children Act preserved the two ways in which guardians might be appointed before it, ie by private appointment or by appointment by the court[5].

Private appointments

Private appointments of guardians may be made by parents with parental responsibility or by guardians and special guardians[6], but not by anyone else, even where they hold parental responsibility. The unmarried father may not appoint a guardian unless he has acquired parental responsibility. One of the effects of conferring parental responsibility automatically on fathers who are registered at the time of the child's birth[7] will therefore be to allow many more, indeed the vast majority of, unmarried fathers to appoint a guardian if they so wish – although in practice the incidence of appointment of guardians is likely to remain insignificant in numerical terms. The extension of the power of private appointment to guardians reflects the general legislative policy of assimilating their position to parenthood. Under the old law, appointments were valid only if made by will or deed, but the Children Act allows a simple appointment by any written document which is dated and signed[8]. The hope is that this will encourage more people, especially younger adults who may have a natural disinclination to contemplate death, to appoint guardians. Having said that, the more formal method of appointment by will is likely to remain the norm. A most common situation is that of joint appointments by parents who are fearful of sudden death together, most obviously in an accident. In many cases, they are likely to discuss together and

---

1   G Douglas and NV Lowe 'Becoming a Parent in English Law' (1992) 108 LQR 414 at 428.
2   But less so since the Inheritance (Provision for Family and Dependants) Act 1975.
3   See Chapter 4 above.
4   Law Com Working Paper No 91 (above) at paras 3.27–3.29.
5   Sections 5 and 6 constitute the new statutory framework for guardianship.
6   Section 5(3) and (4).
7   See Chapter 5 above.
8   Section 5(5).

agree upon a suitable individual or individuals. The Children Act confirms that such appointments may be made jointly by two or more persons[1].

Court appointments

The court may appoint a guardian where there is no parent with parental responsibility, where a deceased parent or special guardian had a residence order in his or her favour at the time of death or where the child's only or surviving special guardian dies[2]. The appointment may be made on the application of the intended guardian or by the court of its own motion, during the course of family proceedings[3].

The first situation could arise where both parents have died, having failed to appoint guardians. The court's intervention might be necessary, for example, to avoid a family wrangle, where more than one relative is asserting the right to look after the children. It could also arise where an unmarried father survives an unmarried mother. The appointment of an unmarried father by either the mother or the court is the only remaining way in which a parent may also become a guardian, and this would also have the effect of conferring parental responsibility on him where he did not otherwise have it.

The second situation most obviously includes the case where a divorced parent with a residence order is survived by the non-residential parent. The implication of this power is that it is not automatically desirable that the latter should be entitled to take over the care of the children which he has not had during the subsistence of the residence order. There must be cases in which a former spouse would be the very last person the deceased parent would have wished to look after the child. Where the court makes an appointment in these circumstances, the guardian will share parental responsibility with the survivor. It may become apparent that the level of actual or potential disagreement between them is such that the court will need to back up the appointment with a s 8 order[4].

The legal effects of guardianship

Guardianship can only take effect on the death of a parent. Its express purpose is to provide a complete replacement for a deceased parent. Where it is thought in the best interests of a child that a living parent be replaced, this can be achieved through adoption by special guardianship, or by a residence order. The Law Commission did float the idea of inter vivos guardianship but it did not attract much support and was not pursued[5]. Subsequently, the interdepartmental *Review of Adoption Law* took up the idea and proposed that it ought to be possible to make the social parent holding parental responsibility under a residence order the guardian of the child. This would enable parental responsibility to be extended to the child's majority, viz up to the child's eighteenth birthday[6]. This could be thought desirable since court orders in relation to children generally cease at 16[7].

---

1 Section 5(10).
2 Section 5(1).
3 Section 5(2).
4 A residence order might, for example, be required to resolve the question of the child's home.
5 Law Com Working Paper No 91 *Guardianship* (1985) at paras 4.4 et seq.
6 Department of Health and Welsh Office *Review of Adoption Law* (HMSO, 1992) at para 6.5, and the White Paper *Adoption: The Future* (1993) (Cm 2288) at para 5.24.
7 Section 9(6).

The Draft Adoption Bill presented in 1996 did not incorporate this proposal as such but did make provision for the extension of residence orders to the child's majority[1]. Now, under amendments to the Children Act 1989 introduced by the Adoption and Children Act 2002, the notion of inter vivos guardianship has been resurrected in the slightly different guise of special guardianship. The reforms are designed to increase, in several ways, the security of long-term carers of children. We discuss the reforms below. For the present, it is sufficient to note the distinction between *guardians*, who act on the death of a parent, and *special guardians*, who act as long-term carers, in most cases during the lifetime of the child's parent or parents.

Before the Children Act 1989, the appointment of a guardian always took effect immediately on the death of the appointing parent. The effect was that the guardian would share parental 'rights', if there was a surviving parent, with that parent. This was a peculiarly English phenomenon. No comparable rule existed in any member country of the Council of Europe. The Law Commission considered that the rule had the potential for creating unnecessary conflict between the guardian and surviving parent, and that a surviving parent should normally be protected from unwelcome interference by an outsider. The Law Commission thought that the general aim of guardianship law should be 'to balance the claims of the surviving parent and the wishes of the deceased in the way which will be best for the child'[2]. To this end, the Children Act established the general rule that a guardian should only take office on the death of the surviving parent[3]. But this rule is displaced where the deceased parent had a residence order at the date of death. Here, the guardianship takes effect immediately[4]. This exception will not apply where *both* parents had residence orders, ie where a joint residence order has been made[5].

The thinking behind these provisions can be called into question. The implication is that while a surviving parent who was living with the deceased in a united household can be trusted to assume the sole care of the children without assistance, the divorced survivor cannot. The primary rule is understandable enough. Few would disagree with the notion that the surviving parent, in what was a united family, should receive help only if this is requested informally and should not have it thrust upon him or her by unwelcome interference from inside or outside the family. The issue is why a non-resident parent should not be similarly protected. The thinking seems to be that the deceased parent should be able, through guardianship, to preserve the 'advantage' of the residence order after his death. It is questionable how far this can be squared with the central principle of continuing parental responsibility of both parents.

---

1   Clause 86.
2   Law Com Report No 172 *Guardianship and Custody* (1988) at para 2.27.
3   Section 5(8).
4   Section 5(7).
5   Section 5(9).

Apart from the residence issue, the non-resident parent is as much a parent as was the deceased resident parent[1]. To make him share parental responsibility with a guardian may seem inappropriate where he has continued, in fact, to be actively connected with the child. It would arguably have been more consistent with the general aims of the legislation to have placed the onus on the guardian to seek immediate appointment where it could be demonstrated that this was in the child's best interests[2]. On the other hand, the view has been expressed that where one person had responsibility for a child under a residence order, it is reasonable that he or she should be able to control the arrangements made for the child immediately following his or her death[3].

Another difficulty is that the rule appears to create uncertainty about who is entitled to take over the physical care of a child. Both the guardian and the surviving parent have parental responsibility and, with it, an equal claim to look after the child. An initial dispute over where the child is to live would, therefore, appear to require a residence order to resolve it. This could have been avoided if the survivor held sole parental responsibility unless and until challenged by the guardian. The rather unsatisfactory outcome is that the onus to commence proceedings will be on 'the person wishing to change the existing arrangements'[4].

Assuming the appointment is operative, what are the essential legal effects of guardianship? The most immediate and significant effect is that the guardian acquires parental responsibility[5]. But, as noted above, the incidents of guardianship extend beyond this. In fact, the guardian occupies a position somewhere between legal parents and social parents who merely have parental responsibility. Like a parent, the guardian (or special guardian) is entitled to object to adoption and to appoint a guardian[6], but unlike a parent (and in common with other social parents with parental responsibility), the guardian is not a liable relative for the purposes of public[7] or private[8] financial responsibility for children. No succession rights arise on the death intestate of either the guardian or the child (although they may, of course, arise expressly by will) and the child cannot derive citizenship from his guardian.

---

1   It should also be recalled that there will be many instances of so-called 'non-resident' parents who survive the parent looking after the child but, because of the no order principle, no residence order will have been made. These 'non-resident' parents will in these cases have *sole* parental responsibility, and the onus will be on the appointed guardian to challenge this position.

2   See A Bainham 'The Children Act 1989: Parenthood and Guardianship' [1990] Fam Law 192 at pp 194–195.

3   R Probert *Cretney's Family Law* (5th edn) (Sweet & Maxwell, 2003) at p 219.

4   Law Com Report No 172 *Guardianship and Custody* (1988) at para 2.28. This rather resembles the law of the jungle since it turns on whether the guardian or the survivor has managed to get to the child first. For other practical difficulties which may arise under the regime, see R Oswald 'The Appointment of Testamentary Guardians and the Children Act 1989' [1992] Fam Law 519.

5   Section 5(6).

6   Adoption and Children Act 2002, s 47, and s 5(4) of the Children Act respectively.

7   Social Security Administration Act 1992, s 78.

8   Section 15 of and Sch 1 to the Children Act.

Revocation, disclaimer and termination of guardianship

An appointed guardian may never take office because the appointment is revoked. He may disclaim his appointment or may be removed by order of the court.

Revocation

An appointment may be revoked in a number of ways[1]. This may be achieved expressly by a written and dated instrument, made by the appointing parent or guardian[2], or impliedly by the destruction of the written document[3], by the later appointment of a guardian unless there was a clear intention to appoint an additional guardian[4], or by subsequent revocation of a will or codicil in which the appointment was made[5]. Following a later amendment, the appointment of a spouse as guardian will be automatically revoked by a subsequent divorce[6].

Disclaimer

The Children Act allowed, for the first time, a guardian to disclaim his appointment in writing within a reasonable time[7]. It is perhaps a surprising feature of the law relating to guardians that the consent of the intended guardian is not required before appointment. There is not even a requirement of notification. Common sense dictates that the appointing parent ought to approach the person concerned and discuss the matter before making the appointment. The right of disclaimer ought to cover the minority of cases in which this sensible approach has not been taken or where, perhaps, a change of circumstances has caused the guardian to change his mind about accepting responsibility.

Termination

Guardianship will automatically terminate on the death of the child[8] or the guardian, or on attainment of majority of the child[9]. It may also be brought to an

---

1 Section 6.

2 Section 6(2). The document must be signed by him, or at his direction, in his presence and in the presence of two witnesses who attest the signature.

3 Section 6(3). It has to be shown that the intention was to revoke the appointment but this may be implied from the destruction.

4 Section 6(1). The intention to appoint an additional guardian might be express or by necessary implication.

5 Section 6(4).

6 Section 6(3A), added by the Law Reform (Succession) Act 1995.

7 Section 6(5). There is provision for the Lord Chancellor to prescribe the manner in which disclaimers are to be recorded. This is analogous to the similar provision for recording parental responsibility agreements. The objective in each case is to resolve any doubt about who has parental responsibility for a child at a given time. At the time of writing, no such regulations had been made.

8 Although it has been argued that a guardian would remain under a duty to bury or cremate the deceased child, unlike a local authority where the child was in care. See *R v Gwynedd County Council ex parte B* [1991] 2 FLR 365, and the evaluation of the decision in *Bromley's Family Law* (9th edn) (Butterworths, 1998) at pp 363–364 and 408.

9 Section 91(7) and (8). Cf parenthood which can, in effect, continue beyond majority for limited purposes such as succession and financial support, where the child is in further education or undergoing training for a trade, profession or vocation.

end by court order[1]. The court may act on the application of anyone with parental
responsibility (including the guardian himself), the child (with the leave of the
court), or of the court's own motion in family proceedings. In all cases, the court
must apply the welfare principle. A termination is likely to be ordered where the
guardian himself wishes to be released (and the allowable time for disclaimer has
elapsed) or where the guardian's continued involvement with the child is
considered undesirable for whatever reason. One example would be where there
is suspicion of abuse. A more likely scenario would be where a guardian and
surviving parent are at loggerheads, although such disputes could also be resolved
in some cases by a lesser order such as a s 8 order, perhaps with directions or
conditions attached. Where the court does remove a guardian, it may need to
consider whether to appoint another guardian, especially where a sole guardian is
involved, since there might otherwise be a hiatus in parental responsibility for the
child.

It has been observed that, apart from the legal framework outlined above, little
is known about the operation of private guardianship appointments in practice,
despite their encouragement in the Children Act[2]. It has been suggested that
research could usefully be carried out into the incidence of such appointments
and disclaimers and to ascertain whether there is any evidence of abuse by
guardians.

STEP-PARENTS

The nature of step-parenthood

Step-parents have not always had a good press. Successive generations of children
have, through fairy-tales, been introduced at an early age to the genre of the
wicked step-parent. The step-mothers of Cinderella, Snow White and Hansel and
Gretel all spring to mind, although, curiously, wicked step-fathers have not
achieved the same degree of prominence. These absurdly unjust stereotypes do,
nonetheless, contain an element of truth – that the step-parent/step-child
relation can often be a difficult one. The step-parent is in a potentially awkward
position from the start[3]. He (or she) is part of a family unit and has a regularised
relationship with the natural parent through marriage, but lacks a regularised
relationship with the children in the family. Thus, while the step-parent
undoubtedly is in most cases in loco parentis and has de facto care of the children,
he lacks in law the parental responsibility which would put him on an equal
footing with his spouse and legitimise his standing to be fully involved in

---

1   Section 6(7).
2   *Bromley's Family Law* (9th edn) (Butterworths, 1998) at p 409. This is arguably the best academic
    treatment of guardianship, and the whole of chapter 12 repays attention. See also G Douglas
    and NV Lowe 'Becoming a Parent in English Law' (1992) 108 LQR 414 at pp 427–430.
3   On how step-families cope with the difficulties of not being a 'normal' family, see J Burgoyne
    and D Clark *Making a Go of it – A Study of Step-Families in Sheffield* (Routledge and Kegan Paul,
    1984), and B Maddox *Step-Parenting* (Unwin Paperbacks, 1980). For more recent discussions of
    the position of step-families see M Smith 'New stepfamilies – a descriptive study of a largely
    unseen group' [2003] CFLQ 185 and R Edwards, V Giles and J Ribbens McCarthy 'Biological
    Parents and Social Families: Legal Discourses and Everyday Understandings of the Position of
    Step-Parents' (1999) 13 IJLPF 111.

upbringing. Mention should perhaps be made at this point of the growing category of cohabitants of natural parents who are sometimes also (inaccurately) referred to as step-parents. While there is a high incidence of 'serial' marriage, equally there are many people who, following divorce, have become disenchanted with the institution of marriage and prefer, thereafter, the more informal relation of cohabitation. These cohabitants of legal parents are in an analogous, but not identical, position to step-parents, since their access to the courts is slightly less assured under the regime of the Children Act.

The step-parent or cohabitant is in no better and no worse position than other de facto carers and has the same powers and obligations[1]. But he is in the unusual position of occupying the same household, potentially permanently, with a person (his spouse) in whom parental responsibility is vested. While the relationship between the adult partners may be viewed as a partnership of equals, the relationship between them and the child is clearly not equal in law. In the event of disagreement, the natural parent (by virtue of parental responsibility) has the sole authority on any issues affecting the children. This is a situation which has all the potential for conflict between the spouses and between the step-parent and the children. Douglas and Lowe have contrasted the strength of the guardian's position with the 'complete lack of legal recognition of step-parenthood'[2]. This weakness of step-parents' legal position led to calls for an upgrading of their status. Recently the courts have shown a greater inclination to recognise the interests of step-parents in the post-divorce context, specifically in relation to applications by the parental spouse to relocate and take the child out of the jurisdiction. In *Re B (Removal from Jurisdiction); Re S (Removal from Jurisdiction)*[3], the Court of Appeal stressed the importance of a reconstituted family to the child's needs and that the necessity for the family to relocate abroad, where the step-parent's employment dictated this, could be the decisive factor on such an application. These cases are discussed further in Chapter 17.

Acquiring a status

The options open to step-parents were, until recently, broadly those which were available to other de facto carers. One option was to apply for a s 8 order. The residence order would give parental responsibility while other orders, especially the contact order, might prove useful if the step-family broke down. Step-parents will usually qualify to apply, as of right, for residence or contact orders, as applications may be made by 'any party to a marriage (whether or not subsisting) in relation to whom the child is a child of the family'[4]. The effect of this provision is to place all step-parents, whether they are married to a widowed, divorced or formerly unmarried spouse, on an equal footing with that spouse, and also to enable an application to be made by the step-parent while his marriage is intact, as well as on its breakdown[5]. The child in question must be a 'child of the family'[6]

---

1   Section 3(5), and see Chapter 2 above.
2   See G Douglas and NV Lowe 'Becoming a Parent in English Law' (1992) 108 LQR 414 at p 430.
3   [2003] 2 FLR 1043.
4   Section 10(5)(a).
5   Under the old law, only those who had married divorced parents could invoke the divorce jurisdiction.
6   Defined in s 105(1) of the Children Act.

which entails 'treatment' of the child by both parties to the marriage as a child of the family[1]. The test is an objective one which should not be difficult to satisfy in most cases of step-parenthood. Alternatively, a step-parent might qualify on the basis of having lived with the child for three years or having the relevant consents[2]. The cohabitant of a parent is in a less favourable position. He will not qualify as a party to a marriage and, if he does not qualify on the other grounds, he will require leave[3]. Whether or not this would be granted might turn on the duration of the cohabitation and the nature of the relationship which the cohabitant has established with the child[4].

An alternative which has, in the past, proved popular with step-parents is to apply to adopt the child. Adoption in this context is, however, controversial because of its traditionally 'exclusive' nature involving termination of the child's legal relationship with one side of his natural family. There has been a policy of discouraging step-parent adoption since the Children Act 1975[5], although the current position is that the court is free to choose between the alternatives of s 8 orders and adoption[6]. These adoption issues are considered in Chapter 7 below, but it should be noted here that the Adoption and Children Act 2002 introduces a much-needed reform in providing that an adoption order may now be made on the *sole* application of a step-parent who is married to the parent of a child[7]. Before this reform, the step-parent and spouse were required to adopt jointly, leading to the bizarre consequence that a natural parent was required to adopt his or her own child.

A number of commentators have argued for greater recognition of the step-parent relationship[8]. In some ways, the debate about step-parents is reminiscent of that regarding unmarried fathers. Generally, the step-father will be part of a reconstituted family following the divorce of a 'resident' mother[9]. The available options for reform were to create an automatic legal status by giving parental responsibility to all step-parents, to allow private arrangements for sharing it, or to continue to require an application to the court.

Judith Masson advocated the first approach. This would involve giving, automatically, to a step-parent or parent's cohabitant, the same status which his

---

1   See *Teeling v Teeling* [1984] FLR 808; *D v D (Child of the Family)* (1981) FLR 93; *W v W (Child of the Family)* [1984] FLR 796; *Carron v Carron* [1984] FLR 805; and *Re A (Child of the Family)* [1998] 1 FLR 347.

2   Discussed above.

3   See fn 4 at p 222 above and accompanying text.

4   See, for example, *G v F (Contact and Shared Residence: Application for Leave)* [1998] 2 FLR 799, which concerned a single-sex cohabitation.

5   The directives to the court in the Children Act 1975 followed the recommendations of the Houghton Committee in the *Report of the Departmental Committee on the Adoption of Children* (1972) (Cmnd 5107).

6   For a critique of the removal of the former statutory directives, see A Bainham 'The Privatisation of the Public Interest in Children' (1990) 53 MLR 206 at pp 214–216.

7   Adoption and Children Act 2002, s 51(2).

8   See, for example, J Masson, D Norbury and SG Chatterton *Mine, Yours or Ours? A Study of Step-Parent Adoption* (HMSO, 1983); J Masson 'Old Families into New: A Status for Step-Parents' in MDA Freeman (ed) *State, Law and Family* (Tavistock, 1984) at ch 14.

9   The expression 'resident mother' is used here in the non-technical sense of the parent with whom the child is living, perhaps with a residence order in her favour but, more likely, under the Children Act, without one.

spouse possesses[1]. Others were less radical. Douglas and Lowe argued that consideration ought to be given to the second alternative, which was adopted for unmarried fathers, of allowing a private agreement by parent and step-parent to share parental responsibility[2]. This was also recommended in the *Review of Adoption Law* and found its way into the Draft Adoption Bill 1996[3].

Adoption and Children Act 2002: an improved status for step-parents

It is this solution which has been adopted by Parliament in the Adoption and Children Act 2002. The 2002 Act amends the Children Act 1989, inserting a new s 4A. This provides as follows:

> '4A (1) Where a child's parent ("parent A") who has parental responsibility for the child is married to a person who is not the child's parent ("the step-parent") –
>
> (a) parent A or, if the other parent of the child also has parental responsibility for the child, both parents may by agreement with the step-parent provide for the step-parent to have parental responsibility for the child; or
>
> (b) the court may, on the application of the step-parent, order that the step-parent shall have parental responsibility for the child.'

The provisions relating to the formalities for parental responsibility agreements and their termination are similar to those which apply to parental responsibility agreements and parental responsibility orders (PROs) in the context of unmarried fathers[4].

The analogy between the step-parent and the unmarried father is therefore a strong one, and we may reasonably expect, in relation to PROs, that the extensive jurisprudence of the courts concerning applications by unmarried fathers will also guide the courts on applications by step-parents[5].

Yet the analogy, though strong, is less than perfect. First, in relation to agreements, it should be noted that in the most common situation of remarriage following divorce, it will be necessary to obtain the consent not only of the spousal parent but also of the non-resident parent. The agreement, unlike the bilateral one involving two unmarried parents, will involve a tripartite sharing of responsibility. It is only likely to be in those post-divorce situations in which there is a high degree of co-operation and understanding between all parties that such an agreement will be made. It is possible therefore to speculate that there may be a greater need for step-parents to apply for PROs than has been the case with unmarried fathers living with the mothers. They have not had to face the opposition of a third party. The second way in which the analogy with unmarried fathers breaks down is in the importance attached to marital status which these new provisions reflect. By definition, marriage is completely irrelevant in the case of applications by unmarried fathers and indeed it is the very lack of marital status which is the *raison d'être* for agreements and PROs. However, in the case of the new step-parent provisions, marriage is centre stage in two respects. First, neither the agreement nor the order may be made in favour of the unmarried cohabitant of a parent, however stable that cohabitation may be. Secondly, the consent of an unmarried father who has not acquired parental responsibility is not required for

---

1   J Masson 'Old Families into New: A Status for Step-Parents' (above) at p 237.
2   G Douglas and NV Lowe 'Becoming a Parent in English Law' (1992) 108 LQR 414 at p 431.
3   See the White Paper, *Adoption: The Future* (1993) (Cm 2288) at para 5.21.
4   Compare s 4(2)–(4) (unmarried fathers), discussed at pp 205–209 above, and s 4A(2)–(4).
5   Ibid.

a parental responsibility agreement. Although, in most cases, the unmarried father will now have parental responsibility by registration, marriage is still significant to the extent that some unmarried fathers will continue not to have it. Whether a private sharing of parental responsibility without the consultation or consent of fathers in this position is consistent with evolving human rights obligations is open to doubt[1].

The other aspect of the reform which should be noted is that it is part of a package of reforms, discussed below, which are designed to act as alternatives to adoption. The aim is to offer security to those with the long-term care of children but without cutting off the legal relationship between the child and the wider birth family. One of the difficulties with step-parent adoption, as noted above, is that it has the effect of terminating the child's legal relationship with the divorced parent and the wider kinship links with that side of the family. The hope must be that the acquisition of parental responsibility will satisfy some step-parents who might otherwise be inclined to apply to adopt the child. Do these reforms reflect a sound policy? A distinction should perhaps be made between the different circumstances of step-parenthood. For, while the spouse of a widowed or formerly unmarried parent would be likely to share parental responsibility *only* with that parent, this is manifestly not the case where the marriage is with a divorced parent. The case for allowing automatic or informal sharing may be stronger where there is no third parental figure on the scene, since this would not entail a tripartite power-sharing arrangement.

There is room for argument about how consistent this sort of arrangement is with the philosophy of the Children Act. On the one hand, this undoubtedly favours an 'inclusive' model of child-rearing which might appear to support the regularisation of the step-parent's position. On the other hand, the principle of continuing parental responsibility might appear to militate against anything which would weaken or detract from the position of the non-resident father who remains, in all respects, a parent. The view expressed in one leading textbook that it is 'unclear why this parent's agreement is thought necessary' and that 'granting parental responsibility to a person does not involve the reduction of the power of others holding it'[2] is questionable. On the contrary, the policy of the Children Act was very clear. The essential philosophy of the Children Act is that parents remain parents and continue to exercise parental responsibility regardless of divorce. It would thus be quite improper to allow a voluntary sharing of parental responsibility by one parent without the other's concurrence or a court order. Moreover, to share decision-making for a child between three rather than two adults is equally clearly a weakening of the position of the parent who is not in the household.

The problem with an enhanced status for step-parents may therefore be that it could be seen as shutting out, or at least diluting, the parental contribution of the non-resident parent, contrary to the spirit of the legislation. There is plenty of evidence that this is precisely what *some* step-families have tried to do by attempting to change the child's surname and/or adopt the child[3]. While a triangular

---

1   For human rights issues affecting unmarried fathers generally, see Chapter 5 above.
2   See SM Cretney, JM Masson and R Bailey-Harris *Principles of Family Law* (7th edn) (Sweet & Maxwell, 2002) at p 562.
3   This is part of the rationale for the former restrictions on step-parent adoptions. See p 234 above.

sharing of parental responsibility may work well where all parties have an interest in the child and wish to enter into a co-operative arrangement, it could be a recipe for conflict where this is not the case. It is also questionable whether the proliferation of parental responsibility which could occur where children are caught up in serial marriages would be in their best interests, or workable at all, on a practical level. There is, therefore, an argument for saying that, contrary to these reforms, any acquisition of parental responsibility by a step-parent should continue to be subject to judicial scrutiny. As Brenda Hale once observed, the step-relation is not the same as the 'normal' family constituted within marriage and 'perhaps we should not pretend that it is'[1].

FOSTER-PARENTS

The nature of foster-parenthood

Broadly speaking, foster-parents are those who look after children on more than a purely temporary basis but who are not related to those children. Yet the expression 'foster-parent' covers a range of different child care arrangements[2]. The principal distinctions are between private and local authority foster-parents and between short-term and long-term fostering arrangements. However, in *R (on the Application of L and Others) v Manchester City Council; R (on the Application of R and Another) v Manchester City Council*[3] Munby J granted judicial review and declared unlawful the local authority's policy of paying short-term foster-carers who were friends and relatives of the child at a much lower rate than that paid to other foster-carers. What all these arrangements have in common is that foster-parenthood does not of itself confer parental responsibility. Thus, unless legal steps are taken to acquire it, foster-parents are in a similar position to other de facto carers. What distinguishes their position is that they are subject to certain legal controls and, in the case of local authority foster-parents, controls which do not apply to other categories of social parents. The controls on the making and conduct of fostering arrangements are considered later under the supervisory functions of local authorities[4]. The concern here is to get a sense of the nature of fostering as one form of social parenthood, and its legal status. The new legal status of special guardianship, which we discuss below, has in mind, inter alia, the need of long-term foster-parents for greater legal security.

There has been a long-standing debate about whether foster-parenthood is best viewed as an exclusive or inclusive arrangement[5]. Exclusive parenting is the

---

1   BM Hoggett *Parents and Children: The Law of Parental Responsibility* (3rd edn) (Sweet & Maxwell, 1987) at p 126. This view does not appear to have been repeated in the fourth edition of the book.

2   For general discussions of fostering, and materials on it, see Hoggett (4th edn) (above) at chs 7 and 9, and B Hale, D Pearl, E Cooke and P Bates *The Family, Law and Society* (5th edn) (Butterworths, 2002) at pp 747–773. For a wide-ranging international and comparative study of the practice of foster-care in both high-income and low-income countries, see S George and N van Oudenhoven *Stakeholders in Foster Care* (IFCO/Garant Publishers, 2002).

3   [2002] 1 FLR 43.

4   See Chapter 10 below.

5   For an excellent discussion of these concepts, see R Holman 'The Place of Fostering in Social Work' (1975) 5 *British Journal of Social Work* 3.

notion that children are better off if they relate to only one set of 'parents' who have their care. Outside involvement with other adults is conceived as undesirable and disruptive of the foster-family. Some foster-parents have evidently held this view and have not welcomed interaction with natural parents. Inclusive fostering, in contrast, recognises the value to foster-children of other family ties and seeks to preserve these through contact arrangements. Some foster-parents have apparently seen their role in this light. There is now no question that the inclusive model is in the ascendant and is the one which accords with the spirit of the Children Act.

Where foster-parents have not acquired parental responsibility through a residence order, they clearly have no authority whatsoever for refusing parental contact or participation in upbringing and are susceptible to an immediate request for the return of the child. Yet, even where they *have* managed to acquire a residence order, parental responsibility must be *shared* with the natural parents, who do not lose it. Foster-parents may, thus, have to accept the idea of greater parental involvement in upbringing, even where they have some security (through a residence order) against removal of the child. It should, of course, be said that the extent to which they will, in practice, have to accommodate parents' views will depend in part on how enthusiastic parents are about being involved, and on the propensity of the courts to regulate the exercise of parental responsibility by the various orders at their disposal[1]. Local authority foster-parents are liable to find themselves in an even more inclusive situation, since they have to concern themselves with the managerial control of the local authority, as well as with the natural parents. Indeed, the greater threat to the security of local authority foster-parents will be from the authority itself if it should decide that the child's future lies elsewhere. Where the child is not in care but is 'looked after' by the local authority under a voluntary arrangement, the local authority will not formally have parental responsibility, but major aspects of its exercise will have been delegated to the authority under an agreement with the parents. Whether the local authority has the child voluntarily or compulsorily, it *must* involve the parents in the child's upbringing. Hence, local authority fostering is bound, at least in theory, to be inclusive in nature. If local authority foster-parents succeed in obtaining a residence order, this has the effect of discharging a care order but not terminating the parental responsibility of the parents[2] which continues to be shared with the foster-parents.

Private foster-parents

The Children Act[3] provides a technical definition of a 'privately fostered child' (and hence of private foster-parents) which is designed to distinguish, by a process of elimination, the private foster-parent from other carers. It is this definition which triggers the provisions of Part IX of the Children Act governing local authority control and support of private fostering[4]. A privately fostered child is

---

1   It should be remembered that, in addition to s 8 orders themselves, courts have a wide power to give directions or attach conditions to their orders (s 11(7)).
2   Sections 91(1) and 2(6) respectively.
3   Section 66, as amended by the Care Standards Act 2000.
4   Also governed in greater detail by the Children (Private Arrangements for Fostering) Regulations 1991, SI 1991/2050.

under 16 years of age[1], is cared for or accommodated in their own home by someone who is *not* a parent, does *not* have parental responsibility, is *not* a 'relative'[2] of his, and is *not* accommodated for a period of less than 28 days where the carer has no intention of accommodating him for a longer period. This last part of the definition excludes temporary carers such as babysitters or day-carers, playgroups and nurseries, friends and others who provide a host of day-to-day child-minding activities[3].

Foster-parents have always been in a precarious legal position. Their principal problem has been, and still is, one of insecurity in the face of demands for the return of the child, from the parents or, in the case of local authority foster-parents, from the authority itself. Their status as foster-parents gives them no right to retain the child where such a request is made, except perhaps for a very short time which is strictly necessary to safeguard the child's welfare[4]. Where the arrangement was always intended to be short-term, perhaps, for example, to provide respite care while a natural parent has a period of illness, the foster-parents may be happy to return the child. The difficulty arises where the arrangement has lasted long enough for an attachment to build up between the child and the foster-parents, and a so-called 'tug of love' situation results. The longer the arrangement has lasted, the more likely it is that foster-parents may be able to demonstrate that it is in the best interests of the child to remain with them. This time factor is reflected in the rules which previously qualified foster-parents to apply under the custodianship procedure and in the current qualifications governing s 8 orders. The basis of these rules is, in part, that it is positively inconsistent with the nature of fostering that applications by foster-parents for parental responsibility should be made in the early years of an arrangement and this applies, a fortiori, to local authority fostering[5].

Private foster-parents qualify to seek a residence or contact order without leave where they have been living with the child for three years or have the consent of those with parental responsibility, usually the natural parents[6]. Otherwise, they must seek leave and this is also required where they wish to apply for one of the other orders. Other alternatives are to apply for adoption[7], to seek an order in wardship proceedings[8] or now to seek to be appointed as special guardians. Whichever proceedings are invoked, the court will have to decide between the alternative claims, and this will always be a difficult and sensitive task. The court will, in particular, be faced with intractable problems about weighing the value of the blood tie to the child against the emotional tie of the foster-parents and the disruption to a settled home[9].

---

1   Where the child is disabled, the age-limit is raised to 18 years (s 66(4)).
2   'Relative' is also defined in the legislation. See p 242 below.
3   Chapter 10 below discusses the controls on day-care arrangements.
4   They would appear to be empowered to do so under s 3(5) of the Children Act as where, for example, they refuse to hand the child over to a drunken parent who has turned up on the doorstep in the dead of night.
5   See below.
6   See Children Act 1989, s 10(5).
7   See Chapter 7 below.
8   Discussed in Chapter 11 below.
9   The classic case was *J v C* [1970] AC 668.

These dilemmas and the uphill struggle faced by some foster-parents are well-illustrated by *Re K (A Minor) (Wardship: Adoption)*[1]. In this case, the natural parents handed over their third child at the age of six weeks to foster-parents, a much older childless couple. The parents' circumstances were far from ideal and there were serious question marks as to their suitability to look after the child. They nonetheless regretted their decision and wanted to resume the care of the baby and to reintroduce her to her two older siblings. The foster-parents sought to prevent this by making the child a ward of court and at first instance succeeded in obtaining care and control with a view to adoption, and an order terminating the mother's access (now contact).

The Court of Appeal allowed the parents' appeal and emphasised that the court was not justified in removing a child permanently from natural parents merely because the child might be better off with the foster-parents. As Butler-Sloss LJ put it: 'The mother must be shown to be entirely unsuitable before another family can be considered, otherwise we are in grave danger of slipping into social engineering'.

While other decisions have been less strident in their support of the blood tie, the case does illustrate the difficulties which will inevitably be faced where private foster-parents, who are essentially conceived as short-term carers, are seeking to make the arrangement permanent against the parents' wishes and in the absence of grounds which would enable the statutory threshold for care proceedings to be crossed[2]. Another important point to emerge from this decision is that the law must not be seen to be allowing private fostering arrangements to slip into compulsion where, if there had been local authority involvement from the outset, it was unlikely that the foster-parents would have succeeded in retaining the child. We now turn to the position of local authority foster-parents.

Local authority foster-parents

Local authority foster-parents occupy a special position in substitute care arrangements and are singled out for peculiar treatment in the legislation[3]. Placement in a foster-family is one of the major options (usually considered the best option) for accommodating a child in the care of a local authority or 'looked after' by it[4] because it provides a family rather than an institutional environment for the child. This 'boarding out' of children is part of the local authority's services to children and families and it is the involvement of social services which makes this a special kind of fostering. Part IX of the Children Act does not apply to these arrangements, which are instead governed by their own set of regulations[5].

It was not thought that local authority foster-parents should have the same access to the courts as other social parents[6]. It was reasoned that to allow them open access might be to interfere unduly with the local authority's ability to make plans for the child and might undermine public confidence in child care services. Before the Children Act, there was a great deal of concern about the way in which

1   [1991] 1 FLR 57.
2   As to which, see Chapter 11.
3   For the official reasoning, see Law Com Report No 172 *Guardianship and Custody* (1988) at para 4.43.
4   Chapter 10 below discusses the options available to authorities.
5   Fostering Services Regulations 2002, SI 2002/57.
6   See Law Com Report No 172 *Guardianship and Custody* (1988) at para 4.43.

children, originally placed in 'voluntary care', could become detained compulsorily under various procedures. It was a major objective of the legislation to
remove the stigma of these public services and encourage a more positive attitude
to local authority assistance. Early applications for s 8 orders by local authority
foster-parents might discourage parents from seeking this assistance. Moreover,
most foster-parents will have no legitimate expectation of acquiring parental
responsibility, especially in the early years of a placement. Many are seen from the
outset as short-term carers and not as long-term foster-parents or prospective
adopters. Thus, even where social services do conclude that a return to the natural
family is no longer in the child's best interests, there is no guarantee that the
existing foster-home will be seen as the best, or even an acceptable, long-term
prospect for the child[1]. Where, however, the local authority is seeking to remove
the child from the foster-parents, and the foster-parents counter with notice of
their intention to apply to adopt the child, the courts are liable to refuse leave to
remove the child before there has been a proper investigation of the merits of the
adoption application[2]. On the other hand, the local authority may succeed in
pre-empting an adoption application by exercising its powers to remove the child
before the foster-parent has made an application to adopt[3]. Because of the special
nature of the role of local authority foster-parents, the Children Act 1989 set up
additional hurdles which they were required to surmount in order to seek leave
for a s 8 order[4]. Until recently they might only apply for leave with the consent of
the local authority if they were relatives of the child or if the child had lived with
them for three years[5]. Most local authority foster-parents, in the early years of an
arrangement, therefore required the consent of the local authority as well as the
leave of the court before an application could even get off the ground, let alone
succeed[6].

---

1 These difficulties are particularly well illustrated by *Re JK (Adoption: Transracial Placement)* [1992]
  2 FLR 340. See also *Re P (Section 91(14) Guidelines) (Residence and Religious Heritage)* [1999] 2 FLR
  573 where the Court of Appeal upheld the judge's decision to make a residence order in favour
  of the local authority foster-parents of a Down's Syndrome child and restricting, by an order
  under s 91(14), further applications for residence by the natural parents. The parents were
  orthodox Jews, and the local authority had attempted without success to find an orthodox
  Jewish family in which to have the child fostered. However, despite important religious and
  cultural issues, the court concluded that the child's welfare was best served by allowing her to
  remain with her non-practising Roman Catholic foster-parents.
2 See *Re C (A Minor) (Adoption)* [1994] 2 FLR 513.
3 In *R (W) v Leicestershire County Council* [2003] 2 FLR 185 Wilson J refused a foster-mother
  permission to apply for judicial review of the local authority's decision to remove twins, whom
  she had fostered for less than six months, under its powers in s 30 of the Adoption Act 1976.
  She had signified her intention to apply to adopt them to the authority. The authority's view
  was that she was not an appropriate adopter, and Wilson J could find no basis for holding that
  this was not a legitimate view.
4 A local authority foster-parent is defined in s 23 of the Children Act 1989. Essentially, he or she
  is someone with whom the child has been boarded by the local authority, which can include a
  relative, but who is not a parent, someone with parental responsibility, or someone who held a
  residence order immediately before a care order was made. The restrictions on applying for
  leave to seek s 8 orders apply to anyone who has been a local authority foster-parent at any time
  within the previous six months.
5 Section 9(3).
6 For a case in which foster-parents succeeded in obtaining leave to seek a residence order with
  the consent of the authority, but in the face of parental opposition, see *C v Salford City Council*
  [1994] 2 FLR 926.

These restrictions on applying for s 8 orders were, however, inconsistent with adoption law in that foster-parents were not prevented from applying for adoption in relation to a child for whom they might have been caring for a very short time. Moreover, the three-year restriction had been known to cause difficulty where a court thought it desirable to grant a residence order to local authority foster-parents who were ineligible to apply for the order because they had cared for the child for less than the requisite three years[1].

The Adoption and Children Act 2002 now amends the Children Act 1989 by reducing the requisite period of care from three years to *one* year. This also harmonises the period for seeking leave with the new adoption law which establishes a probationary period of one year during which the child must have lived with local authority foster-parents before they may give notice of their intention to adopt the child[2]. This reform is part of the package of reforms designed to achieve permanent, secure solutions for children in substitute care where it is apparent that they will not be returning to the natural family. What it means is that it will now be possible for a much earlier decision to be taken where it has already become clear that the best option for the child is to remain in long-term foster care with the existing foster-parents. A residence order will offer security to the foster-parents but will also preserve the link with the natural family which may well be appropriate where, for example, regular contact has been taking place and it is intended that it should continue.

RELATIVES

Definition and problems

The legislation also contains a technical definition of a 'relative'. The expression includes 'a grandparent, brother, sister, uncle or aunt (whether of the full blood or half blood or by affinity) or step-parent'[3]. Relatives are arguably distinguishable from other de facto carers in that the family tie which exists between them and the child makes it reasonably safe to assume that any interest they express in the child will be genuine and not flimsy or fanciful. In some cases, the relative in question may have been looking after the child (temporarily or over a long period), while in others, the relative's concern may be about some aspect of upbringing. Where the child has been looked after for a substantial time, perhaps by a grandparent, the caring relative has a claim for security analogous to that of other long-term carers, such as foster-parents. Yet the existence of a familial connection can also create special problems of its own which surface particularly where a relative wishes to adopt a child. The difficulty here is that to allow an adoption might be to distort existing family relationships. This issue is considered further in Chapter 7 below.

---

1 This was the situation in *Gloucestershire County Council v P* [1999] 2 FLR 61 where the child's guardian ad litem persuaded the court that a residence order in favour of the foster-parents, rather than an order freeing the child for adoption or a residence order in favour of the extended family, would be appropriate. A majority of the Court of Appeal held that there was jurisdiction to make the order of the court's own volition despite the fact that the foster-parents had cared for the child for less than three years; but there was a dissent by Thorpe LJ.
2 Adoption and Children Act 2002, s 42(4).
3 Section 105(1). Cf the much wider definition of 'relative' in Part IV of the Family Law Act 1996 contained in s 63(1) of that Act.

Where a local authority is contemplating an application for a care order, exceptionally difficult questions can arise concerning whether it is, or should be, under a legal obligation to exhaust the resources of the wider, extended family before seeking to place the child in substitute arrangements outside the birth family. Also, wherever a local authority is 'looking after' a child, it is under a statutory obligation to promote contact between that child and the wider family. Indeed the Children Act[1] makes it very plain that the local authority's first duty to children in need is to 'promote the upbringing of such children by their families'. We consider these issues in Part III of the book.

Since adoption by relatives was discouraged, the more traditional course was to resort to wardship, which was often the *only* available procedure[2]. An exception was made specifically for grandparents who were first allowed to intervene to seek access in certain matrimonial proceedings[3] and, later, to participate in care proceedings[4]. Other relatives remained dependent on wardship or, in some circumstances, qualified to apply under the custodianship procedure when this was eventually implemented.

Improved rights of access to the court

It was the policy of the Law Commission[5] to improve the rights of interested persons, including relatives, to access to the courts, and the *Review of Child Care Law* and subsequent White Paper also accepted that they should have greater rights of participation in public procedures relating to care and supervision[6]. It was perhaps questionable whether grandparents ought to have been given preferential treatment. Whilst, undoubtedly, grandparents can often have close emotional ties with their grandchildren, the same may often be true of other relatives such as adult siblings. Moreover, as any parent will testify, grandparents can often have a capacity for interference which may strain relations not simply between grandparent and parent, but also between the parents themselves[7]. Recently, however, the Court of Appeal has stressed that grandparents now enjoy

---

1 Section 17(1)(b). See also s 23(6) and Sch 2, para 10.

2 One of the best examples under the old law was the failed attempt of an uncle, aunt and grandparent to challenge a local authority's plans for a child in care through wardship in *Re W (A Minor) (Wardship: Jurisdiction)* [1985] AC 791. Another example is *Re H (A Minor) (Custody: Interim Care and Control)* [1991] 2 FLR 109 where a maternal grandmother succeeded in gaining interim care and control of a nine-year-old girl as against her divorced natural father, in wardship proceedings. The grandmother and step-father had been appointed testamentary guardians by the deceased mother.

3 Domestic Proceedings and Magistrates' Courts Act 1978.

4 Children and Young Persons (Amendment) Act 1986.

5 Law Com Report No 172 *Guardianship and Custody* (1988), especially at paras 4.40 and 4.41.

6 DHSS, *Review of Child Care Law* (1985) and White Paper *The Law on Child Care and Family Services* (1987) (Cmnd 62). And see *R v Hereford and Worcester County Council ex parte D* [1992] 1 FLR 448 in which Scott Baker J, granting an application for judicial review by the aunt who was also the foster-mother of the child, held that a foster-parent had a legitimate expectation to be consulted by the local authority before the child was removed from her care.

7 As Lord Mackay LC (as he then was) has put it, 'not all interest in a child's life is necessarily benign, even if well-intentioned. Arguably, at least until we have some experience of wider rights of application, the law should provide some protection to children and their parents against unwarranted applications by grandparents, when they occur' (503 HL Official Report, col 1342). And see *Re M (Minors)* [1993] Fam Law 161 in which the Court of Appeal took the view that it was unnecessary and unduly expensive for everyone that grandparents intervene as parties where they had no separate point to make or issue to ventilate.

rights under the ECHR, including the right to a fair hearing under Article 6 and (probably) the right to respect for family life with a grandchild under Article 8. In *Re J (Leave to Issue Application for Residence Order)*[1] Thorpe LJ said that, in the light of the ECHR, the minimum essential protection of a grandparent's rights on an application for leave was that judges should take care not to dismiss the application without a full inquiry. Further, it was important that they should recognise the greater appreciation that had developed of the value of what grandparents had to offer, particularly to children of disabled parents.

Relatives' rights: residence and contact orders

The Children Act did not maintain the preference for grandparents but placed all relatives on an equal footing[2], although most of the reported cases have in fact concerned grandparents. A relative may now apply for a residence or contact order without leave where the child has lived with him for three years or where he has obtained the relevant consents[3]. A few points should be made regarding the latter possibility. First, there is no question of a relative having to obtain the consent of the local authority as is required of local authority foster-parents[4]. Secondly, it is perhaps more likely that relatives (as opposed to outsiders) will have the consent of natural parents to their seeking residence orders, since many situations in which relatives look after children are family arrangements which are made with the full co-operation of the natural parents. A good example is the child of a young unmarried mother being raised by the maternal grandparents while the mother pursues her career or education or generally gets on with her own life. Thirdly, many of these family arrangements will, almost by definition, be inclusive in nature, and this may be one situation in which it is realistic to talk about a genuine sharing of parental responsibility between parents and relatives. Obviously, there will be other situations in which there is a family dispute requiring the court to regulate the exercise of parental responsibility by drawing on the panoply of orders at its disposal.

Where a relative does not automatically qualify to apply under the above rules, an application may be made with leave. Several reported cases have, not surprisingly, concerned grandparents. Here, the problem may be that the input of grandparents may be important to the children following separation or divorce, but family relations between the various adults may be so strained that contact is

---

1 [2003] 1 FLR 114.
2 Step-parents do, however, have slightly better access to the courts in that they may qualify to bring proceedings as parties to a marriage in which the child is a child of the family. 'Child of the family' is defined in s 105(1) of the Children Act.
3 Any person may also apply for variation or discharge of a s 8 order where the order was made on his application or where, in the case of a contact order, he was named in the order (s 10(6)). In *B v B (A Minor) (Residence Order)* [1992] 2 FLR 327, a maternal grandmother succeeded in obtaining a residence order on appeal from the magistrates' decision not to make an order, applying s 1(5). Johnson J held that, although the child was already settled in the care of the grandmother, a residence order would confer parental responsibility on her and would reassure outsiders, such as education authorities, of her authority in relation to the child. Cf *B v B (Interim Contact with Grandparents)* [1993] Fam Law 393 where, unusually, an appeal was allowed against an interim order in favour of grandparents.
4 Section 9(3)(b).

denied[1]. Such was the position in *Re A (Section 8 Order: Grandparent Application)*[2] where the paternal grandmother wanted contact with her young grandson following an acrimonious divorce. She did not, however, have a close or existing relationship with the child, and the mother was fearful of her. In dismissing the grandmother's appeal against refusal of contact, the Court of Appeal rejected her submission that a member of the family should be allowed contact unless there were cogent reasons to the contrary. While there was such a presumption in favour of a parent there was no such presumption, even where a grandparent succeeded in obtaining leave, in favour of other members of the family.

This decision was followed by Hollis J in *Re W (Contact: Application by Grandparent)*[3], a case in which the hostility was between the mother and her own mother. Here, leave had been granted to the grandmother to apply for contact but she failed on the substantive application to obtain the order. It was held that there was no presumption of contact which arose by virtue of crossing the hurdle of leave. Except in the case of the natural parent, anyone applying for contact had to show grounds for it. It was said, however, that it would be nonsense in the long term for a child to be denied contact with his grandmother because of bitterness between her and the mother. Grandparents, it was said, play an important role in children's lives, especially for young children, and their influence could be extremely beneficial if exercised with care and not too frequently. In this case, there was no justification for preventing *indirect* contact between the grandmother and the child through birthday cards and the like[4].

The position of grandparents may perhaps be stronger where they are seeking contact with a child in care rather than contact which is opposed by parents. There is certainly more than a flavour of this in *Re M (Care: Contact: Grandmother's Application for Leave)*[5]. Here, the Court of Appeal, while noting that there is no presumption of reasonable contact in favour of a grandparent where a child is in care[6], said that grandparents should, however, have a special place in any child's affections. Any contact between a child and his natural family should be assumed to be beneficial and the local authority would be required to file evidence to justify

---

1   For an interesting study exploring the contribution of grandparents following divorce see G Douglas and N Ferguson 'Grandparents after Divorce' [2003] Fam Law 653. There is some evidence from this study that *maternal* grandparents tend to be more involved with children both before and after divorce when compared with *paternal* grandparents. See also G Douglas and N Ferguson 'The Role of Grandparents in Divorced Families' (2003) 17 IJLPF 41. The Family Rights Group has also conducted a study of grandparents who are the primary carers of their grandchildren. For a summary of the results, see A Richards 'Second Time Around for Grandparents' [2003] Fam Law 749.

2   [1995] 2 FLR 153.

3   [1997] 1 FLR 793.

4   In another *Re W* case, *Re W (Contact Application: Procedure)* [2000] 1 FLR 263, Wilson J offered the opinion that, although there was no presumption at present in English law that it was in the interests of a child to have contact with a grandparent, this position might have to be reviewed following implementation of the HRA 1998. On the potential of the ECHR and the HRA 1998 for providing strong remedies for members of the extended family to have contact with children, see F Kaganas and C Piper 'Grandparents and Contact: "Rights v Welfare" Revisited' (2001) 15 IJLPF 250.

5   [1995] 2 FLR 86.

6   See Children Act 1989, s 34(1), and Chapter 11 below.

why it was not thought to be consistent with the child's welfare to promote contact with relatives[1].

Applications by other relatives, in particular to be joined as parties to children proceedings, have not fared particularly well – at least in the reported cases[2], and there is a feeling that aunts and uncles and remoter kin would face an even more difficult task than grandparents face where their involvement with the child is opposed by the parents. In *Re N (Residence: Appointment of Solicitor: Placement with Extended Family)*[3], for example, the mother had been killed in a car crash and the youngest of three children had gone to live with an uncle and aunt. Some years later the father, with whom the two older children had been living, sought the return of the child now aged five. The judge made a residence order in favour of the uncle and aunt, but the Court of Appeal remitted the case for rehearing. In its view the judge had failed to give sufficient weight to the father's argument that it was to the benefit of the child to live with a parent and siblings even though it was common ground that the extended family had provided the child with excellent parenting. A similar conclusion was reached by Johnson J in *Re D (Residence: Natural Parent)*[4] where the child concerned had lived with a paternal aunt for three or so months largely because an elder sibling's return to the family home represented a risk to him. The child had settled well in the aunt's care and was doing well at his new school. In these circumstances the family proceedings court made a residence order in the aunt's favour. Johnson J, however, allowed the appeal and remitted the case for rehearing on the basis that there was a strong supposition that the welfare of a child was best served by his continuing to live with his natural parents. The natural parent should be first considered as a potential carer for the child and if there was nothing to displace this supposition a child should remain with the natural parent. Siblings have, however, enjoyed a degree of success in seeking orders to remain in contact with adopted children[5].

These principles relating to the legal relationship between relatives and children must now be set in the context of the ECHR and the HRA 1998. It is entirely possible that some modifications will be required to take account of Convention rights[6], although it may also be necessary to distinguish between Convention rights which members of the extended family may have against the State where a child is in care[7] and those which arise in the *private* sphere where the dispute is between a relative and a *parent.*

Neither the European Commission nor the ECtHR has gone so far as to accept that 'family life', for the purposes of Article 8 of the ECHR arises automatically by virtue of formal kinship links between the child and members of the extended family. A grandparent, uncle or aunt would not therefore, merely by virtue of being a relative, have the right to respect for family life with a child. At the same

---

1 These remarks were made against the background of a statutory obligation under the Children Act, Sch 2, para 15 to promote such contact with relatives.

2 For two unsuccessful applications by aunts, see *G v Kirklees Metropolitan Borough Council* [1993] 1 FLR 805 and *Re A (A Minor) (Residence Order: Leave to Apply)* [1993] 1 FLR 425.

3 [2001] 1 FLR 1028.

4 [1999] 2 FLR 1023.

5 See Chapter 7.

6 See H Swindells, A Neaves, M Kushner and R Skilbeck *Family Law and the Human Rights Act 1998* (Family Law, 1999) at paras 6.50–6.52.

7 See Chapter 11 below.

time there may well be sufficient links between them and the child to give rise to 'family life' between them and thus to trigger Convention rights. In the public law context, the European Commission in *Boyle v United Kingdom*[1] found that an uncle's Convention rights had been violated. He had known the child from birth and had acted as a father figure. There had been an unjustified failure to consult properly with him after the child had been taken into care, bearing in mind the nature of the relationship which he had with the child. In *Z County Council v R*[2], in the context of adoption, Holman J was prepared to accept that 'family life' existed between the child and the extended family by virtue of the blood tie and did not find it necessary to establish that there was an existing social or psychological relationship between them and the child. However, in this case, in which the mother wished to place her child confidentially for adoption, he found that the balance came down in favour of upholding the mother's right to respect for her private life, which was also consistent with the best interests of the child, rather than requiring the relatives to be consulted.

The crucial question under the ECHR, for the engagement of Convention rights will therefore not be the establishment of formal legal ties between relatives and children, but rather an assessment of the quality and nature of the relationship which they have with them.

SOCIAL PARENTS: NEW ALTERNATIVES FOR PERMANENCE

The background

When looking at the legal position of those caring for children on more than a temporary basis there are two conflicting pressures. The first is to find a means of providing security and stability for established relationships and protection from outside interference. The second is to maintain meaningful links, where they exist, with the child's birth family. In many cases there will be ongoing contact of some sort with the child's birth family, and the objective will be to preserve this even where it is recognised that the child will be living permanently away from that family. As we have seen, it is the first responsibility of local authorities where children are living away from home to make every effort to reunite them with their families. Where children cannot live with birth parents authorities must seek a home for them with the extended family or friends before resorting to other substitute carers, provided always that this is consistent with their welfare[3]. For these reasons adoption, which we consider in the next chapter, will often *not* be appropriate since, although it may be seen by some as the most effective way of providing a permanent family for a child, it will have the undesirable consequence of severing the legal ties between the child and the natural family.

Largely because of this, there may be fierce resistance to an adoption proposal from the natural parents or from the welfare professionals involved with the child. It is moreover crucial to grasp that the ECHR will permit only those interferences with Convention rights to respect for the family life between members of the

---

1   (1994) 19 EHRR 179.
2   [2001] 1 FLR 365.
3   See White Paper *Adoption: A New Approach* (Department of Health) (2000) (Cm 5017) at para 5.4.

natural family and the child which are *necessary* and *proportionate* to the legitimate State aim of protecting the child's welfare. Adoption, because it is so final a solution, will in many cases go beyond what is a necessary or proportionate response to the child's situation. If the facts are that a stable and permanent family life can be secured for the child while at the same time preserving valuable contact with the birth family, it may be a violation of Article 8 to press ahead with adoption and to dispense with parental consent to it[1]. This relationship between adoption and the other legal mechanisms for permanence discussed in this chapter should be kept constantly in mind. And, of course, it hardly needs saying that there will be situations in which adoption, despite these human rights limitations, will be the preferred solution and one which is also commensurate with the Convention rights of all concerned.

In its White Paper which preceded the recent radical reform of adoption law, the Government recognised the need to provide a range of options for giving children who are unable to live with their parents a permanent and secure family life[2]. We concentrate below on the changes to the legal options brought about by the Adoption and Children Act 2002, largely achieved by amending the Children Act 1989. Apart from the wholly new concept of 'special guardianship' the reforms merely strengthen the legal provisions which have governed well-established mechanisms. We have already noted two of these reforms which streamline the procedures whereby step-parents and local authority foster-parents respectively may acquire parental responsibility for a child where it is clear that the child is to remain with them on a long-term basis. Those two amendments are specific to particular classes of social parent. In contrast, the new provisions relating to the extension of residence orders to the child's eighteenth birthday and the regime of special guardianship can in principle apply to all those who are acting as social parents.

Before looking at these provisions we should pause to consider the Government's vision of the range of possible options for permanence. This is set out in its White Paper in the following terms:

> 'Looked after children unable to return to their birth parents need new families as quickly as possible. In the short term, a foster family will care for them. In the longer term, the Government must provide a range of options for permanence to deliver high quality outcomes for looked after children. There are many already, including family and friends, residence orders, long-term fostering and adoption. But this list is not complete. There is no status which provides legal permanence, but lacks the complete legal break with birth parents of adoption.'[3]

It is this gap which the new status of special guardian is designed to fill. We need to focus closely on the way in which special guardianship will differ between, on the one hand, the status of someone with a residence order and, on the other hand, adoption. On the spectrum of legal substitute arrangements it sits somewhere between the two.

---

1   See particularly the Court of Appeal's decision in *Re B (Adoption Order)* [2001] 2 FLR 26.
2   *Adoption: A New Approach* (above) at ch 5.
3   Ibid, para 5.2.

The extension of residence orders

As we have seen[1], the effect of a residence order is to confer parental responsibility on the person obtaining it where that person is not a parent. Its effect is also to regulate where the child is to live. Hence, a residence order can provide a measure of legal security for a social carer who will gain through it the right to look after the child and all the decision-making capacities relating to upbringing, except where statute expressly provides otherwise. However, the residence order can be a less than perfect solution for those wishing to provide a permanent home for a child, for several reasons. First, parental responsibility, although acquired under the order, is *shared* with others already holding it – most obviously the parents. Secondly, residence orders are *revocable*[2], in particular on the application of a parent. This is one of the key distinctions between a residence order and an adoption order, which is *irrevocable* other than in wholly exceptional circumstances[3]. It explains why some foster-parents have been inclined to fight tooth and nail for an adoption order rather than a residence order, because of their perception of the threat of disruption to their family life which may be caused by successive applications to court by parents[4]. Restricting further applications without the leave of the court[5] could provide a partial but not completely satisfactory solution to these nagging feelings of insecurity[6]. The new special guardianship regime is designed, inter alia, to tackle these two problems.

A third difficulty with the residence order was that it would usually terminate on the child's sixteenth birthday and might not therefore offer a sufficient sense of permanence[7]. This could leave the long-term carer without parental responsibility, or the local authority to look after the child, in the two years before the child attains majority. The interdepartmental *Review of Adoption Law* expressed concern that residence orders 'are not perceived as being likely to offer a sufficient sense of permanence for a child and his carers'[8]. Accordingly, it proposed that where a court made a residence order in favour of, inter alia, a foster-parent, and it considered that the foster-parent would be responsible for the child's upbringing until he grew up, the court should have a further power to appoint, where appropriate, the foster-parent as the child's inter vivos guardian[9]. The foster-parent obtaining such an order might regard it as giving him 'foster-plus' status but without having to go through the rigmarole of the adoption process[10]. The Draft Adoption Bill did not provide for inter vivos guardianship as such, but would have amended the Children Act to enable the court to direct, with the consent of all those with parental responsibility, that a residence order in favour of a

---

1 See Chapter 4 above.
2 Section 8(2) defines all s 8 orders in such a way as to include orders 'varying or discharging' such orders.
3 See Chapter 7 below.
4 In *Re M (Adoption or Residence Order)* [1998] 1 FLR 570 the foster-parents went so far as to refuse to continue to look after the child unless they were allowed to adopt the child.
5 Under s 91(14). See Chapter 4 above.
6 This was ultimately part of the package of measures produced by the court in *Re M* (above) but had previously been rejected by the foster-parents as an unsatisfactory outcome for them.
7 Section 91(10) and s 9(6).
8 Department of Health and Welsh Office *Review of Adoption Law* (HMSO, 1992) at para 6.4.
9 Ibid at para 6.5.
10 See the White Paper *Adoption: The Future* (1993) (Cm 2288) at paras 5.24–5.25.

non-parent (including for present purposes a foster-parent) should continue in force until the child reaches the age of 18[1]. It would also have been provided that, where such a direction was made, the leave of the court would be required for an application to discharge or vary the order. If enacted, the hope was that this would give greater legal security to long-term foster-parents without severing the legal relationship between the child and the birth family which adoption would entail. This proposal has now resurfaced in two separate reforms – the power to extend residence orders to the child's eighteenth birthday and the introduction of special guardianship. We discuss both of these reforms below.

The Adoption and Children Act 2002 amends the Children Act 1989 to allow extension of the residence order to the child's eighteenth birthday in appropriate circumstances. It is now provided that 'the power of a court to make a residence order in favour of any person who is not the parent or guardian of the child concerned, includes the power to direct, at the request of that person, that the order continue in force until the child reaches the age of eighteen (unless the order is brought to an end earlier); and any power to vary a residence order is exercisable accordingly'[2].

Henceforth therefore it will be possible, in a case in which the formal status of special guardian or adoption are felt not to be appropriate, for the court to provide for prolonged legal security by directing that a residence order should last, or an existing residence order be extended, to when the child attains majority.

Special guardianship

The objective
The central purpose of the introduction of the new regime of special guardian-ship is 'to develop a new legislative option to provide permanence short of the legal separation involved in adoption'[3]. In its White Paper the Government identified a number of situations in which it was thought adoption could be inappropriate to the child's situation. These included the position of older children who might not wish to be legally separated from their birth families[4]; some children being cared for on a permanent basis by members of the wider birth family[5]; some children in minority communities which have religious and cultural difficulties with legal adoption[6]; and asylum-seeking children who, while needing secure, permanent families, have strong attachments to their families

---

1   Clause 86, amending Children Act 1989, s 12.
2   New s 12(5) of the Children Act 1989 as inserted by Adoption and Children Act 2002, s 114(1).
3   White Paper, para 5.9.
4   For a critique of the assessment of birth families as carers themselves in the light of the new special guardianship provisions, see C Talbot and P Kidd 'Special Guardianship Orders – Issues in Respect of Family Assessment' [2004] Fam Law 273.
5   Adoption by relatives has the added disadvantage of the distortion of existing family relationships. See Chapter 7 below.
6   Islamic law in particular does not recognise the concept of adoption and has its own related institution of Kafala recognised by Article 20(3) of the UNCRC.

abroad[1]. The Government's hope for the new option of special guardianship is that it will give clear responsibility for all aspects of upbringing; provide a firm foundation on which to build a lifelong permanent relationship between the carer and the child or young person; be legally secure; preserve the basic legal link between the child and the birth family; and be accompanied by proper access to a full range of support services including, where appropriate, financial support[2].

We now turn to consider the legal framework under which this is to be achieved.

The new law governing special guardianship

The regime of special guardianship is set out in new ss 14A–14G of the Children Act 1989[3]. A 'special guardianship order' may appoint 'one or more persons' to be the child's 'special guardian'[4]. They must be aged 18 or over and must not be a parent of the child[5]. There is no requirement that the applicants be married as used to be, but is no longer, the case with adoption applications.

As with s 8 orders, certain categories of applicant may apply for the order *as of right*, while all other applicants may do so only *with leave* of the court[6]. Those qualified to seek an order as of right are guardians, holders of residence orders, those with whom the child has lived for at least three years, or who have the consent of those with parental responsibility or, where the child is in care, the consent of the local authority[7]. The restrictions on applications by local authority foster-parents which apply to s 8 orders also apply to applications for special guardianship[8]. The order may be made in any 'family proceedings'[9] in which a question arises with respect to the welfare of a child either on application or of the court's own volition[10].

Applicants are required to give at least three months' notice of their intention to apply to the relevant local authority which is looking after the child or in whose area the applicant resides[11]. The authority must then investigate and report to the court on the suitability of the applicant to be special guardian and other relevant matters[12]. It is anticipated that this responsibility will fall on an officer of CAFCASS, and the court is precluded from making a special guardianship order unless it has received such a report[13]. The court is also expressly required, before making the order, to consider whether, if the order were made, a contact order should be made and whether any existing s 8 order should be varied or discharged[14]. This is a clear reflection of the consideration that special guardianship orders will often be expected to be made alongside the preservation of

---

1   White Paper, para 5.8.
2   Ibid, para 5.10.
3   Inserted by the Adoption and Children Act 2002, s 115.
4   Section 14A(1).
5   Section 14A(2).
6   Section 14A(3).
7   Section 14A(5).
8   Section 14A(4) and (5).
9   For the definition of 'family proceedings', see Children Act 1989, s 8(3) and (4), and Chapter 2 above.
10 Section 14A(6).
11 Section 14A(7).
12 Section 14A(8).
13 Section 14A(10) and (11).
14 Section 14B(1)(a).

contact with members of the birth family. This is not to say, of course, that such orders for contact will always be appropriate nor that they will be inappropriate if, instead of special guardianship, an adoption order is made[1]. The court may also give leave for the child to be known by a new surname or for the special guardian to take the child out of the jurisdiction generally or for specified purposes since, without leave, a special guardian will not have authority to do these things without the consent of all those with parental responsibility[2].

The effect of a special guardianship order is set out in s 14C. The special guardian will have parental responsibility for the child and, importantly, will be able to 'exercise parental responsibility to the exclusion of any other person with parental responsibility for the child (apart from another special guardian)'[3]. This right to act exclusively does not affect those rules of law or statutory provisions which require the consent of everyone with parental responsibility such as those above, other issues such as circumcision discussed earlier[4], or a parent's rights in relation to adoption or placement for adoption[5].

Special guardianship orders may in principle be varied or discharged on the application of a special guardian, parent, guardian, holder of a residence order, person with parental responsibility before the order was made, the child himself[6] or the local authority designated in a care order with respect to the child[7]. The court may also vary or discharge the order of its own motion[8]. But it is crucial to note that there are significant restrictions on the circumstances in which an application to vary or discharge may be made and on the circumstances in which the court is permitted to grant the application. These restrictions are a cardinal feature of the new status of special guardian. The first restriction is that, most unusually in family proceedings, there is a general requirement that the leave of the court is necessary for the application. This applies not only to those who are not closely related to the child but also to, inter alia, the parents[9]. Moreover, when the court comes to consider the application for leave, it must *not* grant it (unless the applicant is the child himself) 'unless it is satisfied that there has been a significant change in circumstances since the making of the special guardianship order'[10]. Clearly these restrictions cover some of the ground which has been hitherto covered by the court's jurisdiction to prevent repeat applications by making s 91(14) orders[11]. But the restrictions are more specific and create in effect a presumption against variation, with the onus on the applicant to demonstrate a change of circumstances warranting disruption of what is conceived to be a permanent arrangement.

Sections 14F and 14G are concerned with support services for special guardianship. The details are beyond the scope of this work but the essential features are as follows. Every local authority is required to provide such services

---

1   See Chapter 7 below for discussion of the issues surrounding adoption and contact.
2   Sections 14B(2) and 14C(3).
3   Section 14C(1).
4   See Chapter 4.
5   Section 14C(2).
6   Where the court is satisfied that he has sufficient understanding (s 14D(4)).
7   Section 14D(1).
8   Section 14D(2).
9   Section 14D(3).
10 Section 14D(5).
11 See pp 169 above.

which include counselling, advice and information about special guardianship[1]. The authority may, and in prescribed cases must, carry out an assessment of the needs of individuals, including particularly children themselves and their special guardians, for these support services[2]. Where, as a result of an assessment, the authority concludes that a person has such needs, it must then decide whether to provide any such services to that person[3] and, where it does, it must in prescribed circumstances prepare and keep under review a plan for the provision of such services[4]. The Secretary of State is given power to make provisions in regulations concerning assessments, preparing and reviewing plans which may cover matters prescribed in the legislation[5]. The legislation also requires local authorities to establish a procedure for considering representations, including complaints, made by any person to whom they may provide such services[6].

So what is special about special guardianship?

The obvious question which arises is what precisely is the difference between being appointed special guardian and, on the one hand, holding a residence order (perhaps now extended to the child's majority) and, on the other hand, adopting the child?

So far as residence orders are concerned, the key differences lie in the provisions relating to the exercise of parental responsibility and the circumstances under which orders for variation or revocation can be made. The special guardian will be 'in the driving seat' as far as decisions on the upbringing of a child are concerned and the parent, who it will be recalled retains parental responsibility, will be very definitely in the back seat at best. While this may already be true to an extent in practice with a residence order, it is more explicit in relation to special guardianship. There is perhaps an analogy here with the provision which restricts the exercise of parental responsibility by parents where a child is in care[7]. The objective there is also to prevent interference by the parent with matters relating to the child's upbringing. Yet the special guardianship provision is stronger. It not only gives the special guardian a right to restrict the parent's exercise of parental responsibility; it makes it plain that parental responsibility is to be *exclusively* exercised by the special guardian. The restrictions on variation of the special guardianship order are perhaps even more significant in insulating the special guardian from subsequent challenges by the parent to terminate the arrangement. This will only be allowed under the legislation where there is a clear change of circumstances which makes it reasonable to entertain such a proposal. This contrasts greatly with the residence order regime whereby parents and certain others may apply for variation or discharge of the order *as of right* unless there is a good reason for imposing on them what may be seen as the draconian s 91(14) order. Perhaps, therefore, the real distinction lies in a shift in the requirement that the court be satisfied that a restriction on further applications is justified, to

---

1   Section 14F(1).
2   Section 14F(2) and (3).
3   Section 14F(4).
4   Section 14F(5).
5   Section 14F(6) and (7).
6   Section 14G.
7   Children Act 1989, s 33(3)(b), which allows the local authority to 'determine the extent to which a parent or guardian of the child may meet his parental responsibility for him'.

an onus on the parent, in special guardianship cases, to demonstrate a very good reason for disturbing a largely secure and permanent arrangement.

It seems entirely predictable that these restrictions will in due course be challenged on the basis that they prevent access to the court as required by Article 6 of the ECHR. It remains to be seen whether they will be found sufficiently watertight to survive such a challenge.

What then is the distinction between special guardianship and adoption? The major difference of course is that adoption *terminates* one set of legal family relations and replaces them with another. It is a legal transplant in every sense. Special guardianship in contrast *preserves* such relationships. Succession rights between family members are, for example, unaffected by special guardianship. Despite the restrictions on revocation of special guardianship orders, it is still the case that they are revocable while an adoption order is intended to be irrevocable. At the same time, where an 'open adoption' is contemplated, in which the child will continue to have some limited contact with the birth family, the distinction between special guardianship and adoption may not be huge on the ground. It is, however, fair to say that the assumption of continued contact with the birth family is perhaps stronger in the case of special guardianship than it is in the case of adoption. The new adoption legislation is indeed (controversially) rather silent on that issue[1].

Time will tell whether special guardianship comes to be seen as an important and widely used option for providing a permanent home for a child, or whether instead it suffers the fate of the former 'custodianship' order. This was introduced by the Children Act 1975, took a decade to implement, was little used and rather quickly abolished. Will the perception of foster-carers in particular be that special guardianship is really only a kind of 'second-class adoption'? If so, they may continue to press for what may be seen as the superior adoptive status. However, it is also reasonable to speculate that human rights requirements will have some bearing on the issue. It may well be that in many cases the special guardianship solution will more obviously be a 'proportionate' and 'necessary' one than the more drastic adoption order which has all the potential for obliterating the natural family.

SURROGACY ARRANGEMENTS

The nature of surrogacy

Surrogacy is an arrangement whereby a woman agrees to bear a child for someone else and to hand over that child, on birth, to another person or persons (the 'commissioning parents') with a view to relinquishing parental responsibility in

---

1 Discussed in the context of human rights considerations in Chapter 7 below.

their favour[1]. Contrary to popular belief, the idea of surrogacy is not revolutionary or new but has ancient antecedents. Pinhas Shifman has described how the practice was not unusual in biblical times as a means of compliance with the religious duty to procreate[2]. Such births were, of course, achieved through ordinary sexual intercourse with a concubine or, as Shifman puts it, 'surrogate wife'[3]. Nowadays, while this may still be the method in a small minority of cases, the focus is on assisted reproduction in its various forms[4]. The carrying mother may have been inseminated artificially with the sperm of the commissioning 'father' or she may be genetically unrelated to the child where donated gametes from the commissioning parents or others may be used to create an embryo which is then carried to term by her. Either way, the carrying mother is deemed, in law, to be the mother of the child[5]. The legal determination of paternity in these cases is much more complex, as discussed in Chapter 3.

Surrogacy arrangements, perhaps more than any other kind of familial arrangement, focus our attention on what is meant by being a parent. They might be thought to exemplify the case of the *intentional* parent having claims derived from intending to perform the social role of a parent[6]. Who could be more of an intentional parent than a man and woman who go to the extreme length of commissioning another woman to bear a child for them? Yet, paradoxically, surrogacy will often be inspired by what is thought to be the value of *genetic* parenthood. More often than not, surrogacy will be triggered by a *man's* desire to have his own genetic child where his wife or partner is unable to conceive or bear a child. We shall see that in order to obtain a 'parental order' at least *one* of the commissioning parents must be genetically related to the child. The importance of *marriage* is also underlined by the requirements for this order – perhaps hinting that it is the family unit centred on marriage which really ought to be crucial to the acquisition of parenthood[7]. So in surrogacy we can perhaps observe the deep

---

1   On surrogacy generally, see: D Morgan 'Making Motherhood Male: Surrogacy and the Moral Economy of Women' (1985) 12 *Journal of Law and Society* 219; D Morgan 'Who to be or not to be: The Surrogacy Story' (1986) 49 MLR 358; L Nielsen 'The Right to a Child versus the Rights of a Child'; and M Field 'Surrogate Motherhood' in J Eekelaar and P Sarcevic (eds) *Parenthood in Modern Society* (Martinus Nijhoff, 1993) at chs 13 and 14 respectively. See also E Jackson *Regulating Reproduction: Law, Technology and Autonomy* (Hart Publishing, 2001) ch 6; RG Lee and D Morgan *Human Fertilisation and Embryology: Regulating the Reproductive Revolution* (Blackstone Press, 2001); M Brazier 'Can You Buy Children?' [1999] CFLQ 345; and M Hibbs 'Surrogacy: Who will be left holding the baby?' [2000] Fam Law 736.
2   P Shifman 'A Perspective on Surrogate Motherhood in Jewish and Israeli Law' in A Bainham, DS Pearl and R Pickford (eds) *Frontiers of Family Law* (2nd edn) (John Wiley & Sons, 1995) at pp 65–66.
3   The classic examples being the transaction between Abraham, his wife Sarah, and Hagar the Egyptian, which resulted in the birth of Ishmael (Genesis 16:1–3) and that between Jacob, his wife Rachel, and Bilhah her maid, which led to the births of Dan and Naphtali (Genesis 30: 1, 3).
4   For a readable and succinct description of the principal available methods of assisted conception, see B Dickens 'Reproductive Technology and the "new family"' in E Sutherland and A McCall Smith (eds) *Family Rights* (Edinburgh University Press, 1990) at p 21. For a more recent description of the various techniques, see E Jackson (above) at ch 5.
5   Human Fertilisation and Embryology Act 1990 (HFEA 1990), s 27, and see Chapter 3 above.
6   On the doctrine of intention as it applies to parenthood, see C Barton and G Douglas *Law and Parenthood* (Butterworths, 1995), especially at pp 50–52, and Chapter 3 above.
7   See further Chapter 3 above.

ambivalence in society, reflected in the law, about the true nature of parenthood. We discuss surrogacy in this chapter simply because it will usually (but not invariably) be the case that one or both commissioning parents will be unrelated to the child genetically. Hence it can be regarded as a situation of social parenthood.

The effectiveness of surrogacy arrangements

The current position in English law could be described as an official policy of discouraging surrogacy arrangements whilst providing some 'back-door' mechanisms for indirectly giving effect to them[1]. The matter was considered in depth by the Warnock Committee[2]. The Committee did not recommend either the recognition or the outright prohibition of surrogacy but did propose a ban on commercial arrangements. This recommendation was implemented by the Surrogacy Arrangements Act 1985[3] which makes it an offence to be involved in prescribed ways with assisting, on a commercial basis, the making of surrogacy arrangements. The commissioning parents and surrogate mother are, however, specifically exempted from liability[4]. Following the Surrogacy Arrangements Act 1985, there was uncertainty, and a good deal of speculation, about the enforceability (as opposed to legality) of surrogacy arrangements. The majority view was that they were not enforceable and this was later confirmed by the Human Fertilisation and Embryology Act 1990[5].

Although a criminal offence may conceivably have been committed, and although an agreement may be unenforceable, there remains the question of the destiny of a child born into such an arrangement. Here, the courts and the legislature have shown some ingenuity in dealing pragmatically with the situation. First, it has been the case since before the Surrogacy Arrangements Act that the courts have exercised jurisdiction to determine, in accordance with the welfare principle, who should have the care of the child[6]. This could lead to a decision in favour of the commissioning parents, thereby achieving indirectly the intended result of the agreement. Secondly, the same result might be brought about by allowing the commissioning parents to adopt the child, perhaps turning a blind eye to violation of the rules prohibiting payment for adoption by retrospectively authorising the payments[7]. Thirdly, and more significantly, the Human Fertilis- ation and Embryology Act 1990 provides a means of avoiding the need to resort to

---

1   A succinct summary of the English law and policy relating to surrogacy arrangements may be gleaned from the judgment of Hale LJ in *Briody v St Helen's and Knowsley Area Health Authority* [2001] 2 FLR 1094 at 1098–1102.
2   *Report of the Committee of Inquiry into Human Fertilisation and Embryology* (1984) (Cmnd 9314).
3   Surrogacy Arrangements Act 1985, s 2(1).
4   Ibid, s 2(2).
5   Ibid, s 1A and HFEA 1990, s 36(1).
6   The first such case came before the courts as early as 1978 but was not reported until 1985. See *A v C* [1985] FLR 445. See also *Re C (A Minor) (Wardship: Surrogacy)* [1985] FLR 846 (the 'Baby Cotton' case).
7   *Re Adoption Application (Payment for Adoption)* [1987] Fam 81 and *Re An Adoption Application* [1992] 1 FLR 341.

adoption or the unbridled discretion of the court. It is provided[1] that, where the commissioning parents are married, a so-called 'parental order' may be made 'providing for a child to be treated in law as the child of the parties to a marriage', provided certain conditions are met. These are that at least one of them must be genetically related to the child, the child must be resident with them, there must be no payment involved (although the court can authorise this and the surrogate's reasonable expenses are allowable)[2], and the surrogate mother and the legal father must have agreed unconditionally to the order. In *Re C; Application by Mr and Mrs X under s 30 of the Human Fertilisation and Embryology Act 1990*[3] Wall J authorised retrospectively a payment of £12,000 to the surrogate mother despite agreeing with the justices that this exceeded the £10,000 commonly allowed for expenses in surrogacy arrangements. The agreement had included an element for loss of earnings but it had transpired that the surrogate mother was in fact on income support. The court balanced all the circumstances including the welfare of the child, the fact that the commissioning couple had acted honestly throughout the transaction and that the excess involved was not disproportionately large. The crucial factor was that it was manifestly in the interests of the child that the child be treated in law as the child of the commissioning couple and that they should have parental responsibility. Wall J emphasised the need for both couples and surrogate mothers to be made aware of the need for transparency in the definition and true extent of expenses reasonably incurred.

The case is one of a number which demonstrate the need for clear regulation of surrogacy arrangements as recommended by the Brazier Report, discussed below. The power to make this 'parental order' does not arise where the child was conceived as a result of intercourse between the surrogate and the commissioning father, or where the commissioning couple are unmarried. In these instances, if the parties are in dispute (most obviously where the surrogate mother is refusing to hand over the child), they will have to rely on the inherent jurisdiction or the court's more general discretion to make s 8 orders.

Re MW (Adoption: Surrogacy)[4] is an illustration of the use of adoption where a surrogacy arrangement has gone wrong and the parties are at loggerheads. Here, the initial agreement between the commissioning parents and the surrogate mother was that the former would apply to adopt the child following the birth. The handover took place and for a time there was continued contact between the baby and the surrogate mother. Relations then deteriorated, contact ceased and the mother began a media campaign to draw attention to her situation. She withheld her consent to the adoption and, alternatively, sought post-adoption contact with the child. The court applied the test of whether the advantages of adoption for the welfare of the child were sufficiently strong to justify overriding

---

1 HFEA 1990, s 30 and see the helpful discussion of this provision in *Bromley's Family Law* (9th edn) (Butterworths, 1998) pp 267–269 and in RG Lee and D Morgan (above) at pp 219–221. See also *Re W (Minors) (Surrogacy)* [1991] 1 FLR 385, the case which inspired the introduction of 'parental orders' under s 30. Here, twins born under a surrogacy arrangement were allowed, in wardship proceedings, to remain under the care of the genetic (commissioning) parents on their undertaking to make an application for a parental order, within 28 days of the implementation of s 30 of the HFEA 1990.
2 HFEA 1990, s 30(7).
3 [2002] 1 FLR 909.
4 [1995] 2 FLR 789.

the views and interests of the objecting mother. It also took into account the fact that the mother had been independently advised and had previously given her consent to adoption. In these circumstances, the court dispensed with her consent and denied her contact with the child during the child's minority.

Where it is possible for the court to make a 'parental order', this avoids recourse to adoption but has substantially the same legal effect in treating the successful applicants as parents for all purposes. It is thus wider in its effect than a parental responsibility order[1].

Some policy considerations

Surrogacy cases continue to attract media attention both when there is a successful outcome and when they go drastically wrong. There have been periodic calls for the review of surrogacy legislation and suggestions for a more regulated system[2]. In 1997 a Review team was set up by Health Ministers and asked to report on certain aspects of surrogacy arrangements. The terms of reference included whether payments, including expenses, should continue to be paid to surrogate mothers, whether surrogacy arrangements should be regulated by a recognised body and whether legislative change was required to either the 1985 or the 1990 Act.

The Review team reported in 1998[3]. It found that the failure to implement all the recommendations of the Warnock Committee had created a policy vacuum in which surrogacy had developed in a haphazard fashion. It examined the conflicting considerations involved in balancing the welfare of children with procreative liberty and concluded that the risks of harm, primarily to children but also to adults involved in surrogacy arrangements, justified a degree of regulation. It expressed concern about payments being made to surrogate mothers which exceeded genuine expenses because of the implications regarding the consent of surrogate mothers, the commodification of children and the social norms of British society that, just as bodily parts could not be sold, nor should it be possible to sell such intimate services.

The central recommendations of the Review were that payments to surrogate mothers should be expressly limited to actual expenses occasioned by the pregnancy and that those expenses should be defined in the legislation; that agencies involved in surrogacy arrangements, such as COTS[4], should continue to operate on a non-profit-making basis but should also have to register with the Department of Health; that such agencies should be required to operate within a code of practice setting out minimum standards for surrogacy arrangements; and that contravention of the reasonable expenses restriction on payments should result in ineligibility for a s 30 order. The Review went on to recommend that these changes should be effected by new surrogacy legislation.

---

1   Parental responsibility confers on the non-parent most, but not all, parental powers and duties (not the right to object to adoption or the right to appoint a guardian) and does not make the holder of parental responsibility the child's 'parent'.
2   See M Hibbs 'Surrogacy Legislation – Time for Change?' [1997] Fam Law 564.
3   The Review was chaired by Professor Margaret Brazier. See M Brazier, A Campbell and S Golombok *Surrogacy: Review for Health Ministers of Current Arrangements for Payments and Regulation* (1998) (Cm 4068).
4   'Childlessness Overcome Through Surrogacy', the organisation which has been involved in several of the reported cases in the UK such as the 'Baby Cotton' case (above).

At the time of writing there is no sign of the Government acting on these recommendations. However, there appears to be a perceptible drift towards the acceptance of the phenomenon of surrogacy and a gathering view that regulation, rather than prohibition, is the way forward. Lee and Morgan[1] have gone so far as to describe this shift as a 'metamorphosis'. In particular they believe that the underlying assumption of the Review was that 'public concern had moved on from Warnock, from regarding surrogacy as being an almost offensive offering on the reproductive menu to being a legislative service after all other courses have been sampled and found wanting'[2].

What follows are a few of the author's own observations on the surrogacy issue. English law is frankly ambivalent about surrogacy. On the one hand it is seeking to discourage the making of agreements, whilst on the other it is providing mechanisms for giving effect to a proportion of them. This ambivalence can be explained as follows.

Whilst the initial agreement is not considered to be in the best interests of the *intended* child, when the *actual* child is born it may be, at that point, that it is in his best interests (perhaps as the lesser of two unsatisfactory alternatives) to be with the commissioning parents rather than the surrogate mother. The solutions adopted at this stage are not very different to other substitute care arrangements which the courts can sanction where the natural or 'normal' family fails. Douglas and Lowe, in drawing attention to the debate about whether assisted reproduction is more akin to 'normal' reproduction or adoption, refer to the view of Warnock, rejecting the adoption analogy[3]. According to Warnock:

> 'It is plausible to talk about the good of the child when the child exists and there are alternative futures before it, between which someone must choose. To choose whether or not a baby should be born in the first place is a different kind of choice altogether. The whole undertaking is *in fact* for the sake of the infertile would-be parents. It is *they* who want the baby.'[4]

Herein lies the initial objection to surrogacy. It sits awkwardly with the law's general commitment to the welfare of children since it is predicated on the prioritisation of adult interests. It is difficult to see how it could be argued that surrogacy is designed *primarily* for the benefit of the intended child. But there are unresolved difficulties with this view. The fact is that many 'normal' births in 'normal' families are also the result of decisions by adults who *want* to have a child. These adults are distinguishable from commissioning parents only because their wants can be satisfied in the context of what society currently accepts as 'normal' while this is not so with surrogacy. The distinction can only be sustained if we think of the child having an interest in or, perhaps, a right to a 'normal' start to life. Yet, given the variety of social parenting arrangements examined in this chapter and elsewhere in this book[5], it may be no easy matter to define what 'normality' is, if indeed it exists at all.

---

1 RG Lee and D Morgan *Human Fertilisation and Embryology: Regulating the Reproductive Revolution* (Blackstone, 2001) ch 8, especially at pp 201–211.
2 Ibid at p 206.
3 G Douglas and NV Lowe 'Becoming a Parent in English Law' (1992) 108 LQR 414 at p 416.
4 M Warnock 'The Good of the Child' (1987) 1 *Bioethics* 141 at p 144.
5 See also Chapter 7 below.

Chapter 7

ADOPTION

INTRODUCTION

Adoption has been the subject of a recent major reform in the Adoption and Children Act 2002[1]. This legislation is the culmination of a long process of review which began in the early 1990s[2]. When the Children Act 1989 reformed most of the private and public law affecting children, adoption was not included and has continued to be governed by its own separate legislation, the Adoption Act 1976[3]. A major interdepartmental *Review of Adoption Law* (hereafter the 'Adoption Review') was published in 1992. This was followed by a White Paper in 1993 and a subsequent consultative document, which incorporated a draft Adoption Bill, was presented in March 1996 by the former Conservative administration. Some aspects of this Bill proved controversial and it failed to be introduced into Parliament in the latter days of the Conservative Government.

It did not look as if adoption reform was one of the new Labour Government's priorities but then, in February 2000, the Prime Minister announced that he would personally lead a thorough review of adoption policy. The Performance

---

1 The Act will have a phased implementation while the various sets of regulations made under it are introduced and training of professionals takes place, but it is expected to be fully in force by September 2005. At the time of writing the various court rules to replace the Adoption Rules 1984 were the subject of consultation. See Department of Constitutional Affairs *Draft Court Rules: Adoption and Children Act 2002 – Domestic Adoption and Placement for Adoption* (2004). On the Act generally see C Bridge and H Swindells QC *Adoption: The Modern Law* (Family Law, 2003) and SM Cretney, JM Masson and R Bailey-Harris *Principles of Family Law* (Supplement to the 7th edition) (2003). For an assessment of the Act's impact on the scheme of the Children Act 1989, see J Masson 'The Impact of the Adoption and Children Act 2002, Part I – Parental Responsibility' [2003] Fam Law 580 and 'Part II – The Provision of Services for Children and Families' [2003] Fam Law 644. For a concise description of some of the Act's more important provisions, see D Cullen 'The Adoption and Children Act 2002' [2003] Fam Law 235 and S Mahmood 'Adoption and Children Act 2002: Where are We so Far?' [2004] Fam Law 449. For some commentaries on the background to the Act, see C Bridge 'Adoption Law: A Balance of Interests' in J Herring (ed) *Family Law: Issues, Debates, Policy* (Willan Publishing, 2001); C Barton 'Adoption: The Prime Minister's Review' [2000] Fam Law 731, 'Adoption Strategy' [2001] Fam Law 89 and 'Adoption and Children Bill – Don't let them out of your sight' [2001] Fam Law 431; and S Harris-Short 'The Adoption and Children Bill – A Fast Track to Failure?' [2001] CFLQ 405. For a critique of the political influences on the reforms and of the central policy to increase the use of adoption for children in long-term substitute care, see J Eekelaar 'Contact and the Adoption Reform' in A Bainham, B Lindley, M Richards and L Trinder *Children and Their Families: Contact, Rights and Welfare* (Hart Publishing, 2003).

2 The principal reports and White Papers were Department of Health and Welsh Office, Report to Ministers of the Interdepartmental Working Group *Review of Adoption Law* (1992); Department of Health and Welsh Office, Home Office, Lord Chancellor's Department *Adoption: The Future* (1993) (Cm 2288); Department of Health and Welsh Office *Adoption: A Service for Children, Draft Bill* (1996); and Department of Health *Adoption Now: Messages from Research* (1999).

3 The law under the Adoption Act 1976 is described in Chapter 7 of the second edition of this work and is referred to here only to the extent that it is necessary for an understanding of the new law.

and Innovation Unit of the Cabinet was commissioned and reported in July 2000[1]. This was quickly followed by a White Paper, *Adoption: A New Approach*, which was published in December of that year[2].

The content of the Adoption and Children Act 2002 is therefore the result of two major influences – the Review of the 1990s and the policy initiatives which have resulted from the Prime Ministerial Review and which were embodied in the White Paper. It is fair to say also that certain key provisions in the Act have been significantly affected by political pressures during the parliamentary passage of the Bill, none more so than the new provisions governing those who are entitled to adopt[3]. The influence of the HRA 1998 and the ECHR must also be taken into account in attempting to understand the legislation, although the Act's compatibility with the Convention is something which may be doubted and which will undoubtedly be tested in the years to come.

Perhaps the salient feature of the reforms which is most attributable to the earlier Adoption Review is the attempt to harmonise the principles of adoption law with those of the Children Act 1989. This was, in a sense, a task left over from the earlier wholesale reform of children law in 1989. Accordingly, we discuss below the new central principles which govern adoption law. While, however, these are derived largely from the Children Act 1989 it should be borne in mind that they are tailored in some cases to the special case of adoption. Neither should it be thought that the transplanting of the Children Act principles into the new adoption law is uncontroversial. The application of the welfare principle to the question of dispensing with consent to adoption is especially problematic and likely to give rise to very real tensions with human rights obligations[4].

The White Paper had a very specific agenda – one which focused especially on one type of adoption, public law adoption, or the adoption of children being looked after by local authorities. The Government saw it as the clear responsibility of the State to provide permanent alternative homes for children who were unable to return to their birth parents and that adoption was the most important vehicle for this[5]. Although the White Paper and the Act do visualise a role for alternative options for permanence, such as long-term fostering and the new status of special guardianship[6], it is adoption which has received the emphasis, with the Government's stated intention of increasing by 40 per cent, by 2004/5, the number of adoptions of looked after children and if possible to achieve a 50 per cent increase[7].

There are two fundamental criticisms which can be made of this approach. The first is that adoption is *only one* of the various mechanisms for providing for children who are looked after on a long-term basis by local authorities, and there is

---

1 Performance and Innovation Unit *Prime Minister's Review: Adoption: Issued for Consultation* (Cabinet Office, July 2000).
2 Department of Health *Adoption: A New Approach: A White Paper* (2000) (Cm 5017).
3 Another influence was undoubtedly the report of the Waterhouse Inquiry into the abuse of children in children's homes in North Wales. See *Lost in Care – Report of the Tribunal of Inquiry into the Abuse of Children in the Former County Council Areas of Gwynedd and Clwyd since 1974* (2000).
4 We have already seen that the application of the welfare principle generally does not sit easily with the new human rights obligations. See Chapter 2 above.
5 At para 1.13 of the White Paper it is stated that 'the government believes that more can and should be done to promote the wider use of adoption for looked after children who cannot return to their birth parents'.
6 See White Paper, ch 5.
7 And invest £66.5 million in the improvement of adoption services over a three-year period.

a lack of clear empirical evidence demonstrating that children who are adopted in such circumstances fare better than those who are not adopted[1]. Other European countries resort to adoption much less frequently in such cases and have a stronger commitment of resources to family support and foster care[2]. Secondly, and more importantly, adoption represents the most drastic of all interferences with family life under Article 8 of the ECHR and, as such, requires a much stronger justification. As we have seen, the emphasis of the Convention in relation to children and families in difficulty is on family support services, temporary accommodation away from home where necessary and strong duties to attempt to reunify the child with the family. Where the child *does* need to be away from home permanently, there remain strong human rights obligations to maintain an ongoing link between the child and the birth family. This suggests, contrary to the emphasis in the White Paper, that those measures which will preserve the legal relationship and contact between the child and the birth family should usually be the *preferred* course of action. Adoption should be seen as a *last resort*, rather than the option of choice, after all other attempts to meet the needs of the child have failed. It is only in those circumstances that it can be said with confidence that adoption will pass the test of being 'necessary' and 'proportionate' as required by the Convention.

Those provisions in the new legislation which are therefore designed to facilitate or speed up adoption need to be examined with a critical eye for compliance with the ECHR. This is an issue which will arise both at the placement stage and when the court has to consider whether to make an adoption order in the face of an objecting parent. Even in those cases in which adoption does ultimately prove to be in the best interests of the child, there are still important questions relating to the child's identity rights which need to be accommodated. This may imply a more 'open' system of adoption than has traditionally been the case in England and ongoing contact of some sort with the birth family.

This chapter attempts to set out the essential features of the new adoption law and to identify the core issues. We begin with a brief consideration of the nature and uses of adoption, contrasting this with other measures of providing for children. This is followed by a discussion of the central principles under the Adoption and Children Act 2002. The most controversial use of adoption has been in the context of international or intercountry adoption. We discuss international adoption together with international child abduction and other issues relating to children in the international community in Chapter 17.

The nature of adoption

Adoption in English law is distinguishable from all other forms of social parenthood. It is with limited legal exceptions the only legal mechanism for terminating the legal status of parent and the parental responsibility which goes with it[3]. Adoption is in effect a 'legal transplant' involving the total replacement of one family with a new substitute family. The adoptive parents step into the shoes

---

1   For a review of the evidence see *Adoption Now: Messages From Research* (above) and Eekelaar (above).

2   See pp 306 et seq below.

3   The other mechanism for achieving this in cases of assisted reproduction is s 30 of the Human Fertilisation and Embryology Act 1990, as to which see Chapter 6 above.

of the birth parents. Unlike the residence order under the Children Act 1989 (now the primary order giving parental responsibility to social parents) adoption is permanent and, with rare exceptions, irrevocable. It is precisely this permanence which has so often been seen by adoption applicants as the major advantage of adoption over other solutions, although its advantages in this respect may be somewhat diluted by the introduction of special guardianship[1].

In *Re B (Adoption: Jurisdiction to Set Aside)*[2] the Court of Appeal held that there was no general inherent power to set aside an adoption order on the basis of a mistake. B was the child of an Arab father and Roman Catholic mother and had been adopted and raised in the Jewish faith by an orthodox Jewish couple. On investigating the background, B discovered the truth and, now an adult, sought to have the adoption order set aside. While expressing sympathy for his position, the court thought that its ultimate imperative must be the inviolability of the adoption system. This case should be contrasted with *Re K (Adoption and Wardship)*[3] which provides a rare example of an adoption order being set aside.

In *Re K*, the English foster-parents had adopted a Muslim Bosnian baby found under a pile of bodies during the conflict in the former Yugoslavia. There had, however, been fatal flaws in the adoption process including failure to appoint a guardian ad litem, failure to contact the baby's appointed guardian in Bosnia, failure to serve notice of the proceedings on the Home Office, and the provision of inadequate evidence of the death of the natural parents. The Court of Appeal held that this was a denial of natural justice to the Bosnian guardian and, through him, to the natural parents. The adoption order was therefore set aside and the case remitted for rehearing. At the rehearing in wardship proceedings, care and control was given to the foster-parents, the child was to remain a ward of court and the foster-parents were required to cause the child to receive appropriate instruction in the Bosnian language and Muslim religion. They were also required to report every three months to the Official Solicitor as to the progress of contact with the natural family back in Bosnia.

The case is an excellent illustration of the problems which can arise from international adoption[4]. It also shows the continuing value of wardship in some cases, especially where ongoing judicial control of a situation is thought desirable, and the inter-relationship of legal procedures affecting children.

Purposes of adoption

Although its general effect may easily be described, the purposes of adoption are far from easy to state. First, it is clear that adoption has served different needs at different times and these have differed markedly from society to society. Thus, for example, Duncan[5] notes that in Roman law and in the Code Napoleon of 1804, the primary purpose of adoption was to ensure the continuation of the family line.

---

1 See Chapter 6 above.
2 [1995] 2 FLR 1. See also *Re PJ (Adoption: Practice on Appeal)* [1998] 2 FLR 252 where, despite finding that a step-parent adoption ought not to have been granted, the Court of Appeal refused to set it aside.
3 [1997] 2 FLR 221.
4 See further Chapter 17 below.
5 W Duncan 'Regulating Intercountry Adoption – an International Perspective' in A Bainham, DS Pearl and R Pickford (eds) *Frontiers of Family Law* (2nd edn) (John Wiley and Sons, 1995) at ch 3.

In the Hindu tradition, adoption was mandated by the need for a child to perform certain spiritual tasks for the parent. When adoption was first introduced in England[1], it served the dual purpose of offering a discreet way out of the stigma and economic hardship faced by unmarried mothers and meeting the needs of childless couples. Historically, it can be said that the emphasis in adoption was on satisfying adult needs of one kind or another. The major shift in thinking which has occurred in modern adoption law is that adoption is now supposed to be a 'child-centred' process, a means of finding a family for a child and not a child for a family. Nonetheless, there remains considerable anxiety, especially in the context of intercountry adoption, that the process can still be used to prioritise adult needs without proper regard for the interests of the children involved and their birth families[2].

The circumstances in which adoption is used also differ widely and there have been major changes in the role and incidence of adoption in the last few decades of the twentieth century. Lowe[3] notes that there was a sharp increase in the use of adoption in England between 1927 and 1968 and then a dramatic decline in the last quarter of the twentieth century. Adoption figures reached a peak of 25,000 per year in 1968 but by 1990 had declined to 10,000 and by 1998 to under 5,000. Lowe[4] goes on to distinguish between three sorts of adoption cases as follows.

(1) *Adoption of babies*, viz children under the age of 12 months. In 1968 there were over 12,000 such adoptions representing 51 per cent of the total. By 1998 there were just 195, or 4 per cent of the total. In other words there had been by the 1990s a virtual disappearance of baby adoption in England. The factors contributing to this dramatic decline include the greater effectiveness and availability of contraception, the increase in abortion, the much greater incidence and acceptability of birth outside marriage and the explosion in unmarried cohabitation and births into that situation. These demographic and social changes also largely account for the high demand in the West for babies from the under-developed world and Eastern Europe.

(2) *Step-parent adoption*. There was a sharp increase in the adoption of children by their step-parents between 1951 and 1968. This reflected in large measure the growth in the number of step-parents following the liberalisation of divorce and the consequential increase in remarriage. In 1968 there were about 4,500 step-parent adoptions. By 1998 this had almost halved to about 2,300. The Houghton Report in 1972 officially discouraged step-parent adoption because of its effect of terminating the legal relationship between the now-divorced parent, usually the father, and the child. The Children Act 1975, later consolidated in the Adoption Act 1976, introduced directives that the courts should give specific consideration to alternative solutions in these cases. Step-parent adoptions still account for a substantial proportion of all adoptions although it remains to be seen whether the new provision for

---

1   By the Adoption of Children Act 1926.
2   See Chapter 17 below.
3   NV Lowe 'English Adoption Law: Past, Present and Future' in S Katz, J Eekelaar and M Maclean (eds) *Cross Currents: Family Law and Policy in the US and England* (Oxford University Press, 2000) at ch 14.
4   Ibid, pp 316–323.

step-parents to acquire parental responsibility by agreement or court order will lead to a decline in the use of adoption by step-parents.

(3) *Public law adoption.* The numbers of public law adoptions have, until now, remained reasonably constant at about 2,000–2,500 per year. However, while in 1968 this represented only 8.7 per cent of the total, public law adoptions now account for one-third of all adoptions, and this proportion is likely to rise significantly higher in the light of the reforms ushered in by the Adoption and Children Act 2002.

In the light of the shifting circumstances which may lead to adoption, it has become increasingly evident that a single model of adoption cannot be appropriate in all cases. In particular, there has been a growing appreciation that the traditional 'exclusivity' and secrecy of the adoption process must give way to a more flexible approach which admits of greater 'openness' and *inclusive* relationships. More recently account has had to be taken of human rights obligations, which again militate towards a more inclusive approach. The central question in the context of human rights will be whether it can be convincingly demonstrated that adoption can offer the child something which cannot be offered by the various alternative legal mechanisms at the court's disposal.

CENTRAL PRINCIPLES OF THE NEW ADOPTION LAW

The central principles of the legislation are set out in s 1 of the Adoption and Children Act 2002 and are reminiscent of those in s 1 of the Children Act 1989[1]. They apply 'whenever a court or adoption agency is coming to a decision relating to the adoption of a child'[2] and as such will apply, for example, at both the placement stage and when the court is considering whether or not to make an adoption order.

The welfare principle

Section 1(2) provides that 'the paramount consideration of the court or adoption agency must be the child's welfare, throughout his life'. This brings adoption law into line with both the Children Act 1989 and the UNCRC, Article 21 of which requires States parties that 'recognise and/or permit the system of adoption to ensure that the best interests of the child shall be the paramount consideration'. This is contrary, however, to a long tradition in English adoption law which acknowledged the child's welfare to be the 'first' but not 'paramount' consideration for courts and adoption agencies[3].

There was some disagreement under the old law about whether these apparently different weightings of the child's welfare in the adoption process made any practical difference. The purpose of the 'first consideration' criterion was, however, reasonably clear. It was that the total severance of the parent–child relationship ought not to occur without a thorough examination of the *parent's*

---

1   As to which see Chapter 2 above.
2   Section 1(1). (References within this chapter are to the Adoption and Children Act 2002 unless otherwise stated.)
3   Section 6 of the Adoption Act 1976.

claims and interests as well as those of the child. The welfare principle, as interpreted by the English courts, subsumes any such parental claims into the overall inquiry into the child's welfare[1]. On the contrary, the 'first but not paramount' formulation meant that while the child's welfare was the single most important consideration, it could conceivably be outweighed, at least in theory, by other factors.

In practice, the only context in which this distinction was a serious issue was where the court was considering whether to dispense with a parent's consent to adoption. The Adoption Review recommended that the welfare principle should be extended to adoption law generally to bring it in line with other family proceedings, but this was subject to the important qualification that the child's welfare ought *not* to be paramount in determining this one crucial issue of whether or not adoption should be granted against a parent's wishes. At the time it was put this way:

> 'We are concerned that at present insufficient weight is given to a parent's lack of agreement. Where it is decided that adoption is in a child's interests, there is in practice very little room left for the court to decide to give any weight to parental views. This cannot be regarded as satisfactory in relation to an order which irrevocably terminates a parent's legal relationship with his or her child.'[2]

The test favoured by the Adoption Review was that the court should be 'satisfied that the advantages to a child of becoming part of a new family and having a new legal status are so significantly greater than the advantages to the child of any alternative option as to justify overriding the wishes of a parent or guardian'[3].

This test, if enacted, would have captured the essence of what is required under the ECHR in that it would have required a clear demonstration that adoption was *necessary* and *proportionate* and that the child's best interests could not be served by some alternative form of protection which keeps alive the child's legal links with the birth family. It is, however, the undiluted welfare test which has been favoured by Parliament to apply throughout adoption law and which has also been expressly extended to the question of dispensing with parental consent, whether at the placement stage or at the stage when the court is considering whether to make an adoption order. We consider this all-important issue further below.

It should also be noted that the new test refers to the child's welfare 'throughout his life'. This enables the court or adoption agency to have regard to the benefits of adoption which may extend to the child in adulthood and this is also reflected in the statutory checklist of factors which we discuss below. The essential point is that since adoption entails membership of a new family, the new family links which it generates will not be broken on the attainment of majority. The child will remain a member of the adoptive family for his or her life. All of us remain 'children' of our parents though no longer minors but adults.

The statutory checklist of factors

The new legislation contains, for the first time, a statutory checklist of factors to which the court or adoption agency must have regard. Most of these reflect the

---

1 This is the effect of Lord MacDermott's long-accepted interpretation of the welfare principle in *J v C* [1970] AC 668 discussed in Chapter 2 above.
2 Adoption Review, para 12.1.
3 Ibid, para 12.6.

checklist in s 1 of the Children Act[1] but there are important modifications and additions which adapt the list of factors to the special circumstances of adoption. The list is contained in s 1(4) and is as follows:

'(a)   the child's ascertainable wishes and feelings regarding the decision (considered in the light of the child's age and understanding);

(b)   the child's particular needs;

(c)   the likely effect on the child (throughout his life)of having ceased to be a member of the original family and become an adopted person;

(d)   the child's age, sex, background and any of the child's characteristics which the court or agency considers relevant;

(e)   any harm (within the meaning of the Children Act 1989) which the child has suffered or is at risk of suffering;

(f)   the relationship which the child has with relatives, and with any other person in relation to whom the court or agency considers the relationship to be relevant, including:

(i)   the likelihood of any such relationship continuing and the value to the child of its doing so;

(ii)   the ability and willingness of any of the child's relatives, or of any such person, to provide the child with a secure environment in which the child can develop, and otherwise to meet the child's needs;

(iii)   the wishes and feelings of any of the child's relatives, or of any such person, regarding the child.'

It should be noted that, unlike the position in many other jurisdictions, there is no requirement as to the *consent* to adoption of a child who has attained a particular age, such as 12[2]. The Adoption and Children Act 2002 merely gives to children themselves qualified autonomy to the extent that their wishes are to be taken into account, commensurate with their age and understanding. This formula is, of course, consistent with the general approach of the Children Act 1989 but, again in the special context of adoption, it is open to doubt whether it ought to be possible to make such an order against the express wishes of, for example, a teenager. Factors (c) and (f) are tailored to adoption and require the court or adoption agency to apply their minds to the specific question of what the child may *lose*, as well as what the child may *gain*, from moving, legally, from one family to another. They must consider the value of preserving the child's existing relationships and whether such relationships would be likely to continue if adoption were granted. Specific thought must be given to the resources of the wider family in meeting the child's needs and to the wishes of relatives. In some jurisdictions, notably New Zealand, considerable weight is given to the question of the possibility of the child being looked after by the wider family before adoption by strangers is countenanced[3].

As in the case of the Children Act checklist, the enumerated factors are not exhaustive. The court or agency must have regard to them 'among others'. Failure to take proper account of a factor in the checklist would, however, constitute a ground of appeal. The application of the welfare principle does mean that nothing is in principle excluded from consideration. None of the factors specifically mentioned is weighted more strongly than any other, so that the points made earlier about the wide discretion which this leaves are as valid here as they are in relation to Children Act jurisdictions.

---

1   Children Act 1989, s 1(3), as to which see Chapters 2 and 4 above.

2   The position in Scotland under the Age of Legal Capacity (Scotland) Act 1991, s 2(3).

3   See below.

Culture and religion

It is expressly provided in s 1(5) that 'in placing the child for adoption, the adoption agency must give due consideration to the child's religious persuasion, racial origin and cultural and religious background'. This is again consistent with the Children Act and the duty placed on local authorities, under s 22(5) of that Act, in relation to children looked after by them, which is in exactly similar terms. It is especially important in the context of adoption, indeed crucial where international adoption is contemplated, since the risk to the child of the loss of cultural, linguistic and religious background is all too obvious where the child moves from one family to another permanently. The threat to the child's identity rights, protected by Articles 7 and 8 of the UNCRC, is palpable.

The no delay principle

Section 1(3) enshrines the no delay principle of the Children Act. It is provided that 'the court or adoption agency must at all times bear in mind that, in general, any delay in coming to a decision is likely to prejudice the child's welfare'.

The White Paper was especially concerned about what were seen as delays and inconsistencies in the practice of local authorities and courts at all stages of the adoption process. The Government's conclusion was that for too many children the operation of the system as it was did not provide a chance for a long-term family life[1]. Its proposed solution has a number of aspects to it. First, performance targets would be set for local authorities designed to increase sharply the number of adoptions in relation to children looked after by them. This would be supported by central government investment of £66.5 million over three years to secure sustained improvement in adoption services. Those councils which consistently fail to provide a reasonable level of service on adoption are to risk a range of sanctions[2]. Secondly, the Act establishes a new Adoption and Children Act Register which contains details of children suitable for adoption and of approved prospective adopters[3]. The intention is to enable suitable 'matches' to be made on a national level and thus overcome the problems which can arise where such a match cannot be made within a reasonable time at the local level. Thirdly, the Government has established National Adoption Standards[4], the purpose of which is set out in the White Paper in the following terms:

> 'The National Standards set out what children, prospective adopters, adoptive parents, and birth families can expect from the adoption process, and the responsibilities of adoption agencies and councils, so that all parties receive a fair and consistent service wherever they live. They are underpinned by a set of values, which stress the importance to each child of having a permanent family, where they are safe. They put the child's needs at the centre of the adoption process.'[5]

A central feature of the standards is that they include 'timescales within which decisions for most children should be reached and action taken, to ensure that children are not kept waiting for a family'[6].

---

1   White Paper, paras 1.15 et seq.
2   Ibid, paras 7.21–7.23.
3   Section 125. The Register should not be confused with the Adopted Children Register or with the Adoption Contact Register, both discussed below.
4   Department of Health *National Adoption Standards for England* (2001).
5   White Paper, para 4.5.
6   Ibid, para 4.6.

Accordingly, the Standards provide, inter alia, that the needs of a looked after child for a permanent home must be addressed at a four-month review and a plan for permanence made; that clear timescales must be set for achieving the plan, which must be appropriately monitored and considered at every subsequent review; that, where adoption has been identified as the plan, the adoption panel will make its recommendation within two months; that a match with suitable adoptive parents must be identified and approved by the panel within six months of the agency agreeing that adoption is in the best interests of the child or within six months of the court's decision where adoption is the plan in care proceedings; and so on.

The avoidance of delay in the adoption process, once a decision has been taken to plan for adoption, should not be confused, however, with the process leading up to that decision. It should be remembered that the overwhelming majority of looked after children return home within a short time and that, for those who do not, there are other alternatives to adoption which will need to be carefully explored at the periodic reviews. Indeed, any principle which led to adoption being viewed as the *first* option would be contrary to the ECHR and it is precisely this rush to adoption which has led to multiple violations of the human rights of parents and children in the context of international adoption. Delay, in the sense of a measured consideration of the proportionate response to the child's needs, is therefore not only appropriate but mandated by human rights obligations.

The no order principle

Section 1(6) of the Act enacts the so-called 'no order principle'. As in the Children Act, it provides that 'the court must not make any order under this Act unless it considers that making the order would be better for the child than not doing so'. We considered the interpretation of the principle in the context of the Children Act[1] and there is little to add here except to make the rather obvious point that, given the extreme effect of a placement order or adoption order, the need to demonstrate conclusively that such orders are better for the child than not making them is that much stronger. Along with the requirement to have regard to the range of powers at the court's disposal, this principle really requires that the least intrusive action which is consistent with the best interests of the child should be taken.

The range of powers

Section 1(6) also requires the court or adoption agency to 'consider the whole range of powers available to it in the child's case (whether under this Act or the Children Act 1989)'. Thus, in addition to considering whether or not to make *any* order in accordance with the no order principle, courts and adoption agencies must have express regard to *which* powers or *which* orders are the most appropriate in the individual case. Specifically this requires the court to have regard to the whole range of alternatives to adoption including, especially, the making of a residence order, an order for special guardianship or, in the case of step-parent applications, a parental responsibility order. We considered all these 'alternatives

---

1   See Chapter 2 above.

for permanence' earlier[1], and we consider below some of the reported cases, before and after implementation of the HRA 1998, in which the courts have concluded that some 'lesser' form of order than adoption is the right course of action.

LEGAL CONTROL OF ADOPTION SERVICES AND PLACEMENTS

If adoption is viewed as a process of providing children with the love and security of a family, it follows that great care needs to be taken to ensure the suitability of placements. The process of selection and matching of children with prospective adopters is therefore tightly controlled. This is achieved partly by prohibiting private placements and private arrangements relating to adoption and partly by trying to ensure that a comprehensive adoption service is provided by properly approved adoption agencies. Both of these aspects were features of the Adoption Act 1976. The Adoption and Children Act 2002 takes both further, by strengthening the prohibitions on private activities concerning adoption and by imposing greater duties on local authorities and adoption agencies in relation to the services which they provide.

Prohibition of private adoption

The Act contains a cluster of provisions which prohibit the various kinds of private activities that might occur in connection with the adoption of children[2]. It is a criminal offence for someone other than an adoption agency to be involved in arrangements relating to adoption[3]. This extends to asking a person other than an adoption agency to provide a child, or prospective adopters for a child, offering to find a child for adoption or receiving or handing over a child with a view to adoption. Taking part in negotiations relating to any of those things is also prohibited[4]. The Act prohibits for the first time the preparation of reports about the suitability of a child for adoption or of a person to adopt a child or about the adoption or placement of a child, by those unauthorised to do so under the legislation[5]. The restrictions on advertisements of children for adoption other than those placed by adoption agencies, which were also a feature of the previous law, have been extended by making it explicit that the prohibitions extend to publishing or distributing information to the public by electronic means including, specifically, the internet[6].

There are offences relating to any form of financial reward in connection with the adoption of children. In essence, it is an offence to give or receive any payment in consideration of the adoption of a child, or to obtain a consent to adoption or to remove a child who is a Commonwealth citizen or habitually resident in the UK to

---

1 See Chapter 6 above.
2 See particularly ss 92–97 and ss 123 and 124.
3 Section 92.
4 Section 92(2).
5 Section 94.
6 Section 123, especially s 123(4).

a place outside the British Isles for the purposes of adoption[1]. This latter prohibition is complemented by an offence of bringing into the UK children habitually resident overseas for the purposes of adoption or children adopted by British residents overseas other than in accordance with the Conventions to which the UK is party[2]. There are certain 'excepted payments' which are allowable and which amount to the reimbursement of 'reasonable expenses' incurred by a registered adoption society, such as legal or medical expenses associated with the making of applications for placement or adoption orders[3]. The experience with international adoption and with surrogacy arrangements reveals all too clearly the problematic nature of the concept of 'reasonable expenses' which can be distorted and exceeded in a way that disguises an element of profit.

A problem which arose not infrequently under the old law, and which is bound to resurface under the new law, is the problem of how to deal with breaches of these prohibitions in a way which is consistent with giving effect to the best interests of the child. Under the old law the court had express power to authorise retrospectively what had been illegal payments if, in the court's opinion, making the adoption order was nevertheless, by that time, in the best interests of the child.

This is what happened in *Re C (Adoption: Legality)*[4]. A 39-year-old woman, separated and childless, was rejected as a suitable adopter by two social services departments and one independent adoption agency. She applied to adopt a baby from Guatemala whom she had never seen. She had never been to Guatemala but had arranged a private placement and made illegal payments to Guatemalan lawyers. Johnson J nonetheless made the adoption order on welfare grounds despite these irregularities. The problem has been endemic in international adoption and we discuss it further below.

The adoption service and adoption agencies

The corollary of the prohibitions on private activities relating to adoption is the requirement, which originally followed the recommendations of the Houghton Report[5], that every local authority should provide a comprehensive adoption service designed to meet the needs of children who have been or may be adopted, their parents or guardians and prospective adopters. Local authorities and voluntary adoption societies have long worked in partnership and co-operation to meet local needs in relation to adoption. Some of these societies, such as Barnado's, are national societies while others operate only at local level. This will remain the pattern under the Adoption and Children Act 2002 but the Act goes significantly further than previous legislation in the extent of the service which must now be provided in relation to adoption and especially perhaps in the new requirements to provide 'adoption support services'[6].

The core obligation under the Act is that every local authority:

---

1 Section 95.
2 Section 83.
3 Section 96.
4 [1999] 1 FLR 370.
5 *Report of the Departmental Committee on the Adoption of Children* ('the Houghton Report') (1972) (Cmnd 5107).
6 See White Paper, ch 6.

'must continue to maintain within their area a service designed to meet the needs, in relation to adoption, of:

(a) children who may be adopted, their parents and guardians;

(b) persons wishing to adopt a child; and

(c) adopted persons, their parents, natural parents and former guardians,

and for that purpose must provide the requisite facilities.'[1]

Local authorities provide this service in conjunction with registered adoption societies. These are voluntary organisations registered under Part 2 of the Care Standards Act 2000. Collectively, the services provided by the local authority and these agencies are known under the Act as 'the Adoption Service'[2] and either a local authority or an adoption society may be referred to as an 'adoption agency'[3]. Each local authority must provide the requisite facilities for making and participating in arrangements for the adoption of children and for the provision of adoption support services[4]. The idea of adoption support services is an innovation of the Act and includes such services as advice and counselling, health, education and cultural services. The local authority *must* carry out an assessment of the needs for adoption support services of those mentioned above if requested to do so[5]. Before the Act there was criticism of some councils for unfairly rejecting some would-be adopters on inadequate grounds and of the review mechanisms applying to such decisions. The Act therefore makes provision for the independent review of such determinations. Those in relation to whom a 'qualifying determination' has been made by an adoption agency will henceforth have the right to apply to an independent panel for review of that determination[6].

We have already noted the establishment of the Adoption and Children Act Register and the introduction of National Adoption Standards which together are designed to facilitate the adoption process and to achieve consistency of practice between local authorities. Local authorities are also required to prepare and publish a plan for the provision of adoption services in their area and to keep it under review[7].

QUALIFICATIONS FOR ADOPTION

The question of who may adopt a child is one which has been much affected by the new legislation and was left hanging in the balance as a result of political pressures until the very last moments of the Bill's passage through Parliament. The arguments raged around the central question of whether the necessary link between marriage and adoption should be preserved or severed. The result, at the eleventh hour, is that the legislation breaks this connection and enables, for the first time, unmarried couples whether heterosexual or same sex couples, in principle, to adopt a child together. We consider first which children may be

1 Section 3(1). The details of the support services to be provided by local authorities are beyond the scope of the present work but governed by the Adoption Support Services (Local Authorities) (England) Regulations 2003, SI 2003/1348.

2 Section 2(1).

3 Ibid.

4 Section 3(2).

5 Section 4(1).

6 Section 12.

7 Section 5.

adopted and then turn to this more complex and controversial question of who is eligible to be an adoptive parent.

Which children may be adopted?

English law, unlike that of some other European jurisdictions, does not have a concept of 'adoptable' children so that in principle any child may, with very limited exceptions, be adopted. It should be said that English law, again unlike the law in some jurisdictions, does not permit the adoption of adults except now in the very limited circumstances of an 18-year-old where the proceedings were commenced before his or her eighteenth birthday. Under the old law an adoption could not be granted after the child had attained majority although, because of the benefits of the adoptive status in adulthood, there were occasions when it was thought appropriate to grant an adoption in relation to a child approaching majority. Two reported cases illustrated the advantages of adoption in adulthood.

In *Re D (A Minor) (Adoption Order: Validity)*[1] a severely mentally incapacitated child was adopted six days before his eighteenth birthday. The long-term foster-parents felt harassed by the natural mother who argued that adoption was not necessary to promote the welfare of the child throughout his childhood. The Court of Appeal upheld the judge's adoption order. There was no requirement that benefits during minority were a prerequisite of adoption. It was open to the court to take into account benefits which would accrue to the child after attaining majority and for the rest of his life. Adoption, it was thought, would cement the young man's relationship with his foster-parents. It will be recalled that the checklist of factors now requires the court to take into account the effects of adoption throughout the child's life and not merely during minority. In *Re B (Adoption Order: Nationality)*[2] a teenager from Jamaica was adopted by her grandparents in the UK. Her father was dead and her mother lived in impoverished circumstances back in Jamaica. The House of Lords reinstated the judge's adoption order. Although the courts would not allow adoption to be used as a device for obtaining nationality and the right of abode, in this case the grandparents had assumed parental responsibility, and the girl was doing well in school. The court could not ignore these benefits to her of adoption despite the fact that she was close to majority[3].

The Adoption and Children Act 2002 now provides that the child must be under the age of 19 and must not have been married[4]. As noted above, an adoption order may be made notwithstanding the child's attaining majority provided that the proceedings were commenced, but not concluded, before the child's eighteenth birthday[5].

---

1   [1991] 2 FLR 66.
2   [1999] 1 FLR 907.
3   See also *Re S and J (Adoption: Non-Patrials)* [2004] 2 FLR 111 where Bodey J reached a similar conclusion in relation to two teenage boys from Bangladesh.
4   Section 47(8) and (9).
5   Section 49(4) and (5).

Who may adopt?

The rules governing eligibility in applying to adopt a child are now set out in ss 50 and 51 of the Act. The rules distinguish between adoption by a couple and adoption by one person.

Adoption by a couple

Where a couple apply to adopt both must normally have attained the age of 21 years but, where one of the couple is the mother or father of the child to be adopted, it is sufficient if that parent has attained the age of 18 and the other member of the couple has attained the age of 21[1]. So far as age is concerned English law contains no statutory requirement, such as exists in many jurisdictions, that there should be a minimum age disparity between the child and the adoption applicants.

It is in the definition of 'couple', for these purposes, that we find one of the Act's most contentious changes. A couple is defined to include:

(a) a married couple (as in the previous law); or
(b) two people (whether of different sexes or the same sex) living as partners in an enduring family relationship[2].

The concept of what amounts to an 'enduring family relationship' will require judicial interpretation but it is clearly wider than the heterosexual notion of 'cohabitation' or 'living together as husband and wife'. Neither is there any period specified, as there is in some family legislation, for the length of the relationship, merely that it is 'enduring' – a condition which implies stability without telling us how exactly that stability is to be measured.

This, then, is a major break with traditional adoption law, which was only prepared to countenance joint applications by couples who were married to each other[3]. The Adoption Review had recognised that *some* unmarried couples might make suitable adopters but felt that, on balance, the security and stability required by adopted children was more likely to be met by those who had made the publicly recognised commitment of marriage and who had legal responsibilities to each other[4]. This, of course, was not perceived as a fair argument in relation to same sex couples who, being unable to marry in law, could not give a public commitment through marriage[5]. It was a policy which looked increasingly like one founded on prejudice and discrimination based on sexual orientation[6]. It moreover became

---

1 Section 50(1) and (2).
2 Section 144(4).
3 Adoption Act 1976, ss 14 and 15.
4 Adoption Review, paras 26.9 et seq.
5 For an excellent critique of the provision removing the bar on adoption by same sex couples, which traces the legislative history and also looks at the reform in the context of other legal developments affecting same sex relationships, see A Marshall 'Comedy of Adoption – When is a Parent not a Parent?' [2003] Fam Law 840.
6 It should be noted, however, that in *Fretté v France* [2003] 2 FLR 9, the ECtHR found by a narrow majority that France had not violated the Convention rights of a single homosexual adoption applicant. It was entitled to reject him largely on account of his sexual orientation given the lack of uniformity on the issue among European States, which meant that France had not exceeded its wide margin of appreciation.

clear that the judiciary themselves were increasingly uncomfortable with a blanket prohibition on adoption by unmarried couples and a number of reported cases found ways of circumventing the restrictions where they thought adoption was warranted by the child's best interests.

Re AB (Adoption Joint Residence)[1] concerned an unmarried heterosexual couple who were the long-term foster-carers of a child in care. An adoption order was granted to the foster-father with a joint residence order in favour of both foster-parents. The adoption order could be granted to the foster-father as a single applicant since there was nothing in the legislation preventing this. This solution was not, however, as satisfactory or as tidy as a joint adoption order would have been since its effect was to make the child a full member of the adoptive father's family but only to confer parental responsibility under the residence order on the foster-mother, which itself would be limited in time and would not survive the child's majority. A similar solution was achieved in the case of a same sex couple in *Re W (Adoption: Homosexual Adopter)*[2]. Here Singer J allowed a member of a lesbian couple to pursue an adoption application as a single applicant. He found that there was nothing in the adoption legislation to prevent a single applicant from being a homosexual. The applicant was a 49-year-old childless woman who had been caring for the child who had previously had a succession of unsuccessful foster placements. She was in a stable, long-standing relationship with a professional woman who was herself a grandmother. The case illustrates that in some cases children will already have been in the households of unmarried couples and that the only real issue is whether a settled arrangement should be formalised through adoption. It should also be borne in mind that the new Act merely removes the absolute bar on adoption by the unmarried. The question of whether any *specific* couple should be allowed to adopt a particular child will always ultimately rest on the court's view of the best interests of that child. What is beyond doubt is that it is more logical, where there is a stable cohabitation, to allow that couple to achieve jointly what the courts had previously contrived to allow a single applicant to do.

Adoption by a single applicant

There are several different sets of circumstances set out in the Act in which a single applicant may apply to adopt a child, as follows.

First, there is the general rule that an adoption order may be made on the application of one person who has attained the age of 21 years and is *not* married[3].

Secondly, an adoption order may be made in favour of one applicant who *is* married where the court is satisfied that his or her spouse cannot be found, they have separated and the separation is likely to be permanent, or the other spouse is by reason of ill health, whether physical or mental, incapable of making an application for an adoption order[4]. Unless these circumstances apply, the expectation is that a step as serious as adoption must be undertaken by two spouses together. It is perhaps slightly inconsistent with this notion that there would appear to be nothing in principle to prevent a single application by a member of an unmarried couple, however much the other member of that couple might

---

1   [1996] 1 FLR 27.
2   [1997] 2 FLR 406.
3   Section 51(1).
4   Section 51(3).

disapprove of it. In such a situation the court might in its discretion decide that the adoption was not in the best interests of the child.

Thirdly, the partner of a parent of the child concerned may apply as a sole applicant[1]. This overcomes the previous requirement that a step-parent adoption should necessarily involve a joint application by both spouses, since all applications by married couples had to be joint applications. The unfortunate result was that a natural parent was required to adopt his or her own child. The change in the law means that the application for adoption may now be brought by the step-parent alone. It should be noted that there is again no requirement that the parent and partner should be married so that the unmarried cohabitant of a parent is also eligible to adopt as a sole applicant. This rule may be thought somewhat inconsistent with the new rules governing the acquisition of parental responsibility by step-parents by agreement or court order[2]. In that case the new provisions only apply to step-parents and not to the cohabitants or partners of parents.

Finally, in very limited circumstances, one natural parent may apply to adopt his or her own child to the exclusion of the other parent. If granted, the effect of this type of adoption is to take away rather than give, since the focus is on the *termination* of the parental status of the other parent. The circumstances in which such an order may be made are where the court is satisfied that:

(a) the other natural parent is dead or cannot be found;
(b) there is no other parent by virtue of s 28 of the HFEA 1990; or
(c) there is some other reason justifying the child's being adopted by the applicant alone[3].

In the case of a successful application the court must record that it is satisfied as to the facts in (a) or (b), and where some other reason is thought to justify the application it must record that reason[4].

The corresponding provision under the Adoption Act 1976[5] came up for interpretation by the Court of Appeal and then the House of Lords in one of the most remarkable adoption cases in recent decades. It is a case which raises profound questions about the place of adoption in the modern law and its relationship with human rights. As such we devote considerable space to it and focus more particularly on the decision of the Court of Appeal which, although reversed by the House of Lords, engages more convincingly with the human rights issues presented by the case.

Re B (Adoption: Natural Parent)[6] is one of a number of reported cases in which a woman has become pregnant, not informed the genetic father of the pregnancy or birth and wanted essentially to give the child up for a secret or confidential adoption. In this case there was a sexual relationship lasting less than a year. When

---

1 Section 51(2).
2 Section 112, inserting s 4A into the Children Act 1989. See Chapter 6 above.
3 Section 51(4).
4 Ibid.
5 Adoption Act 1976, s 15(3).
6 *Re B (Adoption: Natural Parent)* [2002] 1 FLR 196 (HL); [2001] 1 FLR 589 (CA). For the author's views in greater detail, see A Bainham 'Unintentional Parenthood: the Case of the Reluctant Mother' [2002] CLJ 288. See also S Harris-Short 'Putting the child at the heart of adoption?' [2002] CFLQ 325.

the baby was born, the mother did not look at her and said that she had no maternal instincts. She had previously given up another daughter for adoption. She told the local authority that the father was working abroad when in fact he was in England. There was then a chance recognition of the father's name in the adoption papers by a secretary working for the local authority. The authority then contacted the father who gave up work to look after the child and in due course wanted to adopt her to the exclusion of the mother. The mother was not opposed to the adoption. She had no direct contact with the child and did not want any beyond an annual photograph and progress report. The judge granted the adoption on the basis that the mother had rejected the child and cited that as the reason. The Official Solicitor appealed on the basis that it was not in the child's best interests for the adoption order to exclude the mother.

The Court of Appeal set aside the adoption order and substituted a residence order in favour of the father to run on to the child's eighteenth birthday. It also gave him power to apply for a passport for the child without the mother's consent and an unfettered right to take the child abroad. The mother was prohibited from applying for orders under the Children Act 1989 without the leave of the court. This package of orders was designed to give the father security against possible interference by the mother, which seemed very unlikely but which bothered the father. Specifically on the adoption question, however, the Court of Appeal took the view that it was generally in the best interests of children to have two legal parents and two legal families and that the exclusion of one could only be justified, under Article 8(2) of the ECHR, if necessary in a democratic society. Hale LJ said that the relationship of mother and child was in itself sufficient to establish 'family life' even where the two were separated at birth. The carrying of and giving birth to a child brings with it a relationship between mother and child which is entitled to respect. Were it otherwise, she said, the State could always interfere without fear of contravening Article 8 by removing children the moment they were born. That only needed stating for it to be clear how wrong that would be. Adoption here would therefore be a disproportionate response to the child's current needs, since to deprive the child entirely of a legal relationship with the mother was not necessary when a package of other measures could achieve the desired result. Under the various orders the court made, the mother would be left with only the remnants of parental responsibility which would come into play only if something serious happened in the father's life and if the court approved the mother's involvement at that stage.

The House of Lords reversed the Court of Appeal's decision and reinstated the adoption order on the narrow, but well-established, ground that the Court of Appeal ought not to have interfered with the exercise of the judge's discretion[1]. In this case it could not be said that the judge had misdirected herself on the proper interpretation of the legislation or that her decision was manifestly wrong. There was no reason for importing into the legislation a requirement that the 'reason' for allowing a sole adoption by one parent must be comparable to the death or disappearance of the other parent. It had therefore been open to the judge to conclude that the child's best interests required adoption. The father's anxiety about the mother's continuing status could perpetuate insecurity for him

---

1   A rule firmly established by the House of Lords in *G v G (Minors: Custody Appeal)* [1985] 1 WLR 647.

and potentially affect the child's stability. There was moreover no inconsistency between the kind of balancing exercise under the ECHR which required that interferences be proportionate. The judge's determination that the child's best interests required adoption identified a pressing social need, and the adoption complied with the principle of proportionality.

This decision raises fundamental questions about human rights in the context of adoption. First, it exposes a distinction in the circumstances in which 'family life' may be said to arise between mother and child on the one hand and father and child on the other. Hale LJ, in the Court of Appeal, was at pains to emphasise the fundamental bond between mother and child which arises at birth and amounts to family life and also to highlight the importance of this for the creation of kinship links between the mother's wider family and the child. It is therefore worth speculating on whether she would have taken the same position if this case had involved the *mother* trying to adopt to the exclusion of the father. How would the bond between the genetic father and child have been viewed in those circumstances and could distinctions sensibly be drawn between the child's interest in the *maternal* family and in the *paternal* family?

Secondly, the case again prompts an evaluation of the theory of intentional parenthood[1]. The corollary of the theory that parentage should be recognised, or parental responsibility awarded, on the basis of a person's *intention* to perform the social role of parent is that parentage should be lost and parental responsibility removed where someone is *unwilling* to perform that social role. The Court of Appeal's approach in this case could be viewed as an emphatic rejection of any such theory. What the Court of Appeal seemed to be saying was that, in the light of human rights considerations, the law ought not to allow a parent simply to drop out of parenthood because that is what that parent wishes to do. Such an approach if carried to its logical conclusion does suggest that the mother's traditional right to give up her child for adoption, which indeed was an important influence on the introduction of adoption in England in the Adoption of Children Act 1926, may be about to be seriously eroded. This case, along with others which we discuss below, challenges the right of mothers to arrange the confidential adoption of their children as a potential breach of both the child's and father's Convention rights, or, conceivably, the Convention rights of the wider maternal or paternal family.

Finally, the case demonstrates again the importance, from a human rights perspective, of balancing the extreme solution of adoption with other less drastic alternatives which may equally well achieve the result needed to protect the welfare of the child but which do not ignore or devalue adult claims. It is submitted that the approach of the Court of Appeal showed a much more sophisticated appreciation of the need to demonstrate that adoption was better than other solutions, and therefore proportionate, than did either the judge or the House of Lords.

The probationary periods

In addition to the above qualifications for applicants, English law also requires the child to live with the prospective adopters for a specified period of time. This was

---

1 As to which see especially C Barton and G Douglas *Law and Parenthood* (Butterworths, 1995).

the case under the Adoption Act 1976[1] and the principle has been preserved under the new legislation[2]. The prescribed periods have, however, been significantly changed by the Adoption and Children Act 2002 and vary markedly depending on the class of applicant. In each case the court must be satisfied that there have been sufficient opportunities to see the child and the applicant/applicants in the home environment together afforded to the adoption agency, or, where the child was not placed by an adoption agency, the local authority within whose area the home is[3].

The requisite periods are as follows.

(1) Where the child was placed by an adoption agency or under the authority of the High Court, the child must have had his home with the applicant/applicants at all times during the period of *ten weeks* preceding the application[4].

(2) Where the applicant, or one of the applicants, is the partner of a parent of the child, the period is *six months*[5].

(3) For local authority foster-parents the period is *one year*[6], a requirement which is consistent with the new period for eligibility, in their case, to seek leave for a s 8 order under the Children Act 1989[7].

(4) In all other cases, which are perhaps most likely to involve relatives of the child, the period is *three years* whether continuous or not during the period of five years preceding the application[8]. This is a very significantly longer period than the corresponding period under the Adoption Act 1976 which was 13 weeks[9]. The reasoning is that it may be more appropriate in such cases for some other order to be sought. Where an adoption order is granted in favour of a relative, such as a grandparent, the effect may be to distort family relationships – in that example by making the grandmother legally the mother of the child, the natural mother the sister, and so on in relation to wider kinship relationships with the extended family. It was for this reason that such adoptions have been discouraged since the Houghton Report, although granted in a minority of appropriate cases. The three-year residence requirement will operate as an automatic break on such adoptions and, where such applications are made, the court will need to consider carefully the other options for permanence such as the making of a residence or special guardianship order.

In all of the above cases, the court may give leave for an application to be made notwithstanding the failure of the applicant to satisfy the relevant probationary period[10]. Probationary periods like this are by no means universally required. The absence of such requirements in the case of jurisdictions which send children for the purposes of international adoption is a continuing cause of concern given the

---

1   Adoption Act 1976, s 13.
2   Adoption and Children Act 2002, s 42.
3   Section 42(7).
4   Section 42(2).
5   Section 42(3).
6   Section 42(4).
7   Section 113, amending s 9(3) of the Children Act 1989. See Chapter 6 above.
8   Section 42(5).
9   Adoption Act 1976, s 13(1).
10 Section 42(6).

importance of being satisfied that an appropriate matching of adoptive parents and child has been made.

THE NEW PLACEMENT REGIME

The Adoption and Children Act 2002 abolishes the former process of 'freeing for adoption' under the Adoption Act 1976 and replaces it with a wholly new placement regime. Placement of a child for adoption will henceforth be possible only with parental consent or where the court is prepared to dispense with that consent and certain other conditions are satisfied. This marks a significant departure from the old law under which there was no such restraint on placing children for adoption and under which the freeing for adoption procedure was only *one* route by which a local authority might seek to arrange the adoption of a child.

The purpose of having a legal process at the stage of placement is essentially twofold. First, it is intended to reduce the uncertainty for prospective adopters who might otherwise face a contested hearing at the stage of the final hearing for an adoption order. Secondly, it is intended to reduce the extent to which birth families are presented with a fait accompli at the final hearing where the child has been placed with prospective adopters for some time. The former process of freeing for adoption had similar aims but was ineffective in achieving them and widely criticised. Before considering the new placement regime, we look briefly at the problems surrounding the former freeing process.

The trouble with freeing for adoption

One of the difficulties prior to the Children Act 1975 was that parents were unable to relinquish their parental rights (as they then were), even though they were in favour of adoption, until the final adoption order was made. This meant that there could be a substantial delay following a parent's decision to give up a child while a suitable placement was found and while the prospective adopters served out the necessary probationary period with the child. The delay could be a source of anxiety also to the prospective adopters and the agency, since natural parents could, and sometimes did, withdraw their consent to adoption at the eleventh hour. The Houghton Committee sought to meet these difficulties by recommending the introduction of a two-stage procedure which could enable the question of parental agreement to be disposed of at a much earlier stage. This became the freeing for adoption procedure[1].

It was, however, only one of two *alternative* routes for adoption agencies and, following the Children Act 1989, could only be used where the child was in the care of the local authority[2]. Much of the time authorities did not resort to the two-stage procedure involving freeing because it added an extra burden and was likely to increase delays in the adoption process. There were other problems. The effect of a freeing order was to confer parental responsibility on the adoption agency and to terminate the parental responsibility of the parents. But this was not

---

1 The freeing regime was contained in ss 18–21 of the Adoption Act 1976.
2 Ibid, s 18(2) and (2A), as amended by Sch 10, para 6 to the Children Act 1989.

necessarily a final termination of parental responsibility since, where within 12 months after the freeing order was made the child had not been placed for adoption, the birth parent might apply for the order to be revoked and, if successful, the effect would be to transfer parental responsibility back to the parent[1].

It soon became apparent, however, that even where the child had not been placed it might well not be desirable for the outcome to be a resumption of responsibility by the parent and this led to litigation in a number of cases. In *Re G (Adoption: Freeing Order)*[2] these issues were brought before the House of Lords, which had to confront the question of the so-called 'statutory orphan' – the child who had not been successfully placed for adoption but who, if the parent's application for revocation of the freeing order to be revoked was rejected, would be left in 'indefinite legal limbo' with no legal parent. In this case the House of Lords held that the powers under the Adoption Act 1976 and under the Children Act 1989 could be exercised in conjunction so that, where the local authority was prepared to seek a care order and the mother was not opposed to this, the freeing order could be discharged and the local authority retain care through the care order.

This was clearly unsatisfactory and a somewhat contrived result which it might not be possible to achieve in other cases. The new placement regime is in part designed to overcome these problems although only time will tell whether it does. The focus of the new regime is on *placement* and, following placement, the parent will retain parental responsibility until such time as a final adoption order is made, although this will be shared with the prospective adopters or the adoption agency where there are no prospective adopters.

The two routes for placement

An adoption agency wishing to place a child for adoption may now only do so *either* where each parent or guardian of the child consents *or* where the court makes a placement order[3]. Placement orders are a new type of order introduced by the Act. So far as placement with parental consent is concerned, the provisions which govern the giving of consent to placement are similar to those which determine the relevant consents and how they must be given in relation to adoption itself, and we consider them below in that context[4]. At this stage we focus only on the placement order route.

The placement order is an order 'authorising a local authority to place a child for adoption with any prospective adopters who may be chosen by the authority'[5]. The circumstances in which the court may make a placement order require the satisfaction of two separate conditions. The first is as follows:

(a) that the child is in the care of the local authority under a care order; or
(b) that the court is satisfied that the threshold conditions for making a care order under s 31(2) of the Children Act 1989 are met; or

---

1 Adoption Act 1976, s 20(1).
2 [1997] 2 FLR 202 and see M Richards 'Relinquishment, freeing or abandonment' [1997] CFLQ 313.
3 Adoption and Children Act 2002, s 18(1).
4 Consent to placement is governed by s 19.
5 Section 21(1).

(c) that the child has no parent or guardian[1].

The second condition is:

(a) that the parent or guardian has consented to placement and that consent has not been withdrawn; or
(b) that the court should dispense with that consent[2].

The Act therefore brings under one umbrella the threshold conditions for compulsory State intervention through a care order with the legal requirements for dispensing with parental consent to adoption. It cannot be emphasised strongly enough that, where a parent or guardian does *not* consent to placement, a placement order may only be made where *both* conditions are satisfied. This was not reflected in the original Bill as drafted but, following widespread criticism, the Bill was amended to make it plain that a local authority should not be able (through the vehicle of a placement order) to obtain compulsory care of a child without meeting the normal threshold conditions. Assuming this first condition is satisfied, the placement order may still only be made if the quite separate grounds are established for dispensing with consent to adoption. As we shall see, this really amounts to a determination at that stage that adoption is in the best interests of the child. We consider the grounds for dispensing with consent in the context of the adoption order itself below.

There are prescribed circumstances in which the local authority *must* seek a placement order where it is satisfied that the child ought to be placed for adoption[3].

A placement order will remain in force until it is revoked, an adoption is made, or the child marries or attains the age of 18 years[4]. A local authority or the child (or a person acting on behalf of the child) may apply to revoke a placement order at any time. Others, including most obviously parents, may only apply for revocation with the leave of the court where the child has not yet been placed for adoption[5]. Leave will only be granted where the court is satisfied that there has been a change of circumstances since the order was made[6].

The legal effects of placement

Parental responsibility
Whether the child is placed by consent or under a placement order, parental responsibility is given to the adoption agency (which will be the local authority or, where placement is by consent, a registered adoption society)[7]. While the child is placed with prospective adopters, parental responsibility is also given to them[8]. In each case, the parents retain parental responsibility up to the time an adoption order is made. The adoption agency, however, 'may determine that the parental responsibility of any parent or guardian, or prospective adopters, is to be

---

1   Section 21(2).
2   Section 21(3).
3   Section 22.
4   Section 21(4).
5   Section 24(1) and (2).
6   Section 24(3).
7   Section 25(2).
8   Section 25(3).

restricted to the extent specified in the determination'[1]. This provision is analogous to s 33 of the Children Act 1989 which applies where a child is in care[2]. Its purpose is to ensure that, notwithstanding the sharing of parental responsibility under the placement regime, the adoption agency remains 'in the driving seat' and able to fulfil its plans for the child without being constantly frustrated in these by the parents or prospective adopters. Where such a determination is made, the retention of parental responsibility may amount to little more than a right of consultation.

Contact

The whole question of contact in the context of adoption has been and remains a hugely debated issue which has been heightened by the greater emphasis which the law now attaches to the rights of the child specifically and to human rights in general. We consider below the question of post-adoption contact. For the moment we are concerned only with contact during placement. The hope and expectation is that contact between the child and the birth family during placement will be agreed between them and the prospective adopters. Where, however, it is not agreed, there is provision for a 'freestanding' application for contact under ss 26 and 27 which constitute a discrete contact code applying only to placement.

The effect of a placement order will be to terminate any existing contact order made under the Children Act, and any other s 8 order, and to *suspend* any existing care order[3]. The broad effect of these provisions as they apply to contact is that applications for contact, where the child is placed for adoption, must be made as an integral part of the placement regime, and not by way of applying for a private contact order under s 8 or a public contact order under s 34 where the child is in care. Subject to that, the provisions governing contact in the placement context are again modelled on the contact code where the child is in care. Where a contact order is sought at the same time as an application for a final adoption order, a s 8 contact order may be made[4].

Restrictions on removal of children during placement

The previous law contained prohibitions on the removal of 'protected children' while an adoption application was pending[5].

Under the new placement regime, there is a general prohibition on removing a child who is placed for adoption from the prospective adopters and this will apply even where the parent has withdrawn his or her consent[6]. Where, however, a child is placed by consent, and that consent is then withdrawn, the prospective adopters are required to return the child to the adoption agency[7]. This is distinguishable from the situation following a placement order. Here there is no automatic right for parents to recover their child, and only the local authority is empowered to

1 Section 25(4).
2 See Chapter 11 above.
3 Section 26(1).
4 Section 26(5).
5 Adoption Act 1976, s 27 et seq.
6 Section 30(1).
7 Section 32.

remove the child where there has been a withdrawal of parental consent[1]. Where a child is being accommodated before any placement order has been made, the agency must return the child to the parents on request within seven days unless an application for a placement order has been made and not yet concluded[2]. Once an application for an adoption order has been made, the child may not be removed by anyone without the leave of the court[3].

CONSENT TO ADOPTION

The question of consent has always been central to the adoption process and, more than anything else, the feature which has distinguished adoption from other legal procedures relating to children[4]. The Adoption and Children Act 2002 makes radical changes to the legal requirements for consent in a number of ways. It makes provision for the giving of an 'advance consent', requires the issue of consent to be addressed in all cases before a child is placed for adoption and, most controversially, openly places the welfare principle at the heart of the judicial decision to dispense with parental consent. In one respect, however, the legislation is less radical than might have been expected in that the consent of *the child*, however old, has not been made a formal legal requirement, despite hints during the long reform process that it would be, as in other jurisdictions, notably Scotland[5]. Under the new legislation, the issue of consent will arise in most cases at the placement stage, but there will continue to be cases – where, for example, the application is by relatives with whom the child has been living – where it will not arise until the application for the adoption order itself. First, we consider the essential conditions in the new legislation regarding consent, including the question of whose consent is legally required. We then consider the grounds for dispensing with consent.

The essential conditions

One of three conditions as to consent must be satisfied before the court may make an adoption order[6]. Only the first two conditions are relevant to a book on English law, since the third relates solely to children who have been freed for adoption under orders made in Scotland or Northern Ireland. The other two conditions are as follows.

The first condition is:

(a) that the parent or guardian consents to the making of the adoption order;
(b) that the parent or guardian has consented under s 20 (and has not withdrawn the consent) and does not oppose the making of the adoption order; or
(c) that the parent's or guardian's consent should be dispensed with[7].

---

1 Section 34.
2 Section 31(1) and (2).
3 Section 37.
4 For background discussion see E Cooke 'Dispensing with parental consent to adoption – a choice of welfare tests' [1997] CFLQ 259.
5 See fn 2 at p 268 above.
6 Section 47.
7 Section 47(2).

The second condition is:

(a) that the child has been placed for adoption by an adoption agency with the prospective adopters in whose favour the order is proposed to be made; and

(b) that either:

  (i) the child was placed for adoption with the consent of each parent or guardian, and the consent of the mother was given when the child was at least six weeks old; or

  (ii) the child was placed for adoption under a placement order; and

(c) that no parent or guardian opposes the making of an adoption order[1].

These are therefore two *alternative* conditions, the first focusing on the issue of consent where the child has not been placed for adoption under a placement order, and the second dealing with cases where there has been a placement under the new placement regime and the parent or guardian does not oppose the adoption. It should be noted that the requirements set out in the first condition are *alternative* requirements whereas those in the second condition are *cumulative* requirements, apart from requirement (b) which deals with the alternatives of placement by consent or placement under a placement order.

Several features relating to the nature of giving consent should be observed. First, it is provided, as it was under the previous law, that the consent of a mother to an adoption order is ineffective if given less than six weeks after the birth of the child[2]. This is in part to comply with the requirements of the European Convention on the Adoption of Children 1967. It would appear that the mother may consent to the *placement* of the child for adoption within six weeks of the child's birth but that, if she were to do so, this would be ineffective for the purposes of the adoption order and consent would need to be given again to adoption itself. The purpose of the restriction is to enable the mother to recover from the effects of giving birth and to receive appropriate counselling. The question of early consent to adoption is an especially controversial one in the context of international adoption where, in some countries, there is clear evidence that expectant mothers have been put under pressure to give up their children for adoption at, or soon after, birth[3].

Secondly, and not unrelated to the first point, it must be established that consent is given 'unconditionally and with full understanding of what is involved'. The consent need not, however, involve knowing the identity of the prospective adopters[4]. The previous legislation required that consent be given 'freely'[5]. This term does not appear in the new legislation although, clearly, it is still implied that the parent must give consent free from external pressure. The explanation for the change given in the White Paper was that the 'decision to agree to adoption is often a very difficult one' and that to say that a parent was agreeing 'freely' might not reflect this. The new wording is supposed to reflect better 'the reality that birth parents have agreed to the adoption on the basis that it is in the best interests of the child'[6]. It is a pity, it is submitted, that it is not made explicit, as it was in

---

1 Section 47(4).

2 Section 52(3).

3 See Chapter 17 below.

4 Section 52(5).

5 Adoption Act 1976, s 16(1)(b)(i).

6 White Paper, paras 8.27 and 8.28.

previous legislation, that consent must be freely given and this adds to the concern that there may be something of a devaluation of parental rights in the legislation. The giving or withdrawing of consent has, however, been formalised and must be given in a form prescribed by rules made under the legislation[1]. It will be the responsibility of CAFCASS officers to advise parents on the implications of giving consent and to ensure that the formalities are properly observed.

Thirdly, the legislation provides, for the first time, for the giving of an advance consent. The Act allows a parent or guardian who consents to a child being placed for adoption by an adoption agency to give an advance consent to an adoption order[2]. He or she may therefore give consent at the same time as consenting to placement, or at any subsequent time, to the making of a future adoption order. The consent may be either in relation to *specific* prospective adopters or to *any* prospective adopters who may be chosen by the agency[3]. This advance consent may subsequently be withdrawn by giving notice to the agency in the prescribed form[4]. This may not be done, however, if by that time an application for an adoption order has already been made[5]. It is possible also to give notice that he or she does not wish to be informed of any application for an adoption order but such a statement may also subsequently be withdrawn[6].

The Act also contains provisions designed to deal with the question of a 'change of heart' by the parent following placement of the child or the giving of an advance consent. In each case it is provided that the parent or guardian concerned may only oppose the making of the adoption order with the leave of the court[7], which may only be granted where the court is 'satisfied that there has been a change in circumstances since the consent of the parent or guardian was given or, as the case may be, the placement order was made'[8]. Given the policy of the legislation to deal expeditiously with the issue of consent, in the interests of certainty, at an earlier stage of the adoption process, it is unlikely that leave will be readily given to oppose adoption at the eleventh hour.

Whose consent is required?

Whether consent is to placement or to adoption, s 52 of the Adoption and Children Act 2002 governs the question of whose consent is required and these provisions also call for some comment on whose consent is *not* required.

Those *required* to consent are parents and guardians[9]. The expression 'guardian' now includes the 'special guardian'[10] appointed by the court under the new regime of special guardianship introduced by the Act, as well as the more obvious guardian who takes over on the death of a parent and whose status is governed by the Children Act 1989[11]. The inclusion of the special guardian among

---

1 Section 52(7).
2 Section 20(1).
3 Section 20(2).
4 Sections 20(3) and 52(8).
5 Section 52(4).
6 Section 20(4).
7 Section 47(3)–(5).
8 Section 47(7).
9 Section 52(1).
10 Section 144(1).
11 Children Act 1989, s 5; and see Chapter 6 above.

those whose consent is required underlines the superior status involved and further distinguishes the special guardian from other substitute carers, especially from those holding residence orders whose consent is *not* required to the child's placement or subsequent adoption. It should not be thought, however, that the inclusion of the special guardian in this privileged category for the purposes of adoption is uncontroversial since, it will be recalled, the other central feature of special guardianship is that it enables the child's legal link with the birth family to be preserved. The effect of adoption is, of course, to extinguish that connection. It should, however, be understood that the consent of the special guardian would not *by itself* be sufficient if the child also has a parent or parents. Their consent would also have to be obtained or the court would have to take the decision to dispense with it.

It should also be noted that the child's consent is *not* required. The Adoption Review had accepted the principle that an adoption order ought not to be made without the consent of a child who had attained the age of 12, an age at which children are required to consent in a number of other jurisdictions including Scotland. It is, of course, the case that the adoption agency and the court are required to ascertain and have regard to the child's wishes, in the light of the child's age and understanding, in accordance with the general principles in the Act[1]. There is no doubt that the wishes of an older child will be highly relevant to the decision and have probably been the decisive factor in the exercise of the court's discretion in some cases[2].

The expression 'parent', as under the Adoption Act 1976, 'means a parent having parental responsibility'[3]. That will clearly include all legal mothers, whether married or not, fathers married to the mother and unmarried fathers who have taken steps to acquire parental responsibility under one of the statutory mechanisms. The change brought about by the Act, whereby parental responsibility may be acquired automatically on registration as the child's father, will (as noted earlier) result in the great majority of unmarried fathers acquiring parental responsibility as opposed to the situation before the Act when the vast majority did not. The Adoption and Children Act 2002 goes on to provide for the situation where an unmarried mother has already given consent to placement of the child for adoption and, subsequently, the legal father acquires parental responsibility. In these circumstances he will be treated as having, at that time, given consent 'in the same terms in which [the mother] gave consent'[4]. The idea is to prevent the father from frustrating or obstructing the arrangement which the mother has entered into with the adoption agency.

The definition of 'parent' thus continues to exclude from the consent requirements a category of unmarried fathers who have not acquired parental responsibility. This does not mean, any more than it did under the old law, that these men will necessarily have no standing in adoption proceedings and no say in the outcome. Indeed, in a whole string of cases since the implementation of the HRA 1998, it has been asserted that human rights obligations require that the father without parental responsibility be notified of the proceedings and allowed

---

1   Section 1(4)(a).
2   See particularly *Re M (Adoption or Residence Order)* [1998] 1 FLR 570.
3   Section 52(6).
4   Section 52(9) and (10).

to participate in them. The result of this litigation has been that in most cases it will be expected that the father is informed and allowed to offer his view, although there will be exceptions where the courts are likely to take the view that his connection with the child is insufficiently close or that he has effectively forfeited his right to participate by his adverse behaviour[1].

Under the Adoption Act 1976, before an order could be made freeing a child for adoption, the court was required to satisfy itself that any person claiming to be the father had no intention of applying for parental responsibility or for a residence order or that if he did apply for such an order it was likely to be refused[2]. The Adoption Rules 1984 also provided that a father contributing to the child's maintenance had the right to be heard on the merits of an adoption application. Beyond that, the court had a discretion whether or not to join him as party to the proceedings. It seems likely that similar provision will be made in the rules to be produced under the new legislation. But, more importantly perhaps, there remains the question of what level of notice and participation is required in order to comply with the ECHR.

A decade ago, the ECtHR signalled its general view on this question in *Keegan v Ireland*[3] when it found Irish law in breach of the father's rights under the Convention by in effect allowing a 'secret' adoption of a child born out of wedlock. Indeed, it is this traditional right of the mother to secrecy or, to put it in a slightly less emotive way, confidentiality which has come under scrutiny from a human rights perspective. The reported cases have been concerned with much the same scenario with variations on the facts. What usually happens is that there is a relatively brief sexual relationship, even a casual encounter in some cases, which results in the pregnancy. The mother decides to give birth but not to inform the genetic father of either the pregnancy or the subsequent birth. Later, when adoption is under consideration, either the father becomes aware of the situation and wishes to establish some sort of relationship with the child or the adoption agency or local authority are concerned about pressing ahead with adoption with the mother's consent without exploring any possible contribution the father might make to the life of the child. In one case, the issue was the mother's desire to keep the facts from her wider family[4].

In these cases, the central principle which has now emerged, and which was expressed most strongly by Dame Elizabeth Butler-Sloss in *Re B (Adoption by One Natural Parent: Exclusion of Other)*[5], is that, although there will be cases where there is a good reason for not joining the father as respondent in adoption proceedings, to do so should be regarded as the norm. Local authorities should therefore be looking to inform the father in the majority of these cases. The desire of the mother for confidentiality (understandable though this is and arguably supported by the mother's right to a respect for her private life under the ECHR) is not in itself a reason for denying to the father an opportunity to be heard as to the future

1 For a review of this case-law, see A Bainham 'Can we Protect Children and Protect their Rights?' [2002] Fam Law 279.
2 Adoption Act 1976, s 18(7).
3 (1994) 18 EHRR 342.
4 *Z County Council v R* [2001] 1 FLR 365.
5 [2001] 1 FLR 589. The decision of the Court of Appeal was subsequently reversed by the House of Lords in *Re B (Adoption: Natural Parent)* [2002] 1 FLR 196, but the principle stated by Dame Elizabeth Butler-Sloss P in the Court of Appeal was not undermined.

welfare of his child. The question therefore must be to identify which sort of cases might justify proceeding without the involvement of the father.

Dame Elizabeth Butler-Sloss herself identified an extreme case in *Re B*, where to inform the father would put the mother's life in danger. In *Re M (Adoption: Rights of Natural Father)*[1], Bodey J also recognised as an exceptional case the situation of a violent father. In that case he was doubtful that the father had done enough to establish at all 'family life' with the child. It was therefore uncertain whether Article 8 rights were engaged and would have to be balanced. But, even if this was the case, he held on the facts that any such interference with the rights of the father would be justified by the proper and legitimate aim of protecting the physical and emotional welfare of the mother and child and the protection of the child's right to family life.

In *Re H; Re G (Adoption: Consultation of Unmarried Fathers)*[2] the Court of Appeal reached different conclusions in the two cases in a consolidated appeal. In each case the respective mothers had placed their children for adoption with the local authorities concerned on the understanding that their confidentiality would be respected. Neither mother was put under pressure to disclose the identity of the father and in neither case had the father acquired parental responsibility but, beyond that, the circumstances were quite different. In the first case there had been cohabitation between the mother and father and indeed they had an elder child together. Nonetheless the pregnancy had been concealed from the father and his family. The mother was concerned that information about the adoption might damage the relationship which she had built up with the father. The local authority sought guidance on whether the father should be joined as respondent and the court held that steps should be taken to identify and consult him. Here there had been cohabitation for several years and a continuing commitment by the father to the elder child. There could therefore be a breach of his Article 8 rights if the child were to be placed for adoption without giving the father notice of this and an opportunity to be heard. In contrast, in the second case the mother and father had never cohabited. They had been engaged at one point but the relationship had broken down and they had lost touch. The mother did not want the father, who was from another country but training for a profession in the UK, to be identified and she did not want her family to know of the birth. In this case, the court confirmed in the inherent jurisdiction that it was lawful for the local authority to place the child for adoption without consulting the natural father. They had not cohabited and their relationship did not show the constancy which was necessary to establish de facto family ties. Hence 'family life' for the purposes of Article 8 had not been shown to exist between the father and the child.

This is one aspect of adoption law, among others, which will continue to give rise to challenges based on human rights arguments. The desire of the courts to exclude from participation in adoption proceedings the man who represents a danger to the mother and the child is understandable enough and consistent with the general approach taken to the refusal of contact. The decisions in the other category of case, in which the father has been unable to establish a relationship with the child because his own relationship with the mother broke down before the child was born, are much more difficult to justify in terms of human rights. It

---

1   [2001] 1 FLR 745.
2   [2001] 1 FLR 646. See also *Re R (Adoption: Father's Involvement)* [2001] 1 FLR 302.

may very well be that the decision to break the relationship in at least some of these cases was the mother's, and that the father, if informed, might have indicated a strong desire to be involved with the child from the start. The view that family life is not established between the father and child in such circumstances is questionable because whether or not the connection is established will depend on whether the mother wants it to be. It is difficult to see how such a decision by her does not amount to a challenge to the human rights of both the father and the child.

Dispensing with consent

The question of dispensing with consent has been at the heart of the conflict which can arise between the professional view of the best interests of the child and the fundamental rights which attach to the relationship of parent and child. While parents might understand that they are unable to look after a child themselves and might be prepared to have the child looked after by others, they might not be willing to accept the complete termination of their legal relationship with the child. Traditionally English law has viewed this as a question which involves the rights of parents and has made provision, through the statutory consent requirements, for the proper accommodation of those rights. Put another way, the approach under previous legislation has been to deny that the welfare of the child should be the sole criterion for determining whether or not an adoption should be granted. This was reinforced by the requirement that consent be either given by the parent or dispensed with on one of the grounds set out in the legislation. The major change brought about by the new legislation is that the welfare of the child has, controversially, been placed centre stage – both by its application throughout the new law and, more specifically, by making it one of only two conditions for dispensing with parental consent and, of these two, by far the more significant. This has led to quite legitimate speculation about what has happened to the rights of parents in the adoption process and is likely to lead to challenges under the ECHR in the coming years.

Before analysing the new grounds for dispensing with parental consent under the Adoption and Children Act 2002, it is necessary to examine the background and the basis for dispensing with consent under the old law.

Dispensing with consent under the Adoption Act 1976

The Adoption Act 1976[1] set out a series of alternative grounds for dispensing with consent, most, but not all, of which focused on parental culpability such as abandonment or neglect of the child, persistent ill-treatment, and so on. But the most significant ground by far numerically was that the parent was withholding agreement unreasonably. This ground, as interpreted by the House of Lords in *Re*

---

1 Adoption Act 1976, s 16(2) provided that the court could dispense with parental agreement (the 1976 Act referred to 'agreement' rather than 'consent') on the grounds that the parent or guardian:
   '(a) cannot be found or is incapable of giving agreement;
   (b) is withholding his agreement unreasonably;
   (c) has persistently failed without reasonable cause to discharge his parental responsibility for the child;
   (d) has abandoned or neglected the child;
   (e) has persistently ill-treated the child;
   (f) has seriously ill-treated the child.'

W (An Infant)[1], did *not* require proof of parental culpability. It was further held that the welfare of the child was a most important element in applying the criterion of reasonableness since a reasonable parent has regard to his or child's welfare. Thus it was that the professional assessment of the child's welfare became accepted as an essential aspect of determining whether or not parental objection to adoption should be overridden by the court. On the other hand, the higher courts continued to vacillate and to disagree over exactly how much weight should be attached to the welfare of the child and how much to the wishes of the parent. There was no argument, however, that it still had to be shown that the parent was unreasonable in the sense that he or she was acting outside the band of reasonable decisions. In other words, the fact that *one* parent might consent to adoption in the circumstances did not lead to the automatic conclusion that it was unreasonable for *the parent in question* to withhold consent.

The tendency after the landmark decision of *Re W* was for the courts to attach more significance to the child's welfare, and thus to dispense with consent more easily, so that it began to be questioned how much practical difference there really was between the approach set out in *Re W* and straightforwardly applying the welfare principle. Nevertheless, there continued to be reported examples of the courts refusing to dispense with parental consent, and judicial disagreement about the proper weight to be attached to the child's welfare vis-à-vis parental claims. Some courts appeared to be taking a more parent-centred approach. Notably, in *Re C (A Minor) (Adoption: Parental Agreement: Contact)*[2] Balcombe LJ expressed the view that the drift towards attaching greater weight to the child's welfare had meant that insufficient weight was being given to the parent's lack of agreement. Neither was it the case, he thought, that because a child had to remain in long-term substitute care, the parent's relationship with that child should be irrevocably terminated. That, in his view, had a flavour of 'social engineering' about it. On the other hand, Steyn and Hoffmann LJJ, in the same case, had taken a more overtly welfare-orientated approach which focused more closely on whether the advantages of adoption from this point of view justified overriding the views and interests of the objecting parent.

These divisions of opinion among the judiciary continued unabated right up to the implementation of the HRA 1998 which, as we shall see, has added a further dimension to the whole question. In late 1997 the Court of Appeal again appeared divided in *Re M (Adoption or Residence Order)*[3]. Here two Oxford academics had expected to adopt the child of an unmarried mother. The girl was nine years old when placed with them and almost 12 by the date of the eventual hearing. As such her views were given considerable weight. The initial expectation on all sides had been for adoption and not just long-term fostering, but both the mother and the child later changed their minds and the local authority, which had originally supported the adoption plan, also withdrew its support for it. The peculiarity of the case was that, despite the strong professional view that a residence order in favour of the foster-carers was the preferred option, the adoption applicants were adamant that they would only continue to care for the child at all if allowed to adopt her. The child was visiting her mother about four times per year and the

---

1   [1971] AC 682.
2   [1993] 2 FLR 260.
3   [1998] 1 FLR 570.

applicants felt insecure about the situation. The judge had granted the adoption order and dispensed with the mother's consent. The Court of Appeal, however, allowed the appeal and substituted a residence order together with a s 91(14) order prohibiting the mother from making further applications without the leave of the court. But the majority in the Court of Appeal (Ward and Judge LJJ) held that the judge had erred in attaching too much significance to the single question of where it was in the best interests of the child to live. The issue of adoption as a change of status had not been adequately addressed, nor whether some other order would adequately safeguard the child's welfare. Accordingly, it could not be said that the mother's consent had been unreasonably withheld. The attitude of the applicants and its implications were relevant in assessing the reasonableness of the mother's refusal since their inflexibility and insecurity raised doubts about the extent to which they would preserve the link between the mother and the child. Simon Brown LJ, however, dissented on the basis of the child's welfare and whether the advantages of adoption, from that point of view, were sufficiently strong to justify overriding the mother's objections.

Re M is an important case because it highlights the need to consider all the alternatives to adoption, something required by the ECHR and the Adoption and Children Act 2002[1]. Meanwhile, several other decisions went the other way and appeared to dispense with the parent's consent almost entirely on the basis of the court's assessment of the child's welfare needs. Such a case was *Re O (Adoption: Withholding Agreement)*[2] which concerned an unmarried father who had had no contact with the child since birth for reasons beyond his control. He had not been informed of the child's existence and, as soon as he became aware of it, he showed a consistent interest in being involved. He was given a parental responsibility order to enable him to participate in the adoption proceedings. The child had, however, been fostered since two months old with devoted foster-parents who were the prospective adopters. The Court of Appeal held here that the judge had been right to conclude that the child's welfare was better safeguarded by an adoption order than by a residence order. Despite the fact that the father could be described as 'blameless' he could nonetheless be said to be withholding agreement unreasonably. The judge had applied the correct test of what a reasonable parent would have done in all the circumstances bearing in mind that a reasonable parent would put the child's welfare first. Adoption was justified in order to provide security for the family arrangement.

This was the situation immediately before implementation of the HRA 1998, with most courts attaching decisive importance to the child's welfare but with some notable examples of a more 'parent-centred' rights-based approach to the question which would attach significance to alternatives for permanence and would be reluctant to find that a parent was unreasonable if such alternatives existed. It was not very long before the question was again before the courts, but this time human rights arguments had to be more directly addressed.

---

1 Moreover, as recently as July 2003, Black J in *Re F (Adoption: Welfare of Child: Financial Considerations)* [2004] 1 FLR 440 reiterated the principle that where there were two opposing reasonable views on the question of adoption, and the parent holds one of them, it could not be said that she was unreasonably withholding her consent.

2 [1999] 1 FLR 451. See also *Re B (Adoption: Father's Objections)* [1999] 2 FLR 215, *Re A (Adoption: Mother's Objections)* [2000] 1 FLR 665 and *Re M (Care Order: Freeing Application)* [2004] 1 FLR 826.

The impact of human rights

As has already been noted many times, the approach under the ECHR requires that for adoption to be justified, and for the interference with Article 8 rights which undoubtedly occurs, it must be a necessary and proportionate response to the child's situation. Put simply, if another alternative will equally well serve the child's interests, adoption would be an unnecessary and disproportionate response and would violate both the Convention rights of the child and those of the parent.

In *Re B (Adoption Order)*[1] the child was in a happy foster placement, having been placed there by his mother, but continued to have a good relationship with his father and his father's family. The father applied for a residence order but the family proceedings court instead made a residence order in favour of the foster-mother buttressed by a s 91(14) order[2]. The father was to be allowed generous contact and was given a parental responsibility order. Everyone was happy with this outcome except the local authority, which encouraged the foster-mother to apply for adoption. The judge granted the adoption order but the Court of Appeal allowed the father's appeal on the basis that the arrangement which had been agreed on all sides was fundamentally inconsistent with an adoption order. The judge had not sufficiently considered whether the interference with the father's right to respect for his family life with the child, which would result from adoption, was a necessary and proportionate response under Article 8(2) given that a completely satisfactory arrangement had already been achieved without an adoption order. The judicial licence to override the sustained objection of a natural parent would be stretched to unjustifiable limits if the father's objections were set aside where adoption was reasonably opposed, not only by the father but by the child's guardian and by a distinguished psychiatrist instructed by him, even though supported by the social worker in the case. Where there were two opposing reasonable views and the parent held one of them, it could not be said that the parent was withholding consent unreasonably.

This was a decision appearing just before the Adoption and Children Act 2002 and which cannot without some imagination be thought consistent with a pure application of the welfare principle to the question of parental consent. It raises serious questions about whether the new legislation, at least on this issue, will be able to withstand challenge under the HRA 1998.

Dispensing with consent under the Adoption and Children Act 2002

The Adoption and Children Act 2002 catapults the welfare principle into the middle of this hugely problematic question. It abolishes all the previous grounds for dispensing with parental consent except for one and replaces them with the undiluted welfare principle which applies elsewhere in the Act.

The all-important provision is now s 52(1), which provides:

> 'The court cannot dispense with the consent of any parent or guardian of a child to the child being placed for adoption or to the making of an adoption order in respect of the child unless the court is satisfied that –
>
> (a) the parent or guardian cannot be found or is incapable of giving consent, or
> (b) the welfare of the child requires the consent to be dispensed with.'

---

1 [2001] 2 FLR 26.
2 Section 91(14) orders are discussed at p 169 above.

Condition (a) is the one ground for dispensing with consent which has been preserved from the old law. It was not much used and is unlikely to be used very often under the new law, but there was a fairly recently reported case involving the use of this ground. In *Re A (Adoption of a Russian Child)*[1] the mother was in Russia and had agreed to the adoption in Russia within six weeks of the child's birth. Her consent was insufficient for the English adoption of the child but the Russian authorities would not co-operate in locating her to obtain her consent to this. The court held in these circumstances that the phrase 'cannot be found' meant that all practicable means must have been employed and all reasonable steps taken to find and communicate with the parent. Charles J was in the circumstances prepared to dispense with her consent on the basis that she could not be found.

Condition (b) will now become the major ground for dispensing with parental consent and will apply in all but a small number of cases. It replaces the former ground of parental unreasonableness which has been swept away by the Act. In one respect it is bound to lead to a change of approach. Under the Adoption Act 1976, there were two distinct stages in the court's decision-making process. At the first stage the court would consider whether adoption would be in the best interests of the child. If this question was answered in the negative then, of course, that would be the end of the matter and the court would opt for some other alternative. But if the court decided that adoption would be in the child's best interests, it would then move to the separate stage of considering whether parental consent should be dispensed with on one of the statutory grounds[2]. Yet, under the new law, it will be the welfare principle which will govern the question of dispensing with consent. It may therefore be that one effect of the move to a welfare test will be to put an end to this two-stage procedure and that the court will face the single question of whether adoption would be in the child's best interests. If it would then, almost by definition, the test for dispensing with consent is satisfied.

This does raise the serious question of what weight, if any, is to be given to parental interests or rights in preserving their legal relationship with the child. What is clear is that if the court's view is that adoption is in the child's best interests, then whether or not the parent is behaving reasonably in objecting to this will have no bearing on the decision. If parental claims are to be fed into this process at all, then it is going to have to happen as an integral part of applying the welfare test as in other contexts in which the welfare principle applies.

It has been argued by Bridge and Swindells that 'some weighting is given to parental rights' by the requirement that the court take into account two of the factors in the checklist[3]. These are factor (c), which refers to 'the likely effect on the child (throughout his life) of having ceased to be a member of the original family and become an adopted person', and factor (f), which refers to 'the relationship which the child has with relatives' and other relevant persons. As noted above, this factor also requires the court to have regard to the likelihood of those relationships continuing and their value to the child, the ability of relatives and others to meet the child's needs and their wishes and feelings. They go on to

---

1 [2000] 1 FLR 539.
2 The two issues could, however, be heard together. See *Re K (A Minor) (Adoption: Procedure)* [1986] 1 FLR 295.
3 C Bridge and H Swindells QC *Adoption: The Modern Law* (Family Law, 2003) at para 8.43.

argue that the wording of the welfare test in s 52 may represent an additional safeguard for parents in that it must be established that the welfare of the child *requires* consent to be dispensed with, as opposed to merely pointing in the direction of adoption, but they conclude that although 'these factors do go some way in giving parents a voice, they are in reality a pale substitute for the more full-blooded protection historically afforded by English law to the parents' rights and interests. Under the former law, notwithstanding the prominence of the child's welfare, the parental decision (provided it fell within a reasonable band of decisions) could be effective as a veto'[1].

The most tantalising question is going to be whether this approach, which attempts to subsume parental rights and interests in a general welfare test, will be sufficient to be compatible with the requirements of Article 8 of the ECHR. This is a point which has already been made regarding the application of the welfare principle in other contexts. But it is particularly acute in relation to adoption because so much is at stake for parents in the adoption decision. The real question, it is submitted, is whether it can demonstrably be shown that *only* adoption, as opposed to other alternative mechanisms, can meet the welfare needs of the child. If the answer to that question is 'no' then adoption ought not to be granted and care should certainly be taken in viewing adoption as an option of preference – certainly in the context of children in long-term care. The Court of Appeal in *Re B (Adoption Order)* hit the nail on the head as far as this was concerned and the decision should serve as a model for applying the new law in a way which respects Convention rights. The real safeguard for parents under the ECHR is the burden which those arguing for adoption will have to discharge when there are available solutions which would preserve the child's legal relationship with those parents and the wider family. We conclude this chapter by commenting briefly on those other options.

THE LEGAL EFFECTS OF ADOPTION

General effects

Adoption fundamentally affects the legal *status* of the child. The Adoption and Children Act 2002 provides that 'an adopted person is to be treated in law as the child of the adopters or adopter'[2]. He or she will also be the 'legitimate' child of the adopter or adopters and, if adopted by a couple or one of a couple under s 51(2), is to be treated as the child of the relationship of the couple in question[3]. The child is then *not* to be treated in law as the child of anyone else except where legislation refers to a person's 'natural parent' or to any other 'natural relationship'[4]. Relationships which are created by adoption may be referred to as 'adoptive relationships'[5], an adopter may be referred to as 'an adoptive parent' or (as the case may be) an 'adoptive father or mother' and other relatives following adoption may be referred to as 'adoptive relatives' of the relevant degree, for

1 C Bridge and H Swindells QC (above) at paras 8.44–8.45.
2 Section 67(1).
3 Section 67(2).
4 Section 67(3).
5 Section 68.

example brother or aunt. Where, however, the adoption has occurred in the context of a same sex relationship the expressions 'adoptive father' and 'adoptive mother' are not thought apposite and instead any reference in that case will instead be to the child's 'adoptive parents'[1]. An adoption order will also operate to extinguish the parental responsibility which anyone other than the adopter or adopters had for the child immediately preceding the making of the order[2]. It will also terminate, as from the date of the adoption order, any maintenance duty in relation to the child whether made by agreement or under a court order[3]. There are rules which govern the interpretation of instruments concerning the disposition of property which are beyond the scope of the present work[4].

Adoption is therefore different from other court orders affecting children, for example s 8 orders under the Children Act, in that it is a legal transplant. Not only does it terminate existing parental responsibility and transfer this to the adoptive parents, it also terminates the very legal relationship of parent and child and the wider family relationships which derive from the relationship of parent and child and replaces these with new parental and family relationships. In short it replaces one legal family with another. There are certain limited exceptions to the transplant principle where the child's relationship with his or her birth parents will continue to be of relevance, the most important of which is that the child remains within the natural family for the purposes of the prohibited degrees of marriage and for the purposes of certain sexual offences within the family[5]. The reasoning here is that the rationale for these prohibitions is largely the perceived genetic objections to intermarriage and sexual relations between close blood relatives. So far as the former is concerned, it should be noted that marriage is prohibited also between the adopted child and his or her adoptive parent but marriage with other adoptive relatives is permitted[6]. So far as the latter is concerned, the principal offence has been incest in its various forms. It should be noted, however, that the Sexual Offences Act 2003 abolishes incest and replaces this offence with new sexual offences which reflect the changing nature of modern families and which take greater account of the need to prevent sexual coercion within the context of adoptive relationships[7]. These new offences do shift the focus somewhat from the genetic concerns of the past – though these still exist – towards the problem of abuse of power in familial relationships. That being the case, the protection afforded to an adoptive person may need to be as strong as that afforded to a natural relative in certain cases.

---

1 Section 68(3).
2 Section 46(2)(a).
3 Section 46(2)(d).
4 Sections 69–73. For a discussion of these rules, see Bridge and Swindells (above) at paras 10.85–10.88.
5 Section 74 which states that s 67 does not apply to a number of enactments including the table of kindred and affinity in Sch 1 to the Marriage Act 1949, ss 10 and 11 of the Sexual Offences Act 1956 (incest), and s 54 of the Criminal Justice Act 1977 (inciting a girl to commit incest). Neither does s 67 apply for the purposes of the British Nationality Act 1981 or the Immigration Act 1971.
6 Marriage Act 1949, Sch 1, as amended.
7 Sexual Offences Act 2003, as to which see Chapter 14 below.

Open adoption?

The Adoption Review recognised the argument for a system which would allow more 'open' adoption while preserving secrecy and confidentiality in those cases in which this was thought appropriate[1]. It was concerned that adoption law and procedure assumed 'a closed model of adoption where this was not always the case, nor always appropriate'. Accordingly it made a cluster of recommendations to promote openness at different stages of the adoption process. These included the proposal that the child should have a statutory right to know that he or she is adopted; that the courts should continue to have power to make a contact order in conjunction with an adoption order[2]; that birth parents' wishes and feelings about such matters as race, religion, language and culture should be taken into account more than had been the case in the past[3]; and that adoption agencies should have power to be proactive in contacting adopted adults and birth relatives to ask whether they would agree to identifying information being passed on to each other[4].

Some thought that the new adoption legislation when it came would signal a clear push towards open adoption as an official policy. It is clear, however, that the Adoption and Children Act 2002 does not embody any clear directives as far as this is concerned. The messages are mixed at best and any policy favouring a more open system of adoption, insofar as it may exist, is implicit rather than explicit. In terms of the provision of identifying information, there is much in the Act which does appear to support greater openness. But this needs to be set against the absence of any express statutory encouragement of post-adoption contact, although the power to make contact orders is preserved. More significantly, perhaps, the effective removal of the parental veto to adoption noted above and the official policy of driving up the adoption figures in relation to children in long-term care will be seen by some as less than unequivocal support for the preservation of the child's links with the birth family.

We focus here on two aspects of the open adoption question: post-adoption contact and the issue of identity.

Adoption and contact

The whole question of contact with parents and other birth relatives in the context of adoption has long been a controversial one and it is fair to say that it continues to be an issue which provokes significant disagreement and, for that reason, some uncertainty in the attitude which the law is taking to the question[5]. We consider elsewhere the particular contact regimes which apply in the private law[6], where

---

1   Adoption Review, para 4.2.
2   Ibid, para 5.5.
3   Ibid, para 28.2.
4   Ibid, para 31.7.
5   On the question of post-adoption contact, see J Eekelaar (fn 1 at p 261 above); C Bridge 'Adoption and Contact: The Value of Openness' [1994] JCL 147; Casey and Gibberd 'Adoption and Contact' [2000] Fam Law 39; J Masson 'Thinking about contact – A social or legal problem' [2000] CFLQ 15; and C Smith and J Logan 'Adoptive parenthood as a "legal fiction" – its consequences for direct post-adoption contact' [2002] CFLQ 281.
6   See Chapter 4 above.

the child is in care[1] and under the placement regime[2]. What we are now concerned with is the question of *post-adoption contact* although clearly this issue should be considered alongside the principles which govern contact more generally in those other contexts.

The traditional view of English adoption law was that it was contrary to the very nature of adoption, which severs irrevocably the tie between the natural family and the child, that there should be continuing contact between the child and the birth family. This was the view which largely prevailed in the courts before the passing of the Children Act 1989. Some relaxation in this position was evidenced by the House of Lords decision in *Re C (A Minor) (Adoption Order: Conditions)*[3]. Here it was held that there was power under the adoption legislation, in appropriate circumstances, to attach conditions to an adoption order and one of those conditions could be designed to preserve contact between the child and the child's siblings. A feature of this decision was, however, that all parties were in agreement and this was to become an important factor, perhaps even the decisive factor, in later cases which considered post-adoption contact.

Under the Children Act 1989 adoption proceedings fall within the definition of 'family proceedings', and the courts have therefore had jurisdiction to make a s 8 contact order when making an adoption order. So far as the underlying policy is concerned, the question of post-adoption contact came to be seen as an important, but by no means the only, aspect of the emerging notion of 'open adoption'. This was rapidly taking the place of the previous closed model of adoption in which secrecy and confidentiality at all stages of the process were the hallmark. It would no longer necessarily be assumed that contact with the birth family was incompatible with the nature of an adoption order. Cases then began to be reported in which such orders were made, but they were characterised by a high level of co-operation between the birth parents and the adoptive parents. In that event, it was recognised that there could be benefits to the child in preserving contact, albeit much more limited contact than the kind associated, for example, with divorce, but it remained open to doubt whether the courts would ever *impose* a contact order against the wishes of adoptive parents.

Thus, in *Re T (Adoption: Contact)*[4] the Court of Appeal was at pains to emphasise, in a case in which adoptive parents had agreed to allow the natural mother some contact, that the mother's security resided in the trust she had in the adopters and not in any court order. The onus should not therefore be on the adoptive parents to go to court in the event of disagreement over contact but should be on the mother who could go back to court with leave. On the other hand, once there has been agreement for some contact, the courts might expect the adoptive parents to adhere to that agreement. Thus, in *Re T (Adopted Children: Contact)*[5] the adoptive parents had resiled from an undertaking to provide annual reports to the adopted child's half-siblings via social services. The Court of Appeal allowed the half-sister's appeal against refusal to grant her leave to seek a contact order. The court took the view that if adoptive parents changed their minds about an informal

---

1 See Chapter 11 below.
2 See p 284.
3 [1988] 2 FLR 259.
4 [1995] 2 FLR 251.
5 [1995] 2 FLR 792.

agreement for contact they ought to give reasons for doing so and that their decision was open to challenge in the courts.

The Adoption and Children Act 2002 is largely silent on the question of post-adoption contact. By no stretch of the imagination can this be said to have been trumpeted either in the White Paper or in the Act itself. About the closest the White Paper came to mentioning it is a reference in two paragraphs to 'Links with the Birth Family'. The first of these paragraphs is concerned with supporting birth families and keeping them fully informed through the adoption process[1]. The second refers to a statement in the then draft Adoption Standards that 'a child's needs to maintain links to their birth family including parents, grandparents, brothers, sisters and other significant people should always be considered'[2]. This is scarcely a ringing endorsement of either open adoption generally or post-adoption contact more particularly. In the light of this it is not perhaps surprising that the power to make post-adoption contact orders is tucked away in a fairly obscure subsection of the Act.

Section 46(6) provides that 'before making an adoption order, the court must consider whether there should be arrangements for allowing any person contact with the child; and for that purpose the court must consider any existing or proposed arrangements and obtain any views of the parties to the proceedings'. There is therefore a statutory *duty* to address the question of contact and to have regard to any existing contact arrangements. In addition, as we have seen, the statutory checklist of factors requires the court to consider the child's existing relationships, the likelihood of their continuing and the value in their doing so. Moreover, it is expressly provided that there is a right, as at present, to apply for a s 8 contact order to be heard together with the application for the adoption order[3]. Yet none of this adds up to *encouragement* of post-adoption contact and there is no implication that, for example, all other things being equal, continuing contact with birth relatives is a good thing which is receiving official approval. This would have been possible, just as the Family Law Act 1996 incorporated a set of principles emphasising Parliament's expectation that contact with both parents should continue post-divorce[4]. Post-adoption contact receives no such official imprimatur.

How consistent this is with human rights obligations is as questionable as are the provisions which facilitate dispensing with parental consent. Will it be a proportionate and necessary response to the child's situation to terminate, or at least not provide for, ongoing contact between the child and members of the birth family? Much will, of course, depend on the particular circumstances of the case, but it is not difficult to predict that this is another issue which is bound to provoke challenges under the HRA 1998 and the ECHR. Bridge and Swindells offer the rather damning assessment that the Act 'does appear to be giving out the signal that the traditional approach of the clean break under the controlling hands of the adoptive parents is intended to stay' and that 'the suspicion is that the Government's "target" approach to adoption ... may have weakened any earlier resolve to change the climate of the closed adoption to a more open approach in

---

1   White Paper, para 6.42.
2   Ibid, para 6.43.
3   Section 26(5).
4   Family Law Act 1996, s 1(c), and see Chapter 4 above.

the interests of the older child'[1]. It is difficult to disagree with this evaluation and it remains to be seen whether it is an approach which will withstand challenge under the Convention.

The issue of identity

As we have seen, the child's identity rights are asserted by Articles 7 and 8 of the UNCRC[2]. Article 8 in particular is concerned with *preservation* of the child's identity 'including nationality, name and family relations'. This issue of identity has surfaced in a number of different contexts including, for example, disputes over paternity and, as we have just seen, the question of post-adoption contact. It also arises where a child was conceived by donated gametes and the issue is whether the child has any right to information concerning the gamete donor who is, of course, the genetic parent[3]. Where the child is adopted, similar concerns arise about the extent to which the adopted person may have access to hitherto confidential information relating to the birth family which was obtained during the adoption process. The issue also arises as to whether members of the birth family should also be able to have access to information about the adopted person. These questions now have to be addressed bearing in mind the identity rights which are internationally protected.

Adoption self-evidently threatens identity rights because its purpose has been to terminate a person's link with one family and replace it with another. Traditionally the adoption process has been a secretive one and it has been usual to preserve the anonymity of adoptive parents and often to shield the child from knowledge about, or contact with, the natural family. Adoption proceedings are heard in private and adoption applicants have been able to apply for a serial number so that birth parents are prevented from discovering their identity[4]. Information collected during the adoption process is confidential and designed to prevent anyone from linking the child's identity before and after adoption. Gradually this view of adoption gave way to recognition, acknowledged in the Adoption Review, that 'a child's knowledge of his or her background is crucial to the formation of positive self-identity, and that adoptive families should be encouraged to be open about the child's adoptive status and the special nature of the adoptive relationship'[5]. It has also begun to be appreciated more that there are serious medical issues about information relating to the birth family where, for example, there is a risk of hereditary disease.

Legislation began incrementally to make greater provision for openness in adoption. Following the recommendations of the Houghton Committee, the Children Act 1975 (quickly consolidated in the Adoption Act 1976) enabled an

---

1 Bridge and Swindells (above) at para 11.18.
2 Chapter 2 above. For recent discussions of the child's right to know genetic origins, see T Callus 'Tempered Hope – A Qualified Right to Know One's Genetic Origins' (2004) 67 MLR 658, and J Wallbank 'The Role of Rights and Utility in Instituting a Child's Right to Know Her Genetic History' (2004) 13 *Social and Legal Studies* 245.
3 As to which see S Maclean and M Maclean 'Keeping Secrets in Assisted Reproduction – the Tension between Donor Anonymity and the Need of the Child for Information' [1996] CFLQ 243, and J Feast and G Brasse 'Embryological Secrecy Syndrome' [2000] Fam Law 897.
4 The details of adoption procedures are beyond the scope of the present work but are discussed in C Bridge and H Swindells (above) at pp 256 et seq.
5 Adoption Review, para 4.1.

adopted person over the age of 18 years for the first time to obtain a copy of his or her original birth certificate[1]. The Children Act 1989 then took the process of disclosure a stage further by establishing an adoption contact register, the purpose of which was to enable adopted persons to discover whether attempts to contact relatives would be welcome and, where this was the case, to provide them with factual information which might enable them to do so[2].

The Adoption and Children Act 2002 builds on these earlier legislative initiatives by placing the primary responsibility for the collection and disclosure of confidential information on adoption agencies, but it also makes provision for restricting disclosure in circumstances which are not thought to be appropriate[3]. The statutory scheme is complex and the details are beyond the scope of the present work[4]. What follows is a description of the salient features relating to disclosure of information under the 2002 Act. The Act distinguishes between adoptions which take place before and after implementation of the Act, but the following discussion is confined to the scheme which will apply in relation to adoptions which take place under the 2002 Act.

The Registers

The Adopted Children Register
The Registrar-General must continue to maintain at the General Register Office a register of adopted children together with an index[5]. The Register is *not* open to public inspection but any person may search the index and have a certified copy of any entry made in the Register[6]. The Act places a duty on the Registrar-General to make necessary connections between the register of live births under the Births and Deaths Registration Act 1953 and other records in which the person concerned has been marked 'Adopted' and the Adopted Children Register[7]. In other words, the legislation requires the preservation of connecting information which makes traceable the link between birth records and the later adoption of a child. One of the most important reasons for these statutory duties is to enable an adopted adult to obtain access to his or her original birth certificate. The means of access has, however, changed under the new legislation. When exercising this right under the Adoption Act 1976, the adopted person applied directly to the Registrar-General[8]. Now, under the 2002 Act, adoption agencies are usually to be the gateway for all confidential information held by the Registrar-General, the court involved in the adoption or the agency itself. Accordingly, the application for access to the original birth certificate will now be made to the adoption agency, and the Registrar-General is obliged to give the necessary connecting information to an adoption agency in relation to any person whose birth record is kept by the

---

1 Adoption Act 1976, s 51(1).
2 Ibid, s 51A, as inserted by Sch 10, para 21 to the Children Act 1989. See also *The Children Act 1989 Guidance and Regulations Vol 9 Adoption* (HMSO, 1991) at ch 3.
3 The principal provisions are ss 56–65 and ss 77–79, but much of the detail is to be consigned to regulations.
4 For a more detailed discussion, see Bridge and Swindells (above) at ch 12.
5 Sections 77(1) and 78(1).
6 Section 78(2).
7 Section 79(1).
8 Adoption Act 1976, s 51(1).

Registrar-General[1]. Provision is made for informing the applicant about the availability of counselling before taking this step[2].

The statutory 'right' to obtain access to the original birth certificate has never been absolute. An adopted person has, prima facie, the right to receive from the appropriate adoption agency:

(a) any information which would enable him to obtain a certified copy of the record of his birth, and

(b) any prescribed information disclosed to the adopters by the agency[3].

This is subject to any order to the contrary made by the High Court on application to the court by the adoption agency[4]. Such an order may be made by the High Court if it is satisfied that the circumstances are exceptional[5]. An illustration of what is likely to amount to exceptional circumstances occurred under the old law in the remarkable case of *R v Registrar General, ex parte Smith*[6]. Here the Court of Appeal upheld the decision of the Registrar-General to refuse access to a Broadmoor patient who had killed his cellmate in Wormwood Scrubs in the mistaken belief that he was killing his adoptive mother. The court held that access to his original birth certificate could be refused on the grounds of public policy if there was evidence to suggest that the applicant might use the information to harm his natural mother.

A number of limitations to this process of disclosing birth records should be noted.

First, the legislation confers no statutory right to be told that one is adopted, despite recommendations in the Adoption Review that there should be such a right. Clearly, it remains possible that an adopted person may go through life in ignorance of the fact that he or she is not the natural child of his or her parents. The problem is even more acute for children conceived by donated gametes who are statistically much less likely to be informed of the true position than are adopted children. It has been good practice in adoption for some time for children to be told of their adoptive status, and the expectation is that the overwhelming majority of adopted children will be told and will thus be able to take advantage as adults of the above tracing procedures. This does, of course, still leave the unanswered question of whether these 'rights' to knowledge of origins should be postponed until adulthood, and what rights, if any, children should have to information *as children* while they grow up. Clearly this issue lies at the heart of the debates about when it is appropriate for courts to direct tests in paternity disputes, whether there should be immediate post-adoption contact, and so on. The short point is that, if there is a right to knowledge of origins, there is a serious question about when that right should bite. And of course it is all too obvious that relationships which might have been encouraged and nurtured *during childhood* will be likely to be that much more difficult, if not impossible, to re-establish in adulthood.

1　Adoption and Children Act 2002, s 79(5).
2　Section 63.
3　Section 60(2).
4　Ibid.
5　Section 60(3).
6　[1991] 2 QB 393.

Secondly, there is a limited right for those under the age of 18 but of an age at which they have the capacity to marry, that is 16 and 17, to be given information about whether or not it appears from the information contained in the relevant birth records that the applicant and the intended spouse may be within the prohibited degrees of relationship[1]. Similar rights are conferred on those conceived by donated gametes under the Human Fertilisation and Embryology Act 1990[2].

Thirdly, these rights of access do not extend to a birth parent wishing to obtain the converse information about the adoption of their natural child. In *D v Registrar General*[3], a mother was seeking to trace her daughter. The Court of Appeal held that only in truly exceptional circumstances would confidential information held by the Registrar-General be ordered to be given to a birth parent. On the other hand, natural relatives, although lacking a statutory right to connecting information, may in some cases be contacted by adopted persons under the scheme in the Adoption Contact Register and may also be able in appropriate circumstances to obtain confidential information from the relevant adoption agency. Thus, in *Gunn-Russo v Nugent Care Society and Secretary of State for Health*[4] there was a successful application for judicial review of an adoption agency's refusal to disclose confidential information in the adoption file it was holding on the applicant. Here the passage of time was an important factor. The claimant had been adopted as long ago as 1948, had managed to trace her natural parents, her adoptive parents were now dead and more than half a century had passed since the adoption. In these circumstances the court's view was that the agency's policy of non-disclosure was too inflexible.

The Adoption Contact Register

As noted above, this was an innovation of the Children Act 1989. The Adoption and Children Act 2002 requires the Registrar-General to continue to maintain this register[5]. The register is in two parts. Part I contains the names and addresses of adopted persons over 18 years of age who have obtained the copies of their birth certificates and who may wish to contact a relative[6]. Part II contains details of the name and present address of any relative who would like to contact an adopted person[7]. 'Relative' for these purposes includes, in relation to an adopted person, 'any person who (but for his adoption) would be related to him by blood (including half-blood) or marriage'[8]. Regulations will govern the disclosure of information where there is a 'match' on the register, and information must not be disclosed except in accordance with these regulations[9]. These provisions therefore go further than mere disclosure of the original birth certificate since they are designed to enable adopted persons and birth relatives to be given

---

1   Section 79(7).
2   Human Fertilisation and Embryology Act 1990, s 31.
3   [1997] 1 FLR 715.
4   [2002] 1 FLR 1.
5   Section 80(1).
6   Section 80(2).
7   Section 80(4).
8   Section 81(2).
9   Sections 80(6) and 81(3).

sufficient information to enable them to make contact with one another where they both want this.

Under the old law the adopted person, but not the relative, might be given the requisite information[1]. Thus, it was for the adopted person to decide whether or not to seek contact. Regulations made under the Act are expected to endorse this approach. The Adoption Review recommended and the Draft Adoption Bill of 1976 provided that adopted persons and relatives should be able to register their wish *not* to be contacted where that is the case[2]. The Adoption Act 1976 had provided only for those who positively wanted to make contact, although there was provision for cancellation of an entry in the register where the relevant person gave the appropriate notice[3]. The Review recognised that it might be deeply disappointing for the adopted person but it was also acknowledged that some birth mothers have suffered grave distress when traced by adopted children, or at the prospect of such an approach being made. While there is no express provision in the Act for registering a desire not to be contacted, the wording, it is submitted, is wide enough to include this situation. The Act talks of adopted persons and relatives 'expressing their wishes *as to* making contact'[4] and not their wishes *for* making contact.

Disclosure of information relating to a person's adoption

The Adoption and Children Act 2002 contains a cluster of provisions in ss 56–65 which regulate, in much greater depth than has been the case under previous legislation, the provision of, or refusal to provide, information relating to a person's adoption. There is a great deal of detail in the Act about this but what follows is no more than a description of some of the salient features of the statutory scheme[5].

Information about the adoption of a person and the various parties involved is held in three separate places – by the Registrar-General, by the court which granted the adoption and by the adoption agency. The policy of the Act is to make the adoption agency in future the principal 'gateway' for access to information from these three sources[6]. The policy has been influenced by human rights concerns about privacy, data protection considerations and by the awareness that the adoption agency is best placed to have access to the detailed information about the adoption which goes beyond some of the basic information held by the Registrar-General or the court. The agency is equally the best place to contact those concerned and to arrange for counselling. The Act therefore introduces a scheme whereby the adoption agency will act as the intermediary for disclosure of the information from these three sources. Information is then divided into different categories which *must* or *may* be disclosed depending on the type of information and the person seeking disclosure. Broadly, these categories are as follows:

---

1 Adoption Act 1976, s 51A(9).
2 Adoption Review, para 31.5, and Draft Adoption Bill 1996, cl 65.
3 Adoption Act 1976, s 51A(7).
4 Section 80(2) and (4).
5 For a closer analysis of the details see Bridge and Swindells (above) at paras 12.31–12.64.
6 White Paper, paras 6.44–6.46.

(a) information which an adoption agency *must* keep in relation to a person's adoption (this includes identifying information and is known as 'protected information')[1];

(b) information which an adoption agency *must* disclose to an adopted adult on request[2];

(c) information which an adoption agency *must* disclose to a prescribed person (this is information which must be released to adoptive adults and adopted persons on request and is essentially s 56 information which is *not* protected information such as background information about the child)[3];

(d) information which adoption agencies *may* disclose to any person in accordance with prescribed arrangements[4].

In all these cases much of the detail is consigned to secondary legislation.

THE PLACE OF ADOPTION IN CHILD PROTECTION AND ALTERNATIVES FOR PERMANENCE

Adoption represents for some children the best solution for long-term care but it is *only one* of the possible solutions. The Adoption and Children Act 2002 recognises this by requiring the court to consider other 'alternatives for permanence', and it is clear that such alternatives must always be explored to comply with the requirements of the ECHR. We considered the different ways in which the Act provides for these alternatives in Chapter 6. As we have seen, these include the new power of the court to extend residence orders to the age of 18; the relaxation of the residential requirement applying to local authority foster-parents, who will now be able to apply for s 8 orders where children have lived with them for *one* year rather than three years as originally required under the Children Act 1989; the provisions enabling step-parents to acquire parental responsibility by agreement with the parent or parents or by obtaining a parental responsibility order; and, above all, the introduction of the new status of special guardianship. All of these alternatives will need to be considered where appropriate.

This does not, of course, answer the question of why the Government appears to view adoption as the *preferred* option for children in long-term care. As we have seen, the Government has specifically targeted a substantial increase in the use of adoption for children in long-term care, and much of the Act is geared up to facilitating adoption. This is an emphasis which is consistent with government policy in the USA enshrined in the Adoption and Safe Families Act 1997[5]. But it is very *inconsistent* with the policies pursued in a number of major European States such as France, Sweden and the Netherlands, and inconsistent too with the

---

1   Section 56.
2   Section 60.
3   Section 58(3).
4   Section 58(2).
5   For a penetrating critique of the Act, see B Bennett Woodhouse 'The Adoption and Safe Families Act: A Major Shift in Child Welfare Law and Policy' in A Bainham (ed) *The International Survey of Family Law (2000 Edition)* (Family Law, 2000) at p 375. On adoption policy in England and Wales over three decades, see J Lewis 'Adoption: The Nature of Policy Shifts in England and Wales, 1972–2002' (2004) 18 IJLPF 235.

approach taken in Australia and New Zealand[1]. In these jurisdictions there is much greater emphasis placed on family support, reunification and the use of long-term fostering. In both France and Sweden, for example, there is a strong emphasis on keeping children with their families and avoiding taking children into care against their parents' wishes wherever possible. And, importantly, there appears to be the necessary commitment of resources by these States to achieve these objectives.

In all of these countries there is less emphasis on adoption. In the Netherlands, domestic adoption is virtually non-existent and such adoption as there is largely consists of the adoption of babies and young children from the developing world[2]. In France there is strong resistance to the adoption of children in long-term care because very great importance is attached to maintaining the legal ties with the birth family which adoption would destroy. The only children likely to be adopted in France are therefore those who might be described as genuinely orphaned or genuinely abandoned and who, consequently, do not have any such links. In both France and Sweden there is a policy of using well-paid, well-trained long-term foster-parents. The evidence from Sweden appears to be that foster-parents do not have great difficulty coming to terms with the idea of providing a home for a child without obtaining parental responsibility, nor with maintaining links with the birth family. Indeed, some of them continue to see the children who have returned home to the birth family following a long period or periods of fostering. There does not seem to be a psychological need among these foster-parents for a legal solution of 'permanence' or a legal transfer of family relationships.

In New Zealand, where the influence of Maori tradition has been felt, there is much greater emphasis placed on the resources of the child's wider or extended family as opposed to substitute care with 'strangers'. There social workers work closely with kinship networks and a 'Family Group Conference' is held for every child at risk of being taken into care to explore whether the wider family can be of assistance, most obviously by providing a home for the child where the child is thought to be unable to return to the parents. In Australia, specifically New South Wales, an attempt to legislate for adoption as the preferred option for children in long-term care was defeated in 2001, apparently for a number of reasons including the problem that adoption legally severs all ties with the birth family; that there are alternatives for achieving permanence without resorting to adoption; that the pro-adoption stance may undermine child protection efforts; and that adoption might leave adopting parents without adequate supports. Commenting on the battle in New South Wales, Patrick Parkinson[3] challenges the polarised nature of the debate surrounding adoption for children in need of protection. This emphasises *either* family support and 'partnership' *or* adoption as the preferred form of permanency planning and something to be championed in the name of children's rights. As he puts it:

---

1   For a very helpful report on the position in these countries, see A Warman and C Roberts *Adoption and Looked After Children – an International Comparison* Working Paper 2003/1, Oxford Centre for Family Law and Policy, Department of Social Policy, University of Oxford (2003).

2   On Dutch adoption policy, see C Van Nijnatten and W de Graaf 'The Legal Management of (Social) Parenthood: Adoption and Dutch family policy' (2002) 24 JSWFL 263.

3   P Parkinson 'Child Protection, Permanency Planning and Children's Right to Family Life' (2003) 17 *International Journal of Law, Policy and the Family* 147.

'the notion that children's rights can be pitted against parents' rights is altogether too simplistic. Families, even dysfunctional and abusive ones, have complex patterns of interrelatedness which make it problematic to conceive of the situation in terms of sharp lines or to conceptualize the issues in oppositional terms.'[1]

And he identifies the unusually significant role which politics and politicians have played in the pro-adoption reforms of the USA and England and the pro-adoption stance taken by politicians in New South Wales which was ultimately defeated. In his words, 'when the issue at stake is decision-making about the future of individual children, it is important that such political initiatives are scrutinized carefully in the light of human rights instruments and available research'[2].

The Adoption and Children Act 2002, with its drive towards adoption, will undoubtedly come in for such scrutiny under the ECHR in the coming years. In taking a pro-adoption stance the Government, not for the first time, appears somewhat out on a limb with the USA and rather isolated from the policies of key European States and those followed elsewhere in the developed world. It will fall to the judiciary to ensure that adoption takes place only where other measures of family support and substitute care will not adequately safeguard the child's welfare[3] and that, even where adoption proves necessary, care is taken to preserve the child's identity rights and interest in maintaining some connection with the birth family.

---

1 Parkinson (above) at p 167.
2 Ibid.
3 For a recent example of long-term foster-care being thought by the court more appropriate than adoption, see the decision of Black J in *Re F (Adoption: Welfare of Child: Financial Considerations)* [2004] 2 FLR 440. See also *Re P (Adoption: Breach of Care Plan)* [2004] 2 FLR 1109, which is also concerned, inter alia, with the relative merits of long-term foster-care and adoption.

Chapter 8

CHILDREN AND MEDICAL DECISIONS

INTRODUCTION

The principles which now govern the relationship between the legal capacities of children, the responsibilities of parents and the limits of State intervention have to a considerable extent been fashioned in the context of medical decision-making. This is not really surprising since the health of children is self-evidently the most basic and essential consideration in protecting their welfare. In this chapter we take a close look at some of the more important decisions of the courts which have determined whether medical procedures should, or should not, be carried out on individual children[1]. These decisions, important in their own right, have a significance which goes beyond this, since they are probably the best practical applications of the theoretical perspectives discussed in Chapter 3. They present acute dilemmas concerning the limits of parents' powers and duties, the extent of children's rights (whether to be protected or to exercise autonomy) and the acceptable limits of State paternalism over children exercised through the courts. It is for this reason that we go into the facts and reasoning of decisions in greater depth than we do elsewhere in the book. Although there are numerous medical issues affecting children, they may perhaps be reduced to two central questions:

(1) who decides what medical procedures or treatment are appropriate for a child?; and

(2) on what criteria ought such decisions to be based?

---

1   There are now several established texts on medical law including: I Kennedy and A Grubb *Medical Law* (3rd edn) (Butterworths, 2000); JK Mason, RA McCall Smith and GT Laurie *Law and Medical Ethics* (6th edn) (Butterworths, 2002); J Montgomery *Health Care Law* (2nd edn) (Oxford University Press, 2002); and J McHale and M Fox with J Murphy *Health Care Law: Text and Materials* (Sweet & Maxwell, 1997). For a collection of essays focusing specifically on medical issues in the family, see E Sutherland and A McCall Smith *Family Rights: Family Law and Medical Advance* (Edinburgh University Press, 1990). For an introduction to the central issues involving medical decisions and children, see MDA Freeman *The Rights and Wrongs of Children* (Frances Pinter, 1983) at ch 7. A very readable account and critique of the relationship between doctors, children and parents is provided in M Brazier *Medicine, Patients and the Law* (3rd edn) (Penguin Books, 2003) at ch 14. Also of use is M Freeman *The Moral Status of Children* (Martinus Nijhoff, 1997), especially ch 15 (which deals with adolescents' rights to take their own decisions) and ch 16 (which deals with sterilisation of the mentally handicapped). Many useful articles may now be found in the *Medical Law Review* also published by Oxford University Press. Among the more recent commentaries are P Lewis 'The Medical Treatment of Children' in J Fionda (ed) *Legal Concepts of Childhood* (Hart Publishing, 2001) and C Bridge 'Religion, Culture and the Body of the Child' in A Bainham, S Day Sclater and M Richards (eds) *Body Lore and Laws* (Hart Publishing, 2002) at p 265. A useful guide published by the British Medical Association is *Consent, Rights and Choices in Health Care for Children and Young People* (BMJ Books, 2001). See also Department of Health *Seeking Consent: Working with Children* (DoH, 2001).

Who decides?

As to the first question, there are any number of possibilities. It would be possible to give parents (or others exercising parental responsibility) an unfettered discretion, although there might need to be a mechanism for resolving disagreements between parents[1]. Equally, decisions could be handed over entirely to children themselves, at least where they have acquired a certain age or level of understanding.

Another alternative might be to allow an outside agency, such as a court, to take the final decision. In that case, the circumstances under which the courts would become involved would need to be addressed. There could, for example, be a mandatory judicial procedure for certain operations[2]. Yet another possibility is that decisions could be left to the medical profession subject to a requirement that they be taken in accordance with accepted medical practice[3].

Yet the English case-law alerts us to the danger of assuming that there must necessarily be a single decision-maker. Whilst it is incontrovertibly true that *someone* has to have the final say, it is equally clear, in the family context, that the law has had to accommodate forms of participatory or inclusive decision-making which take at least some account of *all* the legitimate views involved. The crucial question in any given situation therefore becomes one of determining precisely how this balance should be struck. It is only in the event of serious disagreement that the matter is likely to be brought before the courts.

On what criteria?

As to the second question, there is an argument for saying that, since the facts of no two cases are ever identical, all medical decisions affecting individual children should be taken on an individualistic basis applying the welfare principle. Indeed, this largely represents current practice in England. Even the minority of cases which have reached the higher courts have, on the whole, failed to establish general criteria to determine with any precision such matters as when life-saving treatment should be given or withheld or when the sterilisation of mentally

---

1   For a review of the place that parental opinion has held in the reported decisions on medical treatment for children, see J Loughrey 'Medical Treatment – the Status of Parental Opinion' [1998] Fam Law 146.

2   Such procedures, especially for abortions on minors without parental consent, have been adopted in the USA, but English law has so far stopped short of this, while accepting that for sterilisation of mentally incompetent minors judicial authorisation is required in virtually all cases. See *Practice Note* [1996] 2 FLR 111.

3   This would be in line with the general requirement imposed by the law of tort that doctors act in accordance with the practice accepted by a responsible body of medical men skilled in that particular art. See *Bolam v Friern Hospital Management Committee* [1957] 2 All ER 118. This duty has been the subject of a decision of the House of Lords in *Bolitho v City and Hackney Health Authority* [1997] 3 WLR 1151, a case in which a two-year-old child with acute respiratory difficulties died after a doctor negligently failed to attend him in hospital. Here, the House refined the *Bolam* test by holding that there could be *rare* cases in which it might be demonstrated that professional medical opinion was incapable of withstanding logical analysis. In these rare cases, a judge might be entitled to hold that the body of opinion concerned was not reasonable or responsible. On the facts, however, this was not such a case, since there was good reason to accept the defendant's expert opinion, and it had therefore not been proved that the doctor's failure to attend the child had caused the injuries which had led to his death. For commentary, see J Keown 'Reining in the Bolam test' [1998] CLJ 248.

incompetent young women should be authorised or prohibited. Occasionally, the courts have appeared to go out of their way to deny that general principles of public policy are involved in such cases[1]. Moreover, they will often defer to the expertise of the medical profession on what are seen as clinical matters, preferring to confine themselves to giving broadly defined directions[2]. Indeed, it has been put more strongly by Montgomery (specifically in the context of selective treatment of the newborn) whose assessment is that it has become 'clear that the courts will respect the clinical freedom of doctors and refuse to force them to act against their clinical judgement'[3].

Serious difficulties can arise, of course, where parents fundamentally disagree with the clinical judgment of the medical team and with the regime of treatment proposed for a child. This can result in a complete loss of confidence in the health professionals involved and it may be necessary for the courts to intervene. In a series of cases[4] the courts have set out the principles which should govern such situations. They have emphasised in particular the importance of *consultation* between the doctors and the parents, and the desirability of them reaching agreement wherever possible. Where, however, this is not possible, the specific problems should be brought before the court. The point here is not that the court is likely to order the medical team to act against their clinical judgment but rather that the involvement of the court will *reinforce* those judgments. It may also bring the parents to accept what is proposed even where their natural inclination is to attempt to prolong the life of their child at all cost. As Caroline Bridge has put it, in these situations, 'the court often assumes the role of a compassionate authority, empathising with the parents but leading them to accept what doctors say is best for the child'[5].

Thus, in *R v Portsmouth Hospitals NHS Trust ex parte Glass*[6] there had been a complete breakdown of trust between the hospital team and the family of a severely disabled boy aged 12 with a limited lifespan. The hospital wished to administer palliative care only but the mother wished him to receive whatever medical treatment would prolong his life. She applied for judicial review and sought an anticipatory declaration regarding the course to be taken if the boy were to be admitted for emergency treatment and a disagreement arose. The Court of Appeal upheld the judge's refusal to grant it. It was inappropriate to dictate in advance to the medical team what treatment should or should not be given in circumstances which had not yet arisen. In the event of an irreconcilable conflict, the court would rule in the actual circumstances if and when they arose, on the basis of the child's best interests. However, the case was subsequently taken by the boy's mother to Strasbourg[7]. In an important ruling, the ECtHR held that a decision to impose treatment in defiance of a parent's objections gave rise to an

---

1   A particularly striking example is the speech of Lord Hailsham in *Re B (A Minor) (Wardship: Sterilisation)* [1988] AC 199, in which he offered the view that no general issues of public policy were raised by the proposed sterilisation of a mentally incompetent teenager.

2   See, for example, *Re C (A Minor) (Wardship: Medical Treatment)* [1989] 2 All ER 782.

3   J Montgomery *Health Care Law* (2nd edn) (Oxford University Press, 2002) at p 440.

4   See particularly *R v Portsmouth Hospitals NHS Trust ex parte Glass* [1999] 2 FLR 905; *Re MM (Medical Treatment)* [2000] 1 FLR 224; and *Royal Wolverhampton Hospitals NHS Trust v B* [2000] 1 FLR 953.

5   C Bridge (above) at p 274.

6   [1999] 2 FLR 905.

7   *Glass v United Kingdom* [2004] 1 FLR 1019.

interference with the child's right to respect for his private life, in particular his right to physical integrity, under Article 8 of the ECHR. The interference could not be justified as 'necessary' under Article 8(2) since the earlier disputes between the parent and the hospital team in the event of an emergency highlighted their disagreement and placed a clear onus on the hospital to bring the matter before the court for resolution. Accordingly, there was a violation of Article 8. The key point of this decision is therefore that the obligation is on the medical authorities and not on the parent to bring serious disagreements before the courts (although of course it is also open to the parent to take the initiative and do so).

In *Re MM (Medical Treatment)*[1] there was a disagreement between the medical team and the parents, who were Russian, about the specific treatment regime. The child suffered from immunodeficiency which had been treated in Russia with a programme of immunostimulant therapy. The parents wanted a continuation of this treatment while the local authority, supported by the Official Solicitor, wanted instead a course of replacement immunoglobin administered intra-venously and designed to continue through the child's life. In the event it was possible for an agreement to be reached during the course of the proceedings. It was agreed that the doctors were to determine what course of treatment was appropriate, following consultation with the parents at all stages as far as reasonably practicable, and that there should be consideration of alternative forms of management suggested by the parents. Black J, approving the agreed course, did however indicate that, although the parents' objection to the recommended treatment had been a rational objection, she would have overridden it if necessary since the evidence that it was in the child's best interests was overwhelming.

Finally in *Royal Wolverhampton Hospitals NHS Trust v B*[2] there was a dispute between a consultant paediatrician and the parents of a premature baby with chronic lung disease. The parents favoured ventilation while the medical view was that this would be distressing and risky and allow only a short-term improvement. Again there had been a breakdown in confidence. Bodey J granted the hospital trust a declaration that the child be treated in accordance with the advice of the paediatrician. He held in the face of this disagreement that the best interests of the child were that she had a firm and confident medical team doing all that could be done given the unanimous prognosis that the baby could not survive. He also held that the court should positively make an order rather than say, in effect, that the issue was purely a matter for the clinicians' clinical judgment and that the court declined to play any part. It was right that what appeared inevitable on the evidence should be formally recognised and have the authority of the court.

The practical value of decisions (even those of the House of Lords) as precedents must inevitably be limited. This immediately provokes the question whether a more concerted attempt should be made to formulate, through legislation, legal standards for decision-making[3]. The difficulty with this is that any such attempt would be bound to raise awkward moral questions about the value and quality of life which are, in the end, dependent on individual beliefs and

---

1   [2000] 1 FLR 224.
2   [2000] 1 FLR 953.
3   Such attempts were made in relation to the treatment or non-treatment of severely disabled infants in the USA, as to which see RH Mnookin and DK Weisberg *Child, Family and State* (3rd edn) (Little, Brown and Co, 1995) at pp 590 et seq.

on which there is never likely to be a societal consensus. Yet the consequence of failing to establish reasonably clear criteria is that this can lead to widespread variations in the treatment or non-treatment of children with broadly similar medical conditions and this may be thought to offend principles of formal equality[1]. It is doubtful how far such an approach could be reconciled with a commitment to children's rights.

Who is a child?

The following discussion follows the definition of 'child' in the Children Act 1989 as a person below the age of 18 years. It has been noted that this can cause difficulties at either end of the spectrum, ie the problems of the status of the foetus and the mentally incompetent adult 'child'[2]. Even within this spectrum there is a world of difference between the sort of medical questions which can arise in relation to neonates or young children on the one hand and adolescents on the other. The latter have a capacity for self-help in seeking medical assistance, whilst the former are wholly dependent on the support of interested adults. The general question relating to young children, given that there must be a proxy decision-maker, is when precisely an outside party or agency should be able to challenge parental authority. The general issue regarding adolescents, on the assumption that they themselves have legal capacity, relates to the circumstances in which they may act in conjunction with medical advice and by-pass parental involvement or go ahead with a medical procedure in the face of parental opposition.

We begin by discussing the legal framework within which medical decisions are taken. We then examine the operation of these principles in two key areas which illustrate the particular problems affecting infants and young children and also the special considerations applying to adolescents.

GENERAL PRINCIPLES

The parental consent principle

The consent requirement
As a general proposition it is accepted that the consent of the patient is required for any medical examination or procedure. The principle is rooted in the idea of self-determination. The patient should be left alone to decide what is or is not done to his body[3]. Prima facie, any unauthorised 'touching', which for these purposes includes medical procedures, would constitute an assault or, more accurately, a battery. But provided that the patient has an essential understanding

---

1   The principle entails treating like cases alike. A good theoretical discussion of what is involved in equal treatment is to be found in B Williams 'On Equality' in *Problems of the Self* (Cambridge University Press, 1976).
2   See Chapter 3 above.
3   The consent issue is discussed generally in JK Mason, RA McCall Smith and GT Laurie *Law and Medical Ethics* (6th edn) (Butterworths, 2002) at ch 10, I Kennedy and A Grubb *Medical Law* (3rd edn) (Butterworths, 2000) at ch 6, and J Montgomery *Health Care Law* (2nd edn) (Oxford University Press, 2002) at ch 10. J McHale and M Fox with J Murphy *Health Care Law: Text and Materials* (Sweet & Maxwell, 1997) deal with the consent issue in ch 6 and devote ch 7 specifically to issues involving children. For a view from the Official Solicitor's office, dealing

of what is proposed and consents to it, no assault will have been committed. It is possible that a doctor may be liable in negligence where the patient's consent was induced by his failure to disclose information which any prudent medical practitioner would have disclosed[1]. But beyond this there is no requirement in English law that the patient give an 'informed consent'[2]. The consent requirement throws up an immediate problem in the case of children. The very status of minority has, as its raison d'être, the assumed incapacity of children to act on their own behalf. Thus, as a general rule, the law allows parents (and others in loco parentis) to provide a proxy consent for medical treatment and procedures performed on children.

Who can give consent?

This power, recognised at common law, is now included in the concept of parental responsibility and thus is held by married parents, unmarried mothers, unmarried fathers through the process of birth registration and anyone else (including an unmarried father) who acquires parental responsibility by legal process[3]. The Children Act, as already discussed, allows anyone with de facto care of a child, for however short a time, to 'do what is reasonable in all the circumstances of the case for the purpose of safeguarding or promoting the child's welfare'[4]. The Law Commission specifically instanced the operation of this provision in relation to medical care. It offered the view that it would enable a temporary carer to arrange medical assistance following an accident to the child but would not allow a temporary carer to consent to major elective surgery for the child[5]. While there could be some difficult line-drawing, the essence of the distinction would appear to be that emergency or routine medical care would be covered, but procedures with long-term or irreversible implications would require the consent of a person with parental responsibility. It should also be said that anyone looking after a child might be criminally liable or liable in negligence for failing to secure essential medical aid for a child[6], although there is no wider legal, as opposed to moral, duty on members of the public at large to come to the aid of a distressed child[7].

So far the discussion has assumed that both parents (or all those with parental responsibility) are in agreement. But what is the position where there is a dispute

---

particularly with the problems of incapacity, see M Nicholls 'Consent to Medical Treatment' [1993] Fam Law 30. See also J Montgomery 'Consent to Health Care for Children' (1993) 5 JCL 117. For the view of the British Medical Association, see *Consent, Rights and Choices in Health Care for Children and Young People* (BMJ Books, 2001) ch 2 (English law) and ch 3 (Scots law).

1   See Lord Bridge in *Sidaway v Board of Governors of the Bethlem Royal Hospital and Maudsley Hospital* [1985] 1 All ER 643 at 663.

2   But we discuss below the apparently high level of understanding required of minors wishing to provide their own consent to medical matters.

3   The general principles concerning acquisition of parental responsibility are discussed in Chapter 2 above.

4   Section 3(5).

5   Law Com Report No 172 *Guardianship and Custody* (1988) at para 2.16.

6   Criminal liability arises primarily under the Children and Young Persons Act 1933, s 1.

7   Thus, no criminal offence is committed where an unconnected bystander watches a child drown in a shallow pool, however morally reprehensible this inactivity might be. For a discussion of these principles, see JC Smith and B Hogan *Criminal Law* (10th edn) (Butterworths, 2002) at pp 63–64. In similar vein, there is no mandatory reporting law in England which would require a neighbour or anyone else to inform the relevant authorities of child abuse or neglect.

between parents concerning a medical procedure for the child? This is very unlikely to arise in the context of a united family but could easily occur between divorced or separated parents. This is what happened in *Re C (Welfare of Child: Immunisation)*[1]. Two unmarried fathers who had obtained parental responsibility orders sought specific issue orders that their respective children be vaccinated with the MMR triple vaccine. In each case the mother, who was the primary carer, was vehemently opposed to immunisation. The Court of Appeal upheld the decision of Sumner J authorising immunisation. The court rejected the contention of the mothers that the judge had applied the wrong test. They had argued that he had adopted a two-stage test, asking first what was in the children's best *medical* interests and then asking whether there were sufficient *non-medical* reasons for refusing to order immunisation. In the court's view the judge could not be criticised for making an assessment on the basis of the expert evidence first and he had reached a proper conclusion in accordance with the single welfare test. The court went on to emphasise that a decision concerning immunisation against infectious disease was not one which either parent had the right to take independently. It belonged to a small group of decisions which, despite the provisions of s 2(7) of the Children Act 1989, required the ruling of the court based on the child's best interests in the event of disagreement. Nonetheless, this decision may perhaps be criticised for failing to clarify the significance of best medical interests as opposed to other factors in cases like this.

Wilful neglect

The position of parents as proxies gives rise to both a duty and a discretion, and the primary difficulty is to determine when duty ends and discretion begins. Anyone over the age of 16 years, with 'responsibility' for a child, who 'wilfully assaults, ill-treats, neglects, abandons, or exposes him … in a manner likely to cause him unnecessary suffering or injury to health' commits a criminal offence[2]. The offence specifically includes failure to provide adequate medical aid or failure to take steps to secure it to be provided. This offence of 'wilful neglect' imposes certain minimum standards of medical care on anyone, most obviously a parent, who has the physical care of a child. It has been held that the test of 'wilfulness' is a subjective one, requiring actual appreciation of the risk to the child's health. Consequently, it can be a defence to show that parents of low intelligence did not have this appreciation at the relevant time[3]. On the other hand, the offence may be committed where there is failure to summon medical aid even though *in fact* there was no help which a doctor could have given[4].

---

1   [2003] 2 FLR 1054 (Sumner J) and 1095 (CA). For commentary on the case, see H Baker 'MMR: Medicine, Mothers and Rights' [2004] CLJ 49, and K O'Donnell 'Room to Refuse? Immunisation, welfare and the role of parental decision-making' [2004] CFLQ 213.

2   Children and Young Persons Act 1933, s 1(1). The statute makes it explicit that the suffering or injury to health is widely defined and includes 'injury to or loss of sight, or hearing, or limb, or organ of the body, and any mental derangement'.

3   *R v Sheppard* [1981] AC 394. Failure to satisfy an objective test of reasonableness might, however, give rise to tortious liability.

4   *R v S and M* [1995] Crim LR 486.

When can a parent withhold medical care?

In addition to this special offence, parents and others are, of course, subject to the ordinary criminal law and may, for example, be liable for the death of the child where death was caused by their unwillingness to summon essential aid. Such refusals are sometimes influenced by religious considerations, but while parents may lawfully make martyrs of themselves, they may not make martyrs of their children[1]. Thus, in *R v Senior*[2], a parent's conviction for manslaughter by gross negligence was upheld where for religious reasons he failed to summon medical aid for his dangerously ill child who then died of diarrhoea and pneumonia[3]. It is clear then that parental rights or responsibility 'do not clothe parents with life and death authority over their children'[4]. However, it cannot be concluded from this that in no circumstances is it proper for parents, acting in conjunction with the medical profession, to withhold life-saving treatment from certain children[5]. A fortiori, the extent of the parent's duty to secure medical treatment in *non*-life-threatening situations requires careful examination in individual cases[6].

Therapeutic versus non-therapeutic treatment

Where parents are not under a positive duty to secure medical treatment they nevertheless, as a general principle, have a discretion to consent to or veto it[7]. Although the courts have been loathe to draw rigid distinctions between

---

1   *People (ex rel Wallace) v Labrenz* 104 NE 2d 769 (Ill, 1952). The principle has been illustrated by cases in which the courts have sanctioned blood transfusions for children in the face of religious objections by their parents. See *Re S (A Minor) (Medical Treatment)* [1993] 1 FLR 376 and *Re O (A Minor) (Medical Treatment)* [1993] 2 FLR 149. Moreover, the courts may be prepared to override the *combined* objections of the parents and an adolescent, as in *Re E (A Minor) (Wardship: Medical Treatment)* [1993] 1 FLR 386. In this case, Ward J, while giving full weight to the religious principles accepted by the patient (a boy aged 15) and his parents (all of whom were devout Jehovah's Witnesses), held that the welfare of the patient, objectively judged, led to the inevitable conclusion that blood transfusions should be authorised. The principle was reasserted in *Re A (Conjoined Twins: Medical Treatment)* [2001] 1 FLR 1, where there was an extensive examination of the degree of respect to be accorded to parental views. We consider the case in depth below.
2   [1899] 1 QB 283.
3   The accused belonged to a sect known as the 'Peculiar People' who objected to the use of doctors because of their interpretation of verses 14 and 15 of the Epistle of St James – 'Is there any sick among you? Let him call for the elders of the church and let them pray over him, anointing him with oil in the name of the Lord; and the prayer of faith shall save the sick, and the Lord shall raise him up; and if he have committed sins, they shall be forgiven him.' Accepting evidence that proper medical aid could have prolonged and probably saved the child's life, the judge had pointed out that Christ himself had, according to biblical text, said: 'They that are whole need not a physician but they that are sick.'
4   *Custody of a Minor* 379 NE 2d 1053 (1978).
5   See particularly now *Re T (Wardship: Medical Treatment)* [1997] 1 FLR 502, discussed below. For an examination of the whole issue of parents' powers in relation to the medical treatment of children, see C Bridge 'Parental powers and the medical treatment of children' in C Bridge (ed) *Family Law Towards the Millennium: Essays for PM Bromley* (Butterworths, 1997) at ch 9.
6   This has received much closer examination in the USA than it has in England. See RH Mnookin and D Weisberg *Child, Family and State* (3rd edn) (Little, Brown and Co, 1995).
7   It should be noted, however, that a parent's objection to a scientific test on a child for the purposes of establishing paternity may be overridden by the court if the court considers this to be in the child's best interests: see Family Law Reform Act 1969, s 21(3), as amended, and see further Chapter 5 above. On the question of consent to genetic screening and tests associated with this, see J McHale 'Genetic screening and testing the child patient' [1997] CFLQ 33.

therapeutic and non-therapeutic procedures, it is generally accepted that parents have power to consent to treatment of a therapeutic nature, but their capacity to authorise non-therapeutic treatment is more doubtful[1]. It is thought that they *do* have power to consent to non-therapeutic procedures insofar as they are for the benefit of the child[2]. Thus, they may consent to scientific tests on the child for the purposes of establishing paternity, since it is usually thought to be in the child's best interests for this question to be determined[3]. The Court of Appeal has confirmed that such a direction should not be given where the court is satisfied that it would be *against* the child's interests[4].

Particularly difficult questions can arise where the benefits to the child are less obvious, as where it is proposed that a child should participate in non-therapeutic research or become an organ donor[5]. Such research may be justified on the altruistic basis that it benefits *other* children but may be of no direct benefit to the child undergoing the procedure, which might be hazardous and uncomfortable[6]. Here, the difficult legal issue is whether parents and others are bound by a legal duty to act *only* in the best interests of the child in question[7]. The point is uncertain but it appears to be accepted medical practice that, in *some* circumstances, research on individual children which is intended to benefit other children, may be justifiable. This is subject to significant qualifications concerning the older child's right to object and the need to obtain the consent of the parent or guardian. It is also accepted that parental consent per se should not justify participation in research.

---

1   An illustration of this principle is *Re E (A Minor) (Medical Treatment)* [1991] 2 FLR 585 where it was held that, contrary to normal requirements regarding the sterilisation of mentally incompetent minors, parents might provide a valid consent to a *therapeutic* hysterectomy without obtaining a judicial declaration.

2   It is non-medical benefits which are referred to here, since medical benefits to the child would render the procedure therapeutic in nature.

3   *S v S; W v Official Solicitor* [1972] AC 24.

4   *Re H (Paternity: Blood Test)* [1996] 2 FLR 65.

5   The issue is discussed in JK Mason, RA McCall Smith and GT Laurie *Law and Medical Ethics* (6th edn) (Butterworths, 2002) at pp 595–600, I Kennedy and A Grubb *Medical Law* (3rd edn) (Butterworths, 2000) at ch 14, and J Montgomery *Health Care Law* (2nd edn) (Oxford University Press, 2002) ch 14, especially at pp 363–366. See also British Medical Association *Consent, Rights and Choices in Health Care for Children and Young People* (BMJ Books, 2001) ch 9. See also *Re Y (Mental Incapacity: Bone Marrow Transplant)* [1996] 2 FLR 787. This case concerned organ donation between two adult sisters but there is no reason why the principles should not be extrapolated to children. Connell J held that the test to be applied was the best interests of the prospective donor. Here, there was a closely knit family and it was possible to conclude that it was in the best interests of a severely mentally and physically disabled woman (who was unable to provide a valid consent) that she should donate bone marrow to her elder sister who suffered from leukaemia. For assessments of the decision, see D Feenan 'A good harvest?' [1997] CFLQ 305 and SE Mumford 'Bone marrow donation – the law in context' [1998] CFLQ 135.

6   JK Mason, RA McCall Smith and GT Laurie (above) cite the example of a French project involving lumbar punctures on newborn infants. See also the discussion in J Montgomery *Health Care Law* (2nd edn) (Oxford University Press, 2002) at pp 363–366.

7   This may be the implication of the welfare principle but it has already been noted that the application of this principle to parents is problematic. See Chapter 3 above.

Parents may not validly consent to a procedure which is to the obvious *detriment* of the child and, more generally, it is considered ethically unsound to proceed except where the risks to the child concerned are minimal[1].

Consequences of proceeding without parental consent

We discuss below the circumstances in which parental consent may not be required, but there is a preliminary question. On the assumption that the consent of a parent *is* necessary, what course of action is open to that parent if the doctor or other medical personnel go ahead without his or her consent? Here, it has been established by the Court of Appeal in *F v Wirral Metropolitan Borough Council*[2] that no civil action will lie for interference with parental 'rights' and this principle must surely apply equally to the concept of 'parental responsibility'. Any tortious action a parent has must, therefore, be based on trespass to the *child's* person. The function of parental consent is thus to prevent a tort being committed against the *child* and not to protect any independent parental claim[3]. Where a 'touching' is involved (which would be the case with most medical examinations and procedures), it ought not to be difficult to establish the tort of battery. But the position is much less clear if all that is involved is the giving of advice or the prescription of medication since here there is no obvious physical contact. It is doubtful whether the doctor would be acting unlawfully in those situations although a parent, forewarned of these dealings, might seek to prevent them in wardship, by invoking the inherent jurisdiction or by seeking a prohibited steps order[4].

Exceptions to the parental consent requirement

There are several well-established qualifications to the general rule that the consent of a parent is both a necessary and sufficient consent to treatment for a child. First, the State may, in certain circumstances, restrict the area of parental discretion, either directly through legislation or indirectly through the protective agency of local authorities or the courts. Secondly, the child's own view may prevail over that of a parent in some instances in which they are in conflict. Thirdly, there will be instances in which the medical profession may proceed lawfully without a parent's consent. Some of these instances will arise where no

---

1   The attitude of various medical professional bodies to the issue is discussed by JK Mason, RA McCall Smith and GT Laurie (above) at p 595.
2   [1991] 2 FLR 114.
3   The dangers of the medical profession proceeding with an operation on a child without obtaining parental consent were graphically illustrated in the tragic case of six-year-old Debbie Jenkins which received a great deal of media attention in March 1998. Dr James Taylor, a senior consultant heart surgeon at Great Ormond Street Hospital, was found guilty of professional misconduct by the General Medical Council. The child had died following irreparable brain damage which she sustained when Dr Taylor performed a procedure which involved using a balloon catheter to try to enlarge a narrowed artery. He was fully aware of the lack of the parents' consent to this procedure and had evidently informed them that he would not use it. He was found to have had insufficient medical grounds to undertake the procedure without parental consent. It was also reported that the parents were considering a civil action against the hospital following the ruling of the GMC. (See (1998) *The Times*, March 21.)
4   Section 8(1) of the Children Act 1989. This issue is relevant to other professionals such as teachers, as to which see Chapter 16 below.

consent is either available or required, while in other cases it may be lawful for a doctor, in effect, to choose between the conflicting views of parents and children.

The State as decision-maker

As has been seen, the State may, through the criminal law, cut down the area of parental discretion by imposing duties to ensure certain minimum standards of health for children[1]. An alternative mechanism, used extensively in the USA, is to require compliance with a variety of screening procedures designed to detect particular diseases in children or to require certain immunisations against, for example, diphtheria, whooping cough, tetanus, measles and polio, as a condition of school admission. In the USA, some State legislation has made provision for parents' objections to these procedures, in some cases only on religious grounds, but there has been no consistent pattern[2]. In England, the courts have occasionally exercised their powers to direct that children be tested for HIV infection, although the basis for exercising this jurisdiction is not wholly clear. Such tests should only be directed by the High Court[3]. Interventions like these represent restrictions on parental discretion grounded in the public interest in the prevention of disease.

The State may intervene through the local authority or the court (on the initiative of some interested party) to protect the health of *individual* children. Traditionally, this was achieved in wardship proceedings. While the inherent jurisdiction may remain the appropriate one in sensitive or complex cases, the alternative of applying in family proceedings for a prohibited steps or specific issue order might now be used[4]. A genuine applicant for a s 8 order should not experience difficulty in obtaining leave where a serious medical issue has arisen. Where there is more general concern about the ability of parents or other carers to safeguard the health of a child on an ongoing basis, this will usually be a matter for action by social services. Social services may also, with leave, invoke the court's inherent jurisdiction, where the child is not in care, to resolve a single medical issue of concern[5].

Sterilisation: an illustration of the court's protective role

The court's protective role in relation to children is seen most obviously in life-saving cases. Yet the courts can also be involved other than in life-saving situations, of which the best example is arguably the sterilisation of the mentally incompetent. In this section we concentrate on this controversial issue[6].

---

1 Children and Young Persons Act 1933, s 1.
2 RH Mnookin and D Weisberg *Child, Family and State* (3rd edn) (Little, Brown and Co, 1995) at pp 551–554.
3 See, particularly, *Note: Re HIV Tests* [1994] 2 FLR 116, *Re O (Minors) (Medical Examination)* [1993] 1 FLR 860 and *Re C (HIV Test)* [1999] 2 FLR 1004.
4 As in *Re HG (Specific Issue Order: Sterilisation* [1993] 1 FLR 587.
5 See Chapter 11 below.
6 For a scathing attack on the compulsory sterilisation of the mentally incompetent, see M Freeman 'Sterilising the Mentally Handicapped' in *The Moral Status of Children* (Martinus Nijhoff, 1997) ch 16. See also M Beaupré 'Decision-making and the sterilisation of incompetent children' in A Grubb (ed) *Decision-Making and Problems of Incompetence* (John Wiley & Sons, 1994) at p 89.

The issue first came to the fore in *Re D (A Minor) (Wardship: Sterilisation)*[1] where an educational psychologist invoked wardship in an attempt to prevent the sterilisation of an 11-year-old girl who suffered from an uncommon disorder known as 'Sotos syndrome'. While the principles governing sterilisation have been much refined in later cases, *Re D* arguably remains one of the classic examples of judicial intervention in the medical sphere and repays close attention. The symptoms of the disease in this case included accelerated growth during infancy, epilepsy, generalised clumsiness, emotional instability, aggressive tendencies and the impairment of mental function. The girl's widowed mother, fearful that the girl might become pregnant and give birth to an abnormal child, proposed that she be sterilised. The mother had the support of a paediatrician and a gynaecologist who was prepared to perform the operation. Heilbron J held that it was an appropriate case for wardship and that the procedure should be prohibited. It was not in the girl's best interests, since it involved an irreversible procedure of a non-therapeutic nature, which would entail the deprivation of a 'basic human right to reproduce'. The girl's future role in society and subsequent development could not be accurately predicted but there was medical evidence that her condition was improving and that she might, at some future time, acquire the capacity to make an informed choice about the procedure. Thus, it was not a matter which fell within a doctor's sole, clinical judgment, and the court should intervene.

The decision in this case was no more than a straightforward application of the welfare principle, ie that it was not in this particular girl's best interests to undergo a sterilisation. This is the characteristic approach of the English courts, and later cases have revealed a marked reluctance to lay down any general guidelines or standards[2]. Hence, it was not possible to extract from this decision any general principle against sterilisation of mentally incapacitated minors. It is clear, both from evidence in the case itself, and from later reported cases[3], that sterilisation operations will often be sanctioned where the level of disability is greater than that which was suffered by the girl in *Re D*. Nevertheless, there was, in *Re D*, more than a suggestion that Heilbron J was influenced by what the girl's own view might be on attaining adulthood and making the discovery of what had happened to her whilst a child. This has a flavour of 'substituted judgment' about it, but this was only one

---

1   [1976] Fam 185.
2   Thus in *Re B (A Minor) (Wardship: Sterilisation)* [1988] AC 199 the House of Lords rejected any distinction between therapeutic and non-therapeutic sterilisation on the basis that it would detract from the application of the welfare test.
3   See, particularly: *Re M (A Minor) (Wardship: Sterilisation)* [1988] 2 FLR 497; *Re P (A Minor) (Wardship: Sterilisation)* [1989] 1 FLR 182; *T v T* [1988] Fam 52; *Re F (Mental Patient: Sterilisation)* [1990] 2 AC 1; and *Re W (Mental Patient: Sterilisation)* [1993] 1 FLR 381 (young woman aged 20 suffering from severe epilepsy and minor degree of cerebral palsy). In *Re HG (Specific Issue Order: Sterilisation)* [1993] 1 FLR 587, Peter Singer QC (sitting as a deputy High Court judge) held that, in principle, it was possible for an issue such as sterilisation to be the subject of an application for a specific issue order under the Children Act. But he was of the view that such proceedings ought always to be commenced in a district registry of the High Court and that the Official Solicitor should always be involved. For a case in which leave to perform a sterilisation on a severely disabled 21-year-old was *refused*, the arguments being fairly evenly balanced, see *Re LC (Medical Treatment: Sterilisation)* [1997] 2 FLR 258. See also *Re S (Medical Treatment: Adult Sterilisation)* [1998] 1 FLR 944, where sterilisation of a 22-year-old mentally incompetent young woman, with no understanding of sexuality, was emphatically refused by Johnson J. Here, the risk of sexual exploitation was found to be speculative and not identifiable. Sterilisation was also

element in the judge's thinking[1]. The decision was, in the final analysis for the court, based on what it thought best for the child and this is conceptually distinct from a judicial process which attempts to project what a child would have wanted if she was not suffering from incapacity. The case was significant also from a procedural angle. It revealed that child protection can be dependent on the chance intervention of an interested third party. It thus paved the way for consideration in later cases of the need for a mandatory judicial procedure designed to ensure some consistency in the practice of sterilisation[2].

In *Re B (A Minor) (Wardship: Sterilisation)*[3] (popularly known as '*Jeanette's case*') the more serious case of mental incapacity, visualised in *Re D*, materialised.

Jeanette was 17 years of age and approaching majority. She had a mental age of five or six years. The evidence was that she was unable to appreciate the causal connection between sexual intercourse and childbirth and would be incapable of consenting to marriage. If she should carry a child to term it was predicted that she would need to be delivered by Caesarean section and that she would thereafter be likely to pick at the operational wound. It was also found that she had no maternal instincts and lacked the ability to care for a child. There was, however, evidence that she was becoming sexually aware and that there was a realistic danger of pregnancy resulting from casual sexual activity. Other methods of contraception were found not to be feasible, apart from an oral contraceptive, progesterone. She would be required to take this for the remainder of her reproductive life, the success rate was only 40 per cent, and the long-term side effects were speculative. Sunderland Borough Council, in whose care Jeanette had been since 1973, decided, with the support of her mother, that sterilisation was the best course.

The House of Lords upheld the decision of the judge in wardship proceedings and the Court of Appeal that the operation be sanctioned. The reasoning was again based on the single consideration that the procedure was in her best interests. The House of Lords rejected all other criteria which were considered extraneous to the welfare test. Lord Hailsham stressed that the case involved no general issue of public policy and, in particular, had nothing to do with eugenics. Lord Oliver said that the operation was not sought for social purposes, the convenience of those taking care of Jeanette or to allay family anxieties. The House of Lords specifically rejected as unhelpful a Canadian distinction between therapeutic and non-therapeutic purposes, with only the former being regarded

---

refused by the Court of Appeal in *Re S (Sterilisation: Patient's Best Interests)* [2000] 2 FLR 389 in which it was held that it would be a disproportionate response to the problems of an attractive woman aged 29 with a severe learning disability. The court thought that the insertion of an intra-uterine device called Mirena would be less intrusive, reduce S's periods and offer adequate contraceptive protection. Cf *Re ZM and OS (Sterilisation: Patient's Best Interests)* [2000] 1 FLR 523 in which Bennett J sanctioned a laparoscopic subtotal hysterectomy on a 19-year-old young woman with Down's syndrome on the basis that Mirena would not end her heavy and distressing periods nor wholly remove the risk of pregnancy, both of which were in her best interests.

1 Heilbron J clearly attached significance to the evidence that in later years the girl would be able to make her own choice and that 'the frustration and resentment of realising (as she would one day) what had happened, could be devastating'.

2 Discussed below.

3 [1988] AC 199.

as a legitimate reason for sterilisation in Canada[1]. Lord Hailsham thought that any reference to a 'basic human right to reproduce' was meaningless where an individual lacked the mental capacity to make an informed choice in matters of pregnancy and childbirth. Lord Templeman alone expressed the view that sterilisation, as a procedure of last resort, should only be carried out with the leave of a High Court judge. The House was unanimous that the operation was the only way of averting the 'unmitigated disaster' of pregnancy. Since there was some doubt about whether the court would have jurisdiction once Jeanette reached 18 years of age, it sanctioned performance of the operation without delay[2].

This case rejected the notion that there is any absolute right to reproduce. It showed that, in cases of severe mental incapacity, the court's intervention might be required to protect the child's right *not* to reproduce. It was open to the court to determine that it was in the best interests of a minor not to be denied medical care which would be available to a competent person and which could guarantee a better lifestyle[3]. At the same time, it is questionable whether the objection to sterilisation for contraceptive or social purposes, as opposed to medical purposes, is sustainable in the light of subsequent decisions[4]. The distinction between therapeutic and non-therapeutic sterilisation, rejected by the House of Lords, was specifically utilised in *Re E (A Minor) (Medical Treatment)*[5] where it was held that parents could consent (without the necessity of going to court) to a therapeutic sterilisation occasioned by the need for a hysterectomy.

The courts are likely to take a restrictive approach to applications for male sterilisation by vasectomy. The matter arose in *Re A (Male Sterilisation)*[6] which concerned a man aged 28 with Down's syndrome. His elderly mother was anxious that she would be unable to supervise him and that he might make a woman pregnant. The evidence was that A was sexually aware and active but that he had a high degree of care and supervision which minimised the risk of sexual intercourse. The Court of Appeal upheld the judge's refusal to grant a declaration that sterilisation was in A's best interests. In doing so the court took a somewhat gender-specific approach to the issue. In relation to sterilisation the court's view was that the best interests of a man were not equivalent to the best interests of a woman because of the obvious biological differences. The only direct consequence of sexual intercourse for a man, it was said, was the risk of sexually transmitted diseases. The other consequences which arose from fathering a child

---

1   *Re Eve* (1987) 31 DLR (4th) I; and see CAP Finch-Noyes 'Sterilisation of the Mentally Retarded Minor: The *Re K* Case' (1986) 5 Can J of FL 277. The matter has also exercised the higher courts in Australia a good deal in recent years, as to which see F Bates 'In the Shadow of Change – Australian Family Law in 1995' in A Bainham (ed) *The International Survey of Family Law 1995* (Martinus Nijhoff, 1997) at pp 29 et seq, and F Bates ' "Disputes Do Not Always End Where They Begin": Australian Family Law in 1996' in A Bainham (ed) *The International Survey of Family Law 1996* (Martinus Nijhoff, 1998) at pp 33 et seq.

2   It has since been decided that the courts *do* have jurisdiction to grant declarations as to the lawfulness of sterilisations performed on mentally incompetent adults. See *Re F (Mental Patient: Sterilisation)* [1990] 2 AC 1.

3   This was a matter emphasised by Lord Jauncey at 83. It has more than a suggestion of a right to be sterilised which can conveniently be contrasted with Heilbron J's view of the alleged human right to reproduce in *Re D (A Minor) (Wardship: Sterilisation)* [1976] Fam 185.

4   See fn 3 at p 320 above.

5   [1991] 2 FLR 585.

6   [2000] 1 FLR 549.

would only be psychological, as where his activity might attract disapproval and criticism. In this case the court was not convinced that this would be a major factor because of his mental incapacity and left open the question whether third party interests ought properly to be considered in an assessment of a patient's best interests.

There has remained some doubt about the criteria which should be used in assessing when a sterilisation is justified in individual cases. These concerns were to some extent met by a number of Practice Notes[1]. It is now clear that sterilisation, whether of a minor or of a mentally incompetent adult, requires 'in virtually all cases' the prior sanction of a High Court judge. Applications may be either under the inherent jurisdiction of the High Court or for a specific issue order. The purpose of the proceedings must be to establish whether or not the proposed sterilisation is in the best interests of the patient. The court, accordingly, must be satisfied 'that the patient lacks capacity and that the operation will promote the best interests of the patient rather than the interests or convenience of the claimant, carers or public'. The note goes on to advise that in sterilisation cases there are three particular components to the 'best interests' test. First, the risk of pregnancy arising from the likelihood of sexual activity must be identifiable and not purely speculative. Secondly, there must be clear evidence of potentially damaging consequences deriving from conception and/or menstruation. Thirdly, the court will require a detailed analysis of all available and relevant methods of dealing with the patient's problems. There should be expert evidence explaining each relevant method and listing its advantages and disadvantages for the individual patient, taking into account any relevant aspects of her physical and psychological health.

The statutory role of the local authority

Where it has come to the attention of social services that a child's health may be jeopardised by potential parental abuse or neglect, or because of a parent's inability to cope, there will be a number of options[2]. As a starting point, the local authority will probably wish to explore the possibility of some form of voluntary social work assistance which could include the temporary accommodation of the child away from home. In *F v Wirral Metropolitan Borough Council*[3], for example, the children had been born with phenylketonuria (PKU), a metabolic disease which can lead to severe mental retardation and which calls for skilled dietary management. The parents were persuaded to allow the children to be cared for by social services and to be boarded out with foster-parents.

Where parents are unwilling to co-operate, the local authority may need to take compulsory action for a care or supervision order[4]. Where the authority is merely concerned to secure authorisation for a medical procedure (rather than to assume the overall care of a child), it may apply for leave to invoke the inherent

---

1 See *J v C (Note)* [1990] 3 All ER 735; *Practice Note: Official Solicitor: Sterilisation* [1993] 2 FLR 222; and *Practice Note: Official Solicitor: Sterilisation* [1996] 2 FLR 111. These notes have now been superseded by *Practice Note (Official Solicitor: Declaratory Proceedings: Medical and Welfare Decisions for Adults who Lack Capacity)* [2001] 2 FLR 158. The note covers cases of sterilisation and patients in a permanent vegetative state, each covered by a separate appendix.
2 Public intervention is discussed in greater depth in Chapters 10–12 below.
3 [1991] 2 FLR 114.
4 Under s 31 of the Children Act, discussed in Chapter 11 below.

jurisdiction of the High Court. There have been a number of controversial uses of this jurisdiction, which we discuss in Chapter 11. An alternative for the authority will be to apply for a specific issue order under the Children Act.

In *Re C (HIV Test)*[1] the authority obtained a specific issue order that a baby be tested for the HIV virus. Both parents were opposed to conventional medicine and the mother intended to continue breastfeeding the child until the age of two. The judge found that there was a 20–25 per cent chance that the baby was infected and that breastfeeding increased the risk. The Court of Appeal refused the parents permission to appeal. Although the parents' views on treatment were important they were liable to be overridden in the best interests of the child. In this case it was not in the child's best interests that either the parents or the health professionals should remain ignorant of the child's state of health. The test would provide a comparatively unintrusive way of establishing the child's medical status. All concerned with her future welfare would thereby be better informed of the appropriate avenues of treatment in the event of her illness. The court emphasised that it was only concerned at this stage with testing for information purposes. The issues about the appropriate treatment if the child tested positive, or the risks associated with breastfeeding if the child tested positive, had not yet arisen.

It is important to appreciate the limitations of this decision. While it can be seen as support for the proposition that parental discretion in relation to treatment is limited by the welfare principle this would be an over-simplification. First, it should be borne in mind that this will only be so if someone decides to bring the matter before the court[2]. If the medical authorities or social services do not intervene, then parental discretion is likely to rule even if what might be seen as the optimum medical decision for the child is not taken by the parents. The law does not, for example, *require* that parents consent to the immunisation of their children[3]. Secondly, this was a case in which the intrusion was very minor when compared with the major benefits which would be derived from the test. Where matters are more evenly balanced it is less likely that parental views will be overridden even if a *marginal* benefit to the child might arise by doing so.

Where the local authority is refused access to a child whose health is suspected to be at risk, the local authority may apply for a child assessment order or emergency protection order and may obtain a direction that the child be produced for medical or psychiatric examination[4]. The grounds for these orders are considered later. Suffice it to note here that the definition of 'significant harm' includes within it the impairment of the child's health and, for these purposes, health includes physical or mental health[5]. It has been said that this is wide enough to include such matters as poor nutrition, low standards of hygiene,

---

1 [1999] 2 FLR 1004.

2 Subsequent to this decision, the President of the Family Division issued a Direction indicating that the need to make application to the court for a child to be tested for HIV was likely to arise only rarely. It is *not* necessary where all those with parental responsibility agree to the testing. It *is* necessary where a child of sufficient understanding to make an informed decision opposes the testing. See *President's Direction: HIV Testing of Children* [2003] 1 FLR 1299.

3 See the discussion of *Re C (Welfare of Child: Immunisation)* [2003] 2 FLR 1054 (above).

4 Sections 43 and 44 of the Children Act, discussed in Chapter 12 below. For a general discussion of the medical examination of children under the scheme of the Children Act, see G Brasse 'Examination of the Child' [1993] Fam Law 12.

5 Section 31(9) of the Children Act.

poor emotional care, and failure to seek treatment for an illness or condition[1]. The 'significant harm' test requires a comparison of the state of health of the particular child with that of a hypothetical child with similar attributes[2]. A disabled child, for example, requires a higher standard of care than a normal child. It is not clear how far cultural expectations would be taken into account in applying the test[3].

There was considerable uncertainty before the Children Act concerning the power of local authorities to assume compulsory control of newly born babies whose health was considered to be at risk if left under the control of inadequate or irresponsible parents. The House of Lords had held in *D (A Minor) v Berkshire County Council*[4] that a child requiring intensive care, having been born with drug-withdrawal symptoms, could legitimately be the subject of a care order based, in part, on the mother's abuse of her own body while pregnant. Despite some academic commentary to the contrary[5], it is now reasonably clear that a care order may be made, if necessary, exclusively on the strength of an apprehended risk to the child's health, even where present harm cannot be established. This is because the Act applies where the child is not merely suffering significant harm but is *likely* to suffer significant harm[6]. It is subject to the limitation that the local authority cannot make a pre-emptive strike *before* the birth of the child. A 'foetus' does not fall within the definition of 'child' in the legislation. The local authority cannot insist on supervision and management of the later stages of pregnancy and the birth itself, however concerned it may be about the mother's situation[7]. As soon as the child is born, protective action may be instigated. In *A Metropolitan Borough Council v DB*[8], for example, an emergency protection order was obtained at birth in relation to the child of a 17-year-old crack cocaine addict. The mother herself had undergone a Caesarean birth following an application to the High Court and was later detained in the maternity ward under judicial authorisation[9].

---

1   J Masson *The Children Act 1989 Current Law Statutes Annotated* (Sweet & Maxwell, 1990).

2   Section 31(10) of the Children Act, which provides: 'where the question of whether harm suffered by a child is significant turns on the child's health or development, his health or development shall be compared with that which could reasonably be expected of a similar child'.

3   Cultural considerations gave rise to difficulty under the old law, as to which see particularly *Alhaji Mohammed v Knott* [1969] 1 QB 1. For a thorough examination of cultural and religious issues affecting medical procedures on children, see C Bridge 'Religion, Culture and the Body of the Child' in A Bainham, S Day Sclater and M Richards (eds) *Body Lore and Laws* (Hart Publishing, 2002).

4   [1987] 1 All ER 20.

5   MDA Freeman 'Care After 1991' in D Freestone (ed) *Children and the Law* (Hull University Press, 1990) at ch 6. Cf A Bainham 'Care After 1991 – a Reply' (1991) 3 JCL 99.

6   There will, however, be important human rights requirements to observe where compulsory action is taken in relation to a child at birth. See *P, C and S v United Kingdom* [2002] 2 FLR 631, discussed in Chapter 12 below.

7   Neither may the unborn child be made a ward of court nor, presumably, otherwise the subject of the inherent jurisdiction of the High Court. See *Re F (In Utero) (Wardship)* [1988] 2 FLR 307.

8   [1997] 1 FLR 767.

9   For discussion of this case in the context of the inherent jurisdiction, see Chapter 11 below. On the issues surrounding compulsory Caesarean sections generally, see J Weaver 'Court-ordered Caesarean Sections' in A Bainham, S Day Sclater and M Richards (eds) (above).

The child as decision-maker

Another approach to the whole question of medical decision-making would be to allow older children complete independence of action. The obvious incapacity of young children for rational decision-making precludes this option in their case, but wholly different considerations apply to adolescents. Their factual capacity for self-help prompts the question of how far this should be legally recognised. If the law does recognise the ability of some children to provide or refuse a valid consent to medical treatment, how precisely should this relate to the powers of parents? Should parental consent be viewed simply as a *substitute* consent to be made available only where the child lacks capacity, or should it be viewed as an *alternative* consent remaining available *despite* the child's capacity? If so, we would then have *concurrent* capacities and this would raise the further issue of priority, in the event of a conflict of opinion. Should the law prioritise the view of the child or that of the parent, or should the medical profession be allowed to determine its own ranking order of consents?

These questions may become yet more complicated by ethical considerations of medical confidentiality[1]. Even if the requirement of parental consent is by-passed, it does not necessarily follow that a parent is not entitled to participate at all in the decision-making process. The issues of parental consent and notification have tended to be conflated in England[2], but have been treated as distinct, especially with respect to abortion, in the USA. Certain decisions of the US Supreme Court are thus of considerable interest, provided that due allowance is made for the constitutional setting within which they were made. So far as English law is concerned, there has been no authoritative ruling on the question of when a minor is entitled to have information kept confidential from his parents[3]. Academic commentators seem to be agreed that the *competent* child is entitled to confidentiality to the same extent as an adult patient but opinion is divided on the position of the *immature* or *incompetent* minor[4]. The better view is that 'children are entitled to expect confidentiality, quite independently of their consent to

---

1   The confidentiality issue is treated at length in JK Mason, RA McCall Smith and GT Laurie *Law and Medical Ethics* (6th edn) (Butterworths, 2002) at ch 8, especially in relation to minors at pp 253–256. See also J Montgomery *Health Care Law* (2nd edn) (Oxford University Press, 2002) ch 11 and, specifically in relation to children, at pp 308–311; and British Medical Association *Consent, Rights and Choices in Health Care for Children and Young People* (BMJ Books, 2001) ch 4.

2   This was so in *Gillick v West Norfolk and Wisbech Area Health Authority* [1986] 1 AC 112 where the issue was whether a doctor might lawfully provide contraceptives to an under-age girl without parental knowledge or consent. There was no direct discussion in the case about whether the issues of knowledge and consent could be separated, although Lord Fraser's requirement that the doctor should always seek to persuade the girl to allow him to involve her parents is perhaps some indication of what his thinking was.

3   At the time of writing, however, a legal action is pending to determine whether parents have a right of consultation where an abortion is proposed for a girl under the age of 16. This is in response to a revised guidance issued to doctors by the Department of Health on 29 July 2004 confirming, inter alia, that health professionals must follow *Gillick* when advising girls under 16 on abortion.

4   The arguments either way are rehearsed in J Montgomery *Health Care Law* (2nd edn) (Oxford University Press, 2002) at pp 308–311. Montgomery's discussion also takes account of the obligations under the Data Protection Act 1998. The issues concerning confidentiality of medical information in relation to children have now been thoroughly examined in J Loughrey 'Medical Information, Confidentiality and a Child's Right to Privacy' (2003) 23 *Legal Studies* 510.

treatment'[1]. This is also the position taken by the British Medical Association although there remain some uncertainties[2]. Given the inherent uncertainties surrounding the evaluation of individual competence, this would seem to be a more practical solution than attempting to differentiate between children for the purposes of confidentiality. A final complication is the power of the State, through the courts, to override the wishes of a mature minor.

All these issues are examined in the context of medical problems arising from adolescent sexuality. A large number of the reported cases in England (with the notable exceptions of *Re R* and *Re W*[3]) have been concerned with either contraception, abortion, or sterilisation for young women, most of whom have been below the age of majority. There is, however, no obvious reason why the principles established in these cases should not be extrapolated to other medical questions.

Medical paternalism – the doctor as decision-maker

Under certain circumstances, the decisive say may be left to the medical personnel concerned; where a doctor declines to carry out a medical procedure which either a parent or child is requesting, this may be stating the obvious. The mere fact that a parent or a young woman wishes, for example, that an abortion or sterilisation be performed does not lead to the automatic conclusion that a doctor is obliged to perform it. Any doctor would be acting lawfully in refusing to do so unless it would be negligent not to proceed[4].

These principles were graphically illustrated in *R v Cambridge District Health Authority ex parte B*[5]. Here a 10-year-old girl had received extensive treatment for acute myeloid leukaemia including two courses of chemotherapy, total body irradiation and a bone marrow transplant. Sadly, she suffered a further relapse, and the doctors who had treated her and other experts concluded that she had a very short time to live and that no further treatment could usefully be administered. Her father, unwilling to accept this, secured a further medical opinion which gave his daughter a 10–20 per cent chance of life if further chemotherapy were carried out and successful, and a second transplant were then

---

1 Montgomery (above) at p 311.
2 See *Consent, Rights and Choices in Health Care for Children* (BMJ Books, 2001) ch 4. At p 80 it is stated: 'Children who lack the competence to give consent to treatment are also entitled to confidentiality. These patients should be encouraged to allow their parents to be involved but if they cannot be persuaded, doctors must judge whether disclosure to parents is necessary in the child's medical interests.' The BMA also notes the concern, revealed by research, that 'worries about confidentiality dissuade young people from approaching their doctor about health matters'.
3 *Re R (A Minor) (Wardship: Consent to Treatment)* [1992] Fam 11 and *Re W (A Minor) (Medical Treatment: Court's Jurisdiction)* [1992] 3 WLR 758.
4 There is more than a suggestion in *Re F (Mental Patient: Sterilisation)* [1990] 2 AC 1, however, that a doctor could be under a duty arising from the principle of necessity to perform a sterilisation on a mentally incompetent young woman in certain circumstances. Thus, Lord Brandon said that 'it will not only be lawful for doctors on the grounds of necessity to operate on or give other medical treatment to adult patients disabled from giving their consent: it will also be their common law duty to do so'. This was a view with which Lord Goff specifically concurred. On this point, there would seem to be no good reason for distinguishing between the incompetent adult and the incompetent minor.
5 [1995] 1 FLR 1055.

successfully performed. The initial cost was projected at £15,000, with the cost of the second transplant being £60,000.

The health authority refused to go ahead on the basis: (i) that the proposed treatment would cause considerable suffering and was not in the child's best interests; and (ii) that the substantial expenditure on treatment with such a small prospect of success and being of an experimental nature would not be an effective use of limited resources bearing in mind the present and future needs of other patients. The child applied, through her father as litigation friend, for this decision to be quashed in judicial review proceedings.

At first instance she succeeded. Laws J attached considerable importance to her right to life as a fundamental right. He held that the authority had not put forward a sufficiently substantial objective justification on public interest grounds for its decision which infringed this right. However, on appeal, the Court of Appeal emphasised that, in judicial review proceedings, the court's role was only to rule on the *lawfulness* of the authority's decision and not to substitute its own view of the merits. It could not be said here that the authority had exceeded its powers or acted unreasonably in the legal sense. It had been aware of the family's strongly held views but the treatment proposed was at the frontier of medical science and appropriately described as experimental. The authority was entitled also to have regard to the competing claims on its resources.

Much more difficult legal questions arise where the doctor wishes to go ahead and either no one is available to give the consent normally required or someone, be it the child or parent, objects.

The doctrine of necessity

Perhaps the easiest principle to state (although not the easiest to apply) is that, in limited circumstances, the doctrine of necessity will allow the doctor to proceed without any consent at all. The obvious example is an accident. The law allows not only the doctor, but *anyone*, to render first aid to the child, subject only to the requirement that what is done to the child must not exceed what is required by the exigencies of the situation. It is arguable that a doctor would have a legal duty to assist, as would anyone having the care of the child. The case of accidents is a relatively simple one yet, even here, it might become complicated where a conscious child, or a parent on the scene, is refusing emergency aid[1]. The doctrine is difficult to apply in those cases in which there is time to consult parents and, if necessary, obtain judicial authorisation. A difficult case is that of the opposition of parents to blood transfusions on religious grounds. In a succession of cases[2], the courts have been prepared to override the objections of Jehovah's Witnesses, both parents and children, to life-saving blood transfusions. But would the hospitals

---

1   The better view is, however, that the doctor ought to be empowered to take all essential emergency action on the principle of necessity, whatever the parents' view.

2   *Re E (A Minor) (Wardship: Medical Treatment)* [1993] 1 FLR 386, *Re S (A Minor) (Medical Treatment)* [1993] 1 FLR 376, and *Re O (A Minor) (Medical Treatment)* [1993] 2 FLR 149. And, for the latest case, see now *Re P (Medical Treatment: Best Interests)* [2004] 2 All ER 1117, although in this case there was a hint by Johnson J that there could be a case in which it might be appropriate for the court to follow the wishes of a child. On the facts of the present case, however, the best interests of the patient (a 16-year-old boy) in the widest sense, including medical, religious and social interests, required that leave be granted to the medical authorities to administer blood or blood products if his situation became immediately life-threatening 'unless no other form of treatment [was] available'.

concerned have been covered by the doctrine of necessity if they had decided to go ahead *without* judicial authorisation and in the face of parental opposition? Given the uncertain application of the doctrine, the better view would seem to be that life-saving procedures should be carried out without parental approval only in cases of real emergency in which there is no time to bring the matter to court.

The extent of a doctor's power to act

What, then, is the extent of a doctor's power to act where what is proposed is *not* urgent or necessary but is considered by the doctor to be desirable, and in the best medical interests of the child? In *Re F (Mental Patient: Sterilisation)*[1], the House of Lords held that beneficial medical treatment might be performed on a mentally incompetent *adult* where to do so would save her life or ensure the improvement of, or prevent deterioration in, her mental or physical health. Provided that individual decisions and treatment conformed with medical practice which would be accepted by a responsible body of medical opinion skilled in the particular field, they would be lawful[2]. In earlier cases, it had been suggested that all 'touchings' by the medical profession which conformed to this standard could be lawful on the basis of a general principle that they were not 'hostile' (and therefore non-tortious) if they were 'acceptable in the ordinary conduct of everyday life'[3]. However, in *T v T*[4], Wood J rejected the view that all actions taken in accordance with good medical practice were non-tortious. In his opinion, medical procedures performed without consent were prima facie unlawful unless a justification could be found for them. This position was accepted by the House of Lords in *Re F*. A justification for sterilisation was nevertheless found in the twin concepts of necessity and the best interests of the patient, which appear to have been used interchangeably in this case[5].

---

1   [1990] 2 AC 1.

2   The *Bolam* test: see *Bolam v Friern Hospital Management Committee* [1957] 2 All ER 118 but see now *Bolitho v City and Hackney Health Authority* [1997] 3 WLR 1151 (fn 3 at p 310 above).

3   *Wilson v Pringle* [1987] QB 237 and *Collins v Wilcock* [1984] 3 All ER 374.

4   [1988] Fam 52.

5   Take, for example, the following passage from the speech of Lord Brandon:

> 'In my opinion the solution to the problem which the common law provides is that a doctor can lawfully operate on, or give other treatment to, adult patients who are incapable, for one reason or another, of consenting to his doing so, provided that the operation or other treatment concerned is in the *best interests* of such patients. The operation or other treatment will be in their best interests if, but only if, it is carried out in order to save their lives or to ensure improvement or prevent deterioration in their physical or mental health ... the principle is that when persons lack the capacity for whatever reason to take decisions about the performance of operations on them, or the giving of other medical treatment to them, it is *necessary* that some other person or persons, with the appropriate qualifications, should take such decisions for them.' [Emphasis added.]

It should, however, be noted that this justification can only be used, at least in the case of *adult* patients, where they are *incompetent* to take the particular decision involved. Thus, in *Re C (Refusal of Medical Treatment)* [1994] 1 FLR 31, the court held that it had not been established that a paranoid schizophrenic in Broadmoor lacked the competence to decide whether or not to have his gangrenous leg amputated. An order was therefore made prohibiting the operation without his consent. See also *Re JT (Adult: Refusal of Medical Treatment)* [1998] 1 FLR 48 in which a woman of 25, despite suffering from mental disability involving learning difficulties and extremely severe behavioural disturbances, was found to have the capacity to refuse dialysis for renal failure. As such, Wall J held that it would have been a criminal and tortious assault to

Procedures performed on children without consent

It is not certain how far these principles could be used to justify procedures performed on children without parental consent[1]. It is clear from the *Gillick* case that the medical profession may act in cases of parental abandonment or abuse[2]. It is equally clear that they may obtain the court's authority to act against parents' wishes either under the inherent jurisdiction or by seeking a specific issue order. But it has been pointed out by Lavery that a key objection to this process of obtaining judicial approval is that 'it should not be necessary to invoke the court's authority for medical treatment which is clearly in the child's best interests'[3]. Following *Gillick*, a doctor may be able to act against parental wishes where he has the agreement of the child who is herself competent to produce a valid consent. Even though, following *Re R* and *Re W*, the parent retains a concurrent right to consent, the doctor would appear to be acting lawfully in electing to give priority to the child's view[4]. But what of the immature child who would fail the test of *Gillick* competence? Here, the obvious implication of *Gillick* was that the parent's right to give or withhold consent would remain intact, and this has been confirmed by the later Court of Appeal decisions. Are there, then, any circumstances under which a doctor may act against parental wishes, in non-urgent cases, because he judges it to be in the child's best interests to do so?

It must be said that, as the law stands, this would be a precarious course of action for the medical profession. Much may turn on how far the courts would be prepared to extend the concept of necessity or apply the reasoning in *Re F*, outside the rather special case of sterilisation. Alternatively, some support for such independent action might be found in those cases which have determined that parental responsibility must be exercised *reasonably* and that where parents exceed the bounds of reasonableness they themselves act unlawfully and may, indeed, commit a criminal offence[5]. The difficulty with relying on these principles is that, in the medical context at least, parents do appear to have been allowed considerable latitude in non-life-saving situations. Thus, a refusal to agree to treatment, even if adjudged undesirable, might still be regarded as falling within a band of reasonable decisions and within the scope of parental discretion.

Dispensing with parental consent

Ruth Lavery has argued convincingly that the concept of necessity should be redefined in its application to immature children. She has advocated the adoption of a principle which would enable a doctor to dispense with parental consent

---

perform physically invasive treatment without her consent. The Court of Appeal has now made it very plain in *St George's Health Care NHS Trust v S; R v Collins and Others ex parte S* [1998] 2 FLR 728 that a *competent* adult patient has an absolute right to refuse treatment even if the consequence may be the death of the patient.

1　For an excellent analysis of the implications of *Re F* for the non-emergency treatment of children, see R Lavery 'Routine Medical Treatment of Children' [1990] JSWL 375. A recent article focusing on non-urgent treatment specifically in the context of dental treatment for children is P Booth and S Proud 'Embracing Children – Non-urgent Treatment, Dental Legal Issues and Children' [2002] Fam Law 917.

2　*Gillick v West Norfolk and Wisbech Area Health Authority* [1986] 1 AC 112, although this situation is not entirely unproblematic in practice: see Lavery (above) at pp 378–379.

3　Ibid at p 377.

4　Discussed further in A Bainham 'Non-Intervention and Judicial Paternalism' in P Birks (ed) *The Frontiers of Liability*, Vol 1 (Oxford University Press, 1994), especially at pp 162–166.

5　See, particularly, *R v D* [1984] AC 778 and *R v Rahman* (1985) 81 Cr App R 349.

where there is a clear consensus within the medical profession that treatment is for a child's benefit in a given set of circumstances. This would ensure that particular children would not be denied the benefit of treatment, which is clearly in their best interests, because of parental prejudice, phobia or carelessness. On the other hand, the parent's right to consent, she argues, ought to be preserved where there is a difference of medical opinion as to what is in a child's best interests or where the decision is not a purely medical one but has other social, moral or long-term implications[1].

Lavery saw her proposal as a 'fairly modest inroad' into the parental right to consent. Once a procedure ranges beyond the routine, the prudent course for the doctor would be to seek the sanction of the court. Even where the doctor is dealing with an adolescent, the interaction of the child's competence and parental responsibility is now so uncertain that the doctor could not be confident about whose view should prevail in law, in the event of a clash – although it is perhaps debatable how far the courts would want to question retrospectively the clinical judgment of the medical profession. These doubts must arise, a fortiori, where the child himself is thought to be possibly incapable of providing a valid consent. The courts may have an increasingly important role in resolving these uncertainties.

THE PROBLEM OF INFANTS AND YOUNG CHILDREN: THE SELECTIVE TREATMENT OF THE NEWBORN

The issue of treating, or not treating, newly born infants with serious medical conditions, illustrates the operation of these principles in an extreme context, where life itself is at stake[2]. The reported cases in England have largely been concerned with neonates but there is no good reason why the principles which have emerged from these decisions should not also be applied to young children[3]. The giving or withholding of life-saving treatment for babies or young children, who are self-evidently incapable of expressing any view, gives rise to a multitude of legal and ethical issues[4]. Where, as in the case of the conjoined twins[5], the best medical interests of the child may appear to conflict with those of another, the issues may seem almost incapable of resolution.

When may a parent and/or a doctor be liable under the criminal or civil law *for refusal* to authorise or carry out life-saving treatment or be liable *for performing* such surgery? Can the law realistically distinguish for these purposes between acts and omissions? Is, for example, the decision to withhold life-saving surgery or food to be equated with the positive act of administering a drug which has the effect of hastening death? And, in the case of the latter, does it matter that the primary

---

1 See R Lavery 'Routine Medical Treatment of Children' [1990] JSWL 375 at pp 383–384.

2 See JK Mason, RA McCall Smith and GT Lawrie *Law and Medical Ethics* (6th edn) (Butterworths, 2002) at ch 7, and J Montgomery *Health Care Law* (2nd edn) (Oxford University Press, 2002) at ch 18.

3 In fact, two of the leading Canadian cases did involve young children rather than neonates and repay examination for this reason. See *Re Superintendent of Family and Child Service and Dawson* (1983) 145 DLR (3rd) 610 and *Couture-Jacquet v Montreal Children's Hospital* (1986) 28 DLR (4th) 22.

4 These issues were particularly well identified in M Mulholland 'Neo-Natal Care and Treatment – The Doctor's Dilemma' (1989) 5 *Professional Negligence* 109.

5 *Re A (Conjoined Twins: Surgical Separation)* [2001] 1 FLR 1.

purpose was to relieve pain and suffering and that the acceleration of death was an unavoidable effect of this? Is the duty of the medical profession towards defective newborns the same as it is to 'normal' babies and, if it is not, what are the implications of this for the treatment of disabled adolescents or adults?

Leaving aside the question of criminal liability, the civil law issues are no less complex. What is the extent of parental discretion in this area? How big a part should parents' views play in medical decisions – are doctors bound by them and, if not, how much value ought to be attached to them? When might the State intervene, through the local authority or the court, to impose its own view, and on what basis should it do so? If such intervention does occur, whose responsibility does the child become? Do children have an absolute right to life or ought the quality of life to be taken into account – and who decides, and on which criteria, what *is* a worthwhile life? Ought we, for example, to differentiate between those infants who are terminally ill, those who have reasonable prospects of an appreciable life-span and those where the prognosis is uncertain? Finally, and perhaps most importantly, what is the correct allocation of decision-making responsibility where neither the court nor the local authority is involved? Are the prevailing standards and practices of the medical profession conclusive or are there moral and philosophical questions which ought to be outside the exclusive control of the profession?

English law has given a definite response to some of these questions while others remain shrouded in uncertainty. In order to illustrate the way in which English law approaches these issues, we will now look closely at six of the leading cases. We begin with a much-publicised decision of the Court of Appeal over 20 years ago which authorised life-saving surgery on a Down's syndrome baby. We conclude with the even more publicised case of the conjoined twins which confronted that court with horrendously complex legal and moral issues in the autumn of 2000.

The baby Alexandra case

In *Re B*[1], a baby was born in July 1981 with the double disadvantage of Down's syndrome[2] and duodenal atresia, an intestinal blockage. The latter condition is not uncommon in Down's syndrome infants but, if not operated upon, death by starvation results. The baby's parents, acting with what was accepted to be the best of motives, thought it kinder to let her die in view of her condition. The doctors concerned contacted the local authority which made her a ward of court. Ewbank J gave care and control to the authority and initially authorised the surgery. But when the baby was transferred to another hospital, surgeons there declined to operate in the face of parental objection. The authority then returned to court but, after hearing the parents' views, Ewbank J refused to consent to the operation. The Court of Appeal heard evidence that other surgeons were available who were prepared to operate. There was a good prognosis for success of

---

1   *Re B (A Minor) (Wardship: Medical Treatment)* (1982) FLR 117. This decision should now be compared closely with *Re T (Wardship: Medical Treatment)* [1997] 1 FLR 502 – see pp 338–339 below – and the reasoning in the conjoined twins case.

2   Down's syndrome, often referred to as 'Mongolism', is a chromosomal aberration occurring in an estimated 1 in 700 live births. It produces mental retardation and is often accompanied by other congenital abnormalities of which the most common are gastro-intestinal blockages and congenital heart defects. Corrective surgery is usually required in the first year of life.

the surgery which was thought to give the child a life expectancy of 20 to 30 years – the normal life span of someone with the disorder.

The Court of Appeal, applying the welfare principle, authorised the surgery. Templeman LJ thought that the judge had attached too much weight to parental wishes and was wrong to conclude, in this case, that those wishes should be respected. The issue was what was in the best interests of the child, and the test which ought to be applied was whether her life was demonstrably going to be so awful that she should be condemned to die, or whether it was so imponderable that she should be allowed to live. The evidence here was that the operation would give the child the normal life expectancy of a Down's syndrome child with the disabilities associated with Down's syndrome. He concluded that it was not for the court (on whom the decision devolved) to say that a life of that description ought to be extinguished. He did, however, visualise more serious cases where 'severe proved damage where the future is so certain and where the life of the child is so bound to be full of pain and suffering that the court might be driven to a different conclusion'.

Already in this case, several important principles had emerged. First, it confirmed that, in English law, there was no absolute principle that parents' wishes should be respected in life and death cases. The court in wardship had jurisdiction to override them in appropriate cases. Secondly, it was equally clear that the court rejected any absolute right to life of the child. The court had to make a qualitative assessment of the sort of life the child might lead and balance this with the risks involved in the operation. In this case, where the operation was considered to be relatively routine and where the prognosis was good, the balance was in favour of intervening unless the court was prepared to conclude (which it was not) that a life afflicted by Down's syndrome was not worth living. Thirdly, it was accepted that the responsibility for, and cost of, substitute care for the child should fall on the local authority if the child should ultimately be rejected by the parents following corrective surgery. In this case, adoptive parents were available if necessary[1]. The case left open the question of what the *automatic* legal position might have been had the court not become involved. Since the court here decided that intervention was required by the child's welfare, does this mean that the parents and medical profession, acting in conjunction, would have behaved unlawfully if they had agreed to allow nature to take its course? That no such simple deduction can be made is implicit from the result in the next case.

The trial of Dr Arthur[2]

John Pearson was also born with Down's syndrome, but without any additional complication. He died within three days of birth, and Dr Arthur, a highly respected consultant paediatrician, was charged with his murder – a charge reduced to attempted murder during the course of his trial at Leicester Crown

---

1   It is understood that, in the event, adoptive parents were not required since the natural parents accepted the child.

2   The case never appeared in the official law reports but was reported in (1981) *The Times*, November 6, and at (1981) 12 BMLR 1. Passages from the judge's direction to the jury are extracted in I Kennedy and A Grubb *Medical Law* (3rd edn) (Butterworths, 2000) at pp 2164–2165 and there is a penetrating analysis of the case in MJ Gunn and JC Smith 'Arthur's Case and the Right to Life of a Down's Syndrome Child' [1985] Crim LR 705.

Court[1]. The baby was discovered at birth to have Down's syndrome and was immediately rejected by the mother. After discussion with both parents, Dr Arthur wrote in the casenotes: 'Parents do not wish the baby to survive. Nursing care only.' On the treatment chart, he prescribed the drug dihydrocodeine (DF 118) to be given 'as required' at doses of 5mg every four hours by the nurse in charge. The baby died 57.25 hours after birth. The cause of death was stated to be broncho-pneumonia resulting from Down's syndrome. A member of the 'Life' organisation alleged that the baby had been drugged and starved to death. The pathologist's evidence was that the cause of death was lung stasis produced by DF 118 poisoning. The prosecution case was that this was the result of the defendant's decision to cause the death of the child. The jury acquitted Dr Arthur.

Academic opinion is divided on whether the case of Dr Arthur can be said to have established any principles at all. Since it did not reach the higher courts, what is left is a jury decision which can scarcely have value as a legal precedent. Nevertheless, it has been argued that inferential guidance on the principles of the criminal law, within which these decisions must be taken, can be drawn from the directions which Farquharson J gave to the jury[2]. In particular, the judge regarded the distinction between acts and omissions as crucial. He directed the jury to consider whether 'there was an act properly so-called on the part of Dr Arthur, as distinct from simply allowing the child to die'. The judge contrasted the administration of a deliberately lethal dose of a drug (a positive act) with a decision to decline to operate on an intestinal blockage (an omission). No one, he said, could regard the latter as an act of murder. At the same time, he directed that no one, doctors included, had the right to kill a disabled child any more than they had a right to kill anyone else.

In a powerful critique of this reasoning, Gunn and Smith point out that the criminal law *does* impose liability for omissions where there is a duty to act. Such a duty arises in principle where *anyone*, including a doctor, has physical care of a child. It would include an obligation to provide proper sustenance and medical aid to a 'normal' child[3]. They conclude that the implication of the case is that the duty to an abnormal child must be different from, and lower than, that owed to a normal child. The duty appears to be limited to doing what is reasonable in all the circumstances, something acknowledged by Dunn LJ in the baby Alexandra case, where the parents' decision to allow the child to die was viewed as 'entirely responsible' and could not properly be regarded as an intention to kill[4].

It is difficult to regard the baby Alexandra case and the case of Dr Arthur as reconcilable. What is clear is that, simply because a court might have exercised *its*

---

1   The child was found to have been suffering from certain inherent defects at birth so that the precise cause of death was uncertain. Nonetheless, the prosecution was relying in the murder charge on an intention to kill so that the reduction of the charge was of no relevance to the alleged mental state of the doctor. See *R v Whybrow* (1951) 35 Cr App R 141.

2   JK Mason, RA McCall Smith and GT Laurie *Law and Medical Ethics* (6th edn) (Butterworths, 2002) at pp 477–478.

3   'Arthur's Case and the Right to Life of a Down's Syndrome Child' [1985] Crim LR 705 at pp 709–711.

4   A similar view was expressed by Ward LJ in the case of the conjoined twins (see below) in which he said that if the hospital had bowed to the weight of the parental opposition to surgical intervention 'there could not have been the slightest criticism of them for letting nature take its course in accordance with the parents' wishes': see *Re A (Conjoined Twins: Medical Treatment)* [2001] 1 FLR 1 at 27.

discretion in favour of life, it does not mean that parents and doctors exercising *their* discretion in favour of death would automatically commit an offence[1]. The issue of the limits of decision-making powers under the civil law is a quite separate question from that of criminal liability for homicide. But this leads to the unsatisfactory conclusion that neither case could truly be said to have established standards capable of determining, with any precision, the extent of legal duties owed to disabled infants. And there is a stark incongruity between the life-saving decision for baby Alexandra and the decision to terminate the life of the Pearson baby, who had a comparatively less complicated condition. It is difficult to resist the conclusion that the decisive factor was that the parents and doctors were in agreement in one case but not in the other.

The case of the hydrocephalic baby: *Re C*[2]

Re C (A Minor) concerned the situation of a terminally ill infant. The local authority had decided, before the child's birth, and without knowledge of her medical abnormality, that the parents would be unable to cope. When the child was born, she was found to be hydrocephalic – a condition involving a blockage of cerebral spinal fluid within the brain. In addition, her brain structure was poorly formed[3]. The issue was whether medical staff should seek to prolong her life and whether they should provide treatment appropriate to a child with her condition or appropriate for a child without this disability. The Official Solicitor, acting as guardian ad litem, obtained a report from a foremost paediatrician which stated that the aim of treatment should be to ease suffering rather than achieve a short prolongation of life.

In wardship proceedings, Ward J gave leave to the hospital authorities 'to treat the ward to die; to die with the greatest dignity and the least of pain, suffering and distress'. He also gave specific directions that they should not be required to treat any serious infection or set up an intravenous feeding system. On the Official Solicitor's appeal against these directions, the Court of Appeal held that it was appropriate to authorise treatment for the purpose of alleviating suffering but it would accept the opinions of medical staff if they decided that the aim of nursing care should be limited to this and not to achieve a short prolongation of life. But it was not appropriate for the judge's directions to be worded in that way or to be that specific. The directions concerning infections and feeding were therefore removed and the general direction was amended to authorise the hospital authorities 'to treat the minor to allow her life to come to an end peacefully and with dignity'.

The facts of this case were clearly distinguishable from those in the baby Alexandra case. The child in this case was already dying and no treatment could enable her to have a significant future life. Moreover, the existing 'quality' of her life was far removed from that of the Down's syndrome child. Her brain was

---

1 Gunn and Smith (above).

2 *Re C (A Minor) (Wardship: Medical Treatment)* [1989] 2 All ER 782. See J Stone 'Re C – Any Nearer a Solution to the Problem of Severely Handicapped Newborns?' (1989) 1 JCL 1, and D Morgan 'Severely Handicapped Babies and the Courts' (1989) 139 NLJ 723.

3 The most extreme form of brain malformation occurs in anencephalic infants and this entails the absence of all or most of the higher brain. For an illuminating discussion of this condition, see the materials extracted in I Kennedy and A Grubb *Medical Law* (3rd edn) (Butterworths, 2000) at pp 2225–2233.

incapable of even the most limited intellectual function and she suffered major physical disabilities which *would* render her life demonstrably awful and intolerable. These included a mixture of severe mental incapacity, blindness, probably deafness and spastic cerebral palsy of all four limbs. She was already not absorbing food properly or growing. In these circumstances there was a prognosis of an extremely short life and any treatment could be no more than a temporary palliative.

This decision confirmed that there was no absolute right to life and it provided the classic illustration of the more serious case of disability envisaged in the baby Alexandra case. There were, at the same time, strong echoes of the Dr Arthur case and the refusal of the law to countenance anything which smacks of positive killing.

Hence, the judge's direction required amendment in form if not in substance. While it remains the case that the courts are the final arbiters of what kind of treatment is warranted for a child, the decision in *Re C* revealed that they will usually wish to confine themselves to giving broad directions about the general nature of treatment or non-treatment and will prefer to leave the detailed management of the case to the medical professionals. Beyond this, the case went no further than the baby Alexandra case in articulating, other than indirectly, the scope of parental and medical authority or the standards which should govern these cases.

What then of the child who is *not* terminally ill but whose medical condition is arguably far worse than that of the uncomplicated Down's syndrome child?

The case of the premature baby: *Re J*[1]

Re J concerned a baby born very prematurely at 27 weeks' gestation. At birth, J weighed 1.1 kg. He was not breathing and was placed on a ventilator and given antibiotics on a drip to avoid infection. His pulse rate remained low for the next 10 days and it was touch and go whether he would survive. At three to four months old, he was taken off the ventilator but thereafter suffered repetitive fits and cessations of breathing requiring resuscitation by ventilation. The prognosis was severe brain damage arising from prematurity. The most optimistic neonatalogist thought that there would be serious spastic quadriplegia. It was likely that J would never be able to sit up or hold his head upright, he would probably be blind and deaf and would be most unlikely to develop even the most limited intellectual abilities. On the other hand, since pain was a very basic response, there was evidence that he would be able to feel pain to the same extent as a normal baby. Life expectancy at its highest was late teens and would probably be considerably shorter.

The issue concerned what should be done in the event of J suffering a further collapse which could occur at any time but was not inevitable. Scott Baker J, at first instance, directed that there should be no further ventilation. The Court of Appeal held that the court could, acting in a child's best interests, approve a medical course of action which failed to prevent death. There was *no* absolute rule that life-prolonging treatment should never be withheld except in the case of a terminally ill child. Nor was the 'demonstrably so awful' test propounded in the

---

1 *Re J (A Minor) (Wardship: Medical Treatment)* [1990] 3 All ER 930.

baby Alexandra case to be treated as a quasi-statutory yardstick. While there was a strong presumption in favour of life, the court had to have regard to the quality of life, and to any additional suffering which might be caused by the life-saving treatment itself. In assessing the quality of life if treatment were given, the correct approach was to assess whether such a life *judged from the child's viewpoint* would be intolerable to him. In this case, the court authorised treatment within the parameters of a medical report which advised that, in the event of J requiring further resuscitation, it would not be in his best interests for this to be done unless this seemed appropriate to the doctors caring for him in the prevailing clinical situation. Again, the court was at pains to emphasise that what was at issue was not the right to impose death, but rather the right to choose a course of action which would fail to avert it. Where a patient had full capacity, this choice fell to him, but where, as an infant, he lacked capacity, the choice had to be a co-operative effort between the parents and the doctors or, where a court was involved, between the court and the medical profession, taking into account the views of the parents. In the end, the conclusion might be legitimately reached that it would not be in the *best* interests of a child to subject him to treatment which would cause increased suffering and no commensurate benefit, while giving full weight to the child's desire to survive.

This case was significant for its apparent application of the 'substituted judgment' test. The court emphasised the need for assessments of the quality of life to be made from the *assumed view of the child patient* and not from that of the adult decision-maker. Thus, severely disabled people might subjectively find a quality of life rewarding which to normal people would appear intolerable. The doctrine does not sit well with the traditional English approach which, applying the welfare principle, requires the decision-maker to arrive at his own view of what is best for the child[1]. The court here did, of course, have to apply this principle, but it did so in a way which appeared to equate the best interests of the child with a hypothetical projection of what that child would have wished if fully competent. This approach is, arguably, not merely contrary to the usual application of the welfare principle (which, as has been seen, does not require the actual wishes of competent children to be followed[2]) it also involves the use of a legal fiction. Disabled neonates have never possessed the capacity to express a rational view on anything and there is, therefore, no basis upon which their supposed wishes can be predicted, except that of the individual judgment of the decision-maker. In reality, it is necessary to fall back on what the court itself thinks would be best for a particular child. The decision confirmed that the court must engage in a balancing exercise in determining the quality of life, if prolonged, against the pain and suffering involved in the treatment itself. It was also a further illustration of the court's preference for deferring to the medical profession's clinical judgment within broadly based guidelines.

---

1 Although it fits better with some theories of children's rights which involve retrospective inquiries about what adults would have wished for themselves while children. See Chapter 3.

2 For a critique of the use of the substituted judgment test in cases like this, see Wells, Alldridge and Morgan 'An Unsuitable Case for Treatment' (1990) 140 NLJ 1544.

Later decisions are further evidence of this approach[1]. In _A National Health Service Trust v D_[2] Cazalet J granted a declaration that the medical team should not be obliged to resuscitate a child, now aged 19 months, who had been born prematurely with irreversible brain abnormality and severe chronic disabilities coupled with heart failure, renal and hepatic dysfunction. He was, in short, dying but his committed parents wished him, contrary to the unanimous medical view, to be admitted to paediatric intensive care. Cazalet J took the view that, having regard to the minimal quality of life the child had left in his short life span, any possible short-term extension was not in his best interests, from his assumed standpoint, given the increased pain and suffering involved.

The case is also useful in that the human rights considerations were addressed in it. The parents' argument that the above declaration would involve a breach of the right to life, protected by Article 2 of the ECHR, was rejected on two grounds. First, the court said that there could not be such a breach where the treatment authorised by the court was in the child's best interests as it was here. Secondly, following _D v United Kingdom_[3] the declaration would _protect_ the Article 3 rights of the child which require that he should not be subjected to inhuman or degrading treatment. This includes the right to die.

The resurgence of parental rights: _Re T_

In October 1996, the Court of Appeal handed down its judgment in _Re T (Wardship: Medical Treatment)_[4]. The decision came close to reasserting the concept of parental 'rights' in the medical context and was the subject of much critical academic comment[5]. The baby, C, suffered from a life-threatening liver defect known as biliary artresia. There was a unanimous medical prognosis that without a liver transplant C could not live beyond the age of two-and-a-half years, but the

---

1 See _Re J (A Minor) (Medical Treatment)_ [1992] 2 FLR 165 (not to be confused with the earlier case under discussion). In this later case, the Court of Appeal held that it would be an abuse of judicial power for the court, in the exercise of its inherent jurisdiction, to require a medical practitioner to treat a minor in a manner contrary to his fundamental duty to exercise his best clinical judgment. In this case, the child aged 16 months suffered from severe cerebral palsy, epilepsy and cortical blindness following a fall. He required 24-hour attention and medical opinion was unanimous that his life expectancy was short. The Court of Appeal refused, in these circumstances, to order the health authority to continue with artificial ventilation and other life-saving measures. See also _Re C (A Baby)_ [1996] 2 FLR 3, in which Sir Stephen Brown P said that the courts were ready to assist the medical profession with taking responsibility in cases of grave anxiety. In this case, the baby suffered severe brain damage after developing meningitis. She could not survive without continuing artificial ventilation. This would involve her in increasing pain and distress, and the prognosis was hopeless. The medical experts were agreed that further artificial ventilation was not in her best interests and the court in wardship proceedings granted leave to discontinue it. More recently, it has been held, again by Sir Stephen Brown P, that the court may authorise the withdrawal of ventilation for a terminally ill baby where this is advised by the medical team but opposed by the parents. See _Re C (Medical Treatment)_ [1998] 1 FLR 384, in which the parents were orthodox Jews and did not believe that their religion permitted them to contemplate a course of action which would indirectly shorten life.
2 [2000] 2 FLR 677.
3 (1997) 24 EHRR 423.
4 [1997] 1 FLR 502.
5 See particularly M Fox and J McHale 'In Whose Best Interests?' (1997) MLR 700, and A Bainham 'Do Babies Have Rights?' [1997] CLJ 48.

prospects of success were thought to be good if a donor liver became available. All the medical experts thought it was in C's best interests to undergo such an operation but the parents (who were unmarried[1]) were opposed to it. The case undoubtedly had special features. Both parents were health care professionals with experience of caring for sick children; C had previously undergone unsuccessful surgery which had caused him much pain and distress; and the parents had, albeit against medical advice, gone to a 'distant Commonwealth country'. The issue was whether the mother should be ordered to return to the jurisdiction with C and present him to hospital for liver transplantation assessment.

At first instance, Connell J held that she should, but he appeared to ground his decision on an assessment that the mother's opinion was unreasonable, rather than on a straightforward application of the welfare principle. Allowing the mother's appeal, the Court of Appeal emphasised that the matter was governed by the welfare principle. While there was a strong presumption in favour of life, prolonging life was not the court's sole objective. The judge, it was held, had failed to give adequate weight to certain factors which ought to have been fed into the welfare test. According to Butler-Sloss LJ, he had given insufficient emphasis to 'the enormous significance of the close attachment between the mother and baby' and 'whether it [was] in the best interests of C for [the court] in effect to direct the mother to take on this total commitment where she [did] not agree with the course proposed'. Roch LJ thought that there was a clinical aspect to the bond between mother and child 'because in the absence of parental belief that a transplant [was] the right procedure for the child, the prospects of a successful outcome [were] diminished'.

As we have seen, there is nothing unusual or unprincipled about a court refusing life-saving surgery to a child in an appropriate case. What makes the decision in *Re T* so controversial is the close association which the Court of Appeal was prepared to make between the interests of the mother and the child, and this gave the case a significance which went beyond the fate of the individual child. Here, the focus of the court's attention went beyond the child's best *medical* interests which had, it is submitted, been the decisive factor in the earlier cases. It was prepared to attach significance to the issues surrounding the care of the child in the event of a successful operation – yet nowhere was there the suggestion, as there was in the baby Alexandra case (above), that if necessary the State should be prepared to provide a substitute home. It was sufficient for Butler-Sloss LJ that C's future treatment 'should be left in the hands of his devoted parents'. Waite LJ thought it unhelpful to indulge in 'rights-talk'. This was 'not an occasion – even in an age preoccupied with "rights" – to talk of the rights of the child, or the rights of a parent, or the rights of the court'[2]. Whether or not it is jurisprudentially accurate to assert 'rights' for children or parents, the real criticism of this ruling is that it failed to differentiate sufficiently between the *interests* of the mother and the child which were assumed to coincide but which, it might be argued, were in conflict. In Waite LJ's opinion, 'in the last analysis the best interest of every child incudes an expectation that difficult decisions affecting the length and quality of

---

1 The significance of their being unmarried was that sole parental responsibility was with the mother although it was clear, in any event, that the father agreed with her.

2 On children's rights as a concept, see Chapter 3.

its life will be taken for it by the parent to whom its care has been entrusted by nature'. Yet to take this literally would be to turn the clock back to the nineteenth century and ignore the advances made for children as persons over the last hundred years.

The dilemma of the conjoined twins: *Re A*

In September 2000, ironically perhaps immediately before the implementation of the HRA 1998, the Court of Appeal in *Re A (Children) (Conjoined Twins: Surgical Separation)*[1] was called upon to resolve what many saw as a clash between the fundamental rights and interests of two children. Jodie and Mary were ischiopagus conjoined twins (joined at the pelvis). The medical prognosis should they remain joined was hopeless. The twins shared a common aorta. Mary's heart and lungs were severely deficient and her life was sustained only by this common artery. She was therefore entirely dependent on Jodie for life. It was also known that the death of *both* twins would be inevitable within a few months since Jodie's heart would be unable to cope with the strain. Surgical separation would give Jodie, the stronger twin, a reasonable prospect of a worthwhile life but would be bound to cause the almost immediate death of Mary. The parents were devout Roman Catholics from Malta. They were unwilling to agree to surgery since they took the view that in God's eyes the twins were equal and that morally one could not be sacrificed to save the other.

What was the court to do in a situation like this? The Court of Appeal[2], with much agonising, reached the conclusion that it should uphold the decision of Johnson J who had granted a declaration that the operation might lawfully be performed. This subsequently took place in St. Mary's Hospital, Manchester. Mary, as expected, died during the course of the operation while Jodie survived and is understood to be progressing remarkably well. The issues in the case were immensely complicated but they can be conveniently grouped together as the family law issues and the criminal law issues. There was also an important issue under the ECHR, although this received surprisingly cursory examination by the court.

Taking first the family law issues, what was the correct principle to apply when the interests of two children conflict and what was the proper weight to be attached to the genuinely and firmly held opinions of the parents? As to the conflict of interest between the twins, it should first be acknowledged that there was a division of opinion about whether there was indeed a conflict at all. Johnson J at first instance and Robert Walker LJ in the Court of Appeal both thought that there was not since, as the latter put it, 'continued life, whether long or short, would hold nothing for Mary, except possible pain or discomfort, if indeed she can feel anything at all'[3]. The majority in the Court of Appeal (Ward LJ and Brooke LJ), however, took the view that an invasive procedure which would bring about the sudden death of Mary could not properly be said to be in her best

---

1 [2001] 1 FLR 1.
2 For the author's views on the decision see A Bainham 'Resolving the Unresolvable: The Case of the Conjoined Twins' [2001] CLJ 49. See also M Freeman 'Whose Life is it Anyway?' (2001) 9 *Medical Law Review* 259. For a commentary attacking the decision see S Michalowski 'Sanctity of Life – are some lives more sacred than others?' (2002) *Legal Studies* 377.
3 [2001] 1 FLR 1 at 119.

interests and there was therefore a clash of interests between the twins. The court's obligation in cases like this, as we have seen, is to determine the matter in accordance with the welfare principle. But in a case in which the best interests of two children pull in opposite directions and in which both were the subject of the proceedings[1] the court could not give effect to the paramountcy principle in relation to both children simultaneously. Faced with this impossibility, the majority decided that they could not abdicate from the responsibility of deciding, since to do nothing would in itself be to take a position. They reached the conclusion that they should balance the interests of the two children and choose the least detrimental alternative. This was to sanction the operation since it would offer Jodie the chance of a relatively normal life while not fundamentally affecting the sad condition of Mary whom Ward LJ (controversially) described as 'designated for death'. The court therefore followed what might be seen as a utilitarian approach which maximised the welfare of those whose interests were at stake when taken collectively. There is clearly a tension between such an approach and one which emphasises individual rights. Yet it may well prove less controversial in less emotive contexts in which the issue is not one of life and death. Indeed it is the approach essentially taken by the Law Commission in its Report which preceded the Children Act 1989[2].

The other family law issue was how much weight to attach to the religiously inspired views of the parents. Here the court reiterated the principle that the parental view is not sovereign and that the court's role was not confined to reviewing the reasonableness of a parental decision. The approach in *Re T (Wardship: Medical Treatment)*[3], which many commentators had criticised, was therefore firmly rejected. The court did not in the final analysis attach decisive importance to considerations of respecting the parents' religious views[4] when to do so would jeopardise the life of one child and in this respect the decision reaffirms a long-standing principle[5].

These issues of family law arose within a context in which there was a substantial argument that to authorise the operation would be to bring about the unlawful killing, indeed murder, of Mary. Much of the judgments, especially that of Brooke LJ, are therefore devoted to a close examination of the law of homicide which is beyond the scope of the present discussion. But the essential point is that the criminal law draws a fundamental distinction between *omissions*, such as the withdrawal of life-sustaining treatment[6], and *positive acts* of killing. While the former will not generally be unlawful, it has long been accepted that the latter will, prima facie, amount to homicide. What was proposed here was a surgical intervention which would directly bring about the almost immediate death of a child. It was inevitable too that the doctors who performed it would foresee this

---

1   For other cases in which the courts have had to resolve conflicts of interest between two children and further discussion of this issue see Chapter 2 above.
2   Report No 172, paras 3.13 and 3.14, and clause 1(2) of the Draft Bill appended to that Report.
3   [1997] 1 WLR 242, discussed above.
4   It should be recalled that religious freedom is a fundamental right protected by the ECHR, Article 9 of which upholds the right, inter alia, to 'freedom of thought, conscience and religion ... and freedom ... to manifest ... religion or belief, in worship, teaching, practice and observance'.
5   See Chapter 2 above.
6   See the section on the selective treatment of neonates at pp 331 et seq below.

death as a virtual certainty and hence the inference would be inescapable that they *intended* that death[1]. The altruistic motives of the medical team, to save another life, would not normally exculpate them since the law of homicide, at least in theory, takes no account of motive. The sanctity of life generally means that one life cannot be valued less than another[2].

The issue was therefore whether there could be a defence to what would otherwise be murder. The court found, in the unique circumstances, that the doctrine of necessity applied and, in the case of Ward LJ, that this was a situation of 'quasi self-defence'. So far as necessity was concerned, the court found that the three essential prerequisites were satisfied – the action was needed to avoid inevitable and irreparable evil, no more was proposed than was reasonably necessary for this purpose and the evil inflicted would not be disproportionate to the evil avoided. As to the novel notion of quasi self-defence, Ward LJ relied heavily on the consideration that just as to operate would be to kill Mary, not to operate would kill Jodie. The reality, therefore, 'harsh as it is to state it, and unnatural as it is that it should be happening', was that Mary was effectively killing Jodie. He could 'see no difference between ... resort to legitimate self-defence and removing the threat of fatal harm to her presented by Mary's draining her life blood.' While this formulation has attracted severe criticism, it is one which had the support of the late JC Smith, perhaps the leading criminal lawyer of his generation, who found it unremarkable on the basis that private defence has always been an answer to a charge of murder[3].

A final matter is the question of what human rights, if any, were engaged by the case. Surely this, of all cases, brought sharply into focus the fundamental rights of children. This was not the way in which it was viewed by the Court of Appeal, which decided the matter almost entirely on the traditional basis of applying the welfare principle. The primary focus was therefore on the *best interests* of the twins and not on their *rights*. There were some arguments presented under the ECHR but these were given short shrift by the court. The court's view was that there was nothing in the ECHR or in Strasbourg jurisprudence which would lead to a different conclusion than the one it reached. The arguments, such as they were, revolved around Article 2 of the ECHR which provides that 'everyone's right to life shall be protected by law' and that 'no one shall be deprived of his life intentionally'. Thus, the State is under a *positive* obligation to protect life and a *negative* obligation not to deprive someone of life intentionally. The court quickly rejected the argument for Mary that the negative obligation – not to deprive Mary of life intentionally – was a stronger obligation than the positive obligation to act to save Jodie's life. It took the position that the negative obligation was discharged by the State insofar as it put in place a law against unlawful killing, which was clearly the case in English law. As we have seen, the court's view was that in the very peculiar circumstances of the case the operation would not fall foul of the law of homicide.

Is it really the case that human rights are largely irrelevant in a case such as this? It is submitted that there could have been some benefit to Jodie in a closer concentration on the rights which she might legitimately have asserted in this

---

1 Murder requires an intention to kill or cause grievous bodily harm and the House of Lords in *R v Woollin* [1998] 3 WLR 382 has confirmed that a finding of intention might be made by a jury in these circumstances.

2 A principle with a long history. See especially *R v Dudley and Stephens* (1884) 14 QBD 273.

3 JC Smith *Smith and Hogan: Criminal Law* (10th edn) (Butterworths, 2002) at p 282.

situation. In order to make out this case it is necessary to speculate on what the position would have been if, contrary to the facts, the hospital had agreed, or at least acquiesced in, the parents' wish to allow nature to take its course. Ward LJ was quite definite about this. It would, he said, 'have been a perfectly acceptable response for the hospital to bow to the weight of the parental wish however fundamentally the medical team disagreed with it. Had St Mary's done so, there could not have been the slightest criticism of them for letting nature take its course in accordance with the parents' wishes.' Yet rather contradictorily, elsewhere in his judgment, he emphasises the duty on both the hospital and the parents to act and even speculates that the parents might have been criminally liable for not doing so[1].

A failure to conceptualise the issue in terms of Jodie's *rights* might lead us in the direction of the conclusion that there was no duty to intervene. Yet it is worth considering what would have happened to the human rights of Jodie in that event. Alternatively, if her position were viewed from the perspective of rights, it might have focused attention more clearly on the scope of the duty to intervene, whether the duty of the parents, the hospital or the court.

The case of the conjoined twins provokes considerable disagreement. It is one rather stark demonstration of the lack of a shared morality about these life and death decisions. For the Roman Catholic parents it was morally wrong to kill Mary. For others it was morally wrong not to bring about her death since there was a moral duty to save Jodie.

Quality of life over sanctity of life

These reported decisions have firmly rejected the sanctity of life approach in favour of a *quality* of life approach to the treatment of defective newborns. They establish, beyond question, that there is no absolute duty to save life, either on the part of parents, or the medical profession, and they generally draw a theoretical distinction between acts of positive killing and omissions which do not prevent natural death occurring. The case of the conjoined twins, as indicated above, is to be regarded as wholly exceptional and confined to its own peculiar facts. It is, of course, true that the medical profession has a certain duty to act in the interests of the patient so that the distinction between acts and omissions can be somewhat artificial in this context. It is also true that positive acts, such as the administration of drugs which are designed to alleviate pain and suffering, can have the 'double effect' of also hastening death. The most difficult question is the *extent* of the doctor's duty to act and it seems that this now turns on the notoriously vague notion of 'reasonableness'. The effect of the House of Lords decision in *Airedale NHS Trust v Bland*[2] is that a doctor would be acting lawfully in allowing a patient to die if a responsible body of medical opinion would support that course of action in the circumstances as being in the patient's best interests. This is effectively an application in life-saving cases of the *Bolam* test for medical negligence[3]. A

---

1 See the discussion of wilful neglect at pp 315 et seq above.
2 [1993] 2 WLR 316. For later applications of the *Bland* decision in relation to adults, see *Re D (Medical Treatment)* [1998] 1 FLR 411, *Re D (Medical Treatment: Mentally Disabled Patient)* [1998] 2 FLR 22, and *Re H (A Patient)* [1998] 2 FLR 36.
3 But see now the refinement of the test in *Bolitho v City and Hackney Health Authority* [1997] 3 WLR 1151 (above).

principle of proportionality appears to have emerged whereby a qualitative assessment of the life of the child must be made and this must be balanced with an evaluation of the treatment required to sustain that quality of life.

Yet these principles are themselves problematic and there remain many unanswered questions. It is not obvious that a sensible distinction can really be drawn between acts and omissions. It is even less clear that, if such a distinction can indeed be made, there is a valid moral distinction between failing to keep a child alive and actively helping to hasten death. It may be that a more justifiable moral distinction can be drawn between different kinds of acts and different kinds of omissions. Refusing surgical intervention is arguably of a quite different moral order than withholding food. But the greatest area of concern must be the absence of accepted standards or guidelines to regulate the decisions taken by parents, in conjunction with the medical profession, in the large number of cases which never reach the courts. There is substantial evidence that the decision about whether to treat or not to treat a child is significantly influenced by parental attitudes. A decision to withhold life-saving treatment is much more likely to be taken where parents desire it. Looking at the matter from a children's rights perspective, the question must be whether the unequal treatment of children with like disorders, for example two essentially similar cases of uncomplicated Down's syndrome, can be justified largely, if not entirely, on the basis of parents' preferences[1]. It might be argued that children's rights demand like treatment for like cases, making due allowance for the fact that no two cases are wholly identical.

Children's rights to equality of treatment

The concern to try to ensure a measure of equality of treatment led to successive attempts in the USA, at both the federal and State levels, to formulate legal standards to govern the circumstances under which non-treatment is allowable[2]. It has also led to proposals in England for legislation to regulate, admittedly in a broad way, medical practice in this area[3]. What kind of standards then could be evolved? One possibility is that a relatively plain distinction could be drawn between purely *mental* defects and severe *physical* defects. Selective non-treatment of the latter could be justified, in certain circumstances, since the state of the physical disorder might mean that the child in question would die anyway and that nature should, therefore, take its course. On the other hand, children with purely mental disorders will not die unless encouraged and guided towards death by some positive act and, for these purposes, an instruction to withhold food can be viewed as such. A distinction like this may mean that the non-treatment of an uncomplicated Down's syndrome child could *never* be justified, whereas clearly it could be justified in the case of a hydrocephalic or anencephalic child. Between these extremes there would, undoubtedly, be difficult judgments to be made. What view, for example, ought to be taken of spina bifida and how can the line be

---

1   For children's rights perspectives, see Chapter 3 above.
2   These were triggered by the *Baby Doe* case; as to which see J Dunsay Silver 'Baby Doe: The Incomplete Federal Response' (1986) 20 Fam LQ 173.
3   JK Mason, RA McCall Smith and GT Laurie *Law and Medical Ethics* (6th edn) (Butterworths, 2002), propose, at p 502, the adoption of a single clause Bill and suggest the following draft clause:
    'In the event of positive treatment being necessary for a neonate's survival, it will not be an offence to withhold such treatment if two doctors, one of whom is a consultant

drawn between different levels of severity of particular disorders? The formulation and application of statutory standards would inevitably be contentious but would at least address the inescapable problem that, in numerical terms at least, what happens in the cases which do not reach court is of much greater practical significance than what happens in the few which do.

THE PROBLEM OF OLDER CHILDREN: MEDICAL ISSUES ARISING FROM ADOLESCENT SEXUALITY

Section 8(1) of the Family Law Reform Act 1969 provides that:

> '... the consent of a minor who has attained the age of sixteen years to any surgical, medical or dental treatment ... shall be as effective as it would be if he were of full age; and where a minor has by virtue of this section given an effective consent to any treatment it shall not be necessary to obtain any consent for it from his parent or guardian.'

This provision clarified the position regarding young people of 16 and 17 years of age, by conferring on them legal capacity to provide a valid consent to treatment, and dispensing with the normal requirement of parental consent. The Family Law Reform Act 1969 did not deal directly with the question of a clash between the views of a 16-year-old and his parents, but the implication appeared to be that, at least where the minor was consenting, this could be effective to override any parental objection. The position was somewhat less clear in the converse situation, where the minor was *objecting* and the parent was purporting to consent. The better view seemed to be that the effect of the provision was to confer complete independence in medical decision-making on the 16-year-old – in effect to equate his position with that of an adult. On this interpretation, the objection of the minor would be conclusive. This view now cannot be sustained as a matter of law in the light of the Court of Appeal decisions in *Re R* and *Re W*[1].

Uncertainty surrounded the position of those under 16 years of age where perhaps four major issues are involved:

(1) Can the child under 16 years of age ever have legal capacity to take independent medical decisions?
(2) What are the limits of parental authority?
(3) What is the effect of the child's competence on the legal responsibility of parents? Does the child's view prevail and are parents entitled to be involved at all in the decision-making process?
(4) When may the courts intervene to override the wishes of parents and/or the views of a competent child?

The answer to these questions must be gleaned from three leading cases – the *Gillick* case, *Re R* and *Re W*[2]. *Gillick* was concerned only with the first three

---

paediatrician, acting in good faith and with the consent of both parents if available, decide against treatment in the light of a reasonably clear medical prognosis which indicates that the infant's further life would be intolerable by virtue of pain or suffering or because of severe cerebral incompetence.'

1 [1992] Fam 11 and [1992] 3 WLR 758, respectively.
2 *Gillick v West Norfolk and Wisbech Area Health Authority* [1986] 1 AC 112, *Re R (A Minor) (Wardship: Consent to Treatment)* [1992] Fam 11 and *Re W (A Minor) (Medical Treatment: Court's Jurisdiction)* [1992] 3 WLR 758, respectively.

questions, while *Re R* and *Re W* were directly concerned with the fourth but reopened the debate about the other issues.

The *Gillick* case

Background

In 1980, the then Department of Health and Social Security issued a notice[1] to the effect that, although it would be 'most unusual', a doctor could, in exceptional circumstances, lawfully give contraceptive advice or treatment to a girl under 16 years of age without prior parental consultation or consent. In so doing, he would be required to act in good faith to protect her against the harmful effects of sexual intercourse. Victoria Gillick, a Roman Catholic mother, with five daughters then under 16 years of age, objected to this advice and sought assurances from her area health authority that no minor daughter of hers would receive such advice or treatment without her permission. When she failed to receive a response acceptable to her, she applied for a declaration that the advice in the Circular was unlawful.

In what was arguably to become the most significant twentieth-century decision on the legal relationship between parents and children, Victoria Gillick lost at first instance, won unanimously in the Court of Appeal and eventually lost to a 3 : 2 majority in the House of Lords. Such was the measure of judicial disagreement at the time, and the analysis of the two principal majority speeches of Lord Scarman and Lord Fraser continues to provide a fertile source of argument both academic and judicial[2].

Doctor as secondary party to offence of unlawful sexual intercourse

Victoria Gillick advanced several arguments in support of her claim. The first of these is noted only briefly here, since it concerned the scope of the criminal law and is peripheral to the present discussion[3]. The argument that a doctor who provided contraceptives to a girl under 16 years of age would be a secondary party to the then offence of unlawful sexual intercourse[4] was rejected by four of the five Law Lords, following the reasoning of Woolf J at first instance. This was, in essence, that, while the doctor who provided contraceptives *with the intention* of encouraging the commission of the offence would be liable, the doctor who acted in compliance with the DHSS advice would not necessarily commit the offence. His motives were much more likely to be to protect the girl from the possible

---

1 HN (80) 46.
2 The major academic commentaries include: J Eekelaar 'The Eclipse of Parental Rights' (1986) 102 LQR 4; G Williams 'The Gillick Saga' (1985) 135 NLJ 1156 and 1169; A Bainham 'The Balance of Power in Family Decisions' (1986) CLJ 262; and SM Cretney 'Gillick and the Concept of Legal Capacity' (1989) 105 LQR 356. For an assessment of the issues surrounding adolescent autonomy in the medical arena, see M Brazier and C Bridge 'Coercion or Caring: Analysing Adolescent Autonomy' (1996) *Legal Studies* 84. Judicial disagreement is perhaps best illustrated by the apparent reluctance of Farquharson and Staughton LJJ to associate themselves with the more wide-ranging remarks of Lord Donaldson MR in *Re R* [1992] Fam 11.
3 Chapter 14 below considers the protective function of the criminal law in relation to children.
4 Offences Against the Person Act 1861, s 6. The girl herself does not commit an offence on the basis that the criminal law exists for her own protection: *R v Tyrell* [1894] 1 QB 710. This offence has now been abolished and replaced by other sexual offences relating to children in the Sexual Offences Act 2003. See Chapter 14 below.

adverse consequences of sexual intercourse, including unwanted pregnancy and/or abortion, and not to encourage the offence[1].

Issue 1: capacity of child under 16 years to provide valid consent

The first issue was whether a girl under 16 years old could ever provide a valid consent and thus prevent the commission of the tort of battery by the doctor[2]. The Family Law Reform Act 1969 did not address the position of those under 16 years of age, but it did provide in s 8(3) that 'nothing in this section shall be construed as making ineffective any consent which would have been effective if this section had not been enacted'. The majority held that the cumulative effect of this provision and s 8(1) was simply to avoid doubt in relation to those *over* 16 years old. The child *under* 16 years did not lack capacity by virtue of age alone, but acquired it, according to Lord Scarman, when 'he reaches a sufficient understanding and intelligence to be capable of making up his own mind on the matter requiring decision'. The test propounded by Lord Scarman involves an individualistic assessment of a particular child's level of maturity and intellectual ability. The clear implication is that, if a child fails the test of competence, the doctor will need to look to a person with parental responsibility for a proxy consent and that to go ahead without this will be to risk committing a tort on the child. Further, to make an incorrect assessment of competence will likewise be to run the risk of committing a tort if the matter should subsequently be taken to court. *Gillick* was concerned with the child's capacity to *give* consent and not expressly with the child's capacity to *refuse* it, but many commentators at the time thought that the two must stand or fall together[3].

A key question is what precisely must be understood by the child in order to achieve '*Gillick* competence'? Lord Scarman envisaged that a high level of understanding would be required, extending beyond the purely medical issues. Dealing specifically with contraception, he said:

> 'It is not enough that she should understand the nature of the advice which she is being given: she must have sufficient maturity to understand what is involved. There are moral and family questions especially her relationship with her parents, long-term problems associated with the emotional impact of pregnancy and its termination and there are risks to health of sexual intercourse at her age, risks which contraception may diminish but cannot eliminate. It follows that a doctor will have to satisfy himself before he can safely proceed on the basis that she has at law capacity to consent to contraceptive treatment.'

It will be seen, following *Re R* and *Re W*, that a similarly high level of competence is evidently demanded where a child is *objecting* to a medical procedure.

---

1 While this may have been a sound decision on policy grounds, it is rather more difficult to justify as a correct application of legal principle since the criminal law distinguishes between motive and intention, concerning itself only with the latter. See JC Smith and B Hogan *Criminal Law* (10th edn) (Butterworths, 2002) at pp 95–96.

2 It should be said that while a medical examination involving 'touching' would clearly be tortious without an appropriate consent it is difficult to see how the giving of advice about contraception or the prescription of contraceptive pills could have this tortious character.

3 This has now been exploded by Lord Donaldson's remarks in *Re R* [1992] Fam 11 and by the decision in *Re W (A Minor) (Medical Treatment: Court's Jurisdiction)* [1992] 3 WLR 758, which drew a distinction between *consent* and *refusal.*

Issue 2: the limits of parental authority

The second issue relates to the legal limits on parental authority and, here, the majority in the House of Lords was quite clear that parental power was not absolute. According to Lord Scarman 'parental rights are derived from parental duty and exist only so long as they are needed for the protection of the person or property of the child'. Lord Fraser emphasised that such rights existed for the benefit of the *child* and not for the benefit of the parent.

Issue 3: the clash of views – whose view prevails?

The third issue was the effect of a child achieving competence on the parental 'right' to give or withhold consent. Whose view should be decisive in the event of disagreement? Both Lord Scarman and Lord Fraser were of the opinion that a doctor could, in certain circumstances, proceed on the competent child's consent alone, but Lord Scarman appeared to take a more radical view than Lord Fraser of the effect of the child acquiring capacity[1]. According to Lord Scarman 'the parental right yields to the child's right to make his own decisions when he reaches a sufficient understanding and intelligence to be capable of making up his own mind on the matter requiring decision'[2]. This was interpreted by one commentator quite literally to mean that the attainment of competence by the child would *terminate* parental responsibility over the matter in question and would give to the child an *exclusive* right to decide[3]. Lord Fraser, on the other hand, adopted a more guarded approach. In his view, the mere acquisition of capacity would not, per se, enable a doctor to proceed without parental notification or consent. Lord Fraser laid down five further conditions which would have to be satisfied in order that the doctor could proceed without parental notification or consent:

'(1) that the girl will understand his advice;
(2) that he cannot persuade her to inform her parents or allow him to do so;
(3) that she is very likely to begin or to continue having sexual intercourse with or without contraceptive treatment;
(4) that unless she receives advice or treatment her physical or mental health or both are likely to suffer; and
(5) that her best interests require him to act without consent.'[4]

These extra requirements might have been explained away on the basis that they are not strict legal requirements but rather matters which pertain only to good professional practice[5]. But, equally, Lord Fraser's formulation might have been interpreted as one which supports a *participatory* decision-making process in which neither the parents nor the child would have the sole right to decide. The final decision would rather rest with the doctor who would take into account the girl's own capacity and wishes and, if possible, the views of the parents, and would then make an evaluation of her best medical and other interests before deciding whether to proceed. Such an interpretation would be in keeping with the

---

1 Lord Bridge, unhelpfully for present purposes, simply agreed with both of them.
2 [1986] 1 AC 112 at 186.
3 J Eekelaar 'The Eclipse of Parental Rights' (1986) 102 LQR 4.
4 [1986] 1 AC 112 at 174.
5 J Eekelaar (above).

tradition of medical paternalism in England[1]. Certainly, Lord Fraser did not appear to think that a competent girl was entitled to contraceptives on demand.

The precise inter-relationship of adolescent capacities and parental responsibility was thus the subject of considerable speculation and this has been accentuated by obiter remarks of Lord Donaldson in the Court of Appeal and by the later decision in *Re W (A Minor) (Medical Treatment: Court's Jurisdiction)*.

Issue 4: extent of the courts' powers over adolescents

The *Gillick* case was not directly concerned with the extent of the courts' jurisdiction over adolescents. It has fallen to the Court of Appeal to define the limits of their powers in *Re R* and *Re W*. While *Re R* was concerned with a young person *under* the age of 16, crucially *Re W* involved a young person *over* 16. This gave the court the opportunity of ruling upon the relationship between s 8 of the Family Law Reform Act 1969 and the courts' powers under the inherent jurisdiction.

Re R

Background

Re R[2] was not concerned with issues of adolescent sexuality but with the competence of an adolescent to *refuse* certain medical procedures – in this case the forcible administration of sedative drugs. The principles can nevertheless be applied to questions such as contraception, abortion or sterilisation.

R was a young woman aged 15 years and 10 months at the time of the hearing. Following a history of mental disturbances and a deterioration in her mental health, she entered the care of the local authority and was, in due course, placed in an adolescent psychiatric unit. She had a mental condition which fluctuated between periods of lucidity and rationality, and times when she displayed 'florid psychotic symptoms'. In these latter periods, she was considered a serious suicide risk and 'sectionable' under the Mental Health Act 1983. As part of its regime, the unit used sedative drugs as a last resort. It indicated to the local authority (which had parental responsibility for R) that it was not prepared to retain her unless its whole regime, including medication where appropriate, was accepted by it. Initially, the local authority acceded to this, but later withdrew its consent following a long telephone conversation between R and one of its social workers. R indicated, during this conversation, that the unit were trying to give her drugs which she neither wanted nor needed. The social worker was of the opinion that R was lucid and rational during the conversation, and this view of her mental state was subsequently confirmed by a consultant child psychiatrist. The authority made R a ward of court to resolve the disagreement.

Gillick competence – can it be overridden?

In the proceedings, the unit sought leave to administer such medication as was medically necessary, including anti-psychotic drugs, without R's consent. The

---

1 This is the position taken by A Bainham in 'Growing Up in Britain: Adolescence in the post-*Gillick* Era' (1992) *Juridical Review* 155 and which, it is submitted, is reflected in the later Court of Appeal decisions in *Re R* and *Re W*.

2 *Re R (A Minor) (Wardship: Consent to Treatment)* [1992] Fam 11.

Official Solicitor, acting as guardian ad litem, opposed this. His principal argument was that, where a child had capacity to withhold consent to treatment (based on sufficient understanding and intelligence to comprehend fully what was proposed) any parental right to give or withhold consent terminated. He argued further that, since, in wardship, the court steps into the shoes of a parent, the court could have no greater power to give or withhold consent. The two main issues were, therefore, whether R was '*Gillick*-competent' and, if so, whether the court would have power to override her wishes. These were the only issues directly raised, but Lord Donaldson MR felt it necessary to reopen the whole question of the relationship between the capacity of a competent minor and a parent's right to consent on a minor's behalf.

Competence as a developmental concept

The Court of Appeal upheld the decision of Waite J, that R failed the test of competence and that it was in her best interests for the treatment to be authorised. The court rejected the idea that competence could fluctuate from day to day or week to week. Competence was seen as a developmental concept, although it was acknowledged that a child could be competent for some purposes but not for others. But the *extent* of competence regarding any particular matter (in this case, medication) could not be variable. Farquharson LJ even doubted that *Gillick* could sensibly be applied at all to 'on/off' situations where the impact of a mental illness had to be taken into account. In his view, mental state and capacity could not be isolated from the medical history and background. Lord Donaldson emphasised, as Lord Scarman had in *Gillick*, that the acquisition of capacity was no easy matter. It required not only the ability to understand the procedure of compulsory medication but also 'a full understanding and appreciation of the consequences both of the treatment in terms of the intended and possible side effects and, equally important, the anticipated consequences of a failure to treat'[1]. She would particularly need to be aware of the risk that she might lapse into her former psychotic state, and of the possible harmful consequences of this to herself.

Determination and consent

Despite the court's decision that R was not *Gillick*-competent, Lord Donaldson alone made controversial obiter remarks about what the position would have been had she been adjudged competent. He used the metaphor of keys and locks to illustrate what he took to be the position. Consent was a key which could unlock a door. Both the competent child and the parent were keyholders but neither had a master key. Thus, *either* the child's key *or* the parent's key could unlock the door and open it for the doctor to proceed. He thus drew a distinction between *determination* and *consent*. The former, he said, was a wider concept than the latter since it implied a right of veto. He interpreted Lord Scarman's speech in *Gillick* to mean that it was this right of *determination* which terminated where the child achieved a state of competence. In other words, the parent would, at that point, lose the *exclusive* right to consent. But this did not mean that the parent's independent right to consent would be lost. The parent and child in these circumstances would enjoy *concurrent* rights to consent and it would be open to a

---

1   [1991] 4 All ER 177 at 187.

doctor to act on either consent. Otherwise, said Lord Donaldson, a doctor would be faced with the 'intolerable dilemma' of having to choose between two potentially valid, but also potentially invalid, consents. An incorrect assessment of maturity might then expose the doctor to criminal or tortious liability. He was also of the opinion that the same principles applied to a young person over 16 years, notwithstanding s 8(1) of the Family Law Reform Act 1969. He adopted a literal interpretation of this provision to the effect that, whilst it was unnecessary for a doctor to secure parental consent in relation to a young person of 16 years of age, there was nothing to preclude him from acting on a parent's consent alone.

Power of the court to override objections

The most significant issue in this case, since it had not been addressed in *Gillick*, was whether the court, exercising its protective jurisdiction was empowered to override the wishes of a competent minor[1]. Here, the court held that such a power existed, since the *Gillick* reasoning had no application in wardship proceedings[2]. The court's powers, it was said, were not derived from parents but from the Crown's duties of protection[3]. The court had wider powers than those enjoyed by natural parents including, for example, the power to restrain the publication of information about a child or the power to grant injunctions restraining contact between the child and others. It was also beyond doubt that the court could override the wishes of parents in exercising its powers of protection[4]. By analogy, there was no reason why it should not override the wishes of a competent minor if this was thought to be in her best interests. In wardship, this was the court's sole objective and it was perfectly possible that the application of the welfare test and the *Gillick* test could lead to different results. Whilst the issue had not been directly raised before, there was ample previous authority which had assumed that the court was not obliged to follow the wishes of a mature child[5].

The court's powers to override the objection of a minor have subsequently been dramatically illustrated in the case of *Re M (Medical Treatment: Consent)*[6]. Here a 15-year-old girl required a heart transplant to save her life but she refused to consent. Her reasons were that she did not want to have someone else's heart and did not wish to take medication for the rest of her life. The judge, Johnson J, was faced with an unenviable dilemma given the strength of her feelings and the recognition that she was an intelligent young woman who had thought seriously about the matter. The essence of this dilemma is captured in the notes of the

---

1 The court's decision on this point was, strictly speaking, obiter, since R was adjudged *incompetent*. Nevertheless, it was the principal point of law in the case and one which was unanimously answered by all three judges.

2 Although the court was specifically only concerned with wardship, there is no reason why the logic cannot be applied to other jurisdictions.

3 In fact, the analogy between natural and judicial parenthood was always a rather crude and imperfect one. See A Bainham 'Handicapped Girls and Judicial Parents' (1987) 103 LQR 334.

4 Many examples of this power might be cited, but one in the medical arena is *Re B (Wardship: Abortion)* [1991] 2 FLR 426 where the wish of a 12-year-old girl to have an abortion, supported by a grandparent, was upheld by the court in the face of objection by her mother. The court took the view that the operation was in her best medical interests.

5 See, particularly, the abortion cases of *Re P (A Minor)* [1986] 1 FLR 272 and *Re G-U (A Minor) (Wardship)* [1984] FLR 811.

6 [1999] 2 FLR 1097. For commentary, see R Huxtable '*Re M (Medical Treatment: Consent)* Time to remove the "flak jacket"?' [2000] CFLQ 83.

solicitor who acted as agent for the Official Solicitor and interviewed M in hospital. According to these, M said:

> 'Death is final – I know I can't change my mind. I don't want to die, but I would rather die than have the transplant and have someone else's heart, I would rather die with 15 years of my own heart. If I had someone else's heart, I would be different from anybody else – being dead would not make me different from anybody else. I would feel different with someone else's heart, that's a good enough reason not to have a heart transplant, even if it saved my life …'

Johnson J acknowledged the gravity of the decision to override M's wishes. There were, of course, risks which attached to the operation itself and there were continuing risks thereafter, both in terms of the bodily rejection of the heart and M's own rejection of continuing medical treatment. There was the further risk that she might carry resentment of the court's intervention for the rest of her life. Notwithstanding all this, the risks had to be measured against the certainty of death. M's severe condition of heart failure had developed only very recently and she had been overwhelmed by the decision which she had to make within the time span of a few days. He accordingly authorised the operation as being in her best interests.

The decision is perhaps the best illustration we are ever likely to get of the virtually limitless powers of the courts over children. There was no express finding of competence or incompetence in the case but the court, which had to act quickly, proceeded on the assumption that it could if necessary override the wishes of a competent child. The contrast between the court's powers over children and the much more limited powers over adults is plain to see. Had M been aged 18 and competent, rather than 15, it would have been entirely her decision and there would have been no legal basis for intervention by the court[1]. We have already considered[2] the arguments concerning the legitimate extent of paternalistic interventions from a children's rights perspective and this decision should be evaluated in the light of that discussion.

Re W

The principles governing the role of the courts in relation to adolescents and medical decision-making were further considered in the important decision of the Court of Appeal in *Re W (A Minor) (Medical Treatment: Court's Jurisdiction)*[3]. The decision proved no less controversial than that in *Re R*[4].

In this case, it was held that the High Court could properly exercise its inherent jurisdiction over children[5] to order a 16-year-old girl, suffering from anorexia nervosa, to be transferred, against her wishes, to a London unit specialising in the treatment of eating disorders. The court extended the reasoning in *Re R* to

---

1 *St George's Healthcare NHS Trust v S; R v Collins, ex parte S* [1998] 3 All ER 673.
2 See Chapter 3 above.
3 [1992] 3 WLR 758.
4 It was the subject of extensive critical comment. See, for example, J Eekelaar 'White Coats or Flak Jackets? Doctors, Children and the Courts – Again' (1993) 109 LQR 182, and J Masson 'Re W: Appealing from the Golden Cage' (1993) 5 JCL 37. The decisions of *Re R* and *Re W* were followed in controversial circumstances by Thorpe J in *Re K, W and H (Minors) (Medical Treatment)* [1993] 1 FLR 854 (a case which also raised significant issues of representation of children, which we discuss in Chapter 13 below) and by Douglas Brown J in *South Glamorgan County Council v W and B* [1993] 1 FLR 574.
5 On the distinction between the inherent jurisdiction and wardship, see Chapter 11 below.

'children' over 16 years having prima facie capacity to consent under s 8 of the Family Law Reform Act 1969. It held unanimously that that section had not been designed to confer absolute autonomy on 16-year-olds in medical matters but rather to enable them to provide a consent upon which the medical profession could safely act without incurring legal liability. The court's jurisdiction had not been excluded by the Act and, owing to the serious deterioration in W's health, this was a case in which the court should act. Lord Donaldson (now joined by Balcombe LJ) also reiterated his view in *Re R* that a parent might provide a *concurrent* consent in the case of a '*Gillick*-competent child', although he cast off the metaphor of the 'keyholder' which he had employed in *Re R*, for that of the legal 'flak jacket'. According to this, consent is a flak jacket which protects the doctor from legal actions. He can acquire it from a child over 16 years (under s 8), *or* a *Gillick*-competent child under 16 years, *or* someone with parental responsibility – but he only needs one consent. The decision is in much the same vein as *Re R*, and together the two cases compound the uncertainties about the inter-relationship of adolescent capacities and parental responsibility. The issue must surely return at some point to the House of Lords.

The decisions in *Re R* and *Re W* should now also be read with other recent decisions of the higher courts evincing a greater willingness to make paternalistic interventions in the case of *adults*[1]. If the courts are willing to intervene in the case of adults, the objection to doing so in the case of children (at least if based on the unwarranted differential treatment of children and adults) rather falls apart. The issue of the proper limits of State paternalism in either case, of course, remains[2].

The decision of the Court of Appeal in *St George's Healthcare National Health Service Trust v S*[3] perhaps heralded a new era in which the courts may be less willing to intervene paternalistically in the case of adults. Here, the court held that a pregnant woman could not be forced to undergo a Caesarean section even where her objections were bizarre and irrational and contrary to the views of the overwhelming majority of the community at large. This was so even where her own life depended on receiving medical interventions and where failure to consent would result in the death of her unborn child. The court further held that a person detained under the Mental Health Act 1983 for mental disorder could not be forced into medical procedures unconnected with her mental condition unless

1   See, for example, *Re T (An Adult) (Consent to Medical Treatment)* [1992] FLR 458 in which the Court of Appeal sanctioned a blood transfusion where the patient (who had been raised by her mother as a Jehovah's Witness) had apparently refused consent. In this case the decision was, however, based in part on the view that the patient's purported refusal may have been the product of external influence and thus not a genuine refusal. Nonetheless, the decision is perhaps evidence of a greater willingness to intervene in emergency situations in which the concept of necessity may apply. Intervention in the case of adults now, however, requires a judgment that the adult in question lacks competence, as where they are in a permanent vegetative state, and the court is asked to declare that the withdrawal of life-sustaining treatment would be lawful as being in the best interests of the patient. See, for example, *An NHS Trust v M; An NHS Trust v H* [2001] 2 FLR 367 where such declarations were granted by Dame Elizabeth Butler-Sloss P. Cf *Re SS (Medical Treatment: Late Termination)* [2002] 1 FLR 445, where Wall J refused a declaration that it would be in the best interests of a 34-year-old schizophrenic woman to undergo a termination of pregnancy at 23 weeks. In fact the case did not reach the court until the day before expiry of the 24-week statutory limit for terminations.
2   For further discussion, see A Bainham 'Children, Parents and the Law: Non-Intervention and Judicial Paternalisation' in P Birks (ed) *The Frontiers of Liability* (Oxford University Press, 1993).
3   [1998] 2 FLR 728.

her capacity to consent to such treatment was diminished[1]. It is interesting to speculate on whether the result might have been different here if the person concerned had been an adolescent young woman of, say, 16 or 17. Would the court have been justified in intervening, and, if so, on what basis?

Cumulative effect of the leading cases

What then is the cumulative effect of *Gillick, Re R* and *Re W*? The only principle which can be stated with any confidence is that the court has jurisdiction to overrule the parents, the child, the medical profession or, indeed, all of them in performing its protective functions and, even here, there are arguments about whether it should do so. The distribution of decision-making power which arises by operation of law is now a matter of considerable uncertainty and it is extremely difficult to state the law with any precision. Perhaps this is an inevitable hazard of an appellate system, in which multiple opinions are delivered. Thus, in *Gillick* only three Law Lords were in the majority, two of whom said materially different things and the third of whom simply agreed with the other two. In *Re R*, the then Master of the Rolls gave an opinion which incorporated an arguably idiosyncratic interpretation of the majority decision in *Gillick*, while the other two Lords Justices of Appeal appeared almost anxious to distance themselves from his views[2]. On the other hand, the decision in *Re R* has now been reinforced by that in *Re W* and must be taken to be the law in the absence of a further ruling by the House of Lords.

We will now attempt an evaluation of the present position.

Acquiring legal capacity

It seems reasonably uncontentious that the 16-year-old acquires capacity, is presumed to have capacity for taking medical decisions on attaining that age, and that there is no question of having to engage in an evaluation of individual maturity or intelligence. The sole exception to this will be where the young person is mentally incapacitated and therefore lacks the ability to give a real consent, where the presumption of capacity will be rebutted. Those under 16 years of age must pass the *Gillick* test and, in theory at least, the leading cases require a high level of understanding, extending beyond the mechanics of the medical procedure involved, to the wider medical, moral and family considerations surrounding what is proposed. The British Medical Association has provided

---

1   See also *Re AK (Medical Treatment: Consent)* [2001] 1 FLR 129 in which Hughes J granted a declaration that it would be lawful to discontinue life-sustaining treatment in the case of a 19-year-old patient suffering from motor neuron disease, a progressive, incurable and fatal condition. The patient was only able to communicate through the movement of one eyelid by which he could indicate 'yes' or 'no' to questions. He indicated that he wished his ventilator to be removed and the court held that the refusal to consent to treatment by an adult of full capacity must be observed in law. In *Re B (Consent to Treatment: Capacity)* [2002] 1 FLR 1090 Dame Elizabeth Butler-Sloss P granted a declaration that a hospital had been treating a patient unlawfully and awarded nominal damages against it. The patient, who could not survive without artificial ventilation, was found to have demonstrated a high standard of mental competence, intelligence and ability. A patient with such competence had the right to refuse medical treatment even where this would lead to his or her death.

2   Staughton and Farquharson LJJ confined themselves to the questions of the girl's competence and the power of the court in wardship.

detailed and useful guidance on what is involved in assessing competence in practice[1].

The issues surrounding capacity were illustrated in a life-and-death situation in *Re L (Medical Treatment: Gillick Competency)*[2]. Here a 14-year-old girl had sustained very serious burns from scalding having fallen into a bath. Her condition was life-threatening and she required treatment which would involve blood transfusions. She was, however, a Jehovah's Witness holding sincere religious objections to this. The surgeon responsible made it clear that the transfusion was necessary to save her life and that, without it, she would suffer a horrible death. Gangrene would set in and this would be followed by a very distressing period for both the girl and all those attending her.

In these circumstances Sir Stephen Brown P ordered that the hospital be allowed to go ahead with treatment without the girl's consent. He accepted that her views were sincerely held and derived from strongly held religious beliefs, but he held that there was a distinction between a view of that kind and the constructive formulation of an opinion which occurred with adult experience. It should not be overlooked, he said, that she was still a child or that she had led a sheltered life largely influenced by the Jehovah's Witness congregation. Neither had she been made aware of the actual manner of death. Accordingly, he found that she was not *Gillick*-competent and it was vital that the court should intervene in her best interests to ensure that she receive the treatment despite her lack of consent. He went on to say that *even if she were Gillick-competent* he would still have authorised treatment without her consent because this was an extreme case and she was in a grave situation.

There are, however, several features of this approach to capacity which may be considered unsatisfactory. First, the more that is required of the individual child, the greater is the opportunity for manipulation by adult decision-makers. Someone, whether it be a doctor or the court, has to determine whether an individual child is competent, and there is an obvious danger that the child will be deemed incompetent because his views happen to diverge from the adult assessment of his best interests[3] or that the child's views will simply be overridden under the inherent jurisdiction. Secondly, it is not obvious that the medical profession should be allowed to pass judgment on non-medical matters such as moral and family issues. A young woman's decision to have an abortion may, for example, be seen essentially as a *moral* choice and there may be no decisive medical reason pointing to termination or continuation of the pregnancy[4]. Thirdly, it is arguable that the law is demanding *more* of adolescents in the way of emotional or intellectual maturity than it requires of adults (or, in the case of

---

1   See *Consent, Rights and Choices in Health Care for Children and Young People* (BMJ Books, 2001) ch 5.

2   [1998] 2 FLR 810. For an assessment of the decision, see C Bridge 'Religious Belief and Teenage Refusal of Medical Treatment' (1999) 62 MLR 585.

3   A point forcefully presented in J Eekelaar 'Parents' Rights to Punish – Further Limits after *Gillick*' (1986) 28 *Childright* 9.

4   A similar view of the decision whether or not to make contraceptives available was expressed in the US Supreme Court by Brennan J in *Carey v Population Services International* 431 US 678, 699 (1977). The British Medical Association, however, appears to view competence as the capacity to make a choice and not whether it is a wise choice. See British Medical Association *Consent, Rights and Choices in Health Care for Children and Young People* (BMJ Books, 2001) at p 93.

medical treatment, those over 16 years of age)[1]. Adults, many of whom are not noted for their prudent and cautious approach to sexual involvements, are *not* required to demonstrate (but are rather assumed to have) the necessary maturity to make this all-round judgment of their interests. Many of them make mistakes and this must at least prompt the question, from a civil libertarian and children's rights standpoint, whether those under 16 years should not also have the right to make mistakes.

Finally, the extent of what has to be understood under the *Gillick* formulation has led to some speculation that, in the case of minors, the doctrine of informed consent has been admitted through the back door. This might prompt further speculation about the extent of a doctor's duty of disclosure in the case of young people[2].

Reconciling adolescent capacity, parental responsibility and medical paternalism

There is now considerable uncertainty about when a doctor ought to proceed on either a parent's or a child's consent alone[3]. *Gillick* had ostensibly supported the view that the wishes of a competent child should have priority over those of a parent, at least after suitable attempts had been made to persuade the child to involve her parents. It was apparent from the terms of the original departmental Circular, and from the majority speeches, that it would be seen as unusual for a doctor to deal with a child without parental participation. There was evidently concern that any positive contribution which parents might make in the context of the particular family situation should be explored[4]. It is, however, beyond doubt that both Lord Scarman and Lord Fraser took the position that a doctor would be acting lawfully in dealing exclusively with the child in appropriately defined circumstances. There was no suggestion that a parent's view should be allowed to trump the view of a competent minor.

Montgomery also offers the view that 'in principle it is clear that competence should not be assessed by reference to the outcome of the decision, but the ability to engage in the process of weighing options against each other': *Health Care Law* (2nd edn) (Oxford University Press, 2002) at pp 292–293.

1   It may be argued that the purpose of the test of understanding in both *Gillick* and *Re R* is simply to ensure that minors measure up to adult levels of understanding. Against this it may be argued that the reality is that they are being required to demonstrate more than is demanded of adults. The assessment of the capacity of adolescents also arises in relation to their ability to initiate legal proceedings without a litigation friend or participate in them without a guardian ad litem. We discuss these issues and the relevant case-law in Chapter 13.

2   The point is raised in B Hoggett 'Parents, Children and Medical Treatment: The Legal Issues' in P Byrne (ed) *Rights and Wrongs in Medicine* (1986) 165 at p 173.

3   Although J Montgomery *Health Care Law* (2nd edn) (Oxford University Press, 2002) at pp 299–300 draws attention to an important consideration, relying on the decision of the Court of Appeal in *Northampton Health Authority v The Official Solicitor and the Governors of St Andrews Hospital* [1994] 1 FLR 162. This is that a health authority may find costs awarded against it if it takes a case to court when presented with a child's refusal to consent but where parental consent is forthcoming. In fact, in this case, on appeal, the hospital rather than the health authority was ordered to pay half the Official Solicitor's costs.

4   In *Re R* itself it was the possible contribution of the local authority, which had parental responsibility for the girl, which was at issue. But the principles would appear to be the same whether parental responsibility is held by a parent or by someone else.

The decisions in *Re R* and *Re W* have cast doubt on this analysis. It appears to be envisaged that a doctor would be acting lawfully in relying on parental consent in the face of express objection by a competent child. It could, of course, be argued that whilst *Gillick* was concerned with the child's right to *consent*, *Re R* and *Re W*, by contrast, were concerned with her right to *refuse*, and that this enables them to be distinguished. Yet this is hardly logical. If the competent child's right to consent prevails over a parent's right to object, the converse should be true. This is especially so since a doctor's decision to examine or treat a child against that child's wishes is a potential assault, whereas a doctor's refusal to do so cannot be. The case is, if anything, stronger for giving precedence to the child's views in this situation. Lord Donaldson's distinction between determination and consent cannot overcome the essential reality that, where a doctor is aware of a disagreement between parent and child, he must, of necessity, choose between the two opposing views. If he elects to comply with what the parent wants, then he effectively gives to that parent a veto over the child's wishes, and this would appear to conflict directly with the decision in *Gillick*.

Yet if it is accepted that the competent child ought to have the decisive say in the event of a conflict, this does not necessarily mean that parents should be completely excluded from the process. Can it be said that, although deprived of decision-making capacity, parents yet have a right to be *notified* of dealings between their children and the medical profession? This immediately runs into the problem of medical confidentiality[1]. Of all the matters a young person might want to keep from her parents, those arising from sexual activity are the most likely and, of these, abortion is the one which has generated the greatest amount of litigation in the USA[2]. There, it has been held that States may not constitutionally give to parents an absolute and arbitrary right of veto over abortion[3]. But, in some circumstances, it can be constitutional for a State to require notification of an abortion to parents[4]. States may also act constitutionally in requiring either parental notification or, alternatively, the consent of a judge[5]. The effect of *Gillick* on this would seem to be to preserve the right of the competent child to confidentiality where the doctor is unable to persuade her to inform her parents. The position is less certain in relation to a child who is adjudged incompetent[6]. The question did not arise in *Re R* and *Re W*, and in *Gillick* it was conflated with the consent issue. It may be that this will be an area in which attempts may be made to find a middle course between giving absolute control to either parent or child

---

1 See fn 4 at p 326 above.
2 The leading US Supreme Court decisions on the constitutional framework for abortions on minors are *Planned Parenthood of Central Missouri v Danforth* 428 US 52 (1976); *Bellotti v Baird* 428 US 662 (1979); *Bellotti II* 443 US 662 (1979); *HL v Matheson* 450 US 398 (1981); *Ohio v Akron Center for Reproductive Health* 110 S Ct 2972 (1990); and *Hodgson v Minnesota* 110 S Ct 2926 (1990). A good discussion of the leading cases and the issues raised by them is to be found in RH Mnookin and DK Weisberg *Child, Family and State* (3rd edn) (Little, Brown and Co, 1995) at pp 203–213. For an exploration of the issues surrounding abortions on minors, see J Herring 'Children's Abortion Rights' (1997) 5 *Medical Law Review* 257.
3 *Danforth* and *Bellotti* (above).
4 *HL v Matheson* (above).
5 *Ohio* and *Minnesota* cases (above).
6 See the discussion above and also J Montgomery 'Confidentiality and the Immature Minor' [1987] Fam Law 101.

over a decision which may affect the functioning of the whole family. On balance, the argument for preserving medical confidentiality is probably the stronger[1].

The role of the court

Should the courts have power to override the wishes of a competent child? Staughton LJ warned, in *Re R*, that 'good reason must be shown before the State exercises any power to control the decisions of a competent person whether adult or minor, which only concern his own well-being'. It has, moreover, been argued that, whatever may be the letter of the law, the *spirit* of Gillick requires that the courts should not arrogate to themselves a right to intervene in the lives of children which is denied to natural parents[2]. It should also be said that there must be a danger that a parent might invoke the court's jurisdiction in an attempt, for example, to force an abortion against the wishes of a competent child. This has the potential for driving a coach and horses through the *Gillick* decision. The view which is ultimately taken of these interventions must depend on a judgment as to the appropriate level of paternalism in promoting children's rights. Is this only justified to enable children to become rationally autonomous adults or should the courts continue to exercise a protective jurisdiction in the face of evidence that this rationality has, in fact, been achieved before majority[3]?

The Children Act 1989 gives conflicting messages in this respect. While many of its provisions reject the notion that children's views ought to be decisive[4], it supports the right of a child (in the context of certain proceedings) who 'has sufficient understanding to make an informed decision' to refuse to submit to medical or psychiatric examination or treatment, even where a court is otherwise minded to direct it[5]. The decisions in *Re R* and *Re W* are difficult to reconcile with these provisions, since their underlying principle seems to be that the competent child should have a *conclusive* right of objection.

Yet it is possible to take a more positive view of the role of the courts in these decision-making processes. It can be argued that, since many of these medical decisions are irreversible and of long-term significance to the young people concerned, an objective view is, if not strictly necessary, nevertheless desirable. Given the uncertainty about who in law does have the right to take the final decision, the use of the court is a way of resolving this. In England, there is no mandatory judicial procedure except that judicial authority is considered a necessary precaution before a sterilisation is performed on an incompetent minor. In the USA, greater use is made of judicial procedures for these purposes. A number of States have enacted 'judicial by-pass' procedures which attempt to accommodate the interests of both parents and adolescents. Typically, the legislation will require notification of an abortion decision to one or possibly both parents and will allow a short time, perhaps 48 hours, to elapse after notification

---

1 A convincing defence of confidentiality in all minor cases is to be found in the judgment of Marshall J in *Matheson* (above) at 438–440.
2 J Eekelaar 'The Eclipse of Parental Rights' (1986) 102 LQR 4 at pp 7–8.
3 Chapter 3 above discussed this question. See also A Bainham 'Children, Parents and the Law: Non-Intervention and Judicial Paternalism' in P Birks (ed) *The Frontiers of Liability* (Oxford University Press, 1993). The issue arises particularly in relation to the exercise of the inherent jurisdiction, as to which see Chapter 11 below.
4 See Chapter 2 above.
5 See ss 38(6), 43(8), 44(7) of, and Sch 3, para 4(4) to, the Children Act and the discussion in Chapters 11 and 12 below.

and before the operation is performed. But the notice requirement may be waived, on application to the court, where the court is satisfied that a specified ground is established. The grounds usually include a finding that parents have been guilty of abuse or neglect, that the child is mature and competent to take her own decision, or that the court, for other reasons, finds it to be in her best interest that the abortion should go ahead without parental notification[1]. While parental consent statutes[2] and parental notification statutes without by-pass procedures[3] have been struck down as unconstitutional[4], appropriately drafted notification statutes incorporating adequate by-pass procedures have been held to be constitutional[5].

In England, as in the USA, the challenge is to find a middle course which allows for a degree of autonomy in decision-making for adolescents but which does not exclude the opportunity for potentially beneficial parental involvement[6]. Whether a judicial by-pass could provide the answer depends on the unanswerable question of whether judges are better qualified than others to take what may be seen ultimately as value judgments about the desirability of medical interventions[7].

In 2001 the Department of Health issued a Guidance[8] which recognises the need to involve children and parents fully in the decision-making process. In particular, it states the expectation that children's views should be properly taken into account even where they lack formal legal capacity to decide. In short it supports participatory or shared decision-making in all matters relating to the health of children.

---

1 A particularly good example is the Minnesota legislation reviewed in *Hodgson v Minnesota* 110 S Ct 2926 (1990).
2 As in *Planned Parenthood of Central Missouri v Danforth* 428 US 52 (1976).
3 As in *Bellotti v Baird* 428 US 662 (1979).
4 Except, as in *HL v Matheson* 450 US 398 (1981), where they relate to notification in the case of an immature and unemancipated minor.
5 As in *Ohio v Akron Center for Reproductive Health* 110 S Ct 2972 (1990) and *Minnesota* (above).
6 The arguments for regarding parental involvement as potentially beneficial, rather than negative, are rehearsed in the *Minnesota* decision (above).
7 There may also be seen to be a need for clear principles to govern the activities of the medical profession to avoid the necessity of seeking judicial authorisation in every case.
8 *Seeking Consent: Working with Children* (DoH, 2001).

Chapter 9

CHILDREN, MONEY AND PROPERTY

INTRODUCTION

Historically, children's financial interests have not been well served by the law: there was, in theory, a common law duty on a father to maintain his legitimate children, but no procedure was available to enforce that right[1], while children were not entitled as of right to any share in a deceased parent's property[2]. This chapter first summarises the rules governing children's rights in relation to property, and the evolution of the obligation to provide financial support for children is summarised. The text then outlines some of the most significant features of the welfare benefits system as it affects young people and seeks to summarise the child support legislation. It then analyses the residual role of the courts in making financial orders for children, concluding with some observations on the policy considerations relating to financial responsibility for children.

CHILDREN AND PROPERTY[3]

Children's capacity to own property

Most of the distinctive rules relating to children's interests in property stem from the common law notion that a child has no legal capacity[4]. Although (as has already been seen[5]) the *Gillick* decision[6] means that this denial of legal capacity is no longer absolute, the rules governing children's ownership of property are in general[7] founded on express statutory provisions unaffected by the *Gillick* approach to legal capacity. For example, statute provides that an infant cannot

---

1 A father was not even obliged to reimburse a person who supplied his child with necessary goods or services: *Mortimer v Wright* (1840) 6 M&W 482. However, someone who supplied a wife with goods necessary for a child might be able to recover from the husband under the doctrine of agency of necessity: *Bazeley v Forder* (1868) LR 3 QB 559.

2 The feudal lord became entitled to the profits of land during an heir's minority. The right was abolished by the Tenures Abolition Act 1660.

3 For an extremely helpful article which looks at the various angles of children's interests in property and which incorporates discussion of the Trusts of Land and Appointment of Trustees Act 1996, see E Cooke 'Children and Real Property – Trusts, Interests and Considerations' [1998] Fam Law 349. There is also a useful discussion in D Cowan and N Dearden 'The Minor as (a) Subject: the Case of Housing Law' in J Fionda (ed) *Legal Concepts of Childhood* (Hart Publishing, 2001).

4 See generally Chapter 13.

5 See Chapters 3 and 8.

6 *Gillick v West Norfolk and Wisbech Area Health Authority* [1986] 1 AC 112.

7 But not always. See, for example, the rule that a child cannot give a valid receipt for a legacy paid to him: *Philip v Paget* (1740) 2 Atk 80; *Re Somech; Westminster Bank Ltd v Phillips* [1957] Ch 165. It appears that, as a result of provisions defining parental responsibility contained in the Children Act 1989, s 3(2), any person with parental responsibility may now give such a receipt on the child's behalf. For a discussion of the position before the enactment of the Children Act, see Law Com Working Paper No 91 *Guardianship* (1985) at paras 2.32–2.35.

hold a legal estate in land, nor be registered as the registered proprietor of registered land[1]. Statute denies an infant the right to make a will[2] (unless he[3] is a soldier in actual military service or a mariner or seaman at sea[4]), and a child cannot be appointed a trustee[5], nor act as an administrator[6].

Management of children's property

The rules debarring a child from holding a legal estate are probably of little practical significance. This is because – as a result of legislation[7] and professional practice – most property to which a child is entitled is held by trustees on the child's behalf; and the Trustee Act 1925 contains provisions[8] which facilitate the making of maintenance payments from property which is held in trust for a child[9].

It should also be noted that – in addition to the court's general jurisdiction in respect of the administration of a child's property in wardship[10] – statute[11] specifically empowers the court to approve trust variations on behalf of infants and others incapable of themselves consenting, provided the scheme is beneficial to the persons concerned.

Guardians have parental responsibility for the child, and consequently they have the power to administer a child's property. In certain specified circumstances[12], the Official Solicitor may be appointed to be guardian of a child's estate.

Inheritance rights

English law – in contrast to the law of Scotland and many other legal systems[13] – does not give members of the family any legal right to share in a deceased relative's estate, and, to that extent, English law still embodies the traditional common law

---

1   Law of Property Act 1925, ss 1(6) and 205(1)(v), and see now Sch 1, para 1(1)(a) to the Trusts of Land and Appointment of Trustees Act 1996. However, this does not mean that a child may not hold an equitable interest in land. There is no prohibition on a child disposing of property, but any deed executed by a child is voidable and can be repudiated during minority or within a reasonable time after attainment of full age.

2   Wills Act 1837, s 7.

3   *In the estate of Stanley* [1916] P 192; *In the estate of Rowson* [1944] 2 All ER 36.

4   Wills Act 1837, s 11, as amended by the Wills (Soldiers and Sailors) Act 1918.

5   Supreme Court Act 1981, s 118.

6   *Re Manuel* (1849) 13 Jur 664.

7   See, for example, Sch 1, para 1(1) to the Trusts of Land and Appointment of Trustees Act 1996 (repealing the Law of Property Act 1925, s 19): conveyance of legal estate to a minor takes effect as a declaration of trust; legal estate conveyed to a child jointly with one or more other persons of full age vests in those of full age on trust for the minor.

8   Trustee Act 1925, s 31.

9   This provision will apply where a child is entitled under the statutory trusts arising on an intestacy: see p 363 below. For a consideration of the trustees' broad discretion under the Trustee Act 1925, see *J v J (C Intervening)* [1989] 1 FLR 453.

10   See Chapter 1.

11   Variation of Trusts Act 1958, s 1(1)(a).

12   See s 5(11) of the Children Act; RSC Ord 80, r 13 (as inserted by the Rules of the Supreme Court (Amendment No 4) 1991). Such appointments are made, for example, for the purpose of administering an award to the child under the Criminal Injuries Compensation Scheme where it would be unsuitable for the parents to be involved – for example if they had caused the injuries: see Law Com Working Paper No 91 *Guardianship* (1985) at p 51, note 95.

13   For example, the law of Germany: see *MT v MT (Financial Provision: Lump Sum)* [1992] 1 FLR 362.

principle of freedom of testation. It is true that children do have rights to succeed on the intestacy of a parent, but, in practice, those rights are often not of any real significance. This is because English law treats a surviving spouse generously and treats the deceased's children correspondingly ungenerously. In outline, the rule is that a spouse is entitled to a statutory legacy (currently amounting to £125,000[1]) and to a life interest in one-half of any balance of the estate. Hence, it is only in cases where the deceased had significant means that the children's rights to succeed are likely to prove valuable. The extent of this preference for the surviving spouse may be questioned in an era of high divorce and remarriage. It might be argued that proportionately greater weight should be given to the claims of the deceased's biological children from a former marriage vis-à-vis the claims of the surviving spouse than is so under the existing law[2].

Subject to the interest of the surviving spouse, the deceased's estate is held 'on the statutory trusts' for the deceased's issue[3]. Under the statutory trusts[4], the intestate's children may receive maintenance out of income until they are 18, and any income not applied for their maintenance is accumulated for the children's benefit. On reaching 18 years of age, a child becomes entitled to the appropriate share of the capital. If any of the intestate's children predeceases the intestate (or dies subsequently, but before attaining the age of 18 years) leaving issue, the issue take the child's presumptive share.

Failure to provide for children

There are two situations in which a child may be left without adequate financial provision on the death of a relative. First, the child may be disinherited by a will which makes no provision for him or her and, secondly, the rules of intestacy may (in consequence of the preference they embody for a surviving spouse) leave a child without any provision. For example, in *Re Sivyer*[5], the intestate left a widow, and a 13-year-old daughter by a previous marriage. The widow was entitled, under the rules of intestacy, to the whole of his estate; the child was entitled to nothing.

Even more strikingly, in *Re Collins, dec'd*[6], Mrs Collins had obtained a decree nisi of divorce before her death, but the decree had not been made absolute. In the result, her husband was, at law, entitled on her intestacy to the whole of her estate, and her children – a son of Mr and Mrs Collins and a daughter of hers – were not entitled, under the rules of intestacy, to anything.

Court's power to order that reasonable financial provision be made

The Inheritance (Provision for Family and Dependants) Act 1975 permits certain defined categories of 'dependant' to apply to the court for reasonable financial

---

1 Family Provision (Intestate Succession) Order 1993, SI 1993/2906.
2 For a comparative discussion of the policy underlying the inheritance laws of England, the USA, France and Germany, see MA Glendon *The Transformation of Family Law* (University of Chicago Press, 1989) at pp 238–251. For a critique of the attempts to reform the English law of intestacy, see SM Cretney 'Reform of Intestacy: The Best we can do?' (1995) 111 LQR 99.
3 The term issue now extends equally to those born in wedlock and to those born outside marriage: Family Law Reform Act 1987, s 18(1).
4 See *J v J (C Intervening)* [1989] 1 FLR 453.
5 [1967] 1 WLR 1482.
6 [1990] Fam 56.

provision to be made for them out of the deceased's estate. If the court considers that the will or intestacy does not make such provision, it may make appropriate orders (for example, for periodical income payments, or for payment of a lump sum). The categories of dependant include a child of the deceased, and also:

> 'any person (not being a child of the deceased) who in the case of any marriage to which the deceased was at any time a party, was treated by the deceased as a child of the family in relation to that marriage.'

The term 'child' extends to illegitimate, adopted and posthumous children of the deceased, and there is no restriction of age or marital status so that an adult child is entitled to apply. This is an interesting illustration of the way in which, at least for some purposes, the relationship of parent and child and wider kinship links endure for life and do not end on the child attaining majority.[1]

The category of 'children of the family' is similar to, but not identical with, that in the legislation governing financial provision on divorce[2]: under the divorce legislation, the child must have been treated as a child of the family by *both* parties to the marriage, but under the inheritance legislation, the criterion is treatment *by the deceased* in relation *to the deceased's marriage*. Thus, in *Re Leach*[3], the deceased was the applicant's step-mother who had married the applicant's father at a time when she was aged 32. The applicant had a good relationship with her step-mother and became particularly close to her after her father's death. The judge rejected an argument that the 'treatment' which was required was treatment at or about the time of the marriage; and he did not regard it as directly relevant that most of the treatment in this case had occurred after the end of the marriage.

Exercise of the court's discretion

In deciding whether 'reasonable financial provision' has been made, and if not, what order it should make, the court is given certain guidance. In all cases of applications by children, the court is required to have regard to the following matters[4]:

> '(a) the financial resources and financial needs which the applicant has or is likely to have in the foreseeable future;
> (b) the financial resources and financial needs which any other applicant for an order made under the Act has or is likely to have in the foreseeable future;
> (c) the financial resources and financial needs which any beneficiary of the estate of the deceased has or is likely to have in the foreseeable future;
> (d) any obligations and responsibilities which the deceased had towards any applicant for an order or towards any beneficiary of the estate of the deceased;
> (e) the size and nature of the net estate of the deceased;
> (f) any physical or mental disability of any applicant for an order under the Act or any beneficiary of the estate of the deceased;

---

1   It has also been recognised by the courts and legislature that benefits to a child of being adopted may endure into adulthood and that this may justify the making of an adoption order, even where the child is close to attaining majority. See, for example, *Re D (A Minor) (Adoption Order: Validity)* [1991] 2 FLR 66. The Adoption and Children Act 2002 recognises the benefits of adoption during adulthood in several provisions. See, for example, ss 1(4)(c), 47(9) and 49(4) and (5) and the discussion in Chapter 7 above.
2   See pp 397–398 below, where the scope of the definition is discussed.
3   [1986] Ch 226.
4   Inheritance (Provision for Family and Dependants) Act 1975, s 3(1).

(g) any other matter, including the conduct of the applicant or any other person, which in the circumstances of the case the court may consider relevant',

and the court is also to have regard to the manner in which the applicant was being or in which he might expect to be educated or trained[1].

Where the applicant is someone who makes a claim as a 'child of the family' in relation to the deceased, the court is also required to have regard to the following matters:

'(a) whether the deceased had assumed any responsibility for the applicant's maintenance and, if so, to the extent to which and the basis upon which the deceased assumed that responsibility and to the length of time for which the deceased discharged that responsibility;

(b) whether in assuming and discharging that responsibility the deceased did so knowing that the applicant was not his own child;

(c) the liability of any other person to maintain the applicant.'

These provisions obviously give the court a wide discretion. In respect of applications by children, it has been held that children born outside marriage are to be treated on the same basis as those born within it[2]. In *Re C (Deceased)*[3], for example, the eight-year-old daughter of the deceased was granted permission to make an application for provision out of time through her mother as next friend. The deceased was wealthy whereas the applicant child and her mother lived in humble circumstances. The court held that the fault for delay in making the application lay with the mother and that this should not bar the child, the merits of whose claim were clear – the more so since the estate had not yet been distributed.

What is the position of the 'child' now an adult? On the one hand, it has been held that claims by adults are not exceptional, but it has to be remembered that the policy of the Inheritance (Provision for Family and Dependants) Act 1975 is not to decide how the deceased's assets should be fairly divided. Instead, it is concerned with making reasonable provision for *dependants* and, accordingly, it is not surprising that the courts have adopted the view that claims for maintenance by able-bodied and comparatively young people who are in employment and able to maintain themselves, will be rare and are to be approached with a degree of circumspection[4]. This does not mean that a claim by an adult son or daughter is viewed with disfavour; rather it means that, faced with a claim by a person who is physically able to earn his own living, the court will be inclined to ask 'why should anybody else make provision for you if you are capable of maintaining yourself?'[5]

The leading case is *Re Jennings (Deceased)*[6]. The deceased and his wife had separated as long ago as 1945 when the applicant, their son, was aged two. The applicant had thereafter been raised by his mother and step-father. The deceased left the bulk of his estate to charities and remote relatives. The applicant was married with two children and successfully acquired two companies which provided his family with a comfortable standard of living. He applied for financial provision out of the estate and succeeded at first instance largely on the basis that the deceased had failed to discharge his moral and financial obligations to the

1 Inheritance (Provision for Family and Dependants) Act 1975, s 3(3).

2 *In the estate of McC* (1978) Fam Law 26.

3 *Re C (Deceased) (Leave to Apply for Provision)* [1995] 2 FLR 24.

4 *Re Coventry, dec'd* [1980] Ch 461 at 495.

5 *Re Dennis, dec'd* [1981] 2 All ER 140 at 145.

6 [1994] 1 FLR 536.

applicant during his minority. The Court of Appeal, however, held that the Act could not be construed to include obligations and responsibilities in the distant past but, as a general rule, should be confined to those which the deceased had immediately before his death. The relationship of father and son could not, as such, impose on the deceased a continuing financial obligation up to the time of death. Neither had it been demonstrated that financial provision was reasonably required for the applicant's maintenance since no further provision was necessary to enable the applicant to discharge the cost of his daily living at a standard appropriate to him. The case is an interesting illustration of the way in which the mere presence of a genetic link is not enough, at least under this legislation, to trigger moral and legal financial responsibilities. The position should be contrasted with that under the child support legislation (discussed below), where entirely the opposite is true, albeit in relation to minor, not adult, children. Nevertheless, where such moral obligations to provide do exist at the time of death and where the adult child is in straitened financial circumstances, an order may be appropriate. This was the situation in *Re Goodchild (Deceased) and Another*[1] where the Court of Appeal, although unwilling to find that a father and mother had made effective mutual wills in favour of their son, did find that the father owed a moral obligation to provide for his son out of that part of the estate which he had inherited from his deceased wife. Similarly in *Re Pearce (Deceased)*[2] moral obligations again appeared to weigh heavily in the decision, in this case deriving from the adult son's unpaid work on his father's farm throughout much of his childhood and early adulthood, and his father's (broken) promise to him that he would leave the farm to him on his death. In these circumstances the Court of Appeal upheld an award of £85,000 free of inheritance tax.

At the same time it has been held that a moral obligation on the part of the deceased is not a prerequisite of an order. In *Re Hancock (Deceased)*[3] the Court of Appeal held that an adult son or daughter did not necessarily have to show that the deceased owed him or her a moral obligation or that there were other special circumstances, but that a claim by an adult with an established earning capacity might very well fail in the absence of such factors. In this case there was found to be no moral obligation, but an order for £3,000 per annum was made largely on the basis of the poor financial situation in which the 58-year-old daughter now found herself.

Several reported decisions have concerned adult daughters. An example, involving an adopted daughter, is provided by *Williams v Johns*[4], where the applicant (who was 43, unemployed, impecunious and divorced with no capital beyond the houseboat in which she lived) had had a stormy childhood after being adopted as a baby by the deceased. She was a delinquent, and this caused emotional distress and suffering to her adoptive parents who, nevertheless, continued to assist her financially and morally whenever possible. She had not done anything to help the deceased, and indeed it was suggested that the deceased was afraid of her. The deceased made no provision in her will for the adopted daughter, and left a written statement that she felt no obligation towards

---

1   [1997] 2 FLR 644.
2   [1998] 2 FLR 705.
3   [1998] 2 FLR 346.
4   [1988] 2 FLR 475.

her. The court held that, in these circumstances, it was not unreasonable for the deceased to have made no financial provision for the applicant.

In contrast, in *Re Debenham (Deceased)*[1], the applicant was an unwanted child brought up by her grandparents abroad. When she discovered the facts about her parentage she tried to establish a link with her mother, but these attempts were unsuccessful and the deceased continued to remain aloof, distant and indeed cruel to her daughter. It was held that a legacy of £200 out of an estate of £172,000 was not, in all the circumstances, reasonable provision for the daughter. In particular, the daughter was an epileptic and any mother might have felt some obligation to help her in those circumstances. The court ordered payment of a small capital sum to meet the claimant's immediate needs, and a payment of £4,500 per annum by way of income payments.

More recently, in *Espinosa v Burke*[2] the spotlight was turned on the supposedly adverse conduct of the adult daughter and the effect that this should or should not have on her application[3]. The judge had refused her claim largely on the basis of her behaviour towards the deceased in the final years of his life. She had been married five times and regularly brought male partners into her elderly father's home. In the last year of his life she spent most of her time in Spain with the Spanish fisherman she later married. Meanwhile the deceased was left to be looked after by his grandson and a cleaner. Nonetheless, the Court of Appeal allowed her appeal taking the view that the judge had attached too much significance to the failure of the daughter to discharge her moral obligation to her father and too little to her needs and the promises made to her by the deceased.

Finally, in *Robinson v Bird*[4] Blackburne J refused the claim of an adult daughter for what amounted to a larger share in her late mother's estate. The deceased had by will left the residue of her estate equally to her grandson, the only child of her late son and the claimant. The claimant argued that 80 per cent of the residuary estate to her would better reflect the deceased's wishes at the time of her death. It was held that the fact the claimant's reasonable maintenance requirements could not be satisfied from her own resources did not lead to the conclusion that it was unreasonable that the will did not make greater provision for her. Notwithstanding the closeness of her relationship with the deceased, and the deceased's apparent wish to treat her more favourably than the grandson, there was no sufficient basis for disturbing the equal division of the residuary estate.

Re Abram (Deceased)[5] is an example of a successful claim by an adult son against his mother's estate. Here, the mother had owned a prosperous warehouse business and substantial family home. The applicant was her only son who had, since the age of 17, worked long hours in the business for a minimal wage. He eventually married and broke clear of the home in the face of strong opposition by his mother. The deceased had made a will leaving the whole of her estate to her son but later revoked this, disinheriting him. She never changed this will, although there was evidence that she had intended to do so. Matters were

---

1   [1986] 1 FLR 404.
2   [1999] 1 FLR 747.
3   For a discussion of the relevance of fault in family law generally, see A Bainham 'Men and Women Behaving Badly: Is Fault Dead in English Family Law?' (2001) 21 *Oxford Journal of Legal Studies* 219.
4   [2003] All ER (D) 190.
5   [1996] 2 FLR 379.

complicated following the death of the deceased in that her company had failed and the sole asset was the family home. The applicant had also hit on hard times. His own business had failed and he had entered into an individual voluntary arrangement with creditors under the Insolvency Act 1986.

The court held that these were special circumstances and that the deceased had been under a moral obligation to provide for her son. In view of the arrangement under the Insolvency Act (under which any capital paid to the applicant would have to go to his creditors), the court ordered a settlement under which, inter alia, the income from 50 per cent of the estate would be paid to him for life.

EVOLUTION OF THE OBLIGATIONS TO PROVIDE FINANCIAL SUPPORT FOR CHILDREN

As has been seen, enforcement of the obligation to maintain is governed entirely by statute, and a brief account of the historical development of the law will help put the modern law in context.

The Matrimonial Causes Act 1857 first gave English courts power to dissolve marriages, and it provided that the court granting a decree could make such order as it deemed just and proper with respect to the 'custody, maintenance and education' of children, the marriage of whose parents was in issue[1]. The court's powers to make financial orders in divorce and other matrimonial causes were greatly extended[2] over the years, and courts were given power to make orders for the children in other proceedings.

In 1878, magistrates were given power[3] to make what were, in effect, separation orders where a wife had been the victim of assault by her husband, and they were empowered to give custody of any children under the age of 10 to the wife, and to make financial orders. Magistrates also had power to make financial orders against the father of an illegitimate child in affiliation proceedings[4]. In 1886, the Guardianship of Infants Act[5] empowered the court to make a custody or access order on the application of a child's mother, and legislation[6] subsequently provided that the court could order a father to pay the mother weekly or other periodical sums by way of maintenance.

The Children Act 1989 reformed and assimilated the private law provisions governing financial provision and property adjustment for children, extended the court's powers, and achieved a substantial measure of simplification, rationalisation and harmonisation. The magistrates' court retained its power to make

---

1 Matrimonial Causes Act 1857, s 35.
2 Both in respect of the types of order which could be made and in respect of the class of children eligible to benefit: the Matrimonial Proceedings (Children) Act 1958 gave the divorce court power to make orders for a child of one spouse who had been 'accepted' by the other; and the Matrimonial Proceedings and Property Act 1970 gave the court its present wide powers to make both capital and income payments to, or for the benefit of, any 'child of the family': see p 397 below.
3 Matrimonial Causes Act 1878, s 4.
4 This jurisdiction dates back to the Poor Law Amendment Act 1844: the history of the obligation to maintain is traced in the *Report of the Committee on One-Parent Families* ('the Finer Report') (1974) (Cmnd 5629).
5 Guardianship of Infants Act 1886, s 5.
6 Ibid, s 3.

maintenance orders[1] in matrimonial proceedings, and the divorce court retained its extensive powers to make orders over capital or income for the benefit of children of the family[2]. The Children Act itself[3] provided for a wide range of financial orders to be made in respect of children, on the application of a parent, a guardian, a person who had a child residing with him under a court order, and (in certain circumstances) a child of 18 years or over. The scheme of the legislation was that financial support for a child could be sought as an incident in matrimonal proceedings between the child's parents, and that in other cases – for example, where the unmarried mother of a child wanted an order for financial support for the child – similar relief would be available under the Children Act.

The impact of the Child Support Act 1991 on the private law governing financial provision for children

Although the provisions of the matrimonial legislation and of the Children Act remain on the statute book and in force, their practical importance has been greatly reduced by reason of the coming into force on 5 April 1993 of the Child Support Act 1991 (CSA 1991)[4]. The general principle of the CSA 1991 is that child support should be dealt with by the administrative procedure established by the Act, and that the court's powers should only be exercisable to fill gaps in the statutory child support scheme. In *R (Keyhoe) v Secretary of State for Work and Pensions*[5] there was an unsuccessful challenge to the child support scheme under the HRA 1998. A mother sought to argue that the legislation was incompatible with her Convention rights under Article 6 of the ECHR. She argued that the effect of the scheme was to deny a parent access to the courts in connection with disputes as to whether the non-resident parent had paid or ought to pay the sums due under a maintenance calculation or as to the manner in which maintenance assessment should be enforced. A majority of the Court of Appeal (Ward LJ dissenting in part) held that a deliberate feature of the child support legislation was that it was for the Secretary of State to assess and enforce the maintenance obligation to be owed by a non-resident parent to a child. The mother, as parent with care, did have the right to require the Secretary of State to make an assessment and to request him to take steps to enforce the obligation to pay. However, she had no legal right as against the non-resident parent to a child maintenance payment and, therefore, her civil rights under Article 6 were not engaged. The CSA 1991 provides[6] that in any case where a child support officer would have jurisdiction to make a maintenance assessment, with respect to a qualifying child and an absent parent, on an application duly made by a person entitled to apply for such an assessment with respect to that child, no court shall exercise any power which it would otherwise have, to make, vary or revive any maintenance order (ie an order to make periodical payments – orders for lump sum payments are not within the definition), in relation to the child and absent

---

1 And orders for the payment of small lump sums under the Domestic Proceedings and Magistrates' Courts Act 1978.
2 See pp 396 et seq below.
3 Schedule 1.
4 As amended, first, by the Child Support Act 1995 and then, more radically, by the Child Support, Pensions and Social Security Act 2000. See below.
5 [2004] 1 FLR 1132.
6 Section 8(1).

parent concerned[1]. Hence, the first question to be asked, in any case in which an issue relating to the provision of financial support for a child arises, must be whether the provisions of the CSA 1991 debar the court from proceeding because a child support officer would have jurisdiction to make a maintenance assessment if an application were made under the CSA 1991. Before seeking to explain the provisions of the child support legislation, however, it may be helpful to summarise the relevant provisions governing entitlement to welfare benefits.

WELFARE BENEFITS AND THEIR IMPACT

The Finer Report[2]: welfare benefits as the third system of family law

As long ago as 1974, the Finer Committee on One-Parent Families produced the Finer Report, which made a telling analysis of the inadequacy of the procedures then available to provide financial support for children. The Committee pointed out that there were, in effect, three systems of law governing financial support: the system administered by the divorce court; the system administered by the magistrates' courts in domestic proceedings; and what it described as the 'third system of family law' embodied in the system of welfare benefits, administered by an administrative agency. The Finer Report drew attention to the defects caused by this division of function, and to the hardship thereby caused to one-parent families, and made far-reaching proposals under which many issues relating to the quantification and enforcement of financial support obligations would be dealt with by an administrative agency by reference to clear guidelines rather than by the courts in the exercise of a loosely structured discretion. The Finer Report also proposed the creation of a so-called 'guaranteed maintenance allowance' which was intended to provide an income for single-parent families which was significantly higher than what was then available to them by way of welfare benefits.

Although the Finer Report had a profound impact on opinion, nothing was done to give effect to the Committee's proposals. The law continued to develop in separate compartments.

Changing approaches to the State's role

The State has, ever since the enactment of the Elizabethan Poor Law, assumed some obligation to provide for those persons who would otherwise be completely destitute, but a dramatic change in the philosophy underlying the principles on which provision for the poor should be made took place with the creation of the Welfare State in the period immediately following the end of the Second World War[3]. This change was first manifested in the context of the provision of support

---

1 Section 8(3).
2 *Report of the Committee on One-Parent Families* (1974) (Cmnd 5629).
3 These changes followed the publication in 1942 of the Beveridge Report (the *Report on Social Insurance and Allied Services* (1942) (Cmnd 6404)). For a concise account of the evolution of social security and social policy in Britain, see Wikeley, Ogus and Barendt *The Law of Social Security* (5th edn) (Butterworths, 2002) ch 1.

for the family in the system of family allowances introduced in 1945. That benefit was replaced in 1975 by child benefit, which is now payable to everyone who is responsible for a child under 16 years old (or under 19 years old if certain prescribed conditions are met)[1]. This benefit is tax-free, does not depend on the making of contributions, and is not means-tested. The standard weekly rates of benefit with effect from April 2004 are £16.50 for the first or only child and £11.05 for every other child[2]. The former lone parent benefit payable for the first or only child of a lone parent was abolished from 6 July 1998. Some lone parents receiving it at that time may still be eligible to receive it at the higher rate of £17.55. Child benefit is payable to the mother in the first instance and it has been held that it may not be split in a situation where care of the child is shared[3].

In 2004 Parliament legislated to provide a new universal benefit for children. Under the Child Trust Funds Act 2004, payments will be made by the Government to children which may only be invested in child trust fund accounts, which will be long-term savings and investment accounts. No withdrawals will be allowed until the child attains the age of 18, at which point he or she will be entitled to withdraw the money.

Means-tested benefits for the poor: supplementary benefit and family income supplement

The most important change in policy governing welfare benefits was achieved by the abolition of the Poor Law in 1948 and the creation of the supplementary benefit system under which every person in Great Britain of or over the age of 16 years, whose resources (as defined) were insufficient to meet his requirements (defined, at a modest level, in statute), became entitled to receive a supplementary allowance. At that time, it was the policy of the law to eradicate the stigma attached to the Poor Law, and to insist that supplementary benefits were 'the subject of rights and entitlement and that no shame attached to the receipt of them'[4].

Reducing the burden of welfare benefit provision

Over the years, the supplementary benefit system became increasingly burdensome to the taxpayer. Part of this increase was attributable to the costs apparently caused by family breakdown: the number of lone-parent families in Great Britain rose to over one million in 1986, and such families now constitute about one-fifth of all families with dependent children[5]. It has always been an important principle that, although the State would provide financial support for a family in danger of destitution, the State should be entitled to recover the amounts disbursed from any person legally bound to support the claimant (that is to say the

---

1 For a full description of the current principles and regulations governing child benefit, see Child Poverty Action Group *Welfare Benefits and Tax Credits Handbook* (2004/2005) ch 5.

2 The detailed rules governing entitlement are complex: see Part IX of the Social Security Contributions and Benefits Act 1992, and the Child Benefit (General) Regulations 1976, SI 1976/965, as amended. The rates of benefit are governed by the Child Benefit and Social Security (Fixing and Adjustment of Rates) Regulations 1976, SI 1976/1267, as amended.

3 *R (Barber) v Secretary of State for Work and Pensions* [2002] 2 FLR 1181.

4 *Reiterbund v Reiterbund* [1974] 1 WLR 788 at 797, per Finer J.

5 The percentage has almost doubled since 1981: see *Social Trends 33* (2003) Table 2.4.

so-called 'liable relative'). It should be noted in passing that adult children are no longer legally liable to support their parents[1], but this is not so in every jurisdiction. Singapore, for example, enacted the Maintenance of Parents Act in 1995 which enables parents who are unable to support themselves adequately to apply to the court for maintenance from any or all of their children[2]. In England, such obligations (including obligations to support wider kin) existed under the Poor Law but were finally abolished with the advent of the post-war Welfare State[3]. But with changing attitudes it increasingly came to be said that the law failed, in practice, to give effect to the 'clear moral duty' which all parents have to maintain their children until the children are old enough to look after themselves[4].

In response to these pressures, the supplementary benefit system was replaced by 'income support'[5], and legislation was introduced[6] to reinforce the obligations of parents and others. The CSA 1991 is an ambitious system intended to ensure that absent parents meet their fair share of the cost of supporting their children[7]. Spouses remain liable in public law to maintain *each other* (as well as their children) while separated but this public liability ceases on divorce. Thus, in practice, the Child Support Agency takes responsibility for enforcing the public liability to support *children* while the Department for Work and Pensions (formerly the Department of Social Security) continues to enforce any public liability to maintain a *spouse* under the 'liable relative' procedure governed by the Social Security Administration Act 1992[8].

In 1996 unemployment benefit was replaced by jobseeker's allowance[9], which is divided into income-based and contributory varieties. The contributory jobseeker's allowance is based on national insurance contributions made, while the income-based version is means-tested and has to a large extent replaced income support. It must be claimed, rather than income support, by those who are unemployed, or employed for less than 16 hours per week, and are required actively to seek work. Income support, however, continues to apply to those who are not actively required to seek work including, importantly for present purposes,

---

1 However, in *Bouette v Rose* [2000] 1 FLR 363 an ingenious argument succeeded in the Court of Appeal that a deceased child aged 14 had, at the time of her death, effectively been maintaining her mother for the purposes of s 1(1)(e) and (3) of the Inheritance (Provision for Family and Dependants) Act 1975. The mother succeeded in obtaining leave to apply for financial provision out of her deceased daughter's estate. The daughter had been awarded compensation after suffering severe physical and mental disabilities due to negligence at birth. The Court of Protection had used some of this to pay out capital and regular income to the mother to enable her to buy a house and care for the daughter. The court felt able to characterise this as a situation in which the mother was being maintained by the child.
2 See P de Cruz 'Singapore: Maintenance, Marital Property and Legislative Innovation' in A Bainham (ed) *The International Survey of Family Law 1996* (Martinus Nijhoff, 1998) at p 401.
3 For a concise discussion, see M Maclean and J Eekelaar *The Parental Obligation* (Hart Publishing, 1997), especially at pp 41–44.
4 Per Lord Mackay of Clashfern *Hansard* Vol 526, col 775 (25 February 1991).
5 Social Security Act 1986.
6 Social Security Administration Act 1992, s 106; Income Support (Liable Relative) Regulations 1990, SI 1990/1777.
7 See p 378 below.
8 For a succinct account of the principles and procedures governing the liable relative's contribution to the support of a separated spouse, see Wikeley, Ogus and Barendt's *Law of Social Security* (5th edn) (Butterworths, 2002) at pp 324–327.
9 Jobseekers Act 1995.

those with dependent children, of whom lone mothers are the major category. For this reason we discuss below the basic rules governing income support.

Benefits for school-leavers

A second change of emphasis related to the age at which a person becomes entitled to claim income support in his or her own right. Disquiet came to be expressed about the ease with which (so it was said) young people leaving school at the age of 16 could claim income support and thus be supported by the State rather than seeking work or training for work; and the 1987 Conservative Party election manifesto included a pledge that young persons who chose to be unemployed would be denied benefit[1]. The general rule until 7 October 1996 was that a person did not become entitled to income support in his own right[2] until the age of 18 years[3]. However, there were exceptional circumstances in which a person aged between 16 and 18 would be entitled to income support; and lone parents, persons who were temporarily unemployed but remained available to be re-employed, and persons registered for work who of necessity had to live away from their parents because they were estranged from them, in physical or moral danger, or because there was a serious risk to their physical or mental health[4] were allowed to claim in their own right. The Secretary of State could also direct that income support be paid to a person who would otherwise suffer severe hardship[5].

As from 7 October 1996 the minimum age for claiming income support was reduced again to 16, but to qualify a person must fall within 'a prescribed category'. This change made little difference in practice to those young people eligible for benefit, since it was merely consequential on the replacement of income support by income-based jobseeker's allowance for those required to be available for work as a condition of receiving benefit. To be entitled to the jobseeker's allowance (under the Jobseekers Act 1995, s 3) a person must usually be aged 18, subject to similar (but not identical) exceptions to those which applied to income support[6]. There are, however, special rules which may enable a 16- or 17-year-old to qualify. It is possible that such a young person might qualify for both income-based jobseeker's allowance and income support and thus might have to choose between them[7].

---

1 See Wikeley, Ogus and Barendt's *The Law of Social Security* (above) at pp 287–290. It should be noted that the income support regulations had always required that a claimant be 'available for work'; and in 1986 an additional requirement that a claimant be 'actively seeking' work was introduced: Social Security Contributions and Benefits Act 1992, s 124(1)(d).
2 The benefit entitlement of the parent or other person responsible for a young person in full-time (but not advanced – eg degree level) education was increased to take account of the needs of the young person concerned.
3 Social Security Contributions and Benefits Act 1992, s 124(1)(a).
4 Income Support (General) Regulations 1987, SI 1987/1967, Sch 1A, para 9A.
5 Social Security Contributions and Benefits Act 1992, s 125.
6 See Jobseeker's Allowance Regulations 1996, SI 1996/207, regs 57–68.
7 See Child Poverty Action Group *Welfare Benefits and Tax Credits Handbook* (2004/2005) chs 13 and 15 for the details.

Amount of income support

The income support scheme attributes a so-called 'applicable amount' to each claimant and, in principle, the claimant is entitled to income support to bring the income up to that amount. The necessary calculations are complex: the 'applicable amount' is the aggregate of a prescribed personal allowance, premiums, and housing costs. The Income Support (General) Regulations 1987 prescribe a number of different 'personal allowances' depending on such factors as the claimant's age and whether or not he or she is a lone parent (that is to say 'a member of the family [who] has no partner'). For example, a single claimant or lone parent who is aged less than 18 years has a personal allowance of £33.50 weekly (although this is increased to £44.05 weekly if, for example, the claimant has to live away from his parents for the reasons set out in the previous paragraph)[1]. The personal allowance for a couple is £87.30. To the personal allowance is added £42.27 for each dependent child.

These different rates of personal allowance show considerable flexibility with respect to individual circumstances, but the Regulations, in further pursuance of the policy of targeting benefits without it being necessary to make detailed enquiries into personal needs, provide for the inclusion of weekly *premiums* in the applicable amounts of claimants who satisfy the prescribed conditions. For example, a 'family premium' is payable where at least one member of the family is a child or young person. From April 1997 the family premium was paid at two rates. The higher rate incorporated the former lone parent premium and was paid where the claimant was a lone parent and did not qualify for one of the pensioner or disability premiums. There is now only one rate of family premium for income support purposes set at £15.95. This is part of a deliberate policy begun by the former Conservative Government and continued by the Labour Government of reducing or eroding the additional benefits paid to lone parents. From April 2004 income support no longer includes allowances and premiums for children but a claim may be made instead for child tax credit which will not count as income for income support purposes.

The means test

Income support is a means-tested benefit. The general principle is that the whole of the earnings and other income of members of the family – including maintenance payments made under a court order or child support maintenance paid under the 1991 Act – is calculated on a weekly basis and goes to reduce the amount of benefit entitlement, while a claimant who has capital – other than disregarded capital, such as the house the claimant occupies – worth £8,000 or more, is normally debarred from benefit[2]. A 'tariff' income applies between a threshold, currently £3,000, and the upper limit of £8,000. There is deemed to be an income of £1 per week for each complete £250 or part thereof exceeding the £3,000 threshold. An important change brought about by the recent amendments to the Child Support Act 1991 is, however, the introduction of a £10 disregard in

---

1　Income Support (General) Regulations 1987, SI 1987/1967, Sch 2, Part I, as amended. A single parent aged 18 years or over has a personal allowance of £55.65; as does a single claimant aged 25 years or over.

2　Income Support (General) Regulations 1987, reg 45, as amended.

relation to maintenance. Under the new formula £10 of child support maintenance received is to be disregarded in calculating the entitlement of the 'person with care' of the child to income support or income-based jobseeker's allowance.

The move to tax credits

It is the policy of the Labour Government to shift financial support for children by the State away from the benefits system and in the direction of tax credits administered by the Inland Revenue[1]. This policy is part of a general philosophy that it is better to encourage work than dependency and was reflected particularly by the introduction of a 'working families tax credit' in 1999. Accordingly, those elements in some of the major welfare benefits which have reflected the cost of raising children are to be received instead through a new system of tax credits. Nonetheless it should be borne in mind that certain welfare benefits for children will remain part of the benefit system, most notably child benefit which will not be treated as income for the purposes of calculating tax credits attributable to responsibility for children.

The principal changes took effect from 6 April 2004[2]. Up until that date there were allowances for children as elements in the calculation of income support and income-based jobseeker's allowance. As from that date, these elements were removed and those benefits will comprise only the allowable elements relating to adults plus housing costs. Instead, families with children will now apply for child tax credit in relation to the children. The former working families tax credit has been split, as from April 2003, into two separate tax credits: the 'child tax credit' and the 'working tax credit'. The former is a means-tested, income-based credit for families with children, in or out of employment, who have responsibility for children who are under 16 or under 19 and in full-time, non-advanced education. The latter is a means-tested, income-based credit for working adults who work for more than 16 hours per week and satisfy certain other conditions, one of which is having responsibility for a child. These credits are based only on income and not on capital. They are paid additional to most welfare benefits but may count as income for the purposes of some means-tested benefits.

Child tax credit replaces the elements for children in income support, income-based jobseeker's allowance, together with the working families tax credit, disabled person's tax credit and children's tax credit and was subject to transitional changes between April 2003 and April 2004. The key to eligibility for child tax credit[3] is that the claimant must be 'responsible' for a child or a qualifying young person. It is important to appreciate that those eligible are not confined to parents but could be, for example, a member of the extended family or social parent with primary care of the child. Being responsible for a child essentially involves the application of two tests. First, the child must be 'normally living' with the claimant. Secondly, the claimant must have 'main responsibility' for the child. These are questions of fact for the Inland Revenue. The child may be normally living with the claimant notwithstanding the fact that he or she is *partly* living with someone else. A controversial aspect of the new credit is that it may not

---

1 See generally the Tax Credits Act 2002 and regulations made thereunder.
2 For the details of the new tax credits, see Child Poverty Action Group *Welfare Benefits and Tax Credits Handbook* (2004/2005), Part 6.
3 See the Child Tax Credit Regulations 2002, SI 2002/2007.

be split. Consequently, it is likely to be only the person with whom the child spends the greatest amount of time who will be able to satisfy these two tests and clearly this is capable of bearing harshly on the non-resident parent in whose household the child spends significant amounts of time, albeit less than the time spent with the resident parent. We shall see that the new formula for child support liability does, however, make substantial allowance for time spent with the non-resident parent[1].

Child tax credit comprises a number of elements[2] including a child element (currently set at £1,625 per year), disability element (£2,215 per year), severe disability element (£890 per year) and family element (£1,090 including a 'baby' element, £545 without the baby element). The calculation of the maximum amount of child tax credit then involves adding all these elements which apply to the claimant. The calculation of child tax credit involves comparing the claimant's income with an income threshold figure currently set at £13,480. This threshold figure drops to £5,060 where the claimant is also entitled to working tax credit. Where the claimant's income is less than the threshold income the maximum credit is payable. Where it exceeds the threshold income, it is reduced by 37 per cent of the excess income.

Working tax credit may also be payable to those responsible for one or more children and who work for more than 16 hours per week[3]. A family with children may claim working tax credit especially where they pay for child care and thus qualify for the child care element in the credit. This child care element is paid to the person who is the child's main carer which will be important where a joint claim is made by a couple. If it is not agreed between joint claimants who is the main carer, it will be for the Inland Revenue to decide. The rules relating to eligible children are similar to those which apply to child tax credit. Where the claimant is a member of a married or unmarried couple there must be a joint claim, in line with the aggregation principle applicable to means-tested social security benefits.

Maximising welfare benefits following family breakdown: welfare benefit planning

Lawyers soon began to appreciate that welfare benefits could be a significant resource for families after divorce, and (in particular) could be used to make practicable the 'clean break' philosophy embodied in the divorce legislation after the Matrimonial and Family Proceedings Act 1984. Three features of the welfare benefit legislation were particularly relevant. First, income support (as mentioned above) made allowance for a claimant's 'housing costs' and, subject to certain restrictions, income support payments would cover the interest paid on a mortgage taken out to buy the house or to buy out the interest of a divorced partner. Secondly, although the social security legislation[4] imposed an obligation to maintain the spouse and children, there was no such obligation to maintain a

---

1 See below.
2 Child Tax Credit Regulations 2002, reg 7.
3 See the Tax Credit Act 2002 and the Working Tax Credit (Entitlement and Maximum Rate) Regulations 2002, SI 2002/2005.
4 The relevant provisions are now consolidated in the Social Security Administration Act 1992, ss 78(6) and 105(3).

former spouse. Moreover, although the obligation to maintain children continued notwithstanding divorce and was not affected by the terms of any order made by the divorce court[1], it seemed that, in practice, the DSS did not attach a high priority to seeking to recover income support from parents and others[2]. Thirdly, the courts increasingly began to take account of the availability of State benefits in deciding how to exercise their powers to make financial orders on divorce. In particular, it began to be questioned whether a man should be made to go on paying maintenance out of his own small income when the payments would be of no benefit for the former wife but would merely reduce the amount of income support for which she was eligible. This point of view was put eloquently by Waite J[3]:

> 'no humane society could tolerate – even in the interest of saving its public purse – the prospect of a divorced couple of acutely limited means remaining manacled to each other indefinitely by the necessity to return at regular intervals to court for no other purpose than to thrash out at public expense the precise figure which the one should pay the other – not for any benefit to either of them, but solely for the relief of the tax-paying section of the community to which neither of them has sufficient means to belong.'

The welfare benefit 'clean break'

An appreciation of these factors increasingly led to financial orders being made under which the family home would be transferred to the wife outright. She would give up any claim to periodical maintenance and a small – perhaps even nominal – periodical payment order would be made for the children. In some cases, the wife would increase the mortgage on the house so that she could make a lump sum payment to the husband, sufficient to enable him to pay a deposit on a house for himself and his new family. The outcome would be as follows: the wife would remain eligible for income support, and the costs of meeting interest payments on the mortgage would be added to her basic entitlement. The DSS would have no right to pursue the former husband in respect of income support payments made to the wife; and, although the DSS would be entitled to recover income support paid in respect of the children, it may be that this right would not be vigorously exercised. The husband would have lost his interest in the former matrimonial home but he would have no on-going maintenance liability, and he would be in a position to buy another house on mortgage, and would be eligible for tax relief on the interest.

It seems probable that such planning became common. Certainly a large number of so-called clean break orders were made[4] and, by 1989, less than one-quarter of families on income support were receiving periodical maintenance from the absent parent (whereas one half of such families had received maintenance 10 years earlier)[5].

The reaction to welfare benefit planning

These developments were not welcome to those responsible for the administration of the social security budget. Not only was the financial cost high, it was also

---

1 *Hulley v Thompson* [1981] WLR 159.
2 National Audit Office Report *Support for Lone Parent Families* (1990) HC 328.
3 *Ashley v Blackman* [1988] 2 FLR 278 at 284–285.
4 See *Judicial Statistics Annual Report 1991* at Table 5.5.
5 *Children Come First* (1990) (Cmnd 1263) at para 1.5.

thought that these developments played a part in eroding personal responsibility for the family. In this context, another matter of concern was the growing number of births outside marriage. In 1991, 31 per cent of all live births were outside marriage[1], and it appeared that many children were born to young single mothers who became wholly dependent on welfare benefits, while no sustained effort was made to recover maintenance from the father.

FINANCIAL SUPPORT FOR CHILDREN UNDER THE CHILD SUPPORT ACT 1991

It has been seen[2] that some changes were made to the law to reduce the attractiveness of welfare benefits to young claimants, and attempts were made[3] to increase the effectiveness of the liable relative system. But much more radical change was to come: on 18 July 1990 the then Prime Minister[4] announced that the Government intended to set up a Child Support Agency which would have access to the information necessary to trace absent parents and to make them accept their financial obligations. Shortly afterwards, the Government published a White Paper[5] *Children Come First*, which gave the following diagnosis of the problem:

> 'The present system of maintenance is unnecessarily fragmented, uncertain in its results, slow and ineffective. It is based largely on discretion. The system is operated through the High and county courts, the Magistrates' Courts ... and the offices of the Department of Social Security. The cumulative effect is uncertainty and inconsistent decisions about how much maintenance should be paid. In a great many instances, the maintenance award is not paid or the payments fall into arrears and then take weeks to re-establish. Only 30% of lone mothers and 3% of lone fathers receive regular maintenance for their children. More than 750,000 lone parents depend on income support. Many lone mothers want to go to work but do not feel able to do so.'

The White Paper set out further details about the role of the Child Support Agency which would trace absent parents and assess, collect and enforce maintenance payments. Responsibility for assessing claims for child maintenance was to be removed from the courts, and maintenance assessments would be calculated by reference to a non-discretionary formula intended to produce a level of maintenance reflecting both the day-to-day living costs of raising a child, and the essential living expenses of the person caring for a child and the absent parent.

The White Paper invited comments on its proposals, but the CSA 1991 seems to have been intended to give effect to the proposals in *Children Come First* without any significant change. In particular, it is to be noted that the Act does not seem to reflect the then Prime Minister's statement that 'complicated cases' might still have to be referred to the courts and, in fact, the role of the courts under the English child support system is much less than that in comparable systems

---

1   *Population Trends* No 68 (1992). The figure has continued to rise and is now around 40%. See *Social Trends 33* (2003), Figure 2.18.
2   See p 373 above.
3   See the Maintenance Enforcement Act 1991; the Social Security Administration Act 1992, s 107; and the Income Support (Liable Relatives) Regulations 1990, SI 1990/1777.
4   Mrs Margaret Thatcher.
5   (1990) (Cmnd 1263).

introduced elsewhere in the Commonwealth[1]. The Child Support Act 1995, which introduced the possibility of 'departure directions' in 'exceptional cases', was enacted in an attempt to meet some of the criticisms that the original scheme was too rigid and inflexible. We look more closely at this below.

The passage of the 1991 Act through Parliament was controversial[2] – although, perhaps surprisingly, the official opposition did not question the basic principles underlying the new law – but few amendments were made and the Act was brought fully into force on 5 April 1993[3]. All new cases – ie all cases in which there was no previous court order or maintenance agreement – were taken on by the Child Support Agency with effect from 5 April 1993. Between that date and April 1996, existing cases in which a claimant was on income support or family credit were taken over by the Agency, and by 1997 the Agency had assumed responsibility for all child support cases.

The Child Support Act 1995[4] prescribed a number of cases in which 'departure directions' might be made including costs incurred in travelling to work[5]; costs incurred by an 'absent parent' in maintaining contact with his children; costs attributable to long-term illness or disability; pre-existing debts and financial commitments; and costs incurred in supporting a child of the family who was not the applicant's own child. Another category concerned allowances for property transfers made before the child support scheme came into effect in April 1993, the effect of which had been to reduce the amount of periodical payments which would otherwise have been payable in relation to a child[6]. Other 'additional cases' were prescribed, which included situations in which a person's lifestyle was inconsistent with his level of income or his housing costs or travel were unreasonably high. The 1995 Act reiterated the principle that 'parents should be responsible for maintaining their children whenever they can afford to do so' and

---

1   See, for example, M Harrison 'Child Maintenance in Australia: the New Era' in Weitzman and Maclean (eds) *The Economic Consequences of Divorce* (1991); 'Child Support in Australia: Children's Rights or Public Interest' (1991) 5 Int JL&F 24. On experience in the USA, see I Garfinkel *Assuring Child Support* (New York, 1992). On the scheme in New Zealand, see N Richardson 'The New Zealand Child Support Act' [1995] CFLQ 40. See also JT Oldham 'Lessons from the New English and Australian Child Support Systems' (1996) 29 *Vanderbilt J Transnat'l L* 691. For an academic assessment of the issues surrounding child support in the USA, with some comparative material, see JT Oldham and MS Melli *Child Support: The Next Frontier* (University of Michigan Press, 2000). See also S Altman 'A Theory of Child Support' (2003) 17 IJLPF 173.

2   For more up-to-date commentary on the Act as amended by the Child Support, Pensions and Social Security Act 2000, see R Bird *Child Maintenance: The New Law* (5th edn) (Family Law, 2002). See also N Wikeley 'Child Support – The New Formula' [2000] Fam Law 820. A useful tool for calculation of child support under the old and new formulae is R Bird *Child Support Calculation Kit 2003/2004* (Family Law, 2003). For a penetrating analysis of the work of the Child Support Agency based on empirical research involving privileged access to the Agency's staff, see G Davis, N Wikeley and R Young, with J Barron and J Bedward *Child Support in Action* (Hart Publishing, 1998).

3   The effect of the transitional provisions was complex: see the Child Support Act 1991 (Commencement No 3 and Transitional Provisions) (Amendment) Order 1993, SI 1993/966.

4   For commentary on the changes made by the 1995 Act, see M Horton 'Improving Child Support – A Missed Opportunity' [1995] CFLQ 26. See also the second edition of this work at pp 304–306.

5   Notably not covered in the new system of 'variations'.

6   The transfer of part of a beneficial interest qualified for these purposes. See *Secretary of State for Social Security v Henderson* [1999] 1 FLR 496.

that 'where a parent has more than one child, his obligation to maintain any one of them should be no less an obligation than his obligation to maintain any other of them'. As we shall see, the amendments to the child support scheme introduced by legislation in 2000 give greater effect to this principle by taking account of the presence of children in the non-resident parent's household when calculating his net income on which the new rates of support are based.

It is important to appreciate that there was no rigid 'entitlement' to a departure from the normal liability in any of these cases[1]. The Secretary of State exercised a discretion and issued a departure direction only where it was thought 'just and equitable' to do so, taking into account the financial circumstances of the parties and the welfare of any child likely to be affected by the decision. This discretionary approach has been preserved under the new system of 'variations' allowed under the amended child support scheme[2].

The administration of the child support scheme continued to provoke widespread criticism, indeed hostility, in practice and the new Labour Government published, first, a Green Paper entitled *Children First: A New Approach to Child Support*[3] and then a White Paper, *A New Contract for Welfare: Children's Rights and Parents' Responsibilities*[4]. This paved the way for radical reforming legislation, the Child Support, Pensions and Social Security Act 2000 which has introduced far-reaching changes, especially to the formula for the calculation of child support. These changes are being phased in as from April 2003. It is important to appreciate, however, that the 2000 legislation did not repeal, but only amend, the 1991 Act and did not alter, or even question, many of the fundamental principles and provisions of the CSA 1991. The changes are rather designed to enable the system to work more fairly and expeditiously.

In its White Paper the Government identified what it saw as the major problems with the operation of the scheme. Many parents were not meeting their responsibilities, with only around 40 per cent of non-resident parents paying in full. Moreover, the system was riddled with complexity. It was estimated that it could take more than 100 pieces of information to enable a calculation of child support maintenance to be made. This resulted in a slow and cumbersome system which was prone to errors and open to abuse by unco-operative parents. The Government's proposed solution, to which the 2000 legislation gives effect, comprises a number of elements. First, a much more straightforward formula, based solely on a simple slice of the non-resident parent's income and the number of children concerned, has been introduced. The income of the 'person with care' is ignored, thus removing at a stroke much of the complication of the original formula. This had required a complex calculation which also embraced the needs and resources of the parent with care. The concept of a 'protected income' below which a non-resident parent's income should not fall has also been replaced by a simpler minimum flat rate of payment for those with low incomes or on benefit, and a sliding scale for those with incomes just above the minimum. Secondly, the amendments introduce tougher sanctions for recalcitrant parents who refuse to co-operate including fines and the possibility of more Draconian

---

1 Although there was a right of appeal to a Child Support Appeal Tribunal from a refusal to make a departure direction.
2 See below.
3 (Cm 3992) (The Stationery Office, 1998).
4 (Cm 4349) (The Stationery Office, 1999).

measures used in other jurisdictions, most notably the threat to withdraw a driving licence. Thirdly, the child support service is intended to be transformed into a more 'customer-focused child support service'. This will be expected to make greater use of the telephone and face-to-face discussions. Resources are to be directed away from their previous concentration on the application of complex formulae in calculating benefit, towards making sure that maintenance is paid regularly and on time. Fourthly, more help is given to families on income support through the so-called 'child maintenance premium'. This is something of a misnomer since it is not a payment as such but a disregard of the first £10 of child support maintenance received when calculating benefit. In any event, it is designed to mitigate one aspect of the 'poverty trap' whereby the benefit of any child support received is immediately swallowed up by a corresponding loss of benefit.

The Government is confident that these changes will produce a system which is simple, clear and easy to understand. Non-resident parents will know immediately how much they need to pay for their children and how much they have left to meet other responsibilities. The system, it is claimed, will put the needs of children first and make it clear that parents' legal and moral responsibilities to their children override other day-to-day expenses.

This is an optimistic prognostication and time will tell whether it proves correct.

General principles of the child support legislation

Support for parents, not payments to children
The law governing child support has traditionally been concerned with applications by parents and other adults for financial support in respect of a child's maintenance. Only in exceptional circumstances[1] could a child or young person seek financial support by way of court order and, as has been seen[2], the income support scheme also contains provisions intended to confine eligibility to adults in all save exceptional circumstances. The CSA 1991 follows this traditional policy. It makes no provision for a child to seek support but is concerned to define the liability of each parent of a qualifying child to support that child, to assess the amount of periodical payments of maintenance which will be treated as sufficient to discharge the absent parent's responsibility for maintaining children, and to provide machinery for enforcing that responsibility. In this context, it is interesting to note that in Scotland a qualifying child who has attained the age of 12 years may apply for a maintenance assessment in his or her own right[3].

Child Support Act 1991 concerned only with parent–child obligations
As already noted, the legislation dealing with financial orders relating to children had gradually extended the basis upon which a person was to be treated as having an obligation to support a child, and liability could usually be imposed on anyone who had treated a child as a child of his or her family[4], with the result that a step-parent would, for example, be liable to maintain a step-child. The CSA 1991, however – in this respect following the 'public law' model, whereby welfare

---

1   See p 402 below.
2   See p 373 above.
3   CSA 1991, s 7(1).
4   See p 397 below.

benefits paid in respect of a child's needs can be recovered from a liable relative[1] – is concerned only with the obligations of a parent, and this word is defined to mean any person who is, in law, the mother or father of the child[2]. The CSA 1991 is therefore not directly concerned with the liability of step-parents, or others who may have treated children as children of their family[3]. Since around two-fifths of all marriages are now remarriages for at least one of the partners[4], it is inevitable that there are many cases in which the CSA 1991 has an uneasy relationship with the private law.

Child Support Act 1991 concerned only with income payments

The CSA 1991 is not concerned with capital: it contains no power to require a parent to make capital payments to a child, and it also largely ignores the fact that capital provision – for example, the transfer of a tenancy or other interest in the family home for the benefit of child – may have been made in satisfaction of the child's claims for support[5]. In this respect, the relationship between the new child support system and the older law has become a source of tension.

Two decisions illustrate this concentration on income, and the failure of the CSA 1991 to treat income and capital resources as inter-related.

In *Crozier v Crozier*[6] the divorcing parties had agreed to an all too typical consent order under which the husband was to transfer his interest in the former matrimonial home to the wife in return for being released from any maintenance obligations towards the wife and paying only nominal maintenance for the five-year-old child. The wife had always been in receipt of income support and the Secretary of State for Social Security was content with a contribution of £4 per week in respect of the child from the husband. When the husband subsequently received the documentation from the Child Support Agency it was anticipated that his liability under the CSA 1991 would amount to £29 per week for the child. In these worsened circumstances he applied to have the consent order set aside or varied. Both parties by this time had new partners and, indeed, both had a child of their new relationships.

Booth J refused leave to appeal out of time against the order. The 'clean break' approach which applied in the divorce jurisdiction had no application to *public* obligations to support children arising under the child support legislation. This public liability to maintain children remained on both parents irrespective of their intentions. Although the wife was prepared to assume sole legal liability to maintain the child she could not in fact do so without public assistance. The State was not bound by any agreement between the parties designed to trade off capital provision against liability for child support.

---

1 See p 371 above.
2 CSA 1991, s 54.
3 Although the presence of step-children or other children in the non-resident parent's household will, under the recent amendments to the calculation, have a significant bearing on the extent of liability. See below.
4 *Social Trends 33* (2003) Figure 2.10.
5 See *K v K (Minors: Property Transfer)* [1992] 2 FLR 220, CA.
6 [1994] 1 FLR 26. For other cases exploring the relationship between the clean break and child support, see *Mawson v Mawson* [1994] 2 FLR 985 and *Smith v McInerney* [1994] 2 FLR 1077. Specifically on the relationship between lump sum orders and liability for child support, see *AMS v Child Support Officer* [1998] 1 FLR 955. See also *V v V (Child Maintenance)* [2001] 2 FLR 799.

Crozier illustrated the inflexible nature of an income-based scheme which fails to take proper account of capital transfers which in reality might be viewed as a form of capitalised maintenance. This was only partially ameliorated by the reforms introduced by the Child Support Act 1995 regarding 'departure directions' and by provision for 'variations' following the 2000 reforms. *Crozier* was a case in which the father found himself the worse off for having parted with his capital. *Phillips v Peace*[1] illustrates the opposite problem – the way in which the child support scheme can be artificially generous to a man who has substantial capital but little or no income. Here, the father successfully owned and operated a company which dealt in shares. He lived in a house worth £2.6 million but, applying the child support formula, it was found that he had no actual income. Hence, a child support assessment could not be made against him. Johnson J said it was absurd that the legislation resulted in the father's liability to support the child being assessed at zero. It was, however, open to the court to order a lump sum for the benefit of the child, exercising its jurisdiction under the Children Act, s 15 and Sch 1. It should not, however, do so in a way designed to circumvent the policy of the child support legislation. A lump sum ought only to be ordered to meet the need of the child in respect of a particular item of capital expenditure. A sum of £90,000 was ordered to enable the mother to buy a house plus £24,307.51 for furniture and birth and other expenses.

Child support and the welfare of the child

We noted in Chapter 2 that the 'welfare principle' applies in only a limited number of legal contexts and that the weight to be attached to children's welfare varies depending on the kind of proceedings in question. So far as the child support scheme is concerned, there was a good deal of Government rhetoric about how this was intended to give priority to the interests of children but in fact the statutory commitment on a closer examination is really rather weak. It is provided[2]:

> 'Where, in any case which falls to be dealt with under this Act, the Secretary of State or any child support officer is considering the exercise of any discretionary power conferred by this Act, he shall have regard to the welfare of any child likely to be affected by his decision.'

Hence, welfare is not the 'first' consideration, let alone the 'paramount' consideration, and it is only in cases where there is any *discretion* that the welfare of the child will be relevant at all. As will be seen, there is little discretion in the child support system, which rather involves the mandatory application of rigid rules, albeit somewhat tempered by the possibility of a 'variation'. Thus the welfare of the child is, in practice, unlikely to play much of a part in the calculation and enforcement of child support. Any redress on the basis that the Child Support Agency has failed to give any or proper weight to the welfare of the child will be restricted to the limited possibility of a challenge by way of judicial review[3].

Scheme of the Child Support Act 1991

The underlying principle of the CSA 1991 was said to be that parents have a clear moral duty to maintain their children until they are old enough to look after

---

1   [1996] 2 FLR 230.
2   CSA 1991, s 2.
3   See *R v Secretary of State for Social Security ex parte Lloyd* [1995] 1 FLR 856 and *R v Secretary of State for Social Security ex parte Biggin* [1995] 1 FLR 851.

themselves. Events may change the relationship between the parents but they cannot change their responsibilities towards their children[1]. The CSA 1991 seeks to give effect to this philosophy in several ways: first by providing formulae whereby the liability of parents in respect of their children's maintenance is to be met; secondly by prescribing a nil rate, flat rate and reduced rate where the non-resident parent's income falls below certain prescribed levels; thirdly by conferring wide powers to obtain information on the officials charged with the administration of the CSA 1991; and fourthly by giving wide powers of enforcement and collection in respect of maintenance calculations.

Administration of child support

The Government established a Child Support Agency with the responsibility of administering the provisions of the CSA 1991[2] but the Act itself makes no mention of the Agency: it imposes responsibilities and confers powers on the Secretary of State and provides that he shall appoint persons to be known as 'child support officers' for the purposes of the legislation[3]. The responsibility for the administration of the Act therefore remains with a Minister responsible to Parliament but the actual administration of its provisions has been delegated to a Government Agency.

Liability to maintain: non-resident parents

The underlying principle of the CSA 1991 is that each parent of a 'qualifying child' is responsible for maintaining that child[4], but a child is only a 'qualifying child' if one or both of his parents is, in relation to him, a "non-resident parent"[5]. This provision underscores the fact that the CSA 1991 is concerned with the situation in which child and parent are living apart. The Act is not concerned to define the level of support appropriate to a child living under the same roof with the parents.

1　*Children Come First* (1990) (Cmnd 1263).
2　The Child Support Agency publishes periodic reports. For an assessment of its 2002 Report, see J Pirrie 'Report of the Child Support Agency, March 2002' [2003] Fam Law 105.
3　CSA 1991, s 13(1). The Act, under s 15, also empowered the Secretary of State to appoint persons to act as inspectors who have powers of entry, questioning, etc: see p 392 below. There is a Chief Child Support Officer who must make an annual report which must be published: CSA 1991, s 13(3)–(5).
4　Ibid, s 1(1).
5　Ibid, s 3(1). The language of the Act was amended by the 2000 legislation to replace the term 'absent parent', which was thought to have pejorative connotations, with the more neutral 'non-resident parent'. The parent of any child is a non-resident parent in relation to him if that parent is not living in the same household with the child, and the child has his home with a person who is, in relation to him, a 'person with care': ibid, s 3(2). A person with care is defined as a person with whom the child has his home and who usually provides day-to-day care for the child, whether exclusively or in conjunction with any other person, and who does not fall within a prescribed category of person: ibid, s 3(3). There can be difficult questions of fact concerning which parent is the 'person with care' where the child is at boarding school, as to which see *C v Secretary of State for Work and Pensions and B* [2003] 1 FLR 829.

Who is a parent?

The fact that the CSA 1991 is solely concerned to impose obligations on 'parents' has already been mentioned[1], and the Act states that the term 'parent', in relation to any child, means any person who is, in law, the mother or father of the child[2] (ie the natural parent, an adoptive parent, or a person treated as a child's parent under the Human Fertilisation and Embryology Act 1990[3]). The key to liability is therefore having the status of legal parent[4], and it is to be noted that treating the child as a 'child of the family' for the purposes of the Matrimonial Causes Act 1973 is not sufficient.

Disputes about parentage

We considered in Chapter 5 the general principles governing the resolution of disputes as to parentage. There will seldom be any doubt about the identity of the mother but the question of who is the natural father has often been disputed. In Chapter 5 we noted the growing phenomenon of men wishing to establish paternity with a view to having contact with their children and perhaps playing a parental role. In the context of support for children, a significant number of men have always sought to evade liability by denying paternity.

The resolution of these disputes is governed by s 26 of the CSA 1991. This was extensively amended by the Child Support, Pensions and Social Security Act 2000[5]. The Act provides that no maintenance calculation may be made where parentage is denied unless the circumstances fall within a number of specified cases[6]. Where, however, the case *does* fall within the specified categories, a calculation may be made notwithstanding the denial of parentage. The prescribed cases are as follows[7]:

(i)   where the alleged parent was married to the child's mother at some time between conception and birth;

(ii)   where he has been registered as the child's father on the child's birth certificate[8];

(iii)   where a scientific test reveals that there is no reasonable doubt that he is the father or where he refuses to take such a test;

(iv)   where the alleged parent has adopted the child;

---

1   See p 382 above.
2   CSA 1991, s 54.
3   See *Re M (Child Support Act: Parentage)* [1997] 2 FLR 90. In this case, children who were conceived by AID were born in 1981 and 1986 respectively. The Secretary of State sought a declaration of parentage under s 27 of the 1991 Act in relation to the mother's husband on the basis that he had consented to the procedure. The husband denied that he had consented and argued that he was not therefore the 'parent' of the child. Bracewell J found the issue of consent to be immaterial since the status provisions of the 1990 Act did not have retrospective operation and it was clear that the husband was not the genetic father. If these facts were to recur today the matter *would* turn on whether or not the husband consented or objected to the procedure.
4   See Chapter 3 above.
5   For the detail see N Wikeley 'Child Support, Paternity and Parentage' [2001] Fam Law 125.
6   Section 26(1).
7   Section 26(2).
8   As we noted in Chapter 5, this will now also have the consequence that he will acquire parental responsibility, beyond just financial responsibility, for the child. See Children Act 1989, s 4, as amended by the Adoption and Children Act 2002.

(v) where he is the legal parent of the child by virtue of an order under s 30 of the Human Fertilisation and Embroyology Act 1990[1];

(vi) where the Secretary of State is satisfied that the alleged parent is the parent of the child under the 'status provisions' in ss 27 and 28 of the HFEA 1990[2];

(vii) where there has been a declaration of parentage under s 56 of the Family Law Act 1986[3];

(viii) where the child is in Scotland and one of the presumptions under s 5(1) of the Law Reform (Parent and Child) (Scotland) Act 1986 applies; and

(ix) where the alleged parent has been found or adjudged to be the father of the child in prevous legal proceedings[4].

Where the case does *not* fall within those enumerated above, s 27 of the CSA 1991 provides that the Secretary of State or the person with care may apply to the court for a declaration of parentage under s 55A of the Family Law Act 1986 to establish whether or not the alleged parent is the parent. The court may direct scientific tests and may draw adverse inferences from failure to submit to them[5].

The obligation

The CSA 1991 provides that a non-resident parent is, for the purposes of the Act, to be taken to have met his responsibility to maintain any qualifying child of his by making periodical payments of maintenance with respect to the child, in accordance with the provisions of the Act[6], and it imposes a duty to make such payments on a non-resident parent where a maintenance calculation has been made requiring him to make periodical payments[7].

The maintenance calculation

Before the 2000 amendments, as noted above, the original formulae under the CSA 1991 were extremely complex[8]. They involved first calculating a 'mainten-ance requirement' for the children, a process which was linked to the income support rates payable for the children and the parent with care but deducting the child benefit which was payable to the family. Stage two involved the calculation of the 'maintenance assessment' which required the 'assessable income' of the 'absent parent' less any so-called 'exempt income' to be ascertained. This was then

---

1 See Chapter 6 above.

2 See Chapter 3 above.

3 See Chapter 5 above.

4 See *R v Secretary of State for Social Security ex parte West* [1999] 1 FLR 1233 and *R v Secretary of State for Social Security ex parte W* [1999] 2 FLR 604.

5 For further discussion of the principles applying to the direction of tests, see Chapter 5 above. And for a recent example of such an adverse inference being drawn, see *Secretary of State for Work and Pensions v Jones* [2004] 1 FLR 282. Here it was held by Dame Elizabeth Butler-Sloss P that the justices had erred in concluding that the presumption that the child was the legitimate child of the mother's husband had not been rebutted. Although the mother had become reconciled with her husband, she had also had a relationship with another man and had applied for a maintenance assessment under the Child Support Agency against him. The man had refused to comply with a direction for DNA testing and refused to attend court on any occasion. An extension of the time-limit to appeal against the magistrates' determination was granted.

6 CSA 1991, s 1(2).

7 Ibid, s 1(3).

8 See the second edition of this work at pp 302 et seq.

added to the income of the parent with care, and the aggregate was divided by two. The 'assessable income' was then computed by making allowances for the personal expenditure of the 'absent parent' and adding this to the income support rates for any children living with him plus allowable housing costs. There was also provision for an additional element where the total assessable income exceeded the maintenance requirement, and there was provision for a 'protected income' which was designed to secure that the 'absent parent's' disposable income did not fall below a certain minimum level.

The new rates

As noted above, these complex formulae and calculations have been replaced under the 2000 amendments by much simpler rates of liability which do not involve calculating the resources of the person with care but which concentrate entirely on the income of the non-resident parent[1].

Part I of Sch 1 to the CSA 1991 as amended contains the general rule that the weekly rate of child support maintenance is to be the 'basic rate' unless a 'reduced rate', a 'flat rate' or the 'nil rate' apply[2].

The basic rate

The basic rate is expressed as a percentage of the non-resident parent's net weekly income. This is 15 per cent for one qualifying child, 20 per cent for two qualifying children and 25 per cent where there are three or more qualifying children.

There are a couple of qualifications to the apparent simplicity of this process. First, after some debate, it was conceded that there should be a cap on the amount of weekly income to which these rates apply. The Act sets the maximum net weekly income at £2,000, and anything above that is to be ignored.[3] The courts, however, retain their jurisdiction to make 'top up' orders in wealthy cases where appropriate. Secondly, the Act now makes substantial allowance for 'relevant other children' living with the non-resident parent. It was a widespread criticism of the old formulae that they were insufficiently sensitive to the new obligations which the non-resident parent might have acquired in a reconstituted family in which his new partner had children. The amended scheme takes into account responsibilities for step-children and the children of cohabitants and, in so doing, mirrors the percentages applicable to the non-resident parent's own children[4]. Thus, where there are other relevant children, the appropriate percentages will instead be applied to net weekly income *less* 15 per cent for one relevant other child, 20 per cent for two and 25 per cent where there are three or more relevant other children. In this way the Act attempts to provide some sort of parity in the obligations of natural and social parenthood and some sort of equality of treatment for the various children concerned, although it still results in a relative preference for the natural family. This is perhaps in contrast to the original clearly stated policy which was to the effect that the obligations to the 'first family'and to natural children should receive priority.

---

1   For a brief summary of the changes see A Wormwood 'Countdown to "D-day" for Fathers' [2003] Fam Law 191.
2   Schedule 1, para 1(1).
3   Schedule 1, para 10(3).
4   Schedule 1, para 2(2).

The reduced rate

A reduced rate is payable where the non-resident parent's net weekly income is less than £200 but more than £100, and neither the nil rate nor the flat rate applies[1]. The rate is on a sliding scale and is calculated by adding to the flat rate of £5, the non-resident parent's net weekly income and then applying a percentage to the resulting figure which takes into account both the number of qualifying children and other relevant children[2].

The flat rate

The flat rate[3] of £5 applies where the non-resident parent's net weekly income is £100 or less and the non-resident parent is receiving prescribed benefits or has a partner who is, provided that the nil rate does not apply.

The nil rate

The nil rate[4] applies to certain prescribed categories of non-resident parents, viz students, children under 16, prisoners, 16- and 17-year-olds where they or their partners are in receipt of income support or income-based jobseeker's allowance, patients in hospital, and those in residential care homes or nursing homes who are in receipt of certain benefits. In each case the net weekly income must be less than £5.

The effect of shared care on the rates

We noted above that the amended scheme is more sensitive to the social responsibilities of the non-resident parent towards children in his household. Perhaps in keeping with this, the scheme also makes greater allowance for responsibilities, especially financial responsibilities, arising from the non-resident parent's own children spending substantial periods of time with him. Some allowance for this was made under the old scheme[5] but the new formula takes greater account of shared care[6]. The threshold for the decrease in liability is now 52 nights and the amount of the decrease depends on the number of nights the qualifying child spends with the non-resident parent. The basic or reduced rate is decreased by the following fractions: 52–103 nights, one-seventh; 104–155 nights, two-sevenths; 156–174 nights, three-sevenths and 175 nights or more, one-half.

These decreases go some way to recognising the expense incurred by the non-resident parent while the children are with him and that the parent with care is relieved of some of the financial burden of raising children while they are not with her. It is only possible to speculate on whether the change will result in

---

1   Schedule 1, para 3 and the Child Support (Maintenance Calculations and Special Cases) Regulations 2000, SI 2001/155, reg 3.

2   A useful table is set out at para 3.6 in R Bird *Child Support: The New Law* (5th edn) (Family Law, 2002).

3   Schedule 1, para 4 and SI 2001/155, reg 4.

4   Schedule 1, para 5 and SI 2001/155, reg 5.

5   Maintenance liability was apportioned where each parent cared for the child in excess of 104 nights per annum.

6   Schedule 1, paras 7, 8 and 9, and the Child Support (Maintenance Calculations and Special Cases) Regulations 2001, reg 7A. Shared care is also an issue in relation to the new child tax credit. For a helpful discussion of the question of shared care under both regimes, see J Mitchell 'Shared Care – Shared Benefits?' [2003] Fam Law 321.

greater enthusiasm for exercising contact with children. In any event, it is arguable that the new scheme does give official recognition to the association between contact with and financial responsibility for children. This connection has often been denied, although there is at least some empirical evidence from the USA to suggest that it does exist in fact[1].

Variations

The objective of the child support scheme from the start has been to produce a mathematically fair system for determining individual financial liability for children. At the same time it has been recognised that there would be a small number of exceptional or unusual cases in which justice requires some adjustments of an otherwise rigid formula.

The original scheme had made provision for so-called 'special cases', but where these arose they involved applying another fixed formula. As we have seen, the Child Support Act 1995 introduced 'departure directions'[2] which have been renamed 'variations' under the new scheme[3]. The specified cases under which a variation may be made follow closely the pattern of the former departure directions but are not identical and are somewhat more tightly drafted.

Under s 28F the Secretary of State may agree a variation if he is satisfied that the case falls within those specified and 'it is his opinion that, in all the circumstances of the case, it would be just and equitable to agree to a variation'[4]. In reaching this decision the Secretary of State 'must have regard, in particular, to the welfare of any child likely to be affected if he did agree to a variation' and *must* or *must not* take certain prescribed factors into account[5]. These factors are set out in the regulations[6].

The Secretary of State *must*, for example, take account of whether a variation would be likely to result in a relevant person ceasing paid employment (a clear indication of the priorities which the Government attaches to work as opposed to welfare dependency) and of the extent of liability to pay maintenance under a previous court order or agreement. The list of factors which *must not* be taken into account is fascinating since it is illustrative of the underlying philosophy of the whole scheme. Thus, for example, the Secretary of State[7] must not take into account, in determining what is just and equitable, that the conception of the qualifying child was not planned by one or both of the parents; whether either parent was responsible for the breakdown of the relationship between them; the fact that either of them had formed a new relationship with another person; the existence of particular arrangements for contact with the qualifying child and whether they are being adhered to, and so on. One way of looking at these factors would be to see them as an attempt by the State to be 'morally neutral' as regards

---

1 See J Seltzer 'Child Support and Child Access' in JT Oldham and MS Melli *Child Support: the Next Frontier* (University of Michigan Press, 2000) at p 69.
2 For the then Conservative Government's reasoning, see *Improving Child Support* (1995) (Cm 2745).
3 The details of the new system of variations are to be found in Sch 4B to the CSA 1991, and the Child Support (Variations) Regulations 2000, SI 2001/156.
4 CSA 1991, s 28F(1).
5 Ibid, s 28F(2).
6 Child Support (Variations) Regulations 2000, reg 21.
7 Ibid, reg 21(2).

the making and breaking of relationships and the circumstances surrounding pregnancy. We return to the question of the fundamental basis of liability for child support below[1].

The detail of the specified cases where variations are permitted is beyond the scope of the present work[2]. But in essence they fall into two groups: those which will tend towards a reduction in liability; and those which will tend towards an increased liability. The first category includes so-called 'special expenses'[3] and relates to such things as costs associated with maintaining contact with a child; expenses incurred in relation to another relevant child who has long-term illness or disability; prior debts; boarding school expenses; and mortgage payments in relation to the former family home. It also includes 'property or capital transfers'[4] which took place before the CSA 1991 came into effect on 5 April 1993 and will therefore apply to a decreasing number of cases in future. These are transfers which were made on the understanding that they would relieve a parent of liability to make maintenance payments for the children. The second category, known as 'additional cases'[5], includes the situations where the non-resident parent has assets worth more than £65,000, has a lifestyle which is inconsistent with his declared income, has income which is not taken into account in the calculation, or where he has unreasonably reduced the income which is taken into account in making the calculation.

Revisions

The legislation contains provisions to enable decisions, once made, to be revised periodically and also to be revised if there is a change of circumstances[6].

Assessment will be made only on application

If (but only if) a maintenance calculation has been made, the non-resident parent is required to make payments. It is important to understand that there is no general obligation on a person who has care of children to apply for a maintenance calculation against a non-resident parent[7]: the CSA 1991 does not prevent parents from settling their financial affairs by agreement[8] and, indeed, substantial fees are payable to the Child Support Agency on the making of a calculation[9].

The position is different where the person with care of the child is in receipt of income support, income-based jobseeker's allowance, or another prescribed

---

1   See p 406.
2   For full discussion see R Bird *Child Support: The New Law* (5th edn) (Family Law, 2002) ch 5.
3   See Schedule 4B, para 2, and Child Support (Variations) Regulations 2000, regs 10–15.
4   Schedule 4B, para 3, and SI 2001/156, regs 16 and 17.
5   Schedule 4B, para 4, and SI 2001/156, regs 18–20.
6   CSA 1991, ss 16 and 17, as amended.
7   The obligation to make payments is found in the provisions of the CSA 1991 which state that where a maintenance calculation made under the Act requires the making of periodical payments it is the duty of the absent parent to make those payments (s 1(3)), and payments of child support maintenance under the calculation are to be made in accordance with regulations made by the Secretary of State (s 29(2)).
8   Section 9(2) of the CSA 1991 provides that nothing in the Act should be taken to prevent any person from entering into a maintenance agreement.
9   Child Support Fees Regulations 1992, SI 1992/3094. These fees are payable annually by both parents.

benefit: the CSA 1991 provides[1] that, in those circumstances, the person with care will be treated as having applied for a maintenance calculation unless that person has specifically requested the Secretary of State not to act. She must, so far as she reasonably can, provide information to enable the non-resident parent to be identified or traced, and the amount of child support to be calculated and recovered from him. A refusal to give this information or to take a scientific test to determine paternity will result in the parent being served with notice to give reasons[2]. The Secretary of State must then consider whether there are reasonable grounds for believing that, were the parent to comply, 'there would be a risk of her, or of any children living with her, suffering harm or undue distress as a result of taking such action, or her complying or taking the test'[3]. Where he is not satisfied, he may, except in prescribed circumstances, make a reduced benefit decision[4].

Agreements cannot oust Agency's jurisdiction

Although there is no reason why a couple should not agree on the financial arrangements to be made for their children, it is expressly provided that the existence of a maintenance agreement[5] shall not prevent any party to the agreement (or any other person) from applying for a maintenance calculation with respect to any child to whom or for whose benefit periodical payments are to be made or secured under the agreement. Any provision in an agreement which purports to exclude the right to apply for a maintenance calculaton is void[6]. In practice, therefore, every parent must assume that he or she may be made to support the children by way of periodical income payments up to the amount of any maintenance calculation which could be made under the CSA 1991.

Information

Regulations[7] give the Secretary of State extensive powers to require an absent parent and a person with care to give information on a wide range of matters to enable the absent parent to be identified, and the maintenance calculation computed. There are also powers to require employers, local authorities and others to give information. Inspectors may be appointed[8] who have power to enter at all reasonable times any specified premises (other than premises used solely as a dwelling house) and any other premises used by a specified person for the purpose of carrying on any trade, profession, vocation or business, and to make such examination and enquiry there as the inspector considers appropriate. Any person who is, or has been, an occupier of the premises in question, or an employee, is required to furnish the inspector with all such information and documents as the inspector may reasonably require, and it is a criminal offence intentionally to delay or obstruct any inspector exercising those powers, or

1 By s 6.
2 Child Support Act 1991, s 46(2).
3 Ibid, s 46(3).
4 Ibid, s 46(5). 'Reduced benefit decision' is defined in s 46(10).
5 Defined as any agreement for making or for securing the making of periodical payments by way of maintenance to or for the benefit of any child: s 9(1) of the CSA 1991.
6 Ibid, s 9(4).
7 Child Support (Information, Evidence and Disclosure) Regulations 1992, SI 1992/1812.
8 CSA 1991, s 15(1).

(without reasonable excuse) to refuse or neglect to answer any question or furnish any information or produce any document which is required under the provisions of the CSA 1991. The Act broke a long tradition by providing (in effect) that the child support authorities might obtain information from the Inland Revenue in order to trace the current address of an absent parent or the current employer of an absent parent[1]. These powers enable the Child Support Agency to trace absent parents, investigate their means, and exercise the powers[2] of collection and enforcement given to the authorities by the CSA 1991.

Information held by the Child Support Agency is confidential and not to be disclosed without lawful authority[3]. It has been held that the courts have no power under the Act to give leave to, or direct, the Secretary of State to disclose information to a child as to his father's whereabouts. A court may, however, *request* the Secretary of State to disclose it in the context of an application for a s 8 order[4].

Collection and enforcement

The CSA 1991 contains exceptionally wide powers of collection and enforcement[5]. Among the methods of enforcement, there is power to require a person, from whom payments are due under a maintenance calculation, to make them by way of direct debit or standing order[6], and the Secretary of State may – without having to obtain any court order – require an employer to make deductions from earnings in order to satisfy a maintenance calculation[7]. However, there is a protected earnings rate, below which the employer must not reduce the payments made to the employee.

If there is a failure by a liable person to make a payment of child support and it appears to be 'inappropriate' to make a deduction of earnings order – for example because the person concerned is not in employment, or because such an order has proved ineffective[8] – the Secretary of State may apply to the magistrates for a liability order[9]. The magistrates' court is required to make such an order if the court is satisfied that the payments in question have become payable and have not been paid. Apparently, following the precedent of the community charge legislation, the making of a liability order confers on the authorities a wide range of enforcement powers. In particular, distress may be levied[10], and it appears to be

---

1   CSA 1991, Sch 2, para 1.
2   See below.
3   CSA 1991, s 50.
4   *Re C (A Minor) (Child Support Agency: Disclosure)* [1995] 1 FLR 201.
5   Sections 29–41 of the CSA 1991; and the Child Support (Collection and Enforcement) Regulations 1992, SI 1992/1989, as amended by the Child Support (Collection and Enforcement and Miscellaneous Amendments) Regulations 2000, SI 2001/162. See generally N Wikeley 'Compliance, Enforcement and Child Support' [2000] Fam Law 888.
6   Child Support (Collection and Enforcement) Regulations 1992, SI 1992/1989, Part II.
7   Sections 31–32 of the 1991 Act. It has been held that disputes relating to quantification or validity of a maintenance calculation, in which it is alleged that a deduction of earnings order was defective, are to be dealt with through the review and appeal structure under the child support legislation and are outside the jurisdiction of the magistrates' court. See *Secretary of State for Social Security v Shotton and Others* [1996] 2 FLR 241.
8   CSA 1991, s 33.
9   Such an order was found to be necessary and proportionate for the purposes of the ECHR in *R on the Application of Denson v Child Support Agency* [2002] EWHC 154 (Admin) [2002] 1 FLR 938.
10 CSA 1991, s 35; Child Support (Collection and Enforcement) Regulations 1992, SI 1992/1989, regs 30–32.

the intention to use distress in preference to other procedures[1]. If distress (or other enforcement procedure) fails, the Secretary of State may apply to the magistrates' court for an order committing the liable person to prison, and the court may commit the defaulter to prison if, but only if, it is of the opinion that he has been guilty of wilful refusal or culpable neglect[2].

As noted earlier, one of the objectives of the 2000 reforms is to increase the powers of enforcement in cases of especially recalcitrant defaulters. Two changes to the legislation should be noted in this respect. First, when all else has failed, the Act now provides for the possibility that an application may be made for an order disqualifying the defaulting parent from driving, either by holding or obtaining a driving licence[3]. Secondly, the Act provides[4] for 'penalty payments' to be made where arrears have accumulated but these must not exceed 25 per cent of the amount of child support payable for the week in question. The potential disqualification from driving is a Draconian measure which has been tried in other jurisdictions. Indeed, some have gone further. The city of Buenos Aires, for example, adopted a policy of 'naming and shaming' recalcitrant parents in a public register (the *Registro de Deudores Morosos*)[5]. Consequences of being so named include restrictions on the ability of the debtor to open bank accounts or obtain credit cards. There are undoubtedly civil libertarian objections to such measures, but they do illustrate how far the State might be able to go if it attached a high enough priority to enforcement of child support liability.

The residual role of the court in relation to financial provision for children

The general rule is that where the Secretary of State would have jurisdiction to make a maintenance calculation, the court is debarred from exercising any power which it would otherwise have[6] to make, vary or revive any maintenance order, ie

---

1　A garnishee or charging order may be sought in the county court: CSA 1991, s 36.
2　CSA 1991, s 40(3). The maximum period of imprisonment is six weeks: ibid, s 40(7).
3　Ibid, s 39A(2)(b).
4　Ibid, s 41A.
5　See C Grosman and DB Inigo 'Non-Payment of a Maintenance Obligation: New Rules, Judicial Decisions and Initiatives in Argentina' in A Bainham (ed) *The International Survey of Family Law (2001 Edition)* (Family Law, 2001).
6　In *Department of Social Security v Butler* [1996] 1 FLR 65, the Court of Appeal said that the Child Support Act provided a complete code for assessing and enforcing the financial responsibility of absent parents. This was a comprehensive legislative scheme which left no lacuna to be filled by the High Court's jurisdiction, in this case to grant a *Mareva* injunction. For a recent brief discussion of the relationship between the courts' powers to award child maintenance and the statutory child support scheme, see J Pirrie 'The Courts and Child Maintenance' [2003] Fam Law 431. For the argument in favour of a judicial system of child support, see H Xanthaki 'The judiciary-based system of child support in Germany, France and Greece – an effective suggestion?' (2000) JSWFL 295.

an order for *periodical* payments[1] in relation to the child and non-resident parent concerned[2]. The court may, however, revoke a maintenance order[3], and there are certain circumstances in which the court may still have a role. First, the court has power to make an order if the maximum child maintenance calculation is in force[4], provided that the court is satisfied that the circumstances of the case make it appropriate for the non-resident parent to make, or secure the making of, periodical payments in addition to those under the assessment. Secondly, the court may exercise its powers to make an order in cases where the child is, will be or (if the order were to be made) would be receiving instruction or training requiring provision of some or all of the expenses incurred in connection with the provision of the instruction or training[5]. Thirdly, in cases where a child is disabled, orders may be made to meet some or all of the expenses attributable to the child's disability[6]. Fourthly, the court may exercise its powers to make orders in the case of 17- and 18-year-olds who are not in full-time education[7]; and the bar on making periodical payments orders does not apply if, for any reason, the Secretary of State has no jurisdiction to make a maintenance calculation – perhaps, for example, because the absent parent is not habitually resident in this country. The court may also make periodical payment orders against the parent with care; and the court also has power[8] to make an order giving effect to a written agreement between the parties. It is, therefore, still open to a couple to make an overall financial settlement to be embodied in a consent order, but no such order or agreement can prevent a parent with care subsequently applying for child support maintenance[9].

---

1   Orders for lump sum payments or other capital transfers are not within this definition.
2   Section 8(1) and (3) of the 1991 Act. 'Maintenance order' is defined in s 8(11) of the 1991 Act to mean an order which requires the making or securing of periodical payments under: Part II of the Matrimonial Causes Act 1973; the Domestic Proceedings and Magistrates' Courts Act 1978; Part III of the Matrimonial and Family Proceedings Act 1984; Sch 1 to the Children Act 1989; or any other prescribed enactment.
3   CSA 1991, s 8(4).
4   Ibid, s 8(6).
5   Ibid, s 8(7).
6   Ibid, s 8(8), (9). See *C v F (Disabled Child: Maintenance Orders)* [1998] 1 FLR 151 in which Sir Stephen Brown P upheld a magistrates' order that the father pay £190 per month to the mother for the benefit of the seriously disabled child. This represented the difference between the mother's total monthly expenditure attributable to the child's disability (£820) and what she actually received by way of disability benefit (£630). He held that the magistrates had been right to conclude that jurisdiction to make the order derived from the CSA 1991, although the application itself was made under Sch 1 to the Children Act. Accordingly, he held that the order could not extend beyond the child's nineteenth birthday by virtue of s 55 of the 1991 Act. However, the Court of Appeal, at [1998] 2 FLR 1, allowed the mother's appeal both as to the duration of the order and as to the calculation of the appropriate amount. It held that s 8(8) did not restrict the court to making a 'top-up' order but allowed it to make a freestanding order under the Children Act. The age restriction of 19 which applied under the CSA 1991 did not apply to such Children Act maintenance orders and therefore the order could extend beyond the child's nineteenth birthday. In calculating the appropriate maintenance, the magistrates had taken too narrow a view. They should have taken the broadest view of expenses, including costs associated with, for example, additional help, feeding those providing such additional help, a larger house, heating, clothing, running a car and respite care. The case was remitted to the family proceedings court for reconsideration on this basis.
7   Such persons are not within the CSA 1991 definition of 'child': see s 55(1).
8   CSA 1991, s 8(5); the Child Maintenance (Written Agreements) Order 1993, SI 1993/620.
9   See p 391 above.

Indeed, under amendments introduced by the 2000 legislation[1] it will no longer be possible to prevent an application for a maintenance calculation by the Child Support Agency to be made, because of a court order for maintenance, for more than the period of one year. Private settlements will need to be negotiated in future in the knowledge that there may well be a subsequent application to the Child Support Agency and that child support liability will normally be imposed at the basic rate. This may effectively remove much of the existing latitude to reach private agreements and to determine the level of child support in private cases as part of an overall post-divorce package.

The hiving off of one important component in such settlements in this way has been criticised by Wilson J in *V v V (Child Maintenance)*[2] where he referred to the 'unsatisfactory interface between the jurisdictions' of the Child Support Agency and the courts. The key point is that the level of child support influences the content of other parts of the settlement and that there was an absurdity in the court, which has its 'hard-won' possession of all relevant material, having to leave out of account one vital element in this – namely child support. At least the new simplified rates should mean that the courts will be able to predict child support liability with rather greater certainty, and settlements will need to reflect this.

The court's powers in respect of lump sums and property adjustment

The CSA 1991 does not affect the court's power to make orders for lump sums, or transfers or settlements of property.

THE COURTS' POWERS TO MAKE FINANCIAL ORDERS FOR THE BENEFIT OF CHILDREN

Although the scope for the exercise of the courts' powers to make financial orders in respect of children is now greatly restricted[3], the powers themselves still exist and may, on occasion, be exercised. A brief account must therefore be given here.

The Children Act 1989 introduced a considerable measure of simplification and rationalisation into the law governing the circumstances in which the court may, in the exercise of its discretion, make financial orders intended to benefit children, but the situation is still somewhat complex. It is most easily understood on the basis that the law draws a distinction between divorce and other matrimonial proceedings, on the one hand, and applications by one partner against the other under the provisions of the Children Act, on the other.

Powers exercisable in matrimonial proceedings

Most orders about children were[4], as the Law Commission pointed out[5], made in the course of divorce or other matrimonial proceedings. Since the provisions

---

1 CSA 1991, s 4(10)(aa).
2 [2001] 2 FLR 799.
3 See p 378 above.
4 Ie prior to the coming into force of the CSA 1991.
5 Law Com No 172 *Guardianship and Custody* (1988) at para 1.8.

relating to children could not readily be separated from those relating to adults, the statutory provisions enabling the court to make financial orders for children in divorce and other matrimonial proceedings are still contained in the relevant statutes dealing with the matrimonial proceedings.

Divorce is far and away the most important of these proceedings[1], but it should also be mentioned that either party to a marriage may apply to the court for an order, on the ground that the other spouse has failed to provide or make a proper contribution towards reasonable maintenance for any child of the family[2]. If that ground is made out, the court has power to order either periodical payments (secured or unsecured) or payment of a lump sum. Furthermore, either party to a marriage may apply to the family proceedings court for an order – for periodical payments or a lump sum (not exceeding £1,000) – under the Domestic Proceedings and Magistrates' Courts Act 1978. The grounds are that the respondent: (a) has failed to provide reasonable maintenance for the applicant; or (b) has failed to provide, or make a proper contribution towards, reasonable maintenance for any child of the family; or (c) has behaved in such a way that the applicant cannot reasonably be expected to live with the other party; or (d) has deserted the applicant. It was intended that the last two grounds, which are redolent of the old matrimonial offence doctrine, would be repealed by the Family Law Act 1996. But, as we have seen[3], the divorce aspects of that legislation were never brought into force. Matrimonial offences therefore remain a basis for obtaining a decree of divorce and also for financial orders in the magistrates' court. These provisions are, however, rarely relevant after the coming into force of the CSA 1991[4].

Powers of the divorce court: provision for parents and children

Provision for children may be either direct or indirect. The court has extensive powers to make orders in favour of the parties, and for the benefit of the children. The Matrimonial Causes Act 1973 provides that, in the exercise of these financial powers[5], it is the duty of the court, in deciding to exercise its powers and, if so, in what manner, 'to have regard to all the circumstances of the case … first consideration being given to the welfare while a minor of any child of the family who has not attained the age of 18'[6]. This statutory directive recognises that the financial position of children and their parents is inter-related. It has been said, for example, that it is not in the children's interest that their mother be in straitened circumstances[7] and it may, accordingly, be thought appropriate to make an order for periodical payments in favour of a wife so as to enable her the better to care for the children[8]. Again, the court may consider that this provision

---

1   See below.
2   Matrimonial Causes Act 1973, s 27.
3   See Chapter 4 above.
4   For fuller consideration, see SM Cretney, JM Masson and R Bailey-Harris *Principles of Family Law* (7th edn) (Sweet & Maxwell, 2002) at pp 78 et seq.
5   Ie the power to make financial provision orders (divorce, nullity and judicial separation): s 23; property adjustment orders: s 24; the power to order sale of the property: s 24A; and pension-sharing orders (divorce and nullity only): s 24B.
6   Matrimonial Causes Act 1973, s 25, as substituted by the Matrimonial and Family Proceedings Act 1984, s 3.
7   See *E v E (Financial Provision)* [1990] 2 FLR 233 at 249.
8   See *Waterman v Waterman* [1989] 1 FLR 380, CA.

requires it to ensure that the children's housing needs are protected[1], and this may often best be done by making an order for the transfer of the house to the parent with whom the child is to live, or for settlement of the house on terms that it is not sold during the children's dependency[2].

The fact that orders in favour of parents may indirectly benefit their children assumed a new significance following the coming into force of the CSA 1991. The divorce court is still required, in exercising its financial powers, to give first consideration to the welfare of children of the family who have not attained the age of 18 years, and the CSA 1991 imposes no restriction on the exercise of powers to make orders against parents.

Meaning of 'child of the family'

The court's powers and duties in divorce proceedings[3] arise in respect of any child of the family, and this term is defined, in relation to the parties to a marriage, to mean a child of both those parties, and any other child (not being a child who has been placed with those parties as foster-parents by a local authority or voluntary organisation) who has been treated by both of those parties as a child of their family.

This definition therefore brings within the category of children of the family all children who have been 'treated' as a child of the family – apart from those placed as foster-children[4] – and makes the existence of a biological[5] (or even a formal legal relationship such as adoption) between the child and the parties irrelevant. A step-child living with a married couple is the classic example of a child of the family who is not the child of both spouses. Of course, such a step-child also remains a 'child of the family' in respect of his birth parents, and the broad definition thus accurately reflects the erosion of traditional kinship patterns incidental to increasing divorce and remarriage: a child may have biological and/or factual links with several different marriages and may move in and out of several households[6].

The one limitation which has been placed on the scope of the definition is that it has been held to be impossible to treat an unborn child as a child of the family: if a man marries a woman who is pregnant by someone else, the baby will be a child of their family if the husband treats it as such after birth – even if only for a very short time and even if the wife has deceived him into thinking that he is the father – but if the relationship breaks down before the birth, the child will be outside the

---

1 See, generally, SM Cretney, JM Masson and R Bailey-Harris *Principles of Family Law* (7th edn) (Sweet & Maxwell, 2002) at pp 353 et seq.

2 The so-called *Mesher* and *Martin* orders. Such orders will not, however, be appropriate where it is doubted that the parent with care of the children (usually the mother) will be able to raise sufficient capital to rehouse herself at the end of the period or 'trigger' prescribed by the order for sale of the home. For a recent example, see *B v B (Mesher Order)* [2003] 2 FLR 285.

3 And in most of the other proceedings mentioned in this chapter.

4 The implication is that the local authority or voluntary organisation will be responsible for the provision of financial support for the child.

5 Or a relationship created by law by operation of the provisions of the Human Fertilisation and Embryology Act 1990.

6 For an illuminating study of the nature of the parental obligation as children move between households during the course of their minority, see M Maclean and J Eekelaar *The Parental Obligation* (Hart Publishing, 1997).

definition, whatever the husband may have said about his intentions to treat the baby as his own[1].

Orders the court may make

The court is given wide (but not limitless) powers[2]. It can, subject to the restrictions imposed by the CSA 1991, make periodical payment orders. Those orders may be either in favour of the other party to the marriage[3] or they may direct payments to the child or to someone else on his behalf for the benefit of a child of the family[4] – and they may be either secured or unsecured[5]. The court may also order the payment of a lump sum or sums by one spouse to the other[6] or a payment for the benefit of a child of the family to the child or to someone else on his behalf[7].

The court may also order the transfer of specified property to the other party, or to a child, or to a third party on a child's behalf[8]. It may order the settlement of such property for the benefit of the other party and/or of the children of the family[9] and it may make an order varying any 'ante-nuptial or post-nuptial' settlement made on the parties to the marriage for the benefit of the parties to the marriage and/or of the children of the family[10].

If the court makes a secured periodical payments order, a lump sum, or a property adjustment order, it may also order the sale of any property in which one or both of the parties has a beneficial interest[11].

Factors influencing the exercise of the court's discretion

As has already been seen, the court is required, in the exercise of all these powers, to give first consideration to the welfare, while a minor, of any child of the family who has not attained the age of 18 years. However, notwithstanding this requirement, there was some evidence that, in the past, the courts have underestimated the cost of maintaining children. It seems that orders for conventional sums (rarely exceeding £20 weekly in respect of each child) were often made. In an attempt to remedy this situation, the courts were given details of the income support scale rates for children's requirements, produced by the National Foster Care Association (which were designed to show the actual cost of bringing up a child) and the rates actually paid by local authorities to

---

1　*A v A (Family: Unborn Child)* [1974] Fam 6.
2　For a detailed consideration, see SM Cretney, JM Masson and R Bailey-Harris *Principles of Family Law* (7th edn) (Sweet & Maxwell, 2002) at pp 333–340.
3　Matrimonial Causes Act 1973, s 23(1)(a) and (b).
4　Ibid, s 23(1)(d) and (e).
5　Ibid, s 23(1)(b) and (e).
6　Ibid, s 23(1)(c).
7　Ibid, s 23(1)(f). It is specifically provided that an order for payment of a lump sum to the other spouse may be made for the purpose of enabling that other party to meet any liabilities or expenses reasonably incurred in maintaining any child of the family before making an application for an order, or for meeting any liabilities or expenses reasonably incurred by or for the benefit of the child of the family: ibid, s 23(3)(a) and (b).
8　Ibid, s 24(1)(a).
9　Ibid, s 24(1)(b).
10　Ibid, s 24(1)(c). The court may also make an order extinguishing or reducing the interest of either of the parties to the marriage under any such settlement, s 24(1)(d).
11　Ibid, s 24A.

foster-parents[1]. In practice, however, there will now be little need to refer to such scales since the rates of child support as a proportion of the non-resident parent's income under the amended child support scheme should provide the baseline for any consideration of a child's needs[2].

Limitations on welfare directive

There were limitations on the application of the direction to give first consideration to the welfare of the children and, in particular (as the courts have emphasised), the legislation does not make the welfare of the children the 'paramount' consideration. It has been said that the court must simply consider all the circumstances, always bearing the children's welfare in mind, and then try to make a financial settlement which is *just* as between husband and wife.

For example, in *Suter v Suter and Jones*[3], an order had been made on the basis that the husband should pay the whole of the wife's mortgage outgoings. This was done because preservation of the home was considered necessary to ensure the welfare of the children. The Court of Appeal held that the court should have taken account of the fact that the wife had a cohabitant who could have been expected to make a contribution, and that the court had been wrong to attach overriding importance to the child's welfare.

Since the House of Lords decision in *White v White*[4] it has been the overall objective of the courts in exercising their discretion to achieve 'fairness' and a result which avoids discrimination between husband and wife. Nonetheless, the courts must still apply the statutory criteria which include giving first consideration to the welfare of any minor children. In *Cordle v Cordle*[5] the Court of Appeal held that there was no rule, following *White v White*, that the courts must produce equality of outcome unless there were good reasons to justify departure. Factors relating to children might influence the question of fairness and, in this case, the Court of Appeal found that the circuit judge had erred in failing to recognise the husband's continuing liability to maintain the children. In *B v B (Financial Provision: Welfare of Child and Conduct)*[6] Connell J held that the husband's adverse conduct generally and specifically towards the child (whom he had abducted) justified a departure from equality and a transfer of the entire interest in the former matrimonial home to the wife.

Circumstances to be considered

It is now provided that, as regards the exercise of its powers to make periodical payment orders, transfer of property orders or orders for the sale of property and

---

1   Information about these scales should have been of real value to the court because, as Simon Brown J put it in *Cresswell v Eaton* [1991] 1 All ER 484 at 489, 'although not insubstantial, [the payments] are paid entirely by way of reimbursement of the expense incurred in maintaining children: food, clothing, heating, travel and so forth. The underlying philosophy of the fostering scheme is that it should not be undertaken for gain. There is thus no profit to be made from such payments, no reward for a personal care involved in fostering children'.

2   See p 387 above.

3   [1987] 2 FLR 232.

4   [2001] 1 AC 596.

5   [2002] 1 FLR 207.

6   [2002] 1 FLR 555. Cf *H-J v H-J (Financial Provision: Equality)* [2002] 1 FLR 415 where Coleridge J ordered an equal division of assets and took the view that the judge had given undue weight to the husband's new responsibilities towards the child with his new partner.

pension-sharing orders in relation to a child of the family, the court should have regard to all the circumstances of the case and, in particular, to a list of specific matters which (it has been said) cover almost every conceivable factor[1]. These specified matters are as follows:

> '(a) the financial needs of the child;
> (b) the income, earning capacity (if any), property and other financial resources of the child;
> (c) any physical or mental disability of the child;
> (d) the manner in which he was being and in which the parties to the marriage expected him to be educated or trained;
> (e) the considerations mentioned in relation to the parties to the marriage in paragraphs (a), (b), (c) and (e) of section 25(2) of the Matrimonial Causes Act 1973 [ie their financial resources, financial needs, the standard of living enjoyed by the family before the breakdown and any disability of either party to the marriage].'[2]

Orders against step-parents and others

As pointed out above[3], financial orders may be made against a spouse in respect of any child of the family, and this term is very broadly defined. The legislation seeks to structure the court's discretion by providing that, with regard to the exercise of its financial powers against the party to a marriage in favour of a child of the family who is not the child of that party, the court is also to have regard to the following specified matters:

> '(a) to whether that party assumed any responsibility for the child's maintenance, and, if so, to the extent to which, and the basis upon which, that party assumed such responsibility and to the length of time for which that party discharged such responsibility;
> (b) to whether in assuming and discharging such responsibility that party did so knowing that the child was not his or her own;
> (c) to the liability of any other person to maintain the child.'[4]

Applications by a child in parents' divorce proceedings

The divorce legislation is primarily concerned with applications by one spouse for an order against the other, but it has been held[5] that a child of the family who has attained the age of 18 years may make an application for financial relief by intervening in the parents' matrimonial proceedings – notwithstanding the fact that the decree may perhaps have been granted many years ago. Such a child may also intervene to seek a variation of an existing order[6].

Duration of orders and age limits

The divorce legislation now provides as follows.

(1) Financial provision orders and transfer of property orders cannot be made in respect of a child who has attained the age of 18[7].

---

1 *Mortimer v Mortimer-Griffin* [1986] 2 FLR 315 at 318 per Sir J Donaldson MR.
2 Matrimonial Causes Act 1973, s 25(3).
3 See p 397.
4 Matrimonial Causes Act 1973, s 25(4).
5 *Downing v Downing (Downing Intervening)* [1976] Fam 288. However, the court can make orders continuing after a child's eighteenth birthday only if the child is receiving education or training or there are special circumstances: see below.
6 Matrimonial Causes Act 1973, s 31.
7 Ibid, s 29(1). A child attains a particular age at the commencement of the relevant anniversary of his birth: Family Law Reform Act 1969, s 9.

(2) Periodical financial provision (whether secured or unsecured, and whether in nullity, divorce, judicial separation or failure to maintain proceedings) will not, in the first instance, be ordered beyond the child's attaining the upper limit of compulsory school age[1]. However, the court may extend the obligation to make the payments to a later date (but not beyond the age of 18 years) if it considers that, in the circumstances of the case, the welfare of the child so requires[2].

(3) Periodical orders must terminate when the child attains the age of 18[3].

However, these three restrictions do not apply if: (a) the 'child is, or will be or [if provision extending beyond 18 years of age were made] would be, receiving instruction at an educational establishment, or undergoing training for a trade, profession or vocation, whether or not he is also or will also be in gainful employment'; or (b) there are 'special circumstances which justify' the making of a different order[4].

These restrictions do not apply to the court's powers to order a settlement of property or to vary a nuptial settlement. However, it has been held[5] that a court should not normally exercise the power to order a settlement of property so as to order life-long provision for a child who is under no disability and whose education is secured.

The basic principle of the legislation is thus that special justification must be shown if an order is to be made or continued in respect of an adult child. This justification will often relate to the child's education (which is specifically referred to) but there may be other 'special circumstances', such as disability or ill health, or the fact that a parent had given a child to understand that support would continue until the child had completed a course of professional training.

Finally, it should be noted that periodical payments orders[6] in favour of a child terminate on the death of the payer, whether or not the order so provides[7].

Financial orders for children under the Children Act 1989

Before the coming into force of the Children Act there were a number of ill-related procedures for getting financial provision orders for children outside matrimonial proceedings. Of these, the most commonly invoked was the procedure whereby an affiliation order could be sought against the putative father of an illegitimate child. There were also powers to make orders in guardianship proceedings and in proceedings in which parents simply sought orders about the upbringing of their children and did not seek any order about their own marriage.

---

1 Matrimonial Causes Act 1973, s 29(2).
2 Ibid, s 29(2)(a).
3 Ibid, s 29(1), (2)(b).
4 Ibid, s 29(3). See *B v B (Adult Student: Liability to Support)* [1998] 1 FLR 373 in which a father unsuccessfully argued that his daughter's full maintenance grant while at university and any supplementary income she might make during those substantial parts of the year when she was not required to be in residence should absolve him of any continuing financial liability for her. For a useful round-up of the circumstances under which parents may be liable to provide support for their adult children, see the comment on this decision by S Cretney at [1998] Fam Law 131.
5 *Lilford (Lord) v Glynn* [1979] 1 WLR 78; *Chamberlain v Chamberlain* [1973] 1 WLR 1557.
6 But not a *secured* periodical payments order.
7 Matrimonial Causes Act 1973, s 29(4).

The Children Act reformed and assimilated the various private law provisions relating to the courts' powers to order financial provisions in proceedings which are not connected with the marriage of a child's parents. The Act adopted the divorce legislation as a model and, to a large extent, generalises for all children the benefit of principles which have already been established in the context of particular proceedings[1].

Qualified applicants

The following persons may apply for a financial order in respect of a child[2].

(1) *A parent*: this expression extends to adoptive parents and to parents who are not married to each other. The ordinary meaning of the word is extended so as to 'include any party to a marriage (whether or not subsisting) in relation to whom the child ... is a child of the family'[3]. Hence, it will be possible for a child's biological parent to initiate proceedings claiming support for the child against the child's step-parent[4] or for the step-parent to seek an order against the biological parent.

(2) *A guardian.*

(3) *Any person in whose favour a residence order is in force with respect to a child*: a residence order settles the arrangements to be made about where a child is to live; and accordingly anyone who has been given the right to care for a child by court order can now seek a financial order for the child's support.

(4) *An adult student or trainee or person who can show special circumstances*: anyone from this category may make an application for an order. However, in this case, there are two restrictions on the court's powers. First, no order may be made if the parents are living together in the same household[5], so that it is still impossible for a child to compel parents who are living in a conventional relationship to provide support. Secondly, the court's powers on such an application are limited to making periodical payment or lump sum orders and the power to make periodical payment orders is now severely restricted by the CSA 1991[6].

In addition, there are certain circumstances in which the court may make a financial order even though no application for such an order has been made. It is provided that the court may make a financial order whenever it makes, varies or discharges a residence order[7] – and a residence order may be made in any family proceedings, whether or not applied for, if the court considers that the order should be made. The court can also make financial orders if the child is a ward of court, whether or not any application has been made for such an order[8].

---

1   Law Com No 172 *Guardianship and Custody* (1988) at para 4.63, and Children Act, s 15 and Sch 1.
2   Children Act, Sch 1, paras 1 and 2.
3   Ibid, Sch 1, para 16(2).
4   But a parent's cohabitant is not within this definition, irrespective of the length of time for which he has been in loco parentis to the child: *J v J (A Minor) (Property Transfer)* [1993] 2 FLR 56.
5   Children Act, Sch 1, para 2(4).
6   Ibid, Sch 1, para 2(2).
7   Ibid, Sch 1, para 1(6).
8   Ibid, Sch 1, para 1(7).

Orders which may be made

The range of orders available is now very wide, on the pattern of the range of orders available for children in divorce proceedings. On an application under the Children Act, the court may order the child's parent or parents[1]:

(1) to make periodical payments, secured or unsecured[2];
(2) to pay a lump sum (and it is expressly provided[3] that such an order may be made to enable expenses in connection with the birth or maintenance of the child which were reasonably incurred before the making of the order to be met);
(3) to make a transfer or settlement of specified property to which the parent is entitled either in possession or reversion. This power gives the court greater flexibility in dealing with the home in which an unmarried couple have lived. It has been held that there is power to order the transfer of a secure tenancy to the other parent for the child's benefit[4], and it is possible for the court to order a settlement of such property on trust for the child – perhaps until the child ceases full-time education[5]. Where the issue relates to the competing considerations of sale of a family home jointly owned by unmarried parents as against deferment of the sale during the children's minority, applications may be made under both Sch 1 to the Children Act and s 14 of the Trusts of Land and Appointment of Trustees Act 1996. It has been held that, where this is so, the exercise of the court's powers under both statutes should normally be considered by the same county court at the same time under conjoined applications[6].

Interim orders and variation of orders

The court has wide powers[7] to make interim orders, and to vary periodical payment orders.

---

1 Defined to include step-parents, etc: see above.
2 But there is no jurisdiction under the Children Act jurisdiction or under the inherent jurisdiction to make periodic payments to cover a parent's legal costs. In *W v J (Child: Variation of Financial Provision)* [2004] 2 FLR 300 Bennett J held that such an order would be for the benefit of the *parent* and not for the child.
3 Children Act, Sch 1, para 5(1).
4 *K v K (Minors: Property Transfer)* [1992] 2 FLR 220; but it seems that a cautious approach will be taken to the exercise of this power: *J v J (A Minor) (Property Transfer)* [1993] 2 FLR 56. It should be noted, however, that much wider powers to transfer certain tenancies are now given to the courts under Part IV of the Family Law Act 1996 where an unmarried cohabitation breaks down. These powers may well be exercised in future to provide a continuing home for the children. See Family Law Act 1996, s 53 and Sch 7, and S Bridge 'Transferring Tenancies of the Family Home' [1998] Fam Law 26.
5 Children Act, Sch 1, para 1(1)(d). For examples of the settlement of capital sums to provide homes for children, see *H v P (Illegitimate Child: Capital Provision)* [1993] Fam Law 515 and *Phillips v Peace* [1996] 2 FLR 230.
6 *W v W (Joinder of Trusts of Land Act and Children Act Applications)* [2004] 2 FLR 321.
7 The powers of a (magistrates') family proceedings court in relation to financial orders are limited: such a court cannot make orders for transfer or settlement of property, or for secured periodical payments, and its power to order a lump sum is restricted to a maximum payment of £1,000: Children Act, Sch 1, paras 6 and 7 (variation) and 9 (interim orders).

The exercise of the discretion

The Children Act[1] lays down guidelines for the exercise of the court's powers which largely follow the precedent of matrimonial law[2]. It is provided[3] that, in deciding whether to exercise its powers and if so in what manner, the court shall have regard to all the circumstances including:

(a) the income, earning capacity, property and other financial resources which the applicant, parents[4] and the person in whose favour the order would be made has or is likely to have in the foreseeable future;

(b) the financial needs, obligations and responsibilities which each of those persons has or is likely to have in the foreseeable future;

(c) the financial needs of the child;

(d) the income, earning capacity (if any), property and other financial resources of the child;

(e) any physical or mental disability of the child;

(f) the manner in which the child was being, or was expected to be, educated or trained[5].

The legislation also contains a provision similar to that in the matrimonial legislation dealing with the factors to be taken into account where the 'parent' against whom the order is sought is not the child's mother or father[6].

The scheme of the CSA 1991 has made these provisions somewhat academic, in the vast majority of cases, in relation to the power to order periodical payments. It is only when the question of a payment in excess of the level provided for by the CSA 1991 is a possibility – for example to pay school fees for independent education – that the court will be likely to be asked to exercise its powers to make periodical payments – and, indeed, it is only in such unusual circumstances that it will have jurisdiction to do so[7].

The CSA 1991 does not, however, affect the exercise of the court's powers to make lump sum or property adjustment orders, and it may be that there will be more applications for such orders than in the past – not least because, where a couple are not married, the court has only limited powers to make orders as between the adults concerned in respect of their family home. Accordingly, any such order must usually be sought in proceedings under the Children Act.

---

1 Children Act, Sch 1, para 4(1).

2 Law Com No 172 *Guardianship and Custody* (1988) at para 4.64.

3 Children Act, Sch 1, para 4(1).

4 This states the general effect of Sch 1, para 4(1)(b) to the Children Act; but not the distinction drawn in the Act between applications for orders for persons over 18 and others.

5 There are minor differences between the guidelines for the exercise of the discretion in proceedings instituted under the Children Act and those laid down in relation to divorce and other matrimonial proceedings. The divorce legislation does not require the court (in relation to orders sought for children) to have regard to the contributions which each of the parties has made or is likely, in the foreseeable future, to make to the welfare of the family. In proceedings under the Children Act there is no reference to the standard of living enjoyed by the family before the breakdown of the marriage, and there is no reference to the age of each party to the marriage and the duration of the marriage.

6 Schedule 1, para 4(2) to the Children Act.

7 See p 378 above.

However, in the past, the courts have been reluctant to make capital provision orders in respect of children[1].

For example, in *Kiely v Kiely*[2], the Court of Appeal pointed out that lump sum orders in favour of chidren and, in particular, of children whose parents were of limited means, were rare[3] and stated that the statutory scheme of the divorce legislation was to enable the court to make proper financial provision for children as children or dependants[4].

However, in the unusual circumstances of a lottery win, a lump sum application for a child succeeded in *J v C (Child: Financial Provision)*[5]. The parents were unmarried and their relationship broke down while the mother was still pregnant. After the birth of the child, the father won £1.4 million on the national lottery and the mother applied for financial relief for the child. The father argued that the child was not wanted, a fact disputed by the mother.

Hale J held that this was not crucial since there was nothing in the private or public law which distinguished between wanted and unwanted children. An irresponsible or uncaring attitude should not be allowed to prejudice a child. Although the welfare principle did not govern the matter, the child's welfare was a relevant consideration. On the facts, the child was entitled to be brought up in circumstances which bore some relationship to the father's current resources and standard of living. She therefore made an order requiring the father to purchase a four-bedroomed house for the child to live in together with her mother and two half-sisters, to revert to the father on the child attaining 21 or completing full-time education. She further ordered capital provision to provide a reasonable family car, to cover the mother's past expenditure and provide adequate furnishings for the new property.

Even more dramatic in some ways was the Court of Appeal's decision in *Re P (Child: Financial Provision)*.[6] Here the father of a very young child was a fabulously wealthy international businessman who conceded that he had the resources to pay a lump sum of £10 million if ordered to do so. At first instance the mother was awarded £450,000 for her housing needs, £30,000 for furnishing and annual periodical payments of £35,360 reducing to £9,333 on the child's seventh birthday, together with backdated maintenance of £7,500. On appeal these sums were greatly increased to £1 million for housing, £100,000 for internal decoration, annual periodical payments of £70,000 (less State benefits) and backdated maintenance of £40,000. The court reasoned that the child's needs for a carer required that account be taken of that parent's needs and that the mother's

---

1 In *A v A (A Minor: Financial Provision)* [1994] 1 FLR 657, Ward J held that property adjustment orders should not ordinarily be used to make an outright transfer to a child. They should normally only be made to provide for the child's maintenance during minority or until the child completes education. In this case, the property was settled on trust for the 10-year-old child for a term expiring six months after she attained 18 or completed full-time education (including tertiary education).

2 [1988] 1 FLR 248, CA. Cf *J v J (C Intervening)* [1989] 1 FLR 453. See also *Lilford (Lord) v Glynn* [1979] 1 WLR 78.

3 Ibid at 251 per Booth J.

4 Ibid at 252.

5 [1999] 1 FLR 152.

6 [2003] 2 FLR 865. For a detailed commentary, see S Gilmore '*Re P (A Child) (Financial Provision)*: Shoeboxes and comical shopping trips – child support from the affluent to the fabulously rich' [2004] CFLQ 103.

entitlement to an allowance should not be diminished by her absence of a direct legal claim against the father. The court, it was said, should recognise the responsibility, and often the sacrifice, of the unmarried parent who acted as carer. She should have control of a budget which reflected her position and that of the father, both social and financial.

Clearly the generosity of the award here was largely based on the extreme wealth of the father. It remains the case that the courts are required to maintain a distinction between the child (who is legally entitled to support) and the unmarried parent (who is not). As Bailey-Harris puts it in her commentary on the case[1] 'it remains necessary for the court to guard against unreasonable claims made on behalf of the child but with a disguised element of providing for the mother's independent benefit'.

FINANCIAL RESPONSIBILITY FOR CHILDREN: SOME CONCLUDING POLICY CONSIDERATIONS

Ultimately, the question of financial support for children is about the appropriate apportionment of responsibility between the two parents concerned (or, perhaps more accurately, the two households concerned) and the wider community. The child support legislation shifted the emphasis decisively towards the notion that the *primary* responsibility rests with parents and any obligation on the part of the State is *secondary*. Yet, even if this is accepted, the respective *levels* of responsibility remain a contentious issue as does the view that these obligations of parenthood should fall very largely on biological parents[2] to the exclusion of the legal and moral obligations of social parenthood[3]. It is fair to say, however, that the greater allowance now made for the presence of children in the non-resident parent's household, in calculating his income, does represent a significant shift towards the view that there should be something approaching parity in the obligations towards biological children and those children for whom the non-resident parent has a social, if not legal, responsibility. The fact that almost everyone would agree with the principle that parents have *some* continuing financial responsibility for their children even where they no longer live with them does not mean that there is anything like a consensus about precisely what this responsibility should be. As one policy publication of the Child Poverty Action Group put it: 'the superficial simplicity of support for this principle hides a complex and shifting array of attitudes about family obligations. Public agreement with the general principle does not necessarily mean that people think it should be unconditional or

---

1   At [2003] Fam Law 717, 718.
2   But not entirely, since social parents are regarded as legal parents in the case of adoption and some instances of assisted reproduction under the status provisions of the Human Fertilisation and Embryology Act 1990. See Chapter 3 above.
3   Social parents may have legal, as well as moral, obligations towards children who are treated as 'children of the family'. See p 397 above. It should also be remembered that the presence of a working social father in a household would, under the aggregation rules which apply to social security entitlements, often preclude a mother from making an independent claim for herself and her children for means-tested income support and other benefits. In this sense, there is an assumed indirect legal responsibility on the man concerned to support his 'second' family. For discussion of the aggregation rule, see Wikeley, Ogus and Barendt's *Law of Social Security* (5th edn) (Butterworths, 2002) at pp 291 et seq.

overriding'[1]. The amended scheme certainly reflects in part a widely held perception that some non-resident parents had been required to pay too much and the new rates will result in a lower liability in many cases.

Another angle to this issue is the inconsistency in the legal treatment of the financial obligations of parents in ongoing, intact households as compared with those in separate households. The child support regime applies only where a parent is 'non-resident' and has left the household in which the children are present. The law does not concern itself directly with the management of family finances while the family remains intact[2]. This can lead to the ironic situation in which a 'non-resident' father is legally required to pay more, perhaps much more, for children than he would ever have done had the family remained a going concern. The irony is heightened in those cases in which the man concerned was never in the household at all and whose only link with the child is genetic. As Harry Krause has put it: 'it does not seem at all obvious that the same (or a greater) level of parental responsibility that makes sense in the ongoing family should be grafted (1) onto consanguinity based on what is understood as permissible recreational sex or (2) onto the essentially terminated post-divorce relationship between the typical father and his child' and he urges a search 'for a level of responsibility that is commensurate with the social reality of the situation'[3]. As we have seen[4], the child support scheme is blind to the circumstances of conception, but there is at least an argument that the responsibility which is voluntarily *assumed* for a child in the context of an ongoing relatinship is of a different kind to that which is *imposed* merely because a pregnancy, and in due course a child, results from what may be an isolated act of sexual intercourse. The basis of liability in this case appears to be negligence in relation to the use of contraception[5].

Another issue needs to be confronted when considering whether parenthood and its obligations are principally a matter of genetics or of assumed social responsibility. Whichever it is, there remains something of an inconsistency at the heart of English law, although one which is undoubtedly diluted by the reforms in the Adoption and Children Act 2002. This is that, while genetics is apparently all-important for *financial responsibility*, it is not so regarded for the wider aspects of *parental responsibility*, at least not outside marriage. Neither is it so regarded in applying the test of whether 'family life' comes into being for the purposes of the ECHR[6]. It is difficult to resist the conclusion that the law would command more respect if it made what may appear to some to be necessary connection between the financial and non-financial aspects of parental responsibility.

One way of doing this might have been to remove the financial responsibility of the non-resident parent and to emphasise instead the responsibility of the social parent. The other approach is to recognise, along with financial responsibility, the

---

1   F Bennett *Child Support: Issues for the Future* (CPAG Ltd, 1997) at p 23.

2   For a concise and useful discussion, see M Maclean and J Eekelaar *The Parental Obligation* (Hart Publishing, 1997) at pp 37–44.

3   HD Krause 'Child Support Reassessed: Limits of Private Responsibility and the Public Interest' in Kay and Sugarman (eds) *Divorce Reform at the Crossroads* (Yale University Press, 1990) at p 181. Cf S Sheldon 'Unwilling Fathers and Abortion: Terminating Men's Child Support Obligations' (2003) 66 MLR 175.

4   See above.

5   The point is developed further in A Bainham 'Men and Women Behaving Badly: Is Fault Dead in English Family Law?' (2001) *Oxford Journal of Legal Studies* 219 at 229–231.

6   See Chapter 5 above.

wider parental responsibility of the non-resident, genetic parent. It is this second course which has been pursued by the Government and, to a degree, has been implemented by the Adoption and Children Act 2002[1]. The Lord Chancellor's Department's Consultation paper which preceded the legislation recognised that it was 'a particular source of grievance for some unmarried fathers that they have been forced to support their children financially, whether or not they have acquired parental responsibility under the Children Act'[2]. The great majority of fathers are in future likely to acquire automatic parental responsibility through registration as the father of the child on the child's birth certificate. But there will remain a substantial minority who are not so registered. These men will continue to be automatically liable for child support, on proof of paternity, but will not thereby acquire parental responsibility. There will therefore remain some discordance in the law's treatment of these men for the purposes of the financial and non-financial aspects of being adjudged a legal parent.

A final question relates to the State's obligations towards the costs of raising children. This is a question which relates not just to children whose parents have separated, but also to intact families with children. It has long been accepted, and certainly since the Second World War, that the cost of raising children is something to be met by parents and the State acting in partnership. The public subsidies which the State provides are wide-ranging, the more obvious benefits relating to health and education and, within the social security system, the universal non-taxable child benefit[3]. But it was the burden of social security in a period of widespread family breakdown and a high incidence of lone parenthood which foreshadowed the introduction of the child support legislation in 1991. The Labour Government's particular orientation has been to act in pursuit of a 'welfare to work' philosophy. The principal objective is for the State to support families by a package of measures designed to assist people in moving away from welfare dependency and into work. This approach has been signalled by a shift away from social security benefits and towards a system of tax credits which is sensitive to the costs of raising children.

Nonetheless, beyond the intricacy of the child support scheme, social security system and fiscal policy, there remain fundamental and largely unanswered questions about why it is that liability for the casualties of family breakdown is seen primarily as a matter of *private* rather than *public* responsibility. This is an issue which has not always been well addressed in England, where the tendency has been to assume rather uncritically that the financial support of children and their carers is primarily a private, individual responsibility, rather than a public, collective one. This view has been challenged in the USA by Martha Fineman[4], who sees the child support question as 'merely one component of a complex series of issues surrounding the question of who should bear the economic and social costs of caring for dependent members of society'[5] and who takes the view that

---

1   A Bainham (above).

2   See Consultation Paper *Court Procedures for the Determination of Paternity: the Law on Parental Responsibility for Unmarried Fathers* (Lord Chancellor's Department, March 1998).

3   See p 371 above.

4   M Fineman 'Child Support is not the Answer: The Nature of Welfare Reform' in JT Oldham and MS Melli (eds) *Child Support: The Next Frontier* (The University of Michigan Press, 2000) at p 209.

5   Ibid.

there is 'a fundamental obligation in a just society for the collective to provide for its weaker members'[1]. Within this context, Fineman argues that 'in continuing to allocate dependency automatically to the private sphere, society forgoes the opportunity to develop a theory of collective responsibility for children and other dependents'[2].

When the child support legislation was introduced in 1991, no one doubts that there was a fundamental change of emphasis away from *public* and towards *private* responsibility. This was not debated as well as it might have been then, but the successive changes to the detail and administration of the child support scheme have not wholly managed to disguise the underlying uncertainty about the essential theoretical basis of liability; and that is one thing which is unlikely to change.

---

1   M Fineman (above) at p 211.
2   Ibid at p 212.

PART III
CHILDREN AND LOCAL AUTHORITIES

Part III, 'Children and Local Authorities', is deliberately not called 'Children and the State'. The concept of the State, broadly defined, impinges on children and families in many different ways – through social security and fiscal policy, education and employment, the criminal law, and in a host of other ways. Yet the relationship between local authorities and families is crucial, since it is local authorities which have the primary statutory responsibility for supporting families and for protecting children who are thought to be at risk of abuse or neglect. The historical development of these responsibilities was discussed in Chapter 1.

Chapter 10 analyses the *supportive* functions of local authorities towards children in need and their families. It also deals briefly with the regulation of substitute care arrangements, in relation to which local authorities used to occupy a central role and still perform an important role. This role has, however, been much affected by the Care Standards Act 2000, which has transferred many of the functions previously exercised by local authorities to the new National Care Standards Commission in England and the National Assembly for Wales in Wales. The focus in Chapters 11 and 12 is on *protection* rather than support. Chapter 11 discusses the statutory regime for compulsory action whether through care or supervision. Chapter 12 considers the critical question of short-term protection for children. Here, the emphasis is on immediate legal remedies for dealing with emergencies.

In theory, a sharp distinction can be drawn between *voluntary* assistance governed by Part III of the Children Act 1989 (see Chapter 10) and the *compulsory* measures under Parts IV and V of the Act (see Chapters 11 and 12). Yet, for various reasons, it is not a true reflection of what goes on in practice to postulate so rigid a demarcation. It is important to get some sense of the relationship between voluntary services and more coercive action and this should be constantly kept in mind when reading this Part of the book. The implications of the HRA 1998 and the ECHR should also be kept in mind and these are highlighted throughout the discussion.

Chapter 10

LOCAL AUTHORITY SUPPORT FOR CHILDREN AND FAMILIES

INTRODUCTION

Part III of the Children Act 1989 regulates support services for families and the powers and duties of local authorities towards children looked after by them[1]. In this chapter, we sketch the legal framework of Part III. It is inevitable that the legal boundaries for *compulsory* State intervention in the family should be the subject of close critical evaluation. But to see these compulsory powers as relatively more important, and voluntary services as relatively less important, would be an unbalanced and distorted way of looking at things. In a nutshell, one of the primary purposes of the support services under Part III is to prevent, wherever possible, the circumstances under which it becomes necessary for compulsory action to be taken. Court orders for care and supervision are, in this sense, very much the ambulance at the bottom of the cliff while the support services are the (however inadequate) fence at the top.

This emphasis on voluntary assistance to families in difficulty, or those who would be in difficulty but for that assistance, is consistent with the general thinking behind the Children Act which was identified in earlier chapters[2]. Essentially, it is that first responsibility for children rests with the family. Public support should be viewed as positive, designed to underscore the primary role of parents and not to emphasise their failure. Thus, the local authority's powers should be exercised in *partnership* with parents, implying full participation in decisions, even where the child is looked after by the local authority. Court orders should only be made where they are strictly necessary[3]. Reunification with the family[4] and promotion

---

1 The genesis of the reforms in Part III is the Second Report of the House of Commons Social Services Committee 1983–4, *Children in Care* HC 360 (the 'Short Report'). This was followed by the DHSS *Review of Child Care Law* (1985) Part II and the White Paper *The Law on Child Care and Family Services* (1987) (Cm 62) ch 2. The most detailed academic treatment of the subject is MDA Freeman *Children, Their Families and the Law* (Macmillan, 1992) at ch 4. Also very useful is the account in SM Cretney, JM Masson and R Bailey-Harris *Principles of Family Law* (7th edn) (Sweet & Maxwell, 2002) at pp 691–701, which cites many helpful sources from the social sciences literature. See also R White, P Carr and N Lowe *The Children Act in Practice* (3rd edn) (Butterworths, 2002) ch 6. Many useful materials are extracted in B Hale, D Pearl, E Cooke and P Bates *The Family, Law and Society* (5th edn) (Butterworths, 2002) ch 13. See also J Thoburn 'The Children Act 1989: Balancing Child Welfare with the Concept of Partnership with Parents' [1991] JSWFL 331. For a longer perspective taking in the post-war period, see N Parton *Governing the Family* (Macmillan, 1991) at ch 2. For the official guidance on this part of the legislation, see *The Children Act 1989 Guidance and Regulations Vol 2 Family Support, Day Care and Educational Provision for Young Children* (HMSO, 1991). For much useful information on the implementation of this part of the Act in practice, see Department of Health *Children Act Report 2000* (2001) and Department of Health *Children Act Now: Messages from Research* (2001).
2 See particularly Chapter 2 above.
3 Ibid.
4 See, particularly, s 17(1)(b).

of contact with relatives and friends[1] should be an important objective. There is also a strong presumption that arrangements should be made for a child looked after by a local authority to live with his parents, family or friends[2]. The local authority should be accountable for its actions through an adequate system of internal reviews, there should be procedures for accommodating representations and complaints and access to the courts for aggrieved parents in accordance with the requirements of the ECHR.

These principles, evident in the Children Act itself, are greatly reinforced by the ECHR and the HRA 1998[3]. We will look at the Convention principles as they apply to compulsory and emergency action in Chapters 11 and 12 respectively. In those contexts the issue will often be whether the local authority has resorted to a higher level of intervention than is necessary to protect the child, as where it is seeking to justify the making of a care order and it is argued that a supervision order would be sufficient[4]. We also consider in Chapter 11 the human rights issues surrounding care plans and contact with children in care, two related and fertile areas of dispute which now require engagement with human rights considerations. Why these human rights issues are relevant to the scheme under Part III is precisely because voluntary assistance may be the appropriate level of intervention if the action taken by the authority is to comply with the requirements of the ECHR. If it could be demonstrated that it resorted to coercive measures where sufficient protection of the child's welfare could have been achieved by agreement with the parents, this would constitute, prima facie, a violation of Article 8 Convention rights since it would be disproportionate and unnecessary action.

Yet, there is another side to Convention obligations which should also be borne in mind. This is that the ECHR imposes not merely *negative* obligations not to interfere unjustifiably with family life, but also *positive* obligations to support it. This is an area in which the higher courts and the ECtHR have been very active in recent years, and we consider some of the jurisprudence in this chapter. The essential point is that a *failure* on the part of the State to make sufficient efforts to protect a child will, if that child should subsequently suffer abuse or neglect, leave the local authority exposed to the possibility of a civil action for negligence and the State may be held responsible for violation of the child's Convention rights. The balance between upholding parental autonomy and family integrity while offering sufficient protection to children is a notoriously difficult one for local authorities to strike but suffice it to say that there may be, quite apart from public criticism, legal liability if the authority intervenes too much or too little.

---

1   Schedule 2, para 15.
2   Section 23(6).
3   For a succinct and useful introduction to the Convention principles as they apply to the public law affecting children and adoption, see H Swindells, A Neaves, M Kushner and R Skilbeck *Family Law and the Human Rights Act 1998* (Family Law, 1999), especially ch 6. Chapter 10 of the same work looks more directly at the duties of local authorities and considers the implications of the *positive* obligations imposed on the State by the ECHR.
4   As, for example, in *Re C and B (Care Order: Future Harm)* [2001] 1 FLR 611.

Relationship between voluntary and compulsory action

The legislation differentiates between children 'in care' and children 'looked after' or 'accommodated' by local authorities[1]. It aims to clarify the difference between seeking voluntary help from social services and the circumstances in which compulsion can be justified. It removes from the seeking of voluntary help any pejorative connotation of failure or inadequacy. Any features of the former law which could be interpreted as inconsistent with this ideal were removed[2]. Yet it has been questioned how far this is really a true reflection of what occurs in practice. Judith Masson has argued that the provision of services for children in need can be characterised, not so much as voluntary assistance, but as a form of 'diversion' from the more coercive forms of intervention[3]. She argues that the Childen Act 'contains separate but interlinked frameworks for managing risk with and without court orders'. On this analysis, the primary preoccupation of social services will be with those children who are thought to be at risk. As she puts it:

> 'The fact that there is no order should not be taken as indicating that the relationship between the family and the local authority is entirely voluntary. The local authority has duties to provide services and to protect children; the family accepts services against the coercive backdrop of the authority's powers to take proceedings.'[4]

The Children Act Advisory Committee in its final report[5] commented adversely on the inappropriate use of voluntary accommodation of children under Part III as an alternative to an application for a care or supervision order. Yet, local authority sources are finite and there is evidence that the decisive factor influencing authorities in some cases is the cost involved in taking a child into care[6]. It may well be that the alleged philosophy of 'non-intervention' which is said to permeate the legislation and the 'no order' principle in s 1(5) of the Act have also had some influence in persuading social services to go down the voluntary route where there is doubt that the basis for a care order would be established. And, as discussed above, human rights requirements dictate that the least coercive form of intervention which is consistent with protecting the child's welfare should be the course which is followed. In these ways, the apparently clear distinction between *voluntary* 'services' and *compulsory* 'care' may be less sharp in practice than in theory.

---

1   In fact this is not entirely accurate since the expression 'looked after' is a generic term for both children 'in care' and those in local authority accommodation under voluntary arrangements. Where it is necessary to distinguish the two groups it may therefore be preferable to describe the 'voluntary' children as 'accommodated'. Children must be accommodated for a continuous period of more than 24 hours to fall within the definition of 'looked after' children (s 22(2)).

2   See Chapter 2 above and the discussion below.

3   JM Masson 'Managing Risk Under the Children Act 1989: Diversion in Child Care?' (1992) 1 *Child Abuse Review* 103. The concept of 'diversion' is familiar in the context of juvenile justice.

4   Ibid at p 119.

5   *The Children Act Advisory Committee Final Report June 1997* (Lord Chancellor's Department, 1997) at pp 29–30. See below.

6   See, for example, *Nottinghamshire County Council v P* [1994] Fam 18. See also the discussion, in Chapter 11 below, of the House of Lords decision in *Re C (Interim Care Order: Residential Assessment)* [1997] 1 FLR 1, where financial considerations loomed large at the interim stage of care proceedings.

These concerns about the blurring of the distinction between what is voluntary and what is compulsory do seem to be borne out by research studies[1]. What these reveal is that *short-term* or respite accommodation of children has been successfully used as a family service[2]. Such placements are usually with the same carer, should not exceed four weeks in duration, and the total duration of such placements should not exceed 90 days. On the other hand, *full-time* accommodation tended to be used in the context of a negotiated partnership between the local authority and the parents. The parents were presented with the choice of either agreeing to the provision of accommodation or going to court, an arrangement which 'tests the balance between compulsion and voluntariness'[3]. In such cases any supposed partnership between parents and the local authority may be more illusory than real.

Children in need: eligibility for services

The concept of 'children in need' is central to the operation of Part III of the Children Act[4]. It constitutes an all-important threshold, since it creates an eligibility for a wide range of statutory services. The local authority *must* provide these services to children once it has been determined that a child is in need. The claims of such children are described as an 'eligibility' rather than a 'right' or 'entitlement'. This is because local authorities have very wide discretions in determining how precisely to discharge their many statutory duties. While, therefore, a blanket refusal to provide *any* services to such children could render an authority's decision susceptible to judicial review[5], it will frequently be difficult, perhaps impossible, to argue that the children have a legal right to any *particular* service. The legislation does not give children in need unlimited rights of recipience, and the enforcement of the local authority's duties is highly problematic[6].

This leads us to the 'universality versus selectivity' debate which has so dominated policy-making in the field of social security provision[7]. In the present context, the question is whether publicly provided benefits for children ought to be regarded as available to *all* children on a universal basis or only to *some* children by applying selective criteria. Children are major beneficiaries of State provision of health, education, social security, housing and other welfare needs of the public[8]. In broad terms, it might be said that all children are in need of adequate

---

1   See *Children Act Now: Messages from Research* (2001) at pp 49–52 and the research studies cited there.
2   Ibid at p 49.
3   Ibid at p 51.
4   Defined in s 17(10) and discussed below.
5   For a good discussion of judicial review in this context, see NV Lowe and G Douglas *Bromley's Family Law* (9th edn) (Butterworths, 1998) at pp 604–607. See also R White, P Carr and N Lowe *The Children Act in Practice* (3rd edn) (Butterworths, 2002) at pp 414 et seq. At pp 416–419 there is an exceptionally helpful summary in tabular form of judicial review cases involving children and local authorities between 1999 and 2002.
6   The possibilities are discussed at pp 454 et seq below.
7   As to which, see Wikeley, Ogus and Barendt's *The Law of Social Security* (6th edn) (Butterworths, 2002) at ch 1.
8   Indeed, many of these benefits are specifically geared to children or, at least, to families with children. Obvious examples are child benefit and the 'priority need' which arises where a homeless person has dependent children.

provision in these areas and that, accordingly, they might have a *right* to claim, and society a *duty* to make available, the best possible provision. Universalist claims like these permeate international commitments to children, most obviously in the UNCRC[1]. The concept of 'children in need' in the Children Act is not used in this sense. It has a much narrower and technical definition, the purpose of which is to mark out those families who need the help of specialist services offered by local authorities, in short to target them. Thus, during the parliamentary debates on the Children Bill, the Government rejected the argument that, since nursery education is generally acknowledged to be beneficial to young children, *all* children in the relevant age group could be said to be 'in need' of it, since they could all profit from it[2]. Such an interpretation would have necessitated comprehensive nursery provision which the Conservative Government wanted to resist. The debate highlights the chief dilemma in this area. This is that, however well-intentioned the legislation, and however laudable the efforts of local authorities to implement it, its effectiveness is largely determined by the level of resources committed to it[3]. This has promoted one commentator to conclude thus:

> 'Government policies to improve services but to control local authority spending are in direct conflict. Despite a common legal framework, there are huge differences in provision of children's services nationally which relate to many things including variations in resources. Implementation of legislation relating to children's services involves changes in attitude, reformulation of local policies, and the development of new services ... Without new services, provision will continue to be resource rather than needs-led. ... There is now a wide recognition amongst local authorities that without an adequate level of resources there will be no development of services for children in need.'[4]

A particularly difficult issue is the balance to be struck between providing family support services under Part III and services focused on families where a child is thought to be *at risk*. There is substantial evidence that local authorities have, in the overall context of inadequate funding, prioritised the latter to the detriment of the former[5]. This is, arguably, to put the cart before the horse but, in fairness to those who have to administer these scarce resources, a counter-pressure ought to be identified. This is that there is now more potential for legal liability in negligence or under the HRA 1998 where an authority fails to take appropriate or sufficient action to protect a child at risk who is then subsequently abused or neglected. We consider these developments below. For the moment it is sufficient to comment that local authorities are caught in something of a 'catch-22'

---

1   Take, for example, Article 27(1) which requires States to 'recognize the right of every child to a standard of living adequate for the child's physical, mental, spiritual, moral and social development'.
2   The debate on this provision took an entire session at the Committee Stage of the Children Bill. See *Hansard*, 16 May 1989 (afternoon).
3   On resources for the Children Act generally, see the informative article by JM Masson 'Implementing Change for Children: Action at the Centre and Local Reaction' (1992) 19 *Journal of Law and Society* 320. See also SM Cretney, JM Masson and R Bailey-Harris *Principles of Family Law* (7th edn) (Sweet & Maxwell, 2002) at pp 704–705 and the sources cited there.
4   JM Masson (above) at pp 335–336.
5   See *Children Act Now: Messages from Research* (2001) p 22 at which it is noted that research studies have concluded that there is on the part of local authorities 'a continuing emphasis on linking interpretations of "in need" with eligibility criteria based on risk.' See also the succinct and helpful commentary in SM Cretney, JM Masson and R Bailey-Harris *Principles of Family Law* (7th edn) (Sweet & Maxwell, 2002) at pp 704–705.

situation. They need to divert resources into family support and 'preventative' work, but equally there are dangers in doing so if that means that services to protect children at risk will be left under-resourced.

The Department of Health[1] took the position that these are not, in any event, two entirely separate spheres of activity. It acknowledged that 'early intervention is essential to support children and families before problems, either from within the family or as a result of external factors, which have an impact on parenting capacity and family life escalate into crisis or abuse'[2]. But it recognised also that 'safeguarding children should not be seen as a separate activity from providing for their welfare. They are two sides of the same coin'[3]. The Department issued a framework for the assessment of children in need. This sets out, inter alia, a set of principles which should guide inter-agency, inter-disciplinary work with children in need[4] and it identifies three 'domains' of assessment, namely the child's developmental needs, the parents' or caregivers' capacities to respond appropriately and the wider family and environmental factors. It goes on to advise that the 'interaction between these three domains and the way they influence each other must be carefully analysed in order to gain a complete picture of a child's unmet needs and how to identify the best response to them'[5]. Failure to carry out proper assessments in accordance with the framework may now be a basis for judicial review. In *R (on the Application of AB and SB) v Nottingham City Council*[6] the authority had without good reason failed to identify the child's needs, produce a care plan or provide identified services.

Central and local government: division of functions

Finally by way of introduction, something should be said about the division of functions between central and local government and the important principle of inter-agency co-operation at the local level. This was very much a theme of the reforms and finds expression in several places in the Children Act[7]. Central government responsibility for child care resided in the Department of Health, which took over from the former Department of Health and Social Security in 1989, until 2003. Its brief included the formulation of policy, preparation of legislation and the issuing of guidance[8]. Then, as we noted in Chapter 2, in 2003 responsibility for children's services and child care was transferred from the Department of Health to the Department for Education and Skills under the direction of the First Minister of State for Children. We also noted that the Children Bill 2004 makes provision for the appointment of a Children's

---

1   *Framework for the Assessment of Children in Need and Their Families* (Department of Health, 2000).
2   Ibid at p xi.
3   Ibid, para 1.17.
4   Ibid, para 1.23.
5   Ibid, paras 1.40 and 1.42. On the role of assessment in different contexts and on the development of a 'common assessment framework', under consideration at the time of writing, see C Piper 'Assessing Assessment' [2004] Fam Law 736.
6   [2001] 3 FCR 350.
7   Particularly in s 27.
8   The point was forcefully made that there was no single government department responsible for policies affecting children and that this was one reason why an office of Children's Commissioner was required. See M Rosenbaum and P Newell *Taking Children Seriously* (Gulbenkian Foundation, 1991) (revised edn, 2000) and critique by A Bainham (1992) JSWFL 552.

Commissioner. There is a Social Services Inspectorate which has responsibility for inspecting social services departments[1]. The responsibility for day-care, family support and protection of children is delegated by central government to local authorities. The legislation defines a local authority as a county council, metropolitan district or London Borough[2] or common council of the City of London. These councils are obliged to establish social services departments under the overall control of a Director of Social Services[3]. They replaced the former children departments and have a much wider remit including responsibility for other potentially vulnerable groups such as the mentally ill and the elderly. It should also be noted, however, that many of the duties previously performed by local authorities in relation to the inspection and regulation of children's homes have now been transferred to a new National Care Standards Commission established by the Care Standards Act 2000. The registration and inspection of day-care and child-minding services has also been transferred to Her Majesty's Chief Inspector of Schools by the same legislation. We consider these developments below.

The lack of co-ordination in local services, especially between different departments within individual authorities, was a frequently voiced criticism prior to the Children Act[4]. The Act attempted to address these deficiencies, in part, by creating new duties of inter-departmental co-operation. Hence, the local authority's statutory responsibilities are imposed not simply on its social services department (although clearly this will bear primary responsibility) but also on related departments and authorities, especially those responsible for housing, education and health. These authorities are, subject to limited qualifications, required to co-operate with social services, and social services departments in different authorities are similarly required to co-operate with each other[5]. Local authorities must also co-ordinate the provision of services by themselves and other

---

1 For further discussion of the relationship between central and local government in this field, see JM Masson (above).
2 Section 105(1).
3 Local Authority Social Services Act 1970.
4 Not least in public inquiries into the deaths of children in care – as to which see Chapter 11 below. The importance of inter-agency co-operation was promoted in *Working Together Under the Children Act 1989* (HMSO, 1991). The Government issued a consultation paper, in anticipation of a new edition, entitled *Working Together to Safeguard Children: New Government Proposal for Inter-Agency Co-operation*. See further 'Working Together – a Consultation Paper too Far?' [1998] Fam Law 532. A second edition was published in 1999. See Department of Health *Working Together to Safeguard Children: A guide to inter-agency working to safeguard and promote the welfare of children* (1999). For a critique, see B Lindley and M Richards 'Working Together 2000 – how will parents fare under the new child protection process?' [2000] CFLQ 213. See also R Smith 'The Wrong End of the Telescope: Child protection or child safety?' (2002) 24 JSWFL 247.
5 The House of Lords decision in *R v Northavon DC, ex parte Smith* [1994] 2 AC 402 illustrates the limitations of the legal duty on authorities to co-operate with one another. The housing authority refused to rehouse an 'intentionally homeless' family despite being requested to do so by the social services department. The House of Lords held that it was entitled to refuse given the legal framework of the housing legislation and that the burden fell instead on social services to offer the family assistance, financial or otherwise, under Part III. See G Holgate 'Intentional Homelessness, Dependent Children and their Statutory Rights of Accommodation' [1994] Fam Law 264, which comments on the Court of Appeal decision. See also D Cowan and J Fionda

agencies, particularly voluntary organisations[1]. This is intended to ensure, as far as possible, consistency in the standard of provision and good practice across different regions.

Children's services and the Children Bill 2004

The Children Bill 2004 follows the Victoria Climbié inquiry, the Green Paper *Every Child Matters* and the White Paper *Every Child Matters: Next Steps*. It has the bold general aim of making changes in policy and legislation to maximise opportunities and minimise risks for all children and young people. More specifically, it is designed to focus services more effectively around their needs and those of their families. It seeks to create clearer accountability for children's services to enable better joint working and to produce a better focus on safeguarding children. To this end major organisational changes in responsibility for, and delivery of, children's services are set out in Part II of the Bill.

Some of the central features of Part II are as follows. First, local authorities are placed under a statutory duty to make arrangements through which key agencies co-operate and the Bill empowers them to pool budgets in order to achieve better outcomes for children. Those agencies will be required to have regard to the need to safeguard and promote the welfare of children in discharging their normal functions, the intention being to give priority to the safety of children. Local authorities will be required to establish Local Safeguarding Children Boards which will replace the existing non-statutory Area Child Protection Committees. In order to support professionals working together and sharing information and to enable them to identify difficulties, the Bill permits the creation of databases holding information on all children and young people. In an effort to improve accountability, the Bill requires the local authority to appoint a director for children's services to be accountable, as a minimum, for the authority's education and social services functions insofar as they relate to children. The Bill also requires the designation of a lead member for children's services to mirror the director's responsibility at a local political level. Finally, there will be an integrated inspection framework, and the Bill enables inspectorates to carry out joint reviews of all children's services provided in an area. Part III of the Bill makes similar provision for Wales while also making allowance for implementation in the different context of children's services in Wales.

SERVICES FOR CHILDREN AND FAMILIES

Before the Children Act, local authorities owed a duty to *all* children 'to make available such advice, guidance and assistance' as might promote their welfare 'by diminishing the need to receive children into or keep them in care ... or to bring children before a juvenile court'[2]. More specific powers and duties arose under

---

'Housing Homeless Families – An Update' [1995] CFLQ 66 for comment on the House of Lords decision. Detailed consideration of the housing responsibilities of local authorities is beyond the scope of the present discussion. For an account of these and their relationship with the local authorities' responsibilities under the Children Act, see D Bedingfield *The Child in Need* (Family Law, 1998) at ch 4.

1   Section 17(5). This is another example of the 'partnership' theme in the legislation.
2   Child Care Act 1980, s 1.

other statutes relating to particular groups of children, including the mentally handicapped and the disabled[1]. There was a good deal of regional variation in the quality and extent of services provided to these different groups. The *Review* and the White Paper[2] accepted that it would be in the interests of all the children concerned to unify the relevant parts of child care law and health and welfare legislation, in particular to extend the protection of child care law to handicapped and disabled children. Part III, accordingly, constitutes a single code governing the voluntary services offered by local authorities to children and families, regardless of the particular reason why these services are needed[3].

Reformulation of the general duty

The general duty of local authorities to provide services is now contained in s 17(1) of the Children Act which states:

> 'It shall be the general duty of every local authority (in addition to the other duties imposed on them by this Part) –
>
> (a) to safeguard and promote the welfare of children within their area who are in need; and
> (b) so far as is consistent with that duty, to promote the upbringing of such children by their families, by providing a range and level of services appropriate to those children's needs.'

It is crucial to appreciate that this general duty to safeguard and promote welfare is not the same as being bound by the 'welfare principle' articulated in s 1 of the Act[4]. The Court of Appeal has made this clear in *Re M (Secure Accommodation Order)*[5]. Here, the question was whether the use of secure accommodation under s 25 of the Act was a matter to be governed by the welfare principle. The court held that, although the child's welfare was a relevant factor, the Act prescribed the circumstances under which secure accommodation might be used, including where the child was likely to cause injury to others, and accordingly there might be circumstances in which the exercise of the power would not be consistent with the idea that the child's welfare was paramount. But the court did not stop there. It went on to say that the welfare principle in s 1 did not apply to *any* of the powers and duties arising under Part III of the Act. Thus, while the individual child's welfare is a factor, indeed an important factor, in the exercise of the authority's obligations under Part III, it may be outweighed by other factors and policy considerations which the authority needs to take into account.

---

1   The main statutes were the National Health Service Act 1977, the National Assistance Act 1948 and the Chronically Sick and Disabled Persons Act 1970.
2   DHSS *Review of Child Care Law* (1985) ('the *Review*') and *The Law on Child Care and Family Services* (1987) (Cmnd 62) ('the White Paper').
3   For a comment on how Part III of the Children Act has been affected by the Adoption and Children Act 2002, see J Masson 'The Impact of the Adoption and Children Act: Part 2 – The Provision of Services for Children and Families' [2003] Fam Law 644.
4   For the welfare principle generally, see Chapter 2. It has been held that, while the court may direct a local authority to reconsider the question of the services it should provide for a child, it may not direct it what to decide or direct it to make any *specific* provision for the child. See *Re T (Judicial Review: Local Authority Decisions Concerning Child in Need)* [2004] 1 FLR 601.
5   [1995] 1 FLR 418.

The legal duties towards children in need are imposed on the local authority in relation to those children who are 'within their area'[1]. We have also seen that there is a duty on different authorities to co-operate with one another. Authorities have a statutory obligation to comply with a request for help from another authority 'if it is compatible with their own statutory or other duties and obligations and does not unduly prejudice the discharge of any of their functions'[2]. This has led to some difficult questions concerning the proper boundaries between the statutory obligations of different authorities and especially between social services and housing authorities.

The matter came before the House of Lords in *R v Northavon District Council ex parte Smith*[3] and returned there more recently in *R (G) v Barnet London Borough Council*[4]. In the latter case the principal issue was whether a local authority might, in discharging its statutory duties, accommodate a child *alone* without his or her family. One of the local authorities in the case had adopted a policy of dealing with the accommodation needs of homeless children by making accommodation available to them but not to their parents. The reasoning was that, although the provision of accommodation for the entire family would be at no greater cost to the authority, its experience was that a suggestion that a child might be removed and accommodated separately might lead parents to find family accommodation themselves at no cost to the authority. The House of Lords held by a slim majority that local authorities' duties under s 17 were of a *general* character and the duty to assess the child's needs under s 17 did not crystallise into a specific duty owed to the child as an individual. The services provided might include the provision of accommodation for a child, but the provision of residential accommodation to rehouse a child to enable him to live with his family was not the principal or primary purpose of the legislation. Housing was the function of the local housing authority. Thus, an authority providing a child with accommodation was not under a duty to accommodate the child's family as well. Dissenting, Lord Nicholls of Birkenhead and Lord Steyn took the view that, while it might be reasonable in the case of an older child to accommodate the child but not the parent, where the child was not old enough to understand what was going on and would be likely to be significantly upset at being separated from the parent, the authority could not fulfil its duty to meet the needs of the child by accommodating the child alone.

The duty in s 17 is a substantial recasting of the local authority's preventative role. Before the Children Act, the duty was to endeavour to avert not only compulsory care proceedings but also the need to receive children into voluntary care. The concept of voluntary care was abolished by the Children Act and replaced with the notion of children 'accommodated' or 'looked after' by local

---

1   The child's *physical presence* in the area of the authority is required and is sufficient. See *R, on the Application of S v London Borough of Wandsworth, London Borough of Hammersmith and Fulham, London Borough of Lambeth* [2002] 1 FLR 469 in which there was something of a 'turf war' between the three authorities.

2   Children Act 1989, s 27(2).

3   [1994] 2 AC 402.

4   *R (G) v Barnet London Borough Council; R (W) v Lambeth London Borough Council; R (A) v Lambeth London Borough Council* [2004] 1 FLR 454. For commentary, see D Cowan 'On Need and Gatekeeping' [2004] CFLQ 331. On the interaction of local authorities' powers to accommodate children under the Children Act with the Nationality, Immigration and Asylum Act 2002, see *M v London Borough of Islington and Secretary of State for the Home Department* [2004] 2 FLR 867.

authorities. This voluntary provision of accommodation is now viewed as just one kind of service offered to children and families in difficulty and it was considered important that this should be seen as *positive* assistance and not as a negative or stigmatising procedure. Accordingly, local authorities are no longer required to diminish the need to accommodate children but it remains the case that they must attempt to prevent more coercive measures being required. This other aspect of the local authority's duty has to be ferreted out of Sch 2 to the Children Act, which lists a range of more specific duties. Here, there is a duty to take reasonable steps to reduce the need to bring proceedings for care or supervision orders, criminal proceedings against children, family proceedings which could result in them being placed in a local authority's care, or proceedings under the inherent jurisdiction of the High Court; to encourage childen not to commit criminal offences; and to avoid the need to use secure accommodation[1]. The common characteristic of all these actions is that they are compulsory in nature and stand in contrast to voluntary family support. It is generally agreed that voluntary assistance, where possible, is preferable.

The other respect in which the duty was refashioned was by the addition of the word 'general'. The view of most commentators was that the effect of this was to reverse a decision under the old law that the former preventive duty applied to individual children[2], and this interpretation has been confirmed by the courts[3].

Children in need

The statutory definition of 'children in need' is crucial. While it is true that some of the local authority's more specific duties and powers do extend to *all* children, even these are directed at a more restricted group since they exist 'for the purpose principally of facilitating the discharge of their general duty'[4]. Thus, specific duties like the duty to take reasonable steps to prevent the ill-treatment or neglect of children[5], or the duty to provide 'family centres'[6], are intended to prevent children from *becoming* children in need.

The importance of the classification of 'child in need' is that it operates as a threshold condition or 'passport' to the services offered by the local authority, and these are not simply those services offered by the social services department. The general duty binds all departments within the local authority and it has already been mentioned that they are under an obligation to co-operate with each other. An assessment that a child is, or is not, in need, may therefore have important repercussions, not simply for family support by social services, but in the determination of housing, health and educational priorities. In short, the legislation appears to authorise positive discrimination in favour of childen in need. The negative side of this is that the label 'child in need' can acquire a stigma akin to that which has often been thought to attach to means-tested social security benefits – some of which also have the 'passport' effect of securing entitlement to a range of other benefits. This might become a real danger if local authorities too readily equate 'child in need' with 'child at risk'. The official guidance to this part

---

1 Schedule 2, para 7.
2 *A-G (ex rel Tilley) v London Borough of Wandsworth* [1981] 1 All ER 1162.
3 *R v London Borough of Barnet ex parte B* [1994] 1 FLR 592.
4 Section 17(2).
5 Schedule 2, para 4(1).
6 Schedule 2, para 9.

of the legislation makes it plain that to do so would be unlawful[1], but scarce resources and competing claims on those resources make it inevitable that local authorities will resort to some form of rationing device. We discussed above what can be a blurring of the distinction between voluntary and compulsory action, of which this is perhaps another aspect.

The Children Act defines a child as being in need if:

'(a) he is unlikely to achieve or maintain, or to have the opportunity of achieving or maintaining, a reasonable standard of health or development without the provision for him of services by a local authority under this part;

(b) his health or development is likely to be significantly impaired, or further impaired, without the provision for him of such services; or

(c) he is disabled.'[2]

This definition is rather broad and indeterminate, except insofar as it is clear that we are dealing with a restricted category of children. The Childen Act does, however, go on to define various components in the definition with greater particularity, if not precision. It is evident from the definition itself, that the local authority must concern itself not only with those children who are already in need (in the sense that they already have a low standard of health or development) but also with those who are likely to find themselves in that position unless services are provided. The inclusion of the prospective element emphasises prevention rather than cure and mirrors the reformulated ground for compulsory action[3]. 'Development' for these purposes is expressed to include 'physical, intellectual, emotional, social or behavioural development' and 'health' includes 'physical or mental health'. 'Disabled' means a child who is 'blind, deaf or dumb or suffers from mental disorder of any kind or is substantially and permanently handicapped by illness, injury or congenital deformity or such other disability as may be prescribed'[4]. The use of terminology like this was criticised as unduly stigmatic during the parliamentary debates and it has been said that it is inappropriate today[5]. The reasoning appears to be that Parliament wanted to ensure the specific inclusion of all those categories of children for whom it was intended that the local authority's duty should apply. Direct payments may now be made[6], or in future vouchers issued[7], to a person with parental responsibility for a disabled child of 16 or 17 years of age. The purpose is to enable them to purchase a service which would otherwise have been provided by the authority itself.

It has been held that the local authority's determination that a child is, or is not, in need is not susceptible to challenge except through the judicial review procedure. In *Re J (Specific Issue Order: Leave to Apply)*[8], a 17-year-old boy was refused leave to seek a specific issue order deeming him to be a child 'in need' and requiring the local authority to make appropriate provision for him. Wall J held that Parliament could not have envisaged that the exercise of the duties imposed

---

1 *The Children Act 1989 Guidance and Regulations Vol 2 Family Support, Day Care and Educational Provision for Young Children* (HMSO, 1991) at para 2.4, which states that such a restriction 'would not be acceptable'.

2 Section 17(10).

3 Section 31(2), and see Chapter 11 below.

4 Section 17(11).

5 MDA Freeman *Children, Their Families and the Law* (Macmillan, 1992) at p 57.

6 Children Act 1989, s 17A, inserted by the Carers and Disabled Children Act 2000, s 7(1).

7 Ibid.

8 [1995] 1 FLR 669.

on local authorities under Part III of the Act should be exposed to judicial intervention except where the statute expressly provided for this, for example in relation to secure accommodation. The courts had not been given any power under the legislation to regulate the selection of children in need or to enforce the statutory duty to accommodate such children.

Available services

If the definition of children in need is full of indeterminate concepts, so also is the statutory basis upon which a number of particular services are offered by local authorities. There are duties to 'take reasonable steps' or to make such provision 'as is appropriate'. The combined effect of such provisions (including the definition of 'children in need') is to give local authorities an almost unassailable controlling discretion and to make legal challenges very difficult. However, such a challenge succeeded in *R v Hammersmith and Fulham London Borough Council ex parte D*[1]. Here a Swedish mother had arrived in England with her two sons, having left a situation of domestic violence in Sweden. The local authority accepted that the children were in need, inter alia, by reason of their homelessness. Initially they provided bed and breakfast accommodation and a subsistence allowance but thereafter they wanted to discharge their statutory functions by financial assistance to enable the mother and her children to return to Sweden. They declared that they would terminate the provision of accommodation and financial support in the event that the mother declined this offer. The mother successfully challenged this decision in judicial review. Kay J held that in limiting the use of its statutory powers in this way the authority was in breach of its duties under Part III of the Children Act. It was quite in order for the authority to offer financial assistance to enable the family to return to another country if it thought that the needs of the child would be best met in that way. But it was wrong for it to withdraw further assistance, or threaten to withdraw it, if the offer was declined. In the present case there was no immediate prospect, realistically, that the mother would be able to return to Sweden, and the authority was therefore obliged to continue to provide accommodation and financial support while the mother had no funds to cater for their needs[2].

Services may not only be made directly available to children but also to members of their family. A major aim of the legislation is to promote the upbringing of children within their own families and it is the duty of the local authority to try to give effect to this aim[3]. One aspect of this is that services may be offered to any member of the family of a child in need, provided that this is with a view to safeguarding the welfare of that child[4]. Suppose, for example, that the presence of a severely disabled child within a family is affecting the health or development of other children of the family and putting everyone under strain. The statutory provision would enable extra support to be provided for that child with a view to alleviating the overall family situation. 'Family' for these purposes

---

1 [1999] 1 FLR 642.
2 The mother was not yet eligible for income support because she had not yet become habitually resident in the UK.
3 Section 17(1)(b).
4 Section 17(3).

has an extended meaning and includes 'any person who has parental responsibility for the child and any other person with whom he has been living'[1]. The local
authority is therefore able to concentrate on those who have the actual care of a
child, without having to concern itself with technical questions about who has
parental responsibility.

As under the old law, services may include giving assistance in kind or, in
exceptional circumstances, in cash[2]. Prima facie, it might appear more attractive
for local authorities to spend a relatively small amount of money on improving the
home conditions of a family in which there are children who might otherwise
need to be accommodated by it. There is no question that the cost of
accommodating the child would far exceed any cash assistance given under this
provision. But the issue is politically sensitive, since to make widespread use of
these payments could be seen as usurping the role of the social security system
which, however inadequately, caters for the material needs of families. This is the
true basis of the restriction that such payments may be made in only exceptional
circumstances. Moreover, in keeping with the social security reforms of the 1980s,
the local authority may, in some circumstances, require repayment of its assistance
or its value[3]. It must, however, have regard to the means of parents and there is an
automatic exemption from liability for those in receipt of the principal
means-tested benefits[4].

The principle of inter-agency co-operation has been noted. Another facet of
this is that local authorities are required to facilitate the provision by others of
services which they themselves lack the power to provide, and to make
arrangements for others to act on their behalf in the provision of any service[5]. This
underlines the need for co-operation between the public, private and voluntary
sectors. The specific services which local authorities are required or empowered to
provide are largely contained in Sch 2 to the Children Act.

Specific powers and duties

It is not appropriate in a work of this nature to analyse every detail of Sch 2 to the
Children Act. But it is necessary to gain a general sense of what local authorities
are required to provide beyond their broad umbrella power, and to highlight
some of the more significant services. Freeman has helpfully identified the
general character of the services in question.

> 'Local authorities cannot be expected to meet every individual need, but they are to take
> "reasonable steps" to identify the extent of need in their area and then to use their discretion
> reasonably and sensibly to make decisions about service provision in the light of the information
> they receive and their statutory obligations. They must ensure that a range of services is available

---

1 Section 17(10).
2 Section 17(6). This used to be referred to under the old law as 'section 1 money'.
3 Section 17(7). The obvious analogy is with the abolition of 'single payments' in 1988 and their
   replacement with loans under the newly constituted 'Social Fund'. For a discussion of these
   reforms under the Social Security Act 1986 (implemented in April 1988), see Wikeley, Ogus
   and Barendt's *The Law of Social Security* (6th edn) (Butterworths, 2002) at ch 13.
4 Section 17(8) and (9). The principal means-tested benefits are now income support (formerly
   supplementary benefit), working families tax credit (introduced in 1999 to replace family credit
   which itself replaced family income supplement), disabled person's tax credit and income-
   based jobseeker's allowance. See Chapter 9.
5 Section 17(5)(a) and (b).

to meet the need they identify. What is required will vary from area to area but is likely to include day care, foster care, some provision of residential care. They will need to offer a range of placements to reflect the racial, cultural, religious and linguistic needs of the children of their area (s 22(5)(c)). They will also have to have a range of short-term and longer term accommodation as well as permanent placements.'[1]

We noted above some of the local authority's specific duties. Further duties are listed below, followed by a closer examination of those duties relating to day-care and other services offered to children who are living with their families.

Among the local authority's duties are:

(1) a duty to publicise the services provided by it and by others (particularly voluntary organisations) and to take such steps as are reasonably practicable to ensure that the information is received by those who might benefit from the services[2];

(2) a duty to review its provision of services and, having regard to the review, prepare and publish a plan for the provision of services under Part III[3];

(3) a duty to open and maintain a register of disabled children[4];

(4) a duty to minimise the effects of disability suffered by disabled children[5];

(5) a duty to take reasonable steps to prevent the ill-treatment or neglect of children by the provision of services[6];

(6) a power to assist someone (possibly through cash) with removal expenses and the costs of obtaining alternative accommodation where that person is living with a child and the child is suffering, or is likely to suffer, ill-treatment at the hands of the person in question[7];

(7) a duty to provide family centres at which a child, his parents and others may receive advice, guidance and counselling or take part in various activities of an occupational, social, cultural or recreational nature[8];

(8) a duty, where a child in need is living apart from his family, to take reasonable steps to enable him to live with them or to promote contact with them if, in the authority's opinion, it is necessary to do so to safeguard or promote his welfare[9];

(9) in making arrangements for the provision of day-care or arrangements designed to encourage persons to act as local authority foster-parents, a duty to have regard to the different racial groups to which children in need within its area belong.

---

1 MDA Freeman *Children, Their Families and the Law* (Macmillan, 1992) at p 53.
2 Schedule 2, para 1(2).
3 Schedule 2, para 1A, inserted by the Children Act 1989 (Amendment) (Children's Services Planning) Order 1996, SI 1996/785.
4 Schedule 2, para 2(1).
5 Schedule 2, para 6. The best discussion of the application of the Children Act to disabled children is Freeman (above) especially at ch 11.
6 Schedule 2, para 4.
7 Schedule 2, para 5. This provision should now be taken alongside the provision enabling local authorities to ask for 'exclusion requirements' to be inserted into emergency protection orders and interim care orders under Part IV of the Family Law Act 1996. This followed the recommendations of the Law Commission in (1992) Law Com Report No 207 *Domestic Violence and Occupation of the Family Home*. We discuss this regime in Chapter 12.
8 Schedule 2, para 9.
9 Schedule 2, para 10.

Day-care and pre-school provision

Section 18 sets out the duties and powers of authorities regarding day-care for pre-school children and supervision of school-age children outside school[1]. The matter proved controversial in Parliament and was unusual in being one issue during the progress of the Children Bill which divided the political parties. Contrary to the position elsewhere in Europe, there has been no national plan for day-care and nursery provision in the UK, although there has been an expansion in nursery places under the Labour Government. It has been largely left to the individual discretion of local authorities and its amount and quality varies considerably. The former Conservative Government resisted pressure to impose stronger duties but did eventually accede to a late amendment which placed local authorities under a new duty to review periodically the whole range of day-care facilities provided across the public, private and voluntary sectors within their area[2]. We consider below the new arrangements for the regulation of day-care and child-minding introduced by the Care Standards Act 2000.

Day-care for children in need

Local authorities *must* provide such day-care for children in need 'as is appropriate'[3]. They have power to provide day-care for children in their area who are *not* in need[4]. This reserves a wide discretion to individual local authorities. They are also empowered to provide back-up support for those people who are directly involved in providing day-care facilities[5]. In addition, they have corresponding duties to older children in need, who are attending school, to provide for such care or supervised activities as is appropriate outside school hours or during school holidays. Again, this provision extends to children who are not in need[6]. This is intended to assist working parents, after school hours but before the end of the working day, and during school holidays. It is for individual local authorities to decide how precisely to discharge these responsibilities, but the most obvious examples are day nurseries, playgroups, child-minding, out-of-school clubs, holiday schemes and parent and toddler groups[7]. Despite these provisions, there remains, in many parts of the country, an unmet need. The Labour Government indicated its intentions to make a nursery place available for all four-year-olds, through a partnership between the public and private sectors, as part of its overall strategy for reform of the Welfare State[8].

---

1 For a more detailed discussion, see Freeman (above) at pp 85–88.
2 Section 19. For discussion of the statutory obligations of local authorities in this area, see C Cameron and P Moss 'The Children Act 1989 and Early Childhood' (1995) JSWFL 417. For an excellent comparative critique of the policies relating to child care provision in the context of employment prospects for women and parental employment policies more generally, see S Fredman *Women and the Law* (Clarendon, 1997) at pp 208–224.
3 Section 18(1). Section 18(4) provides that 'day care' means 'any form of care or supervised activity provided for children during the day (whether or not it is provided on a regular basis)'.
4 Section 18(2).
5 Section 18(3).
6 Section 18(5) and (6).
7 Other examples are given in *The Children Act 1989 Guidance and Regulations Vol 2* (above) at paras 3.8–3.17.
8 See Green Paper *New Ambitions for Our Country: A New Contract for Welfare* (March 1998), and Chapter 9 above. Under the School Standards and Framework Act 1998, s 118, LEAs are now under a general duty to 'secure that the provision (whether or not by them) of nursery education for children who: (a) have not attained compulsory school age, but (b) have attained

Assistance for children living with their families
Schedule 2, para 8 to the Children Act requires local authorities to make 'such provision as they consider appropriate' for specified services to be made available for children in need while they are living with their families. The services in question are:

(1) advice, guidance and counselling;
(2) occupational, social, cultural or recreational activities;
(3) home help (including laundry facilities);
(4) travel facilities or assistance with travelling to and from home for the purpose of taking advantage of services;
(5) assistance to enable the child and the family to have a holiday.

This, then, is another duty which encapsulates the ethos of family support. As far as possible, every effort should be made to keep functioning families together. In some cases, for whatever reason, this may not be possible, and it may prove necessary for the local authority to look after a child itself. We now turn to the important duty to provide accommodation.

THE PROVISION OF ACCOMMODATION

Prior to the Children Act, children who were accommodated by local authorities with the consent of parents were 'in care' albeit 'voluntary care'. Yet, although the initial arrangement was voluntary, this could slip into compulsion with the passage of time. 'Voluntary care' began to acquire a negative, even 'threatening'[1], image as local authorities were empowered to pass administrative resolutions assuming parental rights[2]. Parents were required to give 28 days' notice before resuming the care of a child who had been in voluntary care for at least six months. Moreover, it was held that the local authority was not obliged to return the child immediately on demand, even where that child had been in care for less than six months, and that the child remained in care despite the notice having been given[3]. This, it was said, gave the local authority a 'breathing space' to take further action to protect the welfare of the child, usually by passing a resolution to assume parental rights.

All of this was inconsistent with the objectives of the Children Act, in particular the voluntary partnership which is supposed to exist between parents and the local authority. Eekelaar and Dingwall have identified the problem confronted in the *Review* as the 'increasingly sharp distinction between being in and out of care'[4]. If this was the most significant distinction under the old law, the crucial legal distinction following the Children Act is between the children who are formally 'in care' under a court order and those who are not, either because they are at home

---

such age as may be prescribed, is sufficient for their area'. Under s 119, every LEA is required to establish an 'early years development partnership' and, in conjunction with that body, under s 120, prepare 'an early years development plan' for their area. There is extensive provision for the inspection of nursery provision under s 122 and Sch 26 which supersede the Nursery Education and Grant Maintained Schools Act 1996, which previously regulated the matter.

1   The description of J Eekelaar and R Dingwall *The Reform of Child Care Law* (Routledge, 1990) at p 74.
2   Under the Child Care Act 1980, s 3.
3   *London Borough of Lewisham v Lewisham Juvenile Court Justices* [1980] AC 273.
4   J Eekelaar and R Dingwall (above) at pp 74–75. See DHSS *Review of Child Care Law* (1985).

or because they are voluntarily accommodated. Yet, as Eekelaar and Dingwall go on to point out, it was not the intention of the *Review* to create such an obvious demarcation[1]. The *Review* sought to establish 'finer gradations' of voluntary accommodation which would have embraced 'respite care' and 'shared care'. *Respite care* (a concept previously utilised in connection with disabled children) would have been a short-term arrangement of up to one month. Parents would not have been required to give any notice of removal, the local authority would have been wholly dependent on parental delegation, and parental responsibility would not have passed to the local authority[2]. *Shared care* would, in contrast, have involved a transfer of parental responsibility to the authority by agreement[3]. The 28 days' notice would have been preserved and, since it envisaged 'shared' control, the local authority would have been obliged to allow parents to participate in decision-making and plans for the child.

In the event, the Government rejected the distinction between respite care and shared care as unworkable[4]. Hence, *all* children who are not 'in care' under a court order are now not in care at all. Parental responsibility for them does not pass to the local authority, and parents may remove them without notice. There is no longer any power to assume parental rights without a court order. These issues are now governed by formal agreements between authorities and parents, and the law is in retreat from these voluntary arrangements. We now turn to the legal framework under which these agreements operate.

The duty to accommodate

Section 20(1) of the Children Act sets out the circumstances under which local authorities must accommodate children in need[5]. It states:

> 'Every local authority shall provide accommodation for any child in need within their area who appears to them to require accommodation as a result of:
> (a) there being no person who has parental responsibility for him;
> (b) his being lost or having been abandoned; or
> (c) the person who has been caring for him being prevented (whether or not permanently, and for whatever reason) from providing him with suitable accommodation or care.'

---

1 J Eekelaar and R Dingwall (above) at pp 74–75.
2 See DHSS *Review of Child Care Law* (1985) at chs 6 and 7.
3 Ibid, at ch 7.
4 *The Law on Child Care and Family Services* (1987) (Cmnd 62) ('the White Paper') at para 26.
5 It should be noted that under s 21 of the Children Act the local authority has other duties to accommodate children in specified circumstances. These are:
   (i)   where the child is removed or kept away from home under the short-term protective measures in Part V;
   (ii) where the child is in police protection;
   (iii) where the authority is requested to receive the child under s 38(6) of the Police and Criminal Evidence Act 1984 (which generally requires arrested juveniles to be moved to local authority accommodation);
   (iv) where the child is on remand;
   (v)   where the child is the subject of a supervision order imposing a local authority residence requirement under Sch 5, para 6 to the Powers of Criminal Courts (Sentencing) Act 2000.

In simple terms, the duty under s 20 arises in relation to orphaned or abandoned children[1] and children whose parents or carers are prevented by temporary or long-term illness, disability or other reason from properly looking after them. The Children Act Advisory Committee in its *Final Report* commented on what were appropriate and inappropriate uses of the power to accommodate children[2]. The Committee said that accommodation was properly used by the local authorities to work in partnership with parents in a variety of circumstances of need, such as hospital admission of a parent, bereavement, housing difficulties and respite care. But it went on to say that it was crucial that accommodation should not be regarded as an alternative to an application for a care order or supervision order since, if used inappropriately, drift and damaging delay could occur to the detriment of the child. There was evidence in some cases that parents were agreeing to accommodation as an alternative to court proceedings, in return for generous contact with the child. This could lead to delay in decision-making and planning, a failure to address fundamental problems and failure to plan properly for the future. There was also evidence that some parents used accommodation too frequently as a means of crisis resolution, especially in the context of changes of school, resulting in harm to the child from instability.

The relevance of objections

It is the very essence of these arrangements that they are voluntary. This means that they cannot be effected in the face of opposition by parents, although this blanket statement requires some qualification in the case of divorced or unmarried parents. There is no requirement of positive consent since it is obvious that this will be unobtainable in the case of orphaned or abandoned[3] children. Instead, what is required is an absence of *relevant* opposition. Where the arrangement is opposed by someone with the right to oppose it, the local authority will have to resort to compulsory measures if it wishes to take over the care of the child.

Right of objection if suitable alternative accommodation offered

The primary rule is that no child may be accommodated where a person with parental responsibility (most obviously a parent) objects[4]. In *R v Tameside Metropolitan Borough Council ex parte J*[5] it was held that this right of objection

---

1 It should be noted that, since the accommodation of children under s 20 does not confer parental responsibility on the local authority, it may be desirable in the case of an orphan for the authority to seek a care order to enable it to plan for the child's long-term welfare. See *Re SH (Care Order: Orphan)* [1995] 1 FLR 746, and Chapter 11 below.

2 *Children Act Advisory Committee Final Report June 1997* (Lord Chancellor's Department, 1997) at pp 29–30.

3 The concept of abandonment was examined in the context of adoption legislation as long ago as 1955. In *Watson v Nikolaisen* [1955] 2 QB 286 the court defined it to mean 'leaving the child to its fate'. It is certainly not wide enough to include the situation of a parent who allows her child to be looked after by the State only because of poverty or destitution – making proper provision for substitute care does not mean that the child has been abandoned. The concept has been badly distorted and misused in the context of Romania where so-called 'judicial declarations of abandonment' were made in exactly these circumstances in order to pave the way for premature international adoption. See further Chapter 17.

4 Section 20(7).

5 [2000] 1 FLR 942.

extended to the *kind* of accommodation offered to the child. Here a child with severe disabilities was accommodated in a residential home for disabled children under a voluntary arrangement with the local authority. The council later wished to move her to a foster-home believing this to be in her best interests. The parents objected and, when their objections were overruled, applied for judicial review of the decision. Scott Baker J granted a declaration that the authority had no power to place the child with foster-parents without her parents' consent, since they retained parental responsibility and with it the right to decide where the child lived. Neither party to a voluntary arrangement had the right to dictate to the other where the child should live. It was a matter for co-operation between the parents and the authority. The authority under a voluntary arrangement, possessed only day-to-day powers of management. If it wished to secure compulsory control over a child it would need to obtain a care order. Under a voluntary arrangement the only alternative open to the authority, if agreement could not be reached, would be to give parents the choice of accepting its solution or caring for the child themselves. This right of objection is qualified in that it must be shown that the objector is himself willing and able to provide accommodation for the child. It appears that this was inspired by concern that an estranged or 'absent' parent might seek to frustrate an arrangement between the caring parent and the local authority, with no intention of proposing a more suitable alternative. The second, and complementary, rule is that anyone with parental responsibility 'may at any time remove the child from accommodation provided by or on behalf of the local authority'[1]. Both rules are displaced where a residence order is in force and where the person or persons in whose favour it is made has agreed to the arrangement. The same applies where, instead of a residence order, there is an order under the inherent jurisdiction of the High Court[2]. In either case, where more than one person holds a residence order, each of them must agree to the child being accommodated[3].

Operation of provisions in different family situations

How do these provisions operate in the case of the married family, the unmarried family and the divorced family? Where the parents are married and living together, an objection by *either* parent will preclude the arrangement, and either parent may remove a child accommodated originally with the agreement of the other. In practice, it is unlikely that parents will disagree over so fundamental an issue, but it is not impossible, especially where their relationship is breaking down. The normal rule which allows parental responsibility to be independently exercised, even were parents disagree with each other, is clearly superseded by the statutory right of objection.

Where the parents are unmarried, if the father has not acquired parental responsibility[4], the mother alone has parental responsibility. She may thus enter

---

1   Section 20(8). It is, of course, implicit in this that the person with parental responsibility can object to the continuation of an arrangement previously made with his approval.
2   Section 20(9).
3   Section 20(10).
4   This is likely to be the case in only about one in five instances of births to unmarried mothers. The effect of the reforms introduced by the Adoption and Children Act 2002 is that there will henceforth be many fewer instances of unmarried fathers who do not have parental responsibility.

in an arrangement with the local authority, and the father has no right of objection or removal unless he has previously acquired parental responsibility. It has been pointed out that this puts the small minority of unmarried fathers who have actual care of their children but do not have parental responsibility in a peculiarly vulnerable position vis-à-vis social services[1]. It would, of course, be open to an unmarried father to seek a parental responsibility order and/or a residence order, the effect of which would be to authorise removal of the child from the local authority. But where the child is by this time settled, perhaps in a foster-home, the court may be reluctant to upset the status quo.

Where parents are divorced, the primary rule will continue to apply, since a divorced parent, although physically absent, retains equal parental responsibility. This will be the situation in the majority of cases because of the 'no order' principle. In the minority of cases in which a residence order is made, its effect is to displace the primary rule and to 'trump' the non-resident parent's right of objection[2]. How far this is consistent with the notion of continuing parental responsibility has been questioned[3].

Abolition of statutory notice requirement

The abolition of the statutory notice requirement has caused concern. The fear is, as Freeman has put it, that local authorities may become 'dumping grounds'. Children might come in and out of local authority accommodation 'at a parent's whim, with no opportunity for planning, and little attention to the needs of the child for security and stability'[4]. The hope is that this sort of capricious behaviour on the part of parents will be avoided by carefully negotiated agreements which deal specifically with the issue of the child returning home. The possibility of an attempt by parents to remove their child suddenly from local authority care, cannot, however, be discounted, and this had led to widespread speculation about what action the local authority could legally take to forestall such an occurrence[5]. The local authority's general duty to safeguard the child's welfare, and the allied power which de facto carers have to do what is reasonable in the circumstances, ought to be sufficient to resist a summary removal and to fill what might otherwise be a legal vacuum[6]. But if the authority wished to continue to hold the child, it would need to seek a care order, probably preceded by an emergency protection

---

1 A Bainham *Children: The New Law* (Family Law, 1990) at para 4.25, citing the case of *Re L (A Minor)* (1984) *The Times*, June 21.
2 This is not, of course, a situation confined to divorce, but divorce is easily the most significant context numerically.
3 A Bainham (above) at para 4.26.
4 MDA Freeman *Children, Their Families and the Law* (Macmillan, 1992) at p 65.
5 The options are extensively canvassed by Freeman (above) at pp 66–69, and by J Eekelaar and R Dingwall *The Reform of Child Care Law* (Routledge, 1990) at p 77.
6 See ss 17(1) and 3(5). Cretney and Masson took the view that the legal position under the Children Act is uncertain, while it was not in doubt under the old law (see *Krishnan v Sutton London Borough Council* [1970] Ch 181) that local authorities were not under an *absolute* duty to return the child. See SM Cretney and JM Masson *Principles of Family Law* (6th edn) (Sweet & Maxwell, 1997) at p 785. They are now inclined to take the view that this interpretation cannot be sustained. See *Principles of Family Law* (7th edn) (Sweet & Maxwell, 2002) at p 710. This appears to be supported by an unreported decision of Ward J (as he then was) in *Nottinghamshire County Council v J* (26 November 1993). The issue requires resolution by the higher courts.

order[1]. Police protection could be invoked, or a foster-parent might conceivably seek a residence order or care and control in wardship proceedings[2]. Probably the most unsatisfactory aspect of not requiring at least a short period of notice is that this may hinder the legitimate plans of local authorities in trying to ensure a smooth transition back to the family, possibly by means of a phased return. In some cases, the reluctance of social services to hand a child over on demand may simply reflect its wish to be satisfied that the home circumstances have improved sufficiently for the child to return. It would be extremely unfortunate if this wholly reasonable concern were to force the local authority into coercive action. An amendment in the House of Lords which would have required a mere 24 hours' notice was rejected as inconsistent with the voluntary partnership principle[3]. While it is likely that in most cases parents will stick to the agreements they make with social services, and will not try to remove children in inappropriate circumstances, it is still arguable that a statutory requirement would have been desirable.

The child's point of view

How far should children themselves be able to decide whether or not they wish to be admitted to local authority accommodation or, once there, to remain there or leave? The legislation distinguishes between those over 16 years of age and those under that age.

Provision for children over 16 years of age
The position of those over the age of 16 is clear. The Children Act provides that neither the parental right of objection nor the parental right of removal applies where a child of 16 years of age agrees to being provided with accommodation[4]. The authority *must* accommodate any child of 16 years 'in need', whose welfare it considers 'is likely to be seriously prejudiced if they do not provide him with accommodation'[5], and it *may* provide accommodation for any child in its area if it considers that to do so 'would safeguard or promote the child's welfare'[6]. The purpose of these provisions is to cater for teenagers who have a seriously dysfunctional relationship with their parents[7]. The local authority's duty is a very restricted one, although it retains a wider *discretion*. The reason why the local authority's duty is so restricted is not entirely clear, but it may serve as a controlling mechanism for those local authorities which might otherwise be swamped by demands for accommodation from homeless young people in this age group. Again, the relationship between this provision, social security provision and the

---

1   As to which, see Chapters 11 and 12 below.
2   The status of foster-parents is discussed in Chapter 6 above.
3   House of Lords, Official Report, 20 December 1988, col 1335.
4   Section 20(11).
5   Section 20(3).
6   Section 20(4). This applies even though a person with parental responsibility for the child is able to provide him with accommodation.
7   A matter which hit the headlines in October/November 1992 with a string of cases in which children were seeking orders to live elsewhere from their parents. This phenomenon is discussed in Chapter 13 below. See also M Freeman 'Can Children Divorce Their Parents?' in *The Moral Status of Children* (Martinus Nijhoff, 1997) at ch 11.

statutory responsibilities of housing authorities is a politically sensitive one[1]. The legislation does not deal expressly with the issue of a child leaving accommodation but, since the local authority will have no statutory basis on which to retain a 16- or 17-year-old child against his wishes[2], the implication is that the child can discharge himself. The local authority will then have statutory duties to advise and assist that child.

These provisions fell for interpretation in *Re T (Accommodation by Local Authority)*[3]. Here, a 17-year-old girl had been accommodated informally by friends, Mr and Mrs B. She wished to be formally accommodated under s 20, since Mr and Mrs B would, in that event, be eligible for fostering allowances and she herself would be entitled to receive ongoing support from the local authority under s 24 of the Children Act which might otherwise terminate at the age of 18. The director of social services refused to accommodate T, despite a successful complaint by her to the authority's complaints review panel, taking the view that her welfare was not likely to be seriously prejudiced if she was not accommodated. Johnson J quashed this decision in judicial review proceedings. Although it was for the authority and not the court to judge the facts, the director of social services had erred in taking insufficient account of T's *future* needs and in attaching too much weight to its discretionary powers to offer assistance under s 17 of the Act. At the time of taking the decision, the director of social services could not have been sure that the local authority would continue to exercise its supportive discretionary powers.

Provision for children under 16 years of age

The position is less clear where the child is under 16 years of age, since, here, difficult questions arise surrounding the relationship between the wishes of 'competent' minors, parental responsibility and dealings with third parties (in this case social services) which have caused such consternation in other areas[4]. It could be argued that a '*Gillick*-competent' child should have the decisive say. Eekelaar and Dingwall have speculated that parents might lose the legal power to direct where the competent child is to live[5]. This argument probably takes insufficient account of the effect of relevant statutory provisions. It should be remembered that the '*Gillick* principle' must always be subject to express statutory provisions. The most relevant one here states that the local authority, before providing accommodation, shall:

> 'so far as is reasonably practicable and consistent with the child's welfare –
> (a)   ascertain the child's wishes regarding the provision of accommodation; and
> (b)   give due consideration (having regard to his age and understanding) to such wishes of the child as they have been able to ascertain.'[6]

This would appear to fall short of giving the competent child the exclusive right to decide, and it also has to be set against the more concrete parental right of

---

1   But note that housing authorities are required to co-operate with social services under s 27.
2   Neither may the authority make the young person a ward of court for this purpose, s 100(2) effectively reversing the decision in *Re SW (Wardship: Jurisdiction)* [1986] 1 FLR 24.
3   [1995] 1 FLR 159.
4   Most particularly in relation to medical issues. See Chapter 8 above.
5   J Eekelaar and R Dingwall *The Reform of Child Care Law* (Routledge, 1990) at p 78.
6   Section 20(6).

objection. The result seems to be that, where a parent is objecting to the proposed arrangement, the child's wishes cannot prevail, and the local authority would need a court order to accommodate the child. Most obviously, this could be sought where the child is alleging physical or sexual abuse. The converse position is more doubtful, ie where the parents want the child to be accommodated and the child is objecting. Here, the local authority will have to balance the views of parents and child and form its own judgment on whether its duty to accommodate has arisen. The Children Act does not, itself, attach greater weight to either view. The remaining issue is whether a competent child under 16 years of age could discharge himself from accommodation or insist on remaining there. There is a precedent, under the old law, which suggests that the local authority might not be obliged to return an objecting teenager[1]. Freeman discusses whether this might be a case in which the local authority could apply for leave to invoke the inherent jurisdiction of the High Court[2] or, alternatively, to seek a care order on the basis that the child is beyond parental control[3]. The parent's statutory right of removal would seem to prevail, short of compulsory action like this, but the argument for giving greater weight to the child's view is perhaps stronger where the child is already out of the family home than where he is still there. The teenager in local authority accommodation already has a kind of semi-independence.

The use of secure accommodation

In certain circumstances the local authority may wish to make use of secure accommodation in relation to children in its care. Always controversial, the practice must now comply not only with the procedural safeguards of the Children Act 1989 but also with human rights requirements[4].

'Secure accommodation' is defined under the Children Act to mean 'accommodation provided for the purpose of restricting liberty'[5]. The legislation provides that 'a child who is being looked after by a local authority may not be placed and, if placed, may not be kept' in such accommodation:

> 'unless it appears –
> (a) that –

1　*Krishnan v Sutton London Borough Council* [1969] 3 All ER 1367, where the court refused to order the return of a 17-year-old girl, against her wishes, to her father. There would seem to be no reason in principle why, with the current state of the law, this principle could not be applied to significantly younger children.

2　Under s 100(3).

3　Under s 31(2). See MDA Freeman *Children, Their Families and the Law* (Macmillan, 1992) at pp 68–69.

4　The regime under the Children Act is described in depth in R White, P Carr and N Lowe *The Children Act in Practice* (3rd edn) (Butterworths, 2002) ch 9. See also C Smith 'Secure Accommodation' [1995] Fam Law 369; P Bates 'Secure Accommodation – In Whose Interests?' [1995] CFLQ 70; and J Butler and S Hardy 'Secure Accommodation and Welfare' [1997] Fam Law 425. More recently, see A Perry 'Approaches to the Human Rights Act 1998 in Family Law Cases' (2001) *Wales Law Journal* 161, especially at pp 162–166, which considers the human rights implications, M Parry 'Secure Accommodation – the Cinderella of Family Law' [2000] CFLQ 101, and J Fortin 'Children's Rights and Physical Force' [2001] CFLQ 243. Among the earlier reported cases under the Children Act regime, see *Re W (A Minor) (Secure Accommodation Order)* [1995] 1 FLR 692, *Re M (Secure Accommodation Order)* [1995] 1 FLR 418 and *Re D (Secure Accommodation Order) (No 1)* [1997] 1 FLR 197.

5　Section 25(1).

(i) he has a history of absconding and is likely to abscond from any other description of accommodation and;

(ii) if he absconds, he is likely to suffer significant harm; or

(b) that if he is kept in any other description of accommodation, he is likely to injure himself or other persons.'

Regulations[1] prescribe a maximum period beyond which a child may not be kept in secure accommodation without the authorisation of a court. These provide that detention for up to 72 hours in a period of 28 days does not require court approval but anything in excess of this does. The court has power under the regulations[2] to authorise the use of such accommodation for up to three months initially, with extensions of up to six months on a renewal application. Any use of secure accommodation must be necessary and proportionate to a legitimate aim if it is to comply with the ECHR.

In *Re K (Secure Accommodation: Right to Liberty)*[3] an attempt was made to argue that the Children Act regime was incompatible with Article 5 of the ECHR. This provides that everyone has the right to liberty and security of the person. No one may be deprived of this except in the cases specified in the Article and in accordance with a procedure prescribed by law. The fourth of these prescribed cases is in relation to 'the detention of a minor by lawful order for the purpose of educational supervision or his lawful detention for the purpose of bringing him before the competent legal authority'[4].

In *Re K* the child in question had a long history of destructive, aggressive and sexualised behaviour involving fire-setting and sexual assaults. At the age of 11 he was diagnosed as having hyperkinetic conduct disorder and was described as presenting a serious risk to himself and others. He was placed in a secure unit and remained there under a series of secure accommodation orders.

The Court of Appeal rejected the incompatibility argument. The use of secure accommodation did amount to a deprivation of liberty but was justified as detention by lawful order for the purpose of educational supervision within the meaning of the above exception. The court held that 'educational supervision' for the purposes of the ECHR was not to be equated rigidly with the notion of classroom teaching but, especially in the care context, should embrace many aspects of the exercise by the local authority of parental rights for the benefit and protection of the child concerned. It would be a breach of the Convention for the authority to use such an order without providing any educational supervision, but s 25 was not incompatible with the Convention merely because it did not itself mention educational supervision. Thorpe LJ dissented, holding that the use of secure accommodation orders could not be justified on welfare grounds on the basis that the deprivation of liberty was a necessary consequence of an exercise of parental responsibility for the protection and promotion of the boy's welfare. In any event, the clear ruling of the whole court was that the statutory regime was compatible with Convention rights.

Involving as it does the deprivation of liberty, a secure accommodation order is a Draconian order. An application for such an order does not involve a criminal

---

1 Principally the Children (Secure Accommodation) Regulations 1991, SI 1991/1505, as amended under s 25(2).

2 Regulations 11 and 12.

3 [2001] 1 FLR 526.

4 Article 5(1)(d).

charge within the meaning of Article 6(2) and (3) of the ECHR but, in view of the gravity of the application, it has been held by the Court of Appeal[1] that the child should be afforded the five minimum procedural rights in Article 6(3) which are given to those facing criminal charges. These rights are:

(a) to be informed promptly, in a language which he understands and in detail, of the nature and cause of the accusation against him;
(b) to have adequate time and facilities for the preparation of his defence;
(c) to defend himself in person or through legal assistance of his own choosing or, if he has not sufficient means to pay for legal assistance, to be given it free when the interests of justice so require;
(d) to examine or have examined witnesses against him and to obtain the attendance and examination of witnesses on his behalf under the same conditions as witnesses against him;
(e) to have free assistance of an interpreter if he cannot understand or speak the language used in court.

These rights were found not to have been violated in *Re C*, despite the fact that C's new solicitor was informed of the application for a secure accommodation order only on arrival at court. The Court of Appeal took the view that there was an imperative need to protect C, a 15-year-old girl, from herself. She was a heroin and crack cocaine user, and medical problems had resulted from her use of dirty needles. In the circumstances a secure accommodation order was the only management realistically open to the court and the local authority, although with hindsight it was regrettable that there had not been an adjournment for a few days to give C a full opportunity to respond to the application.

Section 25 proceedings are also 'specified proceedings' within the meaning of s 41 of the Children Act 1989[2] and, as such, it will invariably be necessary to appoint a children's guardian in order to safeguard the child's interests.

POWERS AND DUTIES OF LOCAL AUTHORITIES TO CHILDREN LOOKED AFTER BY THEM

The powers and duties which local authorities exercise over children 'looked after' by them are derived in part from the legislation and in part from the agreements made with parents and others with parental responsibility. The expression 'looked after' includes children who are 'in care' and also those 'accommodated' under voluntary arrangements[3], provided that the accommodation is for more than 24 hours[4]. Yet there is a crucial legal distinction between these two groups. Whereas the local authority acquires parental responsibility (albeit shared with parents) over children in care[5], it does not acquire it where

---

1 *Re C (Secure Accommodation Order: Representation)* [2001] 2 FLR 169.
2 See Chapter 13 below.
3 Section 22(1) is in fact somewhat wider than this since it embraces all children 'provided with accommodation by the authority in the exercise of any functions ... which stand referred to their social services committee under the Local Authority Social Services Act 1970' apart from functions under ss 23B and 24B (discussed below).
4 Section 22(2).
5 Section 33(3)(a), discussed in Chapter 11 below.

the children are merely 'accommodated'. Here, it depends for its powers, substantially, on the agreements reached with parents, although some powers are necessarily implied from the existence of its statutory duties. Where the child is in care, the local authority is *not* dependent on parental delegation of responsibility since it has this under the care order. Yet the statutory duties owed to each category of children are broadly similar, as they were under previous legislation[1].

Agreements

The powers which local authorities have by implication from their statutory duties and as a de facto carer are limited and do not, of themselves, provide them with adequate latitude in making their plans. Accordingly, it is vitally important that provision be made for such matters as placement, medical care and schooling. It is now a statutory requirement that local authorities should draw up a written plan for the child and should reach agreement on this with the parents, other persons with parental responsibility, or, where there is no one with parental responsibility, the person caring for the child[2]. Before placing the child, the authority must, so far as is reasonably practicable, make immediate and long-term arrangements for the placement and for promoting the welfare of the child. These agreements are not binding contracts and are not therefore enforceable. To have given them the force of law would, it was thought, have been to detract unacceptably from the voluntary principle.

The regulations and guidance made under the legislation go into considerable detail about what should be incorporated in these agreements[3]. Although each agreement is peculiar to the particular arrangement, most local authorities adopt standard form agreements. Indeed, to do otherwise might lead to unacceptable confusion about the extent of the local authority's powers in relation to different children and equally unacceptable variations in their treatment. The matters over which agreement should be reached include the type of accommodation; the respective responsibilities of the local authority, the parents, the child and others; the services to be provided; contact; the projected length of stay, and the procedure for terminating the arrangements and rehabilitating the child with his family; health and educational considerations[4]. The local authority must produce written copies of the agreement and must provide a copy to everyone with whom the agreement is made, and to the child, in understandable form[5]. The essence of these agreements is that the local authority and the parents should work together for the benefit of the child and this is further underscored by the statutory duties owed to all children looked after by the local authority.

---

1 Child Care Act 1980.
2 Arrangements for Placement of Children (General) Regulations 1991, SI 1991/890, reg 3.
3 *The Children Act 1989 Guidance and Regulations Vol 3 Family Placements* (HMSO, 1991) at paras 2.13 et seq.
4 Arrangements for Placement of Children (General) Regulations 1991, reg 4 and Schs 2, 3 and 4.
5 Ibid, reg 5(3).

Statutory duties

The general duty

The general duty which local authorities owed to children in their care used to be contained in s 18(1) of the Child Care Act 1980[1]. This was substantially recast in the Children Act which provides:

> 'It shall be the duty of a local authority looking after any child –
> (a) to safeguard and promote his welfare; and
> (b) to make such use of services available for children cared for by their own parents as appears to the authority reasonable in his case.'[2]

The former duty under the Child Care Act 1980 expressed the child's welfare to be the 'first consideration' for the local authority[3]. The effect of this formula was thought to be that, although the interests of the child were not the local authority's sole or paramount consideration, they were to receive priority over other competing interests. Under the old law, this was relied on successfully in a number of judicial challenges to the closure of children's homes where the relevant local authorities had failed to give first consideration to the welfare of the individual children affected[4]. While the point is not free from doubt, it would seem that the former duty has been diluted and that similar challenges might fail under the new law[5].

It is not clear how far the local authority's general duty to safeguard and promote the child's welfare is qualified by other considerations, particularly those of administrative convenience. The local authority may have to balance the interests of particular children against those of other children or other potential clients, especially given the pressure of finite resources. One way in which the general duty is certainly limited is that the local authority is permitted to act inconsistently with it where it thinks it is necessary 'for the purposes of protecting members of the public from serious injury'[6]. The Secretary of State may also direct the local authority to act inconsistently and the local authority must comply[7]. It might be necessary, in such a case, to contemplate the use of secure accommodation[8]. Along with the issue of contact with children in care, the use of secure accommodation is unusual in being one type of decision by local authorities which is subject to judicial scrutiny on its merits[9].

---

1   This provided that: 'In reaching any decision relating to a child in their care, a local authority shall give first consideration to the need to safeguard and promote the welfare of the child throughout his childhood ...'.

2   Section 22(3).

3   On the gradations of relevance of children's welfare in different legal contexts, see Chapter 2 above.

4   See, for example, *Liddle v Sunderland Borough Council* (1983) Fam Law 250; *R v Solihull Metropolitan Borough Council ex parte C* [1984] FLR 363; and *R v Avon County Council ex parte K* [1986] 1 FLR 443.

5   Freeman takes the view that the argument, once accepted in *AG v Hammersmith and Fulham London Borough Council* (1979) *The Times*, December 18, that the authority is entitled to consider a child's welfare *after* it has taken a decision to close a home, may again be tenable.

6   Section 22(6).

7   Section 22(7) and (8).

8   Discussed above.

9   This kind of ordinary access to the courts should be contrasted with the more restricted mechanism of judicial review.

Specific duties

Many specific duties are imposed by the legislation. Some are contained in the body of the Children Act, while others are set out in Part II of Sch 2. We discuss below some of the more important specific duties.

The duty to consult

The Children Act made much wider provision for consultation than was the case before it. It states:

'Before making any decision with respect to a child whom they are looking after, or proposing to look after, a local authority shall, so far as is reasonably practicable, ascertain the wishes and feelings of –

(a)   the child;

(b)   his parents;

(c)   any person who is not a parent of his but who has parental responsibility for him; and

(d)   any other person whose wishes and feelings the authority consider to be relevant, regarding the matter to be decided.'[1]

The nature of this duty of consultation came before the courts in *Re P (Children Act 1989, ss 22 and 26: Local Authority Compliance)*[2]. Here the father was in prison having been convicted of rape and buggery of the mother and indecent assault on a child. He continued to represent a significant risk to the children, and the issue arose as to whether the local authority was obliged to continue to consult the father about matters of upbringing and decision-making processes relating to the four children. The children were the subject of care orders and the mother had agreed to care plans which involved their long-term placement outside the family. The father had participated in those care proceedings, but the authority now wished to cut him out of the future decision-making process except to the limited extent of providing him with a basic annual report on the children's general well-being and telling him of any emergencies.

Charles J held that the authority was entitled to follow this course. Its duties of consultation were *directory* rather than mandatory, in the sense that any failure to consult as required would be treated as an irregularity rather than rendering its decisions void. In complying with its duties the authority was entitled to have regard to s 33(3)(b) of the Children Act[3] which allowed it to determine the extent to which a parent could meet his responsibility and also to the case-law under s 91(14)[4] which involved excluding or limiting a parental right. In this case, because of the continuing risk which the father represented, restricted consultation was justified which would be backed up by an order under s 91(14).

This was an exceptional case and should not detract from the central requirement that, in the overwhelming majority of cases, the statutory scheme requires full and continuing consultation.

The local authority must then, after consulting, go on to give 'due consideration' to the views of those consulted, in the case of a child, commensurate with his age and understanding[5]. It must also, in making its decision, give due considera-

---

1   Section 22(4). It was established in *R v North Yorkshire County Council ex parte M* [1989] 1 All ER 143 that where the child has a guardian ad litem (now children's guardian) he should be consulted.

2   [2000] 2 FLR 910.

3   See Chapter 11 below.

4   See Chapter 4 above.

5   Section 22(5)(a) and (b).

tion to the child's 'religious persuasion, racial origin and cultural and linguistic background'[1], a recurrent theme in the legislation[2]. These considerations are probably of greatest relevance to the question of placement. They suggest that, all other things being equal, efforts should be directed to placing children in families of similar race, culture and linguistic background. But clearly this is only a guideline and there will be some instances in which this would be undesirable or impossible having regard to the overriding consideration of the child's welfare. If the only available foster-parents of similar cultural background are considered inappropriate, it may be necessary to place the child elsewhere.

There is no indication in the legislation of the relative weight to be attached to individual views where these conflict, and this must be a matter for the local authority's discretion.

The duty to provide accommodation

The options open to the local authority for accommodating a child who is looked after by the authority are set out in the legislation[3]. They are, to place him with a family, relative or other suitable person (foster-parents), community home, voluntary home, registered children's home, home with special facilities, appropriate children's home or by making such other arrangements as seem appropriate to the authority and which comply with any regulations made by the Secretary of State. The legal regulation of these various placements is considered below.

An important option is to allow the child to remain at home, possibly subject to supervision. The local authority's general rehabilitative objective militates towards this solution but there is always the counter-pressure of adequately protecting the child's welfare[4]. Several provisions in the Children Act reflect these considerations. On the one hand, there is a primary duty to make arrangements for the child to live with his family, unless to do so would not be reasonably practicable or consistent with his welfare[5]. There is a similar duty that accommodation which is not with the family should be near the child's home, and that siblings, who are looked after by the local authority, should be accommodated together[6]. On the other hand, there are regulations[7] which ensure that there are sufficient safeguards where a child is allowed 'home on trial'[8]. The

---

1 Section 22(5)(c).

2 There is a particularly useful discussion of these considerations in MDA Freeman (above) at pp 73–77 and, more generally, on cultural considerations in the context of children's rights, see M Freeman 'Children's Rights and Cultural Pluralism' in *The Moral Status of Children* (Martinus Nijhoff, 1997) at ch 7.

3 Section 23(2).

4 Chapter 11 below discusses these counter-pressures.

5 Section 23(6).

6 Section 23(7).

7 Section 23(5) and Sch 2, para 14, and the Placement of Children with Parents etc Regulations 1991, SI 1991/893, as amended. Under s 23(5A) (inserted by the Courts and Legal Services Act 1990) the regulations apply only where the child lives with the relevant person for a continuous period of more than 24 hours.

8 These provisions are the successors of the Children and Young Persons (Amendment) Act 1986, which legislation was inspired by public anxiety over the deaths of certain children at the hands of parents and others, most notably that of Jasmine Beckford. See *A Child in Trust: Report of the Panel of Inquiry Investigating the Circumstances Surrounding the Death of Jasmine Beckford* (London Borough of Brent, 1985).

regulations govern such matters as notification, consultation, medical and other supervision.

The duty to maintain

The local authority is required to maintain a child looked after by it[1] but may, in certain circumstances, recoup some of the cost by requiring a financial contribution to the child's maintenance or services provided for him from certain other persons[2]. The local authority must charge only what is reasonable, given the financial means of the recipients of the service, but those on the principal means-tested social security benefits are exempt[3]. Contributions towards maintenance are governed by a separate code[4]. These charges have always been controversial and the Children Act brought about a change of emphasis whereby local authorities are required to charge only where they consider it reasonable to do so[5].

The duty to promote contact

Consistent with the primary emphasis on reunification in the legislation, local authorities are required to endeavour to promote contact, so far as is reasonably practicable and consistent with his welfare, between the child, his family, relatives, friends and others connected with him[6]. To this end, the local authority and persons with parental responsibility are obliged to stay in touch with each other. The local authority must take steps to keep them informed of the child's whereabouts and they must keep the local authority informed of their respective addresses[7]. Local authorities must also co-operate among themselves where a child moves into a different area[8].

Other powers and duties

Other powers and duties are set out in Part II of Sch 2 to the Children Act. They include assistance with travelling expenses where visits are made to children in care, the appointment of independent visitors where visits by the family have become very infrequent, assistance in arrangements for the child to live outside England and Wales (subject to significant safeguards), and arrangements for the funeral of a child who dies while being looked after by the local authority.

---

1 Section 23(1)(b).
2 Section 29. Those who may be liable are the child's parents, a child over 16 years of age himself, and, where the service is provided for a member of the child's family, that person (s 29(4)). For the correct approach in assessing a parent's contribution, see *Re C (A Minor) (Contribution Notice)* [1994] 1 FLR 111.
3 Section 29(3) and (3A). This will be likely to be a high proportion, given the close association between poverty and care.
4 Section 29(6) and Sch 2, Part III.
5 Schedule 2, para 21(2).
6 Schedule 2, para 15, which should be read with ss 17(1) and 23(6). Taken together they add up to a strong duty to endeavour to reunite the child with the family – something which, as we have seen, is required by the ECHR.
7 Schedule 2, para 15(2).
8 Section 20(2) and Sch 2, para 15(3) and (4).

Duties to children leaving accommodation and after-care

The Children Act substantially increased the duties of local authorities towards children ceasing to be looked after by them up to the age of 21 years[1]. The purpose was to assist these often vulnerable young people in making the difficult transition to independent living in the community. It was recognised that many of them would have no family on which to rely for support. These duties have been greatly increased by amendments to the Children Act 1989 brought about by the Children (Leaving Care) Act 2000. That Act followed a consultation document published in 1999[2] and reflects the view that far too little was still being done for young people leaving care. The amendments extend the duties of local authorities by requiring them to assess and meet the care and support needs of *eligible* and *relevant* children and young people and to assist *former relevant children*, in particular in relation to their employment, education and training[3]. The legislation is mainly concerned with those over the age of 16 and imposes obligations to support them up to the age of 21 at the level required for the different categories defined in the legislation.

Eligible children are those who are currently being looked after by a local authority and have been so looked after for a period prescribed by regulations[4]. The intention is to exclude certain groups for whom the package of support envisaged by the legislation would be inappropriate, such as those who normally live at home with their families and have been looked after only for short periods of respite care to give their families a break[5]. The authority must for each eligible child carry out an assessment of his needs with a view to determining what advice, assistance and support it would be appropriate for it to provide:

(a) while it is still looking after him, and
(b) after it ceases to look after him[6].

Relevant children[7] are those aged 16 or 17 who meet the criteria for eligible children, but who leave local authority accommodation and cease to be looked after children. *Former relevant children*[8] are those who, before reaching the age of 18, were either eligible or relevant children.

In the case of all three groups, the key obligations on the authority are to appoint a personal adviser[9] for the young person concerned and, with the assistance of the personal adviser, to draw up a Pathway Plan for him or her[10]. The

---

1 Following the recommendations in the DHSS *Review of Child Care Law* (1985) at ch 10; and see generally L Jordan 'Accommodation and Aftercare: Provision for Young People' (1992) 4 JCL 162.
2 *Me, Survive, Out There? – New Arrangements for Young People Living in and Leaving Care* (July 1999).
3 Explanatory notes to the Children (Leaving Care) Act 2000. For judicial examination of these terms see the decision of Sullivan J in *R (Berhe) v Hillingdon London Borough Council* [2004] 1 FLR 439.
4 The Children (Leaving Care) (England) Regulations 2001, SI 2001/2874. Regulations 3 and 4 prescribe that the young person must have been looked after since the age of 14 for a period or periods amounting to 13 weeks ending after the child attained the age of 16.
5 Explanatory notes to the Children (Leaving Care) Act 2000, para 20.
6 Children Act 1989, Sch 2, para 19B.
7 Ibid, s 23A.
8 Ibid, s 23C.
9 Ibid, s 23D.
10 Ibid, s 23E.

details of what is required by the Pathway Plan are set out in regulations[1]. The Plan must be in writing and must set out:

(a) the manner in which the responsible authority proposes to meet the needs of the child and

(b) the date by which, and by whom, any action required to implement the Plan will be carried out.

There are several other instances in child care practice in which plans must be made for children. These include: a 'Children in Need plan' which is made at the conclusion of a core assessment involving the child and family members and the contribution of all relevant agencies; a 'Child Protection plan', which is the decision of an inter-agency child protection conference following enquiries and assessment under s 47[2]; a 'Care Plan for a Child Looked After', which is the result of an assessment that a child will need to be looked after either in the short term or long term and placed in foster or residential care; and, finally, a 'Care Plan' for a child who is the subject of a care or supervision order or for whom the plan is adoption[3]. A general principle in relation to all of these plans is that, wherever possible, they should be drawn up in agreement with the child or young person and key family members and that the commitment of them all to the plan should have been secured[4].

In addition to assisting with the drawing up of the Pathway Plan, the personal adviser must stay in touch with the young person until he or she attains 21 and must ensure the implementation of the Pathway Plan as modified to meet the child's shifting needs.

Young persons qualifying for advice and assistance

A wider category of young persons qualify to receive advice and assistance from local authorities. First, it should be noted that local authorities have a general duty to a child being looked after by them to 'advise, assist and befriend him with a view to promoting his welfare, when they have ceased to look after him'[5]. Secondly, the Children Act imposed additional duties towards young people who are under 21, but who were, while 16 or 17, looked after by a local authority, accommodated by a voluntary organisation or fostered. These duties are to be found in s 24, as amended by the Children (Leaving Care) Act 2000. The essential duty is to advise, befriend and assist such young people and help certain of them with education, employment and training[6].

Consistent with the growth of complaints procedures elsewhere in child care law, the local authority is obliged to establish a procedure for considering representations, including complaints, made by young persons in all the

---

1 Children (Leaving Care) (England) Regulations 2001, SI 2001/2874, reg 8 and Schedule.
2 See Chapter 11 below.
3 Ibid.
4 For further discussion of the principles applying to the various plans, see Department of Health *Framework for the Assessment of Children in Need and their Families* (2000) at paras 4.32–4.37.
5 Originally in the Children Act 1989, s 24, this duty is now to be found in Sch 2, para 19A.
6 The details are beyond the scope of the present work, but are contained in ibid, ss 24, 24A, 24B and 24C.

qualifying categories about the discharge of its functions under this part of the legislation[1].

LEGAL REGULATION OF SUBSTITUTE CARE ARRANGEMENTS

The background

The Children Act 1989 contained a mass of detail on regulating the different kinds of substitute care for children, and a large amount of delegated legislation was introduced under its enabling powers[2]. Much of the framework in Parts VI to XI and some of Part XII still remains, but it has been heavily amended, and to some extent repealed, by the Care Standards Act 2000 and the regulations introduced by that legislation[3]. Much of what was originally in the Children Act was a consolidation of previous law[4]. In general, this section is concerned with the many different kinds of arrangements for looking after children who are living away from home which include residential care, fostering arrangements, child-minding and day-care provision. The major change which has occurred as a result of the Care Standards Act 2000 is a substantial shifting of responsibility for monitoring and supervising these arrangements from local authorities to a new National Care Standards Commission and, in the case of child-minding and day-care, to Her Majesty's Chief Inspector of Schools. That is the position in England. In Wales the transfer of responsibility is largely to a new arm of the National Assembly for Wales.

The Care Standards Act 2000

This Act[5], which received the Royal Assent on 20 July 2000, has as its principal aim the reform of the regulatory system for care services in England and Wales. As such, it is concerned with care services and residential establishments generally and not just those in which children live. Much of what the Act is concerned with is therefore beyond the scope of this work, but an attempt will be made to draw out its salient features as they affect children and the principal changes which the Act has made to the scheme under the Children Act.

Part I of the Act establishes an independent National Care Standards Commission to perform the regulatory function and, in Wales, the National Assembly is established as the equivalent registration authority. These registration authorities are given power in Part II of the Act to issue *national minimum standards*

---

1 Ibid, s 24D.
2 For a detailed discussion of the scheme under the Children Act, see MDA Freeman *Children, Their Families and the Law* (Macmillan, 1992) at ch 9.
3 Most importantly, perhaps, the Children's Homes Regulations 2001, SI 2001/3967.
4 The law before the Children Act was extensively reviewed in MDA Freeman and C Lyon *The Law of Residential Homes and Day Care Establishments* (Sweet & Maxwell, 1984). On the law after the Children Act, see A Bainham *Children: The New Law* (Family Law, 1990) at ch 7 and *The Children Act 1989 Guidance and Regulations Vol 4* (HMSO, 1991).
5 The Act itself and the most important primary and delegated legislation affecting care services are brought together in one place in D Pearl and D Hershman *The Care Standards Legislation Handbook* (Jordans, 2002). See also P Ridout (ed) *Care Standards: A Practical Guide* (Jordans, 2003).

applicable to all services and to which registration authorities and providers must have regard. These arrangements replace the provisions in the Children Act which dealt with the registration of voluntary homes and registered children's homes and regulate community homes for the first time. Voluntary adoption societies fall within the Act, and local authority fostering and adoption services are subject to inspection. The welfare arrangements in all boarding schools and further education colleges which accommodate children are within the Act[1]. The Act's tentacles therefore stretch a long way, and one of its main purposes is to bring the regulation of a wide range of children's services under one regime and to seek to achieve some consistency in the minimum standards of these services.

Children's homes

The Children Act divides children's homes into three categories – community homes, voluntary homes and registered children's homes.

Community homes[2] are further sub-divided. There are 'maintained community homes' which are homes provided and financed by local authorities, 'controlled' and 'assisted' community homes. These are homes provided by voluntary organisations and differ only in the extent to which the local authority is directly involved in their management. Community homes under the Children Act were subject to inspection by the local authority but not to the registration requirements which applied to voluntary homes and registered children's homes.

Voluntary homes[3] were under the Children Act registered with the Secretary of State. They are established and managed by voluntary organisations and the Children Act spells out the general duties of voluntary organisations, to children looked after by them[4].

Registered children's homes were required to register with the local authority[5]. They are now required to register with the Secretary of State. These homes are essentially private homes, set up by individuals and run for profit, and were largely unregulated before the Children Act[6]. The Children Act contains provisions regarding the conduct and management of registered homes and the duties of those persons carrying on or in charge of registered homes[7]. Small private children's homes which accommodate fewer then four children were not required to register and were not inspected. As an interim measure, s 40 of the Care Standards Act 2000 amended the Children Act to require such homes also to register with the local authority pending the establishment of the new regulatory regime under that Act.

The Care Standards Act 2000 now seeks to introduce some uniformity in place of these fragmented regulatory mechanisms by establishing a broad definition of a 'children's home' as an establishment which 'provides care and accommodation wholly or mainly for children'[8]. This definition catches all the categories of home

---

1 See the explanatory notes to the Care Standards Act 2000.
2 Children Act 1989, Part VI and Sch 4.
3 Ibid, s 60(1).
4 Ibid, s 61.
5 Ibid, s 63(1).
6 The Children's Homes Act 1982 did regulate these homes, but the legislation was never implemented.
7 Children Act 1989, Sch 6, Part II.
8 Care Standards Act 2000, s 1(2).

under the Children Act, as well as homes for disabled children. The Act excludes from the definition an establishment where 'a child is cared for and accommodated there by a parent or relative of his or by a foster parent'[1]. Also excluded from the definition are health service hospitals, independent hospitals and clinics, residential family centres and any other exceptions introduced by regulations[2]. On the other hand, it is made explicit that any school which provides accommodation for more than 295 days a year for any individual child must register as a children's home[3].

All children's homes within this definition are now governed by the Children's Homes Regulations 2001[4] and must comply with the national minimum standards produced under the Act and those regulations[5]. Registration with the new registration authorities is mandatory[6] and will be allowed only where that authority is satisfied that the applicant has complied with all relevant requirements in the legislation[7]. Registration may also be cancelled where there has been a failure to comply with the conditions of registration[8]. There is a right of appeal to the Care Standards Tribunal against the refusal to register or cancellation of registration[9].

The Children's Homes Regulations 2001 govern the conduct of children's homes and provide for such matters as the fitness of the registered provider and manager of the home; adequate staffing levels; the fitness of the premises used including suitable and proper equipment and furniture; dietary standards; provision of clothing and pocket money; and inappropriate disciplinary or control management. The regulations also require the registered person, before accommodating a child in a children's home, or as soon as is reasonably practicable thereafter, to prepare a 'child placement plan'. This must set out in particular:

(a) how, on a day-to-day basis, the child will be cared for and his welfare safeguarded and promoted by the home;
(b) the arrangements made for his health and education; and
(c) any arrangements made for contact with his parents, relatives and friends[10].

Given the history of abuse in children's homes, highlighted particularly in the Waterhouse Report[11] which preceded the Care Standards Act and was a major influence on it, the regulations also require the registered person to prepare and implement a written policy which is intended to safeguard children accommodated in a children's home from abuse or neglect and which sets out the procedure to be followed in the event of any such allegation[12]. As noted above,

---

1   Care Standards Act 2000, s 1(3).
2   Ibid, s 1(4).
3   Ibid, s 1(6).
4   SI 2001/3967.
5   Care Standards Act 2000, ss 22 and 23.
6   Ibid, ss 11 and 12.
7   Ibid, s 13.
8   Ibid, s 14.
9   Ibid, s 21.
10 Children's Homes Regulations 2001, reg 12.
11 *Lost in Care – The Report of the Tribunal of Inquiry into the abuse of children in care in the former county council areas of Gwynedd and Clwyd since 1974* (2000).
12 Children's Homes Regulations 2001, reg 16.

there are now published national minimum standards with which establishments must comply[1].

Concern largely arising from the abuse of children in residential establishments has also resulted in legislation under which lists are kept of those thought to be unsuitable to work with children. The principal legislation is the Protection of Children Act 1999[2]. This establishes a register of such persons. It brings together in one place, to produce a 'one stop shop', two previously separate lists of individuals. The first was the Department of Health's 'consultancy index list' which operated as a resource for identifying people unsuitable for employment with children in child care roles. The second was the Department of Education and Employment's so-called 'List 99' which existed on a statutory basis and which had wider criteria for inclusion, for example medical reasons or forms of misconduct other than ones which reflect on suitability for employment in child care positions[3]. The effect of inclusion in the list is that child care organisations, which are obliged to check the list before offering employment, may not offer employment to someone on it[4]. Since inclusion on the list is not dependent on criminal conviction it is especially important that there is a right of appeal to the Care Standards Tribunal[5]. The Care Standards Act 2000 amended the 1999 Act to modify its application to employment businesses and extend its scope to cover persons working in independent schools on the grounds of their unsuitability to work with children. Persons may now be referred to the list by the National Care Standards Commission or the National Assembly for Wales or following the result of an inquiry[6].

Fostering arrangements

The regulatory mechanisms are different as between local authority foster-parents and private foster-parents, yet the local authority has the key role in each case. The difference is that, in the case of local authority foster-parents, the local authority is, by definition, involved from the start, since it makes the arrangements, whereas it is not so involved where private arrangements are effected.

Local authority foster-placements
The definition of local authority foster-parent was noted earlier and the essential status involved was discussed[7]. In the context of increased concern over the standards of care in residential establishments, there has been an associated increase in the use of fostering as the preferred option in most cases. Private agencies are now employed by local authorities to recruit foster-parents, but the responsibility for ensuring the fitness of foster-parents and the welfare of the children looked after by them remains with the authorities. This chapter is

---

1 Standards 7 (Support to Individual Children), 8 (Quality of Care) and 22 (Behaviour Management) are helpfully extracted in B Hale, D Pearl, E Cooke and P Bates *The Family, Law and Society* (5th edn) (Butterworths, 2002) at pp 687–690.
2 See also the Sex Offenders Act 1997 under which those convicted or cautioned for certain sexual offences must keep the police informed of their current address.
3 See the explanatory notes to the Protection of Children Act 1999, paras 8 and 9.
4 Protection of Children Act 1999, s 7.
5 Ibid, s 4.
6 Ibid, ss 2A and 2B.
7 See Chapter 6 above.

concerned with the legal controls on the standard and quality of these placements[1]. These were governed by the Foster Placement (Children) Regulations 1991[2], but these regulations have been revoked and replaced by the Fostering Services Regulations 2002[3]. There are essentially two controlling mechanisms: the approval of the prospective foster-parent, and the *written placement agreement*. Approval may not be given unless the foster service provider[4] has carried out an assessment of the prospective foster-parent. It must obtain[5] references and detailed information concerning such matters as the age, health, personality and marital status of the applicant, particulars of the proposed accommodation, other members of the applicant's family, his religious persuasion, racial origin and cultural background, employment record, previous experience with children and so on. For these purposes the foster service provider must establish a fostering panel[6]. Having approved someone as a foster-parent, the responsible authority must enter into a written agreement with him, governing the detailed aspects of the relationship between local authority, foster-parent and child[7]. The agreement must regulate such matters as: the information to be provided by the local authority to foster-parents about the child's history to enable them to carry out their task; financial support; dental and medical treatment; living and visiting arrangements; contact with parents and others; and the foster-parent's undertaking to co-operate with the authority[8].

Fostering allowances are paid to all local authority foster-parents by the authority. Although the amount paid varies between authorities, the National Foster Care Association annually recommends a minimum fostering allowance which depends on the age of the child and whether the child lives in London or elsewhere. The weekly rates from April 2001 (for children outside London) were: for children aged under 5, £66.64; for those aged between 5 and 10, £82.77; for those aged between 11 and 15, £102.97; and for those aged 16 and over, £133.35. The regulations go on to provide that the approving authority should review at intervals of not more than one year whether the foster-carer and his household continue to be suitable. Where the authority is not so satisfied, the approval is terminated[9].

The regulations impose minimum visiting requirements and also govern such matters as revocation of a placement where it ceases to be suitable, immediate placements in emergencies, registration of children in local authority foster-care, and the maintenance of case records[10].

The fundamental obligation of the foster-parent is 'to care for any child placed with him as if the child were a member of the foster-parent's family and to promote his welfare having regard to the long and short-term plans for the

---

1   For a good general discussion, see MDA Freeman *Children, Their Families and the Law* (Macmillan, 1992), pp 79–85.

2   And see *The Children Act 1989 Guidance and Regulations Vol 3 Family Placements* (HMSO, 1991).

3   SI 2002/57.

4   The term includes the local authority's fostering service and fostering agencies.

5   Fostering Services Regulations 2002, reg 27 and Sch 3.

6   Ibid, reg 24.

7   Known as a 'foster placement agreement' (ibid, reg 34).

8   Ibid, Sch 6.

9   For an unsuccessful attempt by a foster-carer to challenge the authority's decision to terminate his approval as a foster-parent, see *R v Avon County Council ex parte Crabtree* [1996] 1 FLR 502.

10   See MDA Freeman (above) at pp 82 et seq.

child'[1]. The foster-parent is expressly prohibited from administering corporal punishment[2] and must comply with the terms of the foster placement agreement[3]. Most importantly, the foster-parent must undertake to allow the child to be removed from his or her home where the responsible authority considers that termination of the placement would be in the best interests of the child or that its continuation would be detrimental to the child's welfare[4].

Private foster-parents

Again, the definition of private foster-parent has already been discussed[5]. The local authority would not, in the ordinary course of events, have any knowledge of privately arranged placements and this could be a cause for concern. Hence, the chief regulatory mechanism is *notification* rather than registration. The statutory scheme is contained in Part IX of the Children Act together with the Children (Private Arrangements for Fostering) Regulations 1991[6].

A prominent feature of the scheme is the requirement that the local authority should satisfy itself as to the welfare of privately fostered children in its area[7] and, where it is not so satisfied, take further specified action[8]. The notification requirements were tightened significantly by the Children Act. They now extend to parents, persons with parental responsibility and those involved directly or indirectly in making arrangements, as well as the foster-parents themselves. Notification is now required both of the proposal to make the arrangement and of its subsequent cessation[9]. The other key element in the statutory scheme is the *disqualification* of unsuitable persons from private fostering[10]. Those persons who are disqualified include parents whose children have been in care and those convicted of criminal offences against children. The local authority may also prohibit the use of unsuitable premises for private fostering[11]. There is an appeals system, and the disqualification provisions are backed up by criminal offences[12].

---

1 Fostering Services Regulations 2002, Sch 5.
2 Ibid, Sch 5, para 8.
3 Ibid, Sch 5, para 10.
4 Ibid, Sch 5, para 15 and reg 36.
5 See Chapter 6 above.
6 Which replaced the Foster Children Act 1980. The limits on the numbers of foster-children who may be fostered are governed by Sch 7 to the Children Act and apply to children fostered by local authority foster-parents and voluntary organisations as well as those privately fostered.
7 Section 67(1). Under the Children (Private Arrangements for Fostering) Regulations 1991, SI 1991/2050, reg 2(2), the authority must satisfy itself in particular as to such matters as the intended purpose and duration of the arrangement, the child's development, financial arrangements, suitability of the accommodation, health, education, etc: in short, *all* matters relevant to the child's healthy development. Under the Children Bill 2004, the duties of local authorities will be extended to cases where a child is *proposed to be*, but is not yet, privately fostered. The amendment is designed to enable local authorities to carry out proper checks on, and satisfy themselves as to the suitability of, arrangements *before* a child is privately fostered. The Bill also gives the Secretary of State the power to establish through regulations a scheme for the registration of private foster-carers.
8 Section 67(5). It must essentially secure that the child's accommodation is taken over by a parent, person with parental responsibility or relative or, where that is not reasonably practicable, it must consider whether to exercise its functions under the legislation.
9 Children (Private Arrangements for Fostering) Regulations 1991, regs 4–7.
10 Disqualification from Caring for Children (England) Regulations 2002, SI 2002/635, and Disqualification from Caring for Children (Wales) Regulations 2004, SI 2004/2695.
11 Section 69(2)(b).
12 Section 70 and Sch 8, para 8.

Child-minding and day-care for young children

Child-minding and day-care were regulated by Part X of, and Sch 9 to, the
Children Act and regulations made under the Act[1]. These provisions replaced the
previous system of registration under the Nurseries and Child-Minders Regulation Act 1948, which was widely thought to be ineffective. *Registration* is the
essential regulatory mechanism[2]. A major change in the system of registration
introduced by the Children Act was to unify, in one register, all child-minders and
day-carers, where previously separate registers had been maintained for child-
minders and nurseries. The maximum age of children covered by the registration
requirements was unified at eight years. Thus, the system protected mainly
pre-school children but also older children who took part in out-of-school and
holiday activities. The aim of the scheme was to ensure compliance with adequate
standards and to empower the local authority to take action where those standards
were not achieved.

This system has now been replaced by a wholly new regime in Part XA of and
Sch 9A to the Children Act, as inserted by s 79 of the Care Standards Act 2000. The
principal change is that responsibility for the regulation of child-minding and
day-care provision is transferred from local authorities to Her Majesty's Chief
Inspector of Schools for England under a new arm of Ofsted which brings
together the regulation of child care and early years education[3]. In Wales the
regulatory functions are transferred to a new regulatory body for care services
established as part of the National Assembly for Wales. The other significant
change is that regulation in both England and Wales is to be carried out in
accordance with new national standards[4]. All 'registered persons' who act as
child-minders or day-care providers are required to comply with these standards[5].
In other respects, the main features of the regulations are similar to those which
existed under local authority regulation and we therefore refer below to some of
the case-law which arose under the previous regulatory regime. The discussion
below considers only the position in England.

Who must register?

The Chief Inspector is required to keep a register of child-minders and day-care
providers[6]. The distinction is between those who look after children on 'domestic
premises' (child-minders) and those who look after them on 'non-domestic
premises' (day-carers)[7]. The key trigger condition for registration is that the child
should be looked after by someone who is not a parent or relative, or a person with
parental responsibility or a foster-parent, for reward, for more than

---

1   Child Minding and Day Care (Applications for Registration) Regulations 1991, SI 1991/1689;
    Child Minding and Day Care (Registration and Inspection Fees) Regulations 1991,
    SI 1991/2076.
2   Children Act 1989, ss 79A–79X.
3   See Care Standards Act 2000, explanatory notes at para 11. Minor changes to the regime will be
    made by the Children Bill 2004.
4   See the Day Care and Child Minding (National Standards) (England) Regulations 2001,
    SI 2001/1828, and the Child Minding and Day Care (Wales) Regulations 2002, SI 2002/812.
5   See reg 3(2) of the English Regulations.
6   CA 1989, s 79D.
7   Ibid, s 79A(2) and (6).

two hours in any day[1]. 'Nannies' are not child-minders and are not required to register unless they work for more than two employers[2]. There is also an 'occasional facilities' exemption where day-care is provided on any premises for less than six days per year, provided appropriate notice of their use is given to the local authority[3]. Occasional unregistered carers such as baby-sitters, although technically in breach of the regulations, are unlikely to receive enforcement notices[4].

Refusal or cancellation of registrations

The age-limit of eight years for children covered by the registration requirements was a compromise, designed to protect some younger school children but not to be set so high as to prevent any reasonable chance of enforcement. The registration authority may refuse registration on the grounds that the applicant or the premises in question are unfit[5]. There are disqualifications similar to those which apply to private foster-parents[6].

In *London Borough of Sutton v Davis*[7], Anne Davis had been a child-minder under the previous legislation, and she now sought to be registered under the Children Act. The local authority had formally adopted a 'no smacking policy' which entailed an automatic determination of unfitness in relation to any applicant who refused to undertake not to smack a minded child. Anne Davis's position on corporal punishment was that she wished to have the authority to 'smack gently' in accordance with parental wishes. She refused to give the required undertaking whereupon the authority, although satisfied that she met its child-minding criteria in every other respect, refused her registration.

The magistrates allowed her appeal against this refusal, and their decision was upheld by the High Court. Wilson J held that there was nothing in the legislation which required the authority to adopt so inflexible a policy that Anne Davis was, by reason of her views on corporal punishment, per se unfit to be a child-minder. The magistrates had been entitled to look at the applicant's fitness more generally and to reach the conclusion that they did.

The registration authority may also subsequently cancel a registration if it is of the opinion that the person has ceased or will cease to be qualified for registration or has failed to pay the annual fee. There is provision for emergency cancellation

---

1 CA 1989, s 79A(3) and (7).
2 Section 79A(4). The children must be looked after wholly or mainly in the home of either of the employers.
3 Schedule 9A, para 3(1).
4 Contravention of the registration requirement no longer automatically constitutes an offence. An enforcement notice is required (s 79D).
5 Section 79F. It is a prerequisite to registration that suitable premises are available. In *Woodward v North Somerset District Council* [1998] 1 FLR 950, Mrs Woodward failed to be registered as a provider of nursery and other day-care services whereupon she forfeited the lease on the premises in which she had intended to run her business. Her appeal to the magistrates against refusal of registration failed on the preliminary ground that she had no premises in which such services could be provided and, thus, her personal fitness could not be assessed. Bracewell J held that this was the correct interpretation of the legislation, since it contemplated the registration of a person in respect of a particular set of premises.
6 Schedule 9A, para 4.
7 [1994] 1 FLR 737.

of registrations where a child might otherwise be exposed to significant harm[1], and the registration authority has powers of entry and inspection to enable it to carry out its duties[2]. Provision exists for appeals against refusals to register and cancellations of registrations[3], and it is a criminal offence to engage in unregistered activities, to obstruct inspections, to contravene the disqualification requirements or to fail to comply with any registration requirements imposed by the registration authority.

Conditions for registration

Finally, the Children Act introduced important changes affecting the conditions of registration. First, the Act brought in fees for registration[4]. This was a controversial development. The argument in favour was that it would generate much-needed income for local authorities whose responsibilities for scrutiny of arrangements would increase under the legislation. Against this, it was said that the introduction of fees could operate as a disincentive to registration where existing day-care arrangements were already operating on a shoe-string budget. Secondly, authorities were, for the first time, given a *duty* to impose reasonable registration requirements, some of which, such as those relating to the maximum number of children who may be looked after, maintenance of premises, equipment and safety standards, and the duty to keep records of children and day-care assistants, are mandatory[5].

QUESTIONING LOCAL AUTHORITIES' DECISIONS

What redress is available to someone who is aggrieved by a decision of the local authority affecting a child looked after by it? The potential remedies, in theory at least, apply equally to children in care and to accommodated children but, in practice, disputes are most likely to be about children in care, for several reasons. Since the local authority does not have parental responsibility over accommodated children it has less control. Allied to this is the fact that the agreement with the parents may well pre-empt potential areas of disagreement. More fundamentally, if a serious disagreement should arise, it would be open to the parents to demand the return of the child. This is not an option where the child is in care. However, since common principles apply to all children looked after by the local authority, they will be considered here. The general policy of the legislation is to vest managerial control in the local authority, and it was not thought appropriate in the Children Act to expose most areas of decision-making to judicial scrutiny. By way of exception, the decision to commit a child to care[6] or discharge a child from care[7] is left in the hands of the courts, as is the emotive question of contact

---

1 Section 79G.
2 Section 79Q.
3 Section 79M.
4 Then governed by the Child Minding and Day Care (Registration and Inspection Fees) Regulations 1991, SI 1991/2076. See now the Children Act 1989, Sch 9A, para 7.
5 Section 79C, and the Day Care and Child Minding (National Standards) (England) Regulations 2001, SI 2001/1828.
6 Section 31(1).
7 Section 39.

between children in care and their families[1]. As we have seen, this approach now requires substantial re-evaluation in the light of the HRA 1998. We have already considered some of the fundamental principles which apply under the ECHR as it affects State intervention in the family to protect children. In this section we examine more specifically the *remedies* which might be available to parents who allege a breach of their Convention rights. We return to this question in Chapter 11, when we consider possible challenges to the local authority's care plan where the child is in care.

We will now look at the possible avenues of redress[2], but it should be said at the outset that, apart from the statutory procedures for periodic reviews, representations and complaints, most of the other remedies are distinctly 'long-shots', although they do occasionally succeed. The courts have traditionally exhibited a reluctance to interfere with the plans of local authorities, except where they have plainly acted improperly[3].

It should be noted, however, that the local authority must produce a care plan to the court covering such matters as placement and contact with parents *before* the court is able to make a care order in the first place[4]. Until recently, there was no statutory obligation as such to produce a care plan, but this has now been made a formal legal requirement under amendments introduced by the Adoption and Children Act 2002[5]. Under s 31A of the Children Act it is now provided that 'where an application is made on which a care order might be made with respect to a child, the appropriate local authority must, within such time as the court may direct, prepare a plan ("a care plan") for the future care of the child'. We discuss the whole question of care plans, and the extent to which there may be legal challenges arising from them, in Chapter 11. Disputes in relation to care plans are undoubtedly going to be a major source of argument under the HRA 1998. The court also remains in control at the interim stage of care proceedings[6].

Reviews and representations

The local authority is obliged to keep under periodic review the case of each child looked after by it, and it has a complementary duty to establish procedures to deal with representations and complaints[7]. Both are designed to subject local authorities to a measure of accountability and to encourage proper planning for every child. The *Review* was anxious to allow the authority to 'take a grip' on the

---

1 Section 34. The use of secure accommodation is also subject to judicial control under s 25. See above.
2 An informative and detailed discussion of the possibilities is contained in NV Lowe and G Douglas *Bromley's Family Law* (9th edn) (Butterworths, 1998) at pp 596–610. See also R White, P Carr and N Lowe *The Children Act in Practice* (3rd edn) (Butterworths, 2002) ch 13; SM Cretney, JM Masson and R Bailey-Harris *Principles of Family Law* (7th edn) (Sweet & Maxwell, 2002) pp 773–789; and M Hayes 'Challenging Local Authority Decisions' (1993) 5 JCL 107.
3 The *locus classicus* being *A v Liverpool City Council* [1982] AC 363.
4 See *Re J (Minors) (Care: Care Plan)* [1994] 1 FLR 253.
5 Section 121.
6 See *Re C (Interim Care Order: Residential Assessment)* [1997] 1 FLR 1; and confirmed by the House of Lords in *Re S (Minors) (Care Order: Implementation of Care Plans); Re W (Minors) (Care Order: Adequacy of Care Plan)* [2002] 1 FLR 815.
7 Section 26, the Review of Children's Cases Regulations 1991, SI 1991/895, as amended, and the Representations Procedure (Children) Regulations 1991, SI 1991/894, as amended.

case and did not want the courts to intrude into what was seen as the primary responsibility of the local authority. Instead, it recommended a strengthening and improvement of the existing system of reviews and the mandatory introduction of internal complaints procedures with an independent element[1]. The Children Act gave effect to these recommendations.

Reviews

Prior to the Children Act, there were no regulations dealing with the manner or conduct of reviews relating to children in care, although the power existed to make such regulations. The Review of Children's Cases Regulations 1991 now provide that the local authority must review the case of each child being looked after by it. The first review must be within four weeks of the child being accommodated, then within three months after that, and thereafter at not more than six-monthly intervals[2]. These requirements also apply to voluntary organisations and private children's homes[3]. The regulations govern, inter alia, the manner in which reviews are to be conducted, and the considerations to which the local authority is to have regard[4]. Most significantly, for present purposes, the local authority must, before conducting the review, seek and take into account the views of the child, his parents, persons with parental responsibility and any other person whose views it considers relevant[5]. It must also, as far as is reasonably practicable, involve all the persons in the review, where appropriate, by attendance at meetings, and must notify them of the result of the review[6]. Clearly, good practice in the conduct of reviews can go a long way in meeting anxieties and heading off complaints.

Representations and complaints

Local authorities are required to establish procedures for considering representations including complaints[7]. Those entitled to make representations are children being looked after by the local authority, parents, persons with parental responsibility, and local authority foster-parents. Others may be allowed to do so where the local authority considers that they have a sufficient interest in the child to warrant it. The representations may relate to the discharge of any of the local authority's functions under Part III of the Children Act. They could relate to serious issues such as a change of placement or a medical operation, or to relatively trivial matters. The official guidance mentions complaints relating to day-care, support services where the child is at home, accommodation, after-care, and decisions relating to the placement of a child or the handling of a child's case[8]. The local authority must ensure that at least one person who is not a member or officer of the local authority takes part in the procedure[9], but doubts

---

1   *Review*, at para 2.24.
2   Review of Children's Cases Regulations 1991, regs 2 and 3.
3   Ibid, reg 1.
4   Ibid, regs 4 and 5 and Schs 1, 2 and 3.
5   Ibid, reg 7(1).
6   Ibid, reg 7(2) and (3).
7   Section 26(3), and Representations Procedure (Children) Regulations 1991, SI 1991/894, as amended.
8   *The Children Act 1989 Guidance and Regulations Vol 3 Family Placements* (HMSO, 1991) at para 10.8.
9   Section 26(4).

remain about how truly independent any internal procedure can be. The procedure must be publicised by the local authority[1]. Beyond this, the Children Act does not dictate the precise form of procedure to be followed but there are prescribed minimum procedural requirements[2].

Once it has considered a representation, the local authority must have due regard to the findings of those who considered it. It must then take such steps as are reasonably practicable to give written notice of its decision, with reasons, and any action taken or proposed in consequence, to the person making the representation, the child (if the local authority thinks he has sufficient understanding), and such other persons as appear to the local authority to be likely to be affected[3].

As Freeman has said, these procedures are no substitute for good practice, but they may be an integral part of good practice, contributing to a cultural change which encourages clients to express views about services and for these comments to be used as opportunities to improve services, relationships and, ultimately, the image of social services departments[4].

Other potential remedies

The first three possibilities discussed below are what might be called 'public law remedies' in that they are mechanisms for enforcing the proper discharge of public duties. Since local authorities have a vast amount of discretion under the children legislation, it does not follow that, because some third party might disagree with the line a local authority has taken, that authority has acted beyond its powers or otherwise improperly. These remedies should not, therefore, be viewed as offering a great deal of hope to aggrieved individuals, except in the more obvious cases of abuse of power or failure to discharge public duties. We also look at the possibility of obtaining a private order under the Children Act and we conclude by considering the new and potentially important mechanisms for challenge under the HRA 1998.

Judicial review

Despite the restrictive nature of the remedy of judicial review, there has been a steady growth in applications for judicial review in recent years, perhaps initially reflecting the refusal of the courts to entertain wardship applications which were

---

1   Section 26(8). But one research study of the publicity of local authority complaints procedures found them to be insufficiently effective in bringing them to the attention of potential users. See C Williams and H Jordan 'Factors relating to publicity surrounding the complaints procedure under the Children Act 1989' [1996] CFLQ 337. For a recent review of the operation of the complaints procedures, which considers in particular their relationship to judicial review, see C Williams 'The Practical Operation of the Children Act Complaints Procedure' [2002] CFLQ 25.

2   A detailed description of the procedure is to be found in NV Lowe and G Douglas *Bromley's Family Law* (9th edn) (Butterworths, 1998) at pp 599–600.

3   Section 26(7). It is arguable that this lacks teeth in that the complainant has no obvious redress where a complaint is upheld.

4   MDA Freeman *Children, Their Families and the Law* (Macmillan, 1992) at p 145.

designed to challenge local authorities' decisions[1]. In order to succeed, the applicant must show that the local authority has acted in a way in which no reasonable authority would have acted[2], that it has acted *ultra vires*, ie exeeded its statutory powers[3], or that there has been a breach of the rules of natural justice[4]. Permission is required before an application may be brought. Apart from the narrowness of the grounds, the powers of the Divisional Court[5] are limited. It may order the local authority to discharge its statutory duty properly through a mandatory order (formerly the order of mandamus) but, more likely, it will simply quash the local authority's decision through a quashing order (formerly the order of certiorari). It may issue a prohibiting order (formerly prohibition) to prevent a public body from acting unlawfully. It may also grant a declaration that something is unlawful or an injunction to restrain unlawful conduct. The court cannot go on to make orders which it considers to be in the best interests of the child as it can in wardship. The procedure contrasts sharply with the extremely flexible powers which the courts have under the Children Act, and its suitability in individual children cases must be doubted. Where it can prove useful is as a means of challenging *policy* decisions of local authorities. A formal decision, for example, to restrict services for children in need to those considered 'at risk' would clearly be susceptible to challenge. In recent years there have been a number of successful challenges to the policies of local authorities.

A good example is *R v Cornwall County Council ex parte LH*[6]. Here the authority, as a matter of policy, would not permit solicitors to attend child protection conferences except to the extent that they were allowed to read out a prepared statement. Neither would it permit a parent who had attended such a conference to be provided with a copy of the minutes except by order of the court. Scott Baker J granted a declaration that both policies were unlawful. As to the first, although the statutory guidance under the Children Act, *Working Together under the Children Act 1989*, warned of case conferences becoming confrontational and stated that legal representation as such was inappropriate, it nonetheless envisaged a parent being accompanied by a friend or a lawyer. Solicitors could make a useful contribution and should generally be allowed to attend and participate. As to the second policy, this was described by Scott Baker J as 'ludicrous' and a blatant contravention of the statutory guidelines. If an accurate record of the meeting had been taken, nothing in the minutes should be new to anyone who attended it,

---

1   In several cases it was held specifically that judicial review, rather than wardship, was the appropriate remedy. See particularly *Re RM and LM (Minors)* [1986] 2 FLR 205, and *Re DM (A Minor) (Wardship: Jurisdiction)* [1986] 2 FLR 122. For a general discussion, see M Sunkin 'Judicial Review and Part III of the Children Act 1989' (1992) 4 JCL 109. But it has been held that the applicant must exhaust other remedies, particularly the statutory complaints procedure, before resorting to judicial review. See *R v Kingston upon Thames RBC ex parte T* [1994] 1 FLR 798 and *R v Birmingham City Council ex parte A* [1997] 2 FLR 841.
2   See, for example, *R v Lancashire County Council ex parte M* [1992] 1 FLR 109.
3   Good examples of ultra vires action under the old law arose where there was a failure to follow the correct procedure for passing a parental rights resolution, as in *Re L (AC)* [1973] 3 All ER 743. This was a successful challenge in wardship but would now be a matter for judicial review.
4   There have been several notable successes under this head. See, for example, *R v Bedfordshire County Council ex parte C* [1987] 1 FLR 239 and *R v Norfolk County Council ex parte M* [1989] QB 619.
5   The Divisional Court of the Queen's Bench Division. Judges from the Family Division may, however, sit in children cases.
6   [2000] 1 FLR 236.

including the parent, and parents should be trusted to act responsibly with the paperwork.

An inflexible policy by the Prison Service which prohibited children remaining in mother and baby units after attaining the age of 18 months was found to be unlawful[1], and there was a successful challenge in judicial review of the placement of a child on the child protection register where there was insufficient evidence of emotional abuse[2]. On the other hand, there have been a good many unsuccessful applications for judicial review in the child care sphere, some of which turn on the conclusion that the aggrieved applicant should have resorted to the statutory complaints procedures[3] of the local authority rather than the courts. An example is *R v East Sussex County Council ex parte W*[4] where a disabled 13-year-old boy, who had repeatedly run away, failed in a challenge to the local authority's decision not to seek a care order. Another is *Re S (Sexual Abuse Allegations: Local Authority Response)*[5] where the claimant, a consultant gynaecologist, failed to establish that the local authority had acted unreasonably, and therefore unlawfully, in its statutory duty to assess the risk of sexual abuse which he posed to unrelated children living with him in the same house.

Just as the complaints procedure may in some cases be a more appropriate alternative than an application for judicial review, so in future it is likely that, in a significant number of the more serious allegations against local authorities, the HRA 1998 may be invoked rather than judicial review. We consider these remedies below.

The Secretary of State's default powers
The Secretary of State has a number of functions in the child care sphere[6], one of which is the so-called 'default power'. This enables him to intervene in limited circumstances where he is satisfied that a local authority has failed, without reasonable excuse, to comply with any of its duties under the legislation. He may then make an order, giving reasons and declaring the local authority to be in default with respect to the relevant duty[7]. The order may include directions to comply with that duty within a specified period[8], which may be enforced through judicial review and specifically by a mandatory order[9].

It is extremely unlikely that this kind of intervention by central government would be of assistance in individual cases. Again, where it does occur, it is likely to be directed against a policy decision of the local authority with regard to a *class* of children.

---

1 *R, on the Application of P and Q and QB v Secretary of State for the Home Department* [2001] 2 FLR 1122.
2 *R v Hampshire County Council ex parte H* [1999] 2 FLR 359.
3 Under s 26 discussed above.
4 [1998] 2 FLR 1082.
5 [2001] 2 FLR 776.
6 For a general discussion, see A Bainham *Children: The New Law* (Family Law, 1990) at paras 7.71–7.78.
7 Section 84(1) and (2). A similar power exists under the Education Acts, as to which see Chapter 16 below.
8 Section 84(3).
9 Section 84(4).

The local government ombudsman

It is possible to make a complaint to the Commissioner for Local Administration. This requires proof of 'maladministration', and the main disadvantage of the procedure is that it takes too long to be of immediate benefit to individual children, parents, or anyone else directly affected by an authority's decision[1]. Again, it may, if successful, be instrumental in securing the reversal of an ill-conceived policy. In Wales complaints may be made to the Children's Commissioner for Wales, an office which has been functional since 26 August 2001[2]. The Commissioner's role extends, inter alia, to reviewing policy and acts of the National Assembly and other public bodies in Wales, together with giving advice and assistance and considering complaints and representations in respect of any matters relating to the rights and welfare of children[3]. As we have noted, such an office will be created for England under the Children Bill 2004.

Civil actions

In recent years there have been attempts by adults to obtain damages from local authorities in tort for injuries caused to them when children, allegedly resulting from the acts or omission of the authorities concerned[4]. The complaints have ranged from failure to act on reports of abuse made by doctors, teachers, neighbours and others[5]; the separation of a girl from her mother arising from the incorrect identification of an alleged abuser[6]; failure to prevent abuse by a foster-father through inadequate monitoring and supervision of the placement[7]; and failure to act as a reasonable parent would towards a child in care, allegedly resulting in a series of personal catastrophies in adulthood[8]. At first these claims failed whether they were based on common law negligence or breach of statutory duty.

In *X (Minors) v Bedfordshire County Council*[9] the House of Lords, in a consolidated appeal, held that no cause of action arose either in negligence or for breach of statutory duty. The House was much exercised by policy considerations and by the consideration that the existence of a common law duty of care would

---

1 A case in which a complaint was successful was *Re BA (Wardship and Adoption)* [1985] FLR 1008 where the local ombudsman found procedural irregularities in the passing of a parental rights resolution. As a result the local authority agreed to the continuation of wardship proceedings and a sub-committee of the authority recommended that the resolution be rescinded.

2 Created by the Care Standards Act 2000 and the Children's Commissioner for Wales Act 2001. The functions of the Commissioner are further regulated by the Children's Commissioner for Wales Regulations 2001, SI 2001/2783.

3 For more detailed consideration of the Commissioner's role, see J Williams 'The Children's Commissioner for Wales' (2001) 1 *Wales Law Journal* 203 and K Hollingsworth and G Douglas 'Creating a Children's Champion for Wales' (2002) 65 MLR 58.

4 For a thorough and informative critique of the various remedies against local authorities in relation to the discharge of their child care functions, see R Bailey-Harris and M Harris 'Local Authorities and Child Protection – the Mosaic of Accountability' [2002] CFLQ 117. See also C Brennan 'Third party liability for child abuse: unanswered questions' (2003) 25 JSWFL 23, and J Wright 'Local Authorities, the Duty of Care and the European Convention on Human Rights' (1998) 18 *Oxford Journal of Legal Studies* 1.

5 *X (Minors) v Bedfordshire County Council* [1995] 2 AC 633.

6 *M (A Minor) and Another v Newham London Borough Council v Others* [1995] 2 AC 663.

7 *H v Norfolk County Council* [1997] 1 FLR 384.

8 *Barrett v Enfield London Borough Council* [1999] 2 FLR 426.

9 [1995] 2 AC 633.

interfere unduly with the performance of local authorities' statutory obligations to protect children at risk. It was concerned that potential liability might lead to a more cautious and defensive approach to the discharge of those duties and to a multiplicity of law suits[1]. The House of Lords did not close the door completely on civil actions for damages but drew a distinction between *policy* decisions and decisions which were not policy decisions. In the case of the latter, there could be liability if the authority had acted so unreasonably that its decisions went beyond the proper exercise of its statutory discretions.

Having failed in the House of Lords, the aggrieved 'children' and one mother took their cases to Strasbourg. In two landmark decisions in *Z v United Kingdom*[2] and *TP and KM v United Kingdom*[3] the ECtHR found that there had been violations of a number of Convention rights. In *Z v United Kingdom* the Court awarded damages of £32,000 to each child plus costs and expenses. It found that the welfare system had failed to protect the children from serious, long-term neglect and abuse in violation of Article 3 which prohibits torture, or inhuman or degrading treatment or punishment. This imposed on States an obligation to prevent ill-treatment of which the authorities had or ought to have had knowledge. It also found, by a substantial majority of 15:2, a violation of Article 13 which enshrines the right to an effective remedy, in that the children were unable to sue a local authority in negligence for compensation however foreseeable and severe the harm suffered and however unreasonable the conduct of the authority in failing to take steps to prevent the harm[4]. In *TP and KM v United Kingdom* the ECtHR also found a violation of Article 13 and, in this case, held that there had been a breach of the applicants' rights to respect for family life under Article 8 in that the authority had failed to disclose to the mother an interview video with the child or submit the question of the disclosure of the video to the court for its determination. This had deprived the mother of adequate involvement in the decision-making process concerning the care of her daughter and amounted to a failure to respect the family life of both of them. In each case the Court found no violation of Article 6, which guarantees the right to a fair hearing, since there had been no denial of access to the court.

These decisions opened up the possibility of actions under the HRA 1998 or for damages for negligence or breach of statutory duty. In any event, with the backdrop of the European proceedings, the House of Lords had itself already begun to shift its stance dramatically. In *Barrett v Enfield London Borough Council*[5] the House allowed the appeal of a young man who had been continually in the care of the local authority from the age of 10 months through to adulthood. He

---

1 For a scathing attack on the decision, see M Freeman 'The End of the Century of the Child?' (2000) 53 *Current Legal Problems* 505, at 542. See also R Bailey-Harris and M Harris 'The immunity of local authorities in child protection functions – is the door now ajar?' [1998] CFLQ 227.

2 [2001] 2 FLR 612.

3 [2001] 2 FLR 549. For commentary, see J Miles 'Human Rights and Child Protection' [2001] CFLQ 431.

4 See also *E and Others v United Kingdom* [2003] 1 FLR 348 in which the ECtHR similarly found violations of Articles 3 and 13 where the local authority should have been aware of the risk of sexual and physical abuse to the child posed by the step-father and failed to take steps which would have enabled it to discover the exact extent of the problem and, potentially, to prevent further abuse taking place.

5 [2001] 2 AC 550.

brought an action for damages based on psychiatric injury allegedly caused by the authority's negligence and breach of statutory duty. He asserted that it had failed to place him in suitable foster homes or for adoption or to take sufficient steps to reintroduce him to his mother. As a consequence he claimed to have experienced alcohol problems, a tendency to self-harm, behavioural problems and a failed marriage. He argued that the local authority had a common law duty of care to provide him with the standard of care to be expected of a reasonable parent, which it had failed to do.

His claim was struck out by the judge and the Court of Appeal as disclosing no cause of action, but the House of Lords reinstated it holding that it was in principle possible for certain acts done pursuant to a statutory discretion, such as the treatment of a child in care, to give rise to a duty of care. The question would be whether or not they were justiciable actions. The initial decision about whether or not to apply to take a child into care was not justiciable unless it reached the level of being so unreasonable that it was not to be regarded as the proper exercise of a statutory discretion. On the other hand, the treatment of children once in care, the issue here, was one in which it was potentially possible to find a breach of duty. Such a decision did not clearly involve competing policy factors which rendered it non-justiciable. The House went on to hold that it was not necessarily unjust or unreasonable to impose a duty of care on a local authority in relation to a child in its care. While it would be inappropriate to permit a child to sue his parents, it was not necessarily wrong to allow a child to sue the authority whose duties and responsibilities were not identical to those of a parent[1].

The potential existence of the duty was, however, far from the same as establishing liability merely because something had gone wrong. Whether the duty existed and, if so, whether it had been broken depended on the statutory context and the nature of the tasks involved. The court should be careful to have regard to the delicate and difficult factors involved in much local authority work, particularly child welfare work. On the other hand, unless the court exercised its jurisdiction to address these questions, the interests of the child could not be sufficiently protected.

The House of Lords considered related issues in *W v Essex County Council*[2]. Foster-parents made it known to the local authority that they were not prepared to foster any child who was known or suspected of being a child abuser. Despite this the authority placed a boy who was a known sexual abuser with their family without informing them of his history. The foster-parents alleged that he had sexually abused their own children and that, as a consequence, both they and their children had suffered serious psychiatric injury. The Court of Appeal allowed the children's claims to proceed, holding also that the authority could be vicariously liable for the acts of its social worker, but it struck out the parents' claim on the basis that the authority did not owe them a duty of care since they were not primary victims and did not qualify as secondary victims either. The House of Lords reinstated the parents' claim as at least arguable. Whether in the circumstances a duty of care would ultimately be found to have existed or to be breached would depend on an investigation of the full facts known to, and the factors influencing

---

1   For a critique of the view in this case that it is inappropriate for a child to sue a parent, see M Freeman (above) at pp 543–544.

2   [2000] 1 FLR 657.

the decision of, the local authority. It was also impossible to say that the parents' psychiatric injury would necessarily fall outside the range of injury recognised by the law, since the concept of secondary victims was still being developed.

These decisions then established *in principle* that a cause of action could lie in negligence and have been followed by later decisions of the Court of Appeal.

In *S v Gloucestershire County Council; Tower Hamlets London Borough Council and Havering London Borough Council*[1] two adults claimed that they had been sexually abused by their respective foster-fathers while placed with them as children and had as a consequence suffered long-term damage. Both foster-fathers were eventually convicted of sexual offences involving children. The claimants now sought damages against the respective local authorities for negligence in the original placements. Both authorities initially succeeded in having the claims struck out as disclosing no reasonable cause of action. The Court of Appeal, however, distinguished between the two cases. First, it held that it was clear since *Barrett v Enfield* that there might be a viable cause of action against a local authority for negligence in a placement leading to sexual abuse. Accordingly, it reinstated both cases. However, treating the appeals as applications for summary judgment, it held that although a case could disclose a reasonable cause of action it might not necessarily have any reasonable prospect of success on the facts. In the *Tower Hamlets and Havering* case there was no reasonable prospect of success, and summary judgment was given in favour of the council. In the *Gloucestershire* case the court was not prepared to reach that conclusion, and the council's application for summary judgment failed on the facts. That case was therefore allowed to proceed for a determination of whether negligence was in fact established.

In *C v Flintshire County Council*[2] the claimant was abused in a children's home in North Wales. She was severely bullied by other children, without the intervention of staff, in her first placement. In her second placement she was significantly abused by the staff and other residents of the home. This included a serious assault on her by the deputy superintendent of the home, a sexual assault by a care worker, illegal use of a secure unit and persistent verbal abuse and denigration by staff and other residents. She succeeded in obtaining damages for the psychological harm she had suffered. She was awarded £35,000 for pain, suffering and loss of amenities, £20,000 for loss of past earnings, £5,000 for future loss of earnings and over £10,000 for the cost of future psychotherapy. The Court of Appeal upheld these awards, taking the view that it was doubtful whether damages for psychiatric harm caused to children abused by their carers should be constrained by the Judicial Studies Board guidelines on damages for psychiatric damage. The physical, emotional and sexual abuse of children by those who were supposed to care for them, it was said, fell into a wholly different category from psychiatric harm resulting from other personal injury.

This decision may be a significant indication that the damages awarded in a negligence action, if successful, might conceivably be on the high side compared

---

1   [2000] 1 FLR 825. See also *A and B v Essex County Council* [2003] 1 FLR 615 where a negligence action succeeded against the local authority for its failure properly to inform prospective adoptive parents of serious behavioural problems which one of two siblings exhibited. This led to attacks on both prospective adoptive parents and other children, and psychiatric injury to the prospective adoptive mother. On the question of quantum of damages in negligence cases involving child abuse, see *R v Bryn Alyn Community (Holdings) Ltd* [2003] 1 FLR 1203.

2   [2001] 2 FLR 33.

with what an applicant might be awarded under the HRA 1998 where there has been a breach of Convention rights. Both possibilities have now to be considered and it is not at all improbable that actions may be framed in the alternative in future.

ACTIONS UNDER THE HUMAN RIGHTS ACT 1998

Before the HRA 1998 was implemented it was possible for an individual to petition the European Commission and ECtHR alleging a breach by a local authority of the ECHR. Although this was a slow and cumbersome procedure usually taking many years, there were some significant successes notably in relation to contact with children in care[1], parental access to the courts in the context of care procedures[2], and access to case records[3].

The effect of implementation of the HRA 1998, while not removing the 'long stop' remedy of recourse to Strasbourg, is to provide new remedies based on violation of Convention rights which are directly available in the English courts. The framework is contained in ss 6, 7 and 8 of the HRA 1998. The interaction of these provisions was helpfully described by Lord Nicholls of Birkenhead in the leading case of *Re S; Re W*[4] as follows:

> 'Sections 7 and 8 have conferred extended powers on the courts. Section 6 makes it unlawful for a public authority to act in a way that is incompatible with a Convention right. Section 7 enables victims of conduct made unlawful by section 6 to bring court proceedings against the public authority in question. Section 8 spells out in wide terms, the relief a court may grant in those proceedings. The court may grant such relief or remedy, or make such order, within its powers as it considers appropriate. Thus if a local authority conducts itself in a manner which infringes the Art 8 rights of a parent or child, the court may grant appropriate relief on the application of a victim of an unlawful act.'

It is important to appreciate that actions brought under the HRA 1998 can only be based on a breach of the ECHR and must be brought by the *victim*[5]. If the complaint relates to something which does not involve this, then these remedies will be unavailable and the appropriate course of action will be to use one of the other remedies discussed above, such as the complaints procedure, judicial review or a civil action based on negligence. In many cases, however, the alleged unlawful behaviour will *both* constitute a breach of Convention rights and be susceptible to judicial review or an action in negligence. In such cases, there will be a choice of remedy and it is more than likely that in some cases the aggrieved applicant will seek to invoke these remedies in the alternative. The effect of the HRA 1998 is to make available in English law the remedies visualised by Article 13 of the ECHR

---

1   *R v United Kingdom* [1988] 2 FLR 445.
2   *W v United Kingdom* (1987) 10 EHRR 29.
3   *The Gaskin case* [1990] 1 FLR 167. See also *McMichael v United Kingdom* [1995] 2 FCR 718, in which the ECtHR found Scottish child care procedures under the Social Work (Scotland) Act 1968 to be in breach of parents' rights under Article 8(1) in denying them access to reports concerning adoption.
4   *Re S (Minors) (Care Order: Implementation of Care Plan); Re W (Minors) (Care Order: Adequacy of Care Plan)* [2002] 1 FLR 815 at para [45].
5   This precludes an action by a secondary victim such as in *W v Essex County Council* [2000] 1 FLR 657 (discussed above).

and which were found to be lacking in *Z v United Kingdom* and *TP and KM v United Kingdom*.

Actions under the HRA 1998 either may be 'freestanding' in the sense that proceedings are specifically brought for the purpose[1] or may arise in the course of existing proceedings. Thus, someone may rely on a Convention right in the course of family proceedings[2]. In the case of freestanding proceedings, the application must be brought within one year of the alleged unlawful act[3] but the court may at its discretion allow an application within 'such longer period as the court or tribunal considers equitable having regard to all the circumstances'[4]. How this discretion is exercised may clearly have a significant bearing on the availability of these remedies as where, for example, an adult alleges breaches of Convention rights arising from abuse as a child, with which so many of the cases discussed above were concerned.

Reported decisions in which there have been attempts to invoke the HRA 1998 remedies are now beginning to appear. In *Re M (Care: Challenging Decisions By Local Authority)*[5] there was a successful application. The facts are complicated but essentially involved an eventual decision by the authority that reunification of the child with her mother or father was not going to be achievable. This decision was reached at a 'permanency planning meeting' which took place in the absence of both parents and their solicitors. Holman J held, taking Article 8 of the ECHR in conjunction with s 6 of the HRA 1998, that the decision-making process had not involved the parents to the extent required given the seriousness of the decisions to be taken. Accordingly, the decision would be quashed, a new hearing directed for review of the case and consideration of the parents' applications for discharge of the care orders. By contrast, in *C v Bury Metropolitan Council*[6], Dame Elizabeth Butler-Sloss P dismissed an application by a mother under the HRA 1998 and Article 8 of the ECHR. This was another case in which the complaint was the mother's lack of involvement in the authority's decision-making process. In this case it concerned the implementation and revision of the care plan whereby the child was to be moved from a children's home to a residential school many miles from the mother's home. The President found here, however, that the procedural flaws in the management of the case had not, on the facts, had a detrimental effect on the mother's care nor the child's rights. The proposed move was found to be lawful interference with Article 8 Convention rights, since it was necessary to protect the child's best interests and was proportionate to the obvious needs of the child. The question of contact between the mother and the child was governed by s 34 of the Children Act, and the authority was under an obligation to arrange suitable contact and to make travel arrangements to enable the mother to see her child regularly in accordance with the care plan. The parties were accordingly invited to submit an agreement on contact.

---

1   HRA 1998, s 7(1)(a).
2   Ibid, s 7(1)(b).
3   Ibid, s 7(5)(a).
4   Ibid, s 7(5)(b).
5   [2001] 2 FLR 1300.
6   [2002] 2 FLR 868.

This decision reveals an important feature of the new human rights remedies. This is that they are likely to be viewed by the courts as remedies of 'last resort'[1]. The courts are likely to take the view that they should not be invoked where there is an alternative remedy available, in this case the statutory contact regime under s 34 of the Children Act 1989. It is too early to tell how liberal or restrictive the courts are likely to be in this respect.

Private orders

The final possibility is for the aggrieved individual to apply for a s 8 order. Where the child is 'accommodated' by the local authority, all s 8 orders are, in principle, available, subject to the leave requirement[2]. These orders are likely to be sought, if at all, by someone without parental responsibility, since those who have parental responsibility are able to terminate an accommodation arrangement.

Where the child is in care, the jurisdiction of the courts to make private orders is severely curtailed[3], but it is possible to apply for a residence order. This would only be an appropriate course for those persons who are willing and able to offer a home to the child. This course would not be appropriate if the person's grievance related only to some aspect of the local authority's plan for the child. Where the dispute is about contact (as it often is), there is a statutory regime[4]. It was the case prior to the Children Act[5], and it is the case after it[6], that wardship may not be used as an extra-statutory device for challenging local authority decision-making. Although, technically, an application might be made under the inherent jurisdiction of the High Court, it has been argued that this '*Liverpool* principle' would be likely to preclude the court from exercising jurisdiction[7].

Conclusion

Although it is in general likely to remain difficult to challenge successfully the exercise of the local authority's statutory discretions, there is no doubt that there has been a substantial shift in recent years in the direction of greater account-ability and availability of remedies for aggrieved parents and others. For the less serious grievances, the internal procedures of the local authority, including informal negotiation with social workers, the review process and the complaints procedures, will remain the principal means of questioning the local authority's actions in relation to a particular child.

At the same time there is now a keener awareness of the human rights requirements and the importance of procedural fairness in the decision-making process. This was acknowledged by Dame Elizabeth Butler-Sloss P in *C v Bury Metropolitan Borough Council*[8], where she said that the approach of the court to a challenge to the local authority's procedures and care plan should be broader and more investigative than prior to the HRA 1998. There is no question that the

---

1 But for a contrary view, which points out that no such limitation exists in the wording of the statute itself, see R Tolson QC *Care Plans and The Human Rights Act* (Family Law, 2002) at p 10.
2 Reversing, in effect, the House of Lords decision in *M v H* [1988] 3 All ER 5.
3 See Chapter 11 below.
4 Section 34, also discussed in Chapter 11 below.
5 *A v Liverpool City Council* [1982] AC 363 ('the *Liverpool* principle').
6 Section 100(2)(c).
7 NV Lowe and G Douglas *Bromley's Family Law* (9th edn) (Butterworths, 1998) at p 603.
8 [2002] 2 FLR 868.

development of potential liability for negligence has occurred within the context of a greater commitment to human rights. We have noted also that there have been a significant number of successes in judicial review, although counter-balanced perhaps by a comparable number of failures. A key battleground in the future will undoubtedly be the issues surrounding the making and implementation of care plans, in relation to which the House of Lords in *Re S; Re W*[1] has recently had a great deal to say. We consider care plans, and the extent to which they can be questioned, in Chapter 11.

---

1   *Re S (Minors) (Care Order: Implementation of Care Plan); Re W (Minors) (Care Order: Adequacy of Care Plan)* [2002] 1 FLR 815.

Chapter 11
CARE AND SUPERVISION

INTRODUCTION

It would be difficult to visualise a more striking failure of protection under the law than that which occurs when a defenceless young child is killed or seriously injured by an adult in the same household. However, it would be equally difficult to envisage a more serious invasion of family autonomy than that which arises where a child is unjustifiably removed from his family because of unwarranted suspicions of abuse. Here, then, is the dilemma for the law and for those, especially social workers, who have to apply it. The stakes could hardly be higher and, sadly, there have been plenty of examples (often attracting much media attention) of both kinds of failure. There has been a succession of public inquiries into apparent 'agency failure' to prevent the death or abuse of children who have been allowed to remain at, or return to, the family home[1]. In contrast, there have been a number of apparently over-zealous interventions in cases of suspected sexual abuse, most notably in Cleveland in 1987[2] and then in relation to alleged ritualistic abuse in Rochdale[3] and Orkney[4].

Errors on either side of the line usually provoke public outrage, and the difficulty of formulating grounds and procedures which achieve the right balance for compulsory interventions in the family must be apparent to everyone. It is also an issue which has generated substantial academic disagreement. During the 1980s, a number of influential works were published which conveyed the central message that there had been an unacceptable escalation in State intervention which called for the imposition of greater legal controls on social services

---

1 See Chapter 2 above. The most recent such inquiry is the Victoria Climbié Inquiry chaired by Lord Laming and reporting in January 2003. The full report can be downloaded from www.doh.gov.uk. A summary of the inquiry's findings appears at [2003] Fam Law 145. See also H Conway 'The Laming Inquiry – Victoria Climbié's Legacy' [2003] Fam Law 513.

2 See the *Report of the Inquiry into Child Abuse in Cleveland 1987* ('the *Cleveland Report*') (1988) (Cmnd 412).

3 *Rochdale Borough Council v A* [1991] 2 FLR 192; and see the guidelines established for the investigation of such cases in *Re A (Minors) (Wardship) (Child Abuse: Guidelines)* [1992] 1 All ER 153.

4 As to which see R Brett 'Orkney – aberration or symptom?' (1991) 3 JCL 143; EE Sutherland 'The Orkney Case' (1992) *Juridical Review* 93; and A Bissett-Johnson 'Child Protection in Scotland – the Background to the Clyde Report' (1993) 5 JCL 28. The Orkney case was the subject of a major public inquiry: see *Report of the Inquiry into the Removal of Children from Orkney in February 1991* (the *Clyde Report*) (HMSO, 1992). Wide-ranging reforms have since been made to the child protection and children's hearings system in Scotland by Part II of the Children (Scotland) Act 1995. These include reforms which are similar, but not identical, to the reforms introduced in England by the Children Act 1989. The 1995 legislation, inter alia, abolished parental rights resolutions and place of safety orders and introduced child assessment orders, child protection orders and exclusion orders as alternative options for dealing with the short-term protection of children. For further discussion of the Scottish reforms, see EE Sutherland 'Scotland: Child Law Reform – At Last!' in A Bainham (ed) *The International Survey of Family Law 1995* (Martinus Nijhoff, 1997), p 435, at pp 444–452.

departments[1]. This view of child protection practice was seriously challenged by a study in three local authority areas which concluded that these charges were unsupported by hard empirical evidence[2]. The thrust of this research was that child protection agencies operated within a framework of cultural limitations which the authors called the 'rule of optimism'. They argued that the modus operandi of these agencies was to prefer the least coercive form of intervention in family life which was possible in the circumstances. On this analysis, parents would often be given the benefit of any doubt, and only the worst cases of abuse or neglect would be the subject of compulsory action.

The task for the reformers of child care law was to come up with a framework for compulsory action which offered sufficient protection to vulnerable children but which also respected the rights of family members, most obviously those of parents but, increasingly, those of children themselves[3]. The Children Act 1989 attempts to achieve this primarily by rationalising and unifying the statutory ground for care or supervision, by creating more opportunity for participation in care proceedings, and by overhauling procedures for emergency protection. More recently, the Children Act was amended by Part IV of the Family Law Act 1996 to allow for the possibility of 'exclusion requirements' to be inserted into emergency protection orders and interim care orders which, where made, have the effect of removing the alleged abuser rather than the child from the family home[4]. This chapter concentrates on the first two aspects, and emergency and short-term protection is discussed in the next chapter. First it is necessary to say something about the human rights context in which English child protection law has to operate.

Child protection and human rights

As in all other areas of the law affecting children, the public law under the Children Act 1989 must now comply with the requirements of the ECHR and with the extensive jurisprudence of the ECtHR in the field of child protection. Increasingly also the English courts are being confronted with arguments about alleged violations of human rights in the course of care proceedings.

---

1   See, for example, H Geach and E Szwed (eds) *Providing Civil Justice for Children* (1983) and L Taylor, R Lacey and D Bracken *In Whose Best Interests?* (Cobden Trust, 1980).
2   R Dingwall, J Eekelaar and T Murray *The Protection of Children: State Intervention and Family Life* (Basil Blackwell, 1983).
3   The *Cleveland Report* drew public attention to violations of children's rights by child protection agencies, especially in the sphere of repeated medical examination.
4   We discuss these reforms in Chapter 12. It should be noted that Scotland was ahead of England in this respect by making provision in the Children (Scotland) Act 1995 for 'exclusion orders'. See EE Sutherland 'Scotland: Child Law Reform – At Last!' (above).

So what are the fundamental principles which can be extracted from decisions of the ECtHR?[1] As long ago as 1988 the ECtHR in *W v United Kingdom*[2] held that the mutual enjoyment by parent and child of each other's company constituted a fundamental element of family life. Any measures taken by the State which hindered that enjoyment would therefore amount to an interference with the rights protected by Article 8. Such interferences clearly include compulsory removal of children from their parents under an EPO or a care order and later decisions relating to placement, contact and adoption. A key question is the extent to which the ECHR requires the State to allow parents to participate in these decisions, and issues arise here under both Article 8 (right to respect for private life and family life) and Article 6 (right to a fair hearing). Early case law, such as *W v UK* itself, was concerned with procedural protections for parents in care proceedings and with the all-important question of contact with children in care[3]. In future the principal battleground for human rights arguments is likely to be related to the local authority's care plan, before and after a care order is made[4]. In short, *all* major decisions taken by local authorities in relation to children looked after by them are at least potentially susceptible to challenge under the HRA 1998.

Given that all these major decisions amount to interferences with Convention rights, the focus must be on the *justifications* for such interferences provided by Article 8(2)[5]. The process is one of evaluating whether the particular form of intervention is *proportionate* and *necessary* to a *legitimate State aim.* The aims visualised by Article 8(2) are 'the protection of the rights and freedoms of others' and the 'protection of health or morals'. These aims must be 'necessary in a democratic society' which, according to the ECtHR, means that there must be a 'pressing social need' for the relevant interference. In determining this question, the ECtHR has applied the 'fair balance' test. This is that a fair balance must be struck between the legitimate aim and the means to achieve it.

The application of these principles has been considered by the ECtHR in a raft of cases dealing with different decisions in the public law context. Perhaps the leading case is *Johansen v Norway*[6] in which the ECtHR acknowledged that States enjoyed a wide margin of appreciation in pursuing the legitimate aim of protecting the interests of children and assessing the necessity of taking children into care. However, in the Court's view, taking a child into care should normally be regarded as a *temporary measure* to be discontinued as soon as circumstances permit. Moreover, any measures of implementation of temporary care should be

---

1 A good discussion is to be found in H Swindells, A Neaves, M Kushner and R Skilbeck *Family Law and the Human Rights Act 1998* (Family Law, 1999) ch 6, which covers public law and adoption. We consider adoption in Chapter 7 but it should be kept constantly in mind that adoption is an important long-term solution for a significant number of children in care. It is not therefore possible to maintain a strict conceptual segregation of care and adoption and, especially as regards human rights questions, this chapter should be read along with Chapter 7.

2 (1988) 10 EHRR 29.

3 Discussed at pp 513 et seq below.

4 See pp 506 et seq below.

5 Set out at in Chapter 2 above.

6 (1996) 23 EHRR 33.

consistent with the ultimate aim of reuniting the natural parent and the child. This case involved decisions to remove a baby from her mother, removal of her parental rights, termination of access (contact) and a decision to place the baby for adoption. These interferences were found to violate Article 8 in the context of earlier successful contact between mother and child and improvement in the mother's lifestyle. The Court went on to hold that the deprivation of parental rights and access were far-reaching measures, totally depriving the mother of her family life with the child and inconsistent with the aim of reuniting them. Such measures, it was held, should be applied only in exceptional circumstances and could be justified only if they were motivated by an overriding requirement pertaining to the child's best interests. In *Olsson v Sweden*[1] the ECtHR said that good faith on the part of the State in its child protection procedures was not enough. The natural family relationship is not terminated by reason of the fact that a child is taken into public care. Splitting up a family was a very serious interference which must be supported by sound and weighty considerations in the interests of the child. In this case the three children were placed separately in homes and foster accommodation which was a long distance from the parents and each other and contact with the parents was limited. These measures were not supported by sufficient reasons and, in the Court's view, they were not proportionate to the legitimate aim pursued. In *Eriksson v Sweden*[2] the Court again found violations of the Convention arising from restrictions on access between a mother and daughter. The authorities in Sweden had placed a prohibition for an indefinite period on the removal of the child from foster care and had imposed restrictions on access. The Court held that the prohibitions and restrictions were inconsistent with the aim of reunifying parent and child contrary to Article 8. The inability of the mother to challenge the restrictions on access violated her right to a fair hearing under Article 6.

At the heart of these decisions is the obligation on the part of the State to promote reunification of parent and child. It must be emphasised that once the child is looked after away from home, the obligation on the State is a *positive* one, to promote reunification unless there is a very strong justification for not doing so. The whole question of the maintenance of contact between the child and the natural family where the child is looked after by the State is crucial to this reunification effort. We consider in depth below[3] what the ECtHR has had to say about this and also examine the statutory regime applying to contact with children in care under s 34 of the Children Act 1989.

Another aspect of the ECHR's requirements in the context of public care is the requirement in Article 6 that parents and others be granted a fair hearing in care procedures. We noted above the violation of Article 6 in *Eriksson v Sweden*. The matter arose again more recently in the important case of *P,C and S v United Kingdom*[4]. In this case the ECtHR found violations of *both* Article 6 and Article 8

---

1 (1988) 11 EHRR 259.
2 (1989) 12 EHRR 183.
3 See pp 514 et seq.
4 [2002] 2 FLR 631. For the facts and the aspect of the case relating to the emergency removal of the child, see Chapter 12 below. For an article which focuses especially on the participation issue and Article 6 rights, see D Casey, B Hewson and N Mole 'Effective Participation and the European Court' [2002] Fam Law 755. See also *L v Finland* [2002] 2 FLR 118 in which a violation of Article 6 was also found.

where parents were insufficiently able to protect their interests in care proceedings and freeing for adoption proceedings. The Court's decision was based to an appreciable extent on the parents' lack of legal representation in these proceedings. It is not inevitable under the ECHR that publicly funded legal representation should always be made available where Convention rights are at stake. Article 6 does not necessarily guarantee a right to legal aid. But the ECtHR had previously held in *Airey v Ireland*[1] that there might be an obligation on the State to provide it, since the complexity of the issues might make it necessary in order to provide effective access to the courts. In *P, C and S* the Court unanimously held that the complexity of the case, the importance of what was at stake and the highly emotive subject-matter led to the conclusion that the principle of effective access to the court and fairness required that the mother should have received the assistance of a lawyer. The importance of providing this effective access to the courts cannot be under-estimated for the self-evident reason that Convention rights are seriously undermined where there is a lack of an effective remedy.

Almost all of the above decisions have been concerned with protecting the rights of the natural family from unwarranted intrusion by the State and requiring the State to demonstrate strong justifications for taking or keeping a child away from home. It should not be forgotten, however, that there is another equally important side to Convention rights in this public law context. This is that the *child* also has rights to be protected from abuse and neglect. Where the State fails negligently to intervene to protect a child there may be a breach of the child's Convention rights, especially under Articles 3 and 8. We considered this aspect of human rights in Chapter 10[2] but it should be borne in mind when considering the difficult balancing exercises which the Convention requires.

The requirement that the State provide adequate protection for the child from abuse or neglect is enshrined in Article 19 of the UNCRC. This provides:

'1. States Parties shall take all appropriate legislative, administrative, social and educational measures to protect the child from all forms of physical or mental violence, injury or abuse, neglect or negligent treatment, maltreatment or exploitation, including sexual abuse, while in the care of parent(s), legal guardian(s) or any other person who has the care of the child.'

At the same time, there is recognition of the need for family support as well as adequate investigative procedures:

'2. Such protective measures should, as appropriate, include effective procedures for the establishment of social programmes to provide necessary support for the child and for those who have the care of the child, as well as for other forms of prevention and identification, treatment and follow-up of instances of child maltreatment described heretofore, and, as appropriate, for judicial involvement.'

Emphasis on co-operation

The statutory emphasis for social security departments and other authorities to co-operate with each other has been noted, and 'partnership' has been identified as a central theme. The notion of partnership resurfaces here, with the expectation that lawyers, social workers, the police, the NSPCC, education and health personnel, health visitors, probation officers, representatives of voluntary

---

1 (1979) 2 EHRR 305.
2 See pp 460 et seq above.

organisations, and anyone else professionally involved with a child will pool their information and resources in the child's best interests[1].

Procedure before commencement of any action

The starting point for this discussion must be the realisation that compulsory action will not usually be commenced unless the option of voluntary assistance has first been explored. It is very much the philosophy of the legislation that the family should be supported in times of difficulty, that voluntary co-operation with parents is the preferred option, and that compulsory orders should be a last resort. The Department of Health's *Guidance* made this plain when it advised that 'a care or supervision order will be sought only where there appears to be no better way of safeguarding and promoting the welfare of the child suffering, or likely to suffer, significant harm'[2]. Accordingly, before proceeding with an application, social services should always take legal advice about alternative options and about those matters which would inform it as to whether a care or supervision order is really appropriate in the circumstances[3]. This advice should be sought within the context of a multi-disciplinary, multi-agency child protection conference. It is this conference which performs the vital function of preparing the ground work for any application to the court. Still more importantly, the conference is the bridge between voluntary and compulsory action, conceptualised as distinct in the legislation, but, in practice, often blurred as points on a spectrum of possible options to deal with a difficult family situation.

The child protection conference

Inter-agency co-operation is effected through the mechanisms of the child protection conference and the child protection register[4]. Overall planning and the formulation of policy in the different local authority regions is the responsibility of the area child protection committee. Both the committee and the conference are made up of members of the various professions mentioned above. When the Children Bill 2004 is enacted, the non-statutory area child protection committee will be replaced by a new statutory body, the Local Safeguarding Children Board[5]. The effect is to put local arrangements for co-ordinating the work of key agencies in relation to safeguarding children on a statutory footing. The aim is to produce a coherent approach to safeguarding children based on contributions from all the key agencies and to manage this process effectively.

---

1   See, generally, *Working Together – Under the Children Act 1989* (HMSO, 1991), revising the previous 1988 edition. The latest edition is *Working Together to Safeguard Children: A guide to inter-agency working to safeguard and promote the welfare of children* (Department of Health, 1999) (hereafter '*Working Together*'). For commentary, see B Lindley and M Richards 'Working Together 2000 – how will parents fare under the new child protection process?' [2000] CFLQ 213.

2   *The Children Act 1989 Guidance and Regulations Vol 1 Court Orders* (HMSO, 1991) at para 3.2.

3   Ibid, at para 3.12. The relevant matters include such things as whether the criteria for compulsory action would be likely to be satisfied, the implications of opposition to an order, whether the case might need to be transferred to a higher court, what the authority might be required to disclose in advance of the hearing and whether a s 8 order might be appropriate.

4   For a discussion of the role of each, see MDA Freeman *Children, Their Families and the Law* (Macmillan, 1992) at pp 95–97.

5   See Chapter 10 above.

Where, following a preliminary investigation[1], there is reasonable cause to believe that the child is suffering, or is likely to suffer, significant harm there should be a 'strategy discussion' involving social services, the police and other agencies as appropriate'[2]. Where the agencies concerned judge that a child may continue to be at risk, a child protection conference will be called[3]. Its purpose is not to decide the case (which will ultimately be left to the court); it rather 'brings together family members, the child where appropriate, and those professionals most involved with the child and the family'. Its purpose is as follows:

- to bring together and analyse in an inter-agency setting the information which has been obtained about a child's health, development and functioning, and the parents' or carers' capacity to ensure the child's safety and promote the child's health and development;
- to make judgements about the likelihood of a child suffering significant harm in the future; and
- to decide what future action is needed to safeguard the child and promote his or her welfare, how that action will be taken forward, and with what intended outcomes[4].

At the initial conference, a decision will be taken about whether to place the child's name on the child protection register: a register, not of abused children, but of children 'who are considered to be at continuing risk of significant harm and for whom there is a child protection plan'. The aim is to make agencies and professionals aware of children thought to be at risk[5]. The conference must decide on a child protection plan for the child and appoint a 'key worker' whose functions will be to implement that plan to ensure protection for the child, inter-agency co-operation and the participation of parents or other carers in the plan[6]. After the initial conference there will be child protection reviews to monitor the implementation of the plan, the effectiveness of agency co-operation, and to decide whether the child's name should remain on the child protection register[7].

Attendance of family members at child protection conferences

An issue which has caused some controversy is the attendance of parents at child protection conferences. It has been held that it is not a breach of natural justice for parents not to be invited to attend a child protection conference[8], but the latest version of *Working Together*[9] and the spirit of the Children Act require a

---

1 The local authority's investigatory duties are spelled out in s 47 of the Children Act – as to which see Chapter 12 below.
2 *Working Together* at paras 5.28 et seq.
3 Ibid at paras 5.53 et seq.
4 Ibid at para 5.53.
5 Ibid at paras 5.99 et seq.
6 Ibid at paras 5.81–5.84.
7 Ibid at paras 5.90–5.95.
8 *R v Harrow London Borough Council, ex parte D* [1990] Fam 133; and see also *R v East Sussex County Council ex parte R* [1991] 2 FLR 358, and *R v Devon County Council ex parte L* [1991] 2 FLR 541.
9 *Working Together* (above) at para 5.58, which says that exclusion of one or more family members will be 'exceptional' as where, for example, there is a threat of violence or intimidation. Where the parents do not attend it is emphasised that some other way should be found of communicating their views to the conference.

justification for excluding them[1]. While parental involvement and the involvement of older children is a key feature of the legislation, so is the need to ensure that child protection agencies are not unduly inhibited in discharging their statutory functions. The shift brought about by the Children Act is that the onus now appears to be on those who would seek to deny participation since, as June Thoburn has put it:

> 'Practice, wisdom and research lead to the conclusion that the maximum involvement of parents and older children in the work, and honesty at the investigation and case conference stage, can lead to the sort of working together between professionals and family members which is most conducive to the long-term welfare of the children.'[2]

The importance of the child protection conference cannot be overstated. It has, in the recent past, been precisely the absence of this kind of co-ordinated approach and, in particular, the failure of agencies to pool vital information, which has led to some of the worst tragedies.

Working Together[3] also emphasises the importance of the participation of the child of a sufficient age and understanding in the conference. The child, it says, should be given the opportunity to attend and to bring an advocate, friend or supporter. Where the child's attendance is not desired or appropriate, the social services professional who is working most closely with the child should ascertain what his or her wishes and feelings are and make these known to the conference.

THE LEGAL BASIS FOR COMPULSORY ORDERS

Before the Children Act, there were many different routes by which a child might compulsorily enter the care of a local authority[4]. Broadly, these fell into three categories: cases in which children who were initially in voluntary care later became the subject of parental rights resolutions[5]; cases in which the local authority applied to the juvenile court for a care order under the Children and Young Persons Act 1969[6]; and cases where children were committed to care in family proceedings, most notably wardship, but also, for example, divorce,

---

1   For discussions of the issues involved in parents' attendance at conferences, see J Thoburn
'"Working Together" and parental attendance at case conferences' (1992) 4 JCL 11,
P Thomson 'Parents at Case Conferences – a Legal Advisor's Viewpoint' (1992) 4 JCL 15, and
D Savas 'Parental Participation in Case Conferences' [1996] CFLQ 57. It has been held that a
local authority may not adopt a rigid policy of restricting the participation of solicitors in the
conference to reading out a prepared statement and of withholding minutes from parents. See
R v Cornwall County Council, ex parte LH [2000] 1 FLR 236, discussed in Chapter 10 above.

2   J Thoburn (above) at p 14.

3   At para 5.57.

4   For an excellent discussion of the old law, see S Maidment 'The Fragmentation of Parental
Rights and Children in Care' [1981] JSWL 21.

5   The grounds for passing resolutions were largely 'parent-centred' in that they concentrated on
parental failings, such as unfitness arising from the parent's 'habits or modes of life' or
consistent failure 'without reasonable cause to discharge the obligations of a parent'. See the
Child Care Act 1980, s 3. For a critique of the former resolution procedure, see M Adcock,
R White and O Rowlands *The Administrative Parent* (BAAF, 1983).

6   These grounds were 'child-centred' in that they focused on the child's condition, as where the
child was found to be 'exposed to moral danger', or his proper development was 'being
unavoidably prevented or neglected' or he was 'beyond the control of his parent and guardian'.
In each case there was a further test that the child was in need of care and control which he was
unlikely to receive unless the order was made. See the Children and Young Persons Act 1969,
s 1.

adoption or guardianship[1]. This system gave rise to a number of difficulties. The grounds for making a care order differed according to the proceedings in which it was sought[2], the effects of each type of order were far from clear[3], and there was growing concern that local authorities were beginning to rely too heavily on wardship. They were, in effect, invoking an extra-statutory basis for gaining compulsory control of a child where it was doubtful that the statutory grounds could be established[4].

The Children Act met these difficulties head-on by enacting a single ground for all care or supervision orders, by making these orders available in all 'family proceedings' and by closing-off wardship as an extra-statutory option[5]. There were 5,984 care orders and 1,466 supervision orders made in 2001[6]. The abolition of the resolution procedure meant that the new ground was also to be the sole basis for compulsorily *retaining* a child who was initially voluntarily accommodated, and this would also necessitate a court order. It should also be observed that there is no longer any legal means whereby parents may reach a voluntary arrangement that the child should enter the *care* of the local authority as opposed to merely being *looked after* by it. Since care proceedings are also 'family proceedings', the court is bound by the principles in Part I of the Children Act, although the manner of their operation in this child protection context is inevitably somewhat different from their undiluted application in private disputes. The principle that delay is prejudicial also applies and, again, the court must draw up a timetable with a view to expediting matters[7].

Who may apply for an order?

It is the policy of the legislation to locate primary responsibility for child care in local authorities' social services departments. It is they who are under a statutory duty to investigate the circumstances of any child in their area, where they have reasonable cause to suspect that he is suffering, or is likely to suffer, significant harm[8], and it is also they who may be directed by the court, in family proceedings,

---

1 Here, the test was whether there were 'exceptional circumstances making it impracticable or undesirable' for the child to be under the care of a parent or other individual. See, for example, the Matrimonial Causes Act 1973, s 43(1) and the Guardianship Act 1973, s 2(2)(b).

2 See, generally, DHSS *Review of Child Care Law* (1985) at ch 15.

3 See the White Paper *The Law on Child Care and Family Services* (1987) (Cmnd 62) at para 7, which identified the lack of clarity in the mutual rights and responsibilities of parents and local authorities as the most striking defect of the law.

4 On the other hand, a more positive view of this use of the wardship jurisdiction was that it was a necessary 'safety-net' underpinning the statutory regime. See, for example, N Lowe 'Caring for Children' (1989) 139 NLJ 87.

5 But not entirely the use of the inherent jurisdiction of the High Court. See s 100(3)–(5) of the Children Act, and the discussion at pp 532 et seq below.

6 *Judicial Statistics 2001*.

7 Sections 1(2) and 32. See also Chapter 2.

8 Section 47. For fuller discussions of local authorities' investigative duties under the Children Act, see A Bainham *Children: The New Law* (Family Law, 1990) at paras 6.51–6.56 and D Bedingfield *The Child in Need* (Family Law, 1998) at ch 6. For a very helpful recent account, see R White, P Carr and N Lowe *The Children Act in Practice* (3rd edn) (Butterworths, 2002) ch 7, especially at paras 7.5–7.22. And for the official guidance, see Department of Health *Framework for the Assessment of Children in Need and Their Families* (2001).

to conduct an investigation into a child's circumstances[1]. The court ought not to make such a direction, however, unless there is a reasonable prospect that a public law order might be made. In *Re L (Section 37 Direction)*[2] the child concerned had been well looked after by her maternal grandmother and there was no challenge to her as primary carer. The only issue was the amount of contact to be allowed to the father, mother and paternal grandmother. The Court of Appeal held, inter alia, that the judge had been wrong to make a s 37 direction in this case, since the case was nowhere near the threshold in which public law powers could be invoked.

The former power of the courts to make care orders of their own motion has been removed, except with respect to interim orders[3] in deference to this general principle of local authority responsibility. While the court may be concerned enough about a child to trigger an investigation, it is not for the court to usurp the functions of social services by dictating to the local authority, as it sometimes used to in wardship proceedings[4]. Similarly, while other agencies and individuals have their part to play in child protection work, they do not have legal responsibility for initiating action. There is no statutory duty in England which would require individuals to report suspected cases of abuse or neglect[5].

In keeping with this policy, only the local authority or an 'authorised person' may apply for a care or supervision order[6] and, for these purposes, only the NSPCC and its officers, with their historic and substantial contribution to child protection, have been authorised[7]. The police were formerly permitted to bring proceedings based on the so-called 'offence condition', but with the abolition of this ground and the redefinition of local authorities' responsibilities, it was no longer thought appropriate for them to retain the power[8]. Similarly, local education authorities, which used to be able to initiate proceedings based on truancy, are no longer empowered to do so following the abolition of this ground

---

1   Section 37, and A Bainham (above) at paras 5.57–5.61. In *Re H (A Minor) (Section 37 Direction)* [1993] 2 FLR 541, Scott-Baker J adopted a liberal construction of the section. In his view, the statutory phrase 'the child's circumstances' should be widely construed to include any situation which might have a bearing on the child being likely to suffer significant harm in the future. In this case (which involved a lesbian couple in an arrangement analogous to surrogacy) the court was entitled to have regard in particular to the long-term, as well as the short-term, future of the baby concerned. See also *Re CE (Section 37 Direction)* [1995] 1 FLR 26. But a s 37 direction should not be used as a device for appointing a children's guardian where there is no real prospect of a care or supervision order being made, and a local authority may not be made a party to a private law application if it decides, following its investigations, not to seek a public law order (see *F v Cambridgeshire County Council* [1995] 1 FLR 516).
2   [1999] 1 FLR 984.
3   Section 38 discussed at pp 525 et seq below.
4   Particularly good examples of this are *Re E (SA) (A Minor) (Wardship)* [1984] 1 All ER 289, where the court directed a solution not sought by any of the parties; and *Re G-U (A Minor) (Wardship)* [1984] FLR 811, where the authority was reprimanded by the court for not referring back to it an abortion decision concerning a ward of court in its care. It has since been held that where the court is considering making an order not sought by the parties it must give them an opportunity to make submissions on the appropriateness of the order it is proposed to make. See *Devon County Council v S* [1992] 3 WLR 273 and *Croydon London Borough Council v A* [1992] 3 WLR 267.
5   There is such a mandatory reporting law in other jurisdictions, for example in the USA.
6   Section 31(1).
7   Section 31(9)(a).
8   See, generally, DHSS *Review of Child Care Law* (1985) at paras 12.9–12.26.

and its replacement with a new education supervision order[1]. Finally, there is no equivalent under the new law, to the former procedure whereby parents might require the local authority to bring proceedings in relation to a child who is beyond their control[2]. Proceedings must be brought by the 'designated authority', being the local authority in whose area the child is ordinarily resident or, where the child does not reside in any authority's area, the authority in whose area any circumstances arose in consequence of which the order is sought[3]. The Court of Appeal in *C (A Child) v Plymouth County Council*[4] has held that, in all but exceptional cases,[5] the appropriate authority should be determined by applying the simple rules of statutory construction. In this case the child was born and initially lived with her mother in Plymouth. She later spent time in a specialist unit in Cardiff and then lived with her paternal grandmother in Liverpool. At the care proceedings her father argued that Liverpool City Council, rather than Plymouth, should be responsible for any care order made. The judge and the Court of Appeal disagreed. Even if the child's early life did not amount to ordinary residence in Plymouth, a new born baby's ordinary residence must be dependent on the mother's.

Which children?

Care or supervision orders may not be made in relation to a child who has reached the age of 17 years, or a married child who has attained 16 years of age[6]. While this corresponds with the old law, its effect is more dramatic, since there is no longer an option of warding children in this age group and securing care that way[7]. Opinion is divided on whether the removal of the power to take compulsory action, in relation to those older teenagers, was desirable. One view is that it leaves

---

1 Section 36.
2 Children and Young Persons Act 1963, s 3. But being beyond parental control remains an element in one of the alternatives under the statutory ground in s 31(2). See p 505 below.
3 Section 31(8). These provisions can give rise to legal wrangles between local authorities about which of them should be 'designated' and hence have the statutory responsibilities for a child who has moved between areas. See particularly *Re BC (A Minor) (Care Order: Appropriate Local Authority)* [1995] 3 FCR 598, *Gateshead Metropolitan Borough Council v L and Another* [1996] 2 FLR 179, *Re C (Care Order: Appropriate Local Authority)* [1997] 1 FLR 544, and *Re P (Care Proceedings: Designated Authority)* [1998] 1 FLR 80 (in which there were complications arising from the child spending a period of time in interim care).
4 [2000] 1 FLR 875.
5 See *Northamptonshire County Council v Islington London Borough Council* [1999] 2 FLR 881 in which the Court of Appeal emphasised that the judge's function in designating the appropriate authority should involve a rapid and not over-sophisticated review of the child's history in order to make a purely factual determination. It was not to exercise a broad discretion. See also *Re H (Care Order: Appropriate Local Authority)* [2004] 1 FLR 534 and *London Borough of Redbridge v Newport City Council* [2004] 2 FLR 226. For commentaries on the issues, see V Smith 'Which Local Authority Gets the Care Order? The Simple Test' [2004] Fam Law 213, and J Hayes 'The Designated Local Authority in a Care Order: The Far-Reaching Consequences of Re H' [2004] Fam Law 511.
6 Section 31(3).
7 As occurred in *Re SW (A Minor) (Wardship Jurisdiction)* [1986] 1 FLR 24 where the girl in question was 17 years of age. It may, however, be possible for the local authority to exercise control over a 17-year-old by invoking, with leave, the inherent jurisdiction, but not to take the child into care. See below.

a potentially vulnerable group of adolescents unprotected[1]. An opposing view is that coercive orders grounded in non-criminal misbehaviour are open to civil libertarian objections and, in any event, would sit very uneasily with the philosophy of the legislation which finds expression in a number of other provisions[2]. This latter view is partly reinforced by the new provisions allowing troubled teenagers to seek a voluntary 'self-referral' into care[3], unless, of course, it can be argued that some will lack the resourcefulness to engage in self-help. In any event, the Children Act is clear and the embargo on 'public' orders is in line with the corresponding embargo on 'private' orders in relation to this age group[4]. Where both the mother and baby are minors, as we have seen[5], it is the *baby* whose welfare will be paramount in public law proceedings.[6]

Which proceedings and which orders?

It was observed above that care and supervision orders may be made in any family proceedings[7] and not only in what have traditionally been called 'care proceedings'. These latter proceedings, the sole purpose of which is to obtain a care or supervision order, are also now family proceedings for the purposes of the Children Act. Consequently, an application for these orders may be made on its own or during the course of family proceedings which are brought for some other purpose[8]. This, to some extent, corresponds with the old law, except that there is now only one ground for an order, whatever the nature of the proceedings. The statutory test, or threshold criteria, must be crossed, whether an order is requested in care proceedings, divorce proceedings or any other kind of proceedings.

A complementary feature of the Children Act is that, just as 'public' orders may be sought in private family proceedings, so 'private' orders may be sought in public family proceedings. Thus, the court considering an application for a care or supervision order must also consider the alternative of a s 8 order, especially a residence order[9]. There are, however, limitations on the use of s 8 orders in public proceedings, and local authorities will not be allowed to stretch the normal definition and use of such orders, especially where it would clearly be more appropriate for public law orders to be sought[10]. The court will also have at its

---

1   See, for example, N Lowe 'Caring for Children' (1989) 139 NLJ 87.
2   See, for example, J Eekelaar 'Parents' Rights to Punish – Further limits after Gillick' (1986) 28 *Childright* 9. See also the discussion of controversial uses of the inherent jurisdiction in relation to older teenagers below.
3   See Chapter 10 above.
4   Section 8 orders may not usually be made in respect of children who have attained 16 years of age (s 9(6) and (7) and s 91(10)). It should be noted that the court now has power to order the extension of residence orders to 18 years of age in appropriate cases. See Chapter 4 above.
5   See Chapter 2.
6   *Birmingham City Council v H (No 3)* [1994] 1 FLR 224 and *F v Leeds City Council* [1994] 2 FLR 60.
7   Section 8(3) and (4). We discuss the definition in Chapter 2.
8   Section 31(4).
9   In 2000 there were 1,365 residence orders made in public law proceedings and in 2001 there were 1,581 such orders. There were 227 prohibited steps orders in 2000 in public law proceedings. See Department of Health *Children Act Report 2001* (2002).
10 It has, however, been held in *Croydon London Borough Council v A (No 1)* [1992] 2 FLR 341 that the court does not have power to make a prohibited steps order prohibiting a father from having contact with a mother in care proceedings, since contact between spouses is not 'a step which could be taken by a parent in meeting his parental responsibility for a child'. In

disposal its general powers to attach conditions or give directions[1]. The court may also make s 8 orders, unlike care or supervision orders, whether or not they have been requested and, of course, it is not necessary for the statutory threshold criteria for care or supervision to be reached. It has been suggested that this power may be useful where there is doubt that the threshold criteria will be satisfied[2] but it is thought to be in the child's best interests that he lives away from his parents or, perhaps, to effect a 'phased rehabilitation' of the child with his family – a power which is not directly incorporated in the legislation[3]. In fact, it seems likely that the 'lesser' order (ie lesser in terms of its intrusion into family life) may prove valuable in cases at the margins of the statutory grounds[4]. A cautionary note should, however, be sounded. Too great a readiness in the courts to use s 8 orders in these circumstances could be interpreted as arrogating to themselves a wider power than Parliament intended. It could reopen all the old debates about wardship and its relationship to the statutory code – albeit in a rather different guise[5].

It is one thing for a private individual to seek private orders, or for a court to make them of its own volition in public family proceedings, and quite another for the State in the guise of the local authority to be allowed to seek private orders.

---

principle, of course, in appropriate cases, prohibited steps orders are available in public law proceedings. But see also *Nottinghamshire County Council v P* [1993] 2 FLR 134, in which the Court of Appeal held that a local authority had erred in seeking a prohibited steps order instead of a care order in relation to two sisters at risk of sexual abuse by their father. The authority was in reality seeking to exclude the father. The effect of the order would be like that of a 'no contact' order which the authority was precluded from seeking under s 9(2).

1   Section 11(7).

2   NV Lowe and G Douglas *Bromley's Family Law* (9th edn) (Butterworths, 1998) at pp 562–563.

3   This was the issue in the House of Lords decision in *Re E (SA) (A Minor) (Wardship)* [1984] 1 All ER 289.

4   A further example, suggested by NV Lowe and G Douglas (above), is that of an alcoholic or drug-addicted parent. Where there is a relative who could look after the child they suggest that a residence order may be appropriate. But it should be noted that the courts will not, other than in exceptional circumstances, make a residence order in favour of someone who does not want it. In *Re K (Care Order or Residence Order)* [1995] 1 FLR 675, the local authority, having originally applied for a care order, wanted a residence order to be made in favour of the grandparents. The grandparents, however, were getting on in years and did not wish to be exposed to the risk of private law proceedings being brought by the schizophrenic mother. Under a care order they would also be entitled to boarding-out allowances paid to local authority foster-parents. Stuart-White J held that a care order was appropriate in these circumstances to provide the children with the required protection and security.

5   The opposing arguments are extensively probed in Law Com Working Paper No 101 *Wards of Court* (1987), and see the discussion on the inherent jurisdiction below. In *Re RJ (Foster Placement)* [1998] 2 FLR 110 Sir Stephen Brown P refused to entertain an application for a residence order by foster-parents, supported by the guardian ad litem, to preserve the status quo. The foster-father was disqualified from acting as a foster-parent by the newly implemented regulations (the Children (Protection from Offenders) (Miscellaneous Amendments) Regulations 1997) protecting children from individuals convicted of or cautioned in relation to serious offences against children. He held that to have allowed the application would have been contrary to public policy. However, the Court of Appeal reversed this decision in *Re RJ (Fostering: Person Disqualified)* [1999] 1 FLR 605, taking the view that the court had jurisdiction to make a s 8 order and, in exercising its discretion, should weigh all relevant factors including public policy considerations. In an exceptional case such as this a private law application could prevail over a stated policy set out in regulations. The court made the children wards of court to preserve the status quo under which they could continue to live with the foster-parents until the conclusion of the substantive hearing. One week later, in *Re RJ (Wardship)* [1999] 1 FLR 618,

Here, the policy of the legislation is that the local authority should normally be obliged to go down the *public* route, satisfying the threshold criteria and seeking *public* orders. Where the authority has already obtained a care order, the scheme of the Act is that the authority is 'in the driving seat' with parental responsibility for the child and should not normally be allowed to pass this responsibility to the courts by seeking orders in relation to the child's upbringing. In limited circumstances, where the authority's statutory powers are inadequate and the child's welfare requires it, the authority may with leave seek the assistance of the High Court under its inherent jurisdiction. We discuss the inherent jurisdiction below. For the moment we are concerned with the restrictions which the legislation places on the making of private s 8 orders in favour of local authorities, and these are to be found in a cluster of provisions in s 9 of the Act.

First, where the child is already *in care* it is provided that no s 8 order may be made other than a residence order[1]. If a residence order were made in favour of an individual its effect would be to discharge the care order[2]. Such an application challenges the *source* of the authority's parental responsibility rather than its *exercise* and is not therefore inconsistent with the notion that the authority has parental responsibility under a care order. Secondly, no residence or contact order may be made in favour of a local authority[3]. Here, the policy is that if a local authority wishes to look after a child or have involvement with a child it must do so, unless it can secure the voluntary co-operation of the family, by means of the *public* care or supervision orders. As we have seen, a residence order may, of course, be made in favour of an *individual* in care proceedings. So far as contact is concerned, individuals must use the code in s 34 and not seek s 8 contact orders in relation to a child in care. We discuss the statutory contact regime below. Thirdly, no specific issue or prohibited steps order may be made with a view to achieving a result which could be achieved by making a residence or contact order or in any way which is denied to the High Court (by s 100(2)) in the exercise of its inherent jurisdiction with respect to children[4]. These provisions are complex and are not a good advertisement for parliamentary draftsmanship. They have given rise to major difficulties of interpretation, particularly in the case of *Nottinghamshire County Council v P*[5].

Perhaps the restrictions are best understood by concentrating on the limited circumstances in which local authorities *may* seek s 8 orders rather than when they

---

Cazalet J made an order arrived at by consent of all parties that the children should remain wards of court with care and control vested in the foster-parents and a contact order in favour of the mother.

1   Section 9(1).
2   Section 91(1).
3   Section 9(2).
4   Section 100(2) precludes the court from exercising its inherent jurisdiction:
     '(a)   so as to require the child to be placed in the care, or put under the supervision, of a local authority;
     (b)   so as to require a child to be accommodated by or on behalf of a local authority;
     (c)   so as to make a child who is the subject of a care order a ward of court; or
     (d)   for the purpose of conferring on any local authority power to determine any question which has arisen, or which may arise, in connection with any aspect of parental responsibility for a child.'
5   [1993] 2 FLR 134. Cf *Re H (Prohibited Steps Order)* [1995] 1 FLR 638. We consider these cases in the context of the discussion of excluding abusers from the family home in Chapter 12.

may not seek them. The fact of the matter is that when all the restrictions of s 9 are added together there is very little scope left for the granting of private orders at the behest of the local authority. It is clear that residence and contact orders may *never* be made in favour of the local authority and that specific issue and prohibited steps orders may not be made where the child is *in care*. The net result is that the latter two orders may be made in favour of a local authority but not if their effect is to breach the embargo on making the former two orders. They are thus likely only to be used to resolve 'single issues' and, even here, the authority may instead seek leave to invoke the inherent jurisdiction. So, to an appreciable extent, private s 8 orders are beyond the reach of the State.

All applications for care or supervision orders will be made, in the first instance, at the magistrates' level to the family proceedings court, although both the county court and the High Court now have concurrent jurisdiction[1]. There is provision for proceedings to be transferred, vertically or horizontally, to another court in appropriate cases[2].

On what ground?

The statutory ground for care and supervision orders is crucial, as is its interpretation by the courts, since it is now the only basis for compulsory intervention. It is a complex provision with many constituent elements and prompted one commentator to warn:

> 'Each of these elements will require considerable judicial exegesis. Almost every word will require interpretation and analysis. Argument on the meaning of the language contained here (as filled out by later subsections) is likely to rage for as long as this legislation remains in force.'[3]

The all-important provision is s 31(2), but this must be read with *both* the later subsections of s 31 (which define certain elements in the ground), and with the central principles in s 1 of the Children Act.

Section 31(2) provides:

> 'A court may only make a care order or supervision order if it is satisfied –
> (a)   that the child concerned is suffering, or is likely to suffer, significant harm; and
> (b)   that the harm, or likelihood of harm, is attributable to:
> (i)   the care given to the child, or likely to be given to him if the order were not made, not being what it would be reasonable to expect a parent to give to him; or
> (ii)   the child's being beyond parental control.'

Essentially, this is a single composite ground comprising two elements. The first is the presence or risk of significant harm to the child. The second is the attribution of this harm or risk to parental upbringing or to loss of parental control. Close analysis will be needed of these two independent elements, both of

---

1   See Chapter 2 above.
2   Children (Allocation of Proceedings) Order 1991, SI 1991/1677. Detailed discussion of the procedural rules is beyond the scope of the present work, but a useful account is to be found in NV Lowe and G Douglas *Bromley's Family Law* (9th edn) (Butterworths, 1998) at pp 534–536. See also D Bedingfield *The Child in Need* (Family Law, 1998) at pp 355–359.
3   MDA Freeman 'Care After 1991' in D Freestone (ed) *Children and the Law* (Hull University Press, 1990) at p 135.

which must be proved[1], but first it is necessary to explore the relationship between the statutory ground and the principles in Part I of the Children Act.

The threshold criteria and s 1 principles

Care and custody proceedings under the old law

One of the principal distinctions between care proceedings and custody or related proceedings under the old law was that the welfare principle applied in the latter but not in the former. It was not unknown for judges, especially in wardship, to draw attention to this[2]. The point which they were making was that the application of a broad welfare criterion, like the 'best interests' of the child, could allow the court to take almost any action it considered appropriate to safeguard the child's welfare. This was not possible in care proceedings which were hedged about with technical, and arguably restrictive, grounds which could prevent the court from taking the desired action. This, of course, accounts for the popularity of wardship with local authorities in the years leading up to the reforms[3]. Under the Children Act, local authorities may now resort to the inherent jurisdiction only with leave of the High Court.

Rejection of the welfare principle

The *Review*[4] specifically rejected the idea that the welfare principle could be adopted as the basis for compulsory action. The thinking was that this could give rise to widely differing interpretations of welfare and thus expose the family to unrestricted intervention. In short, it would give the State too open-ended a power, and might lead to children being removed from their families simply because someone else could do better in raising them. Instead, it was accepted that, subject to certain minimal acceptable standards, parents should be allowed to continue raising their children in their own way. Hence, the statutory criteria are met only where there has been a failure to measure up to these minimum standards. This is sometimes known as the 'threshold stage'. The ultimate decision on whether to make a care order, supervision order or any other order will then turn on the best interests of the child. Thus, the welfare principle will apply, but only at this second 'welfare stage', as discussed below.

Safeguarding 'the best interests' of the child

The *Review* had proposed the inclusion of a third element in the new ground: that the order would be 'the most effective means available to [the court] of

---

1   In many cases, however, it should be noted that the threshold conditions and indeed the court's order may be agreed by negotiation and the court's investigation of the facts more limited. For a useful discussion, see R White, P Carr and N Lowe *The Children Act in Practice* (3rd edn) (Butterworths, 2002) at p 286. See also, by way of illustration, *Re D (Child: Threshold Criteria)* [2001] 1 FLR 274, which holds that the judge is not bound by such agreements under the principle of issue estoppel, since he must retain his discretion to discharge his principal responsibility to promote the welfare of the child.

2   See, for example, the remarks of Dunn J in *Re D (A Minor) (Justices' Decision Review)* [1977] Fam 158.

3   Local authorities would sometimes 'waive the jurisdictional point' to enable the court to exercise its wardship jurisdiction for this purpose. Good examples of this phenomenon are *A v B and Hereford and Worcester Council* [1986] 1 FLR 289; and *Re JT (A Minor) (Wardship: Committal to Care)* [1986] 2 FLR 107.

4   DHSS *Review of Child Care Law* (1985) at para 15.10.

safeguarding the child's welfare'[1]. In essence, this third element has been grafted on to the statutory ground through the application of the welfare principle in s 1 of the Children Act. Both this and the no order principle in s 1(5) apply, and their cumulative effect is to prevent the making of a care or supervision order where this is not shown to be in the best interests of the child, or where it is not shown to be a better way of safeguarding the child's welfare than any other available option. But these broader considerations of welfare only come into play after the threshold criteria have been satisfied. If the conditions of s 31(2) cannot be proved, that is the end of the matter. If they can be proved, the court must then go on to consider whether care or supervision is the best course of action, which it may not be, given the emphasis on voluntary co-operation. At the welfare stage the court must also engage in the 'vital judicial task' of considering the Convention rights of the adult members of the family and the children under Article 8 of the ECHR. The court is not empowered to sanction such an interference with family life unless it is satisfied that it is both necessary and proportionate and that no less radical form of order will achieve the essential aim of promoting the welfare of the children[2]. Where the court at the threshold stage has been unable to identify which of *two* parents was the perpetrator, the court should proceed at the welfare stage on the basis that *each* of the parents was a possible perpetrator[3]. As Lord Nicholls of Birkenhead put it:

> 'it would be grotesque if such a case had to proceed at the welfare stage on the footing that, because neither parent, considered individually, has been proved to be the perpetrator, therefore the child is not at risk from either of them. This would be grotesque because it would mean the court would proceed on the footing that neither parent represents a risk even though one or other of them was the perpetrator of the harm in question.'[4]

If parents are willing to agree to the local authority's plan for the child, perhaps by allowing the child to be accommodated by the local authority or by not opposing the making of a care order, compulsion may be both unnecessary and undesirable. On the other hand, where there have been serious incidents of violence or sexual abuse, the court may conclude that the local authority requires the additional control which it can get from a care order.

How far can the no order principle be taken?
A final and vitally important preliminary question is how far the courts are likely to take the no order principle in practice. In the private sphere, particularly on divorce, the objection to court orders was that they were often unnecessary, merely upholding the status quo after, at best, a perfunctory investigation of welfare[5]. Care and supervision orders, however, have not been granted routinely but only after a full and often contested hearing before the court. If, therefore, there were to be a similar sharp decline in the number of care orders as there has been in the number of orders on divorce, this would be a matter of major public concern. This is especially so since the wardship procedure, which used to protect a number of children, is now no longer available. In fact, after an initial decline in

---

1   DHSS *Review of Child Care Law* (1985) at para 15.24.
2   See the decision of the Court of Appeal in *Re B (Care: Interference with Family Life)* [2003] 2 FLR 813.
3   See the House of Lords decision in *Re O and N; Re B* [2003] 1 FLR 1169.
4   Ibid at 1177.
5   See Chapter 4 above.

the number of care orders following the implementation of the Children Act in 1991 (when there were only about 1,600 orders in the first year), there has since been a steady increase. In 2000 there were 6,298 care orders and 1,326 supervision orders. In 2001 the figures had remained reasonably constant at 5,984 care orders and 1,466 supervision orders[1].

The first element – significant harm

When must significant harm occur and how it is proved?

An early answer to the question whether the statutory threshold criteria should be interpreted restrictively or liberally was given by the Court of Appeal in *Newham London Borough Council v AG*[2]. The court was concerned with the interpretation of the new prospective element in the statutory threshold – that the child is 'likely to suffer' significant harm. Sir Stephen Brown P held that this was not to be equated with 'on the balance of probabilities' and expressed the hope that the courts would not be asked to perform in every case a strict legalistic analysis of the statutory meaning of s 31. Although the words of the statute had to be considered, Parliament could not have intended them to be unduly restrictive when the evidence clearly indicated that a certain course of action should be followed to protect a child.

The *Newham* case was concerned with what has become a recurrent problem and theme in the reported cases. This is the choice which often has to be made between care in the child's extended family (in this case with grandparents) and substitute care outside the birth family, perhaps leading to the child's ultimate adoption. The broad issue is how far the resources of the birth family must be exhausted before the State is entitled to pursue its preferred choice of substitute care under the force of a care order. In *Newham*, the Court of Appeal accepted the judge's assessment that the grandparents would be unable to offer the child adequate protection from the serious danger which the mother represented (she was seriously ill with a form of schizophrenia which manifested itself in neglect of the child).

The issue was to resurface again in dramatic fashion in *Re M (A Minor) (Care Order: Threshold Conditions)*[3], which is now the leading authority on the interpretation of the statutory threshold. Here, the father had murdered the mother in front of the children in particularly gruesome circumstances. The police took the children into emergency protection[4]. The father was convicted of the mother's murder and was serving a life sentence with a recommendation for deportation (he was Nigerian) on his eventual release. Three of the four children were placed with Mrs W, the mother's cousin, but initially she did not feel able to cope with the youngest child, M. So M, not yet four months old, was placed with a temporary foster-mother. In due course, Mrs W wanted to offer M a home with his half-siblings. It should be noted in passing that there were several different fathers of the children but that the father of M was the mother's husband. Since he was

---

1   Department of Health *The Children Act Report 2001* (2002).
2   [1993] 1 FLR 281.
3   [1994] 3 WLR 558. For commentaries, see J Masson 'Social Engineering in the House of Lords: *Re M*' (1994) 6 JCL 170, J Whybrow '*Re M* – Past, Present and Future Significant Harm' (1994) 6 JCL 88, and A Bainham 'The Temporal Dimension of Care' (1994) CLJ 458.
4   For the powers of the police to protect children in emergencies, see Chapter 12.

married to her, he continued to retain parental responsibility and, indeed, sought to influence the decision from prison on what was to happen to M[1]. The local authority, the guardian ad litem for M and the father all wanted a care order to be made and for M to be placed for adoption outside the extended birth family.

At first instance, Bracewell J made the care order but the Court of Appeal allowed Mrs W's appeal and substituted a residence order in her favour[2]. The House of Lords restored the care order, although by the time of the hearing it was accepted on all sides that M had settled well with Mrs W and her family and should stay with her. The point of law was this. In considering whether a child 'is suffering significant harm' is it permissible to look backwards to the time when the initial protective measures were instigated (in this case police protection) or does this test have to be satisfied at the time of the hearing at which the application is being considered? The significance of the issue was, of course, that by the date of the hearing M was no longer suffering significant harm, nor was he 'likely' to suffer it because he was by this time properly looked after and the danger had passed.

The House of Lords held that there was jurisdiction to make a care order in these circumstances. Lord Mackay LC said that on a correct interpretation of s 31(2)(a) the court was entitled to have regard to the whole period from the instigation of the protective measures until the final disposal of the case. Thus, Bracewell J had been right to look back to the situation as it was when emergency protection was taken. She had been entitled to conclude that *at that time* M was suffering significant harm by being permanently deprived of the love and care of his mother and that this was attributable to the fact that the 'care' given by the parent (the father) was not what it would have been reasonable to expect a parent to give to him[3]. The only limitation on this retrospective process of looking backwards was that the initial protective arrangements had remained continuously in place. The local authority could not, for example, terminate a temporary foster-placement, allow the child home and then, as it were, have a 'second bite at the cherry'. Lords Templeman and Nolan pointed out that to restrict evidence to that which was available at the hearing could mean that *any* temporary measures which removed the risk could preclude the court from making a final care order and that this could not have been Parliament's intention.

The decision raises a number of important questions of policy. First, the reader may wonder why, if the child M had settled happily with Mrs W, the local authority bothered to pursue the chance of obtaining a care order all the way to the House of Lords. Part of the answer to this was of course the need to obtain clarification of the important point of law about when precisely the threshold conditions must be proved to be satisfied. But there was more to it than this. The practical point of a

---

1 There is no statutory power to revoke the parental responsibility of a *married* father short of the ultimate step of adoption. It is questionable whether a father in these circumstances should be able to retain it at all.

2 A particularly good example of the *private* s 8 order being made in *public* family proceedings. See, generally, Chapter 2 for the scheme of the Children Act in this respect.

3 A possible criticism of this logic, but not, it is submitted, a convincing objection, is that the father's behaviour, appalling though it was, had been directed towards the *mother* and not towards the child. This argument will in any event be met, at least in part, by an amendment to s 31 introduced by the Adoption and Children Act 2002 which will include within the concept of 'harm' for the purposes of the threshold, 'impairment suffered from seeing or hearing the ill-treatment of another'. See further p 495 below.

care order in *Re M* itself was that it would enable social services to keep a 'watching brief' on M's situation and intervene quickly to remove him from Mrs W should the need arise. If the residence order in favour of Mrs W had stood, the authority would have had no such right, since parental responsibility would have vested in her and not in the authority. Secondly, there is the broader policy question, alluded to above, about whether the State should have the option of obtaining a compulsory order where the risk *in fact* has passed and there is no obvious future risk to the child. Surely the public law requirement of the Children Act is not intended to allow the State to remove children who are no longer at risk merely because it would have greater confidence in carers outside the family than those within it. The legislation is, after all, supposed to have a commitment to supporting the natural family, and reuniting the child with relatives, wherever possible[1]. In short, State intervention is not about finding the best available home for a child, and children are not to be taken into care merely because someone could make a better job of raising them than their own family. The decision in *Re M* has been subjected to scathing criticism along these lines by Judith Masson[2] and it is impossible here to do justice to the full force of her arguments.

Nevertheless, it is submitted that on balance the positive aspects of the House of Lords ruling in *Re M* outweigh these objections for the following reasons. First, following the Court of Appeal's decision in the *Newham* case, it was important that the House of Lords should adopt a liberal and non-legalistic interpretation of the statutory threshold conditions which allows for some flexibility on the temporal question which had so bedevilled the previous legislation[3]. Secondly, it should be remembered that to cross the threshold is not per se sufficient to found a care order. The court will still need to be convinced, at the welfare stage, that a care order is in the best interests of the particular child, and the authority will have to convince the court in its care plan that this is so. The court is not obliged to make a care order, supervision order or any other order if it sees no need for it at the date of the final hearing. Finally, while it is true that the potential contribution of the extended family must be properly explored, the authority will have to balance this with genuine anxieties it may have about whether the wider family, in which a parent has been shown to be unable to cope with a child, is actually the best environment in which that child should be raised. There is no better illustration of this than the facts of the *Newham* case.

Re M has been applied in several subsequent cases. In *Re K (Care Order or Residence Order)*[4], it was held that the court had jurisdiction to make a care order even though, at the relevant time, the children were well looked after by their grandparents. Although the local authority no longer sought a care order, it had originally applied for one and there was no principle that a care order should only be made in the family context in exceptional circumstances. There would be cases (and this was one) in which a care order would be the only way of protecting children placed with the extended family from significant harm.

What if the initial 'protective measures' envisaged in *Re M* are taken under Part III of the Children Act, ie they are 'voluntary' measures in the sense that they

---

1   See Chapter 10.
2   See fn 3 at p 486 (above).
3   See p 490 below.
4   [1995] 1 FLR 675.

are not opposed by anyone with parental responsibility? Two decisions make it plain that the provision of such services to children, particularly accommodation, may be sufficient to found a care order if in due course the authority feels that it needs the additional security of a care order. In *Re SH (Care Order: Orphan)*[1], the child had had spells of voluntary accommodation with the local authority while his mother was in hospital. There had been allegations of sexual abuse of his half-brother in which the mother was implicated. The mother then died and within months the father also died. At that point, the local authority sought a care order which was opposed by the child's guardian ad litem on the basis that the threshold criteria were not satisfied and that, applying the 'no order' principle, the local authority had ample powers to continue to look after the child under Part III and particularly under its powers to accommodate under s 20. It was held that the words 'is suffering' in s 31(2) meant 'was suffering' significant harm at the time when the 'rescue operation' was instigated, provided that these measures were continuing at the time of the final hearing. The decision confirms that protective measures which start as voluntary accommodation, qualify as the necessary rescue operation. Moreover, a care order offered more than the continuation of voluntary accommodation since it gave the local authority parental responsibility and the legal standing to find an early adoption placement, to authorise medical procedures, to resist applications by relatives, etc. Its voluntary powers were inadequate for these purposes and neither was guardianship (which was the appropriate procedure where an individual wished to take over the care of an orphan) apposite in the case of a local authority.

A similar conclusion was reached in *Re M (Care Order: Parental Responsibility)*[2] which confirms that the threshold conditions may be satisfied in relation to an abandoned baby. Here, a baby of Afro-Caribbean origin was found abandoned on the steps of a health centre when a few days old. It proved impossible to trace the child's family and he was placed with foster-parents. The baby was found to have developmental and other abnormalities and it was likely that medical intervention in the future would be necessary. The local authority was concerned that without a care order its powers were limited in relation, for example, to medical testing. It sought a care order with a view to placing the child for adoption and argued that there was a need for *someone* to have parental responsibility. Cazalet J held that the fact of abandonment, with all the risks it entailed, meant that the baby was suffering from significant harm immediately before he was found. Given his special needs, he was 'likely' to suffer significant harm in the future as a result of being abandoned. It was therefore necessary that someone should have parental responsibility and that the local authority should acquire this through a care order.

The fact that the appropriate date for considering whether the threshold is crossed is the date when the authority first intervenes to protect the child does not mean that the authority may not rely on subsequent evidence or later events. In *Re G (Care Proceedings: Threshold Conditions)*[3] the Court of Appeal held that the authority was entitled to rely on information obtained after the date of intervention, in this case expert assessments, and on later events if those things

---

1 [1995] 1 FLR 746.
2 [1996] 2 FLR 84.
3 [2001] 2 FLR 1111.

were capable of *proving* the state of affairs which existed at the time of the protective action. Hale LJ emphasised that emergency and initial protection measures often had to be taken before the full picture emerged. As a practical matter the authority was bound to be able to rely at the hearing on matters which had come to light since protective action was taken. It did not have to be in possession of all the information on which it intended to rely when it initially intervened. As she put it:

> 'Care cases, like all children cases, look to the future and not to the past. Things are changing all the time while the case progresses. The local authority is not required to plead their case at the outset or indeed at all.'

However, she went on to point to the importance of parents being made aware of the case which they were required to answer by the date of the hearing and approved of the practice in many courts of requiring the authority, before the final hearing, to make a clear statement of the facts it is inviting the court to find and the basis on which it alleges the threshold is crossed[1].

A rather different temporal problem from the one which occurred in *Re M* had caused very considerable difficulty under the old law. A major problem with the former conditions for care orders was that they generally required proof of *existing* harm. The local authority could not usually take a pre-emptive strike to protect a child from apprehended harm[2]. It is true that, in every case, the court had to make an evaluation of future risk when deciding whether to make a care order, but it could not make one *solely* on the strength of this[3]. This restriction caused problems in certain kinds of cases, as where a local authority wished to forestall the removal of a child from a stable foster-home to an uncertain future with parents[4], or where it wished to prevent a new-born baby leaving hospital with parents known to have a propensity for abuse or neglect[5]. The problem, in each case, was that it was very difficult to pin down existing harm, let alone attribute this to parental failings. These difficulties were occasionally circumvented by warding the child or by straining the statutory language as occurred in the well-known *Berkshire* case[6]. It ought now to be possible for cases like this to be resolved, if necessary, exclusively on the strength of the risk to the child's welfare as disclosed by all the surrounding circumstances, although there has been a forceful dissent from this view[7]. It seems clear that purely past conduct will not meet the statutory criteria unless it also points to present or future harm[8] or unless, as discussed above, protective measures have been continuously in place since the conduct in question.

---

1   [2001] 2 FLR 1111 at 1115.
2   By way of exception to this, the old grounds did allow a care order to be made largely on the strength of the risk to one child in the family arising from previous abuse or neglect of *another* child in the household, or risk to the child occasioned by the presence in the household of a child offender. See the Children and Young Persons Act 1969, s 1(2)(b) and (bb).
3   *Essex County Council v TLR and KBR (Minors)* (1978) Fam Law 15.
4   As in the *Essex* case (above).
5   Place of safety orders had, however, been granted, controversially, for this purpose for some considerable time before the Children Act. See MDA Freeman 'Removing Babies at Birth: A Questionable Practice' (1980) Fam Law 131.
6   *D (A Minor) v Berkshire County Council* [1987] AC 317.
7   MDA Freeman 'Care after 1991' in D Freestone (ed) *Children and the Law* (Hull University Press, 1990). Cf A Bainham 'Care After 1991 – A Reply' (1991) 3 JCL 99.
8   Issues raised by the pre-Children Act decision in *M v Westminster City Council* [1985] FLR 325.

The Children Act 1989 Guidance and Regulations Vol 1 Court Orders[1] suggests that most cases of anticipated harm will arise where the child has suffered significant harm at some time in the past and 'is likely to do so again because of some recurring circumstance'. The examples given are:

'where physical abuse of a child is associated with bouts of parental depression; or where a newly-born baby, because of the family history, would be at risk if taken home; or where the welfare of a child who was being looked after by the local authority under voluntary accommodation arrangements . . . would be at risk if the parents went ahead with plans to return him to an unsuitable home environment.'

But the *Guidance* goes on to warn that 'the conditions are intended to place a sufficiently difficult burden of proof upon the applicant as to prevent unwarranted intervention in cases where the child is not genuinely at risk'. There are clearly also, as we have noted, human rights limitations which prevent action that is not proportionate and not necessary from being taken[2].

How then is this difficult burden of proof to be discharged by the local authority? The issue fell to be determined by the House of Lords which found it sufficiently difficult that it was obliged to hand down a 3:2 majority decision. In *Re H and R (Child Sexual Abuse: Standard of Proof)*[3] a 15-year-old girl alleged sexual abuse over a long period by her mother's cohabitant who was subsequently tried for rape but acquitted. The local authority nonetheless wanted to secure care orders in relation to the three younger girls in the household. They invited the judge to find that on the balance of probabilities (viz the lower civil, as opposed to criminal, standard of proof) the man concerned had indeed abused the eldest girl or that there was a substantial risk that he had done so and that, accordingly, the younger girls were 'likely to suffer significant harm' if a care order was not made. The judge was suspicious of abuse and recognised the real possibility that the eldest girl had given true evidence. But he dismissed the application for the care order holding that he could not be sure to the 'requisite high standard of proof' that this was so and that the threshold criteria were not therefore satisfied. The Court of Appeal by majority dismissed the authority's appeal, as did the House of Lords.

The principal majority speech was given by Lord Nicholls (with whom Lord Goff and Lord Mustill agreed) but there were strong dissents by Lord Browne-Wilkinson and Lord Lloyd. The first point was unanimously accepted. Following the Court of Appeal's decision in the *Newham* case, the House confirmed that in order to establish the prospective element in the statutory threshold it was *not* necessary to show that it was *probable* that the child would suffer significant harm in the sense of there being more than a fifty–fifty chance of it occurring. A child might need protection just as much where there was a *real possibility* of harm that could not be ignored having regard to the nature of the harm feared. Where the

---

1   (HMSO, 1991) at para 3.22.

2   It was re-emphasised by the Court of Appeal in *Re O and N (Care: Preliminary Hearing)* [2002] 2 FLR 1167 that the burden of proof rests throughout on the applicant authority to establish its case. It is not for the parent to exculpate himself or herself except to the extent of discharging an evidential burden, namely to provide some explanation for injuries to a child. But that does not amount to a legal burden of proof.

3   [1996] 1 FLR 80. For commentary, see H Keating 'Shifting Standards in the House of Lords' [1996] CFLQ 157, and A Bainham 'Sexual Abuse in the Lords' (1996) CLJ 209.

majority and minority views differed was in what was required in order to establish this real possibility of harm to the court's satisfaction.

The majority held that the standard of proof was the ordinary civil standard of the balance of probabilities, but also took the view that, generally, the truth of specific allegations on which the authority was relying would have to be proved to this standard. More controversially, it was the view of the majority that, in applying this standard, the court should bear in mind that the more serious the allegations the less likely it was that the events had occurred and the stronger the evidence that would be required. The standard of proof itself was not higher in these cases but, since it was inherently unlikely that what was alleged had actually occurred, proportionately more cogent evidence would be required to overcome this improbability[1]. It was further held that in assessing likelihood of harm the court had to determine disputed issues of fact. Suspicion was not enough since the foundation of care orders was 'the language of proof not suspicion'. In this respect, the evidence required to found a care order was greater than that required for short-term orders such as child assessment orders, emergency protection orders or interim care orders where, respectively, 'reasonable cause to suspect', 'reasonable cause to believe' or 'reasonable grounds for believing' that the child is likely to suffer significant harm will suffice[2]. The majority did, however, concede that there would be cases where, although the alleged maltreatment was not proved, the totality of the evidence established a combination of 'profoundly worrying features' which affected the care of the child within the family. It was possible that 'likelihood' of harm could be established in these circumstances even though it could not be said that the child was presently suffering it. In *Re H and R* itself, the difficulty was that the *only* relevant fact was the alleged abuse of the eldest girl, and it could not therefore be said that the younger girls were at risk unless this allegation could be proved. Parents, it was said, should not have their children taken away fom them solely on the basis of suspicion.

The essential difference between the majority and the minority was that the latter, but not the former, were prepared to accept that the eldest girl's evidence remained *evidence* which could be taken into account in making the prognosis of risk. It was not essential to discount it if the truth of the allegations could not be substantiated. Thus, the judge's conclusion that there was a real possibility that her version of events was true was *not* a finding based on suspicion alone but on the *evidence*. Lord Lloyd also commented adversely on the notion that because a risk is

---

1   In *Re ET (Serious Injuries: Standard of Proof)* [2003] 2 FLR 1205 Bodey J, reiterating that the standard of proof was not higher in a case involving very serious allegations, took the view that the difference between the civil and criminal standards of proof in such a case was largely illusory. Cf Hedley J, in *A Local Authority v S, W and T (By His Guardian)* [2004] 2 FLR 129, who emphasised that although very serious issues were raised in family proceedings (in this case whether a father had caused serious injuries to a child by shaking) they remained civil proceedings and subject to civil, not criminal, rules of evidence and the civil law relating to proof; while a jury in a criminal trial were primarily concerned with the defendant and establishing guilt, the family judge was concerned primarily with the child and had to determine the probabilities on the basis of a much wider range of evidence. Finally, in *Re U (Serious Injury: Standard of Proof); Re B* [2004] 2 FLR 263 the Court of Appeal held expressly that it was incorrect to treat the distinction between criminal and civil standards as 'largely illusory' and emphasised again that the material available to the court in a civil case was likely to be much more extensive than that which would be admitted in a criminal trial.

2   See, respectively, s 43(1), s 44(1) and s 38(2). See also the discussion of the inherent jurisdiction below.

serious, it is less likely. As he put it, it 'would be a bizarre result if the more serious the anticipated injury, whether physical or sexual, the more difficult it became for the authority to ... secure protection for the child'.

The majority decision of course represents the law, and it has subsequently been applied by the Court of Appeal which had to consider the appropriate standard of proof at the welfare stage of care proceedings[1]. Having crossed the threshold and found either existing significant harm, or the risk of significant harm to the child, could it be argued that a lesser standard of proof should apply at the welfare stage, viz when the court is deciding whether or not it should make the care order? In *Re M and R*, the Court of Appeal emphatically rejected this argument, again holding that the court can only act on the basis of proven facts rather than suspicion. Here, the judge had made interim care orders on the basis of emotional abuse and neglect of the children but he found that serious allegations of sexual abuse of the children by the mother and two men had not been proved to the requisite standard. He thus refused to make a final care order but adjourned the case for three months. The Court of Appeal was not prepared to accede to the local authority's argument that, because the welfare of the child was paramount at the welfare stage, the standard of proof for establishing likely harm should be less than the preponderance of possibilities. So again, the judge's finding of the real possibility of sexual abuse was not sufficient to found a full care order.

As we have noted, there will be many instances in which parents and others are willing to concede that the threshold criteria are met, thus averting the need for a lengthy trial of the issues. This does not mean, however, that the local authority will necessarily be precluded from leading, or the court from testing, the evidence relating to allegations of abuse. One reason for this is that it may be important to establish whether or not the child has been the victim of a particular kind of abuse in taking future decisions relating to the care of the child. Thus, in *Re M (Threshold Criteria: Parental Concessions)*[2] the adoptive parents of three children conceded that the threshold criteria were met on the basis of their rejection of the child following allegations of sexual abuse by them, their use of inappropriate forms of punishment and their failure to pay reasonable attention to the children's emotional needs. Nonetheless, the authority was allowed to lead evidence of sexual abuse since the concessions made were different in kind and entirely different in importance from the abuse allegations. They did not meet the requirements of justice in this case, since there was the potential for future contact between the adoptive parents and the children. Any care plan, including therapy, ought to take account of the actual harm suffered by the children and any court considering contact should also be aware of it in deciding what approach to take.

The problem of the unborn child
One situation which has caused difficulty is that of the unborn child. Where the pregnant mother is already known to social services, perhaps because of drug or alcohol abuse, or previous difficulties with her other children, the local authority may be genuinely concerned about the welfare of the expected child. If the mother has a medical or psychiatric condition, the local authority may want to ensure that the mother co-operates in the provision of proper ante-natal care and

---

1   *Re M and R (Child Abuse: Evidence)* [1996] 2 FLR 195.
2   [1999] 2 FLR 728.

that the birth itself should be under normal medical supervision. Whatever these anxieties, the legal position is that the foetus is not within the definition of 'child' which means 'a person under the age of eighteen'[1]. Moreover, the foetus may not be made a ward of court[2]. All the authority can normally do is 'offer' voluntary assistance and 'keep its fingers crossed' that the birth will be trouble-free[3]. These limitations reflect, in part, the strong libertarian objections to the coercion of pregnant women who, it is often acknowledged, have complete autonomy over their own bodies. The legal and philosophical difficulty is how to balance any rights the foetus may have against such rights of the mother – an issue which has been hotly debated in the context of abortion[4]. As reflected in abortion law itself, it may well be that different considerations ought to apply to the later stages of pregnancy than in the first or second trimesters[5]. The case for ruling out all judicial intervention where a foetus is close to term is not, it is submitted, a strong one.

The position may, however, be different if the High Court is prepared to exercise its inherent jurisdiction in relation to *the mother* herself, as it did in a number of cases in order to authorise a Caesarean section in the face of opposition by a woman in labour[6]. The courts were careful to avoid saying explicitly that these interventions were designed to protect the health or life of the foetus, and the decisions are at least formally justified on the basis of the best interests of the patient herself. But the effect will nevertheless usually be to ensure the safe delivery of the child. It is now, however, necessary to distinguish between adults and adolescents as far as this issue is concerned. In the case of adults the Court of Appeal in *St George's Healthcare NHS Trust v S*[7] has made it plain that a competent adult patient has the absolute right to refuse a Caesarean even where to do so would jeopardise her own life as well as that of her child. However, where the patient is a minor, the courts have jurisdiction to intervene and may still do so. *A Metropolitan Borough Council v DB*[8] provides perhaps the best illustration of the court's willingness to intervene paternalistically to protect a young mother and her child in the period immediately before and after the birth. It also illustrates

1   Section 105(1), and see Chapter 3 above.
2   *Re F (In Utero)* [1988] Fam 122.
3   The word 'offer' is used since it may well be that social services will attempt to exert pressure to co-operate.
4   As to which, contrast J Jarvis Thomson 'A Defence of Abortion' and J Finnis 'The Rights and Wrongs of Abortion' both in RM Dworkin (ed) *The Philosophy of Law* (Oxford University Press, 1977).
5   For a discussion of English abortion law, see G Douglas *Law, Fertility and Reproduction* (Sweet & Maxwell, 1991) at ch 5. For a useful collection of materials on legal intervention, see J Bridgeman and S Millns *Feminist Perspectives in Law: Law's Engagement with the Female Body* (Sweet & Maxwell, 1998) especially at pp 352–379. See also for a recent thorough examination of the issues involved in balancing maternal rights and foetal welfare, M Brazier 'Parental responsibilities, foetal welfare and children's health' in C Bridge (ed) *Family Law Towards the Millennium: Essays for PM Bromley* (Butterworths, 1997) at ch 8.
6   See, for example, *Re S (Adult: Surgical Treatment)* [1993] 1 FLR 26, *Norfolk and Norwich Health Care (NHS) Trust v W* [1996] 2 FLR 613, and Chapter 8 (above).
7   [1998] 2 FLR 728. See Chapter 8 above. See also J Weaver 'Court-Ordered Caesarean Sections' in A Bainham, S Day Sclater and M Richards *Body Lore and Laws* (Hart Publishing, 2002) at p 229 and E Jackson *Regulating Reproduction: Law, Technology and Autonomy* (Hart Publishing, 2001) at pp 131–140.
8   [1997] 1 FLR 767.

the use of the inherent jurisdiction in conjunction with statutory powers under the Children Act. Here, the mother was a 17-year-old crack-cocaine addict. She had a fear of doctors but her medical condition gave cause for concern since she had suffered eclamptic fits resulting from high blood pressure. A Caesarean section was performed under judicial authorisation, and an emergency protection order was then obtained in relation to the baby once born. The authority then successfully invoked the inherent jurisdiction to keep the mother in the hospital maternity ward, which for these purposes constituted 'secure accommodation', since she had threatened to discharge herself from the ward in life-threatening circumstances. In this case the court found her *incompetent* to consent to medical treatment but, as we have seen in Chapter 8, the courts have reserved to themselves jurisdiction to intervene to protect even competent adolescents. It is therefore submitted that the result could well have been the same if she had been adjudged competent.

What is harm?: the 'Russian doll' provision

The concept of 'harm' is very wide and is the cornerstone of the statutory ground. It has been said that 'the categories of abuse are never closed'[1]. The legislation defines harm[2] as 'ill-treatment or the impairment of health or development' and then provides a definition of each of these components. 'Development' includes 'physical, intellectual, emotional, social or behavioural development'. 'Health' includes 'physical or mental health'. 'Ill-treatment' embraces 'sexual abuse and forms of ill-treatment which are not physical'. It is now provided that harm includes, by way of example, 'impairment suffered from seeing or hearing the ill-treatment of another'[3]. This is a welcome clarification of the doubt which existed about whether abusive actions had to be aimed at the child concerned. It is now clear that they do not. The amendment should bring within the concept of harm many instances of physical harm to children where they witness domestic violence between adults in the same household, most obviously, as in the leading case of *Re M*[4], violence directed at the mother. The kinds of harm contemplated are neglect, physical injury, sexual abuse and emotional abuse[5].

The latest edition of *Working Together*[6] contains helpful definitions of the different forms of abuse and neglect of children, which we set out below.

Neglect

Neglect is not, as such, mentioned in the Children Act but is subsumed within the idea of 'ill-treatment or the impairment of health or development'. Examples of neglect may be failure to summon essential medical attention[7], failure to provide

---

1 MDA Freeman *Children, Their Families and the Law* (Macmillan, 1992), at p 93.

2 Section 31(9).

3 Section 31(9), as amended by the Adoption and Children Act 2002, s 120.

4 *Re M (A Minor) (Care Order: Threshold Conditions)* [1994] 2 FLR 577. See pp 486 et seq above.

5 On the problems of defining child abuse, see C Wattam 'The social construction of child abuse for practical policy purposes – a review of *Child Protection: Messages from Research*' [1996] CFLQ 189, reviewing the Department of Health's overview of research findings (HMSO, 1995). See Department of Health *Child Protection: Messages from Research* (1995).

6 (Above) at paras 2.4–2.7.

7 See Chapter 8.

the child with sustenance or failure to prevent the child coming into contact with foreseeable hazards[1].

Working Together defines neglect as:

> 'the persistent failure to meet a child's basic physical and/or psychological needs, likely to result in the serious impairment of the child's health or development. It may involve a parent or carer failing to provide adequate food, shelter or clothing, failing to protect a child from physical harm or danger, or the failure to ensure access to appropriate medical care or treatment. It may also include neglect of, or unresponsiveness to, a child's basic emotional needs.'

Physical injury and the problem of corporal punishment

Working Together says that physical abuse may involve 'hitting, shaking, throwing, poisoning, burning or scalding, drowning, suffocating, or otherwise causing physical harm to a child. Physical harm may also be caused when a parent or carer feigns the symptoms of, or deliberately causes ill health to a child whom they are looking after. This situation is commonly described using terms such as factitious illness by proxy or Münchausen syndrome by proxy.'

Physical injury is understandable enough, but difficult questions can be asked about the line between corporal punishment and abuse. Some people would outlaw all corporal punishment (as, for example, in the Scandinavian countries, Austria and Cyprus) largely because of the danger that punishment can degenerate into abuse[2]. There is also an argument that to allow parental punishment of children violates Article 19 of the UNCRC, which, inter alia, protects the child from 'all forms of physical or mental violence'. Freeman's view is that 'nothing is a clearer statement of the position that children occupy in society, a clearer badge of childhood than the fact that children alone of all people in society can be hit with impunity'[3].

The whole question of corporal punishment underwent close scrutiny by the Scottish Law Commission[4]. Although the Commission was not addressing the question of when it is or is not abuse, for the purposes of care proceedings, its conclusions were nonetheless an interesting barometer of Scottish public opinion[5]. This seemed to be that, while the spontaneous slap or smack by a loving parent was considered a legitimate exercise of parental control, the striking of a child of any age with an implement was not[6]. The Commission was not prepared to recommend the total abolition of the parental right to administer 'moderate and reasonable chastisement'[7]. We discuss the abolition of corporal punishment in schools when we look at education more generally in Chapter 16. We are concerned here with the legality of parental corporal punishment, and the ECtHR

---

1   See Chapter 15.
2   This is MDA Freeman's view in *Children, Their Families and the Law* (Macmillan, 1992) at p 105. See also *The Moral Status of Children* (Martinus Nijhoff, 1997) especially at pp 116–117 and pp 131–132.
3   (Above) at p 117.
4   Scot Law Com Report No 135 *Family Law* (1992) at paras 2.67–2.105.
5   The Commission conducted a survey through System Three Scotland in September 1991. The results of this are recorded at Scot Law Com Report No 135 (above), at paras 2.100–2.102.
6   While, for example, 83% thought that it ought to be lawful for a parent to smack a three-year-old, only 3% thought that the use of a belt, stick or other object should be within the law.
7   A test established in *R v Hopley* (1860) 2 F&F 202.

had an opportunity to consider this in *A v United Kingdom (Human Rights: Punishment of Child)*[1].

The step-father of a nine-year-old boy repeatedly beat him with a garden cane leaving linear bruises on his thighs and buttocks which remained for up to one week. This was held to amount to 'torture or inhuman or degrading treatment or punishment' contrary to Article 3 of the ECHR. The Court also unanimously held that the United Kingdom could be liable for its failure to take measures which could have prevented the beatings. Matters hinged on the fact that under English law, on a charge of assault, the defendant may rely on the defence of 'moderate and reasonable chastisement'. Where the defence is raised the burden of proof rests on the prosecution to establish that what occurred exceeded those limits. In *A v UK* the step-father was prosecuted for assault occasioning actual bodily harm but was acquitted on a majority verdict of the jury. The ECtHR took the view that the ECHR imposed on States an obligation to implement laws which provide sufficient protection to children and other vulnerable individuals 'in the form of effective deterrence, against such serious breaches of personal integrity'. This the UK had failed to do in making available a defence which could be successfully invoked in circumstances which involved 'punishment' at such a level of severity as to fall within the scope of Article 3.

The Government reacted to the ruling by issuing a Consultation Paper[2] and, for a while, it certainly looked as if it would take steps to legislate by defining more closely the legal limits of corporal punishment by parents. But it also made clear its view that it would not outlaw smacking because 'the overwhelming majority of parents know the difference between smacking and beating'. Others, however, argued strenuously that any attempt to define which applications of physical force to children were acceptable and which were not would be unworkable and argued instead for removal of the defence altogether. The key consideration for the abolitionists is the symbolic power of the law and the message which abolition would deliver in terms of children's rights and the need to remove the official justification for hitting children. It has also been pointed out that the experience in those countries which have taken this course has been that trivial assaults, such as smacking, would not lead to prosecution but that to make all corporal punishment unlawful can have a significant educative effect on social attitudes and promote alternative methods of discipline.

In the event the Government, to the surprise of many, decided not to legislate but to leave the matter in the hands of the judiciary[3]. It has been left to the judges to make clear in their directions in individual cases what are the requirements of the ECHR in the light of the Court's ruling in *A v UK*. In *R v H (Assault of Child: Reasonable Chastisement)*[4] the Court of Appeal identified as factors, the nature of

---

1   [1998] 2 FLR 959. For commentary see C Barton 'The Thirty Thousand Pound Caning – an "English Vice" in Europe [1999] CFLQ 63, and A Bainham 'Corporal Punishment of Children: A Caning for the United Kingdom' (1999) CLJ 291. See also J Rogers 'A Criminal Lawyer's Response to Chastisement in the European Court of Human Rights' [2002] Crim LR 98.

2   *Protecting Children, Supporting Parents: A Consultation Document on the physical punishment of children* (2000).

3   For a full discussion of the arguments, see J Fortin 'Children's Rights and the Use of Physical Force' [2001] CFLQ 243. More recently, see R Smith ' "Hands-off parenting?" – towards a reform of the defence of reasonable chastisement' [2004] CFLQ 261.

4   [2001] 2 FLR 431.

the defendant's behaviour, its duration, its physical and mental consequences in relation to the age and personal characteristics of the child and the reasons given by the defendant for administering punishment. Finally, the Children Bill 2004 does contain a provision which, if enacted, would remove the defence of reasonable chastisement in any proceedings for an offence of assault occasioning actual bodily harm[1], unlawfully inflicting grievous bodily harm[2], causing grievous bodily harm with intent[3], or cruelty to a child[4]. It would also prevent the defence being relied upon in any *civil* proceedings where the harm caused amounted to actual bodily harm. However, the defence would be available in relation to proceedings before a magistrates' court for common assault on a child. It would therefore effectively become unlawful for a parent to cause anything more than temporary pain or discomfort to the child through the infliction of corporal punishment. Although there might clearly be some difficult line-drawing on the facts, smacking would almost certainly not amount to more than a common assault (and the defence of reasonable chastisement would therefore be available) whereas hitting a child with an implement of any kind might well fall on the wrong side of the line. The reform, if enacted, is unlikely to satisfy those children's rights advocates who believe philosophically that *any* form of hitting a child is morally wrong and should be unlawful. It seems clear that parents who operate within these limits[5] (vague though they are) will not have 'ill-treated' the child for the purposes of the legislation, whereas those who exceed them may well have done[6].

Sexual abuse

Sexual abuse is included within the expression 'ill-treatment' but is not otherwise defined in the legislation. *Working Together* states that sexual abuse 'involves forcing or enticing a child or young person to take part in sexual activities, whether or not the child is aware of what is happening. The activities may involve physical contact, including penetrative (eg rape or buggery) ... or non-penetrative acts. They may include non-contact activities, such as involving children in looking at, or in the production of, pornographic material or watching sexual activities, or encouraging children to behave in sexually inappropriate ways'. It would be fair to say that this has been the area of greatest difficulty in recent years. Perhaps this is not so surprising since, as Freeman points out[7], the phenomenon was only recognised to exist at all comparatively recently. While the grosser forms of abuse (rape, and other offences of penetration) are easily recognisable as physical abuse, and serious criminal offences, there is much difficult line-drawing to be done over matters such as 'horseplay' between parents and children[8] or, as Freeman has speculated, the exposure

---

1   Offences Against the Person Act 1861, s 47.
2   Ibid, s 20.
3   Ibid, s 18.
4   Children and Young Persons Act 1933, s 1.
5   Ibid, s 1(7), inter alia, excludes from the offence of cruelty the parental right to administer punishment to a child.
6   For a discussion of the issue of corporal punishment in the context of child-minding, see Chapter 10, and in educational institutions, see Chapter 16.
7   MDA Freeman *Children, Their Families and the Law* (Macmillan, 1992) at p 93 referring to the DHSS circular in 1980 on registers which made no reference to it.
8   In *C v C (Child Abuse: Access)* [1988] 1 FLR 462 the judge found the father to have indulged in 'vulgar and inappropriate horseplay' with his daughter.

of children to pornographic literature[1]. Proof of sexual abuse is often difficult as we have seen. Moreover, the courts may be willing to continue contact arrangements even where sexual abuse is established[2]. These features are perhaps evidence of continuing ambivalence in social and judicial attitudes to the problem[3]. The whole question of the criminal law as it applies to sexual offences, including those involving children, was the subject of a major Home Office Review published in 2000, which was followed by a White Paper in 2002. This culminated in the Sexual Offences Act 2003. We consider these wide-ranging changes to the criminal law in Chapter 14.

Emotional abuse
Emotional abuse undoubtedly comes within the expression 'forms of ill-treatment which are not physical' and it was a recognised form of ill-treatment under the old law[4]. Again, it is not defined in the legislation, but it would seem that it is unlikely to be established without psychiatric evidence pointing to abnormal behaviour on the part of the child[5]. An example of emotional abuse may be the refusal to recognise a child's gender by making the child dress in the clothes of the opposite sex[6].

Working Together defines emotional abuse as:

> 'the persistent emotional ill-treatment of a child such as to cause severe and persistent adverse effects on the child's emotional development. It may involve conveying to children that they are worthless or unloved, inadequate, or valued only in so far as they meet the needs of another person. It may feature age or developmentally inappropriate expectations being imposed on children. It may involve causing children frequently to feel frightened or in danger, or the exploitation or corruption of children. Some level of emotional abuse is involved in all types of ill-treatment of a child, though it may occur alone.'

It goes without saying that the above categorisations should not necessarily be regarded as exhaustive since, sadly, the discovery of new forms of abuse[7], or the rediscovery of old ones, cannot be discounted.

What is significant?
The immense variation in the forms which abuse or neglect can take means that the crucial issue is usually a question of *degree* rather than kind. How much does a child have to suffer, and how much society tolerate, before the 'private realm' of family life can be invaded? The answer given by the legislation is that the harm must be 'significant'. Here, again, we confront one of the many essentially indeterminate concepts which litter the Children Act[8]. The Act, nonetheless,

---

1   MDA Freeman (above) at p 104.
2   See Chapter 4 above.
3   Graphically revealed in the Cleveland crisis and the media attention it received.
4   *F v Suffolk County Council* (1981) FLR 208. For a post-Children Act case of emotional abuse, see the facts of *Re M and R (Child Abuse: Evidence)* [1996] 2 FLR 195.
5   Discussed further by MDA Freeman (above) at p 104.
6   MDA Freeman (above).
7   Eg satanic or ritualistic abuse which, if it does exist, has only periodically been acted upon by child protection agencies.
8   A problem discussed in Chapter 10 above. The question of significant harm must also be related to the likelihood of it occurring. The greater the potential *gravity* of the harm, the stronger will be the case for a care order, as opposed, for example, to a supervision order. The point is well illustrated by *Re D (A Minor) (Care or Supervision Order)* [1993] 2 FLR 423. Here, Ewbank J made a care order, rather than the supervision order which the local authority had itself sought. The circumstances were that the children of the father's previous marriage had

does attempt to provide some guidance on when the requisite level will be reached. Section 31(10) states:

> 'Where the question of whether harm suffered by a child is significant turns on the child's health or development, his health or development shall be compared with that which could reasonably be expected of a similar child.'

While there can be no precise way of measuring the extent of harm, it is agreed that not every minor deficiency in a child's health or development will constitute 'significant harm'. Indeed, it is clear that we are looking for some 'substantial deficit' in the standard of upbringing which could be expected for the child[1]. This can only be ascertained by making a comparison with the hypothetical 'similar child'. But what is a 'similar child' for these purposes? It is generally agreed that the expression was designed to incorporate any subjective or unusual characteristics of the child in question. Thus, disabled children require special care which children who are not disabled do not require. Yet even this may become problematic, and comparisons may need to be more sophisticated. It has been pointed out[2], for example, that a deaf child of deaf parents may not be directly comparable to a deaf child of hearing parents.

Whether it is legitimate to go beyond the inherent characteristics of the child and explore his cultural or social background is more debatable and gave rise to an apparent difference of opinion between the Lord Chancellor and the Department of Health[3], and some academic debate[4]. One view is that cultural pluralism ought to be relevant, especially since the legislation has an ideological commitment to this[5]. According to this view 'Muslim children, Rastafarian children, the children of Hasidic Jews may be different and have different needs from children brought up in the indigenous, white, nominally Christian culture'[6]. The opposing view is that allowances for cultural background ought not to be made, except at the welfare stage of the court process[7], since, by definition, the threshold criteria set minimally acceptable limits of behaviour towards children. As such, society has a right to expect everyone from whatever cultural

---

  suffered non-accidental injuries and a baby in his care had been killed. The need for protection of the children of his present relationship was considered to be the decisive factor as between care and supervision.

1 See the *Review* (above) at para 15(15).

2 MDA Freeman *Children, Their Families and the Law* (Macmillan, 1992) at p 107.

3 In the debates on the Children Bill, Lord Mackay LC suggested that background, as opposed to attributes, should be left out of account (House of Lords, Official Report, col 354). *The Children Act 1989 Guidance and Regulations Vol 1 Court Orders* (HMSO, 1991) at para 3.20, however, states that account may need to be taken of 'environmental, social and cultural characteristics of the child'.

4 Freeman (above). Cf A Bainham 'Care after 1991 – A Reply' (1993) 3 JCL 99. For an extremely helpful discussion of the cultural question in the context of the competing philosophies of relativism, monism and pluralism, see M Freeman 'Children's Rights and Cultural Pluralism' in *The Moral Status of Children* (Martinus Nijhoff, 1997) at ch 7. See also J Brophy ' "Race" and Ethnicity in Public Law Proceedings' [2000] Fam Law 740; J Brophy 'Diversity and Child Protection' [2003] Fam Law 674; and J Brophy, J Jhutti-Johal and C Owen 'Assessing and Documenting Child Ill-Treatment in Ethnic Minority Households' [2003] Fam Law 756.

5 This is Freeman's view, although he would discount social inequality arising from poor socio-economic status.

6 Freeman (above) at p 153.

7 Bainham (above) at p 103. In other words, culture should be relevant when the court decides what order is appropriate.

background to comply[1] and, in any event, allowances for ethnic background take insufficient account of the widely divergent attitudes to child-rearing held among the indigenous population[2]. The matter remains unresolved[3], although in *Re D (Care: Threshold Criteria: Significant Harm)*[4], Wilson J appeared to have greater sympathy for the second view. He made a care order in relation to the child of a Jamaican mother. Although the mother's positive qualities were noted, there had been a history of incidents which together evidenced repeated and gross suppression of the protective instinct at times of stress. These included holding the child out of a window, beating her with a belt which caused bruises and scratches and threatening her with eviction from the home. Wilson J had the following to say about cultural considerations: 'There are many real cultural differences even within ordinary white British society. Today in England and Wales we are not a collection of ghettoes, but one society enjoying the benefit of the composition of very many racial and cultural groups and one society governed by one set of laws. It would concern me if the same event could give rise in one case to a finding of significant harm and in another to a finding to the contrary'. He did, however, concede that 'if a child can say to himself or herself "my brothers, sisters, and friends are all treated in this way from time to time: it seems to be part of life" that child may suffer less emotional harm than a child who perceived himself or herself to be a unique victim'. The matter clearly requires the guidance of the higher courts.

The second element: the attribution of significant harm

The second element has been described as 'causative'[5]. It has been argued, however, that a condition may be 'attributable' to some factor but not 'caused' by it[6]. Yet, the concept of causation in other areas of law is wide enough to embrace indirect influences which contribute to a situation[7]. What is agreed is that parental behaviour does not have to be the sole or direct cause of the child's predicament, as long as it indirectly contributes to it[8]. This might occur as where, for example, a third party, such as a relative or baby sitter, causes harm to the child and the parents were aware of that party's unsuitability to undertake his care.

---

1   Freeman himself would accept that practices such as female circumcision, excessive corporal punishment, refusal of essential medical aid on religious grounds, and so on, ought properly to be regarded as 'significant harm'.
2   For example, on corporal punishment, the Scottish Law Commission survey also revealed that 10% of those questioned thought it *should* be lawful to strike a 15-year-old with a belt, stick or other object, and over two-thirds (68%) thought that smacking a young person of this age should be lawful. See Scot Law Com Report No 135 *Family Law* (1992) at para 2.101.
3   On what is a 'similar child' in the context of truancy, see *Re O (A Minor) (Care Order: Education: Procedure)* [1992] 2 FLR 7, discussed in Chapter 16 below.
4   [1998] Fam Law 657.
5   A Bainham 'Care After 1991 – A Reply' (1993) 3 JCL 99 at 101.
6   MDA Freeman *Children, Their Families and the Law* (Macmillan, 1992) at p 150.
7   A Bainham (above).
8   See SM Cretney, JM Masson and R Bailey-Harris *Principles of Family Law* (7th edn) (Sweet & Maxwell, 2002) at p 733.

Parental upbringing

Here, it must be shown that the harm the child is suffering, or is likely to suffer, is attributable to 'the care given to the child or likely to be given to him . . . not being what it would be reasonable to expect a parent to give to him'[1].

It was said by Lord Mackay LC, during the debates on the Children Bill[2], that the underlying objective of this requirement is to strike a balance between the conflicting pressures of ensuring that intervention in the family occurs only in carefully defined circumstances, and allowing it where harm, or risk of harm, can be traced to a perceptible deficiency in parental care.

It must be shown first, that the harm or risk is indeed attributable, at least in part, to the standard or projected standard of parental care. The view has been offered that harm which is *solely* attributable to disturbing the status quo would not meet the test[3]. This view is questionable. Anxieties about such a move must postulate concern about the standard of care the child is likely to receive at home, if moved. Otherwise, every move of a child from foster-care would be seen as harmful. The reality is that the anxiety fixes not on the move itself but on the risk to the child's welfare on his return home, and this is squarely caught by the reference in the statutory ground to the care *likely to be given* to the child. The *Guidance*[4] states that 'harm caused solely by a third party is . . . excluded (unless the parent has failed to prevent it)'. This might occur, for example, where a parent has a relationship with an undesirable adult, such as a child offender, which exposes the child to contact with that person.

It seems that the test of the adequacy of care is an *objective* one, although all the arguments about social or cultural background resurface again here[5]. The *Guidance* advises that the court will need professional assistance on what it would be reasonable to expect the parents to achieve in the circumstances[6]. But clearly, reasonableness must be assessed in relation to the particular child who is before the court, bearing in mind the needs of that child. The test is, therefore, what would a reasonable parent do for *this* child? Cultural considerations may well be relevant when the court has to apply the ultimate welfare test and decide on what order, if any, it should make. This is because the statutory checklist of factors applies and this includes a reference to the child's background[7].

What is the position if it can be shown that the child is suffering significant harm which is attributable to a deficiency in care, but which cannot be conclusively attributed to either parent or to any other individual? This was the problem which the House of Lords had to address in *Lancashire County Council v B*[8].

---

1   Section 31(2)(b)(i).
2   House of Lords, Official Report, 19 January 1989, col 355.
3   NV Lowe and G Douglas *Bromley's Family Law* (9th edn) (Butterworths, 1998) at p 549.
4   *The Children Act 1989 Guidance and Regulations Vol 1 Court Orders* (HMSO, 1991) at para 3.23.
5   Freeman is in no doubt (above) at p 108, that social deprivation must be discounted:
    'The care given to the child is not what it would be reasonable for *this* parent to give (in her high-rise flat, living on income support, with three children under five and a partner in prison), but what it would be reasonable to expect *a* parent to give.'
6   *The Children Act 1989 Guidance and Regulations Vol 1* (above) at para 3.23.
7   Section 1(3)(d).
8   [2000] 2 WLR 590. For the author's views on the decision, see A Bainham 'Attributing Harm: Child Abuse and the Unknown Perpetrator' (2000) CLJ 458. See also A Perry '*Lancashire County Council v B:* Section 31 – threshold or barrier?' [2000] CFLQ 301.

The case concerned two babies. Child A was looked after partly by her mother and father and partly by a child-minder. This child-minder was the mother of child B. A suffered serious non-accidental head injuries and it was established that these were caused by at least two episodes of violent shaking.[1] The child-minder lived with the father of B but he was exonerated from any blame. The finger of suspicion was therefore pointing at the other three adults in the caring arrangement but the evidence could not establish that any one of them was the perpetrator. The local authority sought care orders in relation to *both* A and B. The judge refused both applications but the Court of Appeal allowed the authority's appeal in relation to A. In the House of Lords there was no further argument about B because the authority accepted that in the absence of evidence establishing that B's mother (the child-minder) was responsible for the injuries to A, it could not be said that he had suffered significant harm or was at risk.

In relation to A, the parents argued in the House of Lords that the phrase 'care given to the child' could only refer to care given by *parents* or other *primary* carers and was not wide enough to cover care given by substitute carers such as a child-minder. Thus, if harm could not be attributed to the standard of care provided by the parents, the court would lack jurisdiction to make the care order. It was argued that this interpretation accorded with the non-interventionist philosophy of the Children Act, encapsulated in the no order principle in s 1(5)[2], and that the best interests of children were generally served by leaving them within the natural family unless it could be demonstrated that there was a serious deficiency in the standard of care *provided by those parents.*

The House of Lords disagreed. It held that the statutory language was wide enough to include situations in which the care of children was *shared,* as it was here between the parents and a child-minder (excluding purely temporary delegations of parental responsibility). Lord Clyde observed that the language of the statute did not expressly require identification of the author of the harm and that the phrase 'not being what it would be reasonable to expect a parent to give to him' merely referred to a *standard* or *level* of care and did 'not restrict the scope of the persons who may be responsible for the care given to the child in the particular case'.

This was the technical basis on which the House was able to find that jurisdiction existed to make the care order but policy justifications were also found for this comparatively liberal interpretation. First, it was said that Parliament could not possibly have intended that a child in the situation of A should remain unprotected. As Lord Nicholls said, a more restrictive interpretation 'would mean that the child's future health, or even her life, would have to be hazarded on the chance that, after all, the non-parental carer rather than one of the parents inflicted the injuries. Self-evidently, to proceed in such a way when a child is proved to have suffered serious injury on more than one occasion could be

---

1   On the evidential difficulties of proving death or injury caused by the violent shaking of babies see *Re A (Non-Accidental Injury: Medical Evidence)* [2001] 2 FLR 657. In this case Bracewell J held that the presence of retinal haemorrhages in a child's body, even in the absence of cerebral haemorrhages, was sufficient for an expert to be able to say, on the balance of probabilities, that the child had suffered a non-accidental death. And see C Cobley and T Sanders ' "Shaken Baby Syndrome": Child protection issues when children sustain a subdural haemorrhage' (2003) 25 JSWFL 101.

2   As to which see Chapter 2 above.

dangerously irresponsible'. These protective concerns outweighed the consideration that 'parents who may be wholly innocent, and whose care may not have fallen below that of a reasonable parent, will face the possibility of losing their child, with all the pain and distress this involves'. Secondly, Lord Clyde pointed out, as the House had done previously in *Re M (A Minor) (Care Orders: Threshold Conditions)*[1], that the question before it was only a *jurisdictional* issue in the sense that the question was whether a care order *could* be made, not whether it *should* be made on the facts. Even if the threshold were crossed, the court would still at the welfare stage have to consider what was the appropriate order to make, if any. So, for Lord Clyde, it was 'reasonable to allow a degree of latitude in the scope of the jurisdictional provision, leaving the critical question of whether the circumstances require the making of an order to a detailed assessment of the welfare of the child'.

The decision again reveals the acute dilemma facing the courts, and indeed child protection agencies, in balancing the fundamental rights of family members, in this case the child A's right to protection as against the parent's right to family integrity[2]. A crucial factor here was that A had already been harmed whereas B had not, but this is open to the objection that the authority ought not to have to wait for a child to be harmed before taking protective action.

The question of the appropriate test to be applied when the court is considering potential perpetrators of non-accidental injury arose for decision in *North Yorkshire County Council v SA*[3]. The child, who was taken to hospital suffering from serious non-accidental injuries, had been injured twice – once within the last 14 hours and once on an earlier unspecified occasion. The judge was unable to establish the perpetrator of either injury, but applying a test that there was 'no possibility that the relevant person injured the child' did not exclude either parent, the maternal grandmother or the night nanny in relation to the latest incident, since all had taken care of the child in the previous 14 hours. Applying this test, there were a large number of possible perpetrators in relation to the earlier injury. The Court of Appeal held that the test the judge had applied was too wide since it could encompass all those who had even a fleeting contact with the child. The correct test, where there was insufficient evidence positively to identify the perpetrator on the balance of probabilities, was 'is there a likelihood or real possibility that A or B or C was the perpetrator or a perpetrator of the inflicted injuries?' Applying this test, the court was able to exclude the maternal grandmother and the night nanny, leaving the real possibility that either of the parents had caused both sets of injuries to the child.

Where it is clear that the child has been harmed by *one* of two parents, but it is not clear which, the threshold criteria will be satisfied. This is the effect of the

---

1   [1994] 2 AC 424.
2   The House of Lords quickly dismissed the parents' argument that to continue care proceedings and leave A in foster-care was a violation of their right to respect for family life under Article 8. Lord Nicholls said that the action taken fell within the permitted exceptions under Article 8(2) as 'no more than ... reasonably necessary to pursue the legitimate aim of protecting A from further injury'.
3   [2003] 2 FLR 849.

subsequent decision of the House of Lords in *Re O and N; Re B*[1]. It held unanimously that where a child clearly had suffered significant harm, but the court was unable to identify which parent was the perpetrator, or whether *both* had been, the threshold criteria were met.

Parental control

The alternative, in the second element, requires that the harm or risk to the child be attributable to 'the child's being beyond parental control'[2]. Under the old law, this was a freestanding ground for a care order, and the former power of parents to initiate proceedings indirectly has already been noted[3]. This was, in essence, a 'status offence' and was open to the objection that compulsory action could be taken against a child for non-criminal misbehaviour. Under the Children Act, a care or supervision order may only be made where the child, being beyond parental control, is suffering significant harm or is exposed to the risk of doing so[4]. Whether the test is objective or subjective is not entirely clear[5] but the *Guidance* advises that it is not necessary to prove fault on the part of the parents[6]. It has been argued that the reference to 'parental' control is wide enough to include non-parents caring for a child, at least where they have parental responsibility[7].

It is possible, but not necessary, for both alternatives to be satisfied at the same time. Indeed, in one reported case[8] the judge indicated that the circumstances established *either* a lack of reasonable parental care *or* the child being beyond parental control.

The welfare stage

If the court finds that the statutory threshold is crossed it must then go on to consider what kind of order, if any, is in the best interests of the child, bearing in mind that human rights considerations require that the action taken should be *proportionate* and no more than is *necessary* to protect the welfare of the child. We discussed the welfare stage of care proceedings above.

Care plans

In order to enable the court to make an informed choice as between care, supervision, a s 8 order or no order at all, it is necessary for the local authority to

---

1   [2003] 1 FLR 1169. For an evaluation of the decision of the Court of Appeal, see J Hayes and M Hayes 'Child Protection in the Court of Appeal' [2002] Fam Law 817. And for a commentary on the House of Lords decision, see E Ryder QC 'Re O and N – Is My Likelihood Your Risk?' [2003] Fam Law 741 and M Hayes 'Uncertain evidence and risk-taking in child protection cases' [2004] CFLQ 63.
2   Section 31(2)(b)(ii).
3   See p 479 above.
4   This would seem to meet the above objections, especially since the order can only be sought in relation to younger teenagers, ie those under 16 years of age.
5   See MDA Freeman *Children, Their Families and the Law* (Macmillan, 1992) at p 100.
6   *The Children Act 1989 Guidance and Regulations Vol 1* (above) at para 3.25.
7   Freeman (above) at p 100. This certainly seems to be confirmed by the decision in *M v Birmingham City Council* [1994] 2 FLR 141 where the teenager concerned was in local authority accommodation but held to be beyond the parental control of her mother and partner. Stuart White J took the view that the statutory conditions could include a state of affairs which might be in the past, present or future.
8   *Re O (A Minor) (Care Order: Education: Procedure)* [1992] 2 FLR 7.

have a care plan to put before the court. The 1987 White Paper[1] acknowledged the importance of care plans. In *Manchester City Council v F*[2] Eastham J said that the care plan delivered by local authorities should accord, as far as is reasonably possible, with the *Guidance* issued under the legislation[3]. This advised that whereas there is no set format for a care plan it should be in writing and should set out the child's and the family's social history. It went on to mention other key elements which should be included in the plan such as identifying the child's needs and how these should be met, the nature of the proposed placement, arrangements for contact and reunification, the duration of the placement and what is to happen if it breaks down, and arrangements for health care and education.

Care plans have now been placed on a statutory footing for the first time by the Adoption and Children Act 2002[4]. This amends the Children Act 1989, inserting a new s 31A. This provides that where any application is made on which a care order might be made, the appropriate local authority must, within such time as the court directs, prepare a care plan for the future care of the child[5]. While the application is pending the authority must keep the care plan under review and where it is of the opinion that some change is required it must revise the plan or make a new one[6]. The plan must include prescribed information which will be set out in regulations[7]. None of these requirements will apply to *interim* care orders[8].

Care plans, human rights and the courts

Since the implementation of the Children Act 1989 there have been disputes about the extent to which the courts are, or should be, able to control aspects of the care plan. Controversies about the proper balance of decision-making between local authorities and the courts have centred on this issue[9]. In a number of cases[10] the courts have exhibited frustration at their inability to direct local authorities to take action in certain circumstances where the authorities concerned were reluctant to do so, but where the court in question felt that action was warranted in the best interests of the children. The matter has been complicated by the issue of the allocation of scarce resources and whether the court or the local authority is best placed to determine these priorities. An authority may, for example, be resisting an expensive assessment of the child and parents at the interim stage of care proceedings because it may feel that it would involve a disproportionate commitment of resources to one family and one or more children. On the other hand, the court may feel that a decision on whether

---

1 *The Law on Child Care and Family Services* (Cm 62) at para 10, where it was said that the 'amount of detail in the plan will vary from case to case depending on how far it is possible for the local authority to foresee what will be best for the child at that time'.
2 [1993] 1 FLR 419.
3 *The Children Act 1989 Guidance and Regulations Vol 3 Family Placements* (HMSO, 1991) at ch 2, para 2.62.
4 Section 121.
5 Section 31A(1). The plan is to be known as a 's 31A plan' (s 31A(6)).
6 Section 31A(2).
7 Section 31A(3).
8 Section 31A(5).
9 See Chapter 2 above.
10 See especially *Nottinghamshire County Council v P* [1993] 2 FLR 134 and *Re C (Interim Care Order: Residential Assessment)* [1996] 3 WLR 1098, discussed at length below.

or not a care order should be made should largely rest on such an assessment. Questions like this have now been given an even sharper focus with the advent of the HRA 1998. Here the essential argument is that an 'unreviewable' care order, or an absence of judicial control over any major decisions taken in relation to children by local authorities, may breach the rights of children, parents or both under Articles 6 and 8 of the ECHR. Since most such decisions will relate to matters in the care plan, the content and implementation of the plan have become a focal point for human rights arguments.

These arguments have so far fixed particularly on two questions. The first is the legitimate extent of the court's control at the interim stage. How far may courts control aspects of the proposed care plan *before* a care order is made by prolonging matters until they are completely satisfied, through the device of successive interim orders? The second issue relates to judicial control over the *implementation* of the care plan *after* a care order has been made. Given the theory and philosophy of the Children Act, that the local authority should be exclusively responsible for the child and not subject to judicial interference once the care order is made[1], is it consistent with this that parents and others should be able to return to court to challenge what the authority has decided? But again, is it consistent with their Convention rights to respect for family life and a fair hearing that they should *not* be able to do so?

Matters came to a head in 2002 in *Re S (Minors); Re W (Minors)*[2]. These two cases, the facts of which were unremarkable and not especially unusual, exemplify the two problems identified above.

In *Re W* the care plan was 'inchoate' or, in simple terms, incomplete. At the interim stage of care proceedings, the future of two boys was rather uncertain. Their mother suffered from mental health problems. There was some prospect, however, of rehabilitation with her, but not for 12–18 months. In the meantime there was the prospect that the grandparents might come from the USA to the UK to look after them in the interim period. Could an interim care order be made and continued in these circumstances? The judge, who wanted to make an interim order, felt bound by authority to make a *final* care order, but the Court of Appeal reversed this decision on the basis that interim orders were available to achieve the required flexibility. This ruling resulted in a change of heart by the grandparents so that, by the time the case reached the House of Lords, they had decided not to come to England, and final care orders were made with the consent of all concerned.

Re S was very different in that a care order had already been made in respect of two children, but similar to the extent that eventual rehabilitation with the mother was also visualised as part of the care plan. The attempt at rehabilitation was to be effected by a package of support measures but, in the event, the authority had failed to deliver on these because of its views of its priorities regarding competing resources. By the time the case reached the House of Lords it was implementing the care plan as it had promised to do.

---

1   See Chapter 2 above. Note that judicial control of contact and the use of secure accommodation, together with judicial control over the making and discharge of care orders, were exceptions to the general principle.

2   *Re S (Minors) (Care Order: Implementation of Care Plan); Re W (Minors) (Care Order: Adequacy of Care Plan)* [2002] 1 FLR 815. For an extremely helpful critique of the House of Lords decision which concentrates, on the human rights implications see R Tolson QC *Care Plans and the Human*

The underlying issues were therefore whether the use of interim orders was a legitimate exercise of judicial control *before* the making of the final care order where the care plan was incomplete and whether there was an adequate mechanism under the Children Act for controlling the implementation of a care plan *after* the making of a care order. It was argued by the respective appellants that, unless the interpretation and application of the Children Act were modified, the Act was incompatible with the ECHR. The Court of Appeal dismissed the appeal in *Re S*, but allowed the appeal in *Re W*. It held that two adjustments were required in the construction and application of the Children Act in order to avoid risking a breach of Convention rights. The first was that judges should enjoy a wider discretion to make interim care orders as opposed to final care orders. The second was that the 'essential milestones' in a care plan should be identified at trial and elevated to starred status. Where the local authority failed to achieve a starred milestone within a reasonable time, this would reactivate the inter-disciplinary process which contributed to the creation of the care plan. As a minimum requirement, the children's guardian would be informed of the failure, and either the guardian or the local authority would then have the right to apply to the court for further directions.

The House of Lords dismissed the mother's appeal against the care order in *Re W*, but allowed the authority's appeal against the proposed 'adjustments' but not against the substantive orders in *Re S*. On the two core issues, the House unanimously held as follows.

(1) Interim orders were a legitimate exercise of the court's discretion in some cases where there were uncertainties within care plans which needed to be resolved before a final care order could be made. It was, however, a question of balance, since some other uncertainties could only be resolved after a care order had been made. Interim care orders were not intended to be used as a means by which the court might continue to exercise a supervisory role over the local authority where it was determined that it was in the best interests of a child that a care order should be made. The court needed always to maintain a proper balance between the need to satisfy itself about the appropriateness of a care plan and the avoidance of over-zealous investigation of matters which fell within the responsibility of the local authority. Lord Nicholls considered that this was already established law and did not amount to a 'major innovation' as the Court of Appeal had appeared to think it was.

(2) 'Starring', on the other hand, was an illegitimate practice, since it crossed the line between what was perfectly proper statutory interpretation and a 'judicial innovation' going well beyond that. In the words of Lord Nicholls it would have 'constituted amendment of the Children Act'. Where a care order was made it was the clear intention of Parliament that responsibility for the child should be with the local authority rather than the court. There was no provision in the Children Act which required starring. Although s 3 of the HRA 1998 required primary legislation to be read and given effect in a way which was compatible with Convention rights, so far as possible, the system of starred milestones would contravene a clear and cardinal principle of the

Rights Act (Family Law, 2002). See also J Herring 'The Human Rights of Children in Care' (2002) 118 LQR 534; and J Harwin and M Owen 'The implementation of care plans and its relationship to children's welfare' [2003] CFLQ 71.

Children Act which could not be interpreted in that way. A declaration of incompatibility could not therefore be made. On the other hand, the House of Lords, crucially, acknowledged the existence of a 'lacuna' or gap in the statutory scheme under the Children Act which could lead to breaches of Convention rights under Articles 6 or 8 and could trigger recourse to the remedies under ss 7 and 8 of the HRA 1998. In particular, the requirements of Article 6 regarding a fair hearing might not be satisfied in relation to 'questions of a fundamental nature regarding the child's future' which 'attract a high degree of judicial control'. Lord Nicholls went on to say that 'one of the questions needing urgent consideration is whether some degree of court supervision of local authorities' discharge of their parental responsibilities would bring about an overall improvement in the quality of child care provided by local authorities'.

The House also noted a problem familiar to family lawyers for at least the last 20 years. This was that there was an absence in the statutory scheme of an effective means of instigating proceedings to protect the civil rights of *young* children, who were unable to engage a lawyer themselves and who had no parent, guardian or other interested adult willing to vindicate their rights on their behalf. But this too was a lacuna and did not mean that the Children Act was thereby incompatible with the ECHR. In the case of both parents and children[1], the House of Lords urged the Government to address the pressing need to attend to the serious practical and legal problems which the starring system had tried to address.

There is therefore some prospect of amending legislation to provide for greater judicial control over major decisions taken by local authorities in relation to children in care. In the meantime there is no reason in principle why all such decisions, whether made before or after a final care order, should not be open to challenge where it is alleged that they have violated Convention rights. Such a case was *Re G (Care: Challenge to Local Authority's Decision)*[2]. Here Munby J emphasised that Article 8 of the ECHR offered not merely substantive protection of rights to respect for family life, but also procedural safeguards. This procedural protection was, moreover, not confined to the trial process but extended to all stages of the decision-making process including the implementation of the care order. Parents had to be properly involved in the decision-making process before, during *and after* care proceedings. Where therefore the authority sought to make significant changes to the care plan (in this case a decision that the children should be removed from parental care), it was under a duty to inform the parents and to give the parents an opportunity, inter alia, to respond to allegations and to make representations. The remedies under the HRA 1998 may be increasingly invoked

---

1 Specifically in relation to young children Lord Mackay said that he did not see 'how a child who has no person to raise the matter on his behalf can be protected from violation of his or her human rights conferred on him or her by our domestic law, other than by reliance on an effective means by which others bring the violation to notice'.

2 [2003] 2 FLR 42.

and it is a near certainty that we shall see many such challenges in the coming years[1].

CARE ORDERS

In some respects, there is considerable similarity between the respective legal positions of those children who are voluntarily accommodated by local authorities and those in care. They are all 'looked after' by the local authority whose general and specific duties apply to both groups[2]. Yet there are also important distinctions. This section looks at the distinctive legal effects of a care order and at the special regime which applies to contact with children in care.

The legal effects of a care order

Section 33 of the Children Act spells out the legal effects of a care order. There is now only one set of criteria for care orders and uniform legal effects whatever the proceedings in which the order was made. One important feature is that the court, having made the care order, retains no residual control over the management of the child's case[3]. The *Review* recommended that the local authority should be able to take a grip on the case by taking firm and early decisions, and should resist the temptation of passing responsibility to another body[4]. Accordingly, the former power of certain courts to give directions to the local authority about strategic plans for the child has been removed[5]. The court has the more limited power of directing an investigation in family proceedings, but it may not act of its own volition in making a care order or dictate to the local authority once an order is made. As we have seen, this principle and indeed philosophy in the legislation now requires substantial re-evaluation in the light of the requirements of the ECHR and especially in relation to challenges to the care plan[6].

Local authorities must receive and keep a child in their care
The first effect of a care order is to require local authorities 'to receive the child into their care and to keep him in their care while the order remains in force'[7]. Although parents do not lose their parental responsibility when a care order is made, they must not exercise this in a way which is incompatible with any order of the court[8]. Thus, they may not remove a child who is subject to a care order, since this would contravene the effect of that order.

---

1 Procedurally, where care proceedings are still afoot, human rights complaints should normally be dealt with in the context of those proceedings. Where they have come to an end, a 'freestanding' application under s 7(1)(a) of the HRA 1998 is the appropriate remedy. See *Re L (Care Proceedings: Human Rights Claims)* [2003] 2 FLR 160, an approach confirmed by the Court of Appeal in *Re V (Care Proceedings: Human Rights Claims)* [2004] 1 FLR 944.
2 See Chapter 10 above.
3 See p 532 below.
4 DHSS *Review of Child Care Law* (1985) at para 2.24.
5 Powers used most frequently, but not exclusively, in wardship.
6 See pp 506 et seq above.
7 Section 33(1).
8 Section 2(8).

Local authorities must assume/share parental responsibility

The second consequence of a care order is prescribed in s 33(3) and is more controversial. It provides:

> 'While a care order is in force with respect to a child, the local authority designated by the order shall –
> (a) have parental responsibility for the child; and
> (b) have the power (subject to the following provisions of this section) to determine the extent to which a parent or guardian of the child may meet his parental responsibility for him.'

The local authority, therefore, has parental responsibility by virtue of the care order and is not dependent, as where a child is voluntarily accommodated, for its legal powers on parental delegation. However, parents do not lose their parental responsibility merely because the local authority also acquires it[1]. Most other people who hold parental responsibility when a care order is made will lose it, since the effect of the order is to revoke a residence order[2]. Guardians and adoptive parents, however, retain parental responsibility, since they do not derive it from a residence order but from their status. The effect of s 33(3) is, therefore, that the local authority must *share* parental responsibility with the parents. This was not the intention in the *Review* or the White Paper which, as Eekelaar has observed, clearly contemplated that a care order would involve a transfer of parental responsibility from the parents to the local authority[3]. It was, for Eekelaar, the Law Commission, which in 1988 'struck out in a new direction'. This sharing of parental responsibility, where the child is in care, has been the subject of trenchant criticism[4] on the ground that it dilutes the local authority's control over the child. In contrast to this, there has also been criticism that parents' participatory rights have been threatened by a late amendment to s 33(3), discussed below.

Sharing parental responsibility

What then does sharing entail? The theory is clear enough. Parents maintain an *equal* say in matters of upbringing and may exercise all aspects of parental responsibility, including, of course, the right of independent action, when the

---

1 Section 2(5) and (6). In *Kent County Council v C* [1992] 3 WLR 808, Ewbank J held that once a care order was made the family proceedings court did not retain the power to direct that the guardian ad litem should continue his involvement with the child. Responsibility passed to the authority under the order. See also *Re B (A Minor) (Care Order: Review)* [1993] 1 FLR 421 in which Thorpe J held that a care order which incorporated provision for a review in six months of the operation of the order, progress in the care plan and contact, was manifestly ultra vires. What both of these cases established is that the court may not make a *conditional* care order. The central effect of a care order is to give the local authority the power to regulate the management of the child's life in care except insofar as the statutory regime makes express contrary provision – for example, in relation to contact or the use of secure accommodation or where respect for rights under the ECHR require it. See the discussion of care plans and contact with children in care at p 513 below.

2 Section 91(2). A care order will also automatically revoke a supervision order (s 91(3)), wardship (s 91(4)), or a school attendance order under the Education Act 1996, s 437(2) (s 91(5)).

3 J Eekelaar 'Parental Responsibility: State of Nature or Nature of the State?' (1991) JSWFL 37 at 43.

4 Ibid, especially at pp 41–42.

child is with them. But since the child will usually *not* be with them, all of this theory probably adds up, in practice, to little more than a right of consultation[1].

While the Children Bill was progressing through Parliament, concern began to be expressed that parents might use the opportunity, where a child was allowed home, to act in ways contrary to the wishes of the local authority[2]. In consequence, an amendment was introduced which is now s 33(3)(b). The intention was to try to ensure that, despite the notional equality of parents and the local authority and the idea of partnership, the local authority would remain in effective control of the situation. Thus, the Children Act gives the local authority power to control the *exercise* of parental responsibility by parents if this would undermine its plan for the child. The *Guidance* euphemistically advises that this power 'allows the local authority to deal with any conflict that may arise between the local authority and the parents in exercising their respective parental responsibilities'[3]. In fact, it allows the local authority to impose its will. As Freeman has put it, 'the local authority has the whip hand'[4]. He is scathing about what he sees as a largely illusory retention of parental responsibility by parents:

'There is concern that we are saying parents have responsibility but giving them no way of challenging the exercise by a local authority of its discretion to take that responsibility away.'[5]

It was envisaged that the power would only be exercised sparingly, and it *can* only be exercised where it is necessary to safeguard or promote the child's welfare[6]. Also, it cannot prevent a parent or guardian with physical care of a child from doing what is reasonable in all the circumstances, for the purpose of safeguarding or promoting that child's welfare[7].

It can be argued that the very idea of sharing parental responsibility, where a child has been compulsorily removed because of parental failings, is an unacceptable intrusion into the managerial control of the local authority. On this view, the concept of a partnership between social services and, for example, parents who are responsible for serious abuse, may be ill-conceived[8]. It is difficult to resist the conclusion that the provision was an unhappy compromise, cobbled together at the eleventh hour, which satisfies neither social services nor the advocates of parents' rights. On the other hand, the continuing involvement of parents through the sharing of parental responsibility may be thought consistent with the ultimate aim of reunification of parent and child, something required by the ECHR.

How much parental responsibility does the local authority acquire?
The parental responsibility which the local authority acquires is not quite as extensive as that of parents since there are some express statutory limitations. The

---

1   Section 22(4) and (5), and see Chapter 10 above. It would not appear that parents are under a concomitant duty to consult the authority and that this is one reason why s 33(3)(b) is required.
2   There could, for example, be arguments about whether what parents proposed to do was incompatible with the care order.
3   *The Children Act 1989 Guidance and Regulations Vol 1 Court Orders* (HMSO, 1991) at para 3.67.
4   See MDA Freeman *Children, The Family and the Law* (Macmillan, 1992) at p 121.
5   Ibid.
6   Section 33(4).
7   Section 33(5), which mirrors s 3(5) in relation to de facto carers.
8   This certainly seems to be the thrust of Eekelaar's position in 'Parental Responsibility: State of Nature or Nature of the State?' (1991) JSWFL 37.

general principle, which also applies to non-parents with parental responsibility[1], is that those legal incidents which are fundamental to the relationship of parent and child ought not to pass to others by any means short of adoption. The powers in question are the right to consent to or refuse an application to place the child for adoption, or a final adoption order, and the right to appoint a guardian[2]. None of these powers pass under a care order. There are also restrictions on changing the child's name and removing him from the country which correspond broadly with those restrictions which apply where a residence order is made[3]. The restriction on changing the child's name will not necessarily apply where the child wishes the change. In *Re S (Change of Surname)*[4] the father of two girls was prosecuted, but acquitted, on sexual abuse charges involving them. He admitted the physical abuse of one of them. The girls, who by this time were the subject of care orders, sought leave of the court to change their surname from that of their father to that of their maternal family. The judge allowed the change only in relation to one of them. The appeal of the other was allowed by the Court of Appeal, which emphasised that, although the welfare principle applied, the judge should give very careful consideration to the wishes, feelings, needs and objectives of the applicant child. The court attached significance to the fact that the young woman was *Gillick*-competent and that a reconciliation with the father was unlikely.

It has also been held by Dame Elizabeth Butler-Sloss P in *Re D, L and LA (Care: Change of Forename)*[5] that no foster-parent or carer should unilaterally change the forename of a child in their care. If the child should subsequently be adopted, however, the adoptive parents would, of course, acquire that right. In addition, the local authority must not 'cause the child to be brought up in any religious persuasion other than that in which he would have been brought up if the order had not been made'[6]. The effect of this is to prevent the local authority itself from unilaterally changing the child's religion. It does not preclude the child from taking his own decision as he grows older.

Contact with children in care

The background
There is no question that the issue of contact between a child in care and parents or relatives has generated more complaints and litigation than any other issue in this area of the law[7]. No doubt this was, in part, a reflection of the largely

---

1 See Chapter 6 above.
2 Section 33(6)(b).
3 Section 33(7) and (8). But the child may be allowed to leave the jurisdiction in accordance with arrangements made under Sch 2, para 19.
4 [1999] 1 FLR 672.
5 [2003] 1 FLR 339.
6 Section 33(6)(a).
7 See *The Children Act 1989 Guidance and Regulations Vol 1 Court Orders* (HMSO, 1991) at paras 3.75–3.86. One view is that the whole problem of contact is more a social one than a legal one and that the law cannot provide solutions to it. See J Masson 'Thinking about contact – a social or legal problem?' [2000] CFLQ 15. For a recent volume devoted almost entirely to issues surrounding contact and which offers socio-legal perspectives, see A Bainham, B Lindley, M Richards and L Trinder (eds) *Children and Their Families: Contact, Rights and Welfare* (Hart Publishing, 2003).

unrestrained power which local authorities used to wield over contact arrange-ments. The absence of effective mechanisms of redress led to a clamour in the early 1980s which culminated in successful challenges under the ECHR[1] and domestic legislation[2]. This legislation provided for judicial control over decisions to 'refuse' or 'terminate' access (as it then was). The current legislation builds on these foundations but goes much further. In particular, it shifts the onus from aggrieved parents to local authorities where local authorities wish to refuse contact to a prescribed category of individuals.

Before turning to the new regime it is as well to put the contact question into perspective. It should be seen alongside the principles of parental responsibility for children, partnership, and the statutory responsibilities of local authorities to endeavour to effect a reunification of the child with his family and, to this end, to promote contact[3]. The contact code in s 34 must be seen in this wider context. The hope is that it will not have to come into play at all, since questions of the nature or extent of contact arrangements will be resolved at the time the care order is made. Indeed, the court is specifically empowered to make a contact order when it makes a care order[4]. More importantly, it must, before making a care order:

'(a)   consider the arrangements which the authority have made, or propose to make, for affording any person contact with a child ... and

(b)   invite the parties to the proceedings to comment on those arrangements.'[5]

Proposals for contact should, therefore, be an important element in the authority's care plan for the child which it puts before the court. The function of the contact code, constituted by s 34 and the Contact with Children Regulations 1991[6], is, therefore, to resolve disputes and to make the local authority accountable for the discharge of its statutory duties.

Contact in care and human rights

The question of the promotion of contact and preservation of contact between a child in care and his natural family is all part of the general aim of reunification which, as we saw, is mandated by the ECHR. The right to contact in this context is a Convention right which both parent and child have as an aspect of the right to respect for their family life together. This implies a continuing relationship between them. Interference with this right must be based on reasons which are relevant and sufficient.

It is important to grasp that the ECtHR has in a number of cases, including *S and G v Italy*[7] and *K and T v Finland*[8] emphasised that it is *more difficult* for the State to

---

1   *R v The United Kingdom* [1988] 2 FLR 445.
2   Health and Social Services and Social Security Adjudications Act 1983, s 6 and Sch 1, adding ss 12A–12G to the Child Care Act 1980.
3   Particularly Sch 2, para 15.
4   Section 34(10).
5   Section 34(11).
6   SI 1991/891. It must be emphasised that the code does not govern contact with 'accommodated' children. Such children could, however, be the subject of a s 8 contact order.
7   [2000] 2 FLR 771.
8   [2000] 2 FLR 79. The case was referred to a Grand Chamber of the ECtHR. The decision of the Grand Chamber is reported at [2001] 2 FLR 707. See also *KA v Finland* [2003] 1 FLR 696 in which the ECtHR emphasised again the *positive* duty on the State to take measures to facilitate family reunification as soon as reasonably feasible. This duty began to weigh on the responsible

justify decisions which would curtail or terminate contact between parent and child than it is to justify the initial decision to take a child into care. 'Very strict scrutiny' is required of decisions which would have this effect. Thus there was a violation of Article 8 in *K and T v Finland* where the State had failed to take sufficient steps to effect a reunification of the family. In *S and G v Italy* the children had been placed in a community which opposed contact and in which two of the community leaders had convictions for sexual offences against children. The ECtHR found a violation of Article 8 on account of the delays and limited number of contact visits the mother was allowed with her children and because the community in question failed to promote the re-establishment of contact between them.

We now turn to the statutory regime under the Children Act governing contact with children in care.

The presumption of reasonable contact

The Children Act broke new ground by creating, for the first time, a presumption of reasonable contact with a child in care[1]. This is in favour of a parent, guardian, person who held a residence order or person who had the care of a child under an exercise of the inherent jurisdiction, immediately before the care order was made[2]. The local authority may refuse contact to these individuals only in very limited circumstances, ie where:

'(a) they are satisfied that it is necessary to do so in order to safeguard or promote the child's welfare; and
(b) the refusal –
    (i) is decided upon as a matter of urgency; and
    (ii) does not last for more than seven days.'[3]

If the local authority then wishes to continue to disallow contact, it must get the court's authorisation, and the onus is on the local authority to bring the application[4]. The court has power to authorise or refuse contact[5]. This is a major shift of emphasis from the pre-Children Act position. Under the old law, the local authority's initial obligations were limited to giving notice of an intended refusal

authorities with 'progressively increasing force' from the commencement of the period of care, subject always to being balanced against the duty to consider the best interests of the child. In this case there had been a categorical statement by one social worker to the parents to the effect that 'they would not get their children back'. The Court took the view that the restrictions on contact, and the failure of the welfare authorities to review them genuinely and sufficiently frequently, not only did not facilitate reunification but contributed to hindering it.

1 It is interesting to note that there is no corresponding statutory presumption in favour of parents in the private law, although the courts have, through their practice, effectively created one. There is such a presumption in Scotland under the Children (Scotland) Act 1995. See Chapter 4 above.

2 Section 34(1).

3 Section 34(6). Under reg 2 of the Contact with Children Regulations 1991 (above), the authority is then required to give written notice with reasons to the child (if he has sufficient understanding) and to any person entitled to the presumption of reasonable contact.

4 Section 34(4). On such an application, the parent must be permitted to call such evidence as he or she sees fit, provided that this is presented in a professional and responsible manner. See *H v West Sussex County Council* [1998] 1 FLR 862.

5 Section 34(2) and (4). The court does not, however, have jurisdiction to make a prohibitory order which would prohibit the authority from exercising its discretion to allow staying contact with a parent. See *Re W (Section 34(2) Orders)* [2000] 1 FLR 502. For a decision illustrating the

or termination of access. Now there are automatic restraints on the local authority's power to refuse contact and it is incumbent on the local authority, subject to emergencies, to justify this to the court.

There is undoubtedly a tension between the two principles, (1) that the courts are *not* allowed under the statutory regime to interfere with the implementation of the local authority's care plan, and (2) that they *are* authorised to regulate the question of contact with a child in care. The short point is that the question of contact with the family is itself a very important integral part of the care plan. The reported cases have given guidance on the proper relationship between these two principles. First, it should be recalled that the court must have regard to the authority's care plan before making a care order[1]. If, therefore, the court is not happy with what is proposed concerning contact, one obvious solution will be for it to refuse to make the care order in the first place[2]. Secondly, once the child is actually subject to a care order, the courts have made it plain that Parliament has given them the right and duty to determine the question of contact in the event of a dispute. Where, therefore, there are any prospects of the link between the child and the family being meaningfully maintained, it falls to the court to decide the reasonableness of continuing contact and either to authorise it or refuse it[3].

Applications for contact

The category of those who benefit from the presumption of contact is limited. Others, such as grandparents or other relatives, may apply, with leave of the court, for a contact order[4]. In *Re M (Care: Contact: Grandmother's Application for Leave)*[5], the Court of Appeal set out in some detail the principles to be applied where the applicant for leave to apply for contact with a child in care is not in the category of those who benefit from the presumption (in this case a grandparent). The court said that, as in private law, grandparents are not entitled to reasonable contact as of right. At the same time, the special place of relatives was acknowledged in the legislation, and grandparents should have a special place in any child's affections. Contact between the child and the birth family should be assumed to be beneficial and the local authority should file evidence to justify why it would not be consistent with the child's welfare to promote contact with relatives. The court went on to hold that, by analogy with private law applications for contact, the criteria in s 10(9)[6] governing applications for leave in that context, were apposite

---

complex relationship between contact and the overall care plan, see *L v London Borough of Bromley* [1998] 1 FLR 709. For some research findings about efforts to promote contact between children looked after by local authorities and their families, see J Masson 'Restoring Contact and Rebuilding Partnerships' [1998] Fam Law 142.

1   *Re J (Minors) (Care: Care Plan)* [1994] 1 FLR 253.
2   *Re T (A Minor) (Care Orders: Conditions)* [1994] 2 FLR 423.
3   See, particularly, the judgment of Hale J in *Berkshire County Council v B* [1997] 1 FLR 171. See also *Re B (Minors) (Termination of Contact: Paramount Consideration)* [1993] Fam 301, *Re T (Termination of Contact: Discharge of Order)* [1997] 1 FLR 517, and *Re D and H (Care: Termination of Contact)* [1997] 1 FLR 841. The court must not, however, attempt to control contact in a way which strikes at the heart of the local authority's care plan. For a case in which the court trespassed unjustifiably on the 'forbidden territory' of the care plan itself, see *Re S (A Minor) (Care: Contact Order)* [1994] 2 FLR 222. For commentary, see C Smith 'Parental powers and local authority discretion – the contested frontier' [1997] CFLQ 243.
4   Under s 34(3)(b) 'any person' may apply with leave.
5   [1995] 2 FLR 86.
6   See Chapter 4.

on applications for leave to seek contact under the public regime. The local authority's general duty to promote contact with the child also extends to 'any relative, friend, or other person connected with him'[1]. It should not, therefore, be difficult for relatives to surmount the leave hurdle, where the application is genuine[2]. It may prove more difficult for those with a less obvious connection with the child. The main difference between this group and those entitled to the presumption of contact is that the onus here is on the applicant and not on the local authority.

Where the issue is not the complete refusal of contact, but rather the level or nature of contact being allowed, the onus will always be on the person affected by the decision to bring the matter to court. The court may then specify the time, place and frequency of contact[3]. Those entitled to the presumption of reasonable contact, together with the local authority and the child, are entitled to apply without leave for defined contact[4]. Others require leave. This power to define contact is again wider than that which existed before the Children Act. Under the old law, the local authority had power to curtail access drastically, perhaps with a view to phasing it out completely, and this was not susceptible to challenge[5]. This is precisely what had happened in the leading wardship case *A v Liverpool City Council*[6] in which a mother's access had been cut to one hour's supervised visit per month at a day nursey. Decisions on the amount of contact are now opened up to judicial scrutiny.

The local authority might itself find it advantageous to apply to the court to define contact where it is anticipating a dispute which could inhibit its ability to make positive plans for the child. The child's standing to make an application may be important, not merely to establish or increase contact but, perhaps more significantly, where the child wishes to have it terminated[7]. When making its orders, the court, as usual, has flexible powers to impose such conditions as it thinks fit[8].

---

1 Schedule 2, para 15(1)(c).
2 The leave requirement was considered necessary to prevent a 'free for all' which could inhibit the authority in executing its plans for children in care. However, in *F v Kent County Council* [1993] 1 FLR 432, Sir Stephen Brown P said that the court should be slow to exercise its discretion under s 91(14) of the Children Act which enables it, on disposing of an application, to order that no application for an order of a specified kind be made without leave of the court. In this case the justices had made an order restricting applications by the parents for contact or discharge of the care order. This had been an improper exercise of their discretion since there was no evidence suggesting that the parents had behaved unreasonably or that their previous applications were vexatious or frivolous. Cf *Cheshire County Council v M* [1993] 1 FLR 463 for a case in which the circumstances justified a refusal to allow a father to seek a contact order where the children were in care. For the operation of s 91(14) in the context of applications for leave to seek private orders, see Chapter 4 above.
3 Section 33(3) allows the court to 'make such order as it considers appropriate'.
4 Section 34(2) and (3)(a).
5 Under the Child Care Act 1980, s 12B(4) it was expressly provided that the authority was not to be taken to have terminated access where it proposed to substitute new arrangements for existing ones.
6 [1982] AC 363.
7 This is an especially pertinent point in the light of the sudden glut of cases in Autumn 1992 in which several children took to the courts in an attempt to secure the right to live apart from their parents. See Chapter 13 below.
8 Section 34(7).

Changes to contact arrangements

The court may vary or discharge a contact order on an application by the local authority, child, or person named in the order[1]. But the regulations[2] also provide for circumstances under which the parties may, by agreement, depart from the terms of a court order or vary or suspend voluntary contact arrangements. Such variations require the child's consent, where he has sufficient understanding, and there are notification requirements relating to those affected. Again, the principle is that it is better to arrive at voluntary arrangements wherever possible. Judicial intervention should be a last resort.

Application of the welfare principle

Since contact proceedings are proceedings under Part IV, the principles in s 1 apply. Thus the court must apply the welfare principle and the statutory checklist, together with the no order principle.

SUPERVISION

Supervision orders were traditionally used for two distinct purposes. One was to provide a measure of local authority control over a family situation, where there was concern that a child might be at risk, but a care order was not thought necessary. The other was to provide short-term assistance to parents, following separation or divorce. The Law Commission wanted to make this distinction clear. Thus the second type of order has now been replaced by the family assistance order, discussed earlier[3]. The first type of order remains as an alternative to a care order and is regulated by s 35 and Parts I and II of Sch 3 to the Children Act. We also discussed earlier the fact that truancy used to be a ground for a care order[4]. The *Review* and the White Paper did not think it an appropriate use of care proceedings where absence from school was the *sole* reason for bringing them[5], although a care order could remain appropriate where absenteeism represented part of a wider family problem[6]. The 'education supervision order' was introduced to deal with truancy as such. Educational supervision will be looked at in the context of education generally[7]. The concern, for the moment, is with the more traditional use of supervision in care proceedings, itself the subject of significant reform[8].

---

1   Section 34(9).
2   Section 34(8)(b), and reg 3 of the Contact with Children Regulations 1991, SI 1991/891.
3   See Chapter 4 above.
4   Children and Young Persons Act 1969, s 1(2)(e).
5   Chapter 16 discusses the position under the Children Act.
6   DHSS *Review of Child Care Law* (1985) at para 15.26, and the White Paper *The Law on Child Care and Family Services* (1987) (Cmnd 62) at para 59.
7   See Chapter 16 below.
8   See, generally, the *Review* (above) at paras 3.87–3.97.

When may a supervision order be made?

A supervision order may be used as an alternative to a care order[1] or may be made on discharging a care order[2]. The threshold criteria of s 31(2) must be satisfied in the ordinary way. Although supervision might be viewed as a less Draconian intervention in the family, the *Review* took the position that nothing less than the minimum conditions for a care order could justify compulsion, even at this lower level[3].

Although the threshold conditions for care and supervision orders are identical, the distinction between the legal effects of the two orders becomes crucial at the welfare stage when the court has to consider which order (if any) to make. We discuss the effects of supervision orders in more detail below. As between a care order or supervision order, the central question for the court will be whether the level of protection which can be offered to the child under a supervision order will be adequate or whether it is necessary to go further and make a full care order. The reported cases provide illustrations of instances in which the courts have felt it necessary to impose a care order and others in which they have decided a supervision order would suffice.

Re V (Care or Supervision Order)[4] is perhaps the best illustration of the first type of case. It reveals that one reason why a care order may be necessary is that it gives to the local authority parental responsibility which it will not acquire under a supervision order. The case concerned an adolescent boy approaching his seventeenth birthday (the age beyond which it becomes impossible to obtain a care order). He suffered from cerebral palsy, had spastic quadriplegia and learning disabilities. His father and mother quarrelled over the specialist school which he attended. The local authority was concerned at his absences and, fearing that his condition was regressing, sought a care order. The judge found that the threshold criteria were satisfied but refused to make the care order on the basis of the strain which this might place on the parents' marriage. Instead, he made a supervision order and attached conditions to it which, inter alia, required the boy to continue to attend the school as a weekly boarder.

The Court of Appeal allowed the guardian ad litem's appeal and substituted a care order. It was held that supervision orders with conditions do not fit into the framework of the Children Act. Requirements and directions in supervision orders could not be enforced other than by returning to court. Supervision orders depended rather on consent and co-operation, failing which the ultimate

---

1 Section 31(1)(b). On the circumstances in which a supervision order can be replaced by a care order, see *Croydon London Borough Council v A (No 3)* [1992] 2 FLR 350.

2 Section 39(4).

3 *Review* at para 18.18. But for an argument that there is a need for an intermediate order between the two in care proceedings, see A Gillespie 'Establishing a third order in care proceedings' [2000] CFLQ 239.

4 [1996] 1 FLR 776. See also *Re S (Care or Supervision Order)* [1996] 1 FLR 753 in which the Court of Appeal held that the judge, in making a supervision order, had not properly adverted to the difference between this and a care order. In this case, the risk of the possibility of sexual abuse of the child justified the making of a care order.

sanction was a care order. In this case, the risk to the parents' marriage was outweighed by the risk of harm to the boy if he was deprived of the specialist facilities at the school.

An example of the second type of case is *Re O (Care or Supervision Order)*[1]. Here, the proceedings concerned six children aged between nine and two. Health professionals and social workers had long been concerned about the children's development and about the neglect of certain specific health needs. On the other hand, it was accepted that their educational needs were largely being met, that their parents loved them and that present standards in the home were satisfactory. The local authority went to the family proceedings court for a supervision order to enable it to monitor the children's progress and continue to work with the family but the guardian ad litem wanted a care order so that the local authority, while leaving the children at home, could share parental responsibility with the parents. The justices made the care order but Hale J allowed the parents' appeal and substituted supervision orders in relation to all the children. She held, inter alia, that the justices had given insufficient weight to the improvements which had taken place in relation to the children's condition, the co-operation of the parents, the intensification of the local authority's efforts and how best to develop that co-operation further. They ought to have looked more carefully at the effect of supervision orders before going on to the most Draconian order (the care order) permitted under the legislation.

Recent case-law has taken account of the requirements of the ECHR that any order made by the court must be a proportionate response to the child's situation and be necessary. This is essentially the approach already taken by the English courts in the above cases but now couched in the language of the ECHR.

The leading case is *Re C and B (Care Order: Future Harm)*[2]. The parents had four children. The two older children were taken into care under orders which were based on actual harm to the elder child and the likelihood of such harm to the younger child. An interim care order was then made in the relation to the third child on the basis of likelihood of significant harm in the future even though all the available evidence was that he was currently doing well. When the fourth child was born, an EPO was made the same day and the two younger children were placed together with foster-parents. The local authority was given permission to refuse contact between the parents and any of the children and an order was made under s 91(14) prohibiting any applications by the parents for contact or discharge of the care orders for a two-year period without the court's permission. The Court of Appeal upheld the orders in relation to the two older children on the basis of past difficulties with contact and the parents' inability to understand the problems which had arisen. But the court had no difficulty in finding that the orders in relation to the two younger children were a disproportionate reaction to

---

1   [1996] 2 FLR 755. See also, in similar vein, *Re B (Care or Supervision Order)* [1996] 2 FLR 693 and *Oxfordshire County Council v L (Care Order or Supervision Order)* [1998] 1 FLR 70, in which Hale J sets out in some detail the reasons why a care order might be preferred over a supervision order and emphasises that although the court is empowered to make an order other than that sought by the local authority it should not make a more Draconian order unless there are cogent and strong reasons for doing so. In this case, the local authority wanted supervision orders while the guardian ad litem pressed for care orders. On the facts, supervision orders were considered sufficient and were substituted for the care orders made by the justices.

2   [2001] 1 FLR 611.

their situation. Although there was a real possibility of future harm to them, there were no long-standing problems of the sort which interfere with the capacity to provide adequate parenting, and the authority could have taken time to explore other options. The principle of proportionality meant that the authority was obliged to work to support and eventually reunite the family unless the risks were so high that the child's welfare required alternative care. The care orders were therefore discharged and the case remitted for re-hearing before a High Court judge. In the court's view, the younger children ought never to have been removed on an interim basis and, accordingly, they were allowed home under an interim supervision order.

This decision was followed in *Re O (Supervision Order)*[1], a case in which the mother had mental health problems and there was some risk of sexual abuse of the children by the father. The parents had, however, been co-operating by residing with the child (the mother's fifth child) in a residential assessment facility. The judge had made a supervision order but the local authority appealed wanting a care order. The Court of Appeal upheld the supervision order. The risk to the child was at the lower end of the spectrum, and a supervision order was the proportionate response. The court emphasised that where this was so the supervision order could and *should* be made to work. There was an obligation on the local authority to deliver the services that were needed and to ensure that other agencies, such as the health services, played their part. The parents also, under a supervision order, were required to co-operate fully.

What is the effect of a supervision order?

A supervision order will automatically terminate any existing supervision or care order[2]. It lasts, in the first instance, for one year but may be extended for up to three years from the date on which it was made[3] and will, in any event, terminate when the child attains 18 years of age[4]. The initial time-limit is designed to enable the court to control the effectiveness of the order.

The chief effect of a supervision order is to place the child under the supervision of a designated local authority[5]. Parental responsibility does not pass to the local authority, as under a care order, but remains exclusively with the parents or those who currently have it. The order places certain duties on the supervisor, the child and, for the first time under the Childen Act, the 'responsible person'[6].

---

1 [2001] 1 FLR 923. See also *Re C (Care Order or Supervision Order)* [2001] 2 FLR 466 which was also adjudged to be a low risk case in which a supervision order rather than a care order was the proportionate response. For a case in which the court considered whether a supervision order was required at all, as opposed to no order, see *Re K (Supervision Order)* [1999] 2 FLR 303.

2 Schedule 3, para 10.

3 Schedule 3, para 6.

4 Section 91(13).

5 Section 31(1)(b). The selection of supervisor is governed by Sch 3, para 9.

6 'Responsible person' is defined in Sch 3, para 1 as '(a) any person who has parental responsibility for the child; and (b) any other person with whom the child is living'.

Role of the supervisor

The supervisor has three duties:

> '(a)   to advise, assist and befriend the supervised child;
> (b)   to take such steps as are reasonably necessary to give effect to the order; and
> (c)   where –
>   (i)   the order is not wholly complied with; or
>   (ii)   the supervisor considers that the order may no longer be necessary,
>   to consider whether or not to apply to the court for its variation or discharge.'[1]

The purpose of the second two duties is to try to prevent the situation of 'drifting' which arose under the old law and tended to discredit supervision orders for their ineffectiveness. Under the Children Act, the supervisor's duties are more specific, and he is obliged to take positive action where the order is proving ineffective. The hope is that local authorities will come to see supervision as a real alternative to care.

Making supervision work

The legislation provides that the order may empower the supervisor to give a range of directions to the child which may include where he is to live for specified periods, requiring him to present himself to a specified person or to take part in specified activities at particular places or times[2]. One of the main difficulties in making supervision work has been that parents or other carers could not be made to comply with the order. The position now is that the court may impose obligations on them but only with their consent. This sounds contradictory, but it should be remembered that supervision depends on co-operation, and, as Freeman has pertinently observed, it is likely that consent 'will be readily obtained where it becomes apparent that the alternative is a care order'[3]. Supervision is only one possible solution, the alternatives being care or, at the other end of the spectrum, voluntary assistance. The order may require the responsible person to take reasonable steps to ensure that the child complies with any requirement in the order or the various directions of the supervisor[4]. It may also require the responsible person to keep the supervisor informed of his own address where it differs from that of the child, and allow the supervisor to visit the child at the address where the child lives[5]. The supervisor has no power to direct the child to undergo medical or psychiatric examination or treatment[6]. The court may do so, subject to the general principle that where a child is capable of giving an informed consent, this must be obtained[7]. Other than in relation to this one matter, the child's consent is not required under the regime of supervision.

'Enforcement'

The 'enforcement' of supervision has always been problematic and, in some ways, it is a contradiction even to talk of enforcement of what is an essentially co-operative programme. However, failure to allow a supervisor access to the child

---

1   Section 35(1).
2   Schedule 3, para 2.
3   MDA Freeman *Children, Their Families and the Law* (Macmillan, 1992) at p 130.
4   Schedule 3, para 3(1).
5   Schedule 3, para 3(3).
6   See Chapters 8 and 12 for further discussion of the issues.
7   Schedule 3, paras 4 and 5.

could be a serious matter and, where this happens, the supervisor may apply to the court for a warrant or possibly take other emergency action, which is discussed in the next chapter[1].

PROCEDURAL FEATURES AND OTHER ORDERS

The minutiae of the procedural rules governing care and related proceedings are beyond the scope of this work[2]. The procedural peculiarities of care proceedings were the source of much discontent and certainly contributed to the impetus for reform. These peculiarities derived from the Children and Young Persons Act 1969 – a piece of legislation which governed both care proceedings and criminal proceedings arising from juvenile delinquency. Most of the defects of care proceedings were the result of the adoption of a quasi-criminal procedure, arguably suited to delinquency cases but certainly not appropriate in cases of alleged abuse or neglect. Under the procedure, only the child and the local authority had party status. Parents were not parties but, initially, might represent the child[3]. This was wholly inappropriate since, by definition, it was their upbringing of the child which was usually in issue[4]. The local authority had no right to appeal against the refusal to make a care order and would sometimes seek to circumvent this restriction by using wardship as an extra-statutory avenue of appeal[5]. Neither did parents have any right of appeal against the making of a care order, at least in their own right[6].

The changes made by the Children Act sought to emphasise the *civil* nature of care and supervision proceedings by procedural changes and also by abolishing the use of care orders in criminal proceedings[7] and the 'offence condition' in care proceedings[8]. We will now look briefly at these changes and at the central features of the law under the Children Act as it applies to interim orders and the discharge and variation of existing orders for care and supervision.

---

1 *The Children Act 1989 Guidance and Regulations Vol 1 Court Orders* (HMSO, 1991) at para 3.95 emphasises that every effort should be made to secure co-operation before taking any such action.

2 The leading practitioner works are *Clarke Hall and Morrison on Children* (Butterworths) now in looseleaf format, and D Hershman and A McFarlane *Children Law and Practice* (Family Law) also in looseleaf format. A useful account of the procedure in care proceedings may also be found in D Bedingfield *The Child in Need* (Family Law, 1998) at pp 355–359.

3 Provision for separate representation for children in care proceedings was first recognised in the Children Act 1975 but those provisions were not brought fully into force until some years after that.

4 Parents themselves had only limited rights of participation in the proceedings, falling short of party status, and this initially meant that they were unable to obtain legal aid (*R v Worthing Justices, ex parte Stevenson* [1976] 2 All ER 194). Under the Children and Young Persons (Amendment) Act 1986, parents did become entitled to party status but only where there had been an order for separate representation of the child.

5 See, for example, *Hertfordshire County Council v Dolling* (1982) FLR 423 and *Re R (A Minor) (Discharge of Care Order: Wardship)* [1987] 2 FLR 400.

6 Although they could exercise the child's right of appeal on his behalf (*B v Gloucestershire County Council* [1980] 2 All 746) but not where a formal order for separate representation of the child had been made (*A-R v Avon County Council* [1985] Fam 150).

7 Section 90(2).

8 Section 90(1).

Procedural changes

Parties

As well as the child and the local authority, parents and others with parental responsibility now automatically have party status in care proceedings[1]. *Anyone* else may apply to the court to be joined as a party[2]. The White Paper had recognised the potential contribution which others might have to make in care proceedings[3]. The most likely candidates are grandparents, foster-parents or members of the extended family, but there is no restriction on those who may be joined. The child has a right to attend court by virtue of his party status, and the court has power to order attendance, where necessary, by authorising the police to bring the child to court[4]. In many cases, however, particularly those involving young children, the child will not attend but will be represented[5].

Representation of the child

Since the Children Act 1975, provision has been made for the separate representation of children in public proceedings[6]. The Children Act extended and reinforced the system of representation by a guardian ad litem ('GAL'), now known as a 'children's guardian'. The court is now required in care and supervision proceedings[7] to appoint a children's guardian for the child 'unless satisfied that it is not necessary to do so in order to safeguard his interests.'[8]. A solicitor will also represent the child. In contrast to private proceedings, independent representation of children is therefore the norm in public proceedings. Later we look at the more general question of the legal representation of children[9].

Disclosure of evidence and discovery of documents

The *Review* recommended that there should be more advance disclosure and discovery of documents in care proceedings[10]. Care proceedings formerly always took place at the level of magistrates' courts (in the juvenile court), and evidence was oral rather than written. This could take parties by surprise, and it was felt that families should know in advance the essential nature of the case for a care order. The legislation now requires that written statements of the substance of the oral evidence which a party intends to adduce at the hearing be submitted in advance[11]. The same applies to copies of any documents upon which a party intends to rely, including experts' reports[12].

---

1 Family Proceedings Courts (Children Act 1989) Rules 1991, SI 1991/1395.
2 Ibid.
3 The White Paper *The Law on Child Care and Family Services* (1987) (Cmnd 62) at paras 55–56.
4 Section 95, but this may often be inappropriate. See *Re G* (1992) *The Times*, November 19.
5 See further Chapter 13 below.
6 Ie care and related proceedings.
7 And in a range of other 'specified proceedings'. See s 41(6).
8 Section 41(1).
9 See Chapter 13 below.
10 DHSS *Review of Child Care Law* (1985), ch 16, especially at paras 16.2–16.29.
11 Rule 17(1)(a) of the Family Proceedings Courts (Children Act 1989) Rules 1991, SI 1991/1395, and r 4.17(1)(a) of the Family Proceedings Rules 1991, SI 1991/1247.
12 Ibid, r 17(1)(b) and r 4.17(1)(b) respectively.

We consider later the question of evidence in children's cases and, more particularly, the evidence of children themselves[1].

Appeals

It was a logical consequence of the peculiar rules which governed party status in care proceedings that appeal rights were very restricted. Only the child had a right of appeal as such, although, initially, parents could (very inappropriately) exercise this on the child's behalf[2]. This right was later removed where there had been an order for the separate representation of the child at first instance[3], but one effect of this was to deny parents any right of appeal *at all* since they had no right independent of the child's.

The Children Act removed these restrictions at a stroke, by ushering in a new rule that *any* party to care proceedings should have an automatic right of appeal[4]. In keeping with the new civil character of care proceedings, the appeal now lies from the family proceedings court (ie the magistrates' court) to the High Court[5] and not as before to the Crown Court, with its almost exclusively criminal jurisdiction. Parents, local authorities and all other parties thus now have *independent* rights of appeal[6].

The legislation makes provision for preserving the status quo, pending an appeal against the court's refusal to make (or decision to discharge) a care or supervision order. The objective is to avoid the risk of unnecessary disruption to the child's current living arrangements. Where the child is already the subject of an interim order (a necessary pre-condition), the court may order that he remain in care or supervision for the 'appeal period'[7].

Interim orders

The old law governing interim orders was criticised in the *Review* for several reasons[8]. First, the orders were apparently routinely granted as part of the package of care proceedings and, in some cases, there could be many such orders before the final care hearing took place. This could result in the child being kept away from home for an indefinite and potentially unlimited time without proof of one of the grounds for a care order. Secondly, the test for granting interim orders was imprecise and inconsistently applied and amounted to no more than showing a prima facie case for a care order. Thirdly, the orders were often made by single

---

1 See Chapter 13 below.
2 See fn 6 at p 523 above.
3 Ibid.
4 Section 94(1), which provides for an appeal against the making or refusing of any order under the Children Act by magistrates.
5 Ibid.
6 For further discussion of the appeals, see NV Lowe and G Douglas *Bromley's Family Law* (9th edn) (Butterworths, 1998) at p 578.
7 Section 40. The 'appeal period' is either the period between the making of the decision and the determination of the appeal or the period during which an appeal might be made against the decision (s 40(6)).
8 See DHSS *Review of Child Care Law* (1985) at ch 17.

justices without an adequate opportunity for parents, or others affected, to be heard.

The Children Act now prescribes the circumstances under which the order may be made[1], restricts their maximum duration[2] and requires them to be sought before a properly constituted court[3]. In keeping with the new image of supervision, it is now possible for the court under the Children Act, for the first time, to make an *interim* supervision order. It *must* do so when making a residence order in care or supervision proceedings, unless it is satisfied that the child's welfare will be satisfactorily safeguarded without the order[4]. The objective is to balance the need to provide the child with necessary protection while proceedings are pending, but not to allow the child to remain in a state of limbo for longer than is necessary[5]. The court has an important power when making an interim order to direct medical or psychiatric examination or other assessments of the child or to prohibit them[6]. This power is, again, subject to the mature child's right of objection.

Difficult questions have arisen concerning the extent to which the courts may direct local authorities to do certain things at the interim stage. The proper division of responsibility between the courts and local authorities under the Children Act is the general context in which this issue has been debated, and there has been speculation about whether the court's function in public cases is meant to be 'adjudicative' or 'participative'[7]. Sometimes the focus of tension between the courts and social services has been the use of limited resources. The authority may be resisting a particular course of action because it does not believe the cost is justifiable in the light of its competing priorities. Is it then open to the court to order it to conduct an expensive investigation against its better judgment? If a full

---

1 Under s 38(1) this is where proceedings for a care or supervision order are adjourned or where the court directs an investigation of the child's circumstances under s 37(1). The court must be satisfied under s 38(2) that there are reasonable grounds for believing that the threshold criteria in s 31(2) are satisfied in relation to the child. The test of whether there are 'reasonable grounds to believe' does not require the court to be satisfied that the threshold conditions are met or to make final findings. See *Oxfordshire County Council v S* [2004] 1 FLR 426. For an application of the test and its relationship to the principles in s 1, see *Humberside County Council v B* [1993] 1 FLR 257. Guidelines on the handling of applications for interim orders were given by Cazalet J in *Hampshire County Council v S* [1993] 1 FLR 559. See also *Re B (A Minor) (Care Order: Criteria)* [1993] 1 FLR 815 especially on the attribution of harm or likely harm at the interim stage.

2 Under s 38(4) this is eight weeks in the first instance, and there are complex rules governing the maximum duration of subsequent orders. A second or subsequent interim order may only last for 'the relevant period' which is defined as eight weeks from the date of the original order or four weeks from the date of a subsequent order, whichever is the longer (s 38(4) and (5)). On the duration of subsequent interim care orders, see *Gateshead Metropolitan Borough Council v N* [1993] 1 FLR 811. See also *Re C (A Minor) (Interim Care Order)* [1994] 1 FCR 447 for some of the difficulties which have arisen.

3 This is implicit in s 38(1). It was held in *W v Hertfordshire County Council* [1993] 1 FLR 118 that the justices must give reasons when making or refusing interim orders. In *S v Oxfordshire County Council* [1993] 1 FLR 452 it was similarly held that reasons must be given when making a supervision order rather than a care order, especially where this conflicts with the recommendations of the child's guardian ad litem.

4 Section 38(3).

5 See *The Children Act 1989 Guidance and Regulations Vol 1 Court Orders* (HMSO, 1991) at para 3.35.

6 Section 38(6) and (7).

7 See J Dewar 'The Courts and Local Authority Autonomy' [1995] CFLQ 15.

care order has already been made the management of the child's care is a matter for the local authority and not for the court. But does this logic hold good for the interim stage? The legal effect of an interim care order is to place the child in care with the legal effects of a care order – most notably that the authority acquires parental responsibility[1]. On the other hand, the court still has to be satisfied about whether the conditions are made out for a full care order.

The question of the court's powers at the interim stage fell to be determined by the House of Lords in *Re C (Interim Care Order: Residential Assessment)*[2]. The narrow issue in this case was a matter of the correct technical interpretation of two subsections of the Children Act, but the broader issue was nothing less than the appropriate balance of power between the courts and local authorities at the interim stage.

The provisions in question (so far as they are relevant) were as follows. Section 38(6) of the Children Act provides:

> 'Where the court makes an interim care order, or interim supervision order, it may give such directions (if any) as it considers appropriate with regard to the medical or psychiatric examination or other assessment of the child ...'

Section 38(7) provides:

> 'A direction under subsection (6) may be to the effect that there is to be –
> (a) no such examination or assessment; or
> (b) no such examination or assessment unless the court directs otherwise.'

The facts were that the local authority had obtained an emergency protection order and interim care order in relation to a baby taken to hospital with serious non-accidental injuries. The parents were very young (father 16, mother 17). Social workers, a clinical psychologist and the child's guardian ad litem all favoured an in-depth assessment of parents and child together at a residential unit. The local authority disagreed. The initial objection appeared to be on the basis of cost which was projected at between £18,000–£24,000. Later, the Assistant Director of Social Services put it differently to the court, arguing that the assessment would expose the child to an unacceptable level of risk. The authority instead pressed for a final care order with a view to adoption.

The judge directed the residential assessment but the Court of Appeal reluctantly allowed the authority's appeal following its own earlier decision in

---

1 Section 31(11).
2 [1996] 3 WLR 1098. For commentary, see A Bainham 'Authority Over the Authority' [1997] CLJ 267. The issue had come before the courts on a number of previous occasions. See, for example, *Re C (Minors) (Care: Procedure)* (1993) Fam Law 288, which held that a local authority might be directed by the court to arrange for a child to be assessed by a suitably qualified social worker. Without this direction, there might have been substantial delay because of pressure on the authority's resources. The court's power to direct assessment by a *named* social worker has also been confirmed by the Court of Appeal in *Re W (Assessment of Child)* [1998] 2 FLR 130. The court held, however, that this should not be encouraged since the court had no means of forcing an unwilling individual to act. The court should take into account the resources of the local authority employing the social worker and any difficulties there might be regarding its responsibility for and duty to supervise that individual. The better direction would be that an assessment be carried out by a 'suitably qualified social worker'. See also *Re O (Minors) (Medical Examination)* [1993] 1 FLR 860 in which Rattee J held that the court had power on making an interim care order to direct the local authority to have the children medically tested for HIV.

Re M (Interim Care Order: Assessment)[1]. The House of Lords allowed the parents' appeal and ordered the assessment.

On the proper construction of s 38(6), the Court of Appeal had adopted a narrow interpretation of the court's power to direct an assessment. It had held that the words 'other assessment of the child' had to be construed *ejusdem generis* with 'medical or psychiatric examination'. It also attached importance to the fact that the statute made no reference to the assessment of anyone other than the child (specifically not the parents), and it thought that to direct the child's residence would be to usurp the local authority's powers to regulate where the child was to reside.

The House of Lords preferred a broader, more purposive interpretation to give effect to the underlying intentions of Parliament. The House accepted that a child in interim care was subject to control by the local authority and that the court had no power to interfere except where specified in the legislation. But the subsections in question created exceptions to this principle. Their purpose was to enable the court to obtain the information necessary for its final decision as to whether the threshold was crossed and a care order was required. The court therefore had power to override the authority to the extent that it was necessary to enable it to reach this decision. It was not for the authority to decide what evidence was to go before the court, and the court should not allow the authority by administrative decision to pre-empt its own judicial decision. Moreover, the prohibition of assessments under subs (7) must have been intended to extend to the prohibition of assessment of *parents* as well as children so that, by analogy, subs (6) ought also to cover assessments of parents.

Re C has been followed or distinguished in a number of cases concerned with what may or may not be within the jurisdiction of the court to order at the interim stage. In *Re B (Psychiatric Therapy for Parents)*[2] the Court of Appeal allowed the local authority's appeal against a judge's order that the authority should be required to support and fund a therapeutic programme for parents recommended by a psychotherapist engaged by the children's guardian as an expert. The court distinguished between an *assessment* and something more appropriately described as *treatment* or *therapy*, and between matters which involved the child alone or the parent–child relationship and those which concerned the parents alone. Since what was proposed was only directed to addressing the parents' disabilities rather than assessing anything in relation to the child, the direction fell outside the scope of s 38(6). The projected cost here was £86,360 and the authority would also have to rent a house. The court held that it would be an order of last resort to impose on the authority an obligation to spend over £100,000 on a single child where the authority was resolutely opposed to this course. Similarly, in *Re D (Jurisdiction: Programme of Assessment or Therapy)*[3] the Court of Appeal held that the judge had lacked jurisdiction to impose on the authority a programme of treatment for a drug-dependent mother at a residential unit since its *primary* aim was treatment for the mother and not an assessment of her parenting abilities. The court acknowledged, however, that a programme in which the primary aim was

---

1   [1996] 2 FLR 464.
2   [1999] 1 FLR 701.
3   [1999] 2 FLR 632.

assessment could be authorised under s 38(6) notwithstanding that it could include a large element of therapy for a parent.

These decisions reveal a sensitivity to the problems which local authorities face in allocating scarce resources, and there can be little doubt that cost was an important factor in all these cases as well as what may be a difficult distinction to draw in practice between assessment and treatment. The desire on the part of the courts to strike a balance between these competing considerations is apparent in *Re M (Residential Assessment Directions)*[1]. Here Holman J directed the authority to participate in and to fund a residential assessment of the mother and her younger child but limited to eight weeks and at a cost of about £14,000. He accepted that at the end of this period the programme would shift to *treatment* as opposed to assessment and that he had no power to direct this treatment or its funding, even if at the end of the eight-week assessment period there was a good prospect of permanent rehabilitation of mother and child. In *Re B (Interim Care Order: Directions)*[2] the Court of Appeal allowed the appeal of parents against the refusal of the judge to direct a residential placement and assessment of the mother and her newborn baby. The authority had previously removed no less than six children from the parents and also wished to remove the seventh permanently when born. The court held that the proposed placement for mother and baby would clearly involve assessment not only of the mother but also the child and therefore fell within the court's jurisdiction. It represented the best course for management of the case in the context of a series of simultaneous assessments designed to illuminate the court's ultimate conclusion[3]. The House of Lords has now confirmed that interim orders are a legitimate exercise of judicial discretion where the care plan is incomplete[4].

Recently the Court of Appeal has returned to the principles governing the direction of residential assessments in *Re G (Interim Care Order: Residential Assessment)*[5]. It held, inter alia, in this case that Holman J's decision in *Re M*[6] should not be regarded as a guidance case[7]. The court reiterated the correct approach to residential assessments established by the House of Lords in *Re C*. The essential question should always be, can what is sought be broadly classified as an assessment to enable the court to obtain the information necessary for its own decision? The court also warned that an application for a s 38(6) direction may now potentially engage both Article 6 and Article 8 of the ECHR, and that the impact of the ECHR on such applications must be recognised. If the local authority wished to resist the assessment on the basis that the cost was excessive or disproportionate, that would need to be substantiated by hard evidence and would not be accepted merely by reference to general budgetary considerations.

---

1   [1998] 2 FLR 371.
2   [2002] 1 FLR 545.
3   As we have noted, the separation of mother and baby at birth is now inevitably sensitive owing to human rights requirements.
4   See pp 506 et seq above.
5   [2004] 1 FLR 876.
6   Above.
7   See D Stuart 'The Slaying of *Re M* – Section 38(6) Directions' [2004] Fam Law 590.

Discharge of care orders and discharge or variation of supervision orders

The defects in the old law which applied to interim orders also applied to care and supervision orders. Only the child or the local authority could apply for a discharge order. The parents had no right to do so except on behalf of the child[1] and this despite a clear conflict of interest between them. After all, what was usually at stake was the question of parental fitness to resume care of the child and the adequacy of the home environment. Recognising these conflicts of interest and providing for separate representation of the child did not offer a complete solution either, since this raised difficult issues about the parents' relationship with the child's guardian. It was not clear how far parents might pursue a discharge application where the guardian opposed it[2], and it was held that parents had no right to exercise the child's appeal against refusal to discharge a care order where the guardian refused to do so[3]. The grounds for discharge were vague. The court simply had to be satisfied that it was 'appropriate' and there was a distinct feeling that the courts were more concerned with issues of parental fitness than with the broader question of the child's welfare[4].

The Children Act increased the category of those persons who are eligible to apply for discharge and made children rather than parents the focus of attention through the application of the welfare principle.

Discharge of care orders

The child himself, the local authority, and anyone with parental responsibility may now apply for discharge of a care order[5]. Variation of care orders (except, indirectly, by substituting supervision orders) is not permitted since this would conflict with the principle that management of the child's case is under the control of the local authority. Parents, unmarried fathers with parental responsibility[6] and guardians (viz guardians taking office on the death of a parent) thus now have independent rights to apply for discharge[7]. Those who do not have parental responsibility may not apply, but may instead apply for a residence order,

---

1 Section 21(2) of the Children and Young Persons Act 1969.
2 *R v Wandsworth West Juvenile Court ex parte S* [1984] FLR 713.
3 *A-R v Avon County Council* [1985] Fam 150.
4 See DHSS *Review of Child Care Law* (1985) at paras 20.11 et seq.
5 Section 39(1). It has been established that a child (in this case a 14-year-old boy) has a statutory right to seek discharge of a care order, and does not require leave as is the case with private law applications for a s 8 order. See *Re A (Care: Discharge Application by Child)* [1995] 1 FLR 599.
6 Unmarried fathers *without* parental responsibility should, under the Family Proceedings Rules 1991, be joined as parties to applications to discharge care orders but the court also has a discretion to discharge any party from the proceedings. In *Re W (Discharge of Party to Proceedings)* [1997] 1 FLR 128, the father was serving a life sentence for the murder of his step-daughter. The mother, who was seeking to discharge a care order in relation to their two children, successfully applied to have the father discharged from the proceedings to prevent him from having any involvement.
7 Non-parents by definition are ineligible since they cannot hold parental responsibility while a care order is in operation. They could only derive it from a residence order, and a care order revokes a residence order (s 91(2)). It is, however, provided that a person to whom an exclusion requirement in an interim care order applies (see Chapter 12 below), where not

the effect of which would be to discharge the care order[1]. As part of its statutory obligations, the local authority must keep under regular review the care of all children looked after by it[2]. An aspect of these reviews is to consider specifically whether an application should be made to discharge a care order[3].

Discharge applications are now governed by the welfare principle and by the other principles in Part I of the Children Act[4]. It should be emphasised that, in contrast to the position where a care order is *sought*, this is an undiluted application of the welfare principle, and the threshold criteria have no part to play. Indeed, it is expressly provided that the statutory criteria do not have to be proved again where the court wishes to substitute a supervision order for the existing care order[5]. Conversely, the substitution of a supervision order with a care order *does* necessitate proof of the threshold criteria, since this involves a higher level of intervention.

The new provisions do not expressly allow a 'phased return' of the child. This was an issue which led, as already seen, to litigation before the Children Act[6]. There has been speculation that, where a phased rehabilitation is considered desirable, the court may be able to sanction this indirectly through its power to control contact decisions[7], or to attach conditions or give directions when making s 8 orders[8]. It would have been preferable if the legislation had confronted the issue directly, both because it is an important matter and because failure to do so may push applicants into inappropriate discharge applications[9].

---

qualified to apply for discharge of the interim order itself, may apply for it to be varied or discharged insofar as it imposes the exclusion requirement (s 39(3A)). The court may also, on the application of such person, vary or discharge the order insofar as it confers a power of arrest (s 39(3B)).

1 Where someone qualifies to apply for either discharge *or* a residence order, the only advantage of the latter would appear to be where there is disunity between two or more eligible applicants such as estranged parents. The residence order would not simply discharge the care order but would also determine the child's residence.

2 Section 26(2), and Review of Children's Cases Regulations 1991, SI 1991/895.

3 Section 26(2)(e), and Review of Children's Cases Regulations, reg 3 and Sch 2.

4 This is because Part I applies to proceedings under Part IV of the Children Act.

5 Section 39(4). In *Manchester City Council v Stanley* [1991] 2 FLR 370 this was done where the local authority had mismanaged the care of two girls committed to its care in wardship proceedings. More recently, see *Re O (Care: Discharge of Care Order)* [1999] 2 FLR 119 where the judge discharged a care order and substituted supervision and residence orders on the basis that the children concerned should not be removed from their mother. The authority's decision to remove them had been shaped by advice based on inaccurate and misleading information. The mother had co-operated with the care plan to the best of her ability, and the major factor in its breakdown had been the authority's failure to provide the agreed support, involving shared care and therapy for the children. There had been a long period with minimal professional input. In these circumstances the care order amounted to an unjustified level of intervention and a supervision order was more appropriate. It might be added, by way of commentary, that the care order in this case would almost certainly not have complied with the requirements of the ECHR.

6 See, particularly, *Re J (A Minor) (Wardship: Jurisdiction)* [1984] 1 WLR 81. Cf *Re M (A Minor)* [1985] Fam 60.

7 Under s 34.

8 Under s 11(7). See NV Lowe and G Douglas *Bromley's Family Law* (9th edn) (Butterworths, 1998) at p 580.

9 This might occur where, for example, parents are unhappy with the pace of a rehabilitative programme.

A final matter is that, where an application (the 'previous application') for discharge of a care or supervision order, or for the substitution of a supervision for a care order, has been disposed of, no further application can be made until six months have elapsed[1]. Again, the thinking is that the local authority should be given a reasonable chance of implementing its plans for the child without the constant interference of court applications.

Variation or discharge of supervision orders

A supervision order may be varied or discharged on the application of the child himself, any person with parental responsibility, or the supervisor[2]. It is also provided that a person who is not entitled to apply for discharge may apply for variation where the child is living with him and where the supervision order imposes a requirement which affects that person[3]. This reflects the obligations which the legislation imposes on 'responsible persons'[4]. Applications in relation to the discharge or variation of supervision orders are also governed by the welfare principle.

WARDSHIP AND THE INHERENT JURISDICTION

One of the aims of the Children Act was to render wardship less necessary by incorporating its more valuable features into the statutory code. The flexible powers given to the court in family proceedings, especially those relating to specific issues and prohibited steps, are designed to have this effect. We have already commented on the possible future use of wardship in private cases[5].

We now turn our attention to the relationship between wardship or the inherent jurisdiction of the High Court and the public law embodied in the Children Act. The effect of the legislation is greatly to reduce the possibilities for recourse to these jurisdictions but, whereas wardship and local authority care are now virtually incompatible, local authorities may still, in limited circumstances, be able to invoke the inherent jurisdiction. What then is the difference between these two jurisdictions? It should be said immediately that wardship is itself one manifestation of the inherent jurisdiction. In essence, the distinction is this: where the court is exercising its wardship jurisdiction, but not where it is otherwise exercising its more general inherent jurisdiction, the court has 'custody' of the child (in the old terminology) or 'parental responsibility' for the child (in the new terminology)[6]. As such, the court has all-embracing, automatic and ongoing control of major issues in the child's life which have to be referred back to the court. This is not the case where the court exercises its inherent jurisdiction in relation to children who are *not* wards of court.

---

1   Section 91(15).
2   Section 39(2).
3   Section 39(3).
4   See p 522 above.
5   Chapter 6 above. There is an extremely informative and detailed discussion of wardship in NV Lowe and G Douglas (above) at ch 16. See also Chapter 17 below for the use of wardship in cases of child abduction which is today, at least numerically, by far the most important use of the jurisdiction.
6   Of necessity, the physical 'care and control' of the child has to be delegated to an individual by the court.

Wardship and local authorities

Wardship proceedings are 'family proceedings' (as are all proceedings under the inherent jurisdiction) for the purposes of the Children Act[1]. It therefore follows that there is no reason, in principle, why the court in wardship proceedings should not make a care or supervision order. But it may *not* do so otherwise than in accordance with the statutory criteria in s 31(2)[2]. It is the wider basis for committing wards to care, based on broad welfare considerations, which had proved so popular with social services, which was abolished by the legislation.

This result was achieved in a number of ways. Where a ward is committed to care, properly applying the statutory criteria, the care order will terminate the wardship[3]. The former power under s 7(2) of the Family Law Reform Act 1969, to place a ward of court in care or under supervision, was repealed[4], as was the court's inherent power to do so[5]. Conversely, no child who is already in care may be made a ward of court[6]. Neither may the inherent jurisdiction be used to require a local authority to accommodate a child[7], nor to confer on it any power to decide questions concerned with any aspect of parental responsibility for the child[8]. These restrictions apply equally to wardship and other exercises of the inherent jurisdiction. The common reasoning behind the restrictions is that local authorities, the courts and everyone else must operate within, rather than outside, the carefully established statutory parameters for compulsory intervention.

It must be emphasised that these restrictions apply only where the child is *in care*. They do not apply where the child is merely 'accommodated'. In principle, wardship is not incompatible with voluntary accommodation arrangements, but it cannot be used initially to bring about such an arrangement[9]. Whether the courts will be prepared to entertain applications to ward accommodated children is highly questionable. There are perhaps two reasons for this. The first reason is that the *Liverpool* principle had been extended by the courts to voluntary cases[10], and it is likely that the courts would follow a similar policy under the Children Act. The second reason is that the courts are very unlikely to allow wardship to be used where they think the purpose can be achieved under the statutory code itself. The important consideration here is that s 8 orders, especially specific issue and prohibited steps orders, are available[11]. It is therefore unlikely that the courts will allow wardship to be used by or against local authorities in voluntary accommodation cases. One view is therefore that wardship as such is redundant in public

---

1 Section 8(3).
2 See, generally, *The Children Act 1989 Guidance and Regulations Vol 1 Court Orders* (HMSO, 1991) at paras 3.98–3.103.
3 Section 91(4).
4 Section 100(1).
5 Section 100(2)(a).
6 Section 100(2)(c).
7 Section 100(2)(b).
8 Section 100(2)(d).
9 Section 100(2)(b). Once a child is accommodated, accommodation and wardship, unlike care and wardship, are not incompatible.
10 *W v Nottinghamshire County Council* [1986] 1 FLR 565.
11 The restrictions in s 9(1) apply only where the child is in care. For an exceptional case in which wardship was continued and a combination of public (supervision) and private (residence) law orders were made at the final hearing of care proceedings, see *Re M and J (Wardship: Supervision*

law cases[1]. This view has, however, been challenged by White, Carr and Lowe[2] who point out that s 8 orders do not cover every situation in which a local authority may be concerned about a child's welfare. They argue that wardship may still be useful to local authorities in those cases in which it is thought to be desirable for the court to exercise a continuing control which is perhaps the hallmark of the wardship jurisdiction. In support they cite cases in which a local authority used wardship to protect a teenage girl from an undesirable relationship with an older man[3]. Other possible uses, they argue, could include protecting 17-year-olds where the normal public law options do not exist, or orphans, and restraining harmful publicity. It should be emphasised again, however, that if the child is in care any such protections could only be obtained either by seeking prohibited steps or specific issue orders[4] or by invoking the inherent jurisdiction, as distinct from wardship, and only then with leave of the court[5].

The inherent jurisdiction and local authorities

The realisation that the High Court has a more general inherent jurisdiction to protect children outside wardship appears to be a comparatively recent phenomenon[6]. The effect of invoking the inherent jurisdiction is not to trigger the extremely wide-ranging effects of wardship but rather to invite the High Court to determine certain specific issues of difficulty. It is in effect a 'single issues' jurisdiction. Local authorities, but not others, require leave for this purpose. It is, prima facie, inconsistent with their primary responsibilities that local authorities should wish to hand over a decision affecting a child in their care. A limited exception to this principle has been allowed because it was appreciated that there

---

and Residence Orders) [2003] 2 FLR 541. In this case Charles J held that as a matter of principle the court should utilise the statutory scheme under the Children Act 1989 wherever possible rather than retreat to an exercise of the inherent jurisdiction. However, there could be exceptional cases such as this in which the structure of wardship, with the opportunity to return to court and the combination of orders, would provide the best solution.

1   See Chapter 10 for possible alternatives to wardship. For a good example of the flexibility which can now be achieved in public cases under the Children Act, see *C v Solihull Metropolitan Borough Council* [1993] 1 FLR 290, in which Ward J indicated that a conditional residence order could be made alongside the interim supervision order. This could avoid the two extremes of a final supervision order or a care order. The court could, in effect, continue to preserve a degree of control over the child's situation where it thought this necessary, by an imaginative use of its statutory powers. But it should be noted that there are *some* limits to the flexibility of the statutory scheme. Thus it was made plain by Booth J in *Hounslow London Borough Council v A* [1993] 1 FLR 702 that care orders and residence orders are incompatible. Where, therefore, the justices had made a care order they were deemed to have dismissed the father's application for a residence order. The proper course, where there remained some uncertainty about the father's role, would have been for the justices to have made an interim care order and adjourned both applications until the authority had had a chance to assess the father as carer.
2   R White, P Carr and N Lowe *The Children Act in Practice* (3rd edn) (Butterworths, 2002) at pp 380–381.
3   *Re R (A Minor) (Contempt)* [1994] 2 All ER 144.
4   See Chapter 4 above.
5   Discussed below.
6   This, at least, is the view of NV Lowe and G Douglas (above) at pp 684–685.

can be some particularly sensitive or complex questions where it may be appropriate for local authorities to seek the assistance of the courts[1].

The Children Act allows the inherent jurisdiction to be invoked by local authorities with leave[2]. This will be granted where the court is satisfied that:

(a) the result which the authority wishes to achieve could not be achieved through the making of any other order available to the authority under the legislation; and

(b) there is reasonable cause to believe that, if the inherent jurisdiction is not exercised, the child is likely to suffer significant harm[3].

There are, thus, two key elements in obtaining leave. The first ought not to be difficult to satisfy since, where the child is in care, the legislation prevents the courts from making specific issue or prohibited steps orders[4]. The inherent jurisdiction will probably be the only mechanism where the local authority wishes to obtain the court's ruling on a 'single issue'. The second requirement is the familiar 'significant harm' test which applies elsewhere in the legislation[5]. Its suitability here as a pre-condition for leave has been thought by some commentators to be unnecessarily restrictive[6]. On the other hand, it might be argued that it is unduly liberal since it effectively lowers the statutory threshold for State intervention. We discuss this further below.

---

1   But the Court of Appeal has held that county courts do *not* have an inherent jurisdiction to grant injunctions to supplement public law orders in favour of local authorities. See *Devon County Council v B* [1997] 1 FLR 591.

2   Section 100(3), and see JM Masson 'Leave, Local Authorities and Welfare' [1992] Fam Law 443. For an illustration of the use of the inherent jurisdiction in this context, see *Nottingham City Council v October Films Ltd* [1999] 2 FLR 347 where the authority sought to restrain the further filming for a Channel 4 documentary of several delinquent children who were either in the care of, or accommodated by, the council. Sir Stephen Brown P, balancing freedom of the press with the need to support caring professionals working with delinquent children, accepted undertakings from the film company in lieu of injunctions restraining its activities which he would otherwise have granted. For commentary, see L Wood 'Fredom of expression and the protection of minors' [2001] CFLQ 470. Cf *Medway Council v BBC* [2002] 1 FLR 104 in which Wilson J refused the authority leave to apply for an injunction restraining the BBC from broadcasting a short interview with a child who had been the subject of an anti-social behaviour order under the Crime and Disorder Act 1998. Significantly, he emphasised that, since the coming into force of the HRA 1998, restrictions on the right to freedom of expression guaranteed by Article 10 of the ECHR had to be based on a strong and pressing social need which did not exist in this case. For a recent case exploring the child's own rights under Articles 8 and 10 of the ECHR in relation to publicity, see *Re Roddy (A Child) (Identification: Restriction on Publication)* [2004] 2 FLR 949.

3   Section 100(4).

4   Section 9(1).

5   Ie in Parts IV and V. But note that whereas under s 31(2) the court must be satisfied that *the child is suffering, or likely to suffer, significant harm*, under s 100(3) it need only be satisfied that *there is reasonable cause to believe* that if the inherent jurisdiction is not exercised with respect to the child, the child is likely to suffer significant harm.

6   See, for example, A Bainham *Children: The New Law* (Family Law, 1990) at para 8.55, and J Eekelaar and R Dingwall 'The Role of the Courts under the Children Bill' (1989) 139 NLJ 217.

What kind of circumstances then might justify leave[1]? It seems to be agreed that the most likely issues will revolve around serious medical procedures[2], restricting harmful publicity[3] or restraining other harmful interferences with the child[4]. There is some doubt as to the precise extent of the court's powers but the view has been expressed judicially that they are co-extensive with the court's powers in wardship[5]. Clearly, these powers extend beyond the court's statutory powers under the Children Act and also exceed the power of a natural parent[6].

It is fair to say that in recent years there have been some controversial uses of the inherent jurisdiction by local authorities which have led to suggestions that it is being used in a way which subverts the intentions of Parliament. We will return to some of this case-law in Chapter 12. For the moment it is sufficient to note that one area of difficulty has concerned the refusal of consent to treatment or medical procedures by young people who have attained the age of 16 but are below the age of majority. We discussed the leading case of *Re W (A Minor) (Medical Treatment: Court's Jurisdiction)*[7] in Chapter 8. This case was followed by the decision of Wall J in *Re C (Detention: Medical Treatment)*[8], another case involving a 16-year-old suffering from anorexia nervosa who was refusing all treatment. Here, it was held that the inherent jurisdiction might be exercised at the behest of the local authority not merely to authorise treatment but also to restrain the young patient in a secure unit[9].

Cases like this raise serious questions about the autonomy aspect of children's rights[10] but they also provoke consideration of the limits of State paternalism under the legislation. Superficially it might appear that intervention via the inherent jurisdiction is, because of the requirement of leave, just as constrained by the threshold test of 'significant harm' to the child as is intervention by means of a care or supervision order. Yet this is not really the case and the decision of the House of Lords in *Re H and R (Child Sexual Abuse: Standard of Proof)*[11] makes this clear. In that case, the House was at pains to emphasise the difference between proof of the statutory threshold conditions and the kind of reasonable suspicions of harm which would be sufficient to found emergency protection orders or

---

1   NV Lowe and G Douglas (above) at pp 710–711; MDA Freeman *Children, Their Families and the Law* (Macmillan, 1992) at pp 161–162.
2   See Chapter 8 for examples.
3   As in *Re L (A Minor) (Wardship: Freedom of Publication)* [1988] 1 All ER 418. See also *Re Z (A Minor) (Freedom of Publication)* [1996] 1 FLR 191. It appears that leave may not be required where the court can exercise its powers to grant injunctions under the Supreme Court Act 1981, s 37. See *Re P (Care Orders: Injunctive Relief)* [2002] 2 FLR 385. In that case Charles J granted the local authority injunctions ancillary to a care order requiring the parents to allow the child to attend a sixth-form college without interference and permitting the authority to monitor the family.
4   As in *Re JT (A Minor) (Wardship: Committal to Care)* [1986] 2 FLR 107.
5   *Re W (A Minor) (Medical Treatment: Court's Jurisdiction)* [1993] Fam 64.
6   A point made plain in relation to wardship in *Re R (A Minor) (Wardship: Consent to Treatment)* [1992] Fam 11, discussed in Chapter 8 above.
7   [1993] Fam 64. See also *A Metropolitan Borough Council v DB* [1997] 1 FLR 67.
8   [1997] 2 FLR 180.
9   He also held that the secure unit in this case did not amount to 'secure accommodation' under s 25 of the Children Act so as to require an application for a 'secure accommodation order' under that section.
10 See Chapters 3 and 8 above.
11 [1996] 2 WLR 8 (discussed above).

interim care orders. When we turn to s 100(4), which governs the criteria for granting leave to invoke the inherent jurisdiction, we find that it is *not* satisfaction of the threshold criteria which is required but *reasonable cause to believe* that the child would otherwise be likely to suffer significant harm. It might be replied that where we are concerned only with a 'single issue' and not with removal of the child from the family, a less stringent test for intervention is justified. But it is also legitimate to reflect on whether the State, through the High Court, is effectively arrogating to itself a wider power of compulsory intervention than that envisaged when the public law affecting children was reformed.

Chapter 12

INVESTIGATION AND SHORT-TERM PROTECTION

INTRODUCTION

This chapter looks at the investigative duties of local authorities where children are suspected to be at risk, and the legal framework within which short-term or emergency protection is undertaken. The connection between investigation and protection is a necessary one since it has been emphasised that no court is likely to grant either a child assessment order or an emergency protection order (EPO) unless there has been a prior investigation of the circumstances[1]. The focus of attention here is on short-term remedies for the purposes of assessment and dealing with emergencies, as distinct from the medium and long-term solutions of care and supervision[2].

Historical background to the reforms

Emergency procedures were arguably criticised even more than other areas of child care law – understandably, since they regulate the initial stages of compulsory intervention in the family. They have, in the past, been associated with Draconian and unceremonious removals of children from their homes, of which the so-called 'dawn raids' in Orkney and Rochdale were glaring examples[3]. Place of safety orders were the chief mechanism for emergency action, but there was much evidence of their misuse. In many instances, orders appeared to be used, not in genuine emergencies, but as a means of gaining control of children for diagnostic or investigatory purposes. The orders were apparently routinely granted, often ex parte, by single magistrates from home[4]. They came to be seen by some social services departments as stage one of a three-stage process leading to a care order[5]. The process lacked elementary procedural fairness, bearing in mind the seriousness of the intrusion. The grounds were based on the applicant's belief that one of the conditions for a care order might be satisfied[6]; the removal of children was authorised for as long as 28 days; and the effects of the order were vague, especially regarding the powers and obligations of the local authority.

---

1   *The Children Act 1989 Guidance and Regulations Vol 1 Court Orders* (HMSO, 1991) at para 4.78. On orders under Part V of the Children Act generally, see ch 4 of the *Guidance*.
2   For a particularly penetrating analysis of the issues in the use of 'apprehension' powers relating to children, which also looks at the human rights requirements, see J Masson 'Human Rights in Child Protection: Emergency Action and its Impact' in P Lødrup and E Modvar (eds) *Family Life and Human Rights* (Gyldendal Akademisk, 2004) at p 457.
3   See, particularly, *Re A (Minors) (Child Abuse) (Guidelines)* [1992] 1 All ER 153.
4   'A Magistrate sitting at home in his pyjamas', in the graphic phrase of Stuart Bell MP (*Hansard*, 23 Oct 1989, col 594).
5   The process would begin with a place of safety order which would be followed up by one or more (usually more) interim care orders and finally the full care order.
6   The test was part objective in the sense that it focused on the *reasonableness* of the applicant's belief, but partly subjective in that it was the *applicant's* belief, not the court's, which was crucial.

The most damning criticism of emergency procedures was the way in which they could be used to ride roughshod over the rights of parents and children. Parents had little input into the process. They had no rights of prior notification, consultation or appeal, and only a limited right to an explanation of the reasons for the order once made. The absence of proper avenues of redress led to applications by parents for interim care orders, as a back-door mechanism for challenging place of safety orders[1]. Even this option was, in due course, removed[2]. It was the large-scale use of place of safety orders in dubious circumstances in Cleveland which was the 'last straw' and led to a clamour for immediate reform[3]. At the same time, there remained widespread anxiety about undetected child abuse in general, and sexual abuse in particular[4].

The emergency protection order

The aim of Part V of the Children Act 1989 is therefore, as the *Guidance* puts it, 'to ensure that effective protective action can be taken when this is necessary within a framework of proper safeguards and reasonable opportunities for parents and others connected with the child to challenge such actions before a court'[5]. The legislation tried to achieve this by revamping the investigative duties of local authorities, by requiring other authorities to co-operate, and by replacing the discredited place of safety order with a new emergency protection order with more stringent grounds, more clearly defined legal effects, and shorter time-limits for detaining children in emergencies.

The need for a 'half-way house': the child assessment order

While the Children Bill was progressing through Parliament, a major issue arose as to whether another type of order for assessment of children was required as an alternative to an EPO. The idea had its origins in the *Carlile Report*[6]. There was concern that there could be many cases in which there was suspicion of abuse, but insufficient evidence to justify emergency action. In such cases, the aim of social services is to make an assessment of the child's situation and, where suspicion of abuse persists, to obtain an accurate diagnosis. This, of course, may require medical and/or psychiatric examination of the child. But what if parents are refusing to co-operate either to let social services see the child at all or to allow the child to be examined? The dilemma for the social worker caught in this situation

---

1   *R v Lincoln (Kesteven) County Justices, ex parte M* [1976] QB 957.

2   *Nottinghamshire County Council v Q* [1982] Fam 94.

3   The evidence in Cleveland was that between 1 January 1987 and 31 July 1987 there were 276 applications for place of safety orders. Of these, 174 were granted by a single justice from home. See *Report of the Inquiry into Child Abuse in Cleveland 1987* (HMSO, 1988) (Cmnd 412) at para 10.9.

4   Considerable media attention was devoted to this, most notably in the BBC television programme 'That's Life' which led to the establishment of 'Childline'.

5   *The Children Act 1989 Guidance and Regulations Vol 1 Court Orders* (HMSO, 1991) at para 4.1. For further discussion of the basis of the reforms in Part V of the Children Act, see the *Review of Child Care Law* (1985) at chs 12 and 13, and the White Paper *The Law on Child Care and Family Services* (1987) at ch 4.

6   *A Child in Mind: Protection of Children in a Responsible Society, Report of the Commission of Inquiry into the Circumstances surrounding the death of Kimberley Carlile* (1987).

has been whether to take highly interventionist emergency action to remove the child, or to do nothing.

It was asserted in Parliament that a 'half-way house' was needed which would require a child to be produced and authorise an assessment but which would not necessarily lead to the removal of the child. There was considerable disagreement about whether the additional order was really required, not least between professional bodies such as the NSPCC and the Association of Directors of Social Services. The opponents of the order were worried about the possible confusion which might arise about when to seek each order and also the potential of the assessment order, as they saw it, for undermining attempts at voluntary co-operation with parents[1]. The proponents of the order stressed that this would not be so, especially since parental responsibility would not pass to the local authority. They argued that the 'lesser' order would allow action to be taken where there was serious, but not urgent, concern for the child's well-being.

It was this view which ultimately prevailed with the introduction of the innovative child assessment order (CAO). The features of the CAO, as it eventually emerged, when compared with those of the EPO, are evidence of the compromise which had to be struck[2]. The extremely short time-limit (seven days), for example, reflects the perceived need to make this shorter than the limit for EPOs (eight days). Both orders can be utilised in 'non-access' cases, and both make provision for medical and psychiatric examination. This is, at least in part, the result of grafting on to the statutory scheme, at the eleventh hour, an alternative mechanism for dealing with some of the difficulties which had already been addressed when formulating the EPO[3]. Nevertheless, conceptually at least, the two orders are quite distinct and, as the *Guidance* says, the CAO 'is emphatically not for emergencies'[4].

Other reforms under the Children Act

The legislation also redefined police powers to protect children and powers of entry and search. These powers should not be underestimated since, in the worst cases of severe violence against children, the police will need to be involved. Finally, the legislation reformed the law governing abduction of children from care, and addressed, for the first time, the legal position of those organisations which provide assistance to young 'runaways'.

---

1 Baroness Faithfull, for example, said in the House of Lords that a court-ordered medical examination would be likely to 'upset an enormous number of good parents who have a finger pointed at them' (House of Lords Official Report, 19 January 1989, col 429).

2 For a further informative discussion of the parliamentary background, see, generally, N Parton *Governing the Family* (Macmillan, 1991) at ch 6. For critical commentary on child assessment orders and their operation in practice, see R Lavery 'The Child Assessment Order – a reassessment' [1996] CFLQ 41, and Dickens 'Assessment and Control of Social Work – analysis or reasons for the non-use of the child assessment order' (1993) JSWFL 88.

3 A point made very well by MDA Freeman in *Children, Their Families and the Law* (Macmillan, 1992) at pp 173–175.

4 *The Children Act 1989 Guidance and Regulations Vol 1 Court Orders* (HMSO, 1991) at para 4.4.

INVESTIGATION[1]

Local authorities, it will be recalled, are required to use the voluntary services offered to families under Part III of the Children Act to 'take reasonable steps ... to prevent children within their area suffering ill-treatment or neglect'[2]. It is not necessary to mention again here the connection between voluntary and compulsory action or the primary focus on the former[3], but what this means is that where social services, because of the information available to them, believe a child may be at risk, they will first have to consider whether this risk can adequately be met through voluntary assistance to the family. A good example of this working is where an alleged abuser can be induced to move out of the home, perhaps with assistance from the local authority[4].

Sources of initial information

How do local authorities get their initial information? There is no single source. Neighbours may hear suspicious noises, or fail to see a child for some time; social services may have had previous dealings with the family and be aware of the problems; the child himself may be sufficiently resourceful to contact social services direct or, more likely, confide in a trusted adult; the family doctor or health visitor may become aware of what looks like a non-accidental injury. Perhaps the most likely source of information in the case of older children is the school. Children spend almost as much time at school as they do at home, and teachers and welfare assistants are in direct contact with them for substantial periods of the day. As such, they are uniquely placed to observe behavioural aberrations (which could point to sexual abuse) or to notice signs of physical injury. Physical education classes and swimming activities provide opportunities for discreet observation, and it is not unknown for a school to hold an impromptu class where a child is suspected to have been abused. It must be stressed, again, that there is no mandatory reporting law in England[5], but various authorities, including local education authorities (LEAs), are required to assist social services with their investigations, unless it would be unreasonable to expect them to do so in all the circumstances[6].

Local authority's investigations

The local authority's investigative duties may arise by direction of the court in family proceedings[7], and also in certain other circumstances specified in s 47 of the Children Act. These circumstances are where the local authority is informed that a child living or found in its area:

(1) is the subject of an EPO;

---

1 A particularly good account of the legislative framework governing the investigative stage of child protection is to be found in R White, P Carr and N Lowe *The Children Act in Practice* (3rd edn) (Butterworths, 2002) at paras 7.1–7.22.
2 Schedule 2, para 4(1).
3 See Chapters 10 and 11 above.
4 Under Sch 2, para 5. The issue of removing adults rather than childen is discussed below.
5 This was not favoured in the DHSS *Review of Child Care Law* (1985) at para 12.4.
6 See p 545 below.
7 Under s 37(1).

(2) is in police protection;
(3) has contravened a ban imposed by a curfew notice within the meaning of Chapter 1 of Part I of the Crime and Disorder Act 1998;
(4) where the local authority has reasonable cause to suspect that the child is suffering, or is likely to suffer, significant harm[1].

In the case of contravention of a curfew notice, the legislation, as amended[2], provides that the enquiries must 'be commenced as soon as practicable and, in any event, within 48 hours of the authority receiving the information'. This provision was inserted by the Crime and Disorder Act 1998 and is part of a package of measures introduced by the Labour Government to combat anti-social behaviour. There has long been a debate about the relationship between delinquency and social deprivation, and this provision recognises that there may be a link between anti-social behaviour and a lack of parental supervision and control[3]. Children engaging in anti-social activities may in short be suffering from abuse or neglect and this should trigger an investigation by the local authority. The enquiries, in this case, must in particular be directed towards whether the authority should make any application to the court under s 11 of the Crime and Disorder Act 1998 for a child safety order which relates to children under the age of 10[4].

This relationship between anti-social or criminal activity by children and child protection is further reflected in a White Paper published in July 2002[5]. This proposed a new power for the *criminal* courts to direct a welfare investigation into a child's circumstances, similar to the power currently available to the courts in family proceedings under s 37 of the Children Act 1989[6]. The direction would require the authority to investigate whether a care order, supervision order or EPO might be justified in the child's case.

Following its investigations, the local authority must make, or cause to be made, 'such enquiries as they consider necessary to enable them to decide whether they should take any action to safeguard or promote the child's welfare'. It is a broader and more positive obligation to conduct enquiries than the pre-Children Act duty. This was limited to making enquiries on receipt of any information which suggested that there were grounds for care proceedings, unless the local authority was satisfied that this was unnecessary[7]. The present duty is more directly focused on the child's welfare. Where the child is already subject to an EPO or in police protection, by definition that child is considered to be at risk and this is an automatic trigger for social services to investigate. Local authorities are required to investigate the circumstances of children in other contexts, especially to

---

1   Section 47(1) as amended. 'Suspicion' as required for an investigation is a lower standard than that required by the tests for making EPOs or interim care orders or taking a child into police protection. It has been said by Hale LJ that the courts should be slow to hold that a local authority does not have reasonable grounds such as will justify it in making inquiries under s 47. See *Gogay v Hertfordshire County Council* [2001] 1 FLR 280 at 294. It has also been held by Scott Baker J that the authority is not required to make a finding on the balance of probabilities as to past conduct before assessing a risk and taking protective steps under s 47. See *Re S (Sexual Abuse Allegations: Local Authority Response)* [2001] 2 FLR 776.
2   Children Act 1989, s 47(1), as amended by the Crime and Disorder Act 1998, s 15(3).
3   See further Chapter 14 below.
4   Section 47(3).
5   *Justice for All* (2002) (Cm 5563).
6   On s 37 directions, see Chapter 2 above.
7   Children and Young Persons Act 1969, s 2(1).

establish whether a child is 'in need' within the meaning of s 17 of the Children Act and following a direction by the court under s 37. We consider these investigative duties elsewhere in the book[1].

Possible courses of action following enquiries

The legislation requires the local authority to decide, following its enquiries, whether to make any application to the court. This will mean that the authority must consider whether to seek a CAO, an EPO, or a care or supervision order or to offer voluntary assistance under Part III[2]. Where a child who is subject to an EPO is not currently in local authority accommodation, the local authority must consider whether the child should be placed there for the duration of the EPO[3]. Where the child is in police protection, the local authority must determine whether it would be in the child's best interests to apply for an EPO[4]. The strongest duty arises where, in the course of the local authority's enquiries, an officer of the authority is refused access to the child or denied information as to his whereabouts. Here, the local authority *must* apply for an EPO, care order or supervision order unless satisfied that the child's welfare can otherwise be satisfactorily safeguarded[5].

Following its investigations, the local authority may conclude that an order is not required. Where it takes the view that no order is necessary, it must still consider whether there should be a later review of the child's circumstances and, if so, it must fix a date for the review to begin[6]. Where it decides that it *should* act to safeguard or promote the child's welfare, it is obliged to take that action, insofar as it is within its power and reasonably practicable for it to do so[7]. Eekelaar has drawn attention to the local authority's 'peculiar position of being allowed to decide whether or not to put itself under additional duties' and has been critical of the absence of a 'clear and unambiguous duty to take action on the basis of the results of the inquiries where the child is likely to be harmed if no such action is taken'[8]. He speculates on whether it could be lawful for the local authority to decide to do no more, for example, because of pressure of resources. And he contrasts the position with the local authority's duty where there has been a s 37 direction to justify to the court a decision to take no action[9]. It is arguable that the local authority is not accountable enough for the proper discharge of these duties.

---

1   See Chapters 2 and 10 above.
2   Section 47(3).
3   Section 47(3)(b).
4   Sections 47(3)(c) and 46(7).
5   Section 47(6).
6   Section 47(7). It should be remembered that the authority may not have decided to do 'nothing', since it may well be offering voluntary assistance under Part III of the Children Act.
7   Section 47(8).
8   J Eekelaar 'Investigation Under the Children Act 1989' [1990] Fam Law 486 at 487.
9   The relevant provision is s 37(3) which requires the authority to inform the court of the reasons for its decision, any service or assistance which it has provided, or intends to provide, for the child and his family and any other action which it has taken, or proposes to take, with respect to the child.

The value of co-operation

The importance of inter-agency co-operation is stressed again at this preliminary investigative stage. Local authorities must co-operate with each other in the investigation of child abuse[1]. Where, as a result of its enquiries, an authority decides that there is an educational issue which requires investigation it must consult the relevant LEA[2]. Housing authorities, health authorities and others specified by the Secretary of State must assist the local authority with its enquiries, if called upon to do so, by providing information and advice[3], unless this would be unreasonable in all the circumstances of the case[4]. Freeman has questioned whether the police should have been left off this list, arguing that some police forces have been obstructive in the past[5]. The spirit of the Act certainly requires police co-operation and, in most cases, no doubt this will be forthcoming.

CHILD ASSESSMENT ORDERS

The *Guidance*[6] describes the CAO as 'a lesser, heavily court-controlled order dealing with the narrow issue of examination or assessment of the child in specific circumstances of non-co-operation by the parents and lack of evidence of the need for a different type of order or other action'. The hope is that the assessment ordered by the court will provide this evidence and enable the local authority to decide what action (if any) is required.

It cannot be emphasised strongly enough that the CAO is not suitable for emergencies, which must be the subject of applications for EPOs. Indeed, the court is precluded from making a CAO where it is satisfied that there are grounds for making an EPO and that it ought to make this order rather than the CAO[7]. It may then treat the application for the CAO as an application for an EPO[8]. The local authority must, in every case, decide whether the case is a genuine emergency or whether there is sufficient doubt about this to push it instead in the direction of a CAO.

Who may apply and on what grounds?

In contrast to the EPO (which may be sought by anyone), the CAO may only be requested by a local authority or 'authorised person' (the NSPCC). The rationale for this distinction is that in *emergencies* anyone should be able to act decisively to protect a child but that, in non-urgent cases, the policy should be to leave action to the primary child protection agencies. The court is empowered to make a CAO where:

---

1   Section 47(12) provides that, where a local authority is making enquiries with respect to a child who appears to it to be ordinarily resident within the area of another authority, it must consult the other authority, which may undertake the necessary enquiries in its place.
2   Section 47(5).
3   Section 47(9) and (11).
4   Section 47(10).
5   MDA Freeman *Children, Their Families and the Law* (Macmillan, 1992) at p 178.
6   *The Children Act 1989 Guidance and Regulations Vol 1 Court Orders* (HMSO, 1991) at para 4.4.
7   Section 43(4).
8   Section 43(3).

'(a)   the applicant has reasonable cause to suspect that the child is suffering, or is likely to suffer, significant harm;

(b)   an assessment of the state of the child's health or development, or of the way in which he has been treated, is required to enable the applicant to determine whether or not the child is suffering, or is likely to suffer, significant harm; and

(c)   it is unlikely that such an assessment will be made, or be satisfactory, in the absence of an order under this section.'[1]

The order is thus designed to enable social services to satisfy themselves about the welfare of children where they have suspicions of abuse or neglect but lack hard evidence. As the *Guidance* at para 4.8 advises:

'The order is for cases where there are suspicions, but no firm evidence, of actual or likely significant harm in circumstances which do not constitute an emergency: the applicant considers that a decisive step to obtain an assessment is needed to show whether the concern is well founded or further action is not required, and that informal arrangements to have such an assessment carried out have failed.'

Rather like the grounds for care and supervision orders, those for CAOs (and for EPOs) involve the satisfaction of minimum threshold criteria, followed by the application of the general principles in Part I of the Children Act. Taking the threshold criteria first, the first element requires the court to be satisfied about the reasonableness of the *applicant's* belief regarding the risk of significant harm to the child. 'Significant harm' for these purposes bears the same meaning as it does in s 31. A more stringent test is required for EPOs where the *court itself* must be satisfied about the risk. This reflects the more intrusive nature of the order. The other two elements in the CAO criteria require the court to satisfy itself that an assessment is really needed and that it cannot be arranged voluntarily. No doubt the court will want to hear evidence of the attempts to persuade parents to co-operate.

As with care and supervision orders, the s 1 principles only come into play once the threshold has been crossed. Ultimately, the court must consider whether a CAO is the right course of action, applying the welfare principle and s 1(5). However, in this context there are two points of distinction. The first is that proceedings under Part V of the Children Act are outside the definition of 'family proceedings' so that the court may not make s 8 orders in lieu of a CAO. The second is that the statutory checklist of factors in s 1(3) does not apply[2]. The reasoning is that Part V is an essentially separate code governing short-term remedies. It would be inappropriate for the court to be inhibited in its ability to act expeditiously, by having to plough through a range of factors in relation to which there may well, as yet, be insufficient information.

An important difference between the CAO and the EPO is that the application for a CAO must be brought before a full court on notice and involves an inter partes hearing[3]. By definition, this is not an emergency and, therefore, parents, those with parental responsibility, anyone with a contact order and the child himself must be given a proper opportunity to participate in the proceedings.

---

1   Section 43(1).
2   Part V proceedings are not within those proceedings specified in s 1(4) as attracting the application of the checklist.
3   Section 43(11).

The *Guidance* suggests that the CAO 'will usually be most appropriate where the harm to the child is long-term and cumulative rather than sudden and severe'[1]. Examples given are of nagging concerns about a child apparently failing to thrive; parents ignorant of, or unwilling to face up to the child's condition; and sexual abuse. In all these cases, the child must not appear to be at immediate risk.

What are the effects of the CAO?

Compulsory production of the child/authorisation of assessment

A CAO has two automatic effects. The first is to require production of the child by anyone able to do so to the person named in the order and thereafter to comply with any directions the court makes regarding assessment[2]. The second effect is to authorise the assessment itself[3]. Parental responsibility does not vest in the applicant. It is expected that the court will spell out with some particularity what the assessment is to involve and, in doing so, it should take advice from those presenting the case and from other professionals. The most obvious directions are likely to relate to medical and/or psychiatric examination, but the assessment may range wider than this to cover other aspects of the child's health and development[4]. Again, a child of sufficient understanding to make an informed decision may refuse to submit to any examinations or form of assessment[5]. The *Guidance* suggests that the child's GAL (now children's guardian), with the assistance of professionals from other disciplines, may advise the court of the child's level of understanding, after talking the matter through with the child, but it emphasises that this process must not result in coercion of the child[6].

The effect of this provision, together with similar provisions which apply to directions made where a court makes an EPO or interim care order[7], is diluted by the power of the High Court to override the child's objections under its inherent jurisdiction[8]. This exercise of the inherent jurisdiction is controversial since it appears to run contrary to the spirit, if not the letter, of the legislation. This appears to give to 'mature minors' a clear right to refuse to submit to such examinations and assessments. The issue is at the heart of the debate about the nature of children's rights[9]. Suppose, for example, there is suspicion that a teenage girl is being sexually abused by her father, and social services succeed in obtaining either an EPO, a CAO or an interim care order. They need to have the girl medically examined in order to determine whether or not there is sufficient evidence of sexual abuse. The court orders the examination but the girl objects to it. Is it her right to do so or is it her right to be protected from the risk of sexual

---

1 *The Children Act 1989 Guidance and Regulations Vol 1 Court Orders* (HMSO, 1991) at para 4.9.
2 Section 43(6).
3 Section 43(7) authorises any person carrying out the assessment, or any part of the assessment, to do so in accordance with the terms of the order.
4 *The Children Act 1989 Guidance and Regulations Vol 1* (above) at para 4.14.
5 Section 43(8).
6 See *The Children Act 1989 Guidance and Regulations Vol 1* (above) at para 4.13, and see further Chapter 13.
7 Sections 44(7) and 38(6) respectively.
8 *South Glamorgan County Council v W and B* [1993] 1 FLR 574. See also (in a rather different context but again involving the court's power to override mature minors) *Re K, W and H (Minors) (Medical Treatment)* [1993] 1 FLR 854.
9 As to which, see Chapter 3.

abuse on the assumption that it may have occurred? The answer to this question must ultimately turn on the view which is taken of children's rights and the balance which is struck between autonomy and protection.

Keeping the child away from home

The CAO, unlike the EPO, is not designed to remove the child from home. As a general proposition, therefore, the child should only be kept away from home where this is strictly necessary for the purposes of the assessment. Overnight stays can be authorised, but this requires a specific direction from the court, and the child may be kept away only for the period or periods specified in the order[1]. The *Guidance* emphasises that this is a 'reserve provision' and that the number of overnight stays should be kept as low as possible[2]. Assessment should be carried out with as little trauma to children and parents as possible, and the CAO should not be regarded as a variant of the EPO. Examples of when an overnight stay might be justifiable are where the child has eating difficulties, seriously disturbed sleeping patterns or other symptoms which might appear to require 24-hour observation and monitoring.

Where the child is kept away from home, the court must give directions about contact between the child and the parents or others[3]. Restrictions on contact can only be justified where contact would unduly interfere with the assessment process. The *Guidance* suggests that consideration should be given to providing facilities for parents to remain overnight with the child[4].

How long does the order last?

Somewhat controversially, the maximum duration of a CAO is seven days from the date specified in the order[5]. But, significantly, there is no power to extend this. A CAO is therefore strictly a 'one-off' order. No further application for a CAO may be made within six months of the disposal of the last, without the leave of the court[6]. Seven days is not a long time and it is imperative that the local authority should make the necessary arrangements for the assessment in advance of the commencement date. The official view is that, if this is done, it should give enough time for an 'initial multi-disciplinary assessment of the child's medical, intellectual, emotional, social and behavioural needs'. It is said that this 'should be sufficient to establish whether the child is suffering, or likely to suffer, significant harm and, if so, what further action is required'[7]. Some scepticism has been expressed about this and about the adequacy of the eight-day limit for EPOs[8]. The argument is that a proper diagnosis of a child's condition may take several weeks and that the rigid time-limit for the CAO might force the local authority to seek an interim care order. This could be seen by everyone as 'a significant escalation in the interventive process'.

1　Section 43(9).
2　*The Children Act 1989 Guidance and Regulations Vol 1 Court Orders* (HMSO, 1991) at para 4.15.
3　Section 43(10).
4　See *The Children Act 1989 Guidance and Regulations Vol 1* (above) at para 4.16.
5　Section 43(5).
6　Section 91(15).
7　See *The Children Act 1989 Guidance and Regulations Vol 1* (above) at para 4.12.
8　J Eekelaar 'Investigation Under the Children Act 1989' [1990] Fam Law 486 at 488.

Finally, to put CAOs in perspective, it should be remembered that a formal order will often not be required, since even the suggestion of an application for this (a fortiori one for an EPO) may bring about voluntary co-operation by the parents.

EMERGENCY PROTECTION ORDERS

The *Guidance* states that the purpose of the EPO is 'to enable the child in a genuine emergency to be removed from where he is, or be kept where he is, if and only if this is what is necessary to provide immediate short-term protection'[1]. It stresses that every aspect of the law governing EPOs whether relating to grounds, duration, effect or opportunities for challenge is different from that which applied to place of safety orders. The EPO, it advises, is an 'extremely serious step' which should not be undertaken lightly or regarded as a routine first step to initiating care proceedings[2]. The order authorises the immediate removal of a child from a dangerous or potentially dangerous environment, or the detention of the child in a safe place, in emergencies.

The human rights context

The removal of children from parents at short notice and possibly without warning represents, unless it can be justified, a clear infringement of the right to respect for family life protected by Article 8 of the ECHR. The Convention rights of both parent and child will be violated unless the action can be justified in accordance with Article 8(2)[3]. The key to this, as always, will be whether the action is *necessary* and *proportionate* to the legitimate aim of protecting the child. The ECtHR has had the opportunity of considering this question in relation to the controversial practice of removing babies at birth.

In *K and T v Finland*[4] the mother was schizophrenic and had been hospitalised many times. While she was pregnant her son, who had behavioural problems, was placed in a children's home for short-term support for the family. When the new baby was born she was immediately removed from the mother under an emergency care order. Both the baby and her elder brother were then placed in provisional public care. The mother and the baby's father were informed of this only *after* the care orders had been made and they were allowed only supervised access to the children. There followed a further period of treatment for the mother, including compulsory psychiatric care. During this period the father was said to have played an important part in looking after the baby, a fact acknowledged by the social welfare authorities. Nevertheless, both children were placed in public foster care together, and the parents' access was restricted. Both parents complained of violations of their Convention rights. They argued that the Finnish authorities had not given them a sufficient chance to try to overcome their problems with the assistance of relatives and other available support measures and

---

1   *The Children Act 1989 Guidance and Regulations Vol 1 Court Orders* (HMSO, 1991) at para 4.28 et seq.
2   Ibid at para 4.30.
3   See Chapter 2 above.
4   [2001] 2 FLR 707.

that they had failed to attach sufficient importance to the aim of reunification of the family.

The Grand Chamber of the ECtHR (by majority) agreed with them about several, but not all, alleged violations of the Convention. The Court held that there had been no violation of Article 8 in relation to the emergency care order concerning the son in the light of his behavioural problems and the fact that he had already been separated from his family. Neither had there been a violation in relation to the normal care orders which had been based on relevant and sufficient reasons. However, Article 8 was violated, both in relation to the emergency care order removing the baby and as a result of the authorities' failure to take seriously the aim of reuniting the family. The Court said that 'extraordinarily compelling reasons' were needed to justify the physical removal of a baby from the care of her mother against her will, immediately after the birth. Here the reasons did not exist and the authorities had failed to consider whether some less intrusive interference would have sufficiently protected the baby. Even allowing for the wide margin of appreciation given to the State in such matters, the level of interference could not be regarded as *necessary* in a democratic society. As to the second violation, the Court found that there was a *positive* duty on the authorities to take measures to facilitate family reunification as soon as reasonably feasible, but in this case there had been no serious or sustained effort to do so. Indeed, the striking feature in the case was the exceptionally firm negative attitude of the authorities.

The decision is reinforced by the later case of *P, C and S v United Kingdom*[1]. The facts are very complex and the ECtHR found violations of Article 6 in relation to several unacceptable procedural irregularities surrounding the obtaining of the various orders. We consider these aspects of the case elsewhere[2]. In the present context we are only concerned with the issue of the removal of the baby from birth under an EPO.

The background was that the mother, an American citizen, had been convicted in California of an offence relating to the care of her first child and had been sentenced to three years' probation and three months in custody by a Californian court. This was based on the allegation that she had been administering laxatives to the child inappropriately. Now in the UK, she gave birth to a second child by her second husband, a qualified social worker with a doctorate the subject of which was women who were wrongly accused of being Münchausen's Syndrome by Proxy (MSBP) abusers. Rochdale Metropolitan Borough Council obtained an EPO at 10.30 am on the day of the birth and at about 4.30 pm social workers took the baby from hospital and placed her with foster-parents. The parents complained, inter alia, that the removal of the baby was not necessary and was disproportionate, arguing that she could have remained with her mother at the hospital under supervision.

The ECtHR distinguished between the obtaining of the EPO and the removal of the child under it. The former was held *not* to violate Article 8 of the ECHR while the latter *did* amount to a violation in the circumstances. The Court recognised

---

1 [2002] 2 FLR 631. For commentary on the case see D Casey, B Hewson and N Mole 'Effective Participation and the European Court' [2002] Fam Law 755.

2 See Chapter 7 (on the adoption issue) and Chapter 11 (on the issue of the right to a fair hearing and access to the court).

that social services were legitimately concerned, and had a duty under s 47 of the Children Act 1989 to investigate where it came to their attention that a mother who was about to have another baby had a conviction for harming one of her other children. The Court refused to accept that there had been a failure to involve the parents in the investigative process and it was apparent that they had been made aware that removal at birth was one of the options under consideration. It also found that there were relevant and sufficient reasons for seeking the EPO in that the mother had been convicted of harming her son and had been found by an expert to suffer from a syndrome which manifested itself in exaggerating and fabricating illness in a child with consequent significant physical and psychological damage to that child. The decision to seek the EPO might therefore be regarded as necessary in a democratic society to safeguard the health and rights of the baby. However, the Court reiterated that the *removal* of a baby at birth required exceptional justification. It was a traumatic step for the mother which put her own physical and mental health under strain. It deprived the newborn baby of close contact with her birth mother and of the advantages of breastfeeding. It also deprived the father of being close to his daughter after birth. The Court was not persuaded that it was impossible for the child to remain in hospital and spend at least some time with her mother under supervision. Even if the mother represented a risk to the child, her capacity and opportunity for causing harm immediately after the birth were limited and there was no suspicion of life-threatening conduct. Thus, the Draconian step of removing the child from her mother shortly after birth was not supported by relevant and sufficient reasons. It was not necessary to safeguard the child and there had been a breach of both parents' rights under Article 8.

What these decisions establish is that local authorities must be able to demonstrate that an emergency measure is really necessary and that no lesser form of intervention would have been sufficient to protect the child. In many cases it may be possible to secure the 'voluntary' co-operation of the parents in agreeing to supervision by social services. The decisions also make it plain that even where an EPO may be warranted to give social services the authority to intervene in an emergency, it should not be assumed that removal of the child from birth is necessarily justified[1].

These principles and considerations of human rights should be constantly borne in mind throughout the following account of the statutory regime. Whether the effect of the rulings of the ECtHR will be to lead to a reduction in the number of EPOs being sought by local authorities remains to be seen.

---

1 In *Re M (Care Proceedings: Judicial Review)* [2003] 2 FLR 171, Munby J dealt in depth with the human rights requirements where a baby is removed from his mother. The least the local authority could do, he said, was to make generous arrangements for contact, including suitable arrangements for the mother who wished to breastfeed. In these cases, contact should be allowed most days of the week for lengthy periods. Nothing less, in his view, would satisfy the requirements of the ECHR. An application to remove a child at birth would moreover require that the court be provided with the fullest possible information and the evidence would need to be full, detailed, precise and compelling. Unparticularised generalities would not be sufficient.

Who may apply and on what grounds?

Applications

Unlike CAOs, care orders or supervision orders, EPOs may be sought by *anyone* and not only by the local authority or NSPCC, except where 'non-access' is the basis of the application[1]. This may also be contrasted with the rules governing standing to apply for private orders. Whilst there is much more flexibility under the Children Act, the applications are, nevertheless, still restricted, either by the class of applicant, or by the requirement of leave. EPOs are the one example in the legislation of wholly unrestricted access to the courts. The reasoning is obvious. Where a child is thought to be in immediate danger, the policy is not to stand on ceremony but to allow any concerned individual to act post haste to protect the child. It is anticipated that this will, in the vast majority of cases, be the local authority or NSPCC but the *Guidance* speculates that in 'dire circumstances' a concerned relative or neighbour (to which we could perhaps add a teacher, doctor or other professional) may find it necessary to seek the order[2]. The police might also wish to apply but are more likely to rely on their independent emergency powers in the legislation[3]. However, regulations provide that, where the applicant is not the local authority, the local authority may take over the order, and the power and responsibilities which go with it, where it considers that this would be in the child's best interests[4]. In deciding whether to do so, the local authority must consult the applicant and must have regard to a range of factors reminiscent of those in the statutory checklist in s 1(3)[5]. It is not thought that these transfer powers will be exercised in relation to the NSPCC, since it is expected that there will be local dialogue and consultation between the NSPCC and the local authority.

Ex parte applications

An important procedural distinction between the EPO and the CAO is that the EPO may, and usually will, be made ex parte[6]. While the court has power to direct an inter partes hearing, 'the very fact that the situation is considered to be an

---

1 Section 44(1) provides that 'any person' may be the applicant. This was the position regarding place of safety orders, and the DHSS *Review of Child Care Law* (1985) found no evidence of abuse (see para 13.7). If someone other than the local authority succeeds in obtaining an EPO, this will trigger the authority's investigative duties under s 47(1). There were 2,565 EPOs and EPO extensions made in 1996 – a fall of 16% from 1995. See *The Children Act Advisory Committee Final Report June 1997* (Lord Chancellor's Department, 1997) at Appendix 2. There was a further small decline to 2,232 in 2000 and 2,127 in 2001. See *Judicial Statistics, 2000* and *2001*.
2 See *The Children Act 1989 Guidance and Regulations Vol 1* (above) at para 4.32.
3 Under s 46 which is discussed at p 569 below.
4 Section 52(3), and the Emergency Protection Order (Transfer of Responsibilities) Regulations 1991, SI 1991/1414.
5 Emergency Protection Order (Transfer of Responsibilities) Regulations 1991, reg 3 provides that the authority must have regard to: the wishes and feelings of the child; his physical, emotional and educational needs; the likely effect of any change of circumstances on him; his age, sex and family background; the circumstances which gave rise to the application for the EPO; any court order or directions; the relationship of the applicant to the child; and any plans which the applicant may have for the child.
6 Family Proceedings Courts (Children Act 1989) Rules 1991, SI 1991/1395, r 4(4).

emergency requiring immediate action will make this inappropriate or impracticable in most cases'[1]. The application must be made in the magistrates' (family proceedings) court and there is no provision for transfer to a higher court[2]. As was the case with place of safety orders, the application may be made to a single justice[3] and in most cases this will be necessary – not least because emergencies arise when courts are not sitting[4]. Time will usually be of the essence. The rules provide that, wherever possible, the application should be made to the court. This reflects concern that place of safety orders were too often requested of single justices where an application to a full court would have been possible. On the other hand, the *Guidance* warns that, in certain instances, to give parents notice of the application might be to place the child in great danger[5].

Where the application is heard ex parte the rules require the applicant to serve a copy of the application and the order within 48 hours on the parties to the proceedings, anyone with the care of the child and the local authority where it is not the applicant[6]. They emphasise the crucial need to inform parents of their rights and responsibilities under the order – something severely neglected in the past.

Identification of the child in the order
Any child may be the subject of an EPO and, wherever practicable, the order should name the child. Where it does not do so, it should identify him as clearly as possible[7]. In some situations, the name of the child who is thought to be in danger will not be known to the applicant.

Grounds
There are three alternative grounds for obtaining an EPO set out in s 44(1), the first of which is open to any applicant. This may be relied on where the court is satisfied that:

> 'there is reasonable cause to believe that the child is likely to suffer significant harm if –
> (i)   he is not removed to accommodation provided by or on behalf of the applicant or
> (ii) he does not remain in the place in which he is then being accommodated.'

Satisfying the court of significant future harm
The first point is that it is the *court* rather than the applicant which must be satisfied that the statutory criteria are met[8]. 'Significant harm' bears the same interpretation as elsewhere in the legislation[9]. Where the application of the statutory test differs in this context is that the grounds for an EPO are *entirely* prospective in nature. Past or present harm will not be sufficient to found an EPO and are relevant only to the extent that they indicate future risk. The court or

---

1   *The Children Act 1989 Guidance and Regulations Vol 1 Court Orders* (HMSO, 1991) at para 4.46.
2   Children (Allocation of Proceedings) Order 1991, SI 1991/1677, arts 3(1)(g) and 7(2).
3   Family Proceedings Courts (Children Act 1989) Rules 1991, r 4(4).
4   Most obviously in the middle of the night or at weekends.
5   See *The Children Act 1989 Guidance and Regulations Vol 1* (above) at para 4.46.
6   Family Proceedings Courts (Children Act 1989) Rules 1991, r 21(8).
7   Section 44(14).
8   Cf the 'non-access' grounds, discussed below, in relation to which it is the *applicant's* belief which is crucial.
9   Ie in relation to care, supervision and child assessment orders.

magistrate must be satisfied of the likelihood of significant harm occurring or recurring.

How likely does 'likely' have to be?

It seems that, in applying this test, the court will need to relate the chance of harm occurring to the gravity of harm if it should occur. Where there is even an outside chance that the child could be exposed to someone convicted of offences against children, this may be seen as an unacceptable risk to run. Equally, where the nature of the possible harm is less grave, it may be that the court should look for a higher risk of its occurrence[1].

Removing or detaining the child

This ground covers two alternative situations. The first is where the intention is to *remove* a child from where he is currently living – most obviously where abuse or neglect is alleged against the parents. Here, it is not necessary for the applicant to prove that the need for the child's removal is *immediate*[2]. The EPO is intended to be flexible enough to cover the situation where, on investigation, the applicant concludes that it is not necessary to remove the child immediately. An example would be where a suspected adult is prepared 'voluntarily' to leave the home and to undertake not to return to it[3]. The EPO allows the local authority to adopt a 'wait and see' policy, albeit over a short period. The power to remove the child remains for the duration of the order. Thus, in the above example, if the alleged abuser agrees to leave immediately, but 24 hours later is still in the home, steps could then be taken to remove the child without having to go back to court.

The second alternative relates to the situation where the child is currently in a safe environment but there is a threat that he may shortly be removed to a potentially unsafe one. Chapter 11 looked at the two most obvious examples, namely where the child is in hospital or settled in a foster-home. In each case, the concern may be that a sudden removal by inadequate parents may expose the child to risk of harm.

No other requirements

It must be appreciated that there is no second element to the test for an EPO corresponding with that which forms part of the test for care and supervision orders. It does *not* have to be shown that the risk of harm is attributable to a likely lack of parental care or the child being beyond parental control. The thinking is that at the emergency stage it is not possible to conduct the kind of forensic inquiry which could determine this issue. Valuable time could be lost and the child might be exposed to unnecessary danger.

---

1   This is rather contrary to what was suggested by the majority of the House of Lords in *Re H and R (Child Sexual Abuse: Standard of Proof)* [1996] 1 FLR 80, where it was suggested by Lord Nicholls that the more serious the allegation the less likely it was that the conduct alleged had occurred. It was suggested in Chapter 11 that this reasoning is less than convincing in the context of applications for full care orders. It is further suggested, a fortiori, that it has no place in relation to EPOs.
2   See Lord Mackay LC, House of Lords, Official Report, 19 January 1989, col 426.
3   See pp 559 et seq below.

Frustrated access: alternative grounds for an EPO

Section 44(1) goes on to prescribe two further alternative grounds for an EPO. They apply to local authorities[1] and authorised persons (the NSPCC)[2] respectively and are designed to cater for emergencies arising from 'frustrated access'. In each case it is provided that an order may be made where:

(1) the applicant is making enquiries into the child's welfare; and
(2) those enquiries are being frustrated by access to the child being unreasonably refused to a person authorised to seek access, and the applicant has reasonable cause to believe that access to the child is required as a matter of urgency.

In the case of the NSPCC, but not local authorities, there is a third requirement that the applicant has reasonable cause to suspect that the child is suffering, or is likely to suffer, significant harm.

EPO or CAO?: degree of urgency

The obvious question is: when should an EPO be requested in non-access cases, given the existence of similar grounds for a CAO and given that the CAO was largely introduced to deal with these situations? The answer lies in the degree of urgency which is felt about the child's situation. Where the circumstances suggest that the child is in imminent danger, the EPO is appropriate. Where this is not the case, but an investigation and assessment of the child's circumstances is required, the CAO will be appropriate. It all depends on the circumstances surrounding the refusal and whether they add up to an emergency[3]. In this context, the test is whether the *applicant*, and not the court, has reasonable cause to suspect that access is required urgently.

Whichever ground is relied on, the principles of s 1 again apply, although the statutory checklist does not. What this means is that the court must ultimately exercise a discretion as to whether the order is really necessary and in the best interests of the child. It is not obliged to make the order. Having said that, unless there is voluntary co-operation to avert the emergency, it is difficult to visualise circumstances in which the court would not feel bound to act to protect a child exposed to imminent danger.

What are the effects of the EPO?

An EPO has three automatic legal effects under s 44(4) while it remains in force. It:

'(a) operates as a direction to any person who is in a position to do so to comply with any request to produce the child to the applicant;

(b) authorises –

---

1 Section 44(1)(b).
2 Section 44(1)(c).
3 As to which see *The Children Act 1989 Guidance and Regulations Vol 1 Court Orders* (HMSO, 1991) at para 4.39. There is evidence, however, that powers which are conceived for emergencies may be used 'to allow intervention without the formalities that ordinary child protection proceedings require'. See J Masson 'Human Rights in Child Protection: Emergency Action and its Impact' in P Lødrup and E Modvar *Family Life and Human Rights* (Gyldendal Akademisk, 2004) at p 457.

    (i)   the removal of the child at any time to accommodation provided by or on behalf of the applicant and his being kept there; or

    (ii)   the prevention of the child's removal from any hospital, or other place, in which he was being accommodated immediately before the making of the order; and

  (c)   gives the applicant parental responsibility for the child.'

Acquisition of parental responsibility by the applicant

This partly reflects the fact that, unlike the position under a CAO, the child will not be at home and will have to be looked after by arrangements made by the applicant[1]. But there are restrictions on the *exercise* of parental responsibility, which reflect the transient nature of the applicant's position. Hence, this may only be exercised 'as is reasonably required to safeguard or promote the welfare of the child (having regard in particular to the duration of the order)'[2]. The applicant must, therefore, ensure that the child is properly looked after while away from home, but should not take major or irreversible decisions which affect the longer-term interests of the child. In keeping with this, the child must not be kept away from home for longer than is strictly necessary. The legislation provides that the child must, accordingly, be allowed to return home or be removed (as the case may be) where it appears to the applicant safe to do so, even though the EPO remains in force[3]. Where this duty arises (which does not involve a return to court) the child must be returned to the care of the person from whom he was removed. Where this is not reasonably practicable, the child must be returned to his parent, a person with parental responsibility or someone else whom the applicant (with the approval of the court) thinks appropriate[4]. Importantly, however, the applicant retains the power, while the order remains in force, to remove the child again if this should prove necessary[5].

Reasonable contact

An EPO gives rise to a presumption of reasonable contact in favour of prescribed individuals, rather like the situation which applies where the child is in care[6]. Subject to any directions by the court, the applicant must allow the child reasonable contact with his parents, persons with parental responsibility, persons with whom he was living before the EPO, those who have contact orders, and any person acting on their behalf[7]. The court may give specific directions about contact[8] when the order is made or while it remains in force[9], and it may impose conditions[10]. What is 'reasonable' will depend on the circumstances, and in many cases it may be necessary to have supervised contact, in view of the nature of the allegations[11]. At the same time there are dangers, well illustrated in Cleveland, of

---

1   Under s 21(1) the local authority is obliged to make provision for the reception and accommodation of children who are removed or kept away from home under Part V of the Children Act.

2   Section 44(5)(b).

3   Section 44(10).

4   Section 44(11).

5   Section 44(12).

6   Under s 34(1), discussed in Chapter 11 above.

7   Section 44(13).

8   Section 44(6)(a).

9   Section 44(9)(a).

10 Section 44(8).

11 See the DHSS *Review of Child Law* (1985) at para 13.17.

depriving parents of contact, only to find that the allegations against them are unsubstantiated. The *Guidance* sees the contact question as largely a matter for the local authority's discretion and for negotiation[1]. In view of the short timescale, it is unlikely that the courts will seek to interfere unduly with this process. The drastic reduction in the allowable period of emergency detention, in itself, goes some way in removing grievances about contact[2].

Other directions which the court can make

These include the power to direct that medical and/or psychiatric examinations or assessments should, or should not, take place[3]. Again, the competent child has a right to refuse to co-operate[4]. It has been pointed out that the applicant, by virtue of having parental responsibility, could, in any event, probably provide a valid consent, and this may not be wholly dependent on the court's direction[5]. But it would be unwise not to seek this in so sensitive a matter – especially bearing in mind the uncertainties involved in establishing the child's level of understanding[6]. It is possible that the EPO may be used *primarily* with a view to securing an examination of some sort where parents are unwilling to co-operate. This can, of course, be achieved under a CAO where the matter is not urgent. The EPO has the advantage that, if the parents should fail to comply with the court's directions, the local authority will have an automatic right to remove the child.

The court may give other ancillary directions to assist with the enforcement of the EPO[7]. First, where it appears to the court that adequate information about the child's whereabouts is not available to the applicant, but is available to someone else, the court may order that person to disclose the information[8]. Secondly, the court may authorise the applicant to enter specified premises and search for the child[9]. This may extend to other children, where the court is reasonably satisfied that there may be another child on the premises with respect to whom an EPO ought to be made[10]. Where a second child is then found on the premises, the court's order may operate as an EPO and authorise removal of *that* child[11], subject to a duty to notify the court[12]. Thirdly, where it appears that the use of force may be necessary, the court may grant a warrant authorising a police constable to assist in

---

1 *The Children Act 1989 Guidance and Regulations Vol 1 Court Orders* (HMSO, 1991) at para 4.62.
2 From 28 days to eight days.
3 Section 44(6)(b) and (8).
4 Section 44(7), and see the discussion in Chapter 8 above. But again, the competent child's refusal may be overridden by the High Court exercising its inherent jurisdiction. See above.
5 N Lowe and G Douglas *Bromley's Family Law* (9th edn) (Butterworths, 1998) at pp 593–594. This is not the case where a CAO is made, since parental responsibility does not pass to the applicant under this.
6 And also the uncertain relationship between adolescent capacities and the exercise of parental responsibility explored in Chapter 8 above.
7 Section 48.
8 Section 48(1).
9 Section 48(3).
10 Section 48(4).
11 Section 48(5).
12 Section 48(6).

the exercise of powers under an EPO, using reasonable force if necessary[1]. When executing the warrant, the constable must allow the applicant to accompany him, unless the court directs otherwise[2], and the court may also direct that the applicant be accompanied by a 'registered medical practitioner, registered nurse or registered health visitor if he so chooses'[3]. None of these directions are automatically part and parcel of an EPO. They must be specifically sought where the applicant, on the strength of information received or his knowledge of the family situation, thinks they may prove necessary.

How long does the EPO last?

One of the most important reforms was the major reduction in the length of time for which emergency orders can last, or remain unchallenged, and in the number of 'extensions' which can be made. As was seen, this is also a feature of interim care orders[4].

The legislation prescribes eight days, rather than 28 days, as the initial maximum duration of an EPO[5]. A limited extension for a further seven days may be granted where the applicant is the local authority or NSPCC, but not where the applicant is an individual[6]. Only one extension is allowed and the maximum period of emergency protection is therefore 15 days[7]. The expectation is that extensions will be uncommon since the initial eight-day period is thought to give the applicant sufficient time in which to decide what further action (if any) to take, and particularly to decide whether to seek an interim care order[8].

There is no appeal, as such, from the making of an EPO, but there is an opportunity for judicial challenge by an application to discharge the order. This may be brought by the child, the parents, persons with parental responsibility and any person with whom the child was living immediately before the order[9], but not before 72 hours has elapsed since the order was made[10]. No discharge application may be made where the potential applicant was given notice of the original hearing and was present at it[11]. In the majority of cases, this will not be the case, since the order will have been made ex parte. But, where it was made following an inter partes hearing, an opportunity for challenge has already arisen. To allow a

---

1   Section 48(9). The court may grant a warrant where it appears to it that a person attempting to exercise power under an EPO has been prevented from doing so by being refused entry to premises or access to the child or that he is likely to be so prevented. These powers are complementary to the general power of the police to act in 'dire emergencies' under the Police and Criminal Evidence Act 1984, ss 17(1)(e) and 25(3)(e) – as to which see *The Children Act 1989 Guidance and Regulations Vol 1 Court Orders* (HMSO, 1991) at para 4.57.
2   Section 48(10).
3   Section 48(11).
4   See Chapter 11 above.
5   Section 45(1). Special provision is made for holidays (s 45(2)). Where the EPO follows police protection, the eight-day period runs from the first day on which the child was taken into police protection (s 45(3)).
6   Section 45(4).
7   Section 45(6).
8   *The Children Act 1989 Guidance and Regulations Vol 1* (above) at para 4.66. See also the DHSS *Review of Child Care Law* (1985) at para 13.23.
9   Section 45(8), (10). For a case in which practical difficulties occurred in applying these provisions, see *Essex County Council v F* [1993] 1 FLR 847.
10 Section 45(9).
11 Section 45(11).

'second bite at the cherry' would be unacceptably disruptive of protection procedures.

The local authority has no right of appeal against the refusal of justices to extend an EPO. *Re P (Emergency Protection Order)*[1] was a disturbing case which illustrates the problems which can arise where there is a refusal to extend the order. Here, a young baby nearly died from what was suspected to be an attempt by his mother to suffocate him. There was clear medical evidence by a paediatrician, later confirmed by a brain scan, that there was no medical cause for what had happened. The local authority did eventually obtain a care order but only after prolonged investigations by experienced paediatricians. Johnson J criticised the justices for their failure to extend the EPO in the face of firm medical evidence pointing to the risk of life-threatening abuse. He considered that there was a lacuna in the legislation and a need for some mechanism of review. Meanwhile, the only options open to a local authority in this situation are to apply immediately for a care order and seek an interim care order or to seek to have the matter transferred to the county court.

Can the alleged abuser be removed instead?

The background: before the Family Law Act 1996
Few people would argue with the general proposition that children are better off left in the family wherever possible. This is, of course, central to the philosophy of the legislation. Removal from home should be confined to those cases in which it is really necessary; something which is now required by the ECHR. One possible solution, and perhaps a better one for the child, may be to remove the alleged abuser from the home. This will be a more viable option where that person's partner or spouse is in agreement with the proposal. It will be much more difficult where this co-operation is not forthcoming and, a fortiori, where there is collusion in the abuse.

As the law stood before 1996 there was no public law remedy which was available to evict an alleged abuser. The options were to try to persuade the abuser to leave voluntarily or to persuade his partner to pursue private law remedies which could at least authorise temporary exclusion. The *Guidance* advised that these options be explored[2]. It stated that the local authority would always want to canvass the possibility of providing voluntary services to the person concerned, perhaps also providing alternative housing or even cash assistance[3]. The same result might be achieved if the non-abusing parent was prepared to apply for an ouster order under the domestic violence legislation[4]. The *Guidance* suggested that this might be particularly appropriate where sexual abuse was alleged. In this instance, the non-abusing parent might have no wish to protect or shield the alleged abuser, but immediate removal of the child might well not be in the child's best interests.

Family law commentators, at least for the purposes of exposition, have been much inclined to put child abuse and domestic violence into different compartments. Yet in reality this distinction has always been somewhat artificial. If a man is

---

1   [1996] 1 FLR 482.
2   *The Children Act 1989 Guidance and Regulations Vol 1 Court Orders* (HMSO, 1991) at para 4.31.
3   Under Sch 2, para 5 to the Children Act.
4   Ie under the Domestic Violence and Matrimonial Proceedings Act 1976, s 1 (county court) or the Domestic Proceedings and Magistrates' Courts Act 1978, s 16 (magistrates' courts).

being violent towards children, or threatening them with violence, this can be viewed both as child abuse which might give rise to *public* care proceedings or domestic violence which could trigger the *private* remedies relating to non-molestation or ouster from the family home. In the years between the implementation of the Children Act 1989 and of Part IV of the Family Law Act 1996[1], local authorities, not wishing to take the ultimate step of seeking a care order, began to explore whether they might exclude an alleged abuser by resorting to the private law orders under s 8 of the Children Act.

The matter came to a head in *Nottinghamshire County Council v P*[2] where the Court of Appeal found, partly for technical reasons arising under the provisions of s 9 of the Children Act and partly on broader policy grounds, that in general local authorities were precluded from invoking *private* s 8 orders, and, in fulfilling their statutory child protection role, ought instead to pursue the *public* remedies which Parliament had provided in the Children Act. Indeed, the court was very critical of Nottinghamshire's failure to do so. What had happened in this case was that there were allegations of sexual abuse against the father of three girls by the eldest girl who claimed that he had been abusing the three of them. The local authority successfully obtained leave to seek a prohibited steps order preventing the father from living in the household and from having contact with the girls. Ward J at first instance held that he was prevented by s 9(5) of the Children Act from making the orders and his decision was upheld by the Court of Appeal.

Sir Stephen Brown P held that in reality the effect of the prohibited steps order (if made) would be for the father to be ordered to have 'no contact' with the children and that a 'no contact' order was equivalent to a contact order. The authority was directly precluded from seeking such a contact order by the provisions of s 9(2) and indirectly by the provisions of s 9(5). From a broader policy perspective, the President said that 'the route chosen by the local authority in this case was wholly inappropriate'. He went on to criticise the authority for not taking steps under Part IV of the Children Act specifically to seek a supervision order to protect the children, and expressed deep concern at 'the absence of any power to direct this authority to take steps to protect the children'.

This decision did not prevent a prohibited steps order being subsequently made by the Court of Appeal (in a case in which the local authority had already obtained a care order in relation to one child and supervision orders in relation to the other children in the household) to restrain a man who was *not* living with the mother and the children from having or seeking to have, contact with the children[3]. The distinction drawn by Butler-Sloss LJ was essentially that this was to prevent an *external* threat to the children and that a 'no contact' order against the man could not be made since he did not live with the children. Local authorities also succeeded in a couple of reported decisions[4] in obtaining ouster orders by invoking the inherent jurisdiction, although the extent of this jurisdiction to protect children was not clear[5]. The distinctions drawn in these cases were often

---

1   Part IV of the 1996 Act was brought into force on 1 October 1997.
2   [1993] 2 FLR 134.
3   *Re H (Prohibited Steps Order)* [1995] 1 FLR 638.
4   *Re S (Minors) (Inherent Jurisdiction: Ouster)* [1994] 1 FLR 623 and *Devon County Council v S* [1994] Fam 169.
5   See particularly *Pearson v Franklin* [1994] 2 All ER 137.

subtle and technical and it was a matter of some doubt whether they could be regarded as at all consistent from a policy perspective.

In 1992 the Law Commission considered the issue[1]. Having rejected the idea that undertakings could provide an adequate solution[2], the Law Commission went on to recommend a new power for the court to make a short-term emergency ouster order when making an EPO or interim care order[3]. The order would be dependent on proof of the criteria for these orders but there would also be additional criteria. First, it would have to be shown that there was reasonable cause to believe that the likelihood of harm to the child would not arise if the named person were to be removed from the household. Secondly, there would have to be another parent or other person in the household who was willing and able to provide reasonable care for the child and that that person consented to the order being made[4]. Importantly, the Law Commission also recommended that the court would have power to attach a power of arrest to the order to offer immediate protection to the child in the event of a breach[5].

Part IV of the Family Law Act 1996
These recommendations have been substantially implemented by Part IV of the Family Law Act 1996[6]. Similar, but somewhat less restrictive, reforms were introduced into Scots law by the Children (Scotland) Act 1995[7]. In a text about children it is inappropriate to go into the intricacies of the scheme governing domestic violence and occupation of the family home. It is, however, possible here to sketch the principal features of the scheme and to draw attention to the way in which the law impacts on the protection of children and interacts with the emergency and short-term protective remedies which are the focus of this chapter.

Essential features of the scheme
Part IV of the Family Law Act 1996 repealed the various statutes which governed domestic violence and occupation of the family home[8] and gathered together in one place a consistent set of remedies obtainable on common criteria, under a

---

1 Law Com Report No 207 *Domestic Violence and Occupation of the Family Home* (1992).
2 Ibid at para 6.15. The Law Commission was particularly bothered by the fact that, since proceedings for EPOs were usually ex parte, there would have to be an adjournment during which time the child might be exposed to risk. It also thought that a power of arrest could not very appropriately be attached to undertakings as opposed to orders.
3 Law Com Report No 207 *Domestic Violence and Occupation of the Family Home* (1992) at para 6.18.
4 Ibid at para 6.20.
5 Ibid at para 6.22.
6 On Part IV of the Act generally, see R Bird *Domestic Violence Law and Practice* (4th edn) (Family Law, 2003). For a concise account of what Part IV is trying to achieve, which takes account of its inter-relationship with the subsequent Protection from Harassment Act 1997, see R Probert *Cretney's Family Law* (5th edn) (Sweet & Maxwell, 2003) at ch 6. For detailed commentary on the individual provisions of Part IV, many of which are technical and complex, see M Freeman *The Family Law Act 1996* (Sweet & Maxwell, 1996).
7 For a concise summary of the 'exclusion order' available to local authorities in Scotland, see E Sutherland 'Scotland: Child Law Reform – At Last!' in A Bainham (ed) *The International Survey of Family Law 1995* (Martinus Nijhoff, 1997) at pp 449–450.
8 The Domestic Violence and Matrimonial Proceedings Act 1976, the Domestic Proceedings and Magistrates' Courts Act 1978 (to the extent that it governed these remedies) and the Matrimonial Homes Act 1983 (MHA 1983).

concurrent jurisdiction exercised by the magistrates' (family proceedings) court, the county court and the High Court[1]. These courts may, at their discretion, make 'non-molestation orders' and 'occupation orders'[2]. The former protect from 'molestation' which, of course, includes violence but is a concept wide enough to cover a range of conduct which can broadly be described as 'pestering' or 'harassment'[3]. Under cl 1 of the Domestic Violence, Crime and Victims Bill 2003 a new s 42A will be inserted into the Family Law Act 1996, the effect of which will be to make it a criminal offence to breach a non-molestation order[4].

Standing to seek a non-molestation order depends on the applicant being 'associated' with the respondent, and the Act contains a definition of 'associated persons'[5], the effect of which is to extend essentially familial or domestic remedies to a very wide range of individuals not before treated as family members for other purposes by English law[6]. For present purposes it is sufficient to note that the definition of 'relevant child' in the legislation is drawn extremely widely and extends to many children who would not, for example, have been regarded as a 'child of the family' as required by some of the earlier legislation[7]. It is hard to visualise any children whose status would preclude the court from making a non-molestation order if it feels inclined to do so. Also of note is that the definition of 'associated persons' includes in relation to a child the two parents of that child, persons with parental responsibility and adoptive (or prospective adoptive) parents[8]. And the term 'relative', which also has the effect of rendering two people 'associated', can surely never have been so widely defined in legislation here or anywhere else[9]. So the scope for protective non-molestation orders being made in relation to children is very considerable. It should be remembered, however, that these orders can only be made on the application of a private

---

1   In this respect it follows the pattern set by the Children Act 1989.

2   In 2001 a total of 20,968 non-molestation orders were made and a total of 9,789 occupation orders: *Judicial Statistics* 2001.

3   It should be noted that the Protection from Harassment Act 1997 has created criminal offences of 'harassment' and putting people in fear of violence. Where these offences are committed or threatened, the victim may have a civil remedy (damages and/or injunction) and a 'restraining order' may be made to prevent a recurrence of the behaviour. The remedies under this Act will be particularly useful where individuals fall outside the definition of 'associated persons' in Part IV of the Family Law Act 1996. The details of the 1997 legislation are beyond the scope of the present discussion, especially since they are more likely to be relevant to the protection of adults than the protection of children.

4   The details are beyond the scope of the present work, but for commentaries on the Bill, see H Conway 'The Domestic Violence, Crime and Victims Bill' [2004] Fam Law 132 and RN Hill 'The Effect of the Domestic Violence Bill on FLA 1996' [2004] Fam Law 442.

5   Section 62(3).

6   For commentary on the significance of this definition in the wider context of conceptual change in family law, see A Bainham 'Changing families and changing concepts: reforming the language of family law' [1998] CFLQ 1.

7   'Relevant child' is defined in s 62(2) as:
    '(a) any child who is living with or might reasonably be expected to live with either party to the proceedings;
    (b) any child in relation to whom an order under the Adoption Act 1976 or the Children Act 1989 is in question in the proceedings; and
    (c) any other child whose interests the court considers relevant.'

8   Section 62(4) and (5).

9   See s 63(1).

individual, usually but not necessarily by the mother, and not by the local authority.

Standing to seek an occupation order is exceedingly complex, as are the criteria which the court must apply. Pressures from the ultra-conservative wing of the Conservative party (then in government) and the tabloid press culminated in a piece of legislation which seeks to draw distinctions between those who have a property interest of some sort in the family home and those who do not; and between spouses and cohabitants. It is a moot point, as Gillian Douglas has observed, whether the purpose 'is as much to stress Parliament's concern for the importance of property rights as it is to emphasise the importance of marriage'[1].

Either way, the Act draws distinctions between so-called 'entitled applicants' and 'non-entitled applicants', the latter category being further sub-divided into 'former spouses' on the one hand and 'cohabitants' and 'former cohabitants' on the other. In essence, 'entitled applicants' are those with 'matrimonial home rights' (which with very limited exceptions will include all spouses who do not otherwise have a proprietary interest in the home) and those 'entitled to occupy a dwelling house by virtue of a beneficial estate or interest or contract or by notice of any enactment giving him the right to remain in occupation'[2]. Entitled applicants may seek an occupation order where the home in question has been the home of the applicant and an associated person or was intended to be their home. Former spouses, cohabitants, and former cohabitants must therefore apply as 'non-entitled' applicants unless they have an interest in the property, and the overall effect in practice will be that the overwhelming majority of spouses will be 'entitled' while very many of those who live together outside marriage will be 'non-entitled'. The criteria for making occupation orders differ depending on the category of the applicant as does the potential duration of any order made[3]. The differential criteria may conceivably be important to the question of the relative weight to be attached to children's interests and we discuss this below in assessing the impact of Part IV on children.

If made, an occupation order, as its name suggests, may regulate the occupation of a home in various ways. In particular (and perhaps most relevant to the current context of child protection), it may oust an alleged abuser from the home, or may go further and exclude him from 'a defined area in which the dwelling-house is included'[4]. An important change brought about by the Act relates to powers of arrest. While it was the case that such powers could be attached to orders under the previous legislation, judges were reluctant to do this unless a pattern of flouting the court's orders had developed. Under the 1996 Act, the court must attach a power of arrest to the order if 'it appears to the court that the respondent has used or threatened violence against the applicant or a relevant child ... unless

---

1   'England and Wales: "Family Values" to the Fore?' in A Bainham (ed) *The International Survey of Family Law 1996* (Martinus Nijhoff, 1998) at p 176.

2   FLA 1996, s 33(1).

3   As to duration, the essential difference is that an order of unlimited duration may conceivably be made in relation to 'entitled applicants' whereas for 'non-entitled former spouses' there may be successive six-monthly orders and for 'non-entitled cohabitants and former cohabitants' the six-month order may be extended only once and is thus bound to be seen as a temporary and not a permanent order.

4   Section 33(3)(g).

satisfied that in all the circumstances of the case the applicant or child will be adequately protected without such a power of arrest'[1].

As in the case of 'non-molestation' orders, it should be carefully noted that occupation orders may be sought only by individuals, usually the mother of the children, and that the local authority has no standing under the legislation to make a 'free-standing' application.

The impact of Part IV on children

Undoubtedly the most innovative and potentially significant reform introduced by Part IV as it applies to children is the amendment of the Children Act to allow local authorities to seek 'exclusion requirements' as adjuncts to emergency protection orders and interim care orders. But before we consider these provisions it may be helpful to highlight two other ways in which the Act is arguably attaching greater weight to the interests of children to be protected. These are, respectively, the reformulation of the statutory criteria for occupation orders, and provision for applications by children themselves.

(i) Reformulation of criteria for occupation orders

One of the matters which caused the greatest amount of difficulty under the former jurisdiction to grant 'ouster orders' was the weight which the court should attach to the welfare of children vis-à-vis other factors, particularly the conduct of the respondent, in deciding whether to make the order. The Court of Appeal had been inconsistent in the guidance which it had given to the lower courts, and the issue eventually came before the House of Lords in *Richards v Richards*[2]. Here, it was held that the matter was governed by the criteria in the Matrimonial Homes Act 1983, which made reference to 'the conduct of the spouses in relation to each other and otherwise to their respective needs and financial resources, to the needs of any children and to all the circumstances of the case'[3]. Hence, it was not permissible for the court to treat the welfare of the children as the 'paramount', or even the 'first', consideration but rather it had to be taken into account alongside the other specified factors with no preconceived weighting as between them.

These criteria have been substantially re-enacted in the Family Law Act 1996[4], but, grafted onto them is a so-called 'balance of harm' test which the court must apply and which may appear to some to be tilting the balance in the direction of children's welfare vis-à-vis the respondent's conduct. It is provided, in the case of applications by 'entitled' applicants and by 'non-entitled former spouses', that where the applicant or any relevant child is likely to suffer significant harm attributable to the conduct of the respondent, the court *must* make the occupation order unless it appears to it that the respondent or any relevant child is likely to

---

1   Section 47(2).

2   [1984] AC 174.

3   MHA 1983, s 1(3).

4   The provision (s 33(6)) which applies to 'entitled applicants' and which, with some controversial additions, applies to the various categories of 'non-entitled' applicants (ss 35(6) and 36(6)) prescribes that the court must have regard to all the circumstances including:

'(a)   the housing needs and housing resources of each of the parties and of any relevant child;

(b)   the financial resources of each of the parties;

(c)   the likely effect of any order, or of any decision by the court not to exercise its powers, on the health, safety or well-being of the parties and of any relevant child; and

(d)   the conduct of the parties in relation to each other and otherwise.'

suffer significant harm if the order is made and that this harm is as great or greater than the harm attributable to the respondent's conduct if the order is not made[1]. This 'balance of harm' must also be considered on applications by 'non-entitled cohabitants and former cohabitants' but, in this case, there is no statutory presumption that the order will be made where the balance weighs on the side of the applicant or children[2].

Not everyone agreed that the provisions of the Act as drafted would be effective if the intention was to emphasise welfare considerations at the expense of conduct in these cases of actual or threatened 'significant harm'. Stephen Cretney[3] argued that since it is only harm 'attributable to the respondent's conduct' which is taken into account under the test 'the effect seems to be to preserve the decision of the House of Lords in *Richards v Richards*'[4]. In other words, 'rubbishy' or 'flimsy' allegations of adverse conduct by the respondent (as occurred in that case) might not be enough to trigger effectively the balance of harm test, if the real problem is just relationship breakdown and/or poor housing conditions. This view certainly seems to be confirmed by the reported cases which have continued to emphasise the Draconian nature of occupation orders rather than the welfare needs of women and children. In *Chalmers v Johns*[5] Thorpe LJ said of the occupation order that it 'remains an order that overrides proprietary rights and ... it is an order that is only justified in exceptional circumstances'[6]. In this case the parties had a tempestuous relationship and the police had been called several times. But there was no evidence that the mother had not given as good as she had received in the matter of assaults[7]. The mother, having moved into temporary council accommodation with the seven-year-old daughter, sought to exclude the father. The Court of Appeal was unwilling to accept that there was a real risk of violence to the mother or child or that they were likely to suffer significant harm if the order were not made. The child had a longer journey to school but that could not amount to harm. There was insufficient evidence therefore to trigger the balance of harm test and, applying the ordinary criteria, the occupation order could not be justified.

This unwillingness to allow occupation orders to operate as a device for alleviating family discord or regulating a difficult housing situation is also evident in the decision of the Court of Appeal in *Re Y (Children) (Occupation Order)*[8]. Here there was a divided family under one roof with two teenage children each

---

1   Sections 33(7) and 35(8).
2   Section 36(7) and (8).
3   SM Cretney *Family Law* (4th edn) (Sweet & Maxwell, 2000) at p 125.
4   The conduct in question is not, however, confined to *intentional* conduct, since it is the *effect* of the conduct on the applicant or child that is the important factor. See *G v G (Occupation Order: Conduct)* [2000] 2 FLR 36. In this case there was an atmosphere of tension and strain in the home after the wife issued divorce proceedings. The circuit judge, while recognising that this had been caused or contributed to by the husband's conduct, refused an occupation order on the basis that, since his conduct was unintentional, the likelihood of harm being suffered could not be attributed to him. The Court of Appeal held that he had erred in this respect but dismissed the mother's appeal on the basis that there was insufficient evidence justifying so Draconian an order.
5   [1999] 1 FLR 392.
6   Ibid at 397.
7   On three of the four occasions when the police were called to the home, it was to investigate an alleged assault by the mother on the father.
8   [2000] 2 FCR 470.

siding with one parent. There was some violence and the recorder concluded that harm was likely to be caused if they remained under the same roof. Taking into account the attitude of the local authority that they might more easily accommodate the mother and her (pregnant) 16-year-old daughter than the father and the 13-year-old child, he ordered the mother to vacate the home on the basis that greater harm would arise from not making the order. The Court of Appeal, however, found that there was insufficient misconduct on the part of the mother to justify the order and that there was no reason, pending divorce, why the matrimonial home could not reasonably be divided to meet the housing needs of all of them. Sedley LJ said that the purpose of an occupation order was 'not to break matrimonial deadlocks by evicting one of the parties, much less to do so at the expense of a dependent, and in this case a heavily pregnant, child'. And he went on: 'To use the occupation order as a weapon in domestic welfare is wholly inappropriate. Parliament has made provision for it as a last resort in an intolerable situation, not as a move in a game of matrimonial chess . . .'.

Rather out of keeping with these decisions, *B v B (Occupation Order)*[1] is one decision which did appear to turn on the interests of a particular child and is one in which housing considerations had a decisive influence. Here the husband had been violent to the wife causing her to leave the family home, council accommodation, for temporary bed and breakfast accommodation provided by the council. She then sought a non-molestation order and an occupation order. The husband had with him in the home a child aged six from his previous marriage. The council's position was that, if excluded, he would be regarded as intentionally homeless and that it would have no duty to rehouse him. In contrast it was clear that the mother and baby would, as matters stood, be rehoused in suitable accommodation in a matter of months if not weeks. The judge made the occupation order, but the Court of Appeal allowed the husband's appeal, finding that the balance of harm test should be resolved in favour of the husband's child. If the father were evicted he would find himself in unsuitable temporary accommodation and the child might have to be separated from him by social services. The court was at pains to emphasise that the decision turned on the highly unusual position of the husband's child. The court emphatically did not wish to convey the message that men who subjected their partners to domestic violence and drove them out could expect to remain in the previously shared accommodation.

Notwithstanding this decision, taken together, the reported cases do not represent the substantial tilting of the balance away from conduct and towards the welfare of mothers and children which appeared to have been the rationale for the introduction of the balance of harm test. As Cretney had astutely predicted, this remains an issue which is influenced more by considerations of the gravity, or otherwise, of misconduct in the family home.

(ii) Applications by children and legal representation
The 1996 Act provided for the first time that children themselves might bring applications for non-molestation orders and occupation orders. Hitherto they had in reality been dependent on applications being brought on their behalf – usually by their mothers. In many, perhaps most, cases of domestic violence, the mother will be seeking orders to protect herself and the children and their

---

1   [1999] 1 FLR 715.

interests will coincide. But there may be instances in which they diverge. An extreme case might be where the mother is herself abusing the child or colluding in abuse by the father. Perhaps social services are unwilling or feel unable to intervene. In circumstances like this, the new standing to bring proceedings might conceivably be very beneficial to a minority of children.

Where the child has attained the age of 16, he or she is able to seek a non-molestation order as an 'associated person'[1]. Where the child is under the age of 16, the 1996 Act follows the pattern of the Children Act 1989 and provides that such a child may not apply for a non-molestation or occupation order 'except with the leave of the court'[2]. Leave may only be granted for these purposes if the court is satisfied that 'the child has sufficient understanding to make the proposed application'[3]. We consider what is involved in this in the context of children's applications for private s 8 orders in Chapter 13.

(iii) Action by the local authority: the exclusion requirements
We have seen that the local authority is precluded from applying for non-molestation or occupation orders under Part IV and to a large extent from resorting to the private s 8 orders of the Children Act. But, following the recommendations of the Law Commission, Part IV of the 1996 Act amended the Children Act to allow the court, in prescribed circumstances, to add 'exclusion requirements' to emergency protection orders and interim care orders[4]. While these requirements are likely to be specifically requested by the local authority concerned, there would appear to be no reason why the court should not insert such a requirement of its own volition. It is important to appreciate that these requirements may only be inserted in the two orders in question and may not, for example, be included in child assessment orders.

The circumstances in which an exclusion requirement may be included in the above orders are:

'(a)   that there is reasonable cause to believe that, if a person ("the relevant person") is excluded from a dwelling-house in which the child lives, the child will cease to suffer, or cease to be likely to suffer, significant harm; and

(b)   that another person living in the dwelling-house (whether a parent of the child or some other person) –

(i)   is able and willing to give to the child the care which it would be reasonable to expect a parent to give him, and

(ii)   consents to the inclusion of the exclusion requirement.'[5]

The exclusion requirement may be one or more of the following:

(a) a provision requesting the relevant person to leave a dwelling-house in which he is living with a child;

(b) a provision prohibiting the relevant person from entering a dwelling-house in which the child lives; and

(c) a provision excluding the relevant person from a defined area in which a dwelling-house in which the child lives is situated[6].

---

1   We looked at the definition of 'relevant child' in fn 7 on p 562 above.
2   Section 43(1).
3   Section 43(2).
4   See ss 38A and 44A of the Children Act 1989.
5   Children Act 1989, s 38A(2). Section 44A(2) is in broadly similar terms.
6   Ibid, ss 38A(3) and 44A(3).

A power of arrest may be attached to the exclusion requirement[1]. The court may provide for this to have effect for a period shorter than the exclusion requirement itself[2]. Breach of the exclusion requirement will amount to contempt of court and may lead to imprisonment[3].

The likely impact of these provisions is hard to assess since much depends on how far social services are prepared to use them. Two limitations on the use of the exclusion requirements should be noted. The first is that since they may only accompany emergency protection orders or interim care orders they are dependent on the authority being able to establish the grounds for those orders[4] and they must cease to have effect when the principal orders themselves expire. They are thus by definition only temporary in nature, and this may give rise to anxiety that an alleged abuser may return to the home once the temporary exclusion requirement has expired. The second is that the requirements may not be included unless 'another person' in the home is able and willing to care for the child and consents to the inclusion of the requirement. Although this category is not confined to the child's parent, in the overwhelming majority of cases we are likely to be talking about the child's mother. There will be concern that the mother in some cases will not be willing to consent in view of the impact this might have on her marriage or relationship with the 'relevant person'.

These are genuine concerns but, it is submitted, they are capable of being exaggerated. Where an interim care order is made, although ultimately limited in time, the relevant person may be excluded for at least some months and in many cases this will help to resolve the problem. As to the mother's consent to the exclusion requirement, it needs to be appreciated that failure to consent may lead to the local authority pursuing a full care order with a view to removing the child from the home. Put crudely, the mother may in some cases have to decide whether she would prefer her husband or partner to be excluded or for her child to be removed. In these circumstances it seems likely that some mothers will be persuaded (albeit reluctantly) to consent.

In this area, as in others, the division between voluntary co-operation and compulsion may be more apparent than real. So far as local authorities themselves are concerned, one attraction in seeking the exclusion requirements will surely be that there will be a considerable saving of hard-pressed resources if the abuser can be removed rather than if a care order, and the extensive ongoing responsibility that goes with it, has to be pursued.

---

1   Children Act 1989, ss 38A(5) and 44A(5). For the procedural requirements, see *President's Direction: Children Act 1989: Exclusion Requirement* [1998] 1 FLR 495.
2   Children Act 1989, ss 38A(4) and 44A(4).
3   For the procedural requirements in enforcing the exclusion requirement, see *Re W (Exclusion: Statement of Evidence)* [2000] 2 FLR 666. Here the father acted in clear breach of a requirement that he should not approach, enter or reside at the property where the mother and children were living. The magistrates made an order committing him to two months' imprisonment suspended for six months. Cazalet J reduced this to a suspended period of one month on the basis that the sentence was excessive. The judgment provides useful guidance on the appropriate formalities for seeking exclusion requirements.
4   Although the amount of evidence required to establish the grounds for an EPO or interim care order is significantly less than is required for a full care order, as to which see particularly *Re B (A Minor) (Care Order: Criteria)* [1993] 1 FLR 815.

POLICE PROTECTION

The police have important powers to protect children in cases of real urgency[1]. The raison d'être of these powers is that the police are able to act *immediately* without a court order where they find a child in need of protection. Thereafter, they must act expeditiously to pass responsibility for the child to the local authority which has the primary statutory responsibility for the child's welfare.

Direct action

Where a police constable has reasonable cause to believe that a child would otherwise be likely to suffer significant harm, he may remove the child to 'suitable accommodation' and keep him there. Alternatively, the constable may take reasonable steps to ensure that the child's removal from a hospital or other place in which he is accommodated is prevented[2]. These powers mirror those conferred by an EPO but, here, the police may take direct action on the basis of their own belief. The powers do not include any rights of entry or search, so that if the police require these rights, they will have to apply to the court for an EPO, together with a warrant where appropriate[3]. These powers can, therefore, only relate to children who are found by the police. Typically, they have been used to pick up and hold runaways[4], glue-sniffers, abandoned children and those found living in unhygienic conditions[5]. Such children are said to be in 'police protection' and may be kept there without legal challenge for up to 72 hours[6]. This is the same period of allowable detention as under an EPO before a discharge application can be made. It is a considerable reduction from the eight days allowed under the old law[7], and is in keeping with the general policy to restrict the length of operation of emergency powers. At the end of this period, the child must either be released or detained further under the authorisation of an EPO[8].

Obligations which the police must fulfil

As soon as practicable after a child is taken into police protection, the constable concerned must ensure that the case is inquired into by a senior officer appointed by the chief officer of the police area[9]. This officer is then known as the 'designated officer' and has independent statutory duties to those of the constable. The constable must, inter alia: inform the local authority of the situation; inform the child (where the child is capable of understanding) of the

---

1   *The Children Act 1989 Guidance and Regulations Vol 1 Court Orders* (HMSO, 1991) at paras 4.71 et seq. For a particularly good example of the exercise of this power, see the facts of *Re M (A Minor) (Care Order: Threshold Conditions)* [1994] 2 AC 424, where the initial protective measures were taken by the police following the murder of the mother by the father. For an academic critique of the use of these powers, see J Masson 'Police Protection – Protecting Whom?' (2002) 24 JSWFL 1.
2   Section 46(1).
3   Section 44(1) and s 48(9).
4   See the discussion of refuges at p 570 below.
5   See *The Children Act 1989 Guidance and Regulations Vol 1* (above) at para 4.71.
6   Section 46(6).
7   Children and Young Persons Act 1969, s 28(4).
8   Children Act 1989, s 46(5).
9   Ibid, s 46(3)(e).

steps being taken, with reasons, and ascertain the child's wishes and feelings; ensure that where the child is not already in local authority accommodation or a refuge, that he is moved to such accommodation; and inform the parents, persons with parental responsibility or others with whom the child was living, of the steps that are being taken, with reasons[1]. The designated officer must inquire into the case. He may, where appropriate, apply for an EPO, whether or not the local authority agrees to it or is aware of it[2]. The *Guidance* states, however, that good effective channels of communication ought to mean that the police never find themselves in this position. No extension of an EPO obtained by the police is possible. The maximum period of police-instigated protection is, therefore, eight days. Thereafter the local authority must be involved if further protection is necessary. The *Guidance* emphasises the importance of inter-agency communication and co-operation between the police and the local authority. This ought to be reviewed and monitored at regular intervals. The aim is to ensure that no child taken into police protection need be accommodated in a police station and that his reception into local authority accommodation is achieved with the minimum of trauma[3].

No parental responsibility

The police do not acquire parental responsibility where a child is in police protection. The designated officer is, however, required to do what is reasonable in all the circumstances for the purpose of safeguarding or promoting the child's welfare (having regard, in particular, to the length of time during which the child will remain under police protection)[4]. Beyond the power of removal and detention, the powers of the police are, therefore, in essence, limited to those held by anyone with the de facto care of a child[5]. The designated officer must also allow prescribed individuals to have such contact with the child as is, in his opinion, reasonable and in the child's best interests[6]. Those concerned are the parents, or others with parental responsibility, contact orders or with whom the child was living before he was taken into police protection[7]. Again, contact under supervision may be the only realistic option during the first 72 hours of an emergency.

ABDUCTION OF CHILDREN AND REFUGES FOR CHILDREN AT RISK

Runaways

We noted above the practice of the police to pick up 'runaways'. The problem of teenage runaways is not a new one but, in recent years, the incidence of

---

1 Section 46(3).
2 Section 46(7) and (8).
3 *The Children Act 1989 Guidance and Regulations Vol 1 Court Orders* (HMSO, 1991) at para 4.77.
4 Section 46(9)(b).
5 Cf s 3(5) and the discussion in Chapter 2 above.
6 Section 46(10). Under s 46(11) this is the obligation of the local authority where a child taken into police protection is in local authority accommodation.
7 Ibid.

homelessness among young people has increased[1]. The legal position of adolescents who run away has never been entirely clear, not least because the law has not set a definite age at which a young person may live independently[2]. Organisations such as the Children's Society, which have habitually given assistance to young runaways, particularly by providing them with temporary accommodation, until the Children Act had a dubious legal basis for doing so. The Children's Society, especially, was concerned to put its activities on a firmer legal footing and to counter any possible charge that they might constitute a criminal offence.

Criminal offence of abduction

The Children Act reaffirmed the criminal offence of abduction relating to children in care, but at the same time exempted from prosecution bona fide organisations, through a process of certification[3]. The starting point is s 49(1), which provides:

> 'A person shall be guilty of an offence if, knowingly and without lawful authority or reasonable excuse, he –
> (a)   takes a child to whom this section applies away from the responsible person;
> (b)   keeps such a child away from the responsible person; or
> (c)   induces, assists or incites such a child to run away or stay away from the responsible person.'

'Responsible person' for these purposes means any person who, for the time being, has care of the child by virtue of a care order, an emergency protection order, or as a result of the child being taken into police protection[4]. The offence is therefore concerned with children absconding from public care as opposed to fleeing the parental home[5]. The court may make a 'recovery order' where it appears that a child has been taken or kept away from the responsible person unlawfully, where the child has run away, is staying away or missing[6]. Recovery orders may not be made in respect of children who are voluntarily 'looked after' by local authorities but the *Guidance* counsels that authorities should also report to the police immediately where these children abscond[7]. The recovery order

---

1   Some years ago the Children's Society estimated that 98,000 young people go missing each year in Britain. For an informative discussion of the work of the Society in relation to runaways, see C Newman *Young Runaways – Findings from Britain's First Safe House* (The Children's Society, 1990). See also C Abrahams 'Understanding "running away" – findings from recent NCH research' (1993) 5 JCL 84.

2   For a discussion of the point, see A Bainham *Children, Parents and the State* (Sweet & Maxwell, 1988) at pp 63–64.

3   For the details see R White, P Carr and N Lowe *The Children Act in Practice* (3rd edn) (Butterworths, 2002) at paras 6.69–6.76.

4   Sections 49(2) and 50(2).

5   Chapter 17 below discusses abduction from parents in the context of international child abduction.

6   Section 51(1). For the first reported decision on the use of recovery orders, see *Re R (Recovery Orders)* [1998] 2 FLR 401, in which Wall J provides detailed guidance on the provisions of s 50. In this case, a recovery order was made where a boy aged 13 was the subject of a care order on the basis that he was beyond his mother's control. He refused to return to the boarding-school which he was required to attend as part of the care plan. The order was made and upheld after the local authority had revised the care plan nominating foster-parents, rather than the boy's mother, to care for him during the holidays – thus making them 'responsible persons' for the purposes of a recovery order.

7   *The Children Act 1989 Guidance and Regulations Vol 1 Court Orders* (HMSO, 1991) at para 4.90.

requires production of the child by any person able to produce him and disclosure of his whereabouts by any person with such information. It also authorises his removal, and authorises a police constable to enter specified premises and search for the child, using force if necessary[1]. The order may be sought by any person with parental responsibility for the child, under a care order or EPO, or by the designated officer where the child is in police protection[2].

Exemption of children's refuges

The legislation exempts from all offences relating to the abduction or harbouring of children, voluntary or registered children's homes which provide a refuge for children who appear to be at risk of harm and which have a certificate from the Secretary of State[3]. Local authority or voluntary organisation foster-parents may also fall within the terms of the certificate where they also provide a refuge[4]. The issue and withdrawal of certificates is governed by the Refuges (Children's Homes and Foster Placements) Regulations 1991[5]. It is not anticipated that such certificates will be readily granted to just *anyone* claiming to assist children, and it was said in Parliament that it would be necessary to separate the 'sheep' from the 'goats'. Without proper scrutiny, there would be a risk of exploitation of vulnerable adolescents by unscrupulous individuals. A key requirement is that, where any child is admitted to, or leaves, a refuge, the police must be notified[6]. Where a refuge fails to measure up to the required standards its certificate may be withdrawn and there is no right of appeal against this[7].

---

1   Section 50(3).
2   Section 50(4).
3   Section 51(1).
4   Section 51(2).
5   SI 1991/1507.
6   Ibid, reg 3.
7   Ibid, reg 4.

PART IV
CHILDREN AND SOCIETY

Part IV of this book is concerned primarily with issues which arise in relation to the child's activities outside the family. This is not an easy distinction to make since the family is often (if not always) affected by these activities. But such a distinction can be made for the purposes of exposition and analysis. It is certainly the case that, whereas Parts II and III have been principally concerned with what might be described as 'mainstream family law', the subjects under discussion in Part IV take the family lawyer into largely uncharted waters. And whereas Parts II and III have been predominantly concerned with the statutory code constituted by the Children Act 1989, Part IV involves an examination of many other pieces of legislation, common law rules and international instruments.

Chapter 13 highlights an issue crucial to the position of children in the legal system – their standing before the courts. This chapter concentrates on the two issues of representation and evidence in children cases including the evidence of children themselves. Chapter 14 discusses the position of children, or more accurately children and young persons, under the criminal law. Chapter 15 does the same in relation to the civil law concentrating, particularly, on the two great areas of the common law, contract and tort, but also pausing to look at the thorny issues surrounding children's employment. Both of these chapters identify, as central features of the law applying to children, the twin concepts of protection and responsibility. Chapter 16 examines education law, so crucial to the rights of children and parents, and undoubtedly a 'boom' area of children law. Finally, Chapter 17 concludes by taking a wider perspective of children's rights within the international community. We considered the UNCRC as a basic source of children law in Chapter 2. Chapter 17 is concerned with other international Conventions and concentrates particularly on those Conventions dealing with the major problems of international child abduction and inter-country adoption.

Chapter 13

CHILDREN IN COURT

INTRODUCTION

The greater awareness of the independent interests and capacities of children, noted elsewhere in this work, has also manifested itself in changes to the legal standing of children in the courts[1]. Indeed, without these changes it might have been difficult to speak with any conviction about children's rights. Rights are arguably of little value, and certainly of less value, where the machinery does not exist for their enforcement[2]. In the case of children, there is an initial difficulty in that the protection of their rights or interests is usually dependent on the intervention of interested adults, most obviously their parents. Children generally suffer from a natural disability, reflected in a legal disability, which prevents them from bringing legal proceedings on their own account. In the case of young children, this factual dependency on adults is self-evident. It is less so in the case of older children, especially adolescents. But whatever the age of the child there is an ever-present danger that there may be a conflict of interest between the child and the adult on whom he or she is dependent for taking action. As has been seen[3], this became apparent in public law cases in the 1970s when the Children Act 1975 first provided for the separate representation of children in care proceedings.

This dependency on adults is illustrated by many features of the legal procedures which govern children cases. In ordinary civil litigation, children are usually required to commence and conduct proceedings through an adult known for these purposes as a 'litigation friend'. In private family proceedings, children are rarely parties, and their independent interests are usually represented, if at all, through welfare reports by children and family reporters (formerly known as court welfare officers). No public official is charged generally with the responsibility of bringing proceedings on behalf of children[4]. Moreover, rules of evidence relating to child witnesses traditionally incorporated warnings about placing too much reliance on children's evidence and were, on the whole, unsympathetic to the special difficulties which they faced when confronting the intimidating environment of the courts[5].

---

1. For a general evaluation of the position of children in family proceedings, drawing on empirical research, see N Lowe and M Murch 'Children's Participation in the Family Justice System – Translating Principles into Practice' [2001] CFLQ 137.
2. This is not to deny the value of international normative standards as reflected in Conventions like the UNCRC, as to which see Chapter 2 above.
3. In Chapter 11 above.
4. It is not, for example, the function of the Official Solicitor to *initiate* wardship proceedings but only to act in existing proceedings. See Heilbron J's remarks in *Re D (A Minor) (Wardship: Sterilisation)* [1976] Fam 185 at 197.
5. Again wardship, with its inquisitorial approach, has been something of an exception.

A new philosophy: the importance of children's views

The new philosophy of the Children Act 1989, with its emphasis on the importance of children's views[1] and the primacy of their interests, necessitated change on several fronts. The Act allows children to commence and conduct certain types of family proceedings in their own right in specified circumstances; they are given party status in a wider range of proceedings and there is much greater provision for their separate representation. Changes to the law of evidence (some in the Children Act and some outside it) were designed to give greater credence to the evidence of children and to make the process of giving evidence a less stressful one for them.

These changes are best seen as incremental. In particular, the greater representation of children in the public sphere has not been extended to private law cases, although the Family Law Act 1996 did empower the Lord Chancellor to provide by regulations for the separate representation of children in certain specified proceedings[2]. The Adoption and Children Act 2002[3] now amends the Children Act 1989 to enable proceedings for the making, variation or discharge of s 8 orders to be included in the list of 'specified proceedings' which may be added by rules of court. There are some who think that the changes to the law of evidence which have been made fall well short of tackling the fundamental problem as they see it – that children should not appear as witnesses in court at all[4]. It is fair to say, however, that the Youth Justice and Criminal Evidence Act 1999 has introduced substantial further reforms, especially by empowering the courts to make 'special measures directions' in children cases[5].

This chapter highlights these changes. We begin by considering briefly the human rights requirements and international obligations which may bear on the general question of children's access to the courts and representation. We then look at the rules governing the way in which legal proceedings involving children are commenced and conducted. We then turn to the crucial question of representation and conclude with a section on the rules applying to child witnesses in legal proceedings both civil and criminal.

INTERNATIONAL OBLIGATIONS AND HUMAN RIGHTS IN THE COURT PROCESS

We noted that one of the most important Articles in the UNCRC is Article 12. This enshrines the right of 'the child who is capable of forming his or her own views . . . to express those views freely in all matters affecting the child, the views of the child being given due weight in accordance with the age and maturity of the child'[6]. Article 12 goes on to be more explicit about the child's right to be heard in the

---

1   See Chapter 2 above. But for a case evincing a more cautious attitude to the significance of children's views in care proceedings, see *Re C (A Minor) (Care: Child's Wishes)* [1993] 1 FLR 832. See also the cases granting leave to children to commence proceedings at pp 581 et seq.
2   Section 64.
3   Section 122(1)(b), inserting s 41(6A) into the Children Act 1989.
4   See, for example, JR Spencer 'Child Witnesses, Video-Technology and the Law of Evidence' [1987] Crim LR 76.
5   See pp 607 et seq below.
6   Article 12(1).

court process, providing that 'the child shall in particular be provided the opportunity to be heard in any judicial and administrative proceedings affecting the child, either directly, or through a representative or an appropriate body, in a manner consistent with the procedural rules of national law'[1].

These are statements of broad principle indicating the international community's commitment to the importance of listening to the child's views in court as elsewhere. It should be noted that the commitment is to a *qualified*, not absolute, level of autonomy. Children have a right to be heard and to have their views taken seriously, but not to take decisions which are properly left to the courts to make in the light not only of the child's views but also of the child's welfare[2]. There is a lack of detail in Article 12 about how precisely the child's views should be presented to the court and what level of representation is mandated. The Council of Europe has attempted to flesh out these procedural obligations towards children in a Convention directly concerned with the *exercise* of children's rights.

The European Convention on the Exercise of Children's Rights 1996

The European Convention on the Exercise of Children's Rights (not yet ratified by the UK) is, as its title suggests, not concerned with creating substantive rights for children but with the practical implementation of their rights[3]. The Convention is the response of the Council of Europe to the perceived need for an instrument to supplement the UNCRC, Article 4 of which requires States parties to 'undertake all appropriate legislative, administrative and other measures for the implementation of the rights recognized in [that] Convention'[4].

The object of the 1996 Convention is set out in Article 1(2) and is:

'... in the best interests of children, to promote their rights, to grant them procedural rights and to facilitate the exercise of these rights by ensuring that children are, themselves or through other persons or bodies, informed and allowed to participate in the proceedings affecting them before a judicial authority.'

The subject-matter of the Convention is therefore procedural rights. It is about the participation of children in family proceedings affecting them – in short, their right to be heard – and, as indicated above, it builds upon Article 12(2) of the UNCRC.

Scope of the Convention

The Convention applies to children under the age of 18[5]. It is concerned with 'family proceedings' before a judicial authority which, for these purposes,

---

1   Article 12(2).
2   See also Chapters 3 and 8.
3   For commentary on the Convention, see M Freeman *The Moral Status of Children* (Martinus Nijhoff, 1997) at pp 57–59; G Van Bueren 'Annual Review of International Family Law' in A Bainham (ed) *The International Survey of Family Law 1995* (Martinus Nijhoff, 1997) at pp 5–8; M Killerby 'The Draft European Convention on the Exercise of Children's Rights' (1995) *International Journal of Children's Rights* 127; and C Sawyer 'One Step Forward, Two Steps Back – The European Convention on the Exercise of Children's Rights' [1999] CFLQ 151.
4   For a more detailed discussion of the initiatives of the Council of Europe in the area of children's rights, see J Fortin *Children's Rights and the Developing Law* (2nd edn) (Butterworths, 2003) at pp 63–65.
5   Article 1(1).

includes an administrative authority having equivalent powers. The Convention contains no definition of 'family proceedings' but it is made explicit that the expression includes 'those involving the exercise of parental responsibilities, in particular, residence and access to children'[1]. Each State is required to specify at least three types of family proceedings before a judicial authority to which the Convention is to apply[2]. As Freeman has rightly pointed out, at the current time it would be much easier for English law to comply with the Convention's requirements in those family proceedings in which care or adoption issues arise than in relation to 'private' family proceedings such as divorce or freestanding applications for residence or contact[3], although new provisions in the Adoption and Children Act 2002 may result in increased representation of children in private proceedings[4].

What then are the requirements of the Convention? The key provisions are Articles 3 and 4. Article 3 gives to the child 'considered by internal law as having sufficient understanding' the rights:

(a) to receive all relevant information;
(b) to be consulted and express his or her views; and
(c) to be informed of the possible consequences of his or her wishes and the possible consequences of any decision.

Article 4 relates to separate representation of children in cases of conflicts of interest which preclude the 'holders of parental responsibilities' from representing the children themselves. It provides that, in these circumstances, the child concerned 'shall have the right to apply in person or through other persons or bodies for a special representative'[5]. Other principles under the Convention strike a chord with English family legislation. There is, for example, a duty on the part of judicial authorities 'to act speedily to avoid any unnecessary delay and procedures [must] be available to ensure that [their] decisions are rapidly enforced'[6]. In urgent cases, judicial authorities are to have power to take decisions which are immediately enforceable and to act of their own motion in 'serious cases' where the welfare of the child is in danger[7]. There is encouragement of mediation but, as Freeman comments, the Convention curiously 'does not extend the procedural rights just listed to this method of dispute resolution'[8]. The position of children in the mediation process remains a matter of considerable uncertainty[9]. A Standing Committee was established to keep under review problems relating to the Convention, to consider any relevant questions concerning its interpretation or implementation, to propose amendments and to provide advice and assistance to the national bodies having functions under the Convention[10].

---

1   Article 1(3).
2   Article 1(4).
3   M Freeman *The Moral Status of Children* (above) at p 58.
4   See below.
5   Under Article 4(2), States are free to limit this right to children who are considered by internal law to have sufficient understanding.
6   Article 7. Cf the 'no delay' principle under the Children Act 1989 discussed in Chapter 2.
7   Articles 7 and 8.
8   Article 13, and M Freeman (above) at p 58.
9   See Chapter 4 above.
10 Articles 16 et seq.

Assessment of the Convention

The Convention has not had an enthusiastic reception from commentators who have been quick to draw attention to its limitations. Van Bueren regrets that more was not done to encourage States 'to begin to develop innovative methods of child participation in family proceedings' and considers some of the language used in the Convention to be unduly restrictive[1]. Freeman describes it as a 'weak document' and thinks it 'toothless' when compared with the ECHR[2]. Fortin[3] has highlighted the restrictive nature of the requirement of 'understanding' on the part of the child when compared with the more liberal requirement in Article 12 of the UNCRC that the child should merely be 'capable of forming his or her own views' on the matter in question. She sees this as having the potential for seriously undermining the requirement of the UNCRC and draws attention also to the problems of formally demonstrating a conflict of interest between the child and others for the purpose of demanding separate representation. At the same time, there is general acknowledgement that the Convention has a symbolic signifi- cance in drawing the attention of States to the procedural rights of children and in recognising that without effective remedies the assertion of rights may be little more than empty rhetoric.

The European Convention on Human Rights

Since the implementation of the HRA 1998, there has also been concern that failure to ensure adequate participation and representation of children in legal proceedings might lead to breaches of the ECHR, especially of Article 6 which guarantees the right to a fair hearing in civil, as well as criminal, proceedings. In principle this applies equally to children as persons under the Convention.

There has as yet been little testing of the extent of the obligations under the ECHR to provide representation for children[4]. There has been an indication by the Grand Chamber of the ECtHR that it would be going too far to say that domestic courts should always hear evidence from a child in court on the question of access (contact). In the cases in question[5] one of the children had been five years old at the relevant time, and the Court held that the German court had been entitled to rely on the findings of an expert whose competence there had been no reason to doubt. There had been no direct contact between the other child and the German court which had been well placed to evaluate her statements and establish whether or not she had been able to make up her own mind. On the other hand, in the criminal context, the ECtHR has emphasised the procedural rights of young children to a fair hearing[6].

As we shall see, the extensive provision for the separate representation of children in public law proceedings in England almost certainly complies with the

---

1   G Van Beuren 'Annual Review of International Family Law' (above).
2   M Freeman (above) at p 39.
3   *Children's Rights and the Developing Law* (2nd edn) (Butterworths, 2003) at pp 198 et seq.
4   But for an evaluation of what may be required under the ECHR, see J Munby 'Making Sure the Child is Heard – Part 2 – Representation' [2004] Fam Law 427.
5   *Sahin v Germany; Somerfeld v Germany* [2003] 2 FLR 671.
6   *V and T v United Kingdom* (1999) 30 EHRR 121.

requirements of Article 6. The doubts revolve around the adequacy of participatory rights in the private law cases in which there is a conflict of interest between
them and the adults involved[1].

COMMENCING AN ACTION

Traditional procedure

The basic rule of civil litigation is that a child is a person under a 'disability'. As
such:

> 'A child must have a litigation friend to conduct proceedings on his behalf unless the court
> makes an order ... permitting the child to conduct proceedings without a litigation friend.'[2]

It is one of the incidents of parenthood that a parent has the prima facie right to
act as the child's litigation friend and the duty to act as his guardian ad litem
(GAL) in legal proceedings[3]. An obvious example might be where the child has
allegedly been injured by the negligence of some third party. The court does,
however, have power to remove a parent and substitute another adult as litigation
friend or GAL where a parent is acting improperly or against the child's best
interests[4].

Exceptions under the Children Act 1989

This normal rule of civil proceedings applies also in 'family proceedings' but is
subject to significant exceptions introduced by the Children Act 1989 and the
rules of court made under it[5]. The starting point is r 9.2 of the Family Proceedings
Rules 1991 which essentially reproduces the general rule that a person under a
disability (a child for present purposes) may only begin and prosecute any family
proceedings by litigation friend and may only defend such proceedings by GAL[6].
But this rule is subject to exceptions in r 9.2A providing that minors who are
entitled to begin, prosecute or defend proceedings under the Children Act 1989
or the inherent jurisdiction of the High Court[7] may do so *without* a litigation friend
or GAL in two alternative sets of circumstances. These are either:

(1) where the leave of the court is obtained[8]; *or*
(2) where a solicitor:

---

1 See pp 593 et seq below and the discussion of *Re A (Contact: Separate Representation)* [2001] 1 FLR
715.
2 CPR 1998, SI 1998/3132, r 21.2(2) and (3).
3 *Woolf v Pemberton* (1877) 6 Ch D 19.
4 *Re Birchall, Wilson v Birchall* (1880) 16 ChD 41; *Re Taylor's Application* [1972] 2 QB 369.
5 Family Proceedings Rules 1991, SI 1991/1247, r 9.2A.
6 It is not necessary for the court to appoint the GAL under this rule. Note that the terminology
of 'guardian ad litem' is retained in this context. The GAL here is not to be confused with the
'children's guardian' (previously also known as a GAL) who represents children in (mainly)
public law cases under the Children Act. See below.
7 Family Proceedings Rules 1991, SI 1991/1247, r 9.1(3).
8 The child does not need to have a litigation friend or GAL in order to apply for leave, which
may be sought by filing a written request or by making an oral request at the hearing (Family
Proceedings Rules 1991, r 9.2A(2)).

(a) considers that the minor is able, having regard to his understanding, to give instructions in relation to the proceedings; *and*

(b) has accepted instructions from the minor to act for him in the proceedings and, where the proceedings have begun, is so acting[1].

The rules go on to provide that a minor may apply for leave to remove an existing litigation friend or GAL where he wishes to prosecute or defend the remaining stages of the proceedings himself[2].

This ability of the child to commence proceedings without a litigation friend is most likely to become relevant where the child obtains the leave of the court to seek a s 8 order. The Act allows a child to seek leave to apply for *any* s 8 order[3]. This may be granted by the court where 'it is satisfied that he has sufficient understanding to make the proposed application'[4]. The same test of 'sufficient understanding' also governs the court's decision whether to allow the child to appear without a litigation friend or GAL[5] and is generally thought to be a statutory application of the *Gillick* test[6]. Where leave is refused, the child may be able to persuade an interested adult to apply for the order. Where leave is given, the child may wish to seek: a residence order preserving his existing home or authorising him to live somewhere else[7]; a contact order or an order prohibiting contact with a relative he does not wish to see; or, perhaps, a prohibited steps or specific issue order to regulate areas of disagreement with his parents or other carers. In this connection, it should be recalled that *Gillick*, subject to its controversial interpretation by the Court of Appeal[8], appears to support the right of the competent child to decide matters within his capacity, thus overriding parental views.

When can a child invoke these procedures?

There has been much speculation about the circumstances in which children might be allowed to invoke these procedures. There was concern that there might be an abuse of the procedures by young people who, following some temporary tiff with their parents, seek a 'divorce' from them[9]. On the other hand, it is not

---

1 On how solicitors go about the task of assessing a child's competence, see C Sawyer 'The competence of children to participate in family proceedings' [1995] CFLQ 180.

2 Family Proceedings Rules 1991, r 9.2A(4). For the principles to be applied on such an application by a child, see *Re S (A Minor) (Independent Representation)* [1993] 2 FLR 437 discussed at p 583 below. See also *Re K (Replacement of Guardian ad Litem)* [2001] 1 FLR 663 in which a father applied unsuccessfully for removal of the child's GAL.

3 Section 10(2)(b).

4 Section 10(8).

5 Family Proceedings Rules 1991, r 9.2A(6), requiring that the court grant leave 'if it considers that the minor concerned has sufficient understanding to participate as a party in the proceedings concerned or proposed without a next friend or guardian ad litem'.

6 *Gillick v West Norfolk and Wisbech Area Health Authority* [1986] 1 AC 112. See, particularly, Chapter 8 above and the cases discussed below for what is involved.

7 On this question, it should also be remembered that minors who have reached 16 years of age may effectively seek a 'self-referral' into local authority accommodation (s 20(3) and (11)), and see Chapter 10 above.

8 In *Re R (A Minor) (Wardship: Consent to Treatment)* [1992] Fam 11 and *Re W (A Minor) (Medical Treatment: Court's Jurisdiction)* [1992] 3 WLR 758, as to which see Chapter 8 above.

9 In fact, the idea is not such a revolutionary one. Legal procedures have long existed in certain jurisdictions, particularly in the USA, for the legal emancipation of certain children, but usually only those who had already achieved de facto independence from their parents. On the

difficult to visualise circumstances in which children who are the alleged victims of physical or sexual abuse could find these procedures an invaluable self-help mechanism. The same might be said of the new right of children to seek orders in cases of domestic violence under Part IV of the Family Law Act 1996 which was discussed in the previous chapter.

On the whole, it is the first view which seems to have characterised the reported decisions of the courts[1]. The case-law has made it plain that even where the court finds that the child has the requisite understanding that is not the end of the matter. The court still retains a discretion in deciding whether or not to grant leave, and the key question has been whether this residual discretion should be exercised restrictively or liberally. Unlike in the case of adults where the Act[2] specifies the criteria the court is to apply, the Act is silent on the considerations which should govern children's applications for leave.

In *Re C (A Minor) (Leave to Seek Section 8 Orders)*[3], a 14-year-old girl who did not get on with her parents went to stay with a friend's family and did not want to return. With the consent of the friend's father, she sought leave to apply for a residence order to enable her to continue living with the family and a specific issue order to allow her to take a holiday with them in Bulgaria. Johnson J refused leave on the specific issue application and adjourned the application relating to residence. In his view, there was no advantage in an order being made at that time in relation to a matter which should be resolved internally within the family. He also took the view that Parliament had intended the jurisdiction only to be exercised in relation to matters of importance and that the issues here were not serious enough to warrant judicial orders. Controversially, he also held that the question of leave was governed by the central principles of the Children Act including the welfare principle. The effect of applying a welfare test to the issue of leave would be, as here, to reserve to the court a wide discretion to refuse leave and to filter out applications by children thought by the courts to be against their best interests. In contrast, two subsequent decisions of the Family Division have held that, on children applications, as on adult applications, for leave to seek s 8 orders, the welfare principle does *not* govern the issue.

In *Re SC (A Minor) (Leave to Seek Residence Order)*[4], another adolescent girl wanted to live with a friend's family but her circumstances were very different. She had been in care for many years and had suffered a number of breakdowns in foster-placements. Her mother was opposed to her obtaining a residence order and wanted her to remain in care, even though she was herself unable to provide a home. Booth J granted the child leave to seek a residence order. In her view, assuming the child passed the test of understanding (which she did here) the court in exercising its discretion should then simply have regard to the likelihood of success of the substantive application. It should be satisfied that this was not a

---

doctrine of emancipation, see A Bainham *Children, Parents and the State* (Sweet & Maxwell, 1988) at pp 67–69 and the sources cited there. For an analysis of the phenomenon of 'divorcing parents', see M Freeman 'Can Children Divorce Their Parents?' in *The Moral Status of Children* (Martinus Nijhoff, 1997) at ch 11 which also cites many useful sources dealing with the position in North America.

1   For a general commentary, see A Bainham ' "See you in Court, Mum": Children as Litigants' (1994) 6 JCL 127. For a more recent and detailed evaluation, see J Fortin *Children's Rights and the Developing Law* (2nd edn) (Butterworths, 2003) at pp 224–233.

2   Section 10(9).

3   [1994] 1 FLR 26.

4   [1995] 1 FLR 96.

'non-starter' doomed to failure. She further held that the child's welfare was *not* paramount on the leave question since the issue of the child's upbringing did not arise at that stage. This case also confirmed that a child was capable of seeking a residence order in favour of an adult since it was Parliament's intention that all s 8 orders should, in principle, be available to children even though the residence order, because of its form, could not be framed in favour of the child herself.

This decision was followed in *Re C (Residence: Child's Application for Leave)*[1]. Here, there had been a long history of proceedings between the two parents since they had separated. The child, another 14-year-old girl, felt that her views had never been properly represented by the court welfare officer. She had a fervent wish to live with her mother but felt under pressure from her father. Stuart-White J held that the welfare principle did not govern the leave question but that applications for leave by children should be treated cautiously. Making a child party in proceedings between warring parents might, for example, expose the child to the evidence of the parents and to matters which it might be better for the child not to hear. However, in this case, he held that the girl had the necessary understanding and leave should be granted. Her application concerned an important matter and it had a reasonable prospect of success.

These latter two decisions perhaps illustrate a more relaxed judicial attitude to children applications, certainly where the issues raised are undeniably serious. On the other hand the courts are likely to refuse leave where they can see no positive benefit to the child in direct involvement in the proceedings. In *Re H (Residence Order: Child's Application for Leave)*[2], for example, a 12-year-old boy applied for leave to seek a residence order in his parents' divorce proceedings. Johnson J found, on the evidence of the solicitors consulted by the boy and that of an educational psychologist, that he had the requisite understanding to instruct a solicitor independently. However, he held, refusing leave, that there would be no advantage to him in doing so and that there could be considerable disadvantages to his being a party. He wanted to live with his father and his wishes in this respect were conveyed to the court in the court welfare officer's report. There was no issue between the wishes of the child and his father, and Johnson J was satisfied that the judge who ultimately decided where the boy should live would be required under the legislation to take full account of his wishes.

It remains the case, of course, that the child concerned must pass the preliminary test of understanding. The leading authority on what is required in this respect is *Re S (A Minor) (Independent Representation)*[3], a case in which a boy aged 11 sought to 'sack' the Official Solicitor who was acting as his GAL in acrimonious proceedings concerned with whether he should live with his father or his mother. Sir Thomas Bingham MR said that the Children Act required a judicious balance to be struck between two considerations. The first was that children were human beings with individual minds, wills, views and emotions which should command serious attention. They should not be discarded merely because they were children. The second was that a child is, after all, a child. The law should be sensitive to the need to protect children who were likely to be

---

1   [1995] 1 FLR 927.
2   [2000] 1 FLR 780.
3   [1993] 3 All ER 36.

vulnerable and impressionable, lacking the maturity to weigh the longer term against the short term amongst other things. In this case, the court concluded that the judge's ruling to the effect that the child lacked sufficient understanding to participate as a party without representation by a GAL, in what were emotionally complex and highly fraught proceedings, was impregnable[1]. It is to the matter of representation that we now turn.

REPRESENTATION

Background

English law has not traditionally given minors a generalised right to representation in legal proceedings or any automatic party status. The process of conferring statutory rights in this area has been an evolutionary one and the changes in the Children Act were another stage in this process. Traditionally, it has been more usual for courts to call for welfare reports on children's 'best interests' rather than for the children themselves or their views to be represented as such. This duty to provide reports has in the past fallen on different people depending on the nature of the proceedings. The welfare test is, as has been seen[2], an indeterminate one, and it has been said that 'the approach taken in each child's case could be as different as the people called upon to discharge the task of representing them to the court'[3]. The notion of more comprehensive reform requiring *every* court in *all* kinds of proceedings to consider whether children should be separately represented or joined as parties has been mooted for a considerable period of time. It was the subject of an abortive private member's Bill introduced by Dr David Owen (now Lord Owen) in the mid-1970s. The idea was closely associated with the establishment of a family court and an independent court welfare service[4].

---

1   See also *Re HB (Abduction: Children's Objections)* [1998] 1 FLR 422 which demonstrates the negative aspects of direct involvement by children in proceedings between parents.
2   See Chapter 2 above.
3   CM Lyon 'Safeguarding Children's Interests? – Some Problematic Issues Surrounding Separate Representation in Care and Associated Proceedings' in MDA Freeman (ed) *Essays in Family Law* (University College, London, 1985) at p 1. Lyon's essay is an excellent introduction to the law on representation of children's interests before the reforms of the Children Act. See also I Robertson 'Acting in Children's Cases – The Future of Specialisation' [1993] Fam Law 103, indicating that the admission of solicitors to The Law Society's Children Panel is carefully controlled to ensure suitability. See further PM Harris 'Procedural problems in representing children' (1995) JCL 49. See also J Masson 'Representations of Children' (1996) *Current Legal Problems* 245, J Fortin *Children's Rights and the Developing Law* (2nd edn) (Butterworths, 2003) at ch 7, and J Masson and M Winn Oakley *Out of Hearing: Representing Children in Care Proceedings* (John Wiley & Sons, 1999). More recently see M Thorpe and J Cadbury (eds) *Hearing the Children* (Family Law, 2004). Much useful information on the practical concerns involved in representing children may be found in the quarterly journal *Representing Children* (formerly *Panel News*) published by the National Youth Advocacy Service.
4   CM Lyon (above) at p 2.

Current trends

This did not materialise, largely, it appears, because of its resource implications, and there remains a patchwork of different kinds of representation. The trend, however, is undoubtedly towards *more* representation[1]. The effect of the reforms first begun in the Children Act 1975 and built upon in the 1989 Act is to increase, very substantially, the provision for representation of children in *public* law cases. The essential feature of child representation in the modern law is that in *public* law cases it is the rule rather than the exception while in *private* law cases it has until now been the exception rather than the rule[2], although in future there is likely to be at least some increased representation of children in private cases[3]. It should be said that, since private law cases vastly exceed public law cases numerically, in most 'family proceedings' the child will be neither a party, nor separately represented[4]. The effect of this divergent policy is to preserve, at least on this issue, a distinct dichotomy of public and private children cases. This might be thought rather contrary to the general thrust of the legislation which has been to harmonise the two through common procedures and common principles[5]. It is thus necessary to take public and private law separately for the purposes of this discussion.

CAFCASS – the reorganisation of representation in family proceedings

Before 2001 there were three separate systems in place for the provision of representation of children in family proceedings which applied in three different contexts. First, there was the Family Court Welfare Service[6] which was responsible for providing welfare services, including welfare reports, conciliation (mediation) and advice in private law cases. 'Court welfare officers' were provided by the Probation Service whose much greater function related to criminal proceedings. The civil court aspect of the work of the Probation Service was under-resourced and jarred somewhat with its principal function in the criminal courts. Secondly, there was the provision of guardians ad litem and reporting officers through local GALRO panels[7] who were appointed in public law and adoption cases. GALs were either self-employed social workers or self-employed probation officers. One of the principal concerns was whether they were sufficiently independent of the local authorities whose responsibility it was to establish these panels, but who were themselves of course involved in child care proceedings, and because the service

---

1 For a useful article exploring the adequacy of the representation of *parents'* views in the family justice system, see J Whybrow 'The Judge, the Lawyer and CAFCASS' [2004] Fam Law 251.
2 The term 'representation' is used here to refer to representation of the *child* as such rather than investigations into the child's *interests*.
3 See p 593 below.
4 This is, of course, principally accounted for by the very high incidence of divorce.
5 See Chapter 2 above.
6 See Chapter 4 above.
7 For discussion of the GAL panel service, see the second edition of this work at pp 453–454.

was partially funded by those authorities[1]. Thirdly, in a small minority of sensitive or complex children cases, the Official Solicitor's Department might provide representation and this could be in either public[2] or private law[3] cases in the High Court or county court.

The advent of CAFCASS

There was a perceived need to provide a more rational and integrated system for delivering welfare services to the courts, including representation, in the various kinds of children proceedings. This led to the establishment in April 2001 of CAFCASS – the Children and Family Court Advisory and Support Service[4]. This was set up under the Criminal Justice and Courts Services Act 2000[5] and is a non-departmental public body, centrally funded and accountable to the Department of Constitutional Affairs. It brings together in one service the previous three disparate forms of provision discussed above, together with some significant changes in terminology. Generically, those providing services under the CAFCASS regime are referred to as 'officers of the service'[6]. This umbrella term now includes 'child and family reporters' who undertake the work formerly done by 'court welfare officers' in private law cases[7]; 'children's guardians' appointed in public law cases to perform the role formerly undertaken by panel guardians (GALs); and 'CAFCASS Legal Services' which have largely, although not entirely, taken over the role of the Official Solicitor's Department in the kinds of difficult children cases in which that Department had previously been involved and in which the child will usually be made a party to the proceedings[8].

The early problems of the new service were legion and were very publicly aired[9]. They included a damaging dispute over the contractual arrangements for

---

1   See, for example, *R v Cornwall County Council ex parte Cornwall and Isles of Scilly Guardians ad Litem and Reporting Officers Panel* [1992] 1 WLR 427.
2   For discussion of the Official Solicitor's former involvement in public law cases, see the second edition of this work at pp 449–450. The lawyers and civil servants who took part in these cases were not qualified social workers (as were GALS) but did have a particular expertise in certain types of case, such as those with a foreign element. For a comparison of the work of the Official Solicitor's staff with that of panel guardians in public law cases, see J Masson 'The Official Solicitor as the child's guardian ad litem under the Children Act 1989' (1992) 4 J Ch L 58.
3   For a discussion of the Official Solicitor's Role in pre-CAFCASS private law cases, see the second edition of this work at pp 457–458. It was not uncommon for the Official Solicitor to be involved in wardship cases and cases under the inherent jurisdiction. Good examples of the kind of cases in which this might occur were disputes over serious medical procedures involving children (see, for example, *Re HG (Specific Issue Order: Sterilisation)* [1993] 1 FLR 587) or cases in which a parent who was herself a minor was seeking an order in relation to her child.
4   The Service has a website at www.cafcass.gov.uk.
5   Sections 11–17 and Sch 2.
6   See, for example, the amended s 41 of the Children Act 1989 which, although concerned with the appointment and role of children's guardians, refers throughout to 'an officer of the service', meaning CAFCASS.
7   Although local authority social workers may continue to provide welfare reports in some cases and, where they do, they (confusingly) continue to be known as 'welfare officers'.
8   It is envisaged that the Official Solicitor's Department will have a residual ongoing role in some children cases. In areas of doubt and, in order to avoid duplication, the staff of CAFCASS Legal are expected to liaise with the Official Solicitor's office to ensure that the most suitable arrangements are made. See *CAFCASS Practice Note (Officers of CAFCASS Legal Services and Special Casework: Appointment in Family Proceedings)* [2001] 2 FLR 151.
9   They were the subject of an investigation by the Constitutional Affairs Select Committee. The Government then published a response to this Committee's report. See *The Response of the Government and the Children and Family Court Advisory and Support Service to the Constitutional Affairs*

guardians, most of whom were self-employed but who were effectively told that self-employment in any form was not compatible with a managed service. This dispute ultimately had to be resolved by the courts[1]. Other problems included an unrealistically short timetable for establishment of the service, unacceptable delays, and a shortage of qualified staff and confused lines of accountability between the then Lord Chancellor's Department and the service. These problems were highlighted in a report by the House of Commons Select Committee on CAFCASS[2].

In response to the many criticisms levelled at the service[3], CAFCASS has introduced the first National Standards relating to its work with children and families in family proceedings, implemented as from April 2003. These are said to incorporate a 'rigorous complaints procedure to ensure that issues regarding the service are reviewed and resolved transparently and efficiently'. Performance against the National Standards will be measured by HM Magistrates' Courts Service Inspectorate and will be the subject of quarterly reports. It remains to be seen whether the quality of performance can be raised sufficiently to enable the proper discharge of the service's responsibilities. A key question is whether the service will be able to cope adequately with what is likely to be an expansion in the separate representation of children in private proceedings alongside the already onerous provision of tandem representation (see below) in public law proceedings.

Public family proceedings

An earlier chapter[4] considered the background to the provision of separate representation for children in care proceedings. The Children Act significantly increased this in two ways. First, it created a presumption of appointment of a GAL (now known as a 'children's guardian' and hereafter referred to as such) in 'specified proceedings' and, secondly, it enlarged the range of proceedings in which the presumption of appointment applies. The child will also automatically be a party in such proceedings.

Appointment of a separate representative
Where the child is separately represented, this is sometimes referred to as 'tandem representation' since it will be by a children's guardian and/or a solicitor. The

---

Select Committee's Report on Children and Family Court Advisory and Support Service (CAFCASS) (Cm 6004) (2003).

1 *The Queen on the Application of National Association of Guardians ad Litem and Reporting Officers v Children and Family Court Advisory and Support Service* [2002] 1 FLR 255. See also *R v Children and Family Court Advisory and Support Service* [2003] 1 FLR 953 in which Charles J dismissed an application in judicial review that CAFCASS was legally obliged to make an officer of the service immediately available to act as guardian on receiving a request from the court for it to do so. The relevant statutory provisions, he held, implied that CAFCASS should respond as soon as possible but there could lawfully be a gap between the request and an appointment.

2 A convenient summary of the findings of this report is set out at [2003] Fam Law 626–627 with a comment by the Right Honourable Alan Beith MP at p 625.

3 As to which see the views of Jonathan Tross, then Chief Executive of CAFCASS in 'CAFCASS – Moving Forward' [2002] Fam Law 829 and, reviewing the next two years of CAFCASS, J Tross 'CAFCASS Present and Future' [2004] Fam Law 731. For the statistics of involvement of CAFCASS in various types of children proceedings between April 2003 and March 2004, see the CAFCASS Annual Report summarised at [2004] Fam Law 760.

4 Chapter 11 above.

relationship between these two kinds of representative is discussed below. The concern for the moment is with the circumstances of appointment.

Appointment of a children's guardian

Section 41(6) of the Children Act 1989 and the accompanying rules of court[1] specify a long list of proceedings in which the court *must* appoint a children's guardian for the child 'unless satisfied that it is not necessary to do so in order to safeguard his interests'[2]. It was envisaged by the Lord Chancellor, during the passage of the Children Bill, that an appointment would need to be made in the vast majority of cases falling within the specified proceedings[3]. The wording of the legislation is a reformulation of the former statutory language and was designed to remove the wide discretion which the courts previously had in deciding whether to appoint a children's guardian[4]. The small minority of cases in which a children's guardian is not appointed are likely to be mainly those in which the child wishes to instruct his own solicitor and is found to be competent to do so. In 'specified proceedings' the child is automatically entitled to be a party[5] and may instruct a solicitor where he has sufficient understanding and wishes to do so[6]. In 'non-specified proceedings', which expression includes mainly private law cases under the Children Act[7], the child is not usually a party but the court has a discretion to join him at his request and also to appoint a children's guardian or solicitor[8]. As we shall see, it is expected that the representation of children in certain private law cases will increase in the future[9].

---

1 Family Proceedings Rules 1991, SI 1991/1247 (FPR 1991) and Family Proceedings Courts (Children Act 1989) Rules 1991, SI 1991/1395 (FPC(CA 1989)R 1991).

2 Section 41(1). On the appointment and functions of children's guardians generally, see *The Children Act 1989 Guidance and Regulations Vol 7 Guardians ad Litem and other Court Related Issues* (HMSO, 1991).

3 House of Lords Official Report, Vol 503, col 408 (19 January 1989). But for a case in which the court held that the appointment of a children's guardian in specified proceedings was unnecessary on the facts, see *Re J (A Minor) (Change of Name)* [1993] 1 FLR 699. Here, a 12-year-old girl in care and living with long-term foster-parents wished to use their name. This was not opposed by the Official Solicitor and there was no longer any contact between the girl and her natural parents following a history of severe abuse. Booth J said that a children's guardian could not have said any more than counsel for the local authority and there was no conflict of interest. Neither was it appropriate here to serve either the parents or the girl or for her to be present in court.

4 In some courts, appointments were evidently made in only a small proportion of cases. See *R v Plymouth Juvenile Court ex parte F and F* [1987] 1 FLR 169 at 178.

5 FPR 1991, r 4.7(1) and App 3, col (iii); FPC(CA 1989)R 1991, r 7(1) and Sch 2, col (iii).

6 Section 41(3), (4)(b).

7 'Relevant proceedings' for these purposes are any proceedings under the Children Act, under any statutory instrument made under it or any amendment made by the Children Act in any other enactment (s 93(1)–(3)).

8 See, for example, *Re CE (Section 37 Direction)* [1995] 1 FLR 26 where a children's guardian appointed following a s 37 direction by a district judge continued to represent a 14-year-old child (who had left her parents to live with her boyfriend's family) even though the local authority decided not to seek a public law order following its investigations. Section 37 should not, however, be used purely as a device to secure the appointment of a children's guardian since the normal course is for the child's views to be presented by the court welfare officer in private proceedings. Neither should wardship be used for the purpose of foisting a children's guardian on a child. See *Re CT (A Minor) (Wardship: Representation)* [1993] 2 FLR 278.

9 See below.

What are 'specified proceedings'?

Essentially, specified proceedings are all proceedings which involve public intervention in the family[1]. They include, most obviously, applications for care or supervision orders and, significantly since the Children Act, applications for the short-term remedies of EPOs and CAOs. Other proceedings included are: those in which a s 37 direction has been made or the court is considering whether to make an interim care order; applications for discharge or variation of care or supervision orders; and applications for residence or contact orders where a child is in care; and appeals against the making or refusal of these orders. Also now included are: secure accommodation applications; applications by a local authority to change the child's name or remove him from the UK; applications to extend supervision orders; proceedings under the HFEA 1990, s 30 in which the court must consider the appointment of a 'parental order reporter'[2]; and appeals in any of these proceedings. In addition, children's guardians will continue to be appointed in adoption proceedings under the Adoption and Children Act 2002.

Although the appointment of a children's guardian can be made at any stage of the proceedings[3], the rules require the court to make the appointment as soon as possible after the commencement or transfer of the proceedings[4]. Children's guardians will thus be involved at an early stage and consequently should be able to advise the court about short-term orders, such as EPOs and interim orders, and directions the court may wish to make in the initial stages of protective intervention[5].

Appointment of a solicitor

It is not the function of the children's guardian to represent the child at the hearing in court. This is undertaken, as one would expect, by a solicitor and, where appropriate, counsel[6]. Where a solicitor has not already been appointed, one of the functions of the children's guardian is to appoint one and thereafter give instructions to him. We consider below the problem of what happens where the instructions of the children's guardian do not accord with the wishes of the child. Where no solicitor has been appointed, the court may itself make an appointment where:

(1) no children's guardian has been appointed for the child;
(2) the child has sufficient understanding to instruct a solicitor and wishes to do so; and
(3) it appears to the court that it would be in the child's best interests for him to be represented by a solicitor[7].

The appointed solicitor must then represent the child in accordance with rules of court[8].

---

1   Children Act, s 41(6).
2   FPR 1991, r 4A.
3   FPR 1991, r 4.10(4) and FPC(CA 1989)R 1991, r 10(4).
4   FPR 1991, r 4.10(1) and FPC(CA 1989)R 1991, r 10(1).
5   As to which see Chapter 12 above.
6   There is much valuable information about the nature of the solicitor's role in representing children in P King and I Young *The Child as Client* (Family Law, 1992).
7   Section 41(3) and (4).
8   Section 41(5), and FPR 1991, r 4.12.

Public funding is available for *all* proceedings under the Children Act 1989[1] and this includes the representation of children. This used to be known as 'legal aid' and, following the Access to Justice Act 1999, is under the control of the Legal Services Commission and the Community Legal Service. The normal 'means and merits' test will apply but this is not so in relation to certain 'special Children Act proceedings'[2]. In these cases, children have a right to non-means, non-merits-tested funding which used to be known as 'free legal aid'. These special proceedings are again confined to *public* family proceedings but are a more restricted class than the 'specified proceedings' for the purposes of representation. Included are cases under s 31 (care and supervision orders), s 43 (CAOs), s 44 (EPOs), s 45 (duration and discharge of EPOs) and s 25 (secure accommodation applications). In 'other public law children cases' falling outside this definition, there is a means test but a more generous one than that which normally applies[3]. In these proceedings, time will often be of the essence, and the special rules mean that a solicitor will be able to get on with the case immediately. A 'free certificate' may also be granted to a person who has been granted legal representation in Special Children Act proceedings, to enable him or her to be represented in 'related proceedings'. This may be so where the two sets of proceedings are being heard together or in which an order is being sought as an alternative to an order in Special Children Act proceedings[4]. An example here is adoption proceedings. In all other children cases, public funding may be applied for in the normal way and it is important to remember that this could include emergency funding over the telephone where necessary. The ability of the solicitor to act quickly is important, not least to avoid offending the general principle in the legislation that delay is prejudicial to children[5].

The specialised nature of the work involved in representing children is recognised by The Law Society which has established a Children Panel with regional branches, in an effort to ensure that solicitors chosen to represent children will have the necessary expertise.

The role of the children's guardian

General

Children's guardians are individuals with qualifications in social work who are required to have a thorough knowledge of both social work theory and child care law. The principal function of the children's guardian system is to ensure that 'the court is fully informed of the relevant facts which relate to the child's welfare and that the wishes and feelings of the child are clearly established'[6]. They were described by the *Guidance*[7] as having a 'proactive role' in relation to the conduct

---

1 Access to Justice Act 1999.
2 See Community Legal Service (Funding) Regulations 2000, reg 3(1)(c), and section 2.2 of the Funding Code made under the Access to Justice Act 1999.
3 Section 2.2 and section 11.8 of the Funding Code.
4 See Funding Code, section 11.8.
5 See Chapter 2 above.
6 *Children Act Advisory Committee Annual Report 1992/3* (Lord Chancellor's Department, 1993) at p 14. See also D Dinan-Hayward 'The Changing Role of the Guardian ad Litem' [1992] Fam Law 555.
7 *The Children Act 1989 Guidance and Regulations Vol 7 Guardians ad Litem and Other Court Related Issues* (HMSO, 1991) at para 2.2.

of the proceedings, including timetabling and advising the court on the range of orders available. The general duty of the guardian, as expressed in the Children Act, is 'to safeguard the interests of the child' in the manner prescribed by rules of court[1]. It should be noted that these rules only govern guardians appointed in 'specified' Children Act proceedings. There are no comparable rules governing the conduct of litigation friends or guardians appointed to represent children in other kinds of proceedings. The rules[2] spell out in some detail the more specific duties of guardians.

Specific duties
The children's guardian is required to attend all directions, appointments and hearings, unless excused by the court, and to advise the court on the following matters:

'(a) whether the child is of sufficient understanding for any purpose including the child's refusal to submit to a medical or psychiatric examination or other assessment that the court has power to require, direct or order;
(b) the wishes of the child in respect of any matter relevant to the proceedings, including his attendance at court;
(c) the appropriate forum for the proceedings;
(d) the appropriate timing of the proceedings or any part of them;
(e) the options available to it in respect of the child and the suitability of each such option including what order should be made in determining the application;
(f) any other matter concerning which the court seeks his advice or concerning which he considers that the court should be informed.'[3]

In addition to this advisory role, the guardian must[4], inter alia:

(1) appoint a solicitor, advise the child as is appropriate having regard to his understanding, and instruct the solicitor;
(2) file a written report advising on the interests of the child, not less than seven days before the date fixed for the hearing; and
(3) make such investigations as may be necessary for him to carry out his duties, including, in particular, interviewing such persons as he thinks appropriate or the court directs, inspecting records and obtaining professional assistance.

Regarding the inspection of records, the Children Act, as amended by the Courts and Legal Services Act 1990[5], gives the guardian access to the records of social services departments which may be inspected and copies taken. This right does not, however, extend to the records of health authorities, except where health records form part of the local authority's own records[6]. As regards the guardian's report, the Act provides that the court may take account of any statement made by the guardian in the report and any evidence given in respect of matters referred to in it where, in its opinion, these are relevant to the issue it is considering[7]. The broad effect of this provision was to disapply the hearsay rule,

---

1   Section 41(2).
2   FPR 1991, rr 4.11 and 4.11A and FPC(CA 1989)R 1991, rr 11 and 11A(3).
3   FPR 1991, r 4.11A(4) and FPC(CA 1989)R 1991, r 11(4).
4   Ibid.
5   Section 42(1), and the Courts and Legal Services Act 1990, Sch 16, para 18.
6   For further analysis of s 42, see MDA Freeman *Children, Their Families and the Law* (Macmillan, 1992) at p 169.
7   Section 41(11).

reflecting the inquisitorial nature of children proceedings[1]. Children cases are, however, no longer distinctive in relation to the hearsay rule since, under the Civil Evidence Act 1995, hearsay is now admissible in civil proceedings generally and its relevance is now only to weight and not to admissibility.

Tandem representation: relationship between the guardian and the child's solicitor
The guardian and the child's solicitor are required to work closely together in the child's best interests[2]. It will usually be the guardian who appoints and instructs the solicitor. Although the solicitor presents the child's case in court, he must act on the guardian's instructions in determining the manner of presentation[3]. Difficulties can arise where the views of the guardian diverge from those of the child, especially if he or she is an older teenager who disagrees strongly with the guardian's view of his or her welfare. A particular problem may be a difference of opinion between the guardian and the solicitor about the competence of the child. It has been suggested[4] that this can lead to acute problems, for example in sexual abuse cases. Here, the solicitor may wish to take instructions from the child direct if, having taken into account the guardian's views and any court directions, he considers that the child wishes to give instructions which conflict with those of the guardian and he has sufficient understanding to do so. The rules allow him to deal directly with the child in these circumstances[5]. In this eventuality, the guardian remains in office and will continue to discharge all his duties other than instructing the solicitor[6].

The child's ability to instruct a solicitor was considered in *Re H (A Minor) (Care Proceedings: Child's Wishes)*[7]. In that case, Thorpe J emphasised that a child must have sufficient understanding and rationality and that this may not be so where the child is suffering from intense emotional disturbance. Where there is any issue as to the child's rationality, the question should be the subject of specific expert opinion from experts already involved in the case. There is evidence that in practice, notwithstanding these provisions, there is a reluctance to accept that

---

1   On the shift towards inquisitorial procedures in children cases under the Children Act, see Chapter 2 above.
2   See, generally, P King and I Young *The Child as Client* (Family Law, 1992) at ch 7, and MR Bell and R Daley 'Social Workers and Solicitors: Working Together?' [1992] Fam Law 257. For a more recent commentary, see J Fortin *Children's Rights and the Developing Law* (2nd edn) (Butterworths, 2003) at pp 233–240. For a summary of research exploring lawyers' views on their relationship with guardians in public law proceedings see G Timmis 'Lawyers' Perspectives on Public Law Cases' [2003] Fam Law 174. For a recent discussion of the relationship between social workers and lawyers in children cases, see J Dickens 'Risks and Responsibilities – the role of the local authority lawyer in child care cases' [2004] CFLQ 17.
3   Detailed guidance on the role of solicitors in public law proceedings, especially where a guardian has not yet been appointed for the child, has been issued by the Law Society. See 'Representation of Children in Public Proceedings: Notice to Children Panel Members Issued by the Law Society, September 2002' [2002] Fam Law 930.
4   MDA Freeman *Children, Their Families and the Law* (Macmillan, 1992) at p 168.
5   FPR 1991, r 4.12(1)(a) and FPC(CA 1989)R 1991, r 12(1)(a).
6   He is entitled to legal representation but not to public funding for this purpose. See *The Children Act Advisory Committee Annual Report 1992/3* (Lord Chancellor's Department, 1993) at p 29. It is for the court to decide how the child should be represented in these circumstances and to rule on any dispute between the guardian and solicitor about whether the child has the necessary capacity to instruct the solicitor. See *Re M (Minors) (Care Proceedings: Child's Wishes)* [1994] 1 FLR 749.
7   [1993] 1 FLR 440.

children may be able to instruct solicitors independently and that this rarely happens[1].

Private family proceedings

The contrast between representation for children in public and private proceedings could hardly be more striking[2]. The issue can be disposed of much more quickly in the private context, since representation of the child, as such, occurs in only a tiny minority of cases. Objective assessments of the child's best interests through welfare reports take place in a larger number of cases, but the proportion of the total is still very small, principally because of the large number of divorce cases in which there is no dispute over children and no need for a court order. Sometimes children's interests are very intimately involved and there is no better illustration of this than divorce. There can be few matters which have the potential for affecting children so deeply as the breakdown of their parents' marriage, yet they are rarely represented in divorce proceedings, and welfare reports are usually ordered only in the small minority of cases in which there is a real contest over the arrangements for the children[3]. In certain other jurisdictions, there is a more systematic investigation of children's interests in private proceedings[4], and there is no doubt that the lack of provision for representation in English law has been influenced, to some extent, perhaps heavily, by resource implications – a fact indirectly acknowledged by the Law Commission[5] in its report which formed the basis of the private law in the Children Act. It is, perhaps, a fair question to pose whether there is any justification, other than pressure on resources, for the preservation of the current distinctions between public and private law on this issue[6].

---

1 J Masson and M Winn Oakley *Out of Hearing: Representing Children in Care Proceedings* (John Wiley & Sons, 1999). See also *Re C (Secure Accommodation Order: Representation)* [2001] 2 FLR 169. Here a secure accommodation order was upheld on appeal despite the very limited opportunities which the 15-year-old child had been given to instruct her solicitor whom she had engaged after being dissatisfied with the children's guardian's approach to her case.

2 There is an extensive discussion of the issues surrounding the representation of children in private proceedings in J Fortin *Children's Rights and the Developing Law* (2nd edn) (Butterworths, 2003) at pp 215–223. For a more recent evaluation of the appointment of guardians for children in private proceedings (which takes account of recent practice directions and notes by, respectively, the President of the Family Division and CAFCASS), see J Whybrow 'Children, Guardians and Rule 9.5' [2004] Fam Law 504. See also the views of Munby J on the lack of appropriate support and representation where *administrative* decisions are being taken in relation to children in 'Making sure the Child is Heard' (2004) 17 *Representing Children* 10, especially at pp 21–22. For the results of some recent research on the extent to which children's wishes were heard and were influential in residence and contact disputes, see V May and C Smart 'Silence in Court? – hearing children in residence and contact disputes' [2004] CFLQ 305.

3 The court is not, however, confined to contested cases. See Chapter 4 above.

4 See, for example, the role of the family advocate in South Africa in I Schäfer 'The Family Advocate in South Africa' in A Bainham, DS Pearl and R Pickford (eds) *Frontiers of Family Law* (2nd edn) (John Wiley & Sons, 1995) at p 30.

5 See Law Com Report No 172 (1988) at para 6.15, where the Law Commission recognised that welfare officers' time was limited and 'must be targeted on the cases in which it will be most valuable'.

6 As noted above, the Adoption and Children Act 2002 also contains an empowering provision which should lead to significantly greater representation of children in private law proceedings.

In recent years there has been increasing pressure from children's rights organisations for the creation of greater opportunities for the representation of children in private family proceedings. This pressure lead to the insertion of an empowering provision in the Family Law Act 1996[1].

There remains the broader policy question of exactly how far it is desirable for children to be independently represented in such proceedings. *L v L (Minors) (Separate Representation)*[2] is a good illustration of the circumstances in which there is a need for the separate representation of children in private law proceedings. Here, the parents and three children aged respectively 14, 12 and 9 were Australian. The parents had separated, the mother having formed a new relationship, and the children remained with their father. There was some suggestion that they might be taken back to Australia. There was a dispute as to residence and the amount of contact with the mother. The children expressed their view to the court welfare officer that existing contact with their mother was inadequate. The welfare officer took the position that she could not adequately reflect the views of the children in court, and the judge therefore ordered the children to be separately represented by a solicitor from the child care panel. The Court of Appeal upheld this decision and also directed that the children be joined as parties to the proceedings. More recently, in *Re A (Contact: Separate Representation)*[3] the Court of Appeal allowed a mother's appeal against the judge's refusal to grant leave for the child's separate representation in private proceedings between her parents who had separated. The mother, inter alia, raised allegations of sexual abuse of the child and approached the charity, the National Youth Advocacy Service (NYAS), which sought leave to intervene and act as guardian to the child. The mother was opposed to contact between the father and the child. The Court of Appeal transferred the case to London but invited the Official Solicitor, rather than NYAS, to act as guardian since the father might have perceived NYAS (albeit wrongly) as acting on the mother's behalf. The court's view was that separate representation was appropriate given the problems facing both parents, the sexual abuse allegations and the potential conflict of interest between each parent and the child. Dame Elizabeth Butler-Sloss P remarked that, following the HRA 1998, there would be likely to be an increased use of guardians in private law cases[4].

See ibid, s 122, adding s 8 orders to the list of proceedings which may be specified under s 41 of the Children Act 1989.

1   Section 64.
2   [1994] 1 FLR 156. See also *Re C (Prohibition on Further Applications)* [2002] 1 FLR 1136 where CAFCASS Legal was directed to represent two younger daughters of four children in a protracted contact dispute.
3   [2001] 1 FLR 715.
4   For a very helpful article discussing the circumstances under which children have been made parties to private law proceedings and guardians appointed for them in one region (Leeds), see C Bellamy and G Lord 'Reflections on Family Proceedings Rule 9.5' [2003] Fam Law 265. The authors identify on the basis of their research a number of factors tending to be relevant to the question of independent representation in private proceedings. These were intractable cases; a significant foreign, ethnic or cultural element; significant health problems; violence and/or sexual abuse; and complex family relationships. The circumstances under which children should be made a party to proceedings which are not specified proceedings and a guardian appointed are now the subject of a Direction by the President of the Family Division. See *President's Direction: Representation of Children in Family Proceedings Pursuant to Family Proceedings Rules 1991, rule 9.5* [2004] 1 FLR 1188.

Other instances in which children might appropriately be parties and separately represented spring to mind. Clearly, this would be so where a child is the applicant for an order under Part IV of the Family Law Act 1996 where, as previously discussed, the division between what is 'public' and what is 'private' is in any event artificial. In acrimonious divorce proceedings in which there is a bitter ongoing battle over the children, it is equally clear that the case for separate representation, which acknowledges the conflict of interest between the parents and the children, is also very strong. But these cases are exceptional. The overwhelming majority of divorce cases are not like this. There is not usually a dispute over the children and in a very high proportion of cases an order in relation to the children is neither sought nor necessary[1]. It would therefore seem right that, unlike in public proceedings in which a conflict of interest between parents and children is rightly presumed, in private proceedings independent representation should continue to be regarded as the exception rather than the rule but nevertheless important in the minority of cases in which there is a real dispute and real conflict.

Welfare reports in private proceedings
Some of the principles applying to welfare reports have already been noted[2] and they will not be repeated here. Instead, we will focus briefly on the essential differences between representation by a children's guardian in public proceedings and the involvement of the child and family reporters[3] in private cases. We also touch upon the role of the Official Solicitor in wardship proceedings, which is somewhat different from that of either guardians or child and family reporters.

The first point to emphasise is that a child and family reporter is *not* the child's representative, and his role is not to represent the child's interest. Rather, it is to provide the court with an objective evaluation, through a report, of the child and his background. There is no reason, in principle, why the court should not appoint a children's guardian *and* seek a welfare report, but the Court of Appeal has warned against unnecessary duplication which might occur where two reports are obtained[4]. Such cases are therefore likely to be rare.

The duty of the child and family reporter is to conduct a thorough investigation of the child's circumstances and prepare a written report for the court. This investigation must extend beyond the child himself, to all other members of the child's family and adult figures in the child's life. This entails interviewing all relevant parties and, perhaps also, inquiries among relatives, the child's school or health authorities. Conciliation is not part of the child and family reporter's

---

1 See Chapter 4 above.
2 Section 7, and Chapter 4 above.
3 Where the officers of local authorities provide reports they continue to be known as 'welfare officers'. Hereafter, the expression 'child and family reporters' will be used in the text to refer to both them and 'welfare officers'.
4 *Re S (A Minor) (Guardian ad Litem/Welfare Officer)* [1993] 1 FLR 110, a *public* case concerning the question of whether an additional report from a welfare officer should be obtained where an appointed guardian already had responsibility to provide a report. Cf *Re W (Welfare Reports)* [1995] 2 FLR 142, discussed in Chapter 4 above, which confirms that the court has an unfettered discretion to order more than one welfare report where it considers this appropriate. For a general comparison of the respective roles of the court welfare officer and the guardian, see C Jackson 'Reporting on Children: The Guardian ad Litem, the court welfare officer and the Children Act 1989' [1992] Fam Law 252.

function and should not be undertaken[1]. The child and family reporter must consider whether it is in the best interests of the child for the child to be made a party to the proceedings[2]. Where he thinks it is, he must notify the court with reasons[3]. When his investigations are completed, the child and family reporter produces a report which must be filed in the time prescribed by the court or, in any event, within 14 days of the hearing[4]. This will then be served on the parties, and on the guardian, where one is appointed. Only the parties, their legal representatives, the guardian, the Community Legal Service, the child and family reporter and an expert whose instruction has been authorised by the court are entitled to have access to the report, without the leave of the court[5]. In due course, the child and family reporter must, unless excused by the court, attend the hearing, and may be questioned about the report by the court or the parties[6]. The influence of welfare reports on the ultimate decision of the court was considered previously[7].

What are the salient differences between the process of obtaining welfare reports and representation by a guardian? In essence, the child and family reporter is an officer of the court with an investigative and reporting role. He is in no sense a representative or witness for the child or any other party. There are, of course, some similarities in what child and family reporters and guardians do, but the functions of the latter are much wider than just investigation and report. It is the representative element of their duties which is the real point of distinction. Apart from the small proportion of private cases in which children are actually joined as parties, as the law stands, they will be unrepresented either by a children's guardian or a solicitor. A further point of distinction is that there is no *presumption* of welfare involvement in private cases which corresponds to the statutory presumption of representation by a children's guardian in public cases. It is certainly arguable that more still needs to be done to ensure an adequate voice for the child and representation of his independent interests and views in the private sphere, and it remains to be seen how far this will be taken under the empowering provisions of the Adoption and Children Act 2002[8].

EVIDENCE

How is evidence obtained in children cases? Are children themselves competent to give evidence and, if so, ought their evidence to be given the same weight as that of adults, or ought allowances to be made for the age of the child witness? Should the legal system make special arrangements for accommodating child witnesses to counteract the ordeal of a court appearance, often arising in connection with alleged abuse of the child concerned? Ought children to attend court at all[9]?

---

1 *Scott v Scott* [1986] 2 FLR 320, and *Re H (Conciliation: Welfare Reports)* [1986] 1 FLR 476.
2 FPR 1991, r 4.13(3A) and FPC(CA 1989)R 1991, r 13(3A).
3 FPR 1991, r 4.13(3B) and FPC(CA 1989)R 1991, r 13(3B).
4 FPR 1991, r 4.13(1) and FPC(CA 1989)R 1991, r 13(1).
5 FPR 1991, r 4.23(1) and FPC(CA 1989)R 1991, r 23(1).
6 FPR 1991, r 4.13(3) and FPC(CA 1989)R 1991, r 13(3).
7 At Chapter 4 above.
8 Children Act 1989, ss 41(6A) and 93(2)(bb), inserted by the Adoption and Children Act 2002, s 122.
9 The most comprehensive treatment of these issues and of children's evidence generally is JR Spencer and R Flin *The Evidence of Children* (2nd edn) (Blackstone Press, 1993), although it

These are some of the questions which law reform agencies have had to face in recent years. In considering the answers which the legal system currently gives to these questions, it is necessary to distinguish between *civil* and *criminal* proceedings.

Family proceedings are civil proceedings, and the dominant principle is that the importance of the child's welfare requires the court to have regard to *all* available evidence[1]. This gave rise to a substantial relaxation in the ordinary rules of evidence, most particularly the hearsay rule. While this had long been a feature of some children proceedings, especially wardship, the effect of the Children Act was to extend the principle more generally to civil cases involving children.

In contrast, in criminal proceedings, the primary focus is not on the welfare of the child victim or witness but on the issue of the guilt or innocence of the accused. That being the case, a balance has to be struck between the needs of children in court as witnesses, whether victims or not, and the traditional safeguards afforded the accused by English criminal procedure, especially the right to confront his accusers through cross-examination. Moreover, these safeguards are now reinforced by Article 6 of the ECHR and the HRA 1998 which require that even more caution be taken in achieving the correct balance[2]. This involves weighing the potential benefits to children of being spared certain aspects of the ordeal of appearing in court against possible prejudice to the accused which might thereby be occasioned. There has been a perceptible shift in thinking in recent years. This reflects a growing appreciation that justice is not served if children are so intimidated by the legal process that their evidence is rendered less reliable or, more seriously, that they feel unable to give evidence at all. The result of excluding the evidence of children may be to deny the court access to the only available evidence of certain offences against children themselves or other children and to allow the perpetrator to escape justice and to continue to represent an ongoing threat to other children.

---

should be borne in mind that many changes to the law governing children's evidence have been implemented since the publication of this edition. See also H Dent and R Flin (eds) *Children as Witnesses* (1992), especially JR Spencer 'Reforming the Law on Children's Evidence in England: The Pigot Committee and After' at ch 7. See JR Spencer, G Nicholson, R Flin and R Bull (eds) *Children's Evidence in Legal Proceedings* (1990), distributed by the Faculty of Law, University of Cambridge. See also the report by the Royal College of Psychiatrists *The Evidence of Children* (1996) Council Report CR 44. A more up-to date discussion is now to be found in IH Dennis *The Law of Evidence* (2nd edn) (Sweet & Maxwell, 2002) especially at pp 451–457 and pp 514–524. For a succinct account of the rules, see H Brayne and H Carr *Law for Social Workers* (8th edn) (Oxford University Press, 2003) at pp 175–187. See also A Levy QC 'Children in Court' in J Fionda (ed) *Legal Concepts of Childhood* (Hart Publishing, 2001) at p 99. Specifically on the changes brought about by the Youth Justice and Criminal Evidence Act 1999, see D Birch and R Leng *Blackstone's Guide to the Youth Justice and Criminal Evidence Act 1999* (2000).

1   For an illustration of this principle, see *Re S (Contact: Evidence)* [1998] 1 FLR 798, where the Court of Appeal granted leave to issue a subpoena duces tecum to compel production of video evidence held by the police. The father wished to challenge allegations of sexual abuse of his five-year-old daughter with whom he had hitherto enjoyed extensive contact but which was now under threat. The court held that it had a duty to decide whether the allegations were true and could not allow the local authority or the police to decide the case. The court needed to have access to the best available evidence, and the parents had to have the opportunity of considering it.

2   Although in *Doorson v The Netherlands* (1996) 22 EHRR 330, the ECtHR accepted that some modification of the normal principle that all evidence should be presented publicly in the presence of the accused was permissible in the case of vulnerable witnesses.

The Youth Justice and Criminal Evidence Act 1999, building on previous legislative initiatives, seeks to make available a raft of measures designed to facilitate the reception of evidence by children. It does this particularly by allowing the court to make 'special measures directions' to lessen what would otherwise be the ordeal of appearing in an ordinary court, daunting enough for adults and, in many cases, impossibly daunting for children.

Civil proceedings

There are perhaps three major issues concerning civil proceedings. The first is the question whether a child is *entitled* to attend court or can be *compelled* to attend as a witness. The second is the question of the *competence* of child witnesses and the weight to be attached to their *own* evidence. The third is how *other* evidence is obtained[1].

Attendance at court and compellability

There are really two sides to this question. The first is whether children are *entitled* to attend family proceedings affecting them when they wish to do so. The second is whether they can be *compelled* to attend as witnesses where they do *not* wish to do so. These issues have been addressed mainly in the context of care proceedings.

It used to be the case that children over the age of five were required to attend care proceedings if an interim care order was to be made[2]. However, now, under the Children Act[3] the court has a discretion which can mean that they may be required to attend where they do *not* wish to do so or may not be allowed to attend where they *do*. The higher courts have generally discouraged the attendance of children, which they generally believe to be a potentially damaging experience to be avoided where possible and prefer to rely on obtaining evidence about the child's situation from adults[4], although children often attend hearings in the magistrates' family proceedings court[5]. Exclusion of children from civil proceedings has been criticised by Masson[6], who contrasts the position with the shift in social work practices towards the participation of children in meetings and case conferences and with the requirement that the child must attend criminal proceedings. She finds it 'paradoxical that children should be excluded when the "benign jurisdiction" is being exercised but required to attend in the punitive atmosphere of the criminal courts'.

The traditional reluctance of the judiciary to allow children to attend court is now having to be re-evaluated in the light of the requirements of Article 6 of the

---

1 For extensive treatment of evidence in family proceedings affecting children, see R White, P Carr and N Lowe *The Children Act in Practice* (3rd edn) (Butterworths, 2002) ch 11.

2 Children and Young Persons Act 1969, s 22.

3 Children Act 1989, s 95(1). The rules of court provide that proceedings may take place in the absence of any party, including the child, where the court considers this to be in the child's best interests and the child is represented by a children's guardian or solicitor. The guardian, solicitor and child (if of sufficient understanding) are all entitled to make representations. See FPR 1991, r 4.16(2) and FPC(CA 1989)R 1991, r 16(2).

4 See, for example, *Re C (A Minor) (Care: Child's Wishes)* [1993] 1 FLR 832 and *Re W (Secure Accommodation Order: Attendance at Court)* [1994] 2 FLR 1092.

5 For a more detailed discussion, see J Fortin *Children's Rights and the Developing Law* (2nd edn) (Butterworths, 2003) at pp 234–237.

6 J Masson 'Representations of Children' (1996) *Current Legal Problems* 245 at pp 259–262.

ECHR. An aspect of this is that the child's right to attend court, in certain cases, may be thought necessary to uphold the child's procedural right to a fair hearing. This is an issue which has arisen in a number of cases in which the courts have been considering whether to make a secure accommodation order under s 25 of the Children Act 1989[1]. These are cases in which the child's liberty is directly threatened, however welfare-based may be the objective of containing the child. As such they have as much, if not more, in common with criminal proceedings as they do with civil proceedings. In this context the initial judicial refusal to allow the attendance at these hearings has given way to an appreciation that, in view of what is at stake for the child, it is normal that the child should attend and be represented[2]. It remains to be seen how far similar arguments may be effectively pressed in other kinds of proceedings in which children's Convention rights may be in issue.

So far as compelling children to attend as witnesses is concerned, the courts have made it plain that a party may not demand as of right that a child attend if this would have an adverse effect on the child and there is an alternative means of introducing the child's evidence into the proceedings. The leading case is *R v B County Council, ex parte P*[3] in which the Court of Appeal upheld the decision of the magistrates not to issue a witness summons against a 17-year-old girl who had accused her step-father of sexually abusing her. In the care proceedings the step-father sought to have her called (the local authority having decided not to do so itself) principally as a way of having her cross-examined. The Court of Appeal held that it was for the local authority to determine what evidence was required to support its case in the care proceedings and that the decision not to call the girl was not amenable to judicial review. A summons should not be issued where its effect would be oppressive or so inimical to the child's welfare as to outweigh the legitimate interest of the person seeking to call her. As Butler-Sloss LJ put it:

> 'Research has shown the adverse effects upon some children of the requirement to give evidence in cases of sexual abuse. In cases of young children, such harm may well be inferred. ... The introduction of the Order of 1990 [now the Children (Admissibility of Hearsay Evidence) Order 1993, SI 1993/621] clearly envisages an alternative to oral evidence and cross-examination and to make it possible for children making allegations of, inter alia, sexual abuse to do so without the additional stress of a court hearing. The philosophy behind the Children Act 1989 would be thwarted by the abuser himself being able to require the attendance of the child at court. A court should be very cautious in requiring the attendance of a child in these cases, reinforced as it must be by considerations as to how to deal with refusal to give evidence after the issue of the summons.'

At the same time, the court did acknowledge one possible disadvantage in the failure of the child to give evidence, namely that this may weaken the case against the alleged abuser because issues will arise about the *weight* which ought to be attached to hearsay evidence. The court warned that magistrates should take great care in assessing how much weight is to be attached to the hearsay evidence of statements from children of mature years making serious allegations against a

---

1 See, for example, *Re W (A Minor) (Secure Accommodation Orders: Attendance at Court)* [1994] 2 FLR 1092.

2 See, for example, *Re C (Secure Accommodation Order: Representation)* [2001] 2 FLR 169, *Re K (Secure Accommodation Order: Right to Liberty)* [2001] 1 FLR 526, and *Re AS (Secure Accommodation Order: Representation)* [1999] 1 FLR 103.

3 [1991] 1 WLR 221.

parent, where there has been no opportunity for cross-examination. It was accepted that different considerations would apply in the case of young children.

The Court of Appeal gave further guidance on the principles applicable to the issue of a witness summons against a child in care proceedings. In *Re P (Witness Summons)*[1] the court made it clear that, in taking into account the great relevance of the child's welfare, the matter was not, however, governed by the 'welfare principle' as such since the issue was not one which related to the child's upbringing[2]. The court went on to say that, in principle, the older the child the more likely it was that the application to call the child would succeed. It was, however, to be expected that in most cases involving a child aged 12 or younger (here, the girl was 12) the court would favour the absence of oral evidence even though that might mean weakening, perhaps even fatally, the evidence against the adult[3].

Children as witnesses: competence

The difficulty with child witnesses before the Children Act was that the common law required them to understand the nature of an oath before being allowed to give evidence. While this was usually assumed in the case of an adult, this was not so with a child. The court would inquire into the *competence* of a child under the age of 14 years who was to be sworn in. The leading case was *R v Hayes*, in which Bridge LJ identified the important consideration as being:

> 'whether the child has a sufficient appreciation of the solemnity of the occasion and the added responsibility to tell the truth, which is involved in taking an oath, over and above the duty to tell the truth which is an ordinary duty of normal social conduct.'[4]

The problem with this test was that, while some children may make competent and credible witnesses[5], they will not necessarily understand abstract concepts like an oath or 'the truth' or the technicalities of the legal system. Dennis[6] has described the *Hayes* decision as 'a policy decision to secularise the common law test'. It was the specifically religious basis of the common law oath which presented a problem to children since it involved an appreciation of the existence of God and the possibility of divine, as well as secular, sanctions for deliberately lying. In *Hayes* itself this would have presented an insurmountable problem since the two boys concerned, aged 11 and 13, both claimed to be ignorant, to have no knowledge of the existence of God and to have received no religious instruction. Rhona Flin has given some colourful illustrations, from a study of child witnesses, of some of the misconceptions which children have about 'law'[7]. Thus, a six-year-old child offered the view that judges 'teach people dancing'; a 10-year-old child said of a jury, 'They ask the criminal questions, then he gives up

---

1   [1997] 2 FLR 447.
2   On the application of the welfare principle generally, see Chapter 2.
3   Even where the child is a teenager, the court may prefer not to hear the child's oral evidence in care proceedings. In *Re O (Care Proceedings: Evidence)* [2004] 1 FLR 161 Johnson J reiterated the principle that it was general practice not to hear oral evidence from children even where, as in this case, the child was a mature boy in his early teens.
4   [1977] 1 WLR 234 at 237.
5   As to which see JR Spencer and R Flin *The Evidence of Children* (2nd edn) (Blackstone Press, 1993) at ch 11, and R Flin 'Child Witnesses: The Psychological Evidence' (1988) 138 NLJ 608.
6   *The Law of Evidence* (2nd edn) (Sweet & Maxwell, 2002) at p 451.
7   R Flin 'Child Witnesses: The Psychological Evidence' (above).

and they sit down'; an eight-year-old child thought that a lawyer 'gives money to the poor'; and some children in a similar US study thought that a lawyer 'loans money', 'sits around', 'plays golf' or 'lies'[1].

The Children Act 1989 sought to overcome these difficulties, by abolishing the competency requirement and admitting the *unsworn* evidence of children, subject to a different test. This test, which formerly governed the admission of unsworn evidence of children of 'tender years' in *criminal* proceedings[2], is based on more general powers of understanding. It allows children with the requisite level of understanding to give unsworn evidence which is not dependent on appreciation of an oath. It provides that a child's evidence may be heard, notwithstanding the child's inability to understand the nature of an oath, where the court is of the opinion that:

'(a) he understands that it is his duty to speak the truth; and
(b) he has sufficient understanding to justify his evidence being heard.'[3]

This provision applies only where a child is, in fact, incapable of understanding an oath under the *Hayes* test. Thus, children may now conceivably give sworn *or* unsworn evidence in civil proceedings depending on their level of understanding. This test of competence in civil proceedings appears to be more stringent than the test in criminal proceedings in two respects. First, the requirement of 'understanding' seems to ask more of the child than the test of 'intelligibility' applying in the criminal law. According to Dennis[4], in the criminal context 'the court will be concerned only with the quality of the child's speech, whereas in civil proceedings the court may have to enquire into the level of the child's mind'. Secondly, in the civil but not the criminal context, the child concerned must still be capable of understanding the duty to tell the truth. Dennis speculates that this may lead to the exclusion of evidence of very young children in civil cases, which might be admitted in a criminal case. However, this may be counter-balanced to some extent by the admission of hearsay and other evidence whereby the evidence of those children may be heard more indirectly. It is younger children who are more likely to give evidence unsworn. There remains the question of the credibility or weight which ought to be attached to the evidence of particular child witnesses, but this is also an issue in relation to adults.

Other evidence in family proceedings

Hearsay
The key feature of civil proceedings involving children is now the disapplication of the hearsay rule, although under the Civil Evidence Act 1995 it has now been disapplied more generally in civil cases. This general rule of evidence, where it applies, renders inadmissible as proof of facts evidence given by someone as to what someone else said or did. If applied in children cases it could prevent the court from relying on evidence in welfare reports and the reports of children's guardians about what children said to the writer of the report, perhaps concerning incidents of abuse.

---

1   R Flin (above) at p 610.
2   Children and Young Persons Act 1933, s 38.
3   Section 96(1) and (2).
4   (Above) at p 457.

The rule was abolished in all *civil* proceedings affecting children[1] before its more general abolition in civil proceedings, the result being that the court can admit a wide range of documentary evidence[2] and simultaneously avert the need for the child to attend court and give oral evidence[3]. While the grounds for challenging the *admissibility* of hearsay have thus been removed, the *weight* to be given to hearsay evidence is a matter within the discretion of the judge, and it is even open to him to disregard it completely[4]. Such weight may well diminish in the case of second or even more remote hearsay. Where it is the child's hearsay evidence, the court will need to take into account factors such as the child's age, the context and circumstances in which the statement was made, the child's previous behaviour, etc. It may also take account of the child's opportunities to have acquired the information elsewhere, and any predilection he may have for fantasising or telling untruths. The courts have also taken the view that, in cases of alleged sexual abuse, the court should rarely be satisfied of the abuse on the balance of probabilities purely on the strength of an unsupported allegation by the child[5].

The rules admitting hearsay are very important in care and other public law proceedings. Prior to the Children Act 1989, care proceedings took place exclusively in the juvenile court – a specialised magistrates' court[6]. Magistrates, subject to limited exceptions, had to apply the hearsay rule and refuse to admit hearsay statements and documentary evidence, such as reports, as evidence of the facts to which they related. The *Review of Child Care Law* recommended an extension of the rules of civil evidence to care proceedings[7]. The broad effect of s 96 of the Children Act was to apply the new rules in *all* civil proceedings affecting children[8], including care proceedings.

The relaxation of the rules of evidence in children cases has other implications. In recent years the courts have made it clear that normal rules of evidence applicable in an adversarial legal system do not necessarily apply in children cases[9]. This is especially so regarding the disclosure of documents[10]. Thus,

---

1   Children (Admissibility of Hearsay Evidence) Order 1993, SI 1993/621, made under the Children Act, s 96(3).
2   Formerly this was largely proved by means of affidavits but these have now been displaced by written statements.
3   On the attendance of children in care proceedings, see pp 598 et seq above.
4   See *Re W (Minors) (Wardship: Evidence)* [1990] 1 FLR 203 and *R v B County Council ex parte P* [1991] 1 FLR 470.
5   Ibid.
6   Now replaced by the youth court. The civil side of the former juvenile court's work has now been taken over by the family proceedings court. On the implications of the change from the juvenile court to the youth court, see the research of C Ball 'Youth justice and the youth court – the end of a separate system?' [1995] CFLQ 196.
7   DHSS *Review of Child Care Law* (1985) at paras 16.30–16.38.
8   The rule is thus also disapplied in civil proceedings which fall outside the definition of family proceedings in the Children Act.
9   For a general discussion of these developments, see C Tapper 'Evidential privilege in cases involving children' [1997] CFLQ 1, L Mendoza 'Confidentiality in Child Proceedings' [1998] Fam Law 30, and J McEwan 'The privilege of parents and the protection of the child – where do priorities lie?' in C Bridge (ed) *Family Law Towards the Millennium: Essays for PM Bromley* (Butterworths, 1997) at ch 5.
10 The issue of disclosure has involved the courts in a delicate balancing exercise involving conflicting considerations of public policy. For particularly good illustrations of the difficult

parents are required to disclose to the court all the documents in their possession, including expert reports commissioned by them, even if they are not favourable to their case[1]. Likewise, the local authority must disclose to the parents all relevant documents in its possession[2].

Criminal proceedings

The three major issues relating to child witnesses in criminal proceedings have been identified as *competence, credibility* and *stress*[3]. Before considering these issues, the preliminary question arises, as it does in relation to civil proceedings, whether a child is a compellable witness in criminal proceedings. The general rule is that a child *can* be compelled to attend and give evidence in any criminal trial. A child's failure to give evidence would, at least in theory, amount to contempt of court unless the child was aged under 10 and thus below the age of criminal responsibility. But, again, in deciding whether to issue a witness summons against the child, the court must balance the interests of justice and fairness to the accused against the possible detriment to the child in having to appear.

In *R v Highbury Corner Magistrates' Court ex parte D*[4] the defendant to an assault charge relating to this former cohabitant sought to have a witness summons issued against their nine-year-old son who saw the incident. The materiality of the witness was accepted but the metropolitan magistrate refused to issue the summons taking the view that the detriment to the boy's welfare if he were obliged to give evidence outweighed the interests of the defendant. His judgment was set aside in judicial review proceedings on the basis that it was premature. The balancing act, it was held, should be performed at the court of trial when the moment arose and a decision had to be taken on whether to call the child. Schiemann LJ pointed out that, by that stage, the picture may have become clearer since something might, or might not, be admitted. It is also evident from the tenor of the judgment that the court in criminal cases should take into account not merely the welfare of children but also their *duties* as citizens to society to an extent appropriate to their age and understanding[5]. This suggests that a witness summons is perhaps more likely to be issued against a child in criminal than in civil proceedings. Fortin has drawn attention to the inconsistency between what she sees as the 'extreme paternalism' of the courts in protecting children from giving evidence in care proceedings and parental disputes and their insistence that children give evidence in criminal trials[6].

---

balance which must be struck and how the courts go about it, see *A County Council v W and Others (Disclosure)* [1997] 1 FLR 574 and *Re R (Disclosure)* [1998] 1 FLR 433.

1 See *Oxfordshire County Council v M* [1994] 2 All ER 269 and *Re L (Police Investigation: Privilege)* [1996] 1 FLR 731.
2 *R v Hampshire County Council, ex parte K* [1990] 2 All ER 129.
3 R Flin 'Child Witnesses: The Psychological Evidence' (1988) 138 NLJ 608.
4 [1997] 1 FLR 683.
5 On the concept of children's duties, see Chapter 3. See also *Re F (Specific Issue: Child Interview)* [1995] 1 FLR 819 and the remarks of Lord Donaldson in *Re R (A Minor) (Wardship: Witness in Criminal Proceedings)* [1991] 2 FLR 95 on which the court relied.
6 J Fortin *Children's Rights and the Developing Law* (2nd edn) (Butterworths, 2003) at p 530. There is also a useful discussion of the extent to which, and the basis upon which, in practice, the CPS takes account of children's concerns in appearing at criminal trials.

Competence

There was, originally, only one way in which a child under 14 years of age could give evidence in civil proceedings (ie sworn). Now, as discussed earlier, there are two ways (ie sworn and unsworn). Confusingly, the converse is true of criminal proceedings. For, whereas before 1991 the child under 14 years of age could give evidence in two ways (sworn and unsworn)[1], now there is only one way (unsworn)[2].

Under the amended provision introduced by the Criminal Justice Act 1991[3] it was feared that the statutory test might operate harshly to exclude the evidence of young children who were incapable of understanding the abstract concepts involved in the duty to tell the truth[4]. These concerns were met by a further amendment to the Criminal Justice Act 1988 made by the Criminal Justice and Public Order Act 1994[5]. Under that provision, an intelligibility test was introduced to govern the issue of competence as follows:

'A child's evidence shall be received unless it appears to the court that the child is incapable of giving intelligible testimony.'

The Court of Appeal in *R v Hampshire*[6] has agreed with the view of John Spencer[7] that this 'appears to be a less rigorous test of competence than that derived from s 38 of the 1933 Act' in that 'it appears to remove the need to determine on a question of competence, whether a child knows the difference between truth and a lie and the importance of speaking the truth'.

The new requirement prescribed no minimum age for competence so that, in principle, a child of any age might pass the test. In *DPP v M*[8] the Divisional Court allowed the prosecution's appeal by way of case stated where, on appeal to the Crown Court, that court had refused to view the video-taped evidence of a four-year-old girl (the victim of an alleged indecent assault by a 12-year-old boy). The Crown Court had taken the view that by reason of her age alone she was not a witness on whom they should rely. The Divisional Court held that the statutory test of intelligibility was mandatory and that the child's evidence *must* be received whatever her age, unless it appeared to the court that she was incapable of giving intelligible testimony. There was no wider discretion to refuse to receive it. In order to make this assessment, the judge should watch any video-taped interviews or ask various general questions of the child, or both, to determine whether she was able to understand questions and to answer them in a coherent and comprehensible manner. In this case, the extreme youth of the complainant properly raised concern as to her competence but it was not of itself conclusive.

It has also been held by the Divisional Court in *G v DPP*[9] that whether or not a child is capable of giving intelligible evidence is a simple test well within the

---

1 Children and Young Persons Act 1933, s 38.
2 Criminal Justice Act 1991, s 52, inserting s 33A into the Criminal Justice Act 1988.
3 Ibid.
4 See, particularly, J Spencer 'Children's Evidence and the Criminal Justice Bill' (1990) 140 NLJ 1750.
5 Section 33A(2A) of the 1988 Act, inserted by Sch 9, para 33 to the 1994 Act.
6 [1995] 2 All ER 1019.
7 *Archbold News* (1994) issue 6. See also M Childs 'Children's Evidence in Criminal Cases' [1996] CFLQ 81.
8 [1997] 2 All ER 749.
9 [1997] 2 All ER 755.

capacity of a judge or magistrate and that it does not require any input from an expert.

The question of competency in criminal proceedings is now governed by the Youth Justice and Criminal Evidence Act 1999[1]. The Act incorporates a general presumption of competence. All persons are (whatever their age) competent to give evidence at any stage of criminal proceedings[2]. This may be rebutted in the case of an individual, however:

> 'if it appears to the court that he is not a person who is able to –
> (a)   understand questions put to him as a witness, and
> (b)   give answers to them which can be understood.'[3]

This is effectively a re-enactment of the test in the Criminal Justice Act 1988 as interpreted by judicial decisions and is not intended to change the law on children's competence. The former provisions are repealed but the effect of this is simply to apply to *adults* the test of competence which had previously been applied only to children.

Where the issue of competence of a child is raised by either a party or the court, the onus to prove competence on the balance of probabilities will be on the party calling the witness and will be for the court to determine[4]. For the purpose of assessing competence, the court must treat the witness as having the benefit of any 'special measures directions' which the court has given, or proposes to give[5]. Thus, for example, a child's competence may be determined bearing in mind that the child may give pre-recorded video-evidence or evidence by live-link, where that child might not have been considered competent if the evidence had to be given in a formal court environment. Any hearing to determine competence will take place in the absence of a jury (if there is one)[6], expert evidence may be received[7] and any questioning of the witness by the court must take place in the presence of the parties[8].

The Act preserves the existing rule that a child under the age of 14 may not give sworn evidence[9]. For sworn evidence the child must be older than this and it must be shown that 'he has a sufficient appreciation of the solemnity of the occasion and of the particular responsibility to tell the truth which is involved in taking an oath'[10]. Those over 14 who are able to give 'intelligible' testimony will be presumed to have a sufficient appreciation of those matters if no evidence is adduced to the contrary[11]. The Act also preserves the rule that those under 14 (and others) who are competent to give evidence but not able to take an oath may give it unsworn[12]. A child giving unsworn evidence will receive an admonition from the court in the following terms: 'Tell us all you can remember of what

---

1   For a comprehensive analysis of the Act, see D Birch and R Leng *Blackstone's Guide to the Youth Justice and Criminal Evidence Act 1999* (2000).
2   Youth Justice and Criminal Evidence Act 1999, s 53(1).
3   Ibid, s 53(3).
4   Ibid, s 54(1) and (2).
5   'Special measures directions' are governed by ss 19 et seq of the Act and discussed at pp 609 et seq below.
6   Ibid, s 54(4).
7   Ibid, s 54(5).
8   Ibid, s 54(6).
9   Ibid, s 55(2)(a).
10   Ibid, s 55(2)(b).
11   Ibid, s 55(3).
12   Ibid, s 56(1) and (2).

happened. Don't make anything up or leave anything out. This is very important.'[1]

Credibility

The next question is, having admitted the evidence of a child, how credible is it? At common law, the judge was required to warn the jury about convicting on the strength of a child's uncorroborated evidence. Similar warnings were, until recent years, given in sexual cases whether the alleged victim was a child or an adult.

The Pigot Committee, reporting in 1989[2], was highly critical of the corroboration rules in sex cases and recommended their abolition. It disapproved of the underlying assumption that women or children were more likely to be untruthful than the ordinary experience and knowledge of jurors might suggest. The corroboration rule as it applied to children was grounded in the notion that children have a propensity for imagining things, lack moral responsibility, have weaker powers of observation and recollection, and are more likely to be open to suggestion. On the last point, similar claims were made for many years in family proceedings and have been used as a reason for discounting, or treating with suspicion, the views of children on residence or contact questions[3]. These claims did not appear to be substantiated by the psychological evidence. Thus, it was asserted by some psychologists[4] that moral understanding is not proved to be a reliable predictor of honesty in *adults* (and hence should not be seen as such for children either), and that moral knowledge should not be equated with intelligence. Moreover, it was said that comparisons between children and adults were often founded on an exaggerated view of adult competence.

The Criminal Justice Act 1988[5] went some way towards meeting these objections, by abolishing the corroboration rule in relation to children. It is provided that:

> 'Any requirement whereby at a trial on indictment it is obligatory for the court to give the jury a warning about convicting the accused on the uncorroborated evidence of a child is abrogated in relation to cases where such a warning is required by reason only that the evidence is the evidence of a child.'[6]

The effect of this reform is that it is at least possible for a conviction to be sustained solely on the basis of the unsworn evidence of a single child, and it also allows the unsworn evidence of one child to be corroborated by the evidence of another child. The 1988 Act did not, however, strike at the rule requiring an official warning regarding the uncorroborated evidence of a *sexual* complainant. In many cases the child might well be the victim of a sexual offence. However, the former mandatory requirement of a warning in sexual cases was abolished by s 32 of the Criminal Justice and Public Order Act 1994.

---

1   For further discussion of the background to this admonition, see Birch and Leng (above) at p 140.
2   *The Report of the Advisory Group on Video Evidence* (Home Office, 1989), as to which see, generally, J McEwan 'In the Box or on the Box? The Pigot Report and Child Witnesses' [1990] Crim LR 363.
3   See Chapter 4 above.
4   See, for example, R Flin 'Child Witnesses: The Psychological Evidence' (1988) 138 NLJ 608.
5   Section 34(2).
6   The provision applies only to 'trials on indictment'. *Quaere* whether magistrates have to apply it by implication.

The effect of the reforms is to remove the obligatory judicial warnings and to leave the question of what warning (if any) is appropriate to the judge's discretion. The Court of Appeal (Criminal Division)[1] has said that whether the judge chooses to give a warning and in what terms will depend on the circumstances of the case, the issues raised, the context and quality of the witness's evidence and whether there is any evidential basis for suggesting that the evidence of the witnesses may be unreliable. Thus Dennis[2] suggests that where there is evidence supporting an allegation that the child's evidence may be fabricated or a fantasy on the part of the child, the judge might think it appropriate to direct the jury to view the child's evidence with caution and to look for supporting evidence. Moreover, where such a warning is given the judge should give it as part of his general review of the evidence and his comments to the jury on how they should evaluate it. Any warning should not be delivered in the traditional manner used when corroboration warnings were mandatory.

Stress and special measures directions

The background

Anyone who has been a witness in court will know that it can be a stressful and worrying experience. These natural anxieties can be magnified in the case of children to such an extent that they may break down in the witness box or become unable to continue at all. Many of the cases will involve highly distasteful sexual allegations. The prospect of the child having to relive the experience in the presence of the alleged offender will be harrowing. It is one reason why many prosecutions for sexual offences against children have in the past either failed to get off the ground at all, collapsed, or resulted in acquittals.

The courts have over the years tried to mitigate the problem through a number of ad hoc devices. As long ago as 1919, in *Smellie's* case[3], the defendant was required by the judge to sit on the stairs leading out of the dock, out of sight of his 11-year-old daughter whom he was alleged to have beaten for stealing[4]. The Court of Appeal dismissed Smellie's appeal, rejecting arguments by defence counsel that the girl might be inclined to say untrue things which she would not have said in her father's presence, and that the jury might be adversely influenced by his removal. Lord Coleridge LCJ laconically responded that there was nothing to prevent the judge from securing the ends of justice by removing the accused from a witness he might intimidate.

In *R v X*[5], the Court of Appeal approved the use of wooden screens to conceal the victims from the defendants during the victims' evidence. In this case, the children in question were alleged to have been abused 'in almost every permutation of sexual perversion'. Counsel could plainly see the children, and the judge expressly warned the jury not to allow the mere presence of the screen to prejudice them in any way against the defendants. In refusing leave to appeal, the court emphasised that the trial judge had to see that justice was done. This meant that he had to ensure that the system operated fairly, not only to the defendants,

---

1 *R v Makanjuola; R v Easton* [1995] 3 All ER 730.
2 (Above) at p 456.
3 (1919) 14 Cr App R 128.
4 The actual conviction was for 'assaulting, ill-treating and neglecting' his daughter.
5 *R v X; R v Y; R v Z* [1990] Crim LR 515.

but also to the prosecution and the witnesses. It was a matter of the balance of fairness, and the judge had been right to conclude that the necessity of trying to ensure that the children were able to give evidence outweighed any possible prejudice to the defendants.

In *R v Smith*[1], the Court of Appeal considered the balance which has to be struck between the need to protect a child witness and the interests of justice and possible prejudice to the defendant. The accused was convicted of rape and gross indecency with a 12-year-old girl. He appealed against his conviction on the basis of alleged procedural irregularities at the trial. During her evidence, a social worker had sat beside the girl. When the girl broke into tears the social worker had comforted her and talked quietly to her. After lunch, and while the jury were present but before the judge returned, the complainant had left court through the judge's door accompanied by, among others, the judge's clerk and the social worker. It transpired that she had been taken to a lavatory to avoid possible confrontation with the defendant's relatives who were outside court.

Dismissing the appeal, the Court of Appeal held that it was the judge's duty to order a procedure which reduces the strain on child witnesses without prejudicing the interests of the defendant. In this case it was clear that there had been no contact between the child witness and the judge and any allegations of procedural irregularity should have been made by counsel at the trial. The court went on to say that in future it was important that anyone providing comfort or support to a child witness should not talk to the child while she is giving evidence and that this should be made clear publicly. To do otherwise would arouse suspicions that something was being said about the evidence. It was therefore desirable that anyone performing that role should say as little as possible to the witness and preferably nothing.

Video technology

The advent of video technology has increased the options open to the courts and was the subject of a report by the Pigot Committee in 1989[2]. Before that, the Criminal Justice Act 1988[3] allowed children under 14 years of age to give evidence from outside the courtroom via closed-circuit television, in sex, cruelty and assault cases. This age-limit was raised to accommodate those under 15 years for offences of violence, and those under 18 years in sex cases, by the Criminal Justice Act 1991[4]. The argument was that the live television link ameliorates the child's

---

1   [1994] Crim LR 458.
2   For some of the earlier writings on the introduction of video technology see *The Report of the Advisory Group on Video Evidence* (Home Office, 1989). See also Department of Health *Memorandum of Good Practice in Video Recorded Interviews with Child Witnesses for Criminal Proceedings* (1992). See also: JR Spencer 'Child Witnesses, Video-Technology and the Law of Evidence' [1987] Crim LR 76; G Smith 'Good practice or yet another hurdle: video recording children's statements' (1993) 5 JCL 21; J Aldridge and K Freshwater 'The preparation of child witnesses' (1993) 5 JCL 25; and J McEwan 'Where the prosecution witness is a child: the memorandum of good practice' (1993) 5 JCL 16. For a discussion of the implications of video technology for *civil* cases, see PM Smith 'Child Witnesses: Implications for Civil Proceedings' [1993] Fam Law 110. For later evaluations of the video-link facilities, see G Davis, C Wilson, R Mitchell and J Milson *Videotaping Children's Evidence: An Evaluation* (Home Office, 1995), *The Child, the Court and the Video* (Social Services Inspectorate, 1994), and H Wescott and J Jones *Perspectives on the Memorandum* (Arena, 1997).
3   Section 32.
4   Section 54(7).

ordeal without an unacceptable risk of prejudice to the defendant. Although the system is recognised to have drawbacks for children[1], there is some evidence that children are less likely to break down under cross-examination and less likely to refuse to give evidence in the first place[2]. The system was reinforced by another provision in the Criminal Justice Act 1991 which prohibited cross-examination by an unrepresented defendant of a child under 14 years, where the offence was one of violence, or a child under 17 years, where it was a sexual offence[3]. The child might be either the victim or simply a witness to the commission of the alleged offence.

The Home Office and Department of Health issued a Memorandum of Good Practice relating the use of video-recorded interviews with children[4]. It was held in *G v DPP*[5] that where the guidelines set out in the memorandum are not followed the evidence of young children may be dangerously suspect. This might result in the evidence not being admitted at all or, depending on the circumstances, the breaches of good practice might merely go to weight rather than to admissibility. A video-recording may be admitted in whole or in part. Where part of it is excluded, it must be edited by the person seeking to introduce it into the proceedings[6].

The drawback with the provision for video-recorded evidence was that the child was required to be available for cross-examination at the trial, if necessary, by live television link. This was a very considerable dilution of what Pigot proposed, since the ordeal of cross-examination is, depending on how extensive the cross-examination is, much worse than examination-in-chief by a supportive and well-disposed lawyer.

The Youth Justice and Criminal Evidence Act 1999 – special measures directions
The Youth Justice and Criminal Evidence Act 1999 introduced a wide range of measures designed to assist vulnerable and intimidated witnesses in giving evidence in criminal proceedings[7]. The Act followed a Home Office report, *Speaking Up for Justice*, published in June 1998[8] and is concerned with other categories of vulnerable witnesses apart from children, as well as those eligible for assistance on the grounds of fear or distress about testifying. We are concerned here only with children.

The Act lists a total of eight special measures which may be directed by the court and which may be directed singly or in combination. The first six measures may be

---

1   By increasing their feeling of isolation, by being intimidated or distracted by the camera or by having difficulty concentrating on a face or voice speaking over a television monitor.
2   G Davies and E Noon *An evaluation of the live-link for child witnesses* (Home Office, 1991).
3   Criminal Justice Act 1991, s 55.
4   *Memorandum of Good Practice on Video Recorded Interviews with Child Witnesses for Criminal Proceedings* (HMSO, 1992). The Court of Appeal made it clear in *Re D (Child Abuse: Interviews)* [1998] 2 FLR 10 that, although the guidelines for interviewing children in the *Memorandum of Good Practice* were primarily designed for criminal trials, the underlying principles were applicable also in care and private law family proceedings.
5   [1997] 3 All ER 755.
6   *Practice Note: Video Recordings of Children's Evidence* [1992] 3 All ER 909.
7   See Birch and Leng (above) at chs 4 and 5, and Dennis (above) at ch 15, especially at pp 514–524. See also D Birch 'A Better Deal for Vulnerable Witnesses' [2000] Crim LR 223 and L Hoyano 'Striking a Balance between the Rights of Defendants and Vulnerable Witnesses' (2000) Crim LR 948.
8   *Speaking Up for Justice, the Report of the Home Office Interdepartmental Working Group on the Treatment of Vulnerable and Intimidated Witnesses in the Criminal Justice System* (1998).

directed in relation to other vulnerable witnesses[1] as well as children, but the final two relate only to witnesses under the age of 17.

The special measures
Special measures in brief are as follows.

(1) **Screens**[2]
   Screens may be used to shield the witness from the defendant. As noted earlier, this practice has been used by the courts for many years. The screen or other arrangement must not, however, prevent the witness from being able to see, and be seen by, the judge, justices, or jury, legal representatives or any interpreter or other person appointed to assist the witness[3].

(2) **Evidence by live link**[4]
   This enables the witness to give evidence during the trial from outside the courtroom by means of a televised link to the courtroom. This may take place either within the court building or outside it. The witness must be able to see, and be seen by, those mentioned in (1) above[5]. The live link has been used especially for cross-examination of child witnesses.

(3) **Evidence given in private**[6]
   The court may direct the exclusion of members of the public and press (except for one named person to represent the press) in proceedings relating to a sexual offence or where there are reasonable grounds for believing that there is a risk of intimidation of the witness[7]. The accused, legal representatives and any interpreter or other person appointed to assist the witness may not be excluded[8].

(4) **Removal of wigs and gowns**[9]
   The court may direct that wigs and gowns be dispensed with by judges and barristers during the giving of the witness's evidence.

(5) **Video-recorded evidence-in-chief**[10]
   The court may direct that a video-recording of an interview with the witness be admitted as evidence-in-chief of the witness[11]. It will not be admitted, however, if the court is of the opinion, having regard to all the circumstances of the case, that in the interests of justice the recording or part of it should not

---

1   The Act (ss 16 and 17) identifies four other categories: witnesses suffering from mental disorder; witnesses significantly impaired in relation to intelligence and social functioning; physically disabled witnesses; and witnesses suffering from fear or distress in relation to testifying in the case.
2   Youth Justice and Criminal Evidence Act 1999, s 23.
3   Ibid, s 23(2).
4   Ibid, s 24.
5   Ibid, s 24(8).
6   Ibid, s 25.
7   Ibid, s 25(4).
8   Ibid, s 25(2).
9   Ibid, s 26.
10 Ibid, s 27.
11 Ibid, s 27(1).

be admitted[1]. Thus, a recording might be excluded if it was of poor quality or, more importantly, if the rules of evidence had been violated in making it – for example, by the interviewer asking too many leading questions of a child[2]. The court must balance any possible prejudice to the accused against the desirability of showing the whole or part of the interview[3].

(6) **Video-recorded cross-examination or re-examination**[4]

The Act makes video-recorded cross-examination or re-examination admissible where there has been a direction for a video-recording to be admitted as evidence-in-chief. Again the video may be excluded if the rules have not been followed in making it. Sometimes known as 'Full Pigot', this is the most significant of the measures introduced by the 1999 legislation. It overcomes the restriction in previous legislation that video-evidence was limited to evidence-in-chief and that the witness had to be available for cross-examination at the trial, if necessary by live television link.

(7) **Examination of the witness through an intermediary**[5]

This is an innovation of the 1999 legislation which applies only to witnesses under the age of 17 and those suffering from incapacity. It enables the court to appoint an interpreter or other person to assist the witness in giving evidence in court.

(8) **Aids to communication**[6]

This enables the court to direct that a witness may, while giving evidence, be provided with 'such device as the court considers appropriate with a view to enabling questions or answers to be communicated to or by the witness despite any disability or disorder or other impairment which the witness has suffered from'. This again applies to witnesses on grounds of age or incapacity.

Eligibility for special measures directions

As noted above, the 1999 Act divides witnesses into two categories for the purposes of eligibility for special measures directions. We are concerned only with the rules which govern the first category, namely those eligible for assistance on the grounds of age or incapacity[7]. Those under the age of 17 at the time of the hearing are automatically eligible for assistance[8]. The general test or 'primary rule' which the court must apply in exercising its discretion on whether it should direct special measures is set out in s 19(2). Where the court is satisfied that a witness is eligible for assistance it must 'determine whether any of the special measures available in relation to the witness (or a combination of them) would, in its opinion,

---

1 Youth Justice and Criminal Evidence Act 1999, s 27(2).
2 The Department of Health issued a *Memorandum of Good Practice in Video Recorded Interviews with Child Witnesses* in 1992. This has now been superseded by the Home Office Guidance, *Achieving Best Evidence in Criminal Proceedings: Guidance for Vulnerable or Intimidated Witnesses including Children* (Home Office, 2001). For a brief summary of the Guidance, see R Langdale 'Children's Evidence in Care (sic) Proceedings' [2003] Fam Law 269.
3 Youth Justice and Criminal Evidence Act 1999, s 27(3).
4 Ibid, s 28.
5 Ibid, s 29.
6 Ibid, s 30.
7 Ibid, s 16.
8 Ibid, s 16(1)(a).

be likely to improve the quality of evidence given by the witness' and then go on to direct them as appropriate.

This primary rule is, however, augmented by special provisions in s 21 in the case of child witnesses which have the broad effect of creating presumptions that special measures will be directed in certain types of proceedings. The scheme of s 21 has been described as 'labyrinthine'[1] and what follows is only a brief description of the essential distinctions drawn in the Act.

Child witnesses are effectively divided by the Act into two categories – those 'in need of special protection' and other child witnesses. The first category of children in need of special protection is further sub-divided depending on the type of offences involved in the proceedings. Where the offence concerned is a sexual offence[2] there is a strong presumption in favour of special measures. Here the court must apply a primary rule that both the child's evidence-in-chief (under s 27) and cross-examination should be by way of video-recording (s 28). The court does not have to apply the normal rule in s 19(2) which would require it to evaluate whether this would be likely to improve the quality of the child's evidence. This is presumed to be the case. The only qualifications to this rule are that such measures are available and that the interests of justice do not dictate that the pre-recorded evidence should not be admitted. Where this results in video-recordings not being admitted, the court is required to direct that the child's evidence at trial be given by live-link[3]. It must then also apply s 19(2) and consider whether any other special measures should be directed as likely to improve the quality of the child's evidence.

The second category of children deemed to be 'in need of special protection' are those involved in proceedings relating to the major non-sexual offences against the person[4]. Here a similar rule to that which applies in relation to sexual offences also applies except that the use of the video-recording is optional rather than mandatory. The normal course will therefore be for evidence-in-chief to be by video-recording but cross-examination via live-link unless, applying s 19(2), the court decides that a video-recording would be likely to improve the quality of the child's evidence.

Outside these cases where the child is deemed to be in need of special protection, the primary rule – that evidence-in-chief should be given by video-recording and cross-examination by live-link – will not apply where the court is satisfied that it would not be likely to maximise the quality of the child's evidence[5].

---

1   Dennis (above) at p 516.
2   As defined in Youth Justice and Criminal Evidence Act 1999, s 35(3)(a).
3   Ibid, s 21(3)(b).
4   Defined in ibid, s 35(3)(b)–(d) to include kidnapping, false imprisonment, child abduction and 'any other offence involving an assault on, or injury or a threat of injury'.
5   Ibid, s 21(4)(c).

Chapter 14

CHILDREN AND THE CRIMINAL LAW

INTRODUCTION

This chapter explores the relevance of the criminal law to children or, more accurately, 'children and young persons'. The civil law does not distinguish between children of various ages as a matter of status. Anyone below the age of majority is a 'child' or a 'minor'[1]. This is not the case with the criminal law where an important distinction is made between minors under the age of 14 years who are known as 'children' and those over 14 but under 18 years who are known as 'young persons'[2]. Collectively, they are referred to as 'juveniles' and sometimes as 'young offenders', although the former 'juvenile court' was renamed the 'youth court' by the Criminal Justice Act 1991[3]. That Act also introduced a very significant reform by bringing within the jurisdiction of the youth court young persons aged 17 years who had previously, although still minors, been treated as *adults* by the criminal law. One of the principal distinctions between 'children' and 'young persons' was that it had been intended, under the Children and Young Persons Act 1969, to abolish criminal prosecutions of 'children' and, instead, to deal with young offenders below the age of 14 years through the more welfare-orientated care procedures. In fact, this never happened[4] for a variety of reasons, some of them political[5]. The distinction is thus not as important as it might have been, but it remains of significance in a number of respects, not least until 1998 in determining criminal responsibility.

It is impossible, in a general introductory work of this nature, to do justice to the multifarious aspects of the criminal justice system as it applies to children and young persons[6]. The aim here is rather to provide an understanding of the various ways in which the criminal law treats children *differently* from adults. It should

---

1   There are, of course, many age-related rules which distinguish between children of different ages for specific purposes.

2   The principal legislation is the Children and Young Persons Acts of 1933, 1963 and 1969, the Criminal Justice Act 1991, the Criminal Justice and Public Order Act 1994, the Crime and Disorder Act 1998 and the Youth Justice and Criminal Evidence Act 1999.

3   Criminal Justice Act 1991, s 70, and see below.

4   Children and Young Persons Act 1969, s 4, now repealed by s 72 of the Criminal Justice Act 1991.

5   For a succinct discussion of the vacillations of policy in juvenile justice, see C Ball 'Young Offenders and the Youth Court' [1992] Crim LR 277, especially at 278–283. For more recent discussions, see L Gelsthorpe 'Recent Changes in Youth Justice Policy in England and Wales' in I Weijers and A Duff *Punishing Juveniles: Principle and Critique* (Hart Publishing, 2002) at ch 3, and C Ball 'Youth Justice? Half a Century of Responses to Youth Offending' [2004] Crim LR 167.

6   See, generally, N Padfield 'Juvenile Justice' in M McConville and G Wilson (eds) *The Handbook of the Criminal Justice Process* (Oxford University Press, 2002) at ch 22; J Fortin *Children's Rights and the Developing Law* (2nd edn) (Butterworths, 2003) at chs 17 and 18; K Doolin 'Youth Justice' in S Uglow *Criminal Justice* (2nd edn) (Sweet & Maxwell, 2002) at ch 11. For a theoretical rights-based perspective on juvenile crime, see MDA Freeman *The Rights and Wrongs of Children* (Frances Pinter, 1983). For more historical perspectives, see J Fionda 'Youth Justice'

always be remembered that children are *people* or citizens and, as such, like everyone else, enjoy the protection of the ordinary criminal law. Conversely, and subject to major qualifications, they are also responsible for their own actions under the criminal law. Children, in the context of criminal prosecution, also have human rights as do adults. These dual ideas of *protection* and *responsibility* are the theme of this chapter, and they are also very much a feature of the *civil* law, which is examined in the next chapter.

The differential treatment of children and adults is a pervasive feature of English criminal law and procedure. Thus, to take *protection* first, there are numerous special offences which relate only to children. Further, those offences which apply more generally to children *and* adults, particularly sexual offences, often have special features in their application to children, which reflect their greater vulnerability. The law and procedure governing the *responsibility* of juveniles is characterised by rules which distinguish them from adults at every stage of the criminal process. The criminal responsibility of 'children' has been determined differently: different factors influence the decision whether to prosecute; there are special protections for children where the police are carrying out their investigations; there is segregation of children and adults while in court or in custody; and, if a finding of guilt is made, the disposal options open to the courts are markedly different in the case of juvenile offenders.

This chapter will endeavour to highlight some of these more important features of the criminal justice system. The chapter begins by looking at the *protection* side of the system. It then looks at the other side, describing first the process of determining *responsibility* or liability for criminal acts, and then examining the criminal process for dealing with juvenile offenders.

PROTECTION

This section is concerned with crimes *against* children which, for the purposes of exposition, can conveniently be put into three categories: those which relate to violence and physical harm; sexual offences; and special offences designed to eradicate or control activities which are thought to be harmful to children. There is a good deal of overlap between these categories. Sexual offences, for example, frequently involve violence and physical harm. Many of the special offences in the third category also involve physical harm but are distinctive in that they are ad hoc legislative responses to particular dangers for children which arise from time to time.

An issue which needs to be confronted immediately is the fact that a high proportion of crimes against children are committed by members of the same family or household. Most instances of child abuse or neglect also involve criminal offences so that, to some extent, child protection agencies face a choice about whether to prosecute or to invoke the civil remedies[1]. In some cases, it may be necessary to take action on both fronts. Until recently, the prospects of bringing a

---

in J Fionda (ed) *Legal Concepts of Childhood* (Hart Publishing, 2001) and HK Bevan *Child Law* (Butterworths, 1989) at chs 9, 10, 12 and 13. For a concise account of the procedures relating to the trial of juveniles, see J Sprack *A Practical Approach to Criminal Procedure* (10th edn) (Oxford University Press, 2004).

1   See Chapters 11 and 12 above.

successful prosecution, especially in cases of sexual abuse, were substantially hindered by the restrictive rules regarding children's evidence. The reforms in this area[1] now render prosecution a more realistic option and it has been argued that in some cases prosecution may serve to remove an abuser (rather than the child) from the family home – and is, in that sense, consistent with the thinking in the Children Act 1989[2].

On the other hand, the Childen Act supports the primary responsibility of parents to raise children, and the principle that the relationship between children and parents should be fostered, except where this is outweighed by considerations of harm to the child. In many cases, child abuse will be the result of stress on parents who themselves have inadequate family backgrounds and who lack sufficient understanding of child development or basic child care techniques. In cases like these, social work support and education may be a more appropriate response than either prosecution or care proceedings[3]. It may also be in the child's best interests for the family unit to be preserved, despite the instances of abuse, and for residential or foster-care to be avoided. In other cases, the abuse may be so serious or abhorrent as to necessitate a prosecution in the public interest. In such cases, it may, in any event, be difficult to conceive of any possible benefit to the child in preserving his 'relationship' with the adult concerned. The broad question, in any given case, must be whether the beneficial consequences of criminal proceedings are likely to outweigh the potential harm to the child and the family[4].

Violent crimes and physical harm

Homicide

The law governing murder and manslaughter applies just as much to child victims as it does to adult victims[5]. However, there are two features in relation to children which deserve special attention. These are deaths of infants within a short time of birth, and deaths of children, of whatever age, as a result of neglect or omission.

Childbirth and the law of homicide

A charge of murder or manslaughter may only be brought in relation to 'any reasonable creature in rerum natura'[6] or, in other words, a human being. There

---

1 See Chapter 13 above.
2 C Cobley 'Child Abuse, Child Protection and the Criminal Law' (1992) 4 JCL 78. The removal of the alleged abuser is possible under the powers to add 'exclusion requirements' to EPOs and interim care orders under Part IV of the Family Law Act 1996, and this may well represent a better alternative than prosecution in some cases. See Chapter 12.
3 See, eg, JG Hall and DF Martin 'Crimes Against Children' (1992) 142 NLJ 902. See also A Wilcznski and A Morris 'Parents who kill their children' [1993] 1 Crim LR 31, and R Mackay 'The consequences of killing very young children' [1993] 1 Crim LR 21.
4 See, for example, C Cobley's argument in 'Child Abuse, Child Protection and the Criminal Law' (1992) 4 JCL 78 at 80, that prosecutions in cases of intra-familial sexual abuse may not always be justified either in the public interest or in the interests of the child victim.
5 For a general analysis of the law of homicide, see Smith and Hogan *Criminal Law* (10th edn) (Butterworths, 2002) at chs 13 and 14, and MJ Allen *Textbook on Criminal Law* (7th edn) (Oxford University Press, 2003) at ch 9. For an incisive academic critique of the underlying principles, see A Ashworth *Principles of Criminal Law* (4th edn) (Oxford University Press, 2003) at ch 7. For its more specific application to child victims, see HK Bevan *Child Law* (Butterworths, 1989) at ch 9, paras 9.06–9.33.
6 Coke, 3 Inst 47.

can be some difficult line-drawing for these purposes. The essential test is that the child should have 'an existence independent of its mother'. This involves expulsion from the mother's body, an independent circulation and breathing after birth[1]. Any killing of a foetus before this constitutes (if anything) the offence of child destruction or falls within the abortion laws. Detailed discussion of the status of the 'unborn child' and the criminal law is beyond the scope of the present work[2].

On the other hand, there may be liability for the homicide of a child where the injury is inflicted on the foetus before birth, the child is born alive and then subsequently dies as a result, at least in part, of the injury. The Court of Appeal so held in *Attorney-General's Reference (No 3 of 1994)*[3] through an ingenious use of the doctrine of transferred malice[4]. In this case, the accused had stabbed his girlfriend, who was 26 weeks' pregnant, cutting the abdomen of the foetus. The child was born prematurely, survived 120 days and then died as a result of stress from operations and immaturity. The accused was acquitted on a charge of murder by direction of the trial judge. The Court of Appeal held that this direction was wrong since the foetus could be regarded as part of the mother's body. The 'malice' towards the mother could thus be transferred to the child at the point where the child was born and became an independent person. An intention to cause serious harm to the mother was an intention to cause serious harm to part of the mother. This could be transferred and there was no requirement that the person to whom it was transferred had to be in being at the time of infliction of the injury. The House of Lords[5] subsequently rejected the application of the doctrine of transferred malice in the circumstances of this case, but held that liability could instead lie in constructive manslaughter. The mother and foetus were to be regarded as 'two distinct organisms living symbiotically, not a single organism with two aspects'. On the other hand, the child, once born, could be regarded as falling within the defendant's mens rea when he stabbed the mother. The decision appears somewhat strained in terms of principle in order to arrive at what was thought to be the right conclusion on policy grounds[6]. In particular, the House declined to hold that murder, rather than manslaughter, could be an appropriate charge.

Where a child was killed by his mother within a short time of birth, there was a traditional reluctance on the part of juries to convict her of murder, and public and professional disapproval of treating these cases as ordinary murders. Many such cases arose, historically, through the fear of unmarried mothers of the stigma of giving birth to an illegitimate child. The special offence of infanticide exists, in essence, to reduce what would otherwise be murder to the equivalent of manslaughter. The offence is committed in the following circumstances:

---

1   For further discussion of the point, see Smith and Hogan (above) at pp 354–356. See also the discussion of the offence of concealment of birth under s 60 of the Offences Against the Person Act 1861, which essentially makes it an offence to conceal the dead body of a child after birth: ibid at pp 391–392.

2   But see ibid at pp 398–409.

3   [1996] 2 FLR 1. For commentary, see J Keown 'Homicide, Fetuses and Appendages' (1996) CLJ 207.

4   On the doctrine of transferred malice, see Smith and Hogan (above) at pp 90–92, and for commentary on this case, see ibid at p 355.

5   [1997] 3 WLR 421.

6   See J Keown 'Homicide by Prenatal Assault Revisited' (1998) CLJ 240.

'Where a woman by any wilful act or omission causes the death of her child being a child under the age of twelve months, but at the time of the act or omission the balance of her mind was disturbed by reason of her not having fully recovered from the effect of giving birth to the child or by reason of the effect of lactation consequent upon the birth of the child.'[1]

There are difficulties in justifying the retention of the offence in the modern law[2]. The causal link between the mother's mental imbalance and the killing may not be easy to establish, the defence of diminished responsibility is now generally available as a defence to murder and the offence may be criticised for being gender-specific[3]. On the other hand, the option of prosecuting for infanticide avoids the need to charge the mother with murder.

Death by neglect or omission

As a general proposition, admittedly subject to significant exceptions, the criminal law does not punish for omission or inactivity[4]. The point was graphically made by Stephen[5] who said that no offence was committed by a person who could save someone from drowning merely by holding out his hand. Morally reprehensible though it would undoubtedly be, it seems that failure to rescue a drowning child from a shallow pool is not homicide on the part of the bystander. It is different for parents and others who have a duty to protect the child. Where a *duty* to act can be established, the criminal law applies[6]. In the case of parents, this duty of protection is an incident of parental responsibility but others who have 'responsibility' for children, in the less technical sense of assuming their physical care, are also bound by this duty[7]. Thus, as long ago as 1918[8], a conviction for murder was upheld where a female cohabitant withheld food from her male cohabitant's child resulting in the child's death. She was held to have assumed responsibility for the child by living with the man and accepting from him money for food. In most cases, manslaughter is more likely to be the charge, but where an *intention* to kill or cause grievous bodily harm can be established, it is murder, in the absence of an exculpatory defence[9].

---

1 Infanticide Act 1938, s 1(1).
2 See Smith and Hogan (above) at pp 396–397. See also D Maier-Katkin and R Ogle 'A rationale for infanticide laws' [1993] Crim LR 903, and R Mackay 'The consequences of killing very young children' [1993] Crim LR 19.
3 See A Ashworth *Principles of Criminal Law* (4th edn) (Oxford University Press, 2003) at pp 286–287. The modern trend, in the light of human rights requirements, is to amend gender-specific criminal offences to make them as far as is practicable gender-neutral. See the discussion of the Sexual Offences Act 2003 below.
4 Discussed, generally, in Smith and Hogan (above) at pp 60–68.
5 *Digest of Criminal Law* (4th edn) (1887) at Art 212.
6 The imposition of liability for inactivity more generally in the criminal law has been the subject of more than one theory, but the duty theory is probably the most convincing and was the basis of the decision in *R v Miller* [1983] 2 AC 161.
7 See below for those who have potential liability for neglect under the Children and Young Persons Act 1933, s 1.
8 *R v Gibbins and Proctor* (1918) 13 Cr App Rep 134.
9 The leading cases are now *R v Hancock* [1986] AC 455, *R v Moloney* [1985] AC 905, *R v Nedrick* [1986] 3 All ER 1, and *R v Woollin* [1999] AC 82.

Non-fatal offences

Assaults under the Offences Against the Person Act 1861

The Offences Against the Person Act 1861 still governs the various criminal offences arising from assault. The main offences are assault occasioning actual bodily harm[1], and wounding or grievous bodily harm with[2] or without intent[3]. Where an injury is intentionally or recklessly inflicted on a child by an outsider who does not have responsibility for him, one of these charges will be appropriate, depending on the extent of the injury and the mental state of the assailant. Again, as with homicide, these are general offences which are not confined to child victims.

Cruelty to childen under 16 years of age

Where, as is more likely, the injury to the child has been caused by one of his 'carers', the offence in s 1(1) of the Children and Young Persons Act 1933 will apply. However, the offence is a good deal wider in its coverage than simply assaults. It extends to various forms of neglect, ill-treatment, abandonment and exposure, as well as to physical assaults[4]. The offence is committed by 'any person who has attained the age of sixteen years' who 'has responsibility for any child or young person under that age'. The concept of 'responsibility' reflects the change of terminology in the Children Act and replaces the former expressions 'custody, charge or care'[5]. The general idea is of either someone who has parental responsibility formally, most obviously a parent or someone with a residence order, but also anyone else who is de facto looking after the child at the relevant time, for example a relative, babysitter or foster-parent.

This potential liability for failure to care adequately for the child is really the obverse of s 3(5) of the Children Act which, as we saw[6], gives to such de facto carers the power to take necessary action to promote the child's welfare. It is also plain that someone who does, formally, have parental responsibility cannot 'contract out' of liability under this offence by delegating responsibility to someone else[7] but, where proper care has been taken to ensure the adequacy of a substitute caring arrangement, it would be unlikely that the parent would have the requisite mens rea. Problems can arise where it is not clear which of more than one person with parental responsibility has caused the injury[8], but there is authority that the court may be able to infer that they are jointly responsible[9]. The Domestic Violence, Crime and Victims Bill 2003, before Parliament at the time of

---

1 Offences Against the Person Act 1861, s 47.
2 Ibid, s 18.
3 Ibid, s 20.
4 For discussion of the offence in the context of failure to summon medical aid for the child, see Chapter 8 above.
5 On the interpretation of these expressions, see HK Bevan *Child Law* (Butterworths, 1989) at paras 9.48–9.55.
6 At Chapter 6 above.
7 Children Act 1989, s 2(11).
8 There may be difficulty here also for the purposes of care proceedings. See the discussion of *Lancashire County Council v B* [2000] 1 FLR 583 in Chapter 11 above.
9 *R v Gibson and Gibson* [1984] Crim LR 615. Cf *R v Aston and Mason* [1991] Crim LR 701. In *R v Young* (1993) 97 Cr App R 280, the Court of Appeal held that as long as the jury were unanimous that cruelty in the sense alleged by the prosecution had been established, it was not necessary for them to agree on the specific evidence which led to a finding of guilt. They might

writing, attempts to address this problem. Under the Bill[1] there would be a new offence of 'causing or allowing the death of a child or vulnerable adult'. This would be committed where:

'(a) a child or vulnerable adult ("V") dies as a result of the unlawful act of a person who –
  (i) was a member of the same household as V, and
  (ii) had frequent contact with him,
(b) D was such a person at the time of that act,
(c) at that time there was a significant risk of serious physical harm being caused to V by the unlawful act of such a person, and
(d) either D was the person whose act caused V's death or –
  (i) D was, or ought to have been, aware of the risk mentioned in paragraph (c),
  (ii) D failed to take such steps as he could reasonably have been expected to take to protect V from the risk, and
  (iii) the act occurred in circumstances of the kind that D foresaw or ought to have foreseen.'

This offence would carry a maximum of 14 years' imprisonment. The essence of the offence would therefore be either to cause *or* to fail to prevent the unlawful killing of a child or vulnerable person where it is unclear which member of the child's household was responsible for his or her death. While the new offence would overcome the problem outlined above, it may also be criticised as another example of an attempt to impose serious criminal liability on the basis of negligence rather than on the basis of the mental culpability required by proof of intention or recklessness.

What is wilful neglect?

The Children and Young Persons Act 1933 goes on to create certain presumptions of neglect which can be applied to parents, guardians and persons who are legally liable to maintain the child. Such persons will be deemed to have neglected the child 'in a manner likely to cause injury to his health' where they have failed 'to provide adequate food, clothing, medical aid or lodging' or have failed to take steps to procure these things for the child[2]. All forms of conduct or omission envisaged by the offence must be committed 'wilfully'. It has been held by a majority of the House of Lords that this requires subjective recklessness[3]. The

---

legitimately differ on the emphasis to place on different incidents. Lloyd LJ said that it might, however, be wrong for the jury to be given the impression that they could convict if some of them were satisfied that *neglect* was established while others were satisfied of *assault* or *ill-treatment*. But there was no evidence in this case that the jury had been given that impression.

1 Clause 4. The issues were considered in depth by the Law Commission, which reported in September 2003. See Law Com Report No 282 *Children: Their Non-Accidental Death or Serious Injury (Criminal Trials)* (2003).

2 Section 1(2)(a) of the Children and Young Persons Act 1933. Section 1(2)(b) also deals with the death of an infant under three years of age by suffocation. Where the suffocation was not caused by disease or a foreign body in the throat or air passages of the infant, and the infant was at the time in bed with someone over 16 years of age, that person is, if he was under the influence of drink when he went to bed, 'deemed to have neglected the infant in a manner likely to cause injury to its health'.

3 *R v Sheppard* [1981] AC 394, and see Chapter 8 above.

unintelligent or inadequate parent who does not appreciate, as would an average person, the health and other needs of the child, will not be liable[1].

How far can parental discipline go?

An issue which arises both in relation to this offence and in relation to ordinary assault is how far a parent might be able to rely on the defence that the conduct in question was a proper exercise of parental discipline. The matter turns on whether the purported chastisement was 'moderate and reasonable'. The issue has already been discussed in the context of 'significant harm' in care proceedings[2] and is discussed in the context of intentional torts in Chapter 15 below.

Prosecutions

Before 1988, prosecutions for wilful neglect were uncommon[3]. This doubtless reflected, in part, the low maximum punishment which, in 1988, was two years' imprisonment. The Criminal Justice Act 1988[4] raised this to 10 years, and there were immediate signs that prosecutions were increasing. This is the maximum and, of course, within it, actual sentences will vary depending on such factors as the extent of the child's injuries and the circumstances surrounding the conduct in question. Where poverty and social deprivation have played a part, this may be expected to have an influence, but not necessarily so in the most atrocious cases of abuse. It has been observed that where a mother and step-father are jointly charged, the tendency has been to impose a more severe sentence on the step-father[5].

Sexual offences

General considerations

The law governing sexual offences has recently been completely reformed by the Sexual Offences Act 2003[6]. Before the Act, there were already a great many sexual offences on the statute book, but the effect of the Act is nonetheless to increase the number of offences. While the Act does bring about some much needed reforms, it also introduces a great deal of complexity and, more alarmingly, extends the reach of the criminal law to many activities which are arguably innocuous, or at

---

1   For a criticism of the case, see HK Bevan *Child Law* (Butterworths, 1989) at para 9.37. Note also that the offence will be committed where there is a failure to summon medical aid even if in fact there was no help which a doctor could have given (*R v S and M* [1995] Crim LR 486). See Chapter 8 above.

2   At Chapter 11 above.

3   In 1987, only 145 persons were sentenced for the offence while, by 1989, 189 women and 192 men were prosecuted and 105 women and 107 men were convicted. See JG Hall and DF Martin 'Crimes Against Children' (1992) 142 NLJ 902.

4   Section 45.

5   A point made by HK Bevan (above) at para 9.57, citing as an example the *Jasmine Beckford* case where the step-father received a 10-year sentence for manslaughter, to run concurrently with an eight-year sentence for cruelty, while the mother was sentenced to only 18 months' imprisonment for wilful neglect.

6   For detailed treatment of the Act, see R Card *Sexual Offences: The New Law* (Jordans, 2004). For a shorter commentary on its principal provisions, see B Brooks-Gordon and A Bainham 'Reforming the Law on Sexual Offences' in B Brooks-Gordon, L Gelsthorpe, M Johnson and A Bainham (eds) *Sexuality Repositioned: Diversity and the Law* (Hart Publishing, 2003). Specifically on the offences relating to children, see J Spencer 'The Sexual Offences Act 2003: Child and Family Offences' [2004] *Criminal Law Review* 347.

least ought not to be the business of the State. This is perhaps especially true of the new offences relating to sexual activity with children which are the concern of this chapter.

The Sexual Offences Act 2003 follows two Reviews by the Home Office – the *Review of Part I of the Sex Offenders Act 1997*[1] and *Setting the Boundaries*[2], published in 2000. These Reviews were followed by a White Paper, *Protecting the Public*[3]. Part II of the Act re-enacts with modifications the law designed to protect the public from sexual offenders. This is beyond the scope of the present work except to note that the Act introduces two new kinds of orders – the sexual offences prevention order and the risk of sexual harm order[4]. The latter order is designed to protect children from coming into contact with paedophiles. It enables the police to apply to the magistrates' court for an order prohibiting an adult from doing certain things where this is 'necessary for the purpose of protecting children generally or any child from the harm of the defendant'[5]. The order may be made where it appears to a chief officer of police that the individual concerned has, on at least two occasions, done certain prescribed acts and 'there is reasonable cause to believe that it is necessary for such an order to be made'[6]. The specified acts are:

(a) engaging in sexual activity involving a child or in the presence of a child;
(b) causing or inciting a child to watch a person engaging in sexual activity or to look at a moving or still image that is sexual;
(c) giving a child anything that relates to sexual activity or contains a reference to such activity; and
(d) communicating with a child, where any part of the communication is sexual[7].

As with so many of the provisions of the Sexual Offences Act 2003, while the motivation for the new powers is clear and laudable, the provision is drawn so widely that it is capable of operating oppressively and is also founded on the same erroneous assumption which pervades the Act – that all sexual activity involving children is wrong. Our principal concern here, however, is with Part I of the Act and the new sexual offences which it introduces. What follows is a necessarily selective account of the principal features of the new code, concentrating on those offences which specifically relate to children and young people. It should, of

---

1 Home Office *Consultation Paper on the Review of the Sex Offenders Act 1997* (July 2001).
2 Home Office *Setting the Boundaries: Reforming the Law on Sexual Offences* (2000). For a critique of the Home Office Review, see N Lacey 'Beset by Boundaries: The Home Office Review of Sex Offences' (2001) *Criminal Law Review* 3.
3 Home Office *Protecting the Public: Strengthening Protection against Sex Offenders and Reforming the Law on Sexual Offences*.
4 See ss 104–113 (sexual offences prevention orders) and ss 123–129 (risk of sexual harm orders). For commentary, see S Shute 'The Sexual Offences Act 2003: (4) New Civil Preventative Orders: Sexual Offences Prevention Orders; Foreign Travel Orders; Risk of Sexual Harm Orders' (2004) *Criminal Law Review* 417.
5 Sexual Offences Act 2003, s 123(6).
6 Ibid, s 123(1).
7 Ibid, s 123(8).

course, be borne in mind that the major sexual offences such as rape[1], assault by penetration[2] and sexual assault[3] apply as much to child victims as they do to adult victims. We comment here on these general sexual offences only insofar as there may be special considerations where the victim is a child. One of the unsatisfactory features of the new legislation is that there appears to be a good deal of overlap, or as it has been put by Spencer, 'overkill'[4], and the boundaries between the various offences are not always clear.

Before coming to the offences themselves, we comment briefly on the aims and objectives of the new code as elaborated in *Setting the Boundaries*. The Home Office Review attempted to identify the proper policy objectives of a sexual offences code. The central principles should be that 'the criminal law should not intrude unnecessarily into the private lives of adults' and that 'most consensual activity between adults in private should be their own affair'. On the other hand, the criminal law 'has a vital role to play where sexual activity is not consensual or where Society decides that children and other very vulnerable people require protection and should not be able to consent'. Herein lies one important distinction between the sexual offences code as it applies respectively to adults and children. With few exceptions, consent will generally be a defence to adult sexual offences[5], whereas the consent of a child will not normally be effective to prevent the commission of an offence. In effect, children under 16 are regarded as incapable of giving a valid consent to sexual activity and, in relation to some offences, and despite the age of consent generally being fixed at 16, there are some instances where the relevant age is 18 and not 16[6]. Important exceptions, however, are rape, the new offence of assault by penetration and sexual assault where the essence of these extremely serious offences[7] is that the victim did not consent. Here it is necessary to distinguish between children *over* the age of 13 and those *under* that age. In relation to those *over* 13, the consent of the child to sexual intercourse, or to penetration with some object other than the penis, will prevent liability for these offences – although some activity will undoubtedly amount to one of the less serious child sex offences *despite* the child's consent. Where, however, the child is *under* the age of 13, the broad effect of ss 5–8 of the Act is to remove the relevance

---

1 Sexual Offences Act 2003, s 1.
2 Ibid, s 2.
3 Ibid, s 3.
4 See fn 6 at p 620.
5 An exception is the new offence of 'sex with an adult relative' in s 64, an offence involving penetrative sexual activities between related adults and replacing the former offence of incest.
6 This is so in relation to the new abuse of trust offences and familial child sex offences discussed below.
7 Rape, for example, is now defined as follows:
   '(1) A person (A) commits an offence if –
      (a) he intentionally penetrates the vagina, anus or mouth of another person (B) with his penis,
      (b) B does not consent to the penetration, and
      (c) A does not reasonably believe that B consents.
   (2) Whether a belief is reasonable is to be determined having regard to all the circumstances, including any steps A has taken to ascertain whether B consents.'

   The consent and mens rea elements are essentially replicated for assault by penetration (s 2) and sexual assault (s 3).

of the child's consent and to create a separate category of offences, of equal seriousness and carrying the same maximum punishments[1].

The view was also taken in *Setting the Boundaries* that a coherent and fair code, which had proper regard for human rights, should also be gender-neutral and ought not to discriminate between men and women, boys and girls, whether as victims or perpetrators of sexual offences, unless there was a good reason for doing so[2]. The new Act gives effect to this principle. It represents a major change from the old law where specific offences relating to children[3] generally applied only to under-age girls and where there was not a single sexual offence specifically enacted to protect boys. In contrast, the new child sex offences and familial child sex offences apply equally to boys and girls, young men and young women. *Setting the Boundaries* also concluded that the law should reflect the 'looser structure of modern families' and, accordingly, the former offence of incest[4] is replaced by new 'familial child sex offences'[5]. The key change is that the new offences move beyond prohibiting sexual activity between blood relations (to which the objections have traditionally been eugenic) to include sexual activity between a range of 'family members' more widely defined. In particular they include step- and foster-relationships and also situations where those concerned have lived in the same household as the victim.

A final general feature of the new law which ought to be highlighted is the distinct shift throughout the Sexual Offences Act 2003 in the direction of criminal liability based on *negligence* rather than on *intention* or *recklessness* which constituted the minimum mental requirement for most sexual offending before the Act. Thus, in relation to the principal offences of rape, assault by penetration and sexual assault, there will now be a requirement of *reasonable* belief in the victim's consent, as opposed to a merely genuine, but unreasonable, one[6]. A similar relaxation in the mental requirement is also apparent in relation to the new child sex offences and familial child sex offences where a mistake as to the child's age must now also be *reasonably* held[7]. Where the child is under the age of 13, there will be strict liability and no mistake as to age, whether reasonable or not, will exculpate the accused.

Rape and other offences against children under 13

It is now an offence where the accused 'intentionally penetrates the vagina, anus or mouth of a child under 13 with his penis'[8]. The new offence mirrors the

---

1 Life imprisonment in the case of rape and assault by penetration, and 14 years' imprisonment in the case of sexual assault.

2 A good reason was thought to exist in relation to rape which, although gender-neutral as to the victim, remains gender-specific as to the perpetrator since it is an offence grounded in the concept of *penile* penetration.

3 Especially unlawful sexual intercourse with a girl under 16 (Sexual Offences Act 1956, s 6) or under 13 (Sexual Offences Act 1956, s 5). Boys were protected as children, but not gender-specifically as boys, under the general law of indecent assault and the Indecency with Children Act 1960.

4 Governed by ss 10 and 11 of the Sexual Offences Act 1956 and discussed in the second edition of this work at pp 480–481.

5 Sexual Offences Act 2003, ss 25–29.

6 Thus overruling the long-standing authority of *DPP v Morgan* [1976] AC 182.

7 Sexual Offences Act 2003, ss 9–12.

8 Ibid, s 5.

re-definition of rape which now includes, for the first time, forced fellatio. Yet, this offence is rather misleadingly referred to as 'rape' in that, first, as noted above, and contrary to the essence of adult rape, the child's consent to the penetration is irrelevant and, secondly, it covers much of the ground previously occupied by the offence of unlawful sexual intercourse with a girl under the age of 13. It is, of course, much broader in that the new offence includes non-vaginal penetration and is gender-neutral and, thus, equally applicable to girls and boys.

It is an offence also to assault by penetration a child of this age[1]. This is a new offence again mirroring the adult offence, except that consent is again irrelevant. These new offences are designed to reflect the gravity of non-penile penetrations carried out by insertion in the vagina, anus or mouth of such objects as fingers or bottles. These violations are considered to be as serious and repugnant as rape and, as with rape, there is a maximum punishment of life imprisonment. Then come the offences of sexual assault of a child under 13[2] and causing or inciting a child under 13 to engage in sexual activity[3]. The concept of sexual assault replaces the former notion of 'indecent assault'[4]. We discuss below the concept of what is 'sexual' for the purposes of the Act. Much of the ground covered by the former offence is duplicated by the lesser offence of 'sexual activity with a child', and the latter offence may be committed also in relation to children over 13, but under 16. The significance of the separate offence seems therefore to turn only on the fact that there is strict liability as to the child's age where that child is under 13.

Child sex offences

Sections 9–15 of the Sexual Offences Act 2003 contain the so-called 'child sex offences'. The principal offence is that of 'sexual activity with a child'[5]. This is committed where a person aged 18 or over (A):

'(a)   intentionally touches another person (B);
 (b)   the touching is sexual; and
 (c)   either –
         (i)   B is under 16 and A does not reasonably believe B is 16 or over, or
         (ii) B is under 13.'

The offence carries a maximum punishment of six months' imprisonment but, where it involves penetration, the maximum punishment is increased to 14 years.

A good deal of criticism may be made of this offence. At one end of the spectrum it catches all the conduct which would have fallen within the former offences of indecent assault and indecency with children, but it also represents a potentially enormous extension of the range of activities which may now be regarded as criminal. It is capable of prohibiting the sort of innocuous, some may even think desirable, sexual experimentation between adolescents which is a

---

1   Sexual Offences Act 2003, s 6.
2   Ibid, s 7.
3   Ibid, s 8.
4   Contrary to ss 14 and 15 of the Sexual Offences Act 1956. The leading authority on the interpretation of indecency was *R v Court* [1988] 2 All ER 221, discussed in the second edition of this work at pp 481–482.
5   Sexual Offences Act 2003, s 9.

normal part of growing up[1]. This is because it is backed up, as are the other child sex offences, by a provision which makes it plain that all of these offences may be committed not merely by adults against children (where the very age disparity may automatically give cause for concern) but also between children and young persons themselves where there is little or no difference in age. Section 13 blandly states that 'a person under 18 commits an offence if he does anything which would be an offence under any of sections 9 to 12 if he were aged 18'. Furthermore, the concept of what is 'sexual' is very widely drawn, as is the notion of 'touching'[2]. 'Sexual' is perhaps the central concept throughout the new code and is defined as follows:

> 'For the purposes of this part of the Act . . . penetration, touching or any other activity is sexual if a reasonable person would consider that –
> (a) whatever its circumstances or any person's purpose in relation to it, it is because of its nature sexual, or
> (b) because of its nature it may be sexual and because of its circumstances or the purpose of any person in relation to it (or both) it is sexual.'[3]

This puts the 'objective' view of the magistrates or jury centre stage. Essentially, that which is sexual is that which a reasonable person, rather than the accused, would deem to be sexual. This is open to the criticism that, along with other provisions in the legislation, it makes criminal liability for sexual offending dependent on negligence alone. It does not require mental culpability as was normally the case before the Act. It is moreover questionable whether the new notion of what is 'sexual' is an adequate replacement for 'indecency' as the chief component in this type of offence. The point is surely that 'indecency' implies wrongdoing whereas 'sexual' is morally neutral and, in many contexts, has a positive connotation. Yet the message of the legislation is that all sexual activity involving children is by definition wrong. It is believed (apparently) by the Government that it is only by criminalising all sexual activity involving children that the law will be sufficiently effective in facilitating the prosecution of paedophiles.

We have noted above the new requirement of reasonableness of belief regarding consent in the context of adult sex offences. Consent is irrelevant in relation to child sex offences, but the issue of negligence raises its head here too. This is because any belief that the child concerned was over the age of 16 must now be *reasonably* held. This effectively overrules two comparatively recent decisions of the House of Lords in *B (A Minor) v DPP*[4] (gross indecency with a girl under 14

---

1 For a compelling defence of the right of adults to have normal associations with children, which may be seen as threatened by the new law, see F Bennion *Sexual Ethics and the Criminal Law: A Critique of the Sexual Offences Bill 2003* (Lester Publishing, 2003).
2 'Touching' as defined by the Sexual Offences Act 2003, s 79(8) includes:
   'touching –
   (a) with any part of the body;
   (b) with anything else,
   (c) through anything,
   and in particular includes touching amounting to penetration.'
3 Ibid, s 78. See F Bennion 'The Meaning of "Sexual" in the Sexual Offences Bill' (2003) 167 *Justice of the Peace* 764.
4 [2000] 2 AC 428. See generally J Horder 'How Culpability Can, and Cannot, be Denied in Under-age Sex Crimes' (2001) *Criminal Law Review* 15.

contrary to the Indecency with Children Act 1960) and *R v K*[1] (indecent assault on a 14-year-old girl). In each case the House of Lords had held that a presumption of mens rea applied, although this was not expressly stated in the legislation. Thus an honest or genuine belief that the girls in question were over age for the purposes of the offences was a defence and it was not necessary to show that such belief was reasonable. More recently, the House of Lords has reasserted the general requirement of mental culpability in the context of serious crime in *R v G and Another*[2]. Here the House of Lords overruled the long-standing authority of *Caldwell*[3] which had introduced an objective version of recklessness into the criminal law. It is worth reflecting on the policy considerations which lie behind the view that conviction for serious crime should require mental awareness of the possibility of wrongdoing. As Lord Bingham of Cornhill[4] said in this case:

> '... it is a salutary principle that conviction of serious crime should depend on proof not simply that the defendant caused (by act or omission) an injurious result to another but that his state of mind when so acting was culpable ... It is clearly blameworthy to take an obvious and significant risk of causing injury to another. But it is not clearly blameworthy to do something involving a risk of injury to another if (for reasons other than self-induced intoxication ...) one genuinely does not perceive the risk. Such a person may fairly be accused of stupidity or a lack of imagination, but neither of those failings should expose him to conviction of serious crime or the risk of prosecution.'

Parliament seems to have lost sight of this principle entirely in the Sexual Offences Act 2003.

Other child sex offences include causing or inciting a child to engage in sexual activity[5], engaging in sexual activity in the presence of a child[6], causing a child to watch a sexual act[7], arranging or facilitating the commission of a child sex offence[8] and meeting a child following sexual grooming[9]. The latter offence is designed principally to meet the modern menace of attempts by paedophiles to seduce children through the internet. It is committed where a person aged 18 or over (A):

> '(a) having met or communicated with another person (B) on at least two earlier occasions ...
>   (i)   intentionally meets B, or
>   (ii) travels with the intention of meeting B in any part of the world,
> (b) at the time, he intends to do anything to or in respect of B, during or after the meeting and in any part of the world, which if done will involve the commission by A of a relevant offence,
> (c) B is under 16, and
> (d) A does not reasonably believe that B is 16 or over.'

'Relevant offence'[10] is defined to include all the offences under the Sexual Offences Act 2003 and some others.

---

1 *R v K (Age of Consent: Reasonable Belief)* [2002] 1 AC 462.
2 [2003] UKHL 50.
3 [1982] AC 341.
4 [2003] UKHL 50 at para 32.
5 Sexual Offences Act 2003, s 10.
6 Ibid, s 11.
7 Ibid, s 12.
8 Ibid, s 14.
9 Ibid, s 15.
10 Ibid, s 15(2)(b).

Again, while the mischief which the offence is trying to address is all too obvious, the breadth of the offence is quite staggering. It must give rise to serious concerns about the extension of criminal liability to situations in which no harm has yet occurred and in which there may be a good deal of equivocality or ambiguity in what may have occurred.

Abuse of a position of trust

The Sexual Offences Act 2003 in ss 16–24 builds on offences relating to the abuse of positions of trust which were introduced by the Sexual Offences (Amendment) Act 2000. The new offences follow the same pattern as child sex offences in that there are specific offences again of sexual activity with a child[1], causing or inciting a child to engage in sexual activity[2], sexual activity in the presence of a child[3] and causing a child to watch a sexual act[4]. What distinguishes these offences is that they are committed by someone in a 'position of trust' in relation to the child and that they apply to young people under the age of 18 and not, as in the case of child sex offences, under 16. Again, any mistake as to age, in this case 18, must be reasonably held for it to operate as a defence. For the purposes of these offences, 'position of trust' is defined[5] to include situations where A 'looks after persons under 18' in various specified institutions including educational establishments, hospitals and certain residential homes. The extension of the previous offence to 16- and 17-year-old 'victims' has been criticised by Spencer[6] as having the sole purpose of criminalising consensual sexual acts between schoolteachers and sixth formers who are over the normal age of consent and whose relationships may sometimes endure and even end in marriage. In his view, these involvements, even if 'unwise and reprehensible, do not look like criminal behaviour punishable with five years' imprisonment'.

Familial child sex offences

The 2003 Act creates two new 'familial child sex offences' which replace incest insofar as that offence applied to children as opposed to sexual activity between adult relatives. These are sexual activity with a child family member[7] and inciting a child family member to engage in sexual activity[8]. The relevant age of the child is again under 18 but the offence may also be committed by a family member who himself or herself is also under 18. The key feature of these offences is that the activity takes place between two people who are in a 'family relationship' as defined by the Act[9]. This includes the relationship of 'parent, grandparent, brother, sister, half-sister, aunt or uncle'. It also includes foster-parents and former foster-parents, together with those 'who live or have lived in the same household' or where the accused 'has been regularly involved in caring for,

---

1 Sexual Offences Act 2003, s 16.
2 Ibid, s 17.
3 Ibid, s 18.
4 Ibid, s 19.
5 Ibid, ss 21 and 22.
6 See fn 6 at p 620.
7 Sexual Offences Act 2003, s 25.
8 Ibid, s 26.
9 Ibid, s 27.

training, supervising, or being in sole charge of' the young person concerned. Step-relationships are included as are relationships between cousins.

The new offences may also be criticised for much the same reasons – they are over-broad, overlap with other offences and catch consensual activity between older teenagers which perhaps should not be the business of the law at all.

Other offences involving children

We should note briefly several other offences in the Sexual Offences Act 2003 which have a specific application to children. First, s 45 amends the Protection of Children Act 1978 so that it applies now to children under the age of 18 as opposed to 16 under the previous law.

Secondly, ss 47–51 of the Sexual Offences Act 2003 create a number of new offences relating to the abuse of children through prostitution or pornography. These latter offences being merely additions to the existing muddled laws regulating prostitution are of doubtful usefulness. After the 2003 Act reached the statute book, the Government announced a wide-ranging review of all laws governing prostitution. It therefore seems likely that we can expect further legislation on this in the foreseeable future.

Concluding remarks

For all its good intentions, the Sexual Offences Act 2003 is a deeply flawed piece of legislation both as it applies to adults and as it applies to children. It is, as it was put by Dominic Grieve MP at the Committee stage of the Bill[1], 'a blunderbuss', a strikingly illiberal piece of legislation which rests on the philosophy that to prosecute successfully harmful sexual misconduct in relation to children it is necessary to criminalise *all* sexual contact with them, whatever the circumstances. John Spencer has rightly lampooned such an approach as 'bad news for Adrian Mole'. Among those activities between consenting teenagers which will now be caught by the Act and its penalties, he identifies 'mouth to mouth kissing', or minor acts of sexual exploration between two 14- or 15-year-olds (five years); two boys giving themselves a sexual thrill by looking at a dirty book (five years); and 'rude games' between two 10-year-olds (14 years, maybe life)[2]. It is, of course, argued by the Government that there is a prosecutorial discretion and that, in practice, prosecutions will not be brought and maximum penalties not imposed except in truly serious cases. This, however, fails to meet the essential requirement of 'fair labelling' in the criminal law or, to put it as strongly as Spencer does, it is an approach which 'runs contrary to the notion of the rule of law'[3].

Special offences relating to children

Restrictions and prohibitions on sale of harmful goods

There are numerous statutory offences regulating various activities which may cause harm to children. Some of these are in the Children and Young Persons Act 1933, while others are scattered about the statute book. Little purpose would be

---

1   House of Commons Standing Committee B, 18 September 2003.
2   J Spencer 'The Shameful Sex Crimes of Adrian Mole aged 13¾' *The Times*, 7 October 2003.
3   See fn 6 at p 620.

served by reproducing a catalogue of these offences[1] but it is important to get a sense of the breadth of coverage of the criminal law. The offences include, most obviously, restrictions on the sale of alcohol[2] and tobacco[3], and road safety regulations[4]. These are widely known to the general public. Also well known are those offences relating to firearms[5], crossbows[6] and explosives, including fireworks[7]. The rationale of these offences is partly to protect the children themselves and partly to protect society from the anti-social conduct which might result from allowing children and traders complete freedom of action.

Offences centred on protection
Other offences are more overtly centred on protection of children. The prohibition on tattooing of minors[8], the restrictions on the employment of children[9] and the offence relating to the exposure of children under 12 years to the risk of burning[10] would all seem to fall into this category. A recent example is the creation of an offence of selling aerosol spray paints to children under 16 by the Anti-social Behaviour Act 2003[11]. The objective is to reduce the incidence of criminal damage caused by acts of graffiti.

Restriction of children's liberty
A feature of many of these special statutory offences is that they restrict not only the activities of adult society towards children but also the liberty of children themselves. This raises the general issue of how far the State has a legitimate interest in imposing these restraints. One of the freedoms which adults enjoy is the right to make mistakes. Many adults are not, for example, conspicuously competent drivers or noted for their restraint with alcohol, tobacco or in sexual matters. Yet the law generally does not step in to prevent them from behaving contrary to their own interests, objectively judged. What then is the case for denying children the right to make mistakes? The justification would seem to reside in the overriding obligation of the State to uphold the public interest in the well-being of children. But ultimately the view which is taken of the proper limits of State paternalism depends on the individual's own stance on the general question of children's rights[12].

---

1 They are examined extensively in HK Bevan *Child Law* (Butterworths, 1989) at chs 9 and 10, and in D Bedingfield *The Child in Need* (Family Law, 1998) especially at paras 5.198–5.216.
2 Licensing Act 1964, s 169.
3 The Protection of Children (Tobacco) Act 1986 and the Children and Young Persons (Protection from Tobacco) Act 1991 which increased the penalties for sale of tobacco to persons under 16 years of age.
4 Thus, persons under 17 years of age are not allowed to drive motor vehicles on public roads.
5 Firearms Acts 1968 and 1982.
6 Crossbows Act 1987.
7 Explosives Act 1875, as amended by the Explosives (Age of Purchase etc) Act 1976.
8 Tattooing of Minors Act 1969.
9 Mainly in the Children and Young Persons Act 1933. See Chapter 15 below.
10 Children and Young Persons Act 1933, s 11, as amended. Another example of such legislation is the Horses (Protective Headgear for Young Riders) Act 1990. The Confiscation of Alcohol (Young Persons) Act 1997 enables a police constable to confiscate intoxicating liquor from young persons under the age of 18 in prescribed circumstances.
11 Section 54.
12 See Chapter 3 above.

RESPONSIBILITY

The Crime and Disorder Act 1998

The Crime and Disorder Act 1998, inter alia, provided the basis for a root and branch reform of the youth justice system[1]. We discuss below some of the reforms, particularly the abolition of the doli incapax presumption and the new parenting orders, and set out the salient features of the Act as it affects youth crime, concluding with a brief comment on its underlying philosophy and how this may relate to the thinking behind other legislation relating to children. The Act introduced a number of new measures, including child safety orders, parenting orders, reprimands and warnings, action plan orders and reparation orders.

The Act essentially reformed the law of juvenile justice in three ways. First, it made what might be called *institutional changes* to the criminal justice system (Part III). Secondly, there were measures for the *prevention* of crime and disorder, many of which related specifically to youth crime (Part I). Finally, there were reforms relating to the options for *dealing with young offenders* (Part IV).

Institutional changes

Part III of the Act set out the aims of the youth justice system, contained provisions relating to youth justice services, and provided for the creation of a new Youth Justice Board and the establishment of local youth offending teams.

The principal aim of the youth justice system was stated to be to prevent offending by children and young persons, and it was henceforth to be the duty of all persons and bodies carrying out functions in relation to the youth justice system to have regard to that aim[2]. Local authorities must ensure the availability of appropriate youth justice services, and police authorities, probation committees and health authorities are required to co-operate in securing that such services are available[3]. The Act goes on to specify and define the meaning of 'youth justice services'[4]. In particular, each local authority must establish one or more youth offending teams[5]. Local authorities, in consultation with the above authorities, must formulate and implement an annual youth justice plan which sets out how youth justice services in their area are to be provided and funded and the composition, funding and functions of the youth offending teams[6]. The Act set up a Youth Justice Board whose function is to monitor the operation of the youth justice system, promote good practice and advise the Home Secretary on the operation of the youth justice system and the setting of national standards[7].

---

1   The Labour Party's proposals for reform of the youth justice system were set out in the consultation paper *Tackling Youth Crime: Reforming Youth Justice* (May 1996). This was followed by other consultation papers culminating in the White Paper *No More Excuses – A New Approach to Tackling Youth Crime in England and Wales* (November 1997) (Cm 3809).
2   Crime and Disorder Act 1998, s 37.
3   Ibid, s 38.
4   Ibid, ss 38–41.
5   Ibid, s 39.
6   Ibid, s 40.
7   Ibid, s 41 and Sch 2.

The Board is located in the Home Office and has 'a wide ranging membership drawn from different backgrounds with expertise in tackling youth offending'[1].

Prevention of youth crime

Part I of the Act contained a number of radical measures designed to prevent crime and anti-social behaviour by adults and young offenders. Our concern here is only with the latter, and we discuss parenting orders below. In addition to these measures to reinforce parental responsibility, the Act introduced a new 'child safety order' which was designed to enable the courts to protect children under the age of 10 (viz below the age of criminal responsibility) who are at risk of becoming involved in crime or have already begun to behave in an anti-social or criminal manner[2]. The order, where made, places the child under the supervision of a specified, responsible officer and requires the child to comply with arrangements aimed at ensuring that he receives appropriate care, protection and support and is subject to proper control. It might, for example, require the child to be home by a certain time or to avoid a certain area. The court, before making such an order, will be required to take into account information about the family circumstances and must explain to the parent in ordinary language the effect and consequences of the order[3].

Allied to the above order, local authorities were given power to make a 'local child curfew scheme' under which a curfew notice may be given banning children of specified ages (below the age of 10) from being in a public place during specified hours unless they are under the control of a responsible adult[4]. The police are required to inform the local authority where they believe the child is contravening a curfew notice, and a police constable is empowered in these circumstances to return the child to his home[5].

Dealing with young offenders

Part IV of the Act contained a number of new measures for dealing with young offenders.

As noted below, the existing system of cautioning young offenders was abolished and replaced with a system of reprimands and final warnings[6]. Where the offence is less serious, the young offender may be reprimanded by a police officer if he has not previously been reprimanded or warned. In those cases where the offence is more serious or where there has been a previous reprimand he will be warned. This final warning may only be given once, since the policy, as set out in the Consultation Paper *Tackling Youth Crime*[7], is that while diversion and an early response is to be encouraged, that response must be 'clear, firm and constructive'. Where the young offender fails to respond to the warning and re-offends, this will normally be followed quickly by prosecution in the courts. The essential scheme

---

1   Consultation Paper *Tackling Youth Crime: Reforming Youth Justice* (May 1996).
2   Crime and Disorder Act 1998, s 11.
3   Ibid, s 12.
4   Ibid, s 14.
5   Ibid, s 15.
6   Ibid, ss 65 and 66.
7   Paragraphs 3 and 7.

therefore is that a young offender should usually be reprimanded for a first offence, warned for a second and prosecuted for a third[1].

Some forces have in recent years pioneered the practice of 'restorative cautioning' whereby the reprimand or warning may be administered at a conference which the young offender, parents and victim may attend. There may then be a discussion about the harm caused and reparation for the victim[2]. This is another manifestation of the notion of 'restorative justice' which is noted elsewhere in this chapter. Where a police constable warns a child or young person, that person will be referred to a youth offending team for assessment and, where appropriate, provision must be made for him to participate in a programme to prevent re-offending, and to secure his rehabilitation[3]. A child who receives a final warning will be given guidance and support to cut down the risks of re-offending, but any further re-offending is then likely to result in a significant punishment from the courts. It is expressly provided that the courts should not, other than in exceptional circumstances, conditionally discharge young offenders convicted of an offence within two years of a warning[4].

Part IV provided for several completely new sentencing options for young offenders. It introduced the 'reparation order' which requires a young offender to make a reparation to the victim of an offence, a person otherwise affected by it or to the community at large[5]. Before making the order, the court is required to consider a written report about the type of reparation and the views of the victim and to explain the order to the young offender[6]. The Act also amended the Children and Young Persons Act 1969 to enable reparation conditions to be attached to supervision orders[7]. It introduced an 'action plan order', a new community penalty requiring a young offender to comply with an action plan intended to address his offending[8]. The order combines reparation, punishment and rehabilitation and involves the offender's parents. The court is required to consider the family circumstances, information about the proposed action plan and the attitude of the offender's parent or guardian. The court must then explain the effect of the order to the young offender and it is empowered to fix a hearing within 21 days of making the order to review its effectiveness and the extent to which it has been implemented[9]. Finally, the Act enables the court to sentence a young offender to a detention and training order (DTO), which requires the offender to be subject to a period of detention and training, followed by a period of supervision[10]. The order is intended to be a generic custodial sentence to replace the various custodial sentences currently available in relation to juveniles as discussed below. The Government made it clear that the DTO

---

1   This at least is Sprack's assessment: see J Sprack *A Practical Approach to Criminal Procedure* (10th edn) (Oxford University Press, 2004) at para 4.12. The conditions under which a juvenile may be reprimanded or warned are also set out there.
2   For further discussion see Doolin (above) at pp 436–437.
3   Crime and Disorder Act 1998, s 66.
4   Ibid.
5   Ibid, s 67.
6   Ibid, s 68.
7   Ibid, s 71.
8   Ibid, s 69.
9   Ibid, s 70.
10 Ibid, ss 73–79.

would be subject to the restrictions on the use of custody laid down in the Criminal Justice Act 1991[1].

Criminal responsibility of children and young persons

The criminal law before the implementation of the Crime and Disorder Act 1998 divided juveniles into three distinct age groups for the purposes of criminal liability[2]. These were: children under the age of 10 who were below the age of criminal responsibility; children aged between 10 and 14 years in relation to whom there was a rebuttable presumption that they were incapable of committing an offence; and children aged 14 and over who were treated as adults for the purposes of criminal liability although differently in terms of criminal procedure and the disposals available to the court. The Crime and Disorder Act 1998[3] abolished the doli incapax presumption in relation to children over 10 but under 14. This controversial reform needs to be assessed alongside what is a very low age of criminal responsibility and the general trend towards a more punitive, less welfarist, approach to juvenile crime over the last decade or so. It is thus now only necessary to distinguish between children below the age of 10 and those of 10 or older, but we will also discuss briefly the reasoning behind the abolition of the doli incapax presumption in relation to children between the ages of 10 and 14.

Children under 10 years of age

Children under the age of 10 years are conclusively presumed to be doli incapax ('incapable of evil') or incapable of committing any offence[4]. They are thus completely immune from prosecution. Historically, at common law, the principle evolved that young children should be exempt from criminal liability and, when an age was first fixed by law, seven years was chosen[5]. This was raised to eight years in 1933 and to 10 years in 1963, where it remains today. Article 40(3) of the UNCRC requires 'the establishment of a minimum age below which children shall be presumed not to have the capacity to infringe the penal law' but does not go on to specify what this should be. Rule 4.1 of the Beijing Rules is a little more prescriptive and provides:

> 'In those legal systems recognising the concept of the age of criminal responsibility for juveniles, the beginning of that age shall not be fixed at too low an age level, bearing in mind the facts of emotional, mental and intellectual maturity.'

The age of criminal responsibility in England is set lower than in most other European countries and has been the subject of extensive criticism[6]. In particular, the British Government has come in for scathing criticism on this and

---

1   For the thinking behind the new order, see the White Paper (fn 1 at p 630 above) at ch 6.

2   See, generally, HK Bevan *Child Law* (Butterworths, 1989) at paras 12.05–12.09, Smith and Hogan *Criminal Law* (10th edn) (Butterworths, 2002) at pp 211–212, and MJ Allen *Textbook on Criminal Law* (7th edn) (Oxford University Press, 2003) at pp 115–119.

3   Section 34.

4   Children and Young Persons Act 1933, s 50, as amended by Children and Young Persons Act 1963, s 16.

5   The historical development of the rule is discussed by HK Bevan (above) at para 12.05.

6   For a particularly helpful discussion, see J Fortin *Children's Rights and the Developing Law* (2nd edn) (Butterworths, 2003) at pp 550–560 and the sources cited there.

on other aspects of its juvenile justice policy in the periodic reports of the UNCRC. In its concluding observations on the UK's report[1], the Committee had this to say:

> 'The Committee ... notes with serious concern that the situation of children in conflict with the law has worsened since the consideration of the initial report. The Committee is particularly concerned that the age at which children enter the criminal justice system is low with the age of criminal responsibility still at 8 years in Scotland and at 10 years in [England], and the abolition of the principle of doli incapax.'

We refer below to other criticisms of the Committee in relation to criminal procedure and the use of custodial measures in the case of juveniles.

Two consequences flow immediately from the rule that a child under the age of 10 is incapable of committing an offence. The first is that, since the child is, in law, incapable of committing a crime, anyone over the age of criminal responsibility who incites a child to commit a criminal act will be liable as principal offender and not as a secondary party. The child is an 'innocent agent' and this can have some unexpected consequences. In *Walters v Lunt*[2], the parents of a boy aged seven years were accused of receiving from him a stolen tricycle. Since the boy himself was incapable of theft, the tricycle was not 'stolen' and the parents had to be acquitted. The second consequence was, where young children committed acts which but for the age rule would be criminal, they could only be dealt with, if at all, through the public law procedures of the Children Act. In many cases, this would involve social services providing the family with voluntary assistance. As has been seen[3], the abolition of the 'offence condition' means that proceedings for compulsory care or supervision may no longer be instigated simply on the strength of delinquency. It has to be shown that the child is also at risk of 'significant harm', applying the statutory criteria and, at the welfare stage, the welfare principle. The options for dealing with behaviour by children under 10 that would be criminal activity but for their age have, however, been greatly extended by New Labour and include the child safety order, the curfew order and the anti-social behaviour order. These measures are considered below.

Children over 10 years of age
Before its abolition by the Crime and Disorder Act 1998[4] the presumption of incapacity applied to children between the ages of 10 and 14 but here it was a *rebuttable* presumption. The prosecution was required to prove that the child had what was termed a 'mischievous discretion'. This was in addition to the normal burden of proof on the prosecution to establish the actus reus and appropriate mens rea which has to be proved for the offence whether committed by a child or an adult. In 1994 there was an attempt by the Divisional Court in *C v DPP*[5] to abolish the common law presumption on the basis that it was outdated, but the

---

1 *Concluding Observations of the United Nations Committee on the Rights of the Child*, 31st session, 9 October 2002, para 59.
2 [1951] 2 All ER 645.
3 Section 90(1) of the Children Act.
4 Section 34 provides that 'the rebuttable presumption of criminal law that a child aged 10 or over is incapable of committing an offence is hereby abolished'.
5 [1994] 3 WLR 888, and for commentary on the Divisional Court's decision, see ATH Smith 'Doli Incapax Under Threat' (1994) CLJ 426.

House of Lords[1] subsequently held that, although reform was desirable, this was a matter for Parliament and not for the courts. It therefore reasserted the existence of the presumption only for the Labour Government to incorporate its abolition as part of a wider package of measures to tackle youth crime in the 1998 legislation[2].

Views were inevitably divided on the merits of the presumption. The Labour Government saw its abolition as an integral part of its more general policy for reinforcing personal and parental responsibility for youth crime[3]. It believed that 'in assuming that children of this age generally do not know the difference between naughtiness and serious wrongdoing, the notion of doli incapax is contrary to common sense'[4]. It also took the view that 'the practical difficulties which the presumption presents for the prosecution can stop children who should be prosecuted and punished for their offences from being convicted or from even coming to court'[5]. Others have pointed out that the existence of the presumption should have been seen alongside the very low age of criminal responsibility in England and that it was perhaps more justifiable in the light of this[6]. It is also questionable how far the abolition of the presumption is consistent with the notion of gradual or gathering independence for children. As was argued in Chapter 3, the notion of children's responsibilities or duties ought to go hand in hand with the extent of their autonomy. The Government appeared to accept this in its White Paper on Youth Crime which states:

> 'As they develop, children must bear an increasing responsibility for their actions, just as the responsibility of parents gradually declines – but does not disappear – as their children approach adulthood.'[7]

Yet this is precisely what the abolition of the doli incapax presumption does not achieve, for instead of a gradual recognition of increasing responsibility of children for crime what we have is the sudden acquisition of responsibility at the age of 10. As Tony Smith has graphically put it, referring to the earlier decision of the Divisional Court in *C v DPP*, 'we now have a law which holds that a person is completely irresponsible on the day before his tenth birthday, and fully responsible as soon as the jelly and ice-cream have been cleared away the following day'[8]. Jane Fortin has also rightly questioned how consistent the age of criminal responsibility is with the often very paternalistic attitude to children as old as

---

1 [1995] 2 WLR 383. For commentary, see ATH Smith 'Reshaping the Criminal Law in the House of Lords' (1995) CLJ 486. For a wider critique of the doli incapax presumption, see G Douglas 'The Child's Right to Make Mistakes: Criminal Responsibility and the Immature Minor' in G Douglas and L Sebba *Children's Rights and Traditional Values* (Ashgate, 1998) at ch 15.

2 For what was involved in establishing a 'mischievous discretion', see the discussion of case-law in the second edition of this work at p 486. It, of course, remains the case that for many offences it will be necessary to establish mens rea and in practice this may prove more difficult in the case of children in this age group depending on their individual level of maturity and understanding.

3 See White Paper *No More Excuses – A New Approach to Tackling Youth Crime in England and Wales* (1997) (Cm 3809) at ch 4.

4 White Paper (above) at para 4.14.

5 Ibid.

6 For a detailed discussion, see J Fortin *Children's Rights and the Developing Law* (2nd edn) (Butterworths, 2003) at pp 550–560.

7 White Paper (above) at para 4.1.

8 ATH Smith 'Doli Incapax Under Threat' (1994) CLJ 426 at 427.

mid-teens in other areas of the law[1]. Moreover, the UNCRC has been critical of the UK's failure to give primacy to the child's welfare in the juvenile justice system of which the very prosecution of children of this age is an important aspect[2].

There used to be a special rule applying to sexual offences and boys under 14 years of age. There was a *conclusive* presumption that a boy of that age was incapable of sexual intercourse and therefore could not commit rape, offences involving sexual intercourse or buggery[3]. Acts which might, but for that presumption, have constituted the above offences might instead have founded a prosecution for indecent assault. It became increasingly appreciated that the presumption did not accord with reality, and it was eventually abolished by s 1 of the Sexual Offences Act 1993.

Responsibility of parents

Should parents be responsible for the criminal acts of their children? The former Conservative administration thought so and, to the surprise of many, New Labour has introduced legislation firmly grounded in the same philosophy. But many commentators on juvenile justice doubted the validity of this[4].

Before 1990, the law was that parents might be made liable for fines imposed on their children. It was the duty of the court to order that a fine, compensation, or costs be paid by a parent or guardian unless it was satisfied that the parent or guardian could not be found, or that the order would be unreasonable in the circumstances. It is understood, however, that the power was rarely used[5].

Enforcing parental responsibility

In a White Paper published in February 1990[6], the Conservative Government expressed its intention to go further in the direction of enforcing parental responsibility in this area. Originally it wanted to make it a criminal offence for parents to 'fail to prevent their children from committing offences'. The proposal was heavily criticised by, among others, the Magistrates' Association and was subsequently dropped. The main criticisms were that most delinquents came from families which were inadequate in some way – often lacking an appropriate father-figure. It was argued that resources could better be diverted to helping the families through education and social work support, and it was further argued that the proposal was likely to be counter-productive in that it might lead to the complete disintegration of already fragile family units. The connection between excessive corporal punishment and child abuse was also noted[7].

---

1   Fortin (above) at pp 551–552; and see Chapters 3 and 8 above.
2   See below.
3   *R v Groombridge* (1836) 7 C&P 582, *R v Waite* [1892] 2 QB 600, *R v Tatam* (1921) 15 Cr App R 132, respectively.
4   For two succinct criticisms of the idea, see JG Hall and DF Martin 'Child Delinquency and Parental Responsibility' (1990) JPN 604, and D Boyd 'Blaming the Parents' (1990) 2 JCL 65.
5   Children and Young Persons Act 1933, s 55. This was the experience at least of JG Hall (a retired circuit judge) and DF Martin (a former principal in the Lord Chancellor's Office) (above).
6   *Crime, Justice and Protecting the Public* (1990) (Cmnd 965).
7   See JG Hall and DF Martin (above) for a neat summary of these objections.

Measures to make parents more accountable

Despite these criticisms, the Conservative Government pressed ahead with a package of measures designed to make parents more accountable. These were incorporated in the Criminal Justice Act 1991[1]. This followed a White Paper in which the Government had expressed its view of the importance of parents attending court and taking responsibility for financial penalties. Accordingly, where a child or young person under 16 years of age *is* charged with a criminal offence, the court must now require a parent to be present in court unless, in all the circumstances, this would be unreasonable[2]. It has a discretion to require a parent's presence where the young person is over 16 years[3]. The court's duty to require parents to pay fines, compensation and costs continues where a child is under 16 years of age but this is now only a *power* in relation to young persons over 16 years[4]. The thinking, similar to that which has inspired reforms in the civil law[5], is that many in this age group will have de facto independence from their parents and, therefore, should be made directly responsible for their own financial penalties. Local authorities were, for the first time, made directly responsible for financial penalties incurred by offenders, under the age of 18 years, who are looked after by them[6]. Where the child is merely accommodated, as opposed to being in the care of the local authority, a parent may not be liable for offences committed by the child if the parent has no control of the child at the relevant time[7].

More controversially, the criminal courts have a duty to bind over the parents of a child or young person under 16 years if satisfied, in the circumstances, that the exercise of this power 'would be desirable in the interests of preventing the commission by him of further offences'[8]. Where the court is not so satisfied, it must give reasons in open court[9], the effect of which is to create a presumption of binding over[10]. There had been a proposal that the power be extended to the parents of children over 16 years in full-time education and living at home, but this was withdrawn. The court may also order a parent or guardian to enter into a recognisance in a sum not exceeding £1,000 to take proper care of the offender and exercise proper control over him[11]. This requires the consent of the parent or guardian, but this is more illusory than real, since the court may fine him where it

---

1 Criminal Justice Act 1991, ss 56–58.
2 Ibid, s 56, creating a new s 34A of the Children and Young Persons Act 1933.
3 Children and Young Persons Act 1933, s 34A(1).
4 Powers of Criminal Courts (Sentencing) Act 2000 (PCC(S)A 2000), s 137.
5 See the discussion of the Age of Legal Capacity (Scotland) Act 1991 in Chapter 15.
6 Criminal Justice Act 1991, s 57, inserting a new s 55(5) into the Children and Young Persons Act 1933 and effectively reversing the decision in *Leeds City Council v West Yorkshire Metropolitan Police* [1983] 1 AC 29. The liability of the local authority will turn in individual cases on whether it has behaved reasonably and properly in its efforts to control the child. See *D (A Minor) v DPP* [1995] 2 FLR 502 and *Bedfordshire County Council v DPP* [1995] Crim LR 962.
7 *TA v Director of Public Prosecutions* [1997] 2 FLR 887.
8 PCC(S)A 2000, s 150(1)(a).
9 Ibid, s 150(1)(b).
10 The Government's intention was clearly to persuade the courts to exercise these powers much more frequently than they had done before the Criminal Justice Act 1991. For an analysis of that Act as it applies to parental responsibility, see M Wasik and RD Taylor *Blackstone's Guide to the Criminal Justice Act 1991* (Blackstone Press, 1991) at paras 4.5–4.8.
11 PCC(S)A 2000, s 150(1) and (2).

considers his refusal unreasonable[1]. The recognisance may then be forfeited if further criminal offences are committed[2]. The controversial bind-over provisions of the Criminal Justice Act 1991 were taken a stage further by the Criminal Justice and Public Order Act 1994. This amended the 1991 Act[3] to empower the courts to bind over parents not merely where their children re-offend but also where they fail to comply with the requirements of a community sentence.

Objections to these powers

These powers come the closest to the Conservative Government's original, more radical, proposal to fix parents themselves with criminal responsibility. There are some formidable civil libertarian objections to these powers, and serious questions about imposing liability for the criminal actions of others. It is not at all clear how well the idea accords with the civil concept of parental responsibility under the Children Act or how far it acknowledges the conflict of interest which may arise between the child and the parent who has done everything in his or her power to control the child but has failed. The trend in the civil law since *Gillick* has been very much away from the notion of parental control and towards independence for adolescents. The binding-over power seems to jar with this. Yet, as we shall see, the effect of recent legislation introduced by New Labout is to extend, rather than reduce, the powers of the criminal courts to take action in relation to parents.

The parenting order

Far from reversing the authoritarian trend towards punishing parents for the sins of their children instigated by the former Conservative Government, the new Labour administration took this policy yet further in the same direction by the introduction in the Crime and Disorder Act 1998 of the 'parenting order'[4]. The Government's thinking was set out in a White Paper which preceded the legislation[5]. Essentially, this was that research had established an association between inadequate parental supervision and juvenile offending. While, therefore, parents of young offenders might not be directly to blame for the crimes of their children, they should be responsible for providing their children with proper care and control. The courts, it was thought, needed powers to help and support parents more effectively to keep their children out of trouble.

The parenting order is generally available in relation to parents of convicted young offenders, parents of children who have been the subject of an anti-social behaviour order, sex offender order or child safety order[6], and parents who have

---

1   PCC(S)A 2000, s 150(2)(b).
2   But interesting questions may arise as to what precisely constitutes a failure 'to take proper care of [the child] and exercise proper control over him'. Can this simply be assumed because the child or young person has committed further offences?
3   Criminal Justice Act 1991, s 58(2), now PCC(S)A 2000, s 150(2)(b).
4   Sections 8–10.
5   See White Paper *No More Excuses – A New Approach to Tackling Youth Crime in England and Wales* (1997) (Cm 3809) ch 4, especially at paras 4.6–4.12. For a useful commentary on the general question of parental responsibility for juvenile crime, see L Gelsthorpe 'Youth Crime and Parental Responsibility' in A Bainham, S Day Sclater and M Richards *What is a Parent?* (Hart Publishing, 1999).
6   See pp 639 et seq below.

been convicted in truancy cases[1]. The order requires parents to attend a counselling or guidance programme for no longer than three months[2]. Where the court thinks it necessary the order may impose additional requirements which may apply for up to one year, for example to ensure that the child attends school every day or that he or she is home by a certain time each night[3]. Parents may be fined for failing without reasonable excuse to comply with any requirement included in the order[4]. Where a person under 16 years of age is found guilty of an offence, the court *must* make a parenting order (if the other conditions for the order exist) or, if no order is made, it must state the reason why it is not in open court[5].

In its White Paper, the Government gave the following example of how the parenting order could work. A 13-year-old boy has committed a number of crimes at night and does not attend school regularly. Here, a parenting order might be imposed which requires his parents to attend training and which might include additional requirements to ensure his attendance at school and that one parent or another responsible adult be at home at night to supervise him.

The Anti-social Behaviour Act 2003: parenting contracts and parenting orders

The Anti-social Behaviour Act 2003[6] extends the circumstances in which parenting orders may be made but also places them within a context in which, as the usual first course of action, parents may 'voluntarily' enter into parenting contracts. The new Act covers the two situations of exclusion from school and truancy[7], and criminal conduct and anti-social behaviour[8]. The essential regime is similar, though not identical, in each set of circumstances. Schools, LEAs and youth offending teams are empowered to enter into parenting contracts with parents, respectively, where a child has been excluded from school or failed to attend regularly[9], or where a child has been referred to a youth offending team and a member of that team has reason to believe that the child has engaged, or is likely to engage, in criminal conduct or anti-social behaviour[10].

The parenting contract consists of a statement by the parent that he agrees to comply with the requirements in the contract for a specified period and a statement by the school, LEA, or youth offending team (as the case may be) that it will provide or arrange support to the parent to help him comply with the requirements. The Act then makes provision for LEAs to apply for parenting

---

1 For the duty of parents to ensure school attendance and the related offences, see Chapter 16 below.
2 Crime and Disorder Act 1998, s 8, as amended by the Anti-social Behaviour Act 2003, s 18. The order may *now* require attendance more than once a week, and there is a new power to require attendance on a residential course.
3 Ibid.
4 Crime and Disorder Act 1998, s 9.
5 Ibid.
6 Part 3. On the Act generally, see M Waddington, H Carr, A Blair and T Baldwin *The Anti-Social Behaviour Act 2003: A Special Bulletin* (Jordans, 2004). On anti-social behaviour orders, see A Pema and S Heels *Anti-Social Behaviour Orders: A Special Bulletin* (Jordans, 2004). For critiques of the Act, see N Padfield 'The Anti-Social Behaviour Act 2003: The Ultimate Nanny-State Act?' (2004) *Criminal Law Review* 712, and A Ashworth 'Social Control and "Anti-Social Behaviour"' (2004) 120 LQR 263.
7 Anti-social Behaviour Act 2003, ss 19 and 20.
8 Ibid, s 25 and 26.
9 Ibid, s 19.
10 Ibid, s 25.

orders in cases of exclusion from school[1], and for youth offending teams to do so in cases of criminal conduct or anti-social behaviour[2]. For these purposes, 'anti-social behaviour' means behaviour which causes, or is likely to cause, harassment, alarm or distress to one or more other persons not of the same household as the child, and 'criminal conduct' includes, significantly, behaviour by children under 10 which would be criminal if they were over that age[3]. In the case of truancy, the Act introduces a new power to enable authorised LEA and school staff and the police to issue fixed penalty notices to parents as an alternative to prosecution[4].

Clearly the intention of this regime is that in most cases parenting contracts will be the option of first choice, backed up by the sanction of parenting orders where necessary. The Act does, however, make it clear that the parenting order may be sought as a *first response* in appropriate cases, as well as in the more obvious situation where a parent has refused to enter into, or has breached, a contract[5]. The requirements laid down in a parenting contract are likely to be similar to those which may be imposed in a parenting order, including now the requirement to attend a residential programme.

The parenting order exists alongside the bind-over powers discussed above. The order might be viewed by some as an attempt to provide support and encouragement to the parents of young offenders, while others may see it as fundamentally authoritarian, an attack on civil liberties and an extraordinary invasion by the State into family autonomy – so richly prized elsewhere in the law[6].

YOUNG OFFENDERS AND THE CRIMINAL PROCESS

Prevention and diversion

The emphasis on inter-agency co-operation in the civil context has already been noted[7]. This is also very much a feature of the criminal processes which may or may not be invoked against young offenders. Local authorities' social services departments have statutory obligations to provide support services to children and families[8]. These include a duty to take reasonable steps designed to reduce the need to bring criminal proceedings against children, to encourage children within their areas not to commit crime, and to avoid the need for children to be placed in secure accommodation[9]. Early local authority involvement is also secured by requiring the prosecuting authorities[10] to give notice of any decision to

---

1 Anti-social Behaviour Act 2003, s 20.
2 Ibid, ss 26–29.
3 Ibid, s 29.
4 Ibid, s 23, and see Chapter 16 below in relation to school attendance requirements.
5 Ibid, s 20.
6 A human rights challenge to parenting orders failed in *R (M) v Inner London Crown Court* [2003] 1 FLR 994 where the Divisional Court found that they did not breach Article 6 of the ECHR and that, although they interfered with family life engaging Article 8, they were a proportionate and justifiable interference. On the facts, however, the particular parenting order was quashed on grounds of irrationality. The pre-sentence report had expressed the view that the mother would not be receptive or suitable for a parenting order, and the offence had involved an isolated attack committed by a child of otherwise exemplary character.
7 See particularly Chapters 10 and 11 above.
8 See Chapter 10 above.
9 Schedule 2, para 7 to the Children Act.
10 The Police, and the Crown Prosecution Service (CPS).

prosecute a juvenile to the relevant local authority. While this ought to, and often will, involve co-operation and consultation *before* the decision to prosecute is taken, there is no statutory requirement to this effect. In practice, there is usually close liaison between the police, social services, education authorities and the probation service.

The use of cautions
The above consultations will be directed in particular to the question whether the offender should be cautioned rather than prosecuted. Cautioning was used extensively as part of a wider strategy of 'diversion' of juveniles from the criminal justice system. This was very much the philosophy behind the unimplemented provisions in the Children and Young Persons Act 1969[1]. If these had been brought into effect, criminal proceedings against children, ie children under 14 years of age, would have been abolished altogether[2] and would only have been brought against those over 14 years as a last resort[3]. The increased preference for cautioning was part of the same thinking, but the practice itself was not on a statutory footing[4]. The Home Office issued guidance on the criteria which should be followed[5]. The caution was a *formal* alternative to prosecution, as contrasted with an informal warning[6]. A caution might, thus, only be administered where guilt was admitted or there was sufficient evidence to give a realistic prospect of conviction, and, importantly, the parent or guardian had to understand the nature of a formal caution and give an informed consent to it.

The Labour Government took the view that the existing system of cautioning was not effective in the prevention of re-offending, especially where there had been repeated cautions. Accordingly, the Crime and Disorder Act 1998 abolished cautioning for young offenders and replaced it with a statutory police reprimand and final warning scheme[7].

Overruling decisions on prosecution
An issue which has come before the courts is whether the decision of the prosecuting authorities is final or susceptible to judicial review. Several cases have established that judicial review could lie in respect of decisions *not* to prosecute[8]. In *R v Chief Constable of Kent*[9] the question was whether a decision to continue a

---

1 Now repealed by the Criminal Justice Act 1991, s 72.
2 Children and Young Persons Act 1969, s 6.
3 Ibid, s 5.
4 The matter was governed by Home Office Circular No 18/1994 *The Cautioning of Offenders.*
5 Ibid at Annex B.
6 Informal warnings or cautions may be given by the police but they do not have the implications of formal cautioning discussed below.
7 Discussed at p 631 above. See R Evans and K Puech 'Reprimands and Warnings: Populist Punitiveness or Restorative Justice' [2001] Crim LR 794.
8 See *R v Metropolitan Police ex parte Blackburn* [1968] 2 QB 118; and *R v Bar Council ex parte Percival* [1990] 3 WLR 323. In *R v DPP ex parte C* [1995] 1 Cr App R 136 the decision of the DPP not to prosecute in a case of alleged non-consensual buggery by a husband on his wife was set aside by the Divisional Court and remitted to the DPP for further consideration. The court said that the power to review the decision not to prosecute was to be exercised sparingly, but in this case there had been a failure to follow the Code for Crown Prosecutors issued by the DPP under s 10 of the Prosecution of Offences Act 1985.
9 *R v Chief Constable of Kent and Another ex parte L* [1991] Crim LR 841. See the commentaries on the case in C Eades 'The Decision to Prosecute Juveniles – No Review of the Actions of the Police and Crown Prosecution Service' (1991) JPN 358, and S Uglow, A Dart, A Bottomley and C Hale 'Cautioning Juveniles – Multi-Agency Impotence' [1992] Crim LR 632.

prosecution, against the advice of the local Juvenile Offender Liaison Team, could be impugned. The Home Office criteria for cautioning were satisfied, but the police, nevertheless, decided to go ahead with the prosecution. This decision received the endorsement of the Crown Prosecution Service (CPS). The decision was reached on the basis that the injuries sustained exceeded the usual incidents of juvenile violence and that it was therefore in the public interest to prosecute[1]. The Divisional Court held that a decision of the CPS to continue or discontinue criminal proceedings was, in principle, susceptible to judicial review but only in very restricted circumstances[2]. It would have to be shown that the decision contravened a settled policy of the DPP, evolved in the public interest. Such instances of a complete disregard of public policy would be rare. The decision, in this case, has been criticised on the basis that it largely ignored the welfare considerations involved in prosecution versus cautioning, making these secondary to legalistic questions of due process, and undermining the role of the non-statutory liaison body[3].

The investigative process

In general, the powers of arrest and detention which the police have are governed by the Police and Criminal Evidence Act 1984 (PACE 1984). Under s 66 there is a Code of Practice[4] regulating the detention, treatment and questioning of persons by police officers. This Code makes special provision for the treatment of young suspects.

The juvenile in police custody

Where a juvenile is arrested, the arresting officer must, where practicable, ascertain the identity of the person responsible for that juvenile's welfare and must notify that person of the arrest[5]. This will normally be the juvenile's parent or guardian or, perhaps, social services, where he is being looked after by the local authority[6]. If the juvenile is then held in custody he must be told of his rights to have someone informed of his whereabouts and he has the right to a solicitor[7]. The 'appropriate adult' must then generally be present at any interview with the juvenile[8]. Any caution must be administered in the presence of the appropriate adult or repeated in his presence later. The juvenile must not be detained in a police cell without good reason and must not be allowed to come into contact with

---

1   The victim had sustained a fracture to the maxillary spine of his nose and had been knocked to the ground. As he lay there it was alleged that the accused had kicked him in the head.

2   It was held that the initial decision of the police was not susceptible to judicial review since their power to prosecute had been severely limited by the setting up of the CPS.

3   Uglow et al (above) at p 199.

4   Revised edition, effective April 2003.

5   Children and Young Persons Act 1933, s 34(2) and (3).

6   Ibid, s 34(5)(b) refers to 'any other person who has for the time being assumed responsibility for his welfare'. And see 'At the Police Station. The Role of the "Appropriate Adult"' (1991) 74 *Childright* 9.

7   PACE 1984, ss 56 and 58.

8   See the *Code of Practice for the Detention, Treatment and Questioning of Persons by Police Officers (Code C)* at para 11. For criticisms of the practice relating to the use of appropriate adults, see J Williams 'The Inappropriate Adult' (2000) 22 JSWFL 43, and H Pierpoint 'How appropriate are volunteers as "appropriate adults" for young suspects? The appropriate adult system and human rights' (2000) 22 JSWFL 383.

adult suspects[1]. As soon as practicable after the arrest, the 'custody officer'[2] must determine whether or not there is sufficient evidence to charge the juvenile. If not, he must be released, with or without bail, unless his further detention is necessary: (1) to secure or preserve evidence relating to an offence for which he is under arrest; or (2) to obtain such evidence by questioning him[3]. The maximum period of detention without charge is 24 hours, but this may be extended on the authority of a superintendent or the court[4].

Further detention of a juvenile

Where the juvenile is charged and further detention is necessary, PACE 1984[5], as amended by the Criminal Justice Act 1991[6], imposes important duties on the custody officer. The central principle is that juveniles who are charged and detained ought, in all but exceptional circumstances, to be looked after by social services in local authority accommodation and not held in police custody. This was the original intention reflected in PACE 1984 itself but there was evidence that the practice of police forces throughout the country differed significantly. The purpose of the amendments made by the Criminal Justice Act 1991 was to reinforce the policy of passing responsibility for the juvenile's accommodation to the local authority[7].

Where the custody officer authorises an arrested juvenile to be kept in police detention, he must now secure that the juvenile is moved to local authority accommodation, unless he certifies:

(1) that, by reason of specified circumstances, it is impracticable for him to do so; or

(2) in the case of an arrested juvenile who has attained the age of 12 years, that no secure accommodation is available and that keeping him in other local authority accommodation would not be adequate to protect the public from serious harm from him[8].

Where an arrested juvenile is charged with a 'violent offence' or a 'sexual offence' there is a statutory definition of 'protecting the public from serious harm'. This means 'protecting members of the public from death or serious personal injury, whether physical or psychological, occasioned by further such offences committed by him'[9].

---

1 Children and Young Persons Act 1933, s 31, which also prescribes that a girl should be under the care of a woman.

2 The 'custody officer' is a designated police officer who is charged with the responsibility of ensuring that the statutory requirements and Code of Practice under PACE 1984 are observed. See PACE 1984, s 36(3), which provides that the officer appointed must be of at least the rank of sergeant.

3 PACE 1984, s 37(2).

4 Ibid, ss 41, 42 and 43.

5 Ibid, s 38(6).

6 Ibid, s 59.

7 For further discussion, see C Bell 'New Criminal Justice Act amends PACE on detention of juveniles' (1991) 79 *Childright* 7.

8 PACE 1984, s 38(6), as amended by the Criminal Justice Act 1991, s 59. For secure accommodation, see p 644 below.

9 Ibid, s 38(6A).

Remands and committals of juveniles

The Criminal Justice Act 1991[1] also amended the law relating to remands and committals of juveniles and applies essentially the same policy regarding their accommodation while in custody. Thus, where a court remands a child or young person charged with or convicted of one or more offences, or commits him for trial or sentence, and he is not released on bail, the remand must be to local authority accommodation[2]. The court is required to designate the relevant authority which will be, where the child is being 'looked after' by an authority, that authority, or the authority in whose area the child resides, or where one of the offences was committed[3]. The court may require the juvenile to comply with any condition which can be imposed under the Bail Act 1976[4], and the relevant authority may be given the responsibility of securing compliance with the conditions imposed[5].

On a remand or committal, the court may, after consultation with the local authority, require it to comply with a 'security requirement' by placing or keeping the juvenile in 'secure accommodation'[6]. This is defined as 'accommodation which is provided in a community home, a voluntary home or a registered children's home for the purpose of restricting liberty, and is approved for that purpose by the Secretary of State'[7]. The Criminal Justice Act 1991[8] requires local authorities to ensure that they have sufficient secure accommodation for these purposes and others. The power to impose a security requirement is, however, carefully restricted. It may be stipulated only where the young person is at least 12 years of age[9] and either:

(1) he is charged with, or has been convicted of, a violent or sexual offence or an offence punishable, in the case of an adult, with at least 14 years' imprisonment; or

(2) he has a recent history of absconding while remanded to local authority accommodation and is charged with, or has been convicted of, an imprisonable offence alleged, or found to have been committed, while he was so remanded.

In either case, the court must be of the opinion that the protection of the public from serious harm justifies the security requirement[10]. Where the court does

---

1 Criminal Justice Act 1991, s 60.
2 Children and Young Persons Act 1969, s 23(1).
3 Ibid, s 23(2).
4 Such conditions typically relate to place of residence, reporting to the police, curfew requirements, etc.
5 Children and Young Persons Act 1969, s 23(9) and (10).
6 Ibid, s 23(4).
7 Ibid, s 23(12).
8 Criminal Justice Act 1991, s 61(1).
9 Section 97 of the Crime and Disorder Act 1998 amended s 23 of the Children and Young Persons Act 1969 to allow courts to remand young persons aged 12 or over direct to local authority secure accommodation. Section 98 amends s 23 to provide for 15- and 16-year-old boys who meet specific criteria to be remanded to prison or a remand centre, and for vulnerable 15- and 16-year-old boys to be remanded to local authority secure accommodation if a place is available.
10 Children and Young Persons Act 1969, s 23(5).

impose a requirement, it must explain the reasons for its decision in open court and in ordinary language which the young person can understand[1].

Consistency of practice
The overall objective of the provisions is to produce consistency of practice between the different police forces and as between detentions while under arrest, on remand or on committal[2].

The criminal courts

Provision for the child's welfare
Since the early part of the twentieth century, the principle has been accepted that there should be a separate system of criminal courts for dealing with juvenile offenders[3]. The objective is to prevent children and young persons coming into contact or associating with adult suspects, while awaiting trial, during the trial itself, and while in custody[4]. The general rule is, therefore, that a juvenile should be tried in the youth court and not in the adult magistrates' court or the Crown Court. Where, exceptionally, it is necessary for the trial of the juvenile to take place in one of the adult criminal courts[5], the principle (again subject to limited exceptions) is that, if convicted, the juvenile should be remitted to the youth court to be dealt with by it[6]. Whichever court is dealing with a child or young person, either as an offender or otherwise, it must have regard to his welfare and must, in a proper case, 'take steps for removing him from undesirable surroundings, and for securing' that proper provision is made for his education and training'[7]. This welfare provision in the criminal context is, however, quite different from the 'welfare principle' which applies in family proceedings[8]. Welfare is not 'paramount' in criminal proceedings but is one important factor in the court's decision-making process. Clearly, there are wider considerations of the public interest at stake here, especially the need to protect the public.

The Crown Court trial of Thompson and Venables, two 11-year-old boys convicted of murdering two-year-old James Bulger, was widely reported in the media and led ultimately to an adverse ruling by the ECtHR[9]. The ECtHR held

---

1   Children and Young Persons Act 1969, s 23(6).
2   For criticisms, see C Bell 'New Criminal Justice Act amends PACE on detention of juveniles' (1991) 79 *Childright* 7.
3   The historical background is traced by HK Bevan *Child Law* (Butterworths, 1989) at paras 12.01 et seq.
4   See the Children and Young Persons Act 1933, s 31.
5   The main exceptions relate to homicide, cases in which the juvenile is jointly charged with an adult or in relation to which an adult is charged as a secondary party or vice-versa or where a young person has committed a serious offence which may merit a longer custodial sentence that may only be imposed after conviction on indictment under the powers in PCC(S)A 2000, s 91. A useful and concise account of the circumstances in which the trial of juveniles may take place on indictment, in an adult magistrates' court and a youth court, is to be found in J Sprack *A Practical Approach to Criminal Procedure* (10th edn) (Oxford University Press, 2004) at paras 10.01–10.19.
6   Children and Young Persons Act 1933, s 56(1), which provides for remission to the youth court unless the adult court is 'satisfied that it would be undesirable to do so'.
7   Ibid, s 44.
8   See Chapter 2 above.
9   *V and T v United Kingdom* (2000) 30 EHRR 121.

that T, one of the two boys, had not received a fair hearing, contrary to Article 6 of the ECHR. He had not been able to participate fully in the three-week public trial. The Court took the view that where a young child was charged with a grave offence, attracting high levels of media and public interest, the hearing must be conducted in a way which reduces, as far as possible, the child's feelings of intimidation and inhibition. It rejected, however, the contention that the trial had subjected him to inhuman and degrading treatment or punishment contrary to Article 3.

Following this ruling, Lord Bingham of Cornhill CJ issued a Practice Note[1] which implemented forthwith changes to the practice of the Crown Courts' conduct of the trials of children and young persons. The overriding principle is now that 'all possible steps should be taken to assist the young defendant to understand and participate in the proceedings' and that 'the ordinary trial process should so far as necessary be adapted to meet these ends'. It is explicitly reasserted that regard must be had to the young defendant's welfare as required by s 44 of the Children and Young Persons Act 1933. Among the changes required are that the trial be held, as far as practicable, in a courtroom in which all the participants are on the same or almost the same level; that a young defendant should be free to sit with a member of his family or others and in a place which facilitates easy, informal communication with legal representatives and others; that robes and wigs should not be worn; that the timetable for the trial should allow for frequent and regular breaks; and that those allowed to attend and report on the trial should be restricted.

While these adaptations are certainly more than cosmetic, they do not come close to addressing adequately the fundamental questions about the criminal responsibility and prosecution of young children.

The youth court

The youth court is a specialised magistrates' court comprised of justices of the peace who are members of the youth court panel for their area. The court will usually be constituted by three members, at least one of whom must normally be a woman. The court abides by the ordinary rules and procedures of magistrates' courts, except where these are expressly modified[2].

Before the Criminal Justice Act 1991, the youth court was known as the juvenile court, and the youth court panel as the juvenile court panel. The change of nomenclature reflected a shift in the demographic make-up of those appearing before the court[3]. In 1988, approximately 90% of those appearing were in the 14- to 16-year age group but it has been predicted that, in future, three-quarters will be 16 or 17 years of age. This shift came about as a result of a number of other changes. First, before the Criminal Justice Act 1991, 17-year-olds were dealt with in the adult court system while 16-year-olds were brought before the juvenile court.

---

1   [2000] 2 All ER 285. See also the Note on *T v United Kingdom* [2000] 2 All ER 1024. The aspect of the decision of the ECtHR dealing with the indeterminacy of the mandatory sentence of detention at Her Majesty's Pleasure is discussed below. For a more detailed discussion of the issues raised by the case see J Fortin *Children's Rights and the Developing Law* (2nd edn) (Butterworths, 2003) at pp 563–566.
2   Magistrates' Courts Act 1980, s 152.
3   See M Wasik and RD Taylor *Blackstone's Guide to the Criminal Justice Act 1991* (Blackstone Press, 1991) at para 4.14.

The Government did not think that this differential treatment of 16- and 17-year-olds could continue to be justified and thought that *both* should be dealt with in the youth court as 'near adults'. The Criminal Justice Act 1991 brought 17-year-olds within the youth court's jurisdiction for most purposes except remand[1]. Alongside this change, the court lost its former substantial *civil* jurisdiction over children in need of care and protection, which was transferred to the 'family proceedings court'[2]. The practical effect of this was to remove from the court's jurisdiction many younger children.

Special procedural rules

Special procedural rules protect the anonymity of children appearing before the youth court[3]. The court must not sit in a room which is used for normal criminal proceedings within one hour either side of such proceedings[4]. There are restrictions on publicity[5], and the categories of those entitled to be present are severely restricted[6]. There is a different form of oath in which the juvenile 'promises' rather than 'swears'. The words 'conviction' and 'sentence' must not be used in relation to juveniles dealt with summarily, and are replaced by the more neutral 'finding of guilt' and 'order made on a finding of guilt'[7]. The juvenile will not go into a dock but will sit on a chair with his parents beside him and the magistrates seated at a table opposite him.

The Crime and Disorder Act 1998

Policies of dealing with young offenders have been the subject of considerable vacillation by governments of different complexion over a great many years. In particular, there has not been a consistent view about how to strike the balance between issues of the welfare of the young offender and considerations of justice or punishment. During the 1960s, within the wider context of the welfare state, it seemed that the welfare model was in the ascendant and, although it can be argued that an increasingly punitive approach has been taken for several decades, there was still, until comparatively recently, an emphasis on diversion from the criminal courts and a preference for community-based rather than custodial sentences[8]. In the 1990s, however, there was a distinctly authoritarian shift, and the sentencing of juveniles took on an increasingly punitive ethos. Once again,

---

1 Criminal Justice Act 1991, s 68.
2 See Chapter 2 above.
3 Children and Young Persons Act 1933, s 47.
4 Ibid, s 47(2).
5 The media must not name the juvenile or report identifying information, although there is power for the court to lift this restriction in order to avoid injustice to the juvenile or where he is unlawfully at large and charged with a violent or sexual or other serious offence (Children and Young Persons Act 1933, s 49). The converse is true in the adult magistrates' court or Crown Court, where the juvenile may be named unless the court orders otherwise.
6 Those allowed are members and officers of the court, the parties, their lawyers and others directly concerned with the case, witnesses, bona fide representatives of newspapers or news agencies and others specially authorised by the court. This contrasts with the position where the juvenile is tried in an adult magistrates' court or Crown Court. The hearings will normally be in open court, although there is power to clear the court in sensitive cases (Children and Young Persons Act 1933).
7 Children and Young Persons Act 1933, s 59(1).
8 On the 'justice' versus 'welfare' debate, see C Ball 'Young Offenders and the Youth Court' [1992] Crim LR 277.

juvenile crime was seen predominantly as a matter of personal responsibility, rather than principally the product of adverse social conditions or a disadvantaged family background. This appears to be the philosophical basis of the Crime and Disorder Act 1998 although there are also aspects of this legislation which are philosophically grounded in the notion of 'restorative justice'. The central tenet of restorative justice has been described by Loraine Gelsthorpe as being that 'crime should be seen primarily as a matter concerning the offender and victim and their immediate families and thus should be resolved by them through constructive effort (restorative measures) to put right the harm that has been done'[1]. The 'reparation order' and 'action plan order', both introduced by the 1998 Act, may be seen as fitting within this model of criminal justice. The Youth Justice and Criminal Evidence Act 1999 gave arguably a more significant push in the direction of restorative justice by introducing the 'referral order' as the mandatory first disposal for most young offenders pleading guilty and making their first appearance before the youth court[2]. There remains some legitimate debate about whether New Labour's youth justice policy can really be said to have embraced the philosophy of restorative justice or whether such measures as have been introduced are insignificant alongside what may be seen as a predominantly punitive approach to juvenile crime[3]. Before coming to this, we will summarise the current range of sentencing options in relation to young offenders. The full range of disposals in the youth court is extensive[4]. Yet this requires qualification, since the alternatives in any individual cases are cut down by various criteria which determine when each can be used. Thus, for example, custodial sentences may only be imposed where the offence is 'so serious' that only a custodial sentence can be justified[5] and, where a community sentence is proposed, it must be shown that the offence is 'serious enough' to warrant such a sentence[6]. Other sentences are restricted by the age of the offender and by whether the offence would be punishable by imprisonment in the case of an adult.

Youth Justice and Criminal Evidence Act 1999 – referral orders

The Crime and Disorder Act 1998 was quickly followed by the Youth Justice and Criminal Evidence Act 1999, Part I of which introduced the new 'referral order'[7]. In 2000 legislation was passed consolidating all the courts' sentencing powers which had previously been dispersed among a large number of statutes. Accordingly, the provisions of the 1999 Act relating to referral orders are now to be found in Part III of the Powers of Criminal Courts (Sentencing) Act 2000 (PCC(SA) 2000).

A referral order is mandatory where a youth court or magistrates' court is dealing with a person under 18 who pleads guilty and is convicted for the first time

---

1   L Gelsthorpe 'Recent Changes in Youth Justice Policy in England and Wales' in I Weijers and A Duff *Punishing Juveniles: Principle and Critique* (Hart Publishing, 2002) at p 57.
2   See below.
3   Cf J Dignan 'The Crime and Disorder Act and the Prospects for Restorative Justice' [1999] *Criminal Law Review* 48, and A Morris and L Gelsthorpe 'Something Old, Something Borrowed, Something Blue, but Something New? A Comment on the prospects for restorative justice under the Crime and Disorder Act 1998' [2000] *Criminal Law Review* 18.
4   See Sprack (above) at paras 10.21–10.28.
5   *Criminal Justice Act 1991*, s 1(2).
6   Ibid, s 6(1).
7   See C Ball 'The Youth Justice and Criminal Evidence Act 1999: Part I: A significant move towards restorative justice, or a recipe for unintended consequences' [2000] Crim LR 211.

in relation to an offence where the sentence is not fixed by law or serious enough to justify imposing a custodial sentence and where the court is not proposing an absolute discharge[1]. A referral order is an order that the young offender be referred to a Youth Offender Panel[2]. The offender is then required to attend all meetings of the panel, and the parent of an offender under 16 is also required to attend all the meetings[3]. The offender is entitled to be accompanied by one person of his choice over the age of 18[4]. The victim may also attend.

The purpose of the order is to try to agree with the offender a programme of behaviour which is aimed to prevent re-offending and to conclude a 'youth offender contract'[5]. Where the order is made the court is prevented from making any principal order which would normally be available to it, such as fines, community sentences, reparation orders or conditional discharges[6]. Neither may the court bind over parents or make parenting orders[7]. The programme of behaviour may include provision for such things as making financial or other reparation to the victim, attending mediation sessions with the victim or others, or carrying out unpaid community work or service. It may also require the offender to be at home at specified times, in attendance at school or a place of work and to participate in specified activities[8]. Finally, it may require the offender to present himself or herself to specified persons at specified times or, conversely, to stay away from specified persons[9]. The programme must not be for a period of less than three months, nor for more than 12 months[10]. In the event that the offender does not agree to a referral order, or acts in breach of it, the panel will refer the offender back to the court[11].

Sentencing options
Sentencing in the criminal courts is largely governed by the principles introduced by the Criminal Justice Act 1991, now consolidated in the PCC(S)A 2000. A key principle in that Act is 'proportionality' – that the sentence or order imposed should be broadly commensurate with the seriousness of the offence[12]. The various disposals can be conveniently categorised into discharges, financial penalties and orders, community sentences, custodial sentences and orders for dealing with mentally disordered offenders.

Discharges
In cases which are perceived by the courts to be at the least serious end of the spectrum, they may either discharge the offender absolutely, or discharge him subject to a condition that he commits no further offences during a specified

---

1   PCC(S)A 2000, s 16.
2   Ibid, s 18.
3   Ibid, s 20.
4   Ibid, s 22(3).
5   Ibid, s 23(1).
6   Ibid, s 19(4).
7   Ibid, s 19(5).
8   Ibid, s 23(2).
9   Ibid.
10 Ibid, s 18(1).
11 Ibid, s 25(2).
12 For a general account of the aims of the Act, see M Wasik and RD Taylor *Blackstone's Guide to the Criminal Justice Act 1991* (Blackstone Press, 1991) at pp 1–9.

period not exceeding three years[1]. If he then re-offends, he will be in breach of the order, and may be brought back before the court and dealt with as the court had power to do originally. Discharges have the advantage that they do not count as convictions against the child or young person, except for limited purposes[2].

Financial penalties and orders

It has already been noted above that it is the duty of the court to order that a parent or guardian be responsible for payment of a juvenile's financial penalties. These penalties broadly divide into fines, compensation and deprivation of property orders.

Fines

Magistrates' courts and youth courts may impose fines subject to maximum levels prescribed by the statutes which create the various offences. The particular fine within the appropriate scale is then fixed in accordance with standard scales. This involves taking into account the gravity of the offence, the means of the person responsible for payment and any mitigating circumstances[3]. Where a juvenile is fined in the magistrates' or youth court there is a maximum fine of £1,000 where he is under 18, and £250 is the maximum in relation to a child aged under 14[4].

Compensation orders

Instead of, or in addition to, dealing with the offender in any other way, the court may order him to pay compensation to the victim for any personal injury, loss, or damage resulting from the offence, or any other offence taken into account[5].

Deprivation of property orders

Deprivation of property orders are designed to ensure that the offender does not profit from his wrongdoing in relation to offences involving property such as theft and related offences. The court may, instead of, or in addition to, dealing with the offender in any other way, make a forfeiture order depriving him of any rights in the property to which the offence relates[6].

Community orders

Community orders, while falling short of custodial sentences, do involve a significant interference with liberty. As such, the criteria for imposing them are more restrictive than for financial penalties but less restrictive than for custodial sentences. Three conditions must be satisfied which are:

(1) that the offence, or the combination of the offence and one or more offences associated with it, was *serious enough* to warrant such a sentence[7];
(2) the particular order or orders comprising or forming part of the sentence is or are the *most suitable* for the offender[8]; and

---

1   Under the PCC(S)A 2000, s 12, the court may grant a discharge where it is of the opinion 'having regard to the circumstances including the nature of the offence and the character of the offender, that it is inexpedient to inflict punishment'.
2   PCC(S)A 2000, s 14.
3   Criminal Justice Act 1991, s 18, now PCC(S)A 2000, s 128.
4   PCC(S)A 2000, s 135.
5   Ibid, s 130.
6   Ibid, s 143.
7   Ibid, s 35(1).
8   Ibid, s 35(3).

(3) the restrictions on liberty imposed are such as are *commensurate* with the seriousness of the offence, or the combination of the offence and other offences associated with it[1].

There are eight community orders[2] which can be made in relation to those aged under 18, as follows:

(a) a community rehabilitation order;
(b) a community punishment order;
(c) a community punishment and rehabilitation order;
(d) a curfew order;
(e) a supervision order;
(f) an attendance centre order;
(g) a drug treatment and testing order; and
(h) an action plan order.

In considering the suitability of the various community orders, the court must obtain and consider a pre-sentence report on the offender[3].

Community rehabilitation order[4]

This was formerly known as the 'probation order' but was renamed by the Criminal Justice and Court Services Act 2000[5]. The order is available in relation to offenders aged 16 and 17 who will be placed under the supervision of a probation officer or member of the youth offending team. It may last for not less than six months nor more than three years. The aim of the order is to secure rehabilitation of the offender, to protect the public from him and to prevent the commission by him of further offences[6]. Standard conditions are attached to community rehabilitation orders which require the offender to keep in touch with the officer concerned. Conditions may also be attached which may, for example, require him to attend approved places from time to time, to take part in various activities or receive various forms of treatment, for example for drug or alcohol dependency.

Community punishment order

Formerly known as the 'community service order', this order was also renamed by the Criminal Justice and Court Services Act 2000[7]. Again it may only be made in relation to offenders aged 16 and over. The order may be made where the offence would be punishable by imprisonment in the case of an adult, and the offender's consent to the order is required. The order entails undertaking specified unpaid work in the community. The order must specify the number of hours to be worked, the minimum being 40 and the maximum 240 hours. The court must be satisfied that provision for such work can be made. The work will be carried out under the supervision of a probation officer or member of the youth offending team. A community punishment order may prove the desirable way of avoiding

---

1   PCC(S)A 2000, s 35(3).
2   Ibid, s 33(1).
3   Ibid, s 36(4).
4   Ibid, s 80.
5   Section 43(1).
6   PCC(S)A 2000, s 41.
7   Section 44(1).

the last resort of a custodial sentence and enable compliance with international obligations as far as that is concerned.

Community punishment and rehabilitation order

This order was previously known as a 'combination order' and is a mixture of the above two orders. Again it was renamed by the Criminal Justice and Court Services Act 2000[1] and again it may only be made in relation to offenders aged 16 and over. The order must be for a minimum of 12 months and a maximum of three years. The punishment element must be for between 40 and 100 hours' unpaid work in the community.

Curfew order

A curfew order requires an offender to remain for specified periods at a place specified in the order[2]. The specified times are between two and 12 hours per day. When originally introduced, the order applied only to offenders over the age of 16 years but, following amendments made by the Crime (Sentences) Act 1997[3], the order has been extended to cover those aged under 16. In the case of the former, the order may not last more than six months, and in the case of the latter, more than three months. The order must include provision for a 'responsible person' to monitor the curfew. Compliance with the order may also be monitored by electronic tagging[4] where such a scheme is in operation. The practice is controversial and it has been questioned whether it is in compliance with Article 40(1) of the UNCRC, which requires States parties to recognise 'the right of every child alleged as, accused of, or recognised as having infringed the penal law to be treated in a manner consistent with the promotion of the child's sense of dignity and worth'[5].

Supervision order

This places the offender under the supervision of a designated local authority or probation officer for a period of not more than three years[6]. There are no restrictions on the kind of offences for which the order may be made and the consent of the offender is not a condition[7]. The local authority will usually be appointed supervisor. The statutory duty of the supervisor is to 'advise, assist and befriend' the offender[8]. The order may impose a range of conditions relating to such matters as residence, education, participation or non-participation in various activities. The order is analogous to a community rehabilitation order but is available in relation to offenders under the age of 16. Together they are known as 'intermediate treatment'.

Attendance centre order

An attendance centre is 'a place at which offenders under 21 years of age may be required to attend, and be given under supervision, appropriate occupation or

---

1 Section 45(1).
2 Criminal Justice Act 1991, s 12. See C Walsh 'Imposing Order: Child Safety Orders and Local Child Curfew Schemes' (1999) 21 JSWFL 135.
3 Section 43.
4 Criminal Justice Act 1991, s 13.
5 J Fortin *Children's Rights and the Developing Law* (Butterworths, 1998) at p 463.
6 Children and Young Persons Act 1969, s 70(1) and s 11.
7 By virtue of amendments made by the Crime (Sentences) Act 1997, parental consent to the imposition of certain requirements is no longer necessary.
8 PCC(S)A 2000, s 64.

instruction'[1]. Often run by police officers, the emphasis is on firm discipline, physical training and handicrafts. The court may make the order where the offence would usually be punishable with imprisonment or where there has been a failure to comply with previous orders of the court, such as breach of conditions of a community rehabilitation order or refusal to pay a fine. The centre must be reasonably accessible to the offender, and the court must specify the number of hours of attendance, which must be at least 12 hours, except that in the case of a child aged under 14 fewer hours may be ordered if the court thinks 12 hours would be excessive[2].

Drug treatment and testing orders

These orders were introduced by the Crime and Disorder Act 1998. The court may make a drug treatment and testing order[3] where it is satisfied that an offender over the age of 16 is dependent on, or has the propensity to misuse, drugs and that this dependency is susceptible to treatment. The order must last for between six months and three years. The order will include a treatment requirement (and will identify the treatment provider) together with a testing requirement the purpose of which is to establish whether or not any drugs are in the body of the offender during the period of the order.

Action plan orders

Introduced by s 69 of the Crime and Disorder Act 1998, the action plan order is a new type of community order for offenders between the ages of 10 and 17[4]. The order is described in the 1997 White Paper *No More Excuses* as a 'short, intensive programme of community intervention combining punishment, rehabilitation and reparation to change offending behaviour, and prevent further crime'. The offender is required for a period of three months to comply with an action plan which prescribes requirements about the offender's actions and whereabouts. He will be placed during this period under the supervision of a probation officer, local authority social worker or member of the youth offending team. The order cannot be combined with most of the other community orders but is instead generally viewed as the first choice of a community order.

Custodial sentences

In the most serious cases of violent or sexual offences there may be no alternative but to pass a custodial sentence, if only to protect the public. As noted above, in recent years there has been an increased use of custodial sentences, particularly in the case of persistent young offenders. This has provoked a barrage of criticism, not least from the UN Committee on the Rights of the Child. The UNCRC is quite explicit that custodial measures should be regarded as a 'last resort' in the case of children and young offenders. The key Article is Article 37(b), the relevant part of which reads:

> 'The arrest, detention or imprisonment of a child shall be in conformity with the law and shall be used only as a measure of last resort and for the appropriate period of time.'

---

1   PCC(S)A 2000, s 62(2).
2   Ibid, s 60(3).
3   Ibid, ss 52–55.
4   Ibid, ss 69–71.

Commenting in 2002 on the UK's performance, the UN Committee had this to say[1]:

> 'The Committee is particularly concerned that since the State party's initial report, children between 12 and 14 years of age are now being deprived of their liberty. More generally, the Committee is deeply concerned at the increasing number of children who are being detained in custody at earlier ages for lesser offences and for longer sentences imposed as a result of the recently increased court powers to issue detention and restraining orders. The Committee is therefore concerned that deprivation of liberty is not being used only as a measure of last resort and for the shortest appropriate period of time, in violation of article 37(b) of the Convention.'

And the Committee went on to recommend[2] that the UK:

> 'Ensure that the detention of children is used as a measure of last resort and for the shortest appropriate period of time and that children are separated from adults in detention, and encourage the use of alternative measures to the deprivation of liberty.'

Neither was the Committee in the least impressed with the UK's record regarding the conditions under which children are detained:

> 'The Committee is also extremely concerned at the conditions that children experience in detention and that children do not receive adequate protection or help in young offenders' institutions (for 15-to-17-year olds), noting the very poor staff–child ratio, high levels of violence, bullying, self-harm and suicide, the inadequate rehabilitation opportunities, the solitary confinement in appropriate conditions for a long time as a disciplinary measure or for protection, and the fact that girls and some boys in prisons are still not separated from adults.'[3]

It went on to recommend[4] that the UK:

> 'Take all necessary measures, as a matter of urgency, to review the conditions of detention and ensure that all children deprived of their liberty have statutory rights to education, health and child protection equal to those of other children.'

This then is the background of international obligations against which the UK has been pursuing a policy involving the greater use of custodial sanctions for juvenile offenders. Conditions in young offenders' custodial institutions also became the subject of domestic litigation in *R (Howard League for Penal Reform) v Secretary of State for the Home Department*[5]. Here Munby J held that an assertion made by the prison authorities[6] to the effect that the Children Act 1989 did not apply to under-18-year-olds in prison establishments was wrong in law. The duties which local authorities owed to 'children in need'[7] do not cease to be owed merely because the child is detained for the time being in a young offender institution. The treatment of children in detention is therefore in principle susceptible to scrutiny both in terms of compliance with human rights and with the regime for child protection in domestic legislation.

---

1   *Concluding Observations on the United Kingdom of Great Britain and Northern Ireland* 9 October 2002, para 59.
2   Ibid, at para 62(e).
3   Ibid, at para 59.
4   Ibid, at para 62(g).
5   [2003] 1 FLR 484.
6   In para 3.1.4 of the Prison Service Order No 4950.
7   As to which see Chapter 10.

The threshold for custodial sentences

The Criminal Justice Act 1991[1] had established a threshold for the making of custodial sentences generally and this applied as much to young offenders as it did to adults. The conditions are now contained in the PCC(S)A 2000[2]. The key concept is that of *proportionality* so familiar in the context of human rights. Before making a custodial sentence the court must be satisfied that either:

(a) the offence, or the combination of the offence and one or more offences associated with it, was *so serious* that only such a sentence can be justified for it; or

(b) that the offence is a violent or sexual offence, and that only such a sentence would be adequate to protect the public from serious harm from the offender.

Assuming this threshold is crossed, the principal custodial option now available to the courts is the detention and training order, although it is also necessary to consider briefly the detention of young offenders under the regime which applies in the small minority of cases where children kill or commit very serious offences.

Detention and training order

The detention and training order was introduced by the Crime and Disorder Act 1998[3]. It is the principal custodial sentence now for offenders between the ages of 10 and 17 and replaces the former detention in a young offender institution (for 15–17-year-olds) and the secure training order (which was available in relation to children aged between 12 and 14 years). In relation to an offender under the age of 15 at the time of conviction, the order may only be made where the court is satisfied that he is 'a persistent offender'[4]. In the case of a child as young as 12–14 years, the order may only be made where the court is satisfied that 'only a custodial sentence would be adequate to protect the public from further offending from him'.

The legislation is quite specific about the possible length of order which may only be for 4, 6, 8, 10, 12, 18 or 24 months[5]. Half of this period will then be spent in custody, detention and training while the other half will be spent under the supervision of a probation officer, social worker or a member of the youth offending team.

Detention for serious offences

Where a young offender aged between 10 and 17 has been *convicted on indictment* of certain very serious offences, a longer custodial sentence may be imposed. Cases such as this represent only a small proportion of the offences committed by young offenders. They were previously governed by s 53(2) of the Children and Young Persons Act 1933. The relevant provision is now found in s 91 of the PCC(S)A 2000. The offences concerned are:

---

1 Criminal Justice Act 1991, s 1(2).
2 Section 79.
3 Sections 73–79, and now governed by PCC(S)A 2000, ss 100–107.
4 PCC(S)A 2000, s 100(2)(a).
5 Ibid, s 101.

(a) an offence punishable in the case of a person aged 21 or over with at least 14 years' imprisonment[1],

(b) an indecent assault on a woman[2] or man[3], or

(c) where the offender is aged at least 14, an offence of causing death by dangerous or careless driving while under the influence of drink or drugs[4].

In each case where 'the court is of the opinion that none of the other methods in which the case may legally be dealt with is suitable, the court may sentence the offender to be detained for such period, not exceeding the maximum term of imprisonment with which the offence is punishable in the case of a person aged 21 or over, as may be specified in the sentence'[5]. The place of detention is determined by the Home Secretary[6] but is likely to be in a young offender institution.

Murder – detention during Her Majesty's Pleasure
Children or young persons convicted on indictment for murder *must* be sentenced to be detained during Her Majesty's Pleasure[7]. The young person concerned must have been under 18 at the time of the commission of the offence. This power has been the subject of extensive criticism and litigation before both the English courts and the ECtHR[8]. The central issue has been the essential indeterminacy of such orders and, as a result of actions brought under the ECHR, the British Government was required to amend the law. A particularly notorious case, which provided the focal point for these concerns, was that of Thompson and Venables.

Before the matter was challenged in the courts, those detained under this provision were detained subject to a minimum initial 'tariff' period followed by a 'post-tariff' period. The period of detention would be reviewed and an assessment of the risk to the public made. The length of both the tariff and the post-tariff periods was ultimately decided by a politician, the Home Secretary, and not by a judge or the Parole Board. As a result of the successful challenge in *Hussain v United Kingdom* the post-tariff period and the question of final release were shifted from the Home Secretary to the Parole Board. Then the decision of Michael Howard, the then Home Secretary, to increase the initial tariff period in the case of Thompson and Venables was quashed by the House of Lords, which took the view, inter alia, that the approach to the tariff in the case of young offenders was not to be equated with the approach in the case of adults. The policy had to be sufficiently flexible that it could take into account, by continuing review, any progress or development of the child in addition to considerations of retribution, deterrence and risk – in other words, welfare considerations. Finally, the decision on the tariff period was wrested from the control of the Home Secretary and given

---

1 PCC(S)A 2000, s 91(1)(a).
2 Ibid, s 91(1)(b).
3 Ibid, s 91(1)(c).
4 Ibid, s 91(2).
5 Ibid, s 91(3).
6 Ibid, s 92.
7 Ibid, s 90, formerly Children and Young Persons Act 1933, s 53(1).
8 See particularly, *Hussain v United Kingdom* (1996) 22 EHRR 1, *R v Secretary of State for the Home Department ex parte Thompson and Venables* [1997] 2 FLR 471 and *V and T v United Kingdom* (2000) 30 EHRR 121. For a more detailed discussion of these cases, see the second edition of this work at pp 502–503, and J Fortin *Children's Rights and the Developing Law* (2nd edn) (Butterworths, 2003) at pp 580–583.

to the judges by the decision of the ECtHR in *V and T v United Kingdom*. However, as Jane Fortin notes[1], the consequence has not been a less punitive approach, in that judges must now, when sentencing child murderers, operate a presumption or starting point of a tariff of 12 years which may be increased or reduced depending on the circumstances. The general question of the incompatibility of this approach with at least the spirit of Articles 37 and 40 of the UNCRC remains unresolved.

Conclusion: New Labour's approach to juvenile crime

The hallmark of the Crime and Disorder Act 1998 as indicated by the title to the White Paper preceding it – 'No More Excuses' – is personal responsibility for crime which is shared between young people themselves and their parents. We have alluded above to the ongoing debates about the appropriate balance between 'justice' and 'welfare' and it must be doubted whether the increasingly punitive, authoritarian approach to juvenile crime, involving as it does Draconian restraints on liberty and family autonomy, is consistent with a commitment to the civil liberties of young people or with international obligations[2].

How far New Labour legislation is consistent with the philosophy embodied in other legislation affecting children, most notably the Children Act 1989, is also open to doubt[3]. On the one hand, the increasing autonomy of adolescents, acknowledged in the Children Act, might be thought consistent with the emphasis on personal responsibility in the Crime and Disorder Act 1998. Indeed, we commented in Chapter 3 on the failure of the law to articulate clearly enough the responsibilities or duties which should go with gathering independence. On the other hand, the Children Act supports the notion of *gradual*, not sudden, emancipation for children as they grow older, and the inflexible imposition of criminal responsibility on children at the age of 10 and the use of custodial sentences for those as young as 12 is hardly consistent with this. Perhaps most striking of all is the notion of *dual* responsibility of children and parents for crime. Elsewhere in the law, the idea is of dwindling parental control as the child gets older. Yet, in the criminal context, the notion persists that parents remain fully in control and responsible for their children. There is little recognition here of the potential for a conflict of interest between the parent and child, and indeed it is not entirely clear who should be regarded as a 'parent' for these purposes[4]. 'Parenting orders' may be made against a 'parent or guardian' but this may well be inadequate to cover the case of many children who are raised not by genetic parents but by social parents such as step-parents. More fundamentally, it is certainly questionable whether a parent, however defined, is actually able to be in control of a teenage child. Making parents legally liable in these circumstances may only serve to exacerbate the tensions between adolescents and parents with which the law has had to grapple in other contexts.

---

1 (Above) at p 582.
2 The UN Committee on the Rights of the Child was, for example, highly critical of the introduction of secure training orders for children as young as 12 and, more generally, of the weight being placed on imprisonment and punishment in the juvenile justice system. See *Concluding Observations of the Committee on the Rights of the Child: United Kingdom of Great Britain and Northern Ireland*, CRC/C/15/Add 34 (January 1995). See also the Committee's 2002 Report and p 634 above.
3 On the philosophy of the Children Act, see Chapter 2 above.
4 On the difficulties of defining parenthood, see Chapter 3 above.

Chapter 15

CHILDREN AND THE CIVIL LAW

INTRODUCTION

We now turn our attention from the criminal law to the civil law. Family law, with which most of this book is concerned, is itself a branch of the civil law but we are concerned in this chapter with those areas which are not directly related to the child's position in the family. We are dealing primarily with those legal issues which can arise from the child's activities outside the home. We have already seen[1] that young people do not acquire capacities and responsibilities all at once, on attaining majority, but at different ages, depending on the activity in question[2], and it has been noted that this can give rise to difficult questions about the relationship between the child's own capacities and the responsibilities of parents[3]. We now concentrate on three key and related areas of the civil law – the law of tort, contract and employment. Little is written on these subjects as they affect children beyond what can be gleaned from the standard texts[4]. Useful comparisons can, however, be made with Scots law where, following a wide-ranging report on the legal capacities and responsibilities of minors and pupils in 1987, there was legislation on the subject in 1991[5].

The central themes of the civil law, like those of the criminal law, are *protection* and *responsibility*. What special protections are afforded children where they are injured by the actions of third parties or where children purport to enter into contracts (whether of employment or otherwise) which are, objectively judged, not in their best interests? To what extent are children responsible for their own actions which lead to the injury of third parties or to commercial loss, as where a trader has dealt fairly with a minor who then defaults? The answers which the law gives reflect a compromise between the desire to protect children, either from themselves or from the exploitation of others, and the need to avoid unnecessary hardship to those who deal with children in good faith.

---

1 At Chapter 3 above.
2 For a good review of the various age limits, see 'At What Age Can I?' published by the Children's Legal Centre.
3 See especially Chapter 8 above in relation to medical issues where most of the difficulties have arisen.
4 An exception is Roderick Bagshaw's excellent treatment of children in the law of torts. See R Bagshaw 'Children Through Tort' in J Fionda (ed) *Legal Concepts of Childhood* (Hart, 2001). For the emerging liability of local authorities towards children in their care or for failure to take action to prevent abuse or neglect, see Chapter 10 above.
5 Scot Law Com No 110 *Report on the Legal Capacity and Responsibility of Minors and Pupils* (1987) implemented by the Age of Legal Capacity (Scotland) Act 1991. For commentary on the Act, see JM Thomson *Family Law in Scotland* (4th edn) (Butterworths, 2002) at ch 9.

CHILDREN AND THE LAW OF TORT

There are two broad aspects of the law of tort which affect children. The first is the question of civil liability for interferences with, or injuries to, children by third parties or by their carers. The second is the issue of the liability which children themselves have for their own tortious acts. In each case, difficult questions arise about the extent of the parental duty to *protect*[1]. Where a child is injured at home, this may be the result of negligence by the parent or other carer or it may be a pure accident. Essentially, this turns on what ought to have been expected of the reasonably prudent parent. Where a child is injured outside the home, this may again be attributable to the negligence of the carer, that of a third party or the negligence of both of them, but again, it may be an accident for which no one is to be held responsible. Conversely, where a child causes injury to someone, this may be solely the responsibility of the child, the result of negligence by the carer or, again, just accidental.

The extent of control, as an aspect of parental responsibility, is also a central feature of the so-called 'intentional torts' involving trespass to the person whether by assault, battery or false imprisonment. It is accepted that the right to control and discipline the child is an element of parental responsibility and, indeed, a failure to exercise that responsibility might conceivably give rise to an action in negligence against the parent. But how far does this go? As the child gets older, the *Gillick* case and the Children Act 1989[2] both support the notion of a gradual relaxation of parental authority and control. Thus, certain purported exercises of parental discipline may themselves be tortious, if they exceed the bounds of reasonableness. A related issue here is the extent to which (if at all) a third party may be held liable for interfering with parents in the discharge of their responsibilities.

Protection of children

Torts based on negligence

The tort of negligence is committed where a duty of care is owed, there is a breach of that duty, and someone (a child for present purposes) is injured as a result[3]. In order to establish this, it needs to be proved, on the balance of probabilities, that the defendant failed to avoid acts or omissions which were foreseeably likely to injure the child. The child will then have a claim for damages.

As a general proposition, the standard of care required *towards* children is higher than that towards adults[4]. Conversely, children themselves (especially

---

1 The duty which is recognised by implication in the Children and Young Persons Act 1933, s 1, as to which see Chapters 8 and 14 above.
2 See Chapter 3.
3 See, generally: WHV Rogers *Winfield and Jolowicz on Tort* (16th edn) (Sweet & Maxwell, 2002) at ch 5; J Murphy *Street on Torts* (11th edn) (Butterworths, 2003) at chs 11–14; and *Salmond and Heuston on the Law of Torts* (21st edn) (Sweet & Maxwell, 1996) at ch 9.
4 The general standard of care was summed up by Alderson B in *Blyth v Birmingham Waterworks Co* (1856) 11 Ex 781 at 784 where he said:
  'Negligence is the omission to do something which a reasonable man, guided upon those considerations which ordinarily regulate the conduct of human affairs, would do, or doing something which a prudent and reasonable man would not do.'

young children) are not expected to exercise the same degree of care as adults[1]. While these are general principles of the law of negligence, they have been applied more specifically by statute in the context of occupiers' liability. This legislation governs the liability of 'occupiers'[2] for injuries caused to those on land or structures under their control. The natural curiosity of children and their propensity for straying into hazardous environments has generated a mass of reported cases over a substantial period of years[3].

The chapter begins by looking at the principles which have emerged in this area of applied negligence. It then considers the tort of negligence itself, in its application to parental failings.

Occupiers' liability

The liability of occupiers is governed by the Occupiers' Liability Acts of 1957 and 1984. The extent of the duty owed depends on whether the injured person was a 'visitor' (the 1957 Act) or a 'non-visitor' (the 1984 Act). Essentially, the distinction is between those persons who were invited onto the property or were otherwise there with the express or implied permission of the occupier, and those who were not – usually, but not always, trespassers[4]. In the case of children, the distinction is not as marked as with adults and many of the cases have, for obvious reasons, involved at least technical trespasses by children[5].

Children as visitors – the Occupiers' Liability Act 1957

The 'common duty of care' owed to visitors is 'a duty to take such care as in all the circumstances of the case is reasonable, to see that the visitor will be reasonably safe in using the premises for the purposes for which he is invited or permitted by the occupier to be there'.

The duty is, therefore, not an unlimited one, but is only to take such precautions as are *reasonable*. In deciding whether there has been a breach of duty, account must be taken of the degree of care, or want of care, which would ordinarily be looked for in the visitor[6]. For these purposes, the Occupiers' Liability Act 1957 singles out children as a special case and provides that 'an occupier must be prepared for children to be less careful than adults'[7].

Clearly, a reasonable man would appreciate the need for greater caution where children are concerned. An obvious example would be child pedestrians.

1   See below. On children's duties generally, see Chapter 3 above.

2   Essentially, the concept of 'occupier' is related to control rather than ownership of property although the two will frequently coincide. The test is laid down in *Wheat v Lacon & Co Ltd* [1966] AC 552.

3   For an excellent review, see R Kidner 'The Duty of Occupiers Towards Children' (1988) 139 *Northern Ireland Legal Quarterly* 150.

4   The Occupiers' Liability Act 1957 abolished the former distinction between 'invitees' and 'licensees'. See *Winfield and Jolowicz on Tort* (16th edn) (Sweet & Maxwell, 2002) at pp 304 et seq, *Street on Torts* (11th edn) (Butterworths, 2003) at pp 333 et seq, and *Salmond and Heuston on the Law of Torts* (21st edn) (Sweet & Maxwell, 1996) at pp 269 et seq. In fact, the position is somewhat more complex than this since there is a category of those who enter by virtue of a legal right, such as the use of a public right of way, who are neither visitors nor trespassers. The effect of the House of Lords ruling in *McGeown v Northern Ireland Housing Executive* [1995] 1 AC 233 is that there is no liability for negligent non-feasance in these circumstances. Thus the occupier is under a duty not to add to the danger but not to take positive steps to avoid it. In this case there was no liability for failure to keep a footpath in good repair.

5   See, for example, *Glasgow Corp v Taylor* [1922] 1 AC 44.

6   Occupiers' Liability Act 1957, s 2(3).

7   Ibid, s 2(3)(a).

What then is the requisite standard of care? It is first established that allowances must be made for the greater vulnerability of children. Something which would not be a danger to an adult might be a danger to a child. This is illustrated by *Moloney v Lambeth Borough Council*[1] where a four-year-old child fell through a balustrade protecting a staircase leading from a ground-floor to a first-floor flat. The gaps in the railings were not wide enough for an adult to fall through but *were* wide enough for a child of the age and size of the plaintiff. The defendant council was held liable on the basis that it ought to have anticipated that young children would use the staircase when unaccompanied by adults. The design of the staircase did not conform with the council's common duty of care owed to a child of that age. A second, long-established, principle is that an occupier may be liable where he has created, or is aware of, an 'allurement' to children, but fails to guard against it. Over 80 years ago, Glasgow Corporation fell foul of this principle[2]. It was held liable to the father of a deceased seven-year-old child who had eaten poisonous 'deadly nightshade' berries from a shrub in public gardens controlled by the Corporation. The berries were attractive and accessible to children, and the Corporation was aware that the area was frequented by them. Yet it took no steps either to fence off the shrub or warn of the danger.

The courts have had to confront the difficulty in the case of young children that virtually anything can be a danger. Is there then an obligation on occupiers to make their premises as safe as a nursery? The courts have avoided this extreme conclusion, first by finding that children were trespassers in some circumstances where unaccompanied by adults[3], and secondly, more realistically, by limiting occupiers' duties to take into account parents' own responsibilities to young children. The essential point is that where a young child comes into contact with a man-made or natural hazard this may be at least as much the fault of the parent, for failing to supervise the child, as it is the fault of the occupier.

In *Phipps v Rochester Corporation*[4], a boy aged five years, out picking blackberries with his seven-year-old sister, broke his leg when he fell into a trench which his sister had safely negotiated. The trench was part of a building site adjoining the plaintiff's home. In exonerating the council, Devlin J held that the council would discharge its duty of care if it reduced the dangers present to those which would either be obvious to a parent or, if not obvious, it warned against them. He emphasised the *primary* duty of parents to ensure that young children did not wander about on their own or that, if they did, they were allowed to go only to safe places. If, on the other hand, an occupier ought to have anticipated the presence of young unaccompanied children, this could impose a duty to take appropriate precautionary measures. These principles were applied to natural hazards in *Simkiss v Rhondda Borough Council*[5]. Here, the seven-year-old plaintiff slid down a Welsh mountainside on a picnic blanket. The mountain had a bluff or steep slope which became very steep at the bottom. The plaintiff sustained a fractured skull when she fell 30 to 40 feet onto the road below. The Court of Appeal held that the council was not obliged either to fence the mountain or to warn of the sharp drop, despite the evidence that unaccompanied children were known to play in the

---

1 (1966) LGR 440.
2 *Glasgow Corp v Taylor* [1922] 1 AC 44. The concept of allurement could have the effect of preventing the child being regarded as a trespasser.
3 The so-called 'conditional licence'.
4 [1955] 1 QB 450.
5 (1983) 81 LGR 460.

vicinity. The prudent parent, it was said, would warn his children of such natural hazards[1]. As Dunn LJ remarked, an occupier was not bound to fence every tree simply because a child might climb it and fall out of it. It should be remembered, however, that this principle applies only to those hazards, natural or unnatural, which would be *obvious* to a prudent parent. Where the danger is latent or concealed, the duty is squarely on the occupier, if he knows of it, to take precautions.

Where the plaintiff is an older child, the occupier's duty will be discharged more easily and the standard of care owed to adolescents may not differ markedly (if at all) from that owed to adults[2]. Nonetheless, even in a case involving teenage children, Lord Hoffmann has said that 'their ingenuity in finding unexpected ways of doing mischief to themselves and others should never be underestimated'[3]. The case was *Jolley v Sutton London Borough Council*[4], which raised the issue of whether the kind of accident, and not merely the injury, to befall the child must be a reasonably foreseeable consequence of the defendant's negligence or breach of statutory duty as an occupier. The defendant council had failed to remove an abandoned and derelict boat from land adjoining a block of flats owned by the council. It was aware of the boat's presence and had made plans to remove it. Two boys aged 13 and 14 began to repair it using a car jack and some wood to prop it up. One of the boys suffered serious spinal injuries, resulting in paraplegia with major complications, when the boat fell off the prop and crushed him. The council argued that the manner of the accident was not foreseeable, despite the fact that it was foreseeable that children might play on the boat and be injured. The claimant's accident, it was argued, was of a *different kind* from that which was foreseeable. This argument prevailed in the Court of Appeal but not in the House of Lords. The risk that had been created and had been conceded by the council was one of injury to children if rotten planking gave way beneath them. The wider risk of more serious injury being caused to children by the condition of the boat fell within its duty of care and the accident which had occurred fell within the general description of the risk.

Children as trespassers – the Occupiers' Liability Act 1984
At common law an occupier was not liable at all to trespassers, except where the injury was caused deliberately or maliciously. No distinction was made between adults and children, and the rule could operate very harshly, as it did in *Addie v Dumbreck*[5]. Here, a four-year-old boy was crushed in the wheel of a haulage system operated at a colliery. The wheel was in a field known to be frequented by children. It was attractive to them but inadequately protected. The House of Lords held that, since the child had no express or implied permission to be on the premises, he had to be classed as a trespasser and hence no duty of care was owed to him. The harshness of the rule was mitigated over the years by several devices,

---

1   The responsibilities of parents to take reasonable steps to prevent accidents, in this case to a baby, also arose in *B v Camden London Borough Council* [2001] PIQR 9. Here, a landlord was held not liable under s 4 of the Defective Premises Act 1972 where a baby fell out of bed and was burnt on uncased heating pipes, in part because the risk was small and in part because the mother should have prevented the accident.

1   See, for example, *Titchener v British Railways Board* [1983] 3 All ER 770.

2   *Jolley v Sutton London Borough Council* [2000] 1 WLR 1082 at 1093.

3   Ibid.

4   *Robert Addie and Sons (Collieries) Ltd v Dumbreck* [1929] AC 358.

including the concepts of allurement and the implied licence, before a more generalised duty of 'common humanity' towards trespassers was fashioned by the House of Lords in *British Railways Board v Herrington*[1]. This extended beyond the duty merely to refrain from deliberately causing injury to a duty to take precautionary measures where there was knowledge of the circumstances of the danger and the actual or likely presence of trespassers. The duty to 'non-visitors', including trespassers, is now contained in the Occupiers' Liability Act 1984[2]. The test for liability now comprises three elements as follows:

(1)   the occupier must be aware of the danger or have reasonable grounds to believe it exists;
(2)   he must have known, or had reasonable grounds to believe, that the non-visitor was in, or might have come into, the vicinity of the danger; and
(3)   the risk of injury must have been one against which, in all the circumstances, the occupier might have been expected to offer the non-visitor some protection.

The duty is then 'to take such care as is reasonable in all the circumstances of the case to see that [the non-visitor] does not suffer injury on the premises by reason of the danger concerned'[3]. The circumstances which give rise to a duty of care do, therefore, have elements of subjectivity and it is also provided that the duty may be discharged in appropriate cases by giving a warning[4]. However, it has been doubted whether, in its application to children, there is any appreciable difference from the common duty of care owed to child visitors. Clearly, the precautions which might be expected of occupiers towards child trespassers are greater than those one would expect for burglars. And it is unlikely that the duty could be discharged merely by giving a warning since this might well be incomprehensible to young children.

Negligence of parents and other carers
As was seen above, the duties of the prudent parent to protect his child might absolve a third party from liability, but under what circumstances might a parent *himself* be liable for the child's injuries, arising from failure to take proper care of him[5]? There is no reason, in principle, why a child should not sue his parent[6], although he would need, as in other ordinary civil actions, to act by a 'litigation

---

1   [1972] AC 877.
2   Occupiers' Liability Act 1984, s 1(3).
3   Ibid, s 1(4).
4   Ibid, s 1(5).
5   See, generally, C McIvor 'Expelling the Myth of the Parental Duty to Rescue' [2000] CFLQ 229, advocating that the law should distinguish more clearly between situations in which the parent has, by his or her conduct, contributed positively to the harm suffered by the child and cases of mere omission. According to this thesis there would be liability in the former situation but not in the latter.
6   Although it was apparently assumed by the House of Lords in *Barrett v Enfield London Borough Council* [1999] 2 FLR 426 that a child could not sue his parent in relation to care-giving decisions. This view has been hotly disputed by Michael Freeman, who questions why there should not be 'an actionable duty of care against a mother who decides to live with a known sex abuser or against parents who smoke in the presence of an asthmatic child or against a mother with HIV who insists on breastfeeding her baby'. See M Freeman 'The End of the Century of the Child?' (2000) 53 *Current Legal Problems* 505 at pp 543–544. Cf R Bagshaw (above) at p 135, who rehearses the concerns, from a public policy perspective, about tortious actions between parents and children.

friend'[1]. However, since the child and his parent will usually be part of a family which constitutes a single economic unit, there will seldom be any point in suing, unless the parent is insured. That exception will, of course, apply where a child is injured through the negligent driving of his parent[2].

Some case-law has been concerned with the liability of foster-parents but the principles can be extrapolated to parents and other carers. Accidents frequently occur at home and the question is: what standard of care is it reasonable to expect the ordinary parent to achieve in the domestic context? The matter arose in *Surtees v Kingston-upon-Thames Borough Council*[3], where the two-year-old plaintiff, while a foster-child, suffered serious foot injuries from immersion in hot water. The facts were disputed, but the court accepted the version of the foster-parents that, while the foster-mother was absent from the bathroom, the child contrived to stick her foot into the wash basin and to turn on the hot water tap. It was not disputed that the foster-mother sought immediate medical attention for the child. A majority of the Court of Appeal held that an injury of the kind suffered was not foreseeable, taking into account the foster-mother's domestic circumstances. The court was mindful of the need to avoid imposing too high a standard of care, given the stress and preoccupation with household tasks which usually characterise parents' domestic circumstances[4].

Clearly, the line must be drawn somewhere, but it ought to be remembered that parents and others with responsibility may be criminally liable for cruelty or neglect and that the circumstances which suffice for this would, almost by definition, also be enough for civil liability[5]. This would also be the case if parents failed to ensure the suitability or adequacy of substitute carers such as babysitters, and the child came to harm as a result[6]. Where the child is injured, partly as a result of the negligence of a third party, and partly as a result of the contributory negligence of a carer, it has been held that the child's damages should not be

---

1 See Chapter 13 above. The child's parent will normally act as litigation friend although this will clearly be impossible where the parent is the defendant.

2 This is also the one exceptional situation in which a child may sue his mother in relation to congenital defects caused before birth. See the Congenital Disabilities (Civil Liability) Act 1976, s 2.

3 [1991] 2 FLR 559.

4 Sir Nicolas Browne-Wilkinson V-C said that the court should be wary to hold parents in breach of a duty of care owed to their children. The duty owed by a foster-parent to a child in care was the same as that owed by the ordinary parent to his or her own children. There were, he thought, very real public policy considerations to be taken into account if the conflicts inherent in legal proceedings were to be brought into family relationships. But see the dissent of Beldam LJ.

5 For a New Zealand decision in which negligence was established against a parent, see *McCallion v Dodd* [1966] NZLR 710 and the analysis of the case in *Bromley's Family Law* (9th edn) (Butterworths, 1998) at p 369. See also *S v Walsall Metropolitan Borough Council* [1986] 1 FLR 397 in which the Court of Appeal upheld the liability of a foster-mother for severe burns to the soles of a child's feet caused by her negligence. The council was held not to be liable since the foster-parents could not be regarded as agents of the local authority. In *S v W and Another (Child Abuse: Damages)* [1995] 1 FLR 862 the 29-year-old plaintiff succeeded in an action for damages against her mother arising from her mother's breach of duty in failing to protect her, while a child, from repeated physical and sexual abuse by her father. Her claim against her father himself (which was based on trespass to the person) was statute-barred. She succeeded against her mother on the basis that she could take advantage of the longer limitation period applicable to negligence claims under the Limitation Act 1980, s 11.

6 See the Children Act 1989, s 2(11).

reduced[1]. Where, of course, the negligence of the carer is the *major* cause of the child's injury, the court may conclude that the third party is not negligent at all.

Intentional torts

Children, as persons, are protected from civil wrongs in the ordinary way, just as they are protected by the criminal law[2]. In the context of the intentional torts of assault, battery and false imprisonment, special considerations apply to parents and others who exercise lawful authority over children. In short, certain bodily interferences with children which would, without doubt, be tortious if carried out on adults *may* be justifiable if they can be regarded as proper acts of parental discipline. Yet, especially after *Gillick*, there are limits to this principle[3]. The responsibility of parents to control the actions of their children also raises the question of whether a third party may commit a tort against the *parent* by interfering.

The limits of parental discipline

Parents will have a defence to the torts of assault and battery where they can show that the physical 'touchings' were proper exercises of parental discipline being moderate and reasonable. Young children, especially, often have to be restrained physically by parents from placing themselves in danger, and some parents resort quite lawfully to low-level corporal punishment, such as smacking. If this does not become excessive, whatever the morality of the practice, it is not tortious[4]. Similarly, parents are known to confine children to the home, or perhaps a bedroom, for misbehaviour. Their special authority deriving from parental responsibility is, again, a defence to what might otherwise amount to false imprisonment.

It is equally well established that, in principle, a parent behaving *unreasonably* may be criminally liable and, by deduction, liable also in tort. In *R v D*[5], the House of Lords held that a parent might be guilty of the common law offence of kidnapping and, in *R v Rahman*[6], a father who tried to take his teenage daughter, by force, to Bangladesh, had his conviction for the common law offence of false imprisonment upheld. Lord Lane CJ said that a parent could act unlawfully where the detention of the child was 'for such a period or in such circumstances as to take it out of the realm of reasonable parental discipline'. The circumstances of the case are instructive and suggest that physical restraints and punishments of older children, especially teenagers, may at best be inappropriate and at worst positively unlawful.

Powers of control and discipline are also exercised by schools, for the purposes of maintaining good order, but these were severely curtailed as regards the use of corporal punishment by legislation in 1986. In *Campbell and Cosans v United*

---

1   *Oliver v Birmingham and Midland Omnibus Co Ltd* [1933] 1 KB 35.
2   See, generally, *Winfield and Jolowicz on Tort* (16th edn) (Sweet & Maxwell, 2002) at pp 827–834, *Street on Torts* (11th edn) (Butterworths, 2003) at pp 649–650, and *Salmond and Heuston on the Law of Torts* (21st edn) (Sweet & Maxwell, 1996) at pp 411–415.
3   *Gillick v West Norfolk and Wisbech Area Health Authority* [1986] 1 AC 112. On the specific issue of consent and potential tortious liability in medical matters, see Chapter 8.
4   The issue of the limits of corporal punishment together with the likely reform of the law in the Children Bill 2004 is discussed in Chapter 11 above.
5   [1984] AC 778.
6   (1985) 81 Cr App R 349.

Kingdom[1], the UK was found to be in breach of the ECHR by failing to respect the philosophical convictions of certain Scottish parents who were opposed to the use of corporal punishment on their children. As a result, corporal punishment was prohibited in all State schools and in relation to State-funded pupils in independent schools[2] by s 47 of the Education (No 2) Act 1986. Although it remained lawful in independent schools, the *Guidance* under the Children Act[3] indicated that its continued use should be regarded as exceptional, and that it should not be used for trivial offences or applied indiscriminately to whole classes of children. It was advised that it should normally only be administered by the head teacher, and should be properly recorded in the school punishment book[4].

Then, in *Costello-Roberts v United Kingdom*[5], the ECtHR, by a narrow 5 : 4 majority, held that corporal punishment inflicted on a seven-year-old pupil in a private boarding school was not a violation of the ECHR. The boy had been struck three times on the buttocks with a rubber-soled gym shoe. The court held that this did not reach the required minimum threshold of severity as to constitute degrading punishment under Article 3 of the Convention. The narrowness of the result and the tone of the judgments, however, necessitated amending legislation which made it explicit that, insofar as corporal punishment was still used in the independent sector, it could not be administered in a way which was 'inhuman or degrading' since this would be in breach of the Convention[6]. The way was paved for the total abolition of corporal punishment in independent schools, and this was achieved by an amendment to the Labour Government's School Standards and Framework Act 1998[7].

The *Guidance* went on to deal with restriction of liberty of children in independent schools. It advised that to restrict the liberty of a child by, for example, locking him in his bedroom, should be regarded as a serious and potentially unlawful step, having regard to the restrictions on the use of secure accommodation imposed on local authorities under s 25 of the Children Act 1989[8]. Schools which resort to locking up children will now run the risk of an action for assault or false imprisonment.

Interference with parental responsibility

If parents have primary responsibility for the care and upbringing of their children (and usually are the only people formally vested with parental responsibility) can it be tortious for an outsider to intervene in their affairs? It

---

1   (1982) 4 EHRR 293.
2   Education (No 2) Act 1986, s 47 applied to all maintained schools (including special schools), grant-maintained schools, non-maintained special schools, independent schools for 'assisted places' pupils and other pupils whose fees were partly or entirely paid out of public funds.
3   *The Children Act 1989 Guidance and Regulations Vol 5 Independent Schools* (HMSO, 1991) at paras 3.9.1 et seq.
4   Ibid at para 3.9.5.
5   [1994] ELR 1.
6   The original provision in the Education Act 1993 was later consolidated in the Education Act 1996, s 584(2). It was also provided in s 549(3) that, in applying the test of whether the punishment was inhuman or degrading, regard was to be had to 'all the circumstances of the case, including the reason given for it, how soon after the event it is given, its nature, the manner and circumstances in which it is given, the persons involved and its mental and physical effects'.
7   Section 131.
8   *The Children Act 1989 Guidance and Regulations Vol 5* (above) at para 3.10.1.

might be thought that, since only the persons with parental responsibility have legal authority to take decisions in relation to the child[1], another person trying to frustrate this would be acting unlawfully as that person would have no legal basis for doing so. Yet, in *F v Wirral Metropolitan Borough Council*[2], the Court of Appeal denied that parents had *independent* rights which were capable of being infringed[3]. The former action which a parent could bring for loss of his child's services[4] had become anachronistic and was abolished by the Administration of Justice Act 1982. Any right a parent possessed, therefore, was subordinate to the welfare of the child. There was no tort of interference with parental rights known to the law.

It should be noted, however, that it may in certain circumstances be possible for what is in reality a financial loss to the parent to be recovered as an element in the child's damages. Thus, in *Donnelly v Joyce*[5], the child's injuries required regular re-bandaging which would normally have been undertaken by a nurse but which was in fact carried out by his mother, herself a nurse. The Court of Appeal allowed the child to recover in damages the cost of the wages which his mother lost by devoting an hour a day to her son's special care. The result could be achieved only by the rather artificial characterisation of the child's loss as the existence of the need for care, rather than the incurring of nursing expenses and this reasoning has been criticised as unconvincing by the House of Lords[6].

Any tortious action by a parent against a third party must, therefore, be grounded in a tort against the *child* and not against the parent. In the case of physical touchings, it may be possible to establish an infringement of the child's rights[7] but this will be very difficult where the complaint is merely that an outsider is acting contrary to parental wishes and encouraging the child to do likewise[8]. In this situation the only option would seem to be for the parent to seek a 'prohibited steps' order under the Children Act or an analogous order under the inherent jurisdiction. But each of these actions would depend on the exercise of the court's discretion in determining what is in the child's best interests; the court would not seek to enforce any independent parental claim. As the law stands, the onus would seem to be on the parent to commence legal action. Arguably, the third party interference should be prima facie unlawful, so that the onus of proof is shifted onto the outsider[9].

---

1 Children Act 1989, ss 2 and 3, and see Chapter 2 above. It should be remembered of course that de facto carers have a limited amount of authority under s 3(5).

2 [1991] Fam 69.

3 For a critique of the decision see A Bainham 'Interfering with Parental Responsibility – A New Challenge for the Law of Torts?' (1990) 3 JCL 3.

4 The former action is discussed at length in *Bromley's Family Law* (6th edn) (Butterworths, 1981) at pp 329 et seq.

5 [1974] QB 454.

6 See *Hunt v Severs* [1994] 2 AC 350. If the parent should also be the tortfeasor the effect of this decision is that the child would be unable to recover the cost of nursing by that parent.

7 See the discussion in the medical context in Chapter 8 above.

8 An example would be various advice agencies. There is nothing tortious about giving advice (unless it amounts to negligent misstatement), but a parent might wish to stop the child from visiting whatever agency it is. See the discussion in Chapter 16 below of the former Conservative Government's circular on sex education and advice given by teachers to individual pupils about sexual matters.

9 See fn 3 above.

Fatal accidents constitute something of an exception. Where a third party has unlawfully brought about the death of a parent or a child, the survivor will have a claim for damages under the Fatal Accidents Act 1976[1].

Congenital Disabilities (Civil Liability) Act 1976

Children born disabled as a result of injuries before their birth caused to their parents may have a cause of action under the Congenital Disabilities (Civil Liability) Act 1976[2]. The action is 'derivative' in that the child must establish that the defendant would have been actually or potentially liable to the *parent* in respect of the injury[3], but it is not necessary to show that the parent did, in fact, sustain injury. Thus, if a pregnant mother takes a negligently manufactured drug which causes her child, when born, to be disabled, an action will lie against the manufacturer, even though the mother suffers no ill-effects[4]. The mother herself is not generally liable where, for example, she neglects her own body through alcohol or drug abuse while pregnant[5]. The exception is where she is driving a car[6], in which case the real defendant will be the insurers. The father does not have the same immunity, and may be liable if, for example, he assaults the mother while she is pregnant. However, it has been pointed out that the mother might be unenthusiastic or unwilling about acting as the child's litigation friend in an action against the father[7].

Since an action under the 1976 Act is derivative in nature, the child's claim may be defeated or reduced by defences available to the parent. Thus, there is no liability for an occurrence preceding the time of conception if, at that time, either or both of the parents knew the risk of the child being born disabled[8]. Similarly, where the responsibility for the child being born disabled is shared by the parent and the defendant, the damages may be reduced as the court thinks just and equitable having regard to the extent of the parent's responsibility[9]. Finally, any term of a contract excluding or restricting liability to the parent binds the child[10].

A major problem for many children who are born disabled is to establish causation and prove that the congenital defects were actually brought about by

---

1 Section 1, as substituted by s 3(1) of the Administration of Estates Act 1982.
2 This Act followed the Law Com Report No 60 *Injuries to Unborn Children* (1974). See, generally, *Winfield and Jolowicz on Tort* (16th edn) (Sweet & Maxwell, 2002) at pp 827 et seq, and *Street on Torts* (11th edn) (Butterworths, 2003) at pp 216–218. The common law position was uncertain until 1992 when, in *Burton v Islington Health Authority* [1993] QB 204, the Court of Appeal held that an action lay at common law for injuries caused to an unborn child by negligence. The action crystallises on the birth of the child. In practice, the common law action will only need to be utilised in respect of births before 1976 since the 1976 legislation governs births after that time. The so-called action for 'wrongful life', where the claimant contends that he or she should never have been born at all, is beyond the scope of the present work but is discussed in *Winfield and Jolowicz* (above) at pp 830 et seq and in *Street* (above) at pp 226–227.
3 Congenital Disabilities (Civil Liability) Act 1976, s 1.
4 The example given in *Winfield and Jolowicz on Tort* (above) at p 828.
5 But this might lead to local authority intervention. See *D (A Minor) v Berkshire County Council* [1987] 1 All ER 20, and Chapter 11 above.
6 See fn 2 at p 665 above.
7 HK Bevan *Child Law* (Butterworths, 1989) at para 9.83.
8 Congenital Disabilities (Civil Liability) Act 1976, s 1(4).
9 Ibid, s 1(7).
10 Ibid, s 1(6).

negligence. The Pearson Committee[1] thought that the Congenital Disabilities (Civil Liability) Act 1976 would benefit only a minute proportion of children born with these defects. In recent years, attention has been focused on group actions by children alleged to have suffered birth defects or developed childhood diseases as a result of local environmental factors[2].

Responsibility for children's acts

Two general principles govern liability for tortious acts committed by children. The first principle is that children themselves are prima facie liable and there is no defence of minority as such[3]. A minor is therefore as liable to be sued as an adult. The second principle is that parents (and others exercising parental responsibility) are not usually liable for torts committed by children. Both of these principles require qualification.

Liability of children

The standard of care required for the tort of negligence is that of the reasonable person. Some torts require proof of malice. In either case, the age of a child may be relevant to show that the child did not possess the requisite mental state. Most of the reported cases have been concerned with the issue of contributory negligence. In many such cases, children have been found not to be negligent where, in similar circumstances, adults would have been. The test appears to be the degree of care for his own safety which it would have been reasonable to expect a child of the particular age reasonably to take[4]. It is not clear whether this test is entirely objective or whether the child's subjective characteristics, such as maturity and understanding, may be taken into account[5].

The standard of care expected of children is illustrated by the Australian case of *McHale v Watson*[6] where a boy of 12 years of age threw a piece of steel welding rod, sharpened to a spike, at a post. The spike glanced off the post hitting a nine-year-old girl who was standing nearby, causing injuries to her eye. It was established that the boy had no intention of hitting the girl or frightening her. The High Court of Australia upheld the judge's decision that this did not amount to negligence, applying the standard of care reasonably to be expected of a child of the same age, intelligence and experience. As Kitto J put it:

> 'It is, I think, a matter for judicial notice that the ordinary boy of 12 suffers from a feeling that a piece of wood and a sharp instrument have a special affinity. To expect a boy of that age to consider before throwing the spike whether the timber was hard or soft, to weigh the chances of being able to make the spike stick in the post, and to foresee that it might glance off and hit the girl, would be, I think, to expect a degree of sense and circumspection which nature ordinarily withholds till life becomes less rosy.'

---

1   *Compensation for Personal Injuries* (1978) (Cmnd 7054).
2   For a good discussion of the issues, see E Palmer 'Children and Toxic Torts' (1992) 4 JCL 156.
3   See, for example, *Gorely v Codd* [1967] 1 WLR 19.
4   *Yachuk v Oliver Blais Co Ltd* [1949] AC 396.
5   Such authority as there is suggests that, although a child's age may be taken into account, the test is otherwise entirely objective. See *Watkins v Birmingham City Council* (1976) 126 NLJ 442.
6   [1966] ALR 513. On the standard of care expected of children, see *Salmond and Heuston on the Law of Torts* (21st edn) (Sweet & Maxwell, 1996) at pp 411–412 and, in the context of occupier's liability, at pp 273–274.

Until comparatively recently, there was no direct English authority on the standard of care required of children, but in *Mullin v Richards*[1] the Court of Appeal addressed the issue and substantially adopted the reasoning of the High Court of Australia in *McHale v Watson*.

Teresa and Heidi were 15-year-old Birmingham schoolgirls. At the end of a maths lesson they were engaged in a mock 'sword-fight' with plastic rulers when tragedy struck. One of the rulers snapped and a fragment of plastic entered Teresa's eye causing her to lose all useful sight in it. Teresa sued Heidi, together with Birmingham City Council, alleging negligence on the part of Miss Osborne, the maths teacher. The judge found that the latter had not been negligent and dismissed the claim against the education authority. But he found that both the girls had been negligent and that Teresa's injury was the foreseeable result. Accordingly, he awarded damages subject to a 50% reduction for contributory negligence.

Allowing the appeal, the Court of Appeal held that where the defendant was a child the test was not that of the ordinary prudent and reasonable adult but that of the ordinary prudent and reasonable child of the same age as the defendant in the defendant's situation. The judge had indeed referred to the fact that the girls were aged 15 but there had been insufficient evidence to justify his conclusion that the accident was foreseeable. There was no evidence of the propensity of such rulers to break, that the practice of playing with rulers was frowned upon or barred by the school or that either of the girls had used excessive or inappropriate violence. All that had occurred was a schoolgirls' game and there was no justification for attributing to the girls foresight of any significant risk of likelihood of injury. Butler-Sloss LJ referred with approval to the judgment of Kitto J in *McHale v Watson* where it was said that 'children, like everyone else, must accept as they go about in society the risks from which ordinary care on the part of others will not suffice to save them. One such risk is that boys of 12 may behave as boys of 12'. And she added that 'girls of 15 playing together may play as somewhat irresponsible girls of 15'.

One of the reasons why there is a shortage of English authority on the standard of care required of children, at least outside the context of contributory negligence, is that a child will generally not be worth suing[2]. One way around this problem, in an appropriate case, is to sue the child's parent or, perhaps, the education authority, where an accident was near the child's school.

Liability of parents and other carers

There are two recognised exceptions to the rule that parents are not liable for the torts of their children. The first exception is where they have specifically authorised the child's actions, or where the child is employed by them. Here, they will be vicariously liable. A similar principle applies to contracts authorised by parents[3].

The second, and more significant, exception arises where the parent *himself* is found to be negligent in failing to prevent the act or omission of the child which

---

1   [1998] 1 All ER 920.
2   This is not, however, inevitably so since the child is capable of owning substantial personal property. See Chapter 9 above.
3   For the child's *own* contractual capacity and liability, see pp 673 et seq below.

has injured a third party[1]. A number of the reported cases have concerned firearms. Thus, a father was held liable where he gave his 15-year-old son an air gun and allowed him to keep it after he had smashed a neighbour's window with it. The son then went on to injure the eye of another boy with the gun[2]. However, a father was held not liable where his 13-year-old son resiled on a promise never to use an air rifle outside the house and did so injuring the plaintiff. It was accepted that the father had taken all reasonable precautions and the son's disobedience was unforeseeable[3].

Similar principles apply to school authorities where the standard of care is that of the reasonably prudent parent[4]. The leading case is the decision of the House of Lords in *Carmarthenshire County Council v Lewis*[5]. Here, the local authority was held liable for the lack of supervision at a nursery school. This led to a young child, not yet four years of age, running out of school and into the road, which caused the death of a lorry driver in the accident which followed. School authorities may also be liable where the child is injured owing to their negligence[6].

It would seem fair to conclude that *anyone* who has assumed responsibility for a child, such as a child-minder taking a child to or from school, could be liable on similar principles if either a child or a third party is injured as a result of their lack of supervision[7]. The employer of someone who injures a child may also vicariously liable if that person was acting within the scope of his or her employment[8].

---

1   As to liability to pay the child's fines and other responsibility for children's crimes, see Chapter 14 above.
2   *Bebee v Sales* (1916) 32 TLR 413. Liability was also established in *Newton v Edgerley* [1959] 1 WLR 1031.
3   *Donaldson v McNiven* [1952] 2 All ER 691.
4   *Ricketts v Erith Borough Council* [1943] 2 All ER 629. For an extensive review of the liability of schools in relation to health and safety, see N Harris *The Law Relating to Schools* (2nd edn) (Tolley Publishing Co Ltd, 1995) at ch 13 and N Harris 'Legal Liability in Respect of School Premises' (1991) 3 *Education and the Law* 125. See also A Ruff *Education Law: Text, Cases and Materials* (Butterworths, 2002) at pp 97–99.
5   [1955] AC 549.
6   As in *Barnes v Hampshire County Council* [1969] 1 WLR 1563. Here, school children were let out of school five minutes earlier than was the normal practice. A five-year-old child was injured when she wandered into the street, her mother having not yet arrived. The local education authority was held responsible, since the injury was foreseeable. Cf *Wilson v Governors of Sacred Heart Roman Catholic School* [1998] 1 FLR 663. Here, a nine-year-old boy was injured at the end of the school day when he was hit in the eye by a coat which had been deliberately whirled around like a lasso by another pupil. The Court of Appeal allowed the school's appeal against a finding of negligence arising from alleged failure to supervise children leaving through the school gates. Supervision was in fact provided during the lunch break when large numbers of children were in the playground. But the lunch period was contrasted with the very short period in which, and very short distance over which, children were engaged in leaving the school. It was not standard procedure to supervise children leaving school and the need for such supervision was not demonstrated. Contrast also *Nwabudike v Southwark London Borough Council* [1997] ELR 35 (where liability was not established on the basis that reasonable precautions to prevent accidents had been taken) with *J v North Lincolnshire County Council* [2000] ELR 245 (where liability was established on the basis that a vulnerable exit gate had not been protected).
7   The principle may extend to failure to control teenagers where there is an expectation of supervision. See *Home Office v Dorset Yacht Co* [1970] AC 1004.
8   See *Lister v Hesley Hall Ltd* [2002] 1 AC 215 where the House of Lords held that a children's home could be liable for the acts of its warden in abusing children in the home. The

CHILDREN AND THE LAW OF CONTRACT

Trietel has observed that the law governing minors' contracts is based on two principles[1]. The first principle is that 'the law must protect the minor against his inexperience, which may enable an adult to take unfair advantage of him, or to induce him to enter into a contract which, though in itself fair, is simply improvident'. The second principle is that 'the law should not cause unnecessary hardship to adults who deal fairly with minors'.

The result of attempting to follow a policy which embraces these two, somewhat conflicting, principles is that the law is complex and, in some respects, quite vague. Some contracts are valid, others are voidable, and yet others are completely unenforceable against the minor. The first principle underlies the general rule that a minor is not bound by his contracts. But this principle is only one of 'qualified unenforceability' since, under the second principle, the minor will be liable under certain types of contract from the outset, while others will bind him unless he takes steps to repudiate them. He may also incur some liability in tort, restitution, or under the Minors' Contracts Act 1987[2]. This section examines the current state of English law regarding the various kinds of contract which a minor may purport to make[3].

It should be appreciated that the practical significance of the issue diminished when the age of majority was lowered from 21 to 18 years of age, by the Family Law Reform Act 1969[4]. Many of the older cases related to young people in this age group such as, for example, undergraduates at the universities of Oxford and Cambridge[5]. Such people are now young adults with full contractual capacity[6]. Having said that, we are witnessing in other areas of the law a gradual

---

defendants had assumed responsibility for the care of the children when they placed them in the home and had entrusted their care to the warden. There was therefore a sufficiently close connection between the actions of the warden and the nature of his employment that the defendants should be liable. For the liability of local authorities for failing to prevent abuse, see Chapter 10 above.

1　GH Treitel *The Law of Contract* (11th edn) (Sweet & Maxwell, 2003) at pp 539–557. See also J Beatson *Anson's Law of Contract* (28th edn) (Oxford University Press, 2002) at pp 215–230. See also Cheshire, Fifoot and Furmston's *Law of Contract* (14th edn) (Butterworths, 2001) at pp 477–492.

2　Following Law Com Report No 134 *Minors' Contracts* (1984).

3　For a discussion of minors' capacity to obtain housing and to rent accommodation, see D Cowan and N Dearden 'The Minor as (a) Subject: the Case of Housing Law' in J Fionda (ed) *Legal Concepts of Childhood* (Hart, 2001).

4　Following *Report of the Committee on the Age of Majority* (the Latey Committee) (1967) (Cmnd 3342).

5　*Nash v Inman* [1908] 2 KB 1 concerned an action by a Savile Row tailor against a Cambridge undergraduate with respect to 11 fancy waistcoats. The action failed since he had not adduced sufficient evidence that the clothes were suitable to the condition in life of the minor or that he was not already adequately supplied with clothes. By contrast, Viscount Middleton, during the second reading of the Infants Contracts Bill 1874, referred to the decisions of juries at Oxford which had found, inter alia, that champagne and wild ducks and studs of emeralds set in diamonds were necessaries for Oxford undergraduates! See (1874) *Hansard*, Vol 219, Ser 3, col 1225.

6　And with full civil capacities for other legal purposes such as making a will or owning real property.

emancipation of older minors[1], and there are certain areas, such as entertainment and sport, in which minors regularly do enter into contracts. Children, sometimes quite young, also routinely engage in everyday transactions, such as purchasing sweets, which, although trivial, have contractual implications.

We conclude this section with a brief look at the position in Scotland where, following a wide-ranging report by the Scottish Law Commission[2], statutory reforms to Scots law have simplified the law on minors' contracts and other civil law capacities. We pose the question whether English law should not be similarly reformed, in pursuit of what the Scottish Commission identified as a third central principle which ought to inform the law: 'that the law should be clear and coherent and should accord with modern social and economic conditions'[3].

Valid contracts

Two kinds of minors' contracts have long been recognised as exceptions to the principle of unenforceability. They are contracts for 'necessaries' and contracts of service. In each case they are only binding on the minor if, on balance, they are *beneficial* to him. Beyond these two special kinds of contract there is no wider principle that a minor is bound by beneficial contracts. Thus, it is equally well established that trading contracts are not binding on a minor, however beneficial the terms might be for him[4].

Contracts for necessaries
A minor is liable to pay for necessaries, whether goods or services, which have been supplied to him under a contract. The concept of necessaries clearly includes the essentials of life such as food, clothing and lodging, but it is wider than this. It extends to what is appropriate to maintain the *particular* minor in his ordinary way of life and this can vary, depending on the lifestyle to which he is accustomed. Pure luxuries are not included, but some of the older cases recognised as necessaries luxurious articles which were also articles of utility[5]. In the case of goods, there is a statutory definition of necessaries, namely 'goods suitable to the condition in life of the minor ... and to his actual requirements at the time of sale and delivery'[6]. The latter part of the definition makes it plain that, as well as being capable of being regarded as necessaries in law, the minor must actually have had need of the items in question[7].

---

1 See Chapter 3 above.
2 Scot Law Com No 110 *Report on the Legal Capacity and Responsibility of Minors* (1987).
3 Ibid at para 2.12. The other two principles broadly corresponded with those identified by GH Treitel (above):
    '(a) that the law should protect young people from the consequences of their immaturity without restricting unnecessarily their freedom of action;
    (b) that the law should not cause unnecessary prejudice to adults who enter into transactions with young people.'
4 See, for example, *Cowern v Nield* [1912] 2 KB 419, although there may be some liability in restitution (see below).
5 See *Chapple v Cooper* (1844) 13 M&W 252.
6 Sale of Goods Act 1979, s 3(3).
7 Thus, in *Nash v Inman* (above) there was no evidence that the minor did not already possess sufficient waistcoats.

The contract will be enforceable against the minor only if it does not contain harsh or onerous terms so that it is, on balance, substantially for his benefit[1]. The concept of necessaries has now been abandoned in Scotland and replaced by a less technical and more wide-ranging notion of 'ordinary transactions' being everyday transactions commonly entered into by a child of the transacting child's age[2].

Contracts of service

It is established that a minor is bound by contracts of apprenticeship or service[3] on the basis that it is 'to his advantage that he should acquire the means of earning his livelihood'[4]. Again, as with necessaries, this will be so only where the contract, construed as a whole, is beneficial to the minor. Where it is not, he is free to repudiate it. The issue is again a question of balance, and the minor will not be able to escape liability merely because some of the terms of the contract are onerous. The standard texts[5] contrast two cases.

De Francesco v Barnum[6]

This case is an example of the oppressive sort of contract which is not binding on minors. Here, a 14-year-old girl entered into an apprenticeship deed to be taught stage dancing for seven years. The agreement prevented her from marrying during the apprenticeship, or from accepting professional engagements without the plaintiff's permission. However, the obligations were one-sided, since the plaintiff did not bind himself to provide the girl with professional engagements or to maintain her, if unemployed, and the stipulated remuneration was very poor. Fry J found the terms of the deed unreasonable and unenforceable since the girl was at the complete disposal of the plaintiff without commensurate obligations on his part.

Clements v London and North Western Railway Co[7]

This case illustrates the kind of contract of service which is regarded as broadly beneficial to minors and hence enforceable. The minor entered the service of the Railway Company as a porter, agreeing to join the company's insurance scheme and to relinquish his right to sue for personal injury under the Employers' Liability Act 1880. This occupational insurance scheme was more favourable to the minor than the statutory scheme, since it provided for compensation in a greater range of accidents but, on the other hand, it fixed a lower scale of compensation. Overall, it was held that the agreement was to the minor's advantage and thus binding on him.

It has also been held that where a term of the contract is repugnant but severable, it may be severed leaving intact the remainder of the contract which is of benefit to the minor[8].

---

1 See *Roberts v Gray* [1913] 1 KB 520.
2 Age of Legal Capacity (Scotland) Act 1991, s 2(1)(a).
3 GH Treitel *The Law of Contract* (11th edn) (Sweet & Maxwell, 2003) at pp 543–545, and Cheshire, Fifoot and Furmston *Law of Contract* (14th edn) (Butterworths, 2001) at pp 481 et seq.
4 Cheshire et al (above).
5 GH Treitel (above) at p 543, and Cheshire et al (above) at p 482.
6 (1890) 45 Ch D 430.
7 [1894] 2 QB 482.
8 *Bromley v Smith* [1909] 2 KB 235.

Voidable contracts

Voidable contracts are those which are valid and binding on minors, unless they repudiate them during minority or within a short time of attaining majority. Four types of such contract have been recognised to exist, namely: contracts concerning land; the acquisition of shares in companies; partnership agreements; and marriage settlements[1]. The basis for placing these contracts in a separate category is not clear. The view of the commentators is that the common factor is the quality of relative permanence which attaches to them. They are all contracts under which the minor acquires an interest in some subject-matter, ie a subject-matter to which continuous or recurring obligations are incident[2]. As such, the obligations continue, unless and until the minor decides to put an end to them. It would then be unjust to allow him to retain his interest in the subject-matter without carrying out his own obligations. Where the minor repudiates the contract in time, he will be freed from future liabilities under it but cannot recover money paid over unless there has been a total failure of consideration[3].

The continued existence of this exceptional category of contracts has been questioned, for it has been said that special treatment has been based on 'social and economic factors which have long since passed away'[4].

Unenforceable contracts: liability under the Minors' Contracts Act 1987, in restitution or in tort

Where a contract does not fall within any of the categories mentioned above, it is unenforceable against the minor. This does not necessarily mean that it has no legal effect. First, the other party remains bound by it and then certain legal consequences for the minor may also flow from it.

Liability under the Minors' Contracts Act 1987

Where the contract is partially carried out, property may pass to the minor under the ordinary principles of contract of sale. It would be unjust to allow the minor to retain this property where he has resiled from his part of the bargain. The issue is now governed by s 3 of the Minors' Contracts Act 1987[5]. This provides:

'(1) Where –
(a) a person ("the plaintiff") has after the commencement of this Act entered into a contract with another ("the defendant") and
(b) the contract is unenforceable against the defendant (or he repudiates it) because he was a minor when the contract was made, the court may, if it is just and equitable to do so, require the defendant to transfer to the plaintiff any property acquired by the defendant under the contract, or any property representing it.
(2) Nothing in this section shall be taken to prejudice any other remedy available to the plaintiff.'

Most obviously, this provision can catch a minor who has obtained goods on credit and is refusing to pay for them, but the remedy is discretionary and there is no guarantee that the court will order the transfer of the property.

---

1 See GH Treitel (above) at pp 545–547, and Cheshire et al (above) at pp 483–488.
2 Cheshire et al (above) at p 483.
3 *Steinberg v Scala (Leeds) Ltd* [1923] 2 Ch 452.
4 GH Treitel *The Law of Contract* (11th edn) (Sweet & Maxwell, 2003) at p 549.
5 For a concise review of the Act, see J Holroyd 'The Minors' Contracts Act 1987' (1987) 84 LS Gaz 2266.

Moreover, the remedy is limited to the property itself transferred under the contract, or 'any property representing it'. In other words, the court does not have carte blanche to order the minor to pay the price of the goods or otherwise to pay out of his wider assets. There may be some difficult 'tracing' issues about whether property really does represent that which was originally transferred[1]. The reasoning for the restriction is that to allow the minor's wider assets to be touched would be to enforce indirectly an unenforceable contract. It has been suggested that, in exercising its discretion, the court will probably wish to take into account the intrinsic fairness of the original contract, such as the price the minor was required to pay. Where this was unreasonable, the court might order the minor to return the property unless he pays a reasonable price for it, fixed by the court[2].

Liability in restitution

The Minors' Contracts Act 1987 preserves any other legal remedy available to the plaintiff. Under the equitable doctrine of restitution, a minor who has obtained goods by fraud may be obliged to disgorge them, if they are still in his possession, on the basis of unjust enrichment. This remedy is not available where the minor has already disposed of the goods and, in this respect, it is more limited than the statutory remedy which allows limited tracing[3]. Moreover, the statutory remedy, unlike the equitable one, is not dependent on proof of fraud.

Liability in tort

The issue here is whether a minor could incur tortious liability for acts directly connected with unenforceable contracts. The general principle is that an unenforceable contract may not be indirectly enforced against a minor by framing the cause of action in tort. Where, however, the wrongful event can be sufficiently divorced from the contract that it can be regarded as an independent wrong, the minor may not escape tortious liability. Two old cases, both involving horse-riding, resulted in different conclusions on this point.

In *Jennings v Rundall*[4], it was held that the minor was not liable in the tort of negligence where he hired a mare for riding and injured her through excessive and improper riding. However, in *Burnard v Haggis*[5], the opposite conclusion was reached where, contrary to the express instructions of the horse's owner, the minor injured the horse while jumping her, having hired her simply for riding. The point of distinction is elusive but is thought to turn on whether or not the wrongful act was contemplated by the contract. In the first case, riding clearly was contemplated (albeit not excessive riding) while, in the second case, jumping was positively excluded under the agreement.

A Scottish solution for England?

The English Law Commission, over a decade ago, considered the possibility of simplifying the law by adopting a general rule that minors of 16 years or over

---

1   These are explored with examples by GH Treitel (above) at pp 552 et seq.
2   Suggested by GH Treitel (above) at p 553.
3   The limitations of the doctrine of restitution are well illustrated by *Leslie Ltd v Sheill* [1914] 3 KB 607.
4   (1799) 8 Term Rep 335.
5   (1863) 14 CB(NS) 45.

should be fully liable on *all* contracts while those under that age would be immune from liability[1]. In the event, it opted for more limited reforms which found their way into the Minors' Contracts Act 1987[2].

Meanwhile, in Scotland, the Scottish Law Commission had embarked on a major examination of the legal capacities and responsibilities of minors and pupils in Scots law[3]. Its review included, but was considerably wider than, the contractual capacity of young people. Its concern was with what, in Scots law, was termed 'active' capacity to perform civil acts having legal effect as opposed to 'passive' capacity simply to hold rights[4]. This active capacity included the capacity 'to enter contracts, make promises, grant conveyances or discharges, make a will, give consent, participate in court proceedings or perform any act of legal significance in the field of private law'[5]. After an extensive consultation, the Scottish Law Commission proposed a two-tier system of legal capacity. Children from the age of 0 to 16 years would, subject to limited but important exceptions, have no legal capacity[6], while those young people from the age of 16 to 18 years would, subject to limited protections, enjoy full legal capacity for all those acts listed above[7]. Transactions purportedly entered into by those under 16 years of age would be void, unless ratified on attaining 16 years, but there would be an important exception, whereby they would have capacity to engage in 'ordinary transactions' – being reasonable transactions of a kind commonly entered into by a child of the same age and circumstances[8]. Transactions entered into by those over 16 years of age would be valid, but the court would have a discretion to set a transaction aside on a young person's application made before attaining 21 years of age, if satisfied that it had caused or was likely to cause him 'substantial prejudice' and was not of a kind 'which a reasonably prudent person acting in the same circumstances, would have entered into'[9]. These recommendations were implemented by the Age of Legal Capacity (Scotland) Act 1991[10].

Effects of the reformed Scots law

The broad effect of the new law was to draw a reasonably clear line for contractual (and other civil) capacity at 16 years of age. This is subject to the very significant exception for 'ordinary transactions'. The gist of this is that the legal capacity of children to do those things which children habitually do is legally recognised, and this varies, depending on the age of the child. The Scottish Law Commission gave

---

1 Law Com Working Paper No 81 *Minors' Contracts* (1982) Part XII.
2 One of these was that minors' contracts should generally be capable of being ratified by the minor on attaining majority.
3 Before the Age of Legal Capacity (Scotland) Act 1991, Scots law distinguished between 'minors' who were boys between the ages of 14 and 18 years and girls between 12 and 18 years and 'pupils' who were boys under 14 and girls under 12 years. For further discussion of the Scottish Law Commission's work and the 1991 legislation, see A Bainham 'Growing Up in Britain: Adolescence in the Post-Gillick Era' (1992) *Juridical Review* 155 at pp 169–172, and JM Thomson *Family Law in Scotland* (4th edn) (Butterworths, 2002) at chs 9 and 10.
4 Scot Law Com No 110 *Report on the Legal Capacity and Responsibility of Minors* (1987) at para 3.22.
5 Ibid.
6 Ibid at paras 3.21 et seq.
7 Ibid at paras 3.97 et seq.
8 Ibid at paras 3.41–3.51.
9 Ibid at paras 3.102 et seq.
10 This Act received Royal Assent on 25 July 1991 and came into force on 25 September 1991.

the examples of the five-year-old child buying sweets and the 15-year-old child purchasing a cinema ticket. Neither of these examples comes within the traditional category of necessaries, but ought to be placed, the Commission thought, on a proper legal footing[1]. The advantage of the 'ordinary transactions' formula was thought to be that it would be flexible enough to cater for children at the two extremes of the age group. Thus, a child of five years would have the capacity to engage in transactions appropriate to his age group, but not those appropriate to an older child. Accordingly, the rule would have built-in recognition of the different levels of understanding of children of different ages[2]. The Commission acknowledged that there might be an element of vagueness, but thought that this would be no worse than that which surrounded the concept of necessaries. It believed that the new formula could cover, inter alia: small shopping transactions; payment of bus or train fares; payment for skating lessons or a haircut; Saturday or holiday jobs; booking accommodation at a Youth Hostel; and the operation of bank deposit accounts[3].

The new scheme also made it possible to sweep away, at a stroke, the existing rules governing the exceptional cases of valid contracts. It thought that it was unnecessary to retain contracts for necessaries as an exception to the general rule of incapacity. It also thought that these items would usually be provided by the parent or guardian and that, where they were not, they would be covered by the ordinary transactions rule[4]. Similarly, the Commission thought that there should be no exemption relating to employment or trading contracts since, where appropriate, they too would fall within the general exception – the most obvious examples being contracts for Saturday or holiday jobs[5].

Reform for England?
Whether such a scheme would be suitable for England is legitimately the subject of debate, but there is no question that Scots law now has a more coherent and rational system. Reform along the lines of the Scottish legislation would also be consistent with the changes in the Children Act 1989 regarding young people over 16 years of age[6]. A comprehensive review of the legal capacities and responsibilities of children and young people is overdue, but at the time of writing there has been no indication from the English Law Commission that it intends to embark on this task.

THE EMPLOYMENT OF CHILDREN AND YOUNG PERSONS

It has been seen that a minor may enter into a valid contract of employment, or other contract whereby he makes a living professionally, if it is substantially for his benefit, but the contractual rules are subject to extensive and complex legislation

---

1 Scot Law Com Report No 110 *Report on the Legal Capacity and Responsibility of Minors* (1987) at para 3.41.
2 Ibid at para 3.42.
3 Ibid at para 3.48.
4 Ibid at paras 3.87–3.88.
5 Ibid at para 3.92.
6 See Chapter 2 above.

which places restrictions on the employment of children. Some of these restrictions are general, while others relate to specific kinds of employment.

Historical background

Legislative intervention can be traced back to the early nineteenth century and was a response to the appalling working conditions and long hours which prevailed in factories, mines and shops during the industrial revolution. This legislation began to impose controls over the hours which children and young people (and women) were permitted to work, at first in textile factories, and later underground or as shop assistants. Other early legislation dealt with health and safety, dangerous and unhealthy industries, and the education of children.

A comprehensive review of this legislation is beyond the scope of the present work[1] but the following were some of the principal landmarks in the nineteenth century. The Factory Act 1833 prohibited the employment of children under nine years of age in textile factories and regulated the employment of older children. The Factory Act 1847 imposed a maximum daily limit of 10 hours' work for women and young persons employed in textile factories. The Factory and Workshop Act 1878, following the report of a Royal Commission, extended the protections to all factories, raised the minimum age of employment to 10 years of age, and limited the hours of children under 14 years of age to half the normal day. The Education Act 1880 introduced compulsory school attendance up to 10 years of age, and this was extended to 13 years of age for those with poor attendance records. The connection between compulsory education and the restrictions on employment is an obvious and significant one and remains a feature of the law today[2].

Further protective legislation continued to be introduced from time to time throughout the twentieth century[3]. The Employment of Women, Young Persons and Children Act 1920, for example, prohibited (with limited exceptions) the employment of women and young persons at night in industrial undertakings and established 14 years of age (the then school leaving age) as the minimum age for employment in such undertakings. The Children and Young Persons Act 1933 imposed the general restrictions on the employment of children under 13 years of age which continue to apply today, although the age restriction has now been raised to 14. The Mines and Quarries Act 1954 consolidated previous legislation regulating the employment of women and children underground in mines, or above ground in quarries, and the Shops Act 1950 was a similar consolidation of legislation, mainly controlling the hours of work of young people in shops. The Education Act 1944 raised the compulsory school leaving age to 15 and this was subsequently raised to 16 (or just under) in 1972, where it remains[4]. More recently, the Employment Act 1989 brought about a substantial 'deregulation' of the employment of young persons (as opposed to children) by sweeping away most of the protective employment legislation applying to this age group.

---

1 There is a detailed review of this legislation in the Department of Employment's Consultative Document *Restrictions on Employment of Young People and the Removal of Sex Discrimination in Legislation* (1987).
2 See also Chapter 16 below.
3 A selective approach is necessary here, but for a full review see the Consultative Document (above) at paras 2.6 et seq.
4 Raising of the School Leaving Age Order 1972, SI 1972/444.

However, in 1994, the Council of the European Union issued a Directive on the Protection of Young People at Work[1] which necessitated some reform of domestic employment legislation affecting children and young people.

International obligations regarding the employment of children and young people

Various international instruments impose obligations on the UK regarding the employment of children and young persons which have as their common themes the objectives of protecting children from economic exploitation, prohibiting the employment of children (with limited qualifications) and ensuring safe and proper conditions of work where they are employed. This is an area in which theory appears to be quite divorced from practice and in which there is an absence of reliable data regarding the actual employment of children and young persons. The detailed provisions are beyond the scope of the present work. What follows is a sketch of the principal instruments[2].

The UNCRC

Article 32 of the UNCRC protects children against economic exploitation. It asserts 'the right of the child to be protected from economic exploitation and from performing any work that is likely to be hazardous or to interfere with the child's education, or to be harmful to the child's health or physical, mental, spiritual, moral or social development'[3]. In particular, States parties are required to provide for a minimum age or minimum ages for admission to employment; appropriate regulation of hours and conditions of employment and appropriate penalties or other sanctions to ensure effective enforcement of these obligations[4].

European Union Council Directive on the Protection of Young People at Work

This Council Directive[5] imposes a wide range of obligations on Member States relating to prohibitions on work by children and the conditions of work affecting young people. It incorporates into English law some of the central requirements of the EU Charter of Fundamental Rights and Freedoms[6]. The following are among the more important provisions. Member States are required to adopt the

---

1 Council Directive No 94/33/EC of 22 June 1994. For a critique of the Directive and of English legislation as it applies to the employment of children in 'family work', see A Bond 'Working for the family? Child employment legislation and the public/private debate' (1996) JSWFL 291. For a review of the issues surrounding children's work in the UK, see B Pettitt (ed) *Children and Work in the UK: Reassessing the Issues* (CPAG, 1998).

2 For more extensive discussions see U Kilkelly 'Economic Exploitation of Children' [2003] *Saint Louis University Public Law Review* 321. This article looks at the issue of the economic exploitation of children from a European perspective. It reviews the provisions of the major international instruments and considers compliance with the relevant standards across the countries of Western and Eastern Europe. See also C Hamilton and B Watt 'The Employment of Children' [2004] CFLQ 135. This article looks at the major international obligations but also includes discussion of the position under English domestic legislation.

3 Article 32(1).

4 Article 32(2). See also the International Labour Organization, Convention No 138 on the Minimum Ages for Employment, discussed by Hamilton and Watt (above) at pp 138–139.

5 Council Directive 94/33/EC.

6 See Article 32 of the Charter. The Charter is not currently part of English law but will become so when the EU Constitution is finally adopted. See Article 5 of the draft Constitution.

measures necessary to prohibit work by children and to ensure that the minimum working or employment age is not lower than the compulsory school leaving age or 15 years in any event[1]. They are obliged to ensure that work by adolescents is strictly regulated and that employers guarantee that young people have working conditions which suit their age. They must also ensure that young people are 'protected against economic exploitation and against any work likely to harm their safety, health or physical, mental, moral or social development or to jeopardize their education'[2]. There are limited exceptions to the prohibitions on employment of children which allow Member States to permit the employment of children aged 13 or 14 in 'light work' and in certain authorised 'cultural or similar activities'[3]. The work undertaken by these children must not be likely to be harmful to their safety, health or development or their attendance at school or participation in vocational guidance or training programmes. The Directive goes on to impose obligations on employers to take the necessary measures to protect the health and safety of young people. They must assess the hazards before young people begin work, inform the young people of them and of the measures adopted concerning their safety and health. They must undergo a similar assessment wherever there is any major change in working conditions[4]. Other provisions of the Directive prohibit employing young people in work which represents a risk to their safety, health and development[5]; limit the number of hours of work for both children and adolescents[6]; subject to limited exceptions, prohibit night work (defined as between the hours of 8 pm and 6 am for children and 10 pm and 6 am or 11 pm and 7 am for adolescents)[7]; and require minimum rest periods, annual rest and minimum break periods[8].

The Council of Europe: the European Social Charter

Article 7 of the European Social Charter governs child labour and has detailed provisions designed to protect children from exploitation. Among the more important obligations which it imposes on the contracting parties are the following[9]:

(i)   a minimum age for employment set at 15, subject to exceptions for children employed in light work which does not harm their health, morals or education;

(ii) a higher minimum age of admission to prescribed occupations regarded as dangerous or unhealthy;

(iii) a prohibition on work which would deprive a person still in full-time education of the full benefit of that education;

(iv) a limit on the working hours of those under 16 bearing in mind their developmental needs and their need for vocational training;

---

1   Council Directive 94/33/EC, Article 1(1).
2   Ibid, Article 1(2) and (3).
3   Ibid, Articles 3, 4 and 5.
4   Ibid, Article 6.
5   Ibid, Article 7.
6   Ibid, Article 8.
7   Ibid, Article 9.
8   Ibid, Articles 10, 11 and 12.
9   There is an extensive and detailed discussion of Article 7 and its requirements in Kilkelly (above) at pp 334–346.

(v) the duty to recognise the right of young workers and apprentices to a fair wage or appropriate allowances.

Other provisions, similar to those of the EU Directive above, regulate such matters as annual holidays and restrictions on night work.

English law: the current situation

The key distinction in current employment law is between 'children' and 'young persons'. This is not, however, the same distinction which exists for the purposes of the criminal law where, as was seen[1], those under 14 years of age are 'children' while those over 14 years of age are 'young persons'. In the employment sphere, the crucial divide is the compulsory school leaving age: those below it are 'children' while those above it are 'young persons'[2]. It would be convenient, for the student's purposes, if a precise age were fixed in this respect, but the position is not quite as straightforward as this. Although 16 years of age is the benchmark, the school leaving age fluctuates slightly depending on the date of the individual pupil's birthday and its relationship to the statutory school leaving dates. In practical terms, this means that it may apply to someone as young as 15 years and eight months or as old as 16 years and seven months[3]. The distinction is, nonetheless, important since there are extensive restrictions on the employment of children but practically none on the employment of young persons.

The employment of children

Restrictions on the employment of children may be divided into two categories – general restrictions and specific restrictions[4].

General restrictions
The general restrictions are contained in the Children and Young Persons Act 1933, as amended[5]. This provides that children may not be employed:

(1) who are under the age of 14 years;
(2) to do any work other than light work;
(3) before the close of school hours on any school day (except where leave to be absent can be, and is, given);

---

1   In Chapter 14 above.
2   Under the Education Act 1996, s 558, any person who is not for the purposes of the Act over compulsory school age is deemed to be a child for the purposes of any enactment relating to the prohibition or regulation of the employment of children or young persons.
3   Education Act 1996, s 8, and the Education (School Leaving Date) Order 1997, SI 1997/1970. On compulsory attendance at school, see Chapter 16 below.
4   For a discussion based on the ages of the children, see Hamilton and Watt (above) at pp 141–146.
5   Children and Young Persons Act 1933, ss 18–21, as amended by the Children (Protection at Work) Regulations 1998, SI 1998/276. The Regulations, which came into force on 4 August 1998, make various amendments to the 1933 Act and the Children and Young Persons Act 1963 to implement in relation to children the EC Directive on the Protection of Young People at Work. In particular, they raise from 13 to 14 years the age at which a child may be employed in any work other than as an employee of his parent or guardian in light agricultural or horti-cultural work on an occasional basis. So far as the latter work is concerned, the relevant age at which children may be employed in such work was raised from 10 to 13 years by the Children (Protection at Work) Regulations 2000 (Nos 1 and 2), SI 2000/1333 and SI 2000/2548.

(4)   before 7 am or after 7 pm on any day;
(5)   for more than two hours on any school day;
(6)   for more than two hours on any Sunday;
(7)   for more than eight hours or, if the child is under the age of 15 years, for more than five hours in any day:
    (i)   on which he is not required to attend school, and
    (ii)   which is not a Sunday;
(8)   for more than 35 hours or, if the child is under the age of 15 years, for more than 25 hours in any week in which he is not required to attend school; or
(9)   for more than four hours in any day without a rest break of one hour; or
(10) at any time in a year unless at that time he has had, or could still have, during a period in the year in which he is not required to attend school, at least two consecutive weeks without employment.

These restrictions may be augmented by other restrictions imposed by local authority bye-laws. Conversely, such bye-laws may allow children under 14 years of age to be employed in limited circumstances[1]. Under the unimplemented Employment of Children Act 1973, the Secretary of State has wide powers to regulate the employment of children, the intention being to remove regional variations and impose uniform standards. It is a criminal offence for an employer to engage a child in breach of any of the above restrictions, but he will have a defence where it can be shown that the contravention was due to the act or default of some other person and that he himself used all due diligence to secure compliance with the statutory requirements[2].

Specific restrictions

Various pieces of legislation impose specific restrictions on children participating in particular kinds of employment. Thus, no child may be employed in an industrial undertaking[3], factory[4], mine or quarry[5], in a shop[6], or aboard a UK registered ship[7].

Children may not, generally, be employed in street-trading[8], but local authorities are empowered to make bye-laws which authorise children of 14 years or over (but not younger children) to be employed by *their parents* in street-trading to a specified extent. The bye-laws may provide for the granting of licences and specify conditions relating to their issue, suspension and revocation. In particular, the bye-laws may determine the days, hours and places during which the children concerned may take part in street-trading[9].

The employment of children in entertainment and performances is strictly regulated by the Children and Young Persons Acts of 1933 and 1963. Detailed discussion of the minutiae of these provisions is not appropriate here[10]. Suffice it

---

1   Children and Young Persons Act 1933, s 18(2).
2   Ibid, s 21(1).
3   Employment of Women, Young Persons and Children Act 1920, s 1(1).
4   Factories Act 1961, s 167.
5   Mines and Quarries Act 1954, s 124.
6   Shops Act 1950, s 74(1) and Part II.
7   Merchant Shipping Act 1995, s 55.
8   Children and Young Persons Act 1933, s 20(1).
9   Ibid, s 20(2).
10 But such a discussion may be found in HK Bevan *Child Law* (Butterworths, 1989) at paras 11.71–11.76. Such children must have attained the age of 12 years to be so trained.

to note that the 1933 Act prohibits the participation by children in dangerous public performances[1]. The training of children to take part in dangerous performances or to be employed outside the UK in singing, playing, performing or being exhibited for profit is controlled by local authority licences[2]. The 1963 Act extended the licensing system to performances more generally, including those on film, television or in broadcasting. Again, a local authority licence must be obtained. This will not be granted unless the authority is satisfied that the child is fit to take part in the performance, that proper provision has been made to secure his health and kind treatment, and that his education will not suffer[3]. These licences apply to all children, namely those under school leaving age, but there are further restrictions on the granting of licences in relation to those under 14 years of age[4].

Enforcement of restrictions

Local education authorities are empowered to institute proceedings in respect of offences under Part II of the Children and Young Persons Act 1933[5]. They may also prohibit or restrict the employment of children where it appears to them that a child is 'being employed in such a manner as to be prejudicial to his health or otherwise to render him unfit to obtain the full benefit of the education provided for him'[6]. The parent or employer may also be required to provide information necessary to ascertain whether the child is being employed in that manner[7]. Failure to comply with a local authority's request for information, or notice of prohibition, constitutes a criminal offence[8].

There is substantial evidence that enforcement of the statutory restrictions is ineffective and that there is widespread contravention of the law[9]. A report by the Low Pay Unit, following a National Child Employment Study[10], found a vast amount of illegal employment of children in Birmingham and concluded that large numbers of children were at risk of economic exploitation, physical risk and educational disadvantage. Among the report's more significant findings were that 43 per cent of children between the ages of 10 and 16 years of age had some sort of job: 74 per cent of these were illegally employed, of which one-quarter were under 13 years of age, and many were employed in work prohibited for children or were working illegal hours; 35 per cent had had an accident including cuts, burns, broken bones and assault; and children were generally underpaid with one-quarter of them earning less than £1 per hour. The report called for immediate implementation of the Employment of Children Act 1973, a thorough review of all

---

1 Children and Young Persons Act 1933, s 23, as amended, refers to any performance in which the child's 'life or limbs are endangered'.
2 Ibid, s 24. For a more up-to-date discussion see Hamilton and Watt (above) pp 142–143.
3 Children and Young Persons Act 1963, s 37(4).
4 Ibid, s 38. Essentially, such a licence may not be granted unless it is for acting or performing in a ballet or opera. It will need to be established that the particular part to be played by the child could not be taken except by a child of about that age.
5 Ibid, s 98.
6 Education Act 1996, s 559(1).
7 Ibid, s 559(2).
8 Ibid, s 559(3).
9 See the assessment of Hamilton and Watt (above) at pp 145–149.
10 C Pond and A Searle *The Hidden Army: Children at Work in the 1990s* Low Pay Pamphlet No 55, and see the summary at (1991) 76 *Childright* 17.

employment legislation affecting children, minimum wage protection for children and young persons and action, at a European level, to provide greater protection for children at work under the European Social Charter.

Family decisions and the employment of children

Children are, of course, members of families as well as individuals, and this raises issues about the application of family law principles in the context of the employment of children[1]. Two problematic and inter-related issues may be identified. The first issue is the impact of parental responsibility on employment decisions. The second issue is the relationship between child autonomy or '*Gillick* competence' and the restrictions on employment.

Employment and parental responsibility

Bevan has noted how, historically, the absolute nature of parental rights was used as a justification for child slavery, whereby a father sold his child to an employer. This influence of parental rights, according to Bevan, also contributed indirectly to the wretched conditions of apprenticeship in the nineteenth century. The father–child and master–servant relationships were considered so closely analogous that, just as the father could make unrestricted demands on the services of his child, so also could the master or employer – thus giving the barbaric conditions of apprenticeship 'an aura of respectability'[2].

Parental rights, now responsibilities, are no longer absolute, as has been shown, but an unresolved question is how far a parent might legally be able to interfere with the relationship of child and employer which does not contravene the statutory restrictions. What, for example, is the legal position if a 14-year-old agrees to take a Saturday job but his parents object? Can they prohibit the potential employer from engaging the child? The one point which is clear is that, if the employer should decide to flout the parents' wishes, no action would lie against him in tort[3]. From a practical point of view this may be all that we need to know, but the theoretical question remains. Does the parent, or the child acting in conjunction with the employer, have the right to decide? The answer would again appear to turn on the uncertain interpretation of *Gillick*. The later Court of Appeal decisions in *Re R* and *Re W* suggest that the employer, if satisfied that the child is '*Gillick*-competent', would be acting lawfully *either* in deciding to employ the child *or* in following the parents' wishes and deciding not to do so[4]. Any disputes could, at least theoretically, be resolved by application to the court, with leave, for a s 8 order.

Gillick competence and employment restrictions

A respectable argument can be mounted for saying that those children who have acquired *Gillick* competence should be liberated from the statutory restrictions on employment and the corresponding requirements of compulsory education. Why should such children not decide to work rather than stay on in school? This is an

---

1   For a damning critique of the law relating to the employment of children by their families, see
    A Bond 'Working for the Family? Child employment legislation and the public/private divide'
    (1996) JSWFL 291.
2   HK Bevan *Child Law* (Butterworths, 1989) at para 11.67.
3   *F v Wirral Metropolitan Borough Council* [1991] Fam 69.
4   *Gillick v West Norfolk and Wisbech Area Health Authority* [1986] 1 AC 112, *Re R (A Minor) (Wardship:
    Medical Treatment)* [1992] Fam 11, and *Re W (A Minor) (Medical Treatment: Court's Jurisdiction)*
    [1993] Fam 64. And see Chapter 8 above.

argument which undoubtedly appeals to some advocates of the liberationist school of children's rights[1]. The opposing argument, in favour of the employment restrictions and compulsory education, is that the child's 'developmental' and 'basic' interests require that he receive a certain level of education and be protected from premature exposure to work[2]. The essence of this argument is that it is only through proper education that a child can acquire the capacity for meaningful independence later in life, and this justifies imposing statutory restrictions before he matures into adulthood.

The employment of young persons

Until comparatively recently, there were innumerable statutory provisions regulating the employment of young persons[3]. Most of these related to night work in industrial undertakings and the number of hours which young people were permitted to work in specified occupations, mainly related to the delivery of goods and the running of errands[4].

Abolition of most protective legislation

The Employment Act 1989[5] swept away practically all the protective legislation applying to young people as distinct from children. Only a few restrictions which were considered necessary, on health and safety grounds, remain. The legislation involved denunciation of part of the European Social Charter, the main provision being Article 7(8) governing night work, which requires contracting parties 'to provide that persons under 18 years of age shall not be employed in night work with the exception of certain occupations provided for by national laws and regulations'. The power of local authorities to make bye-laws governing the employment of young persons was removed, while the Secretary of State was given wide powers to repeal or amend other relevant statutory provisions. The Employment Act 1989 was part of a wider government policy for the 'deregulation' of the labour market by the removal of discriminatory and protective legislation and the relaxation of certain employment protection rights[6]. The position is, for the present, very straightforward. There is effectively no special protective employment legislation and no general legal restrictions on the employment of young persons.

The legislation was controversial and followed a Consultative Document issued by the Department of Employment in 1987. This contended that there was 'no evidence that long hours, shift work or night work have a different effect on young people than on adults'[7]. Another argument in favour of deregulation was that the existing regulations were piecemeal, complex and difficult to understand. As such, they constituted an administrative and clerical burden for employers. It was

---

1 See also the discussion in MP Grenville 'Compulsory School Attendance and the Child's Wishes' [1988] JSWL 4.
2 See A Bainham *Children, Parents and the State* (Sweet & Maxwell, 1988) at pp 166–169.
3 As to which see HK Bevan (above) at para 11.81.
4 The principal legislation was the Employment of Women, Young Persons and Children Act 1920 and the Young Persons (Employment) Acts 1938 and 1964.
5 Employment Act 1989, s 10 and Sch 3.
6 For a critique of the Employment Act 1989, see S Deakin 'Equality Under a Market Order: The Employment Act 1989' (1990) 19 *Industrial Law Journal* 1.
7 Department of Employment's Consultative Document *Restrictions on Employment of Young People and the Removal of Sex Discrimination in Legislation* (1987) at para 1.8.

also said that the legislation was selective in its coverage, without any evidence of greater exploitation in the protected spheres than in the unprotected ones[1]. It was conceded that some form of regulation might need to be retained, on health and safety grounds, or on 'moral' grounds as, for example, to protect young people from exposure to drinking and gambling[2]. The employment of young persons over the age of 16 but under 18 is now subject to special requirements relating to health and safety at work[3]. The regulations require the prospective employer of a young person of that age to undertake a risk assessment relating to his or her health or safety if employed. The regulations specify the factors that must be taken into account in carrying out or reviewing the assessment and these include 'the inexperience, lack of awareness of risks and immaturity of young persons'. The employer must then ensure that such young persons are protected from such risks at work.

Deakin[4] has criticised the legislation for taking away the, admittedly selective, protections for young workers, without making more general provision for maximum hours of work, rest periods and working at weekends. While conceding that there may be no evidence of an extra risk to the health and safety of young workers in the 16–18-year age group, Deakin put forward a more compelling reason for restricting their hours of work, namely 'to facilitate their integration into society'[5]. This, he argued, required that they have positive incentives to train and pursue their education in the transitional period between leaving school and entering fully waged work. The legislation, in his view, 'contributes further to the undervaluing of youth training and education which began with the linking of YTS to a policy of disguising unemployment and coercing the young unemployed into work through cuts in social security'[6]. He concluded that government employment policy in the UK was increasingly out of step with international and European domestic labour standards, which recognise 'that a high level of social protection is a pre-condition of a fair and efficient labour market'[7]. It should be noted that the European Directive applies to 'adolescents' as well as to children, although its requirements are understandably less exacting in relation to the latter. 'Adolescent', for these purposes, is defined by Article 3 as 'any young person of at least 15 years of age but less than 18 years of age who is no longer subject to compulsory full-time schooling under national law'. The Directive prescribes maximum daily working times for adolescents and a prohibition on night work which, despite a partial opt-out for the UK, should require a significant reform of English legislation.

The near abolition of protective legislation applying to young persons and the signal failure to enforce that which applies to children presents us with a curious paradox – that the area of law in which there has perhaps, historically, been the largest amount of legislative intervention is also the one in which the legal system has most emphatically failed to protect children and young people.

---

1   Department of Employment's Consultative Document (1987) (above).
2   Ibid, at para 1.6.2.
3   Health and Safety (Young Persons) Regulations 1997, SI 1997/135.
4   S Deakin (above) at pp 18–19.
5   Citing the Council of Europe *Nightwork, Comparative Study of Legislation and Regulations, Problems and Social Repercussions* (1981) at p 48.
6   These wider aspects of employment policy are beyond the scope of this work.
7   S Deakin (above) at p 19.

Chapter 16

CHILDREN AND EDUCATION

INTRODUCTION

Education law has become an accepted academic discipline in its own right[1]. The fundamental right of children to be educated is recognised in a number of international Conventions. One of the most important is the UNCRC, Article 28(1) of which provides:

> 'States parties recognize the right of the child to education, and with a view to achieving this right progressively and on the basis of equal opportunity, they shall, in particular:
> (a)   make primary education compulsory and available free to all;
> (b)   encourage the development of different forms of secondary education, including general and vocational education, make them available and accessible to every child, and take appropriate measures such as the introduction of free education and offering financial assistance in case of need;
> (c)   make higher education accessible to all on the basis of capacity by every appropriate means;
> (d)   make educational and vocational information and guidance available and accessible to all children;
> (e)   take measures to encourage regular attendance at schools and the reduction of drop-out rates.'

Similarly broad statements about the right of the child to education may be found in the Universal Declaration of Human Rights[2] and the ECHR[3]. Increasingly, also, the education of children has become relevant under the law of the European Union[4].

---

1   On education law generally, see JR McManus (ed) *Education and the Courts* (Jordans, 2004) and O Hyams *Law of Education* (2nd edn) (Jordans, 2004). A useful cases and materials book is A Ruff *Education Law: Text, Cases and Materials* (Butterworths, 2002). For an analytical and more theoretical approach to education law, see N Harris *Law and Education: Regulation, Consumerism and the Education System* (Sweet & Maxwell, 1993). For a children's rights perspective on education law, see J Fortin *Children's Rights and the Developing Law* (2nd edn) (Butterworths, 2003) at chs 6, 11 and 12. For a description of the legislative framework on education, see the chapter by N Harris in S Bailey (ed) *Cross on Local Government* (Sweet & Maxwell).

2   Universal Declaration of Human Rights, Article 26(1) states:
> 'Everyone has the right to education. Education shall be free, at least in the elementary and fundamental stages. Elementary education shall be compulsory. In the exercise of any functions which it assumes in relation to education and to teaching, the state shall respect the rights of parents to ensure such education and teaching in conformity with their own religion and philosophical convictions.'

3   ECHR, Article 2, Protocol 1 provides, inter alia, that, 'No person shall be denied the right to education'.

4   In particular, the children of migrant workers who are employed in the territory of a Member State of which they are not nationals are to be admitted to courses of general education, apprenticeship and vocational training under the same conditions as nationals of that State, provided that they reside in the territory in question (Council Regulation on Free Movement of Workers within the Community, 16/12/68/EEC, Article 12). For further discussion of this and education in EU law more generally, see P Craig and G de Burca *EU Law: Text, Cases and Materials* (3rd edn) (Oxford University Press, 2003) at pp 744–750.

The law relating to education was, until 1996, to be found in a host of Education Acts having as their foundation the Education Act 1944. Education law has, been largely consolidated in the mammoth Education Act 1996 ('the 1996 Act'), and references in the text will usually be to the relevant section of the 1996 Act. There have been several significant pieces of education legislation since this consolidation. The Education Act 1997 made changes, inter alia, to the law governing the LEA, inspection, curriculum authorities and discipline. The Labour Government's first major piece of education legislation was the School Standards and Framework Act 1998. This sought to give effect to the proposals set out in the White Paper *Excellence in Schools*[1], published in July 1997. The cornerstone of the Government's policy was to create 'a greater awareness across society of the importance of education and increased expectations of what can be achieved'. The primary aim was to increase standards of performance[2]. The Special Educational Needs and Disability Act 2001 has made major amendments to the law governing special educational needs, especially by extending disability discrimination protection to schools. Finally, the Education Act 2002 has effected further changes relating to such matters as school government and discipline.

Resources and parental choice

The above provisions are general statements of principle. The particular kind of education which individual children receive is influenced to a large extent by local educational provision and by parental choice. These factors are also acknowledged in international Conventions. Thus, the ECHR requires States parties to 'respect the right of parents to ensure such education and teaching in conformity with their own religious and philosophical convictions'[3]. The UNCRC explicitly recognises the discretion which States have in determining educational provision, provided that it accords with the fundamental principles of the Convention and with the minimum standards of domestic law[4].

Minimum standards

The required minimum standards in English law are contained in s 10 of the 1996 Act which puts the Secretary of State under a general duty 'to promote the

---

1   DfEE (7 July 1997) (Cm 3681).
2   For a summary of the principal provisions see the second edition of this work at pp 571–572.
3   ECHR, Article 2, Protocol 1.
4   Ibid, Article 29(2). The fundamental principles themselves are set out in Article 29(1), which provides that the education of the child shall be directed to:
    '(a) the development of the child's personality, talents and mental and physical abilities to their fullest potential;
    (b) the development of respect for human rights and fundamental freedoms, and for the principles enshrined in the Charter of the United Nations;
    (c) the development of respect for the child's parents, his or her own cultural identity, language and values, for the national values of the country in which the child is living, the country from which he or she may originate, and for civilizations different from his or her own;
    (d) the preparation of the child for responsible life in a free society, in the spirit of understanding, peace, tolerance, equality of sexes, and friendship among all peoples, ethnic, national and religious groups and persons of indigenous origin;
    (e) the development of respect for the natural environment.'

education of the people of England and Wales'. The more specific duty falls on local education authorities (LEAs), and it is to secure that there are sufficient schools available for their area. The 1996 Act provides that they will not be deemed sufficient unless they are sufficient 'in number, character, and equipment to provide for all pupils the opportunity of appropriate education'[1]. 'Appropriate education' for these purposes means:

> 'education which offers such variety of instruction and training as may be desirable in view of –
> (a)　the pupils' different ages, abilities and aptitudes, and
> (b)　the different periods for which they may be expected to remain at school,
> including practical instruction and training appropriate to their different needs.'

The duty is deliberately broad, and legal attempts to challenge the general level of educational provision have usually failed[2]. In particular, the service provided by LEAs is severely constrained by the financial resources available. Indeed, many of the points made earlier about the general duties of social services departments towards children and families are pertinent here[3]. The establishment of a National Curriculum has, however, to some extent defined the basic minimum education which LEAs and individual schools are required to provide[4].

Parental choice

Without question, the dominant ethos of education policy under the former Conservative Governments was consumer choice, the dilution of the role of LEAs and the exposure of the education system to market forces. This was accompanied by greater centralisation in the provision and content of education[5]. The cornerstone of those Governments' policies was parental choice, a principle encapsulated in the so-called 'parents' charter' issued by the then Department of Education and Science in 1991. The Conservative administrations sought to give effect to this principle, directly and indirectly, in many different ways.

The Education Act 1980 tightened the procedures for allowing parents to express a preference as between schools and sought to entrench parental choice[6]. The Education (No 2) Act 1986, following the White Paper *Better Schools*[7], increased parents' representation on governing bodies and stipulated that articles of government require governors to prepare an annual report for parents[8] and to

---

1　Education Act 1996, s 14(2).
2　See, particularly, *Secretary of State for Education and Science v Tameside Metropolitan Borough Council* [1977] AC 1014; and the useful discussion in P Meredith 'Individual Challenge to Expenditure Cuts in the Provision of Schools' [1982] JSWL 344.
3　See Chapter 10 above.
4　See pp 709 et seq below.
5　Such as in the areas of religious and sex education and the ban on political indoctrination, discussed below.
6　See now the Schools Standards and Framework Act 1998, s 86. For reasons of space, the statutory regime governing school admissions is not considered here. The principles are discussed in the first edition of this book, together with the question of parents' statutory rights to information about schools, at pp 555–563. See also A Ruff (above) at ch 3 for a useful collection of materials. The leading case on parental preferences is now *R v Rotherham Metropolitan Borough, ex parte Clark* [1998] ELR 152. See also *R v Sheffield City Council, ex parte H and Others* [1999] ELR 242. Further discussion of the law governing school admissions is to be found in JR McManus *Education and the Courts* (Jordans, 2004) at ch 5.
7　(1985) (Cmnd 9469).
8　Education (No 2) Act 1986, s 30.

hold an annual parents' meeting[1]. The Education Reform Act 1988 took the process further and established the principle of 'open enrolment' (which required schools to admit pupils to the limit of their physical capacity) and 'local management of schools' ('LMS') (which delegated to governing bodies the financial management of the school's budgetary allocation)[2].

Yet more radically, the Education Reform Act 1988 introduced a new category of school, the 'grant-maintained school'. Such schools were given the opportunity to 'opt out' of LEA control altogether and to receive a direct grant from central government[3] although the status of grant-maintained school was subsequently abolished by the Labour Government. The Education (Schools) Act 1992, intending to give effect to the provisions of the 'parents' charter', attempted to increase further the accountability of schools to parents by providing for regular inspections of every State school and increasing the information available to parents about all local schools by requiring the publication of 'performance tables'[4].

The Education Act 1993 gave to parents a statutory right to withdraw their children from sex education classes[5] analogous to their long-standing right to withdraw them from religious education and collective worship[6]. The Labour Government has also adopted as one of its central themes the concept of *partnership*, so familiar elsewhere in children law, in which parents are conceived as working with schools, LEAs and others in the commitment to raise educational standards. Key features of this partnership under the School Standards and Framework Act 1998 are 'home–school agreements', better information for parents and increased representation of parents on governing bodies and LEAs[7].

Rights versus responsibilities

No student of children law, looking at education, can fail to be struck by the contrast between the emphasis on parents' *rights* in education alongside the movement from rights to *responsibilities* elsewhere in the law. However, too much should not be read into this, for it is undoubtedly the case that parents do have *responsibilities* regarding their children's education[8], and many of the reforms in the Children Act, although couched in the terminology of parental responsibility, are founded on the philosophy that parents have primary control of their children. A more valid contrast is perhaps the lack of emphasis which the education legislation seems to place on *children's* rights, particularly (but not exclusively) in the matter of ascertaining and taking into account their views. While this is very much a feature of reforms elsewhere, it is certainly not a

1 Education (No 2) Act 1986, s 31. This has now been put on a direct statutory footing by the School Standards and Framework Act 1998, s 43.
2 Education Reform Act 1988, ss 26 and 36, respectively.
3 Chapter IV of the Education Reform Act 1988. For further discussion, see P Meredith 'Educational Reform' (1989) 52 MLR 215 at pp 224–228.
4 See J Robinson 'The Law of Education in 1992' (1992) 142 NLJ 24.
5 Now contained in the Education Act 1996, s 405.
6 Now contained in the School Standards and Framework Act 1998, s 71.
7 See White Paper *Excellence in Schools* (1997) (Cm 3681) at ch 7.
8 Especially in relation to their registration and attendance at school, discussed below. We also noted in Chapter 14 above the increased emphasis given to parental responsibility for the crimes of children.

prominent feature of education law, much of which seems to be predicated on the assumption of an identity of interests between parent and child.[1] Indeed, one can find examples in the education reforms of a reverse trend, as in the abolition of pupil governors[2]. One question which the student should, therefore, keep constantly in mind when looking at educational issues is the extent to which the *independent* interests or rights of children are being upheld.

It is, of course, true that the interests of children are bound to be affected, albeit indirectly, by every aspect of educational provision whether relating to the kinds of schools provided, their financial and managerial arrangements, the adequacy of teachers and equipment, the role of the governors, and so on. These wider issues cannot be explored here[3]. Instead, this chapter will concentrate on those legal questions which directly relate to the legal rights and obligations associated with the education of children. The following section considers the legal framework governing attendance and discipline. This is followed by a discussion of the *content* of education and the National Curriculum. Two special areas in education law are then examined – religious education and worship, and special educational needs. We conclude with a brief look at reforms introduced by the Children Act 1989 to protect the welfare of children who are being educated in independent schools or have long-term residential placements in various other establishments.

ATTENDANCE AND DISCIPLINE

Attendance

The legal obligation to secure a child's attendance at school is placed on parents and is not an express legal duty of the child himself. The principle of compulsory education is, thus, achieved through a combination of this duty and the statutory obligations of LEAs to provide schools[4]. The UNCRC[5] also requires States parties to: 'Take measures to encourage regular attendance at schools and the reduction of drop-out rates'.

Parents' obligations
The starting point is s 7 of the 1996 Act which provides:

> 'The parent of every child of compulsory school age shall cause him to receive efficient full-time education suitable –
> (a)   to his age, ability and aptitude, and

---

1   But for an interesting critique which challenges the assumption that there is an unjustifiable divergence between children law generally and education law in the matter of children's rights, see D Monk 'Children's Rights in Education – Making Sense of Contradictions' [2002] CFLQ 45 and the many sources cited there. See also P Meredith 'Children's Rights and Education' in J Fionda (ed) *Legal Concepts of Childhood* (Hart Publishing, 2001) ch 12, which concentrates particularly on sex education.

2   Education (No 2) Act 1986, s 15(14), criticised in D Pannick 'School Student Governors – no legal obstacle' (1986) 25 *Childright* 15. Another example is the lack of independent representation and appeal rights against an exclusion. See further p 705 below.

3   But they should be borne in mind throughout this discussion. Clearly, inadequacy of resources can render much of this academic. For an academic treatment of the subject, see N Harris *Law and Education: Regulation, Consumerism and the Education System* (Sweet & Maxwell, 1993).

4   See p 691 above.

5   Article 28(1)(e).

(b)   to any special educational needs he may have,
either by regular attendance at school or otherwise.'

The compulsory school age is from five to 16 years. The child begins to be of compulsory school age essentially when he attains the age of five[1]. He ceases to be of compulsory school age and may leave school on the school leaving date (the last Friday in June since 1998) closest to his sixteenth birthday[2].

Parental discretion over this aspect of upbringing is therefore curtailed to the extent that parents may not decide to withhold from their child an appropriate education. In determining the *manner* of this education, however, they have a considerable say. They are not, strictly speaking, obliged to send the child to school at all if they can meet the statutory requirements by educating the child at home. But it is very unlikely that many attempts to do so would comply with these requirements, especially since the introduction of the more stringent require-ments of the National Curriculum[3]. In any event, it is arguable that to deprive a child of the experience of a school life would, in itself, be a denial of children's rights and a failure to discharge parental responsibility.

Registration and attendance
There are two aspects to the parents' duty. The first is to secure the child's *registration*[4] at a school. The second is to ensure his regular *attendance* thereafter. Failure to comply with the first duty will lead to the invocation of school attendance procedures, and a possible prosecution under s 443 of the 1996 Act. These procedures begin with the LEA serving on the parent a notice which requires the parent to satisfy the education authority, within a specified time of not less than 15 days, that the child is being educated in accordance with s 7[5]. Where the parent does not satisfy the LEA, the LEA must serve a school attendance order (SAO)[6]. If this is not complied with, the parent commits a criminal offence[7] which is punishable by a fine and, where a parent *knows* that his or her child is failing to attend school regularly, by imprisonment for up to three months[8]. It has been held[9] that, once there has been a prosecution in respect of

---

1   In fact, he will be of compulsory school age on a day prescribed by the Secretary of State which will either coincide with his fifth birthday or be the next prescribed day following his fifth birthday – Education Act 1996, s 8(2), as amended by the Education Act 1997, s 52.
2   Ibid, s 8(3), and the Education (School Leaving Date) Order 1997, SI 1997/1970. The Labour Government introduced changes to the rules governing the school leaving date to prevent a child who has attained the age of 16 from leaving school at Easter and hence missing the GCSE examinations which take place just a couple of months later. It was concerned that as many as 17,000 young people left school with no qualifications at all and that this damaged their life-chances. See the White Paper *Excellence in Schools* (1997) (Cm 3681) at p 58. For further guidance on the school leaving date, see DfEE Circular 11/97 (School leaving date for 16-year-olds).
3   LEAs have a right to inspect the education provided at home. See *R v Surrey Quarter Sessions Appeal Committee ex parte Tweedie* (1963) 107 Sol Jo 555.
4   On the significance of the school register, see N Harris *The Law Relating to Schools* (2nd edn) (Tolley, 1995) at p 293. On school attendance more generally, see JR McManus *Education and the Courts* (Jordans, 2004) at pp 293–299.
5   Education Act 1996, s 437.
6   The procedure was amended by the Education Act 1980, ss 10 and 11 to accommodate the then new procedures regarding choice of school.
7   Education Act 1996, s 443.
8   Ibid, s 446, as amended by the Criminal Justice and Court Services Act 2000, s 72.
9   *Enfield London Borough Council v F and F* [1987] 2 FLR 126.

an SAO, no further prosecution may be brought on that order. This has cast doubt on the effectiveness of criminal sanctions in the case of repeated offences, and LEAs may prefer the civil option of the education supervision order, introduced by the Children Act 1989[1]. The more common breach of duty relates to failure to secure the child's regular attendance, which constitutes an offence under s 444 of the 1996 Act[2]. The question here is usually whether parents can avail themselves of one of the prescribed statutory excuses for non-attendance[3]. These are:

(i)   absence with leave;
(ii) sickness or other unavoidable cause[4];
(iii) days of religious observance[5];
(iv) if the school is not within walking distance of the child's home and no suitable arrangements have been made by the LEA or the funding authority for the child's transport to and from the school or for boarding accommodation at or near the school, or for enabling him to become a registered pupil at a school nearer to his home[6].

The last issue has twice been to the House of Lords, not surprisingly, bearing in mind the financial implications of the duty to provide 'free transport'. In reality, the issue is not usually an absence of appropriate transport facilities but rather whether the cost should be borne by the parents or the LEA. In this respect, the LEA has a statutory duty under s 509 of the 1996 Act[7] to make provision for free transport with a view to 'facilitating' the attendance of pupils at school[8]. In discharging this duty, the LEA must be guided by the considerations in s 509(4) of the 1996 Act which provides:

> 'In considering whether or not they are required … to make arrangements in relation to a particular person, a local education authority shall have regard (amongst other things) –
> (a)   to the age of the person and the nature of the route, or alternative routes, which he could reasonably be expected to take, and

---

1   Discussed at p 697 below.
2   It has been held that the offence is one of strict liability and that ignorance of the child's truancy is no defence. See *Crump v Gilmore* (1970) 68 LGR 56. The child's persistent late arrival at school may amount to non-attendance. See *Hinchley v Rankin* [1961] 1 WLR 421.
3   Section 444(3) and (4) of the 1996 Act.
4   This must, however, be an emergency and must relate to the *child's* position rather than the parents'. See *Jenkins v Howells* [1949] 2 KB 218. See also *Bath and NE Somerset District Council v Warman* [1999] ELR 81; and, for a full discussion of the sickness provision, see MP Grenville 'Sickness and Compulsory School Attendance' (1989) 1 *Education and the Law* 113.
5   See, generally, the discussion below of religious issues in schools.
6   Section 444(4).
7   For interpretation of this duty, see *R v Rochdale Metropolitan Borough Council ex parte Schemet* [1994] ELR 89 which inspired an amendment to the legislation to require LEAs in exercising their duty to make transport arrangements to take account of the religious preferences of parents, although it was held in *R on application of T v Leeds City Council* [2002] ELR 91 that this does not amount to a duty to comply with them. See also *R v Essex County Council ex parte C* [1994] ELR 273. Here, it was confirmed by the Court of Appeal that the statutory duty to provide transport only arises where the school (being more than three miles from the child's home) is the authority's choice. In this case, the LEA's choice of school for a child with special educational needs was not that of the parents. The parents chose a school some 14 miles away. While the LEA was willing to accede to the parents' choice of school, it was unwilling to bear the whole cost of the transport. It was held that the LEA was under no obligation to do so since the child's needs could have been met at a closer school.
8   Local education authorities are also empowered under s 509A of the 1996 Act to provide assistance for travel to children receiving nursery education otherwise than at school.

(b)   to any wish of his parent for him to be provided with education or training at a school or institution in which the religious education provided is that of the religion or denomination to which his parent adheres.'

It was the interaction of the respective statutory duties of parents and LEAs which fell for determination by the House of Lords under the former provision in the 1944 Act[1]. 'Walking distance' is defined in the 1996 Act as two miles, or three miles where the child is aged eight years or over, measured by the nearest available route[2]. In *Rogers v Essex County Council*[3], it was held that a route did not cease to be *available* because it would be dangerous for an unaccompanied child. The nearest available route was the nearest along which the child could walk to school with reasonable safety when accompanied by an adult. The House of Lords thought that an interpretation which would render the route unavailable simply because of dangers which could confront an unaccompanied child was too vague. The decision was followed in *George v Devon County Council*[4] where the House held that an LEA exercising its discretion under s 55 of the 1944 Act (now s 444 of the 1996 Act) was entitled to refuse free transport if it was reasonably practicable for the child in question to be accompanied to school. In this case, the child had an unemployed step-father who was in a position to accompany him. The principle underlying these cases is that where a child lives within the statutory limit, the *primary* responsibility for getting the child to school rests with the parent. Normally this will be discharged by the parent accompanying the child to school himself or by making alternative arrangements. The LEA has a discretion, over and above its statutory duty, to give assistance, but this is increasingly unlikely to be exercised given the constraints on public expenditure[5].

Does the child have a duty to attend school?
The child's obligation to go to school arises only by implication from the parent's duty, and the various enforcement procedures. Nowhere is this explicitly laid down in statute[6]. Given the increased autonomy of older children it could be argued that a '*Gillick*-competent' child ought to be able to decide whether or not to stay on in school. The issue is, essentially, the same as that which applies to the restrictions on child employment and the alleged right of the child to work, which was discussed in that context[7]. For the reasons given earlier, it is felt that the compulsory education system is not only compatible with, but positively mandated

---

1   Section 55 of the 1944 Act. See J Matthews 'Free Transport to School within Walking Distance' (1990) 134 Sol Jo 800; and S Luke 'Provision of free school transport (or keep fit by walking 60 miles a week)' (1989) 1 JCL 85. For an extensive discussion of the rights and duties associated with school transport see JR McManus *Education and the Courts* (Jordans, 2004) ch 1.
2   Section 444(5) of the 1996 Act (formerly s 39(5) of the 1944 Act).
3   [1986] 3 All ER 321.
4   [1988] 3 All ER 1002. More recently, in *R v Kent County Council ex parte C* [1998] ELR 108, it was held by McCullough J that the LEA had not acted unlawfully when it refused to provide free transport for a pupil who had been selected for a grant-maintained grammar school on the basis that it was not the nearest 'suitable' school. The fact that the grammar school was *more* suitable for her did not make the nearer wide-ability school unsuitable. See also *R v Vale of Glamorgan County Council ex parte J* [2001] ELR 223.
5   Section 509(3) of the 1996 Act.
6   It can of course be argued that the child *should* be placed under such a statutory duty. On the concept of children's duties, see Chapter 3.
7   At Chapter 15 above.

by, the concept of children's rights. Nevertheless, it has been argued that the independent powers and duties of parent and child are insufficiently defined and ought to be spelled out in legislation[1]. It has also been argued that parents might be able to raise, as a defence to prosecution, the unwillingness of a *Gillick*-competent child to attend school[2]. There are difficulties with this view, not least the short point that *Gillick* governs the common law and cannot be applied in the face of a conflicting statutory provision. Yet, as argued earlier, there would seem to be no reason in principle why explicit legal duties should not be imposed upon children, as the concomitant of the right to act independently.

The enforcement of school attendance – education supervision orders

Where a child is not attending school regularly, the LEA has the option of taking criminal or civil action. It may decide to mount a prosecution for breach of s 444 of the 1996 Act, just as it can for breach of s 443[3], but this has often proved ineffective. Before the Children Act 1989, the LEA was obliged to consider whether it was appropriate, instead of, or as well as, prosecuting, to bring care proceedings based on the truancy condition in the Children and Young Persons Act 1969[4]. It had to be shown, in addition to the fact of failure to attend school, that the child was in need of 'care and control' which he was unlikely to receive unless the court made a care order. Yet this condition was interpreted in such a way that it was virtually redundant since proper 'care' was said to require proper education[5]. At the same time, there was a growing appreciation that taking children into care was not the way to combat the rise in truancy, and in Leeds a system of adjournments in care proceedings was pioneered with the objective of putting parents under pressure to carry out their responsibilities[6]. The legality of the so-called 'Leeds system' had been questioned but the Interdepartmental Committee reviewing child care law concluded that care orders were generally not the way to deal with truancy. The *Review*[7] reasoned that care proceedings were inappropriate where the *only* problem was the child's absenteeism. This was an educational issue, and it was proposed that a new education supervision order (ESO) should be introduced to deal with it. Where the child's absences were part of a wider family problem representing a risk to the child's welfare, the *Review* proposed that care proceedings should remain an available option. Here, the LEA would no longer be the applicant, since these wider problems were properly a matter for social services.

Education supervision orders

The Children Act 1989 gave effect to these recommendations. The LEA may now apply for an ESO simply on the grounds that the child is of compulsory school age and is not being properly educated[8]. The Act provides that this will be so 'only if he is receiving efficient full-time education suitable to his age, ability and aptitude

---

1 MP Grenville 'Compulsory School Attendance and the Child's Wishes' [1988] JSWL 4.
2 Ibid at p 18.
3 See p 694 above, and, more generally, V Smith 'Non-School Attendance after the Children Act 1989' (1992) 156 JPN 387.
4 Children and Young Persons Act 1969, s 1(2)(e).
5 *Re S (A Minor) (Care Order: Education)* [1978] QB 120.
6 As to which, see R Hullin 'The Leeds Truancy Project' (1985) 149 JPN 488.
7 DHSS *Review of Child Care Law* (1985) at para 12.22.
8 Children Act 1989, s 36(3).

and any special educational needs he may have'[1]. Unless proved to the contrary, it will be assumed that the child is not being properly educated where he is the subject of an SAO or where he is not attending regularly the school at which he is registered within the meaning of s 444 of the 1996 Act[2]. An ESO may not be made in relation to a child who is in the care of a local authority, the assumption being that the authority will properly discharge its obligations in relation to the education of children in its care[3]. The effect of an ESO is to place the child under the supervision of the 'designated authority'[4], which must, before applying for the order, consult with the relevant social services department[5]. Before instigating criminal proceedings against parents for offences relating to failure of their child to attend school, the LEA must consider whether it would be appropriate to apply for an ESO. The court, in criminal proceedings against the parents, may also direct the LEA to apply for an ESO. While the LEA is not obliged to follow the direction, it must give reasons to the court for not doing so within eight weeks of the direction being given[6].

Other possibilities
The court has a number of other options instead of making an ESO. Since these are 'family proceedings', the court may wish to consider making a s 8 order to resolve an educational issue. This could be apposite where, for example, parents are at loggerheads over the child's education with the result that he is not attending school at all. Such a dispute might be resolved by a specific issue order or perhaps even by a residence order changing the child's residence to enable the more responsible parent to assume daily responsibility for the child[7]. Another possibility is that the very fact of court intervention might be enough to bring about a more responsible attitude in one or both parents. The general principles in the legislation apply, and the court will not therefore make an ESO, or any other order, unless satisfied that this would do more good than harm, applying the principles in Part I of the Children Act 1989[8]. Another possibility is that the court will take the view that matters are serious enough to satisfy the threshold provisions of s 31(2) of the Children Act 1989 and that it ought to make a care order. This is likely to be an uncommon situation, given the policy of the Act to abandon care orders as a response to purely educational problems. Yet in *Re O (A Minor) (Care Order: Education: Procedure)*[9], Ewbank J upheld the decision of magistrates to make a care order in relation to a 15-year-old girl who had been truanting from school for a three-year period and had only attended on 28 days during the last year. He held that it was open to the justices to conclude that her

---

1   Children Act 1989, s 36(4).
2   Ibid, s 36(5).
3   Ibid, s 36(6).
4   Ibid, s 36(7).
5   Ibid, s 36(8). This is one example of liaison and co-operation between LEAs and social services departments. Another is s 47(5) which provides for reciprocal consultation where it is the social services department which is initially involved with the child, and an educational issue arises.
6   Education Act 1996, s 447.
7   Various options are discussed by V Smith 'Non-School Attendance after the Children Act 1989' (1992) 156 JPN 389. For uses of the specific issue order to resolve educational disputes between parents, see *Re A (Specific Issue Order: Parental Disagreement)* [2001] 1 FLR 121 and *Re P (Parental Dispute: Judicial Determination)* [2003] 1 FLR 286.
8   Children Act 1989, s 1(1) and s 1(5) in particular. See Chapter 2 above.
9   [1992] 2 FLR 7.

social, intellectual and educational development suffered consequential harm which was significant enough to warrant a care order[1].

In recent years the Government has introduced further measures for tackling truancy. On the application of the LEA, the court may make a 'parenting order' when convicting a parent of the offences under s 443 or s 444 of the Education Act 1996[2]. Before doing so it must, however, consider whether instead of or as well as instituting proceedings it should apply for an ESO[3]. The latest options for tackling truancy came into force on 27 February 2004. Under the Anti-social Behaviour Act 2003[4] parents may be requested to enter into 'parenting contracts' which require them to ensure that their child attends school regularly, and there may be a requirement under such contracts to attend a counselling or guidance programme. Secondly, the same Act[5], more radically, authorises a head teacher or an LEA officer to issue a 'penalty notice' to a parent who has failed to secure regular attendance of his child at school. The prescribed penalty is £50 where it is paid within 28 days of receipt of the notice and £100 if paid within 42 days. Where payment is not made the LEA must either institute proceedings or withdraw the notice.

Legal effects of an ESO
Part III of Sch 3 to the Children Act sets out in greater detail the legal effects of an ESO. The ESO will last for one year but the LEA may apply for it to be extended within three months of its expiration[6]. Where the ESO is in force, the duty of parents to secure regular school attendance is superseded by their duty to comply with directions under the ESO[7]. These directions are given by an educational welfare officer or education social worker whose duty under the ESO is to 'advise, assist and befriend' the child and his parents[8]. He should consult with the parents before giving directions and take note of their preferences, especially regarding the place of education[9]. Both parent and child must notify the supervisor of the child's address and must allow visits[10]. Failure to adhere to these directions is a criminal offence[11]. Where the child 'persistently fails to comply with any direction' under the ESO, the LEA must notify the social services department, which then has a duty to investigate the child's circumstances. The ESO may be discharged on an application by the child, the parent or the LEA and will be automatically discharged by a care order or when the child ceases to be of compulsory school age[12].

---

1   On the 'parental failing' limb of s 31(2), see Chapter 11 above.
2   Education Act 1996, s 446. As to parenting orders in the context of criminal offences see Chapter 14 above.
3   Ibid, s 447.
4   Section 19.
5   Section 23, inserting s 444A into the Education Act 1996, and the Education (Penalty Notices) (England) Regulations 2004, SI 2004/181.
6   Children Act 1989, Part III, Sch 3, para 15.
7   Ibid, Part III, Sch 3, para 13.
8   Ibid, Part III, Sch 3, para 12.
9   Ibid, Part III, Sch 3, para 12(2) and (3).
10 Ibid, Part III, Sch 3, para 16.
11 Ibid, Part III, Sch 3, para 18.
12 Ibid, Part III, Sch 3, paras 15(6) and 17(1).

Discipline

Discipline in schools is considered important, partly to protect individual children from bullying, but more generally to create an environment in which education can operate effectively. It is recognised that standards of teaching and learning suffer where there is a breakdown of good order. The whole question of discipline in schools was the subject of a Report by the Elton Committee in 1989[1]. This made a number of significant recommendations which, inter alia, emphasised the importance of striking a balance between punishment and reward. Part II of the Education Act 1997 made a number of important changes to the law on school discipline concerning particularly the power of teachers to use reasonable force to restrain pupils, detention and the procedures relating to exclusions. That Act also gave statutory recognition to so-called 'home–school agreements'. The latter are now included in the School Standards and Framework Act 1998 which, as we have seen, also brought about the abolition of corporal punishment in the independent sector. Further changes to the law governing exclusions have been made by the Anti-social Behaviour Act 2003. This section examines the responsibility of schools for disciplinary matters and the legal limits on punishment. Since we discussed earlier the abolition of corporal punishment in schools[2], this chapter is confined to the other disciplinary measures open to schools.

Responsibility for discipline

As its broadest level, discipline falls within the overall conduct of schools, which in the case of State schools is under the direction of the governing body[3], but, in relation to discipline, the head teacher is given a central role to determine and make known the particular disciplinary regime for the school, and the standards of behaviour which are considered acceptable. The governing body is now under a specific statutory duty to 'ensure that policies designed to promote good behaviour and discipline on the part of its pupils are pursued at the school'[4]. The head teacher must publicise the school's disciplinary regime in a written document and make this available within the school and to parents. At least once a year, he or she must take steps to make the school's disciplinary measures known to parents, pupils, teachers and other employees of the school[5]. The 1996 Act sets out in some detail the general objectives the head teacher should seek to fulfil. The head teacher should determine and enforce measures with a view to:

'(a) promoting, among pupils, self-discipline and proper regard for authority;
(b) encouraging good behaviour and respect for others on the part of pupils and, in particular, preventing all forms of bullying among pupils;
(c) securing that the standard of behaviour of pupils is acceptable; and
(d) otherwise regulating the conduct of pupils.'[6]

In determining disciplinary measures, the head teacher must act in accordance with the current written statement of general principles prepared by the

---

1 *Discipline in Schools: Report of the Committee of Inquiry chaired by Lord Elton* (1989).
2 In Chapter 15 above.
3 School Standards and Framework Act 1998, s 61.
4 Ibid, s 61(1).
5 Ibid, s 61(7).
6 Education Act 1996, s 61(4).

governing body and must have regard to any particular matters arising from the notification of guidance given to him by the governing body[1].

Within these general guidelines, the governing body, and more especially the head teacher, have a good deal of discretion to determine the particular regime of discipline for the school and it is acknowledged that this may need to vary from school to school. The School Standards and Framework Act 1998 also contains a 'reserve power' which enables the LEA to intervene in the case of a complete breakdown in discipline at one of its schools. Thus, the LEA is empowered to 'take such steps in relation to a maintained school as [it considers] are required to prevent the breakdown, or continuing breakdown, of discipline at the school'[2]. It may only do so where, in its opinion (if action is not taken), the 'education of any registered pupils at the school is (or is likely in the immediate future to become) severely prejudiced'[3]. It is not clear what the LEA might do in these circumstances, but it seems likely that it would at least seek to influence the action taken by the governing body to contain the situation.

Disciplinary measures: the legal limits

The limits of teachers' authority over children are largely determined at common law. There was considerable uncertainty both about the legal basis of this authority and its extent, so much so that the Elton Committee recommended that teachers' disciplinary authority be put on a firm statutory footing – a recommendation not immediately acted upon by the Government[4]. By way of exception, we have seen that corporal punishment has for some time been regulated by statute, and this is also the case regarding exclusion, the most serious disciplinary option.

The Education Act 1997 took this process further by clarifying teachers' powers of restraint, putting the practice of detention on a statutory footing and making amendments to the law and procedure governing exclusions. The School Standards and Framework Act 1998 requires all maintained schools to adopt home–school agreements, an important aspect of which will be the school's disciplinary regime[5].

The legal basis of a teacher's authority

The traditional view was that a teacher's authority derived from implied delegation of parental authority. The teacher was, as it were, in loco parentis during the school day and, as such, had the same power and authority as a parent. The modern view is that teachers possess this authority *independently*, by virtue of their status as teachers[6]. The Elton Committee proposed that this latter view be

---

1 School Standards and Framework Act 1998, s 61(7).
2 Ibid, s 62.
3 Ibid, s 62(2).
4 For further discussion, see N Harris 'Discipline in Schools: The Elton Report' (1990) JSWL 110.
5 Under ss 110–111, such agreements are now referred to as 'home–school agreements'. Under the Education Act 1997, s 13 they were previously known as 'home–school partnership documents'.
6 This appeared to some to have been given implied statutory recognition in the Children and Young Persons Act 1933, s 1(7). The subsection provided, in relation to the offence of cruelty to children, that 'nothing in this section shall be construed as affecting the right of any parent, teacher, or other person having the lawful control or charge of a child or young person to administer punishment to him'. Section 1(7), as amended, now provides: 'Nothing in this section shall be construed as affecting the right of any parent, or (subject to section 548 of the Education Act 1996) any other person, having the lawful control or charge of a child or young

made explicit in statute and that there should be a statutory statement of the extent of teachers' disciplinary powers. The Committee thought that this should make clear, inter alia, the general authority of teachers to maintain discipline for educational reasons, to enforce school rules and to impose reasonable punishments (consistent with the school's disciplinary policy and the general law) and to exercise discipline over pupils out of school in certain circumstances[1]. Teachers also, to a degree, derive authority from the Children Act 1989, s 3(5) to the extent that they may, as persons with 'care' of a child, 'do what is reasonable in all the circumstances of the case for the purpose of safeguarding or promoting the child's welfare'. It is clear also under s 2(9) of the Children Act 1989 that while a parent may not surrender parental responsibility he may 'arrange for some or all of it to be met by one or more persons acting on his behalf'. Clearly this occurs where a child is at school and might be seen as consistent with the notion of delegation of authority.

Before turning to the legal framework governing particular disciplinary measures, it is appropriate to begin with a brief description of home–school agreements since these encapsulate the ethos of partnership between schools and parents (and to an extent the children themselves) in securing co-operation over, inter alia, the school's disciplinary regime.

Home–school agreements
The idea of the home–school agreement is that all schools should work in strong partnership with parents. The agreements are not legally binding but are intended to be 'powerful statements of intent'[2]. Although the detail will vary from school to school, 'all agreements are likely to include expectations about the standard of education, the ethos of the school, regular and punctual attendance, discipline, homework, and the information schools and parents will give to one another'[3]. The Government views them as 'important in helping engage parents in raising pupils' achievements and in action to combat truancy, bullying and unacceptable behaviour which undermines pupils' progress'[4].

Under the School Standards and Framework Act 1998[5], such agreements are mandatory in maintained schools, and the governing body is required to take reasonable steps to secure a signed 'parental declaration' by every qualifying parent. The purpose of the declaration is to record that parents 'take note of the school's aims and values and its responsibilities and that they acknowledge and accept the parental responsibilities and the school's expectations of its pupils'[6]. The Act also provides that the governing body may invite the pupil to sign the parental declaration as an indication that he acknowledges and accepts the school's expectations of its pupils but, essentially adopting the test of *Gillick* competence, only where they are satisfied that the pupil 'has a sufficient

---

person to administer punishment to him.' For the implications regarding corporal punishment, see below.

1 *Discipline in Schools: Report of the Committee of Inquiry chaired by Lord Elton* (1989) at para 74, and see N Harris 'Discipline in Schools: The Elton Report' (1990) JSWL 110 at 115–116.
2 White Paper *Excellence in Schools* (1997) (Cm 3681) at p 55.
3 Ibid.
4 Ibid.
5 Sections 110–111.
6 Section 110(2).

understanding of the home–school agreement as it relates to him'[1]. The hope is obviously that the creation of a partnership ethos and co-operation between schools, parents and children will pre-empt the need for the use of the different disciplinary measures discussed below.

General legal constraints on disciplinary action including corporal punishment
The general, albeit rather vague and unhelpful, proposition which can be stated with some confidence is that teachers must, in resorting to any disciplinary measure, act within the law. As with other principles of the common law, this seems, in the end, to come down to proportionality and reasonableness[2]. Subject to this underlying principle, the law does authorise the use of classroom sanctions such as the withdrawal of privileges, confiscation of property and detention. The common law principles are derived, in part, from cases on corporal punishment, decided before its abolition in schools, especially the nineteenth-century case of *R v Hopley*[3]. In this, Cockburn CJ laid down the test, now generally accepted in relation to both parents and schools, that punishment must be moderate and reasonable. This test originally applied specifically to the use of corporal punishment, but it has been argued that the test can be applied, by analogy, to *all* forms of punishment in schools[4]. There is a dearth of direct authority on disciplinary sanctions falling short of exclusion and it has been suggested that this may well reflect a consensus among parents that low-level disciplinary measures are really a matter for individual schools.

There was, however, until comparatively recently, uncertainty concerning the legality of teachers' use of physical restraint. Since 1987, corporal punishment has been outlawed in the State sector and, since 1998, in the independent sector. The effect of the Education Act 1996 is that corporal punishment given by or on the authority of a member of staff 'cannot be justified in any proceedings on the ground that it was given in pursuance of a right exercisable by the member of staff by virtue of his position as such'. The provision covers 'doing anything for the purpose of punishing that child (whether or not there are other reasons for doing it) which, apart from any justification, would constitute battery'. In limited circumstances, however, teachers may be allowed to act in any way which in other circumstances would amount to a battery. The Act[5] provides that:

> 'corporal punishment shall not be taken to be given to a child by virtue of anything done for reasons that include averting –
> (a)   an immediate danger of personal injury to, or
> (b)   an immediate danger to the property of,
> any person (including the child himself).'

The legality of the prohibition on corporal punishment contained in s 548 was unsuccessfully challenged in *R (Williamson) v Secretary of State for Education and Employment*[6] by teachers and parents at certain independent schools specifically established to provide Christian education based on biblical observance. They had argued that the prohibition was incompatible with their right to manifest their

---

1   Section 110(5).
2   This is broadly in line with principles of the tort of negligence, discussed in Chapter 15 above.
3   (1860) 2 F&F 202.
4   N Harris (above) at pp 314 et seq.
5   Section 548(5).
6   [2003] 1 FLR 726.

religion or beliefs under Article 9 and Article 2, Protocol 1 of the ECHR, but this was rejected by a majority of the Court of Appeal. Although a belief that corporal punishment is beneficial is capable of being regarded as a religious and philosophical conviction for the purposes of Article 2, Protocol 1, the majority held that the legislation does not materially interfere with that belief, since corporal punishment by *the parent* is permitted by the national law[1]. The net result is that parents may not delegate any such right as they have to a teacher. The question which has arisen has been how far teachers might be entitled to use physical force in restraining pupils without this degenerating into unlawful corporal punishment. The line was blurred and teachers overstepping it would run the risk of committing a battery on the child. In an effort to clarify the position, the Education Act 1997[2] conferred a new statutory power on members of staff to use 'such force as is reasonable in the circumstances' for the purpose of preventing a pupil from:

'(a)   committing any offence;
 (b)   causing personal injury to, or damage to the property of, any person (including the pupil himself); or
 (c)   engaging in any behaviour prejudicial to the maintenance of good order and discipline at the school or among any of its pupils, whether that behaviour occurs during a teaching session or otherwise.'

It appears that this provision was designed to take away from teachers the fear of prosecution where they use moderate physical restraints, for example to break up fights between pupils. Ultimately, the limits of this power will turn again on the necessarily vague notion of what is reasonable in the particular context.

Detention
There is some authority on the limits of parental control over the physical movements of children which can be applied, by analogy, to schools. In *R v Rahman*[3], Lord Lane CJ held that the detention of a child by a parent could be unlawful and amount to false imprisonment where it was 'for such a period or in such circumstances as to take it out of the realms of reasonable parental discipline'. In the context of schools, detention, when used, should be motivated by proper considerations[4] and should be for a reasonable time. What is reasonable will vary, depending on the circumstances and the ages of the pupils. Detention of whole classes is now of dubious legality and should be avoided since it is insufficiently related to the misdemeanours of individual pupils[5].

The Education Act 1997[6] amended the 1996 Act to give express statutory recognition to the authority of schools to detain badly behaved children after school without their parents' consent thus removing the risk of legal action for false imprisonment. The head teacher must have previously made it known within the school that detention is part of the school's disciplinary regime. Steps must have been taken to bring this to the notice of parents, and the particular pupil's

---

1   On corporal punishment by parents, see Chapter 15.
2   Inserting a new s 550A into the Education Act 1996.
3   (1985) 81 Cr App R 349.
4   Otherwise it may amount to false imprisonment, as to which see *Fitzgerald v Northcote* (1865) 4 F&F 656.
5   See N Harris (above) at p 124.
6   Education Act 1997, s 5, inserting a new s 550B into the Education Act 1996.

parents must have been given at least 24 hours' notice of the proposed detention[1].

The legislation also prescribes the factors which go to determining whether the detention complies with the general test of reasonableness[2]. These are:

'(a)   whether the detention constitutes a proportionate punishment in the circumstances; and
(b)   any special circumstances relevant to its imposition on the pupil which are known to the person imposing it (or of which he ought reasonably to be aware).'

The 'special circumstances' referred to include the pupil's age, any special educational needs he may have, religious factors and transport arrangements.

Confiscation of property

There is no real authority on the legality of this practice, but on general principles it is regarded as lawful[3]. Indeed, in the case of a dangerous object, the teacher might expose the school authorities to a possible negligence action if the item were not confiscated and a child suffered injury as a result[4]. Teachers must operate within the criminal law and civil law, which generally impose liability for permanent taking or destruction of property belonging to others[5]. It has, therefore, been argued that, to avoid any possible legal liability, the confiscated item should be returned to the child or his parent at the earliest opportunity, preferably at the end of the school day[6].

Exclusion

Exclusion is a drastic measure to deal with serious breaches of discipline and is now closely regulated by statute[7] and is the subject of official guidance issued by the Department for Education and Skills[8]. The minutiae of the legal procedures are beyond the scope of this chapter, but the salient features of the law are as follows[9].

The decision whether to exclude a pupil from the school is for the head teacher in the first instance. Where the exclusion is for a fixed term, this must not exceed 45 school days in any one school year[10]. Where he decides to exclude a pupil, the head teacher must inform the child's parents of the decision, giving reasons and the period of the exclusion[11]. He must inform the parents again if he decides to exclude the child permanently. The parents, and the child where he is over 18 years of age, must be informed of their right to make representations to the

---

1   Education Act 1996, s 550B.
2   Ibid, s 550B(4).
3   See N Harris (above) at p 325.
4   Sharp instruments, for example. On the negligence of school authorities, see Chapter 15 above.
5   Particularly theft and related offences and the tort of conversion.
6   N Harris (above).
7   Education Act 2002, s 52, and the Education (Pupil Exclusions and Appeals) (Maintained Schools) (England) Regulations 2002, SI 2002/3178.
8   DfES/0087/2003 – *Improving behaviour and attendance: guidance on exclusion from school and pupil referral units.*
9   A useful collection of materials on exclusions and reinstatement is to be found in A Ruff *Education Law* (Butterworths, 2002) at pp 285–314.
10 Education (Pupil Exclusions and Appeals) (Maintained Schools) (England) Regulations 2002, reg 3. The limit prior to the Education Act 1997 was 15 school days per term. The amendment was designed to give greater flexibility to schools.
11 Education (Pupil Exclusions and Appeals) (Maintained Schools) (England) Regulations 2002, reg 4.

governing body[1]. Whenever a child is excluded for more than five days in total in a single term, or the exclusion would result in the pupil losing the opportunity to take a public examination, the head teacher must inform the governors and LEA without delay[2]. The governing body will in the first instance determine the question of reinstatement and will normally exercise its functions through a discipline sub-committee. The LEA has the right to make representations but has lost its former right to direct reinstatement. Where the governing body directs reinstatement the head teacher must comply with this[3].

The parents have a right of appeal to an independent appeal panel against the decision of the governing body not to reinstate a pupil who has been permanently excluded[4]. The decision of the appeal panel is binding on the parents, governing body, head teacher and LEA[5]. Where it decides in favour of reinstatement the panel may direct that the pupil should be reinstated immediately or by a date specified in the direction[6]. Under an amendment to the exclusions procedure introduced by the Education Act 2002[7], panels are now required, in considering reinstatement, to take into account the interests of other members of the school community and not just those of the excluded pupil.

The Anti-social Behaviour Act 2003 has introduced, as from 27 February 2004, the possibility of 'parenting contracts' and 'parenting orders' in cases where a pupil has been excluded. We saw above[8] that these are also options in truancy cases. As in the case of truancy, under a parenting contract the parent is required to agree to measures designed to improve the behaviour of the pupil, and the LEA is required to provide support to the parent. It is also open to the LEA to apply to the magistrates' court for a parenting order in relation to an excluded pupil[9]. The orders are available only where the exclusion is permanent or where a pupil has been excluded for fixed terms on two or more occasions within the previous 21 months. The LEA must apply within eight weeks of the last exclusion decision or within six months of the date a parenting contract was entered into, whichever is the later. The order may last for up to 12 months and may require the parent to undertake counselling or a guidance programme for up to three months.

It should, however, be noted that the pupil himself, except in the tiny minority of cases in which he is over 18 years of age, has no appeal in his own right, or right of representation – something which is questionable both in terms of children's rights on more general principles of natural justice and now in terms of human rights. It contrasts starkly with the greater legal rights of children in other areas, especially in care proceedings[10]. Indeed, the extent to which the current law on discipline in schools is really 'child-centred' or gets to grips with the independent interests of children (as distinct from those of parents) can be called into question.

---

1   Education (Pupil Exclusions and Appeals) (Maintained Schools) (England) Regulations 2002, reg 4.
2   Ibid, reg 4(3)(a) and (4).
3   Ibid, reg 5(5).
4   Ibid, reg 5(6)(b).
5   Ibid, reg 6(5).
6   Ibid, reg 6(6).
7   Education Act 2002, s 52.
8   See p 699 above.
9   Anti-social Behaviour Act 2003, s 22, and the Education (Parenting Orders) (England) Regulations 2004, SI 2004/182.
10 See Chapters 11 and 13 above.

In its White Paper *Excellence in Schools*[1] the Labour Government recognised that schools need the ultimate sanction of exclusion, but also that the present number of exclusions is too high. It was also concerned about the unjustified variation in exclusion rates across schools, and the disproportionate exclusion of pupils from certain ethnic groups and from children looked after by local authorities.

THE CURRICULUM

Under the 1944 Act, control of the secular curriculum was vested entirely in LEAs. Whether parents had any right even to be consulted was a matter of some doubt[2]. Central control of the curriculum was limited to religious education which was compulsory[3]. The effect of the educational reforms of the 1980s was to wrest control of the curriculum from LEAs and to establish central direction of the curriculum, both secular and religious, while at the same time increasing the influence of governing bodies (and hence parents)[4]. The role of the LEA itself has been marginalised. The central pillar of this policy has been the establishment of a National Curriculum and, alongside this, there has been significant central intervention in specific matters, including religious worship in schools, sex education and political issues. The legal framework may be conveniently examined under three headings: general principles applying to the whole curriculum; the secular curriculum; and religious education. In the case of the latter, consideration must be given not only to the religious education and worship in schools but also to the principles applying to religious upbringing as an aspect of parental responsibility. The statutory framework governing the content of the National Curriculum is now largely contained in the Education Act 2002, which established a separate curriculum for England and Wales.

General principles

Under the 1996 Act we saw that the Secretary of State has a general duty to 'promote the education of the people of England and Wales'[5]. LEAs were given a similarly broad duty to 'contribute towards the spiritual, moral, mental and physical development of the community'. These general promotional duties and underlying aims were fleshed out by the Education Reform Act 1988 (now consolidated in the Education Act 1996). They apply to what is referred to as the 'whole curriculum', which includes the 'basic curriculum' but extends beyond it. The 'basic curriculum' refers to the secular and religious education which schools are bound to provide, while the concept of the 'whole curriculum' includes the essential aims of education which cut across all aspects of the curriculum and other activities of the school. As Harris has put it:

> 'There is an important cross-curricular aspect to the "whole curriculum", involving the inculcation of various skills and emphasising themes such as economic and industrial

---

1　Paragraphs 19–21.
2　Goff J in *Wood v Ealing London Borough Council* [1996] 3 WLR 1209 at 1221 seemed to imply that there was a right of consultation, as a matter of interpretation of s 76 of the 1944 Act.
3　And still is, as discussed below.
4　See P Meredith 'Educational Reform' (1989) 52 MLR 215 at 216–221.
5　Education Act 1996, s 10.

understanding, careers education and guidance, environmental education, health education and citizenship.'[1]

The responsibility for the whole curriculum is shared between the Secretary of State, LEAs, governing bodies and head teachers, who must all have regard to certain guiding principles expressed at a very broad level of generality. Under the Education Act 2002[2], they must exercise their respective functions with a view to securing that the curriculum of a school is 'balanced and broadly based' and that it promotes the 'spiritual, moral, cultural, mental and physical development of pupils at the school and of society' and that it prepares such pupils 'for the opportunities, responsibilities and experiences of later life'.

In addition, certain other responsibilities regarding the curriculum were already in place, having been introduced by the Education (No 2) Act 1986. This Act required LEAs to keep under review their policy in relation to the secular curriculum and to publish and keep up to date a written statement of it[3]. Articles of government were to require governing bodies to consider the LEA's policy and, in the light of their opinion as to the aim of the secular curriculum at the school, consider whether, and if so how, it should be modified in its application to the school[4]. The head teacher was required to ensure that the organisation of the curriculum was compatible with the LEA's policy, as amended by the governors (where relevant) and with the general law. Governing bodies were to have regard to any representations made to them by 'any persons connected with the community served by the school' and particularly any made by the Chief Constable 'and which [were] connected with his responsibilities'[5].

The Education Act 2002[6] requires every maintained school[7] in England and Wales to establish a 'basic curriculum' which must include:

(1) provision for religious education for all registered pupils at the school;
(2) a curriculum for all registered pupils at the school of compulsory school age (to be known as 'the National Curriculum');
(3) in the case of a secondary school, provision for sex education for all registered pupils at the school; and
(4) in the case of a special school, provision for sex education for all registered pupils at the school who are provided with secondary education.

Since religious education needs to be discussed alongside collective worship and parental upbringing (matters falling outside the National Curriculum) it is convenient to begin by looking at the secular curriculum.

---

1 N Harris *The Law Relating to Schools* (2nd edn) (Tolley, 1995) at p 190.
2 Section 78.
3 Education (No 2) Act 1986, s 17.
4 Ibid, s 18.
5 Ibid, s 18(3).
6 Section 80.
7 There are many different categories of maintained schools as opposed to independent schools. These categories were much altered by the School Standards and Framework Act 1998. The former categories of 'county schools', 'controlled schools', 'aided and special agreement schools' and 'maintained special schools' became, respectively, 'community schools', 'voluntary controlled schools', 'voluntary aided schools' and 'community special schools'. The former grant-maintained schools and grant-maintained special schools were re-allocated to different categories depending on their status before becoming grant-maintained, but the governing body could elect to change the indicative category. Such schools might become 'foundation schools', 'voluntary aided schools' or 'foundation special schools'. The organisational

Secular education: the National Curriculum

The origins of the National Curriculum can be traced back at least as far as the White Paper *Better Schools* published in 1985, in which the then Conservative Government signalled its intention to seek a broad consensus on the aims of the secular curriculum. One view of the National Curriculum is that by 1988 this had been achieved, and that the legal framework in the Education Reform Act 1988 '[was] a mere statutory endorsement of the consensus which [had] emerged over the past 10 years or so over the curriculum, and [was] thus a welcome, timely and uncontroversial tidying up measure bringing our practice more into conformity with our European partners where centralised prescription of what is taught in schools is much more advanced'. An alternative view is that it was more a reflection of the desire to by-pass LEAs in the way that has occurred in other aspects of the educational reforms. On this view, the National Curriculum was 'a notable exercise in centralisation and a serious undermining of the role of LEAs and the professional autonomy of teachers'[1]. In any event, LEAs, governing bodies, and head teachers are required to implement the National Curriculum in force at the relevant time[2].

Scheme of the National Curriculum

The content of the National Curriculum is now governed by Part 6 (England) and Part 7 (Wales) of the Education Act 2002. For reason of space only England will be discussed here. In any event the differences are relatively small. Welsh is, for example, a core subject in Welsh-speaking schools and citizenship is not a foundation subject. The 2002 Act introduced a 'foundation stage' in addition to the four 'key stages' that were prescribed by earlier legislation. This approximately covers the age range three to five[3]. The Act specifies 'areas of learning'[4] for the foundation stage which are personal, social and emotional development; communication; language and literacy; mathematical development; knowledge and understanding of the world; physical development; and creative development. The Secretary of State may prescribe 'early learning goals' and 'assessment arrangements' in relation to the foundation stage.

The scheme of the National Curriculum is that there are certain *core*[5] and other *foundation* subjects[6] and in relation to these there are *attainment targets, programmes*

---

framework of schools is therefore complex. For a useful summary of the main types of school, see A Ruff *Education Law* (Butterworths, 2002) at pp 66–69.

1 P Meredith 'Educational Reform' (1989) 52 MLR 215 at 217.
2 Education Act 2002, s 79.
3 Ibid, s 81.
4 Ibid, s 83.
5 Ibid, s 84(2) defines the core subjects as mathematics, English and science.
6 Ibid, s 84(3) defines other foundation subjects to include design and technology, information and communication technology, physical education, history, geography, art and design, and music (in relation to key stages 1–3), and citizenship and a modern foreign language (in relation to key stage 3). Key stage 4 foundation subjects are design and technology, information and communication technology, physical education, citizenship and a modern foreign language.

of study[1] and *assessment arrangements*[2] which are to be promulgated by order from time to time. For each of the core and foundation subjects, the Secretary of State is required to establish a 'complete' National Curriculum and to revise it whenever he considers it necessary or expedient[3]. The attainment targets, programmes of study and assessment arrangements are related to four *key stages* which broadly approximate to the age ranges 6 to 7, 8 to 11, 12 to 14, and 15 to 16 years of age[4]. Standard assessment tasks (SATs) take place at the end of each key stage. Before promulgating orders specifying *attainment targets* and *programmes of study*, the Secretary of State must refer draft proposals to the Qualifications and Curriculum Authority[5], which has responsibility for keeping all aspects of the curriculum for maintained schools under review, advising the Secretary of State, and conducting programmes of research and development[6]. In practice, initial proposals for submission to the Council are first referred to subject working groups, although the Secretary of State has not always followed their recommendations[7]. The LEA, governing body and head teacher of a maintained school are required to publish detailed information about the curriculum and they must establish a complaints procedure relating, inter alia, to curricular matters[8].

Exceptions to these requirements

Limited exceptions to the requirements of the National Curriculum may be specified by the Secretary of State. Pupils with special educational needs and who are 'statemented' under the Special Educational Needs and Disability Act 2001 may be exempted from the whole or part of it[9].

Other specific aspects of the Curriculum are centrally prescribed as follows.

External qualifications and examination entry

Maintained schools are precluded from offering to pupils of compulsory school age courses which lead to qualifications authenticated by outside bodies unless the qualifications have been approved by the Secretary of State or a designated body[10]. Governing bodies must secure that all pupils are entered for *public* examinations for which they are being prepared by the school[11]. Exceptionally, a

---

1   Education Act 2002, s 76 defines attainment targets as 'the knowledge, skills and understanding which pupils of different abilities and maturities are expected to have by the end of [each key stage]', and defines programmes of study as 'the matters, skills and processes which are required to be taught to pupils of different abilities and maturities by the end of that key stage'.

2   Assessment arrangements are defined by Education Act 2002, s 76 as 'in relation to the foundation stage, the arrangements for assessing pupils in respect of that stage for the purpose of ascertaining what they have achieved in relation to the early learning goals, and ... in relation to a key stage, the arrangements for assessing pupils in respect of that stage for the purpose of ascertaining what they have achieved in relation to the attainment targets for that stage'.

3   Ibid, s 87(1).

4   Ibid, s 82(1). Key stages for individual pupils are determined by reference to the age of the majority of pupils in the class.

5   Formerly the School Curriculum and Assessment Authority and before that the National Curriculum Council.

6   Education Act 1997, s 23.

7   See the examples given by P Meredith 'Educational Reform' (1989) 52 MLR 215 at 219.

8   Education Act 1996, ss 408 and 409.

9   Education Act 2002, s 92.

10 Education Act 1997, s 37.

11 Education Act 1996, s 402(1).

particular pupil may not be entered for educational reasons, if his parents request this in writing[1].

Charging for education

Under the Education Act 1944, maintained schools and LEAs were prevented from charging for the education they provided[2]. The principle of 'free education' was largely preserved but the Education Act 1996 does allow charging in certain specified instances involving such things as individual music tuition, the cost of residential trips, 'optional extras' in school, and education provided outside school hours[3].

Political issues

The Education Act 1996 as amended requires the head teachers and governing bodies of all maintained schools to forbid 'the pursuit of partisan political activities' by junior pupils of the school (or such activities off the school premises if organised by a member of staff) and 'the promotion of partisan political views in the teaching of any subject in the school'[4]. Further, LEAs, head teachers, and governing bodies must 'take such steps as are reasonably practicable to secure that where political issues are brought to the attention of pupils' while at school or involved in extra-curricular activities organised for registered pupils, 'they are offered a balanced presentation of opposing views'[5]. These provisions were largely a reaction to what the then Conservative Government saw as political indoctrination by left-wing teachers. It had in mind, in particular, 'Peace Studies'. It has been said that the ban on partisan political activities extends beyond purely *party* political matters and that, for example, environmental issues such as nuclear power could fall within it[6]. It is, of course, a possible criticism of these provisions that they were themselves motivated by partisan political considerations appealing to the government of the day.

Sex education

The law

Much the same point can be made in relation to the attempt to influence the content of sex education in what is now s 403 of the Education Act 1996[7]. The purpose of the legislation is to impose a moral framework on the provision of sex education, now viewed by the Government as 'sex and relationship' education[8]. The Act requires LEAs, governing bodies and head teachers to 'take such steps as

---

1 Education Act 1996, s 402(2).
2 Education Act 1944, s 61, as to which see *R v Hereford and Worcester Local Education Authority ex parte Jones* [1981] 1 WLR 768.
3 Sections 451 et seq.
4 Education Act 1996, s 406(1).
5 Ibid, s 407.
6 N Harris *The Law Relating to Schools* (2nd edn) (Tolley, 1995) at p 199.
7 The initial provision was in the Education (No 2) Act 1986. For a detailed discussion of the legislative framework governing sex education which addresses most of the issues, see P Meredith 'Children's Rights and Education' in J Fionda (ed), *Legal Concepts of Childhood* (Hart, 2001) ch 12, especially at pp 210–220. A useful collection of materials is to be found in A Ruff, *Education Law* (Butterworths, 2002) at pp 467–477.
8 The latest Government circular is so named. See DfEE Guidance 00116/2000 *Sex and Relationship Education*.

are reasonably practicable to secure that where sex education is given to any registered pupils at a maintained school, it is given in such a manner as to encourage those pupils to have due regard to moral considerations and the value of family life'[1]. These requirements were then expanded upon by s 148 of the Learning and Skills Act 2000 which amended the 1996 Act[2]. These amendments place the Secretary of State under a statutory duty to issue guidance (hereafter 'the Guidance') to secure that when sex education is given to registered pupils at maintained schools:

'(a)   they learn the nature of marriage and its importance for family life and the bringing up of children, and
(b)   they are protected from teaching and materials which are inappropriate having regard to the age and the religious and cultural background of the pupils concerned.'[3]

Governing bodies and head teachers must have regard to the Guidance in discharging their functions[4].

As we noted above, sex education is a compulsory element in the basic curriculum for every secondary maintained school[5]. This is explicitly defined to include education about:

'(a)   Acquired Immune Deficiency Syndrome and Human Immunodeficiency Virus, and
(b)   any other sexually transmitted disease.'[6]

The Guidance recommends that sex education should include those subjects which are excluded from the science part of the National Curriculum, and these include (in addition to those above) aspects of human sexual behaviour other than biological aspects. The significance of their exclusion from the National Curriculum is that parents have a statutory right to withdraw their children from some or all sex education, except insofar as it forms part of the National Curriculum[7]. The result is that only instruction about the biological aspects of human sexual development and reproduction are compulsory where parents elect to withdraw their child. The right of withdrawal, like that relating to religious education and collective worship, is *absolute* and parents are not required to give reasons. Compliance with parental wishes is mandatory. Moreover, these rights extend to all registered pupils, which includes those over 16, the age for lawful consensual sexual activity and for marriage with parental consent.

An issue related to the provision of sex education is the matter of what advice it is lawful for teachers to give to individual pupils about sexual matters, including such questions as contraception, abortion and their own sexual behaviour. In 1994 the then Conservative Government issued a circular on sex education[8] which contained some robust statements about this. Schools were warned[9] that dealings between teachers and pupils 'should never trespass on the proper exercise of parental rights and responsibilities', and the advice also hinted at

---

1   Education Act 1996, s 403(1).
2   By adding s 403(1A), (1B), (1C) and (1D).
3   Education Act 1996, s 403(1A).
4   Ibid, s 403(1B).
5   Education Act 2002, s 80(1)(c).
6   Education Act 1996, s 579(1).
7   Ibid, s 405.
8   DFE Circular 5/94 *Sex Education in Schools.*
9   At paras 38–42.

illegality: 'teachers are not health professionals, and the legal position of a teacher giving advice in such circumstances has never been tested in the courts'. The clear implication was that a teacher giving such advice, without parental knowledge or consent, might be acting unlawfully and it was expressly stated that this 'would be an inappropriate exercise of teachers' professional responsibilities'. It was argued in the second edition of this work[1] that the 1994 advice was without legal foundation and that it flew in the face of the House of Lords' decision in *Gillick*[2]. It was difficult to visualise how merely talking to a child could be viewed as unlawful given that parents have no independent cause of action for breach of parental rights[3].

In contrast, the Labour Government's most recent Guidance[4] adopts a distinctly softer touch on this sensitive issue. It makes it plain that trained staff in *secondary* schools 'should be able to give young people full information about different types of contraception, including emergency contraception, and their effectiveness'. Further, 'trained teachers can give pupils – individually and as a class – additional information and guidance on where they can obtain confidential advice, counselling and, where necessary, treatment', and this is something which must be made clear in the school's sex and relationship education policy[5]. On the rare occasions where *primary* school staff are approached, the Guidance recognises that this will always involve child protection issues and requires that arrangements are put in place whereby a designated member of staff 'should make sensitive arrangements in discussion with the child, to ensure that parents or carers are informed'[6]. Finally, where a teacher learns from an under-16-year-old that he or she is having, or contemplating having, sexual intercourse, the Guidance[7] requires that schools should be in a position to take steps to ensure that: wherever possible the young person is persuaded to talk to their parent or carer; any child protection issues are addressed; and that the child has been adequately counselled and informed about contraception, including precise information about where young people can access contraception and advice services.

So is there a right to sex education?

The current law on sex education and the Government's official Guidance do recognise the importance to teenagers of knowledge about and availability of contraception as a means of combating the very high rate of teenage pregnancy in the UK. It is also the case that effective sex and relationship education in secondary schools is officially recognised to play an important role in the Government's strategy to reduce such pregnancies[8]. This has not, however,

---

1 At p 558.
2 See Chapters 3 and 8 above for a more detailed discussion of the *Gillick* case.
3 *F v Wirral Metropolitan Borough Council* [1991] Fam 69. For amplification of the legal arguments see A Bainham 'Sex Education: A Family Lawyer's Perspective' in N Harris (ed) *Children, Sex Education and the Law* (National Children's Bureau, 1996).
4 See fn 8 at p 711 above. For an evaluation, see D Monk 'New guidance/old problems: recent developments in sex education' (2001) 23 JSWFL 271.
5 Guidance, at paras 2.11–2.12.
6 Ibid, para 7.9.
7 Paragraph 7.11.
8 See Guidance, para 2.10. For a most illuminating comparison of the position in the UK, which has a very high rate of teenage pregnancy when compared with the rest of Europe, with that of the Netherlands, which has a very low rate and a strong commitment to universal sex education,

stopped the UN Committee on the Rights of the Child criticising the Government's performance and recommending that it: 'Take further necessary measures to reduce the rate of teenage pregnancies through, inter alia, making health education, including sex education, part of the school curricula, making contraception available to all children, and improving access to confidential and adolescent-sensitive advice and information and other appropriate support'[1].

If sex education is to be viewed as a universal right of children, two principal criticisms can be made of the current law. First, as regards the *content* of sex education, it can be argued that the central directives of Government are over-prescriptive and fail to take account of the diversity of sexual relationships in today's society. The Government's approach, with its emphasis on the value of a stable family life, marriage and the responsibilities of parenthood, has been subjected to scathing criticism by Meredith in the following terms:

> 'Many individuals may argue that the Government's notion of "stable family life" is dangerously and unacceptably narrow, that it has a tendency to reflect and to further the interests of sectors of society that are already disproportionately advantaged, that it signally fails to accord parity of esteem to less advantaged groups and individuals, and that it tends towards the perpetuation of social divisions in society. Above all, it fails to acknowledge the legitimacy of alternative lifestyles and it tends to stigmatise the many children who come from family backgrounds which do not conveniently fit with the Government's perceived ideal model – a tendency which may have profound and lasting detrimental effects upon the educational and social development of the children concerned.'[2]

Secondly, as with the parental right of withdrawal from religious education and collective worship, the absolute right of parents to withdraw their child from sex education may be seen to involve too close an identification of the parents' and the child's interests or, put more bluntly, a denial of the child's right to receive such education. There is no mechanism in the law whereby the child might challenge the parents' decision or whereby it might be challenged by someone else on the child's behalf. This is difficult to square with Article 12 of the UNCRC and the significance attached to children's views elsewhere in the law.

For both of these reasons, any 'right' to sex education of children in general may be seen as less than convincingly established.

What can be said with confidence is that it is not contrary to *parents'* rights under the ECHR for the State to introduce compulsory sex education which covers all aspects, provided that it is not delivered in a way which is intended to indoctrinate, but is objective. The ECtHR so held in *Kjeldsen, Busk Madsen and Pedersen v Denmark* almost 30 years ago[3]. But this decision was not concerned directly with *children's* rights and it cannot be concluded that to allow the parental right of withdrawal is necessarily contrary to children's rights under the Convention. The UNCRC is, moreover, probably too broad and general in its references to education for it to be said that a universal right to sex education is recognised by that Convention[4].

---

see R Ingham 'Sexual Health and Young People: the Contribution and Role of Psychology' in B Brooks-Gordon, L Gelsthorpe, M Johnson and A Bainham (eds) *Sexuality Repositioned: Diversity and the Law* (Hart, 2004) ch 11.

1 *Concluding Observations: United Kingdom of Great Britain and Northern Ireland* (October 2002) at para 44(a).

2 Op cit, p 711, fn 7 (above), at pp 212–213.

3 (1976) 1 EHRR 711.

4 See further, A Bainham (above) at pp 30–33.

From a theoretical and policy perspective, the current position is difficult to defend. The case for all children receiving appropriate sex education in an effort to prevent unwanted teenage pregnancy, abortion and sexually transmitted disease is a strong one, and one which is justified by more than one theory or component of children's rights[1]. Along with the analogous parental right of withdrawal of children from religious education and collective worship[2], the case of sex education brings into sharp focus the problems which can arise where the interests/rights of children are too closely and uncritically identified with those of their parents. At the international level, this is one of a number of areas in which there is likely to be some difficulty in upholding contemporaneously what may be thought to be the fundamental (but perhaps conflicting) rights of parents and children.

Religious education, worship and parental upbringing

Religious education (RE) forms part of the 'basic curriculum' of maintained schools[3]. LEAs, governing bodies and head teachers have statutory responsibilities to ensure that it is provided to *all* pupils, including those over compulsory school leaving age[4]. The matter is now governed by the Education Act 2002[5] which re-enacts the provision in the Education Act 1996[6] listing RE as an element that must be provided in the basic curriculum in addition to the National Curriculum. This requires maintained schools to teach RE in accordance with an agreed syllabus drawn up by a local conference. It must not be 'distinctive of a particular religious denomination'[7]. Special provisions govern the content of religious education in the case of schools which are of a 'religious character'[8]. While religious education at these schools may be in accordance with the agreed syllabus adopted by the LEA, it may instead be taught in accordance with the trust deed for the school or in accordance with the tenets of the religion or religious denomination specified in relation to the school.

The Education Reform Act 1988 also controversially required all agreed syllabuses for RE adopted on or after 29 September 1988 to 'reflect the fact that the religious traditions in Great Britain are in the main Christian whilst taking account of the teaching and practices of the other principal religions represented in Great Britain'[9]. A similar requirement applies to collective worship, and we will consider the issues in that context along with the provision which gives parents a right to insist that their child be excused from RE or worship. Such rights are exercisable in all maintained schools. Maintained schools may also be obliged under the Education Act 1996 to make alternative arrangements for a child to

1 See further, A Bainham (above) at pp 25–28.
2 See below.
3 See, generally, N Harris *The Law Relating to Schools* (2nd edn) (Tolley, 1995) at pp 205–214. See also C Hamilton *Family, Law and Religion* (Sweet & Maxwell, 1995), and C Hamilton and B Watt 'A discriminatory education – collective worship in schools' [1996] CFLQ 28. The matter is also the subject of DFE Circular 1/94 on *Religious Education and Collective Worship*, and the QCA's *Non-statutory Guidance on RE* (February 2000).
4 School Standards and Framework Act 1998, s 69 and Sch 19.
5 Section 80.
6 Section 352.
7 School Standards and Framework Act 1998, Sch 19, para 2(5).
8 Ibid, Sch 19.
9 Education Reform Act 1988, s 8(3), now Education Act 1996, s 375(3).

receive particular denominational instruction during school hours. They must be satisfied that to do so would only interfere with his attendance at the beginning or end of the school day[1].

The 1996 Act[2] requires every LEA to constitute a standing advisory council on religious education (SACRE) which must advise the LEA on all matters relating to the agreed syllabus and collective worship in community schools. Importantly, it must also deal with applications to lift or modify the requirements relating to *Christian* collective worship[3] – a significant role in those areas in which there is a concentration of ethnic minorities. The council is constituted by representatives drawn from school governing bodies, the principal religious traditions in the area, teachers' associations, the LEA and co-opted members.

Collective worship

The provisions in the 1944 Act which required schools to hold a daily act of collective worship[4] were repealed by the Education Reform Act 1988, but only to put in their place more prescriptive requirements. The then Conservative Government had previously made plain its view that religious education and worship had a 'special contribution' to make, in its White Paper *Better Schools*. It proposed that it should continue to receive 'the significance which it deserves within the curriculum', but that this should have a distinctively Christian flavour. Thus, 'within the statutory framework an introduction to the Christian tradition [it thought] remains central to the religious education provided in our schools'. It also indicated that it would look to LEAs and schools to ensure that these requirements were met[5].

The School Standards and Framework Act 1998 now requires (subject to the important parental right of withdrawal) all pupils at maintained schools to 'take part in an act of collective worship' on each school day[6]. This may be a single act of worship for all pupils or different acts for different groups[7]. It must be 'wholly or mainly of a broadly Christian character'[8]. It will be regarded as such 'if it reflects the broad traditions of Christian belief without being distinctive of any particular Christian denomination'[9]. It is not necessary for every act of collective worship to comply with this if, taking the school term as a whole, most of the acts which take place in the school do comply with the principle[10]. It has been held that the broadly Christian character of worship is not lost by the inclusion of elements common to Christianity and other religions which enable children of other faiths to participate[11].

---

1   School Standards and Framework Act 1998, s 71(4).
2   Section 390.
3   School Standards and Framework Act 1998, Sch 20, para 4.
4   Education Act 1944, s 25(1).
5   *Better Schools* at para 55.
6   School Standards and Framework Act 1998, s 70 and Sch 20. See P Cumper 'School Worship and the Education Reform Act 1988' (1989) 139 NLJ 1203; S Poulter 'The Religious Education Provisions of the Education Reform Act' (1990) 2 *Education and the Law* 1; C Hamilton and B Watt (above); and A Bradney 'Christian Worship?' (1996) 8(2) *Education and the Law* 127.
7   School Standards and Framework Act 1998, Sch 20, para 2(2).
8   Ibid, Sch 20, para 3(2).
9   Ibid, Sch 20, para 3(3).
10 Ibid, Sch 20, para 3(4).
11 *R v Secretary of State for Education ex parte R and D* [1994] ELR 495.

These provisions were the result of a House of Lords' amendment to the Education Reform Bill and caused controversy from the outset. The concern seems to have been that schools were failing to get across the principal tenets of Christianity by, as some peers saw it, 'dabbling' in other religions[1]. Of course, this pre-supposes that schools *should* be trying to get across this message, and that there is a proper place for religion in State schools. Other jurisdictions, with different traditions, have exercised great caution to ensure that State schools preserve neutrality as between different religions[2], and the principle of equality of religious belief is also a feature of the decisions of the family courts[3]. The English requirements which seek to elevate in importance one particular religion, Christianity (albeit maintaining neutrality between the many different Christian denominations), do not square with the position elsewhere, and can be a source of antagonism for the ethnic minorities. They are one manifestation of the existence of an established church, binding together church and State, itself something which has been called into question in recent years[4]. As one commentator has pertinently inquired, 'is it not incongruous in our multi-faith society for collective worship in schools to be "wholly or mainly" Christian?'[5]. Further, as has been pointed out[6], a multi-faith approach to both religious education and collective worship may be thought more consistent with the obligations imposed by the UNCRC, Article 29(1)(d) of which requires that the education of the child be directed towards the 'preparation of the child for responsible life in a free society, in the spirit of understanding, peace, tolerance, equality of sexes, and friendship among all peoples, ethnic, national, and religious groups and persons of indigenous origin'. The need for such an approach and the understanding of diversity has never perhaps been more strongly felt than at the present time.

Religious upbringing

There is no legal obligation on parents to raise their children in a particular religion or, indeed, in any religion. They have complete discretion to raise them as atheists, agnostics, or in any religion of their choice, but religion has often been a fertile area of dispute between parents and other carers in proceedings relating, for example, to residence or adoption[7]. Several principles have emerged from the

1 See P Cumper 'School Worship and the Education Reform Act 1988' (1989) 139 NLJ 1203.
2 The approach in the USA is to outlaw religion in State schools. For a review of some of the constitutional cases there, see A Bainham *Children, Parents and the State* (Sweet & Maxwell, 1988) at pp 179–180. For a discussion of the rather different approach to the problem in France, but one which still maintains the principle of equality, see J Bell 'Religious observance in secular schools: a French solution' (1990) 2 *Education and the Law* 121.
3 See below.
4 For an American perspective on the relationship between church and State, see ME Smith 'Relations Between Church and State in the United States: With Special Attention to the Schooling of Children' (1987) 35 Am J Comp Law 1.
5 P Cumper (above) at p 1204.
6 J Fortin *Children's Rights and the Developing Law* (2nd edn) (Butterworths, 2003) at pp 355–356. Fortin also notes that Ofsted (Office for Standards in Education) has encouraged a more multi-faith approach to religion in schools.
7 Reviews of relevant case-law may be found in B Walsh 'Religious Considerations in Custody Disputes' [1988] Fam Law 198 and C Yates 'Religious education and upbringing – child right or parent prerogative?' (1989) 1 JCL 89. See also, more generally, C Hamilton *Family, Law and Religion* (Sweet & Maxwell, 1995) at chs 4 and 5. For an article which explores the relevance of religion and culture on decisions, especially medical decisions, affecting the child's body, see

jurisprudence of the courts on religious issues. The first is that the courts should be reluctant to change the settled religion of a child. This has sometimes resulted in orders for custody (now residence) or adoption being made conditional on the carer or adoptive parent undertaking to secure the continuation of the child's religious upbringing[1]. The courts have in recent years, however, been more willing to recognise the difficulties involved in the child's carer bringing up the child in a religion other than his or her own and that preservation of the child's religion and cultural heritage may not be decisive in determining his or her best interests[2]. The same principle underlies the statutory provisions which preclude local authorities and voluntary organisations from changing the religion of a child in their care[3]. The second principle is that the courts usually do not discriminate between the comparative worth of different religions. They take a neutral stance between them so that the adherence of one parent to a certain religion, or to no religion at all, should not, per se, be decisive as to the child's welfare[4]. A third principle is that they will intervene where the social practices attaching to a particular sect or religion are considered positively harmful to the child. The best example is probably their willingness to intervene to protect the health of children whose parents, for religious reasons, are opposed to certain forms of medical aid[5]. More contentiously, they have occasionally intervened to prevent the child being exposed to what has been seen as 'brainwashing' or social isolation[6]. Disputes between parents themselves specifically over religious issues have not commonly been reported but this was the situation in *Re J (Specific Issue: Child's Religious Upbringing and Circumcision)*[7]. Here a Muslim father, who admitted that he was not devout, sought specific issue orders that his five-year-old son be circumcised and raised as a Muslim. The mother, who was the primary carer, was a nominal Christian and was raising the child in an entirely secular household. The father regarded circumcision as important to the child's Muslim identity but the mother was opposed to the procedure. The Court of Appeal upheld the judge's order refusing the father's application. In the absence of medical necessity, an

C Bridge 'Religion, Culture and the Body of the Child' in A Bainham, S Day Sclater and M Richards (eds) *Body Lore and Laws* (Hart Publishing, 2002) at ch 15. See also Chapter 8 above.

1 For an example of an access dispute revolving around religious questions, see *Re S (Minors) (Access: Religious Upbringing)* [1992] 2 FLR 313. For religious factors in medical cases, see Chapter 8 above.

2 In *Re P (Section 91(14) Guidelines) (Residence and Religious Heritage)* [1999] 2 FLR 573, for example, the Court of Appeal upheld an order that the child, who had Down's syndrome, should not be moved from her nominally Catholic foster parents and returned to her Orthodox Jewish parents. It had proved impossible for the local authority to find a suitable Orthodox Jewish family in which to place her. While acknowledging the importance of religion and cultural background, the judge had been entitled, bearing in mind the child's limited ability to understand and appreciate the Jewish religion, to conclude that this was not an overwhelming factor in determining who should care for the child.

3 See Chapters 10 and 11 above.

4 In *Re Carroll* [1931] 1 KB 317 at 336, Scrutton LJ said:
   'It is, I hope, unnecessary to say that the Court is perfectly impartial in matters of religion, for the reason that it has as a Court no evidence, no knowledge, no views as to the respective merits of the religious views of various denominations.'
   More recently, see *Re R (A Minor) (Residence: Religion)* [1993] 2 FLR 163 in similar vein.

5 Discussed in Chapter 8 above.

6 Perhaps the most striking example of this line of cases is the virtual condemnation of Scientology in *Re B and G (Minors) (Custody)* [1985] FLR 493.

7 [2000] 1 FLR 571.

irreversible operation such as this required the parents to agree, failing which the court should determine the matter on the basis of the welfare principle under which the child's best interests had priority over any religious wishes of a parent. The decisive factor here was that the child was raised in a non-Muslim environment and it was not in his best interests to be circumcised or given a religious upbringing against the wishes of the primary carer.

The courts must be careful, however, not to discriminate between parents in residence and contact disputes purely on the basis of religion, since this might violate parental rights under the ECHR. Article 9 of the Convention protects the individual's right to 'freedom of thought, conscience and religion' and 'this right includes freedom to change his religion or belief'. Religious issues can also arise under Articles 8 and 14. The ECtHR held by a narrow 5 : 4 margin in *Hoffmann v Austria*[1] that the Austrian Supreme Court's decision requiring the mother (who was a Jehovah's Witness) to hand over the children, who had been with her for the last two years, to the father infringed her rights under Article 8 taken in conjunction with Article 14. The majority accepted that there were adverse 'social factors' relating to Jehovah's Witnesses which might tip the balance in favour of the other parent. But crucially in this case the Austrian Supreme Court had attached decisive importance to Austrian federal legislation which prevented either parent from unilaterally changing the religion of the child from the religion shared by both parents. The mother had done this when she had ceased to be a Roman Catholic and had become a Jehovah's Witness. The Supreme Court had essentially based its decision concerning residence (in the English sense) on religion alone and this violated the Convention.

Religious upbringing is, therefore, an area in which parents enjoy a great deal of discretion and this is reflected in the unusual deference which is attached to parental wishes in the education legislation. Whereas the so-called parental choice of school is, in reality, a qualified right to express a preference, the right to withdraw a child from religious education classes and collective worship is a strict legal right, since the educational authorities have an absolute duty to comply[2]. Quite where this leaves the independent rights of the child, especially the '*Gillick*-competent' child, over religious matters is highly questionable[3].

SPECIAL EDUCATIONAL NEEDS

Children with special educational needs (SEN) are entitled to special educational provision under Part IV of the Education Act 1996[4], as amended by the

---

1 (1993) 17 EHRR 293. For commentary, see A Bainham 'Religion, Human Rights and the Fitness of Parents' [1994] CLJ 39.

2 First given to parents in the nineteenth century and now contained in the School Standards and Framework Act 1998, s 71.

3 There is an argument that it amounts to a denial of the child's rights under the ECHR. See A Nelson 'School Religion Law may break Convention' (1988) 44 *Childright* 7. The ECtHR in *Angeleni v Sweden* (1988) 10 EHRR 123 held that Article 9(1) of the Convention prohibits religious indoctrination at school but the Court was here concerned with parents' rights against the State and not with the independent rights of children. Cf the discussion of sex education (above).

4 The Act consolidates the Education Act 1981, as amended by the Education Act 1993, which latter legislation made significant changes to the original scheme under the 1981 Act. See,

Special Educational Needs and Disability Act 2001 (SENDA 2001). The 2001 Act makes changes to the existing scheme. It strengthens the right of children with SEN to be educated in mainstream schools where parents desire this and the interests of the other children can be protected[1]; it requires LEAs to make arrangements for services to provide parents of children with SEN with advice and information[2] and a means of resolving disputes with schools and LEAs[3]; it requires LEAs to comply within specified periods with orders of the Special Educational Needs and Disability Tribunal (renamed SENDIST under the 2001 Act)[4]; it requires schools to inform parents where they are making special educational provision for their child[5]; and it allows schools to request a statutory assessment of a pupil's SEN[6]. But essentially the scheme remains that under the 1996 Act.

Perhaps more significantly, SENDA 2001 also prohibits discrimination against disabled pupils[7]. Statutory duties are placed on LEAs and schools including a duty not to treat disabled pupils less favourably without justification, for a reason which relates to their disability[8], and a duty to make reasonable adjustments so that disabled pupils are not at a substantial disadvantage to pupils who are not disabled[9]. In England and Wales (but not in Scotland) there is also a duty to plan strategically and make progress in increasing accessibility to schools' premises and to the curriculum, and in improving the ways in which written information provided to pupils who are not disabled is provided to disabled pupils[10]. (The details of the legislation as it applies to disabled pupils are beyond the scope of the present work.) Justice cannot be done here to the detail and complexity of the statutory regime now governing SEN but we will attempt to describe its principal features[11].

The purpose of the Education Act 1981 was to reverse the marginalisation of children with SEN, to remove any stigma and to integrate them, wherever possible, into ordinary schools. It sought to achieve this by the creation of legally defined and coherent procedures for assessment of need and special educational

---

generally, N Harris *The Law Relating to Schools* (2nd edn) (Tolley, 1995) at ch 9; S Oliver and L Austen *Special Educational Needs and the Law* (Jordans, 1996); and J Friel *Children with Special Needs: Assessment, Law and Practice* (Jessica Kingsley, 1995). For a study of the role of the special educational needs tribunal (SENDIST) which also contains a concise introduction to the legal principles, see N Harris *Special Educational Needs and Access to Justice* (Jordans, 1997).

1   SENDA 2001, s 1 and Education Act 1996, s 316.
2   SENDA 2001, s 2 and Education Act 1996, s 332A.
3   SENDA 2001, s 3 and Education Act 1996, s 332B.
4   SENDA 2001, s 4.
5   SENDA 2001, s 7 and Education Act 1996, s 317A.
6   SENDA 2001, s 8 and Education Act 1996, s 329A.
7   Part 2 of the Act. For an assessment of the reforms see A Blair and A Lawson 'Disability reforms in education – could do better?' [2003] CFLQ 455.
8   SENDA 2001, ss 11 and 12, inserting ss 28A and 28B into the Disability Discrimination Act 1995 (DDA 1995).
9   SENDA 2001, s 13, inserting s 28C into the DDA 1995.
10   SENDA 2001, s 14, inserting s 28D into the DDA 1995.
11   See the illuminating two-part article, N Harris 'Special Education and the Law: further progress?' (1992) 3 JCL 104 and 147. For a thorough review of the case-law on special educational needs, see N Harris 'Special Educational Needs: the role of the courts' [2002] CFLQ 137. See also JR McManus *Education and the Courts* (Jordans, 2004) ch 4.

provision[1]. Thus, in a nutshell, although children with the most severe learning difficulties are usually expected to attend special schools, those with less severe difficulties (but still having special learning requirements) are expected to be catered for by special provision in mainstream schools[2]. Part IV of the Education Act 1996 must also be read with the Children Act 1989 which, as we saw[3], requires close co-operation between LEAs and social services departments and which places the latter under statutory duties to provide services for 'children in need'. Many children with SEN will also be children in need, and the legislation requires social services to assist any LEA with the provision of services for any child who has SEN[4], and, equally, LEAs are required to assist social services[5]. The legal framework is especially complex because of interlinking and 'relativistic' definitions which broadly require a comparison to be made between the educational requirements of the individual child and ordinary educational requirements[6].

General duties towards children with SEN

The Education Act 1996 requires the LEA to ensure that there are sufficient schools in its area. An aspect of this is that it must have regard 'to the need for securing that special educational provision is made for pupils who have special educational needs'[7]. The Act defines this special educational provision as educational provision of any kind for a child under two years[8] and, for children over that age, 'educational provision which is additional to, or otherwise different from, the educational provision made generally for children of his age in schools maintained by the local education authority (other than special schools)'[9].

The governing body of a community, foundation or voluntary school, and the LEA in relation to a maintained nursery school, have a statutory duty to *identify* children with SEN and use their best endeavours to ensure that special educational provision is made for them[10]. Where the head teacher or appropriate governor is informed by the LEA that a child has SEN, the head teacher or governor must make this known to anyone who is likely to teach the child[11]. The LEA must provide the parent of any child in its area with SEN with advice and information[12].

---

1   N Harris notes that, in 1989, LEAs held statements of SEN in respect of 138,679 pupils or 1.8% of the school population.
2   The policy referred to as 'integration' but more often now as 'inclusion'.
3   At Chapters 2 and 10 above.
4   Education Act 1996, s 322.
5   Children Act 1989, s 27(1) and (3).
6   N Harris 'Special Education and the Law: further progress?' (1992) 3 JCL 104 at 105.
7   Section 14(6).
8   The legislation as it applies to children with special educational needs is not confined to children of school age. For a discussion of local authority obligations regarding day-care and nursery provision for pre-school children, see Chapter 10 above.
9   Section 312(4).
10 Education Act 1996, s 317(1)(a) and (c). See also the Special Educational Needs Code of Practice, approved by Parliament (DfES, 2001). It is the duty of the governing bodies, LEAs and the SENDIST to have regard to the provisions of the Code as revised from time to time (Education Act 1996, s 313).
11 Ibid, s 317(1)(b).
12 Ibid, s 332A, as inserted by SENDA 2001, s 2.

The definition of special educational needs

The Education Act 1996 provides that a child has SEN where he has 'a learning difficulty which calls for special educational provision to be made for him'[1]. 'Learning difficulty' is further defined as either:

(a) 'a significantly greater difficulty in learning than the majority of children of his age'; or
(b) 'a disability which either prevents or hinders him from making use of educational facilities of a kind generally provided for children of his age in schools within the area of the local education authority'.

The Act also provides that a child under five years old has a learning difficulty if he is likely to fall within (a) or (b) (above) after attaining that age or would do so if special educational provision were not made for him[2].

The child's needs are therefore not to be considered in a detached way but must be related to what is considered ordinary and what special educational provision is available, and here there has been some litigation. In *R v Hampshire Education Authority ex parte J*[3], it was held by Taylor J that dyslexia suffered by a highly intelligent child could amount to a 'disability' for these purposes. The argument for the council was that provision for dyslexia could not be 'special educational provision' within the meaning of the legislation since *some* provision was made to deal with the problem in LEA schools through dyslexic units. Taylor J rejected this contention, taking the view that the statutory reference to educational provision 'made generally for children of his age' meant that which was made 'to the general run of normal children, to the normal majority'. Thus, even though each school might have a dyslexic unit or, for example, a deaf unit, this provision could still be special educational provision under the then Education Act 1981[4]. This decision was followed in *R v Lancashire County Council ex parte M*[5] in which the Court of Appeal, casting doubt on an earlier decision to the contrary[6], held that a need for speech therapy was almost always going to constitute SEN calling for special educational provision. It has, however, been held that the requirement of a lift in a school for a disabled pupil would not amount to educational provision[7]. The fact that a child has a disability which prevents or hinders him from making use of educational facilities of a kind generally provided does not necessarily mean that special educational provision is needed if the disability can be overcome in other ways[8].

1　Education Act 1996, s 312(1).
2　Ibid, s 312(2).
3　(1985) 84 LGR 547.
4　For further analysis of the case, see N Harris 'Special Education and the Law: further progress?' (1992) 3 JCL 104 at p 105.
5　[1989] 2 FLR 279, and see T McKevitt 'Speech Therapy as "Special educational provision"' (1990) 2 JCL 45.
6　*R v Oxfordshire County Council ex parte W* [1987] 2 FLR 193.
7　*R v London Borough of Lambeth ex parte MBM* [1995] ELR 374. Cf *City of Bradford Metropolitan Borough Council v A* [1997] ELR 417 in which the provision of a nurse was held to amount to non-educational provision.
8　As McCulloch J put it in *B v Isle of Wight Council* [1997] ELR 279, 'a child with bad sight or hearing has a disability ... but if all he needs is a pair of spectacles or a hearing aid he has no need for special educational provision and therefore he has no "special educational needs"'.

The choice of school

It was noted above that the policy of the legislation is for *inclusion* wherever possible of children with SENs in the ordinary education system by attendance at mainstream schools. This philosophy is given statutory expression in s 316 of the Education Act 1996, as amended by the SENDA 2001. Where a child is not 'statemented' he must be educated in a mainstream school. Where a statement is maintained, he must be educated in a mainstream school unless that is incompatible with (a) the wishes of his parents, or (b) the provision of efficient education for other children. Statemented children are those with the most severe learning difficulties[1].

In principle, also, the policy is that statemented children should follow the National Curriculum except insofar as this is modified to take into account their SEN. All children with SEN, whether statemented or not, are expected to engage in the activities of the school together with those children who do not have SEN[2].

Where, however, the child's needs are especially severe, it may be necessary for him to attend a special school which, since the Children Act 1989, may with public assistance be situated abroad. A special provision was inserted into the legislation to allow local authorities to provide financial and other assistance to families who wished to take advantage in particular of the programme of 'conductive education' at the Peto Institute in Budapest for those suffering from cerebral palsy[3].

Quite protracted legal disputes can arise between parents and LEAs where parents themselves are requesting that a child be educated at a special school at the authority's expense[4] or, conversely, where the parents wish the child to attend a mainstream school and the LEA is pressing for the child to be educated at a special school[5]. The Education Act 1993 conferred on parents the right to express a preference in relation to the school to be named in a statement[6], giving reasons for the preference. Where the LEA decides not to comply with the request it must inform the parents of their right to appeal to the SENDIST[7].

Identification and assessment of children with SEN

The statutory duties of LEAs and schools to identify children with SEN were noted above. These are most likely to become apparent during the teaching process, but might also first come to light through health problems, of which the health

---

1 For the statementing procedure, see pp 724 et seq below.
2 Education Act 1996, s 317(4).
3 Ibid, s 320.
4 As in *R v Hampshire Education Authority ex parte J* (1985) 84 LGR 547. See also *L v Kent County Council and the Special Educational Needs Tribunal* [1998] ELR 140.
5 As in the wardship case *Re D (A Minor) (Wardship: Jurisdiction)* [1987] 1 WLR 1400.
6 See now Education Act 1996, Sch 27, para 3.
7 Ibid, Sch 27, para 8. See further p 724 below.

authorities and National Health Service Trusts are aware. There is, thus, a corresponding duty on health authorities in these circumstances to inform parents in the first instance and then, after giving them an opportunity to discuss the matter, to inform the LEA[1]. Much of the process of identifying and acting upon SEN may be informal and co-operative[2], but the legislation does provide a formal assessment procedure which is designed to safeguard the child's needs and parents' rights, and to make schools and LEAs accountable[3].

This procedure is now laid down in the Education Act 1996 and the regulations made under it[4]. In brief outline the procedure is as follows[5]. The procedure is intended to provide for parental involvement at all stages, and parents may themselves instigate an assessment[6]. Parents must be served with a notice in prescribed form that the authority proposes to assess the child. They must also be informed of the name of the officer within the LEA from whom further advice may be obtained and of their right to make representations and written submissions[7]. The child may be examined as part of the process and it is an offence for parents not to comply with this, although they have a right to attend the examination[8]. If the LEA decides, following the assessment, not to determine special educational provision, parents have a right of appeal to the SENDIST[9]. Where the LEA *does* decide to make such a determination it must maintain a *statement* of the child's SEN in prescribed form, which should include the professional advice on which the assessment was made[10]. Litigation has made two principles clear. The first principle is that LEAs have a wide discretion in the first instance in deciding whether or not a child should be statemented. The second principle is that once LEAs have decided that this is the appropriate course, they must thereafter adhere strictly to the formal requirements in the legislation. Harris, noting that the Code of Practice advises that educational provision should be specified only if adequate provision cannot be made from the school's own resources, says that the decision 'often comes down to the question whether the provision the child requires can, *in the opinion of the LEA*, be met from the resources normally allocated to mainstream schools in the area'[11].

---

1   Education Act 1996, s 332.
2   Informal assessment will be carried out at the school in up to three stages of assessment. See
    S Oliver and L Austen *Special Educational Needs and the Law* (Jordans, 1996) at ch 2 for the
    details.
3   For some robust criticisms of the way the procedure worked under the Education Act 1981, see
    J Robinson 'Reforming the Reforms' (1992) 142 NLJ 685.
4   Education Act 1996, ss 323 and 328–331, and the Education (Special Educational Needs)
    (Consolidation) (England) Regulations 2001, SI 2001/3455. In Wales the regulations are the
    Education (Special Educational Needs) (Wales) Regulations 2002, SI 2002/152.
5   For greater detail, see N Harris *The Law Relating to Schools* (2nd edn) (Tolley, 1995) and S Oliver
    and L Austen (above) at ch 3. See also the materials set out in A Ruff *Education Law*
    (Butterworths, 2002) at pp 345–365.
6   Education Act 1996, s 329. This is what happened in *R v Hampshire Education Authority, ex parte J*
    (1985) 84 LGR 547.
7   Within a time-limit, currently 29 days. See the Education Act 1996, s 323(1).
8   Education Act 1996, Sch 26, paras 4 and 5.
9   Ibid, s 325.
10 Ibid, s 324 and Sch 27.
11 N Harris *Special Educational Needs and Access to Justice* (Jordans, 1997) at p 10.

As to the first principle above, in *R v Secretary of State for Education and Science ex parte Lashford*[1], a distinction was drawn between the finding of fact that a child had SEN and the determination of the LEA that it should itself make provision for those needs through the formal process of statementing. The Court of Appeal upheld the LEA's decision *not* to make a statement, the effect of which was that the girl in question remained in an ordinary school and was not sent to an independent special school as the parents had requested. As to the second principle, the Court of Appeal has held in *R v Secretary of State for Education and Science ex parte E*[2] that where a statement of special educational needs *is* made by the authority, the concomitant statement of special educational provision to be made for those needs must be spelt out precisely, and must deal with each and every educational need that the child has been found to have[3]. Parents have rights of appeal to the SENDIST relating to the various aspects of the statementing process and, from there, appeal to the High Court on a point of law[4]. Appeals may be brought against the decision of the LEA not to make a statement[5], against the description of the statement of the authority's assessment of the child's SEN, against the special educational provision specified in the statement, or against the authority's decision not to name a school in the statement[6]. There is also a right of appeal in relation to a decision by the LEA to cease to maintain a statement[7].

We noted above that the Education Act 1993 gave to parents for the first time the opportunity to express a preference as to choice of school. Where it makes a statement, the LEA must include the name of that school in the statement unless:

(a)   the school is unsuitable to the child's age, ability or aptitude or to his SEN; or
(b)   the attendance of the child at the school would be incompatible with the provision of efficient education for the children with whom he would be educated or the efficient use of resources[8].

The LEA is not required to name a school or institution if the child's parent has made suitable arrangements for the special educational provision specified in the statement[9].

The question of the allocation of scarce resources can loom large in the determination of the choice of school and much of the growing litigation in this area boils down to arguments about whether the cost should be borne by the LEA

---

1   [1988] 1 FLR 72. See also *R v Isle of Wight County Council ex parte RS and ex parte AS* [1993] 1 FLR 634 in which the Court of Appeal held that serving a parent with a *proposed* statement of SEN following an assessment of a child did not give rise to a duty on the part of the LEA to go on to determine special educational provision. The authority was entitled to make a 'no' decision on this at any time up to the issue of the final statement.
2   [1992] 1 FLR 377. See also *L v Clarke and Somerset County Council* [1998] ELR 129 and *Bromley London Borough v SENT* [1999] ELR 260.
3   But it is not required to spell out precisely any non-educational provision. See *R v Hereford and Worcester County Council ex parte P* [1992] 2 FLR 207.
4   Education Act 1996, ss 325 and 326, and the Tribunals and Inquiries Act 1992. A list of the decisions against which there is a right of appeal is set out in A Ruff (above) at p 366.
5   Education Act 1996, s 325.
6   Ibid, s 326(1).
7   Ibid, Sch 27, para 11.
8   Ibid, Sch 27, para 5.
9   Ibid, s 4A.

or by the parents[1]. It has been determined that the fact of naming an independent school in the statement does not necessarily lead to the conclusion that the LEA is liable to meet the fees but this may be so if that particular school is necessary to meet the child's SEN[2].

Review of statements

LEAs are automatically required to review all statements within 12 months of making the relevant statement or when it was last reviewed[3]. In addition, the parent may request the statement to be amended or for the school named to be changed, and has a right of appeal to the SENDIST against the decision of the LEA in relation to these matters[4].

Parents' rights or children's rights?

As elsewhere in education law, a striking feature of the special educational needs regime is the emphasis on the substantive and procedural rights of *parents*[5] and the almost total lack of corresponding rights for the *child* despite the rather obvious point that the entire issue of special needs is about the child and what special educational provision should be made for him. Harris puts this down largely to the 'consumer' culture in education which has depended on 'the provision of parental rights of choice, information, representation and redress while the independent interests of children have generally not been recognised'[6]. The most obvious omission is the absence of an independent right of appeal and there has been judicial confirmation that the child has no right to be a party to a parental appeal to the SENDIST or thereafter to the High Court[7]. On the other hand the regulations[8] do now provide that the child has a right to attend the hearing, and the tribunal may allow him to give evidence and to address it.

CHILDREN ACCOMMODATED IN INDEPENDENT SCHOOLS, LEA SCHOOLS AND OTHER ESTABLISHMENTS

The Children Act 1989 contains a number of provisions which are designed to ensure proper protection of the welfare of children who are accommodated away from home for long periods. We are principally concerned here with children at independent boarding-schools, but the Act also applies to children accommodated by LEAs in special schools, and by health authorities in, for example, long-stay hospitals. It is convenient to discuss all the relevant provisions here.

---

1   See particularly the House of Lords' decision in *R v East Sussex County Council ex parte Tandy* [1998] AC 174.
2   *R v London Borough of Hackney ex parte GC* [1996] ELR 142 and *Staffordshire County Council v J and J* [1996] ELR 418.
3   Education Act 1996, s 328.
4   Ibid, s 326 and Sch 27, paras 8 and 10.
5   'Parent' for these purposes includes a foster-parent who does not have parental responsibility. See *Fairpo v Humberside County Council* [1997] 1 All ER 183.
6   N Harris *Special Educational Needs and Access to Justice* (Jordans, 1997) at pp 4–5.
7   *R v Special Educational Needs Tribunal and the City of Westminster* [1996] ELR 228.
8   Special Educational Needs (Tribunal) Regulations 2001, SI 2001/600.

Children accommodated in health and educational establishments

Section 85 of the Children Act 1989 protects children accommodated for more than three consecutive months by health authorities or LEAs. There was concern about the large numbers of children in long-term accommodation who often had little or no contact with their families. There was also concern that the system for reviewing their position and looking after their welfare needs was too haphazard. Accordingly, the Children Act requires local authorities' social services departments to safeguard their welfare.

Where a health authority, Special Health Authority, Primary Care Trust, National Health Service Trust or LEA now effects a placement intended to last for at least this period, the accommodating authority has a statutory duty to notify the 'responsible authority' of the placement and of when it ceases to accommodate the child[1]. The responsible authority is that in which the child was ordinarily resident before the placement or, where there was no ordinary residence, the authority where the accommodation is situated[2]. On receipt of notification, the local authority must take such steps as are reasonably practicable to determine whether the child's welfare is adequately safeguarded and promoted in his present accommodation. It must also consider the extent to which (if at all) it should exercise of its functions under the Children Act with respect to the child[3].

Corresponding provisions under s 86 relate to children accommodated for similar periods in any care home or independent hospital[4]. Failure to notify the local authority of the child's accommodation is, again, an offence. The authority has powers of entry and it is an offence to obstruct its entry intentionally[5]. When children leave any of the above kinds of accommodation, the local authority has duties regarding their after-care[6].

Children accommodated in boarding-schools and colleges

In the period leading up to the Children Act 1989 there had been considerable media coverage of certain instances of sexual abuse of children in independent boarding-schools. These incidents highlighted the lack of statutory responsibility for the *welfare*, as opposed to the educational, needs of these children. The only existing duties of inspection were vested in HM Inspectorate of Schools and these were restricted to educational and other standards at schools such as the state of the school premises. In keeping with the provisions regarding long-term accommodation of children in State-maintained schools and health establishments, the Children Act imposed similar duties on social services departments to satisfy themselves as to the *social*, as opposed to educational, welfare of children at these schools. These responsibilities have now been transferred to the National Care Standards Commission and in Wales to the National Assembly for Wales. Local authorities must now be proactive, and not merely reactive to those allegations of abuse which might come to their attention. The law is contained in

---

1   Children Act 1989, s 86, as amended by the Care Standards Act 2000.
2   Ibid, s 85(1) and (2).
3   Ibid, s 85(3).
4   Ibid, s 85(4).
5   Ibid, s 86(4) and (5).
6   Ibid, s 24, and see Chapter 10 above.

s 87 of the Children Act, and the Inspection of Premises, Children and Records (Independent Schools) Regulations 1991. There is also a special volume of the *Guidance* on the Children Act devoted to independent schools[1].

Where a school or college provides accommodation for a child, the relevant person[2] must now safeguard and promote the welfare of the child[3]. The duty does not apply to those schools or colleges which fall within the definition of a 'children's home' or 'care home' since they are governed by the provisions applying to those homes[4]. The appropriate authority within whose area the school or college is situated must take reasonable steps to determine whether the child's welfare is being adequately safeguarded and promoted[5]. Where it is of the view that those running the school have failed to discharge the welfare duty properly, it must notify the relevant LEA or Secretary of State. If the breach is serious enough, this could lead to closure or removal of the school from the register of independent schools. Again, there are powers of entry and inspection and offences relating to the intentional obstruction of anyone exercising them[6]. In the case of a genuine emergency, it would be possible to seek an emergency protection order[7].

The *Guidance* and the regulations contain a great deal of information about what is expected of independent schools in discharging the welfare duty and what is expected of those inspecting the schools. Particular emphasis is laid on vigilance in the initial selection of staff and on providing the children with clear and accessible avenues of complaint[8]. Independent schools must now, under the Education Act 2002, Part 10, comply with the minimum national standards as a condition of their registration. In a serious case of failure to comply with these standards causing a serious risk to pupils' welfare there is a fast-track procedure. In other cases, failing schools are required to produce and implement an action plan[9]. There is a right of appeal to the Care Standards Tribunal[10].

THE IMPLICATIONS OF HUMAN RIGHTS

References have been made at various points in this chapter to human rights issues which have arisen in the educational context[11]. A number of articles of the

---

1   *The Children Act 1989 Guidance and Regulations Vol 5 Independent Schools* (HMSO, 1991).
2   The 'relevant person' will be either the proprietor of the school or the person conducting it.
3   Children Act 1989, s 87(1).
4   Ibid, s 87(2).
5   Ibid, s 87(3).
6   Ibid, s 87(6)–(9).
7   See Chapter 12 above.
8   See *The Children Act 1989 Guidance and Regulations Vol 5 Independent Schools* (HMSO, 1991) at ch 3. For an up-to-date exposition of the law governing independent schools, see O Hyams *Law of Education* (2nd edn) (Jordans, 2004) at ch 13.
9   Education Act 2002, s 165.
10 Ibid, ss 166 and 167.
11 Perhaps the most notable impact which the ECHR has had in the context of education has been in the abolition of corporal punishment, first in State schools and then in the independent sector. The Education (No 2) Act 1986, which abolished corporal punishment in the State sector, was the direct result of the decision of the ECtHR in *Campbell and Cosans v United Kingdom* (1982) 4 EHRR 293 in which the ECtHR had held that Article 2, Protocol 1 required that corporal punishment should not be administered contrary to the religious or

ECHR have been invoked in education cases, although, thus far, the tendency both in Strasbourg and in English domestic courts has been to interpret Convention principles restrictively in these cases.

In particular, Article 6 of the ECHR has, thus far at least, failed to be engaged much in cases involving educational decisions and processes of appeal. Article 6, which inter alia provides the individual with the right to a 'fair and public hearing' in the determination of his 'civil rights and obligations', might have been thought relevant to such matters as admissions and exclusions procedures. However, in *Simpson v United Kingdom*[1], a case involving the procedures relating to special educational needs, the European Commission found that no civil right was in issue since the matter fell squarely within the domain of public law and had no private law repercussions for private rights or obligations. This decision has been followed by the English courts in relation to school admissions and exclusion procedures following the enactment of the HRA 1998[2]. More recently, however, the Court of Appeal[3] has taken the view that the right not to be excluded from school without good cause might now be regarded as a civil right for the purposes of Article 6.

Article 8[4] has also been unsuccessfully invoked in a number of cases. In the *Belgian Linguistic Case*[5], for example, the ECtHR did not find a violation of Article 8 where Belgian domestic law did not enable French-speaking children to be educated at local French-speaking schools in accordance with their parents' wishes. The separation of a child from his or her parents by placement at a boarding-school engages Article 8 but was considered justified under Article 8(2) in *CB v London Borough of Merton and Special Educational Needs Tribunal*[6].

Human rights in education arise most directly under Article 2, Protocol 1 which, as we have seen[7], establishes the right to education. The UK Government has, however, made a reservation in Sch 3 to the HRA 1998 as regards the obligation to 'respect the right of parents to ensure such education and training in conformity with their own religious and philosophical convictions'. This is accepted by the UK only insofar as it is compatible with the provision of efficient instruction and training and the avoidance of unreasonable public expenditure. The question then is what the 'right to education' entails and we saw, for example, that it could not be said to provide a universal right to sex education[8]. It has been held by the Court of Appeal in *Holub and Holub v Secretary of State for the Home Department*[9]

---

philosophical convictions of the parents concerned. However, as we have seen, the converse argument that it should be administered in independent schools in accordance with parental beliefs and convictions failed in *R (Williamson) v Secretary of State for Education and Employment* [2003] 1 FLR 726, notwithstanding the rights protected by Article 9.

1   (1989) 64 DR 188.
2   See *R v Richmond London Borough Council ex parte JC* [2001] ELR 21 and *R (on the Application of T) v Head Teacher of Alperton Community School and Others; R (on the Application of T) v Head Teacher of Wembley High School; R (on the Application of C) v The Governing Body of Cardinal Newman High School* [2001] ELR 693.
3   *S, T and P v Brent London Borough Council, Oxfordshire County Council; Head Teacher of Elliott School and Others; Secretary of State for Education and Skills* [2002] ELR 693.
4   Which enshrines the right to respect for private and family life.
5   *Belgian Linguistic Case (No 2)* (1968) 1 EHRR 252.
6   [2002] ELR 401.
7   See fn 3 at p 689.
8   See p 713 above.
9   [2001] ELR 401.

that the right to education comprises four separate rights, none of which is absolute, as follows:

(1) the right of access to such educational establishments as exist;
(2) a right to effective (but not the most effective possible) education;
(3) a right to official recognition of academic qualifications; and
(4) as regards the right to an effective education, for the right to be meaningful the quality of the education must reach a minimum standard.

In trying to predict the future implications of the ECHR and the HRA 1998 for education, it should be remembered that the Convention is a 'living instrument'. It seems entirely likely that the question of 'rights', whether of parents or children, in the context of educational decisions will increasingly be litigated, perhaps with growing success, from a human rights perspective.

Chapter 17

CHILDREN IN THE INTERNATIONAL COMMUNITY

INTRODUCTION

The movement to recognise and protect children's rights has an important international as well as national dimension. In this chapter we look at the attempts which have been made to establish international standards and co-operation between States to uphold the rights of children, whether as persons possessing human rights which apply to everyone, or specifically as children.

The most significant international convention asserting the rights of children is undoubtedly the United Nations Convention on the Rights of the Child. Since this is now widely regarded as a fundamental source of children law, it was discussed in Chapter 2 alongside the Children Act 1989 – the principal source of domestic children law. The reader should therefore read this chapter in conjunction with Chapter 2. We also considered in Chapter 2 the European Convention on Human Rights and Fundamental Freedoms as it applies to children, together with the extensive and ever-growing jurisprudence of the European Court of Human Rights. In Chapter 13 we discussed the principles of the European Convention on the Exercise of Children's Rights, since it was appropriate to look at this Convention in the general context of representation of children. In this chapter we look selectively at some other international conventions concerning children.

We begin by tracing briefly the history of the international children's rights movement[1]. This is followed by a brief discussion of the Hague Protection of Children Convention 1996 and the comparatively recent Council of Europe Convention on Contact concerning Children, adopted in May 2002. We conclude the chapter with a rather more detailed analysis of the Hague Conventions governing respectively international child abduction and intercountry adoption.

THE INTERNATIONAL CHILDREN'S RIGHTS MOVEMENT

There are really two aspects to the protection of children's rights at the international level. The first is the extension to children of those human rights which everyone possesses as a human being. The second is the development of special safeguards for children 'beyond those granted as human rights to adults because of their physical and mental immaturity and consequent dependence and

---

1   For an excellent and informative evaluation of the significance of international law generally and, more specifically of the different kinds of international instruments, in the development of domestic family law (including many major areas affecting children), see G Douglas 'The significance of international law for the development of family law in England and Wales' in C Bridge (ed) *Family Law Towards the Millennium: Essays for PM Bromley* (Butterworths, 1997) at ch 3. A Bainham (ed) *The International Survey of Family Law* (Jordans, published annually) contains an 'Annual Review of International Family Law'. Specifically on human rights, a number of useful essays may be found in P Lødrup and E Modvar (eds) *Family Life and Human Rights* (Gyldendal Akademisk, 2004).

vulnerability'[1]. International law has frequently singled out particular groups and their need for special protection, two of the more obvious examples being civilians in time of war, and refugees. The case of warfare neatly illustrates both the generalised protection of children, along with adults, and also their special protection[2]. While the Geneva Conventions of 1949 generally protect the civilian population (of which children are a part) and individual civilians (which children undoubtedly are), they also contain certain specific Articles which prioritise the needs of children. Thus, for example, the fourth Geneva Convention of 1949 provides, inter alia, that:

> 'Children shall be the object of special respect and shall be protected against any form of indecent assault. The parties to the conflict shall take all feasible measures in order that children who have not attained the age of fifteen years do not take a direct part in hostilities and, in particular, they shall refrain from recruiting them into their armed forces ...'[3]

The primary focus here will be on this special recognition of children in international law but we must also refer to the debate about whether the more humanitarian aspects of international law apply in their entirety *by implication* to children. Here, reference will be made, in passing, to the jurisprudence of the US Supreme Court and the ECtHR – both of which lend support to the notion that, in general, fundamental rights enjoyed by adults also extend to children.

The Declaration of Geneva 1924

International recognition of the claims of children dates back to the early part of the twentieth century and the work of such organisations as the International Committee of the Red Cross, the League of Nations and the International Labour Organization[4]. In 1924 the Fifth Assembly of the League of Nations adopted the First Declaration of the Rights of the Child which became known as the Declaration of Geneva. The Declaration went beyond the earlier, more specific, concerns about the working conditions of children and the problem of slavery. It constituted a more general charter of child welfare dealing with such matters as material and spiritual development, shelter, food, medical aid, relief from distress

---

1   These two strands of protection are brought out particularly well in the seminal article, D Hodgson 'The Historical Development and "Internationalisation" of the Children's Rights Movement' (1992) 6 Aust J Fam Law 252. We draw heavily on this excellent article which should be compulsory reading for anyone with an interest in the position of children under international law. See also G Van Bueren *The International Law on the Rights of the Child* (Martinus Nijhoff, 1995) at chs 1 and 2.

2   See 'Children and the Laws of War' (1989) *Childright* at p 19. See also G Van Bueren (above) at ch 12. For a more detailed examination of the way in which international humanitarian law has been said to have failed to provide effective protection of children in the sphere of armed conflict, see G Goodwin-Gill and I Cohn *Child Soldiers: The Role of Children in Armed Conflicts* (Clarendon, 1994).

3   Article 77, Protocol 1. And see now Article 38 of the UNCRC. Article 38 requires States, inter alia, to respect international humanitarian law; to take all feasible measures to ensure that persons who have not attained the age of 15 years do not take a direct part in hostilities; to refrain from recruiting children under that age and, where recruiting those between the ages of 15 and 18, to give priority to the eldest; and to take all feasible measures to ensure protection and care of children who are affected by armed conflict.

4   D Hodgson 'The Historical Development and "Internationalisation" of the Children's Rights Movement' (1992) 6 Aust J Fam Law 252 at 259 et seq.

and protection against exploitation[1]. Yet the Declaration was limited, both in its concentration on welfare needs and in its lack of binding effect. It has been described as an essentially aspirational document, not requiring, but inviting States which were members of the League of Nations to be guided by its principles in the work of child welfare[2]. It was left to individual States to determine whether, and if so how, to implement its ideals.

Post-war developments

In the period immediately following World War II, several important international humanitarian Conventions and Declarations were adopted. These were, for the most part, aimed at improving international standards of treatment for *all* human beings and not just children. The two most significant were the drawing up of the Charter of the United Nations in 1945[3], and the unanimous adoption by the General Assembly of the Universal Declaration of Human Rights in 1948[4]. This is now generally accepted as the most authoritative statement of the main human rights and fundamental freedoms flowing from the UN Charter. It was noted earlier[5] that, inter alia, the Declaration explicitly recognises the right to education. Another provision also provides:

'Motherhood and childhood are entitled to special care and assistance. All children, whether born in or out of wedlock, shall enjoy the same social protection.'[6]

Beyond this, the Declaration did not expressly mention children, and it is a matter of interpretation how far its other provisions apply to adults and children alike.

The Declaration of the Rights of the Child 1959

There was, at this time, a gathering feeling that the special claims of children required wider, more comprehensive, recognition. This came about in 1959 with the Second Declaration of the Rights of the Child ('the 1959 Declaration')[7]. While the First Declaration (the Geneva Declaration) had focused rather narrowly on the material needs of children following World War I, the second looked more broadly at the claims and entitlements of children across a range of areas including housing, education, recreation, nutrition, medical services and social security. One commentator's assessment of the place of the 1959 Declaration in the internationalisation of children's rights is that it 'reaffirmed and expanded the provisions of the Declaration of Geneva, and applied generally to children in a more specific way the provisions of the Universal Declaration of Human Rights. Unlike the Universal Declaration, however, the 1959 Declaration [was] devoted

---

1 Earlier Conventions dealing with these specific concerns were the Minimum Age (Industry) Convention 1919 and the International Convention for the Suppression of Traffic in Women and Children 1921.
2 D Hodgson (above) at 261. Indeed, the Declaration itself boldly proclaimed that 'Mankind owes to the child the best that it has to give ...'.
3 The Charter does not specifically mention children at any point.
4 Resolution 217A (III), 10 December 1948.
5 See Chapter 16 above.
6 Article 25(2).
7 Resolution 1386 (XIV) adopted 20 November 1959. See D Hodgson (above).

almost exclusively to economic, social and cultural rights, omitting such important civil rights as life and liberty, criminal due process, and freedom from cruel, inhuman or degrading treatment or punishment'[1]. The 1959 Declaration, therefore, while much wider in its scope than what had gone before it, fell short of being comprehensive and, furthermore, did not create binding legal obligations on States which were parties to it[2]. This had to wait 30 years for the adoption of the UNCRC in 1989[3]. The true value of the 1959 Declaration was to establish many of the generally accepted international norms of treatment for children which could then be translated into binding legal obligations on States in the 1989 Convention.

The debate about general application

Between 1959 and 1989 the focus of debate was on whether the general human rights instruments emanating from the United Nations and elsewhere[4] could be applied to children. Those provisions which directly referred to children clearly did apply to children, but the notion gathered ground that most of those which did not specifically refer to children also applied to them as human beings[5].

Meanwhile in the USA, the Supreme Court from the 1960s had begun to accept that the fundamental rights enshrined in the Bill of Rights, as constituted by the various amendments to the US Constitution, were, in principle, available also to children, although their application might be qualified in some cases[6]. The breakthrough came in 1967 when, in *Re Gault*, the court said that 'neither the Fourteenth Amendment nor the Bill of Rights is for adults alone'[7]. This decision was followed by a plethora of decisions extending to children protections enjoyed by adults under the US Constitution[8]. In Europe also, the European Commission and Court of Human Rights made a number of significant decisions protecting the fundamental rights of children under Articles of the ECHR which did not mention children as such[9].

The immediate background to the UNCRC was that the General Assembly designated 1979 as the 'International Year of the Child'[10]. As one of its contributions to this, the Polish Government produced a draft text for a UN Convention, the purpose of which was to translate the principles of the 1959 Declaration into international law. The intention was to create internationally

---

1   D Hodgson (above) at 266.
2   Unless, that is, it could be said to have acquired the status of customary international law.
3   See Chapter 2 above.
4   Debate focused particularly on the so-called 'twin' covenants of 1966 – the International Covenant on Civil and Political Rights and the International Covenant on Economic, Social and Cultural Rights. See D Hodgson (above) at 269 et seq.
5   But international lawyers were not in complete agreement on this. See D Hodgson (above) at 271 et seq.
6   For an excellent collection of materials on the early constitutional breakthroughs for children in the USA, see W Wadlington, CH Whitebread and SM Davis *Children in the Legal System* (Foundation Press, 1983) at ch II.
7   387 US 1, 13 (1967).
8   Such as freedom of speech in *Tinker v Des Moines Independent Community School District* 393 US 503 (1969) and the right to a hearing in school discipline cases where suspension was at stake in *Goss v Lopez* 419 US 565 (1975).
9   We discuss the ECHR in Chapter 2 above.
10 See D Hodgson (above) at 275 et seq.

binding legal obligations and also to extend the coverage of international protections beyond social welfare needs to the more extensive human rights guaranteed to adults. The original Polish draft, which mirrored the 1959 Declaration, was rejected, but in its place, the General Assembly adopted a more wide-ranging document which had been 10 years in the making and which followed extensive consultation. Its adoption on 20 November 1989 was timed to coincide with the thirtieth anniversary of the 1959 Declaration.

We discussed the substance of the UNCRC in Chapter 2 and now turn our attention to several other international conventions which have as their aim the special protection of children. First we describe the Hague Protection of Children Convention, which aims to secure co-operation between States in respect of protective action required for children. Secondly, we look briefly at the Council of Europe's recent Convention on Contact concerning Children. We conclude with an assessment of the international conventions which attempt to regulate international child abduction and intercountry adoption.

THE HAGUE CHILD PROTECTION CONVENTION 1996

The full title of the Hague Child Protection Convention is the Hague Convention on Jurisdiction, Applicable Law, Recognition, Enforcement and Co-operation in Respect of Parental Responsibility and Measures for the Protection of Children[1]. It is a revised and modified version of the little-known and little-used Hague Convention on the Protection of Minors 1961[2]. It would not be an exaggeration to say that few family lawyers had even heard of the 1961 Convention and even fewer knew anything about it. This is not perhaps surprising since both the 1961 and the 1996 Conventions are more the territory of private international lawyers than they are of family lawyers. The Child Protection Convention is concerned with the classic conflicts issues of jurisdiction, applicable law, recognition and enforcement, as its full title makes clear. It is not concerned with substantive rights and there was fierce resistance at The Hague to the incorporation of any such rights in the Convention.

It must also be appreciated that the 1996 Convention is a 'sister' Convention to two other Conventions emanating from the Hague Conference on Private International Law. These are the Hague Child Abduction Convention[3] and the Hague Convention on Inter-Country Adoption[4]. This is important for two reasons. The first is that the Child Protection Convention is not directly

---

1 For a concise and helpful discussion of the Convention, see A-M Hutchinson and MH Bennett 'The Hague Child Protection Convention 1996' [1998] Fam Law 35 and G Van Bueren 'Annual Review of International Family Law' in A Bainham (ed) *The International Survey of Family Law 1996* (Martinus Nijhoff, 1998) at pp 7–10. For an evaluation of the Convention alongside other Hague 'Children's Conventions', see L Silberman, 'The Hague Children's Conventions: The Internationalization of Family Law' in SN Katz, J Eekelaar and M McClean (eds) *Cross Currents* (Oxford University Press, 2000) p 589, especially at pp 597–606. The Convention finally came into force following the ratification by Slovakia, in January 2002.

2 The full title of which was the Convention on the Power of the Authorities and the Law Applicable in Respect of the Protection of Minors. The 1961 Convention was something of a flop having been ratified by just 11 States, all of which were European.

3 Discussed at pp 742 et seq.

4 Discussed at pp 765 et seq.

concerned with these two great international problems of child abduction and intercountry adoption since they are governed by other Conventions. The second is that efforts have been made to avoid clashes between the respective Conventions so that, for example, the Child Protection Convention should not operate in a way which contradicts the fundamental principles under the Abduction Convention governing the return of children wrongfully removed[1]. So far as substantive rights are concerned, the point should also be made that action taken under the 1996 Convention should be consistent with the rights enshrined in the UNCRC.

What is the Convention about?

If the 1996 Convention is not about substantive rights and not (at least not directly) about abduction or intercountry adoption, the reader may legitimately wonder exactly what it *is* about.

Silberman[2] has identified a number of matters which might be covered by the Convention. These include:

'The very simple task of assuring that measures taken with respect to the protection of a child or an order attributing parental responsibility to a particular adult in one country are honoured in another country ... For example, if an order entitles someone to act for a child with respect to a social, education, or medical situation, the Convention requires recognition of that order.'

The Convention thus 'makes possible the recognition of single and straightforward measures taken in one country without necessitating additional action in a second country'. The Convention obligations with respect to co-operation and material assistance might include 'locating a missing child, notification that a child in serious danger is in another State, facilitation through mediation or other means of possible solutions to disputes, and consultation when authorities in one State take steps to place a child in care in another State'[3].

The objects of the Convention are set out in Article 1, and in Article 3 there is a non-exhaustive list of matters in relation to which contracting States may take *protective measures*. This is followed by a list of matters specified in Article 4 which are excluded from the scope of the Convention.

Objects of the Convention

Article 1 describes the objects of the Convention which include determining the State with jurisdiction to take protective measures; the law to be applied; the applicable law governing parental responsibility; providing for the recognition and enforcement of the protective measures taken in all contracting States to achieve the purposes of the Convention.

The Convention in principle applies to both protection of the child's person and the child's property, and 'child' for these purposes includes persons 'from the

---

1   The matter is governed by Article 7, the general principle (subject to limited exceptions) being that the State from which the child has been removed, which will normally be that of the child's habitual residence, should retain the welfare jurisdiction and hence the jurisdiction to take protective measures under the 1996 Convention. See further A-M Hutchinson and MH Bennett (above) at pp 36–37.

2   (Above) at p 597.

3   Ibid at p 605.

moment of their birth until they reach the age of 18 years'[1]. Attempts at The Hague to include the 'unborn child' were resisted.

Included matters
It is clear from Article 3 that, inter alia, States may take protective measures in relation to the attribution, delegation, exercise and termination of parental responsibility; custody rights (which include residence and access issues); guardianship; foster-care or institutional care including the provision of care by Kafala (a form of Islamic guardianship) or care in an analogous institution; supervision by a public authority of the care of a child and the administration, conservation and disposal of a child's property.

Excluded matters
Article 4 contains an exhaustive list of matters which are outside the scope of the Convention. These are establishing or contesting a parent–child relationship; measures relating to adoption; the child's name; emancipation; maintenance; trusts and succession; public educational and health measures; and penal and immigration matters.

It has been suggested[2] that these exclusions fall essentially into three categories:

(1) matters which of themselves cannot be said to be protective of the child;
(2) matters which touch on general public law; and
(3) matters already covered by other Conventions.

General principles under the Convention
The central principle in the operation of the Convention is Article 5. This provides that 'the judicial or administrative authorities of the contracting State of the habitual residence of the child have jurisdiction to take measures directed to the protection of the child's person or property'. Thus, the normal rule is that the child's habitual residence will dictate jurisdiction. It should, however, be borne in mind that this may change where the child leaves one country and establishes a new habitual residence in another.

The test of habitual residence could cause difficulty in the case of internationally displaced children and refugees who 'have severed links with their former State of habitual residence' but 'their situation is too precarious to have established a new State of habitual residence'[3]. The Convention in these circumstances allows the State in whose territory the child now is to take protective measures. In a number of other respects, the Convention allows for flexibility in jurisdictional matters and encourages co-operation between States. Thus, it is possible for the State of the child's habitual residence to relinquish jurisdiction in favour of another State where it considers this appropriate[4], and it is also possible for that other State to request this as being in the child's best interests[5]. In all *urgent* cases, the authority of the State in whose territory the child is present has

---

1 Article 2. The 1996 Convention uses the term 'child' rather than 'minor', which was the term used in the 1961 Convention.
2 A-M Hutchinson and MH Bennett (above) at p 36.
3 G Van Bueren (above) at p 9.
4 Article 8.
5 Article 9.

jurisdiction to take 'any necessary measures of protection'[1]. Finally, there are limited exceptions which allow a State which is not that of the child's habitual residence, but which is exercising a divorce jurisdiction, to take measures of protection[2].

A primary feature of the Convention is to avoid conflicts of jurisdiction and secure co-operation between States in taking necessary measures to protect children. To this end, and in keeping with other Hague Conventions, States are obliged to designate a Central Authority with responsibility for the discharge of their functions under the Convention. Only time will tell whether the Convention is more effective than its predecessor in achieving these aims.

CONVENTION ON CONTACT CONCERNING CHILDREN

The Council of Europe adopted the Convention on Contact concerning Children on 3 May 2002 and opened it for signature on 14 October that year. The Convention is the result of recognition that the question of transfrontier contact with children has become more pressing and its central aim is to improve the machinery for international co-operation in relation to this problem and to establish safeguards for the return of children after a period of contact.

The Convention uses the terminology of 'contact' rather than that of 'access' in order to strengthen the notion that children are holders of certain rights. It was thought to be more consistent with this idea to refer to contact concerning children with different persons rather than just to the rights of certain persons to have access to children. It was also thought that this was more consistent with the jurisprudence of the ECHR[3].

The particular mischief at which the Convention is directed is the fear of the resident parent, in allowing transfrontier contact, that the child may not be returned by the non-resident parent and, conversely, the danger that a non-resident parent allowed little or no contact with the child may abduct the child[4]. The Convention builds on other conventions recognising rights of contact. In particular, it is noted that Article 8 of the ECHR 'guarantees ... the right of a parent and his or her child to maintain regular contact with each other' and that 'the organs of implementation of the ECHR, the European Court of Human Rights and the former Commission of Human Rights, have recognized the existence of this right in their case law and considered that this right could only be excluded on serious grounds in the best interests of the child (eg as a measure necessary to protect the morals or health of the child, etc)'[5]. It is stressed that the Contact Convention supports, but does not affect, the way in which existing international instruments operate. However, since practice had revealed that the provisions of the existing international instruments concerning contact were insufficient and that additional measures might be necessary to improve their effectiveness, the Convention seeks to fill this gap, especially by establishing principles which could be applied in a uniform manner by States.

---

1   Article 11.
2   Article 10.
3   See Council of Europe *Explanatory Report to the Convention on Contact concerning Children*, para 6.
4   Ibid, para 7.
5   Ibid, para 8.

The objectives of the Convention are set out in Article 1 and are:

(a) to determine general principles to be applied to contact orders;
(b) to fix appropriate standards and guarantees to ensure the proper exercise of contact and the immediate return of children at the end of the period of contact; and
(c) to establish co-operation between central authorities, judicial authorities and other bodies in order to promote and improve contact between children and their parents and other persons having family ties with children.

Chapter II of the Convention sets out general principles to be applied to contact orders. It requires States parties to 'adopt such legislative and other measures as may be necessary to ensure that the principles contained in this chapter are applied by judicial authorities when making, amending, suspending or revoking contact orders'.

These general principles include the following.

(1) A child and his or her parents have the right to maintain regular contact with each other[1].
(2) Such contact may only be restricted or excluded where necessary in the best interests of the child[2].
(3) Where it is not in the best interests of a child to maintain unsupervised contact, the possibility of supervised personal contact or other forms of contact with the parent must be considered[3].
(4) Subject to the child's best interests, contact may be established between the child and persons other than his or her parents having family ties with the child[4].
(5) A child considered by the internal law as having sufficient understanding has the right, unless this would be manifestly contrary to his or her best interests, to receive all relevant information, be consulted and express his or her views[5], with due weight being given to those views[6].

The Convention then sets out a further set of principles governing the resolution of contact disputes, the encouragement of agreements over contact and the implementation of contact orders. The more significant include the following.

(1) Judicial authorities are to take all appropriate measures to ensure that both parents are informed of the importance for their child and for both of them of establishing and maintaining regular contact with their child[7].
(2) Judicial authorities are to take all appropriate measures to encourage parents and other persons having family ties with the child to reach amicable agreements with respect to contact[8].

---

1 Article 4(1).
2 Article 4(2).
3 Article 4(3).
4 Article 5(1).
5 Article 6(1).
6 Article 6(2).
7 Article 7(a).
8 Article 7(b).

(3) States parties must take appropriate measures to ensure that contact orders are carried into effect[1].

(4) Each State party must provide for and promote the use of 'safeguards and guarantees'[2]. The intention here is to try to ensure not only that a contact order is carried into effect, but that the child is returned at the end of the period of contact and is not improperly removed. Those safeguards and guarantees for ensuring that the new order is carried into effect include supervision of contact, the provision of travel and accommodation expenses, securities to be deposited and fines. Those for ensuring return of the child or preventing the child's improper removal include the surrender of passports, financial guarantees, charges on property and undertakings. Such measures are to be in writing and form part of the contact order[3].

Chapter III of the Convention is concerned with the measures designed to promote and improve transfrontier contact. Each State party is required to establish a Central Authority to carry out the functions of the Convention in this respect[4]. Among the more important duties of Central Authorities will be to take all appropriate steps to discover the whereabouts of a child, secure the transmission of requests for information and to keep each other informed of any difficulties likely to arise in applying the Convention[5]. It is also provided that the judicial authorities, Central Authorities and the social and other bodies of States parties must co-operate in relation to proceedings regarding transfrontier contact[6]. States parties must also establish a system for the recognition and enforcement of orders for contact and custody made in other States parties[7]. Importantly, where a child is not returned at the end of a period of transfrontier contact, the competent authorities must upon request 'ensure the child's immediate return, where applicable, by applying the relevant provisions of international instruments, of internal law and by implementing, where appropriate, such safeguards and guarantees as may be provided in the contact order'[8]. This Article is significant in illustrating the relationship between the Convention and the other relevant Conventions, for example the Hague Abduction Convention. Where, for example, the principles of the Hague Convention require the return of the child where there has been a 'wrongful taking' or 'retention', that Convention will apply. But where it is difficult to establish that there has been a violation of the Hague Convention, the Contact Convention may come into play and impose a separate obligation to return the child based on breach of the contact order. Ursula Kilkelly[9] summarises this relationship between the Contact Convention and other Conventions as follows:

'The Convention is not intended to affect the operation of other international instruments and, in the event that a child is not returned following arranged contact, it leaves it to the other

---

1 Article 9.
2 Article 10.
3 Article 10(3).
4 Article 11(1).
5 Article 12.
6 Article 13.
7 Article 14.
8 Article 16.
9 U Kilkelly 'Annual Review of International Family Law' in A Bainham (ed) *The International Survey of Family Law (2003 Edition)* (Family Law, 2003) at p 6.

applicable conventions to address the return of the child to the place of habitual residence. Rather, by providing a working framework within which a child and his or her parent's right to contact can be implemented successfully, the Convention aims to avoid the damaging consequences of non-enforcement and breach of contact orders with which the other international treaties are concerned.'

BRUSSELS II AND BRUSSELS II bis

Brussels II or, to give it its full title, Council Regulation EC 1347/2000 on Jurisdiction and the Recognition of Judgments in Matrimonial Matters and in Matters of Parental Responsibility for Children of Both Spouses was not itself a convention, but a Regulation of the European Union. It thus applied, self-evidently, only to Member States in the EU, but there is a considerable overlap in membership between these and Member States of the Council of Europe and European States who are parties to the Hague Abduction Convention[1]. The European Union has not historically been much concerned directly with family law matters, although it has had a strong interest in the family. The Brussels II Regulation was itself best viewed as a by-product of the EU's economic principle of free movement of workers. Brussels II was in effect an extension of Brussels I, the Convention on Jurisdiction and Enforcement of Judgments in Civil and Commercial Matters. Brussels I had excluded from its ambit, inter alia, matters of status and rights arising from marriage. Brussels II extended to civil proceedings relating to divorce, legal separation or marriage annulment and civil proceedings relating to parental responsibility for the children of both spouses on the occasion of the above matrimonial proceedings[2].

The Regulation laid down *exclusive* rules of jurisdiction to determine the competency of the court of a Member State to rule on status and matters relating to parental responsibility. The central governing concept was that of 'habitual residence'[3]. The aim, wherever possible, was to avoid parallel proceedings taking place in Member States. Chapter III of the Regulation governed recognition and enforcement of judgments by Member States. Member States were under a general obligation to recognise judgments given in other Member States without any special procedure being required[4]. In limited circumstances, any interested party might apply for a decision for non-recognition of such a judgment[5] which included situations where recognition would be manifestly contrary to public policy, for procedural defects relating to the judgment or because the judgment was irreconcilable with an earlier judgment given in another Member State or a non-Member State or, importantly, where taking into account the best interests of the child, it was given (except in the case of urgency) without the child being given an opportunity of being heard, contrary to the fundamental principles of procedure in the Member State in question[6].

---

1   For an informative account of the background to the Regulation, its scope and its principal provisions relating to jurisdiction, recognition and enforcement, see G Douglas and N Lowe 'Annual Review of International Family Law' in A Bainham (ed) *The International Survey of Family Law (2002 Edition)* (Family Law, 2002) especially at pp 4–11.
2   Article 1.
3   Articles 2 and 3.
4   Article 14(1).
5   Article 14(3)
6   Article 15(1).

So far as enforcement of judgments relating to parental responsibility are concerned, the Regulation[1] provided that an enforceable judgment on the exercise of parental responsibility made in one Member State could be declared enforceable in another Member State on the application of an interested party.

Brussels II has now been repealed by Brussels II bis, Council Regulation (EC) 2201/2003 concerning Jurisdiction and the Recognition and Enforcement of Judgments in Matrimonial Matters and the Matters of Parental Responsibility[2]. The new Regulation came into force on 1 August 2004 and is to be fully implemented from 1 March 2005. The principal changes brought about by the new Regulation relate to an extension of the scope of the original Regulation rather than a radical revision of it.

These modifications may be described as follows. First, the expression 'parental responsibility' is greatly extended by removing the previous necessary link with matrimonial proceedings and now covers other types of private proceedings as well as public proceedings. Step-children will, for example, now be included where before they were excluded. Secondly, and controversially, the new Regulation now explicitly governs cases of child abduction. Thus, both the Hague Convention and the Regulation may in future be utilised by Member States of the European Union in abduction cases. Thirdly, the new Regulation contains provisions which, in relation to the issue of contact with children, will enable an order in one Member State to be directly enforceable in another Member State. Clearly there will be overlap here with the principles of the Council of Europe's Contact Convention, always remembering that membership of the European Union is not identical with that of the Council of Europe.

THE ABDUCTION CONVENTIONS

Better transport communications across the world have contributed to the growing problem of international child abduction[3]. The English law reports are now replete with cases involving the 'snatching' of children, usually, but not

---

1   Article 21.
2   For an introductory description of the new Regulation, see P Beaton 'Brussels II – The Sequel' [2004] Fam Law 170; P Beaton 'Brussels II bis Encore' [2004] *International Family Law* 4. See also A Schulz 'The New Brussels II Regulation and the Hague Conventions of 1980 and 1996' [2004] *International Family Law* 22; U Rölke and M Busch 'Effect of Brussels II bis on Child Protection and Youth Welfare Services' [2004] *International Family Law* 27.
3   See, generally, *Bromley's Family Law* (9th edn) (Butterworths, 1998) at ch 13; and SM Cretney, JM Masson and R Bailey-Harris *Principles of Family Law* (7th edn) (Sweet & Maxwell, 2002) at ch 21. See also G Van Bueren *The Best Interests of the Child: International Cooperation on Child Abduction* (Queen Mary and Westfield College, London, 1993). A particularly helpful article is D McClean 'International child abduction – some recent trends' [1997] CFLQ 387. See also D Harris 'Is the Strength of the Hague Convention on Child Abduction being Diluted by the Courts? – the English Perspective' [1999] IFL 35. Two books on the subject are P Beaumont and P McEleavy *The Hague Convention on International Child Abduction* (1999) and A-M Hutchinson and H Setright *International Parental Child Abduction* (2nd edn) (Jordans, 2003). See further L Silberman 'The Hague Children's Conventions: The Internationalization of Child Law' in SN Katz, J Eekelaar and M Maclean (eds) *Cross Currents* (Oxford University Press, 2000) at pp 590–596 and J Caldwell 'Child Welfare Defences in Child Abduction Cases – Some Recent Developments' [2001] CFLQ 121. For an evaluation of the principles of the Convention set against the principles in the UNCRC, see R Schuz 'The Hague Child Abduction

invariably, by one parent from the other, either to or from England[1]. We consider here the legal mechanisms for attempting to prevent the unlawful removal of children from England, and the law and procedures which govern attempts to recover abducted children. We also look at the jurisprudence of the English courts when considering requests for the return of children snatched *to* England. This provides some insight into what might be expected of a foreign court in the converse situation of a child taken *from* England[2]. Two international Conventions of 1980, the Hague Convention on the Civil Aspects of International Child Abduction ('the Hague Convention') and the European Convention on Recognition and Enforcement of Decisions concerning Custody of Children and Restoration of Custody of Children ('the European Convention'), regulate the return of children from those States which are parties to the respective Conventions. Both Conventions were implemented in the UK by the Child Abduction and Custody Act 1985. It is therefore necessary to examine not only the position of children taken to a country which is party to either Convention (and those brought to England from such a country) but also the situation of those children taken to or from countries which are not party to either Convention. We also look briefly at abduction *within* the different parts of the UK, a matter regulated by the Family Law Act 1986.

Preventing abduction

It is axiomatic that prevention is better than cure. Where a child is successfully removed from England, it may be difficult even to establish his whereabouts and more difficult still to secure his return. All available means should therefore be utilised to prevent removal in the first place. The matter is complicated by the fact that the Hague Convention can operate only where there has been a *wrongful taking* and, especially since the Children Act 1989, there may be some ambiguity about whether one parent is acting wrongfully in taking a child abroad[3]. Nevertheless, the general principles and procedures of the criminal and civil law can be stated with some confidence.

Convention and the United Nations Convention on the Rights of the Child' in P Lødrup and E Modvar (eds) *Family Life and Human Rights* (Gyldendal Akademisk, 2004) at p 721. The Reunite website in England (www.reunite.org) also contains much useful information.

1   McClean (above) notes, however, that the statistics reveal an important change in the pattern of abductions. Contrary to the public image of abduction by a 'non-custodial' father, two-thirds of abductions were carried out by the mother who was usually also the primary carer of the children. See further the remarks of Hale J in *S v H (Abduction: Access Rights)* [1997] 1 FLR 971 at 977. More recently this figure has risen to 72%, as noted by Hale LJ in *Re TB and JB (Abduction: Grave Risk of Harm)* [2001] 2 FLR 515 at 527, where she emphasised that the abductor in these cases was 'the parent who has always looked after the children, upon whom the children rely for all their basic needs, and with whom their main security lies'.

2   For a discussion of the workings of the Hague Convention in the English courts, see CS Bruch 'Child Abduction and the English Courts' in A Bainham, DS Pearl and R Pickford (eds) *Frontiers of Family Law* (2nd edn) (John Wiley & Sons, 1995) at p 52; and see also CS Bruch 'International Child Abduction Cases: Experience Under the 1980 Hague Convention' in J Eekelaar and P Sarcevic (eds) *Parenthood in Modern Society: Legal and Social Issues for the Twenty-First Century* (Martinus Nijhoff, 1993).

3   See pp 751 et seq.

The criminal law

Under s 1 of the Child Abduction Act 1984 it is an offence for anyone 'connected with a child' to take or send a child under the age of 16 years out of the UK without the appropriate consent[1]. This is the consent of each person who is the child's mother, father (assuming in the case of the unmarried father that he has acquired parental responsibility), guardian, or anyone with a residence order or the leave of the court. There are limited defences available[2]. An exception applies where a residence order is in force – anyone with such an order may unilaterally remove a child for a period of up to one month[3]. Thus, apart from this provision, in the usual case where there is no court order in existence, it is a criminal offence for *one* parent to take a child out of the country without the consent of the other[4]. In the case of unmarried parents (assuming the father has not taken steps to acquire parental responsibility[5]), the mother has authority to act alone. A parent may also commit the common law offence of kidnapping[6], or false imprisonment[7] in removing the child without the appropriate consent, although these charges should not be brought where the facts upon which they are grounded would constitute the statutory offence[8].

Since child abduction is a criminal offence, the assistance of the police may be sought to prevent its commission. In an emergency, when an imminent removal is suspected, informing the police is the best short-term action to take. The police have power to arrest anyone they reasonably suspect of attempting to take a child out of the UK. More importantly, they can effect a 'port stop' through their computerised 'All Ports Warning System'. The effect of a port stop is that immigration officers at all ports and airports will hold the name of the child at risk on an index and will thereafter seek to assist the police in preventing the child's removal. Under a Practice Direction[9], the police will not automatically institute a port alert. They must be convinced that the risk of removal is real and imminent, ie within 48 hours. In order to enable them to act, the police should be given full particulars about the child, the alleged abductor and travel plans where these are

---

1 It is also an offence under the Child Abduction Act 1984, s 2 for anyone who does *not* have parental responsibility or 'custody' of the child to remove a child aged under 16, or keep him, out of the lawful control of the person entitled to lawful control. It is a defence to show that the person concerned acted with lawful authority or had a reasonable excuse, and there is a special defence which can be relied on by the unmarried father or by someone who believes that he is the child's father. This chapter is concerned only with international abductions and the detailed provisions of s 2 are beyond the scope of the present discussion. For a comparatively rare report of a prosecution under s 2, see *O v Governor of Holloway Prison and Government of USA* [2000] 1 FLR 147 in which the Divisional Court held that the section requires proof of mens rea and does not create an offence, as the justices had thought, of strict liability.
2 Child Abduction Act 1984, s 1(5).
3 Children Act 1989, s 13(2).
4 It is not entirely clear whether a positive consent is required or whether an absence of objection on the part of the other parent would suffice. The latter seems more practicable, especially in view of the defences in s 1(5) of the Child Abduction Act 1984.
5 See Chapter 5 above, where we noted that many more such men will now acquire parental responsibility through the process of birth registration.
6 *R v D* [1984] AC 778.
7 *R v Rahman* (1985) 81 Cr App R 349.
8 *R v C (Kidnapping: Abduction)* [1991] 2 FLR 252.
9 *Practice Direction (Child: Removal from Jurisdiction)* [1986] 1 All ER 983 and Home Office Circular 21/1986.

known. The child's name will remain on the stop list for four weeks. After this, a renewed complaint will become necessary if continuing protection is sought. Where the 'child' is aged 16 years or over, the Child Abduction Act 1984 does not apply and a court order is required. But in view of the increased legal autonomy of this age group, it is doubtful how often it will be appropriate to intervene in what may be a joint decision by parent and child to leave the country[1].

The civil law

Passport control
Until 1998 it was possible for children to be added to their parent's passport, but since October of that year this has no longer been possible. The change in the rules was designed to combat the problem of abduction. If the court has made an order prohibiting the removal of the child from the jurisdiction, the Passport Agency may be requested by a concerned person not to issue a passport to the child. The court itself may order the surrender of an existing passport in these circumstances. Under its inherent jurisdiction the court may order the deposit of a foreign passport with solicitors. Thus in *Re A-K (Foreign Passport: Jurisdiction)*[2] the Court of Appeal upheld the order of the judge for the surrender of the father's Iranian passport to his solicitors. The judge had expressly stated that this course would give him easier access to his passport. If a request were unreasonably refused by the mother, the father could make an application to the court and the mother's conduct could be reviewed.

Private court orders
A number of options exist for obtaining orders in the civil courts which have the effect of restraining a child's removal from the jurisdiction. One is to ward the child, since wardship has, as one of its immediate effects, an automatic prohibition on removing the ward from the jurisdiction[3]. A cheaper alternative since the Children Act may be to seek a s 8 order. A residence order will regulate where the child is to live and it will be incompatible with its terms for the *non-resident* parent to take the child abroad even when exercising contact or otherwise discharging parental responsibility[4]. In *Re K (Residence Order: Securing Contact)*[5] the father was (unusually) given a residence order in relation to a two-year-old boy, largely because of the judge's assessment that the mother was untrustworthy, might spirit the child away to India and thereafter deny the father contact. A residence order will also empower the *resident* parent to take the child abroad for up to one month without the non-resident parent's knowledge or consent. Thus, the court should be wary of granting a residence order to a parent if there is the slightest suspicion that that parent might use the apparently innocuous 'holiday provision' as a cloak

---

1 Although Cretney, Masson and Bailey-Harris note that a child of this age could be kidnapped where he is not consenting to leave the country. See SM Cretney, JM Masson and R Bailey-Harris *Principles of Family Law* (7th edn) (Sweet & Maxwell, 2002) at p 672.

2 [1997] 2 FLR 569.

3 Although this is now qualified by the Family Law Act 1986, s 38 as regards removal to another part of the UK.

4 Section 2(8) of the Children Act precludes the exercise of parental responsibility in a way which is incompatible with a court order.

5 [1999] 1 FLR 583.

for a permanent abduction[1]. However, the residence order is more likely to be invoked as a device *against* abduction rather than a vehicle for it, and it is established that a short-term residence order may be granted in exceptional cases ex parte[2]. Perhaps the most appropriate order will be the prohibited steps order, the specific purpose of which can be to restrain removal[3]. As a practical matter, it would still be necessary to instigate a port alert to enforce s 8 orders, but the existence of the orders should certainly secure the ready co-operation of the police.

Parents, especially at the time of divorce, should be alive to the necessity of making formal applications for s 8 orders where there is the slightest risk of abduction. It should be remembered that s 1(5) of the Children Act (the 'no order' principle) is, rightly or wrongly, likely to be interpreted by many courts as creating a legal presumption against court orders. In a large majority of cases, there will, therefore, be no order unless one is specifically sought. Even where it is, the onus will be on the applicant to show that it is necessary. Yet there is now sufficient ambiguity about the authority of parents under the Children Act that the wisest course will be to seek an order whenever there is a hint that one parent may, at some future point, try to take the child abroad. Thus, as Bruch advises[4], residence orders should always be sought 'if there have been threats of abduction, or if the parents come from different countries or either has strong foreign connections (such as lengthy vacations, a second residence, extended family or employment opportunities abroad)'.

Other reasons why civil procedures may be advantageous[5] are that: they may act as a deterrent to abduction; they may secure official assistance in tracing the child; breach of the order will constitute contempt of court and may be punished as such; and passport control, as we have seen, will be facilitated.

Leave to take children out of the jurisdiction

Where a parent who is the child's primary carer (usually but not invariably the mother) wishes to emigrate from the UK, or at least leave for an extended period of time, with the child, the appropriate course of action will be to apply to the court for leave to take the child out of the jurisdiction[6]. Often the courts have had to grapple with a conflict of interest between the mother who wishes to make a new life abroad, with or without a new partner, and the father who wishes to maintain a realistic relationship with the child. The earlier decisions tended to support the

---

1   The danger of the provision being used for a disguised abduction was acknowledged during the debates on the Children Bill, but it was the view of Sir Nicholas Lyell (the then Solicitor-General) that the law should reflect 'normal and reasonable' behaviour. In other words, such cases would be vastly outnumbered by those of parents taking bona fide holidays, and the law should reflect this.

2   *Re B (A Minor) (Residence Order: Ex Parte)* [1992] 2 FLR 1.

3   As in *Re D (A Minor) (Child: Removal from Jurisdiction)* [1992] 1 All ER 892.

4   CS Bruch 'Child Abduction and the English Courts' in A Bainham, DS Pearl and R Pickford (eds) *Frontiers of Family Law* (2nd edn) (John Wiley & Sons, 1995) at p 55.

5   See the discussion in *Bromley's Family Law* (9th edn) (Butterworths, 1998) at pp 481–483.

6   For a recent discussion of the 'relocation' issue in the USA, see S Katz 'Continuity of Relationships in Child Custody' in A Bainham (ed) *The International Survey of Family Law (2004 Edition)* (Family Law, 2004) at p 487. For developments in New Zealand which do not entirely chime with the English approach, see B Atkin 'From Parental Relocation, Rights and Responsibilities to "Relationship" Property' in A Bainham (ed) *The International Survey of Family Law (2003 Edition)* (Family Law, 2003) at p 323.

mother's plan, certainly if it was properly thought out and reasonable[1]. Later decisions, while still attaching considerable importance to the genuineness and reasonableness of the mother's proposals, also showed a greater awareness of the need to take into account the potentially drastic effect of emigration on the child's relationship with the father[2].

The Court of Appeal's decision in *Re T (Removal from Jurisdiction)*[3] perhaps best illustrates the kind of balance which the courts attempted to strike in these cases. Here, following divorce, the mother began a relationship with a man from France and applied for leave to take the three-year-old child of the family there[4]. The child lived with his mother but had overnight weekly contact with the paternal grandparents. The father was suspicious that the mother's proposal was designed to terminate his contact with the child and he countered by seeking a residence order. The mother hinted that she might go to France anyway but later made it clear that she would not go without the child. The judge refused leave on the basis that the proposal was ill-considered, ill-prepared and contrary to the child's interest and made a residence order in favour of the father.

Allowing the mother's appeal against the residence order, the Court of Appeal held that mothers who were generally competent mothers should not be at risk of losing primary care where they made an unsuccessful attempt to obtain leave to take the child out of the jurisdiction. The judge had been entitled to refuse leave on welfare grounds but ought not to have altered the child's residence as a consequence and without seeking the advice of the court welfare officer. There had been a failure to realise that the father's application for a residence order was a purely defensive ploy designed to protect his contact arrangements. The appropriate order was a residence order for the mother with reasonable contact for the father and grandparents, the effect of which was to preserve the status quo[5].

These principles now have to be evaluated in the light of human rights requirements, and the consideration that to allow one parent permanently to leave the jurisdiction with the child is potentially an unjustified invasion of the rights of the other parent and the child to respect for family life under Article 8.

---

1   See particularly the pre-Children Act decision of the Court of Appeal in *Lonslow v Hennig (formerly Lonslow)* [1986] 2 FLR 378, where the mother was allowed to emigrate to New Zealand with the children. The Court of Appeal confirmed in *H v H (Residence Order: Leave to Remove from Jurisdiction)* [1995] 1 FLR 529 that the Children Act has not altered the underlying factors which govern applications for leave.

2   See, for example, *Re K (A Minor) (Removal from Jurisdiction)* [1992] 2 FLR 98 where the mother was refused leave to take a young child to the USA. Her plan to pursue post-graduate education there was considered by the court to be ill-thought out and Thorpe J emphasised the very grave importance of the continuation and development of the relationship between the father and child.

3   [1996] 2 FLR 352.

4   For another case involving France in which the court concluded that, paradoxically, the children's relationship with the father would be better safeguarded by granting the mother leave than by refusing it, see *Re B (Minors) (Removal from Jurisdiction)* [1994] 2 FCR 309.

5   But see also the decision of the Court of Appeal in *Re H (Application to Remove from Jurisdiction)* [1998] 1 FLR 848 in which a father who had been very involved with the care of the child nevertheless failed to prevent the mother from obtaining leave to take the child to Alabama. The mother had by this time married an American, and the court held that there had to be some compelling reason to justify a court preventing the primary carer from taking a reasonable decision to live outside the jurisdiction.

The balancing exercise under Article 8(2) is complicated by the fact that the parent seeking leave (we will assume the mother) also has the right under Article 8 to respect for her *private life*, a notion which embraces such personal decisions as the desire to emigrate[1].

The issue came to a head in *Payne v Payne*[2] where the Court of Appeal, reviewing the courts' jurisprudence on the matter over many years, rejected the father's argument that the settled principle applied by the courts was in breach of the ECHR and in conflict with the Children Act 1989. The argument was essentially that the Convention enshrined a right of contact between parent and child, as an aspect of the right to respect for family life under Article 8, and that the Children Act also required much greater significance to be attached to the preservation of such contact. Mr Payne went on to argue that the effect of the case-law was to create an unwarranted legal presumption in favour of leave which was in breach of his right of contact. The Court of Appeal refused to accept that the courts have applied any such *legal* presumption, reiterating that the matter was governed by the welfare principle. Although the 'reasonable proposal' of the mother did not have the status of a presumption in favour of granting leave, it was nevertheless a factor of 'great weight'. But the court relied in the end on the jurisprudence of the ECtHR which supports the proposition that the best interests of the child may in the final analysis outweigh the Convention rights of a parent[3].

Post-*Payne* decisions have been virtually 'one-way traffic' in favour of granting leave where the proposal is reasonable[4]. *Re B; Re S (Removal from Jurisdiction)*[5] is an important case because the Court of Appeal for the first time emphasised the importance of the interests of the reconstituted family where the need for relocation was brought about primarily because of the employment or nationality of the step-parent or new partner. In the first case the mother wanted to relocate to South Africa having formed a relationship with a South African businessman, while in the second case the mother had repartnered with a citizen of the Philippines who had a right of residence in Western Australia and wished to move to Perth. Both were granted leave subject to agreed contact for the respective fathers. The Court of Appeal held that a mother's attachment to a man whose

---

1　For an illustration of the balancing exercise, see *Re G-A (A Child) (Removal from Jurisdiction: Human Rights)* [2001] 1 FCR 43 where the court balanced the mother's right to decide to take up employment in New York against the father's right to respect for family life, coming down in favour of the mother.

2　[2001] 1 FLR 1052. For a more detailed commentary, see A Bainham 'Taking Children Abroad: Human Rights, Welfare and the Courts' (2001) CLJ 489.

3　The court relied on *Johansen v Norway* (1996) 23 EHRR 33. More recently *Yousef v The Netherlands* [2003] 1 FLR 210 provides further support for this stance.

4　But see *Re C (Leave to Remove from Jurisdiction)* [2000] 2 FLR 457, decided just before *Payne*, for a comparatively rare example of a refusal to grant leave. The Court of Appeal upheld the view of the judge that the mother's reasonable proposal to move to Singapore with her new husband was outweighed on the facts by the severe limitation this would place on the father's contact with the child. See also the recent decision of Hedley J in *Re Y (Leave to Remove from Jurisdiction)* [2004] 2 FLR 330, where the American mother was refused leave to take the child from Wales to the USA. There were, however, special factors in the case which distinguished it from the ordinary run of applications for leave. The child was bilingual, with Welsh as the preferred language, and care was shared more or less equally between the mother and the father. In these circumstances, it was held that, weighing the gains and losses to the child, the least detrimental course would be for the child to remain in Wales.

5　[2003] 2 FLR 1043.

employment required him to live abroad could be a decisive factor. Secondly, the court had to consider the impact of refusal of permission on the new family and on the step-father, which applied with greater force where he was a foreign national. In such circumstances, to frustrate relocation could jeopardise the new family's survival and potential for fulfilment and happiness. This would be manifestly contrary to the child's welfare. It was acknowledged that the court might refuse an application if satisfied that the move was impelled by the mother's selfish desire to pursue a relationship which was injurious to the children. In *L v L (Leave to Remove from Jurisdiction: Effect on Children)*[1] the mother's proposed relocation to the USA with the children was opposed on the basis that the elder child had moderate learning difficulties and special educational needs. The risk to disruption of the child's education was recognised but nonetheless the mother's plan was based on perfectly conventional career advancement. She was an exceptionally committed mother, and Johnson J took the view that to allow her reasonable expectations and those of her husband to be frustrated would seriously impair her emotional security and that of the children.

Finally, in *Re C (Permission to Remove from Jurisdiction)*[2] Charles J reiterated the now familiar principle that there was no legal presumption that once a proposal was shown to be reasonable permission should be granted. That was merely the first hurdle. The court should then ask whether the plan for relocation would promote the welfare of the child. If it could be shown that refusal to grant leave would have a detrimental effect on the primary carer, that would usually outweigh any harm caused to the child by the move. The inevitable reduction in contact with the non-resident parent would not usually be the decisive factor.

What the cases reveal is that, although the courts do not officially endorse a legal presumption in favour of leave where relocation plans are reasonable, in practice the conclusion in most cases reflects something not unlike a presumption to this effect.

Recovery of children

Action under the Hague Convention
The Hague Convention has been widely ratified by countries as far apart as Europe, the Western Hemisphere, Australasia and the Middle East, and remains under consideration in other States[3]. It has a global dimension obviously lacking in the case of the European Convention and Brussels II, which are confined to certain countries within Europe. It is wider, also, in that it may be invoked even

---

1 [2003] 1 FLR 900.
2 [2003] 1 FLR 1066.
3 The list of countries which have ratified or acceded to the Convention is a growing one. Over 70 countries had done so at the time of writing. See M Everall 'Child Abduction after the Hague Convention' [1990] Fam Law 169; and 'The Hague Convention: The Children Act and other recent developments' [1992] Fam Law 164. For an informative commentary on French practice under the Hague Convention, see A Cornec 'The Hague Convention on Abduction and Beyond: Conflicting Aims, Different Solutions – the French Practice' [1993] Fam Law 148. See also D McClean and K Beevers 'International Child Abduction – back to common law principles' [1995] CFLQ 128. For more recent articles on the Hague Convention, see fn 3 at p 742 above. Especially helpful are those by Schuz and Silberman. Specifically on English practice under the Convention, see N Lowe and A Perry 'International Child Abduction – the English Experience' (1999) 48 ICLQ 127.

where there is no prior court order, whereas the European Convention is confined in its operation to the enforcement of court orders. Beyond these distinctions, the two Conventions have similar aims which are to return abducted children promptly to their home countries so that any dispute as to their care is determined *there* and the alleged abductor is denied any tactical advantage from the abduction. In this way, it is also hoped to deter other such removals. As a general proposition, there will be a heavy presumption in favour of returning the child, and only to a limited extent will the court be able or prepared to investigate the merits of disputes over residence or upbringing[1]. Otherwise, the very purpose of the Conventions would be frustrated, but in exceptional cases return of the child may be successfully resisted. Increasingly, it has come to be appreciated that there is a tension between the dual objectives of securing the welfare of the child while upholding the integrity of the system. It must be the case that the best interests of individual children are occasionally sacrificed in the more general interests of the wider class of children in the international community. Since both Conventions are based on reciprocity between nations, the principles apply equally whether the child is taken from, or brought to, England.

Procedural matters – how is the Hague Convention invoked?
The Hague Convention may be invoked in relation to any child under the age of 16 years, habitually resident in one contracting State, who has been wrongfully removed to or retained in another contracting State[2]. The applicant seeking return of a child will probably begin by applying to the 'Central Authority' for the country of the child's habitual residence. Both the Hague and European Conventions require each contracting State to set up a Central Authority to undertake responsibility for the administration and handling of child abduction cases. A Special Commission at The Hague, which met in 2002, has produced a Guide to Good Practice for Central Authorities which also deals with implementation measures[3]. It is the task of the Central Authority to receive applications, collect all relevant information and institute the necessary action, perhaps including judicial proceedings, for recovery of the child. The Central Authority for England and Wales is the Child Abduction Unit, Department of Constitutional Affairs[4], although work is often delegated by it to private firms of solicitors. In practice, the Department will instruct a solicitor to act for the applicant who will

---

1   But undertakings may be required of the aggrieved parent as a condition of the child's return. See particularly *C v C (Minor: Abduction: Rights of Custody Abroad)* [1989] 1 WLR 654. See also *Re O (Child Abduction: Undertakings)* [1994] 2 FLR 349 and *Re M (Abduction: Undertakings)* [1995] 1 FLR 1021. For a critique of the practice of accepting undertakings, see D McClean 'International child abduction – some recent trends' [1997] CFLQ 387 at pp 392–395. The practice of accepting undertakings where there has been a context of domestic violence has been criticised. See M Kaye 'The Hague Convention and the Flight from Domestic Violence: How women and children are being returned by coach and four' [1999] IJLPF 191.
2   Article 4. As to the meaning of the child's habitual residence, see P Stone 'The habitual residence of a child' (1992) 4 JCL 170.
3   See *Guide to Good Practice under the Hague Convention of 25 October 1980 on the Civil Aspects of International Child Abduction, Part I: Central Authority Practice* and *Part II: Implementing Measures* (Hague Conference on Private International Law/Jordans, 2003). See also D Carter 'Child Abduction: The Role of the Central Authorities and Reunite' [2000] *International Family Law* 102.
4   The Child Abduction Unit, Department of Constitutional Affairs, 81 Chancery Lane, London WC2A 1DD. Tel: 020 7911 7045.

then file an application in the High Court, which has exclusive jurisdiction in these cases[1]. As an alternative, the applicant could decide to approach the foreign Central Authority direct, or even institute proceedings in that country. However, at least as far as removals *from* England are concerned, there are distinct advantages in going through the Department of Constitutional Affairs. As well as obtaining the expert assistance of the staff, legal aid will be granted, without regard to the usual means and merits test[2]. The court will then, subject to qualifications, order the child's immediate return to his place of habitual residence, if it finds that the child's removal or retention violated the custody rights of the applicant[3]. It must be emphasised that the circumstances in which the court will refuse to order the return of the child are narrowly defined, and generally restrictively interpreted, since it is an aim of the Hague Convention to prevent the domestic courts of the 'receiving' State from entering into the merits of the matter.

What is a wrongful removal or retention?
The Hague Convention can only be activated where the removal or retention was 'wrongful'. In order to establish this, it must be shown that, according to the law of the child's habitual residence[4], the actions were in breach of rights of custody attributed to a person, an institution or any other body *and* that, at the time of the removal or detention, those rights were actually exercised jointly or alone, or would have been but for the removal or retention[5]. It is *not* necessary for the applicant to hold a court order (as under the European Convention), although clearly the existence of a court order in the applicant's favour, especially a residence order, will help[6].

The question of the child's habitual residence may cause difficulties where the family has lived in more than one jurisdiction in the recent past[7]. This is a question of fact to be determined by the court. The crucial question will be what the child's habitual residence was *immediately before* the alleged wrongful removal or retention[8]. In principle the child's habitual residence will follow that of the

---

1 Child Abduction and Custody Act 1985, s 4.
2 For further discussion, see CS Bruch 'Child Abduction and the English Courts' in A Bainham, DS Pearl and R Pickford (eds) *Frontiers of Family Law* (2nd edn) (John Wiley & Sons, 1995) at pp 53–54.
3 Article 3. In *Re N (Child Abduction) (Habitual Residence)* [1993] 2 FLR 124, the Court of Appeal said that proceedings under the Hague Convention are neither adversarial nor inquisitorial but sui generis. The court has a statutory duty to apply the Convention if the necessary facts are present and, in so doing, it is concerned not only with the interests of the child but also with those of abducted children more generally.
4 See P Stone 'The Habitual Residence of a Child' (1992) 4 JCL 170, and more recently R Schuz 'Habitual Residence of Children under the Hague Child Abduction Convention: Theory and Practice' [2001] CFLQ 1.
5 Article 3.
6 Because of the ambiguities surrounding the concept of wrongfulness as it applies to parental responsibility.
7 See the review of cases under the Hague Convention by P Stone (above), especially at pp 171–172, and the House of Lords decisions in *Re J (A Minor) (Abduction: Custody Rights)* [1990] 2 AC 562 and *Re S (A Minor) (Custody: Habitual Residence)* [1997] 4 All ER 251. See also Schuz (above) who discusses two models for determining a child's habitual residence – the 'parental rights model' and the 'child-centred or objective model', preferring the latter, while acknowledging that it is the former that has held sway in English practice.
8 *Re S (A Minor) (Abduction)* [1991] 2 FLR 1.

person with parental responsibility, usually the parent. But where both have parental responsibility one parent may not change the child's habitual residence by acting independently[1]. The issue of what is wrongful will often be straightforward, but can be difficult in some cases, and the Children Act may have produced some added complications[2]. The action must be in breach of 'custody' rights[3], which for the purposes of English law usually means 'parental responsibility', but, as we have seen[4], parental responsibility may, because of its durability, be held by more than one person or institution jointly, each of which may prima facie be acting lawfully in taking independent action in relation to the child[5]. The matter is complicated further in that in some cases the courts have found a breach of 'custody' rights where the left-behind parent or carer does *not* possess parental responsibility. We discuss these cases below. We need to distinguish those cases in which there is a court order from those where there is none.

Where there is a court order
Where a court order is in existence, the position ought to be clear, since the order will usually make plain where the child is to live and what degree of contact or involvement parents or others are to have with the child. Thus, if the mother has a residence order in her favour, it will be incompatible with that order for the father to take the child abroad[6]. This would be a clear breach of the mother's 'custody' rights, despite the fact that, for many purposes other than residence, parental responsibility continues to be shared by *both* parents. But what if the mother, having obtained a residence order, herself takes the child out of the country? She is entitled under the order to do so, unilaterally, for up to one month, but what is the position if she then *retains* the child abroad for an extended period, perhaps indefinitely? The question is whether that retention is unlawful, given that the initial removal was lawful. The better view, advanced by Bruch[7], is that it is unlawful, since the mother's right to remove the child was a temporary one. The habitual residence of the child would thus remain in England and, according to English law, the retention beyond one month would be wrongful. However, the matter is not wholly free from doubt[8]. Bruch points out that the way around this problem is for the residence order itself to deal expressly with the question of trips abroad, if this appears to be in issue. The point is that the one-month rule will be

---

1   *Re N (Abduction: Habitual Residence)* [2000] 2 FLR 899.
2   CS Bruch 'Child Abduction and the English Courts' in A Bainham, DS Pearl and R Pickford (eds) *Frontiers of Family Law* (2nd edn) (John Wiley & Sons, 1995) at p 55.
3   For a case in which grandparents were found to have joint custodial rights, see *Re O (Child Abduction: Custody Rights)* [1997] 2 FLR 702.
4   At Chapters 2 and 4 above.
5   In particular, there is generally no duty to consult the other parent before taking action.
6   Section 2(8) of the Children Act.
7   See CS Bruch (above) at pp 54 et seq.
8   This is because the House of Lords decision in *Re J (A Minor) (Abduction: Custody Rights)* [1990] 2 AC 562 might suggest that the removal of a child by a parent who is entitled to remove him and who has no intention to return brings about a change in the child's habitual residence. On the other hand, the loss of one habitual residence does not necessarily mean that a new one has been acquired. It is thus possible for a child to have no habitual residence at some point in time. See *Re M (Minors) (Residence Order: Jurisdiction)* [1993] 1 FLR 495. For another case in which wrongfulness was not established because the child could not be said to be habitually resident in the State (Canada) from which the removal took place, see *Re R (Wardship: Child Abduction) (No 2)* [1993] 1 FLR 249.

subject to any express conditions inserted in the court's order. Thus, a s 8 order might prohibit the child's removal by either parent, unless specific consent requirements, court approval or other conditions are satisfied[1]. Even where a 'joint residence order' is granted[2], Bruch argues that 'wrongfulness can be established, inter alia, by acts that are inconsistent with the periods in which the order provides that the child is to live in the respective households'[3].

Where there is no court order

The position may be less clear where there is no court order. It cannot be emphasised strongly enough that this will be so in the overwhelming majority of cases and, in accordance with the 'no order' principle in the Children Act[4], it will also be the usual position following divorce. The 'custody' rights which arise by operation of law are, therefore, crucial. The position of *unmarried* parents will usually be straightforward. Assuming that the father has not acquired parental responsibility by agreement or court order, the mother will be solely entitled to it. She may, therefore, take the child abroad unilaterally for as long as she wishes. The father will generally have no 'custody' rights capable of being breached, as held in the case of *Re J (A Minor) (Abduction: Custody Rights)*[5]. The matter was, however, complicated by the decision of the Court of Appeal in *Re B (A Minor) (Abduction)*[6] in which the father, together with the maternal grandmother, had de facto care of the child before the child was abducted. The majority (Peter Gibson LJ dissenting) drew a distinction between strict legal rights and de facto or 'inchoate' rights and held that the factual care of the child could give rise to 'rights of custody' within the meaning of the Convention. This was, however, an unusual case in which the mother's behaviour was particularly reprehensible and it is clear that mere contact, however extensive, is not sufficient to establish 'rights of custody'[7]. In the vast majority of cases outside marriage, the mother will be the primary carer.

The difficult legal questions which can arise where an unmarried father without parental responsibility is seeking return of a child were the subject of a detailed Practice Note issued by the Child Abduction Unit which also reviewed the state of the authorities[8]. Where the father *has* acquired parental responsibility, the

---

1   The court has a general power to attach conditions to s 8 orders under s 11(7) of the Children Act. For a case illustrating these principles in the 'holiday' context, see *Re D (A Minor) (Child: Removal from Jurisdiction)* [1992] 1 WLR 315.
2   Section 11(4) of the Children Act.
3   CS Bruch (above) at p 55.
4   Section 1(5).
5   [1990] 2 AC 562. A case, in fact, decided under Western Australian law, but the principles would be the same under English law.
6   [1994] 2 FLR 249.
7   See, particularly, the decision of the Court of Appeal in *Re B (Abduction) (Rights of Custody)* [1997] 2 FLR 594.
8   *Practice Note (Hague Convention: Applications by Fathers Without Parental Responsibility)* [1998] 1 FLR 491. See also now the helpful judgment of Hale J in *Re W; Re B (Child Abduction: Unmarried Father)* [1998] 2 FLR 146 in which she gives guidance as to the circumstances in which unmarried parents should be advised that removal by the mother of a child who is habitually resident in England or Wales will be wrongful under the Hague Convention. These are where:
    (a)   the father has parental responsibility either by agreement or court order; or
    (b)   there is a court order in force prohibiting removal; or
    (c)   there are relevant proceedings pending in a court in England and Wales; or

position will be identical to that relating to married parents[1]. It should be remembered that many more such fathers will in future possess parental responsibility by virtue of being registered at the time of the birth. The Adoption and Children Act 2002 is not, however, retrospective in this respect and, in any event, there remain a substantial minority of unmarried fathers who do not acquire parental responsibility[2].

The law reports continue to produce a steady stream of cases exploring exactly when an unmarried father with parental responsibility can be said to have 'rights of custody' for the purposes of the Convention. These cases explore the limitations on the acquisition of 'rights of custody' where parental responsibility has not been acquired. Thus, in *Re C (Child Abduction) (Unmarried Father: Rights of Custody)*[3] the father had *shared* the care of the child with the mother for four months before she left, taking the child to Ireland. Munby J held, inter alia, that sharing the care of a child with the mother as joint primary carer was not enough to generate rights of custody, nor was the mere fact of having contact with the child[4]. The case was distinguishable from those in which the mother was no longer the primary carer as was the case in *Re F (Abduction: Unmarried Father: Sole Carer)*[5]. Here there was a dispute as to the paternity of the youngest child of four children, but no dispute that the mother's former partner had effectively had sole care of all the children for a number of years. In these circumstances Dame Elizabeth Butler-Sloss P held that there were circumstances in which a person who was not related by blood to a child, but who had a 'quasi-parental role' and exclusive care of the child, might be found to have inchoate rights of custody for the purposes of the Convention. Such rights were those which were capable of being affected by court applications in which there was a reasonable prospect of success. The father here, even if proved not to be the natural father, had reasonable prospects of obtaining a residence order and thus had inchoate rights capable of being perfected.

The non-technical and relatively purposive interpretation of 'rights of custody' has been applied to include those situations in which custody rights may be said to be vested in *the court*. The leading authority is *Re H (Abduction: Rights of Custody)*[6]. Here the unmarried father had obtained an interim order for access with the child in the Irish courts. His application for guardianship and access was adjourned. At this point the mother removed the child from Ireland to England, and the father sought summary return of the child under the Convention. The House of Lords

---

(d) the father is currently the primary carer for the child, at least if the mother has delegated such care to him.

The case is also a good illustration of the practical circumstances in which unmarried fathers may, or may not, establish a wrongful taking.

1 The father may also have 'custody rights' where he has interim care and control of the child in wardship proceedings. See *Re S (Abduction: Hague and European Conventions)* [1997] 1 FLR 958. It has been held that imprisonment does not suspend custody rights where the father has parental responsibility. See *Re A (Abduction: Rights of Custody: Imprisonment)* [2004] 1 FLR 1, a case from Australia under which jurisdiction unmarried fathers automatically acquire parental responsibility on the birth of the child.

2 See Chapter 5 above.

3 [2003] 1 FLR 252. See also *Re G (A Child) (Custody Rights: Unmarried Father)* [2002] EWHC 2219 where the mother was the primary carer.

4 See also on this point *S v H (Abduction: Access Rights)* [1997] 1 FLR 971.

5 [2003] 1 FLR 839.

6 [2000] 1 FLR 374.

upheld the decision of the Court of Appeal, which had found that at the relevant time the Irish court had 'rights of custody'. It interpreted the expression 'other body' in Article 8 to include a court. The definition of 'rights of custody' was also wide enough to include the right to determine the child's place of residence, which the court had. The court's rights of custody arose on the date on which the court's jurisdiction was invoked which, at the latest, was the date on which proceedings were served and jurisdiction would continuously be invoked until disposal of the application. It was recognised that jurisdiction could arise before service of the proceedings in special circumstances[1].

It is in relation to married parents that there are some uncertainties. What then amounts to a wrongful taking by a parent who has joint parental responsibility but there has been no court order? Again, wrongfulness must be determined by the statutes and case-law[2] in the country of the child's habitual residence, which in England means the Children Act 1989 and the Child Abduction Act 1984. Section 1 of the Child Abduction Act 1984 makes it a criminal offence for one parent to remove a child without the consent of the other but, perhaps significantly for present purposes, there are a number of defences available. Under s 1(5), no offence is committed where the child is removed:

(1) in the belief that the other person (parent for the present purposes) has consented or would have done had he been aware of all the relevant circumstances; or
(2) after taking all reasonable steps to communicate with the other person, the accused had been unable to do so; or
(3) the other person has unreasonably refused to consent.

While the former Lord Chancellor[3] and certain commentators[4] appeared to think that the regime of the Children Act would not make it more difficult to establish a wrongful taking or retention, others were more doubtful[5]. It is, to say the least, unfortunate that the question of wrongfulness under the civil law would appear to turn on what may be implied from the existence of a criminal offence, itself qualified by defences which are grounded in the nebulous notion of reasonableness. Also, it may not be very easy at all to establish a wrongful *retention* if the initial removal was reasonable under s 1(5) of the Child Abduction Act 1984[6]. Again, the answer would appear to be to obtain a residence or prohibited steps order in advance, but there are practical difficulties with this. First, child abductors are not in the habit of giving notice of their intention to snatch a child, and applying for an order really depends on being forewarned. Secondly, s 1(5) of the Children Act militates against the granting of orders unless it can be positively demonstrated that they are necessary. Thus, unless there is clear evidence of the

---

1 In *Re C (Child Abduction) (Unmarried Father: Rights of Custody)* [2003] 1 FLR 252 the court held that the mere issue of proceedings which had not yet been served did not suffice and that there were no special circumstances justifying the vesting of rights of custody in the court.
2 Central Authorities are authorised under the Hague Convention to provide the court with information on the custody law of the child's habitual residence.
3 See the reference in CS Bruch (above) at p 59, to the Lord Chancellor's speech on 12 October 1991.
4 M Everall 'Child Abduction after the Hague Convention' [1990] Fam Law 169.
5 CS Bruch (above).
6 On the distinction between removal and retention, see the House of Lords decision in *Re H (Minors) (Abduction: Custody Rights); Re S (Minors) (Abduction: Custody Rights)* [1991] 2 AC 476.

risk, the court may simply refuse to make an order. This is one instance in which the courts, notwithstanding the general thinking in the Children Act, should, perhaps, be more ready to make orders.

Wrongfulness may also be established where the taking contravened the defendant's own rights (in the sense that he exceeded them)[1], or those of an institution (such as a local authority where the child is in care, or the court where a child is a ward of court)[2]. Ignorance of the wrongfulness of the removal has been held to be no defence[3]. Finally, one of the objects of the Hague Convention is 'to ensure that ... rights of access under the law of one Contracting State are effectively respected in the other Contracting States'[4], and Central Authorities are required 'to make arrangements for organizing or securing the effective exercise of rights of access'[5]. In the English context this, of course, now means contact. However, the Court of Appeal has held that the duties of the Central Authority under Article 21 are of an *executive* rather than judicial nature, creating no rights in private law which a parent can directly enforce[6].

The Hague Convention has proved to be rather ineffectual in the enforcement of rights of access largely because a mere right of access does not amount to 'custody rights' within the meaning of the Convention[7]. Thus, removal of a child is not a wrongful taking merely because it frustrates the access rights of the aggrieved parent[8]. It may be that this is one area in which the Hague Protection of Children Convention 1996 may have a significant role to play[9], although, for those countries within the Council of Europe, the Convention on Contact concerning Children[10] is likely in future to be the most significant international instrument governing contact issues.

When should the child's return be ordered?
As has been seen, the court is generally precluded under the Hague Convention from becoming embroiled in the merits of rights to custody[11]. The general rule under Article 12 is that, provided the application is brought within 12 months of the removal, the court must order return of the child. This is subject to a number

---

1 *Re H (A Minor) (Abduction)* [1990] 2 FLR 439.
2 *Re J (A Minor: Abduction: Ward of Court)* [1989] Fam 85. See also *B v B (Abduction)* [1993] 1 FLR 238 and see the discussion above as to when a court may possess 'rights of custody'.
3 *C v C (Minors) (Child Abduction)* [1992] 1 FLR 163.
4 Article 1.
5 Article 7(f).
6 *Re G (A Minor) (Hague Convention: Access)* [1993] 1 FLR 669 and *Practice Note (Child Abduction Unit – Lord Chancellor's Department)* [1993] 1 FLR 804. This makes it plain that Article 21 confers no jurisdiction to determine matters relating to access, or to recognise or enforce foreign access orders. It merely provides for executive co-operation in the enforcement of such recognition as national law allows. Thus, the Central Authority should discharge its duty by providing the applicant with solicitors who may act on his behalf in applying for legal aid and instituting proceedings in the High Court under s 8 of the Children Act.
7 See generally N Lowe 'Problems Relating to Access Disputes under the Hague Convention on International Child Abduction' (1994) 8 IJLF 374.
8 See *S v H (Abduction: Access Rights)* [1997] 1 FLR 971.
9 This certainly seems to be the view of A-M Hutchinson and MH Bennett in 'The Hague Child Protection Convention 1996' [1998] Fam Law 35 at p 38. (See further below.) See also NV Lowe 'Problems relating to access disputes under the Hague Convention on International Child Abduction' (1994) 8 IJLF 374.
10 Discussed above at p 738.
11 Article 16.

of limited exceptions under Article 13, although, even where one of these is established, the court retains its discretion to order a return under Article 18.

Consent or acquiescence

The court may refuse to return a child where 'the person, institution or other body having care of the person of a child was not actually exercising the custody rights at the time of removal or retention, or had consented to or subsequently acquiesced in the removal or retention'[1].

Most of the reported cases on Article 13(a) have been concerned with the concept of acquiescence which we discuss below. So far as the notion of consent is concerned, it has been held that consent may be oral and need not be in writing but must be positive and unequivocal[2]. Consent, like acquiescence, may be passive rather than active and inferred from the conduct of the parties[3]. It is not necessary that the party consenting be 'happy' about the move as long as consent may clearly be inferred from what took place. Thus in *Re M (Abduction) (Consent: Acquiescence)*[4] it was possible to establish consent on the part of the Greek father where, according to the mother's evidence, she had made her preparations for leaving Greece openly, had given notice to the nursery and sold her belongings. The father had not at any stage objected to her leaving.

The notion of acquiescence has caused considerable difficulty[5]. It can be active, where some step is taken by the aggrieved parent which is thought to be inconsistent with insistence on summary return of the child, or it may be passive, as where the aggrieved parent allows time to pass by without any words or actions indicating such insistence.

The leading authority is now the decision of the House of Lords in *Re H (Minors) (Abduction: Acquiescence)*[6], where the parties were Orthodox Jews living in Israel. The mother brought the children to England without the father's consent and, initially, he sought relief through the Rabbinical courts in Israel in accordance with his religion. Only when the mother did not comply with a summons issued by the Beth Din did the father, with the approval of the court, take action under the Hague Convention. The Court of Appeal, which had found for the mother, attempted to draw a distinction between the nature of the test to be applied where the alleged acquiescence was passive and that where it was active. It held that only in the case of passive acquiescence could account be taken of the subjective attitude of the aggrieved parent.

The House of Lords rejected any such distinction, holding that under the Hague Convention the concept of acquiescence was always concerned with the subjective state of mind of the wronged parent, whether or not any positive action

---

1 Article 13(a).
2 *Re K (Abduction: Consent)* [1997] 2 FLR 212. See also *Re B (Abduction: Article 13 Defence)* [1997] 2 FLR 573.
3 See *Re R (Abduction: Consent)* [1999] 1 FLR 828. On the relationship between the defence of consent under Article 13 and the notion of wrongful removal, see the Court of Appeal's recent decision in *Re P (Abduction: Consent)* [2004] 2 FLR 1057.
4 [1999] 1 FLR 171.
5 See, for example, *Re A and Another (Minors: Abduction)* [1991] 2 FLR 241; *Re F (A Minor) (Child Abduction)* [1992] 1 FLR 548; *Re AZ (A Minor) (Abduction: Acquiescence)* [1993] 1 FLR 682; *Re S (Minors) (Abduction: Acquiescence)* [1994] 1 FLR 819; and *Re R (Child Abduction: Acquiescence)* [1995] 1 FLR 716. See also *P v P (Abduction: Acquiescence)* [1998] 2 FLR 835, *Re D (Abduction: Acquiescence)* [1998] 2 FLR 335 and *Re S (Abduction: Acquiescence)* [1998] 2 FLR 115.
6 [1997] 1 FLR 872.

had been taken by that parent. Since acquiescence was a question of fact, this subjective intention could be inferred from the outward and visible acts of the wronged parent. The burden of proof was on the abducting parent to show acquiescence. In this case, there was nothing inconsistent in the father pursuing remedies in the courts of his habitual residence, whether religious or civil, and having subsequent recourse to the Hague Convention.

Cases arguing acquiescence continue to be reported. The following two are illustrative of the courts' approach to the question. In *Re B (Abduction: Acquiescence)*[1] an American father was held to have acquiesced in the child's removal from the USA to England, by virtue of his failure to demand the immediate return of the child and his decision to attempt to settle in England and seek contact orders through the English courts. This was so despite the failure on the part of his legal advisers to inform him earlier about his rights under the Hague Convention. In *Re I (Abduction: Acquiescence)*[2] an Australian father was held *not* to have acquiesced in the children's remaining in England (where they had been taken by their mother on holiday) by his willingness to enter into negotiations over their future. It was clear that in writing to the mother's solicitor the father, while wishing the children to return to Australia, was prepared to consider other arrangements in the interests of the family. Hogg J ordered the return of the children in the circumstances.

Grave risk of harm or intolerable situation
The court may also refuse to order the child's return where 'there is a grave risk that his or her return would expose the child to physical or psychological harm or otherwise place the child in an intolerable situation'[3]. Here, the courts have been at pains to stress that it is not just *any* danger which will trigger the defence. They do not have carte blanche to apply the welfare principle as they have in ordinary domestic cases. It must be shown that the risk is a serious one and the harm envisaged must be weighty and not trivial[4]. In *Re C (Abduction: Grave Risk of Psychological Harm)*[5] the Court of Appeal emphasised the very high threshold, which required compelling evidence of a grave risk of harm or other intolerability of a severity that was much more than was inherent in the inevitable disruption, uncertainty and anxiety that followed an unwelcome return to a country of habitual residence. The court will refuse to listen to the argument of the parent who has effected the removal that it would place the child in danger to allow him to return *unaccompanied*. This would be to allow that parent to profit from his wrongdoing. Instead, the court will accept that a degree of discomfort to the child is bound to be involved in a return and will leave it to the parent to decide whether

---

1   [1999] 2 FLR 818.
2   [1999] 1 FLR 778.
3   Article 13(b). For discussion of the scope of Article 13, see J Caldwell 'Child welfare defences in child abduction cases – some recent developments' [2001] CFLQ 121.
4   See, for example, *Re C (A Minor) (Abduction)* [1989] 1 FLR 403; *B v B (Abduction)* [1993] 1 FLR 238; *Re L (Child Abduction: Psychological Harm)* [1993] 2 FLR 401; and *N v N (Abduction: Article 13 Defence)* [1995] 1 FLR 107.
5   [1999] 1 FLR 1145. See also *TB v JB (Abduction: Grave Risk of Harm)* [2001] 2 FLR 515, where a majority of the Court of Appeal held that the mother might be expected to take all reasonable steps to protect herself and the children from her second husband in New Zealand and that therefore the defence had not been established, and *Re W (Abduction: Domestic Violence)* [2004] 2 FLR 499 in which Baron J held, inter alia, that domestic violence will not of itself be sufficient to establish the defence.

he wishes to return with the child. In practice, parents often do return with children, perhaps with the financial support of the parent left behind[1]. Occasionally, however, the defence has succeeded where there has been a history of abuse or violence giving rise to a wholly understandable fear of returning on the part of the children and/or the parent[2] and in one case where there was a dislike and fear of the maternal grandmother who was seeking the child's return[3]. The courts have made it plain that it is the psychological harm to *the child* which is in issue and that a parent may not rely on her own psychological problems in resisting return of the child[4].

The child's wishes

Article 13 of the Hague Convention also provides that the child's return may be refused where the court 'finds that the child objects to being returned and has attained an age and degree of maturity at which it is appropriate to take account of its views'.

It is plain that the views, even of a *Gillick*-competent child, will be accorded less weight than in domestic proceedings[5], again on the principle that to do otherwise would frustrate the principal aim of the Hague Convention – to secure that the substantive issues are determined in the place of the child's habitual residence[6]. Despite this, there is evidence from several reported cases that the courts are prepared to listen to a child's objections, in appropriate circumstances[7], but will not allow the child's wishes to determine the matter[8]. Exceptionally, the court may allow children to be separately represented in proceedings under the Convention[9]. It is clear that something more than just a preference on the part of the child will be required to forestall an order for his return: a mere assertion will not suffice[10]. However, where the child's views accord with the court's own view of

---

1   CS Bruch (above) at p 62 notes that this is common where the abducting parent has alleged abuse or other difficult home circumstances, and the petitioner is prepared to offer undertakings to alleviate the court's concern. See, for example, *Re O (Child Abduction: Undertakings)* [1994] 2 FLR 349.

2   See *Re F (Child Abduction: Risk if Returned)* [1995] 2 FLR 31 and *Re G (Abduction: Psychological Harm)* [1995] 1 FLR 64. See also *Re M (Abduction: Psychological Harm)* [1997] 2 FLR 690.

3   *The Ontario Court v M and M (Abduction: Children's Objections)* [1997] 1 FLR 475.

4   Thus in *Re S (Abduction: Custody Rights)* [2002] 2 FLR 815 a mother could not rely on the argument that her panic and agoraphobia would be exacerbated if she returned to Israel because of the security situation there, since the court was not satisfied that the child was at risk from a breakdown in the mother's health. See also *Re S (Abduction: Intolerable Situation: Beth Din)* [2000] 1 FLR 454 in which an Orthodox Jewish mother failed to establish an intolerable situation based on the alleged lack of impartiality of the Israeli Beth Din and the existence of discrimination against Orthodox Jewish women.

5   Where they must be taken into account as the first item in the statutory checklist. See s 1(3)(a) of the Children Act, and Chapter 4 above.

6   The court may, thus, not be prepared to adjourn proceedings for the purpose of ascertaining the views of the child. See *P v P (Minors) (Child Abduction)* [1992] 1 FLR 155.

7   For a review of some of the earlier cases, see T Sachs 'The Views of the Child in Abduction Cases: *Re R* and *S v S*' (1993) 5 JCL 43.

8   *Re S (Minors) (Abduction: Custody Rights)* [1994] 1 FLR 819. See also *Re M (A Minor) (Abduction: Child's Objections)* [1994] 2 FLR 126, where the child's party status and separate representation were upheld by the Court of Appeal in a case where the dispute was really between the boy and his mother and not between the parents.

9   *Re S (Abduction: Children: Separate Representation)* [1997] 1 FLR 486.

10   See *P v P* (above). See also *Re HB (Abduction: Children's Objections)* [1997] 1 FLR 392 and *Re K (Abduction: Child's Objections)* [1995] 1 FLR 997. For recent cases in which the courts upheld the

his best interests, the court may be prepared to attach greater significance to them[1]. It has been held that, where the court, taking into account the views of two children aged nine and seven respectively, decided not to return them, this may also justify failing to return a younger sibling, too young to express his own views[2].

Absence for more than a year
It has been noted that the principle of the child's return is mandatory (but for the exceptions) where the application is brought within a year of the removal. Where the absence of the child has lasted in excess of a year, the Hague Convention still requires the child's return 'unless it is demonstrated that the child is now settled in its new environment'[3]. The strength of the status quo principle in domestic proceedings has been commented upon[4]. This is displaced in the case of wrongful takings, but there comes a point when the possible harm and disruption to the child of a further move must be taken into account, whatever the rights and wrongs of the original behaviour. Even here, however, the delay may be attributable to the child having been secreted by the abducting parent or may be the result of inadequate or incorrect legal advice being given to the applicant[5].

Violation of human rights and fundamental freedoms
A final defence is that the child's return would be contrary to the fundamental principles of the requested State regarding protection of human rights and fundamental freedoms. As yet, little or no use appears to have been made of the provision. Bruch attributes this, possibly, to the democratic reforms in Eastern Europe and the absence of cases yet raising issues of gender-based or religiously based custody laws[6].

Action under the European Convention

When may the European Convention be invoked?
The European Convention (also known as the 'Luxembourg' Convention or the 'Custody' Convention) is utilised less than the Hague Convention, since it applies only as between certain European countries, and then only if the applicant has a court order in his favour. The Convention is likely to be used even less in the future in the light of the Brussels II Regulation and the Council of Europe Contact Convention, which together cover much of the same ground. The European Convention[7] applies only to 'improper removals', which are defined as those which involve removal across international boundaries in breach of decisions

---

objections of the children, see *Re B (Abduction: Children's Objections)* [1998] 1 FLR 667; *The Ontario Court v M and M (Abduction: Children's Objections)* (above); and *Re L (Abduction: Child's Objections to Return* [2002] 2 FLR 1042.
1   As in *Re R (A Minor) (Abduction)* [1992] 1 FLR 105 and *S v S (Child Abduction: Child's View)* [1992] 2 FLR 492.
2   *B v K (Child Abduction)* [1993] 1 FCR 382. See also *Re T (Abduction: Child's Objection to Return)* [2000] 2 FLR 192 where the Court of Appeal, having attached significance to the clearly expressed fears of an 11-year-old girl in not wishing to return to her alcoholic mother in Spain, also refused the return of her six-year-old brother on the basis that it would be intolerable if he were to be returned to Spain alone.
3   Article 12. The applicant must, however, act expeditiously in the proceedings, which may otherwise be struck out. See *Re G (Abduction: Striking Out Application)* [1995] 2 FLR 410.
4   See Chapter 4 above.
5   Examples given by CS Bruch (above) at p 63.
6   Ibid.
7   Article 1.

relating to custody. These are defined widely enough to embrace orders for residence or contact[1]. The European Convention is really, therefore, about the reciprocal enforcement of court orders in contracting States and, to that extent, it is similar in nature to the Family Law Act 1986 which does the same in relation to orders in different parts of the UK[2]. The Central Authorities perform similar functions under this Convention. The Convention[3] requires the Central Authority in the country of the child's original residence, on receiving a proper application, to act without delay to secure the recognition and enforcement of the custody order. The order must be registered in a court of the contracting State to which the child has been removed. Thereupon, *that* court will have the same powers of enforcement as if it had made the original order[4], and this will enable it to order return of the child.

Can registration be refused?

In limited circumstances, a court may refuse to register an order. The court cannot reopen the merits of the original order, but it may refuse to register or enforce the order if the proceedings were defective, if the order is incompatible with another order which has already been recognised or if the child or defendant has insufficient connection with the State in which it was made[5]. These are matters principally relating to procedural impropriety. Of greater substance is Article 10, which allows a refusal to register 'where it is found by reason of a change of circumstances including the passage of time but not including a mere change in the residence of the child after an improper removal, the effects of the original decision are manifestly no longer in accordance with the welfare of the child'. This, in essence, means that the decision is no longer consistent with the welfare principle[6]. The effect would seem to be to allow the courts to consider the merits of cases more readily than they can under the Hague Convention. Thus, for example, in *Re L (Abduction: European Convention: Access)*[7] Bennett J refused registration and enforcement of a French order for contact between two children and their grandparents. At the time of the order all the parties were in France but the parents had subsequently relocated in England with the children. In these circumstances it was thought to be neither practicable nor in the best interests of the children that they should have to travel twice a month from England to France. Article 8 provides for the virtual mandatory registration of orders, where the application is made within six months of the child's removal, but a number of countries, including the UK, have entered a reservation to this Article[8]. Where registration is refused, other applications can, nonetheless, be made which will be heard on their merits[9].

---

1 Article 1(c).
2 See p 764 below.
3 Article 5.
4 Child Abduction and Custody Act 1985, s 18.
5 Articles 9 and 10, and see *Re M (Child Abduction) (European Convention)* [1994] 1 FLR 551.
6 See, for example, *F v F (Minors) (Custody: Foreign Order)* [1989] Fam 1; *Re G (A Minor) (Child Abduction: Enforcement)* [1990] 2 FLR 325; and *Re R (Abduction: Hague and European Conventions)* [1997] 1 FLR 663.
7 [1999] 2 FLR 1089. And see A-M Hutchinson 'Enforcement of Contact Orders and the Luxembourg Convention' [2000] *International Family Law* 106.
8 The effect is that registration may be refused even where the application is made within six months of the child's removal under the terms of Article 10.
9 Child Abduction and Custody Act 1985, s 20(1).

In view of the greater scope and success of the Hague Convention there will be only limited circumstances in which the European Convention can be invoked where the Hague Convention does not have application. Nonetheless, there will occasionally be such instances, as illustrated by *T v R (Abduction: Forum Conveniens)*[1]. Here the Hague Convention did not apply because the Swedish mother had *sole* custody of the child under a Swedish court order at the time she removed her to England. As such there was no 'wrongful taking or retention' for the purposes of the Hague Convention. However, the father was later awarded sole custody, which he sought to register and enforce in the English courts under the European Convention. Again, however, this was refused by Charles J on the basis of the change of circumstances arising from the mother's now being settled in England. The immediate enforcement of the Swedish order and return of the child to Sweden were not thought to be in the child's best interests.

Despite the more restricted operation of the European Convention, Bromley and Lowe have instanced two situations in which an applicant, having a choice between the two Conventions, might invoke it. The first is where the removal took place *before* implementation of the European Convention by one of the contracting States involved. This is because the European Convention has been held to have retrospective operation, whereas the Hague Convention has not[2]. The second is where the child is taken to a contracting State which has implemented Article 8. Here, an order for the return of the child is a virtual certainty if the application is made within six months of the removal. In practice, they note that there is likely to be little difference, since an order for return under the Hague Convention is also very likely in the circumstances. In any event, where an application is brought under both Conventions, the Hague Convention has precedence.

Non-Convention countries

Although the Hague Convention has been widely ratified, and further ratifications are expected, there are still many countries which fall outside it. In these cases, the prospects for recovery of abducted children may be bleak[3]. Where the English courts become seized of the matter they are liable to order the return of the child on principles similar to those which are applied under the Conventions, as in *Re F (Minor: Abduction: Jurisdiction)*[4]. As a general proposition there is a presumption that, in the absence of good reasons to the contrary, it is in the best interests of the child for questions about his or her future to be determined by the court in the child's country of habitual residence[5]. However, in *C v C (Abduction: Jurisdiction)*[6] Cazalet J applied the principles of the Hague Convention in *refusing* the return of a three-year-old child to Brazil. The decision was based primarily on

---

1　[2002] 2 FLR 544.
2　*Bromley's Family Law* (8th edn) (Butterworths, 1992) at p 494.
3　*Re H (Minors) (Abduction: Custody Rights); Re S (Minors) (Abduction: Custody Rights)* [1991] 2 AC 476. Cf *Re L (Child Abduction: European Convention)* [1992] 2 FLR 178. For a general discussion, see H Setright 'Removals to and from Non-Convention Countries – The Perspective of Courts in England in England and Wales' [2000] *International Family Law* 125.
4　[1991] Fam 25.
5　See, for example, *Re Z (Abduction: Non-Convention Country)* [1999] 1 FLR 1270 where the child was returned to Malta.
6　[1994] 1 FCR 6.

the delay which would be occasioned (over a year) if the case were to be heard in the Brazilian courts. Although the courts will try to act in accordance with the spirit of the Convention, the Court of Appeal has emphasised that the issue of the return of the child in non-Convention cases is governed by the welfare principle. Thus, in *Re P (A Minor) (Child Abduction: Non-Convention Country)*[1] the court refused to order the return of the child to India on the basis that the mother would suffer psychological harm which would affect her ability to care for the child if ordered to return there. Likewise in *Re JA (Child Abduction: Non-Convention Country)*[2] the Court of Appeal held that it would be an abdication of responsibility for the High Court to surrender the determination of its ward's future to a foreign court (in this case the United Arab Emirates) whose regime might be inimical to the child's welfare.

Notwithstanding these decisions, the courts will endeavour to be sensitive as to the child's cultural, religious and ethnic background, although it is fair to say that decisions in the case of non-Convention countries may not appear wholly consistent. There is no principle that return of the child will be refused merely because the country in question applies a different conception of the welfare of the child. Thus, in *Re E (Abduction: Non-Convention Country)*[3] the Court of Appeal held that the welfare principle was the paramount consideration in non-Convention countries, but that what constituted the welfare of the child in an individual case was subject to the cultural background and expectations of the State of habitual residence, in this case the Sudan. Under Islamic law which applied there, the mother, who had remarried, was disqualified from obtaining custody of the children which passed to the grandparents. Nonetheless, upholding the judge's order for return of the children, the court emphasised that it was not permissible to criticise other family justice systems other than in exceptional circumstances, such as cases of persecution or ethnic, sex or other discrimination. In this case the application of Muslim law to a Muslim family was appropriate and acceptable and a solution in accordance with local law was capable of being in the best interests of these children. Similarly, in *B v El-B (Abduction: Sharia Law: Welfare of Child)*[4] the father of two children succeeded in securing their return from England to Lebanon where their fate would also be determined in accordance with Muslim sharia law.

The picture world-wide can only be improved by the process of further ratifications of the Hague Convention. The options for a parent of a child abducted to a non-Convention country are very limited. They boil down to trying to secure the extradition of the abductor, if an extradition treaty exists between the two countries concerned, or trying to pursue civil proceedings in the country to which the child has been taken. In the case of children taken *to* England, an application must be brought in the High Court in wardship or under the inherent jurisdiction[5]. Some parents, in desperation, have, in the past, resorted to extra-legal means, such as attempting to snatch the child back, with or without the assistance of private investigators.

---

1   [1997] 1 FLR 780.
2   [1998] 1 FLR 231.
3   [1999] 2 FLR 642.
4   [2003] 1 FLR 811.
5   The court will only have jurisdiction if the child is habitually resident in England. See *Al Habtoor v Fotheringham* [2001] 1 FLR 951.

Abductions between different parts of the UK

This section is concerned with abductions *within* the UK from one of its constituent jurisdictions to another, ie between England and Wales, Scotland and Northern Ireland[1]. Under the Family Law Act 1986, 'Part I orders' made in one of these jurisdictions are recognised and enforceable in both of the others as if made there[2]. This is with a view to avoiding conflicts of jurisdiction between courts in different parts of the UK[3]. The Family Law Act 1986 applies to orders relating to children under 16 years of age but, since the Children Act, there will, in any event, be few English orders relating to children over this age.

The procedure is that the holder of the order applies to the court in the jurisdiction to which the child has been taken. In England and Wales and Northern Ireland this is the High Court, and in Scotland it is the Court of Session[4]. Registration is achieved by sending to the appropriate court a certified copy of the order. Once the order has been registered, the registering court can enforce it[5]. An interested party may intervene in enforcement proceedings and ask that the application be stayed or dismissed. The grounds for doing so are limited to such cases as where the original court lacked jurisdiction to make the order, or the circumstances have changed such that a variation of the order is justified[6]. The Family Law Act 1986 confers important ancillary powers on the courts which include ordering disclosure of a child's whereabouts, recovery of the child, restricting removal of a child from the jurisdiction and ordering the surrender of passports[7].

The Family Law Act 1986 applies only to moves *between* different parts of the UK and not to moves *within* one of its constituent parts. Thus, it could not be invoked where, for example, a child is moved from London to Swansea, Inverness to Glasgow or Coleraine to Belfast. In such cases, there will be no potential conflict of jurisdiction and, with regard to moves within England and Wales, an application would need to be made for a s 8 order to be granted and enforced. Since parental responsibility is shared between married parents, and it may be exercised independently, moves like this are not unlawful, however distressing they may be to the parent who is left behind. The answer will be to obtain a residence order and enforce it.

1　See Law Com Report No 138 *Custody of Children – Jurisdiction and Enforcement within the United Kingdom* (1984) upon which the legislation was based.
2　Family Law Act 1986, s 25.
3　For an example of a conflict of jurisdiction, see *T v T (Custody: Jurisdiction)* [1992] 1 FLR 43. Courts in one jurisdiction will consider themselves bound by the principle of comity and will not, in effect, purport to act as a Court of Appeal where, for example, an interim order has been made in another jurisdiction. For a post-Children Act decision involving conflicts of jurisdiction between England and Wales and Scotland, turning on the correct habitual residence of the child, see *Re M (Minors) (Residence Order: Jurisdiction)* [1993] 1 FLR 495 and the commentary by G Douglas at [1993] Fam Law 285. See also *S v S (Custody: Jurisdiction)* [1995] 1 FLR 155; *M v M (Abduction: England and Scotland)* [1997] 2 FLR 263; *A v A (Forum Conveniens)* [1999] 1 FLR 1; and *Re B (Court's Jurisdiction)* [2004] 2 FLR 741.
4　Family Law Act 1986, s 32(1).
5　Ibid, s 29.
6　Ibid, ss 30 and 31.
7　Ibid, ss 33–37.

INTERCOUNTRY ADOPTION

Introductory background[1]

The significant decline in the number of babies available for adoption in developed countries has resulted in a situation in which demand from childless couples vastly outstrips the supply. One consequence of this is that there has been an upsurge in applications for intercountry adoption, illustrated most dramatically in the aftermath of the Romanian revolution[2]. The figures for abandoned children across the world, particularly in Latin America, Asia and Africa, have reached staggering proportions[3]. As the *Adoption Review*[4] noted, it is scarcely surprising that some people, especially those unable to have children, should wish to combine the needs of destitute children with their own desire to have a family. Yet in recent years, fears have been expressed across the international community that many of these adoptions have not been child-centred but have had, instead, as their main objective, the satisfaction of adult needs. Often they have been arranged privately and without the professional supervision, support and safeguards which characterise many domestic adoption laws including English adoption law. At their worst, some unregulated adoptions have involved corruption, child-stealing and trafficking. Added to this, there is a further controversy about whether transracial adoptions are in children's best interests.

Some of these problems surfaced in the High Court in *Re M (Adoption: International Adoption Trade)*[5]. The facts of the case, shocking as they are, deserve extensive citation. A white British couple paid £18,500 (of which only US$1,000 was paid to the American birth parents) to adopt a black child. The rest of the money was paid to the lawyers involved, to an American adoption agency, and to

1 See, generally: W Duncan 'Regulating Intercountry Adoption – an International Perspective' in A Bainham, DS Pearl and R Pickford (eds) *Frontiers of Family Law* (2nd edn) (John Wiley & Sons, 1995); C Bridge 'Reforming Intercountry Adoption' (1992) 4 JCL 116; W Duncan 'Hague Convention on the Protection of Children and Co-operation in respect of Intercountry Adoption (29 May 1993)', [1999] *International Family Law* 31. For an assessment of the Hague Convention, see L Silberman 'The Hague Children's Conventions' in SN Katz, J Eekelaar and M Maclean *Cross Currents* (Oxford University Press, 2000) p 589 at pp 606–615. Much useful information on the position of children in sending States is to be found in ED Jaffe (ed) *Intercountry Adoptions: Laws and Perspectives of 'Sending' Countries* (Martinus Nijhoff, 1995). For more up-to-date statements of the law now governing intercountry adoption, see SM Cretney, JM Masson and R Bailey-Harris *Principles of Family Law* (First supplement to the 7th edn) (Sweet & Maxwell, 2003) at pp 46–50, and C Bridge and H Swindells *Adoption: The Modern Law* (Family Law, 2003) at ch 14.
2 See W Duncan 'Regulating Intercountry Adoption – an International Perspective' (above) at p 43. And for a review of the position in the former Soviet Union, see OA Dyuzheva 'Adoption and the Abandonment of Children in the former Soviet Union' [1992] Fam Law 389. For illustrations of the kinds of difficulties which can arise in practice concerning overseas adoptions, see *Re WM (Adoption: Non-Patrial)* [1997] 1 FLR 132 and *Re K (Adoption and Wardship)* [1997] 2 FLR 221. For the immigration difficulties which can occur, see *Re J (Adoption: Non-Patrial)* [1998] 1 FLR 225. Cf *Re B (Adoption Order: Nationality)* [1998] 1 FLR 965. The correct test appears to be whether the adoption is genuinely justified as in the best interests of the child as opposed to a 'status device' designed purely to confer British nationality and the right of abode on the child. The appellate decisions are, however, by no means easy to reconcile on their facts. See the comment by S Cretney at [1998] Fam Law 385.
3 See W Duncan 'Regulating Intercountry Adoption – an International Perspective' (above).
4 Paragraph 46.2.
5 [2003] 1 FLR 1111.

the British so-called 'independent social worker'. The 'home study report' supported the adoption, despite the fact that the adoptive mother had been divorced four times and had six children by four different fathers. One of her children had been on the child protection register, she herself had been diagnosed with cancer and had attempted suicide more than once. Both Barnado's and the local authority had concluded that she was unsuitable to adopt. Despite all this, the adoption went ahead in the USA. Within five months the adoptive parents had separated and three months after that the adoptive mother committed suicide. The adoptive father then abandoned the child, who was placed with foster-parents.

The birth parents sought return of the child to the USA but Munby J concluded that she would be exposed to the risk of significant emotional and possibly physical harm if returned. Instead he made an order freeing her for adoption in the UK. But he went much further than this in his criticisms both of what happened in this case and of the international adoption system more generally. First, he held that the adoption should never have happened. Secondly, the 'independent social worker', Jay Carter, had committed criminal offences under ss 11 and 57 of the Adoption Act 1976, which prohibit private adoptions and illegal payments[1]. Thirdly, the 'home study reports' were deeply flawed, inadequate, positively and dangerously misleading. They rendered the author unfit ever to be involved in such work again. Accordingly, copies of the judgment were to be sent to the Director of Public Prosecutions and the Attorney-General with a view to criminal proceedings. And his verdict on the way in which some international adoptions are carried out was as follows:

> 'It is high time that this evil and exploitative trade was stamped out. It is a trade because, however it is dressed up, it involves the buying and selling of babies by intermediaries who pocket most of the large sums of money which change hands during the course of the transaction. It is evil and exploitative because it battens on would-be adopters who, unable to adopt through more conventional channels, are induced in their desperation to part with large sums of money to intermediaries whose motives are purely mercenary; because it battens on the emotional turmoil of disadvantaged and desperately vulnerable birth mothers who are induced to part with their babies within days of birth, who see little of the large sums of money paid to the intermediaries by the adopters and who too often, as in the present case, soon come to regret their hasty and ill-considered decision; and because it can cause untold harm to children, untold misery to their birth mothers and untold heartache to adopters.'

If this case were uniquely bad it would be serious enough. But sadly it is far from unique, as discussed below in the context of adoptions from Romania.

In an effort to meet these concerns, and to facilitate intercountry adoption only when it is in the best interests of the child concerned, the Hague Conference on Private International Law set up, in 1990, a Special Commission to develop an international Convention on intercountry adoption[2]. The Convention was finalised in May 1993. The principal aims and features of the Convention are considered below, but first we look briefly at the terms of the UNCRC and the recommendations of the *Adoption Review* as they applied to intercountry adoption.

---

1 See Chapter 7.
2 See, generally, W Duncan (above).

The United Nations Convention

The Hague Convention takes, as its starting point, the principles of the UNCRC, and these must also be the yardstick for evaluating domestic law and practice. The all-important provison is Article 21, the relevant part of which requires Member States to:

'(b)　recognise that inter-country adoption may be considered as an alternative means of a child's care, if the child cannot be placed in a foster or an adoptive family or cannot in any suitable manner be cared for in the child's country of origin;

(c)　ensure that the child concerned by inter-country adoption enjoys safeguards and standards equivalent to those existing in the case of national adoption;

(d)　take all appropriate measures to ensure that, in inter-country adoption, the placement does not result in improper financial gain for those involved in it;

(e)　promote, where appropriate, the objectives of this article by concluding bilateral or multi-lateral arrangements or agreements and endeavour, within this framework, to ensure that the placement of the child in another country is carried out by competent authorities or organs.'

The *Adoption Review*

The *Adoption Review*[1] recognised that intercountry adoption, while not a solution to problems arising from world poverty, might, in some cases, represent the *only* opportunity for some children to have a stable home life. Accordingly, those applicants who were assessed as being suitable to offer a home to a child from overseas should be allowed to do so. At the same time, the *Review* took the view that the practice of intercountry adoption should be regulated to ensure that it only takes place where it is in the interests of the child concerned and with safeguards to protect the welfare of the child and to eliminate corrupt practices[2]. The system, it was said, should reflect certain fundamental principles accepted in international statutory instruments. In particular, intercountry adoption should operate as a child-centred service and *not* a child-finding service for adults. It should be allowed only in relation to those children who could not be suitably cared for in their own countries[3]. Other significant recommendations were as follows. It was proposed that children should be admitted to the UK only where authorisation had been granted by the responsible authority in the UK that the adoption proceed, subject to immigration requirements being met[4]. It was also proposed that local authorities should have a duty to provide services in connection with intercountry adoption, or arrange for them to be provided by approved adoption societies. They should be responsible for supervising the placement of children from overseas from the time of their arrival in the UK[5]. Once the new system had been properly developed, it was proposed that it should

---

1　Paragraph 47.1.
2　*Adoption Review* at para 47.1.
3　Ibid at para 47.2.
4　Ibid at para 47.3.
5　Ibid at para 53.

be a criminal offence to bring a child to the UK for adoption without having obtained the prior authorisation of the relevant authority to proceed[1].

The Hague Convention came into force in the UK on 1 June 2003. The enabling legislation was the Adoption (Intercountry Aspects) Act 1999[2]. Most but not all[3] of the provisions of the 1999 Act have now been incorporated into the Adoption and Children Act 2002. The procedures for intercountry adoption in the UK are the subject of detailed guidance issued by the Department of Health[4]. The main provisions of the 1999 Act enabled the UK to ratify the Convention; amended the Adoption Act 1976 to place local authorities under a duty to provide, or arrange to provide, an intercountry adoption service; enabled certain children who are the subject of a Convention adoption to receive British citizenship; and enabled those who adopt children in accordance with the Hague Convention or from a designated country[5] to apply to register the adoption at the Office of the Registrar General for England and Wales.

The effect of the amendments made by the Adoption and Children Act 2002 is to extend the restrictions on bringing children into the UK in connection with intercountry adoption. In particular, the Secretary of State is empowered to make regulations[6] requiring prospective adopters to have their eligibility and suitability to adopt approved and to meet other prescribed conditions. This is backed up by criminal sanctions with a maximum of 12 months' imprisonment and/or an unlimited fine on conviction.

The fundamental objective of the primary and secondary legislation is to try to ensure that the same adoption practice and professional standards are applied to both intercountry and domestic adoptions. Hence, the same requirement to provide an adoption service, specifically in this case for intercountry adoption, is imposed on local authorities and there are similar prohibitions on private adoptions[7]. Only local authorities and voluntary adoption agencies (VAAs) may 'make arrangements' for adoption, and it is made explicit that any arrangement for the assessment of a person's child is considered to fall within this expression[8]. The effect is that home study assessments and reports on the suitability of a person to be an adoptive parent may only be arranged and produced by a local authority or VAA which is registered with the National Care Standards Commission. Other duties imposed on local authorities include the duty to monitor placements for adoption once they have been notified of a prospective adopter's intention to adopt, to prepare reports for courts considering applications for adoption and to

---

1   *Adoption Review* at para 56.2.
2   See D Ranton 'Striking the Balance – Intercountry Adoption in England and Wales' [2001] *International Family Law* 35.
3   Sections 1, 2, 7 and Sch 1 remain.
4   Department of Health *Intercountry Adoption Guide* (May 2003). The guide will be replaced when the Adoption and Children Act 2002 is implemented.
5   There is a list of designated countries in the Adoption (Designation of Overseas Adoptions) Order 1973, as amended. Adoption orders made in these countries are automatically recognised in the UK.
6   The main regulations currently governing intercountry adoption are the Intercountry Adoption (Hague Convention) Regulations 2003, SI 2003/118 and the Adoption (Bringing Children into the United Kingdom) Regulations 2003, SI 2003/1173. The registration of foreign adoptions is governed by the Registration of Foreign Adoptions Regulations 2003, SI 2003/1255.
7   See Chapter 7 for the prohibitions on private adoption in the case of domestic adoptions.
8   Adoption Act 1976, s 72, as amended.

report any breach, or suspected breach, of the legal requirements to the police for investigation. In the case of proposed 'non-Convention adoptions'[1], there are similar requirements[2] that prospective adopters comply with analogous legal conditions regarding, for example, assessment of their eligibility and suitability by the local authority or VAA. Prospective adopters must also give notice of their intention to adopt or not to give the child a home within 14 days of their return to the UK unless they have a recognised adoption order from a designated country.

Where the UK is the State of origin and it is proposed to take a child who is a Commonwealth citizen out of the British Isles with a view to an adoption overseas, those wishing to do so must apply for and obtain a court order authorising a proposed foreign adoption and conferring parental responsibility on them[3].

Therefore, to summarise, where the UK is a 'receiving State' in connection with intercountry adoption, the precise legal regime governing such adoptions will depend on the status of the country of origin[4]. First, there will be adoptions of children from the Hague Convention countries, which must comply with the requirements of the Hague Convention and the Intercountry Adoption (Hague Convention) Regulations 2003. Secondly, there will be adoptions from designated countries, which must comply with the conditions laid down in the Adoption (Bringing Children into the United Kingdom) Regulations 2003. Thirdly, where adoption orders have been made in countries which are neither party to the Hague Convention, nor designated countries, it will be necessary to obtain an adoption order in a UK court having first complied with the above regulations.

The Hague Convention

Objectives
The objects of the Convention[5] are threefold. They are:

(1) to establish safeguards to ensure that intercountry adoptions take place in the best interests of the child and with respect for his or her fundamental rights as recognised in international law;
(2) to establish a system of co-operation amongst contracting States to ensure that those safeguards are respected and thereby prevent the abduction, the sale of, or traffic in children;
(3) to secure the recognition in contracting States of adoptions made in accordance with the Convention.

Encouraging adoption of children within their country of origin
The Convention contains a number of fundamental provisions. One of these, which requires special mention, derives from the important principle of *subsidiarity* in Article 21(b) of the UNCRC[6]. This is that an intercountry adoption

---

1 That is, adoptions of children which will not take place under the Hague Convention because the State of origin is not party to it.
2 See the Adoption (Bringing Children into the United Kingdom) Regulations 2003.
3 Clearly there are likely to be far fewer instances in which the UK is the 'sending State' rather than the 'receiving State'.
4 The various categories are discussed in rather more depth in SM Cretney, JM Masson and R Bailey-Harris *Principles of Family Law* (First supplement to the 7th edn) at pp 48–49.
5 Article 1.
6 Discussed above.

should only take place once the competent authorities in the State of origin have determined, after possibilities for placement of the child within the State of origin have been given due consideration, that an intercountry adoption is in the child's best interests[1]. This is, in many ways, the crux of the matter. The chief concern of the international community is that priority should be given to the fostering of child care services in the developing countries and that, wherever possible, children in difficulty should be kept in their families and, failing that, be placed with families in their own communities.

The purpose of the Hague Convention is, therefore, not simply to facilitate intercountry adoption but to regulate it so that it only takes place when the possibilities for substitute care in the child's country of origin have been exhausted. The difficulty is that, in many developing countries, inadequate child care services exist. Duncan[2] has noted how difficult it is for the child-centred approach to be maintained when, on the international scene, the supply of children available for adoption vastly exceeds the demand. It is his view[3] that the success of the Convention may ultimately be measured 'as much by what it does to encourage and stimulate the growth of child care services in countries of origin as by the number of intercountry adoptions effected under it'.

Once intercountry adoption has been approved

Assuming that it is determined by the State of origin that an intercountry adoption *is* in the child's best interests, the Convention contains a number of other fundamental provisions including the following.

(1) The competent authorities of the State of origin must ensure that the child is adoptable, that all relevant consents (including the child's consent where appropriate) have been given freely and unconditionally after appropriate counselling, and that they have not been induced by payment or compensation[4].

(2) The competent authorities of the State of origin must also ensure, having regard to the age and degree of maturity of the child, that his or her consent has been given freely and unconditionally after appropriate counselling, where the child's consent is required, and that, where it is not, consideration has been given to the child's wishes and opinions[5].

(3) The competent authorities in the receiving State must determine that the prospective adopters are eligible and suited to adopt and that the child will be authorised to enter and reside permanently in that State[6].

(4) There should be no unsupervised contact between the prospective adopters and the natural parents until the fundamental requirements for intercountry adoption have been satisfied[7]. The purpose of this provision will be to

---

1 Article 4(b).
2 W Duncan 'Regulating Intercountry Adoption – an International Perspective' in A Bainham, DS Pearl and R Pickford (eds) *Frontiers of Family Law* (2nd edn) (John Wiley & Sons, 1995) at pp 42–43.
3 Ibid at p 51.
4 Article 4(a) and (c).
5 Article 4(d).
6 Article 5.
7 Article 29.

prevent economic and other pressure being brought to bear on the birth parents.

(5) Transfer of the child to the receiving State is prohibited, until it has been verified by the competent authorities of both States that no bars exist to the adoption under the respective laws of those States and that a permanent placement has been agreed. This is to avoid the situation of 'legal limbo' in which some children arriving in another State currently find themselves[1].

Designation of a Central Authority

Another important feature of the Convention is the requirement that the contracting States designate a Central Authority to discharge their obligations under the Convention[2]. These Central Authorities will be expected to co-operate with one another, especially in the exchange of information and in monitoring the operation of the Convention. Some of their functions may be delegated to 'accredited bodies', which are expected to be, for the most part, approved adoption agencies[3]. Finally, the Convention provides for the automatic recognition in all contracting States of adoptions certified by the competent authority of the State in question as having been made in accordance with the Convention[4].

Recognition of Convention adoptions

Article 23 provides that an adoption certified by the competent authority of the State of the adoption as having been made in accordance with the Convention must be recognised by operation of law in all the contracting States. Such recognition may only be refused if the adoption is 'manifestly contrary to [that State's] public policy, taking into account the best interests of the child'[5].

Romania: a test case for intercountry adoption?

No country epitomises the controversies surrounding intercountry adoption more, perhaps, than does Romania[6]. Before 1990 international adoption from Romania was a very rare occurrence. Then, following the fall of Ceauşescu in December 1989, the world became aware of the situation of large numbers of so-called 'orphans' in large State-run institutions, in many cases in highly unsatisfactory circumstances. In 1990 the international adoption system was liberalised in Romania and this was accompanied by a new law passed in 1993[7]

---

1 Articles 17–19.
2 Article 8. Cf the role of Central Authorities in relation to the international Conventions on Child Abduction, discussed at pp 750 et seq.
3 See Articles 6–13.
4 Article 23.
5 Article 24.
6 The author acted as Special Adviser to Baroness Nicholson of Winterbourne MEP, in her capacity as rapporteur for Romania in the European Parliament. For the author's views on the issues surrounding international adoption from Romania in greater depth, see A Bainham 'International Adoption from Romania: Why the moratorium should not be ended' [2003] CFLQ 223. See also A Bainham 'Child Protection, Adoption and the Moratorium: An Important Crossroads for Romania' (2003) 3 *Romanian Journal of Society and Politics* 54. For a detailed exploration of the issues surrounding the practice of international adoption more generally, see S Dillon 'Making Legal Regimes for Intercountry Adoption Reflect Human Rights Principles: Transforming the United Nations Convention on the Rights of the Child with the Hague Convention on Intercountry Adoption' (2003) 21 *Boston University International Law Journal* 179.
7 Law 47/1993.

which facilitated declarations of 'abandonment', thereby in effect freeing up large numbers of children for adoption. A child looked after by the State could henceforth be declared abandoned where the parents were found not to have contacted the child within a period of six months. It is well-documented and accepted that throughout the 1990s a market in children sprung up in Romania. After 1997 the Romanian authorities made a 'constant offer' of children available for international adoption by maintaining a database. Children on this database would be allocated to agencies specialising in international adoption on a 'points system'. During this period *domestic* adoption was deliberately suppressed and 'fast-track' procedures operated to speed up *international* adoptions. The 'entrust-ment' or probationary period during which the child should live with the prospective adopters was waived for international, but not for domestic, adop-tions. Large sums of money found their way into the pockets of unscrupulous intermediaries arranging such adoptions.

It is worth pausing to reflect on some of the worst excesses of this regime. An Independent Group for International Adoption Analysis[1] was set up by the Prime Minister of Romania and reported on these abuses in March 2002. It highlighted the creation of 'adoption pools' whereby children would be plucked from institutions by agencies, how documents were falsified and how expectant mothers in maternity hospitals had been coerced into surrendering newborn babies at birth. It reached the damning conclusion that Romanian law 'under the appearance of complying with international treaties would stimulate abandon-ment and financial profit from international adoption'[2]. The point about stimulation of abandonment is critical to an understanding of the argument for *prohibiting* intercountry adoption. The statistical evidence exists which establishes a clear association between the availability of intercountry adoption and the abandonment of children in Romania[3]. In other words, it needs to be understood that there is a strong likelihood that a significant number of children would not have been 'abandoned' and would not have been institutionalised at all but for the existence of the international adoption market.

In October 2001, the Romanian government imposed a moratorium on international adoption from the country other than for a category of special cases. Despite this, abuses continued to surface. In January 2004 it was widely reported that 105 children had been despatched to Italy in breach of the various applicable international Conventions following a visit to the country by the Italian Prime Minister[4]. At about the same time a criminal investigation was launched at the Ploiesti Maternity Hospital where it was alleged that the parents of certain babies were informed, without having had an opportunity to see them, that they were stillborn when in fact a number were reported to have been found alive and well several months later.

Romania's response to these abuses involved maintaining the moratorium while, at the same time, embarking on a wide-ranging reform of its entire child

---

1 The IGIAA Report *Re-Organising the International Adoption and Child Protection System* (2002).
2 Ibid at p 26.
3 The author has been provided with statistics from the judets of Cluj and Valcea which show the abandonment rates sharply falling back after the imposition of the moratorium on international adoption from Romania in October 2001.
4 See 'Child traffickers prey on Romania' *The Sunday Times*, 9 May 2004. The same incident was reported in *Ziua*, a leading Romanian newspaper, on 11 May 2004.

protection system, its child protection laws and its laws on adoption[1] in order to comply with the UNCRC, the ECHR and the conditions for Romania's accession to the European Union expected in 2007. Under its new child protection system there is a primary focus on preventive services for the family, closure of the large-scale institutions and their replacement with more suitable 'family-based' alternatives such as smaller family-type homes and the placement of children with 'maternal assistants' (foster carers). The new laws, inter alia, prohibit the placement of a child under two years old in an institution and give priority to placement with the extended family or, failing that, foster care. There are new measures to ensure birth registration and to combat the problem of 'abandonment' of babies by their mothers in maternity hospitals, backed up by criminal sanctions.

Since the Western media is fond of continuing to emphasise the predicament of children in large-scale institutions, despite all the progress made in Romania, it is important to set out the facts on de-institutionalisation[2]. The total number of institutionalised children fell by 34 per cent between January 2001 and December 2003. The number of large-scale institutions (with more than 100 children in care) dropped from 205 at the beginning of 2001 to 85 in December 2003. By the end of December 2003 some 537 alternative services had been created to prevent the separation of children from their families and to support children's re-integration into their birth or extended families.

Romania has, since the commencement of the moratorium, been under relentless political pressure to return to becoming a 'sending State' for the purposes of international adoption. Much of this pressure has emanated from the powerful adoption lobby in the USA and from certain other Western European countries. Often these are countries which are strongly opposed to *domestic* adoption and strongly committed to reunification of children looked after by the State with their birth families, but which have failed (apparently) to see the double standard involved in undermining Romania's own efforts to achieve the same for *its* children. Serious questions must be asked about whether this pressure was 'children-driven' and borne of a desire to help Romanian families and their children, or whether it was 'adult-driven' and has been about finding attractive European children for would-be adopters who have often not been accepted as suitable adopters by their own domestic authorities. If the latter is the correct interpretation, then such pressure runs counter to the whole spirit of modern adoption law. This is about the rights of the child and finding a family for a child. It is not about finding a child for a family, however much sympathy might be felt for those who long for a child.

The Romanian experience raises the fundamental question whether intercountry adoption is better *regulated* (as it is by the Hague Convention) or *prohibited*. While it should be acknowledged that there are of course instances in which children are truly 'orphaned' or 'abandoned', for example in circumstances of war or famine, international obligations require Romania (and those other countries in Eastern Europe which are members of the Council of Europe and

---

1   These laws were passed by the Romanian Parliament in June 2004 and are due to come into force early in 2005.

2   Statistics contained in a paper entitled 'Child Protection in Romania – Accomplishments and Challenges' prepared by the National Authority for Child Protection and Adoption and made available to the author at a conference in Targu Mures in May 2004.

either members of, or aspiring to be members of, the European Union) to operate effective child protection systems which enable them properly to look after all those children who may be in difficulty. The phenomenon of intercountry adoption from such countries is nothing less than an admission of failure on the part of the State to achieve this goal. It is something which, more often than not, under the imprimatur of the Hague Convention, masks multiple breaches by the State concerned of the UNCRC and the ECHR.

CONCLUSION

This discussion of the two Hague Conventions, which deal with the two great international problems of child abduction and intercountry adoption, demonstrates particularly well a central dilemma for the modern law affecting children. Are the *collective* interests of children as a group or class to be given precedence over those of an individual child? In some ways the two Conventions take opposite positions on this. So far as abduction is concerned, we saw that the cardinal principal of peremptory return is founded in the notion that abductors must be deterred and that this is in the interests of children generally. Yet, increasingly there has been a degree of discomfort felt about the return of individual children whose welfare might point in the other direction. In some cases it may be keenly felt that it might be in their best interests to allow them to remain where they now are, especially where the abduction was carried out by the primary carer. In contrast, the Hague Adoption Convention might be criticised from the opposite angle. Arguably there has been too much concern in this context for the regulation of *individual* adoptions and of safeguarding the welfare of the individual children involved (although it is certainly not conceded that the Convention has been successful in this respect), and too little concern for the *collective* interests of children and birth families in the country of origin. The fact that an individual institutionalised child might conceivably benefit from adoption abroad must be weighed against the perpetuation of a system which can, and certainly has in the case of Romania, operated to the detriment of the domestic child protection system in the country of origin. The very existence of intercountry adoption may divert valuable resources, human and financial, into a system which at best can only assist a tiny minority of children in difficulty.

There is no glib answer to this central dilemma. It remains one of the unanswered questions which continue to make children law such a fascinating intellectual challenge.

INDEX

References are to page numbers.